EUROPEAN CRIMINAL LAW

Since their creation, the European Union and the Council of Europe have worked to harmonise the justice systems of their member states. This project has been met with a series of challenges. *European Criminal Law* offers a compelling insight into the development and functions of European criminal law. It tracks the historical development of European criminal law, offering a detailed critical analysis of the criminal justice systems responsible for its implementation. While the rapid expansion and transnationalisation of criminal law is a necessary response to the growing numbers of freely moving persons and goods, it has serious implications for the rights of European citizens and needs to be balanced with rights protections. With its close analysis of secondary legislation and reliance on a wide variety of original sources, this book provides a thorough understanding of European Criminal Law and the institutions involved.

Kai Ambos is Chair of Criminal Law, Criminal Procedure, Comparative Law and International Criminal Law and also Head of the Department of Foreign and International Criminal Law, Institute of Criminal Law and Justice at the Georg-August-Universitat, Göttingen, Germany (GAU). He is the Director of the GAU's Research Centre for Latin American Criminal Law and Procedure (Centro de Derecho Penal y Proceso Penal Latinoamericano, CEDPAL). He has been a Judge at the Provincial Court (Landgericht) of Göttingen from 2006 to March 2017 until his appointment as judge at the Kosovo Specialist Chambers, The Hague. In December 2017 he was selected as adviser (*amicus curiae*), Colombian Special Jurisdiction for Peace, Bogotá. His main research areas lie in comparative, international and European criminal law and procedure. He has worked extensively in Latin America and Eastern Europe on human rights, drug-related issues and criminal law reforms.

EUROPEAN CRIMINAL LAW

KAI AMBOS

Professor of Criminal Law, Criminal Procedure,
Comparative Law and International Criminal Law,
Georg-August-Universität, Göttingen, Germany;
Judge, Kosovo Specialist Chambers, The Hague, NL;
Adviser (amicus curiae) *Colombian Special Jurisdiction for Peace, Bogotá*

CAMBRIDGE
UNIVERSITY PRESS

CAMBRIDGE
UNIVERSITY PRESS

University Printing House, Cambridge CB2 8BS, United Kingdom

One Liberty Plaza, 20th Floor, New York, NY 10006, USA

477 Williamstown Road, Port Melbourne, VIC 3207, Australia

314-321, 3rd Floor, Plot 3, Splendor Forum, Jasola District Centre, New Delhi - 110025, India

79 Anson Road, #06-04/06, Singapore 079906

Cambridge University Press is part of the University of Cambridge.

It furthers the University's mission by disseminating knowledge in the pursuit of education, learning and research at the highest international levels of excellence.

www.cambridge.org
Information on this title: www.cambridge.org/9781107552135
DOI: 10.1017/9781316348628

First published 2018
First paperback edition 2019

A catalogue record for this publication is available from the British Library

ISBN 978-1-107-11969-7 Hardback
ISBN 978-1-107-55213-5 Paperback

To my family

CONTENTS

TABLES AND FIGURES

Tables

Figures

PREFACE

This book pretends to give a systematic and comprehensive overview of European criminal law (ECrL), understood as the law of the European Union (EU) – a highly integrated organisation of (still) twenty-eight Member States with a supranational character – and the law of the Council of Europe (CoE) – an association of forty-seven States. Chapter 1 gives an overview of the history of the European integration process up to its most recent setback with Brexit (which, to be sure, leaves the UK's CoE membership unaffected), the concept and the sources of ECrL. Chapter 2 offers a comprehensive analysis of rights protection in Europe with a view to criminal law distinguishing between the CoE level (ECHR and ECtHR) and the more recent efforts on the EU level (CFREU, especially the European double jeopardy rules). In Chapter 3 the substantive criminal law and in Chapter 4 the procedural law with a focus on police and judicial co-operation are analysed. The final Chapter 5 takes a look at the most important institutions of European criminal law, including the newly established European Public Prosecutor's Office (EPPO).

Given the great importance of the national law of the Member States in various areas of ECrL I have taken into account the national law of some of the most important European jurisdictions (Czech Republic, France, Germany, Greece, Hungary, Italy, the Netherlands, Poland, Portugal, Spain, Sweden, the UK), including one non-EU Member State (Switzerland). This would not have been possible without the help of the following colleagues: I. Zerbes (Austria), P. Šturm (Czech Republic), J. Leblois-Happe, J. Walther (both France), P. Gkaniatsos (Greece), K. Karsai (Hungary), G. Lanza (Italy), A. Klip, J. Vervaele, H. van der Wilt (all Netherlands), A. Świątłowski (Poland), P. Mendes, P. Caeiro (both Portugal), L. Bachmaier-Winter, M. de Hoyos, A. Gil Gil, J. Matia, R. Robles (all Spain), P. Asp (Sweden), F. Meyer (Switzerland), P. Roberts, J. Spencer, F. Stark (all UK). During my sabbatical at the Law Faculty in Cambridge, UK, during the summer of 2016 where I finished writing this book I was warmly welcomed and always assisted by Tony Bottoms,

Antje Du Bois-Pedain and John Spencer. At my Göttingen chair especially Christopher Penkuhn, as well as Panagiotis Gkaniatsos, Luca Petersen (special credit for last-minute efforts!) and Joschka Schlake, assisted in research, and Maximilian Menges and Robert Taeger provided further assistance at proof stage. Margaret Hiley was, as always, extremely helpful in turning my thoughts into more elegant English. Thanks also to Elisabeth Spicer, who was my first contact at CUP, Rebecca Jackaman who was responsible for the production and John Gaunt for thorough copy-editing.

Kai Ambos, Göttingen, February 2018

ABBREVIATIONS

AbfG	Abfallwirtschaftsgesetz (German Waste Management Act)
ACHR	American Convention on Human Rights
AEUV	Vertrag über die Arbeitsweise der Europäischen Union (Treaty on the Functioning of the EU/TFEU)
AfP	*Zeitschrift für Medien- und Kommunikationsrecht* (Germany; formerly *Archiv für Presserecht*)
AG	Advocate General (CJEU) or Amtsgericht (Municipal Court, Germany)
AIDP	Association Internationale de Droit Pénal (France)
AJP	*Actualité Juridique Pénal* (journal, France)
al.	alii
ALF	*Amsterdam Law Forum* (Netherlands)
AmJCompL	*American Journal of Comparative Law*
AO	Abgabenordnung (Tax Statute, Germany)
AP	Additional Protocol
APC	Archives de Politique Criminelle (journal, France)
ARHG	Österreichisches Auslieferungs- und Rechtshilfegesetz (Austrian Law on Legal Assistance)
ARI	Análisis del Real Instituto Elcano (journal, Spain)
Art.	Article
ATCSA	Anti-terrorism, Crime and Security Act 2001 (UK)
AWG	Außenwirtschaftsgesetz (Foreign Trade and Payments Act, Germany)
BayObLG	Bayerisches Oberstes Landesgericht (formerly Bavarian Highest Regional Court)
BB	*Betriebsberater* (journal, Germany)
Benelux States	Belgium, the Netherlands and Luxembourg
BGBl.	*Bundesgesetzblatt* (Federal Law Gazette, Germany)
BGE	*Entscheidungen des Schweizerischen Bundesgerichts* (Decisions of the Swiss Federal Court)
BGH	Bundesgerichtshof (Federal Court, Germany)

BGHSt	*Entscheidungen des Bundesgerichtshofs in Strafsachen* (Decisions of the Federal Court in Criminal Matters, Germany)
BJC	*British Journal of Criminology*
BJCLCJ	*Bergen Journal of Criminal Law & Criminal Justice* (journal, Norway)
BKR	*Zeitschrift für Bank- und Kapitalmarktrecht* (journal, Germany)
BMJ[V]	Bundesministerium der Justiz [und für Verbraucherschutz] (Federal Ministry for Justice [and Consumer Protection], Germany)
BNatSchG	Bundesnaturschutzgesetz (Federal Nature Conservation Act, Germany)
BOE	*Boletin del Estado* (official journal, Spain)
BOMJ	*Bulletin Officiel du Ministère de la Justice* (journal, France)
BR	Bundesrat/Bundesrepublik (German Federal Council [second chamber of Parliament representing the federal states]/ German Federal Republic)
BRAK	Bundesrechtsanwaltskammer (German Bar Association)
BR-Drs.	Bundesratsdrucksache (Printed Matter of the German Federal Council, Germany)
BReg	Bundesregierung (federal government, Germany)
BT	Bundestag (Federal Parliament, Germany)
BT-Drs.	Bundestagsdrucksache (Printed Matter of the Federal Parliament, Germany)
BVerfG	Bundesverfassungsgericht (Federal Constitutional Court, Germany)
BVerfGE	*Entscheidungen des Bundesverfassungsgerichts* (Decisions of the Federal Constitutional Court, Germany)
BVerfGK	*Kammerentscheidungen des Bundesverfassungsgerichts* (Chamber Decisions of the BVerfG)
BVerwG	Bundesverwaltungsgericht (Federal Administrative Court, Germany)
CassP	*Cassazione Penale* (journal, Italy)
CATS	Comité de l'article trente-six du traité UE (Committee of Art. 36 TEU)
CC	Criminal Code
CCP	Code of Criminal Procedure
CDDH	Steering Committee for Human Rights (CoE)
CDDH-UE	CDDH Informal Working Group on the Accession of the EU to the ECHR
CES	Council of Europe Statute

cf.	confer
CFREU	Charter of the Fundamental Rights of the European Union
CFSP	Common Foreign and Security Policy
Ch.	Chapter
CHR	(UN) Commission on Human Rights
CISA	Convention implementing the Schengen Agreement of 14 June 1985 (Schengen II)
cit.	cited
CJEU	Court of Justice of the EU
CJIA	Criminal Justice and Immigration Act 2008 (UK)
CJICL	*Cambridge Journal of International and Comparative Law* (journal, UK)
CLF	*Criminal Law Forum* (journal, international)
CLJ	*Cambridge Law Journal* (journal, UK)
CLP	*Current Legal Problems* (journal, UK)
CLR	*Criminal Law Review* (journal, UK)
CMLR	*Common Market Law Review*
CoE	Council of Europe
col.	column
Conc.	concurring
CP	Code Pénal, Código Penal, Codice Penale (Criminal Code)
CPC	*Cuadernos de Política Criminal* (journal, Spain)
CPP	Code de Procedure Pénal, Código de Procedimiento Penal, Codice di Procedura Penale (Code of Criminal Procedure)
CPS	Crown Prosecution Service
CR	*Computer und Recht* (journal, Germany)
CrAppRep	*Criminal Appeal Reports* (journal, UK)
CrimLSC	*Crime, Law & Social Change* (journal, international)
CYELS	*Cambridge Yearbook of European Legal Studies*
DAR	*Deutsches Autorecht* (journal, Germany)
DenningLJ	*Denning Law Journal* (journal, USA)
DÖV	*Die Öffentliche Verwaltung* (journal, Germany)
DPP	*Diritto Penale e Processo* (journal, Italy)
DRiB	Deutscher Richterbund (German Judges Association)
DRiZ	*Deutsche Richterzeitung* (journal, Germany)
DuD	*Datenschutz und Datensicherheit* (journal, Germany)
DVBl.	*Deutsches Verwaltungsblatt* (journal, Germany)
E. & P.	*International Journal of Evidence and Proof*
EAEC	European Atomic Energy Community
EAW	European Arrest Warrant
EC	European Council/European Community/Communities
ECB	European Central Bank

ECBA	European Criminal Bar Association
ECHR	European Convention on Human Rights
ECJ	European Court of Justice (EU) (now CJEU)/Encyclopedia of Crime and Justice
ECPI	European Criminal Policy Initiative
ECRIS	European Criminal Records Information System
ECSC	European Coal and Steel Community
ECTC	European Counter Terrorism Center
ECtHR	European Court of Human Rights
ed.	editor
EDC	European Defence Community
edn	edition
eds.	editors
EDU	European Drug Unit
EEC	European Economic Community
EEO	European Enforcement Order (EU)
EES	Entry–Exit System
EEW	European Evidence Warrant (EU)
EFTA	European Free Trade Association
EGStGB	Einführungsgesetz zum Strafgesetzbuch (Introductory Act to the Criminal Code, Germany)
EGV	Vertrag zur Gründung der Europäischen Gemeinschaften (Treaty of Rome/Treaty Establishing the European Economic Community)
EHRLR	*European Human Rights Law Review*
EIB	European Investment Bank
EIO	European Investigation Order
EJCCLCJ	*European Journal of Crime, Criminal Law and Criminal Justice*
EJIL	*European Journal of International Law*
EJN	European Judicial Network
ELR	*European Law Reporter*
EMRK	Europäische Menschenrechtskonvention (ECHR)
EP	European Parliament
EPC	Estudios Penales y Criminológicos/European Political Community
EPPO	European Public Prosecutor's Office
ERA Forum	*Europäische Rechtsakademie Forum/Journal of the Academy of European Law*
ESO	European Supervision Order
esp.	especially
et al.	*et alii* ('and others')

ETA	Euskadi Ta Askatasuna (Basque Fatherland and Liberty: basque separatists)
etc.	et cetera
ETS	European Treaties Series
EU	European Union
EuCExt	European Convention on Extradition (CoE)
EuCLR	*European Criminal Law Review*
EuCMACM	European Convention on Mutual Assistance in Criminal Matters (CoE)
EuConst	*European Constitutional Law Review*
eucrim	European Criminal Law Associations' Forum
EuCrL	European Criminal Law
EuGHG	EuGH-Gesetz (German Act on the CJEU)
EuGRZ	*Europäische Grundrechte-Zeitschrift* (journal, Germany)
EU-JZG	(öster.) Bundesgesetz über die justizielle Zusammenarbeit in Strafsachen mit den Mitgliedsstaaten der EU (Austrian Federal Act on judicial co-operation with EU-member states in criminal matters)
EuLJ	*European Law Journal*
EuLRev	*European Law Review*
EUMAC	EU Mutual Assistance Convention
EuPubL	*European Public Law*
EuR	*Europarecht* (journal, Germany)
EURATOM	European Atomic Energy Community
EuR-Bei	*Europarecht-Beilage* (journal, Germany)
EurJCrimPolicyRes	*European Journal on Criminal Policy and Research*
Eurogendfor	European Gendarmerie Force
Europol	European Police Office
EUV	Vertrag über die Europäische Union (European Union Treaty)
EuZW	*Europäische Zeitschrift für Wirtschaftsrecht* (journal, Germany)
EWCA	England and Wales Court of Appeal
EWG	Europäische Wirtschaftsgemeinschaft (European Economic Community)
EWS	*Europäisches Wirtschafts- und Steuerrecht* (journal, Germany)
f.	and the following page/paragraph
FAZ	*Frankfurter Allgemeine Zeitung* (journal, Germany)
FD	Framework Decision (EU)
ff.	and following pages/paragraphs
FG	Festgabe (Festschrift/liber amicorum)/Finanzgericht (Court for Fiscal Offences, Germany)

FIC	Food Information for Consumers (EU Regulation)
FRG	Federal Republic of Germany
FRA	EU Agency for Fundamental Rights
FS	Festschrift (liber amicorum)
GA	General Assembly (UN-Generalversammlung)
GA	*Goltdammer's Archiv für Strafrecht* (journal, Germany)
GASP	Gemeinsame Außen- und Sicherheitspolitik (Common Foreign and Security Policy)
GC	Grand Chamber (CJEU)
GDR	German Democratic Republic
GG	Grundgesetz (Basic Law of the Federal Republic of Germany)
GLJ	*German Law Journal*
GoJIL	*Goettingen Journal of International Law* (journal, Germany)
GRCh	Europäische Grundrechtecharta (Charter of Fundamental Rights of the European Union)
GRECO	Groupe d'États contra la Corruption (CoE)
GS	Gedächtnisschrift (Memorial Publication)
GVG	Gerichtsverfassungsgesetz (Courts Organisational Act, Germany)
HRA	Human Rights Act 1998 (UK)
HRLR	*Human Rights Law Review* (journal, UK)
HRR	*Human Rights Review*
HRRS	*Höchstrichterliche Rechtsprechung Strafrecht* (journal, Germany)
HRW	Human Rights Watch
HumFoR	*Humboldt Forum Recht* (journal, Germany)
IACtHR	Inter-American Court of Human Rights
ICC	International Criminal Court
ICCPR	International Covenant on Civil and Political Rights
ICL	International Criminal Law
ICLQ	*International and Comparative Law Quarterly*
ICLR	*International Criminal Law Review*
id.	*idem* (Lat.: the same)
IJConstL	*International Journal of Constitutional Law*
IJEP	*International Journal of Evidence and Proof*
IJHR	*International Journal of Human Rights*
incl.	including
IntVG	Integrationsverantwortungsgesetz (Implementation Lisbon Treaty in Germany)
IPbpR	Internationaler Pakt über bürgerliche und politische Rechte (ICCPR)
IRA	Irish Republican Army

IRG	Gesetz über die internationale Rechtshilfe in Strafsachen (Act on International Legal Assistance in Criminal Matters, Germany)
IRSG	(Schweizerisches) Bundesgesetz über internationale Rechtshilfe in Strafsachen (Act on International Legal Assistance in Criminal Matters, Switzerland)
ItYIL	*Italian Yearbook of International Law*
JA	*Juristische Arbeitsblätter* (journal, Germany)
JCL	*Journal of Criminal Law* (international)
JCP	*Juris-Classeur Périodique* (journal, France)
JECL	*Journal of European Criminal Law*
JICJ	*Journal of International Criminal Justice* (international)
JIT(s)	joint investigation team(s)
JR	*Juristische Rundschau* (journal, Germany)
JSB	Joint Supervisory Body (Europol)
JSt	*Journal für Strafrecht* (journal, Austria)
Judg.	Judg(e)ment
Jura	*Jurisitsche Ausbildung* (journal, Germany)
JuS	*Juristische Schulung* (journal, Germany)
JZ	*Juristenzeitung* (journal, Germany)
KG	Kammergericht (Higher Regional Court of Berlin)
KJ	*Kritische Justiz* (journal, Germany)
KritV	*Kritische Vierteljahresschrift für Gesetzgebung und Rechtswissenschaft* (journal, Germany)
La Ley	*La Ley – Revista Juridica Española de Doctrina, Jurisprudencia y Bibliografia* (journal, Spain)
LEC	Ley de Enjuiciamiento Criminal (Spanish CCP)
LG	Landgericht (District Court, Germany)
LJIL	*Leiden Journal of International Law* (Netherlands)
LKA	Landeskriminalamt (State Police Office [of the Land], Germany)
LMBG	Lebensmittel- und Bedarfsgegenständegesetz (Foodstuffs and Commodities Act, Germany)
LP	*Legislazione Penale* (Italy)
LuftSiG	Gesetz zur Neuregelung der Luftsicherheitsaufgaben (Aviation Security Act, Germany)
MaastJECompL	*Maastricht Journal of European and Comparative Law* (journal, Netherlands)
MichJIL	*Michigan Journal of International Law* (journal, USA)
mn.	margin number

MOG	Gesetz zur Durchführung der gemeinsamen Marktorganisationen und der Direktzahlungen (Common Market Organisations Implementation Act, Germany)
MR-Int	*Medien und Recht International* (journal, Germany)
MS	Member State(s)
n./nn.	note/notes
NATO	North Atlantic Treaty Organisation
NAW	Nordic Arrest Warrant
NCLR	*New Criminal Law Review* (journal, USA)
NGO(s)	non-governmental organisation(s)
NJ	*Neue Justiz* (journal, Germany)
NJECL	*New Journal of European Criminal Law*
NJIL	*Nordic Journal of International Law* (international)
NJW	*Neue Juristische Wochenschrift* (journal, Germany)
NK	*Neue Kriminalpolitik* (journal, Germany)
NLJ	*New Law Journal* (journal, UK)
no/nos	number/numbers
Nr.	Nummer (number)
NStZ	*Neue Zeitschrift für Strafrecht* (journal, Germany)
NStZ-RR	*Neue Zeitschrift für Strafrecht, Rechtsprechungs-Report* (journal, Germany)
NVwZ	*Neue Zeitschrift für Verwaltungsrecht* (journal, Germany)
NVwZ-RR	*Neue Zeitschrift für Verwaltungsrecht, Rechtsprechungs-Report* (journal, Germany)
NZV	*Neue Zeitschrift für Verkehrsrecht* (journal, Germany)
NZWist	*Neue Zeitschrift für Wirtschafts-, Steuer- und Unternehmensstrafrecht* (journal, Germany)
OJEC	*Official Journal of the European Communities*
OJEU	*Official Journal of the European Union*
ÖJZ	*Österreichische Juristen-Zeitung* (journal, Austria)
OLAF	L'Office européen de lutte anti-fraude (Anti-Fraud Office, EU)
OLG	Oberlandesgericht (Higher Regional Court, Germany and Austria)
OLGSt	*Entscheidungen der Oberlandesgerichte zum Straf- und Strafverfahrensrecht* (Decisions of the Higher Regional Courts in Criminal Matters)
östBMJ	Österreichisches Bundesministerium für Justiz (Austrian Federal Ministry of Justice)
OstEuR	*Osteuropa-Recht* (journal, Germany)
östOGH	Oberster Gerichtshof der Republik Österreich (Austrian Supreme Court of Justice)
p./pp.	page/pages

para(s).	paragraph(s)
PC	Penal Code
PIF	Protection des Intérêts Financiers (Protection of the EC Financial Interests)
PJCCM	Police and Judicial Co-operation in Criminal Matters
PJZ(S)	Polizeiliche und Justizielle Zusammenarbeit (in Strafsachen) (PJCCM)
PNR	Passenger Name Records
PVS	*Politische Vierteljahresschrift* (journal, Germany)
PYIL	*Polish Yearbook of International Law*
RabelsZ	*(Rabels) Zeitschrift für ausländisches und internationales Privatrecht* (journal, Germany)
RbEuHb	Rahmenbeschluss über den Europäischen Haftbefehl (FD European Arrest Warrant)
RC ECtHR	Rules of Court ECtHR
RDCE	*Revisa de Derecho Communitario Europeo* (journal, Spain)
RDFUG	*Revista de la Facultad de Derecho de la Universidad de Granada* (journal, Spain)
RDP	*Revista de Derecho Penal* (journal, Spain)
RDPP	*Revista de Derecho y Proceso Penal* (journal, Spain)
ReDCE	*Revista de Derecho Constitucional Europeo* (journal, Spain)
REDF	*Revista Europea de Derechos Fundamentales* (journal, Spain)
Reg.	Register
Regulations	ICC, Regulations of the Court
Res.	Resolution
Rev.	Revision
RevDPC	*Revue de Droit Pénal et de Criminologie* (journal, France)
RGDP	*Revista General de Derecho Procesal* (journal, Spain)
RIDP	*Revue International de Droit Pénal* (journal, France)
RIDPP	*Rivista Italiana di Diritto e Procedura Penale* (journal, Italy)
RitsumLR	*Ritsumeikan Law Review* (journal, Japan)
Rl	Richtlinie (Directive)
RMC	*Revue du Marché Commun* (journal, France)
RP	*Revista Penal* (journal, Spain)
RP CJEU	Rules of Procedure, Court of Justice of the EU
RPDP	*Revue Pénitentiaire et de Droit Pénal* (journal, France)
RSC	*Revue de science criminelle et de droit pénal comparé* (journal, France)
RW	*Rechtswissenschaft (Zeitschrift für rechtswissenschaftliche Forschung)* (journal, Germany)
SBC	Schengen Borders Code

SDÜ	Schengener Durchführungsübereinkommen (CISA/Schengen II)
Sect.	Section
SED	Sozialistische Einheitspartei Deutschlands (Socialist Unity Party of Germany)
SIRENE	Supplementary Information Request at the National Entry
SIS	Schengen Information System
StatuteLR	*Statute Law Review*
StGB	Strafgesetzbuch (Criminal Code, Germany)
StPO	Strafprozessordnung (Code of Criminal Procedure, Germany)
StraFo	*Strafverteidiger Forum* (journal, Germany)
StrÄndG	Strafrechtsänderungsgesetz (Criminal Law Amendment Act, Germany)
StV	*Strafverteidiger* (journal, Germany)
StVollzG	Strafvollzugsgesetz (Law on the Execution of Sentences, Germany)
SVR	*Straßenverkehrsrecht* (journal, Germany)
SJZ	*Süddeutsche Juristen-Zeitung* (journal, Germany)
SZ	*Süddeutsche Zeitung* (journal, Germany)
TCE	Treaty Establishing a Constitution for Europe
TEC	Treaty Establishing the European Community
TEEC	Treaty of the European Economic Community
TEU	Treaty of the European Union
TFEU	Treaty on the Functioning of the European Union
TransferC	Convention on the Transfer of Sentenced Persons (CoE)
UCLAF	Unité de coordination de la lutte anti-fraude (European Anti-Fraud Unit)
UE	Unión Europea (European Union)
UK	United Kingdom
UKConstLBlog	*UK Constitutional Law Blog*
UKHL	United Kingdom House of Lords
ULR	*Utrecht Law Review* (journal, Netherlands)
UN	United Nations
UNHRC	Human Rights Committee (UN)
UNO	United Nations Organisation
UNTS	United Nations Treaty Series
US	United States (of America)
USA	United States of America
UWG	Gesetz gegen den unlauteren Wettbewerb (Law against Unfair Competition, Germany)
v.	versus
VAT	value added tax

VBlBW	*Verwaltungsblätter für Baden-Württemberg* (journal, Germany)
VCLT	Vienna Convention on the Law of Treaties
VerfV	Vertrag über eine Verfassung für Europa (Treaty Establishing a Constitution for Europe)
VerwArch	*Verwaltungsarchiv* (journal, Germany)
Vol.	volume
VRR	*VerkehrsRechtsReport* (journal, Germany)
VuR	*Verbraucher und Recht* (journal, Germany)
VwGO	Verwaltungsgerichtsordnung (German Code of Administrative Proceedings, Germany)
wistra	*Zeitschrift für Wirtschafts- und Steuerstrafrecht* (journal, Germany)
WpHG	Wertpapierhandelsgesetz (Securities Trading Act, Germany)
WUR	*Wirtschaft und Recht* (journal, Germany)
ZaöRV	*Zeitschrift für ausländisches öffentliches Recht und Völkerrecht* (journal, Germany)
ZAP	*Zeitschrift für die Anwaltspraxis* (journal, Germany)
ZAR	*Zentrum für Angewandte Rechtswissenschaft* (journal, Germany)
ZEuS	*Zeitschrift für europarechtliche Studien* (journal, Germany)
ZfRV	*Zeitschrift für Rechtsvergleichung* (journal, Germany)
ZfW	*Zeitschrift für Wasserrecht* (journal, Germany)
ZfZ	*Zeitschrift für Zölle und Verbrauchsteuern* (journal, Germany)
ZIS	*Zeitschrift für internationale Strafrechtsdogmatik* (journal, Germany)
ZJS	*Zeitschrift für das Juristische Studium* (journal, Germany)
ZLR	*Zeitschrift für das gesamte Lebensmittelrecht* (journal, Germany)
ZP	Zusatzprotokoll (Additional Protocol)
ZP VII	Protokoll Nr. 7 zur Konvention zum Schutze der Menschenrechte und Grundfreiheiten (Additional Protocol No 7 on the Convention for the Protection of Human Rights and Fundamental Freedoms)
ZRP	*Zeitschrift für Rechtspolitik* (journal, Germany)
ZStrR	*Schweizerische Zeitschrift für Strafrecht* (journal, Switzerland)
ZStW	*Zeitschrift für die gesamte Strafrechtswissenschaft* (journal, Germany)
ZUM	*Zeitschrift für Urheber- und Medienrecht* (journal, Germany)
ZVglRWiss	*Zeitschrift für vergleichende Rechtswissenschaft* (journal, Germany)

TABLE OF CASES

1

Foundations

History, Concept and Subject of European Criminal Law

A. The European Integration Process: From the Europe of the Six to the Lisbon Treaty

I. From the Schuman Plan (1950) to Nice (2001)

1 Following the experiences of the Second World War and the growing exacerbation of the conflict between East and West, efforts to establish greater co-operation between the (Western) European States took on a more concrete form in 1945.[1] The general opinion was that a successful European unification process was the prerequisite for a new, independent role of (Western) Europe in world politics and an improvement of economic and social conditions.[2] As early as 1946, Winston Churchill referred to 'a kind of *United States of Europe*' in his famous 'Zurich speech'.[3] Already, the **Council of Europe** had been founded on 5 May 1949.[4] Today, the Council has forty-seven Member States; its most important major agreement probably is the European Convention for the Protection of Human Rights and Fundamental Freedoms (ECHR) of 1950, to be looked at more closely in Chapter 2. Admittedly, as an association of sovereign States, the Council of Europe is only able to advance the process of integration very slowly – for the most part through international law framework agreements, the implementation of which is Member States' responsibility. Thus, the Council cannot itself become a 'motor of integration'.

2 For this reason, a more efficient mechanism of integration was called for, and in 1950 the French foreign minister Robert Schuman suggested uniting the German and French coal and steel industries under a 'common High Authority'. This so-called **Schuman Plan** – which in fact was drafted by Jean Monnet, then a French civil servant – was intended as a first step towards a future European federation based not only on economic integration, but also upon common security interests: the aim was to prevent another war between the major European powers of France and Germany by way of tight economic co-operation in the fields of coal and steel.[5] While the Plan was well received in France, Germany, Italy and the Benelux countries (Belgium, Luxembourg, and the Netherlands),[6] the United Kingdom openly opposed it since it undermined its (alleged) leadership role in Europe.[7] Accordingly, on 18 April 1951 the said countries – without the UK – founded the **European Coal and Steel Community** (ECSC).[8] For the time being, no more was possible. The European Political Community (EPC) and the European Defence Community (EDC), **projects in the field of security policy** going beyond economic policy that would have included the creation of integrated French–German troops, never came about.[9] The French 'sacrifice of sovereignty' proved too great an obstacle to the EDC; in 1954, the French National Assembly refused to ratify the treaty, even though it had already been concluded.[10]

3 Even though efforts for integration in the field of security had thus failed for the time being, the Messina Conference (1955) of foreign ministers initiated by the Benelux States tasked a committee chaired by Belgian foreign minister *Paul-Henri Spaak* with exploring the options for further economic integration.[11] The **Spaak Report** of 1956 suggested complete economic integration, alongside special regulations for the field of nuclear power, which at that time was still seen as a technology of the future.[12] The theory behind this return to the economic sector was that a sectoral integration based upon 'inherent necessity' would set in motion further integration, culminating in the final stage of a European federal state ('spill-over effect').[13] On 25 March 1957, the recommendations of the *Spaak* Report were implemented in the **'Treaties of Rome'**, in which the six founding members of the ECSC agreed to establish the **European Economic Community** (EEC) and the **European Atomic Energy Community** (Euratom).[14]

4 During the 1960s, the process of further political integration was prevented in particular by France under *Charles de Gaulle*, who vetoed British membership in 1963,[15] and whose idea of a *Europe des Patries* ('Europe of Fatherlands') remained focused upon nation states and intergovernmental co-operation[16] – in stark contrast to the integrationist approach pursued by the European Court of Justice (ECJ) – today called Court of Justice of the European Union (CJEU)[17] – since the groundbreaking *Van Gend en Loos* judgment.[18] Only after *De Gaulle's* resignation in 1969 was the 1970 Hague Summit of the EEC Member States' heads of government able to define the realisation of a **European Union**

as a goal for the 1980s.[19] In 1973, the 'Europe of 6' became the 'Europe of 9' following the **'Northern enlargement'**, with Great Britain, Denmark and Ireland joining the EEC.[20] The **'Southern enlargement'** of the 1980s to include Greece (1981), Spain and Portugal (1986) presented a greater challenge to the power of economic integration. However, the admission of these countries also needs to be seen within the context of the political transition process from dictatorship to democracy taking place there, a process that was to be facilitated by their integration into Europe.[21] This shows that enlargement has always been more than just geographic expansion and represented certain policy choices of the Union.[22] In 1995, Austria, Sweden and Finland joined the Union, which thus grew to **15 Members.**[23]

5 In the 1986 **'Single European Act'**, the Member States agreed upon reforms to the Communities, including in particular an expansion of the qualified majority for Council decisions[24] and a strengthening of the position of the European Parliament through the process of co-operation.[25] Furthermore, Members committed themselves to the concept of the internal market.[26] With the **Maastricht Treaty** of 7 February 1992, the EEC was finally renamed the European Community[27] and, more importantly, the **European Union** (EU) was founded.[28] It was designed not as an international organisation possessing legal personality, but as an **association of States.**[29] At this point in time, it represented an **umbrella organisation**, albeit with supranational ambitions,[30] spanning the European Communities (EC, ECSC, EAEC) as a – fundamental – 'first pillar', as well as co-operation in the areas of foreign and security policy (CFSP)[31] and police and justice in criminal matters (PJCCM) as the 'second and third pillars'.[32] This so-called **three-pillar structure** or model is shown in figure 1.

The key difference between the first and the second/third 'pillars' is that only within the former was the EC as a truly supranational organisation, thanks to the transferral of sovereign rights, able to exercise sovereign competencies over the Member States and their citizens. To this extent, one could speak of a 'communitisation' (*communautarisation, Vergemeinschaftung*). By contrast, the second and third pillars operated through intergovernmental co-operation between the Member States, responsible for implementing the decisions taken in these areas.[33] The primary Community law of the TEC took, as a matter of principle, precedence over the Union law of the TEU, since no TEU provisions shall affect the Treaties establishing the European Communities, apart from those necessary for the amendment of the TEEC (in order to

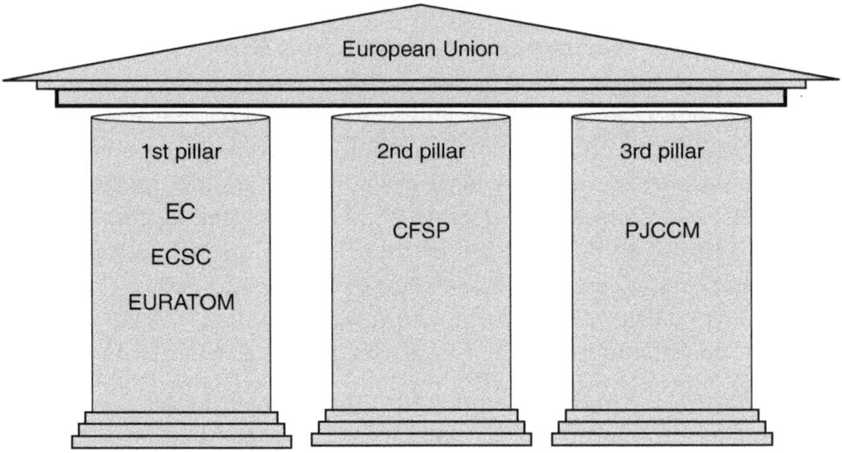

Figure 1 The (former) three-pillar structure

establish the EC) and for the amendment of the Treaties establishing the ECSC and the EAEC.[34] In other regards, however, the pillar structure proved permeable, as is evident in particular from the fact that the institutions of the European Communities (especially the Council and the Commission) were included in the co-operation taking place in the context of CFSP and PJCCM.[35]

6 The revision of the Maastricht Treaty by the **Treaty of Amsterdam** of 2 October 1997 led to a certain strengthening of the parliament's role by expanding the co-decision procedure,[36] and – of particular interest in our present context – transferred the elements of the former (intergovernmental) **co-operation on justice and home affairs** (CJHA) that were *not* related to police and judicial co-operation from the third to the first 'pillar' and thus into EC jurisdiction.[37] By contrast, police and judicial co-operation in criminal matters (PJCCM) remained in the third pillar and thus retained its character as intergovernmental co-operation – for example within the framework of Europol.[38] The so-called **Schengen *acquis***[39] was transferred into the EU framework by a specific Protocol to the Amsterdam Treaty.[40] However, three countries negotiated special regimes: The *UK and Ireland* opted out of the policies regarding visas, asylum, immigration and other matters related to the free movement of persons (Title IV of Part Three TEC),[41] including with regard to the measures necessary to progressively establish the internal market pursuant to Art. 14 TEC.[42] As to the Schengen *acquis* – regardless of its legal base (Title IV [first pillar] or Title VI [PJCCM, third pillar] – the UK and Ireland reserved the right to decide on a case-by-case basis if they wanted to participate in certain measures.[43] *Denmark* also opted out of Title IV of Part Three TEC,[44] but it had no explicit queries regarding the PJCCM given that it remained in the – intergovernmental – third pillar.[45] The **jurisdiction of the ECJ** was expanded to the second and third pillar (Art. 46 TEU);[46] yet the latter was dependent on an explicit acceptance of the Member States, which several, including Denmark, the UK and Ireland, did not submit.[47]

7 Against the backdrop of the Union's above-mentioned expansion,[48] the summit of December 2000 was followed by the **Treaty of Nice** in February 2001.[49] With a view to ensuring that the expanded Union was able to work effectively, a revision of the weighting of votes in the Council (from 1 November 2004[50]) and a certain expansion of the area of qualified majority votes were agreed upon, stipulating a parity of votes between the four large Member States (Germany, France, the United Kingdom and Italy).[51] Furthermore, Art. 31(2) TEU[52] created a basis for a European co-ordination unit of national prosecuting authorities with its headquarters in Brussels (**Eurojust**).[53]

8 Following the European Union's 2004 enlargement in the East and the Mediterranean to include ten further Eastern European states (Estonia, Latvia, Lithuania, Poland, Hungary, the Czech Republic, Slovakia, Slovenia) and Mediterranean states (Malta, Cyprus),[54] the accession of Bulgaria and Romania in 2007 and the accession of Croatia in 2013, the EU has now expanded to twenty-eight States and thus includes **thirty criminal justice systems.**[55] With the Brexit vote in the UK on 23 June 2016 the Union will, however, lose an important member,[56] although the procedure under Art. 50 TEU may be delayed[57] and a possible break-up of the UK may weaken the impact on the Union's composition.[58] As a result of the declarations of Bratislava and Rome, the White Paper on the Future of Europe of 1 March 2017 presents five different scenarios for the EU's political development by 2025 following Brexit.[59]

II. The Failed Constitution and the Lisbon Treaty (2007)

1. The Post-Lisbon EU and Criminal Law

9 As early as 2003, the European Convention presented the draft of a treaty establishing a **Constitution for Europe** (TCE).[60] Following negative referendum results in France and the Netherlands in the summer of 2005, the ratification process was, however, **suspended** and instead it was decided to embark upon **treaty reform** only.[61] Thus the ambitious plan to give Europe a constitution, which was pursued with considerable artificial (and expensive) pathos, has been consigned to history; 'the reality of Europe has brought this normative hubris back down to earth.'[62] The reform treaty was signed on 13 December 2007 in Lisbon,[63] and was last ratified by the Czech Republic on 13 November 2009, coming into effect on 1 December 2009.[64] Yet several parts, including[65] the extended enforcement powers of the Commission and of the CJEU with regard to pre-Lisbon Acts in the area of PJCCM,[66] were suspended for a transitional period of five years and thus were only activated on 1 December 2014.[67] This so-called **Lisbon Treaty** consists of the reformed **Treaty on European Union** (TEU) and the **Treaty on the Functioning of the European Union** (TFEU).[68] The Union replaces the EC as its legal successor (Art. 1, third subparagraph TEU). Its above-mentioned three-pillar structure has been replaced by *two supranational areas* (formerly EC and Justice and Home Affairs) and one *effectively supranational area* (CFSP).[69]

10 The following changes made by the Lisbon Treaty are of significance for criminal law:[70]

- Dissolution of the previous three-pillar structure and instead creation of a (supranational) **area of freedom, security and justice** (cf. Art. 67 TFEU).[71]
- Application of the **ordinary legislative procedure** to (secondary) legal Acts in the area of criminal law,[72] including qualified majority voting in Council as rule;[73] **directives** replace former framework decisions.[74]
- Standardisation of the **principle of mutual recognition** for criminal law (cf. Art. 82(1) TFEU).[75]
- Explicit competence to **approximate the procedural laws**, including the co-operation laws (Art. 82(1) TFEU),[76] of Member States in the areas of mutual admissibility of evidence, and the rights of individuals as well as victims in criminal proceedings (Art. 82(2) TFEU); further 'minimum rules' may be adopted.[77]
- Explicit competence to **approximate the substantive laws** of Member States by way of minimum rules in the areas of terrorism, trafficking in human beings and sexual exploitation of women and children, illicit drug trafficking, illicit arms trafficking, money laundering, corruption, counterfeiting of means of payment, computer crime and organised

Table 1 *Comparison of important rules pre- and post-Lisbon*

Nice (February 2001)	Lisbon (13 December 2007)
No legal personality of EU	Legal personality of EU (Art. 47 TEU)
European Council chaired by the president of the European Council (head of state/government of the country that has the presidency of the EU Council for 6 months)	European Council chaired by a chairperson ('president') who holds this office for two and a half years and can be re-elected once (Art. 15 TEU)
EP has the right to co-decision only in selected policy areas	The EP's right to co-decision is the rule (ordinary legislative procedure, Art. 289(1), 294 TFEU)[i]
Composition of the EP: Germany has 99 MPs (max.), followed by the UK, France and Italy with 72, Spain and Poland with 50 and Malta with 5 (min.)	Composition of the EP: 750 MPs in total, max. 96 (Germany), min. 6 (Malta); France has 74, the UK and Italy 73, Spain 54 and Poland 51; no fixed ratio of distribution (Art. 14 (2) TEU)
Four legislative procedures: co-decision procedure, assent procedure, consultation procedure, co-operation procedure	Two legislative procedures: ordinary and special legislative procedure (Art. 289(1,2) TFEU)[ii]
Unanimous voting in Council	Qualified majority voting in Council as rule (Art. 16(3)TEU, 294 TFEU)[iii]
Competences divided into exclusive and concurrent competences by CJEU and doctrine. No summarising enumeration	Competences divided into 'exclusive' and 'shared' competences, followed by a summarising enumeration and expansion (Art. 2 ff. TFEU)
There is a 'High Representative for the Common Foreign and Security Policy' who does not belong to the Commission, as well as a member of the Commission responsible for foreign policy	There is a 'High Representative of the Union for Foreign Affairs and Security Policy', who at the same time also presides over the Foreign Affairs Council and is a Vice-President of the Commission (Art. 18 TEU).
CFREU: not legally binding	CFREU: legally binding (Art. 6 TEU)
Differences between the jurisdiction of the CJEU and the ECtHR	EU may accede to the ECHR (Art. 6(2) TEU in conjunction with Prot. 14 ECHR)
Withdrawal from the EU not envisaged	Withdrawal from the EU possible (Art. 50 TEU)

Table 1 (*cont.*)

Nice (February 2001)	Lisbon (13 December 2007)
No monitoring by national parliaments	Subsidiarity monitoring (Art. 5(3) third sentence TEU) through opinions during the legislative procedure (Parliament and Subsidiarity Protocol)[iv]

i Kaiafa-Gbandi, *EuCLR*, 1 (2011), 10, regards this as an important measure for the safeguarding of fundamental rights.

ii For more information on this development, with particular reference to criminal law, cf. Meyer, *Strafrechtsgenese* (2012), pp. 327 ff.

iii On the impact of this and other changes on the way negotiations on draft legislation are carried out, cf. Nowell-Smith, *NJECL*, 3 (2012), 381 ff. (arguing that the new rules have made secondary acts longer and more detailed since all parties – i.e., Commission, Council and EP – are interested to clarify the relevant obligations); also de Busser, *ERA Forum*, 16 (2015), 280.

iv Art. 5(3) TEU in conjunction with the Subsidiarity Protocol (Lisbon Treaty, Protocol (No 2) on the Application of the Principles of Subsidiarity and Proportionality, OJ C 326 of 26 October 2012, 206–9) establishes an early warning system (preventive *ex ante* monitoring, including by national parliaments; on their enhanced role see also Art. 12 TEU and Lisbon Treaty, Protocol (No 1) on the Role of National Parliaments in the EU, OJ C 326 of 26 October 2012, 203–5): first of all, the Commission forwards draft legislative acts to the national parliaments (Art. 4 Subsidiarity Protocol), who may then within eight weeks present a reasoned opinion on why they believe that the draft in question does not comply with the principle of subsidiarity (Art. 6 Subsidiarity Protocol). If this so-called subsidiarity objection ('yellow card'; on another 'orange card' mechanism, cf. Art. 7(3) Subsidiarity Protocol) is not successful, then the parliaments may take legal action on grounds of infringement of the principle of subsidiarity with the ECJ (Art. 8 Subsidiarity Protocol – repressive *ex post* monitoring). In **Germany**, this right is exercised by the respective Committee on European Matters of the Bundestag or the Bundesrat. It works essentially like this in all EU MS: for example, in **France** this control is exercised by the Commission des affaires européennes of the Assemblée nationale and by the Sénat (cf. www2.assemblee-nationale.fr/14/autres-commissions/commission-des-affaires-europeennes, last accessed 27 January 2018 and Leblois-Happe, 'Le parquet européen', in Roux-Demare, *L'européanisation de la justice pénale* (2016), 132); in **Italy** by the Camera and Senato applying different procedures (see especially regarding the former Art. 8

Table 1 (*cont.*)

of Law 234 of 24 December 2012 ('Norme generali sulla partecipazione dell'Italia alla formazione e all'attuazione della normativa e delle politiche dell' Unione europea', available at www.politicheeuropee.it/normativa/18408/legge-24-dicembre-2012-n-234, last accessed 27 January 2018)); in **Spain** by the Comisión Mixta para la Unión Europea (it is called 'mixed' because it is composed of members of the Camara de Diputados and the Senat), cf. criticism in Matía Portilla, *ReDCE*, 9 (2012), 95 ff.; in **Sweden** by the committee in charge of the respective matter; if its evaluation is negative, the matter is sent to the plenary (Ch. 9 sect. 20 and Ch. 10 sect. 3 of the Riksdagsordning); in the **UK** by the European Scrutiny Committee of the House of Commons (www.parliament.uk/business/committees/committees-a-z/commons-select/european-scrutiny-committee, last accessed 27 January 2018) and the EU Select Committee of the House of Lords (www.parliament.uk/business/committees/committees-a-z/lords-select/eu-select-committee, last accessed 21 November 2017)); for **Poland** see Pudło, in *Roczniki Administracji i Prawa: Teoria i Praktyka*, 13 (2013), 27 ff.; for **Portugal** see Law 43/2006 as amended by Law 21/2012 of 17 May 2012, available in English at http://www.parliament.uk/business/committees/committees-a-z/lords-select/eu-select-committee-/, last accessed 27 January 2018). Furthermore, an infringement of the principle of subsidiarity may also be objected to as part of a nullity suit, during treaty infringement proceedings or during a preliminary ruling procedure. However, the exact extent of judicial review is debatable. The majority of literature appears to assume that the principle of subsidiarity is fully justiciable, while other opinions see the principle more as a political guideline, so that at most compliance with the obligation to state reasons can be monitored, but not content-related questions themselves; cf. Calliess, in Calliess and Ruffert, *Verfassung der EU*, i (2006), Art. 12 AEUV mn. 10 ff.; cf. also Cygan, *ERA Forum*, 12 (2012), 517 ff.; Kiiver, *ERA Forum*, 12 (2012), 535 ff.; Simon, *NJECL*, 3 (2012), 252–3; Geiger, *Auswirkungen europäischer Strafrechtsharmonisierung* (2012), pp. 49 ff.; Asp, *Substantive Criminal Law Competence* (2012), pp. 183 ff.; Turner, *AmJCompL*, 60 (2012), 580 (calling the parliamentary review a 'welcome innovation'); Esser, *Europäisches und Internationales Strafrecht* (2018), §2 mn. 152 ff.; Mitsilegas, *EU Criminal Law after Lisbon* (2016), pp. 40–1 (national parliaments cannot block); on the other ways in which national parliaments can participate, cf. Meyer, *Strafrechtsgenese* (2012), pp. 319–20, 352 ff.

crime (Art. 83(1) TFEU);[78] this security-driven criminalisation approach[79] may also be expanded.[80]

- Standardisation of an **ancillary competence** that authorises the harmonisation of criminal law if this is 'essential to ensure the effective implementation of a Union policy' in a policy area that has already been harmonised (Art. 83(2) TFEU);[81] this instrumental or functional approach[82] has entailed constitutional concerns, as we will see in a moment.

- Competence to legislate **supranational criminal law** on the EU level, particularly to *protect the financial interests* of the Union (Art. 325 TFEU).[83]
- Introduction of an '**emergency brake procedure**' (Art. 82(3), 83(3) TFEU) – to balance the expanded competences in the area of criminal law[84] – in cases where 'fundamental aspects' of national criminal justice systems are affected thereby, showing deference to national diversity.[85]
- The establishment of a **European Public Prosecutor's Office (EPPO)** together with the creation of a **supranational European criminal procedural law** for this new institution (Art. 86(1,3) TFEU).[86]
- Last, but not least, a strengthening of **individual rights** ('promise of rights')[87] by the explicit recognition of the CFREU (Art. 6 TEU) and a harmonisation competence ('minimum rules') with regard to procedural rights (Art. 82(2)(b) TFEU), which in fact led to the adoption of a series of rights directives as part of the Stockholm programme.[88]

2. Opt-Outs and Constitutional Concerns

11 The *implementation of the Lisbon Treaty* entailed some **conflicts with the national (constitutional) order** of some Member States. As to the PJCCM, **Denmark** negotiated a separate Protocol to the Treaties,[89] pursuant to which it fully abstained from the future Area of Freedom, Security and Justice,[90] unless it decides to opt back in to everything, in which case it will 'apply *in full* all relevant measures then in force taken'.[91] The **UK and Ireland** also negotiated a separate *Protocol (21)*,[92] which likewise gave them the right to fully abstain from any future measures in the area of Freedom, Security and Justice, but also allowed them, unlike Denmark, to *selectively* opt in regarding individual measures.[93] This, in fact, amounts to a reintroduction of the veto, abolished by the Lisbon qualified majority voting, through the back door. In addition, the UK[94] obtained through *Protocol 36* a full *opt-out* option from all (135) police and criminal justice measures adopted under the pre-Lisbon 'third pillar',[95] unless they have been amended ('Lisbonised').[96] As to the EPPO, the UK already made clear at the outset that it will not participate unless there is a national referendum in favour ('referendum lock').[97] The UK has then the possibility of a subsequent selective *opt-in*.[98] On 24 July 2013, the UK made use of the opt-out and the 135 Acts ceased to apply to it on 1 December 2014.[99] Nevertheless, the most relevant acts are still applicable to the UK since, on the one hand, the opt-out does not apply to the amended ('Lisbonised') and the new (post-Lisbon) Acts and,[100] on the other hand, the UK opted back in to thirty-five Acts, including some of the most important ones for police and criminal justice co-operation (e.g. EAW, ECRIS, Europol, Eurojust, ESO, Naples II, JITs, Schengen, SIS II, Art. 54 CISA) with the respective jurisdiction of the CJEU.[101] Thus the whole opt-out–opt-in exercise has been rightly criticised as 'a purely paper one' and as 'gesture politics' with practical consequences amounting to 'nil',[102] although, of course, such a selective approach to a supranational legal system like the EU challenges the coherence of the whole system.[103] At any rate, it remains to be seen what consequences Brexit[104] will have on the UK's participation in police and judicial co-operation in criminal matters at the European level.[105]

12 On the constitutional level, the **Constitutional Courts** of several Member States – the Czech Republic,[106] Germany,[107] Latvia,[108] Poland and,[109] with a slightly different take, France[110] – have taken issue with the compatibility of the Lisbon Treaty with their national constitutions. The most detailed treatment has been given by the German Federal Constitutional Court (*Bundesverfassungsgericht*),[111] declaring the Accompanying Act (*Begleitgesetz*)[112] to the Act approving the Lisbon Treaty (*Zustimmungsgesetz*)[113] unconstitutional.[114] It is worthwhile to take a closer look at the Court's arguments since its detailed analysis is, *mutatis mutandis*, also applicable to other Member States with a similar constitutional framework as Germany.

13 The *Bundesverfassungsgericht* used the example of the right to vote set out in Art. 38(1) of the Fundamental Law (Grundgesetz, GG) as equivalent to a fundamental right, which in its turn serves as the basis for the right to *democratic self-determination*, participation in state authority and compliance with the principle of democracy (*Demokratieprinzip*).[115] The Court argues that the said principle is of fundamental significance particularly for criminal law,[116] as this is a *particularly sensitive area* 'for the ability of a constitutional state to democratically shape itself'.[117] The conditions of punishability are 'depend[ent] on cultural processes of previous understanding that are historically grown and also determined by language' and 'can . . . only partially be normatively derived from values and moral premises that are shared Europe-wide'.[118] In a sensitive area of such extraordinary relevance to fundamental rights, harmonisation is only admissible under highly restrictive conditions; above all, 'substantial freedom of action must remain reserved to the Member States here'.[119]

In the Court's view, the EU's considerably expanded criminal competences are only compatible with these constitutional rules if the following *restrictive conditions* are adhered to: first, the rules regarding competence would need to be interpreted strictly, especially with regard to the principle of culpability (*Schuldgrundsatz*).[120] Thus harmonisation in line with Art. 83(1) TFEU requires that the nature and effects of the crimes make it necessary for these to be combated jointly; the political will to harmonise criminal law is not enough on its own.[121] *Ancillary jurisdiction* to assimilate criminal laws in policy areas that have already been harmonised in line with Art. 83(2) TFEU[122] may only be used if it can be *proven* that 'a serious lack of enforcement actually exists and can only be eliminated through the threat of punishment'.[123] In order to preserve the right to democratic self-determination, the Court also makes the dynamic *blanket authorisation* of Art. 83(1) third subparagraph TFEU, which permits additions to the catalogue of serious crimes through a unanimous Council decision,[124] subordinate to the reservation of statutory powers of Art. 23(1) second sentence GG, so that the federal government's representative on the Council[125] is only permitted to vote in favour of an expansion of EU harmonisation competences if this has previously been approved by the Parliament.[126] Furthermore, the government representative in the Council is only allowed to make use of the *emergency brake provision* in Arts. 82(3), 83(3) TFEU[127] if the German Bundestag and, where applicable, the German Bundesrat have instructed him or her to do so.[128]

The *Bundesverfassungsgericht* has reserved its right to review future EU legal Acts with regard to their compatibility with German (!) constitutional law as concerns the *constitutional identity* and *ultra vires action of the EU*.[129] However, the Court tries hard to interpret European legal acts in a way that makes them compatible with the Grundgesetz.[130] In doing so, the Court is not only failing to refer the matter to the CJEU in line with Art. 267 TFEU (CJEU monopoly on the interpretation of all European legal Acts!), but is also relativising its own rules set down in the ruling on the Lisbon Treaty, as will be seen in the next paragraph.[131]

14 The decisions of the constitutional Courts of the Czech Republic, Latvia and Poland largely follow the Bundesverfassungsgericht but ultimately all confirm the 'constitutionality' of the Lisbon Treaty. The *Czech*

Constitutional Court, while voicing similar concerns regarding the possible threat to State sovereignty as a result of a transfer of competences to the EU, found in both judgments that the Lisbon Treaty is in line with the Czech Constitution.[132] In its earlier 2008 Judgment, the Court held that the 'transfer of powers of bodies of the Czech Republic to an international organization under Art. 10a of the Constitution of the Czech Republic (the "Constitution") cannot go so far as to violate the very essence of the republic as a democratic state governed by the rule of law'.[133] This was also confirmed in its 2009 Judgment, holding that

> in a modern democratic state governed by the rule of law, the sovereignty of the state is not an aim in and of itself – that is, in isolation – but is a means for fulfilling the fundamental values on which the construction of a democratic state governed by the rule of law stands ... [and therefore] that the transfer of certain state competences, that arises from the free will of the sovereign, and will continue to be exercised with the sovereign's participation in a manner that is agreed upon in advance and is subject to review, is not a conceptual weakening of sovereignty, but, on the contrary, can lead to strengthening it within the joint actions of an integrated whole.[134]

With regard to the alleged democratic deficit in the EU, the Court held that the functioning of the Union, 'founded on representative democracy' (Art. 10(1) TEU), shall be directed 'at processes both on the European and the domestic level, not only at the European Parliament'.[135]

15 Similarly, the *Latvian* Constitutional Court considered the Lisbon Treaty in conformity with the Latvian Constitution (*Satversme*), since the 'delegation of competencies to the EU and integration of the legal Acts of the European Community' are compatible with the principles of a democratic State and sovereign people pursuant to Arts. 1 and 2 of the Latvian Constitution.[136] This delegation of competencies 'shall be regarded as the use of sovereignty of people for reaching the aims set forth in the EU treaties rather than weakening the sovereignty of people', since the Lisbon Treaty pursues the same 'values and interests enshrined in the Satversme.'[137]

16 The *Polish* Constitutional Tribunal also found that the Lisbon Treaty is consistent with the Polish constitutional order.[138] It focused on the concept of conferral of competences with a view to State sovereignty, arguing that 'incurring international liabilities and managing them do not lead to the loss or limitation of the state's sovereignty, but are its confirmation, and membership in the European structures does not, in fact, constitute a limitation of the state's sovereignty, but is its manifestation.'[139]

17 Last but not least, the French *Conseil Constitutionnel* took a slightly different approach. It held that the provisions of the Treaty which transfer to the EU 'under the "ordinary legislative procedure" *powers inherent in the exercising of national sovereignty* require a revision of the Constitution.'[140] Such provisions are those regarding the fight against terrorism and related activities, border controls, the fight against trafficking in human beings, judicial co-operation on civil and criminal matters[141] and the EPPO.[142] In addition, the Conseil held that constitutional revision would be necessary for provisions concerning the adoption of qualified majority voting under a subsequent European decision;[143] certain aspects of family law, which have cross-border ramifications for ordinary legislative procedure;[144] and the new powers vested in national parliaments with regard to Union law.[145]

B. The Concept of European Criminal Law (Post-Lisbon)

I. Preliminary Remarks

18 What, then, is to be understood by 'European criminal law'? Taken at face value, this term could refer to a genuinely **supranational criminal law**; that is, to provisions by which the citizens of the Union are directly confronted with the sovereign punitive force – the *ius puniendi* – of the Union as immediately applicable criminal law. However, genuine criminal law legislation by the Union is restricted to a few explicitly defined areas – above all, the protection of the Union's financial interests.[146] Only to this extent can we speak of **European criminal law** in a true, supranational sense, and, arguably, of a European criminal law **system** in a narrow sense; that is, a limited subject matter area where the Union itself is the sole creator of criminal law norms (albeit depending on the MS with regard to their enforcement).[147] Otherwise, the designation 'European criminal law' is a kind of **umbrella term** covering 'all those norms and practices of criminal and criminal procedural law' based on the law and activities of the EU (*European law in the narrower sense*) and the Council of Europe (*European law in the wider sense*) and leading (or aiming to lead) to widespread *harmonisation* of national criminal (procedural) law.[148] Thus, while there is no comprehensive, self-contained European criminal law or justice system of its own,[149] there is, indeed, a system of sorts; that is, 'some sort' of **'umbrella-like' system** that 'connects' the specific areas (which we may call 'micro systems', e.g. the harmonised criminal law, the mutual recognition instruments, the human rights system),[150] and which may, on the operational level, be more aptly characterised as a *Verbund* (compound network/aggregate association) of the different entities and organs in charge of the investigation and prosecution of transnational crimes.[151] In fact, the European criminal justice institutions to be analysed in more detail in Chapter 5, especially Europol and Eurojust, play an increasingly important, albeit hidden and intransparent, role in the shaping of European criminal justice policy in practice.[152]

At any rate, no independent, new (supranational) European criminal law is created beyond the Union's (limited) competence in the area of financial crime; rather, as a rule, national criminal law (either existing laws or those yet to be created) is influenced by European law. Strictly speaking, we are dealing with ***Europeanised*** **criminal law**, which is why any comparison with federal legislation such as that of the USA is necessarily flawed.[153] Besides the supranational criminal law just mentioned we can distinguish **three forms of Europeanisation** of criminal law: through the implementation of treaties and other normative guidelines of the Council of Europe,[154] through the principle of mutual recognition,[155] and through forms and techniques of influence that are specific to European law.[156] This normative Europeanisation goes hand in hand with and is complemented by an **institutionalisation** entailing the creation of different European institutions in the area of criminal law, to be dealt with in more detail in Chapter 5. In regard to the legal disciplines affected, European criminal law represents an **intradisciplinary, cross-sectional subject matter**. While its main focus is criminal law and procedure in a comprehensive form, it cannot dispense with foundations in constitutional, (general) European and international law.[157] Table 2 attempts to cover all (relevant) areas of European Criminal Law.

II. Supranational Criminal Law Legislation

1. Foundations

19 The Treaty of Lisbon has made no difference to the **legal starting point**:[158] according to the **principle of conferral**,[159] *every legislative act* of the Union requires authorisation in primary law. This authorisation has to be explicit or at least possible to establish through interpretation (with reasonable certainty). In this regard, Art. 5(2) TEU, replacing the

Table 2 *Concept and meaning of European criminal law*

In a narrower sense (EU)		In a broader sense
(Former) 1st pillar (EC): • Supranational law • Primacy of EC law • Note: Lisbon (Art. 1 TEU) replaces the EC with the EU	**(Former) 2nd and 3rd pillars:** Formerly intergovernmental co-operation → now 'communitised' PJCCM (Arts. 3(2) TEU, 67 ff. TFEU)	**Council of Europe** International organisation that develops conventions for its Member States
'European' and 'Europeanised' criminal law Collective terms for all criminal and criminal procedural laws and practices based upon the law and activities of the European institutions and leading (or aiming to lead) to a more comprehensive harmonisation of national criminal (procedural) laws		
• Reference of primary law to national criminal law (assimilation), e.g. Art. 30 Statute of the CJEU • Reference of national criminal law to Community law • Instruction to harmonise national laws (Art. 94–5 TEEC = 114–15 TFEU) • OLAF **There is no 'real' supranational criminal law!** **(exception: Art. 325 TFEU)**	• Police and judicial co-operation (e.g. Europol) + • Harmonisation through the approximation of substantive criminal law (e.g. concerning terrorism) → now Arts. 82 ff. + 87 ff. TFEU	Particularly important: • European Convention on Human Rights (ECHR), • Interpretation of the ECHR by the ECtHR, • Further criminal law conventions (e.g. 'Cybercrime' Convention)

earlier Art. 5(1) TEEC, envisages that the Union 'shall act only within the limits of the competences conferred upon it by the Member States in the Treaties'. The principles of **subsidiarity** and **proportionality**[160] confirm the fundamental precedence of Member State competence. The principle of subsidiarity represents a legally binding and justiciable rule for the exercise of competences, forcing the Union to review the *necessity* and (higher) *efficiency* of its activities *ex ante* in order to be able to justify them *ex post*.[161] It follows from the principle of proportionality that action taken on the basis of Union law against the Member States – corresponding to the relationship between state and citizen in national constitutional law – can only then appear legitimate if it is a *suitable, necessary* and *appropriate* means to achieving a Union aim;[162] the measures taken by the Union may not go beyond the minimum intervention necessary to achieve the goal in question.[163]

For every legislative act, the Union has to provide detailed justification for its compliance with these principles[164] and inform the national parliaments,[165] so that they can object to any possible violation of the principle of subsidiarity;[166] where necessary, a complaint can also be made to the CJEU.[167] If criminal law is understood correctly as the expression of a specific legal culture and history and thus of State sovereignty,[168] then subsidiarity and proportionality become condensed in this area, forming an **imperative to use criminal law in the most restrictive form possible** in line with the general principle of *ultima ratio* (*strafrechtsspezifisches Schonungsgebot*).[169] For this reason alone, the 'fundamental aspects' of the criminal justice systems of the Member States represent an insurmountable hurdle for Union law[170] and set the '**emergency brake procedure**'[171] in motion.[172]

20 Against this background, the 'community-friendly' stance formerly advocated, according to which the authorisation to create criminal law can be derived from competences related to specific policy areas – by way of *ancillary competence* and, if necessary, drawing on the idea of *effet utile* or even implied powers pursuant to Art. 352 TFEU[173] – fails to convince.[174] It is also rejected in substance by the German Constitutional Court, which adopts a narrow interpretation of ancillary competence in the area of criminal law in line with Art. 83(2) TFEU.[175] Be that as it may, the Treaty of Lisbon confirms the principle of conferral just mentioned. If the EU is expressly awarded competence to legislate criminal law in individual, selected areas – for example with regard to 'serious crime[s] with a cross-border dimension' pursuant to Art. 83(1) TFEU (so-called eurocrimes) – then there follows by reverse implication (*argumentum e contrario*) that no such competence exists for other areas and can be justified neither via comprehensive ancillary competence nor by invoking expressive or other needs for criminalisation.[176] This competence limitation also extends to legal consequences attached to such crimes, i.e. criminal sanctions *stricto sensu* but also ancillary consequences like confiscation.[177] The Union – unlike a sovereign state – has no *competence-competence* (*Kompetenz-Kompetenz*) on the strength of which it could expand its own competence.[178]

21 When the question of the Union's competence to enact criminal law norms arises, then this question refers to **criminal law in the narrower sense**; that is, to the enacting of punitive norms which threaten sanctions that are referred to as 'punishment'; that is, *prison sentences* or *fines*[179] (and which may also entail the above-mentioned ancillary sanctions). These are to be distinguished from mere regulatory offences (*infractions*), which are routinely punished with an administrative pecuniary sanction.[180] The size of such a pecuniary sanction under Union law, i.e. the financial amount to be paid, does not turn them into criminal-law-type sanctions.[181] For neither does the non-payment of the pecuniary sanction result in a prison sentence, nor does the underlying infringement of a regulatory offence express a 'social and ethical condemnation'[182] or a kind of censure.[183] Such Union competences to create administrative sanctions exist in different sub-areas:[184] Art. 103(2)(a) TFEU authorises the Council to introduce fines for the infringement of competition laws; according to Art. 132(3) TFEU, the European Central Bank may fine companies under certain conditions. However, it is not possible to deduce any *criminal* law competences from these provisions, given that their wording only refers to sanctions outside criminal law (*fines*).

2. Art. 325 TFEU as Authorising Criminal Law Legislation

22 In Art. 325 TFEU, the Lisbon Treaty takes over the old Art. 280 TEC along with its near-classic rule to counter 'fraud and any other illegal activities affecting the **financial interests** of the Union'. However, the new version of paragraph 4 contains a highly significant omittance compared to the earlier version, which appears to make earlier debate on the authorisation to create supranational criminal law legislation[185] somewhat redundant.[186] For while Art. 280(4) TEC made the authorisation of the Council to legislate 'the necessary measures in the fields of the prevention of and fight against fraud' (first sentence) subject to the condition that the measures adopted do 'not concern the application of national criminal law or the administration of justice in the Member States' (second sentence), Art. 325(4) TFEU now dispenses with this second sentence.[187] Thus the main argument against a supranational **criminal law legislation competence** of the Union no longer applies and such a competence, restricted to the area of combating fraud,[188] can be affirmed, even though no use has been made of it to date.[189] Indeed, it is probably safe to assume that the drafters of the Lisbon Treaty were fully aware of the debate on the old second sentence of Art. 280(4) TEC and thus dispensed with it,[190] with the intention of thereby creating the basis for an authorisation to enact area-specific European criminal law by way of regulation.[191] Against this background, it is not convincing to argue that Art. 325 TFEU 'merely regulates the applicability' of the ancillary competence[192] or constitutes an 'external part' of the general harmonisation competence.[193]

3. Further Rules on Competence

23 The possibility to enact supranational criminal law is debated in regard to two further areas. On the one hand, the same rules as in the fight against fraud should apply to **customs matters** because of the deletion of the criminal law caveat of Art. 135 second sentence TEC in the new Art. 33 TFEU.[194] On the other hand, it is also envisaged that the Union will take measures (including the adoption of regulations)[195] in the areas of **illegal immigration and trafficking in human beings**,[196] including combat against the former. However, the fact that Art. 83(1) TFEU contains a special rule on the adoption of *directives* on the harmonisation of the criminal law of the Member States in regard to the combating of human trafficking argues against a supranational criminal law competence; for if such a competence were assumed, then this rule would be unnecessary. Art. 79(2)(c, d) TFEU does not, therefore, constitute the basis for the competence to enact genuine EU criminal law.[197] Independently of this, the 'emergency brake regulation' of Arts. 82(3), 83(3) TFEU can be applied analogously here.[198]

III. Europeanised National Law

1. Within the Framework of the Council of Europe

24 The subject of European criminal law within the framework of the Council of Europe is those norms that result from the consultations of the Council of Europe, particularly the ECHR. We will return to the human rights dimension of the Council of Europe in detail in the next Chapter. While the Council of Europe as a federation of States does not have any power to enact supranational legislation, its aims reveal at least the aspiration to harmonise the law of the Member States. The area of criminal law played an important role here very early on.[199] As early as 1958, the Committee of Ministers created a standing *European Committee on Crime Problems* (CDPC).[200] Under the umbrella of the standing committee, a number of subcommittees deal with a variety of more specific problems.[201] The aim on the one hand is to carry out basic research on criminal law; on the other, it is to draft agreements on criminal law.[202] Of course, looking at the domestic implementation of some Council of Europe conventions, for example in the area of money laundering,[203] one finds that there can be no question of a complete harmonisation of Member State legal systems. As of 17 January 2018, the Council of Europe presented a total of sixty agreements (including the ECHR and Protocols) in the areas of criminal law and procedural law;[204] we will return to these in Chapters 3, mn. 2, and 4, mn. 10.

2. Within the Framework of the EU

a) Foundations, Particularly the Principle of Mutual Recognition

25 The Europeanisation of national criminal law through legislative acts of the EU occurs mainly through the harmonisation of substantive and procedural law and through legislative acts on the mutual recognition of decisions in criminal law. Previously, the regulation of Member State co-operation in criminal law was only possible on an intergovernmental basis in the area of the third pillar of the PJCCM.[205] Through the communitisation of the third pillar by the Treaty of Lisbon,[206] the regulation of the PJCCM now occurs in the **area of freedom, security and justice** at Union level,[207] which enables the European Council to define 'strategic guidelines'.[208]

26 As under previous law of the third pillar, in the area of **substantive criminal law** there is the option of harmonising legislation through passing of minimum requirements defining criminal offences and sanctions in areas of 'particularly serious crime' with a cross-border dimension, the above-mentioned 'eurocrimes';[209] this will be analysed in more detail in Chapter 3.[210] In the area of **procedural law**, judicial co-operation is based on the **principle of mutual recognition**.[211] This principle means that 'judgments and judicial decisions'[212] made in one Member State also have to be recognised in another Member State; that is, ultimately, these decisions have to be directly enforceable and actually enforced in all member States,[213] although this requires a legal basis in secondary law.[214] Of course, mutual recognition in turn presupposes **mutual trust**, which cannot be imposed by legislative fiat but is premised upon mutual respect, rights observance and common values.[215] At any rate, advocating mutual recognition before **harmonising** the (procedural) law of the member States is, in a way, putting the cart before the horse. After all, the recognition of foreign legal acts or decisions is predicated on a certain similarity, if not harmony, of the legal orders concerned. This is, in fact, recognised by Art. 82(1) TFEU, connecting 'mutual recognition' and 'approximation', and by Art. 82(2) TFEU, making approximation by 'minimum rules' a facilitator of mutual recognition.[216] The necessary harmonisation entails in particular the development of a common minimum standard in procedural rights.[217] Chapter 2 will therefore be exclusively dedicated to this matter.

27 The **origin of the principle of mutual recognition** in the Single Market[218] both explains the basic idea, namely that mutually recognised decisions should float in the Union as freely as market goods and services, and, at the same time – despite the above-mentioned requirement for implementation – gives rise to problems for the simple fact that legal decisions are not just finished marked goods. Thus, particularly, evidence cannot be extracted and 'exported' like a 'finished product' from the overall context of its legal system and the specific situation in which it was gathered without its meaning being changed or indeed lost.[219] In fact, in line with their individual character, the 'products' of national criminal law are not traded in a single market like consumer goods, such as Dutch beer, for example, which may or may not be brewed according to German purity law. Furthermore, the procedural principle of immediacy entailing the presentation of evidence before the deciding judge is ultimately abandoned if documentary evidence gathered and valid in other Member States is introduced in the Member State adjudicating the respective case. The mutual recognition of evidence law also forces the national courts of the requested state to apply foreign law, as the lawfulness of the taking of evidence ordered by the requesting State needs to be measured against the latter's law. From a perspective of fundamental rights, the EPPO's 'forum shopping' option, to be explained in Chapter 5,[220] and the ensuing breaking up of national procedural systems, which are each perfectly balanced within themselves in a specific way, can be seen as infringing the principles of fairness and equality of arms.[221] Against this background it is clear that mutual recognition needs to be adjusted if it is to be used as a principle of co-operation in criminal matters.[222] Indeed, being a mere principle – that is, an optimisation requirement[223] or an 'ought-to-follow' rule[224] – it needs to be formed and refined in light of its concrete application in mutual recognition instruments taking into account fundamental reasons and values which may limit its application.[225] In fact, we will see in Chapter 4[226] that mutual recognition does not operate as an automatism since the concrete instruments[227] – especially the Framework Decision on the European Arrest Warrant (FD EAW), which served as a template for several subsequent mutual recognition instruments[228] – provide for a series of mandatory and facultative grounds of refusal.[229] In this context we will also treat the *principle of availability* (*disponibilité, Verfügbarkeit*), which is relevant for the exchange of information.[230]

28 When we speak of '**harmonisation**' in this context, we need to distinguish this term from those of the assimilation and standardisation of criminal justice systems. The difference between harmonisation and '**assimilation**' is that assimilation does not entail or require any harmonisation of the individual criminal justice systems, as their laws are (only) referred to by Union law in order to achieve a similar safeguarding of the legal interests protected by Union law, but without changing the respective national rules.[231] In other words, assimilation focuses on the Union interests and wants the national law of the Member States to protect these interests in the same – or at least similar or analogous – way as they protect their own interests.[232] Thus assimilation is – with regard to the subsidiarity principle – less intrusive than harmonisation; it operates as a 'gap-filling tool',[233] but it also lags behind harmonisation in that the latter serves the broader purpose of creating a unified law of the member States which, in particular, facilitates procedural co-operation.[234] From this perspective, assimilation rather cements differences between national justice systems instead of harmonising them. The difference between harmonisation and **standardisation** is gradual in that harmonisation goes less far than standardisation and aims merely at a *convergence*[235] or **approximation**[236] of national criminal law.[237] We will look at harmonisation and assimilation more specifically in Chapter 3.[238]

b) Forms and Techniques of Influence

29 Union law influences national (criminal) justice systems in a more general fashion through the *aims* of Art. 4(3) TEU as well as through the principles of *primacy* and of the *interpretation of national law in line with Union law*; we will look at these principles more closely in Chapter 3.[239] A national court can also bring a question of European law directly before the CJEU.[240] More concrete forms and techniques of influence, to be analysed in more detail in the following chapters, include:[241]

- The **assimilation** of Union and national interests by way of **references** in Union primary law to national criminal law.[242]
- Conversely, there are **(blanket) references** to Union law in *national criminal laws.*[243]
- In the framework of **police and judicial co-operation** (formerly 'PJCCM') – which is based on the principle of mutual recognition – a higher level of security is to be ensured,[244] on the one hand through the increased *co-ordination and co-operation* of police forces and criminal justice systems,[245] and on the other hand, 'if necessary',[246] through the *approximation of laws*[247] in procedural law[248] and substantive law.[249]

In addition, there are many agreements in the area of **interstate assistance in criminal matters**, including the enforcement of sanctions, such as the European Convention on Mutual Assistance in Criminal Matters (EuCMACM), the Schengen Convention (CISA)[250] and the Convention on simplified extradition procedure between the Member States of the European Union.[251]

C. Sources of European Criminal Law

I. General

30 From a formal perspective, two legal systems have been in existence since the foundation of the EU: the (original) *Community law* of the EC and the (new) *law of the Union*. The Lisbon Treaty not only made the '**Union**' the legal successor of the EC,[252] but also created a **uniform Union law** with the (reformed) 'Treaty on European Union' (TEU) and the 'Treaty of the Functioning of the European Union' (TFEU); the Union is 'founded' upon these treaties.[253] Accordingly, the sources of **primary Union law** are the TFEU and the TEU as the founding treaties of the 'new' Union and their annexes and protocols as **written** (primary) Union law.[254] The earlier law continues to apply until abolished, annulled or amended.[255] Criminal law is now covered in Articles 67, 82 ff. TFEU in particular.[256]

31 In addition, there is the **unwritten** primary law in the form of *customary Union law* and of general principles of law.[257] For example, the option of representation in the Council by deputy ministers (*secrétaires d'État, Staatssekretäre*) is recognised in custom as a supplementary[258] rule of unwritten primary Union law.[259] *General legal principles* as rules of unwritten primary Union law include those laws shared by the legal systems of the Union Member States.[260] The CJEU is to determine these through a value-based comparison of the laws of the Member States.[261] In terms of their content, the general legal principles constitute derivations of the fundamental principles of freedom, democracy, respect for human rights and fundamental freedoms, as well as of the rule of law.[262] They deal with basic rights and principles of the rule of law.[263] The following are recognised as pertinent to the rule of law: proportionality, the protection of legitimate expectation and the rule of legal certainty.[264] The CJEU derives basic rights as part of the general principles of law from Member States' shared constitutional traditions as well as from the **ECHR.**[265] For example, the general principle of equality of treatment, the protection of property, freedom of occupation, freedom of expression and, as basic procedural rights, the right to a fair trial in particular are recognised.[266] With the Lisbon Treaty, the **European Charter of Fundamental Rights**[267] became part of Union law.[268]

32 A number of private initiatives have also taken up the cause of safeguarding the minimum standards of the rule of law. The **Manifesto on Criminal Policy** of the *European Criminal Policy Initiative*[269] should be mentioned in this regard.[270] Taking the basic thought of (European) Enlightenment as their starting point, fourteen scholars from ten EU Member States have developed criteria and demands for a reasonable European criminal policy. The definitive basic principles identified are: the need for a legitimate protective purpose, the principle of last resort, the principle of blameworthiness, the principle of legality, the principle of subsidiarity and the principle of coherence.[271] These suggestions for the development of substantive law have now been supplemented with a **Manifesto on European Criminal Procedure Law**, the particular aim of which is to strengthen the rights of defendants during proceedings.[272] The right to defence[273] is given particular attention by the **Alternative Draft of Penal European Prosecution** presented by a group of European legal academics, which suggests the introduction of a '*Eurodefensor*' to safeguard defendants' rights.[274] The tasks and functioning of the Eurodefensor are described in Articles 32 ff. of the 'Draft regulations for transnational criminal proceedings in the European Union'.[275] A different proposal makes a case for a '**European criminal defence network**' to be secured by European law.[276]

33 **Secondary Union law** is created by the Union institutions. In doing so, the Union is able to use the following legal instruments, which are mentioned in Art. 288(1) TFEU:[277]

- **Regulations.** Regulations are *directly applicable* and *binding* in their entirety. They enjoy *primacy* over national law,[278] so that the application of national law is suspended to the extent that it clashes with a regulation.
- **Directives.** Directives are only binding as to the result to be achieved upon each Member State to which they are addressed.[279] The choice of form and methods to achieve said result is left up to the Member States. The adoption of directives now replaces the framework decisions adopted within the context of the PJCCM.[280] In contrast to the framework decisions, the implementation of directives by Member States[281] is subject to review by the CJEU as part of infringement proceedings.[282] Furthermore, the *ordinary legislative procedure* according to Arts. 289(1), 294 TFEU applies, in which the Council and the EP have equal decision-making powers.[283] Moreover, in the Council a *qualified majority* is usually sufficient,[284] in contrast to the unanimity previously required.[285]
- **Decisions.** According to Art. 288(4) TFEU, decisions are *binding* in their entirety, but only upon those to whom they are addressed.
- **Recommendations/opinions.** According to Art. 288(5) TFEU, recommendations and opinions have *no binding force*.

II. The Schengen Acquis

34 The so-called Schengen *acquis* has developed in parallel with Community and Union law.[286] It consists of the first Schengen agreement on the gradual abolition of border checks of 14 June 1985 (Schengen I),[287] the **Convention Implementing the Schengen Agreement** (CISA, Schengen II, SIS) of 19 June 1990,[288] possible accession protocols and other legal acts.[289] The Convention was incorporated into Union law with the Amsterdam Treaty of 1997,[290] through which the CJEU gained jurisdiction over the interpretation of the Schengen Convention.[291] Through the 'communitisation' of the third pillar, the Court's jurisdiction results from Arts. 267, 67 TFEU.[292]

Protocol 19 to the Lisbon Treaty[293] upholds this legal situation. According to the Protocol, the Schengen *acquis* now applies to thirty States, namely twenty-six EU States[294] (with the exception of the UK and Ireland)[295] and four non-EU States (Iceland, Liechtenstein, Norway and Switzerland).[296] The CISA consists of eight titles and 142 articles. The regulations of particular relevance to police and judicial co-operation are to be found in *Title III* (*'Police and Security'*), particularly in Chapters I to V.[297] From a fundamental rights perspective, the *prohibition of double jeopardy* legally enshrined in Art. 54 CISA is of particular significance.[298] Furthermore, in 2016 the Commission presented a Proposal for a Regulation on a European Travel Information and Authorisation System (ETIAS),[299] the aim of which is to process the data of persons entering the Schengen area to ensure that they can 'cross the borders smoothly'.[300]

35 The Schengen *acquis* 'must be accepted in full by all States candidates for admission'.[301] However, only once the countries joining the agreement have implemented the Schengen standards in their entirety, in particular ensuring the effective protection of their external borders and joining the Schengen Information System,[302] are **border controls** no longer required.[303] And only once the Council of Home Affairs and Justice Ministers of the EU has unanimously decided that the candidate State meets Schengen standards and thus is able to fully implement Schengen law, do identity checks at the new internal borders become unnecessary. This decision is still outstanding for Bulgaria, Croatia, Romania and Cyprus,[304] with Bulgaria and Romania being currently in the process of joining the Schengen area.[305]

36 At any rate, the absence of border controls at internal borders is not without exceptions. Art. 23 of the Schengen Borders Code (SBC)[306] expressly allows the exercise of police powers or security checks on persons within the respective sovereign territory in accordance with national law, as long as these checks do 'not have an effect equivalent to border checks' – which of course gives rise to problematic grey areas.[307] Moreover, Member States may exceptionally temporarily reintroduce border controls for foreseeable events,[308] for cases requiring immediate action,[309] or in exceptional circumstances where the overall functioning of the area without internal border control is put at risk as a result of persistent serious deficiencies relating to external border control.[310] Various Schengen Member States[311] made use of this possibility during the refugee/migrant crisis in 2015–16, carrying out internal border controls, with focus on specific land border sections or specific ports corresponding to the identified migratory routes and threats.[312] Furthermore, the Schengen evaluation and monitoring mechanism – introduced in October 2013 to verify the implementation of the Schengen *acquis* in the participating and candidate States, in order to ensure high security standards as a basis for mutual trust in the Schengen area[313] – identified '[w]ider structural deficiencies in the way the Union's external borders are protected'.[314] As a consequence, the Council recommended certain (Schengen) Member States[315] to maintain controls under Art. 29 SBC for a maximum of six months.[316]

Notes

1. Note, however, that the idea of a 'united Europe' or of a 'European union' (with a lower-case 'u') already appeared in the late seventeenth century; cf. Chalmers, Davies and Monti, *EU Law* (2014), pp. 6–7; Calliess, *EU nach dem Vertrag von Lissabon* (2010), p. 15; on early attempts for European integration, see Streinz, *Europarecht* (2016), mn. 10.
2. Fischer, *Europarecht* (2001), §1 mn. 2; Oppermann, Classen and Nettesheim, *Europarecht* (2016), §2 mn. 2–4; Calliess, *EU nach dem Vertrag von Lissabon* (2010), p. 16; in more detail on the historical development, see Lasok, *Law and Institutions of the EU* (2001), pp. 3 ff.; Dashwood et al., *EU Law* (2011), pp. 1 ff.; Chalmers, Davies and Monti, *EU Law* (2014), pp. 11 ff.; Schorkopf, *Der Europäische Weg* (2015); from an institutional perspective, Craig, in Craig and de Búrca, *The Evolution of EU Law* (2011), pp. 41 ff.; for a short historical overview of EuCrL Miettinen, *Criminal Law and Policy in the EU* (2013), pp. 7 ff.
3. The speech is easily accessible on the Web, for example at www.churchill-society-london.org.uk/astonish.html, last accessed 27 January 2018. Added emphasis.
4. Fischer, *Europarecht* (2001), §1 mn. 2; Oppermann, Classen and Nettesheim, *Europarecht* (2016), §2 mn. 5; Herdegen, *Europarecht* (2017), §1 mn. 7; Lelieveldt and Princen, *Politics of the EU* (2015), p. 6; Streinz, *Europarecht* (2016), mn. 75–6.
5. Cf. Robert Schuman, Declaration of 9 May 1950, available at http://europa.eu/about-eu/basic-information/symbols/europe-day/schuman-declaration/index_en.htm, last accessed 27 January 2018, reprinted in EP, *Selection of Texts Concerning Institutional Matters of the Community for 1950–1982* (1982), p. 47 ('solidarity in production thus established will make it plain that any war between France and Germany becomes not merely unthinkable, but materially impossible.'); see also Chalmers, Davies and Monti, *EU Law* (2014), pp. 11–12; Oppermann, Classen and Nettesheim, *Europarecht* (2016), §2 mn. 9; Calliess, *JZ*, 59 (2004), 1034; Calliess, *EU nach dem Vertrag von Lissabon* (2010), pp. 17–18; Schütze, *EU Law* (2015), p. 7; Lelieveldt and Princen, *Politics of the EU* (2015), pp. 3, 5–8; Streinz, *Europarecht* (2016), mn.17.
6. Fischer, *Europarecht* (2001), §1 mn. 3; Calliess, *Die neue EU nach dem Vertrag von Lissabon* (2010), pp. 17–18; Arndt, Fischer and Fetzer, *Europarecht* (2015), mn. 20; Oppermann, Classen and Nettesheim, *Europarecht* (2016), §2 mn. 10; Lelieveldt and Princen, *Politics of the EU* (2015), pp. 7–8; Streinz, *Europarecht* (2016), mn. 17.

7. See the programmatic book by Dell, *The Schuman Plan and the British Abdication of Leadership in Europe* (1955); see also Chalmers, Davies and Monti, *EU Law* (2014), p. 12; Dashwood et al., *EU Law* (2011), p. 4; Fischer, *Europarecht* (2001), §1 mn. 3.
8. Fischer, *Europarecht* (2001), §1 mn. 3; Herdegen, *Europarecht* (2017), §4 mn. 1; Nicolaysen, *Europarecht*, i (2002), p. 29; Arndt, Fischer and Fetzer, *Europarecht* (2015), mn. 20; Lelieveldt and Princen, *Politics of the EU* (2015), p. 8; Schütze, *EU Law* (2015), pp. 7–10; Streinz, *Europarecht* (2016), mn. 17. This treaty expired after 50 years on 23 June 2002 (Art. 97 ECSC).
9. Fischer, *Europarecht* (2001), §1 mn. 4; Calliess, *EU nach dem Vertrag von Lissabon* (2010), p. 19; Oppermann, Classen and Nettesheim, *Europarecht* (2016), §2 mn. 11; Dashwood et al., *EU Law* (2011), pp. 5–7; Chalmers, Davies and Monti, *EU Law* (2014), pp. 12–13; Lelieveldt and Princen, *Politics of the EU* (2015), pp. 9, 11; Schütze, *EU Law* (2015), pp. 10–12; Streinz, *Europarecht* (2016), mn. 19.
10. Fischer, *Europarecht* (2001), §1 mn. 4; Oppermann, *Europarecht* (2005), §1 mn. 20; Calliess, *EU nach dem Vertrag von Lissabon* (2010), p. 19; Lelieveldt and Princen, *Politics of the EU* (2015), p. 11; Schütze, *EU Law* (2015), p. 12; Streinz, *Europarecht* (2016), mn. 19. The EU reactivated the idea at the beginning of November 2017 with the triggering of the Permanent Structured Co-operation (PESCO); see www.consilium.europa.eu/en/press/press-releases/2017/11/13/defence-cooperation-23-member-states-sign-joint-notification-on-pesco/pdf, accessed 27 January 2018.
11. Calliess, *EU nach dem Vertrag von Lissabon* (2010), pp. 11–12; Oppermann, Classen and Nettesheim, *Europarecht* (2016), §2 mn. 12. On the lukewarm UK participation, see Dashwood et al., *EU Law* (2011), p. 7.
12. Calliess, *EU nach dem Vertrag von Lissabon* (2010), p. 20; Oppermann, Classen and Nettesheim, *Europarecht* (2016), §2 mn. 12; Bieber et al., *Die EU* (2016), §1 mn. 16–17.
13. Fischer, *Europarecht* (2001), §1 mn. 6; Oppermann, Classen and Nettesheim, *Europarecht* (2016), §2 mn. 15, 29; Herdegen, *Europarecht* (2017), §1 mn. 14; Streinz, *Europarecht* (2016), mn. 20.
14. Chalmers, Davies and Monti, *EU Law* (2014), p. 13; Fischer, *Europarecht* (2001), §1 mn. 5; Oppermann, Classen and Nettesheim, *Europarecht* (2016), §2 mn. 12; Herdegen, *Europarecht* (2017), §4 mn. 5; Nicolaysen, *Europarecht*, i (2002), p. 29; Calliess, *EU nach dem Vertrag von Lissabon* (2010), p. 20; Arndt, Fischer and Fetzer, *Europarecht* (2015), mn. 23; Lelieveldt and Princen, *Politics of the EU* (2015), p. 11; Schütze, *EU Law* (2015), pp. 13–14.
15. Dashwood et al., *EU Law* (2011), p. 10; Calliess, *EU nach dem Vertrag von Lissabon* (2010), pp. 23–6; Chalmers, Davies and Monti, *EU Law* (2014), pp. 15, 20; Lelieveldt and Princen, *Politics of the EU* (2015), pp. 12–14; Schütze, *EU Law* (2015), pp. 15–17. On the UK's parallel creation of the European Free Trade Association (EFTA) in 1960, see Dashwood et al., *EU Law* (2011), pp. 9–10; and Chalmers, Davies and Monti, *EU Law* (2014), p. 20. It was, however, considered a 'stepping stone' to future EC membership (Dashwood et al., *EU Law* (2011), p. 9 quoting a UK White Paper) and has indeed been increasingly sidelined by the EU consisting today of only four non-EU Member States (Iceland, Liechtenstein, Norway and Switzerland); cf. also the EFTA website, at www.efta.int, last accessed 27 January 2018.
16. See de Gaulle's press conference on 15 May 1962, where he referred to this phrase, available on video with a transcript at http://fresques.ina.fr/jalons/fiche-media/InaEdu00096/conference-de-presse-du-general-de-gaulle-du-15-mai-1962.html, last accessed 27 January 2018.

17. Cf. Art. 13 (1) TEU; in more detail, see Chapter 5, mn. 23.
18. ECJ, *NV Algemene Transport- en Expeditie Onderneming van Gend & Loos* v. *Netherlands Inland Revenue Administration*, C-26/62, Judgment, 5 February 1963, ECLI:EU:C:1963:1, p. 12: 'The European Economic Community constitutes a new legal order of international law for the benefit of which the states have limited their sovereign rights, albeit within limited fields, and the subjects of which comprise not only the member states but also their nationals'; cf. thereon Calliess, *EU nach dem Vertrag von Lissabon* (2010), p. 22; Lelieveldt and Princen, *Politics of the EU* (2015), pp. 12–13.
19. Calliess, *EU nach dem Vertrag von Lissabon* (2010), pp. 26–7; Oppermann, Classen and Nettesheim, *Europarecht* (2016), §2 mn. 23.
20. Calliess, *EU nach dem Vertrag von Lissabon* (2010), pp. 28; Dashwood et al., *EU Law* (2011), p. 10; Chalmers, Davies and Monti, *EU Law* (2014), p. 20; Fischer, *Europarecht* (2001), §1 mn. 9; Lelieveldt and Princen, *Politics of the EU* (2015), p. 14; Oppermann, Classen and Nettesheim, *Europarecht* (2016), §2 mn. 24–5; Bieber et al., *Die EU* (2016), §1 mn. 36. In light of the recent UK referendum, it is worthwhile noting that the 1974 Labour government renegotiated the agreed terms and put the new agreement to a referendum on 5 June 1975, where it was endorsed. See Dashwood et al., *EU Law* (2011), pp. 10–11.
21. Fischer, *Europarecht* (2001), §1 mn. 11; Lelieveldt and Princen, *Politics of the EU* (2015), p. 15; Oppermann, Classen and Nettesheim, *Europarecht* (2016), §2 mn. 28.
22. For a policy analysis in this sense, see Hillion, in Craig and de Búrca, *The Evolution of EU Law* (2011), pp. 187 ff. (distinguishing between three generations of EU enlargement rules, starting with a simple state-driven procedure to open up the Union to a comprehensive policy especially with regard to Central and Eastern Europe and a recent more cautious approach give a general 'enlargement fatigue'); cf. also Lelieveldt and Princen, *Politics of the EU* (2015), pp. 20–1.
23. Fischer, *Europarecht* (2001), §1 mn. 20; Oppermann, Classen and Nettesheim, *Europarecht* (2016), §3 mn. 7; Lelieveldt and Princen, *Politics of the EU* (2015), pp. 17–18. In Norway, a national referendum voted against membership (Herdegen, *Europarecht* (2017), §4 mn. 18; Bieber et al., *Die EU* (2016), §1 mn. 38; Lelieveldt and Princen, *Politics of the EU* (2015), p. 14).
24. Art. 251 Treaty of the European Economic Community (TEEC).
25. Art. 252 TEEC.
26. Art. 14(2) TEEC describes the situation aimed for as follows: 'The internal market shall comprise an area without internal frontiers in which the free movement of goods, persons, services and capital is ensured in accordance with the provisions of this Treaty.' On the controversial relationship between the internal market and the common market, cf. for example Herdegen, *Europarecht* (2017), §14 mn. 1 ff.; Streinz, *Europarecht* (2016), mn. 807 with further references. See also Dashwood et al., *EU Law* (2011), pp. 12–13; Chalmers, Davies and Monti, *EU Law* (2014), p. 22; Fischer, *Europarecht* (2001), §1 mn. 13; Nicolaysen, *Europarecht*, i (2002), p. 32; Calliess, *EU nach dem Vertrag von Lissabon* (2010), pp. 28–30; Arndt, Fischer and Fetzer, *Europarecht* (2015), mn. 27–8; Lelieveldt and Princen, *Politics of the EU* (2015), p. 16; Schütze, *EU Law* (2015), pp. 20–1; Oppermann, Classen and Nettesheim, *Europarecht* (2016), §2 mn. 29–30; Streinz, *Europarecht* (2016), mn. 36.
27. Art. 1 TEC.

28. Calliess, *EU nach dem Vertrag von Lissabon* (2010), pp. 30–3; Lelieveldt and Princen, *Politics of the EU* (2015), p. 17.
29. BVerfG, Nos 2 BvR 2134/92 and 2 BvR 2159/92, Judgment (12 October 1993), in *BVerfGE*, 89, pp. 155, 181, 188; Calliess, *EU nach dem Vertrag von Lissabon* (2010), pp. 63 ff.; Streinz, *Europarecht* (2016), mn. 39.
30. This is basically reflected in strategies which have come to be known as German, Roman and Greek strategies and encompass collective identity formation, additional competencies and institutional (democratic) reform; cf. van Middelaar, *Passage to Europe* (2013), pp. 223–4; Chalmers, Davies and Monti, *EU Law* (2014), pp. 25–27.
31. On the perspectives of CFSP in reference to the EU constitution, see Vernet, *EuGRZ*, 31 (2004), 584 and Cremer, *EuGRZ*, 31 (2004), 587.
32. Art. 1 subpara. 3 first sentence TEU. Cf. Herdegen, *Europarecht* (2017), §4 mn. 12–13 with graph at p. 6; Nicolaysen, *Europarecht*, i (2002), pp. 32–3; Arndt, *Europarecht* (2004), p. 13; Bieber et al., *Die EU* (2016), §16 mn. 1; Hecker, *Europäisches Strafrecht* (2015), §4 mn. 106 ('temple structure'); Calliess, *EU nach dem Vertrag von Lissabon* (2010), p. 31; Dashwood et al., *EU Law* (2011), p. 14 ('Greek temple facade'); Lelieveldt and Princen, *Politics of the EU* (2015), p. 17; Schütze, *EU Law* (2015), pp. 23–7 ('temple structure'), with figure 1.2. (p. 24).
33. Herdegen, *Europarecht* (2017), §5 mn. 1; Calliess, *EU nach dem Vertrag von Lissabon* (2010), p. 31; Schütze, *EU Law* (2015), pp. 26–7; Arndt, Fischer and Fetzer, *Europarecht* (2015), mn. 30; Lelieveldt and Princen, *Politics of the EU* (2015), p. 17.
34. This follows, *e contrario*, from Art. 47 TEU, earlier version ('Subject to the provisions amending the Treaty establishing the European Economic Community with a view to establishing the European Community, the Treaty establishing the European Coal and Steel Community and the Treaty establishing the European Atomic Energy Community, and to these final provisions, nothing in this Treaty shall affect the Treaties establishing the European Communities or the subsequent Treaties and Acts modifying or supplementing them.'); cf. also Hecker, *Europäisches Strafrecht* (2005), §4 mn. 108, §5 mn. 70.
35. Herdegen, *Europarecht* (2017), §5 mn. 6.
36. Fischer, *Europarecht* (2001), §1 mn. 23; Calliess, *EU nach dem Vertrag von Lissabon* (2010), p. 34; Oppermann, Classen and Nettesheim, *Europarecht* (2016), §3 mn. 3; Dashwood et al., *EU Law* (2011), pp. 15–16; Hilf and Pache, *NJW*, 51 (1998), 710; Schroeder, *Europarecht* (2015), §2 mn. 19; Streinz, *Europarecht* (2016), mn. 50.
37. Fischer, *Europarecht* (2001), §1 mn. 23; Hilf and Pache, *NJW*, 51 (1998), 707; Oppermann, Classen and Nettesheim, *Europarecht* (2016), §3 mn. 3; Nicolaysen, *Europarecht*, i (2002), p. 33; Arndt, *Europarecht* (2004), p. 15; Bieber et al., *Die EU* (2016), §16 mn. 6; Chalmers, Davies and Monti, *EU Law* (2014), pp. 29–30; Vervaele, *RP*, 15 (2005), 176 ff.; Calliess, *EU nach dem Vertrag von Lissabon* (2010), pp. 34–5; Schütze, *EU Law* (2015), pp. 28–9; Schroeder, *Europarecht* (2015), §2 mn. 19; Streinz, *Europarecht* (2016), mn. 52.
38. On the PJCCM, see in detail Chapter 4.
39. Cf. thereon, Section C in this chapter, especially mn. 34 ff.
40. Protocol (No 2) Integrating the Schengen *acquis* into the Framework of the European Union (1997), OJ C 340 of 10 November 1997, 93 = OJ C 321 E of 29 December 2006, 191–5.

41. Protocol (No 4) on the Position of the UK and Ireland (1997), OJ C 321 E, 29 December 2006, 198–200.
42. Protocol (No 3) on the Application of Certain Aspects of Article 14 of the Treaty Establishing the European Community to the United Kingdom and to Ireland (1997), OJ C 321 E of 29 December 2006, 196–7.
43. Art. 4 Protocol 2 (n. 40).
44. Protocol (No 5) on the Position of Denmark (1997), OJ C 321 E of 29 December 2006, 201–2. Those parts of the Schengen *acquis* that were determined to have a legal basis in Title IV of the TEC would apply to Denmark unamended, as before the determination (Art. 3 Protocol 2, n. 40). Denmark also did not want to participate in measures with defence implications (Art. 6 Protocol No 5).
45. Cf. also Art. 3 Protocol 2 (n. 40).
46. On the CJEU and the other relevant institutions, see Chapter 5.
47. While Denmark, the UK and Ireland explicitly declared not to accept (see nn. 41, 44 above), for Bulgaria, Estonia, Malta, Poland and Slovakia no official information is available on whether they submitted a declaration under Article 35(2) EU; cf. CJEU Research and Documentation Service, 'Jurisdiction of the Court of Justice to Give Preliminary Rulings on Police and Judicial Cooperation in Criminal Matters', March 2008 (http://curia.europa.eu/jcms/upload/docs/application/pdf/2008-09/art35_2008-09-25_17-37-4_434.pdf, last accessed 27 January 2018); cf. also information concerning the declarations by the Republic of Cyprus and Romania on their acceptance of the jurisdiction of the Court of Justice of the European Union to give preliminary rulings on the acts referred to in Article 35 of the Treaty on European Union, OJ L 56 of 6 March 2010, 14; de Busser, *ERA Forum*, 16 (2015), 280.
48. See previously mn. 4.
49. Fischer, *Europarecht* (2001), §1 mn. 26; Herdegen, *Europarecht* (2017), §4 mn. 23–4; Dashwood et al., *EU Law* (2011), p. 16; Calliess, *EU nach dem Vertrag von Lissabon* (2010), pp. 36–7; Schütze, *EU Law* (2015), pp. 30–1; Schroeder, *Europarecht* (2015), §2 mn. 20; Streinz, *Europarecht* (2016), mn. 53–5; Arndt, *Europarecht* (2004), pp. 17–19.
50. Arndt, *Europarecht* (2004), pp. 37–8; Calliess, *EU nach dem Vertrag von Lissabon* (2010), p. 36.
51. For an instructive account, see Arndt, *Europarecht* (2004), pp. 37–41; Fischer, *Europarecht* (2001), §1 mn. 26; Herdegen, *Europarecht* (2017), §4 mn. 23–4; Pache and Schorkopf, *NJW*, 54 (2001), 1381 ff.
52. Pache and Schorkopf, *NJW*, 54 (2001), 1385; Bieber et al., *Die EU* (2016), §16 mn. 7.
53. See thereon Chapter 5, mn. 16 ff.
54. On this most recent enlargement, cf. Chalmers, Davies and Monti, *EU Law* (2014), pp. 30–4.
55. The United Kingdom has three different systems: England and Wales, Scotland and Northern Ireland. However, it made use of the opt-out regarding police and judicial co-operation in Art. 10(4) Lisbon Treaty, Protocol (No 36) on Transitional Provisions, OJ C 326 of 26 October 2012, 326, with effect from 1 December 2014 (cf. Council of the EU, 'UK Notification According to Article 10(4) of Protocol No 36 to TEU and TFEU', 12750/13, Brussels, 26 July 2013); on the consequences, cf. Brodowski, *ZIS*, 8 (2013), 458 ff.; cf. also *eucrim*, 8 (2013), 76.

56. The turnout was 72.2%, 51.9% voted to leave and 48.1% to stay; cf. www.bbc.co.uk/news/politics/eu_referendum/results, last accessed 27 January 2018. For an analysis of the post-Brexit options cf. Ambos, *JZ* 72 (2017), 707 ff.; in Spanish in InDret no 4/2017, www.indret.com/pdf/editorial_4.2017.pdf. See also the Brexit issue of *CLF* 28 (2017) 219 ff. with papers by Mitsilegas and – from the perspective of other States – Suominen (Norway), Meyer (Switzerland); Cahn (France); Bock (Germany); Świątłowski and Nita-Świątłowska (Poland) and Jimeno-Bulnes (Spain).
57. The formal notification of the European Council by the respective Member State of its intent to withdraw forms the precondition for the actual negotiations on withdrawal (Art. 50(2) TEU). Prime Minister May notified Council President Tusk of the UK's intent to withdraw from the EU on 29 March 2017 in a six-page letter, cf. http://news.bbc.co.uk/2/shared/bsp/hi/pdfs/29_03_17_article50.pdf, last accessed 27 January 2018. In this letter, among other things she stressed the intention to retain a 'deep and special partnership'. Incidentally, the withdrawal only becomes legally valid, (i) 'from the date of entry into force of the withdrawal agreement', or, (ii) subsidiarily ('failing that') 'two years after the notification' mentioned, unless (iii) the Council in agreement with the MS concerned, 'unanimously decides to extend this period'. Thus, there is by no means, contrary to reports in the media, a fixed two-year deadline but the process may well take a few more years. This explains why UK politicians talked, right after the vote, of 2020 or even later. The High Court decided on 3 November 2016 that the Art. 50 decision must be taken by Parliament (www.theguardian.com/politics/2016/nov/03/parliament-must-trigger-brexit-high-court-rules, last accessed 27 January 2018; confirmed by the Supreme Court on 24 January 2017; on this see the press summary, available at www.supremecourt.uk/cases/docs/uksc-2016-0196-press-summary.pdf, last accessed 27 January 20187). The respective (Notification of Withdrawal) Bill 2016–17 was adopted by the House of Commons on 8 February 2017 and by the House of Lords on 13 March 2017; see for the procedure http://services.parliament.uk/bills/2016-17/europeanunionnotificationofwithdrawal.html, last accessed 27 January 2018.
58. Scotland may, after a second independence referendum, become a new, independent MS (pursuant to Art. 49 TEU) and Northern Ireland may initiate a reunification with the Republic of Ireland, being a MS; cf. Vidmar and Eggett, *EJIL: Talk!*, 27 June 2016.
59. See https://ec.europa.eu/commission/sites/beta-political/files/white_paper_on_the_future_of_europe_en.pdf, last accessed 27 January 2018. The scenarios are: [1] 'Carrying on', [2] 'Nothing but the single market', [3] 'Those who want more do more', [4] 'Less but more efficiently', and [5] 'Doing much more together' (pp. 15 ff.). See also the Joint Declaration on the EU's legislative priorities for 2017, https://ec.europa.eu/commission/sites/beta-political/files/joint-declaration-legislative-priorities-2017-jan2017_en.pdf, last accessed 27 January 2018, which lists six areas of priority: [1] 'Giving a new boost to jobs, growth and investment'; [2] 'Addressing the social dimension of the EU'; [3] 'Better protecting the security of our citizens'; [4] 'Reforming and developing our migration policy in a spirit of responsibility and solidarity'; [5] 'Delivering on our commitment to implement a connected Digital Single Market'; and [6] 'Delivering on our objective of an ambitious Energy Union and a forward looking climate change policy'.

60. Cf. European Convention, 'Draft Treaty establishing a Constitution for Europe', CONV 850/03, Brussels 18 July 2003, available at www.ecb.europa.eu/ecb/legal/pdf/cv00850.en03.pdf, last accessed 27 January 2018. See also Calliess, *EU nach dem Vertrag von Lissabon* (2010), pp. 37–41; Lelieveldt and Princen, *Politics of the EU* (2015), pp. 21–2; Schütze, *EU Law* (2015), pp. 32–5; from a criminal law perspective Hassemer, *ZStW*, 116 (2004), 304 ff.; Kaiafa-Gbandi, *EJCCLCJ*, 13 (2005), 483 ff.; Picotti, in Canestrari and Foffani, *Il diritto penale nella prospettiva europea* (2005), pp. 325 ff.
61. Presidency Conclusions of the Brussels European Council (21–2 June 2007), 11 177/07 CONCL2 of 23 June 2007 (Annex 1), p. 15; cf. also Lelieveldt and Princen, *Politics of the EU* (2015), p. 22.
62. Depenheuer, *SZ*, 17 August 2007, 14 ('die Wirklichkeit Europas hat die normative Hybris auf den Boden der Tatsachen zurückgeholt'); for Streinz, *Europarecht* (2016), mn. 60, one of the reasons why this attempt failed, was the term 'constitution' itself, characterizing it as counterproductive; in a similar vein, Lelieveldt and Princen, *Politics of the EU* (2015), p. 22 ('dared to characterize the Treaty as a constitutional document ... this might have been the element that triggered most opposition'). Thus, the idea of constitutionalization as an alternative to globalisation (Terradillos Basoco, *EPC*, 25 (2004), 395) has also been relegated to history books. Cf. also Haltern, *Europarecht* (2007), §2 mn. 126 ff., esp. 135: 'The symbolic excess ... of the use of the word "constitution" has thus been lost once and for all.' ('Der symbolische Überschuss ... mit der Verwendung des Wortes "Verfassung" ... ist damit endgültig verlorengegangen.'); Meyer, *Strafrechtsgenese* (2012), p. 304: 'U-turn from iconography to iconoclasm' ('Kehrtwende von Ikonografie zu Ikonoklasmus').
63. Treaty of Lisbon amending the Treaty on European Union and the Treaty Establishing the European Community, OJ C 306 of 17 December 2007. On its origins, cf. Streinz, Ohler and Herrmann, *Der Vertrag von Lissabon* (2010), pp. 16 ff.; Fischer, *Der Vertrag von Lissabon* (2008), pp. 47 ff.; Lelieveldt and Princen, *Politics of the EU* (2015), p. 22.
64. For more information on the Lisbon Treaty and its ratification process, cf. also the official website of the EU, available at http://ec.europa.eu/archives/lisbon_treaty/countries/index_en.htm#, last accessed 27 January 2018.
65. On the new voting rules, see Protocol 36 (n. 55), Art. 3 (suspending the provisions concerning qualified majority until 1 November 2014); thereon de Busser, *ERA Forum*, 16 (2015), 278–9.
66. Yet, if they have been amended, this transitional period did not apply, i.e. the new powers of the Commission and CJEU were immediately applicable; cf. Protocol 36 (n. 55), Art. 10(2); and de Busser, *ERA Forum*, 16 (2015), 281 ff. (discussing the ensuing 'Lisbonising' of pre-Lisbon acts and the nature of the relevant amendments).
67. Protocol 36 (n. 55), Art. 10(1), (3); thereto de Busser, *ERA Forum*, 16 (2015), 281 ff. (especially on the 'Lisbonising' of pre-Lisbon acts to subject them immediately to the Commission's enforcement powers); also Fletcher, in Mitsilegas, Bergström and Konstadinides, *Handbook EU Criminal Law* (2016), p. 80.
68. See endnote 63 above. A good overview in regard to its content is provided in Streinz, Ohler and Herrmann, *Der Vertrag von Lissabon* (2010), pp. 27 ff.; Calliess, *EU nach dem Vertrag von Lissabon* (2010), pp. 80 ff.; shorter Dashwood et al., *EU Law* (2011), pp. 19–20; Chalmers, Davies and Monti, *EU Law* (2014), pp. 39–46; Schütze, *EU Law* (2015), pp. 36–9; in a somewhat more anecdotal style, Fischer, *Der Vertrag von Lissabon* (2008), pp. 109 ff.

69. The former second pillar of the CFSP was also transferred into Union law. It continues to enjoy a certain special status (cf. Arts. 23–46 TEU) and now has its own institutions pertaining to Union law, such as the High Representative for Foreign Affairs and Security Policy (Arts. 18, 27 TEU) and the European External Action Service (Art. 27(3) TEU); on this, cf. Dembinski, *Das Parlament, Beilage*, 18 (2010), 9; Brok and Ahumada Contreras, *eucrim*, 5 (2010), 104 ff.
70. For more information on this, cf. Zimmermann, *Jura*, 31 (2009), 844 ff.; Herlin-Karnell, *eucrim*, 5 (2010), 59; Cerizza, *eucrim*, 5 (2010), 65 ff.; Serzysko, *eucrim*, 5 (2010), 69 ff.; Calliess, *ZEuS*, 11 (2008), 34 ff.; Zöller, *ZIS*, 4 (2009), 343–50; Mansdörfer, *HRRS*, 11 (2010), 11 ff.; Beukelmann, *NJW*, 63 (2010), 2081–2; Niemeier, *ERA Forum*, 11 (2010), 198 ff.; Noltenius, *ZStW*, 122 (2010), 607 ff.; Meyer, *EuR*, 46 (2011), 173 ff.; Sieber, in Sieber, Satzger, and Heintschel von Heinegg, *Europäisches Strafrecht* (2014), pp. 76 ff.; Satzger, in Streinz, *EUV/AEUV* (2012), Art. 82 AEUV mn. 1; cf. also Demko and Bock, *JZ*, 65 (2011), 95; Bock, *ZIS*, 6 (2011), 266 ff.; Gleß, *Internationales Strafrecht* (2015), mn. 434–5; Nowell-Smith, *NJECL*, 3 (2012), 382–3; for general information, cf. Sieber, *ZStW*, 121 (2009), 57 ff. Mitsilegas, *EU Criminal Law after Lisbon* (2016), pp. 4 ff., 263, 270, sees a constitutionalisation of EU criminal law, especially because of the new (co-)decision-making procedure and the enhanced roles of the CJEU and the Commission (at 6).
71. Cf. Art. 67 TFEU. For an overview of what this area post-Lisbon entails, cf. Jokisch and Jahnke, in Sieber, Satzger and Heintschel von Heinegg, *Europäisches Strafrecht* (2014), pp. 124 ff. (esp. pp. 131–5, judicial co-operation in criminal matters, and 52–9, police co-operation); Frenz, *Jura*, 34 (2012), 701 ff.; Meyer, *Strafrechtsgenese* (2012), pp. 356–7.
72. See also mn. 33.
73. Art. 16(3)TEU, 294 TFEU.
74. Cf. Art. 82(2) and 83(2) TFEU; and section C main text.
75. Cf. Art. 82(1) TFEU. On the Commission's 'triple C' approach (consolidate, compliment, codify) in this regard, see Salazar, *eucrim*, 9 (2014), 24–5; Herlin-Karnell, *eucrim*, 9 (2014), 30; cf. also mn. 26.
76. Asp, *Procedural Criminal Law Cooperation* (2016), pp. 23–6, 29–31, distinguishes between harmonisation of national criminal procedure (Art. 82(2) TFEU) and national co-operation legislation (Art. 82(1) TFEU), with the former being 'more sensitive' (23–6, 216) and only the latter allowing for supranational rules by way of regulations (33–4, 36–8). While it is correct that Art. 82(2) TFEU only provides for directives while Art. 82(1) does not contain this limitation and therefore, at least theoretically, includes regulations (Art. 288 TFEU, cf. main text, mn. 33), there is no clear-cut distinction between Art. 82(1) and (2) TFEU. In fact, the 'approximation' competence established by para. 1 refers to the areas included in para. 2 and Art. 83 TFEU (cf. Art. 82(1) first sentence *in fine*) and, in addition, national co-operation legislation may be considered as part of national procedural law. On the broad concept of co-operation enshrined in Art. 82(1) TFEU see also Asp, *Procedural Criminal Law Cooperation* (2016), pp. 34–5.
77. Art. 82(2)(d) TFEU provides blanket authorisation to standardise further aspects of criminal procedure (by way of minimum rules) following a unanimous decision of the Council and with the consent of the EP; on this, cf. also Zimmermann, *Jura*, 31 (2009), 845. Mitsilegas, *EU Criminal Law after Lisbon* (2016), pp. 265–6, considers Art. 82(2) TFEU a 'game-changer' since it represents the 'move from mutual recognition to

harmonisation' and thus the acknowledgement that mutual recognition does not work without harmonisation; for more detail on Art. 82(2) TFEU, cf. Chapter 4, mn. 8.

78. Note that the approximation competence regarding substantive law also follows from Art. 82(1) first sentence TFEU, speaking of 'approximation ... in the areas referred to ... in Article 83'.
79. Mitsilegas, *EU Criminal Law after Lisbon* (2016), pp. 58–60, speaks of 'securitised criminalisation'.
80. Art. 83(1) third subpara. TFEU authorises the Council to identify 'other areas of crime' that call for harmonisation. For more detail, cf. Chapter 3, mn. 5 ff. and 37 ff.
81. For more details, cf. Chapter 3, mn. 7–8 and 37 ff.
82. See also Mitsilegas, *EU Criminal Law after Lisbon* (2016), pp. 60–2 ('functional criminalisation').
83. For more details, see mn. 22–3 in this chapter.
84. Cf. also Klip, *European Criminal Law* (2016), pp. 38, 537–8; on the relevance of fundamental rights, cf. Kaiafa-Gbandi, *EuCLR*, 1 (2011), 10.
85. Cf. Mitsilegas, *EU Criminal Law after Lisbon* (2016), pp. 14 ff. (analysing this and other mechanisms as an expression of national resistance to the 'communautarisation' of EU criminal law).
86. For more details, see Chapter 5, mn. 24 ff.
87. Cf. especially Mitsilegas, *EU Criminal Law after Lisbon* (2016), pp. 51, 266 ff. (who sees the individual at the heart of the constitutional project of the Lisbon Treaty and an ensuing 'promise of rights', at 270–1).
88. Cf. Chapter 2, mn. 146 ff.
89. Lisbon Treaty, Protocol (No 22) on the Position of Denmark, OJ C 326 of 26 October 2012, 299–303; on Danish non-participation, cf. Herlin-Karnell, *ALF*, 5 (2013), 100 ff.; Mitsilegas, *EU Criminal Law after Lisbon* (2016), p. 44.
90. The pre-Lisbon instruments are still binding and applicable to Denmark since it did not opt out of the PJCCM measures as long as they belonged to the third pillar; cf. section A with nn. 44 and 45; see also cf. Suominen, *EuCLR*, 1 (2011), 173–4; Herlin-Karnell, *ALF*, 5 (2013), 101; Herlin-Karnell, in Acosta Arcarazo and Murphy, *EU Security and Justice Law* (2014), p. 52; Fletcher, in Mitsilegas, Bergström and Konstadinides, *Handbook EU Criminal Law* (2016), pp. 82–3.
91. Art. 7 Protocol 22 (n. 93, emphasis added); cf. also Herlin-Karnell, *ALF*, 5 (2013), 101 ('Denmark is out unless it "buys" the entire concept').
92. Lisbon Treaty, Protocol (No 21) on the Position of the United Kingdom and Ireland in Respect of the Area of Freedom, Security and Justice, OJ C 326 of 26 October 2012, 295–8.
93. Cf. Protocol 21, Arts. 2–4; see also Ambos, *JZ* 72 (2017), 708 ff.; Walker, *GLJ*, 17 (2016), 126 ('With its opt-outs from the Euro and Schengen, and also from some wider aspects of criminal justice and immigration policy under the Area of Freedom, Security and Justice, the UK was already a major beneficiary – probably *the* major beneficiary – of the EU's variable geometry even before it cut a new "customised membership" deal in February that would have allowed exemption even from the founding Treaty commitment to "ever closer Union"'); de Busser, *ERA Forum*, 16 (2015), 286; Spencer, *Archbold Rev*, issue 7 (2012), 7; Herlin-Karnell, *ALF*, 5 (2013), 100; Fletcher, in Mitsilegas, Bergström and Konstadinides, *Handbook EU Criminal Law* (2016), p. 82; Mitsilegas, *EU Criminal Law after Lisbon* (2016), pp. 44 ff.; Mitsilegas, *CLR*, 63 (2016), 518–19; for more recent UK practice see the 'Decisions' document, updated 30

October 2017 and available at www.gov.uk/government/publications/jha-opt-in-and-schengen-opt-outprotocols–3, last accessed 29 January 2018. Thus Ireland opted in regarding the instruments of the Security, Freedom and Justice Area; cf. Ryan and Hamilton, in Healy et al., *Handbook of Irish Criminology* (2016), pp. 469 ff.

94. Protocol 36 applies only to the UK. Interestingly, Ireland did not express any concerns regarding the extended powers of the Commission and the ECJ regarding PJCCM; cf. de Busser, *ERA Forum*, 16 (2015), 286.
95. Protocol 36 (n. 55), Art. 10 (4) (allowing the UK not to accept the extended powers of the Commission and the CJEU as well as acts re police/justice co-operation in criminal matters), 'shall cease to apply'. On the relevant instruments included, see Spencer, *Archbold Rev*, issue 7 (2012), 7–9; criticizing the UK's opt-out, Spencer, *Archbold Rev*, issue 8 (2013), 6–7; criticizing the UK's pick-and-choose approach as incompatible with a consistent approach to EU law, Mitsilegas, *CLR*, 63 (2016), 522–6 (discussing the EAW, confiscation measures and fraud).
96. Protocol 36 (n. 55), Art. 10 (4) *in fine*, with (2) (the former excluding the application of the opt-out to 'the amended acts which are applicable to the UK as referred to in paragraph 2').
97. EU Act 2011, part 1, sect. 6; thereto Spencer, in Mitsilegas, Alldridge and Cheliotis, *Globalisation, Criminal Law and Criminal Justice* (2015), 142–3; Mitsilegas, *CLR*, 63 (2016), 518.
98. Protocol 36 (n. 55), Art. 10(5) (allowing the UK to 'notify the Council of its wish to participate in acts which have ceased to apply' pursuant to the previous opt-out. This selective (re-)opt-in will need the authorisation of the Commission or Council, i.e. the UK may only request readmission but has no right to be readmitted; see also Spencer, *Archbold Rev*, issue 7 (2013), 6; criticism of Prot. 36, Fletcher, in Mitsilegas, Bergström and Konstadinides, *Handbook EU Criminal Law* (2016), pp. 79 ff.
99. For the UK's letter and notification, see above, endnote 55. On the process and the rhetoric in the UK leading to the opt-out, see Spencer, *Archbold Rev*, issue 8 (2013), 7–8; Fletcher, in Mitsilegas, Bergström and Konstadinides, *Handbook EU Criminal Law* (2016), pp. 86 ff., 94 ff.; briefly Blackstock and Tinsley, *Archbold Rev*, issue 8 (2015), 5.
100. Protocol 36 (n. 55), Art. 10(4) last clause in conjunction with Art. 10(2); on this ('Lisbonising' of pre-Lisbon acts) see already endnote 66.
101. The 'magic' thirty-five measures the UK opted back into are listed in Command Paper 8671, Decision pursuant to Article 10 of Protocol 36 to the TFEU, July 2013, 8–12, available at www.gov.uk/government/uploads/system/uploads/attachment_data/file/235912/8671.pdf, last accessed 27 January 2018; see also Council Decision of 1 December 2014 concerning the notification of the United Kingdom of Great Britain and Northern Ireland of its wish to take part in some of the provisions of the Schengen acquis which are contained in acts of the Union in the Field of police co-operation and judicial co-operation in criminal matters and amending Decisions 2000/365/EC and 2004/926/EC; OJ L 345 of 1 December 2014, 1–5. See also de Busser, *ERA Forum*, 16 (2015), 287; Blackstock and Tinsley, *Archbold Rev*, issue 8 (2015), 5–6; Fletcher, in Mitsilegas, Bergström and Konstadinides, *Handbook EU Criminal Law* (2016), pp. 90–4; Mitsilegas, *CLR*, 63 (2016), 520–2.
102. Cf. Spencer, *Archbold Rev*, issue 8 (2013), 9. In a similar vein Yvette Cooper, Shadow Home Secretary, commented on Cameron's claim to have 'clawed back 100 powers from Brussels': 'We have the power not to do a whole series of things

we plan to carry on doing anyway, the power not to follow guidance we already follow, the power not to take action we already take, the power not to meet standards we already meet, the power not to do things that everyone else has already stopped doing and the power not to do a whole series of things we want to do anyway' (Hansard, House of Commons, 7 April 2015, Column 363).

103. For a fundamental critique, especially with regard to the negative impact on rights protection, cf. Mitsilegas, *EU Criminal Law after Lisbon* (2016), pp. 49–50, 180–1, 266.

104. See above, mn. 8.

105. Criticism of the impact of Brexit on EuCrL Mitsilegas, *CLR*, 63 (2016), 526 ff. (discussing the EAW, EIS and exchange of criminal records, as well as surveillance and police co-operation) but also suggesting possible negotiating options (agreement UK–EU, agreements UK–individual agencies, e.g. Europol, or bilateral agreements EU–MS) at 533–4 (arguing, however, that none of these options will be 'capable of providing to the UK a level of co-operation which is equivalent to the current level of co-operation as a member of the EU'). See also Mitsilegas, *CLF*, 28 (2017), 219 ff., illustrating a double paradox: first, the UK's opt-out approach will become revitalised so that the future co-operation between the UK and the EU leads to a 'collateral damage … in the limited protection of fundamental rights'. Second, 'the UK's willingness to reap the security benefits of EU cooperation after Brexit can be accommodated only if the UK complies fully with the EU *acquis*, including the *acquis* on the protection of fundamental rights … Brexit will thus bring the UK in the paradoxical position to accept *more* EU law than it currently does as an EU Member State' (294–5); also Mitsilegas, in Dougan, *The UK after Brexit* (2017), S. 203 ff.

106. *Constitutional Court of the Czech Republic* (*Ústavní Soud*), 2008/11/26 – Pl. ÚS 19/08, Lisbon Treaty I, Judgment (26 November 2008), available in English at www.usoud.cz/en/decisions/20081126-pl-us-1908-treaty-of-lisbon-i-1, last accessed 27 January 2018; *Constitutional Court of the Czech Republic* (*Ústavní Soud*), 2009/11/03 – Pl. ÚS 29/09: Treaty of Lisbon II, Judgment (3 November 2009), available in English at www.usoud.cz/en/decisions/20091103-pl-us-2909-treaty-of-lisbon-ii-1, last accessed 27 January 2018.

107. BVerfG, 2 BvE 2/08, Judgment (30 June 2009), in *BVerfGE*, 123, pp. 267–437, English translation available at www.bundesverfassungsgericht.de/SharedDocs/Entscheidungen/EN/2009/06/es20090630_2bve000208en.html;jsessionid=67A33469EB624F3A990D068D378D95D0.2_cid361, last accessed 27 January 2018, reprinted in *CMLR*, 3 (2010), 13.

108. *Constitutional Court of the Republic of Latvia* (*Satversmes tiesa*), No 2008-35-01, Judgment on Compliance of the Law 'On Lisbon Agreement Amending the Treaty on European Union and the Treaty Establishing the European Community' with Article 101 of the *Satversme* of the Republic of Latvia (7 April 2009), available in English at www.satv.tiesa.gov.lv/wp-content/uploads/2008/09/2008-35-01_Spriedums_ENG.pdf, last accessed 21 November 2017.

109. *Constitutional Tribunal of the Polish Republic* (*Trybunał Konstytucyjny w Polsce*), K 32/09, Judgment (21 November 2017), available in English at http://trybunal.gov.pl/fileadmin/content/omowienia/K_32_09_EN.pdf, last accessed 27 January 2018.

110. *Conseil Constitutionnel* (*Constitutional Council of the French Republic*), Decision No 2007-560 DC (20 December 2007), available at www.conseil-constitutionnel

.fr/conseil-constitutionnel/francais/les-decisions/acces-par-date/decisions-depuis-1959/2007/2007-560-dc/decision-n-2007-560-dc-du-20-decembre-2007.1166.html, last accessed 27 January 2018; for an English translation, see www.conseil-constitutionnel.fr/conseil-constitutionnel/root/bank_mm/anglais/a2007560dc.pdf, last accessed 27 January 2018.

111. See also Chalmers, Davies and Monti, *EU Law* (2014), p. 45 ('elaborated in most detail').
112. Accompanying Act on the expansion and strengthening of the rights of the two German legislative Chambers (Bundestag and Bundesrat), BT-Drs. 16/8489.
113. Law of 8 October 2008 on the Treaty of Lisbon of 13 December 2007; pursuant to Article 59(2) Grundgesetz (GG – Basic Law).
114. BVerfG, 2 BvE 2/08 (n. 107). For a brief analysis in English, see Chalmers, in Fischer-Lescano, Joerges and Wonka, *The Lisbon Ruling* (2010), pp. 5–9; Craig, *Lisbon Treaty* (2013), pp. 151–4; Mitsilegas, *EU Criminal Law after Lisbon* (2016), pp. 19–21; for a more detailed analysis, cf. Ambos and Rackow, *ZIS*, 4 (2009), 397 ff.; Beukelmann, *NJW*, 63 (2010), 2082–3; Böse, *ZIS*, 5 (2010), 76 ff.; Braum, *ZIS*, 4 (2009), 418 ff.; Folz, *ZIS*, 4 (2009), 427 ff.; Gärditz and Hillgruber, *JZ*, 64 (2009), 872 ff.; Haratsch, *ZJS*, 3 (2010), 122; Heger, *ZIS*, 4 (2009), 406 ff.; Kubiciel, *GA*, 157 (2010), 99 ff.; Oppermann, *EuZW*, 20 (2009), 473; Pache, *EuGRZ*, 36 (2009), 285 ff.; Schorkopf, in Ambos, *Europäisches Strafrecht post-Lissabon* (2011), p. 111; Schünemann, *ZIS*, 4 (2009), 393 ff.; Spemann, *StraFo*, 22 (2009), 499 ff.; Suhr, *ZEuS*, 12 (2009), 687 ff.; Zimmermann, *Jura*, 31 (2009), 844 ff.; Kiiver, *EuLJ*, 16 (2010), 578 ff.; Arato, *EJIL:Talk!*, 9 October 2010; Steinbach, *GLJ*, 11 (2010), 368 ff.; Schmidt, in Fischer-Lescano, Joerges and Wonka, *Lisbon Ruling* (2010), pp. 41, 45–6; Blauberger, in ibid., pp. 47–53; Möller, in ibid., pp. 83 ff.; Wonka, in ibid., pp. 55–62; Liebert, in ibid., pp. 71 ff.; Schütze, *EU Law* (2015), pp. 131–3; from a political-economic perspective, Höpner, in Fischer-Lescano, Joerges and Wonka, *Lisbon Ruling* (2010), pp. 21–6; taking particular account of environmental criminal law, Reiling and Reschke, *wistra*, 29 (2010), 47 ff. On the fundamentally pro-European stance of the German Federal Constitutional Court, cf. Zwingmann, *ICLQ*, 61 (2012), 665 ff.
115. BVerfG, 2 BvE 2/08 (n. 107), para. 208. According to Mylonopoulos, *ZStW*, 123 (2011), 636, the objection of a democratic deficit of the EU has become less important. For a critical view, cf. also Gärditz, in Böse, *Europäisches Strafrecht* (2013), pp. 232 ff.; cf. also Meyer, *Strafrechtsgenese* (2012), pp. 317–18.
116. BVerfG, 2 BvE 2/08 (n. 107), para. 253: 'Instead, the decision on punishable behaviour, on the ranking of legal interests and the meaning and the measure of the threat of punishment, is much more particularly left to the democratic decision-making process' ('Die Entscheidung über strafwürdiges Verhalten, über den Rang von Rechtsgütern und den Sinn und das Maß der Strafdrohung ist vielmehr in besonderem Maße dem demokratischen Entscheidungsprozess überantwortet').
117. BVerfG, 2 BvE 2/08 (n. 107), para. 252: 'for the ability A of a constitutional state' ('für die demokratische Selbstgestaltungsfähigkeit eines Verfassungsstaates'). The following areas are also listed as sensitive: decisions on the police monopoly on the use of force, basic fiscal decisions, the social state's shaping of living conditions and decisions of particular cultural importance, e.g. in family law, school and education law and in dealing with religious communities. Cf. also Landau, *NStZ*, 33 (2013), 194–5; Geiger, *Auswirkungen europäischer Strafrechtsharmonisierung*

(2012), pp. 59–60; Asp, *Substantive Criminal Law Competence* (2012), pp. 76 ff.; Meyer, in Böse, *Europäisches Strafrecht* (2013), pp. 927 ff. On the development of the relationship between sovereignty and criminal law, cf. Capus, *Strafrecht und Souveränität* (2010), pp. 56 ff.

118. BVerfG, 2 BvE 2/08 (n. 107), para. 253: 'depends on cultural processes of previous understanding that are historically grown and also determined by language . . . only partially normatively derived from values and moral premises that are shared Europe-wide' ('von kulturellen, historisch gewachsenen, auch sprachlich geprägten Vorverständnissen . . . abhängig [und] nur eingeschränkt aus europaweit geteilten Werten und sittlichen Prämissen normativ ableitbar'); for an even more critical opinion, cf. Noltenius, *ZStW*, 122 (2010), 622. On European cultures of criminal law, cf. Safferling, in Streng and Kett-Straub, *Strafrechtsvergleichung als Kulturvergleich* (2012), pp. 188 ff.; cf. also Capus, *Strafrecht und Souveränität* (2010), pp. 83 ff.
119. BVerfG, 2 BvE 2/08 (n. 107), para. 253 ('grundsätzlich substantielle mitgliedsstaatliche Handlungsfreiräume'). For a similar view in the Scandinavian states, cf. Suominen, *EuCLR*, 1 (2011), 172; for Sweden's restrictive position, cf. Friman, in Muller and Zouridis, *Law and Justice* (2012), pp. 261 ff.; for Denmark, cf. Baumbach, *EuCLR*, 3 (2013), 300 ff.
120. BVerfG, 2 BvE 2/08 (n. 107), paras. 358 ff.; on the principle of culpability para. 364; in agreement with this, Landau, *NStZ*, 33 (2013), 195 ff.
121. BVerfG, 2 BvE 2/08 (n. 107), para. 359. Vogel is doubtful whether it will be possible to establish these strict criteria in European practice; cf. Vogel, in Ambos, *Europäisches Strafrecht post-Lissabon* (2011), p. 46.
122. Thereon, see also Chapter 3, mn. 10 and 37.
123. BVerfG, 2 BvE 2/08 (n. 107), para. 362: 'that a serious deficit as regards enforcement actually exists and that it can only be remedied by a threat of sanction' ('ein gravierendes Vollzugsdefizit tatsächlich besteht und nur durch Strafandrohung beseitigt werden kann'); in agreement with this, Schützendübel, *EU-Verordnungen in Blankettstrafgesetzen* (2012), p. 41; cf. also Landau, *NStZ*, 33 (2013), 199 ('substantial proof'; orig. 'substantielle Nachweise'); for a critical view, cf. Böse, in Böse, *Europäisches Strafrecht* (2013), pp. 161–2, who grants the Union legislator a margin of discretion; a similar view is taken by Vogel, in Ambos, *Europäisches Strafrecht post-Lissabon* (2011), p. 46.
124. Art. 83(1) second subpara. TFEU.
125. The (old) 'Council' of ministers (Art. 16 TEU) needs to be distinguished from the new, upgraded 'European Council' (Art. 15 TEU). To support its work, the Council has a number of working groups, including the Working Group on Substantive Criminal Law (DROIPEN) or the Committee according to Art. 36 TEU (Comité de l'article trente-six du traité UE = CATS); for more detail cf. Meyer, *Strafrechtsgenese* (2012), p. 308.
126. BVerfG, 2 BvE 2/08 (n. 107), paras. 363, 419; on this, cf. Hahn, *EuZW*, 20 (2009), 760–1; Gärditz, in Böse, *Europäisches Strafrecht* (2013), pp. 244 ff.
127. On this, cf. Chapter 3, mn. 5 ff. and 11.
128. BVerfG, 2 BvE 2/08 (n. 107), paras. 365, 418; on this, cf. Hahn, *EuZW*, 20 (2009), 761–2; Meyer, in Böse, *Europäisches Strafrecht* (2013), p. 941; Meyer, *Strafrechtsgenese* (2012), p. 320; on the role of the German representative on the Council in general: Rathke, in von Arnauld and Hufeld, *Systematischer Kommentar zu den Lissabon-Begleitgesetzen* (2018), mn. 142 ff.

129. BVerfG, 2 BvE 2/08 (n. 107), paras. 240 ff. and 331–2; on this, cf. Zimmermann, *Jura*, 31 (2009), 849; Schorkopf, *EuZW*, 20 (2009), 721; Herdegen, *Europarecht* (2017), §10 mn. 28; Sauer, *ZRP*, 42 (2009), 195; Haratsch, *ZJS*, 3 (2010), 127; Noltenius, *ZStW*, 122 (2010), 611 ff., 622 ff.; for a critical view, cf. Vogel cit. in Bettels, *ZStW*, 124 (2013), 877; cf. also Meyer, *Strafrechtsgenese* (2012), pp. 349–50: 'net . . . with meshes too large for its own demands' (orig. 'Netz . . . das für den eigenen Anspruch zu große Maschen hat') (p. 350). On the frictions between the German and the European understandings of criminal law, cf. Vogel, *JZ*, 67 (2012), 25. Against the background of the ruling on the Lisbon Treaty on the significance of constitutional complaints for defence, cf. Schorkopf, in Ambos, *Europäisches Strafrecht post-Lissabon* (2011), pp. 113 ff.
130. BVerfG, 1 BvR 1215/07, Judgment (24 April 2013), in *BVerfGE*, 133, pp. 277–377, English translation available at www.bundesverfassungsgericht.de/SharedDocs/Entscheidungen/EN/2013/04/rs20130424_1bvr121507en.html, last accessed 27 January 2018, para. 91 ('keine Lesart unterlegt werden [darf], nach de[m] diese[r] offensichtlich als Ultra-vires-Akt zu beurteilen wäre oder Schutz und Durchsetzung der mitgliedstaatlichen Grundrechte in einer Weise gefährdete . . . dass dies die Identität der durch das Grundgesetz errichteten Verfassungsordnung in Frage stellte' ('this decision must not be read in a way that would view it as an apparent *ultra vires* act or as if it endangered the protection and enforcement of the fundamental rights in the member states . . . in a way that questioned the identity of the Basic Law's constitutional order.')). Also see the restriction of the *ultra vires* review to serious infringements of competence in BVerfG, 2 BvR 2661/06, Decision (6 July 2010), in *NJW*, 63 (2010), 3422.
131. For a critical view, cf. also Latzel, *FAZ*, 3 May 2013, 7; on this, cf. also Thym, *NVwZ*, 33 (2013), 890. For a critical view on the general German practice of preliminary references, cf. Vogel, *JZ*, 67 (2012), 26; yet German courts make relatively frequent use of this possibility, cf. Wolter, *Vorabentscheidungsverfahren und Beschleunigungsgebot in Strafsachen* (2011), p. 76; and Ambos, *GA*, 163 (2016), 183. On the relationship between BVerfG and ECJ, see Voßkuhle, *NJW*, 66 (2013), 1330–1; cf. also Landau, *NStZ*, 31 (2011), 546 (Lisbon decision as an 'offer to engage in dialogue'; orig. 'Angebot zum Dialog').
132. See endnote 106 above. See also Krämer, in Fischer-Lescano, Joerges and Wonka, Lisbon Ruling (2010), pp. 12–15; Kruma, in Guild, Carrera and Eggenschwiler, *The Area of Freedom, Security and Justice* (2010), pp. 42 ff.
133. *Ústavní Soud*, 2008/11/26 – Pl. ÚS 19/08, para. 97.
134. *Ústavní Soud*, 2009/11/03 – Pl. ÚS 29/09, para. 147; cf. also Krämer, in Fischer-Lescano, Joerges and Wonka, Lisbon Ruling (2010), pp. 12–15; Kruma, in Guild, Carrera and Eggenschwiler, *The Area of Freedom, Security and Justice* (2010), pp. 42 ff.
135. *Ústavní Soud*, 2009/11/03 – Pl. ÚS 29/09, paras. 137 ff.
136. *Satversmes tiesa*, No 2008-35-01, endnote 108, para. 18.3 (official English translation quoted); on this judgment, cf. also Kruma, in Guild, Carrera and Eggenschwiler, *The Area of Freedom, Security and Justice* (2010), pp. 39 ff.
137. *Satversmes tiesa*, No 2008-35-01 (n. 108) para. 18.3.
138. See *Trybunał Konstytucyjny w Polsce*, K 32/09, n. 109, para. 3.
139. See *Trybunał Konstytucyjny w Polsce*, K 32/09, n. 109, para. 2.1, p. 21.
140. *Conseil Constitutionnel*, Decision No 2007-560 DC, para. 18 (emphasis added) ('des compétences inhérentes à l'exercice de la souveraineté nationale'); thereon,

see also Kruma, in Guild, Carrera and Eggenschwiler, *The Area of Freedom, Security and Justice* (2010), pp. 45–6.

141. *Conseil Constitutionnel*, Decision No 2007-560 DC, n. 140, para. 18.
142. *Conseil Constitutionnel*, Decision No 2007-560 DC, n. 140, para. 19.
143. *Conseil Constitutionnel*, Decision No 2007-560 DC, n. 140, paras. 23–5.
144. *Conseil Constitutionnel*, Decision No 2007-560 DC, n. 140, para. 25.
145. *Conseil Constitutionnel*, Decision No 2007-560 DC, n. 140, paras. 28–32.
146. See main text, mn. 22 ff.
147. For such a limited concept of 'system', see also Asp, *Procedural Criminal Law Cooperation* (2016), pp. 211–13 (with general considerations of the concept of 'system' at 207–8, 213). See also Perron, in Tiedemann et al., *Die Verfassung moderner Strafrechtspflege* (2016), p. 312 ('kind of criminal law order' ('Art von Strafrechtsordnung')).
148. Cf. Ambos, in Joecks and Miebach, *Münchener Kommentar StGB*, i (2011), Vorbemerkung §§3–7, mn. 7; in a similar vein, Klip, *European Criminal Law* (2016), pp. 1–2; Sieber, in Sieber, Satzger and Heintschel von Heinegg, *Europäisches Strafrecht* (2014), pp. 36–7; Satzger, *International and European Criminal Law* (2018), §5 mn. 2–3; Satzger, in Sieber, Satzger and Heintschel von Heinegg, *Europäisches Strafrecht* (2014), pp. 251–2; Satzger, *Internationales und Europäisches Strafrecht* (2016), §7 mn. 2–3; Böse, in Böse, *Europäisches Strafrecht* (2013), pp. 55 ff.; Safferling, *Internationales Strafrecht* (2011), §2 mn. 7, §9 mn. 5 ff.; Flore, *Droit pénal européen* (2009), pp. 11–19; Esser, *Europäisches und Internationales Strafrecht* (2018), §1 mn. 3. On European law in the narrower and wider sense, see e.g. Herdegen, *Europarecht* (2017), §1 mn. 2–11; Hefendehl, *ZIS*, 1 (2006), 229. On the historical development of European criminal law, cf. Asp, *Substantive Criminal Law Competence* (2012), pp. 24 ff.; Nilsson, *EuCLR*, 2 (2012), 106 ff.; Kainer, *EuR-Bei*, 48 (2013), 88 ff.; Böse, in Böse, *Europäisches Strafrecht* (2013), pp. 49 ff.
149. For the relevant arguments against cf. Asp, *Procedural Criminal Law Cooperation* (2016), pp. 209–11.
150. Cf. Asp, *Procedural Criminal Law Cooperation* (2016), pp. 216–17.
151. For a groundbreaking analysis cf. Meyer, in Herzog et al., *GS Weßlau* (2016), pp. 194 ff., understanding the concept of *Verbund*, originating in European administrative law (196–8), in a descriptive–analytical and at the same time critical sense (198) and applying it to the area of European criminal prosecution (the 'EU-Strafverfolgungsverbund', 199) by way of a functional and impact-oriented approach ('funktions- und wirkungsorientierte Herangehensweise', 200), thereby distinguishing between three sorts of *Verbünde* (compound networks): one regarding execution/enforcement ('Vollstreckungs- und Substitutionsverbund'), characterised by mutual recognition and the increasing overlapping of criminal procedure and legal assistance (201–2), another one regarding collection and storage of information/data ('Informationsverbund', 202–4) and a third one regarding investigation/prosecution *stricto sensu* ('Verbundverfolgung im engeren Sinne', 204–10), at 201–10.
152. See again Meyer, in Herzog et al., *GS Weßlau* (2016), pp. 204 ff., identifying a 'surprising' transformation and an increasing influence of the said EU criminal justice agencies (207) with critical implications democratic accountability and rights protection (210–14).

153. For such a (flawed) comparison, see Gómez-Jara Díez, in Bacigalupo and Cancio Meliá, *Derecho penal y política transnacional* (2005), pp. 153 ff., 166 ff.; Gómez-Jara Díez, *EuCLR*, 3 (2013), 170; Gómez-Jara Díez, *European Federal Criminal Law* (2015), pp. 15 ff.; contra, Silva Sánchez, in Bajo Fernández, *Constitución Europea y derecho penal económico* (2006), pp. 258–9. Cf. also the comparison between the USA, Switzerland and the EU in Ouwerkerk, *Mutual Recognition* (2011), pp. 242 ff., 264 ff.
154. See mn. 24 ff.
155. See mn. 25 ff.
156. See mn. 29.
157. Cf. Hecker, *Europäisches Strafrecht* (2015), §1 mn. 9 ff., 39; in a similar vein Flore, *Droit pénal européen* (2009), pp. 14–15; advocating a broader theoretical, argumentative basis instead of a too dogmatic, technical approach Sánchez Lázaro, *GA*, 161 (2014), 663–4.
158. On the previous legal situation, cf. Ambos, *Internationales Strafrecht* (2008), §11 mn. 1 ff.
159. Cf. Art. 5(1), (2) TEU; also Schröder, *Europäische Richtlinien und deutsches Strafrecht* (2002), p. 118; Satzger, *International and European Criminal Law* (2018), §6 mn. 18; Satzger, *Internationales und Europäisches Strafrecht* (2016), §8 mn. 18; Hecker, *Europäisches Strafrecht* (2015), §4 mn. 43; Safferling, *Internationales Strafrecht* (2011), §9 mn. 51 ff.; Esser, *Europäisches und Internationales Strafrecht* (2018), §2 mn. 121; Husemann, *wistra*, 23 (2004), 449; Braum, *wistra*, 25 (2006), 123; Zieschang, in Sieber et al., *FS Tiedemann* (2008), p. 1313; Rosenau, *ZIS*, 3 (2008), 12; Klip, *European Criminal Law* (2016), p. 37 ('principle of conferral'); Meyer, *Strafrechtsgenese* (2012), p. 338, on the threat that competences become watered down, which exists nonetheless, pp. 340 ff.
160. Cf. Art. 5(1), (3) and (4) TEU; Art. 69 TFEU; cf. also Draft Council conclusions 2009, p. 4; Asp, *EuCLR*, 1 (2011), 44 ff.; Asp, *Procedural Criminal Law Cooperation* (2016), pp. 190–1; Zöller, in Baumeister, Roth and Ruthig, *FS Schenke* (2011), pp. 596–7; Safferling, *Internationales Strafrecht* (2011), §9 mn. 58 ff.; Turner, *AmJCompL*, 60 (2012), 562–3; Böse, in Böse, *Europäisches Strafrecht* (2013), pp. 49–50.
161. Cf. Hecker, *Europäisches Strafrecht* (2015), §8 mn. 49; cf. also Klip, *European Criminal Law* (2016), pp. 37–8; Meyer, *Strafrechtsgenese* (2012), pp. 352 ff. On the component of the principle of subsidiarity that protects freedoms, cf. Kubiciel, *ZIS*, 5 (2010), 745; cf. also Bernardi, *RP*, 27 (2011), 23 ff.
162. Generally on a specific model of 'legal reserve', in the sense of *réserve legal* or *Gesetzesvorbehalt*) for the EU, see Muñoz de Morales, *EuCLR*, 2 (2012), 252–3, 274–5, advocating a model based on discursive deliberation (input legitimacy) and accountability (output legitimacy) to be achieved by a transparent, participative and rational legislative process – unfortunately, the paper is written in poor English; on the input, throughput and output legitimacy of European criminal law, also Brodowski, in Tiedemann et al., *Die Verfassung moderner Strafrechtspflege* (2016), pp. 174 ff. (although his understanding of these concepts varies in part).
163. Hecker, *Europäisches Strafrecht* (2015), §8 mn. 52 ff.; cf. also Klip, *European Criminal Law* (2016), pp. 38, 176 ff.; in greater detail, Asp, *Substantive Criminal Law Competence* (2012), pp. 188 ff.; on the competence-limiting function of theories of punishment in the context of the principle of proportionality, cf. Kubiciel, *ZIS*, 5 (2010), 746–7.

164. Art. 5 Subsidiarity Protocol (n. iv).
165. Lisbon Treaty, Protocol (No 1) on the Role of National Parliaments in the European Union, OJ C 326 of 26 October 2012, 203–5 and Art. 4 Subsidiarity Protocol (n. iv).
166. Arts. 6, 7 Subsidiarity Protocol (n. iv). The right to object is restricted to the principle of subsidiarity.
167. Art. 8 Subsidiarity Protocol (n. iv) in conjunction with Art. 263 TFEU. For more detail, see endnote iv.
168. Cf. mn. 13; for further references see also Ambos, *Internationales Strafrecht* (2008), §11 mn. 4, with n. 23.
169. On this, cf. Chapter 3, mn. 37 ff. On the particular demands with regard to subsidiarity in this context, cf. also Klip, *European Criminal Law* (2016), p. 40.
170. For a similar view of this matter, cf. Klip, *European Criminal Law* (2016), pp. 178–80; for a principled approach Silva Sánchez, *RP*, 13 (2004), 138 ff.
171. Arts. 82(3), 83(3) TFEU; see already mn. 10.
172. On this, cf. Chapter 3, mn. 5 ff. and 11–12.
173. In favour of an implied powers competence, however, if the expressive purposes of criminal law (in casu regarding xenophobic and racist crimes) so demand, see Turner, *AmJCompL*, 60 (2012), 576 ff. (proposing strict procedural safeguards and participation of national parliaments).
174. Cf. Satzger, *International and European Criminal Law* (2018), §6 mn. 20 ff.; Satzger, *Internationales und Europäisches Strafrecht* (2016), §8 mn. 20 ff.; regarding secondary legislation, see Chapter 3, mn. 37 ff.
175. BVerfG, 2 BvE 2/08 (n. 107), para. 361.
176. See in this regard Turner, *AmJCompL*, 60 (2012), 557–8, 564 ff., 576 (discussing the EU criminalization of racist and xenophobic crimes to reaffirm 'community values' and for 'expressive purposes' and seeing a legal basis in the Union's implied powers).
177. Cf. Nilsson, *eucrim*, 9 (2014), 19 (confiscation competence only with regard to eurocrimes).
178. Satzger, *Die Europäisierung des Strafrechts* (2001), p. 33; Nicolaysen, *Europarecht*, i (2002), p. 270; Arndt, Fischer and Fetzer, *Europarecht* (2015), mn. 37; Hecker, *Europäisches Strafrecht* (2015), §4 mn. 44; Nuotio, in Müller-Dietz, *FS Jung* (2007), p. 690; on this, cf. also Zweigert, *RabelsZ*, 28 (1964), 604.
179. For more detail on this, cf. Satzger, *Die Europäisierung des Strafrechts* (2001), pp. 72 ff.; Öberg, *EuCLR*, 3 (2013), 273 ff.; also Hecker, *Europäisches Strafrecht* (2015), §4 mn. 61 ff.; Safferling, *Internationales Strafrecht* (2011), §2 mn. 8; Asp, *Substantive Criminal Law Competence* (2012), pp. 61 ff.
180. Musil, *NStZ*, 20 (2000), 68, incl. further references; Asp, *Substantive Criminal Law Competence* (2012), pp. 57 ff. However, cf. also Vermeulen, *Free Gathering and Movement of Evidence* (2011), pp. 28 ff.; on the concept, development and legitimation of administrative sanctions under European law, see Brodowski, in Tiedemann et al., *Die Verfassung moderner Strafrechtspflege* (2016), pp. 142 ff., 166 ff.
181. For example, cf. Vogel, in Dannecker, *Bekämpfung des Subventionsbetrugs im EG-Bereich* (1993), pp. 171 and 175 ff.; on the 'dramatic sanctions', cf. Achenbach, *GA*, 151 (2004), 559, 569 ff. ('dramatischen Sanktionen'); Achenbach, *ZStW*, 119 (2007), 801; cf. also Satzger, *International and European Criminal Law* (2018), §6 mn. 5; Satzger, *Internationales und Europäisches Strafrecht* (2016), §8 mn. 5; Tiedemann, *ZStW*, 116 (2004), 947 ff.; Liebau, *'Ne bis in idem' in Europa* (2005),

pp. 35 ff. For a somewhat different interpretation, cf. Prieto, *ZStW*, 120 (2008), 414 ff., who treats EU sanctions as a 'new type of sanction' (orig. 'neuartigen Sanktionstypus'); in favour of categorising the sanctions as criminal law, especially from the perspective of fundamental rights and regulatory law, see Brodowski, in Tiedemann et al., *Die Verfassung moderner Strafrechtspflege* (2016), pp. 151 ff. (165), 178, 179–80.

182. Satzger, *Die Europäisierung des Strafrechts* (2001), pp. 76–7 ('sozialethischen Unwerturteils'); criticism on the underlying 'romanticised' understanding of criminal law Brodowski in Tiedemann et al., *Die Verfassung moderner Strafrechtspflege* (2016), pp. 158 ff., with further references.

183. On censure as one justification of punishment (apart from prevention), see the seminal contributions by von Hirsch, *Censure and Sanctions* (1995); and von Hirsch and Ashworth, *Proportionate Sentencing* (2005), pp. 12 ff.

184. On EU sanction law on a level below criminal law, cf. Tiedemann, *Wirtschaftsstrafrecht* (2017), mn. 491 ff.; Fromm, *ZIS*, 2 (2007), 280 ff.; Heine, *ZStrR*, 125 (2007), 108 ff., 129–30; Moosmayer, *wistra*, 26 (2007), 91 (on cartel fines); Vogel and Brodowski, in Sieber, Satzger and Heintschel von Heinegg, *Europäisches Strafrecht* (2014), pp. 157 ff.; Vogel and Brodowski, in Sieber, Satzger and Heintschel von Heinegg, *Europäisches Strafrecht* (2014), pp. 178 ff.; on European criminal policy on sanctions in general, cf. Poncela and Roth, *APC*, 27 (2005), 107 ff.

185. On this earlier debate, see Ambos, *Internationales Strafrecht* (2008), §11 mn. 7–13.

186. Cf. also Satzger, *International and European Criminal Law* (2018), §6 mn. 24; Satzger, *Internationales und Europäisches Strafrecht* (2016), §8 mn. 24; Mylonopoulos, *ZStW*, 123 (2011), 634–5; Hecker, in Ambos, *Europäisches Strafrecht post-Lissabon* (2011), p. 27.

187. Notwithstanding, Kubiciel, *ZIS*, 5 (2010), 743, considers the scope of application of Art. 325(4) TFEU to be limited and argues that a (partial) harmonisation of legislation can only be achieved if the General Parts of MS criminal codes are also harmonised. Art. 325(4) TFEU thus also includes the competence – restricted to the area of the fight against fraud – to issue rules on the General Part, although the limitations resulting from the principle of proportionality and the imperative to use criminal law in the most restrictive form possible (*strafrechtsspezifisches Schonungsgebot*) need to be taken into account; cf. also Grünewald, *JZ*, 66 (2011), 975–6; Vogel, in Ambos, *Europäisches Strafrecht post-Lissabon* (2011), p. 53; Weißer, *GA*, 161 (2014), 444–51 (obligation to adopt General Part rules in case of a regulation and, albeit to a minor extent, in case of a directive); in regard to Art. 83(1) TFEU, cf. also Satzger, *ZIS*, 11 (2016), 773; Zöller, in Baumeister, Roth and Ruthig, *FS Schenke* (2011), p. 589. Cf. also the many guidelines on the General Part (incl. attempt, participation and sanctions) in the Commission Proposal for a Directive of the EP and of the Council on the fight against fraud to the Union's financial interests by means of criminal law, COM (2012) 363 final, Brussels, 11 July 2012, which is based on Art. 325(4) TFEU; see Kaiafa-Gbandi, *EuCLR*, 2 (2012), 319, who goes into greater depth on this; also Brodowski, *ZIS*, 7 (2012), 561–2; Kuhl, *eucrim*, 7 (2012), 63 ff.; for a critical view, cf. BR-Drs. 409/12. Jähnke and Schramm, *Europäisches Strafrecht* (2017), §4 mn. 25, also give systematical reasons for a criminal law competence: the codification in Part 6, section 2 TFEU means that 'neither financial nor other administrative regulations' (orig. 'weder um Finanzvorschriften, noch sonst verwaltungsrechtliche Regelungen') are captured. Furthermore, Art. 86(2)

TFEU on the establishment of the EPPO presupposes that the offences falling in its jurisdiction are sufficiently defined, which in turn falls outside the MSs' competence. However, they refuse a competence of the EU to regulate General Part rules (mn. 26). Contra Caeiro, in Kert and Lehner, *FS Höpfel* (2018), p. 660 (distinguishing generally, at 652 ff., between EU core and mere transnational crimes with only the former providing for a broad EU criminal law competence).

188. However, it should be noted that the definition of fraud in European criminal law is broader than definitions in legislations of several MS. See e.g. §263 of the **German** Penal Code (*Strafgesetzbuch, StGB*) according to which the other fraudulent acts encompassed by the European definition are regarded as subsidy fraud (§264 *StGB*) or tax evasion (§370 *Abgabenordnung* (AO)); similarly Art. 326 **Dutch**PC, complemented by Art. 323a PC (embezzlement regarding EU funds); Art. 268 **Polish**PC, complemented by Arts. 297–8 PC and the Tax Criminal Code (*Kodeks karny skarbowy*); also Art. 217 **Portuguese**PC complemented, inter alia, by Art. 36 *Decreto-Lei* no 28/84 of 20 January 1984, as amended by the Act 20/2008 of 21 April 2008 (subsidy fraud); Art. 248 **Spanish**PC (complemented with regard to the EU offence by Art. 306, i.e., fraud against EU budget); Ch. 9 sect. 1 **Swedish**PC (complemented by Ch. 9 sect. 3a regarding subsidy fraud); in **Greece**, pursuant to Art. 4 of Law 2803/2000, fraud against the financial interests of the EU is a *sui generis* crime (so called 'eurofraud') including acts that under ordinary criminal law would constitute fraud (Art. 386 GreekPC), forgery (Art. 216 GreekPC) and so forth; in **Italy**, the ordinary fraud (Art. 640 PC) is complemented by fraud against public property, including of the EU (Art. 640bis PC), and embezzlement of public, including EU, funds (Art. 316bis and ter PC); in **Hungary**, the PC provides for two forms of fraud, a normal one and 'budget fraud' (sect. 373 and 396 PC); also for the ordinary, narrowly defined fraud in **France** see Art. 313-1 CP (*escroquerie*). In **England and Wales**, fraud was codified in a 2006 Statute covering any false information or abuse of a position of trust with the intent to make a financial gain (including affecting the EU's budget); otherwise the common law offence of conspiracy to defraud is still applicable (cf. Simester et al., *Simester and Sullivan's Criminal Law* (2016), pp. 622 ff.). At any rate, the details of the European definition are unclear and remain disputed (for criticism on the harmonisation efforts, see Weißer, *GA*, 161 (2014), 437). For example, it is controversial whether acts such as corruption and money laundering, which only affect the Union's financial interests indirectly, can be seen as fraud in the sense of Art. 325 TFEU; thereon cf. the different approaches taken by Grünewald, *JZ*, 66 (2011), 974; Zöller, in Baumeister, Roth and Ruthig, *FS Schenke* (2011), p. 582; Satzger, *International and European Criminal Law* (2018), §6 mn. 25; Satzger, *Internationales und Europäisches Strafrecht* (2016), §8 mn. 25; Zimmermann, *Jura*, 31 (2009), 846; Tiedemann, *Wirtschaftsstrafrecht* (2017), mn. 126 ff.; Vogel, in Ambos, *Europäisches Strafrecht post-Lissabon* (2011), pp. 48–9. See in more detail below, Chapter 3, mn. 14.

189. Cf. also Grünewald, *JZ*, 66 (2011), 973, incl. further references; but see the Grand Chamber's *Taricco* judgment as discussed in Chapter 3, mn. 45.

190. On the Commission proposals for an Art. 280a TEC and Art. III-415 TCE, cf. Ambos, *Internationales Strafrecht* (2008), §11 mn. 11 ff.

191. Nürnberger, *ZJS*, 2 (2009), 497; Mansdörfer, *HRRS*, 11 (2010), 18; Zimmermann, *Jura*, 31 (2009), 845–6; Satzger, *ZRP*, 43 (2010), 137; Satzger, *International and European Criminal Law* (2018), §6 mn. 24; Satzger, in Streinz, *EUV/AEUV* (2012), Art. 83 AEUV mn. 4; Satzger, in Böse, *Europäisches Strafrecht* (2013), p. 66; Satzger,

Internationales und Europäisches Strafrecht (2016), §8 mn. 24; Calliess, *ZEuS*, 11 (2008), 37; Fromm, *EG-Rechtssetzungsbefugnis* (2009), pp. 64 ff.; Hecker, *Europäisches Strafrecht* (2015), §4 mn. 82, §14 mn. 54; Hecker and Zöller, *Fallsammlung* (2012), pp. 86–7 (Case 8), pp. 111–12 (Case 11); Hecker, in Ambos, *Europäisches Strafrecht post-Lissabon* (2011), p. 27; Safferling, *Internationales Strafrecht* (2011), §10 mn. 41; Esser, *Europäisches und Internationales Strafrecht* (2018), §2 mn. 125; Schramm, *ZJS*, 3 (2010), 615; Noltenius, *ZStW*, 122 (2010), 618; Grünewald, *JZ*, 66 (2011), 973; Vogel and Brodowski, in Sieber, Satzger and Heintschel von Heinegg, *Europäisches Strafrecht* (2014), pp. 155–7; Asp, *Substantive Criminal Law Competence* (2012), pp. 147 ff. (on the limits, pp. 154 ff.); Krüger, *HRRS*, 13 (2012), 311 ff.; Weißer, *GA*, 161 (2014), 438–40, 452 (at 440 ff. advocating a regulation and discussing its contents). For a different opinion, cf. Böse, in Amelung, Günther and Kühne, *FS Krey* (2010), p. 16 ('has no authority . . . to enact sanctions to be applied directly, (even) following the Reform Treaty.'; orig. '(auch) nach dem Reformvertrag nicht befugt . . . unmittelbar anwendbare Strafbestimmungen zu erlassen.'); Böse, in Böse, *Europäisches Strafrecht* (2013), pp. 164–5; Schröder, in Hellman and Schröder, *FS Achenbach* (2011), pp. 496–7; Sturies, *HRRS*, 13 (2012), 273; likewise Sicurella, in Klip, *Substantive Criminal Law of the EU* (2011), p. 236; Schützendübel, *EU-Verordnungen in Blankettstrafgesetzen* (2012), p. 29; Dorra, *Strafrechtliche Legislativkompetenzen der EU* (2013), pp. 278 ff., who assumes that Art. 83(2) TFEU has suspensory effect; Zöller, in Baumeister, Roth and Ruthig, *FS Schenke* (2011), pp. 583 ff., examines the relation to Arts. 75, 82, 83 TFEU; a doubtful view is taken by Caeiro, in Correia, Machado and Loureiro, *Estudos homenagem Gomes Canotilho*, iii (2012), pp. 183 ff. On the relationship between Arts. 325 and 83 TFEU, cf. also Simon, *NJECL*, 3 (2012), 248–9; in detail, Miettinen, *EuCLR*, 3 (2013), 195 ff. Cf. also the debate between the Commission and the Council (Council of the EU, 'Proposal for a Directive of the EP and of the Council on the fight against fraud to the Union's financial interests by means of criminal law', 15309/12, Brussels, 22 October 2012; on this, see Brodowski, *ZIS*, 8 (2013), 464). Heger, *ZIS*, 4 (2009), 416, sees the competence to legislate criminal law emerging only after the establishment of the EPPO and the application of the 'emergency brake' of Arts. 82(3) and 83(3) TFEU.

192. Art. 83(2) TFEU.
193. Art. 83(1) TFEU. This is, however, claimed by Meyer, *EuR*, 46 (2011), 176, 184 ff.; for a more nuanced view, cf. Meyer, *Strafrechtsgenese* (2012), pp. 419 ff. A similar line of argument is taken in Mitsilegas, *EU Criminal Law* (2009), p. 109 (followed by Herlin-Karnell, *eucrim*, 5 (2010), 61).
194. In this vein, Satzger, *International and European Criminal Law* (2018), §6 mn. 25; Satzger, *Internationales und Europäisches Strafrecht* (2016), §8 mn. 25; Satzger, in Böse, *Europäisches Strafrecht* (2013), p. 66; Satzger, in Streinz, *EUV/AEUV* (2012), Art. 83 AEUV mn. 4; Schramm, *ZJS*, 3 (2010), 615; Esser, *Europäisches und Internationales Strafrecht* (2018), §2 mn. 128; Safferling, in Streng and Kett-Straub, *Strafrechtsvergleichung als Kulturvergleich* (2012), p. 203; Safferling, *Internationales Strafrecht* (2011), §10 mn. 43; Reinbacher, *Strafrecht im Mehrebenensystem* (2015), p. 446; for a different opinion, cf. Asp, *Substantive Criminal Law Competence* (2012), pp. 160–1; Böse, in Böse, *Europäisches Strafrecht* (2013), pp. 165–6; Meyer, *Strafrechtsgenese* (2012), pp. 421–2.

195. Art. 288(1) TFEU.
196. Art. 79(2)(c, d) TFEU. Cf. Satzger, *International and European Criminal Law* (2018), §6 mn. 26; Satzger, *Internationales und Europäisches Strafrecht* (2016), §8 mn. 26; Mansdörfer, *HRRS*, 11 (2010), 18; Heger, *ZIS*, 4 (2009), 416; Walter, *ZStW*, 117 (2005), 918–19; Weigend, *ZStW*, 116 (2004), 288; Tiedemann, *Wirtschaftsstrafrecht* (2017), mn. 130.
197. Conc. Zöller, in Baumeister, Roth and Ruthig, *FS Schenke* (2011), p. 585; Esser, *Europäisches und Internationales Strafrecht* (2018), §2 mn. 129; Asp, *Substantive Criminal Law Competence* (2012), pp. 157 ff.; Böse, in Böse, *Europäisches Strafrecht* (2013), p. 25; Meyer, *Strafrechtsgenese* (2012), p. 418; Jähnke and Schramm, *Europäisches Strafrecht* (2017), §4 mn. 24; Grünewald, *JZ*, 66 (2011), 974, albeit with some criticism of the TFEU's lack of conclusiveness; a different view is taken by Schramm, *ZJS*, 3 (2010), 615; Safferling, in Streng and Kett-Straub, *Strafrechtsvergleichung als Kulturvergleich* (2012), p. 203; Safferling, *Internationales Strafrecht* (2011), §10 mn. 44 ff.; arguably also by Satzger, *International and European Criminal Law* (2018), §6 mn. 26; Satzger, in Böse, *Europäisches Strafrecht* (2013), p. 67; Satzger, *Internationales und Europäisches Strafrecht* (2016), §8 mn. 26; however, a different argument is presented by Satzger, in Streinz, *EUV/AEUV* (2012), Art. 83 AEUV mn. 4. The question is left open by Mansdörfer, *HRRS*, 11 (2010), 18.
198. Cf. Chapter 3, mn. 11–12.
199. Vogler, *Jura*, 14 (1992), 587–8; cf. also Schomburg, in Sieber, Satzger and Heintschel von Heinegg, *Europäisches Strafrecht* (2014), pp. 142–3; de Vel, in Muller and Zouridis, *Law and Justice* (2012), pp. 247 ff.
200. Vogler, *ZStW* (79) 1969, 113–14; Vogler, *Jura*, 14 (1992), 586.
201. For example, the Committee of Experts on the Operation of European Conventions in the Penal Field (PC-OC), the Council for Penological Co-operation (PC-CP), the Ad hoc Drafting Group on Dangerous Offenders (PC-GR-DD), the Committee of Experts on Trafficking in Human Organs, Tissues and Cells (PC-TO) or the Ad hoc Drafting Group on Transnational Organised Crime (PC-GR-COT); cf. also www.coe.int/tcj, last accessed 27 January 2018.
202. Vogler, *Jura*, 14 (1992), 586.
203. Cf. Chapter 3, mn. 2 ff.
204. For the full list of (223) CoE Treaties see www.coe.int/en/web/conventions/full-list, last accessed 27 January 2018.
205. Cf. thereon Ambos, *Internationales Strafrecht* (2008), §12 mn. 1 ff.
206. See previously endnote 63 ff. and main text.
207. Art. 67 TFEU. On the EU's aims in this area, cf. Sieber, *ZStW*, 121 (2009), 3 ff. For a critical view on the relationship between those three components in European security policy, cf. Kaiafa-Gbandi, *EuCLR*, 1 (2011), 10. For a linguistic–judicial perspective, Tiberi, in Ruggieri, *Languages* (2014), pp. 9 ff.; Spiezia, in Ruggieri, *Languages* (2014), pp. 23 ff. (stressing both the importance of several languages for the Union's identity and the ensuing problems for co-operation).
208. Art. 68 TFEU. On the (difficult) implementation of Art. 68 TFEU and possible new 'post-Stockholm' guidelines, see Salazar, *eucrim*, 9 (2014), 22 ff.; on key points for a future post-Stockholm programme, Herlin-Karnell, *eucrim*, 9 (2014), 28 ff.; on the need for a framework of principles for European criminal policy, Parisi and Rinoldi, *eucrim*, 10 (2015), 111 ff.; on the need of evidence-based criminal policy but lack of

reliable empirical data, Pérez Cepeda, Benito Sánchez and Gorjón Barranco, *EuCLR*, 3 (2013), 125 ff. In fact, Council and Commission have, long before the Lisbon Treaty, adopted five-year programmes (Tampere (1999), The Hague (2004) and Stockholm (2009)) and respective action plans implementing those programmes. Art. 68 TFEU has complicated matters in giving the Council a kind of prerogative (criticism also in Toscani and Suhr, in Meng, Ress and Stein, *Europäische Integration und Globalisierung* (2011), pp. 584–5).

209. Art. 83(1) TFEU.
210. See Chapter 3, mn. 5 ff.
211. Cf. Art. 82(1) first subpara. TFEU. For a detailed examination, cf. Nalewajko, *Gegenseitige Anerkennung* (2010), pp. 64 ff.; Suominen, *Mutual Recognition in Cooperation* (2011), pp. 17–18, 23 ff., 42 ff., 66 ff., 343 ff.; Mavany, *Die europäische Beweisanordnung* (2012), pp. 3 ff. (history), 33 ff. (concept); Hüttemann, *European Criminal Procedure* (2012), pp. 37 ff.; cf. also de Hoyos, *RDCE*, 9 (2005), 808 ff. (drawing a distinction between mutual recognition in a narrower and a wider sense, 812 ff., 820 ff.); Jégouzo, *RIDP*, 77 (2006), 97 ff.; Bernardi, *RSC*, 72 (2007), 725; Manacorda, *RSC*, 72 (2007), 899 ff., 909; Nilsson, *RIDP*, 77 (2006), 53 ff.; Krüßmann, *Transnationales Strafprozessrecht* (2009), pp. 574 ff., 589 ff.; Fichera, *EAW in the EU* (2011), pp. 48 ff., 59 ff.; Taupiac-Nouvel, *EuCLR*, 2 (2012), 239 ff.; Satzger, in Streinz, *EUV/AEUV* (2012), Art. 82 AEUV mn. 9 ff.; Satzger, *International and European Criminal Law* (2018), §8 mn. 23 ff.; Satzger, *Internationales und Europäisches Strafrecht* (2016), §10 mn. 26 ff.; Asp, *Procedural Criminal Law Cooperation* (2016), pp. 42–4, 46 ff., 59 ff., 76–7; calling for more mutual recognition Valdés, *ERA Forum*, 16 (2015), 291 ff.; on (mutual) recognition as a condition of intercultural discourse on law and intercultural criminal law, cf. Wojciechowski, *Philosophical Approach to the Interculturality of Criminal Law* (2010), pp. 121 ff., 152 ff.; from a Polish point of view, Banach-Gutierrez, *NJECL*, 4 (2013), 154 ff.; for an attempt to 'constitutionalize' mutual recognition, see Burchard, *Konstitutionalisierung der gegenseitigen Anerkennung* (2017).
212. Art. 82(1) TFEU.
213. Nilsson, *eucrim*, 9 (2014), 21; on enforcement as the most important but not the only function of mutual recognition, cf. Asp, *Procedural Criminal Law Cooperation* (2016), pp. 48–50, 60–1; on mutual recognition as the expression of a system of 'global legal pluralism', cf. Mitsilegas, *EU Criminal Law after Lisbon* (2016), pp. 125 ff. (128).
214. Art. 82(1) subpara. 2 TFEU. On the need for implementation (instead of direct applicability as in the law on the single market) Vogel and Eisele, in Grabitz, Hilf and Nettesheim, *Das Recht der EU*, i (2017), Art. 82 AEUV mn. 21; in agreement, Eisele, in Tiedemann et al., *Die Verfassung moderner Strafrechtspflege* (2016), pp. 223, 232; on the implementation in the various instruments Ouwerkerk, *Mutual Recognition* (2011), pp. 82 ff. On the concrete measures see also Chapter 4, mn. 3, 46 ff., 82 ff.
215. On mutual trust and rights observance as basis for mutual recognition, Mitsilegas, *EU Criminal Law after Lisbon* (2016), pp. 125 ff., explaining a lack of trust with 'moral distance' (at 129, 151), and concluding (at 151) that 'this deification of mutual trust . . . poses, however, significant challenges on the effective protection of fundamental rights, which seems to be subordinated to the requirement to respect presumed and uncritically accepted trust'; see also Meyer, *EuR*, 52 (2017), 163, 164 ff., 170 ff., for whom mutual trust is 'one of the great mysteries of

European criminal law' (orig. 'zu den großen Mysterien des eur. Strafrechts', 161) and who, following an instructive overview of the current debate (164–70), identifies a new approach of the ECJ – since its Opinion 2/13 (Chapter 2, mn. 9–10) – towards a 'constitutional principle inherent in the Union' (orig. 'unionsimmanenten Verfassungsprinzip', 173) and a 'cross-policy' concept (183) with an integrative political function (170 ff.). See also Ronsfeld, *Rechtshilfe, Anerkennung und Vertrauen* (2015), pp. 211 ff. (217 ff.) (listing a joint reference system, mutual sympathy and co-ordination, transparency and integrity as trust-founding measures); Jähnke and Schramm, *Europäisches Strafrecht* (2017), §4 mn. 36 (considering the priniciple of mutual recognition as a 'substancial factor of integration' bringing about a certain pressure to harmonise); for a fundamental critical review from the perspective of legitimation theory, Vermeulen, in Tiedemann et al., *Die Verfassung moderner Strafrechtspflege* (2016), pp. 181 ff.; on the relationship between mutual recognition and trust, also Ostropolski, *NJECL*, 6 (2015), 167; on trust resulting from harmonisation, Asp, *Procedural Criminal Law Cooperation* (2016), p. 54; on the indicators for mutual trust, Albers, in Albers et al., *Evaluation Framework* (2013), p. 315; Böse, in Albers et al., *Evaluation Framework* (2013), pp. 357–61; on the weakening of mutual trust by rights violations, BVerfG, No 2 BvR 2735/14, Decision (15 December 2015), in *NJW*, 69 (2016), 1149, paras. 73–5, English translation available at www.bundesverfassungsgericht.de/SharedDocs/Entscheidungen/EN/2015/12/rs20151215_2bvr273514en.html, last accessed 27 January 2018; calling for more mutual trust, Herlin-Karnell, *eucrim*, 9 (2014), 30. Cf. on the project of 'Euro-Justis' (scientific indicators of confidence in justice), www.heuni.fi/en/index/researchareas/confidenceinthecjs/eurojustis-scientificindicatorsofconfidenceinjusticetoolsforpolicyassessment.html, last accessed 27 January 2018.

216. See, on the interdependence between mutual recognition and harmonisation, also Asp, *Procedural Criminal Law Cooperation* (2016), pp. 20–3, 52–5, 73; on Art. 82(2) TFEU in this regard, see already Mitsilegas, *EU Criminal Law after Lisbon* (2016); on the 'profound tension between harmonization ... and the mutual recognition principle', cf. Peers, in Craig and de Búrca, *Evolution of EU Law* (2011), p. 296. See also Ronsfeld, *Rechtshilfe, Anerkennung und Vertrauen* (2015), pp. 233 ff., concluding that the principle of mutual recognition cannot substitute the approximation of laws (240).
217. Rightly focusing on procedural rights, Salazar, *eucrim*, 9 (2014), 24–5, 26.
218. On the historical development of mutual recognition, cf. Mavany, *Die europäische Beweisanordnung* (2012), pp. 3 ff.; Asp, *Procedural Criminal Law Cooperation* (2016), pp. 42–4; 59–62, 76–7; Klimek, *Mutual Recognition of Judicial Decisions* (2017), pp. 41ff.; critical of referring to mutual recognition as a 'principle', Mylonopoulos, *ZStW*, 123 (2011), 640 ff.; see also Nalewajko, *Gegenseitige Anerkennung* (2010), pp. 67 ff.
219. On this, cf. also Chapter 4, mn. 77–8. On the predominantly critical literature, cf. Ambos, *Internationales Strafrecht* (2008), §12 mn. 57a, with n. 340–3; also Sieber, *ZStW*, 121 (2009), 37 ff.; Hecker, *Europäisches Strafrecht* (2015), §12 mn. 63 ff.; Satzger, *International and European Criminal Law* (2018), §8 mn. 26–7; Satzger, *Internationales und Europäisches Strafrecht* (2016), §10 mn. 24–5; Klip, *European Criminal Law* (2016), pp. 435–7; Ambos, *ZIS*, 5 (2010), 557, 559; Nalewajko, *Gegenseitige Anerkennung* (2010), pp. 255 ff.; Gleß, *Internationales Strafrecht*

(2015), mn. 448 ff.; Gleß, in Böse, *Europäisches Strafrecht* (2013), pp. 615–16; Zeder, *EuR*, 47 (2012), 38; Ouwerkerk, *Mutual Recognition* (2011), pp. 76–7; Hinarejos, *EuLRev*, 36 (2011), 425–6 (mutual recognition not automatic); cf. also Zimmermann, Glaser and Motz, *EuCLR*, 1 (2011), 61 ff.; Safferling, *Internationales Strafrecht* (2011), §12 mn. 46; Suominen, *Mutual Recognition in Cooperation* (2011), pp. 62 ff.; Rackow, in Ambos, *Europäisches Strafrecht post-Lissabon* (2011), pp. 120 ff.; with regard to the lack of an effective defence in transnational proceedings, Schünemann, *StV*, 36 (2016), 182–3; for a different opinion, cf. Taupiac-Nouvel, *EuCLR*, 2 (2012), 236 ff.; Mavany, *Die europäische Beweisanordnung* (2012), pp. 49 ff.

220. See Chapter 5, mn. 28.

221. On this, see, in greater detail, Nalewajko, *Gegenseitige Anerkennung* (2010), pp. 244 ff.; Mavany, *Die europäische Beweisanordnung* (2012), pp. 68 ff., who calls for binding rules on jurisdiction; cf. also Bieber et al., *Die EU* (2016), §16 mn. 3 *in fine*, who observe aptly that while the principle of mutual recognition strengthens individual rights in the area of fundamental freedoms, it can weaken them in the area of criminal law. On the consequences this can have on the use of evidence, cf. Krüßmann, *Transnationales Strafprozessrecht* (2009), pp. 676 ff. An approximation of national rules of procedure is demanded by Gleß, in Sieber, Satzger and Heintschel von Heinegg, *Europäisches Strafrecht* (2014), p. 679. Cf. also Dannecker, *ZVglRWiss*, 111 (2012), 69–70; also Erbežnik, *EuCLR*, 2 (2012), 3 ff.; and Thunberg Schunke, *Whose Responsibility* (2013), pp. 69 ff., who examine the effects of mutual recognition on the rights of defendants in general.

222. In a similar vein cf. Asp, *Procedural Criminal Law Cooperation* (2016), pp. 63–4, 68 (arguing that there is 'nothing *per se* wrong' (64) with the use of the principle once it is adjusted to the criminal law context); likewise emphasising the protection of fundamental rights in European co-operation law, Böse, in Tiedemann et al., *Die Verfassung moderner Strafrechtspflege* (2016), pp. 211 ff.

223. Cf. Alexy, *Theorie der Grundrechte* (1986), pp. 71 ff. (English translation by Rivers, *A Theory of Constitutional Rights* (2002), pp. 44 ff.), distinguishing between principles and rules as two types of norms that both give reasons as to what should happen but that differ in a qualitative sense: principles demand that something must be realised to the greatest extent possible, they are 'optimization requirements' (*Optimierungsgebote*) that can only be satisfied to a certain extent, their actual fulfilment depends on the factual and legal possibilities; rules can either be fulfilled or not, they contain determinations (*Festsetzungen*, English translation, at 48: 'fixed points') within the factually and legally possible.

224. Cf. Asp, *Procedural Criminal Law Cooperation* (2016), pp. 65, 66 ff. and the following endnote.

225. For a fundamental treatment cf. Asp, *Procedural Criminal Law Cooperation* (2016), pp. 46 ff., 59 ff., 150–1, considering mutual recognition both as a 'neutral' principle existing in different degrees of strength (48, 50–2) and as a 'legal principle' – that is, as an 'ought-to-follow' rather than a 'shall' rule (65) which as such needs to be balanced with other principles and values (67–9) and summarises reasons to be confronted with other reasons (69–74); all this makes the mutual recognition principle 'fairly weak' (77) with an unstable and unclear content (77–8) so that it must ultimately be formed prospectively in a 'complex interaction with other principles' and taking into account the underlying 'values'

(79) in order to find its 'proper borders' (151). On the principle's neutrality and fundamental rights-based restrictions, see Eisele, in Tiedemann et al., *Die Verfassung moderner Strafrechtspflege* (2016), pp. 223, 224 ff. In favour of a limitation of mutual recognition also ECPI, *ZIS*, 8 (2013), 416 ff.

226. See Chapter 4, mn. 2, 18 ff. and 83 ff.; on proportionality as a limiting factor Chapter 4, mn. 71.
227. On the implementation of mutual recognition in various legal instruments, cf. Ouwerkerk, *Mutual Recognition* (2011), pp. 82 ff.
228. Cf. Peers, in Craig and de Búrca, *The Evolution of EU Law* (2011), p. 295.
229. Criticism in Nilsson, *eucrim*, 9 (2014), 21.
230. Cf. Chapter 4, mn. 4.
231. Cf. also Vogel, *GA*, 150 (2003), 315; Hecker and Zöller, *Fallsammlung* (2012), p. 85 (Case 8); Hecker, in Ambos, *Europäisches Strafrecht post-Lissabon* (2011), p. 17.
232. On the standard-setting Greek maize case in this regard, see Chapter 3, mn. 41. For a profound analysis, see Asp, in Freund et al., *FS Frisch* (2013), pp. 1389 ff.
233. Asp, in Freund et al., *FS Frisch* (2013), p. 1394.
234. For a good comparative analysis, see Asp, in Freund et al., *FS Frisch* (2013), pp. 1394–1400, concluding that assimilation both supplements measures of harmonization – given that the latter will always be fragmentary – and provides a 'fall-back standard' in cases where harmonization is not necessary.
235. Art. 29(2) second subpara. TEU, earlier version.
236. Arts. 67(3), 82(1) and 83(2) TFEU. Klip, *European Criminal Law* (2016), p. 35, sees 'approximation' as a less extensive form of 'harmonisation', but is forced to admit that the two cannot be distinguished completely. See in more detail Chapter 3, mn. 5 ff.
237. For a critical view of the general meaning, functions and effect of harmonisation, cf. Klip and van der Wilt, *Harmonisation and Harmonising Measures in Criminal Law* (2002); Klip, *NStZ*, 20 (2000), 626 ff.; Ramos, in Klip, *Substantive Criminal Law of the EU* (2011), pp. 38 ff.; Weyembergh, *L'harmonisation des législations* (2004), pp. 124–5; Weyembergh, *MaastJECompL*, 12 (2005), 170 ff.; on the problems regarding substantive criminal law cf. Ambos, *MaastJECompL*, 12 (2005), 173 ff.
238. See Chapter 3, mn. 5 ff., 23 ff. and 39 ff.
239. See Chapter 3, mn. 41 ff.; cf. also Ambos, in Joecks and Miebach, *Münchener Kommentar StGB*, i (2017), Vorbemerkung §§3–7 mn. 7; Jung, *JuS*, 40 (2000), 420.
240. Art. 267 TFEU. For more details, cf. Chapter 3, mn. 49–51.
241. Cf. Ambos, in Joecks and Miebach, *Münchener Kommentar StGB*, i (2017), Vorbemerkung §§3–7 mn. 7, incl. further references. On influence and implementation in the United Kingdom, cf. Spencer and Padfield, *RSC*, 71 (2006), 544 ff.
242. Thereon in more detail, see Chapter 3, mn. 22 ff.
243. See Chapter 3, mn. 30 ff.
244. Art. 67(3) TFEU.
245. Art. 82(1) second subpara. TFEU.
246. Art. 67(3) TFEU.
247. Art. 82(1) first subpara. TFEU.
248. Art. 82(2) TFEU; cf. thereon Chapter 4, mn. 8 ff.
249. Art. 83 TFEU. For more details, cf. Chapter 3, mn. 5 ff.

250. See mn. 34 ff.
251. Cf. thereon, Chapter 4, mn. 9 ff. and 29 ff.
252. Art. 1 third subpara. TEU.
253. Art. 1(2) TFEU.
254. Fischer, *Der Vertrag von Lissabon* (2008), mn. 134; Oppermann, Classen and Nettesheim, *Europarecht* (2016), §9 mn. 22 ff.; Herdegen, *Europarecht* (2017), §8 mn. 4–41; Nicolaysen, *Europarecht*, i (2002), p. 38. On the interpretation of EU law, cf. Schroeder, *JuS*, 44 (2004), 180 ff.
255. Protocol No 36 (n. 55) Lisbon Treaty, Art. 9: 'The legal effects of the acts of the institutions, bodies, offices and agencies of the Union adopted on the basis of the Treaty on European Union prior to the entry into force of the Treaty of Lisbon shall be preserved until those acts are repealed, annulled or amended in implementation of the Treaties. The same shall apply to agreements concluded between member states on the basis of the Treaty on European Union.' On the CJEU's jurisdiction on measures of the (former) PJCCM, cf. Chapter 3, mn. 49.
256. See mn. 23 ff.
257. On the basics of this, cf. Zweigert, *RabelsZ*, 28 (1964), 607 ff.; Oppermann, Classen and Nettesheim, *Europarecht* (2016), §9 mn. 26 ff.; Nicolaysen, *Europarecht*, i (2002), p. 38; cf. also Miettinen, *Criminal Law and Policy in the EU* (2013), pp. 93 ff., 102 ff.
258. Art. 16(3) TEU.
259. Oppermann, Classen and Nettesheim, *Europarecht* (2016), §9 mn. 30.
260. Cf. e.g. Art. 340(2) TFEU. See thereon Fischer, *Der Vertrag von Lissabon* (2008), mn. 135; Oppermann, Classen and Nettesheim, *Europarecht* (2016), §9 mn. 33; Herdegen, *Europarecht* (2017), §8 mn. 15 ff.
261. Cf. Jung, *GA*, 152 (2005), 2 ff. ('wertende Rechtsvergleichung'); on the comparative method used when developing European tax law, cf. also Bacigalupo, *CPC*, 83 (2004), 5 ff.
262. Cf. Art. 2 TEU. See also Oppermann, Classen and Nettesheim, *Europarecht* (2016), §9 mn. 39.
263. Fischer, *Der Vertrag von Lissabon* (2008), mn. 135; Schütz, Bruha and König, *Casebook Europarecht* (2004), pp. 857 ff.; cf. also Meyer, *Strafrechtsgenese* (2012), pp. 306–7.
264. Fischer, *Der Vertrag von Lissabon* (2008), mn. 167; Oppermann, Classen and Nettesheim, *Europarecht* (2016), §10 mn. 39 ff.; Herdegen, *Europarecht* (2017), §8 mn. 18 ff., with further references; on this, cf. also ECPI, *ZIS*, 4 (2009), 707–16.
265. Cf. Art. 6(3) TEU. Cf. thereon Fischer, *Der Vertrag von Lissabon* (2008), mn. 149; Oppermann, Classen and Nettesheim, *Europarecht* (2016), §17 mn. 7. On the relationship between the ECHR, the ECtHR and the CJEU, cf. Chapter 2, mn. 6 ff.
266. For more detail, cf. Chapter 2, mn. 17 ff.
267. Thereon, see Chapter 2, mn. 154 ff.
268. Art. 6(1) TEU.
269. Cf. the ECPI website, www.crimpol.eu, last accessed 27 January 2018.
270. ECPI, *ZIS*, 4 (2009), 707–16 (for the English version); ECPI, *EuCLR*, 1 (2011), 86 ff.; on the manifesto cf. Satzger, *ZRP*, 43 (2010), 137–40; Satzger, *International and European Criminal Law* (2018), §7 mn. 34, 53–4; Satzger, *Internationales und Europäisches Strafrecht* (2016), §9 mn. 34, 55–6; Nieto Martín, *RP, 27* (2011), 78 ff.; Prittwitz, in Ambos, *Europäisches Strafrecht post-Lissabon* (2011), pp. 29 ff. A

critical stance on EU criminal policy is taken by Kubiciel, *ZIS*, 5 (2010), 742; Muñoz de Morales, *RP*, 27 (2011), 51 ff.; Wieczorek, *EuCLR*, 2 (2012), 141–2.

271. For a similar view, cf. Asp, *Substantive Criminal Law Competence of the EU* (2012), pp. 164 ff.; cf. also the development of European principles of criminal law in Schaut, *Europäische Strafrechtsprinzipien* (2012), pp. 125 ff.; similarly Miettinen, *Criminal Law and Policy in the EU* (2013), pp. 112 ff.; on mutual recognition, see Suominen, *Mutual Recognition in Cooperation* (2011), pp. 377–8.
272. ECPI, *ZIS*, 8 (2013), 430–46 (for the English version); on this, cf. Satzger and Zimmermann, *ZIS*, 8 (2013), 406 ff.; Löfgren, *EuCLR*, 5 (2015), 54 ff.; Träskman, *EuCLR*, 5 (2015), 60 ff.
273. For an instructive account of defence in transnational European criminal proceedings, cf. Arnold, *HRRS*, 9 (2008), 10 ff.; Nagler, *StV*, 33 (2013), 324 ff.; for more detail, cf. Rackow, in Böse, *Europäisches Strafrecht* (2013), pp. 866 ff.; cf. also the national reports in Cape et al., *Effective Criminal Defence in Europe* (2010), pp. 65 ff.
274. Cf. Schünemann, in Schünemann, *Alternativentwurf europäische Strafverfolgung* (2004), p. 14; Schünemann, *ZStW*, 116 (2004), 388 ff.; Nestler, in Schünemann, *Gesamtkonzept für die Europäische Strafrechtspflege* (2006), pp. 169 ff.; Swarc, in Schünemann, *Gesamtkonzept für die Europäische Strafrechtspflege* (2006), pp. 186 ff.; Arnold, *HRRS*, 9 (2008), 15 ff.; Gleß, *StV*, 33 (2013), 319–20; for further references, cf. Ambos, *Internationales Strafrecht* (2006), mn. 23–32, incl. n. 77.
275. Schünemann, in Schünemann, *Gesamtkonzept für die Europäische Strafrechtspflege* (2006), pp. 4 ff.
276. Vogel, *MaastJECompL*, 12 (2005), 137; Arnold, *HRRS*, 9 (2008), 17 ff.; cf. also Arnold, *StraFo*, 26 (2013), 54 ff.; Ahlbrecht, *StV*, 32 (2012), 491 ff., with further references respectively. See also Bana, Camaldo and Troglia, *eucrim*, 12 (2017), 31 ff., who are in favour of joint rules on (transnational) investigations by the defence based on the Italian model.
277. Fischer, *Der Vertrag von Lissabon* (2008), mn. 136 ff.; Oppermann, Classen and Nettesheim, *Europarecht* (2016), §9 mn. 67 ff.; Herdegen, *Europarecht* (2017), §8 mn. 43–68; Nicolaysen, *Europarecht*, i (2002), p. 38; Ambos and Rackow, *Jura*, 28 (2006), 506; Meyer, *Strafrechtsgenese* (2012), pp. 331 ff.
278. On this primacy, cf. Chapter 3, mn. 46.
279. Art. 288(3) TFEU.
280. Cf. Ambos, *Internationales Strafrecht* (2008), §9 mn. 21.
281. On the serious implementation problems and their causes, see de Busser, *ERA Forum*, 16 (2015), 282–3.
282. Arts. 258 ff. TFEU. On this, cf. also Herlin-Karnell, *eucrim*, 5 (2010), 62; de Busser, *ERA Forum*, 16 (2015), 284–6 (esp. on the meaning of 'infringement'). In greater depth on the changes to the European legal system after the Lisbon Treaty so far, cf. Thiele, *EuR*, 45 (2010), 30, 48 ff. For an in-depth account of the protection of individual rights against Acts of the EU, cf. Schonard, *EuCLR*, 2 (2012), 61 ff. The protection of individual rights is also demanded by Meyer, *Strafrechtsgenese* (2012), pp. 904–5.
283. However, this is modified according to Art. 76 TFEU in that legal Acts can only be adopted on the initiative of a quarter of the MS or the Commission. For a detailed account of the preparatory and follow-up work of the Commission, cf. Meyer, *Strafrechtsgenese* (2012), pp. 312–13.

284. Art. 16(3) TEU.
285. Art. 34(2) second sentence TEU, earlier version. For more details on the legislative procedure following Lisbon, cf. Zimmermann, *Jura*, 31 (2009), 844 ff.
286. Cf. Ambos, *Internationales Strafrecht* (2008), §12 mn. 30.
287. Agreement between the Governments of the States of the Benelux Economic Union, the Federal Republic of Germany and the French Republic on the Gradual Abolition of Checks at Their Common Borders, OJ L 239 of 22 September 2000, 13–18. On the origin in a blockade by French truck drivers and the bilateral French–German agreement of Saarbrücken of 13 July 1984, cf. De Capitani, *ERA Forum*, 15 (2014), 104.
288. Convention Implementing the Schengen Agreement of 14 June 1985 between the Governments of the States of the Benelux Economic Union, the Federal Republic of Germany and the French Republic on the Gradual Abolition of Checks at Their Common Border, OJ L 239 of 22 September 2000, 19 ff.; printed in excerpts in Gleß and Schomburg, in Schomburg et al., *Internationale Rechtshilfe in Strafsachen* (2012), pp. 1648 ff..; also printed in Wasmeier and Möhlig, *Strafrecht der EU* (2008), pp. 109, 250. On Schengen II specifically, cf. Würz, *Das Schengener Durchführungsübereinkommen* (1997).
289. Cf. Gleß, in Schomburg et al., *Internationale Rechtshilfe in Strafsachen* (2012), pp. 1637–8; Safferling, *Internationales Strafrecht* (2011), §12 mn. 71; for a good overview of all changes, see Huybreghts, *ERA Forum*, 16 (2015), 380 ff. (with a table at 403 ff.); summarising, also see De Capitani, *ERA Forum*, 15 (2014), 107–9 (with a very positive assessment focusing on the border regime at 101, 117–18 and *passim*).
290. For the respective Schengen Protocol see already endnote 40 above; cf. also Council Decision of 20 May 1999 (1999/435/EC) concerning the definition of the Schengen *acquis* for the purpose of determining, in conformity with the relevant provisions of the Treaty establishing the European Community and the Treaty on European Union, the legal basis for each of the provisions or decisions which constitute the *acquis*, OJ L 176 of 10 July 1999, 1–16; Council Decision of 20 May 1999 (1999/436/EC) determining, in conformity with the relevant provisions of the Treaty Establishing the European Community and the Treaty on European Union, the legal basis for each of the provisions or decisions which constitute the Schengen *acquis*, OJ L 176 of 10 July 1999, 17–30. On this, cf. Bracke, in Cullen and Jund, *Criminal Justice Co-operation in the EU after Tampere* (2002), pp. 23 ff.; Fischer, *Der Vertrag von Lissabon* (2008), mn. 650; Nicolaysen, *Europarecht*, i (2002), p. 54; Huber, in Wolter et al., *Datenübermittlungen und Vorermittlungen* (2003), pp. 141–2; cf. also Vervaele, *ULR*, 1 (2005), 109; Calliess, *EU nach dem Vertrag von Lissabon* (2010), p. 35; De Capitani, *ERA Forum*, 15 (2014), 110 (pointing to the ensuing trade-offs); Schütze, *EU Law* (2015), pp. 29–30.
291. Art. 35(1) TEU, earlier version. On the (former) caveat on MS declaration of competence ('opt-in', Art. 35(2) TEU, earlier version), cf. Böse, *GA*, 150 (2003), 744 ff.; Radtke and Busch, *NStZ*, 23 (2003), 282.
292. Generally on the Court's jurisdiction, see Art. 19(3) TEU.
293. Lisbon Treaty, Protocol (No 19) on the Schengen *Acquis* Integrated into the Framework of the EU, OJ C 326 of 26 October 2012, 290–2.
294. Pursuant to Art. 2 in conjunction with Art. 1 Protocol 19 (n. 293) these States are: Austria, Belgium, Bulgaria, Croatia, Cyprus, Denmark, Estonia, Finland,

France, Germany, Greece, Hungary, Italy, Latvia, Lithuania, Luxembourg, Malta, Poland, Portugal, Romania, Slovenia, Slovakia, Spain, Sweden, the Czech Republic and the Netherlands. Although **Denmark** has opted out regarding the free movement of persons (cf. the respective Protocols No 5 to the 1997 Amsterdam Treaty and No 22 to the Lisbon Treaty, above mn. 6 and mn. 11), (unamended) Schengen *acquis* measures adopted before the Amsterdam Treaty are still binding and applicable upon Denmark (Art. 3 Protocol 2, n. 40) while it can opt in to measures which build upon the Schengen *acquis* (Art. 3 Protocol 19, in conjunction with Art. 4 Protocol 22). For the still existing border controls regarding **Bulgaria, Croatia, Romania** and **Cyprus** see n. 304–5 with the main text.

295. The **UK** and **Ireland** do not fully participate in the Schengen *acquis* (see already above n. 41 ff. and recital 4 Protocol 19, n. 293) but 'may at any time request to take part in some or all provisions' with the (unanimous) approval of the Council (Art. 4 Protocol 19); note, however, that they may nevertheless opt out within three months (Art. 5(2) Protocol 19); for a summary cf. Huybreghts, *ERA Forum*, 16 (2015), 402. On recent UK practice see the 'Decisions' document of 30 October 2017 at www.gov.uk/government/publications/jha-opt-in-and-schengen-opt-out-protocols–3, last accessed 29 January 2018.

296. These States are associated members: for **Iceland** and **Norway**, see Art. 6 Protocol 19 (n. 293); see also Council Decision 2000/777/EC (1.12.2000) applying the Schengen *acquis* to the countries of the Nordic Passport Union (Denmark, Finland, Iceland, Norway, Sweden). For **Liechtenstein**, see Protocol between the European Union, the European Community, the Swiss Confederation and the Principality of Liechtenstein on the accession of the Principality of Liechtenstein to the Agreement between the European Union, the European Community and the Swiss Confederation on the Swiss Confederation's association with the implementation, application and development of the Schengen *acquis*, OJ L 160 of 18 June 2011, 21, and the associated Council Decision of 13 December 2011, on the full application of the provisions of the Schengen *acquis* in the Principality of Liechtenstein (2011/842/EU), OJ L 334 of 16 December 2011, 27–8. For **Switzerland**, see Agreement between the European Union, the European Community and the Swiss Confederation on the Swiss Confederation's association with the implementation, application and development of the Schengen *acquis*, OJ L 53 of 27 February 2008, 52–9, and the Final Act of 26 October 2004, OJ L 53 of 27 February 2008, 71–3. On these third, non-EU, States, see also Schröder and Stiegel, in Sieber, Satzger and Heintschel von Heinegg, *Europäisches Strafrecht* (2014), pp. 623–5 (Iceland and Norway), 625–6 (Switzerland), 631–2 (Liechtenstein); on Switzerland, cf. also Henzelin and Maeder, *JECL*, 3 (2009), 49 ff.; on the practical work with the associated States, cf. Huybreghts, *ERA Forum*, 16 (2015), 400–1. **Monaco, San Marino, Andorra** and **Vatican City** have not joined the Schengen agreement, but they do not undertake controls of their borders with neighbouring countries (www.schengenvisainfo.com/schengen-visa-countries-list, last accessed 27 January 2018).

297. For more detail, cf. Chapter 4, mn. 5.

298. On this, cf. Chapter 2, mn. 161 ff.

299. COM(2016) 731 final; on this see the critical opinion of the EDPS of 6 March 2017, at https://edps.europa.eu/sites/edp/files/publication/17-03-070_etias_opinion_en.pdf, last accessed 27 January 2018.

300. COM(2016) 731 final, pp. 3–4. On this see also the new Entry–Exit System (EES) to register every entry and exit from the Schengen area by third-state nationals as well as the refusal of access, cf. OJ L 327 of 9 December 2017; see also *eucrim*, 12 (2017), 57–8 and 164–5.
301. Art. 8 Schengen Protocol (n. 40); Art. 7 Protocol 19 (n. 293).
302. On this, see also Chapter 4, mn. 25 ff. In Bulgaria and Romania, the SIS has been operative since 15 October 2010 (Council Decision of 29 June 2010 (2010/365/EU) on the application of the provisions of the Schengen *acquis* relating to the Schengen Information System in the Republic of Bulgaria and Romania, OJ L 166 of 1 July 2010, 17–20).
303. On this, cf. Chalmers, Davies and Monti, *EU Law* (2014), p. 34; Elsen, in Hummer, *Rechtsfragen der Anwendung des Amsterdamer Vertrages* (2001), p. 50; for a critical view of the conditions for its coming into force, cf. Rybicki, *PYIL*, 25 (2001), 112.
304. Cf. the website of the Migration and Home Affairs Directorate-General of the European Commission, available at http://ec.europa.eu/dgs/home-affairs/what-we-do/policies/borders-and-visas/schengen/index_en.htm, last accessed 27 January 2018. On Cyprus and Croatia, cf. www.schengenvisainfo.com/schengen-agreement, last accessed 27 January 2018.
305. On Bulgaria and Romania, cf. also *eucrim*, 5 (2010), 87; *eucrim*, 6 (2011), 3–4, 135–6; *eucrim*, 7 (2012), 3, 143; 8 (2013), 35 and most recently www.schengenvisainfo.com/romania-bulgaria-qualify-join-schengen-area, last accessed 27 January 2018.
306. Regulation (EU) 2016/399 of the EP and of the Council of 9 March 2016 on a Union Code on the rules governing the movement of persons across borders (Schengen Borders Code), OJ L 77 of 23 March 2016, 1–52.
307. For a police perspective on this, cf. Niechziol and Schmucker, *Kriminalistik*, 62 (2008), 105 ff.; a critical view is taken by Mokros, in Lisken and Denninger, *Handbuch des Polizeirechts* (2007), mn. 147 ('Contradictions to the purpose of the Schengen Treaties' (orig. 'Widerspruch zum Zweck der Schengener Verträge')).
308. Arts. 25–7 SBC set the general framework and the procedure for the temporary reintroduction of border controls at internal borders. The reintroduction of border controls is exceptional and for a 'limited period of *up to 30 days* or for the foreseeable duration of the serious threat', and its 'scope and duration . . . shall not exceed what is strictly necessary to respond to the serious threat' (Art. 25(1), emphasis added).
309. Art. 28 SBC: 'Where a serious threat to public policy or internal security in a MS requires immediate action to be taken, the MS concerned may, on an exceptional basis, *immediately* reintroduce border control at internal borders, for a limited period of *up to ten days*' (emphasis added).
310. On the specific procedure (Council Recommendation, after Commission Proposal), the criteria and the duration (up to six months) of the reintroduction of border controls, as a result of that third option, cf. Arts. 29–35 SBC; see also Regulation (EU) No 1051/2013 of the EP and of the Council of 22 October 2013 amending Regulation (EC) No 562/2006 in order to provide for common rules on the temporary reintroduction of border control at internal borders in exceptional circumstances (OJ L 295 of 6 November 2013, 1). See also Esser,

Europäisches und Internationales Strafrecht (2018), §4 mn. 35 ff. and *eucrim*, 6 (2011), 95–6; for more information on the current situation regarding the temporary reintroduction of border control, cf. http://ec.europa.eu/dgs/home-affairs/what-we-do/policies/borders-and-visas/schengen/reintroduction-border-control/index_en.htm, last accessed 27 January 2018.

311. Austria, Denmark, France, Germany, Norway and Sweden.
312. For a full list of MSs' notifications of the temporary reintroduction of border control at internal borders pursuant to Articles 25 ff. of the SBC, cf. http://ec.europa.eu/dgs/home-affairs/what-we-do/policies/borders-and-visas/schengen/reintroduction-border-control/docs/ms_notifications_-_reintroduction_of_border_control_en.pdf, last accessed 27 January 2018.
313. Council Regulation No (EU) 1053/2013 of 7 October 2013 establishing an evaluation and monitoring mechanism to verify the application of the Schengen *acquis* and repealing the Decision of the Executive Committee of 16 September 1998 setting up a Standing Committee on the evaluation and implementation of Schengen (OJ L 295 of 6 November 2013, 27–37). For more information, cf. http://ec.europa.eu/dgs/home-affairs/what-we-do/policies/borders-and-visas/schengen/schengen-evaluation/index_en.htm, last accessed 27 January 2018. Cf. also *eucrim*, 8 (2013), 34–5, 111.
314. Those deficiencies were particularly identified after an on-site visit at the external border of Greece, as part of the annual evaluation programme for 2015 of the Schengen evaluation and monitoring mechanism; cf. Council of the EU, 'Council Implementing Decision Setting Out a Recommendation for Temporary Internal Border Control in Exceptional Circumstances Putting the Overall Functioning of the Schengen Area at Risk', 8835/16, Brussels, 12 May 2016.
315. Austria, Denmark, Germany, Norway and Sweden.
316. Council Recommendation of 12 May 2016 (n. 314); cf. also the list of MSs' notifications of the temporary reintroduction of border control (n. 312). On 11 May 2017, the Council adopted an implementing decision setting out a recommendation to prolong temporary internal border controls in exceptional circumstances; see press release available at www.consilium.europa.eu/en/press/press-releases/2017/05/11/schengen-area-six-month-prolongation-internal-border-controls/pdf, last accessed 27 January 2018; see also *eucrim* 2017, 58 -9. This last possible renewal option expired on 11 November 2017; nonetheless the German federal government declared to extend the border control until May 2018; see press release of the Ministry of the Interior of 12 October 2017, available at www.bmi.bund.de/SharedDocs/pressemitteilungen/EN/2017/extension-border-checks.html, last accessed 27 January 2018. Also, the Commission presented a proposal for a regulation amending regulation (EU) 2016/399 (n. 306) (COM (2017) 571 final), according to which the maximum duration of reintroduced border controls may be up to three years (Art. 27a SBC).

Chapter Bibliography

Achenbach, H., 'Das Strafrecht als Mittel der Wirtschaftslenkung', *ZStW*, 119 (2007), 789–815

'Zur aktuellen Lage des Wirtschaftsstrafrechts in Deutschland', *GA*, 151 (2004), 559–74

Ahlbrecht, H., 'Strukturelle Defizite Europäischer Verteidigung: Gründe und Möglichkeiten ihrer Überwindung', *StV*, 32 (2012), 491–5

Albers, P., 'Results Survey Contact Points of the European Judicial Network in Criminal Matters', in Albers et al., *Evaluation Framework* (2013), 302–317

Alexy, R., *Theorie der Grundrechte* (Frankfurt: Suhrkamp, 1986)

A Theory of Constitutional Rights, translation by J. Rivers (Oxford: Oxford University Press, 2002)

Ambos, K., 'Is the Development of a Common Substantive Criminal Law for Europe Possible? Some Preliminary Reflections', *MaastJECompL*, 12 (2005), 173–91

'Transnationale Beweiserlangung: 10 Thesen zum Grünbuch der EU-Kommission "Erlangung verwertbarer Beweise in Strafsachen aus einem anderen Mitgliedstaat"', *ZIS*, 5 (2010), 557–66

'Vorbemerkung zu den §§3–7', in Joecks and Miebach, *Münchener Kommentar StGB*, i (2011), 115–92

'Zur Zukunft der deutschen Strafrechtswissenschaft: Offenheit und diskursive Methodik statt selbstbewusster Provinzialität', *GA*, 163 (2016), 177–94

Ambos, K., and Rackow, P., 'Erste Überlegungen zu den Konsequenzen des Lissabon-Urteils des BVerfG für das Europäische Strafrecht', *ZIS*, 4 (2009), 397–405

'Institutionelle Ordnung der EU und EG', *Jura*, 28 (2006), 505–12

Arato, J., 'A Preemptive Strike against European Federalism: The Decision of the Bundesverfassungsgericht Concerning the Treaty of Lisbon', *EJIL:Talk!*, 9 October 2010, at www.ejiltalk.org/a-preemptive-strike-against-european-federalism-the-decision-of-the-bundesverfassungsgericht-concerning-the-treaty-of-lisbon, last accessed 27 January 2018

Arnold, J., 'Auf dem Weg zu einem Europäischen Strafverteidiger?', *StraFo*, 26 (2013), 54–62

'Vorschläge zur Verbesserung des Schutzes des Strafverteidigers', *HRRS*, 9 (2008), 10–23

Asp, P., 'The Importance of the Principles of Subsidiarity and Coherence in the Development of EU Criminal Law', *EuCLR*, 1 (2011), 44–54

'(More Than) Two Decades Later: Does the Principle of Assimilation Still Have a Role to Play within European Criminal Law?', in Freund, G., Murmann, U., Bloy, R., and Perron, W., eds., *Grundlagen und Dogmatik des gesamten Strafrechtssystems: Festschrift für Wolfgang Frisch zum 70. Geburtstag* (Berlin: Duncker & Humblot, 2013), 1389–1401

Bacigalupo, E., 'El método comparativo e la elaboración del derecho penal europeo', *CPC*, 83 (2004), 5–22

Bana, G., Camaldo, L., and Troglia, M., 'Feuille de route et droits de la défense', *eucrim*, 12 (2017), 31–4

Banach-Gutierrez, J. B., 'Globalised Criminal Justice in the European Union Centext', *NJECL*, 4 (2013), 154–67

Baumbach, T., 'Danish Criminal Law and the EU', *EuCLR*, 3 (2013), 300–18

Bernardi, A., 'La aproximación constitucional al Derecho Penal frente a las fuentes e instituciones supranacionales europeas', *RP*, 27 (2011), 15–40

'Le rôle du troisième pilier dans l'européanisation du droit pénal', *RSC*, 72 (2007), 713–37

Bettels, T., 'Vertragsrechtliche und verfassungsrechtliche Grenzen des Europäischen Strafrechts nach dem Vertrag von Lissabon', *ZStW*, 124 (2013), 875–80

Beukelmann, S., 'Europäisierung des Strafrechts: Die neue strafrechtliche Ordnung nach dem Vertrag von Lissabon', *NJW*, 63 (2010), 2081–6

Blackstock, J., and Tinsley, A., 'The Arrival of EU Law in Criminal Proceedings', *Archbold Rev*, issue 8 (21 September 2015), 5–6

Blauberger, M., 'Reinforcing the Asymmetries of European Integration', in Fischer-Lescano, A., Joerges, C., and Wonka, A., eds., *The German Constitutional Court's Lisbon Ruling: Legal and Political-Science Perspectives* (Bremen: Zentrum für Europäische Rechtspolitik, 2010), 47–53

Bock, S., 'Tagungsbericht: Europäisches Strafrecht post Lissabon: (Normalisierungs-) Chancen oder (Verstetigungs-)Risiken?', *ZIS*, 6 (2011), 266–71

Böse, M., 'Comparative Overview of the Country Reports and Surveys', in Albers et al., 'Evaluation Framework' (2013), 334–62

'Die Entscheidung des BVerfG zum Vertrag von Lissabon und ihre Bedeutung für die Europäisierung des Strafrechts', *ZIS*, 5 (2010), 76–91

'Der Grundsatz "ne bis in idem" in der Europäischen Union (Art. 54 SDÜ)', *GA*, 150 (2003), 744–63

'Legitimität des europäischen Kooperationsrechts: Menschenrechtliche Standards zwischen Freiheitsschutz und Effektivitätsdenken', in Tiedemann, K., Sieber, U., Satzger, H., Burchard, C., and Brodowski, D., eds., *Die Verfassung moderner Strafrechtspflege: Erinnerung an Joachim Vogel* (Baden-Baden: Nomos, 2016), 211–20

'§1: Einleitung', in Böse, *Europäisches Strafrecht* (2013), 47–59

'§4: Kompetenzen der Union auf dem Gebiet des Straf- und Strafverfahrensrechts', in Böse, *Europäisches Strafrecht* (2013), 149–78

'Verweisungen auf das Gemeinschaftsrecht und das Bestimmtheitsgebot (Art. 103 Abs. 2 GG)', in Amelung, K., Günther, H.-L. and Kühne, H.-H., eds., *Festschrift für Volker Krey zum 70. Geburtstag am 9. Juli 2010* (Stuttgart: Kohlhammer, 2010), 7–25

Bracke, N., 'Amsterdam Treaty Framework with Special Reference to the Incorporation of the Schengen Acquis', in Cullen, P., and Jund, S., eds., *Criminal Justice Co-operation in the European Union after Tampere* (Cologne: Bundesanzeiger, 2002), 23–34

Braum, S., 'Europäische Strafgesetzgebung: Demokratische Strafgesetzlichkeit oder administrative Opportunität?', *wistra*, 25 (2006), 121–5

'Europäisches Strafrecht im Fokus konfligierender Verfassungsmodelle: Stoppt das Bundesverfassungsgericht die europäische Strafrechtsentwicklung?', *ZIS*, 4 (2009), 418–26

Brodowski, D., 'Strafrechtsrelevante Entwicklungen in der EU', *ZIS*, 7 (2012), 558–70

'Strafrechtsrelevante Entwicklungen in der EU', *ZIS*, 8 (2013), 455–72

'Supranationale europäische Verwaltungssanktionen: Entwicklungslinien: Dimensionen des Strafrechts: Legitimität', in Tiedemann, K., Sieber, U., Satzger, H., Burchard, C., and Brodowski, D., eds., *Die Verfassung moderner Strafrechtspflege: Erinnerung an Joachim Vogel* (Baden-Baden: Nomos, 2016), 139–80

Brok, E., and Ahumada Contreras, C., 'Der Europäische Auswärtige Dienst und seine Potentiale in Bezug auf die Gemeinsame Innen- und Justizpolitik', *eucrim*, 5 (2010), 104–11

Burchard, C., *Konstitutionalisierung der gegenseitigen Anerkennung: Die justizielle Zusammenarbeit in Strafsachen der EU-Mitgliedstaaten im Lichte des Unionsverfassungsrechts* (Baden-Baden: Nomos, forthcoming 2017)

Caeiro, P., 'A jurisdição penal da união europeia como meta-jurisdição: em especial, a compêtencia para legislar sobre as bases de jurisdição nacionais', in Correia, F. A., Machado, J. E. M., and Loureiro, J. C., eds., *Estudos em homenagem ao Prof. Doutor José Joaquim Gomes Canotilho*, iii (Coimbra: Coimbra Editora, 2012), 179–210

Caeiro, P., 'Beyond Competence Issues: Why and How Should the EU Legislate on Criminal Sanctions?', in Kert, R. and Lehner, A., eds., *Vielfalt des Strafrechts im internationalen Kontext: Festschrift für Frank Höpfel zum 65. Geburtstag* (Vienna: NWV, 2018), 645–65

Calliess, C., 'Auf dem Weg zu einem einheitlichen Europäischen Strafrecht? Kompetenzgrundlagen und Kompetenzgrenzen einer dynamischen Entwicklung', *ZEuS*, 11 (2008), 3–43

'Europa als Wertegemeinschaft', *JZ*, 59 (2004), 1033–45

Die neue Europäische Union nach dem Vertrag von Lissabon: Ein Überblick über die Reformen unter Berücksichtigung ihrer Implikationen für das deutsche Recht (Tübingen: Mohr Siebeck, 2010)

Cape, E., Namoradze, Z., Smith, R., and Spronken, T., *Effective Criminal Defence in Europe: Executive Summary and Recommendations* (Antwerp, Oxford and Portland: Intersentia, 2010)

Capus, N., *Strafrecht und Souveränität: Das Erfordernis der beidseitigen Strafbarkeit in der internationalen Rechtshilfe in Strafsachen* (Bern: Stämpfli and Baden-Baden: Nomos, 2010)

Cerizza, M., 'Solutions Offered by the Lisbon Treaty', *eucrim*, 5 (2010), 65–9

Chalmers, D., 'A Few Thoughts on the Lisbon Judgment', in Fischer-Lescano, A., Joerges, C., and Wonka, A., eds., *The German Constitutional Court's Lisbon Ruling: Legal and Political-Science Perspectives* (Bremen: Zentrum für Europäische Rechtspolitik, 2010), 5–9

Craig, P., 'Institutions, Power, and Institutional Balance', in Craig and de Búrca, *The Evolution of EU Law* (2011), 41–84

Cremer, H.-J., 'Anmerkungen zur GASP: Eine rechtspolitische Perspektive', *EuGRZ*, 31 (2004), 587–91

Cygan, A., 'National Parliaments within the EU Polity: No Longer Losers but Hardly Victorious', *ERA Forum*, 12 (2012), 517–33

Dannecker, G., 'Le principe de reconnaissance mutuelle en matière pénale dans L'Union européenne', *ZVglRWiss*, 111 (2012), 64–71

de Busser, E., 'The Lisbon After-Burn Effect', *ERA Forum*, 16 (2015), 277–89

De Capitani, E., 'The Schengen System after Lisbon: From Cooperation to Integration', *ERA Forum*, 15 (2014), 101–18

Dell, E., *The Schuman Plan and the British Abdication of Leadership in Europe* (Oxford: Clarendon, 1955)

Dembinski, M., 'EU-Außenbeziehungen nach Lissabon', *Das Parlament, Beilage, aus Politik und Zeitgeschichte*, 18 (2010), 9–15

Demko, D., and Bock, S., 'Tagungsbericht: Europäisches Strafrecht post-Lissabon: (Normalisierungs-)Chancen oder (Verstetigungs-)Risiken?', *JZ*, 65 (2011), 95–7

Depenheuer, O., 'Rechtsstaat, Rechtsstaat über alles', *SZ*, 17 August 2007, 14

De Vel, G., 'Legal and Justice Strategies in the Council of Europe', in Muller, S., and Zouridis, S., eds., *Law and Justice: A Strategy Perspective* (The Hague: Torkel Opsahl Academic EPublisher, 2012), 247–60

Dorra, F., *Strafrechtliche Legislativkompetenzen der Europäischen Union: Eine Gegenüberstellung der Kompetenzlage vor und nach dem Vertrag von Lissabon* (Baden-Baden: Nomos, 2013)

Eisele, J., 'Grundrechtliche Grenzen des Grundsatzes der gegenseitigen: Anerkennung', in Tiedemann, K., Sieber, U., Satzger, H., Burchard, C., and Brodowski, D., eds., *Die Verfassung moderner Strafrechtspflege: Erinnerung an Joachim Vogel* (Baden-Baden: Nomos, 2016), 221–32

Elsen, C., 'Die Übernahme des "Schengen-acquis" im Rahmen der EU', in Hummer, W., ed., *Rechtsfragen der Anwendung des Amsterdamer Vertrages* (Vienna: Manz, 2001), 39–51

Erbežnik, A., 'The Principle of Mutual Recognition as a Utilitarian Solution and the Way Forward', *EuCLR*, 2 (2012), 3–19

Fichera, M., *The Implementation of the European Arrest Warrant in the European Union: Law, Policy* and *Practice* (Cambridge, Antwerp and Portland: Intersentia, 2011)

Fletcher, M., 'EU Criminal Law Flexibility: What Lessons from the UK Protocol No. 36 Saga?', in Mitsilegas, Bergström, and Konstadinides, eds., *Research Handbook on EU Criminal Law* (2016), 78–103

Folz, H.-P., 'Karlsruhe, Lissabon und das Strafrecht: Ein Blick über den Zaun', *ZIS*, 4 (2009), 427–31

Frenz, W., 'Raum der Freiheit, der Sicherheit und des Rechts', *Jura*, 34 (2012), 701–8

Friman, H., 'How to Approach EU Criminal Law', in Muller, S., and Zouridis, S., eds., *Law and Justice: A Strategy Perspective* (The Hague: Torkel Opsahl Academic EPublisher, 2012), 261–70

Fromm, I. E., 'Auf dem Weg zur strafrechtlichen Verantwortlichkeit von Unternehmen/Unternehmensvereinigungen in Europa?', *ZIS*, 2 (2007), 279–91

EG-Rechtssetzungsbefugnis im Kriminalstrafrecht: Der Schutz der finanziellen Interessen der EG nach der neuesten Rechtsprechung des EuGH sowie im Lissabonner Vertrag (Baden-Baden: Nomos, 2009)

Gärditz, K. F., '§6: Europäisierung des Strafrechts und nationales Verfassungsrecht', in Böse, *Europäisches Strafrecht* (2013), 227–68

Gärditz, K. F. and Hillgruber, C., 'Volkssouveränität und Demokratie ernstgenommen: Zum Lissabon-Urteil des BVerfG', *JZ*, 64 (2009), 872–81

Geiger, R., *Auswirkungen europäischer Strafrechtsharmonisierung auf nationaler Ebene: Eine rechtsvergleichende Untersuchung am Beispiel des Rahmenbeschlusses 2004/68/JI zur Bekämpfung der sexuellen Ausbeutung von Kindern und der Kinderpornographie* (Berlin: Duncker & Humblot, 2012)

Gleß, S., 'Ohn(e)macht: Abschied von der Fiktion einer Waffengleichheit gegenüber europäischer Strafverfolgung?', *StV*, 33 (2013), 317–24

'§16: Beweisrechtshilfe', in Böse, *Europäisches Strafrecht* (2013), 611–29

'§38: Europäische Beweisanordnung', in Sieber, Satzger and von Heinegg, *Europäisches Strafrecht* (2014), 677–95

Gómez-Jara Díez,, C., 'Constitución europea y Derecho penal', in Bacigalupo, S., and Cancio Meliá, M., eds., *Derecho penal y política transnacional* (Barcelona: Atelier, 2005), 153–208

European Federal Criminal Law: The Federal Dimension of EU Criminal Law (Cambridge, Antwerp and Portland: Intersentia, 2015)

'European Federal Criminal Law: What Can Europe Learn from the US System of Federal Criminal Law to Solve Its Sovereign Debt Crisis?', *EuCLR*, 3 (2013), 170–93

Grünewald, A., 'Zur Frage eines europäischen Allgemeinen Teils des Strafrechts', *JZ*, 66 (2011), 972–7

Hahn, J.-U., 'Die Mitwirkungsrechte von BT und BR in EU-Angelegenheiten nach dem neuen Integrationsverantwortungsgesetz', *EuZW*, 20 (2009), 758–63

Haratsch, A., 'Anmerkung zu BVerfG, Urt. v. 30.6.2009: 2 BvE 2/08 u.a.', *ZJS*, 3 (2010), 122–8

Hassemer, W., 'Strafrecht in einem europäischen Verfassungsvertrag', *ZStW*, 116 (2004), 304–19

Hecker, B., 'Europäisches Strafrecht post-Lissabon', in Ambos, *Europäisches Strafrecht post-Lissabon* (2011), 13–28

Hefendehl, R., 'Europäisches Strafrecht: bis wohin und nicht weiter?', *ZIS*, 1 (2006), 229–36

Heger, M., 'Perspektiven des Europäischen Strafrechts nach dem Vertrag von Lissabon: Eine Durchsicht des (wohl) kommenden EU-Primärrechts vor dem Hintergrund des Lissabon Urteils des BVerfG vom 30.6.2009', *ZIS*, 4 (2009), 406–17

Heine, G., 'Quasi-Strafrecht und Verantwortlichkeit von Unternehmen im Kartellrecht der EG und der Schweiz', *ZStrR*, 125 (2007), 105–32

Henzelin, M., and Maeder, S., 'Mutual Judicial Assistance between Switzerland and the EU-States', *JECL*, 3 (2009), 49–62

Herlin-Karnell, E., 'All Roads Lead to Rome: The New AFSJ Package and the Trajectory to Europe 2020', *eucrim*, 9 (2014), 27–31

'Constitutional Principles in the Area of Freedom, Security and Justice', in Acosta Arcarazo, D., and Murphy, C. C., eds., *EU Security and Justice Law: After Lisbon and Stockholm* (Oxford and Portland: Hart Publishing, 2014), 38–53

'Denmark and the European Area of Freedom, Security and Justice: A Scandinavian Arrangement', *ALF*, 5 (2013), 95–105

'The Lisbon Treaty', *eucrim*, 5 (2010), 59–64

Hilf, M., and Pache, E., 'Der Vertrag von Amsterdam', *NJW*, 51 (1998), 705–13

Hillion, C., 'EU Enlargement', in Craig and de Búrca, *The Evolution of EU Law* (2011), 187–216

Hinarejos, A., 'Integration in Criminal Matters and the Role of the Court of Justice', *EuLRev*, 36 (2011), 420–30

Höpner, M., 'Disappointment, Some Satisfaction, and a Little Bit of Hope: On the Social Content of the Lisbon Ruling', in Fischer-Lescano, A., Joerges, C., and Wonka, A., eds., *The German Constitutional Court's Lisbon Ruling: Legal and Political-Science Perspectives* (Bremen: Zentrum für Europäische Rechtspolitik, 2010), 21–6

Huber, B., 'Die polizeiliche und justizielle Zusammenarbeit in Europa', in Wolter, J., Schenke, W.-R., Rieß, P., and Zöller, M. A., eds., *Datenübermittlungen und Vorermittlungen: Festgabe für Hans Hilger* (Heidelberg: C. F. Müller, 2003), 141–52

Husemann, S., 'Die Beeinflussung des deutschen Wirtschaftsstrafrechts durch Rahmenbeschlüsse der EU', *wistra*, 23 (2004), 447–54

Hüttemann, S. D., *Principles and Perspectives of European Criminal Procedure* (Florence: European University Institute, 2012)

Huybreghts, G., 'The Schengen Convention and the Schengen Acquis: 25 Years of Evolution', *ERA Forum*, 16 (2015), 379–426

Jokisch, J., and Jahnke, M., '§2: Der Raum der Freiheit, der Sicherheit und des Rechts', in Sieber, Satzger and von Heinegg, *Europäisches Strafrecht* (2014), 124–35

Jung, H., 'Konturen und Perspektiven des europäischen Strafrechts', *JuS*, 40 (2000), 417–24

'Wertende (Straf)Rechtsvergleichung', *GA*, 152 (2005), 2–10

Kaiafa-Gbandi, M., 'The Commission's Proposal for a Directive on the Fight against Fraud to the Union's Financial Interests by Means of Criminal Law', *EuCLR*, 2 (2012), 319–37

'The Treaty Establishing a Constitution for Europe and Challenges for Criminal Law at the Commencement of 21st Century', *EJCCLCJ*, 13 (2005), 483–514

'The Importance of Core Principles of Substantive Criminal Law', *EuCLR*, 1 (2011), 7–34

Kainer, F., 'Strafrecht im Raum der Freiheit, der Sicherheit und des Rechts', *EuR-Beiheft*, 48 (2013), 87–117

Kiiver, P., 'The Conduct of Subsidiarity Checks of EU Legislative Proposals by National Parliaments: Analysis, Observations and Practical Recommendations', *ERA Forum*, 12 (2012), 535–47

'The Lisbon Judgment of the German Constitutional Court: A Court-Ordered Strengthening of the National Legislature in the EU', *EuLJ*, 16 (2010), 578–88

Klip, A., 'Harmonisierung des Strafrechts: Eine fixe Idee?', *NStZ*, 20 (2000), 626–30

Krämer, R. U., 'Looking through Different Glasses at the Lisbon Treaty: The German Constitutional Court and the Czech Constitutional Court', in Fischer-Lescano, A., Joerges, C., and Wonka, A., eds., *The German Constitutional Court's Lisbon Ruling: Legal and Political-Science Perspectives* (Bremen: Zentrum für Europäische Rechtspolitik, 2010), 11–19

Kruma, K., 'Constitutional Courts and the Lisbon Treaty: The Future Based on Mutual Trust', in Guild, E., Carrera, S., and Eggenschwiler, A., eds., *The Area of Freedom, Security and Justice Ten Years On: Successes and Future Challenges under the Stockholm Programme* (Brussels: Centre for European Policy Studies, 2010), 38–48

Krüger, M., 'Unmittelbare EU-Strafkompetenzen aus Sicht des deutschen Strafrechts', *HRRS*, 13 (2012), 311–17

Kubiciel, M., 'Strafrechtswissenschaft und europäische Kriminalpolitik', *ZIS*, 5 (2010), 742–8

'Das "Lissabon"-Urteil und seine Folgen für das Europäische Strafrecht', *GA*, 157 (2010), 99–114

Kuhl, L., 'The Initiative for a Directive on the Protection of the EU Financial Interests by Substantive Criminal Law', *eucrim*, 7 (2012), 63–6

Landau, H., 'Strafrecht in seinen europäischen Bezügen: Gemeinsamkeiten, Diskrepanzen, Entscheidungen und Impulse', *NStZ*, 33 (2013), 194–9

'Strafrecht nach Lissabon', *NStZ*, 31 (2011), 537–46

Latzel, C., 'Eine misslungene Karlsruher Trotzreaktion', *FAZ*, 3 May 2013, 7

Leblois-Happe, J., 'Le parquet européen: Quand, comment, pourquoi?', in Roux-Demare, F.-X., ed., *L'européanisation de la justice pénale* (Paris: Cujas, 2016), 129–42

Lelieveldt, H., and Princen, S., *The Politics of the European Union* (Cambridge: Cambridge University Press, 2nd edn, 2015)

Liebau, T., '*Ne bis in idem*' *in Europa: Zugleich ein Beitrag zum Kartellsanktionenrecht in der EU und zur Anrechnung drittstattlicher Kartellsanktionen* (Berlin: Berliner Wissenschafts-Verlag,Vienna: Neuer Wissenschaftlicher Verlag and Zurich: Schulthess, 2005)

Liebert, U., 'More Democracy in the European Union?! Mixed Messages from the German Lisbon Ruling', in Fischer-Lescano, A., Joerges, C., and Wonka, A., eds., *The German Constitutional Court's Lisbon Ruling: Legal and Political-Science Perspectives* (Bremen: Zentrum für Europäische Rechtspolitik, 2010), 71–81

Löfgren, O., 'A Manifesto for European Criminal Procedure Law: A Prosecutorial Perspective', *EuCLR*, 5 (2015), 54–9

Mansdörfer, M., 'Das Europäische Strafrecht nach dem Vertrag von Lissabon: Oder: Europäisierung des Strafrechts unter nationalstaatlicher Mitverantwortung', *HRRS*, 11 (2010), 11–23

Matía Portilla, F. J., 'Un paso en falso (análisis de la Ley 38/2010, de 20 de diciembre)', *ReDCE*, 9 (2012), 95–129

Mavany, M., *Die europäische Beweisanordnung und das Prinzip der gegenseitigen Anerkennung* (Heidelberg et al.: C. F. Müller, 2012)

Meyer, F., '§25: Demokratische Kontrolle', in Böse, *Europäisches Strafrecht* (2013), 923–46

'Der Grundsatz gegenseitigen Vertrauens: Konzeptualisierung und Zukunftsperspektiven eines neuen Verfassungsprinzips', *EuR*, 52 (2017), 163–86

'Das Strafrecht im Raum der Freiheit, der Sicherheit und des Rechts', *EuR*, 46 (2011), 169–95

Strafrechtsgenese in internationalen Organisationen: Eine Untersuchung der Strukturen und Legitimationsvoraussetzungen strafrechtlicher Normbildungsprozesse in Mehrebenensystemen (Baden-Baden: Nomos, 2012)

'Verbundstrafverfolgung in der EU', in F. Herzog, R. Schlothauer, W. Wohlers and J. Wolter, eds., *Rechtsstaatlicher Strafprozeß und Bürgerrecht: Gedächtnisschrift für Edda Weßlau* (Berlin: Duncker & Humblot, 2016), 193–215

Miettinen, S., 'Implied Ancillary Criminal Law Competence after Lisbon', *EuCLR*, 3 (2013), 194–219

Mitsilegas, V., 'The Uneasy Relationship between the UK and European Criminal Law: From Opt-Outs to Brexit?', *CLR*, 63 (2016), 517–36

Mokros, R., 'Polizei und Justiz auf der Ebene der Europäischen Union', in Lisken, H., and Denninger, E., eds., *Handbuch des Polizeirechts: Gefahrenabwehr, Strafverfolgung, Rechtsschutz* (Munich: C. H. Beck, 4th edn, 2007), 1321–84

Moosmayer, K., 'Die neuen Leitlinien der Europäischen Kommission zur Festsetzung von Kartellgeldbußen', *wistra*, 26 (2007), 91–4

Möller, K., 'After the Lisbon Ruling: Where Is Social Democracy?', in Fischer-Lescano, A., Joerges, C., and Wonka, A., eds., *The German Constitutional Court's Lisbon Ruling: Legal and Political-Science Perspectives* (Bremen: Zentrum für Europäische Rechtspolitik, 2010), 83–91

Muñoz de Morales, R. M., 'Evaluación legislativa y racionalidad en el Ámbito Penal Europeo (y Nacional) ', *RP*, 27 (2011), 51–77

'In Pursuit of Basics for a New Principle of Legal Reserve in Supranational Criminal Law', *EuCLR*, 2 (2012), 252–75

Musil, A., 'Umfang und Grenzen europäischer Rechtssetzungsbefugnisse im Bereich des Strafrechts nach dem Vertrag von Amsterdam', *NStZ*, 20 (2000), 68–71

Mylonopoulos, C., 'Strafrechtsdogmatik in Europa nach dem Vertrag von Lissabon', *ZStW*, 123 (2011), 633–50

Nagler, A., 'Verteidigung gegen im Ausland gewonnene Ermittlungsergebnisse', *StV*, 33 (2013), 324–30

Nalewajko, P., *Grundsatz der gegenseitigen Anerkennung: Eckstein der justiziellen Zusammenarbeit in Strafsachen in der Europäischen Union?* (Berlin: Duncker & Humblot, 2010)

Nestler, C., 'Europäische Verteidigung bei transnationalen Strafverfahren', in Schünemann, B., ed., *Ein Gesamtkonzept für die europäische Strafrechtspflege* (Cologne et al.: Carl Heymanns, 2006), 166–80

Niechziol, F., and Schmucker, M., 'Polizeiliche Bekämpfung der grenzüberschreitenden Kriminalität nach Wegfall der Grenzübertrittskontrollen', *Kriminalistik*, 62 (2008), 105–11

Niemeier, M., 'Nach dem Vertrag von Lissabon: Die polizeiliche Zusammenarbeit in der EU', *ERA Forum*, 11 (2010), 197–206

Nieto Martín, A., 'La armonización del Derecho Penal ante el Tratado de Lisboa y el programa de Estocolmo', *RP*, 27 (2011), 78–82

Nilsson, H. G., 'From Classical Judicial Cooperation to Mutual Recognition', *RIDP*, 77 (2006), 53–8

'25 Years of Criminal Justice in Europe', *EuCLR*, 2 (2012), 106–22

'Where Should the EU Go in Developing Its Criminal Policy in the Future?', *eucrim*, 9 (2014), 19–21

Noltenius, B., 'Strafverfahrensrecht als Seismograph der europäischen Integration: Verfassung, Strafverfahrensrecht und der Vertrag von Lissabon', *ZStW*, 122 (2010), 604–26

Nowell-Smith, H., 'Behind the Scenes in the Negotiation of EU Criminal Justice Legislation', *NJECL*, 3 (2012), 381–93

Nürnberger, S., 'Die künftige Europäische Staatsanwaltschaft', *ZJS*, 2 (2009), 494–505

Nuotio, K., 'Criminal Law of a Transnational Polity', in Müller-Dietz, H., ed., *Festschrift für Heike Jung: Zum 65. Geburtstag am 23. April 2007* (Baden-Baden: Nomos, 2007), 685–98

Öberg, J., 'The Definition of Criminal Sanctions in the EU', *EuCLR*, 3 (2013), 273–99

Oppermann, T., 'Den Musterknaben ins Bremserhäuschen! BVerfG und Lissaboner Vertrag', *EuZW*, 20 (2009), 473

Ostropolski, T., 'The CJEU as a Defender of Mutual Trust', *NJECL*, 6 (2015), 166–78

Ouwerkerk, J., *Quid pro Quo? A Comparative Law Perspective on the Mutual Recognition of Judicial Decisions in Criminal Matters* (Cambridge, Antwerp and Portland: Intersentia, 2011)

Pache, E., 'Das Ende der Europäischen Integration? Das Urteil des BVerfG zum Vertrag von Lissabon, zur Zukunft Europas und der Demokratie', *EuGRZ*, 36 (2009), 285–98

Pache, E., and Schorkopf, F., 'Der Vertrag von Nizza', *NJW*, 54 (2001), 1377–86

Parisi, N., and Rinoldi, D., 'Principles of the European Criminal Policy: Starting from the Protection of the European Union's Financial Interests against Fraud', *eucrim*, 10 (2015), 111–15

Peers, S., 'EU Justice and Home Affairs Law (Non-civil)', in Craig and de Búrca, *The Evolution of EU Law* (2011), 269–97

Perron, W., 'Europäische und transnationale Strafrechtspflege als Herausforderung für eine moderne Strafrechtsdogmatik', in Tiedemann, K., Sieber, U., Satzger, H., Burchard, C., and Brodowski, D., eds., *Die Verfassung moderner Strafrechtspflege: Erinnerung an Joachim Vogel* (Baden-Baden: Nomos, 2016), 307–20

Pérez Cepeda, I., Benito Sánchez, D., and Gorjón Barranco, M.C., 'Study on the Policy-Relevance of Existing Crime Data', *EuCLR*, 3 (2013), 125–51

Picotti, L., 'Diritto penale comunitario e Costituzione europea', in Canestrari, S., and Foffani, L., eds., *Il diritto penale nella prospettiva europea: quali politiche criminali per quale Europa?* (Milan: Giuffre, 2005), 325–76

Poncela, P., and Roth, R., 'Quelles sanctions pour quelle Europe?', *APC*, 27 (2005), 107–24

Prieto, J. V., 'Die juristische Natur der Sanktionen der Europäischen Union', *ZStW*, 120 (2008), 403–17

Prittwitz, C., 'Lissabon als Chance zur kriminalpolitischen Neubesinnung: Das Manifest zur Europäischen Kriminalpolitik', in Ambos, *Europäisches Strafrecht post-Lissabon* (2011), 29–39

Pudło A., 'Przestrzeganie zasady pomocniczości w polskim parlamencie', in *Roczniki Administracji i Prawa. Teoria i Praktyka*, 13 (2013), 27–37

Rackow, P., 'Das Anerkennungsprinzip auf dem Prüfstein der Beweisrechtshilfe', in Ambos, *Europäisches Strafrecht post-Lissabon* (2011), 117–36

'§23: Institutionalisierung der Verteidigung', in Böse, *Europäisches Strafrecht* (2013), 865–86

Radtke, H., and Busch, D., 'Transnationaler Strafklageverbrauch in der Europäischen Union: EuGH, Urteil vom 11.02.2003', *NStZ*, 23 (2003), 281–8

Ramos, J. A. E., 'Towards a European Public Prosecutor's Office', in Klip, *Substantive Criminal Law of the EU* (2011), 38–50

Rathke, H., '6. Abschnitt: Materielle Vertragsänderungen', in von Arnauld, A., and Hufeld, U., eds., *Systematischer Kommentar zu den Lissabon-Begleitgesetzen: IntVG, EUZBBG, EUZBLG* (Baden-Baden: Nomos, 2011), 179–257

Reiling, K., and Reschke, D., 'Die Auswirkungen der Lissabon-Entscheidung des BVerfG auf die Europäisierung des Umweltstrafrechts', *wistra*, 29 (2010), 47–52

Reinbacher, T., *Strafrecht im Mehrebenensystem: Modelle der Verteilung strafrechtsbezogener Kompetenzen* (Baden-Baden: Nomos, 2015)

Ronsfeld, P., *Rechtshilfe Anerkennung und Vertrauen: Die Europäische Ermittlungsanordnung* (Berlin: Duncker & Humblot, 2015)

Rosenau, H., 'Zur Europäisierung im Strafrecht: Vom Schutz finanzieller Interessen der EG zu einem gemeineuropäischen Strafgesetzbuch?', *ZIS*, 3 (2008), 9–19

Ryan, G., and Hamilton, C., 'Criminal Justice Policy and the European Union', in Healy, D., Hamilton, C., Daly, Y., and Butler, M., eds., *The Routledge Handbook of Irish Criminology* (Oxon and New York: Routledge, 2016), 467–85

Rybicki, R., 'Schengen and Poland', *PYIL*, 25 (2001), 97–112

Safferling, C., 'Strafrechtsentwicklung in der EU: Konglomerat oder Synthese?', in Streng, F., and Kett-Straub, G., eds., *Strafrechtsvergleichung als Kulturvergleich: Beiträge zur Evaluation deutschen 'Strafrechtsexports' als 'Strafrechtsimport'* (Tübingen: Mohr Siebeck, 2012), 187–212

Salazar, L., 'EU's Criminal Policy and the Possible Contents of a New Multi-annual Programme', *eucrim*, 9 (2014), 22–6

Sánchez Lázaro, F.G., 'Ein Gespenst geht um in Europa: Auf dem Weg zu einem europäischen Strafrechtsdiskurs', *GA*, 161 (2014), 656–64

Satzger, H., '§2: Grundsätze eines europäischen Strafrechts', in Böse, Europäisches Strafrecht (2013), 61–95

'Das "Manifest zur Europäischen Kriminalpolitik": Eine Antwort auf die (selten gestellte) Frage nach einer vernünftigen Kriminalpolitik der Europäischen Union', *ZRP*, 43 (2010), 137–40

'§9: Europäisierung', in Sieber, Satzger and von Heinegg, *Europäisches Strafrecht* (2014), 251–71

Satzger, H., and Zimmermann, F., 'Europäische Kriminalpolitik "Reloaded": Das Manifest zum Europäischen Strafverfahrensrecht', *ZIS*, 8 (2013), 406–10

Sauer, H., 'Kompetenz- und Identitätskontrolle von Europarecht nach dem Lissabon-Urteil: Ein neues Verfahren vor dem Bundesverfassungsgericht?', *ZRP*, 42 (2009), 195–8

Schaut, A. B., *Europäische Strafrechtsprinzipien: Ein Beitrag zur systematischen Fortentwicklung übergreifender Grundlagen* (Baden-Baden: Nomos, 2012)

Schmidt, S. K., 'Being Wrong but Getting It Right? The Lisbon Judgement of the GCC', in Fischer-Lescano, A., Joerges, C., and Wonka, A., eds., *The German Constitutional Court's Lisbon Ruling: Legal and Political-Science Perspectives* (Bremen: Zentrum für Europäische Rechtspolitik, 2010), 41–6

Schomburg, W., '§3: Überblick über die Aktivitäten des Europarats auf strafrechtlichem Gebiet', in Sieber, Satzger and von Heinegg, *Europäisches Strafrecht* (2014), 136–43

Schonard, P., 'Judicial Review of EU Acts Affecting Criminal Proceedings', *EuCLR*, 2 (2012), 61–76

Schorkopf, F., 'Die EU im Lot: Karlsruhes Rechtsspruch zum Vertrag von Lissabon', *EuZW*, 20 (2009), 718–24

Der Europäische Weg: Grundlagen der Europäischen Union (Tübingen: Mohr Siebeck, 2nd edn, 2015)

'Das Lissabon-Urteil des BVerfG: Die Verfassungsbeschwerde als geschärftes Instrument der Verteidigung', in Ambos, *Europäisches Strafrecht post-Lissabon* (2011), 111–15

Schramm, E., 'Acht Fragen zum Europäischen Strafrecht', *ZJS*, 3 (2010), 615–19

Schroeder, W., 'Die Auslegung des EU-Rechts', *JuS*, 44 (2004), 180–6

Schröder, C., 'Perspektiven der Europäisierung des Strafrechts nach Lissabon: Neues Denken oder alte Fehler?', in Hellmann, U., and Schröder, C., eds., *Festschrift für Hans Achenbach* (Heidelberg et al.: C. F. Müller et al., 2011), 491–507

Schröder J. and Stiegel, U., '§35: Zusammenarbeit mit Drittstaaten', in Sieber, Satzger and von Heinegg, *Europäisches Strafrecht* (2014), 615–35

Schünemann, B., 'Alternativentwurf europäische Strafverfolgung', in Schünemann, B., ed., *Alternativentwurf europäische Strafverfolgung* (Cologne, Berlin and Munich: Carl Heymanns, 2004), 1–42

'Grundzüge eines Alternativ-Entwurfs zur europäischen Strafverfolgung', *ZStW*, 116 (2004), 376–99

'Mindestbedingungen einer effektiven Verteidigung in transnationalen europäischen Strafverfahren', *StV*, 36 (2016), 178–85

'Spät kommt ihr, doch ihr kommt: Glosse eines Strafrechtslehrers zur Lissabon-Entscheidung des BVerfG', *ZIS*, 4 (2009), 393–6

Schützendübel, C., *Die Bezugnahme auf EU-Verordnungen in Blankettstrafgesetzen: Eine Untersuchung zum Phänomen anpassungsbedingter Sanktionslücken bei unionsrechtsakzessorischen Blankettstrafgesetzen* (Baden-Baden: Nomos, 2012)

Serzysko, A., 'European Criminal Justice under the Lisbon Treaty', *eucrim*, 5 (2010), 69–75

Sicurella, R., 'Some Reflections on the Need for a General Theory of the Competence of the European Union in Criminal Law', in Klip, *Substantive Criminal Law of the EU* (2011), 233–49

Sieber, U., 'Einführung', in Sieber, Satzger and von Heinegg, *Europäisches Strafrecht* (2014), 31–101

'Die Zukunft des Europäischen Strafrechts: Ein neuer Ansatz zu den Zielen und Modellen des europäischen Strafrechtssystems', *ZStW*, 121 (2009), 1–67

Simon, P., 'The Criminalisation Power of the European Union after Lisbon and the Principle of Democratic Legitimacy', *NJECL*, 3 (2012), 242–56

Silva Sánchez, J. M., 'Constitución Europea, legalidad y derecho penal económico', in Bajo Fernández, M., ed., *Constitución Europea y derecho penal económico* (Madrid: Ed. universitaria Ramón Areces, 2006), 253–69

'Los principios inspiradores de las propuestas de un Derecho Penal europeo', *RP*, 13 (2004), 138–50

Spemann, T. F., 'Bundesverfassungsgericht zum Lissabon-Vertrag: Überblick unter besonderer Berücksichtigung strafrechtlicher Aspekte', *StraFo*, 22 (2009), 499–505

Spencer, J. R., 'Opting Out of EU Criminal Justice?', *Archbold Rev*, issue 7 (2012), 6–9

'Opting Out of EU Criminal Justice: Withdrawal, or an Exercise in Smoke and Mirrors?', *Archbold Rev*, issue 8 (2013), 6–9

'The UK and EU Criminal Law: Should We Be Leading, Following or Abstaining?', in Mitsilegas, V., Alldridge, P., and Cheliotis, L., eds., *Globalisation, Criminal Law and Criminal Justice: Theoretical, Comparative and Transnational Perspectives* (Oxford: Hart, 2015), 135–52

Spencer, J. R. and Padfield, N., 'L'intégration des droits européens en droit britannique', *RSC*, 71 (2006), 537–50

Spiezia, F., 'Linguistic Regimes and Judicial Cooperation in the Eurojust's Perspective', in Ruggieri, F., ed., *Criminal Proceedings, Languages and the European Union: Linguistic and Legal Issues* (Berlin and Heidelberg: Springer, 2014), 23–42

Steinbach, A., 'The Lisbon Judgment of the German Federal Constitutional Court: New Guidance on the Limits of European Integration?', *GLJ*, 11 (2010), 367–90

Sturies, J., 'Ermächtigt der Vertrag von Lissabon wirklich zum Erlass supranationaler Wirtschaftsstrafgesetze?', *HRRS*, 13 (2012), 273–88

Suhr, O., 'Die polizeiliche und justizielle Zusammenarbeit in Strafsachen nach dem "Lissabon"-Urteil des Bundesverfassungsgerichts', *ZEuS*, 12 (2009), 687–715

Suominen, A., 'The Characteristics of Nordic Criminal Law in the Setting of EU Criminal Law', *EuCLR*, 1 (2011), 170–87

The Principle of Mutual Recognition in Cooperation in Criminal Matters: A Study of the Principle in Four Framework Decisions and in the Implementation Legislation in the Nordic Member States (Cambridge et al.: Intersentia, 2011)

Swarc, A. J., 'Eurodefensor', in Schünemann, B., ed., *Ein Gesamtkonzept für die europäische Strafrechtspflege* (Cologne et al.: Carl Heymanns, 2006), 181–90

Taupiac-Nouvel, G., 'The Principle of Mutual Recognition in Criminal Matters: A New Model of Judicial Cooperation within the EU', *EuCLR*, 2 (2012), 236–51

Terradillos Basoco, J. M., 'La Constitución para Europa: ¿Las bases del derecho penal europeo?', *EPC*, 25 (2004), 361–98

Thiele, A., 'Das Rechtsschutzsystem nach dem Vertrag von Lissabon: (K)ein Schritt nach vorn?', *EuR*, 45 (2010), 30–50

Thunberg Schunke, M., *Whose Responsibility: A Study of Transnational Defence Rights and Mutual Recognition of Judicial Decisions within the EU* (Cambridge et al.: Intersentia, 2013)

Thym, D., 'Die Reichweite der EU-Grundrechte-Charta: Zu viel Grundrechtsschutz?', *NVwZ*, 33 (2013), 889–96

Tiberi, G., 'Multilingualism and Legal Translation of the Sources of Law of the European Union: The Implications for Criminal Law of the New Post-Lisbon Treaty Area of Freedom Security and Justice', in Ruggieri, F., ed., *Criminal Proceedings, Languages and the European Union: Linguistic and Legal Issues* (Berlin and Heidelberg: Springer, 2014), 5–21

Tiedemann, K., 'Gegenwart und Zukunft des Europäischen Strafrechts', *ZStW*, 116 (2004), 945–58

Toscani, S., and Suhr, O., 'Der Raum der Freiheit, der Sicherheit und des Rechts nach Inkrafttreten des Vertrags von Lissabon: Neue Rahmenbedingungen für das Stockholmer Programm', in Meng, W., Ress, G., Stein, T., eds., *Europäische Integration und Globalisierung: Festschrift zum 60-jährigen Bestehen des Europa-Instituts* (Baden-Baden: Nomos, 2011), 581–605

Träskman, P. O., '"A Nordic Academic Perspective" to the European Criminal Policy Initiative: A Manifesto for European Criminal Procedure Law', *EuCLR*, 5 (2015), 60–7

Turner, J. I., 'The Expressive Dimension of EU Criminal Law', *AmJCompL*, 60 (2012), 555–83

van Middelaar, L., *Passage to Europe: How a Continent Became a Union* (New Haven, CT: Yale University Press, 2013)

Valdés, A.R., 'The Mutual Recognition Principle in Criminal Matters: A Review', *ERA Forum*, 16 (2015), 291–303

Vermeulen, G., 'The EU's Mutual Trust and Recognition Bubble: Challenging the Legitimacy of EU Criminal Policy & Judicial Cooperation in Criminal Matters', in Tiedemann, K., Sieber, U., Satzger, H., Burchard, C., and Brodowski, D., eds., *Die Verfassung moderner Strafrechtspflege: Erinnerung an Joachim Vogel* (Baden-Baden: Nomos, 2016), 181–210

Free Gathering and Movement of Evidence in Criminal Matters in the EU: Thinking beyond Borders, Striving for Balance, in Search of Coherence (Apeldoorn, Antwerp and Portland: Maklu, 2011)

Vernet, D., 'Die Union als außenpolitischer Akteur', *EuGRZ*, 31 (2004), 584–7

Vervaele, J. A. E., 'La europeización del Derecho penal y la dimensión penal de la integración europea', *RP*, 15 (2005), 169–83

'The Transnational Ne Bis In Idem Principle in the EU: Mutual Recognition and Equivalent Protection of Human Rights', *ULR*, 1 (2005), 100–18

Vidmar, J., and Eggett, C., ,'Brexit: Is Everything Going to Change in Law, So That Very Little Would Change in Fact?', *EJIL:Talk!*, 27 June 2016, at www.ejiltalk.org/brexit-is-everything-going-to-change-in-law-so-that-very-little-would-change-in-fact, last accessed 27 January 2018

Vogel, J., 'Artikel 82 AEUV', in Grabitz et al., *Das Recht der EU*, i (2014), n.p.

'European Integrated Criminal Justice System and Its Constitutional Framework', *MaastJECompL*, 12 (2005), 125–48

'Harmonisierung des Strafrechts in der Europäischen Union', *GA*, 150 (2003), 314–34

'Die Kompetenz der EG zur Einführung supranationaler Sanktionen', in Dannecker, G., ed., *Die Bekämpfung des Subventionsbetrugs im EG-Bereich* (Cologne: Bundesanzeiger, 1993), 170–87

'Die Strafgesetzgebungskompetenzen der Europäischen Union nach Art. 83, 86 und 324 AEUV', in Ambos, *Europäisches Strafrecht post-Lissabon* (2011), 41–56

'Strafrecht und Strafrechtswissenschaft im internationalen und europäischen Rechtsraum', *JZ*, 67 (2012), 25–31

Vogel, J., and Brodowski, D., '§5: Allgemeiner Teil des supranationalen Sanktionenrechts', in Sieber, Satzger and von Heinegg, *Europäisches Strafrecht* (2014), 153–76

'§6: Besonderer Teil des supranationalen Strafrechts (Überblick)', in Sieber, Satzger and von Heinegg, *Europäisches Strafrecht* (2014), 177–92

Vogler, T., 'Aktuelle Probleme der Auslieferung', *ZStW*, 79 (1969), 163–87

'Die strafrechtlichen Konventionen des Europarats', *Jura*, 14 (1992), 586–93

von Hirsch, A., *Censure and Sanctions* (Oxford: Clarendon Press, 1995)

von Hirsch, A., and Ashworth, A., *Proportionate Sentencing: Exploring the Principles* (Oxford: Oxford University Press, 2005)

Voßkuhle, A., 'Der Rechtsanwalt und das Bundesverfassungsgericht: Aktuelle Herausforderungen der Verfassungsrechtsprechung', *NJW*, 66 (2013), 1329–36

Walker, N., 'The European Fallout', *GLJ*, 17 (2016), 125–30

Walter, T., 'Inwieweit erlaubt die Europäische Verfassung ein europäisches Strafgesetz?', *ZStW*, 117 (2005), 912–33

Weigend, T., 'Der Entwurf einer Europäischen Verfassung und das Strafrecht', *ZStW*, 116 (2004), 275–303

Weißer, B, 'Strafgesetzgebung durch die EU: Nicht nur ein Recht, sondern auch eine Pflicht?', *GA*, 161 (2014), 433–52

Weyembergh, A., 'Functions of Approximation of Penal Legislation within the European Union', *MaastJECompL*, 12 (2005), 149–72

L'harmonisation des législations: Condition de l'espace pénal européen et révélateur de ses tensions (Brussels: Éditions de l'université de Bruxelles, 2004)

Wieczorek, I., 'A Needed Balance between Security, Liberty and Justice: Positive Signals Arrive from the Field of Victims' Rights', *EuCLR*, 2 (2012), 141–57

Wojciechowski, B., *Philosophical Approach to the Interculturality of Criminal Law* (Frankfurt am Main: Peter Lang, 2010)

Wolter, K., *Vorabentscheidungsverfahren und Beschleunigungsgebot in Strafsachen: Unter besonderer Berücksichtigung des Eilvorlageverfahrens zum Gerichtshof der Europäischen Union nach Art. 104b der Verfahrensordnung* (Berlin: Duncker & Humblot, 2011)

Wonka, A., 'Accountability without Politics? The Contribution of Parliaments to Democratic Control of EU Politics in the German Constitutional Court's Lisbon Ruling', in Fischer-Lescano, A., Joerges, C., and Wonka, A., eds., *The German Constitutional Court's Lisbon Ruling: Legal and Political-Science Perspectives* (Bremen: Zentrum für Europäische Rechtspolitik, 2010), 55–62

Würz, K., *Das Schengener Durchführungsübereinkommen: Einführung, Erläuterungen, Vorschriften* (Stuttgart et al.: Richard Boorberg, 1997)

Zeder, F., 'Europastrafrecht, Vertrag von Lissabon und Stockholmer Programm: Mehr Grundrechtsschutz?', *EuR*, 47 (2012), 34–59

Zieschang, F., 'Der Einfluss der Europäischen Union auf das deutsche Strafrecht', in Sieber, U., Dannecker, G., Kindhauser, U., Vogel, J., and Walter, T, eds., *Strafrecht und Wirtschaftsrecht: Festschrift für Klaus Tiedemann zum 70. Geburtstag* (Cologne et al.: Carl Heymanns, 2008), 1303–19

Zimmermann, F., 'Die Auslegung künftiger EU-Strafrechtskompetenzen nach dem Lissabon-Urteil des Bundesverfassungsgerichts', *Jura*, 31 (2009), 844–51

Zimmermann, F., Glaser, S., and Motz, A., 'Mutual Recognition and Its Implications for the Gathering of Evidence in Criminal Proceedings: A Critical Analysis of the Initiative for a European Investigation Order', *EuCLR*, 1 (2011), 56–80

Zöller, M. A., 'Europäische Strafgesetzgebung', *ZIS*, 4 (2009), 340–9

'Neue unionsrechtliche Strafgesetzgebungskompetenzen nach dem Vertrag von Lissabon', in Baumeister, P., Roth, W., and Ruthig, J, ed., *Staat, Verwaltung und Rechtsschutz: Festschrift für Wolf-Rüdiger Schenke zum 70. Geburtstag* (Berlin: Duncker & Humblot, 2011), 579–98

Zweigert, K., 'Der Einfluss des Europäischen Gemeinschaftsrechts auf die Rechtsordnungen der Mitgliedstaaten', *RabelsZ*, 28 (1964), 601–43

Zwingmann, B., 'The Continuing Myth of Euro-Scepticism? The German Federal Constitutional Court Two Years after Lisbon', *ICLQ*, 61 (2012), 665–95

2

The Protection of Fundamental Rights in Europe

A. Introduction, Particularly the Relationship between the EU and the European Convention on Human Rights (ECHR)

1 The protection of fundamental rights in Europe derives from a range of sources.[1] In the first instance, the protection of fundamental rights is guaranteed at the **national level**. If these rights are an expression of the constitutional traditions shared by the EU Member States, they become part of **Union law** as general principles (Art. 6(3) TEU).[2] Besides these principles, there are also the guarantees of the **ECHR**, created by the Member States of the Council of Europe; we will examine them more closely in turn.[3] The EU's fundamental rights system includes the **Charter of the Fundamental Rights of the European Union** (CFREU),[4] which increased in significance after the Lisbon Treaty entered into force.[5] While the Council, EP and Commission were previously only voluntarily bound by the CFREU,[6] Art. 6(1) TEU has now made the CFREU European primary law.[7] Further fundamental rights guarantees can also be found in individual **secondary legislative acts** of the EU,[8] as well as in Art. 54 **CISA**, which establishes a European prohibition of double jeopardy.[9] Of course, all this does not turn the EU from a historically and predominantly economic and market-led organisation into a human rights organisation proper; nevertheless, its ability to embrace human rights as a value-based system which, after all, forms the constitutional basis of its Member States should not be understated.[10]

2 In this European '**multi-level system** of fundamental rights',[11] the relationships between the individual codifications – their respective hierarchies and whether one excludes the other – are ambiguous and complex; the European citizen may even get lost in this complexity.[12] At any rate, the ECHR's **relation to the national law** of the Member States is determined by this multi-level system.[13] In some States the ECHR enjoys, formally or at least effectively, *constitutional status*,[14] in others it has *supralegal* status,[15] in still others only *legal* status.[16]

3 In the **UK**, the 1998 *Human Rights Act* has given 'further effect to rights and freedoms guaranteed under the ECHR'.[17] It puts the ECHR on the level of ordinary primary legislation and UK courts have to 'take into account' the Court's jurisprudence.[18] Given its rank, a subsequent Act of Parliament may repeal the HRA and the Conservatives indeed promised to do so in the 2015 election campaign,[19] but so far the proposed British Bill of Rights is on hold.[20] According to one leading expert on the matter, 'the HRA is likely to be around for some time to come, noises about a Bill of Rights notwithstanding'.[21] Apart from that, it is controversial whether the derogation of the HRA would entail a loss of rights (protection) or whether the proposed Bill of (common law) Rights would fully account for the rights protected by it.[22] At any rate, matters are not that dramatic given that, on the one hand, the UK's compliance with and implementation of ECtHR judgments is high;[23] on the other hand, it seems as if the Court has taken a more cautious approach with regard to the UK in the last years, considering far fewer cases, delivering fewer judgments and striking out almost all cases.[24] In substance, human rights critics in the UK have been upset[25] especially by the *Hirst* case, where the Court ruled that the British law banning all convicted persons from voting[26] violates Art. 3 of Protocol 1 to the ECHR.[27] Interestingly, the same ruling by the Court in *Anchugov and Gladkov* against **Russia**[28] resulted in an amendment of the law on the Constitutional Court of the Russian Federation giving this Court the power to declare decisions of a human rights body – i.e. not only of the ECtHR – 'impossible to implement' if their implementation were inconsistent with the Russian Constitution.[29]

4 The consequence of a mere legal status of the ECHR – that is, its equivalence in rank to national (primary) law – is, as we have just seen with regard to the UK HRA, that a *lex posterior* may derogate the ECHR as *lex prior*.[30] To prevent such an outcome, **German** case law pursues an interpretation *that conforms to the Convention*, using the ECtHR's case law as an *aid to interpretation*,[31] but without interpreting the guarantees of the ECHR and the *Grundgesetz* (Basic Law) in a schematically parallel manner.[32] Similarly, the **UK** HRA orders judges 'to take into account' the relevant case law of the ECHR;[33] also, any legislation 'must be read and given effect in a way which is compatible with the Convention rights'.[34] Thus judges should interpret – 'so far it is possible to do so'[35] – statutory and common law in line with the Convention,[36] coming close to the German conformity interpretation approach just mentioned. In concrete terms, given the HRA's equal rank to primary legislation, if found incompatible with the Convention such legislation remains valid, and the domestic courts may only make a declaration of incompatibility; only *subordinate* legislation is invalid to the extent of the incompability.[37] As to *common law*, it has been argued that it may have to be overruled if incompatible with the ECHR.[38] The **Russian** approach mentioned above goes, of course, in a radically different direction, for it gives clear precedence to Russian over ECHR law and ultimately entails the non-implementation of ECtHR judgments against Russia.

5 At any rate, an ECHR-oriented interpretation is not permitted to restrict in any way the scope of the constitutional protections given that they may go beyond the Convention guarantees.[39] Moreover, ECtHR decisions that entail a reinterpretation of the constitutional guarantees are considered legally relevant changes to the factual and legal situation that set aside the finality of a Constitutional Court judgment – its effect of *chose jugée* (*res judicata*) – so that the Court is able to address the matter in question a second time.[40] However, constitutional complaints cannot be based directly on an infringement of the Convention, since ordinary law cannot be applied as a legal test by a constitutional court.[41] As a consequence, a law that contravenes the ECHR, albeit illegal and against international law, is not unconstitutional.[42]

6 The various codifications may also clash[43] or interact on the **European level**. Thus, on the one hand, the ECtHR referred explicitly

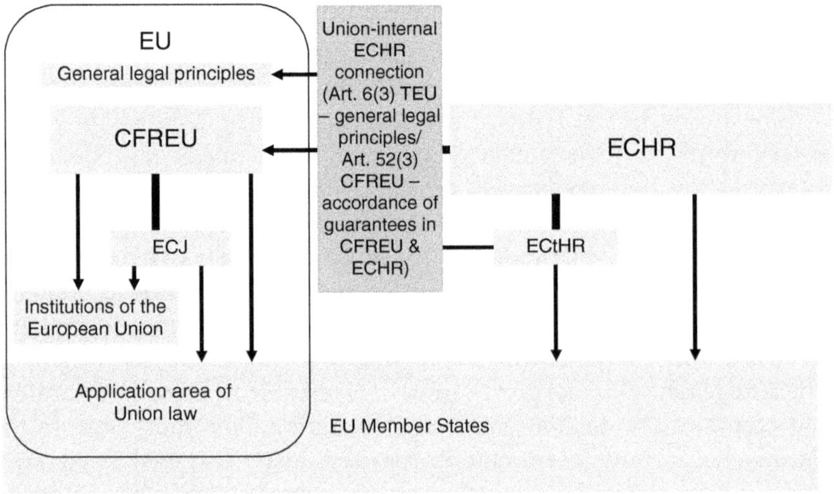

Figure 2a The protection of fundamental rights in the current European multi-level system

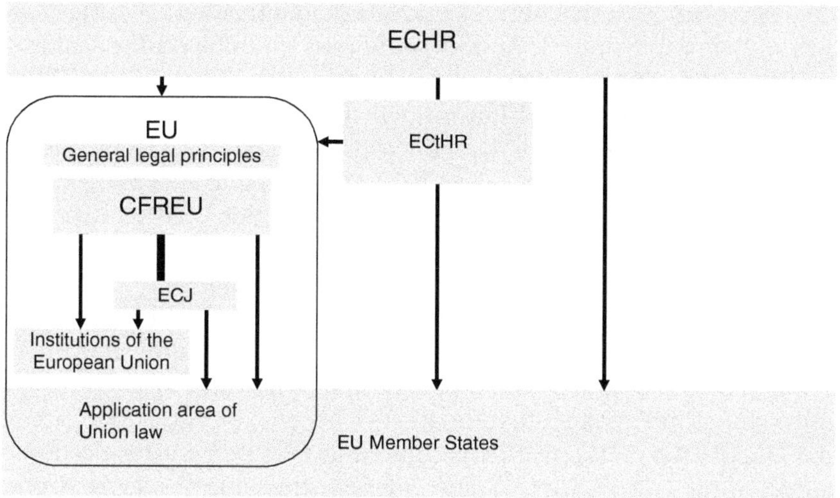

Figure 2b The protection of fundamental rights in the current European multi-level system after a possible EU accession to the ECHR

to Art. 49 I CFREU and CJEU case law on the prohibition of retroactive legislation[44] in its *Scoppola* judgment of 17 September 2009.[45] On the other hand, the ECHR and the standards developed by the ECtHR have been incorporated into the case law of the CJEU.[46] This recourse to the **ECHR as a source for human rights law** has now been taken up explicitly in Art. 6(3) TEU, which grants the ECHR's fundamental rights the status of general principles of Union law.[47] Furthermore, the *CFREU* has aligned itself with the ECHR in decreeing that the fundamental rights it contains shall have the same '*meaning and scope*' as respective rights laid down in the ECHR (Art. 52(3) CFREU).[48] Thus reference is also made to the case law of the ECtHR,[49] which, accordingly, also needs to be taken into account when interpreting the CFREU.[50] This reference is particularly important in the field of criminal procedure, as the respective rules in the CFREU and the ECHR correspond to a large extent,[51] and so far the CJEU has not developed a sophisticated case law in this field.[52] Art. 52(3) CFREU thus makes an important contribution to the **coherence of the protection of fundamental rights** in Europe.[53]

7 Despite all of these links and overlaps, at present the EU is not (yet) bound by the ECHR's guarantees.[54] Before *Lisbon*, legal grounds prevented the EU itself becoming a contracting party to the ECHR alongside the EU Member States.[55] Now, with the Lisbon Treaty, the Union has

legal personality[56] and is able to conclude or join treaties.[57] Furthermore, Art. 6(2) first sentence TEU both authorises and obliges the Union to **accede to the ECHR.**[58] While this option was so far only available to members of the Council of Europe, which consists only of States,[59] this obstacle was overcome with the ratification of ECHR AP XIV by Russia[60] and its entry into force on 1 June 2010. According to Art. 59(2) ECHR, the EU is now also able to 'accede to this Convention'; further details are regulated in Protocol No 8 on Art. 6(2) TEU.[61] In June 2010, the Council conferred a mandate on the Commission to negotiate with the Member States in this matter and prepare the respective draft agreement. The negotiations, which commenced on 7 July 2010,[62] culminated in the submission of a draft accession agreement in June 2013.[63] Among other things, it envisages that the EU will become a contracting party of the ECHR (Art. 1(1)), will be permitted to take part in the election of judges at the ECtHR (Art. 6), and will be included in the scope of state (Art. 4) and individual applications.[64]

8 The further, highly complex, treaty agreement procedure on the part of the EU is set out in Art. 218 TFEU, which still represents a significant obstacle to the EU's accession to the ECHR.[65] Thus the Council, among others, has to reach a unanimous decision on the accession.[66] This decision again only enters into force when ratified by all Member States.[67] As soon as the accession has taken place, the ECHR will become part of the Union's legal system.[68] In the hierarchy of legal sources, the ECHR would then take on an *intermediate position* below the EU treaties (and thus below the CFREU), but above European secondary law,[69] so that this secondary law would have to be measured against the ECHR.[70] With this, the EU places itself under the jurisdiction of the ECtHR, as do all States that are party to the ECHR.[71] However, this does not alter the fact that the CJEU remains responsible for the interpretation of Union law[72] and thus also for the interpretation of the ECHR, which has been transferred into Union law. Accordingly, both the CJEU and the ECtHR will be tasked with ensuring the effective protection of fundamental rights in the EU.[73] However, as the ECtHR has the ultimate responsibility for interpreting the ECHR, the necessary coherence of legislation relevant to fundamental rights needs to be ensured.[74] Moreover, it can also be anticipated that existing gaps in legal protection, such as in the protection of individual rights against so-called self-executing norms – that is, directly applicable binding legal acts – will be closed. This is to be welcomed, especially in light of the EU's – already mentioned[75] – competence to enact directly applicable criminal laws created through the Lisbon Treaty.[76]

9 However, all these developments have been abruptly brought to an end by **Opinion 2/13 of the CJEU of 18 December 2014**[77] – sitting as full Court[78]– holding that the draft accession agreement is incompatible both with Art. 6(2) TEU and with Protocol No 8 EU.[79] As a consequence, 'the agreement may not enter into force unless it is amended or the Treaties are revised'.[80] To fully understand the Court's opinion it is important to note that Art. 6(2) TEU allows the accession only upon the condition that it does 'not affect the Union's competences as defined in the Treaties'.[81] Similarly, but more specifically, Protocol No 8 EU stipulates that the agreement 'shall make provisions for preserving the specific characteristics of the Union and Union law',[82] 'ensure that accession of the Union shall not affect the competences of the Union or the powers of its institutions',[83] and not 'affect' Art. 344 TFEU.[84] Against this background it is not surprising that the Court invokes the autonomy of the EU legal order and the particularities of the Union and its law,[85] which, in its view, are not sufficiently taken into account by the agreement.[86] It is equally plausible that the Court emphasises the autopoetic character of the dispute settlement system pursuant to Art. 344 TFEU[87] and the Member States' obligation, derived from their duty of loyalty pursuant to Art. 4(3) TEU, to respect this system and the ensuing exclusive jurisdiction of the Court.[88] In the Court's view this system would be undermined by an EU accession to the ECHR since this would make the latter 'an integral part of EU law',[89] which therefore would be subject to the exclusive jurisdiction of the CJEU but its jurisdictional claim would conflict with the ECtHR's exclusive jurisdiction over ECHR matters pursuant to Art. 33 ECHR.[90] Thus, to guarantee the precedence of the CJEU's jurisdiction,

> only the express exclusion of the ECtHR's jurisdiction under Art. 33 of the ECHR over disputes between Member States or between Member States and the EU in relation to the application of the ECHR within the scope ratione materiae of EU law would be compatible with Art. 344 TFEU.[91]

Otherwise, the accession would entail the possibility of an external control of the Union by the ECHR with regard to the Convention guarantees.[92] Further, in the Court's view, the agreement does not sufficiently account for the EU law principle of mutual trust which is predicated on the assumption that the fundamental rights are respected throughout the EU and therefore an external control is not necessary.[93] Also the agreement does not address the problem that the preliminary referral procedure under Art. 267 TFEU does not allow for the concurring procedure before the ECHR pursuant to its Protocol 16.[94] Last but not least, under the agreement the ECtHR would be empowered to rule on matters pertaining to the Common Foreign and Security Policy (CFSP) disregarding the CJEU's limited jurisdiction therein.[95]

10 While all these arguments of the CJEU are formally plausible, it is striking that the Court seems to conceive the EU's accession to the ECHR as essentially a problem of institutional relationship (EU/ECHR) and conflicting competence (CJEU/ECtHR) with the underlying tone of the Opinion making unambigously clear that it does not accept a subordinate role vis-à-vis the ECtHR but rather wants to control it and subject the ECHR to the finality of integration so characteristic of its – the CJEU's – own case law.[96] As a consequence, the CJEU does not deal with the material issue at stake; that is, the rights dimension of the accession as expressed in the explicit Treaty obligation of Art. 6(2) TEU ('The Union *shall* accede to the ECHR')[97] and the ensuing challenge to interpret the draft accession agreement in a way that makes it possible to bring it into line with the EU constitutional legal order.[98] It is fair to say that such a more flexible approach, as indeed suggested by Advocate General *Kokott*,[99] would have been possible if the CJEU had not sacrificed the rights dimension of the accession idea on the altar of its excessive preoccupation with institutional precedence and primacy, accompanied by the overstatement of purely normative claims such as the ideology of mutual trust in particular.[100] Thus the CJEU missed the chance to place the Union at the centre of a broader pan-European human rights polity, that is, a value-based European community of nations with human rights at its core.[101]

B. The Protection of Fundamental Rights within the Framework of the Council of Europe

I. *The Council of Europe*

11 The Council of Europe is a regional confederation of States. With its 47 Member States (current as of 27 January 2018), which include Russia and Turkey,[102] it extends far beyond the EU itself. The Council acts through its institutions, the *Committee of Ministers* and the *Parliamentary Assembly*.[103] If the Council of Europe recommends that its Member States conclude an agreement, this happens based on a *decision* of the Committee of Ministers.[104] The Council of Europe has a large number of agreements that focus on inter-state co-operation in criminal matters. The agreements on extradition and on (general) mutual legal assistance[105] should be mentioned here, as should the many agreements in the field of substantive criminal law.[106] The Council's most important convention is, however, the European Convention on Human Rights (ECHR) of 4 November 1950.

II. *The ECHR and Criminal Law*

1. Preliminary Remarks: ECHR and the ECtHR, Particularly the Binding Effect of Decisions

12 The ECHR is an international law treaty whose States Parties de facto are the Member States of the Council of Europe; therefore, there are – as of January 2018 – 47 States Parties. The ECHR is supplemented by a number of *Additional Protocols*.[107] From a criminal law perspective, Protocol No 6 on the Abolition of the Death Penalty of 28 April 1983 (AP VI),[108] on the one hand, and Protocol No 13 on the Complete Abolition of the Death Penalty of 3 May 2002 (AP XIII), on the other, are of particular interest.[109]

13 The ECtHR monitors compliance with the ECHR. To that effect it may even 'undertake an investigation',[110] including fact-finding missions on the territory of the State Party concerned, although this possibility is reserved, given the limited resources of the Court, for especially serious rights violations.[111] Today, it operates in **four** different **formations.**[112] As a rule, **individual applications**[113] are first reviewed by a *single judge*, who in clear-cut cases is able to declare the matter inadmissible or strike it out of the list of cases.[114] By contrast, if the single judge considers the application admissible, he or she forwards it to a committee or chamber.[115] The *committees*, which consist of three judges, decide unanimously on the admissibility of the individual application and are also able to render a judgment on its merits if the underlying question in the case is already the subject of well-established case law of the Court.[116] The *chambers*, which are made up of seven judges, examine the individual applications that have not been settled by the single judges or committees, as well as the – rare – **inter-state applications**[117] in regard to their admissibility and merit.[118] The *Grand Chamber* of seventeen judges decides, on the one hand, on individual or inter-state applications of particular importance that have been referred by a chamber;[119] on the other hand, it represents a kind of appellate court against judgments of a

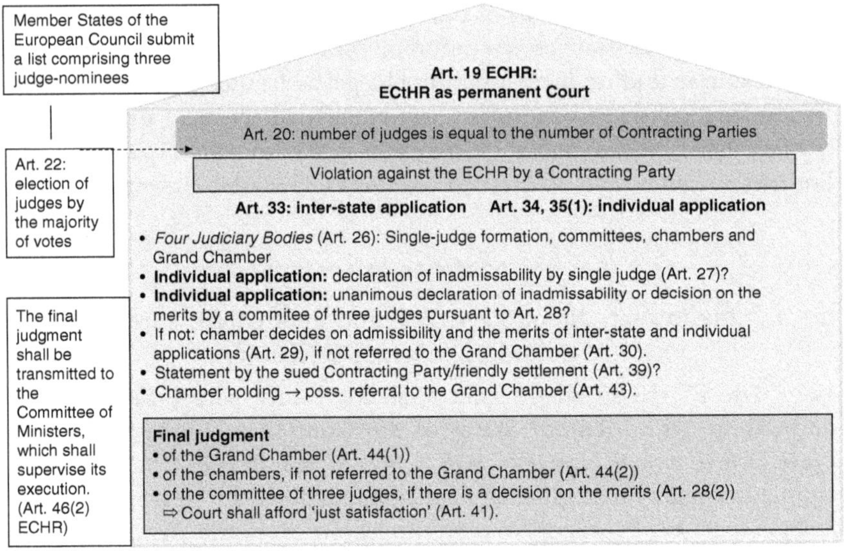

Figure 3 Overview of the European Court of Human Rights

chamber if the parties to the case request that the matter be referred.[120] The *Committee of Ministers* is responsible for the **supervision** of the execution of the Court's judgments.[121]

14 If the (Grand) Chamber's **final judgment** rules that a **violation** of the Convention[122] has taken place,[123] the chamber awards the injured party fair *compensation* in line with Art. 41 ECHR if the internal law of the State Party concerned allows only partial reparation to be made.[124] However, the Court does *not* have the authority to *quash* domestic judgments.[125] From the wording of Art. 46 ECHR ('to which it is a party') it also follows that judgments **only** take effect ***inter partes***,[126] but this does not argue against the general binding force of the interpretation of the Convention by a particular judgment.[127] Indeed, the ECHR – as a supranational Constitution of fundamental rights[128] – holds significance for the whole of Europe; its importance transcends European borders[129] and it represents an autonomous, objective legal system, the substantive content of which arises from the overall analysis of the ECtHR's case law, independent of the parties to the case.[130] Against this background, it serves as an orientation and possesses an appeal function for all States Parties of the ECHR and in this sense has an ***erga omnes, intra partes* effect**.[131] From a criminal law perspective, it is fair to say that the ECHR constitutes *the* central human rights instrument of a pan-European criminal procedure law,[132] and, as recognised in the EU Green Paper on Procedural Safeguards,[133] represents *the* minimum rule-of-law standard for European criminal procedure.

15 At the national level the importance of the Convention, as interpreted by the case law of the ECtHR, is recognised in certain procedural rules. Thus, in several jurisdictions a Convention violation as acknowledged by the Court represents a *ground of revision*.[134] Of course, the option of invoking an ECtHR judgment to reopen domestic proceedings should be available not only to the person who has obtained the judgment, but also to all citizens affected by the law that violates the Convention.[135] For it neither makes sense nor is procedurally economic that every further person affected has to go all the way to Strasbourg, even though – at least in the case of laws that have been declared in violation of the Convention – no different decision is to be expected. Nor does it make any sense that another State Party wait to be convicted in a similar case before correcting the legal situation that violates the Convention.[136] Taking the common human rights space created by the ECHR seriously, one may even go a step further and advocate a broader view giving any ECtHR judgment the said effect with regard to the question decided and the respective provisions in the legal systems of the States Parties.[137]

2. ECHR Rights of Relevance to Criminal Law

16 The ECHR's fundamental rights can be divided[138] into rights of **liberty**,[139] rights of **equality**,[140] **political** rights,[141] and **judicial** rights.[142] From the perspective of criminal law, a division into rights that are relevant to **substantive criminal law** and rights relevant to **criminal procedure** suggests itself, with the procedural rights meriting more attention due to their greater practical importance. They have a particularly marked effect on domestic law, as the constitutional guarantees are usually less differentiated and less criminal-procedure-specific. The most important *procedural right* is the principle of *fair trial* (Art. 6 ECHR), which in turn gives rise to many further, more specific rights. Furthermore, the right to liberty and security (Art. 5 ECHR) merits closer attention in regard to arrests and pre-trial detention, and the protection of private and family life (Art. 8 ECHR) and freedom of expression (Art. 10 ECHR) deserve a closer glance with respect to the coercive measures used in criminal procedure. The prohibition of double jeopardy included in Art. 4 AP VII will be discussed in conjunction with the corresponding guarantees of the Schengen Convention and the

Art. 6: **fair trial, equality of arms + *individual procedural rights*: para. 3**	**Other procedural rights**	**Rights pertaining to substantive criminal law**
(a) Right to be informed (b) Preparation of defence (c) Effective defence (d) Right to examine (e) Interpreter	**Art. 5**: Right to liberty and security **Art. 8**: Right to respect for private and family life **Art. 10**: Freedom of expression	**Art. 2**: Right to life **Art. 3**: Prohibition of torture **Art. 7**: No punishment without law

Figure 4 ECHR rights relevant to criminal law

CFREU.[143] As far as the guarantees relevant to *substantive criminal law* are concerned, the right to life (Art. 2 ECHR), the prohibition of torture (Art. 3 ECHR) and the principle of legality (Art. 7 ECHR) merit particular attention.[144] As we will see below, most of these Convention rights contain explicitly prescribed restrictions, but these 'shall not be applied for any purpose other than those for which they have been prescribed'.[145]

a) Art. 6: Fair trial, equality of arms and individual procedural rights

Case 1a

17 A confidential informant of the German police, an Italian citizen, approached his countryman B regarding an insurance issue. The informant then shifted the conversation to the topic of drugs and asked B whether he could get hold of a kilogram of cocaine. B refused, stating he was not involved in the drug business. The informant approached B three further times, promising him a profit of 5,000 DM (German marks). Finally, B agreed; he had an acquaintance whom he knew to take drugs and put the confidential informant in contact with this acquaintance's dealer, who subsequently procured the kilogram of cocaine.[146] → mn. 98.

Case 1b

18 Textile worker T, who had no criminal record, was approached by undercover investigators of the Portuguese police. They had been referred to him by a small-time criminal and asked whether he could supply them with 20 grams of heroin. T agreed and procured the drugs through a third party. He was arrested at the handover of the drugs to the sham buyers.[147] → mn. 98.

Does Art. 6(1) represent an obstacle to the punishment of B and T, as they were incited to carry out the crime by confidential informants?

Case 2

19 B was given a suspended prison sentence in 1991. Five years later, the District Court (*Landgericht*) in question revoked the suspension on the grounds that B had committed crimes during the period of probation. B immediately appealed against this decision; however, the Higher Regional Court (*Oberlandesgericht*) rejected his appeal. In doing so, it also focused on a pending trial against B, in which the – for the new charge – competent municipal court (*Amtsgericht*) had not yet reached a verdict on B's guilt. The Higher Regional Court had previously examined witnesses, and had assured *itself* of B's guilt. It did not wait for the verdict of the local court. The Federal Constitutional Court (*Bundesverfassungsgericht*) did not accept B's constitutional complaint. Does the revocation of probation because of a new crime on which judgment has not yet been passed violate Art. 6(2) ECHR?[148] → mn. 99.

Case 3

20 V.M. and four other defendants were given long prison sentences for robbing a post office, a crime they had carried out with exceptional criminal energy. During the investigation, police officers had testified anonymously, as it was feared that the defendants would instigate reprisals against the officers and their families. The anonymous witnesses had been examined by an investigative judge in a separate room in the presence of a court recorder; there was only an acoustic link to the defendants, defence lawyers and members of the prosecution. Can the information provided by the police offers, who are testifying anonymously, be used in the trial?[149] → mn. 100.

Case 4

21 Among other things, the complainant was sentenced as an accessory to attempted murder in connection with the hijacking of the Lufthansa aeroplane *Landshut* in 1977. The Higher Regional Court relied mainly on the statement of a witness imprisoned in Lebanon who could not be examined at trial, as well as on information provided by anonymous informants. Does this constitute a violation of the Convention?[150] → mn. 101.

Case 5 a

22 A French citizen reported a conspiracy (to commit murder) to a police officer and suggested calling the person in question and engaging him in conversation. He then placed a telephone call to the person in question from the inspector's office, without the approval of the investigative judge. During the conversation the person called incriminated himself, and was prosecuted and sentenced on the basis of this phone call.[151] → mn. 102.

Case 5b

23 At the suggestion of the police, a Dutch woman called the criminal attorney of her imprisoned husband to try and get him to talk about sexual advances that she had reported to the police. Once again, the sentence was passed on the basis of the information gained through this 'listening trap'.

In both of these cases, the question arises whether it is compatible with Art. 8 if private individuals co-operate with the police in leading suspects to make (incriminating) statements.[152] → mn. 102.

Case 6

24 In Spain, a newspaper and a television broadcaster were shut down on judicial order. Pro-Basque statements in the news published had led to the suspicion that the press institutions were co-operating with the terrorist organisation ETA. In both cases, the order to close down for a fixed term of five years was given during the pre-trial investigation procedure. Was this course of action necessary within the meaning of Art. 10(2) ECHR? → mn. 103.

i) *Fair Trial and Equality of Arms*

25 The principle of the right to a fair trial[153] enshrined in the first sentence of Art. 6(1) ECHR – 'fair and public hearing'[154] – represents both the core and the main umbrella term covering procedural rights.[155] It subsumes a large number of other rights, the totality of which aims to safeguard a criminal procedure which is overall fair and in line with the rule of law.[156] Of all Convention rights, Art. 6 ECHR has surely the greatest practical relevance. In 2016, the ECtHR issued 829 judgments with at least one violation, identifying 322 cases in which Art. 6 ECHR was violated. Some 106 decisions were based on the (excessive) duration and 176 on the general fairness of proceedings.[157] Whereas there is a decrease in the number of Art. 6 violations compared to 2014 (313 convictions) and 2015 (280 convictions), what does not change, with some exceptions from year to year, is which States are responsible for the majority of those violations. More than half of the convictions for Art. 6 violations in 2016 concerned only five States, with Russia leading in the respective statistics (69 convictions), followed by Ukraine (31), Romania (25), Greece and Hungary (each with 19).[158] The same goes for 2014 and 2015, where Turkey and Russia (each with 71), Hungary and Greece (each with 54), Romania (50), Ukraine (27) and Italy (24) dominate the statistics of the Court regarding convictions for Art. 6 violations.[159]

26 One of the main components of fair trial is the principle of the **equality of arms.**[160] By equality of arms, we do not so much refer to the formal procedural equality of prosecution and defence,[161] but rather to a kind of material equality in the sense that the one party must be able to present the case under conditions that do not place it at a disadvantage to the other party.[162] The Court further infers from the fairness principle the right to an **adversarial procedure** without limiting this right *a limine* to the trial proceedings.[163] In substance, this means that prosecution and defence are familiar with their respective positions and evidence and must be able to respond to them.[164] The bench needs to start the trial free of any influence, with no 'preconceived idea',[165] and the examination of the witnesses has to be contradictory.[166] Such an adversarial reading of Art. 6(1) ECHR is difficult to reconcile with an investigative judge (*juge d'instruction*), at least if this judge acts impartially in a truth-seeking manner.[167] While the Court expressly leaves the **question of the system** open,[168] its demands are closer to the adversarial ('contradictory') procedural system than to the judge-led (reformed) inquisitorial system,[169] although the adversarial/inquisitorial concepts suggest a greater divide than actually exists in procedural practice.[170]

27 As far as the **temporal application** of Art. 6 ECHR is concerned, the terms 'criminal charge' and 'everyone charged with a criminal offence' in paras. (1) and (3) should not lead to the conclusion that this rule only applies once a charge has been brought; that is, after the investigation phase has come to an end.[171] In fact, equality of arms needs to be guaranteed from the earliest possible point in time in order to allow the suspect to actively participate in the results of the investigation[172] that will determine the outcome of his or her trial.[173] The right to a fair trial thus applies from the moment the defendant is notified of the criminal charge against him or her during the investigation, up to the final conclusion of the trial (including a possible appeal procedure).[174] The enforcement of final decisions is, in principle, not covered by Art. 6(1) ECHR, although it can come within the article's scope if the enforcement was the subject of an agreement in the trial.[175]

28 The **material scope** of Art. 6(1) ECHR covers civil and criminal proceedings; for the latter, paras. (2) and (3) also apply. The term '*criminal* charge' is interpreted autonomously and broadly by the ECtHR, so that it does not depend on its understanding in the domestic jurisdictions of the States Parties.[176] In the *Engel* case,[177] the question thus arose of whether Art. 6 also applies in a trial that – according to the legal understanding of the State in question – is **disciplinary in nature**. When classifying the matter at hand, the Court takes national law as its starting point, but then focuses on the 'nature of the offence' and the 'degree of severity of the penalty that the person concerned risks incurring', setting aside the national understanding of the term.[178] In this vein, the ECtHR classifies German administrative offences as '*criminal*' within the meaning of Art. 6 ECHR.[179]

As far as the applicability of Art. 6(1) to **civil proceedings** is concerned, the Court accepts that such proceedings fall in principle within the scope of Art. 6,[180] recognising an, albeit limited, victims' right to a fair trial.[181] The complicated case law and the uncertainty surrounding the issue were simplified in *Perez*,[182] where the Court developed some criteria on the applicability of Art. 6 in civil-party proceedings.[183] Accordingly, Art. 6 applies to proceedings (i) when there is a claim for financial reparation, or – even in the absence of a claim for financial reparation – (ii) if the outcome of the proceedings is decisive for the 'civil right' in question,[184] or – even if the criminal proceedings are determinative only of a criminal charge and not a civil right – (iii) if the civil component remains closely connected with the criminal component (the criminal proceedings affect the civil component).[185] Pending or potential proceedings in the civil courts do not preclude the application of Art. 6, which also covers the relevant proceedings (proceedings involving civil-party complaints) even during the preliminary investigation stage.[186] However, civil proceedings for purely punitive purposes are excluded from the protective scope of the provision,[187] since 'the Convention does not confer any right ... to "private revenge" or to an *actio popularis*.'[188]

ii) *Examples: Excessive length of proceedings and crime provocation*

29 Among the concrete groups of cases that are discussed within the context of Art. 6(1) and thus concern the principle of fairness, procedures on grounds of excessive length of proceedings and on grounds of crime provocation merit special mention.[189] The former make up a large quantity of ECtHR cases, amounting to 210 in 2015–16[190] and to 5,541 for the 1959–2016 period.[191] Most of the cases for 2015–16 concern Hungary (37) and Greece (36), followed by Russia (21), Ukraine (18), Portugal (17), Romania (15) and Turkey (12).[192] In contrast, cases for crime provocation are relatively rare,[193] but they deserve special interest given the criminal energy of the State agents involved and the controversy about the adequate remedy to compensate the wrong produced in such cases.

30 The ECtHR identifies the appropriateness of the **length of proceedings** in a *procedural or factual analysis*, the main aim of which is to investigate which delays are to be attributed to domestic authorities;[194]

this does not include, for example, delays that are due to the defence's delaying tactics[195] or delays caused by the authorities of another State.[196] As a consequence, the right to expedient proceedings must not be invoked against the accused in order to restrict his defence rights,[197] especially regarding the presentation and examination of evidence.[198] The Court does not set an abstract temporal threshold or limit, but checks the reasonableness of the length of the proceedings on a case-by-case basis by reference to different criteria like the complexity of the case, the conduct of the applicant or the authorities and the importance of what is at stake for the applicant.[199] Thus expediency or delay are relational, context-based concepts.[200] The Court's method of procedure differs from that of national courts that, like the German Federal Court of Justice[201] or the UK Supreme Court (previously the House of Lords),[202] make an overall evaluation taking into account, inter alia, the stress caused by the delay and the defendant's guilt.

31 It is mainly the *consequences* of overly long proceedings that are controversial: must this excessive length necessarily lead to a termination or stay of proceedings given the seriousness of the fairness violation – the so-called *procedural solution*[203] – or can the violation be compensated by a mere mitigation of the punishment – the so-called *fixing-of-penalty solution*?[204] For one thing, the correct solution certainly depends on the concrete undue delay: the longer it is, the stronger or more radical the procedural consequence must be. Indeed, where the delay has made a fair trial for the accused impossible a permanent stay may result from the abuse of process doctrine.[205] On the other hand, if there is only a little delay, it may be sufficient as a compensation to name the delay in the grounds of the judgment or sentence.[206] In case of serious delays amounting to a violation of the respective human right and thus to a serious fair-trial violation, both the procedural and the fixing-of-penalty solution come into play. Yet the more radical former approach leading to a termination of proceedings will often appear unreasonable given that it entails impunity, which may be inacceptable in light of the seriousness of the offence and the defendant's guilt.[207] Yet mitigation solutions also have the problem that it is difficult to explain why an undue procedural delay should influence the length of the punishment. After all, punishment is determined according to the wrong caused by the defendant and his guilt and therefore procedural issues, unrelated to these considerations, should not matter.[208] The so-called *execution solution* attempts to account for this by leaving the length of the punishment as pronounced in the judicial verdict – in line with the defendant's guilt – intact, but considering – as a kind of fiction – a part of the sentence to have been executed to compensate for the excessive length of proceedings.[209] In more concrete terms, a court would issue a certain sentence it considers commensurate with the convict's guilt, e.g., four years, but would then state that it considers a part of this sentence to be executed, e.g. one-quarter, leaving it effectively at three years. Of course, this model only works if there is a sentence to be executed in the first place – which is, for example, not the case if the sentence is suspended[210] – and if there is no mandatory sentence which does not allow for any reduction of the sentence effectively to be executed.[211]

32 A violation of Art. 6(1) ECHR in the case of excessive length of proceedings can go hand in hand with a violation of the **right to an effective remedy** (Art. 13 ECHR) if no effective legal remedy is available preventively to speed up the ongoing proceedings, or to obtain a compensation after the fact.[212] In *Rumpf*, the ECtHR noted that there was no effective legal protection against excessively long proceedings and that legislative efforts in this regard had been insufficient and hesitant.[213] Accordingly, the Court tasked Germany with adapting its system of legal protection to the requirements of Art. 13 ECHR within one year.[214] At the time of the judgment, a corresponding draft law had been presented by the federal government.[215] This was explicitly welcomed by the ECtHR[216] and entered into force in November 2011.[217] In a combination of preventive and compensatory elements, the new provision envisages that a party to the proceedings may make a **complaint on grounds of delay** if there is reason for concern that proceedings may not be completed in an appropriate time period. If there is an undue delay, notwithstanding, then the defendant has the right to material and/or immaterial compensation.[218] In line with the broad reading of Art. 6(1) ECHR this is a general remedy going beyond criminal proceedings.[219] In criminal proceedings, the provision adopts the execution (mitigation) solution discussed above;[220] if this is insufficient – for example when the defendant is acquitted – then financial compensation may also be considered. Other EU jurisdictions have similar rules regarding a remedy,[221] or at least compensatory rules in case of undue delay in proceedings.[222]

33 The issue of **crime provocation** often arises in the context of the fight against drug-related crime: as seen in our cases 1a and 1b, persons with links to the drug scene are often encouraged by undercover investigators or police informants to engage in drug transactions, with the initiative coming *solely* from the investigators or informants, meaning that the drug-related crimes are ultimately initiated by the police.[223] The ECtHR has, in such a situation, in the seminal *Teixeira de Castro* case, held that the trial against the person so incited is unfair 'right from the outset'.[224] All depends on the circumstances of the concrete case, of course.[225] However, if the person incited has not been involved – in line with the Court's 'substantive test of incitement'[226] – in the illicit drug trade himself and has never committed a criminal act before,[227] the unfairness of the whole (police) operation is obvious and flagrant, leaving an independent and impartial court no other choice than to stop proceedings. Any lesser consequence, e.g. a mitigation of the punishment, as in the case of an undue delay discussed above,[228] cannot reasonably explain why the evidence gained in proceedings that are unfair *ab initio* should be admitted at all, and how the compensation prescribed by the ECHR can be achieved if not through the exclusion of this evidence.[229] Only in this way can the ECtHR's clear position be accounted for,

> that, although the admissibility of evidence is primarily a matter for regulation by national law, the requirements of a fair criminal trial under Art. 6 entail that the public interest in the fight against crime cannot justify the use of evidence obtained as a result of police incitement.[230]

iii) *The systematics of Art. 6 ECHR*

34 The defendants' rights enshrined in Art. 6(3) ECHR are part of the general principle of fairness included in Art. 6(1),[231] but cannot always be clearly distinguished from it. There is also some overlap between the various rights.[232] They can be subsumed under the umbrella term of the right to an **effective and appropriate defence**, which is listed separately under para. (c);[233] here, two levels can be distinguished: first, the basic conditions of an effective defence are safeguarded by the requirement to *inform the defendant* of the charges brought against him or her according to Art. 6(3)(a) and give him or her *adequate time* to prepare the defence according to Art. 6(3)(b). Then the focus shifts to the actual practice of defence *stricto sensu*, which includes the *right to examine witnesses* in Art. 6(3)(d) and the *use of an interpreter* according to Art. 6(3)(e). It should also be noted in this context that the catalogue of procedural rights developed in case law to date is not exhaustive; rather, Art. 6 'repeatedly brings to light new facets of what constitutes a fair trial'.[234] If the Court has not yet issued a statement on an individual question, then it is to be addressed in light of case law to date; in doing so, the principle of the **equality of arms** is a particularly significant maxim of interpretation.

35 Art. 6(2) ECHR stipulates the **presumption of innocence**:[235] 'Everyone charged with a criminal offence shall be presumed innocent until proved guilty according to law.' For an accused to be 'proved guilty', a conviction at first instance is not sufficient, but it must be final (*res judicata*); that is, upheld on appeal.[236] The presumption of innocence – to be distinguished from presumptions of fact and law which operate in every legal system[237] – only applies in criminal matters[238] and requires the judge to carry out the trial without any preconceived opinion on the defendant's guilt.[239] From Art. 6(2) it also follows that the burden of proof rests with the prosecution[240] and any doubts work in the defendant's favour.[241] Furthermore, the presumption of innocence binds State authority beyond the area of judicature;[242] accordingly, Art. 6(2) calls upon a State party to prevent any *prejudgment* in the media that pre-empts the judicial determination of guilt.[243] The binding force of the presumption of innocence does not even end with the defendant's death, but continues to be effective, so that, for example, a court is not permitted to make any statements on a defendant's guilt after his suicide without this guilt having been ascertained in a formal trial.[244]

36 Further, according to the so-called *Cleve rules*,[245] the presumption of innocence prohibits statements indicating the guilt of the accused in a judgment of acquittal. From the previous *Karaman* judgment it follows that the same applies with regard to statements referring to a separately prosecuted suspect which are contained in a separate (earlier) judgment against his co-suspects.[246] As to the protective scope of the presumption of innocence in such cases, the *Cleve* court distinguishes between 'some reasoning suggesting' that the accused is guilty – which is inadmissible – and the mere description of a 'state of suspicion' – which is admissible.[247] The final assessment depends on the 'true sense of the impugned statements', which in turn depends on the 'nature and context of the particular proceedings' in which they were made.[248] The delimitation between reasoning suggesting real guilt and the expression of mere suspicions is, of course, tricky,[249] and the Court's approach has everything of a decisionist case-by-case solution. In fact, the underlying distinction between a 'formal finding of guilt' and a sort of factual guilt[250] by ascriptive statements calls for a conceptual clarification of the latter; that is, a clarification of what factual guilt exactly means.[251] At any rate, the importance of the judgment cannot be overestimated.

37 The other side of the presumption of innocence is the **right to remain silent and not incriminate oneself** (*nemo tenetur se ipsum accusare*),[252] for a person who must be presumed innocent should not have to contribute to proving otherwise. The Court includes this right among the core elements of a fair trial.[253] It is not restricted to cases in which force was used against the defendant, but constitutes a general protection of a suspected person's freedom to make statements. This freedom of decision is effectively undermined if the authorities elicit confessions or other incriminatory statements from the defendant through deceit although he has decided to remain silent during the examination.[254] The right to a fair trial and the presumption of innocence are also intrinsically linked to the **principle of culpability or guilt**, for although this principle is procedural and substantive in nature, the (procedural) presumption of innocence presupposes that (substantive) culpability must and can be proved.[255] Other areas for which the guarantee of Art. 6(2) ECHR can also be of relevance include *costs orders* without formally ascertaining the defendant's guilt and the partial *reversal of the burden of proof* in criminal proceedings onto the defendant (which the ECtHR does not categorically exclude, however).[256]

38 Germany was convicted of violating Art. 6(2) ECHR in a case where a suspended sentence was revoked as the convicted person had committed a crime (case 2, above, mn. 19). German prevailing opinion – based on constitutional court case law of the time[257] – assumed that it was compatible with the presumption of innocence if, according to Art. 56(1) no 1 StGB,[258] the probation was revoked due to an offence committed during the period of probation without this further offence having been tried.[259] The ECtHR[260] has taken the stance that a probation revocation – in regard to the presumption of innocence – presupposes that the new offence has already been tried or that the person convicted (in the original trial) confessed to the (new) crime in the presence of his defence counsel.[261] As a consequence of this case law German appeals courts now require the new offence to have been given a *final* sentence.[262] However, this goes too far, for the ECtHR regards all sentences – including first-instance sentences – as sufficient.[263] In light of ECtHR case law, any decision or order based on the probation revocation, such as the issuing of a warrant of arrest,[264] may also only be made after the new offence has been tried.[265] The same applies when a disciplinary measure is to be imposed upon a prisoner[266] for committing an unlawful and culpable criminal offence.[267] However, Art. 6(2) ECHR does not

constitute an obstacle to the non-suspension of the remaining sentence within the early release procedure,[268] as this rule only requires a favourable social prognosis, but not the commission of a criminal offence (determined by a court) during the period of probation.[269]

iv) *Individual Rights*

(1) Information of the Nature and Cause of the Accusation (Art. 6(3)(a) ECHR)

39 The right to prompt information of the 'nature and cause' of the accusation[270] serves as protection against 'being taken by surprise'.[271] If the principle of the equality of arms is taken seriously, then the defendant must be sufficiently, comprehensively and truthfully informed, *as early as possible*, of the charges and their legal classification[272] so that he or she does not trail behind the investigative authorities in terms of information.[273] Thus the obligation to inform arises as soon as investigations into a person are launched, i.e. a concrete suspect exists,[274] although this suspicion may still have to mature further to turn into a precise charge or charges.[275] However, this information may be denied if there is reason to believe that the defendant will frustrate the investigation through means other than exercising procedural rights.[276] Unfortunately, no duty of admonition regarding the rights due to the defendant can be derived from Art. 6(3)(a). Hopefully, this gap in protection will be closed by the 'letter of rights' called for in the EU Green Paper on Procedural Safeguards to be discussed below.[277]

40 Comprehensive information presupposes that the incriminating evidence is **disclosed**; this also includes, for example, statements on the trustworthiness of a witness for the prosecution.[278] The duty of disclosure is a typical consequence of an adversarial procedure, which strives hard to balance out the prosecutor's superiority and investigative advantage.[279] It thus targets first and foremost the prosecutorial authorities. Of course, there are opposed interests, especially reasons of national security and witness protection.[280] However, any restriction of the duty of disclosure needs to be proportionate and must be balanced out in the course of proceedings if possible.[281]

41 The 'inquisitorial' counterpart to disclosure is the right to comprehensive **access to the case file** (*dossier*).[282] The Court indeed speaks of 'access to the case file'[283] and thus includes the *inspection* of records as one possible form of access. This right is not explicitly stated in the

ECHR, but can be deduced from the principle of equality of arms,[284] the right to a fair hearing[285] and Art. 6(3)(b).[286] It also follows from Art. 6(3)(a), for comprehensive information also includes knowledge of the file. Mere oral information on the content of a case file is usually insufficient.[287] Although so far the Court has not fixed the time of the access to the file, there can be little doubt that this right *already applies during the investigation phase.*[288] This follows not only from the principle of the equality of arms, but also more specifically from the fact that the effective exercise of the individual rights in Art. 6(3) ECHR requires the defendant to have been comprehensively informed, through access to files if applicable. However, like the duty of disclosure, the right to file access is *not absolute.* Individual pieces of evidence may be withheld to protect conflicting interests, for example for reasons of national security, witness protection or risk to the purpose of the investigation.[289] The person charged has the right that all evidence is kept available until the trial has reached its final conclusion; this also applies to telecommunication surveillance records.[290]

42 Tension can arise between the right to access files and the right to an effective defence when the defendant is allocated a defence counsel (possibly against her will) and the exercising of the right to access files is left to the counsel, who then neglects to inform the defendant of the file's content or does not even make use of the right to access the file. From a fairness perspective this situation calls for an approach whereby the right to access files may only be restricted to the defence counsel where the person charged already has one (whom she trusts!) or can be allocated one in line with Art. 6(3)(c) ECHR.[291]

(2) Adequate Time and Facilities for the Preparation of the Defence (Art. 6(3)(b) ECHR)[292]

43 Here the underlying concept of equality of arms entails that the defendant is to have as much time to prepare his or her defence as the prosecution to prepare the charge(s).[293] This also includes the time necessary to sufficiently examine the case file.[294] Accordingly, this right already applies during the pre-trial investigation phase.[295] 'Short trials' are to be avoided.[296] From this, it also follows that the prosecutorial authorities are not allowed to hinder the suspect in the preparation of his defence as long as he is acting within the law; documents produced by the suspect for the obvious purpose of defence may not be confiscated.[297]

(3) Effective Defence (Art. 6(3)(c) ECHR)

44 Strictly speaking, this rule guarantees *three rights*, namely the right to defend oneself, the right to legal assistance of the defendant's choice and the right to legal counsel assigned free of charge.[298] The right to effective defence can thus be exercised either by the defendant herself (alternative 1) or by the defence counsel (alternative 2). This distinction shows that the defence counsel does not replace the defendant but only assists him – assistance or representation does not mean replacement or substitution! Thus Art. 6(3)(c) does not provide – contrary to a widespread broad interpretation of the ECtHR's case law[299] – for a right to a trial *in absentia*, and the defendant can be ordered to appear in person.[300]

45 In principle, the *appointment of the defence counsel* has to take place during the *investigation*, as due to the investigation's prejudicial significance[301] the lack of a defence counsel can lead to an irreparable imbalance between the prosecuting authority and the suspect.[302] In concrete terms the question thus arises whether an investigative act interferes with the suspect's defence position to such an extent that the lack of a defence counsel would lead to an irreparable disadvantage. This has indeed been assumed by the ECtHR in a case where a suspect lacked legal assistance in the first interrogation by the police or the investigative judge.[303] This case law informed the EU directive on the right of access to a lawyer which will be analysed below.[304]

46 The right to an effective defence requires the *participation* of the defendant and/or the defence counsel in any hearing and interrogation, if applicable. This makes clear that this right is based on the right to a *fair hearing*.[305] The defendant and the defence counsel have the right to *confidential* and *unrestricted contact* with one another, and this right already applies during the pre-trial proceedings.[306] The confidentiality of contact is a fundamental prerequisite of the *practical effect* of Art. 6(3)(c) ECHR in regard to the effective preparation of the defence.[307] While the extent of contact is not defined exactly in the ECHR and the measures for its realisation are also a matter of domestic discretion, it always has to be measured against the practical effect of the right to defence.[308]

47 The right to defence continues to hold even if the defendant chooses not to be present or flees.[309] If the defendant is absent from the trial without leave although duly summoned, the court must allow the defence counsel to defend the defendant in his absence.[310] This issue has been the object of a row between the ECtHR and several German appeals courts. The ECtHR has declared §329(1) of the German CCP (StPO) – which allowed to dismiss an appeal due to the defendant's absence, even though the defence counsel is present – to be incompatible with Art. 6(3)(c) ECHR.[311] However, German appeals courts have rejected the ECtHR's interpretation and continued with their earlier practice.[312] The Higher Regional Court of Celle expressed this rejection particularly clearly and openly, holding that the verdict of the ECtHR 'fundamentally disregards the legal situation in Germany' and that the 'defendant's interest in letting himself be represented by a defence counsel in the main appeal proceedings ... is not legally protected by Art. 6(3)(c) ECHR'.[313] Finally, the legislator amended the controversial provision to bring it into line with the ECtHR case law.[314]

48 The Court also derived a state *duty of care* from Art. 6(3)(c) ECHR, which requires intervention in the case of an (obvious) lack of defence where necessary.[315] In this regard, the defendant's *proper responsibility* is to be taken into account, for example with respect to the chosen defence counsel's appearance in the main trial.[316] Serious violations of the Convention exist only if a domestic court does nothing despite obvious violations of the duties of the defence.[317] On the other hand, the defence strategy and the exercising of the rights of the defence are the sole responsibility of the defence counsel.[318] The right to an effective defence is also violated if the time between the appointment of the defence counsel and the beginning of the main proceedings is too short for an adequate preparation of the defence (the appropriate length of time depending on the scope and difficulty of the case in question). If the defence counsel applies for the trial to be suspended for additional preparation, the Court must grant this application.[319]

49 The defendant has the right to a defence counsel free of charge if he or she is without means and pro bono defence is in 'the interests of justice'.[320] The second condition depends on the severity of the crime, the complexity of the case and the personal circumstances of the defendant.[321] This condition only refers to the free provision of an assigned defence counsel, not to the right to legal assistance in general, for of course a wealthier defendant can use a defence counsel he trusts.[322]

(4) The right to examine witnesses (Art. 6(3)(d))

50 This rule refers to witnesses both for the prosecution and for the defence, and thus adopts an Anglo-Saxon understanding of procedure and witnesses.[323] Nevertheless, the concept of the witness is to be interpreted autonomously; it includes any statement that can form the foundation of a conviction – regardless of whether this statement was made by a witness or by a co-defendant in court or before another authority.[324] In this matter, 'full **equality of arms**' is guaranteed,[325] so that the defendant must at *some* time have an appropriate and suitable **opportunity to examine** witnesses of the prosecution[326] and summon witnesses for the defence.[327] Even though this confrontation can take place 'at any time', the rule already applies during the investigation.[328] Although the wording ('the right to . . . have examined') seems to imply that the defence counsel can replace the defendant, as with the right to access files[329] the defendant's greater knowledge of the matter at hand cautions against this.[330] More than the mere right to ask questions is concerned here; we are dealing with the **right to 'question'**,[331] to **confrontation** with the opportunity for active and comprehensive examination.[332] Even though it might not seem possible to derive this from the wording of Art. 6(3)(d) ECHR itself,[333] it does follow from the right to 'full equality of arms'. For it is only possible to speak of full equality of arms if the defendant is able to rigorously examine the witnesses for the prosecution.[334] This shows clearly that the concern here is with *testing the witness's reliability* in the sense of 'tested evidence'.[335] For this reason, domestic courts have to make an effort to ensure the witnesses appear in the main trial. There should be no premature recourse to surrogate evidence; that is, to written records of earlier examinations or even the statements of a person who examined the witness.[336]

51 The accused needs to know the entire **content of the witness statement** in order to be able to examine the witness on all the incriminating aspects of his statement.[337] If, following the (first) examination, the defendant is incriminated further by the same witness but using *new information*, then – in line with the equality of arms – there must be the option of a new confrontation.[338] Conversely, the equality of arms prohibits one party carrying out an *additional* cross-examination of a witness.[339] The confrontation can take place without the defence counsel if the accused is able to exercise his rights adequately himself.[340]

52 In principle, the right to examine witnesses extends to *all witnesses*, including independent witnesses, as the equality of arms requires access to all of the evidence.[341] In the case of **expert witnesses**, Art. 6(3)(d) ECHR gives the defendant the right to submit an opinion if the expert's opinion constitutes significant evidence against him,[342] although being a member of an authority that is party to the proceedings does not automatically make the expert a witness of the prosecution.[343]

53 The right to confrontation and to examine witnesses is subject to **restrictions.**[344] Where there are justified interests in witness and victim protection, an overall view of the fairness of proceedings[345] needs to weigh these against the interests of the defence.[346] Recognised exceptions to the right to examine witnesses are inaccessible and anonymous witnesses, but strict conditions regarding inaccessibility and preserving anonymity need to be met and,[347] at any rate, the relevant witness evidence has to be assessed with great caution and care.[348] While the ECtHR does not see using the statements of anonymous witnesses as inadmissible *a limine*, it does require that the defendant – as the essence of Art. 6(3)(d) ECHR, so to speak[349] – is afforded **some form of confrontation** – which was missing in the *Van Mechelen* case (case 3) due to police officers' lack of objectivity.[350] With this in mind, the lack of the opportunity to examine a prosecution witness because of his right to remain silent needs to be taken into account when evaluating the evidence.[351] In the *Haas* case (case 4), the ECtHR decided that the rights of the defence had been sufficiently observed, as the information provided by anonymous informants of the German security services **was not key evidence** and the Frankfurt am Main Higher Regional Court had evaluated this information with great care and within the context of other evidence.[352] The Court emphasised this line even more strongly in *Sapunarescu*:[353] while the Frankfurt am Main District Court had 'at no point in time' given the defendant, the applicant or his defence counsel 'an opportunity to cross-examine the anonymous main witness for the prosecution in person' during this drug trial,[354] the conviction 'cannot be considered to have been based to a decisive extent on the depositions' of the inaccessible anonymous witness.[355] However, these principles were qualified by the ECtHR Grand Chamber in *Al-Khawaja/Tahery*, giving more room to an effective prosecution: a conviction may also be based decisively on the statement of a witness who has not been interrogated during the main proceedings if the restriction of the right to confrontation is compensated for by procedural safeguards and is taken into consideration in the evaluation of evidence.[356] Although the Court

has as yet not issued any statement on **audiovisual examinations** via a *live video link*, one can assume this is compatible with Art. 6(3)(d) ECHR – given sufficient justification for eschewing the direct examination of witnesses is provided – since the option of directly questioning the witness is retained, even though the examination is transmitted by audiovisual means.[357]

54 A **cross-examination by the judge** in the presence of the defence counsel is also sufficient if he is able to question the witness thoroughly.[358] Yet the formulation of *written questions* that are subsequently posed by the interrogator is insufficient,[359] as is the *transmission via a sound link* of the cross-examination (by the judge) to another room, from which the defendant and his defence counsel can ask questions.[360] By contrast, it is compatible with Art. 6(3)(d) ECHR if the accused and the defence follow the examination of child witnesses in cases of abuse using a one-way mirror and are able to ask questions of the judge at any time.[361]

(5) Assistance of an Interpreter (Art. 6(3)(e) ECHR)

55 This rule supplements the right to an effective defence, adding the right to the free assistance of an interpreter during the *entire trial* in regard to *all documents and statements* that have an influence on the charge.[362] A comprehensive **'right to communication'** is thus guaranteed, which is not – as might be assumed based on the wording ('language used in court') – restricted to the court proceedings, but includes the pre-trial proceedings and even preparatory conversations between defendant and defence counsel.[363] The early application of this right follows from Art. 6(3)(e) and Art. 5(2) ECHR, according to which the suspect or arrested individual must be informed of the charge 'in a language which he understands'.[364]

56 In the opinion of the German Federal Constitutional Court,[365] Art. 6(3)(e) ECHR does not prohibit the defendant being made liable for the **cost of the interpreter** arising from the translation of telephone surveillance records from his native language. The purpose of Art. 6(3)(e) is only to ensure that defendants involved in criminal proceedings in a foreign language can follow these proceedings so that their rights are guaranteed. This is to be distinguished from the prosecutorial authorities' interest in the translation of telephone surveillance records. This is convincing in light of the protective purpose of Art. 6(3)(e) ECHR but it is not entirely clear why defendants should have to pay for the costs of interpretation and translation that have only arisen due to the interests of the prosecution.[366]

(6) Consequences of Violations of Art. 6 ECHR, the So-Called Overall Assessment or Fairness Test

57 A violation of the above-mentioned rights does not lead automatically to a conviction of violating the fairness principle. Rather, the ECtHR performs a quite unique – and in other human rights systems thus far unknown[367] – **two-levels test or analysis:**[368] at the first level, it determines whether an individual rights violation has been committed; at the second level, it then carries out an *overall assessment of the entire proceedings* in order to determine whether the violation in question was so serious that the proceedings as a whole have to be considered unfair within the meaning of Art. 6 ECHR, the so-called doctrine or test of overall assessment/examination (*appréciation globale, Gesamtbetrachtungslehre*).[369] Thus a prognosis must be made on whether a certain violation of the rights of the accused in the pre-trial proceedings is serious enough to render the **trial as a whole** (the entire trial) **unfair.**[370]

58 Such an overall unfairness may follow from a particularly serious individual violation, for instance if police agents – crime provocation as discussed above – 'persuade' a fully law-abiding citizen to commit a crime (turning the subsequent adjudication unlawful 'right from the outset'),[371] if a confession is obtained by torture,[372] or if the suspect is completely deprived of legal representation while in police custody.[373] If no such flagrant violation, affecting the principle of equality of arms[374] or the core of defence rights,[375] has taken place, the violation may be remedied at a different procedural phase, for example a violation at the investigation stage may be remedied at trial or appeal.

59 The Court is particularly 'flexible' in regard to the use of evidence obtained in a manner that violates the Convention, e.g. by sidestepping the right to confrontation (Art. 6(3)(d) ECHR) or,[376] going beyond fair-trial rights, the right to respect for private and family life (Art. 8 ECHR).[377] On the one hand, it grants national legislative authorities a broad *margin of appreciation*,[378] especially with regard to the law of evidence, and limits its judicial control to cases of blatant abuse.[379] On the other hand, such (unlawfully obtained) evidence can still, albeit with 'extreme care', be used;[380] an overall fair-trial violation in the sense of the above-mentioned test can only be considered if the conviction was 'based either *solely or to a decisive extent*' on this tainted evidence and proceedings were not conducted with thorough scrutiny and without 'sufficient *counterbalancing factors*'.[381] Thus the ensuing 'sole or decisive rule'[382] is not absolute[383] given that a thorough conduct of the proceedings and 'sufficient counterbalancing factors' may ultimately rule out an overall fair-trial violation. Concretely speaking, for example, a transcript of a declaration of a witness, who invokes his right to refuse testimony in open court, is admissible if that written declaration is corroborated by further evidence and does not constitute the only evidentiary basis of the judicial decision.[384]

60 The fairness considerations of Art. 6 ECHR are, as clarified by the ECtHR in *Stojkovic*,[385] also to be taken into account in the context of **mutual assistance procedures**, where the overall assessment doctrine may also play an important role.[386] In the case at hand, the suspect had been interrogated in Belgium following a French legal assistance request. Although both the French authorities and the suspect himself had asked for legal assistance, this interrogation took place without it, as it is in fact admissible under Belgian law. The French court later used the so-obtained statement in the trial without taking into account that the interrogation in Belgium was taken without legal assistance. The ECtHR considered this to be a violation of Art. 6(3)(c) ECHR.[387] It affirmed that the States Parties to the ECHR must, according to Art. 1 ECHR, secure to everyone within their jurisdiction the rights and freedoms of the Convention. From this it follows that the French courts would have had to check whether the right to a fair trial had been violated overall; that is, taking into account Belgium's acts of legal assistance, especially the suspect's interrogation without counsel.[388] The French courts failed to fulfil this obligation; in particular, no measures were taken to balance out the restriction of the right to assistance by counsel. Unfortunately, this isolated approach in the context of mutual assistance procedures is not uncommon in domestic jurisdictions.[389] It should be countered by a 'refined *lex fori* approach' according to which foreign evidence should, in principle, be admissible if the evidentiary rules of the *lex fori* are met unless its use would violate fundamental fair-trial rights.[390]

61 In sum, an overall fair-trial violation on the ground of unlawfully obtained or regularly inadmissible evidence may be prevented by taking recourse to other (incriminating) evidence, which corroborates this evidence or generally supports the prosecution case. Thus the overall-assessment doctrine may undermine the fair-trial performance of domestic courts given that individual rights violations have no immediate consequences and may, at any rate, be compensated by other procedural measures.[391] In fact, the doctrine turns thereby into a mere *balancing* *exercise* weighing fair-trial rights against prosecutorial or public order interests but without providing for precise contours.[392] On a more conceptual level, the Court's overall fairness evaluation constitutes a challenge to the very understanding of 'fairness' or 'fair trial' as concepts whose aim is to protect suspect rights. In fact, the Court dilutes this rights-based understanding by subsuming under its 'overall fairness' concept the rights of victims and the interest of the general public in expedient criminal proceedings.[393]

62 Notwithstanding these concerns, it should not be forgotten that the overall assessment test may also work in the defendant's favour. On the one hand, it takes into account all the developments during the entire proceedings, including further violations, which may then aggravate the overall fair-trial violation. On the other hand, it has a transnational, cross-border potential of fair-trial protection since it includes in the fair-trial analysis all investigatory activities, independent of their geographical location or temporal point of reference, as long as they concern the proceedings object of the human rights litigation.[394] From this perspective, the overall assessment doctrine promises to set fairness constraints even to the mutual recognition of evidence and coercive measures, to be analysed in more detail below.[395] Ultimately, it must be determined on a case-by-case-basis whether the individual fair-trial restrictions taken all together amount to an overall unfair trial.

b) Other Procedural Rights

i) *Art. 5 ECHR: The Right to Liberty and Security*

63 Leaving aside the term 'security', Art. 5 is concerned with **protection from illegitimate imprisonment**.[396] This acts as a counterpart to or the reverse of all cases of legitimate (valid) imprisonment according to para. 1(a)–(f) and covers all cases not mentioned there.[397] Art. 5 protects only the (physical) liberty to **move away** from a given location. It should not be seen as guaranteeing general freedom of action, nor does it contain any guarantees regarding the circumstances of a given deprivation of liberty, as this is covered by Arts. 3 and 8 ECHR.[398] Finally, mere restrictions to the freedom of movement must be distinguished from the *deprivation* of liberty; the overall context is decisive here, and may turn, for example, internment in a transit zone into a deprivation of liberty.[399]

64 According to Art. 5 **second sentence**, the deprivation of a person's liberty is admissible 'in the following cases and in accordance with a procedure prescribed by law'. From this, we can deduce several preconditions that have to be met for deprivation of liberty to conform to the Convention: first of all, there needs to be a (national) **legal basis**;[400] that is, a (sufficiently precise[401]) substantive or procedural law.[402] Further, the formulation 'in accordance with a procedure *prescribed by law*' leads to the conclusion that State actions must conform to the respective legal basis *in concreto*,[403] the national law being the standard against which decisions should be measured.[404] Yet the ECtHR also examines whether the national legal basis actually *conforms to the Convention* in terms of its content.[405] Any State intervention must comply with the purpose of Art. 5, namely **protection from arbitrariness** in the execution of arrests.[406] Finally, one of the **grounds** for detention listed in Art. 5(1)(a)–(f) ECHR – to be interpreted restrictively and constituting an exhaustive list[407] – needs to be present.[408]

(1) Grounds for Detention (Art. 5(1)(a)–(f) ECHR)

Art. 5(1)(a) ECHR

65 According to Art. 5(1)(a) ECHR deprivation of liberty is justifiable following **conviction by a competent court**. A broad concept of what constitutes a court applies here.[409] The decisive factors are that it is independent of the executive power and that the verdict is reached in a fair and transparent procedure.[410] Both criminal and disciplinary offences can form the basis of the conviction.[411] In any case, the deprivation of liberty must occur '*after*' the conviction. This does not only mean that the deprivation of liberty must follow the conviction in temporal terms; there must also be a '*sufficient causal connection*' between them.[412]

66 It is disputed whether the term *conviction* presupposes **guilt** (blameworthiness, *culpa*) and thus the ensuing social and ethical disapproval (censure) of the respective offence on which punishment is predicated.[413] The fact that the purpose of Art. 5 (only) lies in the protection from arbitrary deprivation of liberty[414] speaks in favour of including custodial measures that impose a deprivation of liberty based solely on the threat posed by the offender (his dangerousness) independent of his guilt.[415] However, it should be noted that Art. 5(1)(e) offers more appropriate grounds for detention in such cases. Furthermore, in cases concerning the imprisonment of offenders who are not criminally responsible, there is no causal relationship between the deprivation of liberty and the conviction.[416] Accordingly, the ECtHR only applied Art. 5(1)(e) in *Luberti*, where the defendant was acquitted on grounds of mental illness and an order was simultaneously issued that he be committed to a psychiatric hospital.[417]

67 At any rate, the ECtHR classified the so-called *Sicherungsverwahrung* – a **preventive detention** for the purpose of the incapacitation of particularly dangerous offenders, existing in Germany[418] and other civil law jurisdictions[419] (as opposed to the imposition of an aggravated or indeterminate sentence, more common in common law jurisdictions)[420] – as a conviction in line with Art. 5(1)(a) ECHR. The Court saw the sufficient causal connection as established since preventive detention is always ordered in connection with a criminal conviction; that is, a decision on the guilt of the person concerned.[421] By contrast, if the preventive detention is ordered *retrospectively* (subsequent custodial measure, e.g. an incapacitation order), then this does not include any decision on the affected person's guilt. Accordingly, it is not issued as a causal result of a conviction so that Art. 5(1) is not relevant.[422]

68 The judgment entailing the deprivation of liberty does not have to be final.[423] Nor does imprisonment become a deprivation of liberty that violates the Convention because a higher court later rescinds the decision of the lower court. The *correctness of national judgments* is not the object of the Court's examination.[424] It will thus only hear a prisoner's submission that a judgment is factually or legally defective if the decision is based on a flagrant denial of justice.[425]

Art. 5(1)(b) ECHR

69 The grounds for detention in Art. 5(1)(b) follow on from a **failure to comply** with a legitimate court order (first alternative) or a failure **to fulfil** a legal obligation (second alternative). The first alternative implies that the person concerned has not met the obligations laid upon him by court order, such as payment of a fine.[426] Examples of this include the various measures to compel witnesses to appear before court 'under threat of punishment', which ultimately may entail arrest or detention.[427] In distinction to para. (1)(a), the deprivation of liberty on the basis of para. (1)(b) only has the 'character of a *surrogate or substitute sanction*', the imposition of which is connected to the failure to comply with the preceding order;[428] 'court order' is thus not to be understood in the sense of 'conviction'.

70 On the other hand, '*legal obligation*' within the meaning of the second alternative of subpara. (b) should not be understood as already constituting a general duty to conduct oneself in a manner that complies with the law,[429] for this understanding would obviously render the grounds for detention highly uncertain.[430] Rather, it is necessary that a person is deprived of their liberty on a legal basis in order to enforce compliance with certain specific legal obligations imposed on her.[431] Deprivation of liberty for the purposes of enforcing the obligation to carry out military or alternative service represents one example of this.[432] However, a legal ruling envisaging deprivation of liberty on grounds of debts would run counter to Art. 1 AP IV and thus would not constitute viable grounds for detention.[433]

Art. 5(1)(c) ECHR

71 Art. 5(1)(c) permits **provisional arrest and pre-trial detention**, as well as **preventive detention**(!),[434] 'when it is reasonably considered necessary to prevent [a person] committing an offence'. Pre-trial detention can be mandated for the purposes of bringing a person before a judge if there are sufficient grounds for suspicion or there is a risk of the person fleeing;[435] that is, even when there is only reasonable suspicion that the person in question has committed a crime.[436] *Reasonable suspicion* exists when there are sufficient facts that, following an objective *ex ante* evaluation, lead to the conclusion that the person in question carried out the criminal offence pursuant to the applicable domestic law.[437] National law thus constitutes the legal test to be applied.[438] If national law sets out further conditions for pre-trial detention – thus going beyond Art. 5(1)(c) ECHR – such as a higher level of suspicion or the risk of suppression of evidence,[439] then these must be met, otherwise the deprivation of liberty would not occur 'in accordance with a procedure prescribed by law' within the meaning of Art. 5(1).[440] While reasonable suspicion may suffice for arresting a person, it cannot justify without further ado the *continuation* of pre-trial detention. After a certain period has elapsed, further grounds for detention need to have emerged so that the continued deprivation of liberty remains *proportional*.[441] This follows directly from Art. 5(3) ECHR, which we will examine more closely below.[442]

72 In regard to '**preventive detention**', it is obvious that the grounds for detention of Art. 5(1)(c) ECHR need to apply restrictively,[443] seeing as they regard the mere 'risk of carrying out a crime' as sufficient[444] and potentially permit – in accordance with the respective national law – the detention of completely innocent individuals. Within the context of the threat of terrorism, it should be stressed that the preventive detention of persons considered 'abstractly dangerous' by the respective authorities – there even exists special terminology[445] – is prohibited by Art. 5(1)(c).[446] There must be *concrete and reliable informations or indicia*[447] that justify the assumption that someone will carry out 'sufficiently concrete and specific', not just 'potential further', offences, 'as regards, in particular, the place and time of their commission and their victims'.[448] Moreover, the ECtHR has recently explicitly stated that Art. 5(1)(c) on no account can justify a preventive detention of indeterminate duration, as the deprivation of liberty in these cases does not serve 'the purpose of bringing [a person] before the competent legal authority'. Accordingly, a subsequent custodial measure, already mentioned above, cannot be based on Art. 5(1)(c) ECHR.[449]

Art. 5(1)(d) ECHR

73 Art. 5(1)(d) permits the **detention of a minor** by lawful order for the purpose of educational supervision, or his lawful detention for the purpose of bringing him before the competent legal authority (for matters of education).[450] Educational supervision refers to measures in line with *juvenile criminal law* on the one hand and *welfare law* on the other.[451] The systematics of Art. 5(1)(d) lead to the conclusion that the second alternative must be concerned with bringing those minors before the competent authority for whom 'educational supervision' is the right option.[452]

Art. 5(1)(e) ECHR

74 According to Art. 5(1)(e), persons can be detained to prevent the spreading of infectious diseases, as can persons of unsound mind, alcoholics, drug addicts or vagrants.[453] On the one hand, we are dealing here – where the first group is concerned – with the prevention of the spread of **infectious diseases**, so that quarantine regulations can be based on Art. 5(1)(e) ECHR.[454] However, according to ECtHR case law, it is mandatory that the illness be attested by medical certificate.[455] On the other hand, the detention of the second group of persons, especially those of **unsound mind**, while primarily serving to protect the public,[456] may also be necessary to prevent such a person causing harm against himself.[457] The following reference to 'alcoholics'

is more controversial. '**Alcoholics**' can be detained, independent of their being diagnosed as such, when they 'pose a threat to public order or themselves', but not merely for the fact that they consume alcohol.[458] The following references to '**drug addicts**' and '**vagrants**', equally or even more controversial, must also be interpreted restrictively.[459]

75 The most important ground is the one referring to '**unsound mind**'. While the definition of this concept is dynamic given the development of psychiatric research, a detention of such a person presupposes three minimum conditions: (i) a true mental disorder – equivalent to an 'unsound mind'[460] – must be demonstrated by medical expertise; (ii) it must warrant compulsory confinement; (iii) the validity of continued confinement depends on the persistence of such a disorder.[461] The detention must take place in a hospital, clinic or another appropriate institution.[462]

76 Under these strict conditions, a retrospective custodial measure (subsequent incapacitation order) could also be seen as complying with the Convention.[463] Of course, in line with the minimum conditions set out above, the detention of persons of unsound mind must take place within an **appropriate institution**. Thus the Court held in various cases against Germany that 'normal' (German) prisons or separate wings thereof do not meet this condition as in their case the required connection between mental illness and detention is lacking.[464] Yet, in *Bergmann*, the Chamber acknowledged, and indeed welcomed, the German efforts to clearly separate, in line with the domestic case law and legislation,[465] ordinary prisoners from mentally disordered inmates[466] and provide for the latter a differentiated treatment 'similar to that in a psychiatric hospital'.[467] The Chamber also considered that the continued detention of the applicant was also lawful, i.e. not arbitrary, within the meaning of Art. 5(1)(e) ECHR.[468]

Art. 5(1)(f) ECHR

77 The last ground for detention permitted by Art. 5(1)(f) is the arrest and detention of a person to '**prevent his effecting an unauthorised entry into the country**'. One relevant practical example of measures taken based on this ground is the detention of asylum seekers at airports and border crossings.[469] The detention of persons 'against whom action is being taken with a view to deportation or extradition' is also covered.

In this case, it is only relevant whether a case is pending, not whether the detention serves to prevent a person from escaping or committing a crime.[470] The unlawfulness of the extradition occurring within the context of this procedure as such does not lead to a violation of Art. 5(1)(f); however, this rule at least requires the interests of the person to be extradited and of the extraditing State to be weighed up against one another.[471]

78 It is to be welcomed that the (former) House of Lords regarded the *detention of non-British suspected terrorists* for an indefinite period without a trial under the Anti-terrorism, Crime and Security Act 2001 (ATCSA)[472] in conjunction with the 'Derogation Order' (de facto rescinding Art. 5(1)(f) ECHR)[473] as a violation of the Convention.[474] Section 23(1) ATCSA provided for the possibility of arrest and detention of a 'suspected international terrorist' even though there were legal obstacles – based on international treaties or on practical considerations[475] – to his deportation; this (continued) detention – without action being taken with a view to deportation or extradition – would be impermissible under Art. 5(1)(f) ECHR, and thus a Derogation Order from the UK's obligations under Art. 5(1)(f) ECHR had to be issued. According to the Law Lords, the preconditions for a 'derogation in times of emergency' listed in Art. 15 ECHR[476] are not present in Art. 5(1)(f), as the order referred to draws on the affected persons' foreign nationality in a discriminatory manner (as British nationals are not included).[477]

(2) Control and Duration of Pre-trial Detention (Art. 5(3) ECHR)

79 In conjunction with the fairness principle as embodied in Art. 6 ECHR, Art. 5 considerably strengthens the legal position of suspects in pre-trial detention.[478] Art. 5(3) offers individuals who are detained on the basis of Art. 5(1)(c) ECHR two different procedural safeguards:[479] on the one hand, they have the right to 'be brought promptly before a judge or other officer authorised by law to exercise judicial power'. On the other hand, conviction or release must take place 'within a reasonable time'. Art. 5(3) stands in the tradition of the English *Habeas Corpus Act* of 1679, according to which arrests had to be ordered by a judge and the prisoner brought before a judge within three days.[480]

80 The purpose of the first-mentioned guarantee – **prompt judicial control** – is to ensure the independent, non-partisan monitoring of pre-trial detention by an independent judicial authority which decides in a professional and fair manner.[481] There must not exist any doubt as to the independence of the relevant adjudicatory authority.[482] The judicial intervention must be prompt, i.e. within a strict time constraint, moving between 'immediacy' (as expressed by the French term *aussitôt*) and the broader 'promptly'.[483] In any case, the scope for flexibility in interpreting and applying the notion of 'promptness' is very limited,[484] even though it has to be assessed on a case-by-case basis taking into account the respective case's special features.[485] Thus, while the Court has regarded in *McKay* that 'the strict time constraint imposed for detention without judicial control is a maximum of four days',[486] it held in other cases that 'three days and twenty-three hours after [the person's] arrest . . . [do] not appear prompt'[487] or that four days and six hours – even in a terrorist case – fall 'outside the strict constraints as to time permitted' by Art. 5(3).[488] Furthermore, the judicial intervention has to be automatic, i.e. not dependent upon previous application by the detained person.[489]

The second guarantee – trial within a **reasonable time** or release from pre-trial detention – is at least as significant. Above all, Art. 5(1), (3) ECHR limits the **duration** of pre-trial detention.[490] According to the ECtHR, besides continued suspicion, the grounds for detention must be valid and the authorities must facilitate the progress of the trial. Otherwise, the right to freedom, which gains in importance as the length of detention increases, turns the detention into an unlawful one in light of the Convention.[491] Thus the widespread domestic practice of ordering the continuation of detention using formulaic grounds represents a violation of the Convention.[492]

81 The **appropriate length** of the pre-trial detention cannot be determined in the abstract but depends on the **circumstances of the individual case.**[493] Thus the ECtHR has both judged pre-trial detention of more than four years to be in line with the Convention and one of over two years as inappropriate.[494] In principle, the ECtHR applies stricter standards to the length of pre-trial detention than to the length of the trial.[495] This is to be welcomed given the greater intensity of the intervention to personal freedom. The decision on the admissible length is based on the *weighing up* of the public interest in the continuation of the detention and the individual's interest in his freedom.[496] In particular, the punishment threatened must be compared to the length of the pre-trial detention and the effects of the detention on the detainee are to be taken into consideration.[497] Furthermore, the *terrorist background* of an offence giving rise to pre-trial detention may in individual cases legitimate a longer period of detention.[498] The factor of time, which plays a particularly significant role in the deprivation of liberty, is taken into account by the ECtHR through the fact that it examines in a separate step whether the responsible authorities have conducted the trial in a speedy manner.[499] If there are avoidable *delays to the procedure*, for example because the whole original file was sent instead of photocopies of relevant documents, the extended pre-trial detention must be deducted from any period of imprisonment the defendant is sentenced to.[500]

82 Any violation of Art. 5(3) first sentence must be reviewed separately from a violation of Art. 6(1) ECHR and restitution must be made that goes beyond the compulsory deduction of time in line with domestic law.[501] If national law allows for release from pre-trial detention on **bail**, State authorities are required to review this option.[502] If – besides suspicion – the length of detention is based (only) on flight risk, then release on bail is to be ordered in accordance with national law.[503] However, if the ECtHR finds that the requirement of a special speed in matters of detention has been infringed, then the applicant may not be considered a victim within the meaning of Art. 34 ECHR, if the national courts have (already) explicitly noted a violation of Art. 5(3) ECHR on the one hand and compensated for this by granting sufficient mitigation on the other hand.[504]

(3) Information of the Factual Basis of Detention (Art. 5(2) ECHR)

83 Combining equality of arms and Art. 5(2) it follows that the suspect must be appropriately *involved* and *informed* of the facts that form the basis of the detention.[505] This right to information serves to prepare the legal remedies of Art. 5(4) ECHR. The arrested person must be informed, in a language which she understands, of the factual and legal reasons for the detention; this also includes information on evidence.[506] He need not be informed immediately upon being imprisoned, but the wait must not be overly long (ten days).[507] If the individual is not able to understand the information, then his legal representative must be informed.[508] Within the context of the pre-trial detention, too, the 'benefit of an adversarial procedure',[509] especially being present at a hearing[510] and the possibility to respond to a submission by the prosecution,[511] must be guaranteed.

(4) Judicial Review (Art. 5(4) ECHR) and Compensation (Art. 5(5) ECHR)

84 The guarantees of Art. 5(4) differ from those of Art. 5(3) – analysed above – in two ways: first, Art. 5(3) applies only to pre-trial detainees whose detention is based on Art. 5(1)(c), while Art. 5(4) applies to *any person* 'who is deprived of his liberty by arrest or detention'. Second, Art. 5(3) contains a substantive guarantee with the entitlement to trial within a reasonable time, while Art. 5(4) has the nature of a **procedural guarantee**,[512] granting the individual affected the right to a judicial review of the lawfulness of his deprivation of liberty.[513] In case of an unlawful detention, the 'enforceable right to **compensation**' of Art. 5(5) is triggered.[514]

A paradigmatic example of a violation of Art. 5(3) and (4) ECHR constitutes the practice of the '*enforced disappearance*' of prisoners.[515] The same applies to the practice of so-called 'extraordinary renditions' carried out on the initiative of the CIA after 11 September 2001; that is, the transfer of a prisoner to another state outside normal mutual assistance procedures, entailing the concrete risk of torture and inhuman treatment.[516] Here, ECHR States Parties can be held responsible for rights violations by the receiving state (*in casu* the USA) on the basis of their duty to protect the right to liberty under Art. 5 ECHR.[517]

(5) Access to Files (Art. 6 in Conjunction with Art. 5(4) ECHR)

85 From Art. 6 in conjunction with Art. 5(4), the accused can deduce an almost full right to access files.[518] According to the case law, the defence counsel is to have access to all documents and information in the case file necessary to evaluate the lawfulness of the arrest and thus indispensable for effectively challenging the lawfulness of the detention.[519] The prosecuting authorities' legitimate needs for secrecy need to be taken into consideration, but cannot justify substantial restrictions of the right to defence.[520] However, the ECtHR will only confirm a violation of Art. 5(4) ECHR if the applicant has been denied access to material that was decisive for the evaluation of his imprisonment.[521]

86 More extensive access to the case file can be derived from the principle of (formal) **equality of arms**, for if defence and prosecution are to possess the same level of information, then the defence must have full knowledge of the file. Understood in this strict a manner, the right to access files comes close to the disclosure obligation in an adversarial trial already discussed above.[522] By contrast, if a more substantive understanding of equality of arms is taken – in line with the structure of the inquisitorial (judge-led) procedure[523] – then access remains restricted to the information decisive for challenging the detention.[524] At any rate, under this case law access to the case file cannot be denied lightly invoking an ongoing (secret) investigation.[525]

ii) *Art. 8 ECHR: The Right to Respect for Private and Family Life*

87 Art. 8 limits the type and scope of coercive measures in regard to **private and family life, home** and **correspondence.**[526] Home searches, confiscation of documents and surveillance of communication in particular constitute State interventions in these areas.[527] If a home is entered to be searched and if objects are confiscated in doing so, then the confiscation as such represents an infringement of Art. 8(1) and of the safeguarding of property according to Art. 1 AP I ECHR.[528] Searches and confiscations need to correspond to 'a pressing social need' and to be proportionate, which may particulary not be the case if the criminal charge is comparatively minor.[529] If press products are confiscated, then this may constitute, in addition, a violation of the freedom of opinion guaranteed in Art. 10 (to be looked at more closely in the next section).[530] Beyond this, Art. 8 protects the home from being entered by State officials for any reason, even if they are not effecting entrance to search the property but to enforce civil law claims, for example.[531]

88 Correspondence within the meaning of Art. 8(1) includes not only written correspondence, but also – in line with the protective purpose of Art. 8 – *telephone*[532] and *electronic* communication; that is, the 'confiscation' of data, for example.[533] **Telephone surveillance** constitutes a particularly serious interference with Art. 8.[534] The Court requires that the exceptions provided for in Art. 8(2) shall be 'in accordance with the law', which

> must be sufficiently clear in its terms to give citizens an adequate indication as to the circumstances in which and the conditions on which public authorities are empowered to resort to this secret and potentially dangerous interference with the right to respect for private life and correspondence.[535]

State interference exists independently of whether the conversation was conducted from a private line – that is, whether the protected interest of 'private life' is (also) affected – or whether the conversation's content deals with family matters and thus represents protected 'family life'; rather, every kind of telephone communication enjoys comprehensive protection from State surveillance measures.[536]

89 The situation is more difficult where the **involvement of private persons** in concerned; that is, when a *private* individual records telephone conversations with suspects under directions from, at the instigation of, or at least with the help of the police in order to make the recordings available to the prosecution (**so-called 'listening traps'**, as represented by our cases 5a and 5b).[537] From the point of view of Convention law, the problematic aspect of these cases is that the actions of private individuals can, in principle, only violate the ECHR[538] if they can be *attributed to State authorities.*[539] In this sense, accountability already exists for the ECtHR when private actions are *in some manner* encouraged or instigated by State authorities.[540] Relevant case law tends towards a positive State obligation to act to protect private life. State interventions requiring justification can thus be assumed to exist already when private actions have merely been brought about in some way by the State, without, for example, the police (actively) making bugging devices being a decisive issue.[541]

90 Art. 8 also applies to the **surveillance of written correspondence**, particularly that of pre-trial detainees.[542] Monitoring, failing to pass on and censoring the letters of prisoners represents an interference in the person's right to respect for their correspondence (Art. 8(1)).[543] Art. 8(2) permits such interferences if they are **prescribed by law** and '**necessary** in a democratic society', including to uphold national security, public safety, the economic well-being of the country[544] or health. Accordingly, case law assumes that interfering with the correspondence of convicts does not violate the Convention in principle.[545] However, *in concreto* there need to be sufficient grounds for such monitoring.[546] Necessity, within the meaning of Art. 8(2), is more than mere expediency; State actions must be *proportionate*[547] and there must be an *urgent need* for the specific restriction.[548] In essence, we are dealing with a decision that requires the **balancing of interests**, which will be more likely to go against the admissibility of an intervention the weaker or more diffuse the grounds for interference asserted are (morals! public order!) on the one hand, and the stronger the interference on the other hand.[549] Thus, in the *Erdem* case, which dealt with a prisoner suspected of terrorism, the ECtHR decided that the control of defence correspondence complied with the Convention.[550] By contrast, in *Dudgeon* the ECtHR demanded weighty grounds for the confiscation of objects that affected a person's most intimate sphere.[551]

91 Given the explicit requirements of Art. 8(2), there are no immanent limitations justifying an intervention.[552] Rather, always a **legal basis** is required, albeit not necessarily a parliamentary law.[553] Orders and directives can only be considered a sufficient legal basis if they are *accessible* to the public or *in concreto* for the imprisoned persons they affect.[554] In this regard, the ECtHR – in line with Art. 7 ECHR[555] – demands that possible restrictions to the guarantees be *predictable* and sufficiently *clear*.[556] Of course, these requirements may also be met by orders, directives and regulatory statutes (which render the legal basis more specific), as well as by the 'substantial body of case law'.[557] The requirements of Art. 8(2) are also met– as the ECtHR ruled in the *Pretty* case[558] – by a statutory prohibition of assisted suicide, as found in the English Suicide Act or §216 StGB, for example; while it cannot be ruled out[559] that the prohibition of assisted suicide touches upon the protective scope of Art. 8(1), given the risk of abuse particularly in the field of assisted suicide, this prohibition meets the requirements of Art. 8(2).[560]

92 The Grand Chamber was also quite generous with regard to the French ban on the wearing of a **full-face veil** in public,[561] holding that respect for the conditions of 'living together' ('vivre ensemble') in 'a democratic and open society' ('d'une société démocratique et ouverte') was a legitimate aim for the (penal) measure at issue, given the particular 'wide margin of appreciation' in such questions of culture and religion.[562] One may well, however, question this finding of the Court given the woolly justification of the measure and its penal nature.[563] The Court has been, in a previous decision, similarly generous with the German criminalisation of **sibling incest**,[564] holding that there exists 'a pressing social need' for the measure in question and a wide margin of appreciation in such 'sensitive moral or ethical issues', since 'State authorities are, in principle, in a better position than the international court to give an opinion, not only on the "exact content of the requirements of morals" in their country, but also on the necessity of a restriction intended to meet them.'[565] In such a situation, the Court will only have to assess whether the alleged aims of the measure 'appear not to be unreasonable'.[566]

iii) *Art. 10 ECHR: Freedom of Expression*

93 Art. 10 guarantees the freedom of expression; this includes the **freedom of the press.**[567] According to Art. 17 (prohibition of abuse of rights), the *denial of the Holocaust*[568] already falls outside the area protected by Art. 10, for Art. 17 aims to prevent ECHR guarantees being used to undermine the value order upon which the Convention is based.[569] **Interventions** include publication bans, press censorship[570] and the confiscation of press products,[571] but also the refusal of Internet access in prison.

94 Art. 10(2) places certain restrictions upon the guaranteed protected areas of para. (1).[572] Despite particularities in the article's wording – such as the statement that exercising the freedom of expression 'carries with it duties and responsibilities' – similar conditions apply as to other limiting provisions: on the one hand, a **legal basis** is required ('prescribed by law'), while on the other hand the intervention has to be **necessary**; that is, serve a legitimate purpose and be proportionate (on this, cf. case 6).[573] In *Rodriguez Ravelo*, the Court rejected a sort of contempt-of-court sanction against a lawyer who used expressions attributing blameworthy conduct to a judge. While the Court acknowledged that the imposition of a criminal sanction may have a *dissuasive effect* with regard to other lawyers, thereby serving the legitimate purpose of maintaining the authority of the judiciary,[574] *in casu* the measure was considered disproportionate and therefore not necessary in a democratic society.[575] The ECtHR also affirms that a legal basis exists even when confiscation is clearly not envisaged according to the wording of the law, but there is a legal basis for a *more serious* intervention.[576] If the confiscation of press products is carried out on the basis of a suspected national offence, then the ECtHR only examines whether national law has been correctly applied to the matter.[577] As far as the **proportionality** of state actions is concerned, the prosecuting authorities must take into account the fact that freedom of expression represents the 'cornerstone of every democratic society'.[578] During election season, the right to press freedom is to be interpreted in a manner that takes the right to free elections according to Art. 3 AP I ECHR into account. On the one hand, it is thus particularly important that opinions and information of any kind can circulate freely in the time before an election, but on the other hand it is possible to allow for certain restrictions to the freedom of expression during this time that would not be acceptable otherwise in order to safeguard the citizens' very freedom of expression in the election of their parliament.[579]

95 Interferences with freedom of expression on the grounds of **national security** (listed in Art. 10(2)) are of particular significance. On the one hand, this justifies the punishing of the publication of military secrets.[580] On the other hand, the ECtHR saw this as legitimate grounds for confiscating a magazine that had published the confidential report of an intelligence service.[581] For that reason, even the confiscation of the entire edition may be legitimate if necessary.[582] In this regard, the ECtHR focuses on the sensitivity of the information contained, which derives from the currency of the report, its degree of confidentiality and its purpose. Confiscating an entire edition is not necessary if the information in question has already become public knowledge.[583]

96 Besides this, Art. 10(2) permits press products to be confiscated 'for the **prevention of disorder**'. By 'order', the ECtHR understands not only public order, but also the 'internal order' of a particular social group or institution.[584] Accordingly, a State intervention in the freedom of the press for the purposes of maintaining order in the army is legitimate in principle.[585] Member States can make the publication of tobacco advertisements subject to penalty, with the amount of the fine determined by the circulation and the distribution of the magazine in question.[586]

iv) *Art. 2/4 Additional Protocol VII*

97 AP VII[587] provides for several important procedural rights. First, its Art. 2(1) specifies the right to *review* by a 'higher tribunal', thus envisaging a cassation-like review and going beyond Art. 6 ECHR.[588] Art. 3 AP VII grants the right to *compensation* for wrongful conviction as long as the lack of timely information of the facts justifying the wrongful conviction is not the convicted person's own fault.[589] Last but not least, Art. 4 AP VII contains the *prohibition of double jeopardy*, which also appears in Art. 54 CISA and Art. 50 CFREU and will therefore be discussed below.[590]

Solution, Cases 1a and 1b

98 Here we are dealing with cases of provocation to commit an offence. In **case 1a**, the German Federal Supreme Court identified a violation of the principle of fair trial (Art. 6(1) ECHR), but concluded that this did not constitute a procedural obstacle or lead to an exclusion of evidence.[591] Instead, it was only necessary and sufficient to compensate for this violation of the Convention by mitigating the sentence; *in casu* a 'sanction close to the minimum sentence' thus suggested itself.[592] In contrast to this *fixing of penalty or mitigation solution*, the ECtHR takes the stance that in constellations such as that in **case 1b** there is a lack of fair trial *ab initio* and a conviction is thus impossible; the trial must be terminated (*procedural or termination solution*). The consistency of the ECtHR's solution speaks in its favour, for it hardly makes sense that the State be allowed to punish acts that would not have taken place without the very State's provocation (cf. above, mn. 33).[593]

Solution, Case 2

99 For the ECtHR, it follows from the *presumption of innocence* that the revocation of a suspended sentence because of the commission of a new offence during the probation period can only take place if the convict has already been reconvicted for the new offence. Thus the ECtHR demands that either the new offence has been tried, resulting in a conviction, or that the convict has confessed to it in the presence of his defence counsel. *In casu*, it thus found a violation of Art. 6(2) ECHR (cf. above, mn. 38).

Solution, Case 3

100 The case's focal point is the *right to confrontation*. The accused must be given the opportunity to confront the witnesses of the prosecution in some way (Art. 6(3d) ECHR). As far as keeping witnesses' identities secret during the trial is concerned, account needs to be taken first of the fact that police officers cannot be equated with independent witnesses, as policemen and -women are answerable to the executive and have links to the prosecutor. While in principle it must be accepted that the State will not reveal the identities of police undercover investigators, the rights of the defence can only be curtailed in this manner if this is strictly necessary.[594] In the *Van Mechelen* case the protective measures went too far for the ECtHR (cf. above, mn. 53).

Solution, Case 4

101 Like in the *Van Mechelen* case, a Convention violation could result from a violation of the right to confrontation. Once again, the ECtHR makes it clear that the right to confrontation is by no means exempt from being weighed up against the interests of the conflicting party. It all depends on the circumstances of the case. In the *Haas* case, the ECtHR denied a violation of the Convention had taken place, as the German authorities, first, had made an effort to enable the witness (who was imprisoned in Lebanon) to take part in the trial, and second, the Higher Regional Court had evaluated his information as well as that provided by the anonymous witnesses very carefully (cf. mn. 53 above).

Solution, Cases 5a and 5b

102 As to a possible violation of *Art. 8(1) ECHR*, in these cases the decisive factor is whether the actions of private individuals setting 'listening traps' is to be attributed to the State Parties concerned (here France and the Netherlands). The ECtHR confirmed this for both applications and thus assumed a violation of Art. 8 ECHR. In *A.* v. *France* the officer made a 'crucial contribution' by making his office, telephone and recording equipment available.[595] In *M. M.* v. *The Netherlands* a significant contribution was also made by the police officers, even though the person pressing charges had made the call from her private line (cf. above, mn. 89).[596]

Solution, Case 6

103 A key criterion in evaluating the proportionality of the measure is the *severity of the intervention*, particularly the nature and extent of the sanction applied. In the present case, a violation of Art. 10 ECHR can be confirmed. While the duration of the closures was limited, in real terms this measure had the same effect as a permanent closure, given the fast-moving nature of the news business and the need for press companies and their staff to make economic plans. Moreover, there would have been the option to ban individual reports, namely those with terrorist content, as a milder measure (cf. above, mn. 94).

c) Substantive Criminal Law Rights

Case 7

104 T sees from a window that O is destroying his (T's) expensive sports car with a sledgehammer. When O fails to react to a call and to a warning shot, instead continuing his work of destruction, T has no other way of defending his property than shooting at O with the aim of incapacitating him. T is aware of the possibility that O could be hit by a deadly shot but accepts that this may occur. T shoots at O, who dies then and there of the gunshot wound. Are T's actions justified by self-defence, or does Art. 2 ECHR impede the defence of property?[597] → mn. 137

Case 8

105 British authorities allowed the IRA members McCann, Farrell and Savage to enter Gibraltar unchallenged under secret surveillance, even though they (*correctly*) assumed that they intended to carry out an assassination there. Over the next days, McCann, Farrell and Savage continued to be watched by British security, including by soldiers of the 'Special Air Service' (SAS) special forces. When the SAS men (*incorrectly*) thought that the suspects were in the process of remotely setting off a hidden bomb, they shot them. In the case of an (inevitable) erroneous assumption of the direct threat of a terrorist attack, can the use of deadly force amounting to a 'targeted killing' be reconciled with Art. 2 ECHR?[598] → mn. 138

Case 9

106 Plainclothes policemen arrested the applicant upon suspicion of drug trafficking. He proceeded to swallow a plastic bag which later was found to contain cocaine. Instead of waiting for the bag to pass through the body naturally, the prosecution ordered the applicant be given an emetic. Does this treatment constitute a violation of Art. 3 ECHR? Does it result in exclusion of evidence?[599] → mn. 139

Case 10

107 Following German reunification, Fritz Streletz, former GDR minister of defence, Heinz Keßler, his deputy, and Egon Krenz, member of the SED's

Politbüro and the National Defence Council, had been convicted of manslaughter by German criminal courts as persons holding (joint) responsibility in the GDR's 'border regime' for the deadly shots fired by border guards at so-called *Republikflüchtlinge* (citizens attempting to flee the GDR) at the GDR–FRG border. In principle, the justification of §27 of the GDR Border Law could have been applied, but the German courts did not do so due to its 'incompatibility with human rights' (*Menschenrechtswidrigkeit*).[600] Following an unsuccessful constitutional complaint,[601] the defendants made an application to the ECtHR on the grounds of a violation of Art. 7 ECHR. Does the conviction of responsible GDR functionaries for the shots fired at the Berlin Wall violate Art. 7?[602] → mn. 140

Case 11

108 In 1986, M, who had previously already been convicted of several offences, was sentenced to a prison term of five years for attempted murder in coincidence with robbery. Furthermore, the competent domestic court ordered M to be placed in preventive (custodial) detention (*Sicherungsverwahrung*) after the prison term was served. At the time the sentence was passed, preventive detention was limited to a maximum period of ten years by law. After serving his prison sentence and ten years of detention, M applied for suspension of the preventive detention. This was rejected on the ground that M continued to pose a threat. As the legal maximum for preventive detention had already been rescinded in 1998, including for existing cases, the court did not regard M's release as imperative in legal terms. Is the retroactive repeal of the ten-year limit a violation of Art. 7 ECHR?[603] → mn. 141

i) *Art. 2 ECHR: The Right to Life*

109 Art. 2 not only imposes a duty on a State Party to refrain from the 'intentional' taking of life (**negative obligation**), but also contains the obligation to ensure *actively* the lives of those within its jurisdiction (**positive obligation**).[604] As a consequence, no human right to a 'dignified' death ('right to die') can be derived from Art. 2(1) by a kind of *e contrario* inference.[605] The positive obligation addresses all three State powers.[606] States Parties may create, for example, a legal framework that deters attempts on their citizens' lives, or provide a legal and administrative structure to prevent, investigate and punish relevant violations of the respective norms.[607] States Parties are, in particular, under the procedural limb of Art. 2, under an obligation to conduct an **effective investigation** into the – non-natural – death of persons under their jurisdiction.[608] However, this obligation does not arise naturally from Art. 2 since an investigation after the fact cannot undo this fact (i.e. the death) and thus is not life-protecting.[609]

110 At any rate, States Parties have to be granted a *margin of appreciation* in how to fulfil this positive obligation,[610] in particular in the complex area of the continuation or withdrawal of life-sustaining treatment.[611] Thus the Court considers three factors: (i) the existence of a domestic regulatory framework compatible with Art. 2, (ii) whether the wishes of the person concerned and of persons close to him have been sufficiently taken into account, and (iii) whether there was the possibility to approach the national courts.[612] In the case of abortions based upon medical negligence, the ECtHR has left the question whether the embryo already comes under the protective scope of Art. 2 open.[613] In exceptional cases, there may be a violation of Art. 2 even if the victim has not died, but was (only) subjected to life-threatening treatment.[614]

111 According to **Art. 2(2)** ECHR, the killing of a human being is not seen as a violation of the right to life

> when it results from the use of force which is no more than absolutely necessary: (a) in defence of any person from unlawful violence; (b) in order to effect a lawful arrest or to prevent the escape of a person lawfully detained; (c) in action lawfully taken for the purpose of quelling a riot or insurrection.[615]

The particular restriction of the second paragraph always presumes a **legal basis**, as can be deduced from the phrases 'lawfully' in (b) and (c); furthermore, one of the **grounds for intervention** listed at the end of the article must be given, and finally the measure has to be 'no more than **absolutely necessary**'.[616] Besides the restriction in para. (2), it should also be noted that by recognising 'the execution of a sentence', the first paragraph, second sentence does not *a limine* exclude the death penalty.[617] However, AP VI abolishes capital punishment in times of peace[618] and AP XIII strives to abolish it completely.[619] Occasionally, the observation of a violation of Art. 2 and its attribution to State organs can be problematic, as seen particularly in cases of *enforced disappearance*.[620]

112 The scope of the restriction of para. (2) is controversial in regard to self-defence in cases of manslaughter committed in **defence of property or other material assets** (as in our case 7),[621] and on a fundamental level in regard to the use of deadly force as ultimate means to rescue a third innocent person (so-called '**final rescue shot**' cases (*finaler Todesschuss/Rettungsschuss*)). For one opinion, the ECHR is not concerned with relations between citizens but only restricts State interventions, so that Art. 2 does not apply to the law on self-defence.[622] Another opinion takes a broader view as to the *ratione materiae* application of Art. 2(2) and argues that it indeed prohibits manslaughter in defence of material assets.[623] A third, intermediate opinion takes the same broad *ratione materiae* view of Art. 2 but argues that it must not unduly limit the national law; that is, it must respect self-defence with regard to property attacks.[624]

113 Apart from that, it is generally assumed that Art. 2 only prohibits the intentional,[625] or at least the either **intentional** or **conscious**,[626] killing of a person who is attacking a material asset; that is, it would in any case not cover a mere reckless or negligent killing. However, the fact that the Convention's main aim is to (closely) restrict State attacks on or abuse of citizens speaks against this.[627] Thus the ECtHR has clarified explicitly, with regard to State interferences in the right to life, that the protective scope of Art. 2 not only applies to intentional killings, but also covers the use of violence leading – albeit unintentionally – to the victim's death.[628] The English and French versions of Art. 2 ECHR ('intentionally' and *intentionellement*), suggesting a volitional *mens rea* element, also argue against differentiating according to the kind of intent.[629] The ECtHR has not produced a statement on this issue, but that is probably due to the fact that any justification for killing an assailant in defence of material assets *in praxi* usually fails because of the restrictions on the deadly use of *weapons* developed in most EU jurisdictions (quite contrary to the US law and practice).[630]

114 In regard to the problem of the deadly use of force as ultimate means to rescue the victim ('**final rescue shot**', case 8), the ECtHR takes the stance that it is certainly permitted to intentionally kill an assailant if this is a proportionate measure within the meaning of Art. 2(2)(a) ECHR to protect third persons from unlawful violence.[631] In the Court's view, it is even justified to kill an attacker if it emerges only *ex post* that actually there was no attack, but the competent State authority had to presume *ex ante* that innocent third parties could only be saved by killing the supposed assailants.[632]

115 Art. 2(2) does not aim to restrict national **state-of-emergency rules** that permit killing in defence of human life.[633] Thus the German Aviation Security Act[634] did *not* constitute a violation of the ECHR although its §14(3) permitted shooting down hijacked passenger planes – that is, intentionally killing their passengers and crew – if (as was the case in the attacks of 11 September 2001) 'it can be assumed that the intention is to use the aeroplane against the lives of human beings, and [the direct use of armed force] . . . is the only way to avert this present threat'.[635] Interestingly, the German Federal Constitutional Court has declared the regulation unconstitutional, basically arguing (in a *Kantian* fashion) that human beings (*in casu* the passengers and crew of the respective airplane) cannot be regarded or treated as objects (so-called *Objektformel*).[636] The German legislator never adopted a new law on the matter.

ii) *Art. 3 ECHR: The Prohibition of Torture*

116 The prohibition of torture – which uses the same wording as Art. 4 CFREU[637] – acts as a safeguard against inhuman or degrading punishment or treatment, with torture constituting the more serious violation of Art. 3.[638] Similar to Art. 2 it imposes on States Parties a *positive obligation* 'to take measures designed to ensure that individuals within their jurisdiction are not subjected to torture or inhuman or degrading treatment or punishment, including such ill-treatment administered by private individuals.'[639] This obligation arises in particular with regard to children and other vulnerable individuals.[640]

117 The ECtHR stresses the *distinction between torture and inhuman treatment* in order to highlight the former's particular reprehensibility.[641] Accordingly, torture requires that inhuman or degrading treatment causes **very serious and cruel suffering.**[642] It is also required that the victim is caused pain and suffering **purposefully**, 'for the purpose of . . . making [the victim] confess to the offence which [he is] suspected of having committed'.[643] In this regard, the ECtHR[644] draws on the legal definition of Art. 1(1) of the UN Convention against Torture.[645]

118 The prohibition of torture reveals the ECHR's **dynamic character** particularly well.[646] In the inter-state application proceedings *Ireland* v. *the UK*[647] of 1978 the ECtHR qualified specific British methods of interrogating suspected IRA members[648] 'only' as inhuman treatment, not as torture. In the *Selmouni* case 21 years later,[649] France was convicted of torture, as the applicant – who had been given a prison sentence of several years for drug dealing – had been beaten and kicked while in police custody. Last but not least, the 'enhanced interrogation techniques' – including waterboarding, beating by the use of a collar, confinement in a box, exposure to cold temperature and food deprivation – used in the context of the infamous 'extraordinary renditions'[650] carried out mostly by the CIA, have been qualified as torture.[651] The Court considered decisive not 'exclusively . . . the infliction of physical pain', but also the 'mental suffering, which is caused by creating a state of anguish and stress by means other than bodily assault' (so-called 'white torture').[652] These cases show the difficulty in delimitating torture from the less serious **inhuman treatment or punishment**.[653] The latter exists when intense physical or mental suffering is intentionally caused to someone,[654] although it is controversial whether this distinction is to be made purely objectively or whether the particular purpose of the torture (especially forcing a confession) should be taken into consideration.[655] The **degrading treatment** of a person constitutes the weakest form of State violations of Art. 3. In contrast to torture and inhuman treatment, the focus here lies not on the infliction of physical pain, but on the humiliation of a human being, the violation of her dignity.[656] There is no violation of Art. 3 when **slight injuries** have been incurred during an arrest or a flight attempt, even if the circumstances cannot be clarified completely.[657] The prohibition of assisted suicide in the case of seriously ill persons who wish to die does not represent degrading treatment.[658] Yet a deportation of a severely ill person violates the guarantee of Art. 3 ECHR.[659]

119 The **'punishment' limb** of Art. 3 ECHR differs from the 'treatment' limb in that it refers to an institutional imposition of a punitive harm which is prima facie legitimate because of its very institutionality.[660] This legitimacy claim is, however, rebutted if punishment turns out to be 'inhuman' or 'degrading'; that is, where an additional 'distress or hardship exceeding the unavoidable level of suffering inherent in detention'[661] is caused[662] or the punishment as such is grossly disproportionate.[663] As to the latter, the Grand Chamber held in *Vinter* that Art. 3 prohibits a **mandatory life sentence** which is 'irreducible' in law and fact[664] since *human* punishment presupposes the possibility to regain freedom before death ('right to hope').[665] Thus, to be compatible with Art. 3, a criminal justice system imposing life sentences must provide for 'both a prospect of release and a possibility of review';[666] that is, there must be an *adequate review mechanism* which allows for early release on penological grounds.[667] Yet this does not exclude continued imprisonment due to the continued dangerousness of the convict,[668] nor a life sentence in especially serious offences such as terrorism.[669] This mechanism must, in principle, exist at the outset of the enforcement of the life sentence so that the prisoner knows what he has to do to be considered rehabilitated and thus obtain early release.[670] It is, of course, in line with the Court's doctrine of margin of appreciation, in the discretion of the competent national authorities to set up and develop such a review mechanism.[671] It is against this background that the ECtHR in *Hutchinson* accepted the UK Appeals Court's interpretation of the English regime for reviewing whole-life sentence, especially the Secretary of State's early-release power, as being compatible with Art. 3 ECHR, for it 'did provide to an offender sentenced to a whole life order hope and the possibility of release in the event of exceptional circumstances which meant that the punishment was no longer justified'. [672] Clearly, it is difficult, if not impossible, for the ECtHR to fully understand the different and complex national regimes of review and early release, let alone to assess if they actually provide for a 'realistic and discernible prospect of release.'[673]

120 The *Selmouni* decision is also significant because of the statements it makes on the **burden of proof for charges of state abuse**. The Court made the applicant's account the basis of its decision, and justified this by the fact that the French State was unable to provide any plausible explanation for the injuries identified.[674] The State authorities are obliged to explain why a person exhibits injuries after a detention that did not exist beforehand.[675] Similarly, if there are serious injuries after the use of force by State authorities, it is up to the State to prove that the use of force was admissible; otherwise, a violation of Art. 3 can be assumed.[676] The Court has confirmed this approach in the notorious *El-Masri* (extraordinary rendition) case.[677] As a consequence, there is a strong presumption of a State's responsibility if a person dies or suffers injury in its custody – or, for that matter, suffers serious injury at the hand of State authorities – and there are no other plausible explanations of the State's (unlawful) use of force.[678] The ECtHR has thus created a *relaxation of the burden of proof*[679] intended to break the (police) wall of silence concerning the abuse of detainees.[680]

121 The ECtHR applies a **mandatory exclusion of evidence** gained through torture that incriminates the defendant (our case 9).[681] Evidence gathered abroad is already inadmissible if there was a real risk of torture being used in the gathering of this evidence in the foreign State, and if its criminal justice system does not guarantee that torture charges are followed up as part of an independent, impartial and serious investigation.[682]

122 The distinction between torture and inhuman and degrading treatment is also evident in the fact that any justification for the former is inadmissible even when a **state of emergency** exists: Art. 15(2) ECHR explicitly prohibits any exception to the prohibition of torture, even during times of 'public emergency'.[683] In addition, Art. 3 – unlike Art. 2(2) ECHR – does not contain any **restriction** as to its scope of protection.[684] Yet ECtHR case law recognises *immanent restrictions* in regard to inhuman and degrading treatment, which are of significant practical relevance in regard to *detention conditions*.[685] The ECtHR considers inhuman treatment of prisoners to be admissible if this serves to create order in prison and 'the prisoner's conduct renders the use of violence absolutely necessary'.[686] Before this, the Court had judged the detention conditions of German left-wing terrorists in Stuttgart-Stammheim during the 1970s to comply with the Convention, as they had, in the estimation of the European Commission of Human Rights, sufficient opportunity to access information and contact.[687] Similarly, the ECtHR judged the international terrorist 'Carlos's' solitary confinement of more than eight years as complying with the Convention in regard to Art. 3 ECHR.[688] This does not mean, of course, that long-term isolation cannot amount to a violation of Art. 3.[689]

123 By contrast, the ECtHR judged the administering of **emetics** (our case 9) to force a drug trafficking suspect to egest a swallowed pack of drugs to constitute inhuman, degrading treatment within the meaning of Art. 3 ECHR. Administering the emetic by force was not 'absolutely necessary'; instead, it would have been possible for the pack of drugs to be passed naturally.[690] However, this decision should not be misunderstood as meaning that the ECtHR regards the use of emetics in criminal proceedings as violating the Convention per se; rather, the decisive factor is whether the threshold of Art. 3 has been exceeded in the circumstances of the respective individual case.[691]

124 Finally, the guarantees of Art. 3 ECHR are relevant where the **deportation** of foreigners is concerned.[692] Consequently, a deportation must not take place if there is a risk that in the receiving State the person concerned will be subjected to treatment that violates Art. 3. The deporting State is to be held responsible for this treatment, as it was the deporting State that delivered the person into the receiving State's clutches while fully aware of the risks involved.[693] Thus a State Party to the ECHR cannot escape its human rights responsibility by deporting persons to States outside the Convention area known to commit human rights violations.[694] This is one of the reasons why **extraordinary rendition** – extrajudicial transfer entailing harsh interrogation, up to torture, in the receiving State – gives rise to the human rights responsibility of the sending State.[695] If there is a risk of torture or inhuman treatment, then deportation is not permitted even – because of the absolute nature of the torture prohibition – when serious reasons of national security are invoked in its favour.[696]

125 At any rate, to adduce the ECHR as a barrier to deportation requires the threat of a sufficiently concrete risk or danger to the foreign citizen to be deported in the receiving State.[697] This may also be the case for deportations within the EU.[698] Yet generally insecure living conditions and so on are not sufficient. The person in question has to show that his situation would be worse than that of other persons in the receiving State.[699] When examining whether there is a real risk of torture or abuse, any assurances given by the receiving State to the deporting (sending) State on the respective individual's further treatment must be taken into account. Their significance depends on the circumstances of the individual case, for example on whether assurances given in the past have been kept and whether it can be verified that the individual is being treated in a manner that conforms to the Convention.[700]

iii) *Art. 7 ECHR: No Punishment without Law (Principle of Legality)*

126 Art. 7 contains the principle of legality (*nullum crimen, nulla poena sine lege*).[701] The first paragraph safeguards against **retroactive punishment** (*lex praevia*) and against punishment by **analogy** (*lex stricta*),[702] requires criminal laws to possess sufficient **certainty** (*lex certa*),[703] and provides for the *lex mitior* principle. However, Art. 7 does not constitute an obstacle to punishment on the basis of unwritten law (*nulla poena sine lege scripta*).[704] It only requires 'a criminal offence under national or international law'. It does not require that the offence be codified in national (or international) law. Thus common law crimes or customary international law crimes do not contravene Art. 7(1) ECHR.

127 Moreover, the **prohibition of analogy** contained in Art. 7(1) should not be understood strictly to mean that the literal meaning of the words marks the limits of every admissible interpretation;[705] nor does the use of highly normative terms such as 'immoral' or 'indecent' automatically indicate a violation of Art. 7(1).[706] Rather, according to ECtHR case law, it is more important for the preservation of the principle of legality that a certain behaviour can be subsumed in a non-arbitrary manner – if appropriate, including the consideration of the relevant case law – under an offence definition, so that each citizen is able to

foresee the legal consequences of his conduct and adapt it to the law.[707] Not only the threat of punishment, but also the maximum penalty must be defined and foreseeable,[708] as well as 'the manner of choice of jurisdiction, as this reflected on the penalty that the offence in question carried'.[709] Thus the Court focuses on individual foreseeability, enshrining thereby the **principle of culpability** in Art. 7(1) and giving it a subjective connotation.

128 On the basis of the said principles, the ECtHR, in the famous case of *S. W.* v. *the UK*, confirmed a 1991 conviction for marital attempted rape in the UK, which was issued at a time in which the (unwritten) common law defence of '**marital immunity**' dating from 1736(!) gave husbands the right to force their wives to have sexual intercourse against their will without being held criminally responsible because they could invoke the said defence.[710] The House of Lords, taking account of societal changes and a heated reform debate on the abolition of this 'marital privilege', convicted the husband in question of attempted rape and assault occasioning actual bodily harm,[711] whereupon he appealed to the ECtHR on the grounds of a violation of the prohibition of retroactive legislation within the meaning of Art. 7(1) ECHR given that the Law Lords revoked the said defence retroactively to his detriment.[712] However, the ECtHR upheld the conviction basically arguing that it was – taking into account the changed societal conditions and the reform debate – 'consistent with the essence of the offence' and could 'reasonably' be foreseen.[713]

129 The **border guard cases** (our case 10) also dealt with the retroactive repeal of a defence, namely the justification of the use of deadly force – under certain strict conditions – against GDR citizens attempting to cross the border ('border violators').[714] The ECtHR denied a violation of Art. 7 ECHR,[715] arguing that the shots fired at 'border violators' and the firing order constituted a punishable offence even if the law of the GDR was taken as a legal basis. The border regime practice, instructing border guards to stop 'border violators' even at the cost of human lives, violated the guarantee of the right to life in the GDR's Constitution; thus the order to shoot could not even be justified by the GDR Constitution.[716] Furthermore, the killings also violated international law, such as the right to life guaranteed in Art. 6 ICCPR, ratified by the GDR.[717] In the Court's view, the fact that the GDR law was not so interpreted at the time of the commission of the relevant acts is of no relevance since Art. 7 does not demand that earlier interpretations of laws be adhered to, even if there has been a regime change. Accordingly, the convictions were *foreseeable* (for the applicants).[718]

130 The ECtHR opted for a **pro-human rights reading of GDR law**, apparently to avoid the application of the controversial Art. 7(2) ECHR, the notorious *Nuremberg clause*,[719] according to which conduct is punishable if at the time it took place 'it constituted a criminal offence according to the legal principles recognised by civilised nations'.[720] With this the Court further avoided taking a stance with regard to the **human rights** or even natural law[721] **compliance of the GDR border regime**, especially the cause of justification of §27 GDR Border Law (which effectively has been declared invalid by the German Supreme and Constitutional Court).[722] However, the ECtHR's line of argument is open to attack: the Court's downgrading of the offence of *Republikflucht* (the attempt to flee the 'German Democratic *Republic*') to a misdemeanour, thus rendering the felony of §213(3) GDR StGB and accordingly §27 GDR Border Law inapplicable,[723] raises the question whether a retroactive revocation of §27 GDR Border Law can be reconciled with Art. 7(1) ECHR. In fact, the Court ignores that according to GDR practice *at the time of the events*, border violations were already regarded as serious cases when simple tools were used and thus upgraded to felonies.[724] Thus the **gist of the issue** is whether it is permissible to declare a cause of justification, valid at the time of the event, ex post and thus retroactively inapplicable or even invalid. In this regard, it would seem more honest and consistent to inquire whether (naturalistic) reasons of justice demand punishment – in the sense of a natural law and human rights 'normativisation' of the legality principle brought about by the Nuremberg ICL and converting it into a *nullum crimen sine iure* (instead of *sine lege*)[725] – than to reinterpret the positive law in a manner in which it was not understood at the time the events took place.[726] Of course, while Art. 7(2) is indeed predicated on the said (*objective*) human rights-oriented approach, this approach does not answer the question whether the defendants could – pursuant to the *subjective* reading of the prohibition of retroactivity that forms the basis of Art. 7 – envisage that their actions could at some point be judged criminal offences and thus were able to *foresee* – in the sense of a 'fair warning' – the punishability of their former conduct.[727] A nuanced approach requires that we distinguish here between high-ranking perpetrators (that is, the members of the political decision-making bodies – *in casu:* Nation Defence Council, the SED's Central Committee, Politbüro) and the mere executioners of the orders within the framework of the border regime (that is, the border guards) exempting only the latter from punishment.[728]

131 In *Vasiliauskas* the Grand Chamber delivered a fundamental judgment concerning the general issue of how new regimes should deal with **past grave human rights violations** in the light of Art. 7's principle of legality. *In casu*, the question was further aggravated by the fact that the former regime was the Soviet occupation force in the territory of the Baltic States and the new regime (Lithuania) came into existence with the dissolution of the former Soviet Union as one of the many consequences of the fall of the Berlin Wall. The Chamber had to decide whether the killings of two members of the Lithuanian partisan movement by the applicant as agent of the Soviet secret service in 1953 could be qualified as **genocide**, as done by the domestic courts. The Chamber held, with a slim majority of nine to eight votes, that this conviction violated Art. 7 ECHR.[729] While it was beyond dispute between the majority and the dissenting judges 'that the crime of genocide was clearly recognised as a crime under international law in 1953',[730] i.e. at the time of the commission of the relevant acts, the majority interpreted the applicable offence definition more narrowly, in particular excluding political groups.[731] Thus the applicant's conviction under the broader definition violated Art. 7 ECHR, turning it unforeseeable, even if assisted by a lawyer.[732] The majority also rejected the argument that the victims belonged to a national group within the accepted meaning of the genocide offence since this amounted to a (prohibited) analogy to the detriment of the accused (applicant) which rendered his conviction equally unforeseeable.[733] Last but not least, in the majority's view, the conviction could not be justified under para. 2 of Art. 7 either,[734] since this para. does not allow for a general exception of the non-retroactivity rule but is 'only a contextual clarification of the liability limb of that rule, included so as to ensure that there was no doubt about the validity of prosecutions after the Second World War in respect of the crimes committed during that war'.[735]

Dissenting Judges *Villiger et al.*[736] admited that social and political groups are not covered by the genocide offence as internationally recognised and thus an attack on 'a purely political group *per se*' could not constitute genocide.[737] However, they considered it 'excessively formalistic' to consider the partisans 'exclusively through the prism of a "political group"' and instead argued that their destruction would have affected 'the survival of the national or ethnic group [of the Lithuanians] as a whole'.[738] Accordingly, in the view of the dissenting judges, 'there is considerable force in the argument that J.A. and A.A. [the partisan-victims], as ethnic Lithuanians, were targeted specifically for their membership of the partisan movement whose members were, simultaneously, a significant and emblematic part of the national group', turning the applicant's conduct into 'an act of genocide on an ethno-national basis'.[739] I have argued elsewhere why the arguments of the majority appear to be more convincing.[740]

132 In a seminal decision of 2009, which was subsequently confirmed several times, the ECtHR judged the (*retroactive*) extension of the length of **preventive (custodial) detention** (*Sicherungsverwahrung*) from 10 years to an indefinite period[741] to constitute a violation of the prohibition of retroactivity within the meaning of Art. 7 ECHR,[742] as the offence giving rise to the detention decision had been committed before the extension was decreed in law (our case 11).[743] The German mainstream position so far has been that the principle of legality, including its prohibition of retroactivity, does not apply to custodial measures since they do not constitute penal sanctions. Preventive (custodial) detention in particular is independent of guilt, focuses on the threat posed by the offender, and is a purely preventive measure, so that any change in its duration is not covered by the prohibition of retroactivity.[744] By contrast, the ECtHR interpreted the term of punishment in Art. 7 ECHR autonomously[745] and focused upon the fact that preventive detention also constitutes a *form of deprivation of liberty*, the enforcement of which hardly differs from that of a prison sentence.[746] The Court was unable to identify any fundamental difference between preventive detention and prison terms in regard to their aims. In the Court's view, detainees were not treated in a special way aimed at reducing the threat they posed to the general public.[747] Furthermore, both forms of deprivation of liberty serve both to protect the public from criminal offenders and to reintegrate the persons affected into society.[748] Given the lack of a time limit for preventive detention, it constitutes one of the most serious sanctions, if not *the most serious sanction*, available in German law.[749] In sum, the Court viewed preventive detention as a punishment within the meaning of Art. 7[750] and thus found that the retroactive repeal of the maximum period violated this Article.[751]

133 In reaction to this ECtHR judgment, the German legislator revised the Law on Preventive (Custodial) Detention as of 1 January 2011,[752] adopting, inter alia, the Act on Therapy and Detention of Mentally Disturbed Violent Offenders ('Therapy Detention Act'), which permitted dangerous criminals to be placed in closed (therapeutic) facilities.[753] Yet the German Federal Constitutional Court (BVerfG) quickly declared a large part of the reformed rules unconstitutional[754] and a new Law on Preventive Detention was adopted on 5 December 2012.[755] The BVerfG now took the human rights dimension of preventive detention much more seriously. It held that preventive detention constitutes a serious interference in the right to liberty[756] which 'can only be justified in accordance with a strict evaluation of its proportionality, ensuring that the decisions that form the sentence's basis and the structuring of its enforcement meet strict requirements'.[757] Each individual case needs to weigh up the public's need for security against the detainee's right to freedom,[758] taking account of the affected person's legitimate expectation that the preventive detention will come to an end or will not in fact be imposed.[759] Referring explicitly to the ECtHR's reflections on the issue, the BVerfG stressed that the enforcement of preventive detention must differ substantially from the enforcement of ordinary prison sentences (*Abstandsgebot*, or **differentiation/distinction requirement**).[760] The BVerfG considered the restriction of liberty linked to preventive detention as disproportionate since the said requirements had not been sufficiently met.[761] As to the new regulation, the BVerfG made quite an extensive list of requirements to be observed by the legislator: it had to be ensured that preventive detention would only be applied as a last resort, that its enforcement would be structured according to preventive and therapeutic considerations and that its continuation would be regularly reviewed in court.[762]

134 In *Bergmann*, the ECtHR distinguished between preventive detention under the Preventive Detention Act and confinement under the Therapy Detention Act, the latter not being 'a measure imposed following and together with conviction for a criminal offence' but one 'ordered by the civil courts, outside the criminal law context, and aimed at the medical and therapeutic treatment of persons suffering from a mental disorder'.[763] The Chamber also acknowledged the separate detention of the applicant in a separate detention centre[764] under much better conditions with a focus on medical and therapeutic treatment.[765] In the Chamber's view, 'as a result of the changes, adequate treatment of persons in preventive detention with a view to reducing their dangerousness is now at the heart of preventive detention.'[766] The Chamber also sees a difference between the (former) imposition of preventive detention by a trial court as 'additional punishment' and the 'new precondition for the prolongation' of preventive detention in the form of the establishment of a mental disorder.[767] Further, the Chamber stresses the focus on medical treatment and the 'high level of individualised care' in the Rosdorf Preventive Detention Centre.[768] Thus the Chamber concludes that while preventive detention 'as a rule' still constitutes a penalty within the meaning of Art. 7 ECHR, its prolongation with the specific purpose to treat a mental disorder and the specific treatment focus mentioned above entails that 'the punitive element, and its connection with his criminal conviction, is eclipsed to such an extent that the measure is no longer to be classified as a penalty within the meaning' of Art. 7 ECHR.[769]

135 The consequences the ECtHR judgment in *M.* had for around 70 parallel cases[770] – also affected by the retroactive repeal of the maximum period – were highly controversial. Would all the persons concerned have to be released? Case law was not uniform.[771] While in some cases the persons concerned were indeed ordered to be released immediately,[772] the majority of courts judged the continuation of detention to be admissible given the State's duty to protect its citizens until the legal situation was (completely) clarified.[773] In its decision of May 2011, the German Constitutional Court then decreed that in existing cases continued preventive detention was only admissible '*if the detainee's specific circumstances or his or her conduct suggest a high risk of very serious violent or sexual criminal acts*'[774] and if there is evidence of a psychological disorder within the meaning of §1(1) No 1 of the – above-mentioned – Therapy Detention Act.[775] At the same time, the Court (BVerfG) ordered the immediate review of whether these requirements were met in the cases of the persons affected.[776]

136 As to the ***lex mitior* rule**, the ECtHR affirmed in *Scoppola* that Article '7 §1 of the Convention guarantees not only the principle of non-retrospectiveness of more stringent criminal laws but also, and implicitly, the principle of retrospectiveness of the more lenient criminal law.'[777] There are no general exceptions to the latter principle since Art. 7(2) ECHR serves 'only [as] a contextual clarification of the liability limb' of the general rule of non-retroactivity entailed in Art. 7(1).[778] In determining the more lenient criminal law, an abstract comparison of the maximum or minimum limits of the penalties *in abstracto* or on the basis of the domestic court's intention to impose a sentence closer to the maximum or the minimum does not suffice.[779] Rather, as reiterated in *Maktouf and Damjanović*, Art. 7(1) presupposes an *in concreto* test of the applicable penal laws against the specific facts of the case in order to identify the presumed penalties according to each of them and apply the one most favourable to the defendant.[780] Applying this test *in casu*, the Court found that while (*in abstracto*) the applicants' sentences were 'within the latitude' of both provisions in question – and therefore it could not 'be said with any certainty that either applicant would have received lower sentences' had the other provision been applied – there existed (*in concreto*) a '*real possibility*' that the retroactive application of the one provision did operate to the applicants' disadvantage in terms of sentencing, entailing a violation of Art. 7.[781] While this seems to be the correct result, it has been criticised that the majority did not apply the proclaimed test in its concrete terms – test the two provisions against the facts of the case, find the presumed penalties and apply the one most favourable to the defendant – and thus its finding remains 'speculative'[782] and abstract.[783]

Solution, Case 7

137 According to prevailing opinion, the ECHR *cannot be applied* to relationships between citizens as it only operates as a bulwark against human rights violations by the State. Even if a broader view is taken and Art. 2 applied to the conflicts of private individuals, then the wording to Art. 2(1) ('intentionally') could still be used to show that killings in self-defence with a lower mental element than direct intent, e.g. *dolus eventualis* or recklessness, are not subject to its restrictions (cf. above, mn. 112–13).

Solution, Case 8

138 The ECtHR made a distinction between the SAS men's actions and the planning and implementation of the anti-terror operation. There was both a *legal basis* and one of the (conclusive) *grounds for intervention* listed in Art. 2(2).[784] The issue of absolute *necessity* was decisive: as far as the soldiers were concerned, their actions were *ultimately* accepted as justified since they had acted under the (erroneous) assumption that by shooting to kill they were preventing the direct threat of a car bomb being triggered.[785] However, the violation of Art. 2 arose from the manner in which the operation was organised, more specifically from the fact that the British authorities had not prevented the victims from entering Gibraltar even though they were aware of their plan to carry out an attack; thus they had not done everything in their power to prevent the deaths of the alleged terrorists (cf. above, mn. 114).[786]

Solution, Case 9

139 The ECtHR judged the actions of the German investigative authorities to constitute inhuman and degrading treatment within the meaning of Art. 3 ECHR. It took an *individual perspective weighing up the interests involved* as the basis of its judgment. Accordingly, no right not to have to suffer interference by force in one's physical integrity that is not subject to such appraisal can be deduced from Art. 3 ECHR. Nor does the use of evidence gathered in this way violate the right not to incriminate oneself (Art. 6(1)). However, in the *Jalloh* case, the administering of an emetic was *not absolutely necessary*, as it would have been possible to wait until the drugs swallowed had passed through the body. This violation of the Convention results in the exclusion of evidence (cf. above, mn. 121, 123).

Solution, Case 10

140 The ECtHR reached the same decision as the German higher courts (BGH and BVerfG), denying a violation of the prohibition of retroactivity. However, unlike the German courts it referred mainly to the GDR law in force at the time of events: while §27 of the GDR Border Law permitted the use of firearms in the case of crimes, the cases of *Republikflucht*, in which young, unarmed individuals were attempting to escape from the GDR using simple tools such as ladders, did not represent a threat, so that – even according to the existing GDR law at the time – these were not serious cases of illegal border crossing that could have constituted a crime within the meaning of §213(3) GDR StGB.[787] Thus the shots fired were already punishable according to the law of the time (cf. above, mn. 129–30).

Solution, Case 11

141 While the German Constitutional Court denied the applicability of the prohibition of retroactivity to custodial measures, arguing that they do not entail criminal sanctions (penalties), the ECtHR interpreted the term 'punishment' in Art. 7 ECHR autonomously. As preventive detention (as one form of a custodial measure) also represents a form of deprivation of liberty, the implementation of which does not differ significantly from that of a punishment (neither in regard to its concrete execution nor in regard to its enforcement aim), it should be assessed as such. Accordingly, retroactively extending it by repealing the legal maximum period that originally applied constitutes a violation of the prohibition of retroactivity within the meaning of Art. 7 ECHR (cf. above, mn. 132).

C. The Protection of Fundamental Rights by the EU

I. Efforts to Protect Fundamental Rights at the EU level

142 The protection of fundamental rights at the EU level is (indirectly) influenced by the ECHR on the one hand, while on the other hand there are proper efforts at the EU level itself to guarantee and improve the protection of basic rights. In addition to the CFREU, already mentioned at the beginning of this chapter, these efforts focus particularly on safeguarding procedural rights through instruments of secondary law.[788] In particular, the 'exporting' of evidence (made possible by the principle of mutual recognition) risks undermining accused rights through so-called 'forum shopping'; that is, the choice of the jurisdiction with the less developed fair-trial rights.[789] This further worsens the already difficult situation of suspects abroad, who are confronted with a foreign language and an unfamiliar legal system.[790] The ECHR's relevant procedural guarantees – if they are adhered to in practice – offer only a quite general minimum level of protection and do not guarantee consistent standards across EU Member States.[791] Moreover, the ECtHR can only be appealed to once domestic remedies have been exhausted. In this regard, the protection of fundamental rights at the EU level proves itself stronger, as a case can be refered to the CJEU[792] while proceedings are still ongoing and thus national practice can already be monitored at an early stage.[793]

1. Commission Proposal for a Framework Decision on Procedural Rights

143 On the basis of the **Green Paper on Procedural Safeguards**, in 2004 the Commission submitted a 'Proposal for a Council Framework Decision on Certain Procedural Rights in Criminal Proceedings with the Aim of Standardising Defendants' Rights throughout the EU'.[794] This proposal envisaged some minimum guarantees (which fell well below those of the Green Paper), such as the right to legal representation both before and during the main proceedings, the use of interpreting and translation services free of charge, the right to contact consular authorities and the right to be properly informed ('letter of rights').[795] Despite these modest suggestions, the framework decision was never adopted by the Member States.[796]

2. The Stockholm Programme and Its Follow-Up

144 Following the failure of the Commission's Green Paper proposal, the Swedish Council Presidency made the standardisation and strengthening of defendants' rights part of the Stockholm Programme passed on 10–11 December 2009 by the European Council.[797] It defines Union guidelines for the areas of domestic and security policy for **2010 to**

2014. As the first of six items, it plans to '[promote] citizenship and fundamental rights' and as part of this create minimum standards for procedural law.[798] In consultation with the Commission, the implementation process for these goals was given concrete form in a 'roadmap'.[799] This roadmap plans to strengthen the procedural rights of suspects and charged persons through measures – directives based on Art. 82(2)(b) TFEU[800] – in the areas of translation and interpreting services, right to be informed, legal assistance and legal aid, communication with relatives and consular authorities and the creation of special safeguards for suspects who are particularly vulnerable. On 20 April 2010, the Commission presented an 'Action Plan Implementing the Stockholm Programme',[801] which includes a specific schedule in its annex. It led to several directives to be examined in the next section.

145 A '**Post-Stockholm Programme' (PSP)** was meant to succeed the Stockholm Programme but was never adopted.[802] It should have focused on the consolidation and application of the legislative acts adopted so far and further (complementing) codification.[803] Yet several Member States, in particular the UK, made clear at the outset that they will not support any concrete legislative acts to improve defence rights – in line with the opt-outs with regard to the PJCCM already discussed in Chapter 1.[804] In an interim evaluation of the Stockholm Programme the strengthening of suspects' rights and the progressive harmonisation in the area of criminal law was praised.[805] On a private level, with its Agenda 2020 the ECBA[806] recently presented a proposal with a catalogue of minimum guarantees for criminal proceedings.[807]

3. Concrete Legislative Acts (Directives)

146 The first Commission Proposal for a Framework Decision on the **Right to Interpretation and to Translation** in Criminal Proceedings[808] entered into force on 20 October 2010.[809] It has to be interpreted in accordance with the relevant guarantees in the ECHR and the CFREU.[810] Its scope of application covers all criminal proceedings (including those without a cross-border dimension),[811] proceedings for the execution of a European Arrest Warrant[812] and appeals against certain regulatory sanctions (Art. 1(1)–(3)).[813] The directive becomes applicable the moment the person is informed of the suspicion against him by the authorities;[814] it remains applicable until any potential appeal has come to a conclusion (Art. 1(1), (2)). In terms of content, the directive requires Member States to make interpreting services available free of charge (Art. 4) to persons suspected or charged who are not sufficiently familiar with the language of the criminal proceedings throughout the entire proceedings and especially for their contact with their legal counsel (Art. 2(1), (2)). The directive also gives the suspects the right to have all essential documents translated (Art. 3).[815]

147 The directive on the **right to information** in criminal proceedings was adopted in May 2012.[816] Its scope of application essentially is the same as that of the directive on interpretation. Art. 3 requires Member States to ensure that suspects or accused persons are provided promptly with information concerning certain rights, including the right of access to a lawyer, the right to interpretation and the right to remain silent.[817] If an arrest is made, the person charged is to be provided with a letter of rights (Art. 4(1)). This explanation must also include information on further rights, such as the right of access to case materials or the right to have consular authorities informed.[818] Besides this, suspects or accused persons are to be provided with information about the criminal act they are suspected or accused of having committed in such a way that they can effectively exercise the rights of the defence (Art. 6(1)).[819] Detailed information must be provided on the accusation at the latest on submission 'of the merits of the accusation to a court' (Art. 6(3)). According to Art. 7, the person charged must also be granted the right to access the case materials.

148 The third directive of 22 October 2013, resulting from a complex process of negotiations,[820] deals with the **right of access to a lawyer** and the right to have a third party informed and to communicate with third persons and with consular authorities while deprived of liberty.[821] Given the controversies surrounding the directive it has many more recitals (59) than articles (18).[822] The directive applies to persons suspected or accused in criminal and certain administrative proceedings from the time that they are informed of the charges brought against them, as well as to persons arrested to execute an EAW from the time of their arrest (Art. 1).[823] These persons have the right of access to a lawyer (Art. 3)[824] and to the confidentiality of communication with her (Art. 4).[825] Arrested persons must also be given the opportunity to inform a person of their choosing of their arrest (Art. 4), to communicate with third parties while deprived of liberty (Art. 6) and if necessary to communicate with their consular authority (Art. 7).[826] According to Art. 8, these rights can be restricted (though any such derogation must be proportionate and must not prejudice the fairness of proceedings).[827]

This directive should have been implemented by 27 November 2016, but by February 2018 Bulgaria has still not taken the respective implementing measures.[828]

149 This first phase of the implementation of the Stockholm Programme has been criticised as insufficient since, inter alia, the rights guaranteed become effective too late; moreover, some of the individual guarantees are described so vaguely that there is a risk of their being undermined in practice.[829] However, it should not be ignored that the new directives can contribute to a clear improvement of the current situation.[830] Accordingly, if they are implemented inadequately, the Commission may bring the matter before the CJEU according to Art. 258 TFEU.[831] After the transposition time limit has expired, persons affected may invoke the directives directly if needs be.[832] In part, the guarantees contained in the directives also go beyond existing guarantees at the European level.[833] Thus, for example, neither the ECHR nor the CFREU include the right to information set out in Directive 2012/13/EU.[834] In the long term, the standardisation of the procedural guarantees for accused persons should make interstate co-operation between defence counsels easier within the EU, as the procedural guarantees in the various Member States will become more coherent.[835] Even though there is still a need for further regulation, especially in regard to institutional strengthening of the defence, these first steps of the EU towards strengthening the rights of defendants are thus to be welcomed on the whole.[836]

150 In a second phase, the Commission presented a **Green Paper** on the application of EU criminal justice legislation in the field of **detention** in June 2011,[837] in which it focuses particularly on detention conditions in the Member States. The consultation process initiated may result in the introduction of minimum standards for detention conditions and shared prisoners' rights in the EU.[838] Moreover, by 27 November 2013 the Commission had proposed three further **draft directives** on the following themes: strengthening the presumption of innocence and of the right to be present at trial,[839] procedural safeguards for children suspected or accused in criminal proceedings,[840] and legal aid.[841] Subsequently, the proposals have been adopted as Directive 2016/343,[842] Directive 2016/800[843] and Directive 2016/1919.[844]

151 Directive 2016/343 'on the strengthening of certain aspects of the **presumption of innocence** and of the **right to be present at the trial** in criminal proceedings'[845] repeats in Art. 3 the provisions of Arts. 6(2) ECHR and 48(1) CFREU. Accordingly, the *presumption of innocence* only applies to natural persons and to criminal proceedings, as interpreted by the CJEU, but without prejudice to the case law of the ECtHR.[846] The right is triggered at the earliest stages of the proceedings, even before the persons concerned have been made aware that they are suspects or accused persons.[847] There is a general exception allowing public authorities to publicly disseminate information on certain criminal proceedings if this is strictly necessary for reasons relating to the criminal investigation.[848] Moreover, presumptions of facts or law are also allowed.[849]

As far as the *right to be present at the trial* is concerned, this is not an absolute right in the directive.[850] Thus, under certain circumstances, a trial can be held in the accused person's absence, if she has been duly informed of this possibility or is represented by a mandated lawyer.[851] If these conditions are not met, the person concerned has the right to request a new trial in line with the applicable national law.[852] The right to be present can, of course, only be exercised if there are hearings to be held in the first place.[853] National proceedings conducted in a simplified manner following, exclusively or in part, a written procedure (with an optional hearing),[854] or a procedure without any hearing, are permitted in principle, as long as they comply with the right to a fair trial as interpreted by the CJEU and the ECtHR.[855]

The scope of Directive 2016/800/EU on **procedural safeguards for children who are suspects or accused persons in criminal proceedings** applies from the time of arrest to the termination of any appeal proceedings (Art. 2(1) and (2)); 'child' is defined as a person under the age of 18 (Art. 3(1)). The child is granted a range of procedural rights (right to information, right to inform the holder of parental responsibility, right to individual assessment and medical examination, right to be accompanied by the holder of parental responsibility or another 'appropriate adult' during the proceedings, right to appear in person at, and participate in, their trial (Arts. 4 ff., 14 ff.)). The directive furthermore considers the particular strain trials place upon children by (albeit vaguely) limiting any deprivation of liberty – which is only to be applied as a last resort in any case following the consideration of alternative measures – to the 'shortest appropriate period of time' (Art. 10 f.). Furthermore, in situations of deprivation of liberty, specific treatment and accommodation are envisaged (Art. 12) and criminal proceedings must be treated 'as a matter of urgency and with due diligence' (Art. 13).

Directive 2016/1919/EU on **legal aid** contains a definition of legal aid in Art. 3, while Art. 2 includes a comprehensive definition of the directive's scope, which requires in all cases that the person in question has 'a right of access to a lawyer pursuant to Directive 2013/48/EU'; the directive always applies when a decision on detention is taken, and during detention (Art. 2(4) subpara. 2). In criminal proceedings the Member States must guarantee the right to legal aid 'when the interests of justice so require' (Art. 4(1)), whereby Member States are explicitly granted the right to apply a means test, a merits test, or both (Art. 4(2)). According to Art. 4(4), the merits test is deemed to have been met if a person is brought before a competent court or judge in order to decide on detention (lit. a) or is already in detention (lit. b). Furthermore, a person arrested pursuant to an EAW also has a right to legal aid until she is surrendered, or until the decision not to surrender her becomes final (Art. 5(1)).

4. Data Protection

152 Given its importance the – recently adopted – **General Data Protection Regulation**[856] should, albeit briefly and with a criminal law focus, be mentioned here.[857] It is based on Art. 16 TFEU and explicitly invokes Art. 8 CFREU.[858] It calls for an 'equivalent' level of data protection in all Member States.[859] Yet restrictions on the broad data protection regime are permissible in the context of crime prevention/prosecution and the execution of criminal penalties.[860] Personal data may be processed 'for archiving purposes', in particular with regard to the commission of international crimes under (former) totalitarian regimes.[861] Data related to criminal convictions or offences shall be processed 'only under the control of official authority' or, when authorised by (Union or domestic) law, with 'appropriate safeguards for the rights and freedoms of data subjects'.[862] On the enforcement side the Regulation provides for criminal penalties – besides administrative fines – in case of infringement of its rules, including the deprivation of profits which result from the infringement; these 'shall' be laid down by the Member States and shall be 'effective, proportionate and dissuasive'.[863]

153 Apart from that, data protection within the context of crime prevention and criminal prosecution is left to a specific legal Act,[864] adopted the same day, namely the **Police and Criminal Justice Authorities Data Protection Directive.**[865] It sets a common regulatory framework for data processing, trying to keep a balance[866] between the 'free flow of personal data between competent authorities'[867] and the protection of the data subject[868] in the police and criminal justice context. Thus the directive provides for and regulates a set of rights for the data subject; that is, the right to information, to access and to rectification or erasure, as well a right to lodge a complaint, to an effective judicial remedy and to compensation.[869] Yet these rights do not apply 'in the course of an activity which falls outside the scope of Union law',[870] nor to processing 'by the Union institutions, bodies, offices and agencies'.[871] Further, the directive provides for the establishment of an independent State authority responsible for the monitoring of its application in the respective Member State.[872]

II. The Charter of Fundamental Rights (CFREU)

1. Foundations, Particularly the Binding Effect of the CFREU

154 Guarantees relevant to criminal law are to be found in Arts. 47–50 CFREU, essentially modelled after the relevant provisions of the ECHR (as we will see in a moment),[873] but subject to a *general* limitation clause (Art. 52(1) CFREU).[874] While the Charter rights have originally been of secondary importance within the framework of the European system of rights protection, the CJEU's case law has increasingly attached **more importance** to the Charter,[875] and its importance for the future EU criminal law cannot be overestimated.[876] According to Art. 51(1) first sentence CFREU, the Charter applies to the institutions, bodies and other authorities of the EU – and thus also to agencies like Europol and Eurojust, which are involved in the field of criminal prosecution.[877] For the EU Member States – apart from Poland and the UK[878] – the Charter is **binding,**[879] albeit – pursuant to Art. 51(2) second sentence – 'only' insofar as 'they are implementing' EU law[880] and their actions are thus occasioned by Union law.[881] For the transposition of *directives*, this means that the national legislator is bound to the Charter to the extent that the directive determines the national implementation, interpreting any discretion in that regard in line with Union fundamental rights.[882] Apart from this, the protection of fundamental rights is determined in line with national law.[883] By contrast, when transposing *regulations* the Member States are comprehensively bound to the Charter.[884] Issues of detail that go beyond these principles are unclear and remain disputed.[885]

155 In *Åkerberg Fransson*,[886] the CJEU declared itself in favour of a broad interpretation of Art. 51(1) CFREU.[887] *In casu*, the application of

Art. 50 CFREU (prohibition of double jeopardy) was at stake.[888] The Swedish citizen *Fransson* was alleged to have evaded a considerable sum of income and value added tax, following which the Swedish authorities had imposed surtaxes. In addition to this, he was charged with the respective criminal offence by the public prosecution department. The Swedish Court called upon the CJEU to clarify whether criminal prosecution in addition to surtax violated the prohibition of double jeopardy of Art. 50 CFREU.[889] As the charges against *Fransson* also concerned value added tax, which is regulated by Union law (cf. Directive 2006/112/EC[890]), the CJEU determined that the imposition of tax-related sanctions and initiation of proceedings for tax fraud implemented Union law, even though the national rules in question had not been issued to transpose the VAT Directive 2006/112/EC.[891] In the matter itself, the CJEU approved the criminal prosecution alongside the tax sanction as long as the tax penalties were not 'of a criminal nature'.[892] From this decision follows that Member States should also implement Union law when national norms were not issued to transpose directives, but only serve Union law indirectly.[893] The decisive issue is whether a national provision *actually* falls within the scope of application of Union law.[894] At any rate, it seems to be clear that the Charter does not apply to cases that are not shaped by Union law.[895]

156 There is a certain contradiction between the expansion of the scope of application of Union law and of the Charter in the *Fransson* case and the CJEU's decisions in *Radu* and *Melloni*, where the CJEU reduced the Charter's scope of application *within* the system of Union law.[896] Here, the CJEU had to resolve the question whether a Member State could refuse to execute a European Arrest Warrant (EAW)[897] with a view to the obstacles to legal assistance that could possibly arise from the ECHR or the Charter.[898] The CJEU denied this, arguing that the possible reasons to refuse are conclusively dealt with in Arts. 3, 4, 4a of the EAW Framework Decision (FD).[899] The CJEU reasoned that according to Art. 1(2) of the EAW FD, Member States are in principle obliged to execute an EAW.[900] This view, which boils down to an '*enumerative protection of fundamental rights*',[901] is, however, unconvincing. The Charter constitutes primary Union law,[902] and thus should determine the interpretation of secondary Union law, such as the FD EAW, and not the other way around.[903] Moreover, the CJEU has placed – in line with its already above-criticised too integrationist stance[904] – too much emphasis on the interest in an effective administration of criminal justice as expressed by the EAW FD to the detriment of an effective protection of individual rights.[905] Accordingly, the CJEU's interpretation only takes limited account of the nature of the FD EAW.[906] While the CJEU takes Art. 1(2) of the FD EAW into consideration, it ignores Art. 1(3), according to which it shall not have the effect of modifying Member States' obligation to adhere to and respect fundamental and human rights.[907] An interpretation of the EAW FD that obliges arrest warrants to be executed despite serious rights violations, would potentially also be a case for an *ultra vires* (esp. in regard to Art. 6 TEU) or *identity review* by the constitutional courts of Member States.[908] Recent case law of the CJEU seems to have taken into account this criticism. In *Aranyosi and Căldăraru*, the Grand Chamber held that detention conditions in the requesting State must be taken into account by the requested State within the framework of an EAW surrender procedure.[909] If there is 'objective, reliable, specific and properly updated evidence' which indicates that these detention conditions amount to inhuman or degrading treatment,[910] the executing judicial authority must request supplementary information from the issuing judicial authority and postpone its surrender decision until the risk of the said treatment can be 'discounted'. If 'that risk cannot be discounted within a reasonable time', the executing judicial authority may stop the surrender proceedings.[911]

2. Specific Guarantees of Relevance to Criminal Law

a) Procedural Rights

157 Art. 47(1) CFREU guarantees everyone whose rights and freedoms, as guaranteed by Union law, are violated the **right to an effective remedy**.[912] Unlike the above-mentioned Art. 13 ECHR, which only guarantees access to a 'national authority', the Charter requires that the person affected be able to apply to a Court, which need not necessarily be a national one.[913] Beyond this, Art. 47(2) CFREU – once again corresponding to Art. 6 ECHR,[914] but without the latter's limitations to the determination of civil rights and obligations or criminal charges[915] – establishes the right to a **fair and public hearing within a reasonable time**.[916] Furthermore, Art. 47(3) CFREU guarantees the right to be 'advised, defended and represented'. Although this right is not noted explicitly in the ECHR,[917] as far as the right to an effective and adequate defence documented in Art. 6(3)(c) ECHR is concerned, the question arises whether this constitutes any real improvement. Art. 47(3) CFREU provides clarification in that it contains the right to legal aid.[918] The individual guarantees listed in Art. 6(3) ECHR are, in addition, indirectly referred to through Art. 48(2) CFREU (right to respect for the rights of the defence).[919] Using exactly the same wording as Art. 6(2) ECHR, Art. 48(1) CFREU sets out the **presumption of innocence**, 'until proved guilty according to law'.[920]

b) Substantive Criminal Law Rights

158 Similarly to the ECHR, the Charter also protects the right to **life** in Art. 2, but in its para. (2) also explicitly contains the prohibition of capital punishment.[921] Even though Art. 2 CFREU diverges from the wording of the ECHR and its AP VI, a coherent protection of fundamental rights is guaranteed through Art. 52(3) first sentence CFREU – mentioned above. In this way, the drafters of the Charter avoided taking an explicit stance on controversial topics such as euthanasia and abortion,[922] or the admissibility of targeted killings.[923] In this regard, the current case law on the ECHR applies accordingly.[924] At the same time, this approach also incorporates the exceptions of Art. 2(2) ECHR and the emergency clause of Art. 15(1), (2) ECHR into the Charter.[925]

159 The **prohibition of torture** of Art. 4 CFREU is identical with that of Art. 3 ECHR, in terms of both wording and content.[926] Furthermore, Art. 19(2) CFREU explicitly prohibits extradition to States where the person affected is at risk of capital punishment, torture or inhuman treatment.[927] Art. 6 CFREU guarantees – in accordance with Art. 5 ECHR, which is much more strongly differentiated in terms of content[928] – the right to **liberty** and security. Art. 7 CFREU guarantees the right to respect for **family life**. This forms the equivalent to Art. 8 ECHR,[929] with Art. 8 CFREU as a *lex specialis* which additionally places personal data under its protection[930] and thus serves as a rights foundation of the above-mentioned data protection regime.[931]

160 Just like Art. 7 ECHR, the Charter includes the **principle of legality** (*nullum crimen sine lege*) in Art. 49(1), (2).[932] In addition to this,[933] Art. 48(1) third sentence CFREU contains the *lex mitior* rule, which – like the criminal justice systems of many European countries[934] – specifies that the most lenient law be applied between the time of the offence and the sentence. Furthermore, Art. 49(3) CFREU for the first time explicitly[935] sets out the principle of **proportionality**. Neither the (abstract) legally threatened punishment nor the specific sanction applied in each individual case may be disproportionate to the offence committed.[936] Further, Art. 52(1) provides that any limitation to the rights of the Charter shall be prescribed by law and, subject to the principle of proportionality, be necessary and genuinely meet objectives of general interest recognised by the Union or the need to protect the rights and freedoms of others.[937]

III. Special Focus: The European Prohibition of Double Jeopardy

Case 12

161 German citizen S was arrested breaking into a holiday flat in Austria. A trial followed, at the end of which S was given a one-year prison sentence, which he served. After his return the prosecutor's office in his place of residence[938] charged him with a misdemeanour.[939] Does the Austrian sentence represent an obstacle to this new charge?[940] → mn. 193

Case 13

162 The German citizen Brügge is accused in Belgium of having caused bodily injury to a Belgian citizen. After the investigation carried out in Germany at Brügge's place of residence[941] was stopped following payment of a fine,[942] the Rechtbank van Eerste Aanleg Veurne raised the question whether Art. 54 Schengen Convention constitutes a barrier to proceedings against Brügge because of the (anticipated) termination of prosecution in Germany. Will the German termination of proceedings block the prosecution in Belgium?[943] → mn. 194

Case 14

163 The Belgian citizen Van Esbroeck exported drugs from Belgium (in violation of Belgian law) and imported them to Norway the following day (in violation of Norwegian law). Van Esbroeck was apprehended and sentenced in Norway and served part of his prison sentence. Later the Belgian prosecutor's office responsible brought charges against him for exporting narcotics. Was this in line with Art. 54 Schengen Convention?[944] → mn. 195

Case 15

164 During the Second World War, T was in charge of a unit of the Wehrmacht that murdered eight civilians as part of retaliatory action. In 2006, an Italian military tribunal sentenced T *in absentia* to life imprisonment. Can he be prosecuted again in Germany?[945] → mn. 196

1. Legal Bases (Articles 50 CFREU, 54 CISA, 4 AP VII ECHR)

165 The prohibition of double jeopardy is regulated in Art. 54 CISA, Art. 50 CFREU and Art. 4 AP VII ECHR.[946] However, the last only prohibits renewed criminal proceedings in the *same* State and thus has no inter-state effect.[947] By contrast, according to Art. 54 CISA and Art. 50 CFREU every conviction in an EU Member State acts as a barrier to renewed prosecution or conviction in *every other* Member State, i.e. both Art. 54 CISA and Art. 50 CFREU have a transnational effect and are not applicable in merely domestic proceedings.[948] While this is clearer from the wording of Art. 54 CISA (referring to 'one' and 'another' Contracting Party) than that of Art. 50 CFREU ('within the Union'), the rationale of both provisions is clearly to 'Europeanise' – supported by the principle of mutual recognition – the otherwise merely domestic prohibition of double jeopardy,[949] thereby deviating from a human rights provision like Art. 4 AP VII ECHR imposing legal obligations with a mere domestic effect.[950] The guarantee protects against the double or multiple imposition of *penal sanctions*, not merely administrative ones.[951] In substance, Art. 54 CISA and Art. 50 CFREU differ only in that the former requires that 'the penalty has been imposed, it has been enforced, is actually in the process of being enforced or can no longer be enforced under the laws of the sentencing Contracting Party', while Art. 50 CFREU omits the latter enforcement element. We will return to this below.

166 Beyond this, both rules have a different scope of application. While the CISA applies to all Schengen States,[952] the Charter is aimed at the EU and its Member States, although special rules apply to Poland and the United Kingdom.[953] In addition, the *European Convention on the Transfer of Proceedings in Criminal Matters* of 1972[954] and bilateral supplementary agreements on the EU Convention on mutual assistance in criminal matters and area-specific regulations – such as Art. 7 PIF Convention[955] and Art. 10 of the Convention on the Fight against Corruption[956] – refer to the threat of European double jeopardy.[957]

2. Art. 54 CISA

a) Introduction

167 Chapter 3 (Arts. 54–8) CISA is titled 'Application of the **ne bis in idem principle**' (double jeopardy).[958] Its central Art. 54 specifies that a person 'may not be prosecuted in another Contracting Party for the same acts' if her 'trial has been finally disposed of in one Contracting Party', 'provided that, if a penalty has been imposed, it has been enforced, is actually in the process of being enforced or can no longer be enforced under the laws of the sentencing Contracting Party'.[959] However, Art. 55 (1) CISA gives the Contracting Parties the option to declare Art. 54

inapplicable in certain situations and for certain crimes: if the acts took place in whole or in part in their own territory, if the acts constitute an offence against essential interests of the Contracting Party, or if the acts were committed by officials of that Contracting Party in violation of the duties of their office. Germany and Austria have made statements to this effect.[960] In particular, if Art. 55 leads to further prosecution becoming barred due to double jeopardy, then any period of deprivation of liberty is to be **deducted** (Art. 56 CISA).[961] Art. 57 sets out a consultative mechanism between Contracting Parties.

168 It is sometimes assumed that the reservations linked to Art. 55 CISA have become ineffective with the transposition of the Schengen *acquis* into Union law. This view is based mainly on the argument that the Schengen Protocol that regulated the transposition did not refer to the statements made in Art. 55.[962] However, the fact that the Schengen Protocol only aims to transpose the *acquis* into Union law, but not change its content, argues against this. Otherwise, the statements on hot pursuit[963] (which the Protocol also fails to mention) would also have to have become obsolete. This would lead to the highly undesirable result that it would no longer be possible to comprehensively exercise the rights of pursuit and arrest.[964] Thus, as long as Art. 55 CISA is not explicitly repealed, its continued validity should be assumed.[965]

169 As the prohibition of double jeopardy in the Schengen states (with the exception of the Netherlands) only applies to **internal judgments**,[966] the increasing danger of multiple prosecution for the same offence in a 'Europe without borders' represents a significant problem, in both practical and human rights terms.[967] Transnational multiple prosecution and punishment become less and less acceptable the more progress is made in the harmonisation of substantive criminal law.[968] For this reason, the embedding of the prohibition of double jeopardy in **Arts. 54–8 CISA** and **Art. 50 CFREU** is a welcome development in principle.[969] However, we should not ignore that this right only becomes active comparatively late, after a first legally binding decision, and thus does not protect the person accused from multiple parallel investigations.[970]

170 Art. 54 CISA – also to be applied if the CISA has not yet entered into force in the country where the first sentence was issued[971] – requires that a **final judgment** be passed for '**the same act**' and thus requires that a penalty has been enforced or is not possible to enforce ('**enforcement**

element').[972] In case 12, these requirements were met without any problem or complication, as S was sentenced in Austria for a crime he had committed there and served his prison sentence there as well. Thus, while the German double jeopardy prohibition would not help S here (being only applicable to German judgments), Art. 54 CISA 'blocks' the new prosecution and thus operates as a **procedural obstacle** for the whole Schengen area.[973] Moreover, **Art. 50 CFREU** clarifies that not only a renewed conviction, but also *renewed prosecution*, is prohibited.[974]

171 Art. 54 CISA thus has the following requirements:

- final judicial decision ('finally disposed of'),
- the same act ('same acts'),
- the enforcement of the penalty or the impossibility of it (note, once again, that this so-called enforcement element is missing in Art. 50 CFREU and Art. 4 AP VII ECHR!).

b) Final Judicial Decision within the Meaning of Art. 54 CISA ('Finally Disposed Of')

172 It is beyond doubt that a **judgment on the merits of the case by a court** represents a 'final disposition' of the matter within the meaning of Art. 54 CISA and thus further prosecution is barred in the CISA Member States.[975] However, when we venture outside this clearly defined field, the question of what is to be understood by 'finally disposed of' becomes controversial and delimitations are blurred.[976] Thus, for example, the German BGH takes a more *restrictive approach*, stating that 'only verdicts – or at least **judicial decisions** – have the effect of barring further criminal prosecution',[977] which also includes *acquittals*[978] or (judicial) termination of proceedings according to Art. 153(2) StPO.[979] Similarly, the Austrian Supreme Court demanded 'decisions by the prosecutor's office that terminate proceedings have the character of a penalty and are equivalent [to a verdict].'[980] By contrast, the Higher Regional Court of Cologne left the question open whether 'a decision reached with judicial authorisation' falls within the scope of Art. 54 CISA.[981] In academic writings, one can find broader approaches accepting any legally binding **final decision** – for example by the prosecution – with judicial participation[982] or even without judicial participation.[983]

173 The **CJEU** has dealt with this issue within the context of preliminary references – with regard to the conditional termination of proceedings[984] – made by the Higher Regional Court of Cologne

(*Gözütok* case)[985] and the Belgian Rechtbank van Eerste Aanleg Veurne (*Brügge* case, case 13).[986] The CJEU joined both reference proceedings and took a **broad interpretation** of Art. 54 CISA:

> the ne bis in idem principle . . . also applies to procedures whereby further prosecution is barred, such as the procedures at issue in the main actions, by which *the Public Prosecutor* in a Member State discontinues, *without the involvement of a court*, a prosecution brought in that State once the accused has fulfilled certain obligations and, in particular, has paid a certain sum of money determined by the Public Prosecutor.[987]

174 However, in a later decision the CJEU clarified that a termination of proceedings was not sufficient if it had only been ordered because an investigation had already been initiated in another country.[988] While this seems reasonable as otherwise impunity would be the result,[989] the crucial issue is whether the **conditional termination of proceedings**, to be provided for in virtually all criminal justice systems of the Member States, can be understood as a '**final disposition**' within the meaning of Art. 54 CISA. This issue needs to be analysed by way of a grammatical, systematic and teleological interpretation of the relevant part of Art. 54 ('finally disposed of').[990] A **grammatical interpretation** of the term 'disposed of'[991] first highlights the issue that even the authentic-language versions (German, French and Dutch), which are all equally binding,[992] allow for *different interpretations*: while the German and Austrian term *Aburteilung* suggests a judgment on the merits that brings proceedings to conclusion, the French *jugement* and Dutch *vonnis* can be understood more broadly as general (judicial) 'decisions'.[993] If the other official EU languages are also taken into consideration – as they also became binding (though not equally ranking!) with the transposition of the Schengen *acquis* into Union law[994] – then the problems of interpretation multiply but the tendency appears to be that a judicial decision is required.[995] Finally, we should consider that the true meaning of foreign legal terms ultimately is only really accessible within the context of the respective legal systems.[996] Given the continued differences between the legal systems of the Member States and the lack of a 'European procedural law' or common procedural law doctrine, it is not possible to fall back upon a pan-European concept of judgment or judicial decision.[997] A more colloquial interpretation of the concept of judgment in the sense of an 'evaluative decision on a person or matter' does not really lead to a restriction to judicial verdicts.[998] Overall, the wording 'disposed of' thus seems to suggest the requirement of a judicial decision, but this interpretation cannot be taken as absolute given the interpretational difficulties described.[999]

175 Nor can any clear restriction of Art. 54 CISA to judicial verdicts be derived from a **systematic interpretation.**[1000] The German Supreme Court (BGH) deduces from the relationship between Arts. 54 and 58 CISA that the former only prescribes *minimum standards* for a sub-area of the judicial decisions able to end proceedings, namely decisions taken by a judge, as Art. 58 contains a superordinate term with 'judicial decisions taken abroad'.[1001] However, for several reasons this perspective is *not conclusive*. First of all, the term 'judicial decision taken abroad' is unclear as it is not defined in the Schengen Convention, so that nothing can be deduced from it in reference to the (equally undefined) term 'finally disposed of'.[1002] We cannot even exclude the possibility that both terms are referring to the same thing, especially as Art. 58 CISA refers not only to Art. 54, but also to the other rules of Chapter 3 CISA.[1003] Furthermore, the Dutch version of Art. 58 mentions '*rechterlijke* beslissingen', and thus – unlike the BGH – does not restrict Art. 58 to non-judicial decisions ending proceedings.[1004] Lastly, it should be noted that the CISA is based on the *Convention between the Member States of the European Communities on Double Jeopardy*,[1005] the preamble of which refers to the superordinate term 'foreign judicial decisions' as the exclusive focus of the international prohibition of double jeopardy.[1006]

176 If we approach our issue from the perspective of a **teleological interpretation** of Art. 54 CISA, then the question of the purpose of the prohibition of double jeopardy arises. On the one hand, this purpose consists of ensuring **effective transnational prosecution** by dealing with matters that fall under the jurisdiction of several Member States in one of them only; that is, concentrating and effectively utilising the capacity of resources for prosecution through the *mutual recognition* of decisions that end proceedings[1007] within the Schengen area.[1008] On the other hand, this *objective* purpose is countered by a *subjective* one that focuses on the **human rights** limb of Art. 54 CISA: accordingly, the prohibition of double jeopardy – entirely in line with Art. 50 CFREU[1009] – protects citizens from the increased possibility of interferences with their fundamental rights arising from ever closer police and judicial co-operation.[1010] While as broad an interpretation of Art. 54 CISA as necessary is needed to realise this purpose, *efficient* transnational prosecution requires not only resources to be concentrated, but also a kind of '**guarantee of correctness**' (*Richtigkeitsgewähr*), i.e. certainty that the decisions terminating proceedings are correct.[1011] For only when the second prosecuting State is convinced of the correctness of the first prosecuting State's final decision will its need for security be adequately accounted for, and only then will it be able to readily refrain from renewed prosecution. Now, it cannot be denied that the correctness of prosecutors' decisions to terminate proceedings does not carry the same degree of certainty as that of judicial judgments on the merits.[1012]

177 How, then, can the ensuing **conflict in purpose** arising between the objective and the subjective reading of Art. 54 CISA be solved?[1013] According to one view,[1014] a narrow, *substantive offence definition* should be used that restricts the scope of prohibition of further prosecution only for the actual offence referred to by the measure terminating proceedings. This kind of restricted barring then entails a *restricted* transnational *prohibition of double jeopardy*, namely with regard to the concrete offence covered by the terminating decision. Another view is to demand a *substantively (real) final* decision;[1015] that is, a decision that truly terminates proceedings in substantive terms and thus has the effect of acting as a true barrier to a second prosecution. Of course, these proposals suffer from the lack of agreement on the exact meaning and content of a pan-European or part-European definition of *res judicata* (*chose jugée, materielle Rechtskraft*).[1016] Yet another view calls for a 'form of "qualified termination of proceedings" ..., after which – to put it in psychological terms – the individual's confidence that he will have no cause to fear international prosecution within the Schengen area must be adequately protected', this (only) being the case when 'the object of proceedings has been assessed thoroughly by an institution following on from the investigating authority' and thus independent of it.[1017] Concretely speaking, following this approach, decisions in German *Klageerzwingungsverfahren* (procedure to force criminal prosecution) and French *ordonnance de non-lieu* would come within Art. 54 CISA (as long as the suspect has been heard)[1018] but not the Dutch *transactie*.[1019] In a similar vein, but focusing on the parties' perspective, another view suggests that 'a final decision is a decision which is presented to the interested party as being final'.[1020] The finality of the decision shall solely depend upon its presentation to the interested party; that is, whether it was 'presented ... without an express indication that it is only a provisional resolution', regardless of whether it was given by a judge, after a detailed investigation, after a hearing or on recognition of guilt or whether it may be subject to appeal.[1021] Consequently, if the provisional character of the decision is expressly indicated to the defendant it cannot be 'final'.[1022] Thus, under this view, the above-mentioned German and French termination decisions would be considered final.

178 As an **interim result** we can thus note that neither the grammatical nor the systematic interpretation of 'finally disposed of' in Art. 54 CISA provide clear results. While the teleological considerations, as informed by the subjective, rights-oriented reading, suggest a rather broad interpretation of the rule, account needs also to be taken of its objective, prosecution-oriented reading which leads to an at least slight restriction of its otherwise overly broad scope.[1023] Returning to the **CJEU's decision** in *Gözütok/Brügge* following these reflections, the Court's assumption of a final decision within the meaning of Art. 54 CISA ('finally disposed of') seems to go **too far** in regard both to the Dutch *transactie* and to any conditional termination of proceedings (along the lines of §153a StPO). The CJEU considers it decisive that in both cases prosecution was 'discontinued by the decision of an authority required to play a part in the administration of criminal justice in the national legal system concerned',[1024] and that, because the termination of proceedings is dependent on the defendant performing certain obligations, 'the unlawful conduct which the accused is alleged to have committed [is penalised]'.[1025] In contrast, the Court considers the fact that 'no court was involved' and that the decision did 'not take the form of a judicial decision' to be irrelevant, as these formal matters 'do not impinge' on the punitive 'effects of the procedure' described above.[1026] In addition, two things need to be taken into consideration here in the Court's view: on the one hand, Member States' mutual trust in each other's legal systems must be taken as a 'necessary implication'.[1027] On the other hand, anticipated termination is usually only an option for less serious crimes, so that a restrictive interpretation of Art. 54 CISA would privilege those defendants who have committed more serious and extremely serious crimes, for only these usually entail a final disposition by way of a proper judgment on the merits.[1028]

179 While the Court's view that the Art. 54 CISA decision is not necessarily taken by a judge is agreeable,[1029] it is regrettable that the criteria developed by the Court to define the feature of final disposition in Art. 54 CISA, namely action taken by a responsible authority and (punitive) sanctioning[1030] of the person concerned, remain unclear and do not cover the substantive content of the double jeopardy rule exhaustively. In fact, the Court does not positively state the criteria that lead to the barring of further prosecution, but rather merely equates final judgment (final disposition) with double jeopardy.[1031] As far as the requirement of a (punitive) sanction is concerned, the question arises whether this really can constitute a mandatory requirement of European double jeopardy, seeing as there are a series of situations – as, for example, in the refusal to open main proceedings in German law,[1032] French *non-lieu* termination or Dutch formal termination of proceedings by the prosecution – that do not envisage such sanctions but for which double jeopardy can still be assumed, as proceedings can only be continued based on new facts or evidence becoming available.[1033] This criticism of the CJEU's reasoning leads us to reject its result if we are unwilling to regard anticipated termination of proceedings as a truly final disposition within the meaning of Art. 54 CISA due to the above espoused understanding of a true (real) termination of proceedings in substantive terms.[1034] This rejection of the Court's result is, of course, not absolutely compelling, especially not in regard to the subjective, rights-oriented reading of Art. 54 CISA, which the CJEU in fact alludes to when it rejects the privileging of serious offenders.[1035] A more convincing criterion would appear to be whether proceedings can only be reopened if new facts emerge which nullify the initial decision to terminate proceedings. Accordingly, when determining whether double jeopardy in the sense of a true termination of proceedings in substantive terms has actually occurred, it is decisive that the offence can only be prosecuted anew based on new material evidence or facts;[1036] that is, under very limited circumstances as known from revision proceedings.[1037] In other words, Art. 54 CISA does not become applicable, due to the lack of such a substantive (anticipated) termination of proceedings, in all cases where an investigation or prosecution can easily be reopened.[1038] The CJEU took a similar approach in *M.*, where it considered a judicial termination decision for lack of evidence as sufficient since it would allow for a new prosecution only if new (incriminating) facts arose.[1039] In *Kossowski* the Court complemented the requirement of the finality of the decision convincingly with the more substantive criterion of a 'determination . . . as to the merits of the case',[1040] which comes close to the qualified termination of the proceedings mentioned above.

c) The Same Act within the Meaning of Art. 54 CISA

180 Art. 54 CISA also refers to the 'same acts'. Interestingly, the authentic-language versions (German, French and Dutch) use the concept either in the singular (*Tat*) or in the plural (*mêmes faits, dezelfde feiten*). At any rate, here too, **national law** can hardly serve as orientation given the existing differences:[1041] on the one hand 'act' is understood broadly taking recourse to the factual concept of 'continuing relationship' between the acts (*Fortsetzungszusammenhang*) and the normative concept of 'evaluation unit' (*Bewertungseinheit*); on the other hand, double jeopardy is extended to undetected offences for which material is 'on file'; moreover, highly different criteria are adopted in specific areas of criminality, e.g. with regard to offences linked to membership in a criminal organisation or 'organised crime'.[1042] This **legal fragmentation** also argues against a definition of the same act by the first prosecuting State and the subsequent recognition of this definition by the following States based on the principle of mutual recognition.[1043] This would only cement the differences across Europe and thwart the equal treatment of Schengen citizens that is the very aim of Art. 54 CISA. Furthermore, Art. 54 defines the legal consequence of a conviction 'for the same acts' itself and thus constitutes an autonomous European law regulation which also needs to be interpreted autonomously. Accordingly, here again an autonomous **European concept** of 'the same acts' is required, which is to be determined through the recognised methods of interpretation already employed above.[1044]

181 In this respect, the **grammatical** interpretation reveals that the act concept in Art. 54 CISA should not only be understood in factual terms, but that normative aspects should also be taken into consideration.[1045] A **systematic** interpretation is unproductive.[1046] Once again, the **teleological interpretation** is key, and once again we find *a conflict of purpose* between the objective (prosecution-oriented) and subjective (rights-oriented) reading of Art. 54 CISA: while the *subjective* view calls for a broad enough definition in order to offer citizens comprehensive protection from renewed prosecution, the *objective* perspective cautions against an overly broad definition of 'acts' since it can represent an obstacle to effective transnational prosecution.[1047] It should be noted in this context that the notion of a transnational *ne bis in idem* idea is predicated on the *fundamentally* equal protection of legal interests in the respective criminal justice systems. The recognition of the first prosecuting State's decision requires that it protect the interests of all other (Member)

States as effectively as it protects its own. However, recognising this decision is not mandatory in cases where the second prosecuting State has a justified interest *of its own* in renewed prosecution since the legal interests that make it initiate new proceedings have not been sufficiently taken into account by the proceedings in the first State.[1048]

182 This concept of act, which is oriented towards and **guided by the (legal) interests** to be protected, cannot be derived purely factually,[1049] but must take into consideration *normative criteria* which are informed by the State interests to be protected. These interests are expressed by the penal provisions applied by the first prosecuting State for these provisions themselves pursue the protection of certain interests. As a consequence, the second prosecuting State can only legitimately launch a (second) **prosecution of its own** if thereby **legal interests of particular significance** to this State are protected which have not already been covered and thus protected by the penal provisions applied in the proceedings in the first prosecuting State. In regard to the comparison of the respective penal provisions and the legal interests protected, it is sufficient that 'the affected legal interest and the type of attack (e.g. injury or abstract threat) are basically identical in both defined offences'.[1050]

183 In the *Van Esbroeck* case[1051] (case 14), the CJEU[1052] took a decidedly *naturalistic approach* when defining what is meant by 'act' in Art. 54 CISA.[1053] According to this, 'the only relevant criterion for the application of Art. 54 of the CISA is identity of the material acts, understood in the sense of the existence of *a set of concrete circumstances which are inextricably linked together*'.[1054] While in the case to be decided – the inextricably linked illegal export of narcotics from Belgium and their immediate importation to Norway – this approach led to a convincing result, this is not the case in a number of other cross-border constellations: thus it would certainly not make sense if the organisers of Europe-wide major fraud ultimately could choose to turn themselves in for criminal proceedings only in that State where the least damage was caused and in which they cannot be charged with damage caused in a different State according to national law of the former (forum) State. The CJEU's *Van Esbroeck* decision fails to meet the requirement of such constellations as its understanding of the act concept is too formal.[1055]

184 This can already be seen in the follow-up decision *Van Straaten*: here, the issue was export of narcotics from Italy to the Netherlands.

The case was unusual in that the (proven) amount exported (five kilogrammes of heroin) was *not identical* with the (proven) amount imported (one kilogramme of heroin). The CJEU does not seem to challenge this when it decrees apodictically[1056] that in order for Art. 54 CISA to apply, 'the quantities of the drug that are at issue in the two Contracting States concerned or the persons alleged to have been party to the acts are not required to be identical'. Of course, the question arises whether this can really apply when there are greater differences between amounts, for example when the proven exported amount is five kilogrammes but the amount imported is only five grammes and the offender is then only sentenced to a small fine in a liberal country of importation (such as the Netherlands).[1057] Should the (perhaps more repressive) country of exportation be prevented from prosecuting the export of the five kilogrammes (in a manner proportionate to the unlawfulness and blameworthiness of the act), merely because 4,995 grammes of the drug were mysteriously 'blown away' on the perpetrator's journey? Moreover, the CJEU's approach can lead to significant loopholes in prosecution as it does not take the different (*ratione loci*) jurisdictional reach of national courts sufficiently into account.[1058] Thus we can easily imagine that a national court's competence might be limited to single parts of events due to a restrictive *ratione loci* jurisdictional regime. In such a situation it would be unreasonable, however, if this court's judgment then resulted in pan-European double jeopardy even for those aspects of the relevant 'act' (conduct) that have not even been tried, let alone finally disposed of.[1059]

d) The Enforcement Component

185 The enforcement component of Art. 54 CISA consists of **three alternatives** regarding a penalty that 'has been imposed', namely the penalty (i) '*has been* enforced', (ii) 'is actually *in the process of* being enforced' or (iii) 'can *no longer* be enforced under the laws of the sentencing Contracting Party'. While the first alternative, whether the penalty has been enforced through serving a prison sentence, payment of a fine or, for example, through a suspended sentence[1060] or meeting certain set conditions,[1061] is comparatively unproblematic,[1062] it can certainly be an issue for debate when enforcement begins; that is, when the penalty 'is in the process of being enforced' (alternative 2); the third alternative (enforcement 'no longer' possible) entails its own problems as we will see at the end of this subsection.

186 As we have already said above, this enforcement component is missing in **Art. 50 CFREU**, giving rise to the difficult question of the **relationship** between this provision and Art. 54 CISA.[1063] According to one opinion, Art. 50 CFREU as comprehensively binding primary law should supersede Art. 54 CISA, so that the enforcement component is no longer required within the Charter's scope of application.[1064] This opinion relies mainly on the wording of Art. 50 CFREU that is deliberately based upon Art. 4 AP VII, aiming at a parallel interpretation of both guarantees.[1065] Besides this, the fact that the drafter did not simply copy the enforcement clause of Art. 54 CISA into Art. 50 CFREU must be seen as a conscious legislative decision against restricting the prohibition of double jeopardy under the Charter.[1066] Given the effective system of mutual legal assistance within the EU it is furthermore guaranteed that the convicted person can be transferred to the forum State for the purpose of enforcement of the sentence. The enforcement component that makes a new trial and conviction in the State of residence possible is thus unnecessary to prevent enforcement loopholes.[1067]

187 However, it is doubtful whether the formulation used in Art. 50 CFREU can really be seen as a *conscious* decision to forgo the enforcement component. After all, the *travaux* of Art. 50 CFREU refer explicitly to Art. 54 CISA.[1068] More importantly still, the omission of the enforcement component could have dubious legal and political consequences, as even the EU's highly developed mutual legal assistance instruments still have loopholes. One needs only recall the reasons for refusal to execute a request under the EAW FD.[1069] The risk that the convicted person will try to escape the enforcement of his sentence by fleeing to another Member State thus still remains.[1070] Furthermore, the Charter's character must be taken into account when defining the relationship between Art. 50 CFREU and Art. 54 CISA. Art. 50 CFREU is a broadly phrased judicial right, which is rendered more concrete and restricted in scope by the CISA constituting a 'law' within the meaning of Art. 52(1) CFREU.[1071] In other words, Art. 54 CISA is to be understood as a **limiting provision of Art. 50 CFREU**, so that the scope of the European prohibition of double jeopardy continues to be defined by Art. 54 CISA – including its enforcement component.[1072] This has been confirmed by the CJEU (Grand Chamber) in *Spasic*, where the enforcement limb of Art. 54 CISA was seen as a (inherent) limitation of Art. 50 CFREU and therefore subjected to the proportionality test of Art. 52(1) CFREU.[1073] The Chamber held that the enforcement component ('execution condition') of Art. 54 CISA is appropriate for attaining the objective pursued and does not go beyond what is necessary to prevent the impunity of persons definitively convicted and sentenced in an EU Member State.[1074] As to our case 15, this means that Art. 54 CISA continues to be applicable, so that due to the earlier sentence's lack of enforcement renewed prosecution is possible.

188 Where **prison sentences** are concerned, it is sometimes required that these have actually been served,[1075] while sometimes a suspended sentence, where the probationary period has begun, is regarded as sufficient.[1076] The latter opinion is to be endorsed, as the *purpose of the enforcement component*, namely preventing an obstruction of justice through fleeing to another European State,[1077] can also be accommodated by a conditional prison sentence. In such a case, the suspension of enforcement is made subject to certain conditions and/or directions.[1078] If the convicted person violates these, then the suspension can be revoked[1079] and the first prosecuting State can apply to the State of residence for the extradition of the convicted person for the purposes of enforcement[1080] or for the transfer of enforcement.[1081] Renewed prosecution would mean that the second prosecuting State would basically 'equally take power over the first sanction away from the first sentencing State'.[1082] Accordingly, the CJEU decided that a penalty is 'in the process of being enforced' (Art. 54 CISA) when the sentence has become enforceable and that the penalty 'has been enforced' following the expiry of the probation period.[1083] Controversy also surrounds the issue of whether the **failure to pay a fine** – that has been issued in addition to a (suspended) custodial sentence – means that the 'enforcement component' is missing, as the fine and prison sentence are to be seen as one overall sanction, the enforcement of which within the meaning of Art. 54 CISA can only be seen as executed once both partial sanctions have been carried out.[1084] However, the purpose of Art. 54 CISA and of the enforcement component demands a more favourable interpretation for the individual concerned, as the risk of an 'obstruction of enforcement' is countered sufficiently if at least the more severe sanction – the prison sentence – is carried out.[1085]

189 The **third alternative** of the enforcement component is based on the assumption that a penalty '**can no longer be enforced** under the laws of the sentencing Contracting Party', for example due to a statute of limitations, amnesty or pardon.[1086] It covers every State discontinuation of enforcement, for example through extradition of the convicted person, if the continuation of enforcement depends only on the convict's will, such as her choice to return to the country in question.[1087] Ultimately the decision of the first prosecuting State is thus accepted.[1088] Art. 54 CISA also applies when the penalty to which the accused person has been sentenced was never enforceable in the sentencing State due to specific features of procedure. Thus, in *Bourguain*, the CJEU held that a penalty – imposed in the defendant's absence – 'can no longer be enforced' if it had expired because of a statute of limitation.[1089]

e) Alternative Proposals

190 It is clear that multiple prosecutions and thus double jeopardy problems may be avoided at an earlier stage, namely at the level of determining the competent jurisdiction to prosecute the relevant conduct. Along these lines, there have been various initiatives within the EU to combine rules of competence with double jeopardy rules. The **Commission** presented a **Green Paper on Conflicts of Jurisdiction** and *ne bis in idem* towards the end of 2005.[1090] According to this Green Paper, once a certain procedural stage has been reached, a suspension mechanism should be triggered, halting all prosecutions in other Member States.[1091] The Green Paper also proposes creating a list of objective criteria to determine which State should lead the prosecution.[1092]

191 Following on from a **Greek initiative**[1093] and the Green Paper,[1094] the **Framework Decision on Conflicts of Jurisdiction** represents a first general attempt to mitigate positive conflicts of jurisdiction,[1095] at least within the EU.[1096] Its objective is to prevent parallel criminal proceedings against the same person by achieving consensual solutions (cf. Art. 1). The FD is not concerned with setting out a binding hierarchy of criteria for determining jurisdiction,[1097] but with improving Member State co-operation by introducing a '*conflict resolution mechanism* at Union level'.[1098] According to Art. 5(1) FD, all authorities are obliged to contact the competent authorities of another Member State if they have sufficient grounds to assume that said authorities are conducting parallel proceedings in the same matter.[1099] If this is indeed the case, then the authorities of the States in question shall enter into direct consultations in accordance with Art. 10, leading to the concentration of the criminal proceedings in one Member State as appropriate. If no consensus can be achieved, the matter shall be referred to Eurojust if it falls within Eurojust's competence,[1100] and Eurojust can suggest a solution to the conflict of jurisdiction to the Member States. This suggestion is not binding.[1101] However, if a Member State does not wish to follow this suggestion, it needs to give reasons for doing so.[1102] The fact that an obligation to inform and consult is established, but not an obligation to reach consensus, considerably detracts from the effectiveness of this conflict resolution mechanism.[1103] Accordingly, there is no possibility of forcing a State to waive its investigation or prosecution.[1104] If the Member States are unable to reach a consensus, parallel criminal proceedings are still possible. Given the fact that avoiding conflicts of jurisdiction is now an **objective of harmonisation,**[1105] it remains to be seen whether the EU will use its competencies to establish a binding hierarchy of legitimate (genuine) jurisidictional links at some point in the foreseeable future.

192 On a private level, the '**Freiburg Proposal** on concurrent jurisdictions and the prohibition of multiple prosecutions in the EU'[1106] suggests a **three-stage solution.**[1107] At the *first stage* (§§1–5), double jeopardy should be avoided *a limine* through the co-ordination of the Member States responsible;[1108] certain legitimate jurisdictional links are suggested (§1). If this co-ordination fails and multiple prosecutions ensue, the *ne bis in idem* rule set out in §6 intervenes at the *second stage* (§§6–10). According to this rule, a further prosecution is prohibited if the act in question has already been 'finally disposed of' in a Member State or by a European organ. This is the case if the State in which the first prosecution took place has issued a decision that 'bars future prosecutions and makes reopening subject to exceptional circumstances' (§6(2)(d)). A reopening is only permissible in the State in which the case was first disposed of (§10). If multiple prosecutions occur nonetheless, an 'accounting principle' kicks in at the *third stage*, according to which sanctions that have already been enforced must be taken into account (§11).

Solution, case 12

193 Art. 103(3) Grundgesetz – as many other double jeopardy provisions in domestic jurisdictions – does not prevent double jeopardy as this guarantee (according to prevailing opinion) only applies to internal judgments. However, Germany and Austria are Contracting States of the CISA and thus Art. 54 CISA fully applies here: A was given a final judgment (in Austria), his sentence has been served, and he is to be charged again (in Germany) for the same act (mn. 167 ff.).

Solution, case 13

194 The decisive issue when determining whether a conditional termination of proceedings (here according to §153a German StPO) constitutes a barrier to a (new) prosecution according to Art. 54 CISA is whether the matter has been *finally disposed of*. The CJEU has taken the stance that the punishment of the conduct charged by an authority responsible under national law triggers a European prohibition of double jeopardy. However, these criteria are very formal, as they provide no independent definition of the nature and content of the final decision required. It seems preferable, in line with the considerations above (mn. 173 ff.), to focus on whether the object of the proceedings has been dealt with in *substantive* terms.

Solution, case 14

195 In this case, it was doubtful whether the import and following export of narcotics constituted *the same act* within the meaning of Art. 54 CISA. As in the *Brügge* case, the CJEU affirmed this, using an overly formal line of argument and assuming that an '*idem*' always already exists when the respective charges refer to an identical set of concrete circumstances which are inextricably linked together (for more detail, cf. above, mn. 183–4).

Solution, case 15

196 The European prohibition of double jeopardy of Art. 50(1) CFREU could act as a barrier to renewed criminal proceedings in Germany. However, this rule is not applicable for two reasons: on the one hand, the trial makes no reference to Union law, which is why the Charter does not apply (Art. 51(1) CFREU; see above, mn. 154–5).[1109] On the other hand, the person charged has not served the prison sentence yet, so that a new conviction is possible due to the continued applicability of Art. 54 CISA (for more detail, cf. above, mn. 185).

Notes

1. On some of the earliest attempts regarding human rights protection in the process of European integration, see de Búrca, in Craig and de Búrca, *Evolution of EU Law* (2011), pp. 467 ff.
2. On the origins, cf. CJEU, *Internationale Handelsgesellschaft mbH* v. *Einfuhr- und Vorratsstelle für Getreide und Futtermittel*, No C-11/70 (ECLI:EU:C:1970:114), Judgment (17 December 1970), paras. 3–4 ('respect for fundamental rights forms an integral part of the general principles of law protected by the Court of Justice. The protection of such rights, whilst inspired by the constitutional traditions common to the Member States, must be ensured within the framework of the structure and objectives of the Community'); cf. also Pache and Rösch, *EuR*, 44 (2009), 771–2; Schütze, *EU Law* (2015), pp. 433 ff.; critical of the differences in the constitutional traditions of the Member States and the ensuing fragmentation, Douglas-Scott, *HRLR*, 11 (2011), 669–73.
3. Main text, mn. 16 ff.
4. Main text, mn. 154 ff.

5. On this development, cf. Niedobitek, in Merten and Papier, *Handbuch der Grundrechte*, vi/1 (2010), p. 923 mn. 1 ff.; generally Chalmers, Davies and Monti, *EU Law* (2014), pp. 35–6; on the CFREU's importance for the work of the Commission, cf. European Commission, *Strategy for the Effective Implementation of the CFREU* (2010), pp. 5 ff; Jähnke and Schramm, Europäisches Strafrecht (2017), §9 mn. 57. The EU's increased focus on fundamental rights is also reflected in the creation of the European Union Agency for Fundamental Rights (Council Regulation (EC) No 168/2007 of 15 February 2007 establishing a European Union Agency for Fundamental Rights, OJEU L 53 of 22 February 2007, 1–14), the task of which is to support the institutions, authorities and agencies of the Union and its Member States in regard to fundamental rights. On this, cf. Härtel, *EuR*, 43 (2008), 489 ff.; von Bogdandy and von Bernstorff, *EuR*, 45 (2010), 141 ff.; von Bogdandy, in Merten and Papier, *Handbuch der Grundrechte*, vi/1 (2010), p. 1241 mn. 4 ff.; Sokhi-Bulley, *HRLR*, 11 (2011), 683 ff.; all incl. further references.
6. Pache and Rösch, *EuR*, 44 (2009), 774; Schweitzer and Dederer, *Staatsrecht III* (2016), mn. 592; cf. also Mayer, *EuR*, 44 (2009), *Beiheft 1*, 89 ('political declaration with no legally binding effect', orig. 'politische Erklärung ohne rechtliche Bindungswirkung'); and Schorkopf, in Grabitz, Hilf and Nettesheim, *Das Recht der EU*, i (2017), Art. 6 EUV mn. 21; on using the CFREU as an aid for interpretation, cf. Kokott and Sobotta, *EuGRZ*, 37 (2010), 265; Peers, *ERA Forum*, 11 (2011), 573.
7. Fassbender, *NVwZ*, 29 (2010), 1049; Pache and Rösch, *EuR*, 44 (2009), 774; Satzger, *International and European Criminal Law* (2018), §9 mn. 16; Satzger, *Internationales und Europäisches Strafrecht* (2016), §11 mn. 15; Schorkopf, in Grabitz, Hilf and Nettesheim, *Das Recht der EU*, i (2017), Art. 6 EUV mn. 28; Kingreen, in Callies and Ruffert, *EUV/AEUV-Kommentar* (2016), Art. 6 EUV mn. 12; Naumann, *EuR*, 43 (2008), 424; Kokott and Sobotta, *EuGRZ*, 37 (2010), 267; Douglas-Scott, *HRLR* 11 (2011), 651; Schütze, *EU Law* (2015), pp. 448–9.
8. Cf. Main text, mn. 142.
9. Cf. Main text, mn. 165 ff. On the nature of the prohibition of double jeopardy as a fundamental right, cf. Bieber et al., *Die EU* (2016), §16 mn. 15.
10. For a more critical view, cf. Douglas-Scott, *HRLR*, 11 (2011), 678–80 ('no clearly developed, substantive sense of human rights'; 'EU cannot be constructed as a human rights organisation merely on the back of dimensions of human rights protection necessary to ensure economic integration'; 'The EU's very design reveals its limited capability as a human rights organisation').
11. Thus Lindner, *EuR*, 42 (2007), 160 incl. further references (orig. 'grundrechtlichen Mehrebenen-System'). For a similar stance, cf. Schorkopf, in Grabitz, Hilf and Nettesheim, *Das Recht der EU*, i (2017), Art. 6 mn. 13 ('pluralism of legal sources in the protection of fundamental rights', orig. 'Rechtsquellenpluralismus beim Grundrechtsschutz') and Mehde, *EuGRZ*, 35 (2008), 269.
12. Cf. Van der Heyning, *Fundamental Rights Lost in Complexity* (2011); Douglas-Scott, *HRLR*, 11 (2011), 648, 682 ('complexity, rather than human rights protection itself, which has increased most').
13. Cf. also the overview provided in Satzger, *International and European Criminal Law* (2018), §9 mn. 11 ff.; Satzger, *Internationales und Europäisches Strafrecht* (2016), §11 mn. 10 ff.; Schorkopf, in Grabitz, Hilf and Nettesheim, *Das Recht der EU*, i (2017), Art. 6 EUV mn. 18; Postberg, *Zusammenwirken von EMRK,*

Grundgesetz und EU-Grundrechtecharta (2008), p. 453; in particular on the relationship between the GG (German Basic Law) and Art. 6 CFREU, see Brunhöber, *ZIS*, 5 (2010), 761 ff.; in more detail, cf. Ambos, *Internationales Strafrecht* (2008), §10 mn. 8.

14. In **Austria**, the ECHR is a federal constitutional law with 'constitutionally guaranteed rights' (Art. 144 Austrian Federal Constitutional Law). In **Switzerland**, violations of the ECHR can be contested directly – as constitutional rights within the meaning of Art. 189(1a) Federal Constitution – through constitutional appeals. On this, cf. Thurnherr, in Keller and Stone Sweet, *A Europe of Rights* (2008), pp. 311 ff.; Grabenwarter and Pabel, *EMRK* (2016), §3 mn. 2–3; previously Ambos, *ZStW*, 115 (2003), 588–9 with further references in nn. 38–9, 42.
15. Cf. Art. 55 **French** Constitution; on this, cf. also Mellech, *Die Rezeption der EMRK* (2012), pp. 13 ff., 81 ff., 111 ff.; Lambert, Abdelgawad and Weber, in Keller and Stone Sweet, *A Europe of Rights* (2008), pp. 115 ff.; Grabenwarter and Pabel, *EMRK* (2016), §3 mn. 4. Cf. also Art. 117(1) **Italian** Constitution, as interpreted by the Italian Constitutional Court (*Corte Costituzionale*), No 348/2007, Sentenza (24 October 2007), para. 4.7 and No 349/2007, Sentenza (24 October 2007), para. 6.2, granting the ECHR rules an intermediate rank between constitutional and national law (*norme interposte*); cf. thereon, Caligiuri and Napoletano, *ItYIL*, 20 (2010), 134 ff.; in the same vein, cf. Arts. 10(2), 96(1) and 95(1) **Spanish** Consitution; on Italy and Spain, see also Candela Soriano, in Keller and Stone Sweet, *A Europe of Rights* (2008), pp. 393 ff. In **Greece**, pursuant to Art. 28(1) Constitution, the ECHR is 'an integral part of domestic Greek law and shall prevail over any contrary provision of the law'; see thereon Billis, in Sieber, Jarvers and Silvermann, *National Criminal Law in a Comparative Legal Context*, 1.2 (2013), pp. 216–17. Cf. also Arts. 9 and 91(1) and (2) **Polish** Constitution (thereon see Garlicki and Kondak, in Motoc and Ziemele, *Impact of the ECHR in Central and Eastern Europe* (2016), pp. 306 ff.; also Krzyżanowska-Mierzewska, in Keller and Stone Sweet, *A Europe of Rights* (2008), pp. 531 ff.); Arts. 8 and 16 **Portuguese** Constitution (thereon Martinico, *EJIL*, 23 (2012), 403–4, 407–8, 416) and Ch. 2, Art. 23 **Swedish** Constitution (thereto Nergelius, *Constitutional Law in Sweden* (2011), pp. 99–101; also Wiklund, in Keller and Stone Sweet, *A Europe of Rights* (2008), pp. 165 ff.).
16. Cf. Art. 59(2) **German** Basic Law (*Grundgesetz*); thereon BVerfG, No 2 BvR 1481/04, Decision (14 October 2004), in *BVerfGE* 111, 307; available in English at www.bundesverfassungsgericht.de/SharedDocs/Entscheidungen/EN/2004/10/rs20041014_2bvr148104en.html, last accessed 27 January 2018; BGH, Nos 5 StR 394/10, 5 StR 440/10, 5 StR 474/10, Judgment (9 November 2010), in *NStZ*, 31 (2011), 149–50; Lambert Abdelgawad and Weber, in Keller and Stone Sweet, *A Europe of Rights* (2008), pp. 107 ff.; cf. also Satzger, *International and European Criminal Law* (2018), §9 mn. 13; Satzger, *Internationales und Europäisches Strafrecht* (2016), §11 mn. 12; Quarthal, *Jura*, 33 (2011), 496–7; Schramm, *JuS*, 53 (2013), 1095; Grabenwarter and Pabel, *EMRK* (2016), §3 mn. 8 ff.
17. UK Human Rights Act 1998, 9 November 1998 (HRA), preamble, available at www.legislation.gov.uk/ukpga/1998/42/pdfs/ukpga_19980042_en.pdf, last accessed 27 January 2018. On the genesis of the ECHR from a British perspective, see Simpson, *Human Rights* (2004), pp. 91 ff. (offering a detailed account of the negotiations and the ratification process (pp. 649 ff., 711 ff., 808

ff.) as well as of the previous attempts of rights protection (pp. 91 ff., 157 ff., 221 ff., 390 ff., 597 ff.)).

18. Cf. HRA, Sect. 2; crit. Douglas-Scott, *HRLR*, 11 (2011), 657; Clayton in Ziegler, Wicks and Hodson, *The UK and European Human Rights* (2015), pp. 98 ff. (crit. of the qualified 'mirror principle'); cf. also Grabenwarter and Pabel, *EMRK* (2016), §3 mn. 6–7.
19. Conservative Party, *Protecting Human Rights in the UK* (2015). On the conservative government's announced withdrawl from the ECHR in times of armed conflict cf. Milanovic, *EJIL:Talk!*, 5 October 2016.
20. Cf. the annual Queen's Speech for 2016 (18 May 2016), available with background notes at www.gov.uk/government/uploads/system/uploads/attachment_data/file/524040/Queen_s_Speech_2016_background_notes_.pdf, last accessed 27 January 2018. Reference is made to the 'Bill of Rights' to '[r]eform the UK human rights framework' with a view to 'better protect against abuse of the system and misuse of human rights law' and 'restore common sense to their application'. The rights of this bill would be based on the ECHR, 'while also taking into account our common law tradition'. Yet, there is no concrete date when a draft bill will be proposed. On this see also Dickson in Ziegler, Wicks and Hodson, *The UK and European Human Rights* (2015), pp. 115 ff.; and Gearty, *On Fantasy Island* (2016); for a historical perspective cf. Bates, in Ziegler, Wicks and Hodson, *The UK and European Human Rights* (2015), pp. 42 ff.
21. Elliott, *Public Law for Everyone*, 18 May 2016.
22. For a nuanced analysis cf. Elliott, *CLP*, 68 (2015), 85 ff., comparing the common law and HRA/ECHR rights protection in light of three interdependent factors, i.e. the normative reach of each system, its protective rigour in terms of effective judicial protection and the constitutional resilience in the face of legislative or administrative incursion; and concluding that the HRA, despite the common law's potential and dynamic development, has made a difference, having 'invigorated' and highlighted 'the capacity' of the former (115–17). See also Dickson in Ziegler, Wicks and Hodson, *The UK and European Human Rights* (2015), pp. 120 ff. (concluding at 132 that a statutory system replacing the HRA 'will not be as protective as the HRA has been').
23. Cf. Anagnostou and Mungiu-Pippidi, *EJIL*, 25 (2014), 215–20, 221–2 (the UK performing best in comparison to Austria, Bulgaria, France, Germany, Greece, Italy, Romania and Turkey, using a sample of 754 judgments); generally on implementation in the UK cf. Donald, in Ziegler, Wicks and Hodson, *The UK and European Human Rights* (2015), pp. 141 ff.
24. Cf. Wagner and Hacker, *Rights Info*, 18 May 2016.
25. Cf. Leach and Donald, *EJIL:Talk!*, 19 December 2015.
26. It is noteworthy in this context that within the framework of the CoE/ECHR, 18 Member States allow prisoners to vote without restriction, 13 States (including the UK) bar prisoners from voting and 12 others limit the right to vote in some way (cf. ECtHR, *Hirst* v. *the UK*, No 74025/01, GC Judgment (6 October 2005), para. 33).
27. ECtHR, *Hirst*, 74025/01. Art. 3 AP I ECHR guarantees the right to free elections, which in the Court's view, however, is not an absolute right but may be restricted due to security or other public policy reasons, leaving a wide margin of appreciation to States Parties (ibid., paras. 60–1, 82). *In casu*, the Court considers that the respective provision (§3 of the Representation of the People Act 1983), while

pursuing a legitimate aim (paras. 74–5), entails a disproportionate restriction of prisoners' voting rights (paras. 76 ff., upholding the Chamber's judgment): 'section 3 of the 1983 Act remains a blunt instrument. It strips of their Convention right to vote a significant category of persons and it does so in a way which is indiscriminate. The provision imposes a blanket restriction on all convicted prisoners in prison. It applies automatically to such prisoners, irrespective of the length of their sentence and irrespective of the nature or gravity of their offence and their individual circumstances. Such a general, automatic and indiscriminate restriction on a vitally important Convention right must be seen as falling outside any acceptable margin of appreciation, however wide that margin might be, and as being incompatible with Article 3 of Protocol No. 1' (para. 82). Thereto from a UK perspective cf. Bates, in Ziegler, Wicks and Hodson, *The UK and European Human Rights* (2015), p. 65.

28. ECtHR, *Anchugov and Gladkov* v. *Russia*, Nos 11157/04 and 15162/05, Judgment (4 July 2013), paras. 101–12, holding that 'the circumstances [*in casu*] are, on their face, very similar to those examined in the Hirst (no. 2) [GC] judgment' (para. 101). '[D]isenfranchisement . . . concerns a wide range of offenders and sentences, from two months . . . to life and from relatively minor offences to offences of the utmost seriousness' and therefore 'Article 32 §3 of the Russian Constitution imposes a blanket restriction [of their right to vote] on all convicted prisoners serving their prison sentence' (para. 105), 'irrespective of the length of their sentence and irrespective of the nature or gravity of their offence and their individual circumstances' (para. 101). Thus, 'although the margin of appreciation is wide, it is not all-embracing' (para. 103) and consequently, 'the respondent Government have [has] overstepped the margin of appreciation afforded to them [it] in this field and have [has] failed to secure the applicants' right to vote guaranteed by Article 3 of Protocol No 1' (para. 110).
29. Cf. Chaeva, *EJIL:Talk!*, 26 April 2016; generally on the relationship between Russia and the ECtHR Chernishova, in Ziegler, Wicks and Hodson, *The UK and European Human Rights* (2015), pp. 401 ff.; Bowring, in Ziegler, Wicks and Hodson, *The UK and European Human Rights* (2015), pp. 415 ff. See also Marchuk, *EJIL:Talk!*, 13 February 2017.
30. On this threat of derogation due to the *lex posterior derogat legi priori* rule, cf. previously Ambos, *Internationales Strafrecht* (2008), §10 mn. 9.
31. BVerfG, No 2 BvR 2365/09, Judgment (4 May 2011), in *BVerfGE* 128, 367–8: 'The text of the Convention and the case-law of the European Court of Human Rights serve, on the level of constitutional law, as interpretation aids to determine the contents and scope of fundamental rights and of rule-of-law principles of the Basic Law, provided that this does not lead to a restriction or reduction – which the Convention itself does not intend' (orig. 'Der Konventionstext und die Rechtsprechung des EGMR dienen . . . auf der Ebene des Verfassungsrechts als Auslegungshilfen für die Bestimmung von Inhalt und Reichweite von Grundrechten und rechtsstaatlichen Grundsätzen des Grundgesetzes, sofern dies nicht zu einer – von der Konvention selbst nicht gewollten – Einschränkung oder Minderung des Grundrechtsschutzes nach dem Grundgesetz führt'). BVerfG, 2 BvR 1481/04, *BVerfGE* 111, 323 is not clear enough: 'The principle that the judge is bound by statute and law (Article 20(3) of the Basic Law (Grundgesetz – GG)) includes taking into account the guarantees of the ECHR and the decisions of the

ECtHR as part of a methodologically justifiable interpretation of the law' (orig. 'Zur Bindung an Gesetz und Recht gehört aber auch die Berücksichtigung der Gewährleistungen der EMRK und der Entscheidungen des Gerichtshofs im Rahmen methodisch vertretbarer Gesetzesauslegung'). Cf. also BVerfG, No 2 BvR 589/79, Judgment (26 March 1987), reprinted in *BVerfGE* 74, 370; BVerwG, No 4 CN 9.98, Judgment (16 December 1999), in *JZ*, 55 (2000), 1052; BGH, No 1 StR 493/06, Judgment (29 November 2006), in *NStZ*, 27 (2007), 167: 'Account is to be taken of the Convention of Fundamental Rights in its interpretation through the case law of the ECtHR when applying German criminal procedural law' (orig. 'Bei der Anwendung des deutschen Strafprozessrechts ist die EMRK in der Auslegung, die sie durch Rechtsprechung des EGMR erfahren hat, zu berücksichtigen'). Cf. also BGH, No 1 StR 554/09, Judgment (9 March 2010), in *NStZ*, 30 (2010), 384; BGH, 5 StR 394/10 et al. (n. 16), pp. 149–50; Kirchhof, *NJW*, 64 (2011), 3683; Pösl, *ZJS*, 4 (2011), 139–40; Grabenwarter, *EuGRZ*, 39 (2012), 509 ff.; Quarthal, *Jura*, 33 (2011), 497; Renzikowski, *ZIS*, 6 (2011), 539; Safferling, *Internationales Strafrecht* (2011), §13 mn. 21; Schramm, *JuS*, 53 (2013), 1095.

32. BVerfG, 2 BvR 2365/09 (n. 31), pp. 367–8.
33. HRA, Sect. 2(1)(a).
34. HRA, Sect. 3(1).
35. HRA, Sect. 3.
36. Simester et al., *Simester and Sullivan's Criminal Law* (2016), pp. 36–41 (discussing the power to reinterpret domestic law and the review of legislation 'on the face').
37. Cf. HRA, Sect. 3(2)(b) and (c); also Simester et al., *Simester and Sullivan's Criminal Law* (2016), pp. 36–36.
38. Simester et al., *Simester and Sullivan's Criminal Law* (2016), pp. 35–6.
39. BVerfG, 2 BvR 2365/09 (n. 31), p. 368. This corresponds to Art. 53 ECHR: 'Nothing in this Charter shall be interpreted as restricting or adversely affecting human rights and fundamental freedoms as recognised, in their respective fields of application, by Union law and international law and by international agreements to which the Union, the Community or all the Member States are party, including the ECHR, and by the Member States' constitutions.'
40. BVerfG, 2 BvR 2365/09 (n. 31), p. 326; Mayer, in Karpenstein and Mayer, *EMRK* (2015), p. 19 mn. 86; Grabenwarter and Pabel, *EMRK* (2016), §3 mn. 12.
41. BVerfG, No 2 BvR 243/60, Judgment (14 January 1960), reprinted in *BVerfGE*, 10, 271, 274; BVerfG, No 2 BvR 731/80, Judgment (17 May 1983), reprinted in *BVerfGE*, 64, 135, 157; BVerfG, No 2 BvR 209/84, Judgment (13 January 1987), reprinted in *BVerfGE*, 74, 102, 128; Bernhardt, *EuGRZ*, 23 (1996), 339–41; Hoffmann-Riem, *EuGRZ*, 29 (2002), 474; Grabenwarter and Pabel, *EMRK* (2016), §3 mn. 8; Esser, *StV*, 25 (2005), 348 ff.; Hirsch, in Griesbaum, Hannich and Schnarr, *FS Nehm* (2006), pp. 61–2.
42. Schmitt, in Meyer-Goßner and Schmitt, *StPO* (2017), Vor Art. 1 MRK, mn. 3–4.
43. For an in-depth discussion of this, cf. Lindner, *EuR*, 42 (2007), 160; cf. also Klip, *European Criminal Law* (2016), pp. 250 ff.; on the different interpretations given the term 'criminal charges' by the CJEU and the ECtHR, cf. Badea, *ERA Forum*, 13 (2012), 308–9; Mylonopoulos, *ZStW*, 121 (2009), 69 ff.; Mylonopoulos, *ZStW*, 123 (2011), 644.

In particular on the controversial relationship between Arts. 54 CISA and 50 CFREU, cf. main text, mn. 186–7.

44. CJEU, *Berlusconi et al.*, Nos C-387/02, C-391/02, C-403/02 (ECLI:EU:C:2005:270), GC Judgment (3 May 2005), paras. 67–9.
45. ECtHR, *Scoppola* v. *Italy*, No 10249/03, Judgment (17 September 2009), para. 38; on this, cf. Bohlander, *CLR*, 58 (2011), 630; ECtHR, *Ullens de Schooten and Rezabek* v. *Belgium*, Nos 3989/07 and 38353/07, Judgment (20 September 2011), paras. 33–4, 56; ECtHR, *Tomasović* v. *Croatia*, No 53785/09, Judgment (18 October 2011), para. 26; ECtHR, *Nada* v. *Switzerland*, No 10593/08, GC Judgment (12 September 2012), paras. 82 ff. On the citation of Union law by the ECtHR in general, cf. Gundel, in Müller-Graff, *FS Scheuing* (2011), pp. 66 ff.; cf. also Saiz Arnaiz and Torres Pérez, *Case Law of the CJEU and ECtHR* (2012), pp. 99 ff.
46. E.g. in CJEU, *Pupino*, No C-105/03 (ECLI:EU:C:2005:386), Judgment (16 June 2005), para. 59, or more recently CJEU, *Aranyosi and Căldăraru* v. *Generalstaatsanwaltschaft Bremen*, Nos C-404/15 and C-659/15 PPU (ECLI:EU:C:2016:198), GC Judgment (5 April 2016), paras. 86–7. For more detail, cf. Polakiewicz, *EuGRZ*, 37 (2010), 14, who even states that the CJEU follows 'the case law of the ECtHR in well-nigh exemplary fashion' (orig. 'Rechtsprechung des EGMR in geradezu exemplarischer Weise'); Saiz Arnaiz and Torres Pérez, *Case Law of the CJEU and ECtHR* (2012), pp. 97 ff.; Krommendijk, *MaastJECompl*, 22 (2015), 812 ff.; cf. also Klip, *European Criminal Law* (2016), p. 250.
47. Satzger, *International and European Criminal Law* (2018), §9 mn. 17; Frenz, *Europarecht*, iv (2009), §2 mn. 37; Kokott and Sobotta, *EuGRZ*, 37 (2010), 266; Schütze, *EU Law* (2015), p. 436.
48. For greater detail, cf. Naumann, *EuR*, 43 (2008), 425 ff.; Niedobitek, in Merten and Papier, *Handbuch der Grundrechte*, vi/1 (2010), p. 923 mn. 95 ff.; Postberg, *Zusammenwirken von EMRK, Grundgesetz und EU-Grundrechtecharta* (2008), pp. 465–6; Ziegenhorn, *Einfluss der EMRK* (2009), pp. 19 ff.; Grewe, *EuR*, 47 (2012), 290 ff.; also Douglas-Scott, *HRLR*, 11 (2011), 655 ('ECHR as minimum standard'); in the same vein, Schütze, *EU Law* (2015), p. 450 ('Convention rights will thus offer a baseline – a minimum standard – for Charter rights', but crit. of the 'highly ambivalent' wording of Art. 52(3) CFREU).
49. On this, cf. Naumann, *EuR*, 43 (2008), 425–6 incl. references on the opposing view. For the same result also Polakiewicz, *EuGRZ*, 37 (2010), 14; Frenz, *Europarecht*, iv (2009), §2 mn. 57–8; Borowsky, in Meyer, *Charta der Grundrechte der EU* (2014), Art. 53 mn. 37; also Kokott and Sobotta, *EuGRZ*, 37 (2010), 267; Schneiders, *Die Grundrechte der EU und die EMRK* (2010), pp. 241, 259.
50. On whether the CJEU is able to provide a stronger or broader protection of fundamental rights in the CFREU's area of application as compared to the ECHR, cf. Naumann, *EuR*, 43 (2008), 430; Frenz, *Europarecht*, iv (2009), §2 mn. 65 ff.
51. Cf. Arts. 13 ECHR and 47 first sentence CFREU; Arts. 7 ECHR and 49 CFREU, and so forth; on the individual fundamental rights, cf. main text, mn. 157–60.
52. Polakiewicz, *EuGRZ*, 37 (2010), 14.
53. Frenz, *Europarecht*, iv (2009), §2 mn. 49; Polakiewicz, *EuGRZ*, 37 (2010), 14.
54. Frenz, *Europarecht*, iv (2009), §2 mn. 39; Hecker, *Europäisches Strafrecht* (2015), §3 mn. 76; Postberg, *Zusammenwirken von EMRK, Grundgesetz und EU-*

Grundrechtecharta (2008), pp. 463–4; Wiethoff, *Das konzeptionelle Verhältnis von EuGH und EGMR* (2008), p. 21.

55. CJEU, *Opinion 2/94 of the Court*, Accession by the Community to the European Convention for the Protection of Human Rights and Fundamental Freedoms (ECLI:EU:C:1996:140) (28 March 1996), paras. 27, 36; CJEU, *Opinion 2/13 of the Court (Full Court)* (ECLI:EU:C:2014:2454) (18 December 2014), paras. 153 ff.
56. Cf. Art. 47 TEU.
57. For example, on 23 December 2012 the EU ratified the United Nations Convention on Rights of Persons with Disabilities; cf. http://europa.eu/rapid/press-release_IP-11-4_en.htm, last accessed 27 January 2018.
58. Schorkopf, in Grabitz, Hilf and Nettesheim, *Das Recht der EU*, i (2017), Art. 6 EUV mn. 40; Pache and Rösch, *EuR*, 44 (2009), 779. Cf. also European Commission, *Strategy for the Effective Implementation of the CFREU* (2010), p. 3.
59. Cf. Art. 59(1) first sentence ECHR and Art. 4 CES.
60. In more detail, see Bowring, *GoJIL*, 2 (2010), 589 ff.
61. Protocol No 8 relating to Article 6(2) of the Treaty on European Union on the accession of the Union to the ECHR, OJEU C 83 of 30 March 2010, 273. Among other things, the protocol requires an 'agreement' on the accession. Therefore the EU cannot accede to the Convention with a mere declaration of accession; on this, cf. Uerpmann-Wittzack, *EuR*, 47 (2012), *Beiheft 2*, 175–6.
62. Cf. *eucrim*, 5 (2010), 39. On the history of the negotiations, cf. Obwexer, *EuR*, 47 (2012), 123 ff.; Spaventa, *MaastJECompL*, 22 (2015), 35 ff.; cf. also the website of the Council of Europe with the working documents in question: www.coe.int/en/web/human-rights-intergovernmental-cooperation/accession-of-the-european-union-to-the-european-convention-on-human-rights, last accessed 27 January 2018.
63. Cf. the draft revised agreement on the accession of the European Union to the Convention for the Protection of Human Rights and Fundamental Freedoms in the '47+1' Group, *Final Report to the CDDH* (10 June 2013), pp. 4–12, available at www.coe.int/t/dghl/standardsetting/cddh/cddh-documents/47_1%282013%29008rev2_EN.pdf, last accessed 27 January 2018; for a summary see Raba, *ERA Forum*, 14 (2013), 557 ff.; Spaventa, *MaastJECompL*, 22 (2015), 44–5. On the first draft of June 2011, cf. CDHH, *Report to the Committee of Ministers on the Elaboration of Legal Instruments for the Accession of the EU to the ECHR* (CDDH (2011)009), 14 October 2011, pp. 5–13; CDDH-UE, *Draft Legal Instruments on the Accession of the EU to the CHR* (CDDH-UE(2011)16), 19 July 2011, pp. 2–10; on this, cf. Uerpmann-Wittzack, *EuR*, 47 (2012), *Beiheft 2*, 167.
64. On this, cf. '47+1' Group, *Final Report to the CDDH* (2013), p. 16 para. 5 ('As a result of the accession, any person, non-governmental organisation or group of individuals will have the right to submit the acts, measures and omissions of the EU, like those of every other High Contracting Party, to the external control exercised by the Court in the light of the rights guaranteed under the Convention'). If, in the future, lawsuits can be brought both against the EU and against EU Member States (which implement Union law), it will be necessary to examine in each individual case to which party (the EU or the Member State) the queried act of public authority is to be attributed; on this, cf. Obwexer, *EuR*, 47 (2012), 120; Arndt and Schubert, in Karpenstein and Mayer, *EMRK* (2015), Art. 59 mn. 17 ff.; in detail, Vondung, *Architektur des europäischen Grundrechtsschutzes*

(2012), pp. 172 ff.; cf. also Grewe, *EuR*, 47 (2012), 299 ff. Cf. also Art. 3(3) of the draft agreement which authorises the EU and Member States to become 'co-respondents' to proceedings ('47+1' Group, *Final Report to the CDDH* (2013), p. 7).

65. Cf. also Satzger, *International and European Criminal Law* (2018), §9 mn. 15; Satzger, *Internationales und Europäisches Strafrecht* (2016), §11 mn. 14; Hecker, *Europäisches Strafrecht* (2015), §3 mn. 76; Pache and Rösch, *EuR*, 44 (2009), 782–3; Pache and Rösch, *EuZW*, 19 (2008), 521; Douglas-Scott, *HRLR*, 11 (2011), 660.
66. Art. 216(8) TFEU.
67. Schorkopf, in Grabitz, Hilf and Nettesheim, *Das Recht der EU*, i (2017), Art. 6 EUV mn. 38; Uerpmann-Wittzack, *EuR*, 47 (2012), *Beiheft 2*, 174; Schütze, *EU Law* (2015), pp. 455–6. For a critical stance on this, cf. Obwexer, *EuR*, 47 (2012), 118, according to whom the decision to accede to the ECHR should be within the exclusive competence of the EU.
68. Pache and Rösch, *EuR*, 44 (2009), 785.
69. Satzger, *International and European Criminal Law* (2018), §9 mn. 15; Satzger, *Internationales und Europäisches Strafrecht* (2016), §11 mn. 14; Pache and Rösch, *EuR*, 44 (2009), 785; Obwexer, *EuR*, 47 (2012), 143; a similar view is taken by Uerpmann-Wittzack, *EuR*, 47 (2012), *Beiheft 2*, 173 ('second-level primary law'; orig. 'Primärrecht zweiter Stufe'); cf. also de Búrca, in Craig and de Búrca, *Evolution of EU Law* (2011), pp. 486–90 (pointing out the Union's emphasis on the autonomy and primacy of its own system of human rights protection).
70. Schorkopf, in Grabitz, Hilf and Nettesheim, *Das Recht der EU*, i (2017), Art. 6 EUV mn. 48; Frenz, *Europarecht*, iv (2009), §2 mn. 115; Obwexer, *EuR*, 47 (2012), 118.
71. Frenz, *Europarecht*, iv (2009), §2 mn. 106, 116, 119; European Commission, *Strategy for the Effective Implementation of the CFREU* (2010), p. 3; cf. also de Búrca, in Craig and de Búrca, *Evolution of EU Law* (2011), p. 487 ('EU accountability to the regional human rights system', i.e., to the ECHR).
72. Art. 19(1) TEU.
73. Frenz, *Europarecht*, iv (2009), §2 mn. 117. On the relationship between the CJEU and the ECtHR prior to the accession, cf. Satzger, *International and European Criminal Law* (2018), §9 mn. 17–18; Satzger, *Internationales und Europäisches Strafrecht* (2016), §11 mn. 17–18. On subsequent questions arising from the EU's accession to the ECtHR, cf. Klip, *European Criminal Law* (2016) pp. 258–60; on the legal process, cf. Arndt and Schubert, in Karpenstein and Mayer, *EMRK* (2015), Art. 59 mn. 17; on the joint declaration issued by the presidents of the CJEU and the ECtHR, *eucrim*, 6 (2011), 18–19. On the possible effects on the protection of fundamental rights, cf. Vondung, *Architektur des europäischen Grundrechtsschutzes* (2012), pp. 323 ff.
74. Frenz, *Europarecht*, iv (2009), §2 mn. 117–18; Pache and Rösch, *EuR*, 44 (2009), 786. On the relationship between the ECtHR, the CJEU and the national courts, cf. Hentschel-Bednorz, *Derzeitige Rolle und zukünftige Perspektive des EuGH* (2012), pp. 123 ff., 341 ff.
75. Cf. Chapter 1 above, mn. 20–1.
76. This view is shared by Vondung, *Architektur des europäischen Grundrechtsschutzes* (2012), p. 159; cf. also '47+1' Group, *Final Report to the CDDH* (2013), p. 16 para. 5.
77. Cf. Art. 218(11) first sentence TFEU, according to which the CJEU may deliver an opinion on the compatibility of an agreement with the Treaties at the request of a Member State, the EP, the Council or the Commission.

78. On the different composition of the CJEU, cf. Chapter 5 below, mn. 23.
79. CJEU, *Opinion 2/13*, para. 258. For a mostly critical discussion, see Tomuschat, *EuGRZ*, 42 (2015), 133 ff.; Schorkopf, *JZ*, 69 (2015), 781 ff.; Wendel, *NJW*, 68 (2015), 921 ff.; Nanopoulos, *CLJ*, 74 (2015), 185 ff.; Mitsilegas, *eucrim*, 10 (2015), 91–3; Mitsilegas, *EU Criminal Law after Lisbon* (2016), pp. 140–2 (sacrificing 'individualised case-by-case assessment ... in the name of uncritical presumed mutual trust'); Halleskov Storgaard, *HRLR*, 15 (2015), 485 ff.; Swoboda, *ZIS*, 10 (2015), 362–3, 371–3; Caunes, *ERA Forum*, 16 (2015), 459 ff., esp. 463–6; Krenn, *GLJ*, 16 (2015), 147 ff.; Johansen, *GLJ*, 16 (2015), 169 ff.; Łazowski and Wessel, *GLJ*, 16 (2015), 179 ff.; Peers, *GLJ*, 16 (2015), 213 ff.; Editorial Comments, *CMLR*, 52 (2015), 1 ff.; Douglas-Scott, *UKConstLBlog*, 24 December 2014; Spaventa, *MaastJECompL*, 22 (2015), 45 ff.; crit. of the underlying 'problematic attitude of "European exceptionalism"', Isiksel, *EJIL*, 27 (2016), 565 ff.; defending the *Opinion* Halberstam, *GLJ*, 16 (2015), 105–8, 113 ff., 144–6; generally on the relationship between the ECtHR and the CJEU Kargopoulos, *eucrim*, 10 (2015), 96 ff., arguing in particular that the CJEU deviates from ECHR standards in criminal matters, giving precedence to the efficient administration of criminal justice (96–7).
80. Art. 218(11) second sentence TFEU.
81. Cf. Art. 6(2) TEU second sentence.
82. Protocol No 8 EU, Art. 1 (referring 'in particular' to 'the specific arrangements for the Union's possible participation in the control bodies of the European Convention' and 'the mechanisms necessary to ensure that proceedings by non-Member States and individual applications are correctly addressed to Member States and/or the Union as appropriate').
83. Protocol No 8 EU, Art. 2. The article further requires the agreement to 'ensure that nothing therein affects the situation of Member States in relation to the European Convention'.
84. Protocol No 8 EU, Art. 3.
85. CJEU, *Opinion 2/13*, paras. 157 ('the founding treaties of the EU ... established a new legal order, possessing its own institutions, for the benefit of which the Member States thereof have limited their sovereign rights') and 179 ff. Previously thereon, Douglas-Scott, *HRLR*, 11 (2011), 662–4.
86. CJEU, *Opinion 2/13*, paras. 179–200, concluding that 'the draft agreement is liable adversely to affect the specific characteristics of EU law and its autonomy' (para. 200) and 'does not ensure coordination between Article 53 of the ECHR and Article 53 of the Charter, does not avert the risk that the principle of Member States' mutual trust under EU law may be undermined' (para. 258 first indent).
87. CJEU, *Opinion 2/13*, para. 201.
88. CJEU, *Opinion 2/13*, para. 202.
89. CJEU, *Opinion 2/13*, para. 204.
90. CJEU, *Opinion 2/13*, paras. 204–14.
91. CJEU, *Opinion 2/13*, para. 213; also para. 258 second indent ('does not preclude the possibility of disputes ... being brought before the ECtHR').
92. CJEU, *Opinion 2/13*, paras. 181 ff., 208 ('very existence of such a possibility undermines ... Art. 344 TFEU'); on the reinterpretation of Art. 344 TFEU in Opinion 2/13, see Johansen, *GLJ*, 16 (2015), 169 ff.
93. CJEU, *Opinion 2/13*, paras. 168, 191–5, 258 (para. 192: 'Thus, when implementing EU law, the Member States may, under EU law, be required to presume that

fundamental rights have been observed by the other Member States, so that not only may they not demand a higher level of national protection of fundamental rights from another Member State than that provided by EU law, but, save in exceptional cases, they may not check whether that other Member State has actually, in a specific case, observed the fundamental rights guaranteed by the EU'; para. 193: agreement treats EU merely 'as a State' and thus 'disregards the intrinsic nature of the EU'; para. 258 first indent: 'does not avert the risk that the principle of Member States' mutual trust under EU law may be undermined'). On this also see Meyer, *EuR*, 523 (2017), 173 ff., who sees this as a new understanding of mutual trust on the ECJ's part that is informed by an integrationist approach (cf. Chapter 1 above, mn. 26).

94. CJEU, *Opinion 2/13*, paras. 196 ff., 258 first indent ('makes no provision in respect of the relationship between the mechanism established by Protocol No 16 and the preliminary ruling procedure provided for in Article 267 TFEU').
95. CJEU, *Opinion 2/13*, paras. 249 ff., 258 fourth indent ('fails to have regard to the specific characteristics of EU law with regard to the judicial review of acts, actions or omissions on the part of the EU in CFSP matters in that it entrusts the judicial review of some of those acts, actions or omissions exclusively to a non-EU body'). On the CJEU's limited jurisdiction, see Art. 24 TEU and Art. 275 TFEU; thereon also Plaza Garcia, *ERA Forum*, 16 (2015), 481 ff.; crit. of the CJEU's failure to see the rights dimension of the CFSP, Tomuschat, *EuGRZ*, 42 (2015), 137; Nanopoulos, *CLJ*, 74 (2015), 187.
96. For a fundamental critique, see Tomuschat, *EuGRZ*, 42 (2015), 133–6. On the current relationship between the ECtHR and the CJEU and on the maintenance of the Bosphorus Doctrine according to which there is a presumption of the lawfulness of a State action which interferes in Convention rights and at the same time complies with Union law, as long as the Union's fundamental rights standard corresponds to that of the ECHR (ECtHR, *Avotiņš* v. *Latvia*, No 17502/07, GC Judgment (23 Mai 2016)); on this Glas and Krommendijk, *HRLR*, 17 (2017), 586 ('the tone of the dialogue has thus become a bit harsher on both sides, albeit in a subtle way, for the courts continue to listen, defer, show respect and prevent conflict').
97. Emphasis added.
98. See also Schorkopf, *JZ*, 69 (2015), 784 ('Leerstelle im Gutachten').
99. *View of Advocate General Kokott*, ECLI:EU:C:2014:2475, Opinion Procedure 2/13 (13 June 2014), paras. 130–3, while seeing some room for improvement, endorsing the compatibility of the draft agreement with the Treatise by interpreting Art. 3(6) Draft agreement more broadly ('the powers of the Courts of the EU are by no means limited to examination of the legality of provisions of EU law, but, crucially, extend also to their interpretation' (para. 130), 'to limit the subject-matter of prior involvement to questions of pure legality or validity would be to blatantly disregard the powers of the Courts of the EU' (para. 131), 'the reference to the assessment of compatibility in Article 3(6) of the draft agreement as such is sufficiently broad to include questions of interpretation of EU law and to enable this Court to avail itself of the prior involvement procedure in order to ensure that provisions of EU law are interpreted in conformity with the ECHR' (para. 132).
100. Crit. in this context also Tomuschat, *EuGRZ*, 42 (2015), 137; Mitsilegas, *eucrim*, 10 (2015), 91–2, 94 ('extreme view of presumed mutual trust leading to automatic mutual recognition' which can only be rebutted by overcoming a 'high threshold of systemic deficiency' and thus operates to the detriment of individual rights,

standing in marked contrast to the ECtHR's position, in particular in *Tarakhel* v. *Switzerland* (No 29217/12, GC Judgment (4 November 2014): thorough and individualised examination of fundamental rights of asylum seekers; 'uncriticial acceptance of . . . enforcement aims of the system of mutual recognition'). See also Meyer, *EuR*, 52 (2017), 171 ff., according to whom the principle of mutual trust may well be derived from the principle of loyal co-operation, but was introduced by the ECJ without any further justification, thereby creating 'an important lever through which both the Court itself and the Commission will be able to monitor and steer Member States' loyalty to the Union more closely' (183–4). For a general critique on the concept of mutual trust and recognition, see previously Chapter 1, mn. 25 ff., esp. 27.

101. In a similar vein Nanopoulos, *CLJ*, 74 (2015), 187–8; Wendel, *NJW*, 68 (2015), 923 (damaging the human rights credibility of the Union), 926 (exaggerated concerning own autonomy); Halleskov Storgaard, *HRLR*, 15 (2015), 520 ('excessive autonomy concerns . . . take precedence over the interest in ensuring EU law compliance with international human rights law and European fundamental rights coherence'); Favreau, *eucrim*, 11 (2016), 104 ff. (esp. 108: 'double Europe qui ne le protégeait qu'insuffisament').
102. Cf. Art. 26 CES.
103. Art. 10 CES.
104. For more detail on this, cf. Ambos, *Internationales Strafrecht* (2008), §10 mn. 1–5.
105. On this, cf. Chapter 4 below, mn. 10.
106. For more detail, cf. Chapter 3 below, mn. 2.
107. There are currently 17 Protocols, all available (with further information on their current status) at www.coe.int/en/web/conventions/full-list/-/conventions/webContent/en_GB/7435985, last accessed 27 January 2018.
108. Protocol No 6 to the Convention for the Protection of Human Rights and Fundamental Freedoms concerning the abolition of the death penalty, 28 April 1983 (ETS No 114), as amended by Protocol No 11 to the Convention for the Protection of Human Rights and Fundamental Freedoms, Restructuring the Control Machinery Established thereby, 11 May 1994 (ETS No 155), as from its entry into force on 1 November 1998.
109. Protocol No 13 to the Convention for the Protection of Human Rights and Fundamental Freedoms, concerning the abolition of the death penalty in all circumstances, 3 May 2002 (ETS No 187), entry into force on 1 July 2003.
110. Cf. Art. 38 ECHR.
111. For a good analysis, see Meyer, in Stuckenberg and Gärditz, *Strafe und Prozess* (2015), pp. 796–8; on the relationship with the 'right to truth', cf. ibid., pp. 806–8; in general on this right in recent ECtHR case law (especially the 'extraordinary rendition' cases), ibid., pp. 810–14; also Sweeney, *The ECtHR in the Post-Cold War Era* (2012), pp. 73–8; Fabbrini, *HRLR*, 14 (2014), 99 ff.; Ambos, *EuCLR*, 5 (2015), 108, 111–14.
112. Art. 26 ECHR. On the court's earlier structure cf. Ambos, *Internationales Strafrecht* (2008), §10 mn. 11. On the elections of the judges cf. Drzemczewski, *EHRLR*, 16 (2010), 377 ff.
113. Individual applications can be brought by *any person* or an NGO claiming to be 'the victim of a violation' by a State Party (cf. Arts. 34, 35 ECHR); that is, to be 'directly affected' by the measure complained of (cf. ECtHR, *Lambert et al.* v. *France*, No 46043/14, GC Judgment (5 June 2015), para. 89; also Grabenwarter and Pabel, *EMRK* (2016), §13 mn. 2 ff.; Peters and Altwicker, *EMRK* (2012), §1

mn. 25 ff., §35 mn. 1 ff.; Meyer-Ladewig, *NJW*, 48 (1995), 2815 and Graph 21); Schorkopf, *Staatsrecht* (2017), §8 mn. 55–6. The Court has taken a more flexible approach regarding violations of Arts. 2, 3 and 8 ECHR, allowing for indirect victims (family members or even legally entrusted agencies) to bring an application (cf. ECtHR, *Lambert et al.*, 46043/14, paras. 90–5); in the case of a terminally ill patient, family members may bring an application claiming a violation of *own* rights with regard to Art. 2 (ibid, paras. 112, 115). On the procedure, cf. Meyer-Ladewig and Petzold, *NJW*, 62 (2009), 3752–3; Safferling, *Internationales Strafrecht* (2011), §13 mn. 108–9, 117 ff.; Esser, *Europäisches und Internationales Strafrecht* (2018), §9 mn. 20 ff.; on possible reforms, cf. Keller, Fischer and Kühne, *EJIL*, 21 (2010), 1025 ff.

114. Art. 27 ECHR in conjunction with Rule 49 RC ECtHR.
115. Cf. also Meyer-Ladewig and Petzold, *NJW*, 62 (2009), 3752; Esser, *Europäisches und Internationales Strafrecht* (2018), §9 mn. 23.
116. Art. 28(1) ECHR. See also Grabenwarter and Pabel, *EMRK* (2016), §13 mn. 2; Meyer-Ladewig, *NJW*, 48 (1995), 2815; Oppermann, Classen and Nettesheim, *Europarecht* (2016), §17 mn. 93.
117. Inter-state applications can be brought by Member States on the grounds of a violation of the Convention by other Member States (Art. 33 ECHR). One of the rare examples is the 1967 application of Denmark, Norway, Sweden and the Netherlands against the Greek military regime of the time (cf. Grabenwarter and Pabel, *EMRK* (2016), §10 mn. 1–3; Peters and Altwicker, *EMRK* (2012), §36; Schorkopf, *Staatsrecht* (2017), §8 mn. 57). On 26 March 2007, the Georgian government brought an inter-state application against the Russian Federation because of the alleged arbitrary repression of Georgians living in Russia; for an overview of the case (from Georgia's application to the Grand Chambers Judgment (ECtHR, *Georgia* v. *Russia (I)*, No 13255/07, GC Judment (3 July 2014)), cf. the press release by the ECtHR Registrar, ECHR 196 (2014) (3 July 2014), available at http://hudoc.echr.coe.int/engi=001-145546, last accessed 27 January 2018.
118. Art. 29 ECHR. See also Grabenwarter and Pabel, *EMRK* (2016), §13 mn. 2; Meyer-Ladewig, *NJW*, 48 (1995), 2816.
119. Art. 31(a) 1st alternative in conjunction with Art. 30 ECHR.
120. Art. 43, 31(a) 2nd alternative ECHR.
121. Art. 46(2) ECHR. See also Meyer-Ladewig, *NJW*, 48 (1995), 2814; Hentschel-Bednorz, *Derzeitige Rolle und zukünftige Perspektive des EuGH* (2012), p. 301. On the **national implementation of or compliance with** ECtHR decisions, cf. Hillebrecht, *HRR*, 13 (2012), 279 ff., who assumes a 'compliance rate' of at least 49 per cent (282); also Anagnostou and Mungiu-Pippidi, *EJIL*, 25 (2014), 205 ff. (examining the implementation of 754 judgments in nine countries (see above endnote 23) and finding that 'implementation performance is closely linked to the overall legal infrastructure capacity and government effectiveness of a state'); for a more nuanced approach Voeten, *EJIL*, 25 (2014), 229 ff. (while capacity is certainly an important factor, a more comphrehensive empirical analysis is necessary, inter alia taking into account the nature and contents of the judgments to be implemented); for implementation by national case law cf. Schaiko, Lemmens and Lemmens, in Gerards and Fleuren, *Implementation of the ECHR* (2014), pp. 95 ff.; Lageot, in ibid., pp. 145 ff.; Klein, in ibid., pp. 185 ff.; Gerards and Fleuren, in ibid., pp. 217 ff.; Cameron and Bull, in ibid., pp. 261 ff.;

Masterman, in ibid., pp. 297 ff.). Russia is seen as a particularly problematic case, as it pays compensation following judgments, but fails to make the structural changes necessary to prevent future violations of the Convention, cf. Stewart, *Russland und der Europarat* (2013), pp. 19–20; Hillebrecht, *HRR*, 13 (2012), 287; cf. also Paramonova and Bogush, *ZStW*, 125 (2013), 718–19. At present, Azerbaijan's conduct is particularly problematic, giving rise to discussions whether to launch infringement proceedings (Art. 46 ECHR) that would ultimately lead to the expulsion of the violating state (Art. 8 in conjunction with Art. 3 CoE Statute), cf. Remezaite, *EJIL:Talk!*, 22 March 2017. In detail on the infringement proceedings, see de Londras and Dzehtsiarou, *ICLQ* 66 (2017), 467 ff., who emphasise the effect that the non-execution of ECtHR judgments has on the overall efficacy of the human rights system, but at the same time note that non-execution is primarily a political problem and thus requires a political solution (482 ff.); this is taken up by Donald, *EJIL:Talk!*, 28 April 2017.

122. On the extraterritorial validity of the ECHR in regard to extraterritorial conduct of States Parties (depending ultimately on effective authority and control), with a good overview of the case law ('spatial' and 'personal' models), cf. Milanovic, *EJIL:Talk!*, 27 November 2013; see also Szydlo, *JICJ*, 12 (2012), 276 ff., 283 ff.; Besson, *LJIL*, 25 (2012), 857 ff. On the more restrictive position of the UK Investigatory Powers Tribunal (regarding the right to privacy), cf. Milanovic, *EJIL:Talk!*, 18 May 2016.
123. Art. 44 ECHR.
124. For greater detail on this, cf. Grabenwarter and Pabel, *EMRK* (2016), §15, mn. 1–12; Oppermann, Classen and Nettesheim, *Europarecht* (2016), §17 mn. 95; Peters and Altwicker, *EMRK* (2012), §37 mn. 1 ff.; Hentschel-Bednorz, *Derzeitige Rolle und zukünftige Perspektive des EuGH* (2012), p. 290; on the internal effects of ECtHR case law, see Eisele, *JA*, 37 (2005), 392 ff.
125. Ambos, *NStZ*, 22 (2002), 628, incl. further references; Ambos, in Radtke and Hohmann, *StPO Kommentar* (2011), Art. 6 mn. 5; Hentschel-Bednorz, *Derzeitige Rolle und zukünftige Perspektive des EuGH* (2012), p. 320; Oppermann, Classen and Nettesheim, *Europarecht* (2016), §17 mn. 95; Hecker, *Europäisches Strafrecht* (2015), §3 mn. 29; Jähnke and Schramm, *Europäisches Strafrecht* (2017), §3 mn. 32.
126. Cf. Peters and Altwicker, *EMRK* (2012), §37 mn. 1; Renzikowski, in Strafrechtsprofessoren et al., *GS Keller* (2003), p. 199; Ruffert, *EuGRZ*, 34 (2007), 249–50; Satzger, *Jura*, 31 (2009), 760; Brunhöber, *ZIS*, 5 (2010), 763; Hentschel-Bednorz, *Derzeitige Rolle und zukünftige Perspektive des EuGH* (2012), pp. 100–1, 290 ff.; Hecker, *Europäisches Strafrecht* (2015), §3 mn. 30.
127. Cf. Ambos, *ZStW*, 115 (2003), 589 ff. incl. further references.
128. Ambos, in Radtke and Hohmann, *StPO Kommentar* (2011), Art. 6 mn. 2.
129. It is not only highly relevant for other (regional) human rights systems (for Latin America, for example, cf. Woischnik, *Untersuchungsrichter und Beschuldigtenrechte in Argentinien* (2001), p. 126) but also for the defence rights before international criminal tribunals (regarding the ICC, cf. Croquet, *HRLR*, 11 (2011), 91 ff., affirming, somewhat exaggerated, a 'deferential attitude' of the ICC (94, 122 ff.); also Ambos, *Treatise ICL III* (2016), pp. 57 ff.).
130. On the 'autonomous' interpretation of the ECtHR, cf. Frowein, in Frowein and Peukert, *EMRK-Kommentar* (2009), Einführung mn. 9 and, in detail, Letsas, *EJIL*, 15 (2004), 279, esp. 281 ff., 295 ff.; also Renzikowski, in Strafrechtsprofessoren et al., *GS Keller* (2003), p. 200 and in summary Eisele, *JA*, 37 (2005), 391.

131. Papier, *EuGRZ*, 33 (2006), 1 ff.; Ruffert, *EuGRZ*, 34 (2007), 249 ff.; Esser, *Europäisches Strafverfahrensrecht* (2002), pp. 839 ff.; Kieschke, *Praxis des EGMR* (2003), pp. 69 ff., 237; Bleckmann, *EuGRZ*, 22 (1995), 387–8; Masuch, *NVwZ*, 19 (2000), 1267; Chryssogonos, *EuR*, 36 (2001), 61; Jung, *GA*, 150 (2003), 193; Hecker, *Europäisches Strafrecht* (2015), §3 mn. 30; Ambos, in Radtke and Hohmann, *StPO Kommentar* (2011), Art. 6 mn. 6; a similar view is taken in Beulke and Witzigmann, *NStZ*, 31 (2011), 255; Hentschel-Bednorz, *Derzeitige Rolle und zukünftige Perspektive des EuGH* (2012), pp. 299–300; McGoldrick, *ICLQ*, 65 (2016), 31 ('in effect . . . *erga omnes* effect'); cf. also Andenas and Bjorge, *National Implementation of ECHR Rights* (2011), p. 4; Jähnke and Schramm, *Europäisches Strafrecht* (2017), §3 mn. 32; from a Polish point of view Brodzisz, *ZIS*, 4 (2009), 110.
132. Cf. Esser, *Europäisches Strafverfahrensrecht* (2002), pp. 7, 10, 18 and *passim*; for the same result Busse, *NJW*, 53 (2000), 1074 ff.; cf. also Kühne, *Strafprozessrecht* (2015), §3 mn. 43: 'a kind of European criminal procedure law' (orig. 'eine Art europäisches Strafverfahrensrecht'); Wohlers, *GA*, 152 (2005), 23 ff.; Hörnle, *ZStW*, 117 (2005), 825.
133. EU, *Green Paper on Procedural Safeguards* (2003), pp. 16 ff.
134. Cf. Art. 363a **Austrian** StPO; Art. 457(1)(b) **Dutch** CPP; Arts. 622-1 **French** CPP ('réexamen d'une décision pénale définitive . . . lorsqu'il résulte d'un arrêt rendu par la Cour européenne des droits de l'homme que la condamnation a été prononcée en violation de la convention européenne'); §359 No 6 **German** StPO; Arts. 525(1) No 5 and 525A **Greek** CCP; Art. 540(3) **Polish** CCP (more broadly referring to a 'decision of an international authority'); Art. 954(3) **Spanish** LEC; for **Hungary**, see Karsai and Szomora, *Criminal Law in Hungary* (2015), pp. 215–16. In **Italy**, the Constitutional Court has interpreted Art. 630 Italian CPP – the norm for a revision – to allow for a revision in the case of an ECtHR judgment (*Italian Constitutional Court (Corte Costituzionale)*, No 113/2011, Sentenza (4 April 2011) demanding 'la riapertura del processo, quando ciò sia necessario, ai sensi dell'art. 46, paragrafo 1, della Convenzione per la salvaguardia dei diritti dell'uomo e delle libertà fondamentali, per conformarsi ad una sentenza definitiva della Corte europea dei diritti dell'uomo'). In the **UK**, albeit there is no explicit provision of that kind, a person can go to the Criminal Cases Review Commission and request this body to re-refer his case to the Court of Appeal, which may quash it if it considers it 'unsafe' (for this test see §2 of the Criminal Appeals Act 1968); thereto Donald, in Ziegler, Wicks and Hodson, *The UK and European Human Rights* (2015), pp. 141–7. From a scholarly perspective see Kühl, in Müller-Dietz, *FS Jung* (2007), p. 438; from an English perspective the Rt Hon the Lord Kerr of Tonaghmore, in Ziegler, Wicks and Hodson, *The UK and European Human Rights* (2015), pp. 32–7; from a French perspective Lafourcade, *La réouverture des procédures juridictionnelles* (2014); Grewe, in Ziegler, Wicks and Hodson, *The UK and European Human Rights* (2015), pp. 341 ff.; from a Russian perspective Chernishova, in Ziegler, Wicks and Hodson, *The UK and European Human Rights* (2015), pp. 401 ff.; and Bowring, in Ziegler, Wicks and Hodson, *The UK and European Human Rights* (2015), pp. 415 ff.; for a detailed account from an Italian and a comparative perspective, cf. Mangiaracina, *RIDPP*, 49 (2006), 982 ff.; Parlato, *RIDPP*, 49 (2006), 1010 ff. On the relationship between the ECtHR and the Italian Constitutional Court, see Pollicino, in Ziegler, Wicks and Hodson, *The UK and European Human Rights* (2015), pp. 361 ff.; on the

relationship between the ECtHR and the German Federal Constitutional Court, see Rackow, in Ziegler, Wicks and Hodson, *The UK and European Human Rights* (2015), pp. 379 ff. Of course, the ECHR violation may not lead to a reopening of the case if the respective judgment was not based on this violation; cf. Kühne, *GA*, 152 (2005), 214; for a critical stance, cf. Selbmann, *ZRP*, 39 (2006), 125.

135. The same view has been taken by the *Supreme Court of the Republic of Poland (Sąd Najwyższy)*, No I KZP 14/14, Judgment (26 June 2014). In the same vein previously, Weigend, *StV*, 20 (2000), 388; Ambos, *ZStW*, 115 (2003), 591; a similar stance is taken by Bernhardt, in Geiger, *Völkerrechtlicher Vertrag* (2000), pp. 147, 153; contra the mainstream opinion in Germany: Schmidt, in Hannich, *Karlsruher Kommentar StPO* (2013), §359 mn. 40 (referring to BT-Drs. 12/10 333, pp. 4–5); also Meyer-Goßner, in Meyer-Goßner and Schmitt, *StPO* (2017), §359 mn. 52; Esser, *Europäisches Strafverfahrensrecht* (2002), p. 869; Esser, *Europäisches und Internationales Strafrecht* (2018), §9 mn. 124; crit. of the mainstream view Kieschke, *Praxis des EGMR* (2003), pp. 156 ff.

136. In a similar vein Masuch, *NVwZ*, 19 (2000), 1267 (prevention of similar Convention violations); Okresek, *EuGRZ*, 30 (2003), 170–1; Kühne, *Strafprozessrecht* (2015), §2 mn. 38; Bernhardt, in Geiger, *Völkerrechtlicher Vertrag* (2000), p. 154.

137. In this line, Nita, *Europejski Przegląd Sądowy*, 5 (2010), No 9, 4 ff.

138. In the same vein Peters and Altwicker, *EMRK* (2012), §1 mn. 15–16; conc. Satzger, *International and European Criminal Law* (2018), §9 mn. 26; Satzger, *Internationales und Europäisches Strafrecht* (2016), §11 mn. 25.

139. Arts. 2, 3, 8, 9, 12 ECHR and Arts. 1 and 2 AP I.

140. Art. 14 ECHR, Art. 5 AP VII and AP XII.

141. Arts. 10, 11 ECHR and Art. 3 AP I.

142. Arts. 5, 6 ECHR, Arts. 2–4 AP VII.

143. Cf. main text, mn. 161 ff.

144. Moreover, Hecker, *Europäisches Strafrecht* (2015), §3 mn. 19, mentions Arts. 4(1)–(3) (prohibition of slavery and forced labour), 9 (freedom of thought, conscience and religion), 11 (freedom of assembly and association), 13 (right to an effective remedy) and 14 CFREU (prohibition of discrimination), but does not discuss them in further detail.

145. Art. 18 ECHR. So far this provision has not been given an autonomous role but has only been applied in conjunction with the rights referred to in it in order to avoid their excessive (illegitimate, disproportional) restriction (see e.g. ECtHR, *Gusinskiy* v. *Russia*, No 70276/01, Judgment (19 May 2004), para. 73; ECtHR, *Khodorkovskiy* v. *Russia*, No 5829/04, Judgment (31 May 2011), para. 254; and ECtHR, *Tymoshenko* v. *Ukraine*, No 49872/11, Judgment (30 April 2013), para. 294; for a summary of the case law, see Satzger, Zimmermann and Eibach, *EuCLR*, 4 (2014), 92–109). Yet the provision may attain importance of its own in the context of politically motivated restrictions of rights for the purpose of political persecution (cf. ibid., 91–2, 109–13; on the procedural implications, esp. the standard of proof required to demonstrate that the respective State authorities acted in bad faith, see Satzger, Zimmermann and Eibach, *EuCLR*, 4 (2014), 249 ff., esp. 255–8); on Art. 18 in regard to Azerbaijan, see also Remezaite, *EJIL:Talk!*, 22 March 2017.

146. BGH, No 1 StR 221/99, Judgment (18 November 1999), in *BGHSt* 45, 321.

147. ECtHR, *Teixeira de Castro* v. *Portugal*, No 44/1997/828/1034, Judgment (9 June 1998).
148. ECtHR, *Böhmer* v. *Germany*, No 37568/97, Judgment (3 October 2002); on this, cf. also Hecker, *Europäisches Strafrecht* (2015), §3 mn. 56.
149. ECtHR, *Van Mechelen et al.* v. *the Netherlands*, Nos 21363/93 et al., Judgment (23 April 1997), with concurring notes by Wattenberg and Violet, *StV*, 17 (1997), 620 ff.
150. ECtHR, *Haas* v. *Germany*, No 73047/01, Judgment (17 November 2005).
151. ECtHR, *A.* v. *France*, No 14838/89, Judgment (23 November 1993).
152. ECtHR, *M. M.* v. *the Netherlands*, No 39339/98, Judgment (8 April 2003).
153. On the importance of this guiding principle, cf. Weigend, *ZStW*, 113 (2001), 276; Demko, *'Menschenrecht auf Verteidigung'* (2014), pp. 99 ff. ('process principle at the highest level', orig. 'Verfahrensprinzip auf höchster Ebene'); with regard to Swiss and Austrian criminal procedure in particular, cf. Minelli, in Europäische Anwaltsvereinigung, *Das faire Verfahren* (2005), pp. 29 ff.; Schaerz, in Europäische Anwaltsvereinigung, *Das faire Verfahren* (2005), pp. 51 ff.; Rech, in Europäische Anwaltsvereinigung, *Das faire Verfahren* (2005), pp. 77 ff.; on the historical development, cf. Banach-Gutierrez, *NJECL*, 3 (2012), 89 ff. On the effect of cultural differences in legal systems on the fairness of trials, cf. Krüßmann, *Transnationales Strafprozessrecht* (2009), pp. 149 ff.
154. On the public limb, see e.g. Morscher and Christ, *EuGRZ*, 37 (2010), 272 ff.
155. For a comprehensive analysis of the fair trial as a guiding principle in the European multi-level system see Jahn, *ZStW*, 127 (2015), 549 ff.
156. Ambos, in Radtke and Hohmann, *StPO Kommentar* (2011), Art. 6 mn. 9; Demko, *'Menschenrecht auf Verteidigung'* (2014), pp. 236–7. On the full application of the right with regard to terrorists, see Ambos and Poschadel, *ULR*, 9 (2013), 109 ff.
157. ECtHR, *Violations by Article and by State* (2016), http://echr.coe.int/Documents/Stats_violation_2016_ENG.pdf, last accessed 27 January 2018. On the statistics regarding the length of the proceedings, see also main text, mn. 29.
158. At the other end of the list, one can find more than half of the MS with *no* conviction for an Art. 6 violation (Andorra, Bosnia and Herzegovina, Cyprus, Denmark, Finland, Iceland, Ireland, Luxembourg, Monaco, Norway, San Marino), just *one* (Czech Republic, Georgia, the Netherlands, Poland, Sweden, Switzerland), *two* (Belgium, Estonia, Germany, Latvia, Liechtenstein, Malta, Montenegro, Slovenia) or *three* (France, Italy, the UK).
159. ECtHR, *Violations by Article and by State* (2015), available at www.echr.coe.int/Documents/Stats_violation_2015_ENG.pdf; and ECtHR, *Violations by Article and by State* (2014), available at www.echr.coe.int/Documents/Stats_violation_2014_ENG.pdf, both last accessed 27 January 2018.
160. ECtHR, *Ofner and Hopfinger* v. *Austria*, Nos 524/59 and 617/59, Committee of Ministers Decision (5 April 1963); ECtHR, *Neumeister* v. *Austria*, No 1963/63, Judgment (27 June 1968), para. 22; ECtHR, *Delcourt* v. *Belgium*, No 2689/65, Judgment (17 January 1970), para. 28; ECtHR, *Bulut* v. *Austria*, No 1735/90, Judgment (22 February 1996), para. 44; ECtHR, *Lanz* v. *Austria*, No 24430/94, Judgment (31 January 2002), para. 57; ECtHR, *Fischer* v. *Austria*, No 33382/96, Judgment (17 January 2002), para. 18. Cf. also Demko, *'Menschenrecht auf Verteidigung'* (2014), pp. 255–6, 356 ff. ('rechtliches Gehör und des Rechtsprinzips der Waffengleichheit als der

"Kernausübungselemente" des Menschenrechts des Angeklagten auf Verteidigung im Strafverfahren'); Rzepka, *Fairness* (2000), p. 83; Braitsch, *Gerichtssprache für Sprachunkundige* (1991), p. 124; Kohlbacher, *Verteidigung und Verteidigungsrechte* (1979), pp. 25–6; Wasek-Wiaderek, *The Principle of 'Equality of Arms'* (2000), p. 23; Viering, in Van Dijk et al., *Theory and Practice of the ECHR* (2006), pp. 580 ff.; Satzger, *International and European Criminal Law* (2018), §9 mn. 80; Satzger, *Internationales und Europäisches Strafrecht* (2016), §11 mn. 70; Gundel, in Merten and Papier, *Handbuch der Grundrechte*, vi/1 (2010), p. 349 mn. 105 ff.; Fedorova, *Equality of Arms* (2012), pp. 36 ff. On the significance of equality of arms from a Polish perspective, cf. Brodzisz, *ZIS*, 4 (2009), 109 ff.

161. ECtHR, *Ofner and Hopfinger*, 524/59 and 617/59, para. 1 ('procedural equality of the accused with the public prosecutor'). Cf. also Demko, *'Menschenrecht auf Verteidigung'* (2014), pp. 357 ff. Cf., on the concept of 'prosecution', Sidhu, *Equality of Arms* (2017), pp. 91–4 (considering 'an opponent of the accused ... as one who is not a judge, juror or witness, but is directly part of the prosecution team or, like an *avocat géneral* or similar officer, is a party joined to the proceedings whose position or observation cannot be regarded as neutral').

162. ECtHR, *Borgers* v. *Belgium*, No 12005/86, Judgment (30 October 1991), para. 33; also ECtHR, *Dombo Beheer B V* v. *the Netherlands*, No 14448/88, Judgment (27 October 1993), para. 33; ECtHR, *Bulut*, 1735/90, para. 44; ECtHR, *Lanz*, 24430/94, para. 57; ECtHR, *Fischer*, 33382/96, para. 18; ECtHR, *A. B.* v. *Slovakia*, No 41784/98, Judgment (4 March 2003), para. 55; ECtHR, *Öcalan* v. *Turkey*, No 46221/99, Judgment (12 March 2003), para. 159; on civil proceedings: ECtHR, *Nideröst-Huber* v. *Switzerland*, No 18990/91, Judgment (18 February 1997), para. 23; ECtHR, *Ankerl* v. *Switzerland*, No 17748/91, Judgment (23 October 1996), para. 38. Cf. also Demko, *'Menschenrecht auf Verteidigung'* (2014), pp. 243, 334 ff., 363 ff. ('antithetical participation', orig. 'antithetische Teilnahme'); Haefliger and Schürmann, *Die EMRK und die Schweiz* (1999), pp. 185, 223; Haefliger, *Die EMRK und die Schweiz* (2008), mn. 31–2; Villiger, *Handbuch der EMRK* (1999), p. 307; Merrills, *Development of International Law by the ECtHR* (1993), p. 166; Harris, O'Boyle and Warbrick, *Law of the ECHR* (2014), pp. 413–14; Gleß, *Internationales Strafrecht* (2015), mn. 76; Gleß, *StV*, 33 (2013), 318; Sommer, in Brüssow et al., *Strafverteidigung in der Praxis* (2007), pp. 833, 838–9; Schilling, *Internationaler Menschenrechtsschutz* (2016), §20 mn. 621. On the significance of the principle of fairness when handling evidence from internal investigations, cf. Knauer and Gaul, *NStZ*, 33 (2013), 193–4. On the fundamental elements of equality of arms, Sidhu, *Equality of Arms* (2017), pp. 94–113 (quoting 'Arms', 'Equality' and 'Disadvantage').

163. Cf. ECtHR, *García Alva* v. *Germany*, No 23541/94, Judgment (13 February 2001), para. 1; ECtHR, *Lietzow* v. *Germany*, No 24479/94, Judgment (13 February 2001), para. 6; ECtHR, *Schöps* v. *Germany*, No 25116/94, Judgment (13 February 2001), para. 11; ECtHR, *Öcalan*, 46221/99, para. 166. Cf. also Rzepka, *Fairness* (2000), pp. 85–6; Esser, *Europäisches Strafverfahrensrecht* (2002), p. 401, incl. references in n. 70; Esser, *Europäisches und Internationales Strafrecht* (2018), §9 mn. 225; Sommer, in Brüssow et al., *Strafverteidigung in der Praxis* (2007), pp. 839–9, 841.

164. ECtHR, *Öcalan*, 46221/99, para. 166; ECtHR, *Natunen* v. *Finland*, No 21022/04, Judgment (31 March 2009), para. 39; Tochilovsky, *Jurisprudence* (2014), pp. 443–4; on the right of victims to fair trial, which can also be deduced from this principle, cf. Bock, in Barton and Kölbel, *Ambivalenzen der Opferzuwendung des Strafrechts* (2012), pp. 69 ff.
165. ECtHR, *Barberà et al.* v. *Spain*, Nos 10588/83, 10589/83 and 10590/83, Judgment (6 December 1988), paras. 76–7; Esser, *Europäisches Strafverfahrensrecht* (2002), pp. 624–5. On the issue of the compatibility of **military courts** with the right to a fair trial, cf. Bucherer, *Vereinbarkeit von Militärgerichten mit dem Recht auf ein faires Verfahren* (2005), pp. 37 ff. and, on ECtHR case law in this regard, pp. 43 ff.; and Grabenwarter, *ECHR* (2014), Art. 6 mn. 48.
166. Cf. for example ECtHR, *Kostovski* v. *the Netherlands*, No 11454/85, Judgment (20 November 1989), para. 41; ECtHR, *Windisch* v. *Austria*, No 12489/86, Judgment (27 September 1990), para. 26; ECtHR, *Barberà et al.*, 10588/83, 10589/83 and 10590/83, paras. 67, 78; also ECtHR, *Bönisch* v. *Austria*, No 8658/79, Judgment (6 May 1985), para. 32. On this, cf. also Esser, *Europäisches Strafverfahrensrecht* (2002), pp. 632 ff.
167. Cf. ECtHR, *Pandy* v. *Belgium*, No 13583/02, Judgment (21 September 2006), para. 51 ('juge d'instruction, chargé d'instruire tant à charge qu'à décharge, réponde à des critères d'impartialité'); on this, cf. Kuty, *RevDPC* 87 (2007), 365 ff.
168. ECtHR, *Öcalan*, 46221/99, para. 166. Cf. also Kohlbacher, *Verteidigung und Verteidigungsrechte* (1979), pp. 1, 24; Spaniol, *Recht auf Verteidigerbeistand* (1990), p. 127.
169. Cf. also Demko, *'Menschenrecht auf Verteidigung'* (2014), p. 348; Spaniol, *Recht auf Verteidigerbeistand* (1990), p. 126; Matscher, *ÖRiZ*, 71 (1993), 154 ff.; Sommer, in Brüssow et al., *Strafverteidigung in der Praxis* (2007), pp. 838–9; Jung, *GA*, 150 (2003), 203; Ambos, in Radtke and Hohmann, *Strafprozessordnung* (2011), Art. 6 EMRK mn. 12; Fedorova, *Equality of Arms* (2012), pp. 92 ff., 121 ff.
170. For a fundamental treatment, cf. Trüg, *Lösungskonvergenzen trotz Systemdivergenzen* (2003), pp. 72 ff., 104 ff., 203 ff., 480 ff. Cf. also Jung, *StV*, 10 (1990), 510; Fairchild and Dammer, *Comparative Criminal Justice* (1993), pp. 128–9; Jörg, Field and Brants, in Fennell et al., *Criminal Justice in Europe* (1995), pp. 41 ff.; Tulkens, in Delmas-Marty, *Criminal Process and Human Rights* (1995), pp. 8–9; Sanders and Young, *Criminal Justice* (2010), pp. 13 ff.; Ambos, *ICLR*, 3 (2003), 2 ff.
171. For more detail, cf. Ambos, *ZStW*, 115 (2003), 595; Gaede, *Fairness als Teilhabe* (2005), pp. 191 ff.; Gleß, *Internationales Strafrecht* (2015), mn. 68; Gundel, in Merten and Papier, *Handbuch der Grundrechte*, vi/1 (2010), p. 349 mn. 58; Esser, in Sieber, Satzger and von Heinegg, *Europäisches Strafrecht* (2014), p. 1072; cf. Tiwisina, *Rechtsfragen überlanger Verfahrensdauer* (2010), p. 25; ECtHR, *Pandy*, 13583/02, para. 50, both incl. further references to ECtHR case law and literature. Cf. also ECtHR, *Salduz* v. *Turkey*, No 36391/02, Judgment (27 November 2008), para. 50.
172. Cf. ECtHR, *Murray* v. *the UK*, No 18731/91, Judgment (8 February 1996), para. 66 ('paramount importance'); see also Wasek-Wiaderek, *The Principle of 'Equality of Arms'* (2000), p. 21; Walischewski, *Akteneinsichtsrecht* (1999), p. 87; Braitsch, *Gerichtssprache für Sprachunkundige* (1991), pp. 129–30; Sommer, in Brüssow et al., *Strafverteidigung in der Praxis* (2007), p. 839; Schleiminger, *Konfrontation*

(2001), p. 291; Nack, in Boetticher, *NJW-Sonderheft Schäfer* (2002), p. 51. On these grounds, Ambos, *ZStW*, 115 (2003), 617 ff.; Wohlers, *GA*, 152 (2005), 26 ff. argue in favour of a 'participatory' investigation; Schünemann, in Triffterer, *GS Vogler* (2004), p. 92, is in favour of a 'contradictory balanced pre-trial investigation' (orig. 'kontradiktorisch ausbalancierte[s] Ermittlungsverfahren').

173. Frister, *StV*, 18 (1998), 160 incl. n. 15; Schünemann, *StV*, 18 (1998), 394–5; Schünemann, *StV*, 20 (2000), 159 ff.; Däubler-Gmelin, *StV*, 21 (2001), 361; Braitsch, *Gerichtssprache für Sprachunkundige* (1991), p. 130; Arquint, in Schindler and Schlauri, *Auf dem Weg zu einem einheitlichen Verfahren* (2001), p. 195.
174. Satzger, *International and European Criminal Law* (2018), §9 mn. 70; Satzger, *Internationales und Europäisches Strafrecht* (2016), §11 mn. 60; Satzger, *Jura*, 31 (2009), 766; Esser, *Europäisches und Internationales Strafrecht* (2018), §9 mn. 209.
175. ECtHR, *Bijen* v. *Germany*, No 27804/05, Judgment (1 April 2010), paras. 40 ff.
176. ECtHR, *J. B.* v. *Switzerland*, No 31827/96, Judgment (3 May 2001), para. 44 ('the concept of "criminal charge" within the meaning of Article 6 is an autonomous one'); cf. also Gaede, in Gaede, Meyer and Schlegel, *HRRS-FG Fezer* (2008), p. 24; Ambos, in Radtke and Hohmann, *StPO Kommentar* (2011), Art. 6 mn. 8; Satzger, *International and European Criminal Law* (2018), §9 mn. 69; Satzger, *Internationales und Europäisches Strafrecht* (2016), §11 mn. 59; Bock, in Müller-Graff, *FS Scheuing* (2011), p. 269; Grabenwarter, *ECHR* (2014), Art. 6 mn. 18 ff., goes into greater detail, focusing particularly on the EC's cartel fines; in detail, Gaede, *Fairness als Teilhabe* (2005), pp. 79 ff., esp. 98 ff. as well as Mylonopoulos, *ZStW*, 121 (2009), 70.
177. ECtHR, *Engel et al.* v. *the Netherlands*, Nos 5100/71 et al., Judgment (8 June 1976). On this, cf. Barrot, *ZJS*, 3 (2010), 701–2.
178. ECtHR, *Engel et al.*, 5100/71 et al., para. 82; ECtHR, *J. B*, 31827/96, para. 44. In the *Engel* case, however, the applicability of Art. 6 was rejected due to the brevity of the two-day disciplinary prison term Engel was sentenced to; on the *Engel* case and autonomous interpretation, cf. Letsas, *EJIL*, 15 (2004), 297; Mayer, in Karpenstein and Mayer, *EMRK* (2015), Art. 6 mn. 23 ff.; Grabenwarter and Pabel, *EMRK* (2016), §5 mn. 9 ff. incl. further references; Grabenwarter, *ECHR* (2014), Art. 6 mn. 29; Bock, in Müller-Graff, *FS Scheuing* (2011), p. 270; Maffei, *European Right to Confrontation* (2006), p. 63; Gärditz, in Menzel, Pierlings and Hoffmann, *Völkerrechtsprechung* (2005), pp. 530 ff.; Grabenwarter and Pabel, in Dörr, Grote and Marauhn, *EMRK/GG*, i (2013), Kapitel 14 mn. 20 ff.; Sommer, in Brüssow et al., *Strafverteidigung in der Praxis* (2007), pp. 846–7; Trechsel, *Die EMRK und die schweizerischen Strafprozessrechte* (1974), pp. 16 ff.; Lorenzmeier, *ZIS*, 3 (2008), 23 ff. On the *procedure of taxation* as a criminal charge within the meaning of Art. 6, see Morsch, in Müller-Dietz, *FS Jung* (2007), pp. 612 ff.; cf. also the examples in Mayer, in Karpenstein and Mayer, *EMRK* (2015), Art. 6 mn. 28 ff.
179. ECtHR, *Öztürk* v. *Germany*, No 8544/79, Judgment (21 February 1984), paras. 51 ff.
180. ECtHR, *Perez* v. *France*, No 47287/99, Judgment (12 February 2004), para. 71; thereon Helmken, *StV*, 36 (2016), 457 ff.
181. See e.g. ECtHR, *Mocanu et al.* v. *Romania*, Nos 10865/09, 45886/07 and 32431/08, GC Judgment (17 September 2014), paras. 359 ff., where the Court found that the civil party's right to fair trial was violated due to excessively long proceedings. The

protection this right offers, however, does not amount to the one guaranteed for an accused person; cf. ECtHR, *Perez*, 47287/99, para. 72; and Helmken, *StV*, 36 (2016), 461.

182. ECtHR, *Perez*, 47287/99, paras. 54–6, with an overview of the previous case law in paras. 47–53.
183. ECtHR, *Perez*, 47287/99, paras. 57 ff.; Helmken, *StV*, 36 (2016), 458 ff.
184. ECtHR, *Perez*, 47287/99, para. 65.
185. ECtHR, *Perez*, 47287/99, para. 67 ('where criminal proceedings are determinative only of a criminal charge, the decisive factor for the applicability of Article 6 §1 is whether, from the moment when the applicant is joined as a civil party until the conclusion of those criminal proceedings, the civil component remains closely connected with the criminal component . . . in other words whether the criminal proceedings affect the civil component').
186. ECtHR, *Perez*, 47287/99, para. 66.
187. ECtHR, *Perez*, 47287/99, paras. 69, 71.
188. ECtHR, *Perez*, 47287/99, para. 70; crit. Helmken, *StV*, 36 (2016), 460. In favour of so-called punitive damages (compensation with a punitive character), cf. however, Pinto de Albuquerque and Van Aaken, in Van Aaken and Motoc, *ECHR and General International Law* (forthcoming, https://papers.ssrn.com/sol3/papers.cfm?abstract_id=2781397), pp. 14 ff., arguing that they are already used by the ECtHR (pp. 3 ff. with case law references).
189. On the length of proceedings, cf. Grabenwarter and Pabel, in Dörr, Grote and Marauhn, *EMRK/GG*, i (2013), Kapitel 14 mn. 113 ff. incl. further references; Grabenwarter, *ECHR* (2014), Art. 6 mn. 92 ff.; Esser, *StraFo*, 9 (2003), 336; cf. also BayObLG, No 5 St RR 301/02, Judgment (12 December 2002), in *StV*, 23 (2003), 375 ff. with a commentary by Roxin, *StV*, 23 (2003), 377–9. For more detail on provocation, cf. Renzikowski, in Strafrechtsprofessoren et al., *GS Keller* (2003), pp. 197 ff.; also Korn, *Defizite bei der Umsetzung der EMRK* (2005), pp. 102 ff.; Trechsel, *Die EMRK und die schweizerischen Strafprozessrechte* (1974), pp. 111 ff.; Hecker, *Europäisches Strafrecht* (2015), §3 mn. 55; cf. also the case solution in Ambos, *Fälle* (2010), p. 30 (case 3); previously Ambos, *NStZ*, 22 (2002), 629 ff., 632.
190. ECtHR, *Violations by Article and by State* (2015) and (2016), available respectively at www.echr.coe.int/Documents/Stats_violation_2015_ENG.pdf, www.echr.coe.int/Documents/Stats_violation_2016_ENG.pdf, both last accessed 27 January 2018.
191. ECtHR, *Violations by Article and Respondent State 1959–2016* (2016), available at www.echr.coe.int/Documents/Stats_violation_1959_2016_ENG.pdf, last accessed 27 January 2018.
192. Cf. ECtHR, *Violations by Article and by State* (2015) and (2016).
193. There are not even case statistics by the ECtHR.
194. Cf. Herdegen, *Völkerrecht* (2017), §58 mn. 5 ff.; on the question of attribution, cf. also Mansdörfer, *GA*, 157 (2010), 160 ff. The requirement for proceedings without undue delay applies to the State Party as a whole, so that delays by all State agencies need to be taken into account and not only those caused by the judicial authorities, cf. BGH, No 5 StR 253/09, Decision (4 August 2009), in *NStZ*, 30 (2010), 230–1 (delays caused by the registry offices); BGH, No 2 StR 600/10, Decision (7 September 2011), in *StV*, 32 (2012), 82–3 (delays caused by

the recording clerks). In contrast, delays caused by the temporary suspension and resumption of the proceedings (pursuant to §154 StPO) are not attributable to domestic authorities, cf. BGH, No 2 StR 344/10, Decision (21 December 2010), in *NStZ*, 31 (2011), 651–2.

195. Cf. ECtHR, *Peterke and Lembcke* v. *Germany*, No 4290/03, Decision (3 February 2009), p. 5 ('the reasonableness of the length of proceedings must be assessed in the light of the circumstances of the case and with reference to the following criteria: the complexity of the case, the conduct of the applicant and the relevant authorities and what was at stake for the applicant in the dispute . . . in the present case is the conduct of the applicant . . . which even raises doubts as to whether the applicant can in fact claim to be a victim on account of the length of the proceedings'). For an instructive account of the criteria, cf. Satzger, *International and European Criminal Law* (2018), §9 mn. 74; cf. also Safferling, *Internationales Strafrecht* (2011), §13 mn. 82; Grabenwarter, *ECHR* (2014), Art. 6 mn. 94; more critically Baumanns, *Der Beschleunigungsgrundsatz im Strafverfahren* (2011), pp. 109 ff.
196. Cf. BGH, No 1 StR 153/11, Decision (23 August 2011), in *BGHSt* 57, 1 (delay in Austrian investigation not to be attributed to Germany).
197. On this worrying tendency cf. Roxin, *GA*, 157 (2010), 428 ff.; Wohlers, *NJW*, 63 (2010), 2470–1; Franke, *StV*, 30 (2010), 433–6.
198. See, for instance, BGH, No 1 StR 32/07, Decision (9 May 2007), in *BGHSt* 51, 333–4; BGH, No 1 StR 484/08, Decision (23 September 2008), in *BGHSt* 52, 355.
199. For the leading case, see ECtHR, *König* v. *Germany*, No 6232/73, Judgment (Merits) (28 June 1978), para. 99; see also ECtHR, *Deumeland* v. *Germany*, No 9384/81, Judgment (29 May 1986), paras. 78 ff.; more recently ECtHR, *Lazariu* v. *Romania*, No 31973/03, Judgment (Merits) (13 November 2014), para. 147. The IACtHR pursues a similar approach, cf. IACtHR, *Genie Lacayo* v. *Nicaragua*, Series C 21, Judgment (29 January 1997), paras. 77 ff. and IACtHR, *Juan Humberto Sánchez* v. *Honduras*, Series C 99, Judgment (7 June 2003), paras. 129, 132; thereon Medina, *ACHR* (2014), pp. 201 ff.; see also McDermott, in Sluiter et al., *International Criminal Procedure* (2013), p. 817 (with references to ICL case law).
200. Cf. Paeffgen, *GA*, 161 (2014), 278–9 ('relationaler Begriff').
201. BGH, No 5 StR 376/03, Decision (13 November 2003), in *NStZ*, 24 (2004), 641; BGH, No 3 StR 89/09, Decision (18 June 2009), in *StV*, 30 (2010), 228, 230 with a commentary by Stuckenberg, *StV*, 30 (2010), 231–2; also BVerfG, No 2 BvR 49/09, Judgment (10 March 2009), reprinted in *StV*, 29 (2009), 673–5; OLG Saarbrücken, No 1 Ws 263/06, Decision (18 January 2007), in *StV*, 27 (2007), 178, 180; BGH, No 2 StR 31/14, Decision (4 June 2014), in *StV*, 35 (2015), 172 (blatant procedural error entails procedural delay); BGH, No 5 StR 411/11, Decision (13 March 2012), in *StV*, 32 (2012), 596 (lack of relaxed detention regime for a first offender as additional hardship with regard to procedural delay); BGH, No 5 StR 537/10, Decision (11 January 2011), in *StV*, 31 (2011), 365 (having to report to the police station twice a week for almost two years as a considerable burden to be considered in the context of a compensation for a procedural delay); on previous case law see also Ambos, *NStZ*, 22 (2002), 630–1; Waßmer, *ZStW*, 118 (2006), 171 ff.; Kraatz, *JR*, 78 (2006), 408–9.

202. Cf. e.g. House of Lords, *Attorney General's Reference*, No 2/2001, No [2003] UKHL 68, Opinions of the Lords of Appeal for Judgment (11 December 2003), para. 24.
203. On this, cf. incl. further references Baumanns, *Der Beschleunigungsgrundsatz im Strafverfahren* (2011), pp. 307 ff., 311 ff.
204. On the foundations of this approach, cf. BGH, No 2 StR 492/71, Decision (10 November 1971) in *BGHSt* 24, 239 (*Strafzumessungslösung*). On the legal situation in Spain, where excessive length of proceedings was recognised in law as a ground for mitigation, cf. Ramos Tapia, *eucrim*, 5 (2010), 168 ff.
205. Cf. Spencer, *CambLJ*, 73 (2014), 14, describing the 'common law power to stay a prosecution as an abuse of process' as 'surely . . . one of the most astonishing developments in the history of English criminal justice.'
206. Cf. Grand Senate of the German Federal Court, BGH, No GSSt 1/07, Decision (17 January 2008), in *BGHSt* 52, 124; BGH, No 4 StR 364/08, Judgment (21 October 2008), reprinted in *StV*, 29 (2009), 682–3; BGH, No 3 StR 173/09, Judgment (16 June 2009), reprinted in *StV*, 29 (2009), 638–9; BGH, No 1 StR 551/11, Decision (24 January 2012), *NStZ*, 32 (2012), 470; BGH, No 5 StR 410/14, Decision (23 September 2014), in *StV*, 35 (2015), 154. Crit. of this merely rhetorical reaction, Roxin, *GA*, 157 (2010), 426 ff.
207. Cf. BGH, 5 StR 376/03 (n. 201), p. 641; BGH, No 3 StR 166/06, Judgment (22 June 2006), in *NStZ*, 27 (2007), 53–4; cf. also OLG Rostock, No 1 Ss 8/10, Decision (24 March 2010), in *StV*, 31 (2011), 220–2 (procedural obstacles after seven-year proceedings); Reich, *Überlange Verfahrensdauer* (2011), pp. 100–1.
208. There are, however, jurisdictions which consider an undue delay as an explicit substantive ground of mitigation when determining the sentence, see e.g. Art. 21(6) Spanish CP; thereon Oubiña Barbolla, *Eunomia*, 10 (2016), 261–2.
209. ECtHR, *Kaemena and Thöneböhn* v. *Germany*, Nos 45749/06 and 51115/06, Judgment (22 January 2009), para. 86 ('under the new so-called "execution approach" the criminal courts would also be able . . . to afford redress to litigants in cases . . . in which a mandatory life sentence had to be imposed . . . by declaring that a specified part of the life sentence . . . had to be considered as having been served'); BGH, GSSt 1/07 (n. 206), p. 124 (*Anrechungs- oder Vollstreckungslösung*); thereon Gaede, *JZ*, 63 (2008), 422–4; based on BGH, No 3 StR 50/07, Decision (23 August 2007), in *NJW*, 60 (2007), 3294–8; thereon Peglau, *NJW*, 60 (2007), 3298–9; Roxin, *StV*, 28 (2008), 14–18; Salditt, *StraFo*, 13 (2007), 513; Weber, *JR*, 80 (2008), 36 ff.; cf. also Tepperwien, *NStZ*, 29 (2009), 4; Hecker, *Europäisches Strafrecht* (2015), §3 mn. 62; Mayer, in Karpenstein and Mayer, *EMRK* (2015), Art. 6 mn. 88. On the separate contestability of the claim to compensation in appeals, cf. BGH, No 3 StR 250/09, Judgment (27 August 2009), in *NJW*, 62 (2009), 3734–5 with further references; Maier, *NStZ*, 30 (2010), 651; BGH, 3 StR 89/09 (n. 201), p. 230. On the compatibility of the execution solution with the ECHR, cf. Reich, *Überlange Verfahrensdauer* (2011), pp. 84 ff.
210. On the problematic use of the execution solution in brief custodial sentences, cf. Çelik and Stief, *StV*, 30 (2010), 657 ff.; with regard to juvenile sentence OLG Düsseldorf, No III-4 RVs 191/09 IV, Decision (4 March 2010), in *NStZ*, 31 (2011), 525–7.

211. Satzger, *International and European Criminal Law* (2018), §9 mn. 76; Mayer, in Karpenstein and Mayer, *EMRK* (2015), Art. 6 mn. 89–90; in detail on the application of the execution solution to life sentences, Reich, *Überlange Verfahrensdauer* (2011), pp. 111 ff.
212. Cf. ECtHR, *Kudla* v. *Poland*, No 30210/96, Judgment (26 October 2000), paras. 146 ff., 159; ECtHR, *Kirsten* v. *Germany*, No 19124/02, Judgment (15 February 2007), paras. 53 ff. (noting that a constitutional complaint is not a suitable legal remedy for the excessive length of pending civil proceedings, paras. 33–4). For further information, cf. on *Kudla* Bien and Guillaumont, *EuGRZ*, 31 (2004), 462 ff.; Demko, *HRRS*, 6 (2005), 403 ff.; on the relationship between Arts. 6 and 13, cf. Tiwisina, *Rechtsfragen überlanger Verfahrensdauer* (2010), pp. 49 ff.
213. ECtHR, *Rumpf* v. *Germany*, No 46344/06, Judgment (2 September 2010), paras. 68, 72.
214. ECtHR, *Rumpf*, 46344/06, para. 73.
215. Federal Government Draft Bill on Legal Protection in Excessively Long Court Proceedings and Criminal Investigations (Gesetzentwurf der Bundesregierung über den Rechtsschutz bei überlangen Gerichtsverfahren und strafrechtlichen Ermittlungsverfahren, 12 August 2010); on this, cf. Steinbeiß-Winkelmann, *ZRP*, 43 (2010), 205 ff.; Beukelmann, *NJW-Spezial*, 7 (2010), 632–3; for a critical stance, cf. Roxin, *StV*, 31, 2 (2011), Editorial; on the development in Spain, cf. Ramos Tapia, *eucrim*, 5 (2010), 168 ff.
216. ECtHR, *Rumpf*, 46344/06, para. 72.
217. Act on Legal Protection in Excessively Long Court Proceedings and Criminal Investigations (Gesetz über den Rechtsschutz bei überlangen Gerichtsverfahren und strafrechtlichen Ermittlungsverfahren), 24 November 2011 (*BGBl.* I 2011, 2302 ff.) adding new §§198–201 to the German Courts Organisational Act (GVG); thereon Sommer, *StV*, 32 (2012), 107 ff.
218. §198 GVG.
219. Thus the protection afforded by Art. 6(1) also applies to civil lawsuits brought in an ECHR State against a non-Member State for damages inflicted through torture in said non-Member State; however, according to ECtHR case law, the principle of state immunity effectively restricts Art. 6(1) in these cases; cf. ECtHR, *Al-Adsani* v. *the UK*, No 35763/93, Judgment (21 November 2011), paras. 46 ff. and 52 ff.; ECtHR, *Fogarty* v. *the UK*, No 37112/97, Judgment (21 November 2001), paras. 24 ff. and 32 ff. and ECtHR, *McElhinney* v. *Ireland*, No 31253/96, Judgment (21 November 2001), paras. 23 ff. and 33 ff. Thereon also Grabenwarter, *ECHR* (2014), Art. 6 mn. 71 ff., 74.
220. Art. 199(3) first sentence GVG.
221. In **the Netherlands**, for example, the suspect has a remedy against protracted procedure after the trial has started (Article 12 CCP (Wetboek van Strafvordering)); further, the suspect can request the Court to pronounce an official declaration that the case has ended (Article 36 CCP). In **Greece**, Law No 4239/2014 introduced a compensatory remedy in cases of undue delay in proceedings before criminal and civil courts and the Audit Court, following the ECtHR's recommendations in *Michelioudakis* and *Glykantzi* (cf. ECtHR, *Michelioudakis* v. *Greece*, No 54447/10, Judgment (3 April 2012) and *Glykantzi* v. *Greece*, No 40150/09, Judgment (30 October 2012)). For **Hungary**, see

Art. 262/A CCP; and Karsai and Szomora, *Criminal Law in Hungary* (2015), p. 194; for **Italy**, see Legge no 89 of 24 March 2001, Chapter II, Art. 1*bis* and 1*ter*; for **Poland**, see 'Act on the complaint for breach of the right to hear the case without undue delay' of 17 June 2004 (free translation by A. Swiatlowsky); for **Portugal**, see Art. 23 no 1 Constitution (complaint before the *Provedor de Justiça*) and Art. 108 CCP (application to accelerate proceedings).

222. For **France**, see Art. L 144–1 Code de l'organisation judiciaire (compensation in case of 'fonctionnement défectueux du service de la justice'); for **Italy**, see Legge no 89 of 24 March 2001, Chapter II, Art. 2; in **Spain** a right to reparation has been developed through case law of the Constitutional Court, cf. Oubiña Barbolla, *Eunomia*, 10 (2016), 250 ff. In **Sweden**, the sentence may be mitigated for reasons of equity, up to a total renunciation of punishment (cf. Chapter 29, §§5 and 6 CC). In the **UK**, the House of Lords held that, while an unreasonable delay does not give rise to an anticipated termination of the process under the abuse-of-process doctrine, a remedy might be 'a reduction in the penalty imposed on a convicted defendant or the payment of a compensation to an acquitted defendant' (House of Lords, *Attorney General's Reference*, 2/2001 (n. 202), para. 24).

223. ECtHR, *Bannikova* v. *Russia*, No 18757/06, Judgment (4 November 2010), paras. 32 ff.; on this, cf. Esser, Gaede and Tsambikakis, *NStZ*, 32 (2012), 619 ff.; cf. also Grabenwarter, *ECHR* (2014), Art. 6 mn. 83.

224. ECtHR, *Teixeira de Castro*, 44/1997/828/1034, para. 39; ECtHR, *Ramanauskas* v. *Lithuania*, No 74420/01, Judgment (5 February 2008), para. 52; ECtHR, *Bugallo* v. *Spain*, No 21218/09, Judgment (18 October 2011), para. 27; ECtHR, *Furcht* v. *Germany*, No 54648/09, Judgment (23 October 2014), para. 64 (exclusion of the affected evidence); thereon, Penkuhn and Brill, *JuS*, 56 (2016), 685–6.

225. For example, in ECtHR, *Bugallo*, 21218/09, paras. 29 ff., the Court considered the undercover operation in line with Art. 6, inter alia because 'the agreement to purchase the drugs and the intent to organise its shipment to Spain *had already existed prior* to the undercover officers' intervention' (emphasis added) and therefore 'the activity of the police officers involved in the case cannot be regarded as having instigated the drug trafficking on which the applicant's conviction was based. Accordingly, their activity did not go beyond that of an undercover officer' (para. 29).

226. ECtHR, *Bannikova* v. *Russia*, No 18757/06, Judgment (4 November 2010), para. 37 ('the Court will attempt, as a first step, to establish whether the offence would have been committed without the authorities' intervention'), citing the definition of police incitement in *Ramanauskas*, 74420/01, para. 55 ('Police incitement occurs where the officers involved – whether members of the security forces or persons acting on their instructions – do not confine themselves to investigating criminal activity in an essentially passive manner, but exert such an influence on the subject as to incite the commission of an offence that would otherwise not have been committed, in order to make it possible to establish the offence, that is, to provide evidence and institute a prosecution'); for the determination whether the investigation was 'essentially passive' the Court will apply two criteria: it 'will examine the reasons underlying the covert operation [objective suspicions for the applicant's involvement in or predisposition to criminal activity] and the conduct of the authorities carrying it out' (ECtHR, *Bannikova*, 18757/06, para. 38); that is, 'whether the undercover agents merely "joined" the criminal acts or instigated

them' (ibid., para. 43); for examples of indicators of the first criterion, see ibid., paras. 39–42, and for the second, ibid., paras. 43 ff., both with further case law references. Thereto Sinn and Maly, *NStZ*, 35 (2015), 380; for criteria of delimitation between police incitement and permissible investigation actions, cf. also Meyer and Wohlers, *JZ*, 70 (2015), 765–7, 769.

227. Cf. ECtHR, *Constantin and Stoian* v. *Romania*, Nos 23782/06 and 46629/06, Judgment (29 September 2009), para. 55 (prior criminal convictions are not by themselves indicative of predisposition to commit a crime); ECtHR, *Bannikova*, 18757/06, para. 41. However, 'the applicant's demonstrated familiarity with the current prices for drugs and ability to obtain drugs at short notice' may be indicative; cf. ECtHR, *Shannon* v. *the UK*, No 67537/01, Decision (6 April 2004); ECtHR, *Bannikova*, 18757/06, para. 42.
228. BGH, 1 StR 221/99 (n. 146), pp. 326 ff.; BGH, 3 StR 50/07 (n. 209), p. 3298; also BVerfG, Nos 2 BvR 209/14, 240/14 and 262/14, Decision (18 December 2014), in *NJW*, 68 (2015), 1083–6; thereon also Esser, *Europäisches und Internationales Strafrecht* (2018), §9 mn. 233; for a rightly critical stance, cf. Korn, *Defizite bei der Umsetzung der EMRK* (2005), pp. 146 ff.; Sinn and Maly, *NStZ*, 35 (2015), 381 ff. More recently, the second Chamber (Zweiter Senat) of the BGH has adopted the position of the ECtHR opting for a stay of proceedings (BGH, No 2 StR 97/14, Judgment (10 June 2015), in *BGHSt* 60, 276, 290 ff.); conc. Meyer and Wohlers, *JZ*, 70 (2015), 770; for the BVerfG, 2 BvR 209/14 et al., in *NJW*, 68 (2015), 1084; this is only possible in 'extreme exceptional cases' ('extreme Ausnahmefälle'); in the same vein with examples, Zieschang, in Stuckenberg and Gärditz, *Strafe und Prozess* (2015), pp. 436–7.
229. In favour of the exclusion of evidence, also Satzger, *International and European Criminal Law* (2018), §9 mn. 90; Satzger, *Internationales und Europäisches Strafrecht* (2016), §11 mn. 79; Sinn and Maly, *NStZ*, 35 (2015), 382–3; Meyer and Wohlers, *JZ*, 70 (2015), 769 (stressing the binding effect of the ECtHR's case law).
230. ECtHR, *Edwards and Lewis* v. *the UK*, Nos 39647/98 and 40461/98, Judgment (22 July 2003), para. 49; on this, cf. Esser, *StraFo*, 9 (2003), 338.
231. Cf. Rzepka, *Fairness* (2000), pp. 25–6, 57; Meyer-Ladewig, Harrendorf and König, in Meyer-Ladewig, Nettesheim and von Raumer, *EMRK* (2017), Art. 6 mn. 221; both include references to case law. In detail Gaede, *Fairness als Teilhabe* (2005), pp. 159 ff.; Tochilovsky, *Jurisprudence* (2014), pp. 443 ff.
232. Cf. also Haefliger and Schürmann, *Die EMRK und die Schweiz* (1999), p. 227 (letters (b) und (c)); Villiger, *Handbuch der EMRK* (1999), p. 327 (letters (b) und (e)).
233. On Art. 6(3b) as the 'mother right' (orig. 'Mutterrecht'), see Trechsel, in Schweizer, Burkert and Gasser, *FS Druey* (2002), p. 995.
234. Villiger, *Handbuch der EMRK* (1999), p. 301 (orig. 'immer wieder neue Facetten eines fairen Gerichtsverfahrens zu Tage [fördert]'); a similar stance is taken by Peukert, in Strafverteidigervereinigungen, *Reform oder Roll-Back?* (1997), p. 243.
235. On this, cf. the case law overview in Barrot, *ZJS*, 3 (2010), 701 ff.
236. ECtHR, *Konstas* v. *Greece*, No 53466/07, Judgment (24 May 2011), para. 36 ('the presumption of innocence cannot cease to apply in appeal proceedings simply because the accused was convicted at first instance. To conclude otherwise would contradict the role of appeal proceedings, where the appellate court is required to re-examine the earlier decision submitted to it as to the facts and the law. It would

mean that the presumption of innocence would not be applicable in proceedings brought in order to obtain a review of the case and have the earlier conviction set aside'); see also Grabenwarter, *ECHR* (2014), Art. 6 mn. 154; Reid, *A Practitioner's Guide to the ECHR* (2011), p. 217. However, it has been said earlier that the presumption of innocence, depending on 'the special nature of these proceedings', may cease to apply in the appeal proceedings; cf. ECtHR, *Callaghan et al.* v. *the UK*, No 14739–89, Commision Decision (9 May 1989), pp. 5–6, para. 2; Reid, *A Practitioner's Guide to the ECHR* (2011), p. 127.

237. ECtHR, *Salabiaku* v. *France*, No 10519/83, Judgment (7 October 1988), para. 28 (allowing such presumptions but calling for an application 'within reasonable limits which take into account the importance of what is at stake and maintain the rights of the defence').
238. On the autonomous interpretation of the concept of 'criminal charges', see above, main text, mn. 28.
239. Barrot, *ZJS*, 3 (2010), 701 ff.; Mayer, in Karpenstein and Mayer, *EMRK* (2015), Art. 6 mn. 162.
240. On this, cf. ECtHR, *Barberà, Messegué and Jabardo* v. *Spain*, No 10590/83, Judgment (6 December 1988), para. 77; and Satzger, *International and European Criminal Law* (2018), §9 mn. 92; Satzger, *Internationales und Europäisches Strafrecht* (2016), §11 mn. 80; Mayer, in Karpenstein and Mayer, *EMRK* (2015), Art. 6 mn. 161.
241. ECtHR, *Barberà et al.*, 10588/83, 10589/83 and 10590/83, para. 77.
242. Peters and Altwicker, *EMRK* (2012), §21 mn. 6; Gundel, in Merten and Papier, *Handbuch der Grundrechte*, vi/1 (2010), p. 349 mn. 137. On the prohibition of accusatory statements before and during a trial, cf. Barrot, *ZJS*, 3 (2010), 703 ff.; for a broader normative understanding focusing on the relationship between citizens and the State, cf. Ferguson, *CLF*, 27 (2016), 131 ff. (with references to the importance of the principle in constitutional law at 132–3).
243. ECtHR, *Allenet de Ribemont* v. *France*, No 15175/89, Judgment (10 February 1995), paras. 11, 41; on this, cf. Peters and Altwicker, *EMRK* (2012), §21 mn. 10; Grabenwarter, *ECHR* (2014), Art. 6 mn. 158–60; Mayer, in Karpenstein and Mayer, *EMRK* (2015), Art. 6 mn. 163 ff.; ECtHR, *Borovský* v. *Slovakia*, No 24528/02, Judgment (2 June 2009), para. 46; Stapper, *AfP*, 27 (1996), 350 ff.; on the presumption of innocence in German, French and English criminal procedure, cf. Gleß, *Beweisrechtsgrundsätze* (2006), pp. 203 ff.
244. ECtHR, *Vulakh* v. *Russia*, No 33468/03, Judgment (10 January 2012), paras. 34 ff.; Rui, *ERA Forum*, 13 (2012), 356–7; a different opinion is put forward by Grabenwarter, *ECHR* (2014), Art. 6 mn. 3.
245. ECtHR, *Cleve* v. *Germany*, No 48144/09, Judgment (15 January 2015); thereon Penkuhn and Brill, *JuS*, 56 (2016), 683–4.
246. Cf. ECtHR, *Karaman* v. *Germany*, No 17103/10, Judgment (27 February 2014), para. 42 ('presumption of innocence may in theory also be infringed on account of premature expression of a suspect's guilt made within the scope of a judgment against separately prosecuted co-suspects'). *In casu*, the Court rejected, by five votes to two, a violation by Germany since the District Court (Landgericht Frankfurt a.M.) 'made it sufficiently clear that it was not also implicitly determining the applicant's guilt' (ibid., para. 67), i.e., in the majority's view, the innocence of the separately prosecuted applicant was not affected by the judgment against

the co-accused. For a critical analysis ('borderline case' [*Grenzfall*]), see Esser, in Stuckenberg and Gärditz, *Strafe und Prozess* (2015), pp. 514 ff.

247. ECtHR, *Cleve*, 48144/09, para. 53. See also BGH, No 1 StR 56/15, Decision (14 October 2015), in *NStZ*, 15 (2016), 560–1, where the Court underlines that the *Cleve* rules are not in conflict with the requirement of gravamen for the admissibility of appeal; in the same vein BVerfG, No 2 BvR 2282/16, Decision (8 March 2017), paras. 12–13.

248. ECtHR, *Cleve*, 48144/09, para. 55. *In casu*, the accused had been acquitted of the charge of sexual abuse with regard to his daughter, but the District Court (*Landgericht*) nevertheless found in the reasoning of the judgment 'that the accused actually carried out sexual assaults on his daughter in his car' and thus suggested that he was guilty (ibid., paras. 56 ff.). For the ECtHR this amounted to a reasoning suggesting guilt; contra Rostalski, *HRRS*, 16 (2015), 324–6 (mere expression of suspicion).

249. For possible criteria, cf. Rostalski, *HRRS*, 16 (2015), 323–6; Stuckenberg, *StV*, 36 (2016), 5–6.

250. ECtHR, *Cleve*, 48144/09, para. 63 ('formal finding of guilt') versus para. 61 ('was in fact guilty').

251. Cf. Stuckenberg, *StV*, 36 (2016), 5 ff., who, while concurring with the Court's result in *Cleve*, criticizes its conceptual confusion and tries to clarify the meaning of factual guilt.

252. Cf. ECtHR, *Krumpholz* v. *Austria*, No 13201/05, Judgment (18 March 2010), para. 30; Gleß, *Internationales Strafrecht* (2015), mn. 90; Mayer, in Karpenstein and Mayer, *EMRK* (2015), Art. 6 mn. 127–30. For an application to legal persons, see Dannecker, *ZStW*, 127 (2015), 370 ff., 991 ff.

253. ECtHR, *Murray*, 18731/91, para. 45; ECtHR, *Saunders* v. *the UK*, No 19187/91, Judgment (17 December 1996), para. 68; ECtHR, *Heaney and McGuinness* v. *the UK*, No 34720/97, Judgment (21 December 2000), para. 40; ECtHR, *J. B.*, 31827/96, para. 64; ECtHR, *Krumpholz*, 13201/05, para. 31; cf. also ECtHR, *Weh* v. *Austria*, No 38544/97, Judgment (8 April 2004), para. 46; cf. also Grabenwarter, *ECHR* (2014), Art. 6 mn. 152; Meyer-Ladewig, Harrendorf and König, in Meyer-Ladewig, Nettesheim and von Raumer, *EMRK* (2017), Art. 6 mn. 129; Mayer, in Karpenstein and Mayer, *EMRK* (2015), Art. 6 mn. 127; Walter, in Roth, *Europäisierung des Rechts* (2010), pp. 303–4; fundamentally cf. Moscarini, *RIDPP*, 49 (2006), 611 ff. For a critical stance on this, cf. Matt, *GA*, 153 (2006), 327–8.

254. ECtHR, *Allan* v. *the UK*, No 48539/99, Judgment (5 November 2002), para. 50 (elicitation of statements by police informants); this is somewhat relativised by ECtHR, *Bykov* v. *Russia*, No 4378/02, Judgment (10 March 2009), paras. 99 ff. (no violation of the *nemo-tenetur* principle if prior to an arrest a conversation between an informant and the defendant was secretly recorded; the defendant has not yet invoked the right to remain silent and he is not subject to any pressure to make statements). The same conclusion is reached in BGH, No 1 StR 701/08, Judgment (29 April 2009), in *BGHSt* 53, 294 ff.; BGH, No 3 StR 400/10, Decision (31 March 2011), in *NStZ*, 31 (2011), 596–8; cf. also Mayer, in Karpenstein and Mayer, *EMRK* (2015), Art. 6 mn. 129 ff., 137 ff.; for a monographic analysis of the use of undercover agents to elicit confessions cf. Wang, *Einsatz Verdeckter Ermittler* (2015). Originally, the German Federal Supreme

Court did not invoke the *nemo-tenetur* principle in a similar situation – the secret tapping of a conversation between a pre-trial detainee and his wife in an unsupervised prison visiting room – but rather confirmed that a violation of the right to a fair trial had taken place after an overall assessment (BGH, 1 StR 701/08, in *BGHSt* 53, 294 ff.; crit. Walter, in Roth, *Europäisierung des Rechts* (2010), p. 302; Hauck, *NStZ*, 30 (2010), 19 ff.); however, on more recent German case law influenced by the ECtHR decisions in *Allan* and *Bykov*, see Bock, in Leblois-Happe and Stuckenberg, *Was wird aus der Hauptverhandlung?* (2014), pp. 113 ff.; Kasiske, *StV*, 34 (2014), 423 ff.

255. Thus Gollwitzer, *Menschenrechte im Strafverfahren* (2005), Art. 6 MRK mn. 103, 105; on the principle of culpability in community law, cf. Heine, *ZStrR*, 125 (2007), 117.
256. On this, cf. Peters and Altwicker, EMRK (2012), §21 mn. 9–10.
257. BVerfG, No 2 BvR 796/86, Judgment (4 December 1986), reprinted in *NStZ*, 7 (1987), 118; BVerfG, No 2 BvR 1741/89, Judgment (6 December 1989), reprinted in *NStZ*, 11 (1991), 30; BVerfG, No 2 BvR 1706/92, Decision (21 April 1993), in *NJW*, 47 (1994), 377–8.
258. According to this provision the court 'shall order the suspended sentence to take effect if the convicted person . . . commits an offence during the operational period showing that the expectation on which the suspension was based has been disappointed' (translation by M. Bohlander).
259. Cf. Hubrach, in Laufhütte, Rissing-van Saan and Tiedemann, *Leipziger Kommentar StGB*, iii (2008), §56f mn. 6; Stree and Kinzig, in Schönke, Schröder and Eser, *StGB Kommentar* (2014), §56f mn. 7.
260. ECtHR, *Böhmer*, 37568/97, paras. 65 ff.; on this, cf. Peglau, *NStZ*, 24 (2004), 248–9; Pauly, *StV*, 23 (2003), 85; Neubacher, *GA*, 151 (2004), 402 ff.; Krumm, *NJW*, 58 (2005), 1832 ff.; Diehm, *Die Menschenrechte der EMRK* (2006), pp. 479 ff.; Kraus, *Bewährungswiderruf* (2007), pp. 103 ff., 163 ff.
261. This second constellation formed the basis for the decision of the European Commission of Human Rights, ECtHR, *S.* v. *Germany*, No 15871/89, Commission Decision (9 October 1991); and OLG Köln, No 2 Ws 209/04, Decision (9 June 2004), in *NStZ*, 24 (2004), 685–6. The German Federal Constitutional Court also mentions, invoking the ECtHR's *Böhmer* decision (*Böhmer*, 37568/97), the requirement of a credible confession, BVerfG, No 2 BvR 2314/04, Decision (9 December 2004), in *NJW*, 58 (2005), 817; a critical stance is taken by Seher, *ZStW*, 118 (2006), 149 ff.
262. OLG Celle, No 1 Ws 250/03, Decision (23 July 2003), in *StV*, 23 (2003), 575; OLG Thüringen, No 1 Ws 163/03, Decision (07 May 2003), in *StV*, 23 (2003), 575; conc. Seifert, *Jura*, 30 (2008), 685; a more doubtful view is taken by OLG Schleswig, Nos 2 Ws 463, 465 and 479/03, Decision (9 December 2003), in *NStZ*, 24 (2004), 628.
263. Cf. also Peglau, *NStZ*, 24 (2004), 251; Kühl, in Müller-Dietz, *FS Jung* (2007), p. 441 ('final sentence by the trial court', orig. 'rechtskräftige Verurteilung durch das erkennende Gericht'); Kreicker, in Sieber, Satzger and von Heinegg, *Europäisches Strafrecht* (2014), p. 911; going beyond that and requiring, in line with the case law cited, a final judgment, Pauly, *StV*, 23 (2003), 86; and Neubacher, *GA*, 151 (2004), 412. The ECtHR's line is more or less taken (with some differences in detail) by OLG Düsseldorf, No III-3 Ws 469/03, Decision

(19 December 2003), in *NStZ*, 24 (2004), 269; OLG Stuttgart, No 4 Ws 180/04, Decision (26 July 2004), in *NJW*, 58 (2005), 83–4; OLG Köln, 2 Ws 209/04 (n. 261), p. 686; OLG Zweibrücken, No 1 Ws 343/04, Decision (15 September 2004), in *NStZ-RR*, 10 (2005), 8; see also BVerfG, 2 BvR 2314/04 (n. 261), p. 817. For an instructive take on this as a whole cf. Krumm, *NJW*, 58 (2005), 1833 ff., esp. 1834; for a detailed discussion of this problem cf. Seher, *ZStW*, 118 (2006), 101 ff.; cf. also Scheffler, in Joerden and Szwarc, *Europäisierung des Strafrechts* (2007), p. 100.

264. According to §453c (1) StPO.
265. Klinger, *NStZ*, 32 (2012), 75 (who calls for a *final* judgment, however).
266. Cf. §102 German Law on the Execution of Sentences (StVollzG).
267. OLG Hamm, No 1 Vollz (Ws) 323/12, Decision (17 July 2012), in *StV*, 33 (2013), 451–2; the Court makes it clear at the same time that Art. 6(2) ECHR is not affected if the incident in question would entail disciplinary measures regardless of whether it constituted a criminal offence or not.
268. Cf. §57 StGB (conditional early release after two-thirds or half of a fixed-term sentence have been served).
269. ECtHR, *M. M.* v. *Germany*, No 23091/93, European Commission of Human Rights Decision (30 November 1994); correctly therefore OLG Hamm, No 2 Ws 168/04, Decision (12 July 2004), in *NStZ*, 24 (2004), 685; OLG Düsseldorf, No 3 Ws 376/91, Decision (10 July 1991), in *StV*, 12 (1992), 287–8; on this, cf. also Peglau, *ZRP*, 36 (2003), 243 in reference to ECtHR, *M. M.*, 23091/93.
270. Cf. Simon, *Beschuldigtenrechte* (1998), pp. 7 ff.; Rzepka, *Fairness* (2000), pp. 8 ff.; Esser, *Europäisches Strafverfahrensrecht* (2002), pp. 437 ff.; Braitsch, *Gerichtssprache für Sprachunkundige* (1991), pp. 137 ff.; Frister, *StV*, 18 (1998), 159 ff.; Villiger, *Handbuch der EMRK* (1999), pp. 322 ff.; Meyer-Ladewig, Harrendorf and König, in Meyer-Ladewig, Nettesheim and von Raumer, *EMRK* (2017), Art. 6 mn. 223.
271. Trechsel, *ZStrR*, 96 (1979), 343 (orig. 'Überraschung und Überrumpelung'); conc. Villiger, *Handbuch der EMRK* (1999), pp. 322–3; cf. also Cape et al., *Effective Criminal Defence in Europe* (2010), p. 33.
272. Grabenwarter, *ECHR* (2014), Art. 6 mn. 125.
273. Kreicker, in Sieber, Satzger and von Heinegg, *Europäisches Strafrecht* (2014), pp. 911–12.
274. Simon, *Beschuldigtenrechte* (1998), pp. 9–10; Villiger, *Handbuch der EMRK* (1999), p. 323; Sommer, in Brüssow et al., *Strafverteidigung in der Praxis* (2007), p. 829; for a different view, see Esser, *Europäisches Strafverfahrensrecht* (2002), p. 440.
275. In the same vein, Safferling, *Towards an International Criminal Procedure* (2003), pp. 115, 120–1; Zappalà, *Human Rights in International Criminal Proceedings* (2005), pp. 48–50.
276. Cf. Gillmeister, *StraFo*, 2 (1996), 115–16; Simon, *Beschuldigtenrechte* (1998), pp. 10–11; Sommer, in Brüssow et al., *Strafverteidigung in der Praxis* (2007), p. 829; see generally Alamuddin, in Khan, *Evidence* (2010), p. 272 (arguing that especially suspected senior government officials may hamper the investigation); conc. de Meester, Pitcher, Rastan and Sluiter, in Sluiter et al., *International Criminal Procedure* (2013), p. 235.
277. EU, *Green Paper on Procedural Safeguards* (2003), pp. 37–8, see main text, mn. 143. The letter of rights is an information leaflet containing all the fundamental rights

the persons charged are due and which should be handed out to them by the police. In agreement Bachmaier, in De la Oliva Santos and Calderón, *Garantías fundamentales* (2007), pp. 56 ff., 68; cf. also Illuminati, in Arangüena Fanego, *Garantías procesales* (2007), pp. 361 ff.; Allegrezza, in ibid., pp. 368 ff.; Sommovigo, in ibid., pp. 381 ff.; on the different ways of proceeding in the Member States, cf. Spronken, *An EU-Wide Letter of Rights* (2010), pp. 11 ff.

278. ECtHR, *Jespers* v. *Belgium*, No 8403/78, Report of the European Commission of Human Rights (14 December 1981), para. 58; ECtHR, *Edwards* v. *the UK*, No 13071/87, Judgment (16 December 1992), para. 36; ECtHR, *Rowe and Davis* v. *the UK*, No 28901/95, Judgment (16 February 2000), para. 60; ECtHR, *Natunen*, 21022/04, para. 39; cf. also Esser, *Europäisches Strafverfahrensrecht* (2002), pp. 403 ff.; Sommer, in Brüssow et al., *Strafverteidigung in der Praxis* (2007), p. 829; Plowden and Kerrigan, *NLJ*, 151 (2001), 735–6; Wohlers and Schlegel, *NStZ*, 30 (2010), 489–90.
279. From a comparative and supranational perspective, see Ambos, *Treatise ICL III* (2016), pp. 520 ff.
280. On witness protection on the European level, cf. Enikö, *RIDP*, 77 (2006), 313 ff.
281. Esser, *Europäisches und Internationales Strafrecht* (2018), §9 mn. 225.
282. In detail Walischewski, *Akteneinsichtsrecht* (1999), pp. 71 ff. and passim; Esser, *Europäisches Strafverfahrensrecht* (2002), pp. 424 ff.; Braitsch, *Gerichtssprache für Sprachunkundige* (1991), pp. 152 ff.
283. Cf. e.g. ECtHR, *Öcalan*, 46221/99, paras. 158 ff.
284. Thus Esser, *Europäisches Strafverfahrensrecht* (2002), pp. 425 ff.; also ECtHR, *Öcalan*, 46221/99, para. 159; Wohlers and Schlegel, *NStZ*, 30 (2010), 489. For a critical stance on this, cf. Trechsel, in Schweizer, Burkert and Gasser, FS Druey (2002), p. 996.
285. Haefliger and Schürmann, *Die EMRK und die Schweiz* (1999), p. 188; Esser, *Europäisches und Internationales Strafrecht* (2018), §9 mn. 225; from the perspective of constitutional law, Walischewski, *Akteneinsichtsrecht* (1999), pp. 11 ff.
286. Cf. ECtHR, *Öcalan*, 46221/99, para. 163. In the same vein Trechsel, in Schweizer, Burkert and Gasser, FS Druey (2002), p. 994; Simon, *Beschuldigtenrechte* (1998), pp. 29, 30 ff.; Walischewski, *Akteneinsichtsrecht* (1999), p. 86; Villiger, *Handbuch der EMRK* (1999), p. 326; Sommer, in Brüssow et al., *Strafverteidigung in der Praxis* (2007), pp. 830–1.
287. ECtHR, *Mooren* v. *Germany*, No 11364/03, Judgment (13 December 2007), para. 96; cf. Beulke and Witzigmann, *NStZ*, 31 (2011), 257.
288. Thereon above, mn. 27. Cf. also Walischewski, *Akteneinsichtsrecht* (1999), pp. 93–4, 97, 140; Trechsel, in Schweizer, Burkert and Gasser, *FS Druey* (2002), pp. 1006 ff.; Esser, *Europäisches Strafverfahrensrecht* (2002), p. 430; Braitsch, *Gerichtssprache für Sprachunkundige* (1991), p. 154; Sommer, in Brüssow et al., *Strafverteidigung in der Praxis* (2007), pp. 830–1; Beulke and Witzigmann, *NStZ*, 31 (2011), 256.
289. For more detail, cf. Ambos, in Radtke and Hohmann, *StPO Kommentar* (2011), Art. 6 mn. 42; Beulke and Witzigmann, *NStZ*, 31 (2011), 259.
290. ECtHR, *Natunen*, 21022/04, paras. 46 ff. On extending the right to access files to summaries of the content of telephone conversations tapped by the police, cf. BGH, 3 StR 89/09 (n. 201), p. 230; with concurring commentary by Stuckenberg, *StV*, 30 (2010), 231–2.
291. In a similar vein, Esser, *Europäisches Strafverfahrensrecht* (2002), pp. 428–9.

292. Cf. in detail Simon, *Beschuldigtenrechte* (1998), pp. 27 ff.; Rzepka, *Fairness* (2000), pp. 60 ff.; Esser, *Europäisches Strafverfahrensrecht* (2002), pp. 447 ff.; Braitsch, *Gerichtssprache für Sprachunkundige* (1991), pp. 146 ff.; Haefliger and Schürmann, *Die EMRK und die Schweiz* (1999), pp. 221 ff.; Villiger, *Handbuch der EMRK* (1999), pp. 325 ff.
293. Braitsch, *Gerichtssprache für Sprachunkundige* (1991), p. 146; Haefliger and Schürmann, *Die EMRK und die Schweiz* (1999), p. 223; Kühne, in Pabel and Schmahl, *Internationaler Kommentar zur EMRK* (2013), Art. 6 EMRK mn. 499–500, 521 ff.; Sidhu, *Equality of Arms* (2017), pp. 165 ff.; cf. also Esser, *Europäisches und Internationales Strafrecht* (2018), §9 mn. 245–6. On the tension between the right to sufficient time for preparation and the guarantee of an appropriate length of proceedings, cf. Ambos, in Radtke and Hohmann, *StPO Kommentar* (2011), Art. 6 mn. 43.
294. ECtHR, *Öcalan*, 46221/99, GC Judgment (12 May 2005), paras. 146–8; also BGH, No 1 StR 355/13, Decision (11 February 2014), in *NStZ*, 34 (2014), 347, 349 (mn. 28).
295. Cf. also Rzepka, *Fairness* (2000), p. 60.
296. Villiger, *Handbuch der EMRK* (1999), p. 325 (orig. 'kurzer Prozess'). For more detail in reference to the Öcalan case, cf. Ambos, *ZStW*, 115 (2003), 603.
297. Esser, *Europäisches und Internationales Strafrecht* (2018), §9 mn. 247; cf. also BVerfG, No 2 BvR 2248/00, Decision (30 January 2002), in *NJW*, 55 (2002), 1410–11; BGH, No 3 StR 490/97, Decision (25 February 1998), in *NStZ*, 18 (1998), 309–11; Joecks, in Radtke and Hohmann, *StPO Kommentar* (2011), §97 mn. 31 incl. further references.
298. Cf. Grabenwarter, *ECHR* (2014), Art. 6 mn. 131 ff.; Esser, in Sieber, Satzger and von Heinegg, *Europäisches Strafrecht* (2014), pp. 1071–3; Rzepka, *Fairness* (2000), pp. 64 ff.; Esser, *Europäisches Strafverfahrensrecht* (2002), pp. 450 ff., 466 ff.; Braitsch, *Gerichtssprache für Sprachunkundige* (1991), pp. 155 ff.; Sommer, in Brüssow et al., *Strafverteidigung in der Praxis* (2007), p. 831; Villiger, *Handbuch der EMRK* (1999), pp. 327 ff., 333–4; EU, *Green Paper on Procedural Safeguards* (2003), pp. 20 ff.; Demko, *HRRS*, 7 (2006), 250 ff.; Demko, in Gaede, Meyer and Schlegel, *HRRS-FG Fezer* (2008), p. 1. Cf. also Art. 47(2) CFREU: 'Everyone shall have the possibility of being advised, defended and represented.'
299. See recently Frisch, in Stuckenberg and Gärditz, *Strafe und Prozess* (2015), pp. 601 ff., who therefore severely criticises the judgment in ECtHR, *Neziraj* v. *Germany*, No 30804/07, Judgment (8 November 2012); also crit. Hüls and Reichling, *StV*, 34 (2014), 244 ff.; admittedly, however, dissenting judges Power-Forde and Nussberger also read the majority's view in that way, arguing that one should 'distinguish the right to legal assistance from the right to be absent from trial . . . Thus, we do not share the Court's view that the accused would lose his right to be defended by a lawyer as guaranteed by Article 6 §3 (c) of the Convention. He is merely denied the right to be replaced by a lawyer, a right which is not guaranteed by the Convention.' Cf. ECtHR, *Neziraj*, 30804/07, Joint Concurring Opinion of Judges Power-Forde and Nussberger, recital 6; on Neziraj, Penkuhn and Brill, *JuS*, 56 (2016), 684–5.
300. Haefliger and Schürmann, *Die EMRK und die Schweiz* (1999), p. 228; Ambos, *ZStW*, 115 (2003), 604 (with various further references); Böse, in Stuckenberg and Gärditz, *Strafe und Prozess* (2015), pp. 571–2, 586. On the limits to sanctioning the

defendant's absence without leave, cf. Esser, Gaede and Tsambikakis, *NStZ*, 31 (2011), 147–8.

301. Cf. above, mn. 27. On the situation in *Switzerland*, cf. Schlegel and Wohlers, *StV*, 32 (2012), 307 ff. Schumann, Bruckmüller and Soyer, *NJECL*, 3 (2012), 31 ff. provide an overview of the regulations in Germany, Croatia, Austria and Slovenia.

302. Cf. ECtHR, *Salduz* v. *Turkey*, 36391/02, paras. 50 ff.; ECtHR, *Dayanan* v. *Turkey*, No 7377/03, Judgment (13 October 2009), para. 31; ECtHR, *Boz* v. *Turkey*, No 2039/04), Judgment (9 February 2010), paras. 33–6; ECtHR, *Nechiporuk and Yonkalo* v. *Ukraine*, No 42310/04, Judgment (21 April 2011), paras. 262–7; ECtHR, *Huseyn et al.* v. *Azerbaijan*, Nos 35485/05 et al., Judgment (26 July 2011), paras. 170–3; ECtHR, *Bandaletov* v. *Ukraine*, No 23180/06, Judgment (31 October 2013), paras. 55–7; ECtHR, *A. T.* v. *Luxembourg*, No 30460/13, Judgment (9 April 2015), paras. 63–4; ECtHR, *Dvorski* v. *Croatia*, No 25703/11, GC Judgment (20 October 2015), paras. 77–8; ECtHR, *Borg* v. *Malta*, No 37537/13, Judgment (12 January 2016), paras. 56–63; *Ibrahim et al.* v. *UK*, Nos 50541/08 et al., GC Judgment (13 September 2016), paras. 367 ff., esp. 373 ff. with critical comment by Castorf, *HRRS*, 18 (2017), 169. See also Weigend, *StV*, 20 (2000), 385 incl. n. 24; Esser, *Europäisches Strafverfahrensrecht* (2002), pp. 476–7; Haefliger and Schürmann, *Die EMRK und die Schweiz* (1999), p. 328; Simon, *Beschuldigtenrechte* (1998), pp. 55–6; Meyer-Ladewig, Harrendorf and König, in Meyer-Ladewig, Nettesheim and von Raumer, *EMRK* (2017), Art. 6 mn. 230; Wohlers, *GA*, 152 (2005), 35 with n. 174; Ambos, in Radtke and Hohmann, *StPO Kommentar* (2011), Art. 6 mn. 44; Kreicker, in Sieber, Satzger and von Heinegg, *Europäisches Strafrecht* (2014), p. 913; Giannoulopoulos, *HRLR*, 16 (2016), 105 ff. (with further remarks on the Irish Supreme Court's position in *DDP* v. *Gormley*); Sidhu, *Equality of Arms* (2017), pp. 221 ff.; also CJEU, *Hoechst* v. *European Commission*, Nos 46/87 and 227/88 (ECLI:EU:C:1989:337) (21 September 1989), according to which the right to legal assistance is already to be observed in the preliminary examination; EU, *Green Paper on Procedural Safeguards* (2003), pp. 22–3. On the right to consular assistance, cf. Ambos, *Internationales Strafrecht* (2008), §10 mn. 27 incl. n. 160; on the right of the defence counsel to be present at police interrogations, cf. Esser, Gaede and Tsambikakis, *NStZ*, 31 (2011), 144.

303. On police interrogations: ECtHR, *Murray*, 18731/91, para. 81; concurring ECtHR, *Öcalan*, 46221/99, para. 140; more restrictively, ECtHR, *Salduz*, 36391/02, para. 52, according to which restrictions to the right to legal assistance may be justified in individual cases; on examinations by the investigative judge: ECtHR, *Quaranta* v. *Switzerland*, No 12744/87, Judgment (24 May 1991), para. 36.

304. See main text, mn. 148.

305. On the basics of this, cf. Spaniol, *Recht auf Verteidigerbeistand* (1990), pp. 212 ff., 219 ff.; conc. Walther, *GA*, 150 (2003), 222; also Meyer-Ladewig, Harrendorf and König, in Meyer-Ladewig, Nettesheim and von Raumer, *EMRK* (2017), Art. 6 mn. 113 with n. 160; cf. also Ambos, *ZStW*, 115 (2003), 605.

306. Esser, in Sieber, Satzger and von Heinegg, *Europäisches Strafrecht* (2014), p. 1074; Simon, *Beschuldigtenrechte* (1998), pp. 30, 53 ff.; Rzepka, *Fairness* (2000), pp. 72–3; Esser, *Europäisches Strafverfahrensrecht* (2002), pp. 501 ff.; Haefliger and Schürmann, *Die EMRK und die Schweiz* (1999), p. 223–4; Villiger, *Handbuch der EMRK* (1999), pp. 333–4; Meyer-Ladewig, Harrendorf and

König, in Meyer-Ladewig, Nettesheim and von Raumer, *EMRK* (2017), Art. 6 mn. 235; Braitsch, *Gerichtssprache für Sprachunkundige* (1991), pp. 147–8 (in conjunction with Art. 6(3)(b)); Gundel, in Merten and Papier, *Handbuch der Grundrechte*, vi/1 (2010), p. 349 mn. 143; Sidhu, *Equality of Arms* (2017), pp. 225 ff.; on confidentiality of correspondence, cf. Ambos, *NStZ*, 23 (2003), 15–16; on the right to refuse to give evidence applicable to all foreign lawyers, cf. Wessing, *wistra*, 26 (2007), 173–4.

307. ECtHR, *Öcalan*, 46221/99, para. 146 incl. further references.
308. ECtHR, *Öcalan*, 46221/99, para. 153 incl. further references.
309. ECtHR, *Poitrimol* v. *France*, No 14032/88, Judgment (23 November 1993), paras. 33–5; ECtHR, *Lala* v. *the Netherlands*, No 14861/89, Judgment (22 September 1994), paras. 26, 31–3; ECtHR, *Pelladoah* v. *the Netherlands*, No 16737/90, Judgment (22 September 1994), paras. 33, 38–40; ECtHR, *Van Geyseghem* v. *Belgium*, No 26103/95, Judgment (21 January 1999), paras. 34–6; ECtHR, *Kari-Pekka Pietiläinen* v. *Finland*, No 13566/06, Judgment (22 September 2009), paras. 31 ff.; Esser, *Europäisches Strafverfahrensrecht* (2002), pp. 463 ff.; Villiger, *Handbuch der EMRK* (1999), pp. 329 ff.; Sommer, in Brüssow et al., *Strafverteidigung in der Praxis* (2007), p. 832; Paul, *Abwesenheitsverfahren als rechtsstaatliches Problem* (2007), pp. 247 ff. incl. further discussion of ECtHR case law.
310. ECtHR, *Kari-Pekka Pietiläinen*, 13566/06, paras. 31 ff.; ECtHR, *Neziraj*, 30804/07, paras. 49 ff.; for a different opinion, cf. OLG Celle, No 32 Ss 29/13, Decision (19 March 2013), in *NStZ*, 33 (2013), 615–16; Mosbacher, *NStZ*, 33 (2013), 313. On case law, cf. Gerst, *NStZ*, 33 (2013), 310 ff.; Zehetgruber, *HRRS*, 14 (2013), 399–400; Engel, *ZJS*, 6 (2013), 339 ff.
311. ECtHR, *Neziraj*, 30804/07, paras. 49 ff. The core finding of the judgment, i.e. the violation of Art. 6(3)(c) ECHR by allowing the dismissal of an appeal despite the presence of a defence counsel willing and able to defend, has received widespread support in the scholarly literature: Waszczynski, *NStZ-RR*, 19 (2014), 18 ff.; Esser, *StV*, 33 (2013), 334–5; Esser, *Europäisches und Internationales Strafrecht* (2018), §9 mn. 255; Gerst, *NStZ, 33* (2013), 310 ff.; Böse, in Stuckenberg and Gärditz, *Strafe und Prozess* (2015), pp. 570 ff.; Frisch, in Stuckenberg and Gärditz, *Strafe und Prozess* (2015), pp. 596 ff.
312. OLG Celle, 32 Ss 29/13 (n. 310), pp. 615–16; OLG München, No 4 StRR (A) 18/12, Decision (17 January 2013), in *NStZ*, 33 (2013), 358–9 with a critical discussion by Zehetgruber, *HRRS*, 14 (2013), 402; OLG Düsseldorf, No III-2 RVs 11/12, Decision (27 February 2012), in *StV*, 33 (2013), 299–301 with a critical discussion by Esser, *StV*, 33 (2013), 331 ff. ('lack of knowledge of human rights standards in criminal procedure', orig. 'Ignoranz gegenüber menschenrechtlichen Standards in Strafverfahren', 338); Mosbacher, *NStZ*, 33 (2013), 313–15, essentially agrees with the courts ('There is no methodologically acceptable way of incorporating the results desired by the ECtHR into the structure of established law', orig. 'Es gibt keinen methodisch vertretbaren Weg, das vom EGMR gewünschte Ergebnis in die Struktur des geltenden Rechts einzupassen'). A more doubtful view is put forward by Waszczynski, *NStZ-RR*, 19 (2014), 19–21; for still another view, see Esser, *StV*, 33 (2013), 338–9; and Zehetgruber, *HRRS*, 14 (2013), 403–4, who believe it possible to interpret §329(1) in a way that conforms to the Convention

(admissible representation by a defence counsel demanded by human rights law); cf. also Engel, *ZJS*, 6 (2013), 344.

313. OLG Celle, 32 Ss 29/13 (n. 310), p. 615 (orig. 'an der deutschen Rechtslage fundamental vorbei', 'Interesse des Angeklagten, sich von einem Verteidiger in der Berufungshauptverhandlung vertreten zu lassen ... von Art. 6 IIIc EMRK nach sachgerechter Interpretation dieser Vorschrift rechtlich nicht geschützt').
314. Act on Strengthening the Right of the Accused to be Represented in Appeal and on Recognition of in Absentia Judgments in Mutual Assistance (Gesetz zur Stärkung des Rechts des Angeklagten auf Vertretung in der Berufungsverhandlung und über die Anerkennung von Abwesenheitsentscheidungen in der Rechtshilfe, *BGBl.* I 2015, 1332) (representation of defendant by defence counsel, presence of defendant only in legally prescribed cases and new paras. (2)–(4) of §329 StPO); crit. *Böhm NJW*, 68 (2015), 3132–6; Spitzer, *StV*, 36 (2016), 48 ff.
315. Esser, *Europäisches Strafverfahrensrecht* (2002), pp. 457–8, 472–3, 490–1; Villiger, *Handbuch der EMRK* (1999), p. 330; Sommer, in Brüssow et al., *Strafverteidigung in der Praxis* (2007), pp. 841–2 (derived from fair trial); Toney, *IJEP*, 5 (2001), 56; cf. also Gaede, in Gaede, Meyer and Schlegel, *HRRS-FG Fezer* (2008), p. 28; rightfully critical of the German Federal Court's inconsistent case law in this regard, cf. Beulke and Barisch, *StV*, 26 (2006), 569 ff.
316. Cf. Peukert, in Frowein and Peukert, *EMRK-Kommentar* (2009), Art. 6 mn. 293; Sommer, in Brüssow et al., *Strafverteidigung in der Praxis* (2007), pp. 831–2.
317. Sommer, in Brüssow et al., *Strafverteidigung in der Praxis* (2007), p. 831; Mayer, in Karpenstein and Mayer, *EMRK* (2015), Art. 6 mn. 197 ('manifest' grave defence errors', orig. 'gravierende Fehlerhaftigkeit des Verteidigerhandelns offensichtlich ist').
318. Sommer, in Brüssow et al., *Strafverteidigung in der Praxis* (2007), pp. 831–2.
319. BGH, No 5 StR 181/09, Judgment (24 June 2009), in *StV*, 29 (2009), 565–6.
320. ECtHR, *Pakelli* v. *Germany*, No 8398/78, Judgment (25 April 1983), para. 31; ECtHR, *Boner* v. *the UK*, No 18711/91, Judgment (28 October 1994), para. 36; ECtHR, *Maxwell* v. *the UK*, No 18949/91, Judgment (28 October 1994), para. 33. Cf. in detail Esser, *Europäisches Strafverfahrensrecht* (2002), pp. 474 ff.; Simon, *Beschuldigtenrechte* (1998), pp. 48–9; 56 ff.; Haefliger, *Die EMRK und die Schweiz* (2008), p. 35; Villiger, *Handbuch der EMRK* (1999), pp. 330–1; Sommer, in Brüssow et al., *Strafverteidigung in der Praxis* (2007), pp. 832–3; Demko, in Gaede, Meyer and Schlegel, *HRRS-FG Fezer* (2008), pp. 1 ff.; Grabenwarter, *ECHR* (2014), Art. 6 mn. 142.
321. ECtHR, *Quaranta*, 12744/87, para. 35. Cf. also Simon, *Beschuldigtenrechte* (1998), pp. 57 ff.; Esser, *Europäisches Strafverfahrensrecht* (2002), pp. 477 ff. In greater detail, Demko, in Gaede, Meyer and Schlegel, *HRRS-FG Fezer* (2008), pp. 3 ff.
322. For more detail overall, cf. Ambos, *ZStW*, 115 (2003), 606–7. On the problem of money laundering by way of legal fees and its tension with Art. 6(3)(c) ECHR, see Bermejo and Wirtz, *ZIS*, 2 (2007), 398 ff.
323. See the classic example of the Fourth Amendment of the US Constitution: 'to be confronted with the witnesses *against* him; to have compulsory process for obtaining witnesses *in his favour*' (author's italics). Cf. also Haefliger and Schürmann, *Die EMRK und die Schweiz* (1999), p. 239; Simon, *Beschuldigtenrechte* (1998), pp. 103–4; Wasek-Wiaderek, *The Principle of 'Equality of Arms'* (2000), p. 27; Sommer, in Brüssow et al., *Strafverteidigung in der Praxis* (2007), pp. 833–4;

Beulke, in Hanack et al., *FS Riess* (2002), p. 6 with n. 12; Schleiminger, *Konfrontation* (2001), p. 143. From the perspective of international criminal procedure, see Ambos, *Treatise ICL III* (2016), pp. 84 ff., 466–7.

324. Gaede, in Gaede, Meyer and Schlegel, *HRRS-FG Fezer* (2008), p. 24; Gundel, in Merten and Papier, *Handbuch der Grundrechte*, vi/1 (2010), p. 349 mn. 147; Ambos, in Radtke and Hohmann, *StPO Kommentar* (2011), Art. 6 mn. 48 incl. further references. Cf. also Demko, *'Menschenrecht auf Verteidigung'* (2014), pp. 414 ff.; Sidhu, *Equality of Arms* (2017), pp. 123–4.
325. ECtHR, *Engel et al.*, 5100/71 et al., para. 91; ECtHR, *Vidal* v. *Belgium*, No 12351/86, Judgment (22 April 1992), para. 33. Cf. also Esser, *Europäisches Strafverfahrensrecht* (2002), p. 633; Villiger, *Handbuch der EMRK* (1999), p. 334; Braitsch, *Gerichtssprache für Sprachunkundige* (1991), p. 163; Sidhu, *Equality of Arms* (2017), pp. 117 ff. On the implementation in Poland (Arts. 185 A–B Polish CCP) cf. Pływaczewski et al., in Pływaczewski and Guzik-Makaruk, *Current Problems of the Penal Law and Criminology* (2017), pp. 204 ff.
326. Cf. Grabenwarter, *ECHR* (2014), Art. 6 mn. 146; also Krauß, *V-Leute im Strafprozess und die EMRK* (1999), pp. 103 ff., 108 ff., 120; Simon, *Beschuldigtenrechte* (1998), p. 106; Rzepka, *Fairness* (2000), pp. 74–5; Villiger, *Handbuch der EMRK* (1999), p. 305; Gaede, *Fairness als Teilhabe* (2005), pp. 278 ff.; Beulke, in Hanack et al., *FS Riess* (2002), pp. 14, 21; Schleiminger, *Konfrontation* (2001), p. 33; Wohlers, *ZStrR*, 123 (2005), 164–5; Velten, *StV*, 27 (2007), 100. For German case law, cf. BGH, No 5 StR 472/06, Decision (14 December 2006), in *StV*, 27 (2007), 226–7 and BGH, 1 StR 493/06 (n. 31), pp. 166–7.
327. More detail is provided in Demko, *'Menschenrecht auf Verteidigung'* (2014), pp. 445 ff.; Sidhu, *Equality of Arms* (2017), pp. 158 ff.; Schleiminger, *Konfrontation* (2001), pp. 31 ff.; Braitsch, *Gerichtssprache für Sprachunkundige* (1991), pp. 165–6; on the defendant's burden of proof, cf. ECtHR, *Garaudy* v. *France*, No 65831/01, Judgment (24 June 2003); on the particular issues raised in transnational criminal procedure with regard to applicability, cf. Krüßmann, *Transnationales Strafprozessrecht* (2009), pp. 685 ff. On the distinction between witnesses for the prosecution and for the defence, cf. Krausbeck, *Konfrontative Zeugenbefragung* (2010), pp. 65 ff.
328. Simon, *Beschuldigtenrechte* (1998), p. 106; Schleiminger, *Konfrontation* (2001), p. 291; arguably also Wohlers, *GA*, 152 (2005), 32; cf. also Stoffers, *NJW*, 66 (2013), 1496–7, who seeks to derive a general right of the defence counsel to be present at all witness examinations (including police examinations) from Art. 6(3)(d) ECHR.
329. See main text, mn. 42.
330. For a convincing argument, cf. Schleiminger, *Konfrontation* (2001), pp. 291, 320–1; for a different opinion, cf. Wohlers, *ZStrR*, 123 (2005), 164 incl. further references.
331. Demko, *'Menschenrecht auf Verteidigung'* (2014), pp. 445 ff., esp. 449 ff.; Walther, *GA*, 150 (2003), 215.
332. ECtHR, *Saïdi* v. *France*, No 14647/89, Judgment (20 September 1993), para. 44 as well as the – already mentioned – Fourth Amendment of the US Constitution: 'to be *confronted*' (author's italics); Demko, *'Menschenrecht auf Verteidigung'* (2014), pp. 445 ff.; Esser, *Europäisches Strafverfahrensrecht* (2002), p. 643; Tochilovsky, *Jurisprudence* (2014), p. 540; Cornelius, *NStZ*, 28 (2008), 244, 247; cf. also Krausbeck, *Konfrontative Zeugenbefragung* (2010), pp. 24–5 and Jung, *GA*, 156 (2009), 236.

333. Walther, *GA*, 150 (2003), 212–13; cf. also Gollwitzer, *Menschenrechte im Strafverfahren* (2005), Art. 6 MRK mn. 225 with n. 632.
334. Cf. also Walther, *GA*, 150 (2003), 214 ff., 220: 'fundamental procedural right of the highest order' (orig. 'Prozessgrundrecht allerhöchsten Ranges'); Walther, *JZ*, 59 (2004), 1110 incl. n. 50. Cf. also Schleiminger, *Konfrontation* (2001), p. 17.
335. Cf. also Beulke, in Hanack et al., *FS Riess* (2002), pp. 15, 21; Gleß, in Zöller et al., *FS Wolter* (2013), p. 1356; cf. also BGH, No 4 StR 662/08, Judgment (17 March 2009), in *StV*, 29 (2009), 346–7 (on the evaluation of evidence when the witness for the prosecution invokes the right to remain silent). Generally Ambos, *ICLR*, 3 (2003), 23 ff.; Ambos, in Bohlander, *International Criminal Justice* (2007), pp. 481 ff. On international criminal procedure, see Ambos, *Treatise ICL III* (2016), pp. 86, 481.
336. ECtHR, *Makeyev* v. *Russia*, No 13769/04, Judgment (5 February 2009), para. 42; Kreicker, in Sieber, Satzger and von Heinegg, *Europäisches Strafrecht* (2014), p. 914.
337. ECtHR, *Bricmont* v. *Belgium*, No 10857/84, Judgment (7 July 1989), para. 81. Cf. also Esser, *Europäisches Strafverfahrensrecht* (2002), p. 644.
338. Conc. Esser, *Europäisches Strafverfahrensrecht* (2002), p. 646; Villiger, *Handbuch der EMRK* (1999), p. 305 incl. n. 23; Beulke, in Hanack et al., *FS Riess* (2002), p. 15; for a view against, cf. Schlothauer, *StV*, 21 (2001), 128; regarding audiovisual presentation of evidence (§255a StPO), see BGH, 1 StR 221/99 (n. 146), pp. 326 ff.; BGH, No 1 StR 64/03, Decision (15 April 2003), in *BGHSt* 48, 268, 271, 274; BGH, 1 StR 493/06 (n. 31), p. 166; restrictively also Swiss Federal Court, *X., Y. and Z.* v. *Kanton Bern*, Judgment (18 March 1987), in *BGE* 113 Ia, 412, 422.
339. On parallels in international criminal procedure, see Ambos, *Treatise ICL III* (2016), pp. 86, 466.
340. Cf. Esser, *Europäisches Strafverfahrensrecht* (2002), p. 645; Schleiminger, *Konfrontation* (2001), p. 16.
341. Cf. Chand, *NLJ*, 150 (2000), 1666.
342. ECtHR, *Bönisch*, 8658/79, para. 32; ECtHR, *Mantovanelli* v. *France*, No 21497/93, Judgment (18 March 1997), para. 36; Krausbeck, *Konfrontative Zeugenbefragung* (2010), pp. 79–80. Cf. also Wasek-Wiaderek, *The Principle of 'Equality of Arms'* (2000), pp. 31–2.
343. ECtHR, *Brandstetter* v. *Austria*, Nos 11170/84 et al., Judgment (28 August 1991), paras. 44 ff.
344. On this issue in general, cf. Demko, *'Menschenrecht auf Verteidigung'* (2014), pp. 457 ff.; Brunhöber, *ZIS*, 5 (2010), 767–8. On the lack of a confrontational defence in case of the use of intelligence information (with special regard to the Spanish law) Jimeno-Bulnes, *NJECL*, 8 (2017), 171ff. (arguing that use of such evidence conflicts with the right to confrontation).
345. For more detail, cf. main text, mn. 57 ff.
346. In BGH, No 4 StR 461/08, Decision (9 June 2009), in *StV*, 30 (2010), 57 a co-defendant made incriminating statements when examined by the court, but when subsequently examined critically by the defence invoked his right to remain silent. When reviewing whether this violation of the right to confrontation had jeopardised fair trial, the German Federal Court focused on whether the fact that the defendant had no opportunity to carry out a confrontative examination could be attributed to the judiciary; for a detailed analysis see Dehne-Niemann, *HRRS*, 11 (2010), 189 ff. On the non-attributability of procedural errors of *foreign* judicial institutions, cf. BGH, No 2 StR 397/09, Decision (17 March 2010), in *NStZ*, 30 (2010), 410–12; for more detail, cf. mn. 60 with n. 389.

347. On this, cf. BGH, No 2 StR 156/04, Decision (3 December 2004), in *NStZ*, 25 (2005), 224–5; BGH, 1 StR 493/06 (n. 31), pp. 166–7 (holding that the issue of the inaccessibility of the witness in the trial is no longer relevant if there are errors in the investigation); the latter was confirmed by BVerfG, No 2 BvR 547/08, Decision (8 October 2009), in *StV*, 30 (2010), 337–42. For more detail on this, cf. Esser, *Europäisches Strafverfahrensrecht* (2002), pp. 648 ff., 657 ff., 678; Gaede, *StV*, 26 (2006), 602 ff.; more critically Maffei, *European Right to Confrontation* (2006), p. 95 ('confrontation is too easily surrendered'); Trechsel, *Die EMRK und die schweizerischen Strafprozessrechte* (1974), pp. 314 ff.; cf. also Demko, *ZStrR*, 122 (2004), 418 ff.; Schleiminger, *Konfrontation* (2001), pp. 11 ff.; Haefliger and Schürmann, *Die EMRK und die Schweiz* (1999), p. 241. On anonymous and police witnesses, cf. Ambos, *ZStW*, 115 (2003), 609 with n. 203; Safferling, *NStZ*, 26 (2006), 77 ff.; Gaede, *Fairness als Teilhabe* (2005), pp. 281 ff.; Krausbeck, *Konfrontative Zeugenbefragung* (2010), pp. 243–4.
348. For a discussion with case law references, see Wohlers, *StV*, 34 (2014), 563 ff.
349. Schleiminger, *Konfrontation* (2001), pp. 17–18.
350. ECtHR, *Van Mechelen et al.*, 21363/93 et al., paras. 56–62; also ECtHR, *S. N.* v. *Sweden*, No 34209/96, Judgment (2 July 2002), para. 44. On undercover investigators' basic obligation to testify according to Art. 252 Austrian CCP in conjunction with Art. 6(3)(d) ECHR, cf. Austrian Supreme Court of Justice (ÖstOGH), No 13 Os 153/03, Decision (18 February 2004), in *NStZ*, 25 (2005), 346–7. On using the statements of a *witness deceased* in the meantime (in line with the Convention), cf. BGH, 2 StR 156/04 (n. 347), pp. 224–5.
351. Cf. BGH, No 5 StR 71/04, Decision (7 July 2004), in *NStZ*, 24 (2004), 691–2 with reference to BGH, No 1 StR 169/00, Judgment (25 July 2000), in *BGHSt* 46, 93, 106.
352. ECtHR, *Haas*, 73047/01. BGH, No 4 StR 345/06, Decision (4 April 2007), *NStZ*, 28 (2008), 51 also follows along these lines, holding that the witness statement in question may not be the only piece of evidence and must be confirmed by other important aspects; in the same vein, BGH, No 1 StR 638/13, Decision (16 April 2014), in *StV*, 35 (2015), 142–3.
353. ECtHR, *Sapunarescu* v. *Germany*, No 22007/03, Judgment (11 September 2006) with critical commentary by Sommer, *StraFo*, 13 (2007), 109.
354. ECtHR, *Sapunarescu*, 22007/03, para. 30.
355. ECtHR, *Sapunarescu*, 22007/03, paras. 32–3; cf. also the case ECtHR, *Bracci* v. *Italy*, No 36822/02, Judgment (13 October 2005), paras. 54 ff., where the defence was also unable to examine the prosecution witnesses 'X' and 'Y'. The ECtHR, in *Bracci* (ibid., paras. 57–8 and 59 ff.) differentiates between the statement given by witness X to the police, which was corroborated by further evidence and the use of which thus conformed to the Convention, and that of witness Y, which was not supported by further evidence and the use of which accordingly constituted a violation of Art. 6(1) and (3)(d) ECHR. From an Italian perspective thereon, cf. Zacchè, *Indice Penale*, 9 (2006), 427 ff. Crit. on the lack of judicial review of *Sperrerklärungen*, i.e. formal executive acts that block witness testimony of undercover or other secret agents, cf. Mahler, *HRRS*, 14 (2013), 333 ff.
356. ECtHR, *Al-Khawaja and Tahery* v. *the UK*, Nos 26766/05 and 22228/06, Judgment (15 December 2011), para. 147 ('sufficient counterbalancing factors . . . including measures that permit a fair and proper assessment of the reliability of that

evidence') with commentary by Du Bois-Pedain, *HRRS*, 13 (2012), 120 ff.; and (critically) Meyer, *HRRS*, 13 (2012), 117 ff.; on this, cf. also Esser, Gaede and Tsambikakis, *NStZ*, 32 (2012), 148; Widder, *CJICL*, 3 (2014), 1084 ff. Confirmed in ECtHR, *Hümmer* v. *Germany*, No 26171/07, Judgment (19 July 2012), para. 37; on this, cf. Grabenwarter, *ECHR* (2014), Art. 6 mn. 158; cf. also Esser, *Europäisches und Internationales Strafrecht* (2018), §9 mn. 268.

357. Cf. Esser, *Europäisches Strafverfahrensrecht* (2002), pp. 670–1, 677; Schleiminger, *Konfrontation* (2001), pp. 318–19; Wohlers, *ZStrR*, 123 (2005), 166; Mayer, in Karpenstein and Mayer, *EMRK* (2015), Art. 6 mn. 207. For this view see also ECtHR, *S. N.*, 34209/96, para. 49 where the ECtHR argued that the defendant could have demanded that the police examination of a child witness was recorded on video. The same view is taken by Krausbeck, *Konfrontative Zeugenbefragung* (2010), p. 314.

358. ECtHR, *Doorson* v. *the Netherlands*, No 20524/92, Judgment (26 March 1996), paras. 73–5; Esser, *Europäisches Strafverfahrensrecht* (2002), pp. 666 ff.; Villiger, *Handbuch der EMRK* (1999), p. 306.

359. Cf. Simon, *Beschuldigtenrechte* (1998), p. 135; Schleiminger, *Konfrontation* (2001), p. 15; and Ambos, *NStZ*, 23 (2003), 16–17 incl. further references.

360. ECtHR, *Van Mechelen et al.*, 21363/93 et al., para. 59; Esser, *Europäisches Strafverfahrensrecht* (2002), pp. 668 ff.; Schleiminger, *Konfrontation* (2001), p. 16; Wohlers, in Donatsch, Forster and Schwarzenegger, *FS Trechsel* (2002), p. 816.

361. Cf. ECtHR, *Accardi et al.* v. *Italy*, Nos 30598/02 et al., Judgment (20 January 2005). On particularly vulnerable witnesses, cf. Krausbeck, *Konfrontative Zeugenbefragung* (2010), pp. 306 ff.

362. ECtHR, *Kamasinski* v. *Austria*, No 9783/82, Judgment (19 December 1989), para. 74. Cf. also Simon, *Beschuldigtenrechte* (1998), pp. 142 ff.; Rzepka, *Fairness* (2000), pp. 80 ff.; Esser, *Europäisches Strafverfahrensrecht* (2002), pp. 508 ff.; Kieschke, *Praxis des EGMR* (2003), pp. 72 ff.; Braitsch, *Gerichtssprache für Sprachunkundige* (1991), pp. 166 ff.; Haefliger and Schürmann, *Die EMRK und die Schweiz* (1999), pp. 188, 234 ff.; Sommer, in Brüssow et al., *Strafverteidigung in der Praxis* (2007), p. 837; Grabenwarter and Pabel, in Dörr, Grote and Marauhn, *EMRK/GG*, i (2013), Kapitel 14 mn. 161; on the criteria for the parts of the proceedings that require interpretation, cf. EU, *Green Paper on Procedural Safeguards* (2003), pp. 26 ff. (p. 30, Question 10).

363. This used to be controversial; cf. Peukert, in Frowein and Peukert, *EMRK-Kommentar* (2009), Art. 6 mn. 317; Braitsch, *Gerichtssprache für Sprachunkundige* (1991), p. 183; Haefliger and Schürmann, *Die EMRK und die Schweiz* (1999), p. 235 with n. 81; Sommer, in Brüssow et al., *Strafverteidigung in der Praxis* (2007), p. 837.

364. Cf. Esser, *Europäisches Strafverfahrensrecht* (2002), pp. 511 ff.; Haefliger and Schürmann, *Die EMRK und die Schweiz* (1999), pp. 220, 234–5; Villiger, *Handbuch der EMRK* (1999), p. 324.

365. BVerfG, No 2 BvR 2118/01, Decision (7 Octobert 2003), in *BVerfGK* 2, 36, 44.

366. Thus Mayer, in Karpenstein and Mayer, *EMRK* (2015), Art. 6 mn. 220.

367. In the ACHR system, the Court only examines the individual violation; see e.g. more recently IACtHR, 19 *Comerciantes* v. *Colombia*, Judgment (5 July 2004), para. 186 (adequate facilities for preparation of defence); IACtHR, *Tibí* v. *Ecuador*, Judgment (7 September 2004), para. 198 (torture to obtain confession

as fair-trial violation); IACtHR, *Mohamed* v. *Argentina*, Judgment (23 November 2012), paras. 86 ff. (right to review by a higher tribunal). The same applies to the ICCPR system; see HRC, *Polay Campos* v. *Peru*, No 577/1994 (CCPR/C/61/D/577/1994) (6 November 1997), para. 8.8 (trial by 'faceless' judges). In more recent judgments regarding the military justice system, the IACtHR has, however, analysed the overall impact of military proceedings on certain fair trial rights, cf. especially IACtHR *Arguelles et al.* v. *Argentina*, Serie C No 288, Judgment (20 November 2014), para. 166 (looking at the process in its integral form ('de manera integral'), especially the review of the military court's judgment by an ordinary court, and denying a violation of Articles 8 (1) and 25 (1) ACHR).

368. On the two-levels test instructively, see Krauß, *V-Leute im Strafprozess und die EMRK* (1999), pp. 141 ff.; see also Satzger, *International and European Criminal Law* (2018), §9 mn. 79.

369. Cf. Haefliger and Schürmann, *Die EMRK und die Schweiz* (1999), pp. 180, 219; Villiger, *Handbuch der EMRK* (1999), p. 302; Zwaak, in Van Dijk et al., *Theory and Practice of the ECHR* (2006), p. 318; Rzepka, *Fairness* (2000), pp. 102 ff.; Schleiminger, *Konfrontation* (2001), pp. 8, 21; Meyer-Ladewig, Harrendorf and König, in Meyer-Ladewig, Nettesheim and von Raumer, *EMRK* (2017), Art. 6 mn. 92; Demko, *HRRS*, 6 (2005), 283 ff.; Gaede, *Fairness als Teilhabe* (2005), pp. 427 ff.; Vogel and Matt, *StV*, 27 (2007), 209 (critically 211); Kreicker, in Sieber, Satzger and von Heinegg, *Europäisches Strafrecht* (2014), pp. 907–8; Gleß, *Internationales Strafrecht* (2015), mn. 85–6; crit. Walter, in Roth, *Europäisierung des Rechts* (2010), p. 306; on the differentiation between violations of whole and partial rights, using the example of the freedom to self-incrimination: Hauck, *NStZ*, 30 (2010), 20 ff.; on the prohibition of the use of evidence derived from partial rights of Art. 6 in reference to particular groups of cases, cf. Gaede, *JR*, 81 (2009), 495–6.

370. Cf. e.g. ECtHR, *Öcalan*, 46221/99, paras. 140, 153; ECtHR, *Haas*, 73047/01; ECtHR, *Bugallo*, 21218/09, paras. 37 ff.; ECtHR, *Bandaletov* v. *Ukraine*, No 23180/06, Judgment (31 October 2013), para. 58; ECtHR, *Ibrahim et al.* v. *UK*, Nos 50541/08 et al., GC Judgment (13 September 2016), paras. 387 ff. For a critical stance on this when the rights of the defence are impaired in the investigation, cf. Gaede, *Fairness als Teilhabe* (2005), pp. 455 ff.

371. ECtHR, *Teixeira de Castro*, 44/1997/828/1034, paras. 35–6, 39; cf. also ECtHR, *Vanyan* v. *Russia*, No 53203/99, Judgment (15 December 2005), paras. 46–7; ECtHR, *Ramanauskas*, paras. 54, 60; ECtHR, *Pyrgiotakis* v. *Greece*, No 15100/06, Judgment (21 February 2008), paras. 16–17; ECtHR, *Bannikova*, 18757/06, paras. 34–5, 56.

372. Cf. ECtHR, *Gäfgen* v. *Germany*, No 22978/05, Judgment (30 June 2008), paras. 97 ff. (confirmed by the Grand Chamber, *Gäfgen* v. *Germany*, No 22978/05, GC Judgment (1 June 2010)), where, however, no violation of the Article 6 was found by the court ('only' inhuman treatment, para. 70); in the same vein Greer, *HRLR*, 11 (2011), 77 (at 79–80 also agreeing with the ECtHR's result regarding Art. 6).

373. ECtHR, *Öcalan*, 46221/99, paras. 140 ff.; ECtHR, *Ibrahim*, 50541/08 et al., paras. 387 ff.; against a restriction of the right to legal representation in general, Spaniol, *Recht auf Verteidigerbeistand* (1990), pp. 164 ff., 173; concurring, Walther, *GA*, 150 (2003), 222.

374. Cf. ECtHR, *De Haes and Gijsels* v. *Belgium*, No 19983/92, Judgment (24 February 1997), paras. 58–9 ('substantial disadvantage'); Toney, *IJEP*, 5 (2001), 47.
375. ECtHR, *Magee* v. *the UK*, No 28135/95, Judgment (6 June 2000), paras. 44–5 (defence rights 'irretrievably prejudiced'); ECtHR, *Öcalan*, 46221/99, para. 143; see also Spaniol, *Recht auf Verteidigerbeistand* (1990), pp. 164 ff., 173.
376. In depth and with further references, see Ambos, *Beweisverwertungsverbote* (2010), pp. 102 ff. On the developments in the case law, see Lubig and Sprenger, *ZIS*, 3 (2008), 433 ff. and Du Bois-Pedain, *HRRS*, 13 (2012), 120 ff.
377. ECtHR, *Bykov*, 4378/02, para. 91 ('the Court . . . found the use of covert listening devices to be in breach of Article 8 since recourse to such devices lacked a legal basis in domestic law and the interferences with those applicants' right to respect for their private life were not "in accordance with the law". Nonetheless, the admission in evidence of information obtained thereby did not in the circumstances of the cases conflict with the requirements of fairness guaranteed by Article 6 §1'); for a critical view, see Jung, *GA*, 156 (2009), 655; Gaede, *JR*, 81 (2009), 500.
378. This doctrine, originally developed by the case law (ECtHR, *Handyside* v. *the UK*, No 5493/72, Judgment (7 December 1976), para. 48), has now been taken up in AP XV (Protocol No 15 amending the Convention for the Protection of Human Rights and Fundamental Freedoms of 24 June 2013 (ETS No 213)), which provides in Art. 1 for the doctrine to be included in the ECHR's preamble ('At the end of the preamble to the Convention, a new recital shall be added, which shall read as follows: "Affirming that the High Contracting Parties, in accordance with the principle of subsidiarity, have the primary responsibility to secure the rights and freedoms defined in this Convention and the Protocols thereon, and that in doing so they enjoy a *margin of appreciation*, subject to the supervisory jurisdiction of the European Court of Human Rights established by this Convention"' (emphasis added)). The doctrine received widespread support by States Parties, especially in the UK-sponsored 'Brighton Declaration' on the Future of the ECHR of 19/20 April 2012, available at www.echr.coe.int/Documents/2012_Brighton_FinalDeclaration_ENG.pdf, last accessed 27 January 2018. For a recent systematic analysis of the doctrine in the Court's case law, cf. McGoldrick, *ICLQ*, 65 (2016), 21 ff. (explaining its justification, at 32–7, and advocating its universal use – that is, by the UN HRC – at 52 ff.); from a methodological perspective, cf. Jung, in Callies, *Herausforderungen an Staat und Verfassung* (2015), pp. 976 ff.; for an analysis of the Court's deeper understanding of the doctrine ('deeper subsidiarity') in relation to national parliaments cf. Saul, *HRLR*, 15 (2015), 745 ff., concluding (772) that the Court is increasingly 'taking account of the quality of the processes of national authorities in its determination of the margin of appreciation to be afforded states'. On the development of the Court's subsidiarity concept which is the basis of the margin of appreciation doctrine (the latter being its normative offspring), Mowbray, *HRLR*, 15 (2015), 313 ff.
379. Cf. e.g. ECtHR, *S. N.*, 34209/96, para. 44; cf. also Sommer, in Brüssow et al., *Strafverteidigung in der Praxis* (2007), pp. 834, 841. On the margin of appreciation doctrine in general, cf. Tulkens and Donnay, *RSC*, 2006, 3 ff.
380. ECtHR, *Doorson*, 20524/92, para. 76; ECtHR, *S. N.*, 34209/96, para. 53; ECtHR, *Krasniki* v. *the Czech Republic*, No 51277/99, Judgment (28 February 2006), para. 77; ECtHR, *Jakubczyk* v. *Poland*, No 17354/04, Judgment (10 May 2011), para. 45.

381. ECtHR, *Al-Khawaja and Tahery*, 26766/05 and 22228/06, para. 147 ('At the same time where a conviction is based solely or decisively on the evidence of absent witnesses, the Court must subject the proceedings to the most searching scrutiny . . . the admission of such evidence . . . would require sufficient counterbalancing factors, including the existence of strong procedural safeguards'); ECtHR, *Karparenko* v. *Russia*, No 5605/04, Judgment (13 March 2013), para. 61; ECtHR, *Matytsina* v. *Russia*, No 58428/10, Judgment (27 March 2014), para. 152. For previous case law, see ECtHR, *Windisch*, 12489/86, para. 31; ECtHR, *Doorson*, 20524/92, para. 76; ECtHR, *Van Mechelen et al.*, 21363/93 et al., para. 55; ECtHR, *P. S.* v. *Germany*, No 33900/96, Judgment (20 December 2001), para. 153; cf. also Schleiminger, *Konfrontation* (2001), p. 19; Jung, *GA*, 150 (2003), 203; Esser, *Europäisches Strafverfahrensrecht* (2002), pp. 647–8; on German case law cf. Krausbeck, *Konfrontative Zeugenbefragung* (2010), pp. 178 ff.
382. See also ECtHR, *Al-Khawaja and Tahery*, 26766/05 and 22228/06, para. 119 ('when a conviction is based solely or to a decisive degree on depositions that have been made by a person whom the accused has had no opportunity to examine or to have examined, whether during the investigation or at the trial, the rights of the defence may be restricted to an extent that is incompatible with the guarantees provided by Article 6 (the so-called "sole or decisive rule")'); in favour of this flexible approach, Widder, *CJICL*, 3 (2014), 1095 ff. (advocating its adoption also by the HRC and the IACtHR, at 1097); crit. on the 'sole or decisive rule' Heffernan, *E. & P.*, 20 (2016), 108 ff.
383. See also ECtHR, *Al-Khawaja and Tahery*, 26766/05 and 22228/06, para. 119 ('Court will examine below whether the latter rule is to be considered as an absolute rule the breach of which automatically leads to a finding that the proceedings have not been fair').
384. ECtHR, *Asch* v. *Austria*, No 12398/86, Judgment (26 April 1991), paras. 28–31; cf. also Esser, *Europäisches Strafverfahrensrecht* (2002), pp. 652 ff.
385. ECtHR, *Stojkovic* v. *France*, No 25303/08, Judgment (27 October 2011).
386. On this, cf. also Gleß, *ZStW*, 125 (2013), 576 ff.; Renzikowski, in Hellmann and Schröder, *FS Achenbach* (2011), pp. 373 ff.; Nagler, *StV*, 33 (2013), 325 ff.
387. ECtHR, *Stojkovic*, 25303/08, paras. 55–7.
388. ECtHR, *Stojkovic*, 25303/08, para. 55.
389. In a similar vein, for example, the German Federal Court of Justice has assumed that acts of mutual assistance that comply with the national law of the requested state cannot be attributed to the requesting state in general (BGH, 2 StR 397/09 (n. 346), pp. 410–12). This restrictive approach does not deserve approval, as it ultimately makes it possible for States to shrug off responsibility for human rights violations, which is particularly worrisome in light of the increase in transnational prosecution in Europe (cf. Gleß, in Zöller et al., *FS Wolter* (2013), pp. 1366–7; similarly Sommer, *StraFo*, 16 (2010), 284–5; for a change in the case law also Nagler, *StV*, 33 (2013), 326). Ultimately the question of which State is responsible for the Convention violation cannot be decisive as long as the violation has an effect in the use of the respective evidence in the requesting State (cf. Gleß, in Zöller et al., *FS Wolter* (2013), p. 1363).
390. Cf. Gleß, *ZStW*, 125 (2013), 592 ff (607: exclusion if 'superordinate individual interests that should be protected by exclusion of evidence have been violated'; orig. 'übergeordnete Individualinteressen verletzt worden sind, die durch ein Beweisverwertungsverbot geschützt werden müssen').

391. For a critical view, see also Esser, *Europäisches Strafverfahrensrecht* (2002), pp. 404, 468; Beulke, in Hanack et al., *FS Riess* (2002), p. 9; Schleiminger, *Konfrontation* (2001), pp. 8 ff.; for this reason the suggestions for solution presented in Villiger, *Handbuch der EMRK* (1999), pp. 324–5 are questionable.
392. In a similar vein, Walther, *GA*, 150 (2003), 218; on conflicting guarantees also Smet, *HRLR*, 17 (2017), 499 ff. (advocating a balancing solution on the basis of the distinction between 'absolute rights function as rules' and 'relative rights function as principles'); for a different view, see Wohlers, *GA*, 152 (2005), 26; for more detail, incl. references, cf. Ambos, *ZStW*, 115 (2003), 613.
393. Cf. eg. ECtHR, *Al-Khawaja and Tahery*, 26766/05 and 22228/06, para. 118 ('proceedings as a whole having regard to the rights of the defence but also to the interests of the public and the victims that crime is properly prosecuted ... and, where necessary, to the rights of witnesses '). For a critical discussion, cf. Jung, in Heger, Kelker and Schramm, *FS Kühl* (2014), pp. 915 ff.
394. In a similar vein, Krausbeck, *Konfrontative Zeugenbefragung* (2010), p. 52.
395. Cf. Chapter 5, mn. 20 ff.; generally already Chapter 1, mn. 26 ff.
396. On its scope, cf. ECtHR, *Amnur* v. *France*, No 19776/92, Judgment (25 June 1996); on this, see Demko, *HRRS*, 5 (2004), 171 ff.; cf. also Satzger, *International and European Criminal Law* (2018), §9 mn. 53; Satzger, *Internationales und Europäisches Strafrecht* (2016), §11 mn. 49; and the evaluation model in Esser, *Europäisches und Internationales Strafrecht* (2018), §9 mn. 166; from a Polish point of view, Morgenstern, *ZIS*, 6 (2011), 243 ff. On the classification of house arrest, cf. Hochmayr, *NStZ*, 33 (2013), 14–15.
397. Esser, *StraFo*, 9 (2003), 338; Grabenwarter, *ECHR* (2014), Art. 5 mn. 1; Schmitt, in Meyer-Goßner and Schmitt, *StPO* (2017), Art. 5 MRK mn. 1; Demko, *HRRS*, 5 (2004), 95–6.
398. Grabenwarter, *ECHR* (2014), Art. 5 mn. 1; Unfried, *Freiheits- und Sicherheitsrechte EMRK* (2006), p. 30; Ambos, in Radtke and Hohmann, *StPO Kommentar* (2011), Art. 6 mn. 4.
399. ECtHR, *Amnur*, 19776/92, paras. 44–5; Gärditz, in Menzel, Pierlings and Hoffmann, *Völkerrechtsprechung* (2005), pp. 527 ff.; Elberling, in Karpenstein and Mayer, *EMRK* (2015), Art. 5 mn. 7; Esser, *Europäisches und Internationales Strafrecht* (2018), §9 mn. 168.
400. Meyer-Ladewig, Harrendorf and König, in Meyer-Ladewig, Nettesheim and von Raumer, *EMRK* (2017), Art. 5 mn. 14 ff.; Peters and Altwicker, *EMRK* (2012), §18 mn. 21; Elberling, in Karpenstein and Mayer, *EMRK* (2015), Art. 5 mn. 18.
401. Gollwitzer, *Menschenrechte im Strafverfahren* (2005), Art. 5 MRK mn. 27, 29; Peters and Altwicker, *EMRK* (2012), §18 mn. 21; Grabenwarter, *ECHR* (2014), Art. 5 mn. 8.
402. Cf. ECtHR, *M.* v. *Germany*, No 19359/04, Judgment (17 December 2009), para. 90 with case law references.
403. ECtHR, *Mooren*, 11364/03, paras. 72 ff., 83 ff.; ECtHR, *M.*, 19359/04, para. 90; Esser, Gaede and Tsambikakis, *NStZ*, 31 (2011), 79–80; Gollwitzer, *Menschenrechte im Strafverfahren* (2005), Art. 5 MRK mn. 32; Meyer-Ladewig, Harrendorf and König, in Meyer-Ladewig, Nettesheim and von Raumer, *EMRK* (2017), Art. 5 mn. 16; Peters and Altwicker, *EMRK* (2012), §18 mn. 22.
404. Eiffler, *NJW*, 52 (1999), 763; Satzger, *International and European Criminal Law* (2018), §9 mn. 53. This observation of national law was lacking, for example, in ECtHR, *K.-F.* v. *Germany*, No 25629/94, Judgment (27 November 1997), where in

a case of arrest for the purposes of identification the *legally* defined twelve-hour time limit of §163(3) StPO was exceeded by 45 minutes. However, not every procedural error automatically leads to the deprivation of liberty in question becoming unlawful. Rather, a Convention violation only exists in cases of severe and obvious violations of national law, ECtHR, *Mooren*, 11364/03, paras. 74–5, 84 ('a gross and obvious irregularity'). On this case, cf. also Satzger, *International and European Criminal Law* (2018), §9 mn. 63; Esser, Gaede and Tsambikakis, *NStZ*, 31 (2011), 81–2.

405. ECtHR, *Mooren*, 11364/03, para. 76; ECtHR, *M.*, 19359/04, para. 90; Meyer-Ladewig, Harrendorf and König, in Meyer-Ladewig, Nettesheim and von Raumer, *EMRK* (2017), Art. 5 mn. 17–18; Peters and Altwicker, *EMRK* (2012), §18 mn. 21.
406. ECtHR, *K.-F.*, 25629/94, para. 63; ECtHR, *Mooren*, 11364/03, paras. 72, 77 ff.; ECtHR, *M.*, 19359/04, para. 90; ECtHR, *Bergmann* v. *Germany*, No 23279/14, Judgment (7 January 2016), para. 102; on this, cf. Eiffler, *NJW*, 52 (1999), 762–3.
407. ECtHR, *Guzzardi* v. *Italy*, No 7367/76, Judgment (6 November 1980), para. 98; ECtHR, *Assanidzé* v. *Georgia*, No 48787/99, Judgment (8 July 2004), para. 170; ECtHR, *McKay* v. *the UK*, No 543/03, Judgment (3 October 2006), para. 30; ECtHR, *Bergmann*, 23729/14, para. 95; also Esser, in Erb et al., *Löwe-Rosenberg StPO*, xi (2012), Art. 5 EMRK mn. 39.
408. ECtHR, *Radu* v. *Germany*, No 20084/07, Judgment (16 May 2013), para. 86; Meyer-Ladewig, Harrendorf and König, in Meyer-Ladewig, Nettesheim and von Raumer, *EMRK* (2017), Art. 5 mn. 17; Peters and Altwicker, *EMRK* (2012), §18 mn. 12 ff.; Kreicker, in Sieber, Satzger and von Heinegg, *Europäisches Strafrecht* (2014), p. 919.
409. Gollwitzer, *Menschenrechte im Strafverfahren* (2005), Art. 5 MRK mn. 39.
410. ECtHR, *De Wilde, Ooms and Versyp* v. *Belgium*, Nos 2832/66, 2835/66 and 2899/66, Judgment (18 June 1971), para. 78 ('independence of the executive and of the parties to the case . . . but also the guarantees of judicial procedure'); ECtHR, *Engel et al.*, 5100/71 et al., para. 68; cf. also Grabenwarter, *ECHR* (2014), Art. 5 mn. 12.
411. Grabenwarter, *ECHR* (2014), Art. 5 mn. 12; Meyer-Ladewig, Harrendorf and König, in Meyer-Ladewig, Nettesheim and von Raumer, *EMRK* (2017), Art. 5 mn. 28.
412. ECtHR, *M.*, 19359/04, para. 88 with further references; Grabenwarter, *ECHR* (2014), Art. 5 mn. 12.
413. Cf. von Hirsch, *Censure and Sanctions* (1995) and von Hirsch and Ashworth, *Proportionate Sentencing* (2005), pp. 12 ff.
414. Cf. Meyer-Ladewig, Harrendorf and König, in Meyer-Ladewig, Nettesheim and von Raumer, *EMRK* (2017), Art. 5 mn. 1.
415. Gollwitzer, *Menschenrechte im Strafverfahren* (2005), Art. 5 MRK mn. 42 incl. further references; arguing against this, Grabenwarter, *ECHR* (2014), Art. 5 mn. 12, referring to ECtHR, *Guzzardi*, 7367/76, para. 100; also Elberling, in Karpenstein and Mayer, *EMRK* (2015), Art. 5 mn. 29.
416. Cf. in detail Esser, *Europäisches Strafverfahrensrecht* (2002), pp. 212 ff.
417. ECtHR, *Luberti* v. *Italy*, No 9019/80, Judgment (23 February 1984), paras. 10, 25; cf. also Esser, *Europäisches Strafverfahrensrecht* (2002), p. 215.

418. §66 StGB. §66a StGB provides for a deferred incapacitation order ('vorbehaltene Sicherungsverwahrung') and §66b StGB for a subsequent one; thereon see the main text.
419. Cf. e.g. Arts. 69–70 **Greek** PC (security measures in therapeutic institution for criminally not responsible, but dangerous offenders); §78 **Hungarian** CC (security measures); Arts. 119 ff., 215 **Italian** CC ('misure di sicurezza'); Arts. 93 ff. **Polish** CC ('środki zabezpieczające'). In **Portugal** the CC provides for the internment in a psychiatric institution (Arts. 91 ff. CC, 'medida de segurança de internamento') and offenders with diminished ability to understand the unlawfulness of their acts may be subject to security measures (Art. 20(4) CC); it is further argued that the 'relatively indeterminate' sentence applicable to *inimputáveis* (Arts. 83 ff. CC) is similar to a preventive custodial measure (Antunes and Caeiro, in Michaelsen, *Comparative Perspectives on the Theory and Practice of Preventive Detention* (2017) (forthcoming)).
420. See e.g. for **England and Wales** (protective sentencing regarding dangerous offenders, i.e. continued detention after expiry of tariff due to dangerousness) von Hirsch, *Doing Justice* (1986), pp. 124 ff., arguing that such 'variations from the deserved sentence' as 'predictive restraint might be necessary for a few especially violent defendants', but they shall be permitted 'only in narrowly delineated special cases' (p. 131); Floud, *BJC*, 22 (1982), 213 ff. (advocating bringing 'protective sentencing under statutory control', 220). But see also for civil law jurisdictions: **Greece** (Arts. 90–92 Greek PC (increase [indefinitely] over the limits prescribed for the particular offence, for *habitual or professional* offenders or *habitual or professional* recidivists, who are a danger for public security), and Arts. 38–41 (confinement in psychiatric institutions for indeterminate maximum duration for dangerous offenders with diminished responsibility), thereon Billis, in Sieber, Jarvers and Silvermann, *National Criminal Law in a Comparative Legal Context*, 1.2 (2013), p. 251); **Hungary** (§§89, 90 CC (increase in case of recidivicism), thereon Karsai and Szomora, *Criminal Law in Hungary* (2015), pp. 132–3); and **Sweden** (Ch. 31 sect. 3 CC).
421. ECtHR, *M.*, 19359/04, para. 96; confirmed in ECtHR, *Grosskopf* v. *Germany*, No 24478/03, Judgment (21 October 2010), paras. 46–7; following on from ECtHR case law, BVerfG, No 2 BvR 1048/11, Decision (20 June 2012), in *BVerfGE* 131, 268, 296 (thereon Merkel, *ZIS*, 7 (2012), 521 ff.; conc. Satzger, *StV*, 33 (2013), 247). In the *M.* case, the ECtHR affirmed a violation of Art. 5(1) ECHR, as the deprivation of liberty exceeded the maximum period of ten years valid at the time of conviction (§67d (1) StGB old version) and thus could no longer be seen as the result of the first conviction (cf. ECtHR, *M.*, 19359/04, paras. 97 ff.; on this, cf. Kinzig, *NStZ*, 30 (2010), 235 ff.; also Freund, *GA*, 157 (2010), 206 ff.; crit. as to the reasoning Hörnle, in Bernsmann and Fischer, *FS Rissing-van Saan* (2011), pp. 242 ff.). By contrast, the German Constitutional Court had confirmed the compatibility of the maximum period with the Basic Law, including for the 'old cases' ('Altfälle') (BVerfG, No 2 BvR 2029/01, Decision (21 October 2003), in *BVerfGE* 109, 133, 187). The infringement of the right to liberty in Art. 2(2) GG resulting from preventive detention must be weighed up against the public's need for security. For more detail on the *M.* case and case 11, cf. main text, mn. 108, 132, 141; see also the case solution presented in Hecker and Zöller, *Fallsammlung* (2012), pp. 147 ff. (case 15).

422. The ECtHR stated this in an *obiter dictum* in ECtHR, *M.*, 19359/04, para. 96; it was confirmed in ECtHR, *Haidn* v. *Germany*, No 6587/04, Judgment (13 January 2011), paras. 84 ff. and ECtHR, *Bergmann*, 23279/14, para. 104; for a critical stance on this, cf. Schöch, in Heinrich et al., *FS Roxin*, ii (2013), p. 1204; see also BGH, No 5 StR 60/10, Decision (21 July 2010), in *NStZ*, 30 (2010), 565–7; OLG Hamm, No 4 Ws 171/10, Decision (22 July 2010), in *NStZ-RR*, 15 (2010), 388–9; Drenkhahn and Morgenstern, *ZStW*, 124 (2012), 150–1; Renzikowski, *ZIS*, 6 (2011), 535; Elberling, in Karpenstein and Mayer, *EMRK* (2015), Art. 5 mn. 36; Grabenwarter, *ECHR* (2014), Art. 5 mn. 12. Cf. also Kinzig, *NStZ*, 30 (2010), 235, 239 (considering also the deferred preventive detention/incapacitation order as incompatible with Art. 5 ECHR) and Müller, *StV*, 30 (2010), 211; on its justification based on Art. 5(1)(c), see main text, mn. 72.
423. Schmitt, in Meyer-Goßner and Schmitt, *StPO* (2017), Art. 5 MRK mn. 2a; Meyer-Ladewig, Harrendorf and König, in Meyer-Ladewig, Nettesheim and von Raumer, *EMRK* (2017), Art. 5 mn. 28; Vogler, *ZStW*, 89 (1977), 761, 770.
424. Grabenwarter, *ECHR* (2014), Art. 5 mn. 12; Meyer-Ladewig, Harrendorf and König, in Meyer-Ladewig, Nettesheim and von Raumer, *EMRK* (2017), Art. 5 mn. 32; Gollwitzer, *Menschenrechte im Strafverfahren* (2005), Art. 5 MRK mn. 48.
425. ECtHR, *Douiyeb* v. *the Netherlands*, No 31464/96, Judgment (4 August 1999), para. 45; ECtHR, *Radu*, 20084/07, para. 88; Meyer-Ladewig, Harrendorf and König, in Meyer-Ladewig, Nettesheim and von Raumer, *EMRK* (2017), Art. 5 mn. 32; on this, cf. also Thunberg Schunke, *Whose Responsibility?* (2013), pp. 85 ff.
426. Meyer-Ladewig, Harrendorf and König, in Meyer-Ladewig, Nettesheim and von Raumer, *EMRK* (2017), Art. 5 mn. 35.
427. Esser, *Europäisches Strafverfahrensrecht* (2002), p. 218; Schmitt, in Meyer-Goßner and Schmitt, *StPO* (2017), Art. 5 MRK mn. 3. Cf. also the examples in ECtHR, *Gatt* v. *Malta*, No 28221/08, Judgment (27 July 2010), para. 37.
428. ECtHR, *Steel et al.* v. *the UK*, No 24838/94, Judgment (23 September 1998), paras. 68 ff.; Esser, *Europäisches Strafverfahrensrecht* (2002), p. 217–18 (imprisonment after an unsuccessful request to keep the peace, following a breach of the peace).
429. ECtHR, *Lawless* v. *Ireland*, No 332/57, Judgment (1 July 1961), para. 9; Peukert, in Frowein and Peukert, *EMRK-Kommentar* (2009), Art. 5 mn. 55; Meyer-Ladewig, Harrendorf and König, in Meyer-Ladewig, Nettesheim and von Raumer, *EMRK* (2017), Art. 5 mn. 36; Prill, *Präventivhaft zur Terrorismusbekämpfung* (2010), pp. 269 ff. (276); Schilling, *Internationaler Menschenrechtsschutz* (2016), §10 mn. 240.
430. Grabenwarter, *ECHR* (2014), Art. 5 mn. 13.
431. ECtHR, *Engel et al.*, 5100/71, para. 69; Grabenwarter, *ECHR* (2014), Art. 5 mn. 13; Meyer-Ladewig, Harrendorf and König, in Meyer-Ladewig, Nettesheim and von Raumer, *EMRK* (2017), Art. 5 mn. 36; Peukert, in Frowein and Peukert, *EMRK-Kommentar* (2009), Art. 5 mn. 69.
432. ECtHR, *Johansen* v. *Norway*, No 10600/83, Judgment (14 October 1985); on this, cf. Peukert, in Frowein and Peukert, *EMRK-Kommentar* (2009), Art. 5 mn. 56 (detention to enforce civilian service as alternative to military service).
433. Grabenwarter, *ECHR* (2014), Art. 5 mn. 13.
434. Grabenwarter, *ECHR* (2014), Art. 5 mn. 15–16; Esser, in Joerden and Szwarc, *Europäisierung des Strafrechts* (2007), pp. 238 ff.; for the contrary view Meyer-Ladewig, Harrendorf and König, in Meyer-Ladewig, Nettesheim and von Raumer,

EMRK (2017), Art. 5 mn. 38; on the issue of a violation of Art. 7 (*nulla poena sine lege*) and the option of derogation in regard to preventive detention in light of the case ECtHR, *Lawless*, 332/57, cf. Schneider, in Menzel, Pierlings and Hoffmann, *Völkerrechtsprechung* (2005), pp. 524 ff.

435. Peters and Altwicker, EMRK (2012), §18 mn. 16; Elberling, in Karpenstein and Mayer, *EMRK* (2015), Art. 5 mn. 52.
436. Grabenwarter, *ECHR* (2014), Art. 5 mn. 17; Schilling, *Internationaler Menschenrechtsschutz* (2016), §10 mn. 241–2; on particularities of trials on the grounds of suspicion of terrorist crimes, cf. Demko, *HRRS*, 5 (2004), 95, 98 ff.
437. ECtHR, *Erdagöz* v. *Turkey*, No 127/1996/945/746, Judgment (22 October 1997), paras. 51–2; ECtHR, *Fox, Campbell and Hartley* v. *the UK*, Nos 12244/86, 12245/86 and 12383/86, Judgment (30 August 1990), paras. 32 ff.; Grabenwarter, *ECHR* (2014), Art. 5 mn. 17; Peters and Altwicker, EMRK (2012), §18 mn. 13; Demko, *HRRS*, 5 (2004), 95, 97–8; Esser, *Europäisches und Internationales Strafrecht* (2018), §9 mn. 178.
438. ECtHR, *Loukanov* v. *Bulgaria*, No 21915/93, Judgment (20 March 1997), paras. 42–6; Peukert, in Frowein and Peukert, *EMRK-Kommentar* (2009), Art. 5 mn. 64 (stating that an objective observer must be convinced that the suspect could have committed the offence in question); Grabenwarter, *ECHR* (2014), Art. 5 mn. 17; Peters and Altwicker, *EMRK* (2012), §18 mn. 16.
439. Cf. e.g. Arts. 137 and 143–1 ff. **French** CPP (esp. 144); §§112 ff. **German** StPO; Arts. 282(3) 296 **Greek** CPP; Arts. 280, 380 ff., 384 **Italian** CPP; Arts. 489 ff., 502 ff. **Spanish** LEC. For an analysis of the minimum standards in pre-trial detention in the EU Member States, cf. also the country reports in van Kalmthout, Knapen and Morgenstern, *Pre-trial Detention in the EU* (2009).
440. ECtHR, *Kemmache* v. *France*, No 17621/91, Judgment (24 November 1994), para. 42; Meyer-Ladewig, Harrendorf and König, in Meyer-Ladewig, Nettesheim and von Raumer, *EMRK* (2017), Art. 5 mn. 40.
441. ECtHR, *W.* v. *Switzerland*, No 14379/88, Judgment (26 January 1993), para. 30; Grabenwarter, *ECHR* (2014), Art. 5 mn. 17; Peters and Altwicker, *EMRK* (2012), §18 mn. 16. On compensation for excessively long detention, cf. Reich, *Überlange Verfahrensdauer* (2011), pp. 174 ff.
442. Cf. main text, mn. 79–82.
443. ECtHR, *Haidn*, 6587/04, para. 90.
444. Grabenwarter, *ECHR* (2014), Art. 5 mn. 20.
445. In Germany the police authorities speak of *Gefährder* (dangerous offender, 'endangerer'), cf. Böhm, in Duttge and Lee, *The Law in the Information and Risk Society* (2011), pp. 145 ff. On the 'prevalent but elusive' concept of dangerousness in English criminal justice, cf. Floud, *BJC*, 22 (1982), 214–15.
446. On terrorist offences, cf. Grabenwarter, *ECHR* (2014), Art. 5 mn. 18, arguing that they fall into a special category.
447. ECtHR, *Makarov* v. *Russia*, No 15217/07, Judgment (12 March 2009), para. 134 ('specific facts supporting their finding that there existed a risk of the applicant's reoffending').
448. ECtHR, *M.*, 19359/04, para. 102; ECtHR, *Guzzardi*, 7367/76, para. 102 (no 'general prevention directed against . . . individuals who, like mafiosi, present a danger on account of their continuing propensity to crime', but 'a means of preventing a concrete and specific offence'); ECtHR, *Haidn*, 6587/04, para. 90; Grabenwarter,

ECHR (2014), Art. 5 mn. 20; Meyer-Ladewig, *EMRK* (2011), Art. 5 mn. 39. For more detail on preventive detention for the purposes of combatting terrorism, cf. Prill, *Präventivhaft zur Terrorismusbekämpfung* (2010), pp. 279 ff.; cf. also Macken, *Counter-terrorism* (2011), pp. 53 ff.

449. ECtHR, *Haidn*, 6587/04, para. 90; cf. also Müller, *StV*, 30 (2010), 211; Drenkhahn and Morgenstern, *ZStW*, 124 (2012), 152; Renzikowski, *ZIS*, 6 (2011), 536. In ECtHR, *M.*, 19359/04, para. 102, the ECtHR focused on the fact that in the case in question the risk of new crimes had not become sufficiently clear yet; thereon Kinzig, *NStZ*, 30 (2010), 236. In detail on retrospective preventive detention (subsequent incapitation order), taking account of a range of constellations, Greger, *NStZ*, 30 (2010), 678 ff. Its compatibility with Art. 5 has always been controversial: arguing against it already, Renzikowski, *JR*, 76 (2004), 273–4 (purely preventive detention not covered by Art. 5(1)(c) ECHR); Ullenbruch, *NJW*, 61 (2008), 2609, 2613–14; von Freier, *ZStW*, 120 (2008), 273, 326 with n. 184; for the same conclusion, Wollmann, *NK*, 19 (2007), 154–5; for a different view, see Trechsel, *Die EMRK und die schweizerischen Strafprozessrechte* (1974), pp. 225 ff.
450. Esser, *Europäisches und Internationales Strafrecht* (2018), §9 mn. 184; Grabenwarter, *ECHR* (2014), Art. 5 mn. 22.
451. ECtHR, *Bouamar* v. *Belgium*, No 9106/80, Judgment (29 February 1988), paras. 50 and 52; Grabenwarter, *ECHR* (2014), Art. 5 mn. 22.
452. Peukert, in Frowein and Peukert, *EMRK-Kommentar* (2009), Art. 5 mn. 75; Grabenwarter, *ECHR* (2014), Art. 5 mn. 22.
453. On this, cf. the overview of case law provided in Ambos, in Radtke and Hohmann, *StPO Kommentar* (2011), Art. 5 mn. 17.
454. Grabenwarter, *ECHR* (2014), Art. 5 mn. 23.
455. ECtHR, *Winterwerp* v. *the Netherlands*, No 6301/73, Judgment (24 October 1979), para. 39; ECtHR, *Luberti*, 9019/80, para. 27; ECtHR, *Ashingdane* v. *the UK*, No 8225/78, Judgment (28 May 1985), para. 37; Grabenwarter, *ECHR* (2014), Art. 5 mn. 23.
456. On this, cf. BGH, 1 StR 554/09 (n. 31), pp. 383 (subsequent incapacitation order following sentencing to juvenile punishment); crit. Kreuzer, *NStZ*, 30 (2010), 477; Bartsch, *StV*, 30 (2010), 521, 524; Renzikowski, *NStZ*, 30 (2010), 507–8; cf. also Ostendorf and Petersen, *ZRP*, 43 (2010), 245 ff.
457. ECtHR, *Guzzardi*, 7367/76, para. 98; ECtHR, *Litwa* v. *Poland*, No 26629/95, Judgment (4 April 2000), para. 60; ECtHR, *Herz* v. *Germany*, No 44672/98, Judgment (12 June 2003); ECtHR, *Bergmann*, 23279/14, para. 97.
458. ECtHR, *Bergmann*, 23279/14, para. 100.
459. For a general restrictive interpretation cf. ECtHR, *Bergmann*, 23279/14, para. 95; ECtHR, *Shimovolos* v. *Russia*, No 30194/09, Judgment (21 June 2011), para. 51; ECtHR, *Winterwerp*, 6301/73, para. 37 ('Only a narrow interpretation of the exhaustive list of permissible grounds for deprivation of liberty is consistent with the aim of Article 5, namely to ensure that no one is arbitrarily deprived of his liberty').
460. 'Unsound mind' is to be understood more restrictively than 'mental disorder', i.e., as a serious, true mental disorder; cf. ECtHR, *Bergmann*, 23279/14, paras. 113–14.
461. ECtHR, *Bergmann*, 23279/14, para. 96 (with references to earlier case law); for the application to the case see ibid., paras. 106 ff., concluding that the continued

detention was lawful under Art. 5(1)(e) ECHR (paras. 133–4 and main text above).

462. ECtHR, *Hutchison Reid* v. *the UK*, No 50272/99, Judgment (20 February 2003), para. 48; ECtHR, *Haidn*, 6587/04, para. 94; ECtHR, *Kallweit* v. *Germany*, No 17792/07, Judgment (13 January 2011), para. 46; ECtHR, *Bergmann*, 23279/14, para. 99. Crit. of the lack of such appropriate institutions in Germany Renzikowski, *NStZ*, 30 (2010), 508.

463. Thus BVerfG, 2 BvR 2365/09 (n. 31), p. 326; BGH, No 5 StR 52/11, Judgment (21 June 2011), in *NStZ*, 31 (2011), 631–2; cf. also ECtHR, *M.*, 19359/04, para. 102; on this, cf. Greger, *NStZ*, 30 (2010), 678 and OLG Hamm, 4 Ws 171/10 (n. 422), p. 389; for a different view, Elberling, in Karpenstein and Mayer, *EMRK* (2015), Art. 5 mn. 69.

464. ECtHR, *Haidn*, 6587/04, para. 94; ECtHR, *Kallweit*, 17792/07, para. 46; ECtHR, *B.* v. *Germany*, No 61272/09, Judgment (19 April 2012), paras. 81–2; ECtHR, *Radu*, 20084/07, para. 83; more or less in agreement Drenkhahn and Morgenstern, *ZStW*, 124 (2012), 152; Grabenwarter, *ECHR* (2014), Art. 5 mn. 24; Esser, Gaede and Tsambikakis, *NStZ*, 32 (2012), 558.

465. Art. 2 Therapieunterbringungsgesetz (ThUG, Act on Therapy and Detention of Mentally Disturbed Violent Offenders, see main text, mn. 133). However, it remains unclear which criteria are to apply when determining the existence of mental illness and whether the ThUG meets the requirements of Art. 5(1)(e) in this regard; crit. Satzger, *StV*, 33 (2013), 248; Renzikowski, *ZIS*, 6 (2011), 537–8; on this, cf. also Ullenbruch, *StV*, 32 (2012), 47; Ullenbruch, *StV*, 34 (2014), 174 ff. (incl. a critical analysis of the implementation practice); Elberling, in Karpenstein and Mayer, *EMRK* (2015), Art. 5 mn. 70–1 and BVerfG, No 2 BvR 1516/11, Decision (15 September 2011), in *BVerfGK*, 19, 72, discussed in Morgenstern, *ZIS*, 6 (2011), 975.

466. ECtHR, *Bergmann*, 23279/14, para. 123 ('Court welcomes the extensive measures which have been taken in the defendant State on judicial, legislative and executive levels with a view to adapting preventive detention to the requirements, in particular, of the fundamental right to liberty'). The Chamber concretely analyses the situation in the Preventive Detention Centre of Rosdorf (ibid., paras. 3, 34 ff., 119 ff.), close to the town of Göttingen, which was constructed as a separate building on the premises of the Rosdorf prison complex, in order to host mentally ill inmates under the German custodial detention regime in compliance with the *Abstandsgebot* ('differentiation/distinction requirement') to be explained in the main text, mn. 133 with n. 759. From September 2015 to February 2017 the author was in charge of this section of the prison as part-time judge at the District Court Göttingen.

467. ECtHR, *Bergmann*, 23279/14, paras. 125 ('this staffing situation, which was similar to that in a psychiatric hospital run in the same *Land*, put the authorities in a position to address the applicant's mental disorder'), 127 ('it transpires from the Rosdorf centre's treatment plan that the applicant was successfully encouraged to participate in group therapy'), 128 ('applicant was offered the therapeutic environment appropriate for a person detained as a mental-health patient and was thus detained in an institution suitable for the detention of such patients').

468. ECtHR, *Bergmann*, 23279/14, paras. 129–32.

469. Peters and Altwicker, *EMRK* (2012), §18 mn. 20. Elberling, in Karpenstein and Mayer, *EMRK* (2015), Art. 5 mn. 81 incl. further references. In the context of the refugee movement via the so-called Balkan route, the ECtHR judged the detention of refugees in the border regions on Hungarian territory without any formal legal

basis to constitute an unlawful deprivation of liberty and a violation of Art. 5(1)(f) (ECtHR, *Ilias and Ahmed* v. *Hungary*, No 47287/15, Judgment (14 March 2017), paras. 65–8).

470. ECtHR, *Saadi* v. *the UK*, No 13229/03, Judgment (29 January 2008), para. 72.
471. Grabenwarter, *ECHR* (2014), Art. 5 mn. 26.
472. Available at www.legislation.gov.uk/ukpga/2001/24/pdfs/ukpga_20010024_en.pdf, last accessed 27 January 2018; Sect. 21–32 ATCSA were repealed by Prevention of Terrorism Act 2005 (14 March 2005).
473. Human Rights Act 1998 (Amendment No 2) Order 2001 (S I 2001/3644).
474. House of Lords, *A. and Others* v. *Secretary of State for the Home Department*, No [2004] UKHL 56, Opinions of the Lords of Appeal for Judgment (16 December 2004).
475. Sect. 23 (1) ATCSA 2001: 'despite the fact that his removal or departure from the United Kingdom is prevented (whether temporarily or indefinitely) by – (a) a point of law which wholly or partly relates to an international agreement or (b) a practical consideration.'
476. On the preconditions and procedures of derogation, cf. Grabenwarter and Pabel, *EMRK* (2016), §2 mn. 8 ff., who use the term 'suspension' (*Suspendierung*).
477. House of Lords, *A. and Other*, [2004] UKHL 56, paras. 73 ('section 23 of the Anti-terrorism, Crime and Security Act 2001 is incompatible with articles 5 and 14 of the European Convention insofar as it is disproportionate and permits detention of suspected international terrorists in a way that discriminates on the ground of nationality or immigration status'), 84 ('Unwanted aliens who cannot be deported, as much as nationals, are not to be detained indefinitely without charge or trial'), 97 ('a power of detention confined to foreigners is irrational and discriminatory'), 139 ('section 23 of the Anti-terrorism, Crime and Security Act 2001 is incompatible with the right to liberty in article 5 of the ECHR on the ground that it is not proportionate, and that it is incompatible with article 14 of the Convention on the ground that it discriminates against the appellants in their enjoyment of the right to liberty on the ground of their national origin'), 160 ('the Order is not compliant with article 15 of the ECHR'), 189 ('the detention of the foreign suspects cannot be strictly required . . . to meet the comparable threat that they pose. The second requirement of article 15(1) is accordingly not satisfied. Equally, it follows that there has been a breach of article 14 and that the third of the requirements for a valid derogation under article 15(1) is not satisfied either').
478. Previously thereon, Ambos, *NStZ*, 23 (2003), 14–15; Ambos, *ZStW*, 115 (2003), 583, 601 ff.
479. Grabenwarter, *ECHR* (2014), Art. 5 mn. 31.
480. Peters and Altwicker, *EMRK* (2012), §18 mn. 27.
481. On this, cf. Gollwitzer, *Menschenrechte im Strafverfahren* (2005), Art. 5 MRK mn. 108; examples from practice (a Swiss district prosecutor can act as a judicial officer, but not a Dutch military auditor) in Peukert, in Frowein and Peukert, *EMRK-Kommentar* (2009), Art. 5 mn. 107.
482. Grabenwarter, *ECHR* (2014), Art. 5 mn. 31; on the lack of judicial monitoring of pre-trial detention in Eastern European states, cf. Pellonpää, in Donatsch, Forster and Schwarzenegger, *FS Trechsel* (2002), pp. 84 ff.
483. ECtHR, *Brogan et al.* v. *the UK*, Nos 11209/84, 11234/84, 11266/84 and 11386/84, Judgment (29 November 1988), para. 59; cf. also Grabenwarter, *ECHR* (2014), Art. 5 mn. 32.

484. ECtHR, *Brogan et al.*, 11209/84 et al., para. 62; ECtHR, *Aquilina* v. *Malta*, No 25642/94, GC Judgment (29 April 1999), para. 48; ECtHR, *Kandzhov* v. *Bulgaria*, No 68294/01, Judgment (06 November 2008), para. 65.
485. ECtHR, *De Jong, Baljet and Van den Brink* v. *the Netherlands*, Nos 8805/79, 8806/79 and 9242/81, Judgment (22 May 1984), paras. 51–2; ECtHR, *Brogan et al.*, 11209/84 et al., para. 59; ECtHR, *Aquilina*, 25642/94, para. 48; ECtHR, *Kandzhov*, 68294/01, para. 65.
486. ECtHR, *McKay*, 543/03, para. 47; ECtHR, *İpek et al.* v. *Turkey*, Nos 17019/02 and 30070/02, Judgment (3 February 2009), para. 36; cf. also ECtHR, *Aquilina*, 25642/94, para. 51 (appearance before a magistrate two days after the person's arrest was regarded as 'prompt').
487. ECtHR, *Kandzhov*, 68294/01, para. 66. On the interrelationship between the ECHR guarantees, esp. Art. 6, and the EU rights Directives (main text, mn. 146 ff.) see Wahl, ERA *Forum*, 18 (2017), 311 ff. (concluding that the Directives, on the one hand, go beyond the ECHR, and, on the other, fall short of the ECHR minimum standard requiring further elaboration by case law.
488. ECtHR, *Brogan et al.*, 11209/84 et al., para. 62; cf. also ECtHR, *Harkmann* v. *Estonia*, No 2192/03, Judgment (11 July 2006), para. 39 (a period of fifteen days 'is incompatible with the requirement of "promptness"').
489. ECtHR, *De Jong, Baljet and Van den Brink*, 8805/79 et al., para. 51; ECtHR, *Aquilina*, 25642/94, para. 49; ECtHR, *Harkmann*, 2192/03, para. 36; ECtHR, *McKay*, 543/03, para. 34. Cf. aslo Grabenwarter, *ECHR* (2014), Art. 5 mn. 31.
490. On the excessive use and length of pre-trial detention in many EU Member States, Cf. EU, *Green Paper on Detention* (2011), pp. 14 ff. (Annexes); thereon, Anagnostopoulos, *ERA Forum*, 15 (2014), 22.
491. ECtHR, *Erdem* v. *Germany*, No 38321/97, Judgment (5 July 2001), paras. 39 ff.; ECtHR, *Cevizovic* v. *Germany*, No 49746/99, Judgment (29 July 2004), paras. 38 and 41; cf. also OLG Hamm, No III-3 Ws 37/12, Decision (1 March 2012), in *StV*, 33 (2013), 166; OLG Koblenz, No 2 Ws 383/10, Decision (26 August 2010), in *StV*, 31 (2011), 167–9; Renzikowski, in Joerden and Szwarc, *Europäisierung des Strafrechts* (2007), pp. 344–5.
492. Cf. ECtHR, *Bykov*, 4378/02, para. 66 as well as BVerfG, No 2 BvR 388/09, Judgment (13 May 2009), in *StV*, 29 (2009), 481; cf. also Peters and Altwicker, *EMRK* (2012), §18 mn. 30; a critical view is also taken by Tiedemann, *ZRP*, 23 (1992), 108, who suggests fixed terms for pre-trial detention. A critical stance is also taken by Unfried, *Freiheits- und Sicherheitsrechte* (2006), pp. 77, esp. 118–19.
493. ECtHR, *Cevizovic*, 49746/99, para. 37; Esser, in Joerden and Szwarc, *Europäisierung des Strafrechts* (2007), p. 240; Grabenwarter, *ECHR* (2014), Art. 5 mn. 35; Meyer-Ladewig, Harrendorf and König, in Meyer-Ladewig, Nettesheim and von Raumer, *EMRK* (2017), Art. 5 mn. 83; Peters and Altwicker, *EMRK* (2012), §18 mn. 30; Esser, *Europäisches und Internationales Strafrecht* (2018), §9 mn. 194; in detail on the relevant case law: Reindl, *Untersuchungshaft und Menschenrechtskonvention* (1997), pp. 121 ff.; cf. also Tochilovsky, *Jurisprudence* (2014), pp. 1225 ff.; Gialuz and Spagnolo, *EuCLR*, 3 (2013), 222 ff.
494. In ECtHR, *Toth* v. *Austria*, No 11894/85, Judgment (12 December 1991), paras. 66 ff., a detention period of two years, one month and two days was deemed unreasonably long due to the lack of 'special diligence' by the national authorities in the conduct of the proceedings; cf. also Peters, *Einführung in die EMRK* (2003),

p. 99. On the other hand, in *Cevicovic*, the Court deemed four years, nine months and three days of pre-trial detention inappropriate (ECtHR, *Cevicovic*, No 49746/99, Judgment (29 July 2004), paras. 34, 53 ff.).

495. Meyer-Ladewig, Harrendorf and König, in Meyer-Ladewig, Nettesheim and von Raumer, *EMRK* (2017), Art. 5 mn. 83; cf. also BGH, No 1 StR 238/08, Judgment (9 October 2008), in *StV*, 28 (2008), 633–4; OLG Nürnberg, No 1 Ws 28 – 30/09, Judgment (11 February 2009), in *StV*, 29 (2009), 367–8.
496. ECtHR, *Cevizovic*, 49746/99, para. 37; ECtHR, *Labita* v. *Italy*, No 26772/95, Judgment (6 April 2000), paras. 152–3; ECtHR, *Kudla*, 30210/96, para. 110; ECtHR, *Erdem*, 38321/97, para. 39; cf. also BVerfG, No 2 BvR 109/05, Decision (22 February 2005), in *NStZ*, 25 (2005), 456–7; BVerfG, No 2 BvR 1315/05, Decision (23 September 2005), in *StV*, 25 (2005), 615 and BVerfG, No 2 BvR 1964/05, Decision (5 December 2005), in *NJW*, 59 (2006), 672; OLG Hamm, No 2 Ws 56/06, Decision (2 March 2006), in *StV*, 26 (2006), 481–2; on this, cf. Jahn, *NJW*, 59 (2006), 653; Esser, in Joerden and Szwarc, *Europäisierung des Strafrechts* (2007), p. 234; cf. also Grabenwarter, *ECHR* (2014), Art. 5 mn. 35.
497. ECtHR, *Letellier* v. *France*, No 12369/86, Judgment (26 June 1991), para. 43; Mansdörfer, *GA*, 157 (2010), 158 ff.
498. ECtHR, *Brogan et al.*, 11209/84 et al., para. 61; for a detailed account of this, cf. Klugmann, *EMRK und antiterroristische Maßnahmen* (2002), pp. 109 ff.; for a critical view of the *Brogan* case, cf. Tanca, *EJIL*, 1/2 (1990), 269, 273 ff.; cf. also Grabenwarter, *ECHR* (2014), Art. 5 mn. 35.
499. ECtHR, *Toth*, 11894/85, paras. 64 ff., esp. 76–7; ECtHR, *Kudla*, 30210/96, paras. 110–11; Meyer-Ladewig, Harrendorf and König, in Meyer-Ladewig, Nettesheim and von Raumer, *EMRK* (2017), Art. 5 mn. 85; Grabenwarter, *ECHR* (2014), Art. 5 mn. 36; Peters and Altwicker, *EMRK* (2012), §18 mn. 30.
500. ECtHR, *Toth*, 11894/85, para. 77; Peters and Altwicker, *EMRK* (2012), §18 mn. 30.
501. ECtHR, *Dzelili* v. *Germany*, No 65745/01, Judgment (10 November 2005), para. 83; BGH, No 5 StR 363/09, Decision (22 September 2009), in *NStZ*, 30 (2010), 229–30 (referring to deduction of time in line with §51(1) first sentence StGB).
502. ECtHR, *Wemhoff* v. *Germany*, No 2122/64, Judgment (27 June 1968), paras. 14–15; on this, cf. Meyer-Ladewig, Harrendorf and König, in Meyer-Ladewig, Nettesheim and von Raumer, *EMRK* (2017), Art. 5 mn. 91. Cf. also ECtHR, *Mangouras* v. *Spain*, No 12050/04, Judgment (28 January 2010), para. 79; Grabenwarter, *ECHR* (2014), Art. 5 mn. 37.
503. ECtHR, *Letellier*, 12369/86, para. 46; ECtHR, *Neumeister*, 1936/63, para. 14; Grabenwarter, *ECHR* (2014), Art. 5 mn. 37.
504. ECtHR, *Dzelili*, 65745/01, paras. 82 ff.; on this, cf. Pauly, *StV*, 26 (2006), 480–1.
505. Cf. Esser, *Europäisches Strafverfahrensrecht* (2002), pp. 342 ff.
506. Meyer-Ladewig, Harrendorf and König, in Meyer-Ladewig, Nettesheim and von Raumer, *EMRK* (2017), Art. 5 mn. 69. Cf. also Satzger, *International and European Criminal Law* (2018), §9 mn. 60; Satzger, *Internationales und Europäisches Strafrecht* (2016), §11 mn. 50.
507. ECtHR, *Van der Leer* v. *the Netherlands*, No 11509/85, Judgment (21 February 1990), para. 30.
508. ECtHR, *Van der Leer*, 11509/85, paras. 25 ff., esp. 28; Meyer-Ladewig, Harrendorf and König, in Meyer-Ladewig, Nettesheim and von Raumer, *EMRK* (2017), Art. 5 mn. 70.

509. ECtHR, *Sanchez-Reisse* v. *Switzerland*, No 9862/82, Judgment (21 October 1986), paras. 51; ECtHR, *Keus* v. *the Netherlands*, No 12228/86, Judgment (25 October 1990), para. 28; ECtHR, *Nikolova* v. *Bulgaria*, No 31195/96, Judgment (25 March 1999), para. 58. On this, cf. also Esser, *Europäisches Strafverfahrensrecht* (2002), p. 346; Sommer, in Brüssow et al., *Strafverteidigung in der Praxis* (2007), p. 855.
510. Esser, *Europäisches Strafverfahrensrecht* (2002), p. 349 (arguing that the application for the review of a detention entails the applicant being present at the hearing).
511. Cf. ECtHR, *Toth*, 11894/85, paras. 83–4; Esser, *Europäisches Strafverfahrensrecht* (2002), pp. 347–8.
512. Peters and Altwicker, *EMRK* (2012), §18 mn. 27 ff., 34; Ambos, in Radtke and Hohmann, *StPO Kommentar* (2011), Art. 5 mn. 27. Cf. also Grabenwarter, *ECHR* (2014), Art. 5 mn. 39.
513. ECtHR, *V.* v. *the UK*, No 24888/94, Judgment (16 December 1999), para. 122 (violation of Art. 5(4) on the grounds that 'the applicant has been deprived . . . of the opportunity to have the lawfulness of his detention reviewed by a judicial body'); ECtHR, *T.* v. *the UK*, No 24724/94, Judgment (16 December 1999), para. 121.
514. Cf. Brockhaus and Ullrich, *StV*, 36 (2016), 678 ff.
515. ECtHR, *Kurt* v. *Turkey*, No 15/1997/799/1002, Judgment (25 May 1998), paras. 122 ff.; ECtHR, *Mooren*, 11364/03, para. 124; cf. also Hoffmann, in Menzel, Pierlings and Hoffmann, *Völkerrechtsprechung* (2005), p. 513; Schilling, *Internationaler Menschenrechtsschutz* (2016), §10 mn. 233. On enforced disappearance as a crime against humanity, see Ambos, *Treatise ICL II* (2014), pp. 108–12.
516. ECtHR, *El-Masri* v. *the FYROM*, No 3963/09, GC Judgment (13 December 2012), paras. 236 ff., 240; also ECtHR, *Al Nashiri* v. *Poland*, No 28761/11, Judgment (24 July 2014), paras. 453 ff.; ECtHR, *Husayn (Abu Zubaydah)* v. *Poland*, No 7511/13, Judgment (24 July 2014), paras. 451 ff.; ECtHR, *Nasr and Ghali* v. *Italy*, No 44883/09, Judgment (23 February 2016), paras. 172 ff.; thereon also Fabbrini, *HRLR*, 14 (2014), 85; Ambos, *EuCLR*, 5 (2015), 107 ff.; Staffler, *EuGRZ*, 43 (2016), 344 ff. On the European discussion and treatment of the CIA rendition flights, see Heinz, in Müller, Sander and Válková, *FS Eisenberg* (2009), pp. 39 ff.
517. ECtHR, *El-Masri*, 3963/09, para. 239; ECtHR, *Al Nashiri*, 28761/11, paras. 517–19; ECtHR, *Husayn (Abu Zubaydah)*, 7511/13, paras. 521–3; ECtHR, *Nasr and Ghali*, 44883/09, paras. 301–2; thereon Ambos, *EuCLR*, 5 (2015), 108, 110, 115–16, 119.
518. Cf. Simon, *Beschuldigtenrechte* (1998), pp. 31–2, 42–3; Walischewski, *Akteneinsichtsrecht* (1999), pp. 71 ff., 84, 141; Esser, *Europäisches Strafverfahrensrecht* (2002), pp. 351 ff.; Ambos, *NStZ*, 23 (2003), 14; Jung, *GA*, 150 (2003), 201–2; Unfried, *Freiheits- und Sicherheitsrechte* (2006), pp. 121 ff., esp. 129; for a critical stance, see Trechsel, in Schweizer, Burkert and Gasser, *FS Druey* (2002), pp. 1004–5.
519. Cf. ECtHR, *Mooren*, 11364/03, paras. 91–2; ECtHR, *Shishkov* v. *Bulgaria*, No 38822/97, Judgment (9 January 2003), para. 77; ECtHR, *Nikolova*, 31195/96, para. 97; cf. also Renzikowski, in Joerden and Szwarc, *Europäisierung des Strafrechts* (2007), pp. 326 ff. incl. further references; ECtHR, *Kunkel* v. *Germany*, No 29705/05, Decision (2 June 2009).
520. ECtHR, *Mooren*, 11364/03, para. 92; ECtHR, *Shishkov*, 38822/97, para. 77.
521. ECtHR, *Falk* v. *Germany*, No 41077/04, Decision (11 March 2008).
522. Above, main text, mn. 40.

523. On this substantive understanding of equality of arms, cf. Ambos, *ZStW*, 115 (2003), 615–16.
524. Similarly Esser, *Europäisches Strafverfahrensrecht* (2002), pp. 352–3.
525. Ambos, in Radtke and Hohmann, *StPO Kommentar* (2011), Art. 5 mn. 28. On the reform of the respective provision in the German CCP (§147(2) StPO) to bring it more into line with the ECHR, Jahn, in Schulz, Reinhart and Sahan, *FS Imme Roxin* (2012), pp. 586 ff., 590 ff.
526. For an overview, cf. Meyer-Ladewig and Nettesheim, in Meyer-Ladewig, Nettesheim and von Raumer, *EMRK* (2017), Art. 8 mn. 35 ff., 114–15, 94 ff., appendix to Art. 8 mn. 4 ff.; Ambos, in Radtke and Hohmann, *StPO Kommentar* (2011), Art. 8 mn. 4 ff. On the challenges of Article 8 decisions in the UK's judicial practice cf. Ockelton, in Ziegler, Wicks and Hodson, *The UK and European Human Rights* (2015), pp. 218–20.
527. Art. 8 may also be violated if state authorities set up databases containing the DNA of offenders for the purposes of prosecution; ECtHR, *S and Marper* v. *the UK*, Nos 30562/04 and 30566/04, Judgment (4 December 2008), paras. 119 ff.; cf. also Grabenwarter, *ECHR* (2014), Art. 8 mn. 29–30.
528. Cf. in detail on the issue of the confiscation of objects, Esser, *Europäisches Strafverfahrensrecht* (2002), pp. 126 ff. In the case of ECtHR, *Bosphorus Hava Yollari Turizm ve Ticaret Anonim Sirketi* v. *Ireland*, No 45036/98, Judgment (30 June 2005), para. 150, the ECtHR decided that the confiscation (which lasted several years) of an aeroplane on the basis of an EC order served significant public interest and denied any violation of Art. 1 AP I; for more detail, cf. Winkler, *EuGRZ*, 34 (2007), 641 ff.; Schorkopf, *Staatsrecht* (2017), §8 mn. 108.
529. ECtHR, *Buck* v. *Germany*, No 41604/98, Judgment (28 April 2005), paras. 44, 47, 52 in a case dealing with the charge of road traffic offence. On the lack of proportionality, cf. also ECtHR, *Keegan* v. *the UK*, No 28867/03, Judgment (9 August 2006), with a commentary by Roberts, *JCL*, 70 (2006), 481.
530. Esser, *Europäisches Strafverfahrensrecht* (2002), p. 126.
531. ECtHR, *McLeod* v. *the UK*, No 72/1997/856/1065, Judgment (23 September 1998), para. 36; Esser, *Europäisches Strafverfahrensrecht* (2002), p. 125; cf. also Grabenwarter, *ECHR* (2014), Art. 8 mn. 37.
532. ECtHR, *Weber and Saravia* v. *Germany*, No 54934/00, Decision (29 June 2006), para. 77; ECtHR, *Malone* v. *the UK*, No 8691/79, Judgment (2 August 1984), para. 64.
533. Gollwitzer, *Menschenrechte im Strafverfahren* (2005), Art. 8 MRK mn. 37; Grabenwarter, *ECHR* (2014), Art. 8 mn. 28; on email communication cf. de Hert, *ULR*, 1 (2005), 74; ECtHR, *Copland* v. *the UK*, No 62617/00, Judgment (3 April 2007), paras. 41–2; on the confiscation of data cf. ECtHR, *Robathin* v. *Austria*, No 30457/06, Judgment (3 July 2012), paras. 38; Schilling, *Internationaler Menschenrechtsschutz* (2016), §12 mn. 355.
534. Grabenwarter, *ECHR* (2014), Art. 8 mn. 40, 61. From an empirical perspective, cf. Albrecht, Dorsch and Krüpe, *Rechtswirklichkeit und Effizienz der Überwachung der Telekommunikation* (2003).
535. ECtHR, *Malone*, 8691/79, paras. 67, 79 ('the law of England and Wales does not indicate with reasonable clarity the scope and manner of exercise of the relevant discretion conferred on the public authorities. To that extent, the minimum

degree of legal protection to which citizens are entitled under the rule of law in a democratic society is lacking'), finding a violation of Art. 8 (para. 80).

536. Cf. in detail Esser, *Europäisches Strafverfahrensrecht* (2002), pp. 145 ff.
537. Cf. in detail on this topic Gaede, *StV*, 24 (2004), 46 ff.; Esser, *Europäisches Strafverfahrensrecht* (2002), pp. 148 ff. Cf. also Schilling, *Internationaler Menschenrechtsschutz* (2016), §12 mn. 358 ff.
538. See, however, main text, mn. 112 ff., on the controversial issue of whether Art. 2 ECHR limits the national regulations on self-defence.
539. Gaede, *StV*, 24 (2004), 46 ff.
540. ECtHR, *A.*, 14838/89; ECtHR, *M. M.*, 39339/98.
541. Esser, *Europäisches Strafverfahrensrecht* (2002), p. 149.
542. Cf. also Ambos, in Radtke and Hohmann, *StPO Kommentar* (2011), Art. 8 mn. 15; Schilling, *Internationaler Menschenrechtsschutz* (2016), §12 mn. 362 ff.
543. Cf. Peters and Altwicker, *EMRK* (2012), §30 mn. 2.
544. This restriction applies for example to measures governing the use of living space (Esser, *Europäisches und Internationales Strafrecht* (2018), §9 mn. 299).
545. ECtHR, *Silver et al.* v. *the UK*, Nos 5947/72 et al., Judgment (25 March 1983), paras. 26, 93, 98; ECtHR, *Pfeifer and Plankl* v. *Austria*, No 10802/84, Judgment (25 February 1992), para. 46; ECtHR, *Campbell* v. *the UK*, No 13590/88, Judgment (25 March 1992), para. 45; Grabenwarter, *ECHR* (2014), Art. 8 mn. 69.
546. ECtHR, *Puzinas* v. *Lithuania*, No 44800/98, Judgment (14 March 2002), para. 21; Grabenwarter, *ECHR* (2014), Art. 8 mn. 69.
547. ECtHR, *Erdem*, 38321/97, para. 61; on this, see Ambos, *NStZ*, 23 (2003), 15–16.
548. Meyer-Ladewig and Nettesheim, in Meyer-Ladewig, Nettesheim and von Raumer, *EMRK* (2017), Art. 8 mn. 110. Cf. Grabenwarter, *ECHR* (2014), Art. 8 mn. 69.
549. Cf. Esser, *Europäisches und Internationales Strafrecht* (2018), §9 mn. 303 ff.
550. ECtHR, *Erdem*, 38321/97, paras. 62 ff., 64, 67 (referring to §148(2) StPO); on this, see Ambos, *NStZ*, 23 (2003), 15–16.
551. ECtHR, *Dudgeon* v. *the UK*, No 7525/76, Judgment (22 October 1981), paras. 33, 41, 52; on this, cf. Esser, *Europäisches Strafverfahrensrecht* (2002), p. 135–6 (comparing this to the similar position of the BGH regarding the confiscation of diaries and similar highly personal records).
552. ECtHR, *Golder* v. *the UK*, No 4451/70, Judgment (21 February 1975), para. 44; Esser, *Europäisches Strafverfahrensrecht* (2002), p. 317.
553. ECtHR, *De Wilde, Ooms and Versyp*, 2832/66, 2835/66 and 2899/66, para. 39 (royal decree on monitoring correspondence sufficient); ECtHR, *Golder*, 4451/70, paras. 17, 43, 45 (the 1964 Prison Rules based on the 1952 Prison Act as forming the basis for monitoring correspondence); cf. also Esser, *Europäisches Strafverfahrensrecht* (2002), p. 317. In greater depth on Art. 8(2), cf. Ambos, in Radtke and Hohmann, *StPO Kommentar* (2011), Art. 8 mn. 17 ff.
554. ECtHR, *Silver et al.*, 5947/72 et al., paras. 26, 86–7, 93; cf. in detail Esser, *Europäisches Strafverfahrensrecht* (2002), p. 318.
555. Cf. main text, mn. 126 ff.
556. Cf. ECtHR, *Bykov*, 4378/02, para. 76.
557. ECtHR, *Chappell* v. *the UK*, No 10461/83, Judgment (30 March 1989), para. 56; thereon Esser, *Europäisches Strafverfahrensrecht* (2002), pp. 318–19.
558. ECtHR, *Pretty* v. *the UK*, No 2346/02, Judgment (29 April 2002).

559. Cf. the cautious formulation in ECtHR, *Pretty*, 2346/02, para. 67 ('The Court is not prepared to exclude').
560. ECtHR, *Pretty*, 2346/02, paras. 68 ff.; conc. ECtHR, *Lambert et al.*, 46043/14, para. 142. On this, cf. Müller-Terpitz, in Menzel, Pierlings and Hoffmann, *Völkerrechtsprechung* (2005), pp. 494–5.
561. Loi No 2010–1192 (11 October 2010) interdisant la dissimulation du visage dans l'espace public, which makes it a 'contravention' to wear 'dans l'espace public . . . une tenue destinée à dissimuler son visage'.
562. ECtHR, *S.A.S.* v. *France*, No 43835/11, GC Judgment (1 July 2014), paras. 113 ff., esp. 154 ff. (157: 'having regard in particular to the breadth of the margin of appreciation afforded to the respondent State in the present case, the Court finds that the ban imposed by the Law of 11 October 2010 can be regarded as proportionate to the aim pursued, namely the preservation of the conditions of "living together" as an element of the "protection of the rights and freedoms of others"', 158: 'The impugned limitation can thus be regarded as "necessary in a democratic society"').
563. Crit. ECtHR, *S.A.S.*, 43835/11, Dissenting Opinion of Judges Nussberger and Jäderblom; also Jung, *GA*, 162 (2015), 35 ff.; Berry, *EJIL:Talk!*, 2 July 2014.
564. §173 StGB.
565. ECtHR, *Stübing* v. *Germany*, No 43547/08, Judgment (12 April 2012), paras. 55 ff. (esp. 58, 60, 66).
566. ECtHR, *Stübing*, 43547/08, para. 65. The Court found that the aims are reasonable enough (para. 66, essentially referring to the decision of the German Constitutional Court); conc. Kubiciel, *ZIS*, 7 (2012), 282 ff.; Hwang, *EuR*, 48 (2013), 307 ff.; crit. Jung, *GA*, 159 (2012), 617 ff. (no need for a criminal law prohibition).
567. Esser, *Europäisches Strafverfahrensrecht* (2002), p. 136; Gollwitzer, *Menschenrechte im Strafverfahren* (2005), Art. 10 MRK mn. 10; Grabenwarter, *ECHR* (2014), Art. 10 mn. 2, 11–12; Peters and Altwicker, *EMRK* (2012), §10 mn. 22.
568. On this recently Heger, in Pływaczewski and Guzik-Makaruk, *Current Problems of the Penal Law and Criminology* (2017), pp. 74 ff.
569. ECtHR, *Garaudy*, 65831/01; this is rejected in Grabenwarter, *ECHR* (2014), Art. 10 mn. 7, who considers that the line between the level of the scope of protection and the level of restriction is at risk of beoming blurred, resulting in a contradiction to case law that also permits hurtful, shocking and disturbing statements. On the ban on the symbols of former regimes, cf. Buyse, in Buyse and Hamilton, *Transitional Jurisprudence and the ECHR* (2011), pp. 133 ff.
570. Peters and Altwicker, *EMRK* (2012), §10 mn. 2; on the ban on so-called scalping in this regard, cf. Gaede and Mühlbauer, *wistra*, 24 (2005), 16–17.
571. Esser, *Europäisches Strafverfahrensrecht* (2002), p. 136; Grabenwarter, *ECHR* (2014), Art. 10 mn. 17. ECtHR, *Jankovskis* v. *Lithuania*, No 21575/08, Judgment (17 January 2017), paras. 52–64; on this Bode, ZIS, 12 (2017), 348 ff. (arguing for a right to Internet access in prison notwithstanding security concerns).
572. Grabenwarter, *ECHR* (2014), Art. 10 mn. 16 ff. In greater depth on this, cf. Ambos, in Radtke and Hohmann, *StPO Kommentar* (2011), Art. 10 mn. 6 ff.
573. Cf. in criminal case law ECtHR, *Guja* v. *Moldova*, No 14277/04, Judgment (12 February 2008), para. 56; ECtHR, *TV Vest AS and Rogaland Pensjonistparti* v. *Norway*, No 21132/05, Judgment (11 December 2008); ECtHR, *Rodriguez*

Ravelo v. *Spain*, No 48074/10, Judgment (12 January 2016), paras. 36–8. Cf. also Grabenwarter, *ECHR* (2014), Art. 10 mn. 22 ff.

574. ECtHR, *Rodriguez Ravelo*, 48074/10, para. 45 ('l'infliction d'une peine d'emprisonnement à un avocat emporte, par sa nature même, un "effet dissuasive", non seulement pour l'avocat concerné, mais aussi pour la profession dans son ensemble . . . un facteur important à prendre en compte pour ménager un juste équilibre entre les tribunaux et les avocats dans le cadre d'une bonne administration de la justice').
575. ECtHR, *Rodriguez Ravelo*, 48074/10, para. 51 ('la condamnation du requérant, qui impliquait même un risque d'emprisonnent, n'était pas proportionnée au but légitime poursuivi et n'était, dès lors, pas "nécessaire dans une société démocratique". Il y a donc eu violation de l'article 10 de la Convention').
576. For a critical stance on this, cf. Esser, *Europäisches Strafverfahrensrecht* (2002), pp. 137–8.
577. ECtHR, *Vereniging Weekblad Bluf!* v. *the Netherlands*, No 16616/90, Judgment (9 February 1995), para. 32; Esser, *Europäisches Strafverfahrensrecht* (2002), p. 137.
578. Esser, *Europäisches Strafverfahrensrecht* (2002), p. 139 (orig. 'Grundpfeiler jeder demokratischen Gesellschaft'); Mensching, in Karpenstein and Mayer, *EMRK* (2015), Art. 10 mn. 1. Cf. also ECtHR, *Ressiot et al.* v. *France*, No 15054/07, Judgment (28 June 2012), para. 101; and ECtHR, *Bayev et al.* v. *Russland*, Nos 67667/09 et al., Judgment (20 June 2017), paras. 61ff., where the Court stated that the Russian Law on 'Protection of Children's Rights in the Ryazan Oblast' of 3 April 2006, which prohibits public activities to promote homosexuality among minors, constitutes a disproportionate interference with freedom of expression because the national legislature has only limited discretion in regulating matters relating to personal and, in particular, sexual identity; conc. Istrefi and Irving, *EJIL:Talk!*, 27 June 2017.
579. ECtHR, *TV Vest AS and Rogaland Pensjonistparti*, 21132/05, para. 61.
580. Grabenwarter, *ECHR* (2014), Art. 10 mn. 25.
581. ECtHR, *Vereniging Weekblad Bluf!*, 16616/90, paras. 33–4; Grabenwarter, *ECHR* (2014), Art. 10 mn. 25.
582. ECtHR, *Vereniging Weekblad Bluf!*, 16616/90, paras. 35–6; Esser, *Europäisches Strafverfahrensrecht* (2002), p. 139.
583. ECtHR, *Vereniging Weekblad Bluf!*, 16616/90, paras. 41, 44–5; Esser, *Europäisches Strafverfahrensrecht* (2002), p. 140–1.
584. Esser, *Europäisches Strafverfahrensrecht* (2002), p. 138; Gollwitzer, *Menschenrechte im Strafverfahren* (2005), Art. 10 MRK mn. 23; Grabenwarter, *ECHR* (2014), Art. 10 mn. 25.
585. ECtHR, *Vereinigung demokratischer Soldaten Österreichs and Gubi* v. *Austria*, No 15153/89, Judgment (19 December 1994), para. 32; Grabenwarter, *ECHR* (2014), Art. 10 mn. 25.
586. ECtHR, *Hachette Filipacchi Presse Automobile and Dupuy* v. *France*, No 13353/05, Judgment (5 March 2009), paras. 43 ff.
587. Protocol No 7 to the Convention for the Protection of Human Rights and Fundamental Freedoms, 22 November 1984 (ETS No 117), entered into force with the seventh ratification on 1 November 1988 (cf. www.coe.int/en/web/conventions/full-list/-/conventions/treaty/117, last accessed 27 January 2018).
588. Peters and Altwicker, *EMRK* (2012), §24 mn. 3; Meyer-Ladewig, Harrendorf and König, in Meyer-Ladewig, Nettesheim and von Raumer, *EMRK* (2017), Art. 2 AP

VII mn. 1, 3; Satzger, *International and European Criminal Law* (2018), §9 mn. 107; Satzger, *Internationales und Europäisches Strafrecht* (2016), §11 mn. 94; Grabenwarter, *ECHR* (2014), Art. 6 with Art. 2 ZP VII mn. 1.

589. On this, cf. Meyer-Ladewig, Harrendorf and König, in Meyer-Ladewig, Nettesheim and von Raumer, *EMRK* (2017), Art. 3 AP VII; Breuer, in Karpenstein and Mayer, *EMRK* (2015), Art. 3 ZP VII mn. 2 ff.
590. Main text, mn. 161 ff.
591. BGH, 1 StR 221/99 (n. 146), pp. 333 ff.
592. BGH, 1 StR 221/99 (n. 146), p. 342.
593. On the different stances taken by the German Federal Court and ECtHR, cf. Ambos, *Fälle* (2010), p. 30 (case 3 mn. 5 ff.).
594. Cf. also Ambos, *Fälle* (2010), p. 30 (case 3 mn. 15 ff.).
595. ECtHR, *A.*, 14838/89, para. 36.
596. ECtHR, *M. M.*, 39339/98, paras. 38 ff.; however, cf. also ibid., Dissenting Opinion of Judge Palm, who puts emphasis on the interests of the (alleged) victim of a sexual offence, whose word stands against that of the person charged – in this case, against that of the husband's defence counsel(!). However, this consideration was unable to establish itself: Gaede, *StV*, 24 (2004), 47, explains accurately that *ex ante* in regard to the purpose of the Convention neither the (*alleged*) offender 'can be granted a position that is worse per se, nor the (*possible*) victim a position that is better per se in terms of human rights' (orig. 'eine per se schlechtere, noch dem *(möglichen)* Opfer eine per se bessere menschenrechtliche Position').
597. Case cited according to Eisele, *JA*, 32 (2000), 427; cf. also the case in Satzger, *International and European Criminal Law* (2018), §9 mn. 29, 33; for an instructive analysis of the problem, cf. Kindhäuser, *Strafgesetzbuch, Lehr- und Praxiskommentar* (2017), §32 mn. 48 ff.
598. ECtHR, *McCann, Farrell and Savage* v. *the UK*, No 18984/91, Judgment (27 September 1995).
599. ECtHR, *Jalloh* v. *Germany*, No 54810/00, Judgment (11 July 2006); cf. also the case solution in Safferling, *Internationales Strafrecht* (2011), §13 mn. 57.
600. Cf. in detail Ambos, *JA*, 29 (1997), 983.
601. BVerfG, Nos 2 BvR 1851/94 et al., Decision (24 October 1996) in *BVerfGE* 95, 96.
602. ECtHR, *Streletz, Kessler, Krenz* v. *Germany*, Nos 34044/96, 35532/97 and 44801/98, Judgment (22 March 2001).
603. ECtHR, *M.*, 19359/04; on this, cf. the case solution provided in Hecker and Zöller, *Fallsammlung* (2012), pp. 147 ff. (case 15).
604. Cf. ECtHR, *Lambert et al.*, 46043/14, para. 117 with further references. See also the ECtHR Judgment on the hostage-taking in Beslan in September 2004, in which the Court established that a violation of Art. 2 ECHR had occurred due to the high number of casualties caused by the Russian security services' insufficiently professional intervention (ECtHR, *Tagayeva et al.* v. *Russia*, Judgment (13 April 2017, paras. 481 ff.; on this also cf. Milanovic, *EJIL:Talk!*, 13 April 2017). For a fundamental study of the ECtHR's approach to positive obligations (entailing criminalisation, investigation, prosecution and sanctioning obligations in case of serious human rights violations) and its difficult compatibility with the case law of the Spanish Constitutional Court cf. Tomás-Valiente Lanuza, *InDret*, 17 (2016), issue 3. See also the Kunduz decision of the German Constitutional Court where the Court affirmed, in line with the ECtHR case law, a subjective right to have

prosecuted the perpetrators of serious offences (e.g. against life), BVerfG, No 2 BvR 987/11, Decision (19 May 2015), reprinted in *StV*, 37 (2017), 373 ff., esp. 376 ff.; thereto Esser and Lubrich, *StV*, 37 (2017), 418 (at 421 with n. 49).

605. ECtHR, *Pretty*, 2346/02, paras. 39–40 (the very seriously ill and paralysed applicant had unsuccessfully attempted to obligate the UK Attorney General not to prosecute her husband according to Section 2(1) of the Suicide Act if he helped her to commit suicide in line with her express wish). For an instructive account of the *Pretty* case, cf. Müller-Terpitz, in Menzel, Pierlings and Hoffmann, *Völkerrechtsprechung* (2005), pp. 489 ff.; Alleweldt, in Dörr, Grote and Marauhn, *EMRK/GG*, i (2013), mn. 30 ff.; Pedain, *CLJ*, 62 (2003), 182 ff.; Keown, *IJConstL*, 1 (2003), 722 ff.; crit. Hilgendorf, in Joerden and Szwarc, *Europäisierung des Strafrechts* (2007), pp. 180 ff.; summarising similar cases, *Lambert et al.*, 46043/14, para. 137; cf. also Puppinck and de La Hougue, *IJHR*, 18 (2014), 737 ff. Thus it is subject to Member States' discretion whether or not to prohibit (active) assisted dying and render it punishable, cf. Zwaak, in Van Dijk et al., *Theory and Practice of the ECHR* (2006), p. 392. On the other hand, Art. 2(1) does not contain any obligation to live, cf. Schilling, *Internationaler Menschenrechtsschutz* (2016), §7 mn. 135.

606. Cf. Zöller, in Esser et al., *FS Kühne* (2013), pp. 632 ff. (with a systematic analysis of the ECtHR case law).

607. ECtHR, *Makaratzis* v. *Greece*, No 50385/99, Judgment (20 December 2004), para. 57; ECtHR, *Usta et al.* v. *Turkey*, No 57084/00 (21 February 2008), para. 45; ECtHR, *Isaak* v. *Turkey*, No 44587/98, Judgment (24 June 2008), para. 106; Satzger, *Jura*, 31 (2009), 761–2; in detail, cf. Grabenwarter, *ECHR* (2014), Art. 2 mn. 16 ff.; on Member States' duty to initiate criminal investigations of (alleged) violations of Art. 2, cf. Ariav, *GoJIL*, 4 (2012), 857–8; Grabenwarter, *ECHR* (2014), Art. 8 mn. 22–3, 25. Cf. also Schilling, *Internationaler Menschenrechtsschutz* (2016), §7 mn. 145 ff. (who also touches upon the problems ensuing as part of regime change (mn. 147)).

608. Cf. recently ECtHR, *M. Tunç and F. Tunç* v. *Turkey*, No 24014/05, GC Judgment (14 April 2015), paras. 169 ff. (171: 'Article 2 imposes a duty on that State to secure the right to life . . . [and] requires by implication that there should be some form of effective official investigation when there is reason to believe that an individual has sustained life-threatening injuries in suspicious circumstances, even where the presumed perpetrator of the fatal attack is not a State agent'). The Chamber took an outcome-oriented approach with regard to the independent nature of the investigation focusing on its efficiency (ibid., para. 223 ('Article 2 does not require that the persons and bodies responsible for the investigation enjoy absolute independence, but rather that they are sufficiently independent'), and para. 225 ('compliance with the procedural requirement of Article 2 is assessed on the basis of several essential parameters . . . which, taken jointly, enable the degree of effectiveness of the investigation to be assessed. It is in relation to this purpose of an effective investigation that any issues, including that of independence, must be assessed')), thereby deviating from the absolutist approach of the former case law (e.g. ECtHR, *Al-Skeini et al.* v. *the UK*, No 55721/07, GC Judgment (7 July 2011), paras. 166–7 (167: 'it is necessary for the persons responsible for and carrying out the investigation to be independent from those implicated in the events. This means not only a lack of hierarchical or institutional connection but also a practical independence'); ECtHR, *Mocanu et al.*, 10865/09, 45886/07 and 32431/08, paras. 320 ff.); thereon Kukavica and Fikfak, *CLJ*, 74 (2015), 415 ff. The German Constitutional Court,

while generally rejecting a State constitutional duty to prosecute, recognises such a duty for serious crimes, in particular unlawful killing (BVerfG, No 2 BvR 1568/12, Decision (6 October 2014), paras. 10 ff., reprinted in *NJW*, 68 (2015), 150–1). On the complex issues of the ***ratione temporis* jurisdiction** of the Court in case of deaths before the entry into force of the Convention for the State concerned, cf. ECtHR, *Janowiec et al.* v. *Russia*, Nos 55508/07 and 29520/09, GC Judgment (21 October 2013), paras. 127 ff. (141); ECtHR, *Mocanu et al.*, 10865/09, 45886/07 and 32431/08, paras. 200 ff.; on the UK Supreme Court's approach thereon in *Keyu and Others* v. *Secretary of State for Foreign & Commonwealth* [2015] UKSC 69 Moynihan, *EJIL:Talk!*, 24 December 2015.

609. For a profound doctrinal critique, cf. Zöller, in Esser et al., *FS Kühne* (2013), pp. 639–40.
610. ECtHR, *Lambert et al.*, 46043/14, para. 144.
611. ECtHR, *Lambert et al.*, 46043/14, paras. 148 ('States must be afforded a margin of appreciation, not just as to whether or not to permit the withdrawal of artificial life-sustaining treatment and the detailed arrangements governing such withdrawal, but also as regards the means of striking a balance between the protection of patients' right to life and the protection of their right to respect for their private life and their personal autonomy'), 181 ('primarily for the domestic authorities to verify whether the decision to withdraw treatment was compatible with the domestic legislation and the Convention'). Thus, for example, Art. 2 as interpreted by the Court does not provide for a specific procedure to be followed to take a decision on the continuation or termination of the treatment (ibid., para. 162).
612. ECtHR, *Lambert et al.*, 46043/14, para. 143 with further references. *In casu*, the Court found, by twelve votes to five (Judges Hajiyev, Šikuta, Tsotsoria, De Gaetano and Gritco dissenting), that the French authorities complied with their positive obligation under Art. 2 (ibid., paras. 149–82).
613. ECtHR, *Vo* v. *France*, No 53924/00, Judgment (8 July 2004), para. 85 (holding that at least the French State did not violate its procedural duty to protect, as the injured party was able to take action against the hospital in the administrative courts). For an instructive account of the *Vo* case, cf. Blau, *ZEuS*, 8 (2005), 424 ff.; Jung, in Hoyer et al., *FS Schroeder* (2006), p. 809. On the applicability of Art. 2 on unborn life, cf. Satzger, *International and European Criminal Law* (2018), §9 mn. 30. On the status of the dispute, cf. Lagodny, in Pabel and Schmahl, *Internationaler Kommentar zur EMRK* (2013), Art. 2 mn. 46; Esser, in Erb et al., *Löwe-Rosenberg StPO*, xi (2012), Art. 2 EMRK mn. 7–8; Paeffgen, in Wolter, *Systematischer Kommentar StPO*, x (2012), Art. 2 EMRK mn. 5 ff.; Frenz, *Europarecht* (2009), p. 273.
614. ECtHR, *Makaratzis*, 50385/99, paras. 49 ff., 55; Zöller, in Esser et al., *FS Kühne* (2013), p. 630.
615. Cf. e.g. Gollwitzer, *Menschenrechte im Strafverfahren* (2005), Art. 2 MRK mn. 17 ff.
616. Peters and Altwicker, *EMRK* (2012), §5 mn. 14; for ECtHR criminal case law, cf. ECtHR, *Khatsiyeva et al.* v. *Russia*, No 5108/02, Judgment (17 January 2008), para. 129 incl. further references; on necessity in particular, cf. ECtHR, *Usta et al.*, 57084/00, para. 46.
617. Rosenau, *ZIS*, 1 (2006), 338; cf. also Last, in Menzel, Pierlings and Hoffmann, *Völkerrechtsprechung* (2005), pp. 498–9; and Eisele, *JA*, 37 (2005), 902, which both refer to ECtHR, *Öcalan*, 46221/99. On this case, cf. also Aras, *ZEuS*, 10 (2007), 239–40.

618. See AP VI (ETS No 114), n. 108, ratified by all CoE MS, except Russia (www.coe.int/en/web/conventions/full-list/-/conventions/treaty/114/signatures?p_auth=4kJOJjXj, last accessed 27 January 2018). Art. 2 permits 'the death penalty in respect of acts committed in time of war or of imminent threat of war'.

619. See AP XIII (ETS No 187), n. 109, ratified by 44 CoE MS. Russia and Azerbaijan neither signed nor ratified it; Armenia has signed, but not yet ratified it (as of 10 August 2016, www.coe.int/en/web/conventions/full-list/-/conventions/treaty/187/signatures?p_auth=4kJOJjXj, last accessed 27 January 2018).

620. Thereon see above, mn. 84. See also Hoffmann, in Menzel, Pierlings and Hoffmann, *Völkerrechtsprechung* (2005), pp. 515–16; Jötten, *Enforced Disappearances und EMRK* (2012), pp. 132 ff. The failure to clarify the circumstances of a person's death can also constitute a violation of Art. 2 ECHR, cf. Esser, *Europäisches und Internationales Strafrecht* (2018), §9 mn. 137.

621. See e.g. Art. 122–5(2) **French** CP ('pour interrompre l'exécution d'un crime ou d'un délit contre un bien, accomplit un acte de défense'); §32 **German** StGB; Art. 22(2) **Greek** CC; Art. 52(1) **Italian** CP ('difendere un diritto proprio od altrui'); Art. 25 §1 **Polish** CC ('any legally protected interest'); Art. 20(4) **Spanish** CP. In **England and Wales**, the law is more complicated because of the complex relationship between common law as (re)stated by the case law and more recent statutory law (cf. §76 Criminal Justice and Immigration Act 2008, CJIA, which attempts to 'clarify' the available defences of subsect. (9) but rather complicates the situation; cf. Simester et al., *Simester and Sullivan's Criminal Law* (2016), pp. 88–90). Defence of property was recognised as early as 1924 by the case law, when it was held in *Hussey* that defence actions may also be directed against assaults on property (cf. *Rex* v. *Hussey*, in *CrAppRep*, 18 (1924), 160) but the case is of limited value for the *general* property defence since the attack occurred in the victim's home. Apart from that, the problem of these so-called household cases is that the actual attack on the property is often confused with attack on other values, especially the life or bodily integrity of the houseowner, and thus we are no longer faced with a mere defence of property (cf. Leverick, *Killing in Self-Defence* (2006), pp. 137–41; Horder, *Ashworth's Principles of Criminal Law* (2016), pp. 132–3). At any rate, while the test applied is always that of the *reasonable* use of force (cf. §3(1) Criminal Law Act 1967, referred to in §76(2)(b) CJIA 2008, which itself tries to clarify the reasonableness standard in subsects. (3) to (8)), the use of *deadly* use of force will normally be assumed to be unreasonable for the protection of property (cf. Leverick, *Killing in Self-Defence* (2006), pp. 131, 134, 136, 142). In light of Art. 2 ECHR this is even admitted by those who take a more flexible view (as Simester et al., *Simester and Sullivan's Criminal Law* (2016), pp. 814, 821–2). For a comparative perspective on self-defence, see also Ambos, *Treatise I* (2013), pp. 331–4; for a comparative study on Art. 2(2) ECHR cf. Perron, in Arnold et al., *FS Eser* (2005), p. 1019.

622. Bockelmann, in Bockelmann, *FS Engisch* (1969), pp. 456, 463; Eisele, *JA*, 37 (2005), 902; Gollwitzer, *Menschenrechte im Strafverfahren* (2005), Art. 2 MRK mn. 19; Kindhäuser, in Kindhäuser, Neumann and Paeffgen, *Nomos Kommentar StGB*, i (2013), §32 mn. 96; Rönnau and Hohn, in Laufhütte, Rissing-van Saan and Tiedemann, *Leipziger Kommentar StGB*, ii (2006), §32 mn. 235 ff.; Hecker, *Europäisches Strafrecht* (2015), §3 mn. 68 ff., 73; for a more reticent view, cf. Perron, in Arnold et al., *FS Eser* (2005), pp. 1024–5; Safferling,

Internationales Strafrecht (2011), §3 mn. 73; and also Kühl, in Müller-Dietz, *FS Jung* (2007), p. 440; also Bülte, *GA*, 158 (2011), 163.

623. Cf. e.g. Frister, *GA*, 132 (1985), 564–5; Koriath, in Ranieri, *Die Europäisierung der Rechtswissenschaft* (2002), pp. 52 ff.; a similar view is taken by Kühl, *ZStW*, 100 (1988), 624 ff.; Kreicker, in Sieber, Satzger and von Heinegg, *Europäisches Strafrecht* (2014), p. 928; Perron, in Schönke, Schröder and Eser, *StGB Kommentar* (2014), §32 mn. 62; cf. also Schroeder, in Schroeder and Zipf, *FS Maurach* (1972), pp. 127, 138–9; Bisson, *Die lebensgefährliche Verteidigung von Vermögenswerten* (2002), pp. 149 ff., 210 (thus arguing that §32 StGB represents a violation of the Convention and accordingly is unconstitutional). The same view is taken by Diehm, *Die Menschenrechte der EMRK* (2006), pp. 338–9.

624. Cf. esp. Bernsmann, *ZStW*, 104 (1992), 306–7, 323; Alleweldt, in Dörr, Grote and Marauhn, *EMRK/GG*, i (2013), mn. 66–7 (fails to take sufficiently into account, however, that the ECHR as an international law convention addresses the State as a subject of international law, and that accordingly the State is particularly bound by it).

625. Cf. e.g. Schmitt, in Meyer-Goßner and Schmitt, *StPO* (2017), Art. 2 MRK mn. 3.

626. In the sense of the civil law *dolus directus*; e.g. Jescheck and Weigend, *Lehrbuch des Strafrechts: Allgemeiner Teil* (1996), pp. 349–50; Krey, *JZ*, 34 (1979), 709; Roxin, *Strafrecht: Allgemeiner Teil*, i (2006), §15 mn. 88; Zieschang, *GA*, 153 (2006), 418–19; arguing against a restriction to deliberate killings, Frister, *GA*, 132 (1985), 560–1; Bisson, *Die lebensgefährliche Verteidigung von Vermögenswerten* (2002), pp. 126 ff., 137.

627. Cf. Eisele, *JA*, 32 (2000), 428 incl. further references.

628. ECtHR, *Wasilewska and Kalucka* v. *Poland*, Nos 28975/04 and 33406/04, Judgment (23 February 2010), para. 42 ('The text of Article 2, read as a whole, demonstrates that it covers not only intentional killing but also situations where it is permitted to 'use force' which may result, as an unintended outcome, in the deprivation of life'); cf. also ECtHR, *Isaak*, No 44587/98, para. 104; ECtHR, *Vachkovi* v. *Bulgaria*, No 2747/02, Judgment (8 July 2010), para. 70. A similar view is taken by Safferling, *Internationales Strafrecht* (2011), §13 mn. 46; Perron, in Schönke, Schröder and Eser, *StGB Kommentar* (2014), §32 mn. 62 (who wants to apply this case law to interferences by private persons).

629. See also Rönnau and Hohn, in Laufhütte, Rissing-van Saan and Tiedemann, *Leipziger Kommentar StGB*, ii (2006), §32 mn. 236.

630. Cf. also Perron, in Arnold et al., *FS Eser* (2005), p. 1025; Perron, in Schönke, Schröder and Eser, *StGB Kommentar* (2014), §32 mn. 62.

631. ECtHR, *McCann, Farrell and Savage*, 18984/91, paras. 194, 200. For a detailed account, cf. Peters and Altwicker, *EMRK* (2012), §5 mn. 22.

632. ECtHR, *McCann, Farrell and Savage*, 18984/91, para. 200 ('To hold otherwise would be to impose an unrealistic burden on the State and its law-enforcement personnel in the execution of their duty, perhaps to the detriment of their lives and those of others'). On this, cf. Klugmann, *EMRK und antiterroristische Maßnahmen* (2002), p. 66; Peters and Altwicker, *EMRK* (2012), §5 mn. 22; Reid, *A Practitioner's Guide to the ECHR* (2011), p. 747; Zwaak, in Van Dijk et al., *Theory and Practice of the ECHR* (2006), p. 398. According to German law, in cases of self-defence or defence of others in the context of an 'apparent threat', which possibly has been duly examined, according to prevailing opinion an error regarding the factual basis of the defence (*in casu* the permission following from self-defence) is to be assumed.

633. Thus Frowein, in Frowein and Peukert, *EMRK-Kommentar* (2009), Art. 2 mn. 11–12; Gollwitzer, *Menschenrechte im Strafverfahren* (2005), Art. 2 MRK mn. 19; also Sinn, *NStZ*, 24 (2004), 590.
634. *Luftsicherheitsgesetz* (LuftSiG, 11 January 2005, *BGBl.* I 2005, 78).
635. Cf. Sinn, *NStZ*, 24 (2004), 592–3 (who incidentally regards §14 Abs. 3 LuftSiG as a special regulation that takes precedence over §34 StGB). Kühne, *GA*, 152 (2005), 209 and Alleweldt, in Dörr, Grote and Marauhn, *EMRK/GG*, i (2013), mn. 63, are doubtful whether it is compatible with the ECHR. On the regulation's character as criminal law in wartime or as criminal law governing the treatment of enemies, cf. Lüderssen, *StV*, 25 (2005), 106–7. In favour of an extra-legal ground of duress/necessity, cf. Roxin, in Arnold et al., *FS Eser* (2005), p. 469.
636. BVerfG, No 1 BvR 357/05, Judgment (15 February 2006), in *BVerfGE* 115, 118, 153–4 (English translation available at www.bundesverfassungsgericht.de/SharedDocs/Entscheidungen/EN/2006/02/rs20060215_1bvr035705en.html;jsessionid=AEA8D1C6CE54AC78FFBFEFF7DB560972.2_cid393, last accessed 27 January 2018). The Constitutional Court noted, inter alia, a violation of Art. 2(2) in conjunction with Art. 1(1) Basic Law, but did not analyse the relevant ECHR provisions. On this, cf. also Hirsch, *NJW*, 60 (2007), 1188–9; Geiß, *MichJIL*, 27 (2005/2006), 227 ff.; Bohlander, *CLR* (2006), 579 ff.; Lepsius, *GLJ*, 7 (2006), 762 ff.; Ladiges, *ZIS*, 3 (2008), 129 ff.; Beltrán de Felipe and Rodríguez de Santiago, *EuPubL*, 14 (2008), 565 ff.; crit. Schenke, *NJW*, 59 (2006), 738; Rogall, *NStZ*, 28 (2008), 1 ff. From a philosophical perspective, see Hörnle, *NCLR*, 10 (2007), 582 ff.
637. Thereon see main text, mn. 159.
638. Peters and Altwicker, *EMRK* (2012), §6 mn. 2; Satzger, *International and European Criminal Law* (2018), §9 mn. 35; in detail on the protective scope, cf. Ackermann, in Donatsch, Forster and Schwarzenegger, *FS Trechsel* (2002), pp. 839 ff.; also Pabel, in Menzel, Pierlings and Hoffmann, *Völkerrechtsprechung* (2005), pp. 517–18; Mavronicola, *HRLR*, 15 (2015), 723–6. ECtHR case law on Art. 3 has entered into the case law of the international criminal tribunals; on this, cf. de Frouville, *JICJ*, 9 (2011), 637 ff.; Ambos, *Treatise ICL III* (2016), pp. 96, 161, 519 (esp. overall unfairness and exclusionary rule in case of torture); generally on the definition in ICL, Ambos, *Treatise ICL I* (2013), p. 296; Ambos, *Treatise ICL II* (2014), pp. 89 ff.
639. ECtHR, *A* v. *the UK*, No 100/1997/884/1096, Judgment (23 September 1998), para. 22; ECtHR, *Cestaro* v. *Italy*, No 6884/11, Judgment (7 April 2015), paras. 204 and 206; on this Caroeli, ICLR, 17 (2017), 567 ff.; ECtHR, *Z and Others* v. *the UK*, No 29392/95, Judgment (10 May 2001), para. 73; ECtHR, *E. et al.* v. *the UK*, No 33218/96, Judgment (26 November 2002), para. 88; ECtHR, *M. C.* v. *Bulgaria*, No 39272/98, Judgment (4 December 2003), para. 149; ECtHR, *Ubilanzila Mayeka and Kaniki Mitunga* v. *Belgium*, No 13178/03, Judgment (12 October 2006), para. 53; ECtHR, *Members of the Gldani Congregation of Jehovah's Witnesses et al.* v. *Georgia*, No 71156/01, Judgment (3 May 2007), para. 96; cf. also Grabenwarter, *ECHR* (2014), Art. 3 mn. 8.
640. ECtHR, *A*, 100/1997/884/1096, para. 22. Yet the mere attribution of criminal responsibility to an eleven-year-old child does not entail a violation of Art. 3, cf. ECtHR, *V.*, 24888/94, paras. 72–4; ECtHR, *T.*, 24724/94, paras. 70–2.
641. ECtHR, *Selmouni* v. *France*, No 25803/94, Judgment (28 July 1999), para. 96; ECtHR, *Gäfgen*, 22978/05, para. 66; ECtHR, *Gäfgen*, 22978/05, GC Judgment, para. 90; ECtHR *Cestaro* v. *Italy*, No 6884/11, Judgment (7 April 2015), para. 171

('Ainsi que la Cour l'a déjà relevé, cette distinction paraît avoir été consacrée par la Convention pour marquer d'une spéciale infamie des traitements inhumains délibérés provoquant de fort graves et cruelles souffrances').

642. ECtHR, *Saadi*, 37201/06, para. 136; ECtHR, *Selmouni*, 25803/94, paras. 96–7; ECtHR, *Aksoy* v. *Turkey*, No 21987/93, Judgment (18 December 1996), para. 64; ECtHR, *Ireland* v. *the UK*, No 5310/71, Judgment (18 January 1978), para. 167; ECtHR, *El-Masri*, 3963/09, paras. 196 ff.; ECtHR, *Al Nashiri*, 28761/11, para. 508; ECtHR, *Husayn (Abu Zubaydah)*, 7511/13, para. 500; ECtHR, *Nasr and Ghali*, 44883/09, para. 282; cf. also Prosenjak, *Folterbegriff* (2011), pp. 38 ff., 81–2, 92 ff.; Grabenwarter, *ECHR* (2014), Art. 3 mn. 3; Meyer-Ladewig and Lehnert, in Meyer-Ladewig, Nettesheim and von Raumer, *EMRK* (2017), Art. 3 mn. 20–1; Peters and Altwicker, *EMRK* (2012), §6 mn. 2, 5 ff. On the concept of torture, cf. also Ambos, *JICJ*, 6 (2008), 266–70.

643. ECtHR, *Selmouni*, 25803/94, para. 98; ECtHR, *Al Nashiri*, 28761/11, para. 508; ECtHR, *Husayn (Abu Zubaydah)*, 7511/13, para. 500; ECtHR, *Nasr and Ghali*, 44883/09, para. 282; cf. also ECtHR, *Gäfgen*, 22978/05, GC Judgment, para. 90; on this, cf. also Herrmann, *ZIS*, 2 (2007), 302; Prosenjak, *Folterbegriff* (2011), pp. 157 ff.

644. ECtHR, *Selmouni*, 25803/94, para. 97; ECtHR, *Gäfgen*, 22978/05, GC Judgment, para. 90; ECtHR, *Al Nashiri*, 28761/11, para. 508; ECtHR, *Husayn (Abu Zubaydah)*, 7511/13, para. 500; ECtHR, *Nasr and Ghali*, 44883/09, para. 283; ECtHR *Cestaro* v. *Italy*, No 6884/11, Judgment (7 April 2015), para. 171; Peters and Altwicker, *EMRK* (2012), §6 mn. 11; Safferling, *Jura*, 30 (2008), 102.

645. 'For the purposes of this Convention, torture means any act by which severe pain or suffering, whether physical or mental, is intentionally inflicted on a person for such purposes as obtaining from him or a third person information or a confession'.

646. Grabenwarter, *ECHR* (2014), Art. 3 mn. 3. On the understanding of the Convention as a 'living instrument', cf. ECtHR, *Tyrer* v. *the UK*, No 5856/72, Judgment (25 April 1978), para. 31; ECtHR, *T.*, 24724/94, para. 70; ECtHR, *V.*, 24888/94, para. 82; Frowein, in Frowein and Peukert, *EMRK-Kommentar* (2009), Einführung mn. 7; Letsas, *EJIL*, 15 (2004), 298 ff.; Schuhr, *NJW*, 59 (2006), 3538–9; Safferling, *Jura*, 30 (2008), 102; Satzger, *Jura*, 31 (2009), 760.

647. ECtHR, *Ireland*, 5310/71, paras. 162 ff.; on this, cf. Peters and Altwicker, *EMRK* (2012), §6 mn. 12; Reid, *A Practitioner's Guide to the ECHR* (2011), pp. 794–5; Herrmann, *ZIS*, 2 (2007), 303.

648. They had to stand leaning against a wall for up to 30(!) hours; sleeping, drinking and eating were reduced to a minimum.

649. ECtHR, *Selmouni*, 25803/94, paras. 82 ff.; on this, cf. also Peters and Altwicker, *EMRK* (2012), §6 mn. 4; Gaede, in Camprubi, *Angst und Streben nach Sicherheit* (2004), p. 162; Reid, *A Practitioner's Guide to the ECHR* (2011), p. 795; Herrmann, *ZIS*, 2 (2007), 303.

650. For a definition see Ambos, *EuCLR*, 5 (2015), 107, 115; also Staffler, *EuGRZ*, 43 (2016), 344.

651. ECtHR, *Al Nashiri*, 28761/11, para. 516; ECtHR, *Husayn (Abu Zubaydah)*, 7511/13, para. 511; ECtHR, *Nasr and Ghali*, 44883/09, paras. 287–90.

652. ECtHR, *Husayn (Abu Zubaydah)*, 7511/13, para. 510; cf. also Ambos, *EuCLR*, 5 (2015), 114–15, 119; Ambos, *Treatise II* (2014), p. 243; Grabenwarter and Pabel, *EMRK* (2016), §20 mn. 42; Staffler, *EuGRZ*, 43 (2016), 349–50. The origin of the term 'white torture' appears to be unclear. 'Some use it because many of the solitary cells in Iran are freshly painted white so that the prisoners cannot leave

messages for one another or write on the walls. Others believe the term refers to a technique that is as effective as physical torture but leaves no physical evidence' (HRW, *Like the Dead in Their Coffins*, 2004, Vol. 16, p. 19 n. 42).

653. On this cf. Ambos, *JICJ*, 6 (2008), 267–8; and Ambos, *ZStW*, 122 (2010), 517–18.

654. ECtHR, *Stoica* v. *Romania*, No 42722/02, Judgment (4 March 2008), para. 60; Grabenwarter, *ECHR* (2014), Art. 3 mn. 4; Meyer-Ladewig and Lehnert, in Meyer-Ladewig, Nettesheim and von Raumer, *EMRK* (2017), Art. 3 mn. 22; on the relevance threshold, cf. ECtHR, *Al-Saadoon and Mufdhi* v. *the UK*, No 61498/08, Judgment (2 March 2010), para. 121. Cf. also ECtHR, *Gäfgen*, 22978/05, para. 66, where the ECtHR noted that the treatment threatened would have been classed as torture had it been carried out (para. 69). The Grand Chamber also emphasised that the threat of *physical* torture can in principle constitute *mental* torture, but that the threats in the case at hand had not been serious enough to warrant being classed as torture; ECtHR, *Gäfgen*, 22978/05, GC Judgment, para. 108; for greater detail on this case, cf. Satzger, *International and European Criminal Law* (2018), §9 mn. 40 ff.; Satzger, *Internationales und Europäisches Strafrecht* (2016), §11 mn. 39 ff.; Schiedermair, *JuS*, 50 (2010), 993 ff.; Grabenwarter, *NJW*, 63 (2010), 3128 ff.; Esser, Gaede and Tsambikakis, *NStZ*, 31 (2011), 78–9; crit. Greer, *HRLR*, 11 (2011), 79 ff. (considering the Grand Chamber's judgment as 'deeply flawed methodologically, substantively and morally'). On the significance of Art. 3 and the CPT standards for juvenile detention in particular, cf. Pollähne, *StV*, 27 (2007), 554–5.

655. Objectively, differentiating on the basis of the severity of treatment, Grabenwarter, *ECHR* (2014), Art. 3 mn. 3; arguing in favour of including the purposefulness characteristic of torture, Peters and Altwicker, *EMRK* (2012), §6 mn. 11; Esser, *Europäisches und Internationales Strafrecht* (2018), §9 mn. 152. Cf. also Gaede, in Camprubi, *Angst und Streben nach Sicherheit* (2004), p. 162; Bank, in Dörr, Grote and Marauhn, *EMRK/GG*, i (2013), Kapitel 11 mn. 16 ff.

656. ECtHR, *Stoica*, 42722/02, para. 61; Grabenwarter, *ECHR* (2014), Art. 3 mn. 6; Grabenwarter and Pabel, *EMRK* (2016), §20 mn. 48–50 incl. further references; Gaede, in Camprubi, *Angst und Streben nach Sicherheit* (2004), p. 162; Schilling, *Internationaler Menschenrechtsschutz* (2016), §8 mn. 180; Mavronicola, *HRLR*, 15 (2015), 725 ('qualitative' distinction between 'inhuman and degrading').

657. ECtHR, *Klaas* v. *Germany*, No 15473/89, Judgment (22 September 1993), paras. 29–30 (forcible arrest and handcuffing of a drunk driver); Meyer-Ladewig and Lehnert, in Meyer-Ladewig, Nettesheim and von Raumer, *EMRK* (2017), Art. 3 mn. 54; Peters and Altwicker, *EMRK* (2012), §6 mn. 15; Reid, *A Practitioner's Guide to the ECHR* (2011), p. 796. On the exclusion of slight injuries see also ECtHR, *Paposhvili* v. *Belgium*, No 71738/10, GC Judgment (13 December 2016), para. 174 ('Such treatment has to attain a minimum level of severity').

658. ECtHR, *Pretty*, 2346/02, paras. 54–5.

659. ECtHR, *Paposhvili* v. *Belgium*, No 71738/10, GC Judgment (13 December 2016), para. 206; on this Anderson, *EJIL Talk!*, 21 February 2017.

660. Cf. Mavronicola, *HRLR*, 15 (2015), 726.

661. ECtHR, *Kafkaris* v. *Cyprus*, No 21906/04, Judgment (12 February 2008), para. 96; also ECtHR, *Ramirez Sanchez* v. *France*, No 59450/00, GC Judgment (4 July 2006), para. 119. But see also ECtHR, *V.*, 24888/94, para. 98 and ECtHR, *T.*, 24724/94, para. 97, where it was held that the punitive element in the 'tariff approach' itself does not give rise to a breach of Article 3. On the 'tariff' policy adopted over the years in

England and Wales by the Secretary of State in exercising his discretion as to the release of offenders sentenced to life imprisonment, see ECtHR, *V.*, 24888/94, para. 40 and ECtHR, *T.*, 24724/94, para. 38 ('the tariff approach involves breaking down the life sentence into component parts, namely retribution, deterrence and protection of the public. The "tariff" represents the minimum period which the prisoner will have to serve to satisfy the requirements of retribution and deterrence'); for a comparative perspective on *V.* and *T.*, see Dyer, *HRLR*, 16 (2016), 572–5.

662. Discussing the factors causing such an illegitimate additional distress or hardship, Mavronicola, *HRLR*, 15 (2015), 727–32, 734–5.

663. Such a finding would, however, only be made 'on rare and unique occasions'; cf. ECtHR, *Vinter et al.* v. *the UK*, Nos 66069/09, 130/10 and 3896/10, GC Judgment (9 July 2013), para. 102; for a discussion of disproportionality in this context, Mavronicola, *HRLR*, 15 (2015), 733–4.

664. ECtHR, *Vinter et al.*, 66069/09, 130/10 and 3896/10, paras. 107 ff.; with commentary by Van Zyl Smit, Weatherby and Creighton, *HRLR*, 14 (2014), 59 ff.; see also ECtHR, *Hutchinson* v. *the UK*, No 57592/08, Judgment (3 February 2015), para. 19; for a good summary of the discussion, see Hart, *CLJ*, 74 (2015), 205 ff.; recently also ECtHR, *Hutchinson* v. *the UK*, No 57592/08, GC Judgment (17 January 2017), para. 42; see also Dyer, *HRLR*, 16 (2016), 572 ff., highlighting the positive role 'strong human rights guarantees within a jurisdiction', such as the ECHR or a Bill of Rights, can play in changing the criminal justice system as far as the 'procedural safeguards for life sentence prisoners' are concerned (582–4).

665. ECtHR, *Vinter et al.*, 66069/09, 130/10 and 3896/10, paras. 109 ('to ascertain whether a life prisoner can be said to have any prospect of release'), 113 (conc. with the German CC's right to hope approach based on human dignity); in the same vein Mavronicola, *HRLR*, 15 (2015), 737–8, 740, 742; cf. also Grabenwarter, *ECHR* (2014), Art. 3 mn. 5; crit. on the human dignity argumentation and demanding a better reasoning with a view to the functioning of punishment Lippke, *HRLR*, 17 (2017), 395 ff.

666. ECtHR, *Vinter et al.*, 66069/09, 130/10 and 3896/10, para. 110; conc. ECtHR, *Hutchinson*, 57592/08, para. 20.

667. ECtHR, *Vinter et al.*, 66069/09, 130/10 and 3896/10, para. 119.

668. ECtHR, *Vinter et al.*, 66069/09, 130/10 and 3896/10, para. 108; ECtHR, *Hutchinson*, 57592/08, para. 21; cf. also ECtHR, *V.*, 24888/94, para. 98 and ECtHR, *T.*, 24724/94, para. 97 ('It does not consider ... that the Convention prohibits States from subjecting a child or young person convicted of a serious crime to an indeterminate sentence allowing for the offender's continued detention or recall to detention following release where necessary for the protection of the public').

669. Cf. ECtHR, *Trabelsi* v. *Belgium*, No 140/10, Judgment (4 September 2014), para. 127 (in terrorist cases, 'discretionary life sentence would not be grossly disproportionate').

670. ECtHR, *Vinter et al.*, 66069/09, 130/10 and 3896/10, para. 122 ('would be capricious to expect the prisoner to work towards his own rehabilitation without knowing whether, at an unspecified, future date, a mechanism might be introduced which would allow him, on the basis of that rehabilitation, to be considered for release'); conc. ECtHR, *Hutchinson*, 57592/08, para. 20(d). Stressing the rehabilitation focus of *Vinter*, also Mavronicola, *HRLR*, 15 (2015), 736, 740, 742.

671. ECtHR, *Hutchinson* v. *the UK*, No 57592/08, GC Judgment (17 January 2017), para. 42; ECtHR, *Vinter et al.*, 66069/09, 130/10 and 3896/10, para. 120.

672. ECtHR, *Hutchinson*, 57592/08, paras. 22 ff. (23), also para. 25 ('national court has specifically addressed those doubts and set out an unequivocal statement of the legal position, the Court must accept the national court's interpretation of domestic law'); confirmed by ECtHR, *Hutchinson*, No 57592/08, GC Judgment, para. 50 ('executive nature of a review is not in itself contrary to the requirements of Article 3').
673. Crit. of the 'uncritical acceptance' of the UK's regime by the *Hutchinson* Court, Hart, *CLJ*, 74 (2015), 207.
674. ECtHR, *Selmouni*, 25803/94, para. 87.
675. ECtHR, *Selmouni*, 25803/94, para. 87.
676. ECtHR, *Rehbock* v. *Slovenia*, No 29462/95, Judgment (28 November 2000), para. 72; ECtHR, *Altay* v. *Turkey*, No 22279/93, Judgment (22 May 2001), para. 54.
677. ECtHR, *El-Masri*, 3963/09, paras. 152 ff. ('where the events in issue lie within the exclusive knowledge of the authorities, as in the case of persons under their control in custody, strong presumptions of fact will arise in respect of injuries and death occurring during that detention. The burden of proof in such a case may be regarded as resting on the authorities to provide a satisfactory and convincing explanation'); in the same vein ECtHR, *Husayn (Abu Zubaydah)*, 7511/13, paras. 395–6.
678. Cf. Ambos, *EuCLR*, 5 (2015), 108, 110–11, 114–15, 118; crit. Meyer, in Stuckenberg and Gärditz, *Strafe und Prozess* (2015), pp. 800–3.
679. A final *shifting of the burden of proof* requires that the human rights violations in question have been proven 'in the form of concordant inferences', cf. ECtHR, *El-Masri*, 3963/09, para. 153; also Ambos, *EuCLR*, 5 (2015), 111, 118.
680. Cf. also Peters and Altwicker, *EMRK* (2012), §6 mn. 4; Meyer-Ladewig and Lehnert, in Meyer-Ladewig, Nettesheim and von Raumer, *EMRK* (2017), Art. 3 mn. 56.
681. ECtHR, *Jalloh*, 54810/00, para. 105; continued in ECtHR, *Harutyunyan* v. *Armenia*, No 36549/03, Judgment (28 June 2007), para. 63. For more detail, cf. Safferling, *Jura*, 30 (2008), 100 ff.; Grabenwarter, *NJW*, 63 (2010), 3131 ff.; Ambos, *StV*, 29 (2009), 151 ff.; Ambos, *Beweisverwertungsverbote* (2010), pp. 100 ff.
682. ECtHR, *El Haski* v. *Belgium*, No 649/08, Judgment (25 September 2012), paras. 86 ff. with a commentary by Schüller, *ZIS*, 8 (2013), 245 ff.; Heine, *NStZ*, 33 (2013), 680.
683. ECtHR, *Jalloh*, 54810/00, para. 99; ECtHR, *Gäfgen*, 22978/05, para. 63; Gaede, *HRRS*, 7 (2006), 242; ECtHR, *Gäfgen*, 22978/05, GC Judgment, paras. 87 ff. The inalienability of the prohibition of torture was reaffirmed in prevailing opinion in connection with the *Daschner* case, cf. Diehm, *Die Menschenrechte der EMRK* (2006), pp. 369 ff. incl. further references; Kinzig, *ZStW*, 115 (2003), 791–2; Gaede, in Camprubi, *Angst und Streben nach Sicherheit* (2004), pp. 166 ff.; Saliger, *ZStW*, 116 (2004), 41 ff.; Jeßberger, *Jura*, 25 (2003), 711 ff.; Perron, in Heinrich et al., *FS Weber* (2004), pp. 143 ff.; Grabenwarter, *ECHR* (2014), Art. 3 mn. 7; Roxin, in Arnold et al., *FS Eser* (2005), pp. 468–9; Roxin, in Griesbaum, Hannich and Schnarr, *FS Nehm* (2006), p. 216 (supra-legal duress in extreme cases as appropriate); Norouzi, *JA*, 37 (2005), 309–10; Eisele, *JA*, 37 (2005), 903; Peters and Altwicker, *EMRK* (2012), §6 mn. 3. In favour of excuse in liminal cases, see Ambos, *JICJ*, 6 (2008), 261 ff.; *Hecker/Zöller*, S. 163 ff.
684. Ackermann, in Donatsch, Forster and Schwarzenegger, *FS Trechsel* (2002), p. 846; Grabenwarter, *ECHR* (2014), Art. 3 mn. 1, 7.

685. In detail Ackermann, in Donatsch, Forster and Schwarzenegger, *FS Trechsel* (2002), pp. 844 ff. and Pohlreich, *NStZ*, 31 (2011), 560 ff., 567 ff. Cf. also Grabenwarter, *ECHR* (2014), Art. 3 mn. 11.

686. ECtHR, *Tekin* v. *Turkey*, No 22496/93, Judgment (9 June 1998), paras. 52–3; cf. also Peters and Altwicker, *EMRK* (2012), §6 mn. 15 incl. references on the case law. On improvements to the protection of prisoners' human rights through an Additional Protocol, cf. Jung, in Donatsch, Forster and Schwarzenegger, *FS Trechsel* (2002), pp. 864–5.

687. ECtHR, *Ensslin, Baader and Raspe* v. *Germany*, Nos 7572/76 et al., European Commission of Human Rights Decision (8 July 1978), paras. 6–10; in a similar vein, ECtHR, *Öcalan* v. *Turkey* (No 2), Nos 24069/03, 197/04, 6201/06 and 10464/07, Judgment (18 March 2014), para. 148 (*Öcalan's* detention conditions rendered to be in conformity with Art. 3 because of 'the improvement in the applicant's access to news and information . . . the substantial reinforcement of communication and collective activities . . . the increased frequency of visits authorised and the quality of the applicant's conversations with his family, without any glass barrier . . . and the provision of facilities mitigating the effects of the relative social isolation'); cf. also Meyer-Ladewig, Harrendorf and König, in Meyer-Ladewig, Nettesheim and von Raumer, *EMRK* (2017), Art. 5 mn. 37.

688. ECtHR, *Ramirez Sanchez*, 59450/00; thereon cf. Irmscher, *EuGRZ*, 34 (2007), 135 ff.; Moliner-Dubost, *AJP*, 4 (2007), 161 ff.; cf. also Vermeulen, in Van Dijk et al., *Theory and Practice of the ECHR* (2006), p. 422; Grabenwarter, *ECHR* (2014), Art. 3 mn. 11. Cf., however, ECtHR, *Ilascu et al.* v. *Moldova and Russia*, No 48787/99, GC Judgment (8 July 2004), paras. 438 ff.

689. Cf. e.g. ECtHR, *Ilascu et al.*, No 48787/99, GC Judgment (8 July 2004), paras. 438 ff., where it was held that the isolation conditions of the applicant ('no contact with other prisoners, no news from the outside – since he was not permitted to send or receive mail – and no right to contact his lawyer or receive regular visits from his family'), applied for the same period (eight years) as in *Ramirez Sanchez* (n. 687), violate Art. 3.

690. ECtHR, *Jalloh*, 54810/00, paras. 75 ff., esp. 77; on this, cf. Gaede, *HRRS*, 7 (2006), 242–3; Safferling, *Jura*, 30 (2008), 101; Satzger, *International and European Criminal Law* (2018), §9 mn. 43 ff.

691. Schumann, *StV*, 26 (2006), 663–4; for a critical stance in this regard, cf. Schuhr, *NJW*, 59 (2006), 3539.

692. Generally on the ECHR and its APs as barriers to *extradition*, cf. Chapter 4, mn. 34 ff.

693. ECtHR, *Trabelsi*, 140/10, paras. 110 ff. (119: 'In so far as any liability under the Convention is or may be incurred, it is incurred by the extraditing Contracting State by reason of its having taken action which has the direct consequence of exposing an individual to proscribed ill-treatment'); ECtHR, *Mamatkulov and Askarov* v. *Turkey*, Nos 46827/99 and 46951/99, GC Judgment (4 February 2005), para. 67; summarising ECHR case law, Komrey and Morgenstern, *ZIS*, 9 (2014), 708 ff.

694. Cf. ECtHR, *Al-Saadoon and Mufdhi*, 61498/08, para. 123; ECtHR, *K.R.S.* v. *the UK*, No 32733/08, Decision (2 December 2008), where the ECtHR decided that when a citizen of a third State is deported to a transit State which is also a signatory of the ECHR, it must be ensured that the deported person is able to appeal in the

transit State against his further deportation. See also Grabenwarter, *ECHR* (2014), Art. 3 mn. 13–14; Satzger, *International and European Criminal Law* (2018), §9 mn. 48–9; Esser, *Europäisches und Internationales Strafrecht* (2018), §9 mn. 162.

695. Cf. Ambos, *EuCLR*, 5 (2015), 107 ff. (discussing *El Masri* and *Husayn*). The USA itself would violate Art. 5(2) ACHR (prohibition of torture and inhuman treatment) if, as part of its war on terrorism, it transfered detainees to States that have been proven to use methods of interrogation that violate human rights.
696. Hoffmann, in Menzel, Pierlings and Hoffmann, *Völkerrechtsprechung* (2005), pp. 510–11 in reference to ECtHR, *Chahal* v. *the UK*, No 22414/93, GC Judgment (15 November 1996).
697. ECtHR, *Al-Saadoon and Mufdhi*, 61498/08, para. 123 ('real risk'); on this in detail Lorz and Sauer, *EuGRZ*, 37 (2010), 396–403; in a similar vein insofar, CJEU, *Aranyosi and Căldăraru*, C-404/15 and C-659/15 PPU, as quoted in the main text, mn. 156 *in fine*.
698. ECtHR, *M.S.S.* v. *Belgium and Greece*, No 30696/09, Judgment (21 January 2011), paras. 358; on this, cf. Grabenwarter, *ECHR* (2014), Art. 3 mn. 14.
699. ECtHR, *H.L.R.* v. *France*, No 24573/94, Judgment (29 April 1997), para. 41; Meyer-Ladewig and Lehnert, in Meyer-Ladewig, Nettesheim and von Raumer, *EMRK* (2017), Art. 3 mn. 70.
700. ECtHR, *Othman (Abu-Qatada)* v. *the UK*, No 8139/09, Judgment (17 January 2012), paras. 187–8; on this, cf. Michaelsen, *ICLQ*, 61 (2012), 759 ff.; Grabenwarter, *ECHR* (2014), Art. 3 mn. 14.
701. On the legal–philosophical and historical perspective, cf. Renzikowski, in Amelung, Günther and Kühne, *FS Krey* (2010), pp. 407 ff.; for a brief overview, see Tamietti, *eucrim*, 10 (2015), 116–17; from a comparative perspective, Karsai, *ZIS*, 8 (2013), 24–5; from an Italian perspective, see di Martino, *ZStW* 128 (2016), 270 ff.
702. Cf. ECtHR, *Kononov* v. *Latvia*, No 36376/04, Judgment (17 May 2010), para. 185; also Peters and Altwicker, EMRK (2012), §6 mn. 6.
703. Cf. ECtHR, *Kononov*, 36376/04, para. 185; also Satzger, *International and European Criminal Law* (2018), §9 mn. 96; Satzger, *Internationales und Europäisches Strafrecht* (2016), §11 mn. 84.
704. Ambos, *KritV*, 86 (2003), 41; Peters and Altwicker, *EMRK* (2012), §6 mn. 4–5; Frowein, in Frowein and Peukert, *EMRK-Kommentar* (2009), mn. 4; Gollwitzer, *Menschenrechte im Strafverfahren* (2005), Art. 7 MRK mn. 9; Vest, *Gerechtigkeit für Humanitätsverbrechen* (2006), pp. 149 ff.; Satzger, *International and European Criminal Law* (2018), §9 mn. 96. But see on the importance of *lex scripta* and *certa* for EU criminal law, Karsai, *ZIS*, 8 (2013), 26.
705. Ambos, *KritV*, 86 (2003), 41; Arnold, Karsten and Kreicker, *NJ*, 55 (2001), 562. For a recent theoretical foundation of the prohibition of analogy in the context of European criminal law, see Greco, *GA*, 163 (2016), 138 ff., 195 ff. (determining the limits of the letter of the law by taking recourse to the theories of ordinary, colloquial use of language (145–9) and focusing on the language of the place of commission and the *lex fori* (205 ff., 216)).
706. Cf. ECtHR, *O'Carroll* v. *the UK*, No 35557/03, Decision (15 March 2005), on reconciling the punishability of importing 'indecent' photographs according to §170(2b) of the British Customs and Excise Act of 1979 with Art. 7(1) ECHR; on

this, cf. Gillespie and Bettinson, *JCL*, 70 (2006), 127 ff. On the sufficient certainty of the term *verwerflich* ('reprehensible') in §240(2) StGB, cf. ECtHR, *Witt* v. *Germany*, No 18397/03, Decision (8 January 2007).

707. Cf. e.g. ECtHR, *Žaja* v. *Croatia*, No 37462/09, Judgment (4 October 2016), para. 90; ECtHR, *Vasiliauskas* v. *Lithuania*, No 35343/05, GC Judgment (20 October 2015), para. 154; ECtHR, *Sunday Times* v. *the UK*, 6538/74, para. 49; ECtHR, *Kafkaris*, 21906/04, paras. 139–40; ECtHR, *Kononov*, 36376/04, para. 185; see also Ambos, *KritV*, 86 (2003), 38 ff.; Peters and Altwicker, *EMRK* (2012), §23 mn. 5; similarly, on the basis of an 'interacción entre el poder legislativo y el judicial', Silva Sánchez, in Bajo Fernández, *Constitución Europea y derecho penal económico* (2006), p. 253.

708. Esser, *Europäisches und Internationales Strafrecht* (2018), §9 mn. 283.

709. ECtHR, *Camilleri* v. *Malta*, No 42931/10, Judgment (22 January 2013), para. 40; cf. thereon Mitsilegas, *EU Criminal Law after Lisbon* (2016), pp. 93–4; for a fundamental treatment of the relationship between the principle of legality and jurisdictional rules, Asp, *Procedural Criminal Law Cooperation* (2016), pp. 123 ff., 151 ff. (arguing that jurisdiction has a dual nature with a procedural focus but, notwithstanding, legality may 'have a bearing on the legal assessment' of the respective conduct (160), especially in cases of extraterritorial jurisdiction where the jurisdictional claim of a certain State is hardly foreseeable for the citizen (167); at any rate, the jurisdiction regime within the EU, albeit not 'unproblematic', is not in conflict with the legality principle (173)).

710. Cf. ECtHR, *S. W.* v. *the UK*, No 20166/92, Judgment (22 November 1995), para. 10; thereon, cf. Lawrence, *DenningLJ*, 18 (2006), 37 ff.; Conaghan, *Law and Gender* (2013), pp. 48 ff.

711. House of Lords, *Regina* v. *R*, No [1991] UKHL 12, Judgment (23 October 1991).

712. Cf. Ambos, *KritV*, 86 (2003), 35 ff., esp. 40 incl. further references; Peters and Altwicker, *EMRK* (2012), §23 mn. 5.

713. ECtHR, *S. W.*, 20166/92, para. 36; ECtHR, *C. R.* v. *the UK*, No 20190/92, Judgment (22 November 1995), para. 34. Cf. also Demko, *HRRS*, 5 (2004), 20–1; for a critical stance, cf. Mylonopoulos, *ZStW*, 121 (2009), 82.

714. Cf. §27 GDR Border Law (DDR-Grenzgesetz) allowing for the use of firearms against a person 'where resort to physical force [*körperliche Einwirkung*], with or without the use of mechanical aids, has been unsuccessful or holds out no prospect of success', where 'shots aimed at objects or animals have not produced the result desired' (§27(1)), in order 'to prevent the imminent commission or continuation of an offence [*Straftat*] which appears in the circumstances to constitute a serious crime [*Verbrechen*]' or 'in order to arrest a person strongly suspected of having committed a serious crime' (§27(2)). It must 'be preceded by a shouted warning or warning shot, save where imminent danger may be prevented or eliminated only through targeted use of the firearm' (§27(3)), 'Firearms must not be used when the life or health of third parties may be endangered; the persons appear, from their outward aspect, to be children; or the shots would impinge on the sovereign territory of a neighbouring State' (§27(4)) (cf. ECtHR, *Streletz, Kessler, Krenz*, 34044/96, 35532/97 and 44801/98, para. 38). For a thorough analysis, cf. Kreicker, *Art. 7 EMRK und die Gewalttaten an der deutsch-deutschen Grenze* (2002).

715. ECtHR, *Streletz, Kessler, Krenz*, 34044/96, 35532/97 and 44801/98. In agreement with this, Werle, *NJW*, 54 (2001), 3001 ff.; Peters and Altwicker, *EMRK* (2012), §23 mn. 10; Kühl, in Müller-Dietz, *FS Jung* (2007), pp. 442–3; cf. also Demko, *HRRS*, 5 (2004), 22 ff.; Cornils, in Menzel, Pierlings and Hoffmann, *Völkerrechtsprechung* (2005), pp. 537 ff.; Eisele, *JA*, 37 (2005), 907; Sweeney, *The ECtHR in the Post-Cold War Era* (2012), pp. 51 ff.; a critical stance is taken by Vest, *Gerechtigkeit für Humanitätsverbrechen* (2006), pp. 78 ff., 174–5. Ultimately the same decision was reached by the *UN Human Rights Committee* (UNHRC) in regard to the former GDR chief of border troops and deputy minister of defence, Klaus Dieter Baumgarten, UNHRC, *Baumgarten* v. *Germany*, No 960/2000 (UN Doc. CCPR/C/78/D/960/2000), Decision (31 July 2003), para. 9.4 ('even when used as a last resort lethal force may only be used, under article 6 of the Covenant, to meet a proportionate threat . . . the disproportionate use of lethal force was criminal according to the general principles of law recognised by the community of nations already at the time when the author committed his acts').
716. ECtHR, *Streletz, Kessler, Krenz*, 34044/96, 35532/97 and 44801/98, paras. 67 ff.
717. Similarly UNHRC, *Baumgarten*, 960/2000, paras. 9.4, 9.5. Moreover, the right to freedom of movement guaranteed in Art. 12(2) ICCPR and Art. 2(2) AP IV ECHR had also been violated (ECtHR, *Streletz, Kessler, Krenz*, 34044/96, 35532/97 and 44801/98, paras. 92 ff.). On the evaluation of the shootings as crimes against humanity, cf. Vest, *Gerechtigkeit für Humanitätsverbrechen* (2006), pp. 152 ff., 175.
718. ECtHR, *Streletz, Kessler, Krenz*, 34044/96, 35532/97 and 44801/98, paras. 87 ff.
719. On Art. 7(2), cf. ECtHR, *Kolk and Kislyiy* v. *Estonia*, Nos 23052/04 and 24018/04, Decision (17 January 2006); conc. Cassese, *JICJ*, 2 (2006), 414 ff.; Frowein, in Frowein and Peukert, *EMRK-Kommentar* (2009), Art. 7 mn. 11; Gollwitzer, *Menschenrechte im Strafverfahren* (2005), Art. 7 MRK mn. 10; Schmitt, in Meyer-Goßner and Schmitt, StPO (2017), Art. 7 MRK mn. 2. See further ECtHR, *Kononov*, 36376/04; on this, cf. Kleinlein, *EuGRZ*, 37 (2010), 547; in greater detail, see Gil Gil, *ADPCP*, 63 (2010), 131 ff.
720. Germany issued a reservation on this clause in 1952 (*BGBl.* II 1954, 14); Ambos, *StV*, 17 (1997), 41 with n. 40; Frowein, in Frowein and Peukert, *EMRK-Kommentar* (2009), mn. 12), which was only withdrawn on 5 October 2001 (Peters, *Einführung in die EMRK* (2003), p. 6); cf. also Safferling, *Internationales Strafrecht* (2011), §13 mn. 66, who considers the regulation 'superfluous', as punishability according to international law is already covered by para. (1).
721. Cf. the 'critical natural law' approach advanced by Naucke, in Donatsch, Forster and Schwarzenegger, *FS Trechsel* (2002), pp. 513–14 ('critical natural law . . . the only content of which is to protect individual citizens from State or State-like acts of violence'; orig. 'kritische[s] Naturrecht . . . das den einzigen Inhalt hat, den einzelnen Bürger vor staatlichen oder staatsähnlichen Gewaltakten zu schützen'). In a similar vein, cf. Cassese, *JICJ*, 2 (2006), 417, arguing in favour of a precedence of (international values upholding) human dignity over foreseeability.
722. Cf. on the one hand, BGH, No 5 StR 370/92, Decision (3 November 1992), in *BGHSt* 39, 1, 14–15, according to which the interpretation of §§213 GDR-StGB, 27 Border Law practised in the GDR is not authoritative 'because of the violation of superordinate legal principles that the GDR was also bound to observe and because of an extreme violation of the principle of proportionality'. On the other hand cf. BVerfG, 2 BvR 1851/94 et al., in *BVerfGE* 95, 133, according to which

there was no violation of the prohibition of retroactive legislation as 'in this very special situation ... the imperative of material justice, which also includes the observance of international human rights, [does not permit] such a cause of justification [§27 GDR Border Law] to be applied'.

723. For a critical stance on this, cf. Ambos, *KritV*, 86 (2003), 42.
724. Arnold, Karsten and Kreicker, *NJ*, 55 (2001), 563; Arnold and Kühl, *JuS*, 32 (1992), 994; a critical stance is also taken by Cornils, in Menzel, Pierlings and Hoffmann, *Völkerrechtsprechung* (2005), p. 539 (criticising the only apparent positivist reasoning of the German High Courts).
725. Thereon with further references Ambos, *Treatise ICL I* (2013), pp. 88–9.
726. Ambos, *KritV*, 86 (2003), 42–3; in a similar vein Vest, *Gerechtigkeit für Humanitätsverbrechen* (2006), pp. 183–4 and passim; cf. also Kadelbach, in Dörr, Grote and Marauhn, *EMRK/GG*, i (2013), Kapitel 15 mn. 34; Renzikowski, in Amelung, Günther and Kühne, *FS Krey* (2010), pp. 409–10.
727. Ambos, *KritV*, 86 (2003), 42; Renzikowski, in Amelung, Günther and Kühne, *FS Krey* (2010), pp. 409–10.
728. In this regard, the conviction of border guards, as in the case of *K.-H. W.*, is a cause for concern (ECtHR, *K.-H. W.* v. *Germany*, No 37201/97, Judgment (22 March 2001)); at least the assumption of an inevitable mistake of law would have seemed logical (Ambos, *KritV*, 86 (2003), 43; for a different view see Naucke, in Donatsch, Forster and Schwarzenegger, *FS Trechsel* (2002), pp. 506 ff., esp. p. 508).
729. ECtHR, *Vasiliauskas*, 35343/05, paras. 165 ff.
730. ECtHR, *Vasiliauskas*, 35343/05, para. 168; also para. 172; dissenting opinion Villiger, Power-Forde, Pinto de Albuquerque and Kūris, para. 6.
731. ECtHR, *Vasiliauskas*, 35343/05, paras. 170 ff. (170, 175), 178.
732. ECtHR, *Vasiliauskas*, 35343/05, para. 181.
733. ECtHR, *Vasiliauskas*, 35343/05, para. 183 with references; also paras. 185, 186.
734. ECtHR, *Vasiliauskas*, 35343/05, paras. 188–90.
735. ECtHR, *Vasiliauskas*, 35343/05, para. 189; also para. 188 with further references (inter alia stating that para. 2 has only once been applied in the context of post-Second World War and Soviet deportations).
736. The dissent of Judges Sajó, Vučinić and Turković does not deal with the merits but considers the application to be inadmissible since the Lithuanian Constitutional Court has provided a remedy; ECtHR, *Vasiliauskas*, 35343/05, Joint Dissenting Opinion of Judges Sajó, Vučinić and Turković, p. 93.
737. ECtHR, *Vasiliauskas*, 35343/05, Dissenting Opinion Villiger et al., para. 9.
738. ECtHR, *Vasiliauskas*, 35343/05, Dissenting Opinion Villiger et al., para. 11; reaffirmed by *Vasiliauskas*, 35343/05, (additional) Dissenting Opinion of Judge Power-Forde, p. 94.
739. ECtHR, *Vasiliauskas*, 35343/05, Dissenting Opinion Villiger et al., para. 16; in the same vein ECtHR, *Vasiliauskas*, 35343/05, (additional) Dissenting Opinion of Judge Kūris, para. 4 and Dissenting Opinion Of Judge Ziemele, para. 14; also para. 23.
740. Ambos, *HRLR*, 17 (2017), 179–84; conc. with the majority (albeit critical of its reasoning) also Vest, *ZIS*, 11 (2016), 489 ff.
741. §67d(3) StGB.
742. On the violation of Art. 5 ECHR, see already main text, mn. 67 with n. 421.
743. ECtHR, *M.*, 19359/04, paras. 122 ff., 136; confirmed in ECtHR, *Schummer* v. *Germany*, Nos 27360/04 and 42225/07, Judgment (13 January 2011), paras. 65

ff.; ECtHR, *Mautes* v. *Germany*, No 20008/07, Judgment (13 January 2011), paras. 52 ff.; ECtHR, *Kallweit* v. *Germany*, No 17792/07, Judgment (13 January 2011), paras. 65 ff.; ECtHR, *Haidn*, 6587/04, and through the judgment of BVerfG, 2 BvR 2365/09 (n. 31), p. 326; on this, cf. Satzger, *International and European Criminal Law* (2018), §9 mn. 93, 83; Kinzig, *NStZ*, 30 (2010), 237; Grosse-Brömer and Klein, *ZRP*, 43 (2010), 172 ff.; Radtke, *NStZ*, 30 (2010), 537 ff.; Bachmann and Goeck, *NJ*, 64 (2010), 457; Pollähne, *KJ*, 43 (2010), 255 ff.; Laue, *JR*, 82 (2010), 198 ff.; Grabenwarter, *JZ*, 65 (2010), 857 ff.; Jung, *GA*, 157 (2010), 639 ff.; Peglau, *jurisPR-StrafR*, 4 (2010), No 2; Klesczewski, *HRRS*, 11 (2010), 394 ff.; Müller, *EuR*, 46 (2011), 423; Esser, Gaede and Tsambikakis, *NStZ*, 31 (2011), 79 ff.; Esser, Gaede and Tsambikakis, *NStZ*, 32 (2012), 555–6; Pösl, *ZJS*, 4 (2011), 132 ff.; Drenkhahn and Morgenstern, *ZStW*, 124 (2012), 145 ff.; Michaelsen, *HRLR*, 12 (2012), 155 ff.; Rissing-van Saan, in Heinrich et al., *FS Roxin*, ii (2011), pp. 1177 ff.; Müller, *StV*, 30 (2010), 207 ff.; crit. on the ECtHR's reasoning Hörnle, in Bernsmann and Fischer, *FS Rissing-van Saan* (2011), pp. 242 ff.

744. BVerfG, 2 BvR 2029/01, in *BVerfGE* 109, 133, 167 ff.; for a different view see Bock, in Müller-Graff, *FS Scheuing* (2011), p. 272 incl. further references; in detail on the rules in constitutional law governing preventive deprivation of liberty in Germany Radtke, *GA*, 158 (2011), 648 ff.
745. ECtHR, *M.*, 19359/04, para. 126; ECtHR, *Bergmann*, 23279/14, paras. 150, 155 (stressing in particular the imposition of the measure after conviction for a 'criminal offence'); on the criteria cf. Satzger, *StV*, 33 (2013), 244; cf. also ECtHR, *del Rio Prada* v. *Spain*, No 42750/09, Judgment (21 October 2013), paras. 81 ff. (violation of Art. 7 due to the retroactive change of the basis upon which prison sentences are calculated, leading to a longer prison term).
746. ECtHR, *M.*, 19359/04, para. 127.
747. ECtHR, *M.*, 19359/04, para. 128.
748. ECtHR, *M.*, 19359/04, para. 130.
749. ECtHR, *M.*, 19359/04, para. 132.
750. However, the German Federal Supreme Court continues not to regard preventive detention as a punishment in matters of juvenile crime given its educational purposes (BGH, 1 StR 554/09 (n. 31), p. 384); crit. Renzikowski, *NStZ*, 30 (2010), 507; Kreuzer, *NStZ*, 30 (2010), 477; Bartsch, *StV*, 30 (2010), 523–4; Frommel, *NK*, 22 (2010), 82 ff.
751. ECtHR, *M.*, 19359/04, para. 135.
752. Reorganisation of the Law of Preventive Detention and Accompanying Rules Act of 22 October 2010 (Gesetz zur Neuordnung des Rechts der Sicherungsverwahrung und zu begleitenden Regelungen, *BGBl.* I 2010, 2300); cf. Drenkhahn and Morgenstern, *ZStW* 124 (2012), 180 ff.; cf. also Ambos, *Internationales Strafrecht* (2011), §10 mn. 88; Pollähne, *ZJS*, 4 (2011), 218.
753. 'Gesetz zur Therapierung und Unterbringung psychisch gestörter Gewalttäter' (ThUG). Thereon, cf. Beukelmann, *NJW-Spezial*, 7 (2010), 696–7; Esser, Gaede and Tsambikakis, *NStZ*, 31 (2011), 81; Kinzig, *NJW*, 64 (2011), 177 ff.; Kreuzer, *StV*, 31 (2011), 122 ff. with a critical commentary on the ThUG's compatibility with the ECHR (131–2); also commenting on the ThUG's compliance with the ECHR: Ullenbruch, *StV*, 32 (2012), 47. The BVerfG refused to accept a constitutional complaint directed against the ThUG (BVerfG, No 2 BvR 94/11, Decision (13 January 2011), in *BVerfGK*, 18, 343, 344); cf. also OLG Saarbrücken, No 5 W

212/11-94, Decision (30 September 2011), in *StV*, 32 (2012), 31 ff. and Ullenbruch, *StV*, 33 (2013), 268 ff.

754. BVerfG, 2 BvR 2365/09 (n. 31), p. 326 (legislative revision by 31 May 2013); thereon Kreuzer and Bartsch, *StV*, 31 (2011), 472 ff.; Eisenberg, *StV*, 31 (2011), 480; Hörnle, *NStZ*, 31 (2011), 488; Schöch, *GA*, 159 (2012), 14 ff. On the practical consequences: Peglau, *NJW*, 64 (2011), 1924–7; cf. also Dessecker, *ZIS*, 6 (2011), 706; Pösl and Dürr, *EuCLR* 2 (2012), 173.
755. Act on establishment, at federal level, of a difference between the provisions on preventive detention and those on prison sentences ('Gesetz zur bundesrechtlichen Umsetzung des Abstandsgebotes im Recht der Sicherungsverwahrung'), 5 December 2012, *BGBl.* I 2012, 2425; Rissing-van Saan, in Heinrich et al., *FS Roxin*, ii (2011), p. 1185; on the changes to enforcement cf. Schäferskϋpper and Grote, *NStZ*, 33 (2013), 447 ff.; crit. Renzikowski, *NJW*, 66 (2013), 1638 ff.; Höffler, *StV*, 34 (2014), 173–4.
756. Art. 2(2) in conjunction with Art. 104(1) GG.
757. BVerfG, 2 BvR 2365/09 (n. 31), p. 372 ('nur nach Maßgabe einer strikten Verhältnismäßigkeitsprüfung und unter Wahrung strenger Anforderungen an die zu Grunde liegenden Entscheidungen und die Ausgestaltung des Vollzugs zu rechtfertigen').
758. BVerfG, 2 BvR 2365/09 (n. 31), p. 373 ('Dem Freiheitsanspruch des Untergebrachten ist das Sicherungsbedürfnis der Allgemeinheit entgegenzuhalten; beide sind im Einzelfall abzuwägen').
759. BVerfG, 2 BvR 2365/09 (n. 31), pp. 388–9.
760. BVerfG, 2 BvR 2365/09 (n. 31), pp. 374 ff. See also for more case law and more details regarding the differentiated treatment of preventively detained persons, Schäferskϋpper and Grote, *NStZ*, 36 (2016), 197–201.
761. BVerfG, 2 BvR 2365/09 (n. 31), pp. 366, 378, 389–90, 398–401.
762. BVerfG, 2 BvR 2365/09 (n. 31), pp. 379–80; on this, cf. also Pösl and Dürr, *EuCLR* 2 (2012), 176; Beck, *HRRS*, 14 (2013), 9 ff.
763. ECtHR, *Bergmann*, 23279/14, para. 158.
764. On the respective unit of the Rosdorf Preventive Detention Centre, see already above endnote 466.
765. ECtHR, *Bergmann*, 23279/14, paras. 166–9.
766. ECtHR, *Bergmann*, 23279/14, para. 174.
767. ECtHR, *Bergmann*, 23279/14, para. 176.
768. ECtHR, *Bergmann*, 23279/14, para. 177.
769. ECtHR, *Bergmann*, 23279/14, para. 182.
770. ECtHR, *M.*, 19359/04, para. 67.
771. On the background, Radtke, *NStZ*, 30 (2010), 539 ff.; cf. also Gaede, *HRRS*, 11 (2010), 329 ff.; Greger, *NStZ*, 30 (2010), 676–7; Kreuzer, *StV*, 31 (2011), 125–6; Hörnle, in Bernsmann and Fischer, *FS Rissing-van Saan* (2011), pp. 248 ff. The Act on Safeguarding the Uniformity of Case Law in Preventive Detention Decisions, 24 July 2010 (*BGBl.* I 2010, 976), introduced a requirement for courts to make a submission to the German Federal Court if they wished to deviate from previous case law on the matter (a so-called *Divergenzvorlage*; §121 (2) No 3 GVG).
772. OLG Frankfurt a.M., No 3 Ws 485/10, Decision (24 June 2010), in *NStZ*, 30 (2010), 573–4; OLG Frankfurt a.M., No 3 Ws 539/10, Decision (1 July 2010), in *NStZ-RR*, 30 (2010), 321–2; OLG Karlsruhe, Nos 2 Ws 458/09 and 2 WS 22/10,

Decision (15 July 2010); cf. also BGH, 5 StR 60/10 (n. 422), p. 567 with commentary by Ahmed, *StV*, 30 (2010), 574; a different decision was reached by the 5th Senate of the German Federal Court, which submitted an enquiry on this issue to the other senates (BGH, 5 StR 394/10 et al. (n. 16), p. 149–51 with commentary by Bachmann and Goeck, *ZIS*, 6 (2011), 44). On this, cf. also Gaede, *HRRS*, 11 (2010), 329 ff.; Pösl, *ZJS*, 4 (2011), 141 and Drenkhahn and Morgenstern, *ZStW* 124 (2012), 175 ff.; Rissing-van Saan, in Heinrich et al., *FS Roxin*, ii (2011), p. 1187.

773. Cf. OLG Celle, No 2 Ws 169/10, Decision (25 May 2010), in *NStZ-RR*, 15 (2010), 322; OLG Köln, No 2 Ws 431/10, Decision (14 July 2010); OLG Nürnberg, No 1 Ws 404/10, Decision (4 August 2010), in *NStZ*, 30 (2010), 574–6; OLG Hamm, No 4 Ws 114/10, Decision (12 May 2010); OLG Koblenz, No 1 WS 108/10, Decision (7 June 2010); OLG Nürnberg, Nos 1 Ws 315/10 and 2 Ws 78/10, Decision (24 June 2010); OLG Stuttgart, No 1 Ws 57/10, Decision (1 June 2010). Cf. also OLG Hamm, 4 Ws 171/10 (n. 422), p. 388 and BVerfG, No 2 BvR 769/10, Decision (19 May 2010), in *NJW*, 63 (2010), 2501.

774. BVerfG, 2 BvR 2365/09 (n. 31), p. 332. Following on from this, BVerfG, Nos 2 BvR 2122/11 and 2705/11, Decision (6 February 2013), in *BVerfGE* 133, 40, 51; BGH, 5 StR 52/11 (n. 463), pp. 631–2.

775. BVerfG, 2 BvR 2365/09 (n. 31), p. 332; BVerfG, 2 BvR 2122/11 (n. 774), para. 27; on the concept of 'psychological disorder', cf. Dessecker, *ZIS*, 6 (2011), 711 and, in greater detail, Höffler and Stadtland, *StV*, 32 (2012), 239 ff.; for a critical perspective on the application of the ThuG to existing cases, cf. Höffler, *StV*, 34 (2014), 174.

776. BVerfG, 2 BvR 2365/09 (n. 31), p. 332; cf. also BGH, 5 StR 394/10 et al. (n. 16), pp. 149–51.

777. Cf. ECtHR, *Scoppola*, 10249/03, para. 109; cf. also ECtHR, *Maktouf and Damjanović* v. *Bosnia and Herzegovina*, Nos 2312/08 and 34179/08, GC Judgment (18 July 2013), Concurring Opinion of Judge Pinto de Albuquerque, joined by Judge Vučinić, p. 43. On the general recognition of *lex mitior* in the EU MS, see Karsai, *ZIS*, 8 (2013), 27.

778. ECtHR, *Tess* v. *Latvia*, No 34854/02, Decision (12 December 2002); ECtHR, *Kononov*, 36376/04, para. 186; *Maktouf and Damjanović*, 2312/08 and 34179/08, para. 72 ('the two paragraphs of Article 7 are interlinked and are to be interpreted in a concordant manner'); see also Damnjanovic, *ZIS*, 9 (2014), 636; Tamietti, *eucrim*, 10 (2015), 116.

779. *Maktouf and Damjanović*, 2312/08 and 34179/08, Concurring Opinion Pinto de Albuquerque and Vučinić, p. 44.

780. *Maktouf and Damjanović*, 2312/08 and 34179/08, para. 65 and Concurring Opinion Pinto de Albuquerque and Vučinić, p. 44; cf. also Damnjanovic, *ZIS*, 9 (2014), 634–5.

781. ECtHR, *Maktouf and Damjanović*, 2312/08 and 34179/08, para. 70.

782. ECtHR, *Maktouf and Damjanović*, 2312/08 and 34179/08, Concurring Opinion of Judge Kalaydjieva, p. 38; Damnjanovic, *ZIS*, 9 (2014), 634.

783. Damnjanovic, *ZIS*, 9 (2014), 633 ff., 637, calling for an exhaustive analysis of the respective provisions and thus criticising the *Maktouf and Damjanović* judgment for limiting its assessment to an abstract comparison of the maximum or minimum limits of the applicable penalties; in the same vein, ECtHR, *Maktouf and Damjanović*, 2312/08 and 34179/08, Concurring Opinion of Judge Pinto de Albuquerque, Joined by Judge Vučinić, p. 44.

784. Peters and Altwicker, *EMRK* (2012), §5 mn. 16.
785. ECtHR, *McCann, Farrell and Savage*, 18984/91, para. 200.
786. ECtHR, *McCann, Farrell and Savage*, 18984/91, para. 213.
787. ECtHR, *Streletz, Kessler, Krenz*, 34044/96, 35532/97 and 44801/98, para. 63; on this, cf. Arnold, Karsten and Kreicker, *NJ*, 55 (2001), 563; Kreicker, *Art. 7 EMRK und die Gewalttaten an der deutsch-deutschen Grenze* (2002), pp. 16–17; cf. also UNHRC, *Baumgarten*, 960/2000, para. 9.5.
788. On private initiatives, cf. Chapter 1, mn. 32; on the structure of the EU's system of rights protection generally Schorkopf, *Staatsrecht* (2017), §8 mn. 70–3.
789. Chapter 1, mn. 27. See also Satzger, *International and European Criminal Law* (2018), §8 mn. 92; Kaiafa-Gbandi, *ZIS*, 1 (2006), 532; Schünemann, *StV*, 23 (2003), 116 ff.; Roger, *GA*, 157 (2010), 29; calling for an '[e]arly and active participation of the affected individuals' with a view to prevent possible forum shopping. Anagnostopoulos, *ERA Forum*, 15 (2014), 14–15.
790. On six 'handicaps' of transnational defence and its minimum conditions, Schünemann, *StV*, 36 (2016), 181, 184–5.
791. Satzger, *StV*, 23 (2003), 141; Satzger, *International and European Criminal Law* (2018), §8 mn. 92; Gleß, *Replies to Green Paper on Obtaining Evidence in Criminal Matters from One Member State to Another and Securing Admissibility*, p. 2; also the 'Memorandum by the European Commission, Directorate-General for Justice and Home Affairs', printed in UKHL EU Committee, *HL Paper*, 28 (2005); for a differentiated, more detailed account, cf. Polakiewicz, *EuGRZ*, 37 (2010), 12 ff.; a different view is taken by Vogel and Matt, *StV*, 27 (2007), 208–9.
792. On the varying use of this preliminary reference procedure across the Member States, see, however, Chapter 5, mn. 23.
793. Douglas-Scott, *HRLR*, 11 (2011), 657.
794. FD Proposal on Certain Procedural Rights (COM(2004), 328 final); on this, cf. Esser, in Sieber, Satzger and von Heinegg, *Europäisches Strafrecht* (2014), pp. 965–7; Piattoli, *DPP*, 13 (2007), 548 ff.
795. Cf. FD Proposal on Certain Procedural Rights (COM(2004), 328 final), para. 25; on this, cf. Ahlbrecht, *NStZ*, 26 (2006), 74–5; Kirsch, *StraFo*, 14 (2008), 456; Polakiewicz, *EuGRZ*, 37 (2010), 12; more critically Brandts, in Vervaele, *European Evidence Warrant* (2005), p. 105.
796. Satzger, *International and European Criminal Law* (2018), §8 mn. 93; for an overview, cf. Kirsch, *StraFo*, 14 (2008), 456–7; and Vogel and Matt, *StV*, 27 (2007), 206 ff.; also Polakiewicz, *EuGRZ*, 37 (2010), 14–15; on the UK's 'lack of support', see UKHL EU Committee, *HL Paper*, 84 (2009), p. 6.
797. European Council, *Stockholm Programme* (2010), 1–38.
798. European Council, *Stockholm Programme* (2010), 1, 4, 10; on this, cf. Brodowski, *ZIS*, 5 (2010), 377–8; Beukelmann, *NJW*, 63 (2010), 2083–4; Nieto Martín, *RP*, 27 (2011), 80–2; Caeiro, *The EU Agenda on Procedural Safeguards* (2015), p. 15 (highlighting the interpretation given by para. 2.4 of the Stockholm Programme of the 'minimum rules' pursuant to Art. 82(2) TFEU 'as minimum rights of the individuals'); on its genesis, Mitsilegas, *EU Criminal Law after Lisbon* (2016), pp. 154–60 (Art. 82(2)(b) as legal basis).
799. Resolution of the Council 2009/C 295/01 of 30 November 2009 on a Roadmap for Strengthening Procedural Rights of the Suspected or Accused Persons in Criminal Proceedings, OJEU C 295 of 4 December 2009, 1–3; cf. also the development of a

schedule in the 'Action Plan Implementing the Stockholm Programme' (COM(2010), 171 final); thereon, cf. also Brodowski, *ZIS*, 5 (2010), 378–80; Jimeno-Bulnes, *eucrim*, 4 (2009), 157 ff.; Pabel, in Grabenwarter, *Europäischer Grundrechteschutz* (2014), pp. 807–8; Anagnostopoulos, *ERA Forum*, 15 (2014), 12; Caeiro, *The EU Agenda on Procedural Safeguards* (2015), pp. 15 ff.; for a more critical view, cf. de Bondt and Vermeulen, *eucrim*, 5 (2010), 163 ff.

800. This, of course, requires a 'cross-border dimension' of the relevant criminal matter; crit. insofar of the Commission's jurisdictional claim de Bondt and Vermeulen, *eucrim*, 5 (2010), 164; Meysman, *EuCLR*, 4 (2014), 183–7; see also Chapter 4, mn. 8.
801. Action Plan Implementing the Stockholm Programme (COM (2010), 171 final), cf. also *eucrim*, 5 (2010), 2.
802. On the negotiations, see Labayle and de Bruycker, www.europarl.europa.eu/RegData/etudes/etudes/join/2013/493015/IPOL-LIBE_ET%282013%29493015_EN.pdf, 26–7, 32 ff. (refering to institutional tension between the EP and the Council); Herlin-Karnell, *eucrim*, 9 (2014), 28.
803. Cf. Herlin-Karnell, *eucrim*, 9 (2014), 29 ('consolidate, codify, and complement'). See also the German Ministry of Interior, *Position Paper of the Federal Government on the Post-Stockholm Programme* (21 January 2014) (available at http://ec.europa.eu/dgs/home-affairs/what-is-new/public-consultation/2013/pdf/0027/authorities/german_moi_en.pdf, last accessed 27 January 2018), p. 1. (closing of gaps and consolidation); Finnish Ministry of the Interior, *Non-paper on the Future Development of the EU Home Affairs Area After 2014* (Helsinki, 29 November 2013) (available at http://ec.europa.eu/dgs/home-affairs/what-is-new/public-consultation/2013/pdf/0027/authorities/finland-moi_en.pdf, last accessed 27 January 2018), p. 1.
804. Chapter 1, mn. 6, 11; see also the references regarding the relevant directives, main text, mn. 146 ff.
805. EP, *Report on the Mid-term Review of the Stockholm Programme* (4 March 2014) (2013/2024(INI), p. 10 ('Recognises the progress made to date with the roadmap for strengthening the procedural rights of suspects and accused persons in criminal proceedings'); thereon Brodowski, *ZIS*, 8 (2013), 456–7; cf. also Mitsilegas, *EU Criminal Law after Lisbon* (2016), pp. 176–80 (harmonising impact of directives by way of autonomous concepts to be ultimately interpreted by the CJEU).
806. Cf. Chapter 5, mn. 1.
807. Cf. on this Matt, *eucrim*, 12 (2017), 1.
808. COM (2009), 338 final, becoming a Proposal for a Directive (COM (2010), 82 final) following the Lisbon Treaty's entry into force COM (2010), 82 final.
809. Directive 2010/64/EU of the EP and Council on the Right to Interpretation and Translation in Criminal Proceedings, OJEU L 280 of 26 October 2010, 1–7; on this, cf. Brodowski, *ZIS*, 12 (2017), 19–20; Brodowski, *ZIS*, 5 (2010), 382; Cras and De Matteis, *eucrim*, 5 (2010), 153 ff.; Ahlbrecht, *StV*, 32 (2012), 493; Blackstock, *EuCLR*, 2 (2012), 25–6; Payter et al., in Atkinson, *EU Law in Criminal Practice* (2013), p. 107; Smith, *NJECL*, 4 (2013), 91 ff.; Mitsilegas, *EU Criminal Law after Lisbon* (2016), pp. 161–2; on its development, cf. Esser, in Sieber, Satzger and von Heinegg, *Europäisches Strafrecht* (2014), pp. 976–7; on the implementation in Germany see Christl, *NStZ*, 34 (2014), 376 ff.; on the opt-in of the UK, see Hinarejos, Spencer and Peers, *CELS Working Paper*, 1 (2012), 3; crit. on the implementation in France Gros, *eucrim*, 12 (2017), 27 ff.

810. Recital 13 Directive 2010/64/EU.
811. Cras and De Matteis, *eucrim*, 8 (2013), 23. Art. 82(2) subparagraph 1 TFEU limits the EU's harmonisation competence to constellations in which the introduction of shared minimum standards is necessary for co-operation in criminal matters '*having a cross-border dimension*'. It has been argued that this provision gives, de facto, the EU the competence to regulate purely national criminal matters since it is virtually impossible to draw a clear distinction between these and proceedings with a cross-border dimension; cf. Vogel and Eisele, in Grabitz, Hilf and Nettesheim, *Das Recht der EU*, i (2017), Art. 82 TFEU mn. 96.
812. Thereon, cf. Chapter 4, mn. 43 ff.
813. For a critical stance on this, cf. Blackstock, *EuCLR*, 2 (2012), 25; ECPI, *ZIS*, 8 (2013), 445; crit. also Esser, in Zöller et al., *FS Wolter* (2013), p. 1339 (arguing that the level of protection offered by the Directive is lower than that of the ECHR).
814. However, the Directive does not state at which point the suspect has to be informed of the suspicion. Ultimately this is thus left to the Member States; cf. Esser, in Zöller et al., *FS Wolter* (2013), p. 1341; for a critical view of the vagueness of these rules, cf. Miettinen, *Criminal Law and Policy in the EU* (2013), p. 217.
815. However, no general right to the complete translation of judgments that goes beyond Art. 6 ECHR can be derived from this; cf. OLG Köln, No 2 Ws 589/11, Decision (30 September), in *NStZ*, 32 (2012), 471–2.
816. Directive 2012/13/EU of the European Paliament and of the Council on the Right to Information in Criminal Proceedings, OJEU L 142 of 1 June 2012, 1; on this, cf. Gatzweiler, *StraFo*, 17 (2011), 295; Ahlbrecht, *StV*, 32 (2012), 493; Brodowski, *ZIS*, 12 (2017), 19–20; Brodowski, *ZIS*, 7 (2012), 565; Payter et al., in Atkinson, *EU Law in Criminal Practice* (2013), p. 110; Mitsilegas, *EU Criminal Law after Lisbon* (2016), pp. 162–5; on the development of the Directive, cf. Cras and De Matteis, *eucrim*, 8 (2013), 22 ff.; Blackstock, *EuCLR*, 2 (2012), 27–9; crit., cf. Esser, in Zöller et al., *FS Wolter* (2013), p. 1338; see also Ruggeri, *ZStW*, 128 (2016), 581–8 (including the right to access to the case file and to linguistic assistance). On the implementation in Germany (inter alia amendments of §§114b, 136 and 168b StPO) Christl, *NStZ*, 34 (2014), 382–3; on the UK's opt-in, cf. Hinarejos, Spencer and Peers, *CELS Working Paper*, 1 (2012), 3; crit. on the implementation in France Gros, *eucrim*, 12 (2017), 27 ff.
817. On this, cf. also Esser, in Zöller et al., *FS Wolter* (2013), pp. 1345–6, and the special arrangements for arrests in EAW proceedings in Art. 5.
818. On this, cf. the model Letter of Rights in the Annex of the Directive 2012/13/EU, OJEU L 142 of 1 June 2010, 8–10.
819. For a critical stance on the vagueness of this clause, cf. Miettinen, *Criminal Law and Policy in the EU* (2013), p. 218. In CJEU, *Tranca*, *Reiter* and *Opria*, Nos C-188/16 et al. (ECLI:EU:C:2017:228), Judgment (22 March 2017), paras. 40 ff., the Court has stated that it does not infringe Art. 6(1) if required by national law 'that the accused person who neither resides in that Member State nor has a fixed place of residence in that State or in his Member State of origin is required to appoint an agent for the purposes of service of a penalty order concerning him and that the period for lodging an objection to that order, before it becomes enforceable, runs from service of that order on that agent'. At the same time, Art. 6 'requires that when the penalty order is enforced, as soon as the person concerned has actually

become aware of the order, he should be placed in the same situation as if that order had been served on him personally and, in particular, that he have the whole of the prescribed period for lodging an objection, where necessary, benefiting from having his position restored to the *status quo ante*' (para. 51).

820. Cf. Cras, *eucrim*, 9 (2014), 33–5 (initial rejection by France, Ireland and the UK for the too-high standard of protection of the proposal and rejection by Italy and Spain for the too-low standard). Thus Denmark, Ireland and the UK did not opt in (for the UK, cf. UKHL EU Committee, *HL Paper*, 159 (2013), 41; for Ireland, see Irish Council for Civil Liberties, *Implementation of the Right of Access to a Lawyer* (2016), p. 5).
821. Directive 2013/48/EU of the EP and of the Council on the Right of Access to a Lawyer in Criminal Proceedings and in European Arrest Warrant Proceedings, and on the Right to have a Third Party Informed upon Deprivation of Liberty and to Communicate with Third Persons and with Consular Authorities while Deprived of Liberty, OJEU L 294 of 6 November 2013, 1; on this, cf. Soo, *EuCLR*, 6 (2016), 284 ff.; Blackstock, *EuCLR*, 2 (2012), 29 ff.; Brodowski, *ZIS*, 7 (2012), 565; Corell and Sidhu, *StV*, 32 (2012), 248; Esser, in Esser et al., *FS Kühne* (2013), pp. 550 ff.; Amnesty International et al., *NJECL*, 4 (2013), 332 ff.; Smith, *NJECL*, 4 (2013), 93–5; Cras, *eucrim*, 9 (2014), 35 ff.; Anagnostopoulos, *ERA Forum*, 15 (2014), 13; Symeonidou-Kastanidou, *EuCLR*, 5 (2015), 68 ff.; Mitsilegas, *EU Criminal Law after Lisbon* (2016), pp. 165–71; in Germany, with the entry into force of the Act of 27 August 2017 (*BGBl.* I 2017, 3295), a right to presence of defence lawyers during police interrogation has been recognized; crit. on the implementation in France Gros, *eucrim*, 12 (2017), 27 ff.
822. See also Cras, *eucrim*, 9 (2014), 35.
823. On the controversy surrounding this EAW amendment, see Cras, *eucrim*, 9 (2014), 42–3.
824. There is a special regulation in Art. 10 with regard to the execution of a European Arrest Warrant.
825. On this, cf. also Amnesty International et al., *NJECL*, 4 (2013), 337.
826. The communication rights of Arts. 4–7 incorporate Measure D ('Communication with Relatives, Employers and Consular Officials') of the Roadmap (above endnote 799).
827. Thereon Cras, *eucrim*, 9 (2014), 40–2.
828. Cf. http://eur-lex.europa.eu/legal-content/EN/NIM/?uri=celex:32013L0048, last accessed 29 January 2018. Note that Denmark, Ireland and the UK have not opted in; above n. 820.
829. ECPI, *ZIS*, 8 (2013), 445.
830. Cf. Cras and De Matteis, *eucrim*, 8 (2013), 31; Corell and Sidhu, *StV*, 32 (2012), 250.
831. Blackstock, *EuCLR*, 2 (2012), 25.
832. Cf. CJEU, *Ratti*, C-148/78 (ECLI:EU:C:1979:110), Judgment (5 April 1979); on the requirements, cf. also Biervert, in Schwarze, *EU-Kommentar* (2012), Art. 288 AEUV mn. 29.
833. In the same vein, Mitsilegas, *EU Criminal Law after Lisbon* (2016), pp. 171–6 (horizontal and vertical impact of directives as 'autonomous, self-designed project' going beyond ECHR standard (175) and also applying to domestic cases (183)).

834. Cras and De Matteis, *eucrim*, 8 (2013), 27; on the need for reform in Germany through the Directive on interpretation, cf. Kotz, *StV*, 32 (2012), 627.
835. Gatzweiler, *StraFo*, 17 (2011), 298; Banach-Gutierrez, *NJECL*, 3 (2012), 97.
836. A similar opinion is voiced by Ahlbrecht, *StV*, 32 (2012), 493.
837. EU, *Green Paper on Detention* (2011); on this, cf. Payter et al., in Atkinson, *EU Law in Criminal Practice* (2013), p. 117; for a summary of the replies to the Green Paper after the public consultation period, see 'Analysis of the Replies to the Green Paper on the Application of EU Criminal Justice Legislation in the Field of Detention' available at http://ec.europa.eu/justice/newsroom/criminal/opinion/files/110510/summary_gpreplies_ms_ongs_en.pdf, last accessed 27 January 2018; on this Smith, *NJECL*, 4 (2013), 95 ff.
838. But for a mixed system combining fixed time limits with a flexible approach ('hybridisation'), see Gialuz and Spagnolo, *EuCLR*, 3 (2013), 221–2, 229–31.
839. Proposal for a Directive on the Strengthening of certain aspects of the presumption of innocence and of the right to be present at trial in Criminal Proceedings (27 November 2013, COM (2013), 821).
840. Proposal for a Directive on Procedural Safeguards for Children Suspected or Accused in Criminal Proceedings (27 November 2013, COM (2013), 822). Calling for an 'integrated approach' covering all mentally impaired persons in general, Meysman, *EuCLR*, 4 (2014), 179, 188–94.
841. Proposal for a Directive on Provisional Legal Aid for Suspects or Accused Persons Deprived of Liberty and Legal Aid in European Arrest Warrant Proceedings (27 November 2013, COM (2013), 824).
842. Directive (EU) 2016/343 of the EP and of the Council of 9 March 2016 on the Strengthening of Certain Aspects of the Presumption of Innocence and of the Right to be Present at the Trial in Criminal Proceedings, OJEU L 6 of 11 March 2016, 1–11. Denmark, Ireland and the UK did not opt in, cf. Brodowski, *ZIS*, 12 (2017), 18; Cras and Erbežnik, *eucrim*, 11 (2016), 26.
843. Directive (EU) 2016/800 of the EP and of the Council of 11 May 2016 on procedural safeguards for children who are suspects or accused persons in criminal proceedings, OJEU L 132 of 21 May 2016, 1–20. On this Brodowski, *ZIS*, 12 (2017), 18–19; Cras, *eucrim*, 11 (2016), 109 ff.
844. Directive (EU) 2016/1919 of the EP and of the Council of 26 October 2016 on legal aid for suspects and accused persons in criminal proceedings and for requested persons in European arrest warrant proceedings, OJEU L 297 of 4 November 2016, 1–8. On the proposal Brodowski, *ZIS*, 12 (2017), 19; crit. on the implementation in France, Gros, *eucrim*, 12 (2017), 27 ff.
845. On genesis, negotiations and content, Cras and Erbežnik, *eucrim*, 11 (2016), 25 ff.; Kraml and Zeder, *JSt*, 3 (2016), 357 ff. (criticising the possibility of developing different standards when implementing the Directive from those applied in the area of mutual recognition, 361); also crit. Schünemann, *StV*, 36 (2016), 179–80 (not going beyond ECtHR case law); crit. for the lack of application to legal persons Lamberigts, *eucrim*, 11 (2016), 36 ff.; crit. on the implementation in France Gros, *eucrim*, 12 (2017), 27 ff.; for an overview, cf. Villamarín López, *ERA Forum*, 18 (2017), 335 ff.
846. Directive (EU) 2016/343, recital 11.
847. Directive (EU) 2016/343, recital 12.
848. Directive (EU) 2016/343, Art. 4(3), and recital 18.
849. Directive (EU) 2016/343, recital 22; Cras and Erbežnik, *eucrim*, 11 (2016), 35.

850. Directive (EU) 2016/343, recital 35; crit. insofar, Ruggeri, *eucrim*, 11 (2016), 50; for a general analysis of the right to personal participation in EU law cf. Ruggeri, *ZStW*, 128 (2016), 581–93 (distinguishing between certain information and linguistic guarantees and the right to an active involvement in the proceedings); crit. of the Directive ibid., 597–600, 603–5.
851. Directive (EU) 2016/343, Art. 8(2).
852. Directive (EU) 2016/343, Art. 9.
853. Directive (EU) 2016/343, recital 41. See also Cras and Erbežnik, *eucrim*, 10 (2016), 33; regarding presence and in absentia proceedings in Italy, see Pierini, *ZStW*, 125 (2013), 951 ff.
854. On this kind of *in absentia* proceedings (more precisely *inaudito reo* proceedings), where the possibility of a hearing depends on a complaint (objection) to be filed by the suspect (e.g. the German procedure of a penal order (*Strafbefehl*) with a very short two-week period for filing the complaint), cf. Ruggeri, *eucrim*, 10 (2016), 42 ff.; Ruggeri, *ZStW*, 128 (2016), 601–5 (discussing critically the CJEU's judgment in *Covaci*, No C-216/14 (ECLI:EU:C:2015:686), Judgment (15 October 2015), which concerns a German penal order).
855. Directive (EU) 2016/343, Art. 8(6).
856. Regulation (EU) 2016/679 of the EP and of the Council of 27 April 2016 on the protection of natural persons with regard to the processing of personal data and on the free movement of such data, and repealing Directive 95/46/EC (General Data Protection Regulation), OJEU L 119 of 4 May 2016, 1–88.
857. On the earlier discussion on this issue Braum, *ZRP*, 42 (2009), 174 ff.; Simitis, *NJW*, 62 (2009), 1782 ff.; Terhechte, *EuZW*, 20 (2009), 199 ff.; Gundel, *EuR*, 44 (2009), 536 ff.; Zeitzmann, *ZEuS*, 14 (2011), 433 ff.; also Ambos, *JZ*, 64 (2009), 468 ff. incl. further references. For an overwiew of the law on data protection, analysing the data exchange between the police, judicial authorities and intelligence services, Beckerhoff, *eucrim*, 12 (2017), 88 ff.
858. Regulation (EU) 2016/679, recital (1). It also provides for the infamous 'right to be forgotten' as 'right to erasure' (Art. 17).
859. Regulation (EU) 2016/679, recital (10).
860. Regulation (EU) 2016/679, recital (73) and Art. 23(1)(d).
861. Regulation (EU) 2016/679, recital (158); see also generally e.g. recital (50) ('processing for archiving purposes in the public interest') and Art. 89.
862. Regulation (EU) 2016/679, Art. 10; also recital (75), (80), (91), (97).
863. Regulation (EU) 2016/679, Art. 84 and recitals (148), (149). In detail on the data protection sanction law Bülte, *StV*, 37 (2017), 460 ff. (on the development at 461–2 and on the General Data Protection Regulation at 462 ff.).
864. Regulation (EU) 2016/679, recital (19) and Art. 2(2)(d).
865. Directive (EU) 2016/680 of the EP and of the Council of 27 April 2016 on the protection of individuals with regard to the processing of personal data by competent authorities for the purposes of prevention, investigation, detection or prosecution of criminal offences or the execution of criminal penalties, and the free movement of such data and and repealing Council Framework Decision 2008/977/JHA, OJEU L 119 of 4 May 2016, 89–131; on the *travaux*, see de Hert and Papakonstantinou, *NJECL*, 7 (2016), 7–9.
866. De Hert and Papakonstantinou, *NJECL*, 7 (2016), 11.

867. Directive (EU) 2016/680, recital 4; de Hert and Papakonstantinou, *NJECL*, 7 (2016), 11 ('the Directive aims at institutionalising and streamlining such data flows').
868. Directive (EU) 2016/680, recital 1: 'The protection of natural persons in relation to the processing of personal data is a fundamental right.'
869. Directive (EU) 2016/680, Arts. 12–18 and 52–57; de Hert and Papakonstantinou, *NJECL*, 7 (2016), 12–13. Cf. also Stief, *StV*, 37 (2017), 473 ff., demanding a consent of the person concerned which, albeit not excluded by the Directive, is to be regarded as an 'exceptional case'.
870. For instance, data processing for national security reasons; see de Hert and Papakonstantinou, *NJECL*, 7 (2016), 10.
871. Directive (EU) 2016/680, Art. 2.
872. Directive (EU) 2016/680, Arts. 41 ff.; de Hert and Papakonstantinou, *NJECL*, 7 (2016), 13–14.
873. On the parallels, cf. also the joint statement of the presidents of the ECtHR and the CJEU, *eucrim*, 6 (2011), 18; also Pabel, in Grabenwarter, *Europäischer Grundrechteschutz* (2014), p. 809. For a critical stance on the lack of order, cf. Eser, *RitsumLR*, 26 (2009), 169; on the classification of Arts. 47–50 CFREU as fundamental rights in distinction to principles (cf. Art. 52(5)), see Sagmeister, *Die Grundsatznormen in der Europäischen Grundrechtecharta* (2010), p. 379; crit. on the principles/rights distinction also Douglas-Scott, *HRLR*, 11 (2011), 652; Schütze, *EU Law* (2015), pp. 444–6.
874. Crit. Douglas-Scott, *HRLR*, 11 (2011), 652. There should be, however, no substantive difference with regard to the explicit and implicit limitations of the ECHR, cf. Pabel, in Grabenwarter, *Europäischer Grundrechteschutz* (2014), pp. 811–12. On 'limitations on limitations' to fundamental rights, see Schütze, *EU Law* (2015), pp. 437–8, 446–8.
875. Douglas-Scott, *HRLR*, 11 (2011), 656; Thym, *NVwZ*, 32 (2013), 890; cf. also Thunberg Schunke, *Whose Responsibility?* (2013), p. 118.
876. Cf. Meyer, *ZStW*, 128 (2016), 1089ff., stressing the transnational–vertical importance of the CFREU towards the EU and its transnational–horizontal importance towards several MS (at 1090) and at the same time critical of the insufficient consideration of its potential by the national prosecutorial authorities (at 1138 ff.); for a more restrictive view, Herlin-Karnell, *eucrim*, 9 (2014), 30.
877. Fassbender, *NVwZ*, 29 (2010), 1049; Pabel, in Grabenwarter, *Europäischer Grundrechteschutz* (2014), p. 809; Schallmoser, *EJCCLCJ*, 22 (2014), 138–40 (advocating, apart from the obligation to omit infringements, also the positive obligation to secure fundamental rights, even by the EU legislator itself, 151 ff.).
878. Insofar the **Protocol 30** to the Lisbon Treaty on the Application of the Charter of Fundamental Rights of the European Union to Poland and to the United Kingdom, OJEU C 306 of 17 December 2007, 156–7, limits the jurisdiction of the CJEU and generally the application of Charter rights. According to Art. 1(1), the CJEU (or any court or tribunal of **Poland** and the **UK**) has no jurisdiction to find that the national law or practices of Poland and the UK are inconsistent with the Charter rights; according to Art. 1(2), Title IV CFREU does not create justiciable rights applicable to both countries except in so far as they have provided in their domestic law; according to Art. 2 references to national laws and practices in the Charter are only applicable to Poland and the UK if the relevant rights or principles are recognised in these countries. See thereon also

Lindner, *EuR*, 43 (2008), 786; Pache and Rösch, *EuZW*, 19 (2008), 520–1; Mehde, *EuGRZ*, 35 (2008), 289; Mayer, *EuR*, 44 (2009), *Beiheft 1*, 90 ff.; Zöller, in Amelung, Günther and Kühne, *FS Krey* (2010), pp. 520–1; Peers, *ERA Forum*, 11 (2011), 575; Douglas-Scott, *HRLR*, 11 (2011), 653–5; Schütze, *EU Law* (2015), pp. 464–6. In 2011, the Czech government submitted a proposal to the Council for a further Protocol to the TEU and TFEU, which would provide that Protocol 30 also applies to the **Czech Republic** (thereon Zöller, in Amelung, Günther and Kühne, *FS Krey* (2010), p. 521, but Declaration 53 mentioned there is not relevant in this context since it does not give any additional rights); however, on 7 March 2014 (after political changes), the Czech Republic requested the discontinuation of the procedure for the conclusion of this new Protocol (on the background of that process, cf. 'Withdrawal of the Recommendation for a European Council Decision on the examination by a conference of representatives of the governments of the Member States of the amendment to the Treaties proposed by the Czech Government in the form of a Protocol on the application of the CFREU to the Czech Republic, to be annexed to the TEU and to the TFEU, and not to convene a Convention', 8 April 2014, Doc. 8385/14). On the other hand, see also **Protocol 35** which ensures that the protection of the right to life of the unborn child by Art. 40.3.3 of the **Irish** Constitution remains unaffected.

879. According to CJEU, *Åklagaren* v. *Åkerberg Fransson*, No C-617/10 (ECLI:EU:C:2013:105), GC Judgment (26 February 2013), para. 48, this means that a national court has directly 'to disapply any provision contrary to a fundamental right guaranteed by the Charter' (without referring this question to a national high court), thereby complementing the CJEU; thereon Scalia, *eucrim*, 10 (2015), 105–6; Schütze, *EU Law* (2015), pp. 461–2; Meyer, *ZStW*, 128 (2016), 1139.

880. The term is to be interpreted broadly as follows from the German version (*Durchführung* = 'execution'; thereon Lindner, *EuR*, 43 (2008), 790 ff.; Stalberg, *Art. 50 der Charta der Grundrechte* (2013), pp. 53 ff.; Schorkopf, *Staatsrecht* (2017), §8 mn. 125 ff.; Jähnke and Schramm, *Europäisches Strafrecht* (2017), §3 mn. 8 ff., esp. 13; cf. also Lenaerts, *EuR*, 47 (2012), 3 ff.; Heger, in Esser et al., *FS Kühne* (2013), pp. 569 ff.) and the *travaux* ('when they act in the scope of Union law', cf. Explanations Relating to the Charter of Fundamental Rights, OJEU C 303 of 14 December 2007, 17, 32); for a detailed analysis of the binding effect of the CFREU in the context of transnational criminal proceedings within the EU, see Meyer, *ZStW*, 128 (2016), 1089 ff.; for the same terminology, CJEU, *ERT AE et al.* v. *Dimotiki Etairia Pliroforissis et al.*, No C-260/89 (ECLI:EU:C:1991:254), Judgment (18 June 1991), para. 42 ('within the scope of Community law'), which includes derogation from EU law by Member States (thereon Schütze, *EU Law* (2015), pp. 459–60); in the same vein, Douglas-Scott, *HRLR*, 11 (2011), 652–3; for a broad definition cf. also CJEU, *Siragusa* v. *Regione Sicilia*, No C-206/13 (ECLI:EU:C:2014:126), Judgment (6 March 2014), para. 25 ('In order to determine whether national legislation involves the implementation of EU law for the purposes of Article 51 of the Charter, some of the points to be determined are whether that legislation is intended to implement a provision of EU law; the nature of that legislation and whether it pursues objectives other than those covered by EU law, even if it is capable of indirectly affecting EU law; and also whether there are specific rules of EU law on the matter or capable of affecting it'). With a special focus on criminal law, see also Gaede, in Böse, *Europäisches*

Strafrecht (2013), mn. 25–6; Scalia, *eucrim*, 10 (2015), 102–3 (invoking AG Sharpston's reference to the 'existence and scope of a material EU competence' as basis of application of Art. 51).

881. Schonard, in Lenz and Borchardt, *EU-Verträge Kommentar* (2013), Art. 51 GRCh mn. 2; Borowsky, in Meyer, *Charta der Grundrechte der EU* (2014), Art. 51 mn. 25; Fassbender, *NVwZ* 29 (2010), 1049. Cf. also Kokott and Sobotta, *EuGRZ*, 37 (2010), 268 ff., who focus particularly on CJEU case law on interpretation in consistency with fundamental rights.

882. Hatje, in Schwarze, *EU-Kommentar* (2012), Art. 51 GRCh mn. 16–19; Jarass, *Charta der Grundrechte der EU* (2016), Art. 51 mn. 21; Jarass, *EU-Grundrechte* (2005), §4 mn. 13; Meyer, *ZStW*, 128 (2016), 1100 ff. (pointing to examples from the harmonisation of criminal law and the assimilation of procedure by way of the principle of mutual recognition); cf. also Sagmeister, *Die Grundsatznormen in der Europäischen Grundrechtecharta* (2010), pp. 316 ff.; for another view see, Kingreen, in Callies and Ruffert, *EUV/AEUV-Kommentar* (2016), Art. 51 GRCh mn. 12 (only the directive is to be interpreted in compliance with Union fundamental law); Matz-Lück, in Matz-Lück and Hong, *Grundrechte und Grundfreiheiten* (2012), p. 184.

883. Schonard, in Lenz and Borchardt, *EU-Verträge Kommentar* (2012), Art. 51 GRCh mn. 6. On the relationship between the CFREU and the national rights (which are applicable in parallel) in light of the approach of the BVerfG, cf. Meyer, *ZStW*, 128 (2016), 1095 ff., 1127 ff.

884. Hatje, in Schwarze, *EU-Kommentar* (2012), Art. 51 GRCh mn. 19; Kingreen, in Callies and Ruffert, *EUV/AEUV-Kommentar* (2016), Art. 51 GRCh mn. 7 ff.; cf. also Schallmoser, *EJCCLCJ*, 22 (2014), 141 ff. ('division of labour' between EU and MS: either EU regulates rights or leaves it with margin of appreciation to the MS).

885. On this, cf. Wegner, *HRRS*, 14 (2013), 127; Huber, *NJW*, 64 (2011), 2387; Lenaerts, *EuR*, 47 (2012), 3 ff.; in detail Stalberg, *Art. 50 der Charta der Grundrechte* (2013), pp. 53 ff., 61 ff. incl. further references; Meyer, *ZStW*, 128 (2016), 1099 ff.

886. CJEU, *Åkerberg Fransson*, C-617/10, paras. 23–9 with a commentary by Dannecker, *JZ*, 68 (2013), 616 ff.; Eckstein, *ZIS*, 8 (2013), 220 ff.; Rabe, *NJW*, 66 (2013), 1407 ff.; Ogorek, *JA*, 45 (2013), 956 ff.; Streinz, *JuS*, 53 (2013), 568–71; Wegner, *HRRS*, 14 (2013), 125 ff.; cf. Ohler, *NVwZ*, 32 (2013), 1433 ff.; Thym, *NVwZ*, 32 (2013), 889 ff.; Weiß, *EuZW*, 24 (2013), 289; Esser, *Europäisches und Internationales Strafrecht* (2018), §6 mn. 10; Vervaele, *ULR*, 9 (2013), 223.

887. Also in favour of a broad interpretation, Spaventa, *Article 51 CFREU* (2016), pp. 1, 32 ff. (at p. 1: 'a more courageous approach should be taken at EU level when examining national implementing measures of EU law raising fundamental rights issues, notably until these are not evenly and properly guaranteed across the EU', and concluding at p. 35 that 'there is also the need for a more courageous use of the Charter in those situations that fall in any event within the scope of EU law, such as citizenship cases, and those that demand thorough fundamental rights scrutiny'). On the controversial question of whether the Union legislator aimed to diverge from CJEU case law in the formulation of Art. 51(1) CFREU, cf. Wegner, *HRRS*, 14 (2013), 127; Huber, *NJW*, 64 (2011), 2387; Lenaerts, *EuR*, 47 (2012), 3 ff.; in detail on this dispute, cf. Stalberg, *Art. 50 der Charta der Grundrechte* (2013), pp. 53 ff., 61 ff. incl. further references.

888. Thereon cf. main text, mn. 165–6.

889. CJEU, *Åkerberg Fransson*, C-617/10, para. 14.

890. Arts. 2, 250 I, 273 D Council Directive 2006/112/EC of 28 November 2006 on the Common System of Value Added Tax, OJEU L 347 of 11 December 2006, 1–118. On Member States' duty according to Art. 325 TFEU to protect the Union's financial interests, which is also relevant here, cf. Chapter 3, mn. 41 ff. incl. n. 322.
891. CJEU, *Åkerberg Fransson*, C-617/10, para. 27.
892. CJEU, *Åkerberg Fransson*, C-617/10, paras. 32 ff.
893. CJEU, *Åkerberg Fransson*, C-617/10, paras. 24–7; on this, cf. also BVerfG, No 1 BvR 1215/07, Judgment (24 April 2013), in *BVerfGE* 133, 277, 316 with a commentary in Bülte and Krell, *StV*, 33 (2013), 713 ff. According to the BVerfG, 'this decision must not be read in a way that would view it as an apparent *ultra vires* act or as if it endangered the protection and enforcement of the fundamental rights in the Member States in a way that questioned the identity of the Basic Law's constitutional order. The decision must thus not be understood and applied in such a way that absolutely any connection of a provision's subject matter to the merely abstract scope of Union law, or merely incidental effects on Union law, would be sufficient for binding the Member States by the Union's fundamental rights set forth in the EUCFR.' Arguing against the classification of the CJEU decision as an *ultra vires* act, cf. Ohler, *NVwZ*, 32 (2013), 1436; Weiß, *EuZW*, 24 (2013), 287, 288–9; cf. also Thym, *NVwZ*, 32 (2013), 891.
894. CJEU, *Åkerberg Fransson*, C-617/10, paras. 27–8; on this, cf. also Esser, *Europäisches und Internationales Strafrecht* (2018), §6 mn. 11; a critical stance is taken by Nestler, *HRRS*, 14 (2013), 341 and Safferling, *NStZ*, 34 (2018), 548, 550–1.
895. CJEU, *Åkerberg Fransson*, C-617/10, para. 19; this is emphasised particularly in BVerfG, 1 BvR 1215/07, in *BVerfGE* 133, 277 ('applicable in all situations governed by European Union law, but not outside such situations', orig. 'nur in "unionsrechtlich geregelten Fallgestaltungen, aber nicht außerhalb derselben Anwendung finden"'). Accordingly, purely hypothetical connections to Union law are not sufficient; cf. Jarass, *Charta der Grundrechte der EU* (2016), Art. 51 mn. 27.
896. CJEU, *Ministerul Public* v. *Radu*, No C-396/11 (ECLI:EU:C:2013:39), GC Judgment (29 January 2013); CJEU, *Melloni* v. *Ministerio Fiscal*, No C-399/11 (ECLI:EU:C:2013:107), GC Judgment (26 February 2013); on both decisions, cf. Thunberg Schunke, *Whose Responsibility?* (2013), pp. 58 ff.; crit. thereof, Xanthopoulou, *NJECL*, 6 (2015), 38–45 (*Radu*), 45–7 (*Melloni*); also Anagnostopoulos, *ERA Forum*, 15 (2014), 17–20; Swoboda, *ZIS*, 10 (2015), 364–8; Schütze, *EU Law* (2015), pp. 462–4 (invoking the principle of pre-emption according to which 'a higher national human rights standard will not be pre-empted by a lower European standard as regards the validity of national law'); on the issue of the preliminary reference in *Radu*, cf. Tinsley, *EuCLR*, 2 (2012), 338 ff.; on the preliminary reference in *Melloni*, Tinsley, *NJECL*, 3 (2012), 19 ff.
897. For an analysis of the EAW, cf. Chapter 4, mn. 43 ff.
898. Furthermore, in the *Melloni* decision the CJEU took the stance that persons affected in proceedings according to the EAW FD could only invoke national fundamental rights 'provided that the level of protection provided for by the Charter, as interpreted by the Court, and the primacy, unity and effectiveness of EU law are not thereby compromised'; CJEU, *Melloni*, C-399/11, paras. 57 ff., 60; confirming this, Gaede, *NJW*, 66 (2013), 1281.
899. CJEU, *Radu*, C-396/11, para. 36; CJEU, *Melloni*, C-399/11, para. 38.
900. CJEU, *Radu*, C-396/11, paras. 36, 40; CJEU, *Melloni*, C-399/11, para. 38.

901. Gaede, *NJW*, 66 (2013), 1279 (orig. 'enumerativen Grundrechtsschutz').
902. Schorkopf, in Grabitz, Hilf and Nettesheim, *Das Recht der EU*, i (2017), Art. 6 EUV mn. 28.
903. Ambos and Poschadel, in Ambos, König and Rackow, *Rechtshilferecht* (2015), pp. 84–5.
904. See the discussion of CJEU, *Opinion 2/13*, at the beginning of this Chapter.
905. CJEU, *Radu*, C-396/11 (ECLI:EU:C:2012:648), Advocate General Sharpston Opinion (18 October 2012), mn. 69 ff., 73 ff.; in the same vein, Mitsilegas, *eucrim*, 10 (2015), 90–1; Xanthopoulou, *NJECL*, 6 (2015), 38–45 (in favour of a strict proportionality test with a balancing of the respective interests, concluding that the seriousness of the rights violation should be taken into account and 'the executing authority may not surrender the person unless it secures that the issuing authority will definitely provide for a remedy', at 44–5); on the importance of proportionality in this context cf. Chapter 4, mn. 71. Generally crit. of the lack of a human rights approach by the CJEU, Swoboda, *ZIS*, 10 (2015), 361, 373–4 ('shadow side', 'missing perspective').
906. Ambos and Poschadel, in Ambos, König and Rackow, *Rechtshilferecht* (2015), pp. 84–5.
907. Gaede, *NJW*, 66 (2013), 1280; a similar opinion is voiced by Vogel, *StV*, 33, issue 5 (2013), Editorial; cf. also Xanthopoulou, *NJECL*, 6 (2015), 45–7 (arguing that the rights' protection – in *Melloni* the right to appeal against an *in absentia* decision which resulted in the EAW – is more highly ranked and more important than mutual recognition which is only a means but not an end in itself and therefore lacks a legitimate objective entailing a violation of the first stage of the proportionality test); on the structure of the proportionality test cf. Chapter 4, mn. 71 with n. 531.
908. Cf. recently BVerfG, No 2 BvR 2735/14, Decision (15 December 2015), in *NJW*, 69 (2016), 1149, paras. 34, 41–7; English translation available at www.bundesverfassungsgericht.de/SharedDocs/Entscheidungen/EN/2015/12/rs20151215_2bvr273514en.html, last accessed 27 January 2018 (nature and control of identity reviews), holding that the principle of individual guilt, rooted in the guarantee of human dignity enshrined in Art. 1(1) GG, lies within the identity core of the Grundgesetz and therefore shall be protected, unconditionally and in any individual case, according to Art. 23(1) sentence 3 in conjunction with Art. 79(3) and Art. 1(1) GG, through a constitutional identity review by the Constitutional Court, possibly entailing a restriction of the primacy of EU Law (paras. 36, 48–9); yet this review has to be exercised with restraint and in a manner open to European integration. It follows from the recognition of a national constitutional identity and the respective identity review that the German court deciding on the admissibility of a surrender request has a *Gewährleistungsverantwortung* (ibid., para. 59) with respect to the requesting MS; that is, it has to make sure that the surrender does not entail or facilitate a rights violation in the requesting State (paras. 59 ff., summarising para. 101). For an identity review with regard to the right to silence also BVerfG, No 2 BvR 890/16, Decision (6 May 2016, interim injunction), in *StV*, 36 (2016), 586 (suspension of extradition to the UK because of possible violation of right to silence); but note that the Court finally granted the extradition since it considered the possible rights violation as not fundamental enough to block extradition; cf. BVerfG, No 2 BvR 890/16, Decision (6 September 2016), paras. 30 ff. Generally crit. Kühne, *StV*, 36 (2016), 302, arguing that the fundamental rights standard enshrined in the GG is too vague and therefore the

BVerfG could, by way of this standard, subject practically every EU law decision to an identity review, thereby undermining the efficiency of the Union law and of the EAW FD; also crit. regarding the consequences for the primacy of EU Law and the efficiency of the EAW FD, Sauer, *NJW*, 69 (2016), 1134 ff. (esp. 1137); also crit. Brodowski, *JR*, 88 (2016), 415 ff. (unnecessary activation of the identity review, questionable emphasis of the culpability principle, serious social–ethical burden of criminal law by marginalising alternative approaches); see also Satzger, *NStZ*, 15 (2016), 521–2, arguing that the national identity control is limited to exceptional cases ('Eine eigenständige Bedeutung erlangt die "Verfassungsidentitätskontrolle" allenfalls in einem ganz engen Raum, nämlich dort, wo keine positiv-rechtlichen Ausnahmen von der Anerkennungspflicht im Unionsrecht vorgesehen sind und der durch das BVerfG skizzierte Kern der deutschen Grundrechte – orientiert am Menschenwürdegehalt und insbesondere als Ausdruck des strafrechtlichen Schuldprizips – im engen "europäischen ordre public" ... keine Entsprechung hat'); for a compromise approach, Paulus, in Bouffier, *Grundgesetz und Europa* (2016), pp. 276–82 (criticising both the appeal to national identity reviews as an argument for non-compliance in the sense of the US Supreme Court's 'option of non-compliance' (*Medellín* v. *Texas*, 552 U.S. 491, 511 (2008)), and the ignorance of the national constitutional identity by international courts, instead advocating a compromise approach with an identity review limited to the core of the national constitution and respectful of international/EU law); crit. also Safferling, *NStZ*, 34 (2014), 551; Swoboda, *HRRS*, 15 (2014), 15 (discussing a recent BGH decision (BGH, No 1 StR 310/12, Decision (21 November 2012)) where the European *ordre public*, including individual rights, is, in sharp contrast to the CJEU, invoked as a barrier to an unlimited mutual assistance on the basis of mutual recognition). Cf. also Thunberg Schunke, *Whose Responsibility?* (2013), p. 65 ('disaster for human rights enforcement'), who does not consider it possible to generalise the CJEU's case law; Thunberg Schunke, *EuCLR*, 5 (2015), 46 ff. (esp. 49 ff.); also in favour of a human rights bar in EAW proceedings, Anagnostopoulos, *ERA Forum*, 15 (2014), 18–19. Identity reviews are also recognised in the constitutional law of **other Member States**, such as the Czech Republic, Denmark, Estonia, France, Ireland, Italy, Latvia, Poland, Spain and the UK (BVerfG, No 2 BvR 2735/14, para. 47 with references to case law from those States); in fact, there is a conflict between the Italian Constitutional Court and the CJEU regarding the Taricco case (thereto Ch. 2 mn. 45; see also Brodowski, *ZIS*, 12 (2017) 691).

909. JEU, *Aranyosi and Căldăraru*, C-404/15 and C-659/15 PPU, ruling (after para. 105). Thereon cf. Satzger, *NStZ*, 15 (2016), 519 ff.; Brodowski, *JR*, 88 (2016), 429 ff.; Brodowski, *ZIS*, 12 (2017), 22; Niblock, *NJECL*, 7 (2016), 250–1; Zeder, *JSt*, 14 (2016), 262 ff. (265: 'milestone'); in a similar vein, Böhm, *NJW*, 69 (2016), 1713–14. Following this judgment, OLG Stuttgart, No 1 Ausl. 321/15, Decision (21 April 2016), and OLG Stuttgart, No 1 Ausl. 321/15, Decision (8 June 2016), making the surrender dependent upon assurances from the Greek authorities on the detention conditions in Greece.

910. Böhm, *NJW*, 69 (2016), 1714 (refusal to surrender when striking violations of the proportionality principle or the ECHR).

911. CJEU, *Aranyosi and Căldăraru*, C-404/15 and C-659/15 PPU, ruling (after para. 105) ('must decide whether surrender procedure should be brought to an end');

OLG Stuttgart, 1 Ausl. 321/15 (n. 909); cf. also Zeder, *JSt*, 14 (2016), 265; Brodowski, *JR*, 88 (2016), 430; Niblock, *NJECL*, 7 (2016), 251.

912. Pabel, in Grabenwarter, *Europäischer Grundrechteschutz* (2014), pp. 819 ff.; Shelton, in Peers et al., *The EU Charter* (2014), pp. 1200 ff.; Hofmann, in Peers et al., *The EU Charter* (2014), pp. 1211 ff.
913. Eser, *RitsumLR*, 26 (2009), 177; Eser, in Meyer, *Charta der Grundrechte der EU* (2014), Art. 47 mn. 3, 11; cf. also Heine, *Rechtsstellung des Beschuldigten* (2009), p. 173; Magiera, in Merten and Papier, *Handbuch der Grundrechte*, vi/1 (2010), p. 1031 mn. 69; Pabel, in Grabenwarter, *Europäischer Grundrechteschutz* (2014), pp. 808–9, 813.
914. Heine, *Rechtsstellung des Beschuldigten* (2009), p. 174. On the relationship between Art. 47(1) and (2), see Pabel, in Grabenwarter, *Europäischer Grundrechteschutz* (2014), pp. 814–15.
915. Explanations Relating to the CFREU, OJEU C 303 of 14 December 2007, 17, 34; Pabel, in Grabenwarter, *Europäischer Grundrechteschutz* (2014), p. 815; Shelton, in Peers et al., *The EU Charter* (2014), pp. 1210–11; Pech, in Peers et al., *The EU Charter* (2014), pp. 1250 ff.
916. Pabel, in Grabenwarter, *Europäischer Grundrechteschutz* (2014), pp. 830–1; Shelton, in Peers et al., *The EU Charter* (2014), pp. 1205–6.
917. As emphasised by Eser, *RitsumLR*, 26 (2009), 182; Eser, in Meyer, *Charta der Grundrechte der EU* (2014), Art. 47 mn. 37; Pabel, in Grabenwarter, *Europäischer Grundrechteschutz* (2014), p. 831.
918. Cf. Eser, *RitsumLR*, 26 (2009), 182; Pabel, in Grabenwarter, *Europäischer Grundrechteschutz* (2014), pp. 826–7; Holopaien, in Peers et al., *The EU Charter* (2014), pp. 1269 ff.
919. Eser, *RitsumLR*, 26 (2009), 185 ff.; Eser, in Meyer, *Charta der Grundrechte der EU* (2014), Art. 48 mn. 24; Heine, *Rechtsstellung des Beschuldigten* (2009), p. 174; Magiera, in Merten and Papier, *Handbuch der Grundrechte*, vi/1 (2010), p. 1031 mn. 80; Jarass, *NStZ*, 32 (2012), 614; Pabel, in Grabenwarter, *Europäischer Grundrechteschutz* (2014), pp. 835–6.
920. On this, cf. Szczekalla, in Heselhaus and Nowak, *Handbuch der Europäischen Grundrechte* (2006), mn. 20; Eser, in Meyer, *Charta der Grundrechte der EU* (2014), Art. 48 mn. 16–17; Heine, *Rechtsstellung des Beschuldigten* (2009), p. 174; Pabel, in Grabenwarter, *Europäischer Grundrechteschutz* (2014), p. 833–5; explanation of Art. 28 in Note of the Praesidium – Draft Charter of Fundamental Rights of the European Union – Text of the Explanations Relating to the Complete Text of the Charter as set out in Charte 4487/00 Convent 50, 11 October 2000 (Charte 4473/00); Banach-Gutierrez and Harding, *EJCCLCJ*, 20 (2012), 256.
921. The relationship between the two paragraphs is controversial. In favour of two independent subjective rights, e.g. Borowsky, in Meyer, *Charta der Grundrechte der EU* (2014), Art. 2 mn. 26; in favour of a unified fundamental right with the prohibition of the death penalty as a limitation of the statutory exceptions to Art. 2(1), Jarass, *EU-Grundrechte* (2005), §9 mn. 2. This makes, however, no difference in substance.
922. Borowsky, in Meyer, *Charta der Grundrechte der EU* (2014), Art. 2 mn. 1.
923. On this, see above, mn. 114; Borowsky, in Meyer, *Charta der Grundrechte der EU* (2014), Art. 2 mn. 34.
924. On this, see also Borowsky, in Meyer, *Charta der Grundrechte der EU* (2014), Art. 52 mn. 29 ff.; a similar stance is taken by Klip, *European Criminal Law* (2016),

p. 270, who, however, also accords the right to security an independent scope of application.
925. Borowsky, in Meyer, *Charta der Grundrechte der EU* (2014), Art. 2 mn. 38–9.
926. Heine, *Rechtsstellung des Beschuldigten* (2009), p. 171; cf. also CJEU, *Aranyosi and Căldăraru*, C-404/15 and C-659/15 PPU, paras. 86–7.
927. On this, cf. Beltran de Felipe and Adán Nieto, *JICJ*, 10 (2012), 583 ff., who refer to the *Soering* case law of the ECtHR (pp. 585–6) that forms the basis for this rule (cf. Chapter 4, mn. 36).
928. Cf. above, mn. 63 ff. See also explanations on Arts. 6 and 52(3) in Note from the Praesidium, Charte 4473/00; also Heine, *Rechtsstellung des Beschuldigten* (2009), p. 172 doubts whether Art. 5(2)–(5) ECHR can be transferred into the scope of application of Art. 6 CFREU.
929. Explanations on Art. 7 in Note from the Praesidium, Charte 4473/00.
930. Bernsdorff, in Meyer, *Charta der Grundrechte der EU* (2014), Art. 8 mn. 13; on this, see also Reding, *eucrim*, 5 (2010), 25 ff.
931. See above, main text, mn. 152–3.
932. On the slightly differently worded Nuremberg clause in Art. 49(2) CFREU, which, however, does not entail any change in content, cf. Eser, *RitsumLR*, 26 (2009), 172; Eser, in Meyer, *Charta der Grundrechte der EU* (2014), Art. 49 mn. 4; Pabel, in Grabenwarter, *Europäischer Grundrechteschutz* (2014), pp. 838–9.
933. Eser, *RitsumLR*, 26 (2009), 171, speaks of 'further human rights improvement' in this regard.
934. Cf. explanations on Art. 49(a) in Note from the Praesidium, Charte 4473/00; Kaiafa-Gbandi, *EuCLR*, 1 (2011), 29–30. For Germany, cf. §2(3) StGB; for a comparison of StGB and CFREU, cf. Gaede, *wistra*, 30 (2011), 365 ff.
935. Pabel, in Grabenwarter, *Europäischer Grundrechteschutz* (2014), pp. 839–40; Nevertheless, this principle is still established beyond the CFREU within its scope as characteristic of the rule of law: Eser, *RitsumLR*, 26 (2009), 176; Eser, in Meyer, *Charta der Grundrechte der EU* (2014), Art. 49 mn. 5; Heine, *Rechtsstellung des Beschuldigten* (2009), pp. 175–6 incl. further references; Banach-Gutierrez and Harding, *EJCCLCJ*, 20 (2012), 258–9.
936. On this, CJEU, *Melloni*, C-399/11; CJEU, *Louloudakis* v. *Elliniko Dimosio*, No C-262/99 (ECLI:EU:C:2001:407), Judgment (12 July 2001), mn. 67, 71; also Jarass, *NStZ*, 32 (2012), 615; Blanke, in Callies and Ruffert, *EUV/AEUV-Kommentar* (2016), Art. 49 GRCh mn. 6; Jarass, *EU-Grundrechte* (2005), §42 mn. 21.
937. The somewhat awkward wording is based on the case law of the CJEU in *Wachauf* v. *Bundesamt für Ernährung und Forstwirtschaft*, No C-5/88 (ECLI:EU:C:1989:321), Judgment (13 July 1989), para. 18 ('The fundamental rights recognised by the Court are not absolute, however, but must be considered in relation to their social function. Consequently, restrictions may be imposed on the exercise of those rights, in particular in the context of a common organisation of a market, provided that those restrictions in fact correspond to objectives of general interest pursued by the Community and do not constitute, with regard to the aim pursued, a disproportionate and intolerable interference, impairing the very substance of those rights'); see also CJEU, *Kjell Karlsson and Others*, No C-292/97 (ECLI:EU:C:2000:202), Judgment (13 April 2000), para. 45 ('correspond to objectives of general interest pursued by the Community and do not constitute, with regard to the aim pursued, disproportionate and unreasonable interference

undermining the very substance of those rights'). On the application of Art. 52(1) CFREU in *Spasic* by the CJEU, see main text, mn. 187.

938. On the competence, see cf. §8(1) StPO.
939. According to §244(1) No 3 StGB.
940. Case based on the BGH, No 4 StR 105/69, Judgment (30 April 1969), reprinted in *NJW*, 22 (1969), 1542.
941. On the competence, cf. §7(2) No 1 StGB and §8(1) StPO.
942. Cf. §153a in conjunction with §153(1) second sentence StPO.
943. CJEU, *Gözütok and Brügge*, Nos C-187/01 and C-385/01 (ECLI:EU:C:2003:87), Judgment (11 February 2003).
944. CJEU, *Van Esbroeck*, No C-436/04 (ECLI:EU:C:2006:165), Judgment (9 March 2006).
945. BGH, No 1 StR 57/10, Decision (25 October 2010), in *NJW*, 64 (2011), 1014–18.
946. For an instructive account, cf. Zöller, in Amelung, Günther and Kühne, *FS Krey* (2010), p. 501. On Art. 4 AP VII, cf. Coffey, *NJECL*, 4 (2013), 65 ff.; Helenius, *EuCLR*, 1 (2011), 203 ff.; on the relationship between Art. 4 AP VII and Art. 50 CFREU, cf. Vervaele, *ULR*, 9 (2013), 218; on the relationship between Art. 4 AP VII and Art. 54 CISA, cf. ECtHR, *Zolothukin* v. *Russia*, No 14939/03, Judgment (10 February 2009), paras 78–84; and Mitsilegas, *EU Criminal Law after Lisbon* (2016), p. 87. For a historical account, cf. Lelieur, *ULR*, 9 (2013), 199 ff.; Schomburg, *ERA Forum*, 13 (2012), 312 ff.; cf. Neagu, *LJIL*, 25 (2012), 955 ff.; on the rationale of the principle, see Asp, *Procedural Criminal Law Cooperation* (2016), pp. 98 ff. (distinguishing between the national and international level and focusing on the legal certainty produced by a final decision).
947. BVerfG, No 2 BvR 148/11, Decision (15 December 2011), in *NJW*, 65 (2012), 1202; Satzger, *International and European Criminal Law* (2018), §9 mn. 109; Satzger, *Internationales und Europäisches Strafrecht* (2016), §11 mn. 96; Zöller, in Amelung, Günther and Kühne, *FS Krey* (2010), p. 503; Schramm, *JuS*, 53 (2013), 1096; a more differentiated view is presented by Brodowski, *StV*, 33 (2013), 342–3, according to whom the renewed prosecution made possible by extradition represents an interference with the protective scope of Art. 103(3) GG, although in certain cases this may be justified. The prevailing view, however, does not grant any inter-state effect to Art. 103(3) GG; see also main text below.
948. For another view with regard to Art. 50 CFREU, however, Tomkin, in Peers et al., *The EU Charter of Fundamental Rights* (2014), Art. 50 mn. 50.02; Eser, in Meyer, *Charta der Grundrechte der EU* (2014), Art. 50 mn. 6; Jarass, *Charta der Grundrechte der EU* (2016), Art. 50 mn. 10. These authors do not give convincing reasons, if any at all, for their position.
949. Cf. Eser, in Meyer, *Charta der Grundrechte der EU* (2014), Art. 50 mn. 1; Ligeti, *eucrim*, 4 (2009), 38; cf. also explanations on Art. 50 CFREU in Note from the Praesidium, Charte 4473/00.
950. Cf. in this context also CJEU, *M.*, No C-398/12 (ECLI:EU:C:2014:1057), Judgment (5 June 2014), para. 37: 'Second, it must be noted that, according to the explanations relating to Article 50 of the Charter, which have to be taken into consideration for the purpose of interpreting it . . . "[a]s regards the situations referred to by Article 4 of Protocol No 7, namely the application of the [*ne bis in idem*] principle within the same Member State, the guaranteed right has the same meaning and

the same scope as the corresponding right in the ECHR".' From this it follows, *e contrario*, that Art. 50 CFREU does not have an internal effect.

951. Cf. regarding the exclusion of administrative sanctions, regarding common agricultural policy, CJEU, *Bonda*, No C-489/10 (ECLI:EU:C:2012:319), Judgment (5 June 2012), para. 28 ('penalties laid down in rules of the common agricultural policy, such as the temporary exclusion of an economic operator from the benefit of an aid scheme, are not of a criminal nature'). See also CJEU, *Orsi* and *Baldetti*, Nos C-217/15 and C-350/15 (ECLI:EU:C:2017:264), Judgment (5 April 2017), paras. 14 ff., according to which the double jeopardy rule only applies to either a natural or a legal person, so that administrative proceedings against the legal person do not preclude criminal proceedings against natural persons belonging to this legal person.
952. Cf. Chapter 1, mn. 34–5.
953. See above, mn. 154 with endnote 878.
954. European Convention on the Transfer of Proceedings in Criminal Matters, 15 May 1972 (ETS No 73).
955. Council Act of 26 July 1995 drawing up the Convention on the Protection of the European Communities' Financial Interests, OJEU C 316 of 27 November 1995, 48.
956. Convention Drawn Up on the Basis of Article K.3 (2) (c) of the Treaty on European Union on the Fight against Corruption Involving Officials of the European Communities or Officials of Member States of the European Union, OJEU C 195 of 25 June 1997, 2. On Art. 10 *ne bis in idem*, cf. esp. No 10 of the explanatory report on said Convention, OJEU C 391 of 15 December 1998.
957. The prohibition of double jeopardy is not (yet) recognised in international customary law; cf. Ambos, *Treatise ICL I* (2013), pp. 401–2.
958. For an instructive account thereon, see Huybreghts, *ERA Forum*, 16 (2015), 386 ff. (Title III), and esp. 391–2 (*ne bis in idem*).
959. On this, cf. case 12, main text, mn. 161, 170, 193.
960. Cf. Schomburg, in Schomburg et al., *Internationale Rechtshilfe in Strafsachen* (2012), Art. 55 SDÜ mn. 1–2; for a critical view of the room to manoeuvre created by Art. 55 CISA, cf. Stein, *ZStW*, 115 (2003), 984–5; for reflections that the exceptions based on Art. 55 CISA 'might become obsolete with the creation of a balanced mechanism for the choice of jurisdiction', cf. EU, *Green Paper on Conflicts of Jurisdiction* (2005), p. 9 (on this, cf. Ambos, *Internationales Strafrecht* (2008), §12 mn. 55 incl. further references). See also the Council Framework Decision 2009/948/JHA of 30 November 2009 on prevention and Settlement of Conflicts of Exercise of Jurisdiction in Criminal Proceedings, OJEU L 328 of 15 December 2009, 42–47.
961. On this, cf. Bacigalupo, *ZStW*, 116 (2004), 330–1; Sanz Hermida, *RP*, 21 (2008), 135.
962. Cf. the Annex to the Protocol Integrating the Schengen Acquis into the Framework of the European Union, OJEC C 340, 10 November 1997, 93, 96; Hecker, *Europäisches Strafrecht* (2015), §13 mn. 67; Plöckinger and Leidenmühler, *wistra*, 22 (2003), 83; Hackner, *NStZ*, 31 (2011), 427; a similar stance is taken by Vervaele, *ULR*, 9 (2013), 227.
963. On this, cf. Chapter 4, mn. 5.
964. Böse, in Esser et al., *FS Kühne* (2013), p. 523.
965. Böse, in Esser et al., *FS Kühne* (2013), p. 519; Radtke, in Böse, *Europäisches Strafrecht* (2013), mn. 34; arguably also Eser, in Sieber, Satzger and von Heinegg, *Europäisches Strafrecht* (2014), p. 653; for a detailed account of the validity of these reservations in the light of Art. 50 CFREU, cf. Böse, in Esser

et al., *FS Kühne* (2013), pp. 524 ff. Insofar, however, the AG in *Kossowski* v. *Generalstaatsanwaltschaft Hamburg*, No C-486/14 (ECLI:EU:C:2015:812), argued that the reservation provided for by Article 55(1)(a) CISA 'does not respect the essence of the ne bis in idem principle as expressed in Article 50 of the Charter of Fundamental Rights of the European Union and must therefore be declared invalid' (Opinion of AG Bot, 15 December 2015, para. 85(a); thereon Asp, *Procedural Criminal Law Cooperation* (2016), pp. 88–9, leaving the question, however, open). The GC did not reply to that question (the validity of this reservation) in its judgment; it concurred, however, with the AG in the result (holding that a decision of the public prosecutor terminating criminal proceedings and finally closing the investigation against a person, without any penalties having been imposed, cannot be characterised as a final decision when it is clear from the statement of reasons for that decision that the procedure was closed without a detailed investigation having been carried out). Cf. CJEU, *Kossowski* v. *Generalstaatsanwaltschaft Hamburg*, No C-486/14 (ECLI:EU:C:2016:483), GC Judgment (29 June 2016), paras. 55–6; on this Brodowski, *ZIS*, 12 (2017), 12.

966. Radtke and Busch, *EuGRZ*, 27 (2000), 423; cf. also Bacigalupo, *ZStW*, 116 (2004), 330; de Hoyos Sancho, *Diario La Ley*, 6330 (2005), 1 ff.; Vervaele, *ULR*, 1 (2005), 100; from a German perspective (Art. 103(2) GG), see in particular BVerfG, No 2 BvL 17/60, Judgment (17 January 1961), in *BVerfGE*, 12, 62, 66; BVerfG, No 2 BvM 2/86, Decision (31 March 1987), in *BVerfGE*, 75, 1, 15–16; on the prohibition of double jeopardy after transnational requests for proceedings, cf. Ambos and Poschadel, *GA*, 158 (2011), 95.
967. Radtke and Busch, *NStZ*, 23 (2003), 282; Schomburg, in Arnold et al., *FS Eser* (2005), pp. 842–3; Vervaele, *ULR*, 9 (2013), 211–12.
968. Satzger, *Europäisierung des Strafrechts* (2001), p. 688; Satzger, *International and European Criminal Law* (2018), §8 mn. 60; also Ligeti, *eucrim*, 4 (2009), 38; Asp, *Procedural Criminal Law Cooperation* (2016), pp. 109 ff. (considering the development of an extensive *ne bis in idem* protection within the EU as as result of the internal market, as 'market-driven criminal law rights', p. 113).
969. On Arts. 1–5 EC Convention between the MS of the European Communities on Double Jeopardy, 25 May 1987 (the forerunner of Arts. 54 ff. CISA), cf. Ambos, *Internationales Strafrecht* (2008), §12 mn. 21 n. 115 and mn. 39 n. 209. On *ne bis in idem* in the international criminal courts, cf. Ambos, *Treatise ICL I* (2013), pp, 401 ff.
970. ECPI, *ZIS*, 8 (2013), 435; cf. also van Bockel, *ERA Forum*, 13 (2012), 331.
971. CJEU, *van Esbroeck*, C-436/04, paras. 23–4, 43.
972. In this regard, it goes beyond many national *ne bis in idem* provisions; see e.g. Art. 103(3) GG.
973. Schomburg, in Schomburg et al., *Internationale Rechtshilfe in Strafsachen* (2012), Art. 54 SDÜ mn. 18. According to OLG München, No OLG Ausl. 14 Ausl. A 1156/12(274/12), Decision (7 December 2012), in *StV*, 33 (2013), 313–14, extradition does not constitute prosecution within the meaning of Arts. 54 CISA and 50 CFREU; for a different opinion, cf. Schomburg and Suominen-Picht, *NJW*, 66 (2013), 1192.
974. Zöller, in Amelung, Günther and Kühne, *FS Krey* (2010), p. 517; Alber, in Tettinger and Stern, Kölner Gemeinschaftskommentar GRCh (2006), Art. 50 mn. 9.

975. BGH, No 5 StR 596/96, Decision (13 May 1997), in *NStZ*, 18 (1998), 149, 151–2; BGH, No 2 StR 458/00, Decision (28 February 2001), in *BGHSt* 46, 307; Austrian Supreme Court of Justice (östOGH), No 12 Os 23/04, Decision (17 June 2004), in *NStZ*, 25 (2005), 344–5; Radtke and Busch, *NStZ*, 23 (2003), 287; Thym, *NStZ*, 23 (2003), 334; Böse, *GA*, 150 (2003), 745–6 incl. further references; Dannecker, in Hirsch, Wolter and Brauns, *FS Kohlmann* (2003), p. 607; Gleß, *ZStW*, 116 (2004), 363–4; Hecker, *Europäisches Strafrecht* (2015), §13 mn. 23. Cf. also I No 5 of the Draft Resolution of the AIDP Preparation Colloquium (2003), in Biehler, *ZStW*, 116 (2004), 260. On the fact that this principle should only be applied to individuals that have been given a final sentence *by a Contracting Party*, cf. CJEU, *Gasparini et al.*, No C-467/04 (ECLI:EU:C:2006:610), Judgment (28 September 2006), para. 37.
976. This is not changed by the different phrasing used in Art. 50 CFREU ('acquitted or convicted'), as this does not entail any substantive change in the scope of application of the prohibition of double jeopardy; cf. Eser, in Meyer, *Charta der Grundrechte der EU* (2014), Art. 50 mn. 8; Zöller, in Amelung, Günther and Kühne, *FS Krey* (2010), p. 517; Esser, *Europäisches und Internationales Strafrecht* (2018), §7 mn. 39; Schramm, *JuS*, 53 (2013), 1097; a more differentiated view is presented by Heger, in Esser et al., *FS Kühne* (2013), p. 576, who claims that the scope of Art. 50 CFREU is restricted to *judicial* verdicts and acquittals.
977. BGH, 5 StR 596/96 (n. 975), p. 151; BGH, No 5 StR 596–96, Decision (2 February 1999), in *NStZ*, 19 (1999), 250–1 (Belgian *transactie*): 'a traditional interpretation leads to the conclusion that ... only verdicts – or at least judicial decisions – should have the effect of barring further criminal prosecution'; BGH, No 4 StR 87–98, Decision (10 June 1999), in *BGHSt* 45, 123 (French *ordonnance de non-lieu*): only foreign 'verdicts', not the 'mere discontinuation of a case due to lack of evidence'; similarly BayObLG, No 1 St RR 67/00, Decision (26 May 2000), in *StV*, 21 (2001), 263 (final decision of a court verdict or ruling). On the *Lacour* case, cf. Nehm, in Pilgermair, *FS Steininger* (2003), pp. 373–4 and Appl, in Triffterer, *GS Vogler* (2004), pp. 114–15. For a summary of the restrictive view taken in case law, cf. Böse, *GA*, 150 (2003), 745.
978. BGH, 4 StR 87–98 (n. 977), p. 123 (*obiter*); BGH, No 1 StR 534/06, Decision (28 December 2006), in *NStZ-RR*, 12 (2007), 179; BGH, 2 StR 458/00 (n. 975), p. 309; see also (acquittal due to statute of limitations) CJEU, *Gasparini et al.*, C-467/04 and CJEU, *Van Straaten* v. *Staat der Nederlanden and Republiek Italië*, No C-150/05 (ECLI:EU:C:2006:614), Judgment (28 September 2006), paras. 59 ff. (acquittal due to lack of evidence); conc. with the BGH Radtke, *NStZ*, 21 (2001), 662–5; also Nehm, in Pilgermair, *FS Steininger* (2003), p. 372 and Mansdörfer, *Ne bis in idem im europäischen Strafrecht* (2004), p. 179; Kniebühler, *Transnationales 'ne bis in idem'* (2005), pp. 224–5; on the CJEU, cf. Wasmeier, *RIDP*, 77 (2006), 126.
979. Cf. §153(2) StPO and BGH, No 5 StR 145/03, Decision (26 August 2003), in *BGHSt* 48, 331. Whether this can be seen as moving away from the more reticent line taken so far is unclear, as termination according to §153(2) StPO requires a court decision, unlike the case of §153(1) first sentence (court consents to a prosecutorial termination decision) or second sentence (exclusive prosecutorial decision); by contrast, Kühne, *JZ*, 59 (2004), 744, claims that the Federal Court's

line of argument is also suitable for decisions according to §153(1) first sentence StPO.

980. ÖstOGH, No 12 Os 23/04 (n. 975), pp. 344–5: *not* mere termination due to lack of suspicion on the basis of §170(2) StPO.

981. OLG Köln, No 2 Ws 590/97, Decision (30 March 2001), in *NStZ*, 21 (2001), 558–60 (Dutch *transactie*).

982. Regarding the termination of proceedings according to §153(2) StPO in this regard, Plöckinger and Leidenmühler, *wistra*, 22 (2003), 83 (n. 52) quote Tribunal de première instance Eupen, No 37.22.1.1157.94, Judgment (27 January 1999) reprinted in *wistra*, 18 (1999), 479–80. On final judgments in summary (*Strafbefehl*) proceedings and administrative fine proceedings (*Bußgeldverfahren*), cf. Hecker, *Europäisches Strafrecht* (2015), §13 mn. 60, 63 ff.

983. Cf. e.g. Lagodny, *NStZ*, 17 (1997), 266; Specht, *Die zwischenstaatliche Geltung des Grundsatzes 'ne bis in idem'* (1999), p. 139; also Böse, *GA*, 150 (2003), 744.

984. The conditional termination of proceedings was based in the first case on a Dutch *transactie* and in the second case on §153a StPO.

985. OLG Köln, 2 Ws 590/97 (n. 98), p. 558.

986. See generally on this, Anagnostopoulos, in Herzog and Neumann, *FS Hassemer* (2010), pp. 1123 ff.; Eser and Burchard, in Derra and Träger, *FS Meyer* (2006), pp. 514 ff.; cf. also the case law overview in Ligeti, *eucrim*, 4 (2009), 39–40.

987. CJEU, *Gözütok and Brügge*, C-187/01 and C-385/0, para. 48 (emphasis added); for a critical stance on this, cf. Nehm, in Pilgermair, *FS Steininger* (2003), pp. 381 ff.; Appl, in Triffterer, *GS Vogler* (2004), pp. 118 ff.; Schomburg, in Arnold et al., *FS Eser* (2005), p. 835; Conway, *EJCCLCJ*, 13 (2005), 281–2; a positive view is taken by Eicker, *Transstaatliche Strafverfolgung* (2004), pp. 119 ff.; Degenhard, *StraFo*, 11 (2005), 68; Vervaele, *ULR*, 1 (2005), 114; Vervaele, in Vervaele, *European Evidence Warrant* (2005), pp. 149–50; Dannecker and Bürger, in Dannecker and Jansen, *Steuerstrafrecht in Europa und den Vereinigten Staaten* (2007), pp. 69–70; Vogel, in Hoyer et al., *FS Schroeder* (2006), p. 889 with the argument that 'nobody would embark on settling a matter according to §153a StPO or *transactie* if he or she had to fear being prosecuted in another responsible State despite this' (orig. 'niemand . . . sich auf eine Erledigung nach §153 a StPO oder durch transactie einlassen [würde], wenn er befürchten müsste, gleichwohl von einem anderen zuständigen Mitgliedstaat verfolgt zu werden'); also Kniebühler, *Transnationales 'ne bis in idem'* (2005), pp. 218 ff., esp. 223; Zöller, *Jura*, 27 (2005), 554; Esser, *Europäisches und Internationales Strafrecht* (2018), §7 mn. 18 ff., who refers to the principle of mutual recognition in this regard. On the 'scope' left open by the CJEU, cf. Kühne, *GA*, 152 (2005), 213; on the case law, cf. Neagu, *LJIL*, 25 (2012), 964 ff.

988. CJEU, *Miraglia*, No C-469/03 (ECLI:EU:C:2005:156), Judgment (10 March 2005), para. 35.

989. As accurately pointed out by Mangiaracina, *LP*, 26 (2006), 638.

990. A historical interpretation is unproductive here; cf. Radtke and Busch, *EuGRZ*, 27 (2000), 425; Böse, *GA*, 150 (2003), 747; however, Wasmeier, *RIDP*, 77 (2006), 125, argues against the CJEU for this reason.

991. On the significance of the grammatical interpretation, cf. Radtke and Busch, *NStZ*, 23 (2003), 283–4.

992. Cf. Art. 33(1) VCLT in conjunction with Art. 142(2) fourth sentence CISA.
993. Specht, *Die zwischenstaatliche Geltung des Grundsatzes 'ne bis in idem'* (1999), p. 136; conc. Plöckinger and Leidenmühler, *wistra*, 22 (2003), 84; Böse, *GA*, 150 (2003), 748; similarly Radtke and Busch, *NStZ*, 23 (2003), 284; Schomburg, *StV*, 17 (1997), 384; Schomburg, in Schomburg et al., *Internationale Rechtshilfe in Strafsachen* (2012), Art. 54 SDÜ mn. 31; in regard to the French and Dutch terms, Kniebühler, *Transnationales 'ne bis in idem'* (2005), p. 179; Safferling, *Internationales Strafrecht* (2011), §12 mn. 90; on the Dutch version, cf. also BGH, 5 StR 596/96 (n. 977), p. 151; for pertinent case law cf. OLG Hamburg, No 1 Ws 316/95, Decision (8 March 1996), in *wistra*, 16 (1996), 193, 195.
994. Specht, *Die zwischenstaatliche Geltung des Grundsatzes 'ne bis in idem'* (1999), pp. 135 and 102, n. 270; Böse, *GA*, 150 (2003), 747.
995. This follows particularly from the Portuguese version (*julgado por um tribunal*); for an analysis of all official languages, cf. Böse, *GA*, 150 (2003), 748. Kühne, *GA*, 152 (2005), 212–13, emphasises that pursuant to the English text prosecutorial decisions would also suffice.
996. The bindingness of the official EU languages for the interpretation of CISA (Specht, *Die zwischenstaatliche Geltung des Grundsatzes 'ne bis in idem'* (1999), pp. 134–5, 137; Böse, *GA*, 150 (2003), 748; Dannecker, in Eser and Rabenstein, *Neighbours in Law* (2001), pp. 176–7) does not automatically make them authentic treaty languages within the meaning of Art. 33(2) WCLT; rather, a (later) official language needs to orient itself towards the authentic (original) treaty language (accurately pointed out by Hecker, *Europäisches Strafrecht* (2015), §13 mn. 30).
997. Specht, *Die zwischenstaatliche Geltung des Grundsatzes 'ne bis in idem'* (1999), pp. 134–5; Böse, *GA*, 150 (2003), 748; Plöckinger and Leidenmühler, *wistra*, 22 (2003), 84; cf. also Mosiek, *StV*, 28 (2008), 97.
998. Specht, *Die zwischenstaatliche Geltung des Grundsatzes 'ne bis in idem'* (1999), p. 137 (orig. 'wertenden Entscheidung über eine Person oder eine Sache'); in agreement Böse, *GA*, 150 (2003), 748–9, who regards a 'broad' interpretation of 'judgment' to flout the Portuguese treaty text (above endnote 995).
999. The same conclusion is reached by Böse, *GA*, 150 (2003), 749; Plöckinger and Leidenmühler, *wistra*, 22 (2003), 84; Radtke and Busch, *EuGRZ*, 27 (2000), 424; Radtke and Busch, *NStZ*, 23 (2003), 284; Kniebühler, *Transnationales 'ne bis in idem'* (2005), p. 184; Schomburg, in Schomburg et al., *Internationale Rechtshilfe in Strafsachen* (2012), Art. 54 SDÜ mn. 9; Hecker, *Europäisches Strafrecht* (2015), §13 mn. 31. Stein, *NJW*, 56 (2003), 1163, welcomes that the CJEU (in *Gözütok and Brügge*, C-187/01 and C-385/0) 'courageously overrode'(!) the law's wording, but also recognises the 'guarantee of correctness' (*Richtigkeitsgewähr*) that results from the involvement of a court. For a critical stance on the CJEU's handling of the grammatical interpretation, cf. Vogel and Norouzi, *JuS*, 43 (2003), 1061; Appl, in Triffterer, *GS Vogler* (2004), pp. 118–19; and Wasmeier, *RIDP*, 77 (2006), 125.
1000. Cf. in detail Böse, *GA*, 150 (2003), 749–50; also Plöckinger and Leidenmühler, *wistra*, 22 (2003), 85; another opinion is put forward by Stein, *Zum europäischen ne bis in idem* (2004), pp. 52 ff., who deduces from an overview of Arts. 54, 55 and 58 CISA that the latter (only) covers final judgments; a similar stance is taken by Appl, in Triffterer, *GS Vogler* (2004), pp. 119–20: 'Art. 55 SDÜ, which refers to Art. 54, explicitly uses the term foreign judgment' (orig. 'Art. 55 SDÜ, der sich auf Art. 54 bezieht, [gebrauche] explizit den Begriff ausländisches Urteil').

1001. BGH, 5 StR 596/96 (n. 975), p. 151; OLG Hamburg, 1 Ws 316/95 (n. 993), p. 195; this is also more or less the line of argument adopted in Vogel and Norouzi, *JuS*, 43 (2003), 1062; Stein, *Zum europäischen ne bis in idem* (2004), p. 53.
1002. Thus Safferling, *Internationales Strafrecht* (2011), §12 mn. 92.
1003. Specht, *Die zwischenstaatliche Geltung des Grundsatzes 'ne bis in idem'* (1999), p. 142; in the same vein, Plöckinger and Leidenmühler, *wistra*, 22 (2003), 85; Hecker, *Europäisches Strafrecht* (2015), §13 mn. 32; for a different opinion, see Stein, *Zum europäischen ne bis in idem* (2004), p. 54, who sees a 'clear contrast between Arts. 54 and 58', 'general inconsistencies in the language' notwithstanding, as 'consistent usage of words cannot be expected given the difference in the scope of the concepts' content in the individual languages' (orig. 'deutlichen Kontrast zwischen Art. 54 und 58 ... allgemeiner sprachlicher Inkonsistenzen ... eine konsistente Wortverwendung auf Grund der Unterschiede in der Reichweite der Begriffsinhalte in den einzelnen Sprachen von vornherein nicht erwartet werden').
1004. Accurately stated by Böse, *GA*, 150 (2003), 749; also Kniebühler, *Transnationales 'ne bis in idem'* (2005), pp. 185–6.
1005. See also above endnote 977.
1006. Plöckinger and Leidenmühler, *wistra*, 22 (2003), 85.
1007. EU, *Communication from the Commission to the Council and the EP: Mutual Recognition of Final Decisions in Criminal Matters*, 26 July 2000 COM(2000) 495 final.
1008. Cf. Specht, *Die zwischenstaatliche Geltung des Grundsatzes 'ne bis in idem'* (1999), p. 148; Plöckinger and Leidenmühler, *wistra*, 22 (2003), 85; Böse, *GA*, 150 (2003), 750; cf. also Lagodny, in Donatsch, Forster and Schwarzenegger, *FS Trechsel* (2002), p. 262.
1009. Cf. Dannecker, in Eser and Rabenstein, *Neighbours in Law* (2001), p. 156.
1010. Specht, *Die zwischenstaatliche Geltung des Grundsatzes 'ne bis in idem'* (1999), pp. 148 ff.; Plöckinger and Leidenmühler, *wistra*, 22 (2003), 85; Böse, *GA*, 150 (2003), 750–1; a narrower view is taken by the Spanish Constitutional Court, which sees the principle's rationale in maintaining proportionality and the principle of culpability (cf. Sanz Hermida, *RP*, 21 (2008), 135); cf. also van Bockel, *ERA Forum*, 13 (2012), 333–4.
1011. Cf. Böse, *GA*, 150 (2003), 752–3.
1012. This can be seen in German law, for example, where §153a StPO only has a limited terminating effect (only for misdemeanours, not crimes; §153a(1) fifth sentence). Thus the prevailing opinion convincingly assumes it is certainly possible that a misdemeanour (*Vergehen*) for which proceedings were terminated according to §153a StPO can become the subject of renewed prosecution following its 'upgrade' to a crime or felony (*Verbrechen*), even without new facts coming to light (Loos, *JZ*, 33 (1978), 598; Schmitt, in Meyer-Goßner and Schmitt, *StPO* (2017), §153 a mn. 52, 54).
1013. For other (earlier) opinions in the literature, cf. Ambos, *Internationales Strafrecht* (2008), §12 mn. 46, small print.
1014. Cf. Böse, *GA*, 150 (2003), 756; similarly, Hecker, *Europäisches Strafrecht* (2015), §13 mn. 61–2.
1015. Radtke and Busch, *NStZ*, 23 (2003), 284 ff. ('materielle rechtskräftige Entscheidung').

1016. As recognised by Radtke and Busch, *NStZ*, 23 (2003), 288; and Bohnert and Lagodny, *NStZ*, 20 (2000), 640.
1017. Mansdörfer, *Ne bis in idem im europäischen Strafrecht* (2004), pp. 168 ff., 248 (orig. 'Form "qualifizierter Verfahrensbeendigung" ... von dem bzw. von der ab – psychologisierend formuliert – das Vertrauen des Individuums, innerhalb des Schengen-Raums keine internationale Strafverfolgung mehr befürchten zu müssen, hinreichend geschützt werden muss ... der Verfahrensgegenstand von einer der ermittelnden Behörde nachgeschalteten Institution eingehend gewürdigt wurde').
1018. Cf. eg. OLG Innsbruck, *NStZ*, 20 (2000), 663 (at 665: a decision rejecting the complaint against a termination of proceedings corresponds to a final judgment). This has, however, been ignored by the French Cour de cassation in the infamous *Krombach* (K) case (Cour de cassation, *M. Dieter X.*, No 1515 (13–80.474) (ECLI:FR:CCASS:2014:CR01515), Chambre criminelle arrêt (2 April 2014): the proceedings against K have been terminated in Germany by a prosecutorial no-case-to-answer decision (§170(2) StPO) which was confirmed by the Munich Appeals Court after a *Klagerzwingungsverfahren* (§§172–4 StPO). Extradition, as well as surrender, of K was refused based on double jeopardy reasons, including Art. 54 CISA, but K was later abducted and brought against his will to France, where he already had been convicted *in absentia*. The Cour de cassation saw no procedural problems, neither with the abduction nor with the second prosecution in violation of Art. 54 CISA; cf. crit. Lelieur, *AJP*, 11 (2014), 365 ff. ('leçon d'unilatéralisme égoïste', 367).
1019. Mansdörfer, *Ne bis in idem im europäischen Strafrecht* (2004), pp. 171 ff.; for a different view Van den Wyngaert, *NStZ*, 18 (1998), 153 (arguing that a Belgian, Dutch or French *transactie* has the same effect as a judgment since the person can no longer be prosecuted).
1020. Lelieur-Fischer, *Comments on the Green Paper on Conflicts of Jurisdiction* (March 2006), p. 22 ('and he could reasonably believe to be the final solution to the dispute in question').
1021. Lelieur-Fischer, *Comments on the Green Paper on Conflicts of Jurisdiction* (March 2006), pp. 22–3.
1022. Lelieur-Fischer, *Comments on the Green Paper on Conflicts of Jurisdiction* (March 2006), p. 24.
1023. Cf. also Stein, *Zum europäischen ne bis in idem* (2004), pp. 468 ff., 476 ff., 504; for more information, cf. Ambos, *Internationales Strafrecht* (2008), §12 mn. 47 n. 263.
1024. CJEU, *Gözütok and Brügge*, C-187/01 and C-385/01, para. 28.
1025. CJEU, *Gözütok and Brügge*, C-187/01 and C-385/01, para. 29.
1026. CJEU, *Gözütok and Brügge*, C-187/01 and C-385/01, para. 31.
1027. CJEU, *Gözütok and Brügge*, C-187/01 and C-385/01, para. 33. However, the idea of mutual trust is not unanimously shared by all domestic authorities throughout the Union; cf. e.g. OLG Hamburg, 1 Ws 316/95 (n. 993), p. 195, where the barring effect of 'national legal special features' such as Belgian *transactie* is decidedly rejected and the necessity of punishing offences committed within one's own territory is emphasised. Crit. also Stein, *NJW*, 56 (2003), 1163; and Weyembergh, *CMLR*, 42 (2005), 1582 ('tendency merely to declare or proclaim the existence of mutual trust').

1028. CJEU, *Gözütok and Brügge*, C-187/01 and C-385/01, paras. 39–40.
1029. Plöckinger, *JSt*, 4 (2003), 129; Radtke and Busch, *NStZ*, 23 (2003), 283; Hecker, *Europäisches Strafrecht* (2015), §13 mn. 36; Stein, *NJW*, 56 (2003), 1163–4; however, a stricter view is taken in Stein, *Zum europäischen ne bis in idem* (2004).
1030. Asp, *Procedural Criminal Law Cooperation* (2016), pp. 93–8, advocates the application of both Art. 54 CISA and Art. 50 CFREU in administrative proceedings resulting in 'sanctions having a criminal character', although admitting that such an application would be 'far-reaching' and 'a big step ahead' (p. 96); for a different view regarding Art. 50 CFREU, see Kargopoulos, in Bergström and Jonsson Cornell, *European Police and Criminal Law Co-operation* (2014), pp. 101–6; and Kargopoulos, *eucrim*, 9 (2015), 96, arguing that it does not cover punitive administrative proceedings.
1031. Radtke and Busch, *NStZ*, 23 (2003), 283 ff. A critical stance is also taken by Appl, in Triffterer, *GS Vogler* (2004), p. 121, who draws attention to the fact that in regard to §153a StPO (1) fifth sentence the CJEU ignores that the offence can still be prosecuted as a felony (*Verbrechen*). Above, endnote 1012.
1032. §204 StPO.
1033. Stein, *NJW*, 56 (2003), 1164; a different conclusion is reached in BGH, No 4 StR 87/98, Decision (10 June 1999), in *StV*, 19 (1999), 478–81 (no 'final disposition' within the meaning of Art. 54 CISA); Kühne, *StV*, 19 (1999), 480–1 right argues against this; cf. also Stein, *ZStW*, 115 (2003), 984. Therefore, Art. 54 CISA offers protection not only from double punishment, as argued by Sanz Hermida, *RP*, 21 (2008), 134, 137, but also from double prosecution (as in the cases mentioned in the present text).
1034. Cf. Radtke and Busch, *NStZ*, 23 (2003), 287–8.
1035. Cf. above endnote 1030 and main text.
1036. Bohnert and Lagodny, *NStZ*, 20 (2000), 639–40; Ambos, in Joecks and Miebach, *Münchener Kommentar StGB*, i (2011), Vorbemerkung §§3–7 mn. 68; Nehm, in Pilgermair, *FS Steininger* (2003), p. 384, also takes this line of argument. Cf. also Liebau, *'Ne bis in idem' in Europa* (2005), p. 290: 'Only those decisions are final, the proceedings of which cannot be taken up again and continued, or [can] only [then been taken up and continued] after the more difficult preconditions for reopening cases under revision rules have been met' (orig. 'Rechtskräftig sind solche Entscheidungen, deren Verfahren nicht mehr oder nur unter den erschwerten Voraussetzungen der Wiederaufnahme erneut aufgegriffen und fortgeführt werden können').
1037. On revision from a comparative and international perspective, see Ambos, *Treatise ICL III* (2016), pp. 576 ff.
1038. This would apply to §170(2) StPO (cf. ÖstOGH, No 12 Os 23/04 (n. 975), pp. 344–5; similarly Kniebühler, *Transnationales 'ne bis in idem'* (2005), p. 244), §154(1) StPO (cf. OLG Nürnberg, No 1 OLG Ausl. 130/07, Decision (23 June 2009), in *StV*, 31 (2011), 401–2), §153(1) StPO (cf. Hecker, *Europäisches Strafrecht* (2015), §13 mn. 62; Esser, *Europäisches und Internationales Strafrecht* (2018), §7 mn. 19; Jähnke and Schramm, *Europäisches Strafrecht* (2017), 9 mn. 69; Hackner, *NStZ*, 31 (2011), 429) and – to a lesser extent – to §153a StPO (cf. above endnotes 1011–12 and text).
1039. CJEU, *M.*, C-398/12, paras. 26 ff. (para. 29: 'a decision of the judicial authorities of a Contracting State by which an accused person is definitively acquitted because of the inadequacy of the evidence must be considered to be based on

such a determination [as to the merits of the case]', and thus 'constitutes a decision finally disposing of the case against a person, within the meaning of that Article [Art. 54 CISA]', para. 28); conc. Gaede, *NJW*, 67 (2014), 2992.

1040. CJEU, *Kossowski*, C-486/14, para. 42, 52 (thereby effectively proposing a twofold test: finality of national decision and more detailed investigation with determination as to merits).

1041. On an autonomous interpretation of the term, cf. CJEU, *Mantello*, No C-261/09 (ECLI:EU:C:2010:683), Judgment (16 November 2010), para. 38; on this, cf. Ligeti, *KritV*, 93 (2010), 380 ff. and Böse, *HRRS*, 13 (2012), 19 ff. This decision refers directly to Art. 3 EAW FD (on this, cf. Chapter 4, mn. 46 ff.), but the CJEU points to the similarity to the phrasing used in Art. 54 CISA; on the concept of 'act' see also Stuckenberg, in Meng et al., *FS Europa-Institut* (2011), pp. 569 ff.

1042. Schomburg, in Schomburg et al., *Internationale Rechtshilfe in Strafsachen* (2012), Art. 54 SDÜ mn. 50; cf. also Plöckinger and Leidenmühler, *wistra*, 22 (2003), 87; Böse, *HRRS*, 13 (2012), 22. See also the case in Ambos, *Fälle* (2010), p. 40 (case 4 mn. 8 ff.).

1043. For a critical stance on this, cf. Radtke, *NStZ*, 28 (2008), 164.

1044. The same conclusion is reached by Böse, *GA*, 150 (2003), 757–8; also Mansdörfer, *Ne bis in idem im europäischen Strafrecht* (2004), pp. 177–8; for a different opinion, cf. LG Hannover, No 33 Qs 65/02, Decision (15 September 2004), in *NStZ-RR*, 9 (2004), 378–9, which focuses on the 'systematic structure of the participating legal systems' (orig. 'Systematik der beteiligten Rechtsordnungen').

1045. For a detailed account see Böse, *GA*, 150 (2003), 758–9; a different opinion is voiced by Kniebühler, *Transnationales 'ne bis in idem'* (2005), pp. 275–6, whose analysis of the wording produces 'an understanding of the concept of "act" oriented towards the facts'; Plöckinger and Leidenmühler, *wistra*, 22 (2003), 86 (however, they only look at the German, French and Dutch versions); for a different opinion in regard to fines, Dannecker, in Eser and Rabenstein, *Neighbours in Law* (2001), pp. 175–6.

1046. Böse, *GA*, 150 (2003), 760; Stuckenberg, in Meng et al., *FS Europa-Institut* (2011), pp. 575–6.

1047. Cf. the instructive account in Böse, *GA*, 150 (2003), 760–1; going too far, LG Hannover, 33 Qs 65/02 (n. 1044), pp. 378–9, according to which it only has to be 'the same act' according to the law of *one* of the States involved.

1048. Böse, *GA*, 150 (2003), 760.

1049. A different opinion is put forward by Plöckinger and Leidenmühler, *wistra*, 22 (2003), 87 and Degenhard, *StraFo*, 11 (2005), 68, 70, who focus upon the 'historical and social concept of an act' ('historischer Lebenssacherhalt'). Similarly also I. 3 of the Draft Resolution of the AIDP Preparation colloquium (2003), cf. Biehler, *ZStW*, 116 (2004), 259; also Mansdörfer, *Ne bis in idem im europäischen Strafrecht* (2004), pp. 178–9. For a different view, cf. Kniebühler, *Transnationales 'ne bis in idem'* (2005), pp. 288–9, who stresses as decisive 'the first State's understanding of the offence'.

1050. Thus Böse, *GA*, 150 (2003), 762, drawing on the idea of offence in EU competition law (orig. 'das betroffene Rechtsgut sowie ggf. die Art des Angriffs (z.B. Verletzung oder abstrakte Gefährdung) in beiden Tatbeständen im Wesentlichen identisch sind'); similarly Dannecker, in Hirsch, Wolter and

Brauns, *FS Kohlmann* (2003), p. 604; rightly arguing in favour of allowing 'normative corrections' to the historical and social definition of an act, Vogel, in Hoyer et al., *FS Schroeder* (2006), pp. 879–80; also focusing on the respective protected legal interest, Ligeti, *Strafrecht und strafrechtliche Zusammenarbeit in der EU* (2005), pp. 107–8.

1051. CJEU, *van Esbroeck*, C-436/04; on this, cf. Wasmeier, *RIDP*, 77 (2006), 127 ff.; Mangiaracina, *LP*, 26 (2006), 635.
1052. An overview over pertinent CJEU case history is provided in Radtke, in Schneider et al., *FS Seebode* (2008), pp. 306 ff.
1053. Cf. Kühne, *JZ*, 61 (2006), 1020; cf. also van Bockel, *CMLR*, 45 (2008), 238 ('"strictly the facts" test'); in agreement Radtke, *NStZ*, 28 (2008), 162–4; Radtke, in Schneider et al., *FS Seebode* (2008), pp. 309–10; Lelieur, *ULR*, 9 (2013), 205.
1054. CJEU, *Van Esbroeck*, C-436/04, para. 36 (emphasis added); cf. also CJEU, *Van Straaten*, C-150/05 with a critical commentary by Kühne, *JZ*, 62 (2007), 247; and CJEU, *Gasparini et al.*, C-467/04, paras. 53 ff., on the constellation of marketing olive oil in one Member State following its importation into another Member State, on the grounds of which the defendant was acquitted there; CJEU, *Kraaijenbrink*, No C-367/05 (ECLI:EU:C:2007:444), Judgment (18 July 2007), para. 26; CJEU, *Kretzinger*, No C-288/05 (ECLI:EU:C:2007:441), Judgment (18 July 2007), para. 29; CJEU, *Mantello*, C-261/09, para. 39. Cf. also OLG München, No OLGAusl. 262/06 (92/06), Decision (4 December 2006), in *NStZ*, 27 (2007), 412; in agreement Radtke, *NStZ*, 32 (2012), 483–4; Böse, *GA*, 158 (2011), 511; Esser, *Europäisches und Internationales Strafrecht* (2018), §7 mn. 27; also Stuckenberg, in Meng et al., *FS Europa-Institut* (2011), p. 576.
1055. For a rightly critical stance, cf. Kühne, *JZ*, 61 (2006), 1020; Van Bockel, *CMLR*, 45 (2008), 238–9. Böse, *EWS*, 18 (2007), 204, quite rightly draws attention to a contradiction between the broad interpretation of 'act' in Art. 54 CISA and competition law, where the criterion of the identity of protected legal interests is focused upon. On this issue, cf. also Van Bockel, *CMLR*, 45 (2008), 241 ff. At the same time, in the CJEU, *Kretzinger*, C-288/05, para. 31 (reference by BGH, No 5 StR 342/04, Decision (30 June 2005), in *NStZ*, 26 (2006), 106–9), the CJEU stresses that the identity of material acts 'must be made irrespective of the legal interest protected'; conc. Karakosta, *KritV*, 91 (2008), 81.
1056. CJEU, *Van Straaten*, C-150/05, para. 49.
1057. Variation of the case in Kühne, *JZ*, 62 (2007), 247.
1058. Stuckenberg, in Meng et al., *FS Europa-Institut* (2011), pp. 576–7.
1059. Stuckenberg, in Meng et al., *FS Europa-Institut* (2011), p. 577.
1060. Schomburg, in Schomburg et al., *Internationale Rechtshilfe in Strafsachen* (2012), Art. 54 SDÜ mn. 53.
1061. CJEU, *Gözütok and Brügge*, C-187/01 and C-385/01, para. 30.
1062. Plöckinger and Leidenmühler, *wistra*, 22 (2003), 87; Hecker, *Europäisches Strafrecht* (2015), §13 mn. 42.
1063. On this, cf. the detailed account in Böse, *GA*, 158 (2011), 505 ff.; and Stalberg, *Art. 50 der Charta der Grundrechte* (2013), pp. 168 ff.; see also Mitsilegas, *EU Criminal Law after Lisbon* (2016), pp. 84 ff. with an interesting discussion of the case law, especially CJEU, *Kretzinger*, C-288/05, CJEU, *Spasic*, No C-129/14 PPU (ECLI:EU:C:2014:586), GC Judgment (27 May 2014); and ECtHR, *Zolothukin*, 14939/03.

1064. In this vein Reichling, *StV*, 30 (2010), 237; Heger, *ZIS*, 4 (2009), 408; Heger, in Esser et al., *FS Kühne* (2013), p. 575; the same conclusion is reached by Zöller, in Amelung, Günther and Kühne, *FS Krey* (2010), p. 518; Zöller, *GA*, 163 (2016), 328, 332–5; Böse, *GA*, 158 (2011), 505 ff. (although he wants to transfer the restrictions according to Art. 55 CISA to Art. 50 CFREU); Böse, in Tiedemann et al., *Die Verfassung moderner Strafrechtspflege* (2016), pp. 215–16; Merkel and Scheinfeld, *ZIS*, 7 (2012), 212; Stalberg, *Art. 50 der Charta der Grundrechte* (2013), p. 179; Walther, *ZJS*, 6 (2013), 19–20; more or less the same argument is presented in Swoboda, *JICJ*, 9 (2011), 266; Schomburg, in Schomburg et al., *Internationale Rechtshilfe in Strafsachen* (2012), Art. 54 SDÜ mn. 14; Schomburg, *ERA Forum*, 13 (2012), 316; Radtke, in Böse, *Europäisches Strafrecht* (2013), p. 482; and Radtke, *NStZ*, 32 (2012), 481 (primacy of Art. 50 CFREU within the scope of application of Union law, but outside this scope Art. 54 CISA, including the enforcement component, continues to apply).
1065. Böse, *GA*, 158 (2011), 506–7.
1066. Schomburg, in Schomburg et al., *Internationale Rechtshilfe in Strafsachen* (2012), Art. 54 SDÜ mn. 14; Schomburg, *ERA Forum*, 13 (2012), 316; Schomburg and Suominen-Picht, *NJW*, 65 (2012), 1191; Zöller, *GA*, 163 (2016), 328, 333; a similar stance is taken by Stalberg, *Art. 50 der Charta der Grundrechte* (2013), pp. 170–1.
1067. Zöller, in Amelung, Günther and Kühne, *FS Krey* (2010), p. 519; Zöller, *GA*, 163 (2016), 328, 333; Stalberg, *Art. 50 der Charta der Grundrechte* (2013), pp. 175–6.
1068. Declaration concerning the explanations relating to the Charter of Fundamental Rights, OJEU C 310 of 16 December 2004, 453 ('In accordance with Article 50(2), the "non bis in idem" rule applies not only within the jurisdiction of one State but also between the jurisdictions of several Member States. That corresponds to the *acquis* in Union law; see Articles 54 to 58 of the Schengen Convention'); cf. also CJEU, *Spasic*, C-129/14 PPU, para. 55; thereon, Lelieur, *AJP*, 11 (2014), 425–8; crit. Gaede, *NJW*, 67 (2014), 2990–1, 2992; Swoboda, *ZIS*, 10 (2015), 368–71; Asp, *Procedural Criminal Law Cooperation* (2016), pp. 85–7; cf. also BGH, 1 StR 57/10 (n. 945), pp. 1014–15; Satzger, *Jura*, 31 (2009), 759 ff.; Satzger, in Heinrich et al., *FS Roxin*, ii (2011), p. 1524; for a critical stance on this argument, cf. Böse, *GA*, 158 (2011), 506; Nestler, *HRRS*, 14 (2013), 339; Stalberg, *Art. 50 der Charta der Grundrechte* (2013), pp. 170 ff.; Walther, *ZJS*, 6 (2013), 19. On the significance of the travaux, cf. Gaede, in Böse, *Europäisches Strafrecht* (2013), mn. 29.
1069. Thereon cf. Chapter 4, p. 112.
1070. Nestler, *HRRS*, 14 (2013), 338. Cf. also Satzger, in Heinrich et al., *FS Roxin*, ii (2011), pp. 1522–3; Satzger, *International and European Criminal Law* (2018), §8 mn. 66; Satzger, *Internationales und Europäisches Strafrecht* (2016), §10 mn. 57; criticism of this argument in regard to proportionality is voiced by Böse, in Ambos, *Europäisches Strafrecht post-Lissabon* (2011), pp. 73–4. Against this background, cf. also the more differentiated suggestion made by Safferling, *Internationales Strafrecht* (2011), §12 mn. 84–5, who wants to retain the enforcement component when no Union-wide (legal remedy) measures exist that guarantee punishment will be enforced.
1071. CJEU, *Spasic*, C-129/14 PPU, para. 56.
1072. In detail Burchard and Brodowski, *StraFo*, 16 (2010), 179 ff.; Satzger, *International and European Criminal Law* (2018), §8 mn. 65; Satzger, *Internationales und*

Europäisches Strafrecht (2016), §10 mn. 57; Ambos, in Joecks and Miebach, *Münchener Kommentar StGB*, i (2017), Vorbemerkung §§3–7 mn. 75 with n. 537; Esser, *Europäisches und Internationales Strafrecht* (2018), §7 mn. 43–4; Koch and Dorn, *Jura*, 33 (2011), 694; a similar stance is taken by Eckstein, *ZStW*, 124 (2012), 521–5; Eckstein, *ZIS*, 8 (2013), 220 ff. (who wants to restrict the effect of Arts. 54 ff. CISA through the principles of subsidiarity and proportionality); also BGH, 1 StR 57/10 (n. 945), pp. 1014–15, discussed in Böse, *GA*, 158 (2011), 505 ff.; BGH, No 2 StR 420/10, Decision (1 December 2010), with a commentary in Koch and Dorn, *Jura*, 33 (2011), 690 ff.; Walther, *ZJS*, 6 (2013), 16 ff.

1073. CJEU, *Spasic*, C-129/14 PPU, paras. 51 ff. (at 74 holding 'that Article 54 CISA ... is compatible with Article 50 of the Charter, in which that principle is enshrined').

1074. CJEU, *Spasic*, C-129/14 PPU, paras. 61–4 (appropriate), 65–72 (necessary), 74. Crit. of the Court's focus 'on the security aspect thereby turning the area of freedom, justice and security in fact into a European area of collective combat against impunity', Swoboda, *ZIS*, 10 (2015), 368–71 (370).

1075. Thus OLG Saarbrücken, No Ss 90/95–122/95, Decision (6 December 1996), in *StV*, 17 (1997), 359–60; Specht, *Die zwischenstaatliche Geltung des Grundsatzes 'ne bis in idem'* (1999), pp. 166–7; the same conclusion is reached by Liebau, *'Ne bis in idem' in Europa* (2005), p. 123, who assumes that no barring effect occurs 'if the State in which the first sentence was passed does not (completely) enforce the penalty imposed, thus causing an obstruction of justice' (orig. 'der Ersturteilsstaat die verhängte Strafe gar nicht oder nicht vollständig vollstreckt und so eine Strafvereitelung herbeigeführt wird'). On the question of the extent to which an **SIS alert** following an Italian conviction *in absentia* can be considered **enforcement** within the meaning of the second alternative in Art. 54 CISA, cf. Zöller, *Jura*, 27 (2005), 555 (in regard to the *Friedrich Engel* case).

1076. Thus BGH, No 2 StR 274/00, Decision (3 November 2011), in *BGHSt*, 46, 187, 189; conc. Nehm, in Pilgermair, *FS Steininger* (2003), p. 372; also Schomburg, in Arnold et al., *FS Eser* (2005), p. 836; Vogel, in Hoyer et al., *FS Schroeder* (2006), p. 890; Schomburg, in Schomburg et al., *Internationale Rechtshilfe in Strafsachen* (2012), Art. 54 SDÜ mn. 53; Hecker, *Europäisches Strafrecht* (2015), §13 mn. 43–5; Safferling, *Internationales Strafrecht* (2011), §12 mn. 102.

1077. Specht, *Die zwischenstaatliche Geltung des Grundsatzes 'ne bis in idem'* (1999), p. 166; Plöckinger and Leidenmühler, *wistra*, 22 (2003), 87; Mansdörfer, *Ne bis in idem im europäischen Strafrecht* (2004), p. 182.

1078. By way of example see §§56 b, 56 c StGB.

1079. Cf. §56 f StGB.

1080. Cf. Art. 1 European Convention on Extradition (ETS No 24, 13 December 1957).

1081. Arts. 68, 69 CISA. Thereon also Safferling, *Internationales Strafrecht* (2011), §12 mn. 102.

1082. Schomburg, in Schomburg et al., *Internationale Rechtshilfe in Strafsachen* (2012), Art. 54 SDÜ mn. 53 (orig. 'dem Ersturteilsstaat die Erstsanktion ... gleichermaßen aus der Hand' schlagen).

1083. CJEU, *Kretzinger*, C-288/05, para. 42. By contrast, Art. 54 CISA does not already cover police or pre-trial detention which is to be deducted from a prison sentence (ibid., para. 52).

1084. CJEU, *Spasic*, C-129/14 PPU, para. 85 ('the mere payment of a fine by a person sentenced by the self-same decision of a court of another MS to a custodial sentence that has not been served is not sufficient to consider that the penalty "has been enforced" or is "actually in the process of being enforced" within the meaning of that provision'); see also OLG Saarbrücken, Ss 90/95–122/95 (n. 1075), pp. 359–60; conc. Zöller, *GA*, 163 (2016), 332; Hecker, *Europäisches Strafrecht* (2015), §13 mn. 45 (deviation from his view in the previous edition, see the following note).

1085. Specht, *Die zwischenstaatliche Geltung des Grundsatzes 'ne bis in idem'* (1999), p. 167; Plöckinger and Leidenmühler, *wistra*, 22 (2003), 88; Hecker, *Europäisches Strafrecht* (2012), §13 mn. 45; Gaede, *NJW*, 67 (2014), 2991 (invoking proportionality considerations).

1086. Plöckinger and Leidenmühler, *wistra*, 22 (2003), 88; Hecker, *Europäisches Strafrecht* (2015), §13 mn. 46.

1087. Hecker, *Europäisches Strafrecht* (2015), §13 mn. 47 ff.

1088. Cf. also Satzger, *International and European Criminal Law* (2018), §8 mn. 84; Satzger, *Internationales und Europäisches Strafrecht* (2016), §10 mn. 73.

1089. CJEU, *Bourquain*, No C-297/07 (ECLI:EU:C:2008:708), Judgment (11 December 2008): In 1961 B was sentenced *in absentia* by a French court. However, according to French law this sentence could only be enforced if B was tried again when present. After 20 years, the sentence issued in his absence expired by limitation. The CJEU confirmed that Art. 54 CISA was applicable, even though the French conviction *in absentia* was never enforceable. On this, cf. also Satzger, *International and European Criminal Law* (2018), §8 mn. 83; Hecker, *Europäisches Strafrecht* (2015), §13 mn. 52.

1090. EU, *Green Paper on Conflicts of Jurisdiction* (2005); thereon Rekate, *Vermeidung von Jurisdiktionskonflikten* (2015), pp. 194 ff.; Wasmeier, *ZeuS*, 9 (2006), 35–6; Mangiaracina, *LP*, 26 (2006), 642 ff.; crit. Braum, in Joerden and Szwarc, *Europäisierung des Strafrechts* (2007), pp. 17 ff.; cf. on this Seitz, in Schöch, *FS Böttcher* (2007), pp. 677–8.

1091. EU, *Green Paper on Conflicts of Jurisdiction* (2005), pp. 6–7. See also Rekate, *Vermeidung von Jurisdiktionskonflikten* (2015), p. 197, who welcomes the referral process but criticises the lack of detail concerning the procedural position of the accused.

1092. EU, *Green Paper on Conflicts of Jurisdiction* (2005), p. 8.

1093. Greece had presented a Draft FD on resolving the problem of *ne bis in idem* in Europe (Initiative of the Hellenic Republic with a View to Adopting a Council Framework Decision Concerning the Application of the 'ne bis in idem' Principle, OJEU C 100 of 26 April 2003, 24–7); in detail Kniebühler, *Transnationales 'ne bis in idem'* (2005), pp. 318 ff.; briefly Henzelin, *ZStrR*, 123 (2005), 369–70; Mangiaracina, *LP*, 26 (2006), 640–1. However, due to numerous inconsistencies, such as the enforcement clause or concerning the reopening of proceedings, as well as a range of reservations, this initiative was not pursued any further. Thereon Bogensberger, in Moos, Jesionek and Müller, *FS Miklau* (2006), pp. 104–5; Rekate, *Vermeidung von Jurisdiktionskonflikten* (2015), pp. 191 ff.; Vervaele, *ULR*, 1 (2005), 114–15.

1094. Cf. Rekate, *Vermeidung von Jurisdiktionskonflikten* (2015), p. 193.

1095. Hecker, in Sinn, *Conflicts of Jurisdiction* (2012), p. 95.

1096. FD 2009/948/JHA on Conflicts of Jurisdiction; see also the Report on the Implementation of the Council Framework Decision 2009/948/JHA by the General Secretariat of the Council of 22 July 2015 (5881/4/15 REV 4/15); see *de lege ferenda* also the consensual jurisdiction model based on the FD in Sinn, *Conflicts of Jurisdiction* (2012), pp. 601 ff.; thereon Sinn, *ZIS*, 8 (2013), 4 ff.
1097. Crit. Böse and Meyer, *ZIS*, 6 (2011), 336 ff.; Fikarova, in Sinn, *Conflicts of Jurisdiction* (2012), p. 105; Sinn, *ZIS*, 8 (2013), 4; ECPI, *ZIS*, 8 (2013), 440–1; Lelieur, in Brach-Thiel and Fourment, *Questions de droit pénal* (2014), p. 262; Hecker, in Sinn, *Conflicts of Jurisdiction* (2012), p. 96, thinks this is unproblematic, as the affected person's interest in avoiding multiple prosecutions is also taken into full account in the consensual solution. This approach already formed the basis for the EU, *Green Paper on Conflicts of Jurisdiction* (2005), Nos 2.1. ff., which suggested a 'mechanism . . . to allocate cases' to an appropriate national court, but based this on co-ordination and consultation at an early stage and, concerning the criteria for choosing the State of prosecution (2.5.), focused more upon flexible criteria such as appropriateness and fair trial than on a hierarchy based upon international law (cf. also Questions 10–13). Crit. thereon with an emphasis on procedural rights, ECBA, *Response to the Green Paper on Conflicts of Jurisdiction* (2006), pp. 2 ff. See also the development of criteria to determine the best jurisdiction in Art. 13 of the model proposed in Sinn, *Conflicts of Jurisdiction* (2012), pp. 603 ff.
1098. Hecker, in Sinn, *Conflicts of Jurisdiction* (2012), p. 95 (italics by the author); see also Fikarova, in Sinn, *Conflicts of Jurisdiction* (2012), p. 104.
1099. Crit. of the broad wording used here Eisele, *ZStW*, 125 (2013), 18; see also Lelieur, in Brach-Thiel and Fourment, *Questions de droit pénal* (2014), p. 269.
1100. Thereon Chapter 5, mn. 16.
1101. A different proposal is made in Art. 14 of the agreed-jurisdiction model in Sinn, *Conflicts of Jurisdiction* (2012), p. 604, who recommends making the Eurojust Decision (Council Decision 2009/426/JHA of 16 December 2008, thereon Chapter 5 mn. 17) obligatory; in greater depth *Eisele, ZStW*, 125 (2013), 23 ff.
1102. Cf. Art. 8 Eurojust Decision (n. 1101). In detail on Eurojust's role in the settlement or avoidance of conflicts of jurisdiction, Herrnfeld, in Sinn, *Conflicts of Jurisdiction* (2012), pp. 142 ff.; see also Lelieur, in Brach-Thiel and Fourment, *Questions de droit pénal* (2014), pp. 272 ff.
1103. See also the criticism in Schomburg, in Schomburg et al., *Internationale Rechtshilfe in Strafsachen* (2012), Art. 54 SDÜ mn. 22 ('vague suggestions for action'); Sinn, *ZIS*, 8 (2013), 4 and ECPI, *ZIS*, 8 (2013), 435–6, who call for clear rules to prevent conflicts of jurisdiction (432).
1104. Hecker, in Sinn, *Conflicts of Jurisdiction* (2012), p. 95; Eisele, *ZStW*, 125 (2013), 18; ECPI, *ZIS*, 8 (2013), 435; see also Brodowski, *ZIS*, 5 (2010), 384.
1105. Art. 82(1)(b) TFEU. Crit. on the lack of implementation Klip, *European Criminal Law* (2016), p. 217, calling for a common Union approach on the allocation of jurisdiction (pp. 531–3).
1106. Biehler, Kniebühler, Lelieur-Fischer and Stein, *Freiburg Proposal* (2003); thereon Gropp, in Sinn, *Conflicts of Jurisdiction* (2012), pp. 51–2; Stein, *ZStW*, 115 (2003), 986–7; Weitzmann, *ZStW*, 116 (2004), 268, referring to *Biehler*; Vervaele, *ULR*, 1 (2005), 115–16.

1107. Similar thoughts are presented in Schomburg, in Arnold et al., *FS Eser* (2005), pp. 843–4.
1108. On the consensus at the AIDP preparation colloquium in this regard, Biehler, *ZStW*, 116 (2004), 257.
1109. This line of argument is taken by BVerfG, 2 BvR 148/11 (n. 947), p. 1204. Another opinion is voiced by Stalberg, *Art. 50 der Charta der Grundrechte* (2013), pp. 179–87, who regards Art. 82(1) TFEU as an 'implemented' legal norm and thus considers the Charter's scope of application to apply; on this, cf. also Schramm, *JuS*, 53 (2013), 1097.

Chapter Bibliography

Aalto, P., Hofmann, H. C. H., Holopainen, L., Paunio, E., Pech, L., Sayers, D., Shelton D., and Ward, A., 'Article 47', in Peers et al., *The EU Charter*, 1197–1200

Ackermann, J.-B., 'Disziplinarstrafen in Züricher Gefängnissen und EMRK', in Donatsch, A., Forster, M., and Schwarzenegger, C., eds., *Strafrecht, Strafprozessrecht und Menschenrechte: Festschrift für Stefan Trechsel zum 65. Geburtstag* (Zurich: Schulthess, 2002), 835–59

Ahlbrecht, H., 'Der Rahmenbeschluss – Entwurf der Europäischen Beweisanordnung – eine kritische Bestandsaufnahme', *NStZ*, 26 (2006), 70–5

'Strukturelle Defizite Europäischer Verteidigung: Gründe und Möglichkeiten ihrer Überwindung', *StV*, 32 (2012), 491–5

Ahmed, A., 'Anmerkung zu BGH, Beschluss v. 12.5.2010 – 4 StR 577/09', *StV*, 30 (2010), 574–5

Alamuddin, A., 'Collection of Evidence', in Khan, K. A. A., Buisman, C., and Gosnell, C., eds., *Principles of Evidence in International Criminal Justice* (Oxford: Oxford University Press, 2010), 231–305

Alber, S., 'Artikel 50', in Tettinger and Stern, *Kölner Gemeinschaftskommentar zur Europäischen Grundrechte-Charta* (2006), 751–8

Albrecht, H.-J., Dorsch, C., and Krüpe, C., *Rechtswirklichkeit und Effizienz der Überwachung der Telekommunikation nach den §§100 a, 100 b StPO und anderer verdeckter Ermittlungsmaßnahmen* (Freiburg i.Br.: Ed. iuscrim, 2003)

Allegrezza, S., 'Formal Aspects of the Letter of Rights', in Arangüena Fanego, C., ed., *Garantías procesales en los procesos penales en la Unión Europea* (Valladolid: Ed. Lex Nova, 2007), 367–73

Alleweldt, R., 'Kapitel 10: Recht auf Leben', in Dörr, Grote, and Marauhn, *EMRK/GG*, i (2013), 491–536

Ambos, K., 'Anmerkung zu EuGH, Urteil v. 10.2.2009 – C-301/06', *JZ*, 69 (2009), 468–71

'Artikel 5, 6, 8, 10', in Radtke and Hohmann, *StPO Kommentar* (2011), 2507–45

'Artikel 7 EMRK, Common Law und die Mauerschützen', *KritV*, 86 (2003), 31–43

'Cesare Beccaria und die Folter: Kritische Anmerkungen aus heutiger Sicht', *ZStW*, 122 (2010), 504–20

'The Crime of Genocide and the Principle of Legality under Article 7 of the ECHR', *HRLR*, 17 (2017), 175–86

'Der Europäische Gerichtshof für Menschenrechte und die Verfahrensrechte: Waffengleichheit, partizipatorisches Vorverfahren und Art. 6 EMRK', *ZStW*, 115 (2003), 583–637

'Europarechtliche Vorgaben für das (deutsche) Strafverfahren (Teil I)', *NStZ*, 22 (2002), 628–33

'Europarechtliche Vorgaben für das (deutsche) Strafverfahren (Teil II)', *NStZ*, 23 (2003), 14–17

'The European Court of Human Rights and Extraordinary Renditions', *EuCLR*, 5 (2015), 107–21

'International Criminal Procedure: "Adversarial", "Inquisitorial" or Mixed?', *ICLR*, 3 (2003), 1–37

'May a State Torture Suspects to Save the Life of Innocents?', *JICJ*, 6 (2008), 261–87

'Nuremberg Revisited: Das BVerfG, das Völkerstrafrecht und das Rückwirkungsverbot', *StV*, 17 (1997), 39–43

'The Structure of International Criminal Procedure: "Adversarial", "Inquisitorial" or Mixed?', in Bohlander, M., ed., *International Criminal Justice: A Critical Analysis of Institutions and Procedures* (London: Cameron May, 2007), 429–503

'Die transnationale Verwertung von Folterbeweisen', *StV*, 29 (2009), 151–61 (English version: 'The Transnational Use of Torture Evidence', *Israel Law Review*, 42 (2009), 362–97).

'Vorbemerkung zu den §§3–7', in Joecks and Miebach, *Münchener Kommentar StGB*, i (2011), 115–92

'Zur Rechtswidrigkeit der Todesschüsse an der Mauer', *JA*, 29 (1997), 983–90

Ambos, K., and Poschadel, A., '1. Hauptteil: Grundlagen', in Ambos, K., König, S., and Rackow, P., eds., *Rechtshilferecht* (2015), 57–95

'Terrorists and Fair Trial: The Right to a Fair Trial for Alleged Terrorists Detained in Guantánamo Bay', *ULR*, 9 (2013), 109–26

'Transnationales Strafverfolgungsersuchen: Verfolgungshindernis im ersuchenden Staat?', *GA*, 158 (2011), 95–102

Amnesty International, European Criminal Bar Association, Fair Trials International, Irish Council for Civil Liberties, JUSTICE, and Open Society Justice Initiative, 'Joint Briefing on the Directive on the Right Access to a Lawyer in Criminal Proceedings and the Right to Inform a Third Party upon Deprivation of Liberty', *NJECL*, 4 (2013), 332–9

Anagnostopoulos, I., 'Criminal Justice Cooperation in the EU after the First Few "Steps": A Defence View', *ERA Forum*, 15 (2014), 9–24

'Ne bis in idem in der EU: Offene Fragen', in Herzog, F., and Neumann, U., eds., *Festschrift für Winfried Hassemer zum 70. Geburtstag am 17. Februar 2010* (Heidelberg et al.: C. F. Müller, 2010), 1121–40

Anagnostou, D., and Mungiu-Pippidi, A., 'Domestic Implementation of Human Rights Judgments in Europe: Legal Infrastructure and Government Effectiveness Matter', *EJIL*, 25 (2014), 205–27

Andenas, M., and Bjorge, E., *National Implementation of ECHR Rights: Kant's Categorical Imperative and the Convention* (Oslo: University of Oslo, Faculty of Law Research Paper Seriers No 2011–15, 2011)

Antunes, M. J., and Caeiro, P., 'Preventive Custodial Measures in Portuguese Law', in Michaelsen, ., ed., *Comparative Perspectives on the Theory and Practice of Preventive Detention*, Onati International Series in Law and Society (Oxford et al.: Hart Publishing 2018), XX–XX (forthcoming)

Appl, E., 'Ein neues "ne bis in idem" aus Luxemburg?', in Triffterer, O., ed., *Gedächtnisschrift für Theo Vogler* (Heidelberg: C. F. Müller, 2004), 109–23

Aras, N., 'Die Bedeutung der EMRK für den Grundrechtsschutz in der Türkei', *ZEuS*, 10 (2007), 219–46

Ariav, R., 'National Investigations of Human Rights between National and International Law', *GoJIL*, 4 (2012), 853–71

Arndt, F., and Schubert, A., 'Artikel 59', in Karpenstein, U., and Mayer, F. C., *EMRK: Konvention zum Schutz der Menschenrechte und Grundfreiheiten: Kommentar* (Munich: C. H. Beck, 2nd edn, 2015), 719–30

Arnold, J., and Kühl, M., 'Forum: Die Probleme der Strafbarkeit von "Mauerschützen"', *JuS*, 32 (1992), 991–7

Arnold, J., Karsten, N., and Kreicker, H., 'Menschenrechtsschutz durch Art. 7 Abs. 1 EMRK', *NJ*, 55 (2001), 561–9

Arquint, S., '"Anwalt der ersten Stunde"? Ein Positionspapier!', in Schindler, B., and Schlauri, R., eds., *Auf dem Weg zu einem einheitlichen Verfahren* (Zurich: Schulthess, 2001), 175–202

Bachmaier, L., 'Proceso penal y protección de los derechos fundamentales del imputado en Europa', in De la Oliva Santos, A., and Calderón, C. M. P., eds., *Garantías fundamentales del proceso penal en el espacio judicial europeo* (Madrid: Ed. Colex, 2007), 41–69

Bachmann, M., and Goeck, F., 'Anmerkung zu OLG Celle, Beschluss v. 3.8.2010 – 2 Ws 264/10', *ZIS*, 6 (2011), 44–5

'Das Urteil des EGMR zur Sicherungsverwahrung und seine Folgen', *NJ*, 64 (2010), 457–64

Bacigalupo, E., 'Bemerkungen zu strafrechtlichen Fragen des Verfassungsentwurfs', *ZStW*, 116 (2004), 326–31

Badea, C., 'Shaping Fundamental Principles of EU Law in the Area of Freedom, Security and Justice: The ne bis in idem Challenge for the CJEU', *ERA Forum*, 13 (2012), 307–9

Banach-Gutierrez, J., 'Some Reflections on the Concept of Due Process: What Kind of "Doing Justice" Is Emerging in Contemporary Criminal Proceedings?', *NJECL*, 3 (2012), 83–101

Banach-Gutierrez, J., and Harding, C., 'Fundamental Rights in European Criminal Justice: An Axiological Perspective', *EJCCLCJ*, 20 (2012), 239–64

Bank, R. 'Kapitel 11: Das Verbot von Folter, unmenschlicher oder erniedrigender Behandlung oder Strafe', in Dörr, Grote, and Marauhn, *EMRK/GG*, i (2013), 537–606

Barrot, J., 'Die Unschuldsvermutung in der Rechtsprechung des EGMR', *ZJS*, 3 (2010), 701–6

Bartsch, T., 'Anmerkung zu BGH, Urteil v. 9.3.2010 - 1 StR 554/09', *StV*, 30 (2010), 521–4

Bates, E., 'The UK and Strasbourg: A Strained Relationship: The Long View', in Ziegler, K. S., Wicks, E., and Hodson, L., eds., *The UK and European Human Rights: A Strained Relationship?* (Oxford and Portland: Hart, 2015), 39–69

Baumanns, S., *Der Beschleunigungsgrundsatz im Strafverfahren* (Baden-Baden: Nomos, 2011)

Beck, S., 'Strafe oder Nicht-Strafe? Zur Umsetzung des Abstandsgebots in der bisherigen Praxis der Sicherungsverwahrung', *HRRS*, 14 (2013), 9–15

Beltrán de Felipe, M., and Adán Nieto, M., 'Post 9/11 Trends in International Judicial Cooperation: Human Rights as a Constraint on Extradition in Death Penalty Cases', *JICJ*, 10 (2012), 581–604

Beltrán de Felipe, M., and Rodríguez de Santiago, J. M., 'Shooting Down Hijacked Airplanes? Sorry, We're Humanists: A Comment on the German Constitutional Court Decision of 2.15.2006, Regarding the Luftsicherheitsgesetz (2005 Air Security Act)', *EuPubL*, 14 (2008), 565–84

Bermejo, M. G., and Wirtz, G., 'Strafverteidigerhonorar und Geldwäsche aus europäischer Perspektive', *ZIS*, 2 (2007), 398–406

Bernhardt, R., 'Die Entscheidungen des EGMR im deutschen Rechtsraum', in Geiger, R., ed., *Völkerrechtlicher Vertrag und staatliches Recht vor dem Hintergrund zunehmender Verdichtung der internationalen Beziehungen* (Baden-Baden: Nomos, 2000), 147–55

'Die Europäische Menschenrechtskonvention und die deutsche Rechtsordnung', *EuGRZ*, 23 (1996), 339–41

Bernsdorff, N., 'Artikel 8', in Meyer, *Charta der Grundrechte der EU* (2014), 239–50

Bernsmann, K., 'Überlegungen zur tödlichen Notwehr bei nicht lebensbedrohlichen Angriffen', *ZStW*, 104 (1992), 290–327

Berry, S., 'SAS v France: Does Anything Remain of the Right to Manifest Religion?', *EJIL:Talk!*, 2 July 2014, at www.ejiltalk.org/sas-v-france-does-anything-remain-of-the-right-to-manifest-religion, last accessed 27 January 2018

Besson, S., 'The Extraterritoriality of the European Convention on Human Rights: Why Human Rights Depend on Jurisdiction and What Jurisdiction Amounts to', *LJIL*, 25 (2012), 857–84

Beukelmann, S., 'Europäisierung des Strafrechts: Die neue strafrechtliche Ordnung nach dem Vertrag von Lissabon', *NJW*, 63 (2010), 2081–6

'Gesetz über den Rechtsschutz bei überlangen Verfahren', *NJW-Spezial*, 7 (2010), 632–3

'Der Kabinettsentwurf zur Neuregelung der Sicherungsverwahrung', *NJW-Spezial*, 7 (2010), 696–7

Beulke, W., 'Konfrontation und Strafprozessreform: Art. 6 Abs. 3 lit. d EMRK und ein "partizipatorisches" Vorverfahren anstelle einer Hauptverhandlung in ihrer bisherigen kontradiktorischen Struktur', in Hanack, E.-W., Hilger, H., Mehle, V., and Widmaier, G., eds., *Festschrift für Peter Riess zum 70. Geburtstag am 4. Juni 2002* (Berlin et al.: de Gruyter, 2002), 3–29

Beulke, W., and Barisch, K.-T., 'Beweiswürdigung, rechtmäßige Inanspruchnahme der Eilkompetenz der StA', *StV*, 26 (2006), 569–71

Beulke, W., and Witzigmann, T., 'Das Akteneinsichtsrecht des Strafverteidigers in Fällen der Untersuchungshaft', *NStZ*, 31 (2011), 254–61

Biehler, A., 'Thema IV: Konkurrierende nationale und internationale strafrechtliche Zuständigkeit und das Prinzip ne bis in idem', *ZStW*, 116 (2004), 256–64

Biehler, A., Kniebühler, R., Lelieur-Fischer, J., and Stein, S., *Freiburg Proposal on Concurrent Jurisdictions and the Prohibition of Multiple Prosecutions in the European Union* (Freiburg i. Breisgau: edition iuscrim, 2003), available at www.mpicc.de/files/pdf2/fa-ne-bis-in-idem.pdf, last accessed 27 January 2018

Bien, F., and Guillaumont, O., 'Innerstaatlicher Rechtsschutz gegen überlange Verfahrensdauer', *EuGRZ*, 31 (2004), 451–66

Billis, E., 'National Characteristics, Fundamental Principles, and History of Criminal Law in Greece', in Sieber, U., Jarvers, K., and Silvermann, E., eds., *National Criminal Law in a Comparative Legal Context, 1.2: Introduction to National Legal Systems: Australia, Côte d' Ivoire, Greece, South Korea* (Berlin: Dunckler and Humblot, 2013), 187–290

Bisson, F., *Die lebensgefährliche Verteidigung von Vermögenswerten: Eine Untersuchung über die Vereinbarkeit des Notwehrrechts gemäß §32 StGB mit Art. 2 Abs. 2 lit. a der Europäischen Menschenrechtskonvention* (Frankfurt a.M.: Peter Lang, 2002)

Blackstock, J., 'Procedural Safeguards in the European Union: A Road Well Travelled?', *EuCLR*, 2 (2012), 20–35

Blau, K., 'Neuere Entwicklungen in der Schutzpflichtdogmatik des EGMR am Beispiel des Falles "Vo/Frankreich"', *ZEuS*, 8 (2005), 397–440

Bleckmann, A., 'Bundesverfassungsgericht versus Europäischer Gerichtshof für Menschenrechte', *EuGRZ*, 22 (1995), 387–90

Bock, D., 'Strafe und Grundrechtseingriff: Zum Begriff der strafrechtlichen Anklage i.S.d. Art. 6 I EMRK', in Müller-Graff, P.-C., ed., *Europäisches Recht zwischen Bewährung und Wandel: Festschrift für Dieter H. Scheuing* (Baden-Baden: Nomos, 2011), 263–78

Bock, S., 'Beweisverbote aus deutscher Sicht im Lichte der Rechtsprechung des EGMR', in Leblois-Happe, J., and Stuckenberg, C.-F., eds., *Was wird aus der Hauptverhandlung* (Göttingen: V&R unipress, Bonn University Press, 2014), 99–115

'Opferrechte im Lichte europäischer Vorgaben', in Barton, S., and Kölbel, R., eds., *Ambivalenzen der Opferzuwendung des Strafrechts* (Baden-Baden: Nomos, 2012), 67–88

Bockelmann, P., 'EMRK und Notwehrrecht', in Bockelmann, P., ed., *Festschrift für Karl Engisch zum 70. Geburtstag* (Frankfurt a.M.: Klostermann, 1969), 456–67

Bogensberger, W., 'Die Anwendung des transnationalen Ne-bis-in-idem-Prinzips in Europa', in Moos, R., Jesionek, U., and Müller, O. F., eds., *Strafprozessrecht im Wandel: Festschrift für Roland Miklau zum 65. Geburtstag* (Innsbruck et al.: StudienVerlag, 2006), 91–107

Bohlander, M., 'In Extremis: Hijacked Airplanes, "Collateral Damage" and the Limits of Criminal Law', *CLR*, 53 (2006), 579–92

'Retrospective Reductions in the Severity of Substantive Criminal Law: The Lex Mitior Principle and the Impact of Scoppola v Italy No. 2', *CLR*, 58 (2011), 627–41

Böhm, K., 'Anmerkung: EuGH (Große Kammer), Urteil vom 5.4.2016- C-404/15, C-659/15 PPU (Pal Aranyosi und Robert Cildararu)', *NJW*, 69 (2016), 1713–14

Böhm, K. M., 'Die strafrechtlicher Abwesenheitsverhandlung im Berufungsverfahren', *NJW*, 68 (2015), 3132–6

Böhm, M. L., 'Endanger Law: War on Risk in German Criminal Law', in Duttge, G., and Lee, S. W., eds., *The Law in the Information and Risk Society* (Göttingen: Göttingen University Press, 2011), 145–64, available at http://univerlag.uni-goettingen.de/bitstream/handle/3/isbn-978-3-86395-012-5/GJS10.pdf?sequence=1&isAllowed=y, last accessed 27 January 2018

Bohnert, J.-F. and Lagodny, O., 'Art. 54 SDÜ im Lichte der nationalen Wiederaufnahmegründe', *NStZ*, 20 (2000), 636–40

Börner, R., 'Das Verwerfungsverbot aus §329 Abs. 1 S. 1 StPO i.V.m. Art. 6 Abs. 1, Abs. 3 lit. c) EMRK in der Revision', *HRRS*, 15 (2014), 132–4

Borowsky, M., 'Artikel 2, 51, 52, 53', in Meyer, *Charta der Grundrechte der EU* (2014), 137–59, 743–826

Böse, M., 'Art. 6 Abs. 3 lit. c EMRK und die Verteidigung des abwesenden Angeklagten in der Berufung', in Stuckenberg, C.-F., and Gärditz, K. F., eds., *Strafe und Prozess im freiheitlichen Rechtsstaat: Festschrift für Hans-Ulrich Paeffgen zum 70. Geburtstag am 2. Juli 2015* (Berlin: Duncker & Humblot, 2015), 567–87

'Ausnahmen vom grenzüberschreitenden "Ne bis in idem"? Zur Fortgeltung der Vorbehalte nach Art. 55 SDÜ', in Esser, R., Günther, H.-L., Jäger, C., Mylonopoulos, C., and Öztürk, B., eds., *Festschrift für Hans-Heiner Kühne zum 70. Geburtstag* (Heidelberg et al.: C. F. Müller, 2013), 519-30

'Der Grundsatz "ne bis idem" und der Europäische Haftbefehl: Europäischer ordre public vs. gegenseitige Anerkennung', *HRRS*, 13 (2012), 19–23

'Der Grundsatz "ne bis in idem" im Wettbewerbsrecht der Gemeinschaft und Art. 54 SDÜ', *EWS*, 18 (2007), 202–11

'Der Grundsatz "ne bis in idem" in der Europäischen Union (Art. 54 SDÜ)', *GA*, 150 (2003), 744–63

'Der Grundsatz der gegenseitigen Anerkennung unter dem Vertrag von Lissabon', in Ambos, *Europäisches Strafrecht post-Lissabon* (2011), 57–75

'Legitimität des europäischen Kooperationsrechts: Menschenrechtliche Standards zwischen Freiheitsschutz und Effektivitätsdenken', in Tiedemann, K., Sieber, U., Satzger, H., Burchard, C., and Brodowski, D., eds., *Die Verfassung moderner Strafrechtspflege: Erinnerung an Joachim Vogel* (Baden-Baden: Nomos, 2016), 211–20

'Die transnationale Geltung des Grundsatzes "ne bis in idem" und das "Vollstreckungselement"', *GA*, 158 (2011), 504–13

Böse, M., and Mayer, F., 'Die Beschränkung nationaler Strafgewalten als Möglichkeit zur Vermeidung von Jurisdiktionskonflikten in der Europäischen Union', *ZIS*, 6 (2011), 336–44

Bowring, B., 'The Russian Federation and the Strasbourg Court: The Illegitimacy of Sovereignity?', in Ziegler, K. S., Wicks, E., and Hodson, L., eds., *The UK and European Human Rights: A Strained Relationship?* (Oxford and Portland: Hart, 2015), 415–37

Bowring, B., 'The Russian Federation, Protocol No. 14 (and 14 bis), and the Battle for the Soul of the ECHR', *GoJIL*, 2 (2010), 589–617

Braitsch, T., *Gerichtssprache für Sprachunkundige im Lichte des 'fair trial'* (Frankfurt a.M. et al.: Peter Lang, 1991)

Brandts, C., 'Procedural Safeguards in the European Union: Too Little, Too Late?', in Vervaele, *European Evidence Warrant* (2005), 103–19

Braum, S., 'Das Haager Programm der Europäischen Union: Falsche und richtige Schwerpunkte europäischer Strafrechtsentwicklung', in Joerden and Szwarc, *Europäisierung des Strafrechts* (2007), 11–22

'"Parallelwertungen in der Laiensphäre": Der EuGH und die Vorratsdatenspeicherung', *ZRP*, 42 (2009), 174–7

Breuer, M. 'Artikel 3 ZP VII', in Karpenstein, U., and Mayer, F. C., *EMRK: Konvention zum Schutz der Menschenrechte und Grundfreiheiten: Kommentar* (Munich: C. H. Beck, 2nd edn, 2015), 469–72

Brockhaus, M., and Ullrich, I., 'Ungeahnte Möglichkeiten in Haftsachen: Eine Erinnerung an Art. 5 Abs. 5 EMRK', *StV*, 36 (2016), 678–81

Brodowski, D., 'Die drohende Verletzung von Menschenrechten bei der Anerkennung Europäischer Haftbefehle auf dem Prüfstand: Die zweifelhafte Aktivierung der Verfassungsidentität durch das BVerfG und eine Kurskorrektur in der Rechtsprechung des EuGH', *JR*, 88 (2016), 415–32

'Ne bis in idem im europäisierten Auslieferungsrecht', *StV*, 33 (2013), 339–46

'Strafrechtsrelevante Entwicklungen in der Europäischen Union', *ZIS*, 5 (2010),376–86

'Strafrechtsrelevante Entwicklungen in der Europäischen Union', *ZIS*, 7 (2012), 558–70

'Strafrechtsrelevante Entwicklungen in der Europäischen Union: Ein Überblick', *ZIS*, 8 (2013), 455–72

'Strafrechtsrelevante Entwicklungen in der Europäischen Union', *ZIS*, 12 (2017), 11–27

Brodzisz, Z., 'Der Grundsatz der Waffengleichheit und seine Bedeutung für das Ermittlungsverfahren in Polen: Staatsanwaltschaft und kontradiktorisches Vorverfahren', *ZIS*, 4 (2009), 109–19

Brunhöber, B., 'Für ein Grundrecht auf ein faires Verfahren in der strafprozessualen Praxis', *ZIS*, 5 (2010), 761–71

Bucherer, J., *Die Vereinbarkeit von Militärgerichten mit dem Recht auf ein faires Verfahren gemäß Art. 6 Abs. 1 EMRK, Art. 8 Abs. 1 AMRK und Art. 14 Abs. 1 des UN-Paktes über bürgerliche und politische Rechte* (Berlin et al.: Springer, 2005)

Bülte, J., 'Der Verhältnismäßigkeitsgrundsatz im deutschen Notwehrrecht aus verfassungsrechtlicher und europäischer Perspektive', *GA*, 158 (2011), 145–66

Bülte, J., and Krell, P., 'Grundrechtsschutz bei der Durchführung von Unionsrecht durch Strafrecht: Zugleich Besprechung von BVerfG, Beschl. v. 24.4.2013-1 BvR 1215/07 (Antiterrordateigesetz) = StV 2013, 673', *StV*, 33 (2013), 713–19

Burchard, C., and Brodowski, D., 'Art. 50 Charta der Grundrechte der Europäischen Union und das europäische ne bis in idem nach dem Vertrag von Lissabon', *StraFo*, 16 (2010), 179–86

Busse, C., 'Die Geltung der EMRK für Rechtsakte der EU', *NJW*, 53 (2000), 1074–9

Buyse, A., 'The Truth, the Past and the Present: Article 10 ECHR and Situations of Transition', in Buyse, A., and Hamilton, M., eds., *Transitional Jurisprudence and the European Convention on Human Rights* (Cambridge et al.: Cambridge University Press, 2011), 131–50

Caeiro, P., 'Introduction (or: Every Criminal Procedure Starts with a Bill of Rights)', in Caeiro, P., ed., *The EU Agenda on Procedural Safeguards for Suspects or Accused Persons: The 'Second Wave' and Its Predictable Impact on Portuguese Law* (Coimbra: Universidade de Coimbra, 2015)

Caligiuri, A., and Napoletano, N., 'The Application of the ECHR in the Domestic Systems', *ItYIL*, 20 (2010), 125–59

Cameron, I., and Bull, T., 'Sweden' in Gerards, J., and Fleuren, J., eds., *Implementation of the European Convention on Human Rights and of the Judgments of the ECtHR in National Case-Law: A Comparative Analysis* (Cambridge, Antwerp and Portland: Intersentia, 2014), 261–95

Candela Soriano, M., 'The Reception Process in Spain and Italy', in Keller, H., and Stone Sweet, A., eds., *A Europe of Rights: The Impact of the ECHR on National Legal Systems* (Oxford: Oxford University Press, 2008), 393–452

Cape, E., Namoradze, Z., Smith, R., and Spronken, T., *Effective Criminal Defence in Europe* (Antwerp et al.: Intersentia et al., 2010)

Cassese, A., 'Balancing the Prosecution of Crimes against Humanity and Non-retroactivity of Criminal Law: The *Kolk and Kislyiy v. Estonia* Case before the ECHR', *JICJ*, 2 (2006), 410–18

Castorf, C., 'Die Anforderungen an die Beschränkung des Zugangs zu einem Verteidiger im Ermittlungsverfahren nach der EMRK', *HRRS*, 18 (2017), 169–73

Caunes, K., 'La protection des droits fondamentaux dans l'Union européenne', *ERA Forum*, 16 (2015), 159–466

Çelik, O., and Stief, M., 'Kurze Freiheitsstrafen, §47 StGB und die Vollstreckungslösung des BGH', *StV*, 30 (2010), 657–61

Chaeva, N., 'The Russian Constitutional Court and Its Actual Control over the ECtHR Judgement in Anchugov and Gladkov', *EJIL:Talk!*, 26 April 2016, at www.ejiltalk.org/the-russian-constitutional-court-and-its-actual-control-over-the-ecthr-judgement-in-anchugov-and-gladko, last accessed 27 January 2018

Chand, D., 'Independent Witness', *NLJ*, 150 (2000), 1666

Chernishova, O., 'Russia's Response to the European Court of Human Rights' Systematic Findings: Words or Actions?', in Ziegler, K. S., Wicks, E., and Hodson, L., eds., *The UK and European Human Rights: A Strained Relationship?* (Oxford and Portland: Hart, 2015), 401–14

Christl, E., ,'Europäische Mindeststandards für Beschuldigtenrechte: Zur Umsetzung der EU-Richtlinien über Sprachmittlung und Information im Strafverfahren', *NStZ*, 34 (2014), 376–83

Chryssogonos, K., 'Zur Inkorporation der EMRK in den nationalen Rechtsordnungen der Mitgliedstaaten', *EuR*, 36 (2001), 49–61

Clayton, R., 'Should the English Courts under the HRA Mirror the Strasbourg Case Law?', in Ziegler, K. S., Wicks, E., and Hodson, L., eds., *The UK and European Human Rights: A Strained Relationship?* (Oxford and Portland: Hart, 2015), 95–113

Coffey, G., 'Resolving Conflicts of Jurisdiction in Criminal Proceedings: Interpreting Ne bis in idem in Conjunction with the Principle of Complementarity', *NJECL*, 4 (2013), 59–81

Conaghan, J., *Law and Gender* (Oxford: Oxford University Press, 2013)

The Conservatives, *Protecting Human Rights in the UK: The Conservatives' Proposals for Changing Britain's Human Rights Laws* (2015), available at http://news.bbc.co.uk/2/shared/bsp/hi/pdfs/03_10_14_humanrights.pdf, last accessed 27 January 2018

Conway, G., 'Judicial Interpretation and the Third Pillar', *EJCCLCJ*, 13 (2005), 255–83

Corell, C., and Sidhu, K., 'Das Recht auf Rechtsbeistand nach dem europäischen Fahrplan zur Stärkung der Verfahrensrechte in Strafverfahren', *StV*, 32 (2012), 246–50

Cornelius, K., 'Konfrontationsrecht und Unmittelbarkeitsgrundsatz', *NStZ*, 28 (2008), 244–8

Cornils, M., '91. EGMR v. 22.3.2001: Streletz, Kessler und Krenz', in Menzel, Pierlings, and Hoffmann, *Völkerrechtsprechung* (2005), 537–40

Cras, S., 'The Directive on Procedural Safeguards for Children Who Are Suspects or Accused Persons in Criminal Proceedings', *eucrim*, 11 (2016), 109–20

'The Directive on the Right of Access to a Lawyer in Criminal Proceedings and in EAW Proceedings', *eucrim*, 9 (2014), 32–44

Cras, S., and De Matteis, L., 'The Directive on the Right to Information', *eucrim*, 8 (2013), 22–32

'The Directive on the Right to Interpretation and Translation in Criminal Proceedings', *eucrim*, 5 (2010), 153–62

Cras, S., and Erbežnik, A., 'The Directive on the Presumption of Innocence and the Right to Be Present at Trial', *eucrim*, 11 (2016), 25–36

Croquet, N. A. J., 'The ICC and the Treatment of Defence Rights: A Mirror of the ECtHR's Jurisprudence?', *HRLR*, 11 (2011), 91–131

Damnjanovic, V., 'Nullum crimen sine lege praevia: Das Rückwirkungsverbot des Art. 7 EMRK vor dem EGMR im Fall Maktouf und Damjanovic gegen Bosnien und Herzegowina', *ZIS*, 9 (2014), 629–37

Dannecker, C., 'Konturierung prozessualer Gewährleistungsgehalte des nemo tenetur-Grundsatzes anhand der Rechtsprechung des EGMR, *ZStW*, 127 (2015), 991–1017

'Der nemo tenetur-Grundsatz: prozessuale Fundierung und Geltung für juristische Personen', *ZStW*, 127 (2015), 370–409

Dannecker, G., 'Anmerkung zu CJEU, Judgment 26 February 2013, No. C-617/10 (ECLI:EU:C:2013:105): "Åkerberg Fransson"', *JZ*, 68 (2013), 616–20

'Community Fines and Non-Member State Sanctions: The Effect of the Principle ne bis in idem', in Eser, A., and Rabenstein, C., eds., *Neighbours in Law: Are Common Law and Civil Law Moving Closer Together? Papers in Honour of Barbara Huber on Her 65th Birthday* (Freiburg i.Br.: Ed. iuscrim, 2001), 153–86

'Die Garantie des Grundsatzes "ne bis in idem" in Europa', in Hirsch, H. J., Wolter, J., and Brauns, U., eds., *Festschrift für Günter Kohlmann zum 70. Geburtstag* (Cologne: Schmidt, 2003), 593–616

Dannecker, G., and Bürger, S., 'Generalbericht', in Dannecker and Jansen, *Steuerstrafrecht in Europa und den Vereinigten Staaten* (2007), 15–92

Däubler-Gmelin, H., 'Überlegungen zur Reform des Strafprozesses', *StV*, 21 (2001), 359–63

de Bondt, W., and Vermeulen, G., 'The Procedural Rights Debate', *eucrim*, 5 (2010), 163–7

de Búrca, G., 'The Evolution of EU Human Rights Law', in Craig, P., and de Búrca, G., *The Evolution of EU Law* (Oxford: Oxford University Press, 2nd edn, 2011), 465–97

de Frouville, O., 'The Influence of the European Court of Human Rights' Case Law on International Criminal Law of Torture and Inhuman or Degrading Treatment', *JICJ*, 9 (2011), 633–50

de Hert, P., and Papakonstantinou, V., 'The New Police and Criminal Justice Data Protection Directive: A First Analysis', *NJECL*, 7 (2016), 7–19

de Hert, P. J. A., 'Balancing Security and Liberty within the European Human Rights Framework', *ULR*, 1 (2005), 68–96

de Hoyos Sancho, M., 'Eficacia transnacional del non bis in idem y denegación de la Euroorden', *Diario La Ley*, 6330 (2005), 1–22

de Londras, F., and Dzehtsiarou, K., 'Mission Impossible? Adressing Non-execution through Infringement Proceedings in the ECtHR', *ICLQ*, 66 (2017), 467–90

De Meester, K., Pitcher, K., Rastan, R., and Sluiter, G., 'Investigation, Coercive Measures, Arrest, and Surrender', in Sluiter, G., Friman, H., Linton, S., Vasiliev, S., and Zappalá, S., eds., *International Criminal Procedure* (2013), 171–379

Degenhard, K., 'Das Europäische Doppelverfolgungsverbot', *StraFo*, 11 (2005), 65–70

Dehne-Niemann, J., '"Nie sollst du mich befragen": Zur Behandlung des Rechts zur Konfrontation mitbeschuldigter Belastungszeugen (Art. 6 Abs. 3 lit. d EMRK) durch den BGH', *HRRS*, 11 (2010), 189–207

Demko, D., 'Das Fragerecht des Angeklagten nach Art. 6 Abs. 3 lit. d EMRK aus Sicht des Europäischen Gerichtshofs für Menschenrechte, der schweizerischen sowie der deutschen Rechtsprechung', *ZStrR*, 122 (2004), 416–35

'Die gerichtliche Fürsorgepflicht zur Wahrung einer "tatsächlichen und wirksamen" Verteidigung im Rahmen des Art. 6 Abs. 3 lit. c EMRK', *HRRS*, 7 (2006), 250–9

'Der hinreichende Tatverdacht nach Art. 5 Abs. 1 lit. c EMRK bei "conventional" und "terrorist crime"', *HRRS*, 5 (2004), 95–102

'Keine Strafe ohne Gesetz', *HRRS*, 5 (2004), 19–25

'Das Recht auf Verfahrensbeschleunigung gemäß Art. 6 Abs. 1 S. 1 EMRK in Strafverfahren und dessen Verhältnis zum Recht auf wirksame Beschwerde gemäß Art. 13 EMRK in der Rechtsprechung des EGMR', *HRRS*, 6 (2005), 283–96 (Teil I) and 403–9 (Teil II)

'Das Recht des Angeklagten auf unentgeltlichen Beistand eines staatlich bestellten Verteidigers und das Erfordernis der "interests of justice"', in Gaede, K., Meyer, F., and Schlegel, S., eds., *HRRS-Festgabe für Gerhard Fezer zum 70. Geburtstag am 29. Oktober 2008* (Hamburg 2008), www.hrr-strafrecht.de/hrr/archiv/hrrs-fezer-festgabe.pdf, last accessed 27 January 2018, 1–20

'Zum Begriff der "Freiheitsentziehung" des Art. 5 Abs. 1 EMRK im Fall Amuur gegen Frankreich', *HRRS*, 5 (2004), 171–7

Dessecker, A., 'Die Sicherungsverwahrung in der Rechtsprechung des Bundesverfassungsgerichts', *ZIS*, 6 (2011), 706–13

di Martino, A., 'Das Gesetzlichkeitsprinzip "zwischen zwei Welten": Formelles nationales vs. materielles Gesetzlichkeitsprinzip der EMRK in der jüngsten Rechtsprechung Italiens', *ZStW*, 128 (2016), 270–82

Dickson, B., 'Repeal the HRA and Rely on the Common Law?', in Ziegler, K. S., Wicks, E., and Hodson, L., eds., *The UK and European Human Rights: A Strained Relationship?* (Oxford and Portland: Hart, 2015), 115–33

Diehm, D., *Die Menschenrechte der EMRK und ihr Einfluss auf das deutsche Strafgesetzbuch* (Berlin: Logos, 2006)

Donald, A., 'The Implementation of European Court of Human Rights Judgments against the UK: Unravelling the Paradox', in Ziegler, K. S., Wicks, E., and Hodson, L., eds., *The UK and European Human Rights: A Strained Relationship?* (Oxford and Portland: Hart, 2015), 135–62

'Tackling Non-implementation in the Strasbourg System: The Art of the Possible?', *EJIL:Talk!*, 28 April 2017, at www.ejiltalk.org/tackling-non-implementation-in-the-strasbourg-system-the-art-of-the-possible, last accessed 27 January 2018

Douglas-Scott, S., 'The EU and Human Rights after the Treaty of Lisbon', *HRLR*, 11 (2011), 645–82

'Opinion 2/13 on EU Accession to the ECHR: A Christmas Bombshell from the European Court of Justice', *UKConstLBlog*, 24th December 2014, at https://ukconstitutionallaw.org/2014/12/24/sionaidh-douglas-scott-opinion-213-on-eu-accession-to-the-echr-a-christmas-bombshell-from-the-european-court-of-justice, last accessed 27 January 2018

Drenkhahn, K., and Morgenstern, C., 'Dabei soll es uns auf den Namen nicht ankommen: Der Streit um die Sicherungsverwahrung', *ZStW*, 124 (2012), 132–203

Drzemczewski, A., 'Election of Judges to the Strasbourg Court: An Overview', *EHRLR*, 16(2010), 377–83

du Bois-Pedain, A., 'Artikel 6 Abs. 3 lit. d EMRK und der nicht verfügbare Zeuge: Weist der modifizierte Lucà-Test den Weg aus der Sackgasse?', *HRRS*, 13 (2012), 120–38

Dyer, A., 'Irreducible Life Sentences: What Difference Have the European Convention on Human Rights and the United Kingdom Human Rights Act Made?', *HRLR*, 16 (2016), 541–84

Eckstein, K., 'Grund und Grenzen transnationalen Schutzes vor mehrfacher Strafverfolgung in Europa', *ZStW*, 124 (2012), 490–527

'Im Netz des Unionsrechts: Anmerkung zum Fransson-Urteil des EuGH', *ZIS*, 8 (2013), 220–5

Editorial Comments, 'The EU's Accession to the ECHR: A "NO" from the ECJ!', *CMLR*, 52 (2015), 1–15

Eicker, A., *Transstaatliche Strafverfolgung: Ein Beitrag zur Europäisierung, Internationalisierung und Fortentwicklung des Grundsatzes ne bis in idem* (Herbolzheim: Centaurus, 2004)

Eiffler, S.-R., 'Die Überprüfung polizeilicher Maßnahmen durch den EGMR', *NJW*, 52 (1999), 762–3

Eisele, J., 'Die Bedeutung der EMRK für das deutsche Strafverfahren', *JA*, 37 (2005), 390–5

'Die einzelnen Beschuldigtenrechte der EMRK', *JA*, 37 (2005), 901–8

'Internationale Bezüge des Strafrechts', *JA*, 32 (2000), 424–9

'Jurisdiktionskonflikte in der Europäischen Union: Vom nationalen Strafanwendungsrecht zum Europäischen Kollisionsrecht?', *ZStW*, 125 (2013), 1–33

Eisenberg, U., 'Sicherungsverwahrung: Anmerkung II', *StV*, 31 (2011), 480–2

Elberling, B., 'Artikel 5 EMRK', in Karpenstein, U., and Mayer, F. C., *EMRK: Konvention zum Schutz der Menschenrechte und Grundfreiheiten: Kommentar* (Munich: C. H. Beck, 2nd edn, 2015), 108–51

Elliott, M., 'Beyond the European Convention: Human Rights and the Common Law', *CLP*, 68 (2015), 85–117

'The 2016 Queen's Speech and the Constitution', *Public Law for Everyone*, 18 May 2016, at https://publiclawforeveryone.com/2016/05/18/the-2016-queens-speech-and-the-constitution, last accessed 27 January 2018

Engel, D., 'Berufungsverwerfung aufgrund Säumnis des Angeklagten im Lichte der jüngsten Rechtsprechung des EGMR sowie des OLG München', *ZJS*, 6 (2013), 339–45

Enikö, F., 'The Rising Importance on the Protection of Witnesses in the EU', *RIDP*, 77 (2006), 313–22

Eser, A., 'Artikel 47, 48, 49, 50', in Meyer, *Charta der Grundrechte der EU* (2014), 652–717

'Human Rights Guarantees for Criminal Law and Procedure in the EU-Charter of Fundamental Rights', *RitsumLR*, 26 (2009), 163–90

'Konkurrierende nationale und transnationale Strafverfolgung: Zur Sicherung von "ne bis in idem" und zur Vermeidung von positiven Kompetenzkonflikten', in Sieber, U., Satzger, H., Heintschel von Heinegg, B., eds., *Europäisches Strafrecht* (2014), 636–60

Eser, A., and Burchard, C., 'Interlokales "ne bis in idem" in Europa?', in Derra, H.-J., and Träger, M., eds., *Freiheit, Sicherheit und Recht: Festschrift für Jürgen Meyer zum 70. Geburtstag* (Baden-Baden: Nomos, 2006), 499–524

Esser, R., 'Artikel 2' and 'Artikel 5', in Erb, V., Esser, R., Franke, U., Graalmann-Scheerer, K., Hilger, H., and Ignor, A., eds., *Löwe-Rosenberg StPO*, xi (2012), 100–24, 193–332

'Europäische Initiativen zur Begrenzung der Untersuchungshaft', in Joerden and Szwarc, *Europäisierung des Strafrechts* (2007), 233–54

'Garantien in der EU', in Sieber, U., Satzger, H., and Heintschel von Heinegg, B., eds., *Europäisches Strafrecht* (2014), 950–88

'Initiativen der EU zur Harmonisierung der Beschuldigtenrechte: Zugleich eine kritische Analyse der Richtlinie 2012/13/EU zum Recht auf Belehrung und Unterrichtung in Strafverfahren', in Zöller, M. A., Hilger, H., Küper, W., and Roxin, C., eds., *Gesamte Strafrechtswissenschaft in internationaler Dimension: Festschrift für Jürgen Wolter zum 70. Geburtstag am 7. September 2013* (Berlin: Duncker & Humblot, 2013), 1329–54

'Mindeststandards einer Europäischen Strafprozessordnung unter Berücksichtigung der Rechtsprechung des EGMR', *StraFo*, 9 (2003), 335–44

'(Nichts) Neues aus Straßburg: Effektive Verteidigung bei Nichterscheinen des Angeklagten zu Beginn der Hauptverhandlung in der Berufungsinstanz (§329 Abs. 1 S. 1 StPO)', *StV*, 33 (2013), 331–9

'Die Umsetzung der Urteile des Europäischen Gerichtshofs für Menschenrechte im nationalen Recht: Ein Beispiel für die Dissonanz völkerrechtlicher Verpflichtungen und verfassungsrechtlicher Vorgaben?', *StV*, 25 (2005), 348–55

'Unschuldsvermutung (Art. 6 Abs. 2 EMRK) bei Verfahrenstrennung', in Stuckenberg, C.-F-, and Gärditz, K. F., eds., *Strafe und Prozess im freiheitlichen Rechtsstaat: Festschrift für Hans-Ulrich Paeffgen zum 70. Geburtstag am 2. Juli 2015* (Berlin: Duncker & Humblot, 2015), 503–26

'Verteidigungsrechte', in Sieber, U., Satzger, H., and Heintschel von Heinegg, B., eds., *Europäisches Strafrecht* (2014), 1070–84

'Zur Bereitstellung des Verteidigers im Ermittlungsverfahren: Plädoyer für eine Reform des §141 Abs. 3 StPO im Lichte der EMRK und der EU-Richtlinie zum Recht auf Rechtsbeistand', in Esser, R., Günther, H.-L., Jäger, C., Mylonopoulos, C., and Öztürk, B., eds., *Festschrift für Hans-Heiner Kühne zum 70. Geburtstag* (Heidelberg et al.: C. F. Müller et al., 2013), 539–63

Esser, R., Gaede, K., and Tsambikakis, M., 'Übersicht zur Rechtsprechung des EGMR in den Jahren 2008 bis Mitte 2010', *NStZ*, 31 (2011), 78–82 (Teil I) and 31 (2011), 140–8 (Teil II)

'Übersicht zur Rechtsprechung des EGMR in den Jahren 2010 bis 2011', *NStZ*, 32 (2012), 554–9 (Teil I) and 32 (2012), 619–25 (Teil II)

Esser R., and Lubrich, F., 'Anspruch des Verletzten auf Strafverfolgung Dritter: Der Kunduz-Beschluss des Bundesverfassungsgerichts', *StV*, 37 (2017), 418–24

European Commission, *Strategy for the Effective Implementation of the Charter of Fundamental Rights by the European Union* (19 October 2010), COM (2010) 573

European Criminal Policy Initiative, 'A Manifesto on European Criminal Procedure Law', *ZIS*, 8 (2013), 430–46

Fabbrini, F., 'The European Court of Human Rights, Extraordinary Renditions and the Right to the Truth: Ensuring Accountability for Gross Human Rights Violations Committed in the Fight against Terrorism', *HRLR*, 14 (2014), 85–106

Fairchild, E., and Dammer, H. R., *Comparative Criminal Justice Systems* (Belmont et al.: Wadsworth and Thomson Learning, 1993)

Fassbender, B., 'Der einheitliche Gesetzesvorbehalt der EU-Grundrechtecharta und seine Bedeutung für die deutsche Rechtsordnung', *NVwZ*, 29 (2010), 1049–54

Favreau, B., 'L'Europe à la poursuite des droits fondamentaux', *eucrim*, 11 (2016), 104–9

Fedorova, M., *The Principle of Equality of Arms in International Criminal Proceedings* (Cambridge et al.: Intersentia, 2012)

Ferguson, P. R., 'The Presumtion of Innocence and Its Role in the Criminal Process', *CLF*, 27 (2016), 131–58

Fikarova, D., 'Prospects of the Council Framework Decision 2009/948/JHA of 30 November 2009 on Prevention and Settlement of Conflicts of Exercise of Jurisdiction in Criminal Proceedings', in Sinn, A., ed., *Conflicts of Jurisdiction in Cross-border Crime Situations: A Comparative Law Study on International Criminal Law* (Göttingen: V & R Unipress, 2012), 103–8

Floud, J., 'Dangerousness and Criminal Justice', *BJC*, 22 (1982), 213–28

Franke, U., 'Ambivalente Wirkungen des Beschleunigungsgebotes nach Art. 6 Abs. 1 S. 1 EMRK', *StV*, 30 (2010), 433–6

Freund, G., 'Gefahren und Gefährlichkeiten im Straf- und Maßregelrecht', *GA*, 157 (2010), 193–210

Frisch, W.,'Zum Recht des abwesenden Angeklagten auf Verteidigung, insbesondere in der Berufungsinstanz', in Stuckenberg, C.-F., and Gärditz, K. F., eds., *Strafe und Prozess im freiheitlichen Rechtsstaat: Festschrift für Hans-Ulrich Paeffgen zum 70. Geburtstag am 2. Juli 2015* (Berlin: Duncker & Humblot, 2015), 589–619

Frister, H., 'Der Anspruch des Beschuldigten auf Mitteilung der Beschuldigung aus Art. 6 Abs. 3 lit. a EMRK', *StV*, 18 (1998), 159–64

'Zur Einschränkung des Notwehrrechts durch Art. 2 der EMRK', *GA*, 132 (1985), 553–65

Frommel, M., 'Reform der Sicherungsverwahrung: Nach dem rechtskräftigen Urteil des EuGH vom 10.5.2010', *NK*, 22 (2010), 82–8

Frowein, J. A., 'Artikel 2, 7', in Frowein and Peukert, *EMRK-Kommentar* (2009), 28–42 and 269–78

'Einführung', in Frowein and Peukert, *EMRK-Kommentar* (2009), 1–9

Gaede, K. 'Anmerkung zu BGH, Beschluss v. 17.1.2008 - GSSt 1/07 (LG Oldenburg)', *JZ*, 63 (2008), 422–4

'Beweisverbote in der Rechtsprechung des EGMR zur Wahrung des fairen Verfahrens insbesondere bei verdeckten Ermittlungen', *JR*, 81 (2009), 493–502

'Deutscher Brechmitteleinsatz menschenrechtswidrig: Begründungsgang und Konsequenzen der Grundsatzentscheidung des EGMR im Fall Jalloh', *HRRS*, 7 (2006), 241–9

Fairness als Teilhabe: Das Recht auf konkrete und wirksame Teilhabe durch Verteidigung gemäß Art. 6 EMRK (Berlin: Duncker & Humblot, 2007)

'Die Fragilität des Folterverbots', in Camprubi, M., ed., *Angst und Streben nach Sicherheit in Gesetzgebung und Praxis* (Zurich: Schulthess, 2004), 155–90

'Grund- und Verfahrensrechte im europäisierten Strafverfahren', in Böse, *Europäisches Strafrecht* (2013), 97–153

'Minimalistischer EU-Grundrechtsschutz bei der Kooperation im Strafverfahren', *NJW*, 66 (2013), 1279–82

'Rückwirkende Sicherungsverwahrung: Art. 7 Abs. 1 Satz 2 EMRK als andere gesetzliche Bestimmung i. S. d. §2 Abs. 6 StGB', *HRRS*, 11 (2010), 329–39

'Schranken des fairen Verfahrens gemäß Art. 6 EMRK bei der Sperrung verteidigungsrelevanter Informationen und Zeugen', *StV*, 26 (2006), 599–607

'Transnationales "ne bis in idem" auf schwachem grundrechtlichen Fundament', *NJW*, 67 (2014), 2990–2

'Ungehobene Schätze in der Rechtsprechung des EGMR für die Verteidigung', in Gaede, K., Meyer, F., and Schlegel, S., eds., *HRRS-Festgabe für Gerhard Fezer zum 70. Geburtstag am 29. Oktober 2008* (Hamburg 2008), www.hrr-strafrecht.de/hrr/archiv/hrrs-fezer-festgabe.pdf, last accessed 27 January 2018, 21–51

'Das Verbot der Umgehung der EMRK durch den Einsatz von Privatpersonen bei der Strafverfolgung', *StV*, 24 (2004), 46–53

'Zeitgesetze im Wirtschaftsstrafrecht und rückwirkende geschlossene Ahndungslücken', *wistra*, 30 (2011), 365–73

Gaede, K., and Mühlbauer, T., 'Wirtschaftsstrafrecht zwischen europäischem Primärrecht, Verfassungsrecht und der richtlinienkonformen Auslegung am Beispiel des Scalping', *wistra*, 24 (2005), 9–17

Gärditz, K. F., '88. EGMR v. 25.6.1996: Amuur', in Menzel, Pierlings, and Hoffmann, *Völkerrechtsprechung* (2005), 526–30

'89. EGMR v. 8.6.1976: Engel', in Menzel, Pierlings, and Hoffmann, *Völkerrechtsprechung* (2005), 530–3

Garlicki, L., and Kondak., I 'Poland: Human Rights between International and Constitutional Law', in Motoc, I., and Ziemele, I., eds., *The Impact of the ECHR on Democratic Change in Central and Eastern Europe: Judicial Perspectives* (Cambridge: Cambridge University Press, 2016), 305–29

Gatzweiler, C., 'Die neuen EU-Richtlinien zur Stärkung der Verfahrensrechte (Mindestmaß) des Beschuldigten oder Angeklagten in Strafsachen', *StraFo*, 17 (2011), 293–8

Gearty, C., *On Fantasy Island: Britain, Europe and Human Rights* (Oxford: Oxford University Press, 2016)

Geiß, R., 'Civil Aircraft as Weapons of Large-Scale Destruction: Countermeasures, Article 3bis of the Chicago Convention, and the Newly Adopted German "Luftsicherheitsgesetz"', *MichJIL*, 27 (2005/2006), 227–56

Gerards, J., and Fleuren, J., 'The Netherlands', in Gerards, J., and Fleuren, J., eds., *Implementation of the European Convention on Human Rights and of the Judgments of the ECtHR in National Case-Law: A Comparative Analysis* (Cambridge, Antwerp and Portland: Intersentia, 2014), 217–60

Gerst, H.-J., 'Die Konventionsgarantie des Art. 6 III c und die Abwesenheitsverwerfung gemäß §329 I 1 StPO: Ein kleiner Schritt für Straßburg, ein zu großer für Deutschland?', *NStZ*, 33 (2013), 310–12

Gialuz, M., and Spagnolo, P., 'Reasonable Length of Pre-trial Detention: Rigid or Flexible Time Limits?', *EuCLR*, 3 (2013), 220–31

Giannoulopoulos, D., 'Strasbourg Jurisprudence, Law Reform and Comparative Law: A Tale of the Right to Custodial Legal Assistance in Five Countries', *HRLR*, 16 (2016), 103–29, available as 'free access' at http://hrlr.oxfordjournals.org/content/16/1/103.full.pdf+html, last accessed 27 January 2018

Gil Gil, A., 'La excepción al principio de legalidad del número 2 del artículo 7 del Convenio Europeo de Derechos Humanos', *ADPCP*, 63 (2010), 131–63

Gillespie, A., and Bettinson, V., '"Indecent" Images: ECHR, Article 7', *JCL*, 70 (2006), 127–30

Gillmeister, F., 'Rechtliches Gehör im Ermittlungsverfahren', *StraFo*, 2 (1996), 114–18

Gleß, S., 'Grenzüberschreitende Beweissammlung', *ZStW*, 125 (2013), 573–608

'Ohn(e)macht: Abschied von der Fiktion einer Waffengleichheit gegenüber europäischer Strafverfolgung?', *StV*, 33 (2013), 317–24

'Das Recht auf Konfrontation eines Auslandsbelastungszeugen: Eine europäische Perspektive aus Karlsruhe', in Zöller, M. A., Hilger, H., Küper, W., and Roxin, C., eds., *Gesamte Strafrechtswissenschaft in internationaler Dimension: Festschrift für Jürgen Wolter zum 70. Geburtstag am 7. September 2013* (Berlin: Duncker & Humblot, 2013), 1355–70

'Replies to Green Paper on obtaining evidence in criminal matters from one Member State to another and securing admissibility', http://ec.europa.eu/justice/news/consulting_public/0004/civil_society/sabine_gless_en.pdf, last accessed 27 January 2018

'Zum Prinzip der gegenseitigen Anerkennung', *ZStW*, 116 (2004), 353–67

Grabenwarter, C., 'Androhung von Folter und faires Strafverfahren: Das (vorläufig) letzte Wort aus Straßburg', *NJW*, 63 (2010), 3128–32

'Die deutsche Sicherungsverwahrung als Treffpunkt grundrechtlicher Parallelwelten', *EuGRZ*, 39 (2012), 507–14

'Wirkungen eines Urteils des EGMR: am Beispiel des Falls M. gegen Deutschland', *JZ*, 65 (2010), 857–69

Grabenwarter, C., and Pabel, K., 'Kapitel 14: Der Grundsatz des fairen Verfahrens', in Dörr, Grote, and Marauhn, *EMRK/GG*, i (2013), 742–838

Greco, L., 'Analogieverbot und europarechtliches Strafgesetz. Teil 1 und Teil 2', *GA*, 163 (2016), 138–52, 195–216

Greer, S., 'Should Police Threats to Torture Suspects Always Be Severely Punished? Reflections on the Gäfgen Case', *HRLR*, 11 (2011), 67–89

Greger, A., 'Herausforderung Sicherungsverwahrung: Wie die Praxis mit der Entscheidung des EGMR (M. gegen Deutschland) umgehen kann', *NStZ*, 30 (2010), 676–80

Grewe, C., 'Beitritt der EU zur EMRK und ZP 14: Wirksame Durchsetzung einer gesamteuropäischen Grundrechteverfassung?', *EuR*, 47 (2012), 285–309

'The ECHR in French Law: Status, Implementation and Debates', in Ziegler, K. S., Wicks, E., and Hodson, L., eds., *The UK and European Human Rights: A Strained Relationship?* (Oxford and Portland: Hart, 2015), 341–59

Gropp, W., 'Kollision nationaler Strafgewalten: Nulla prosecutio transnationalis sine lege', in Sinn, A., ed., *Conflicts of Jurisdiction in Cross-border Crime Situations: A Comparative Law Study on International Criminal Law* (Göttingen: V & R Unipress, 2012), 41–63

Gros, F., 'The EU Directives on the Rights of Suspects', *eucrim*, 12 (2017), 27–30

Grosse-Brömer, M., and Klein, O., 'Sicherungsverwahrung als Verfassungsauftrag', *ZRP*, 43 (2010), 172–5

Gundel, J., 'Verfahrensrechte', in Merten, D., and Papier, H.-J., eds., *Handbuch der Grundrechte in Deutschland und Europa*, vi/1: *Europäische Grundrechte I* (Heidelberg et al.: C. F. Müller, 2010), 349–62

'Vorratsdatenspeicherung und Binnenmarktkompetenz: Die ungebrochene Anziehungskraft des Art. 95 EGV', *EuR*, 44 (2009), 536–48

'Der wachsende Einfluß des EU-Rechts auf die Auslegung der EMRK: und seine strukturellen Grenzen', in Müller-Graff, P.-C., ed., *Europäisches Recht zwischen Bewährung und Wandel: Festschrift für Dieter H. Scheuing* (Baden-Baden: Nomos, 2011), 58–78

Hackner, T., 'Das teileuropäische Doppelverfolgungsverbot insbesondere in der Rechtsprechung des Gerichtshofs der Europäischen Union', *NStZ*, 31 (2011), 425–30

Haefliger, A., *Die Europäische Menschenrechtskonvention und die Schweiz* (Bern: Stämpfli, 2008)

Haefliger, A., and Schürmann, F., *Die Europäische Menschenrechtskonvention und die Schweiz: Die Bedeutung der Konvention für die schweizerische Rechtspraxis* (Bern: Stämpfli, 2nd edn, 1999)

Halberstam, D., '"It's the Autonomy, Stupid!": A Modest Defense of Opinion 2/13 on EU Accession to the ECHR, and the Way Forward', *GLJ*, 16 (2015), 105–46

Halleskov Storgaard, L., 'EU Law Autonomy versus European Fundamental Rights Protection: On Opinion 2/13 on EU Accession to the ECHR', *HRLR*, 15 (2015), 485–521

Hart, N., 'Whole-Life Sentences in the UK: Volte-Face at the ECtHR?', *CLJ*, 74 (2015), 205–8

Härtel, I., 'Die Europäische Grundrechteagentur: Unnötige Bürokratie oder gesteigerter Grundrechtsschutz?', *EuR*, 43 (2008), 489–513

Hatje, A., 'Artikel 51 GrCh', in Schwarze, *EU-Kommentar* (2009), 2320–4

Hauck, P., 'Lauschangriff in der U-Haft: Anmerkungen zu BGH, Urt. v. 29.4.2009 (1 Str 701/08): und Versuch einer dogmatischen Klärung', *NStZ*, 30 (2010), 17–22

Hecker, B., 'Die rechtlichen Möglichkeiten der Europäischen Union zur Lösung von Kompetenzkonflikten', in Sinn, A., ed., *Conflicts of Jurisdiction in Cross-border Crime Situations: A Comparative Law Study on International Criminal Law* (Göttingen: V & R Unipress, 2012), 85–102

Heffernan, L., 'Calibrating the right to confrontation', *E. & P.*, 20 (2016), 103–11

Heger, M., 'Das europäische Doppelbestrafungsverbot nach Art. 50 GRCh', in Esser, R., Günther, H.-L., Jäger, C., Mylonopoulos, C., and Öztürk, B., eds., *Festschrift für Hans-Heiner Kühne zum 70. Geburtstag* (Heidelberg et al.: C. F. Müller et al., 2013), 565–78

'Perspektiven des Europäischen Strafrechts nach dem Vertrag von Lissabon', *ZIS*, 4 (2009), 406–17

Heine, G., 'Quasi-Strafrecht und Verantwortlichkeit von Unternehmen im Kartellrecht der EG und der Schweiz', *ZStrR*, 125 (2007), 105–56

Heine, H., *Die Rechtsstellung des Beschuldigten im Rahmen der Europäisierung des Strafrechts* (Frankfurt a.M.: Peter Lang, 2009)

Heine, S., 'Zur Verwertbarkeit von Aussagen im Ausland möglicherweise gefolterter Zeugen', *NStZ*, 33 (2013), 680–3

Heinz, W. S., 'Die europäische Diskussion über CIA-Rendition-Flüge: Erfahrungen mit strafrechtlicher und politischer Aufklarung: Eine Zwischenbilanz', in Müller, H. E., Sander, G. M., and Válková, H., eds.,

Festschrift für Ulrich Eisenberg zum 70. Geburtstag (Munich: C. H. Beck, 2009), 35–67

Helenius, D., 'The Finnish Supreme Court on "ne bis in idem"', *EuCLR*, 1 (2011), 203–8

Helmken, K., 'Ein Recht des Tatopfers auf ein faires Strafverfahren? Zum Anwendungsbereich des Art. 6 EMRK', *StV*, 36 (2016), 456–61

Hentschel-Bednorz, M., *Derzeitige Rolle und zukünftige Perspektive des EuGH im Mehrebenensystem des Grundrechtsschutzes in Europa* (Cologne et al.: Carl Heymanns, 2012)

Henzelin, M., '"Ne bis in idem", un principe à géométrie variable', *ZStrR*, 123 (2005), 345–82

Herlin-Karnell, E., 'All Roads Lead to Rome: The New AFSJ Package and the Trajectory to Europe 2020', *eucrim*, 9 (2014), 27–31

Herrmann, J., 'Implementing the Prohibition of Torture on Three Levels: United Nations: Council of Europe: Germany', *ZIS*, 2 (2007), 299–306

Herrnfeld, H.-H., 'Die Rolle von Eurojust bei der Beilegung von Jurisdiktionskonflikten', in Sinn, A., ed., *Conflicts of Jurisdiction in Cross-border Crime Situations: A Comparative Law Study on International Criminal Law* (Göttingen: V & R Unipress, 2012), 141–62

Hilgendorf, E., 'Sterbehilfe in Europa: Vom Schutz des Lebens zur Pflicht zum Leiden? Skeptische Anmerkungen zum Fall Diane Pretty', in Joerden and Szwarc, *Europäisierung des Strafrechts* (2007), 173–90

Hillebrecht, C., 'Implementing International Human Rights Law at Home: Domestic Politics and the European Court of Human Rights', *HRR*, 13 (2012), 279–301

Hinarejos, A., Spencer, J. R., and Peers, S., 'Opting out of EU Criminal Law: What Is Actually Involved?', CELS Working Paper, 1 (2012), available at www.statewatch.org/news/2012/oct/eu-cels-uk-opt-out-crim-law.pdf, last accessed 27 January 2018

Hirsch, B., 'Zum Verbot des Rettungstotschlags', *NJW*, 60 (2007), 1188–9

Hirsch, G., 'Grundrechtswidrige Menschenrechte: Ein Paradoxon?', in Griesbaum, R., Hannich, R., and Schnarr, K. H., eds., *Strafrecht und Justizgewährung: Festschrift für Kay Nehm zum 65. Geburtstag* (Berlin: Berliner Wissenschafts-Verlag, 2006), 61–72

Hochmayr, G., 'Elektronisch überwachter Hausarrest: Gegenwart und Zukunft in Deutschland und Österreich', *NStZ*, 33 (2013), 13–19

Höffler, K., 'Das Therapieunterbringungsgesetz und der verfassungsrechtliche Strafbegriff', *StV*, 34 (2014), 168–74

Höffler, K., and Stadtland, C., 'Mad or Bad? Der Begriff "psychische Störung" des ThUG im Lichte der Rechtsprechung des BVerfG und des EGMR', *StV*, 32 (2012), 239–46

Hoffmann, J., '84. EGMR v. 25.10.1996 – Chahal' and '85. EGMR v. 25.5.1998 – Kurt', in Menzel, Pierlings, and Hoffmann, *Völkerrechtsprechung* (2005), 509–16

Hoffmann-Riem, W., 'Kohärenz der Anwendung europäischer und nationaler Grundrechte', *EuGRZ*, 29 (2002), 473–83

Hörnle, T., 'Einige kritische Bemerkungen zum Urteil des EGMR vom 17.12.2009 in Sachen Sicherungsverwahrung', in Bernsmann, K., and Fischer, T., eds., *Festschrift für Ruth Rissing-van Saan zum 65. Geburtstag am 25. Januar 2011* (Berlin and New York: de Gruyter, 2011), 239–57

'Hijacked Airplanes: May They Be Shot Down?', *NCLR*, 10 (2007), 582–612

'Der Streit um die Sicherungsverwahrung', *NStZ*, 31 (2011), 488–93

'Unterschiede zwischen Strafverfahrensordnungen und ihre kulturellen Hintergründe', *ZStW*, 117 (2005), 801–38

HRW, *Like the Dead in Their Coffins* (June 2004), vol. 16, p. 19 n. 42, available at www.hrw.org/reports/2004/iran0604/iran0604.pdf, last accessed 27 January 2018

Huber, P. M., 'Auslegung und Anwendung der Charta der Grundrechte', *NJW*, 64 (2011), 2385–90

Hubrach, J., '§56 f', in Laufhütte, Rissing-van Saan, and Tiedemann, *Leipziger Kommentar, StGB*, iii (2008)

Hüls, S., and Reichling, T., 'Der abwesende Angeklagte in der (Berufungs-) Hauptverhandlung nach der EGMR-Entscheidung Neziraj vs. Deutschland: Zugleich Anmerkungen zu OLG Bremen, Beschl. v. 10.06.2013 - 2 Ss 11/13 = StV 2014, 211, und OLG Celle, Beschl. v. 19.03.2013 - 32 Ss 29/13 = StV 2014, 209', *StV*, 34 (2014), 242–7

Huybreghts, G., 'The Schengen Convention and the Schengen *Acquis*: 25 Years of Evolution', *ERA Forum*, 16 (2015), 379–426

Hwang, S.-P., 'Grundrechtsschutz unter der Voraussetzung des europäischen Grundkonsenses?', *EuR*, 48 (2013), 307–23

Illuminati, G., 'The Letter of Rights: The Lack of Guarantees in the European Approach to a Common Criminal Justice System', in Arangüena Fanego, C., ed., *Garantías procesales en los procesos penales en la Unión Europea* (Valladolid: Ed. Lex Nova, 2007), 361–5

Irish Council for Civil Liberties, *Implementation of the Right of Access to a Lawyer - Training Manual* (Dublin, Irish Council for Civil Liberties, 2014)

Irmscher, T. H., 'Einzelhaft und Folterverbot', *EuGRZ*, 34 (2007), 135–41

Isiksel, T., 'European Exceptionalism and the EU's Accession to the ECHR', *EJIL*, 27 (2016), 565–89

Jackson, M., 'Freeing Soering: The ECHR, State Complicity in Torture and Jurisdiction', *EJIL*, 27 (2016), 817–30

Jahn, M., 'Fair trial als strafprozessuales Leitprinzip im Mehrebenensystem', *ZStW*, 127 (2015), 549–615

'"Parität des Wissens"? Die konventionskonforme Auslegung der Neuregelung des Akteneinsichtsrechts (§147 StPO)', in Schulz, L., Reinhart, M., and Sahan, O., eds., *Festschrift für Imme Roxin* (Heidelberg: C. F. Müller, 2012), 585–600

'Stürmt Karlsruhe die Bastille? Das BVerfG und die überlange Untersuchungshaft', *NJW*, 59 (2006), 652–4

Jarass, H. D., 'Strafrechtliche Grundrechte im Unionsrecht', *NStZ*, 32 (2012), 611–16

Jeßberger, F., 'Wenn Du nicht redest, füge ich Dir große Schmerzen zu', *Jura*, 25 (2003), 711–15

Jimeno-Bulnes, M., 'The EU Roadmap for Strengthening Procedural Rights of Suspected or Accused Persons in Criminal Proceedings', *eucrim*, 4 (2009), 157–61

Joecks, W., '§97 – [Beschlagnahmefreie Gegenstände]', in Radtke and Hohmann, *StPO Kommentar* (2011), 335–42

Johansen, S. Ø., 'The Reinterpretation of TFEU Article 344 in Opinion 2/13 and Its Potential Consequences', *GLJ*, 16 (2015), 169–78

Jörg, N., Field, S., and Brants, C., 'Are Inquisitorial and Adversarial Systems Converging?', in Fennell, P., Harding, C., Jörg, N., and Swart, B., eds., *Criminal Justice in Europe: A Comparative Study* (Oxford: Clarendon Press, 1995), 41–56

Jötten, S., *Enforced Disappearances und EMRK* (Berlin: Duncker & Humblot, 2012)

Jung, H., 'Faires Verfahren und menschenrechtswidrige Beweiserhebung', *GA*, 156 (2009), 651–6

'"Funktionsfähigkeit der Strafrechtspflege" contra "schützende Formen": ein prozessualer "Klassiker" im Lichte der Rechtsprechung des Europäischen Gerichtshofes für Menschenrechte', *GA*, 150 (2003), 191–203

'Das Inzestverbot oder der Europäische Gerichtshof für Menschenrechte auf den Spuren des Bundesverfassungsgerichts', *GA*, 159 (2012), 617–20

'Neues zum Konfrontationsrecht?', *GA*, 156 (2009), 235–40

'"Overall Fairness": Anmerkungen zu einer verfehlten Begriffsbildung', in Heger, M., Kelker, B., and Schramm, eds., *Festschrift für Kristian Kühl zum 70. Geburtstag* (Munich: Beck, 2014), 915–22

'Die Rechte von Gefangenen im Lichte der EMRK', in Donatsch, A., Forster, M., and Schwarzenegger, C., eds., *Strafrecht, Strafprozessrecht und Menschenrechte: Festschrift für Stefan Trechsel zum 65. Geburtstag* (Zurich: Schulthess, 2002), 861–8

'Die Sicherungsverwahrung auf dem Prüfstand der EMRK: Zugleich Besprechung von EGMR, Urteil vom 17.12.2009', *GA*, 157 (2010), 639–44

'Status und Schutz des Embryos: Anmerkungen zur Entscheidung des Europäischen Gerichtshofes für Menschenrechte im Falle Vo/Frankreich', in Hoyer, A., Müller, H. E., Pawlik, M., and Wolter, J., eds., *Festschrift für Friedrich-Christian Schroeder zum 70. Geburtstag* (Heidelberg: C. F. Müller, 2006), 809–18

'Strafverteidigung in Europa', *StV*, 10 (1990), 509–17

'Upgrade für die margin of appreciation?', in Callies, C., ed., *Herausforderungen an Staat und Verfassung: Liber Amicorum für Torsten Stein zum 70. Geburtstag* (Baden-Baden: Nomos, 2015), 976–87

'Zum Verbot der Vollverschleierung', *GA*, 162 (2015), 35–41

Kadelbach, S., 'Kapitel 15: Keine Strafe ohne Gesetz', in Dörr, Grote, and Marauhn, *EMRK/GG*, i (2013), 839–67

Kaiafa-Gbandi, M., 'Aktuelle Strafrechtsentwicklung in der EU und rechtsstaatliche Defizite', *ZIS*, 1 (2006), 521–36

'The Importance of Core Principles of Substantive Criminal Law for a European Criminal Policy Respecting Fundamental Rights and the Rule of Law', *EuCLR*, 1 (2011), 7–34

Karakosta, C., 'Das Prinzip ne bis in idem (gemäß Artikel 4 des Protokolls Nr. 7 zur EMRK): Ein Recht mit ungewisser Reichweite', *KritV*, 91 (2008), 73–81

Kargopoulos, A.-I., 'ECHR and the CJEU', *eucrim*, 10 (2015), 96–100

'Ne Bis In Idem "in Criminal Proceedings"', in Bergström, M., and Jonsson Cornell, A., eds., *European Police and Criminal Law Co-operation* (Oxford, Portland: Hart, 2014), 85–126

Karsai, K., 'The Legality of Criminal Law and the New Competences of the TFEU', *ZIS*, 8 (2013), 24–39

Karsai, K., and Szomora, Z., *Criminal Law in Hungary* (Alphen aan den Rijn: Kluwer, 2nd edn, 2015)

Keller, H., Fischer, A., and Kühne, D., 'Debating the Future of the ECHR after the Interlaken Conference: Two Innovative Proposals', *EJIL*, 21 (2010), 1025–48

Keller, H., and Stone Sweet, A., eds., *A Europe of Rights: The Impact of the ECHR on National Legal Systems* (Oxford: Oxford University Press, 2008)

Keown, J., 'European Court of Human Rights: Death in Strasbourg: Assisted Suicide, the Pretty Case, and the European Convention on Human Rights', *IJCL*, 1 (2003), 722–30

The Rt Hon the Lord Kerr of Tonaghmore, 'The Relationship between the Strasbourg Court and the National Courts: As Seen from the UK Supreme Court', in Ziegler, K. S., Wicks, E., and Hodson, L., eds., *The UK and European Human Rights: A Strained Relationship?* (Oxford and Portland: Hart, 2015), 31–7

Kieschke, O., *Die Praxis des EGMR und ihre Auswirkungen auf das deutsche Strafverfahrensrecht* (Berlin: Duncker & Humblot, 2003)

Kindhäuser, U., '§32', in Kindhäuser, Neumann, and Paeffgen, *Nomos Kommentar StGB*, i (2013), 1490–1534

Kinzig, J., 'Die Neuordnung des Rechts der Sicherungsverwahrung', *NJW*, 64 (2011), 177–82

'Not kennt kein Gebot?', *ZStW*, 115 (2003), 791–814

'Das Recht der Sicherungsverwahrung nach dem Urteil des EGMR in Sachen M. gegen Deutschland', *NStZ*, 30 (2010), 233–9

Kirchhof, F., 'Grundrechtsschutz durch europäische und nationale Gerichte', *NJW*, 64 (2011), 3681–6

Kirsch, S., 'Schluss mit lustig!', *StraFo*, 14 (2008), 449–58

Klein, E., 'Germany', in Gerards, J., and Fleuren, J., eds., *Implementation of the European Convention on Human Rights and of the Judgments of the ECtHR in National Case-Law: A Comparative Analysis* (Cambridge, Antwerp and Portland: Intersentia, 2014), 185–216

Kleinlein, T., 'Der EGMR und das Völkerstrafrecht im Rahmen von Art. 7 EMRK', *EuGRZ*, 37 (2010), 544–60

Klesczewski, D., 'Strafen statt Verwahren! Besprechung von EGMR, Mücke v. Deutschland, Urt. v. 17. 12. 2009, Az. 19359/04 = HRRS 2010 Nr. 1/65.', *HRRS*, 11 (2010), 394–403

Klinger, M., 'Der Sicherungshaftbefehl gem. §453c StPO im Lichte der Rechtsprechung des EGMR zum Widerruf der Strafaussetzung', *NStZ*, 32 (2012), 70–6

Klugmann, M., *Europäische Menschenrechtskonvention und antiterroristische Maßnahmen* (Frankfurt a.M. et al.: Peter Lang, 2002)

Knauer, C., and Gaul, M., 'Internal Investigations und Fair Trial: Überlegungen zu einer Anwendung des Fairnessgedankens', *NStZ*, 33 (2013), 192–4

Kniebühler, R. M., *Transnationales 'ne bis in idem': Zum Verbot der Mehrfachverfolgung in horizontaler und vertikaler Dimension* (Berlin et al.: Duncker & Humblot et al., 2005)

Koch, A., and Dorn, V., 'Verurteilung eines ehem. SS-Mannes vor dem Hintergrund deutschen und europäischen Rechts', *Jura*, 33 (2011), 690–7

Kohlbacher, U., *Verteidigung und Verteidigungsrechte unter dem Aspekt der Waffengleichheit* (Zurich: Schulthess, 1979)

Kokott, J., and Sobotta, C., 'Die Charta der Grundrechte der EU nach dem Inkrafttreten des Vertrags von Lissabon', *EuGRZ*, 37 (2010), 265–71

Koriath, H., 'Einschränkung des deutschen Notwehrrechts (§32 StGB) durch Art. 2 II a EMRK?', in Ranieri, F., ed., *Die Europäisierung der Rechtswissenschaft: Beiträge aus der Universität des Saarlandes* (Baden-Baden: Nomos, 2002), 47–60

Korn, D., *Defizite bei der Umsetzung der EMRK im deutschen Strafverfahren: V-Leute, Lockspitzel und Telefonüberwachung von Rechtsanwälten* (Berlin: Duncker & Humblot, 2005)

Kotz, P., 'Anspruch auf Dolmetsch- und Übersetzungsleistungen im Strafverfahren', *StV*, 32 (2012), 626–31

Kraatz, E., 'Gedanken zur Strafzumessungslösung bei rechtsstaatswidriger Verfahrensverzögerung', *JR*, 78 (2006), 403–9

Kraml, B., and Zeder, F., 'Die vierte Richtlinie über Beschuldigtenrechte: Unschuldsvermutung und Recht auf Anwesenheit in der Verhandlung (Richtlinie 2016/343)', *JSt*, 3 (2016), 357–61

Kraus, K., *Der Bewährungswiderruf gem. §56 f Abs. 1 Satz 1 Nr. 1 StGB und die Unschuldsvermutung: Das Urteil des Europäischen Gerichtshofs für Menchenrechte im Fall Böhmer und seine Auswirkungen* (Münster: Lit., 2007)

Krausbeck, M., *Konfrontative Zeugenbefragung: Vorgaben des Art. 6 Abs. 3 lit. d EMRK für das deutsche Strafverfahren* (Tübingen: Mohr Siebeck, 2010)

Krauß, K., *V-Leute im Strafprozess und die Europäische Menschenrechtskonvention* (Freiburg i.Br.: Ed. iuscrim, 1999)

Kreicker, H., *Art. 7 EMRK und die Gewalttaten an der deutsch-deutschen Grenze: Zu den Urteilen des Europäischen Gerichtshofs für Menschenrechte* (Baden-Baden: Nomos, 2002)

'Strafrechtliche Garantien der EMRK' in Sieber, U., Satzger, H., and Heintschel von Heinegg, B., eds., *Europäisches Strafrecht* (2014), 903–36

Krenn, C., 'Autonomy and Effectiveness as Common Concerns: A Path to ECHR Accession after Opinion 2/13', *GLJ*, 16 (2015), 147–68

Kreuzer, A., 'Neuordnung der Sicherungsverwahrung', *StV*, 31 (2011), 122–32

'Sicherungsverwahrung nach Jugendstrafrecht angesichts divergierender Urteile des BGH und EGMR: Zugleich eine Besprechung des Urteils des BGH vom 9. 3. 2010 – 1 StR 554/09', *NStZ*, 30 (2010), 473–9

Kreuzer, A., and Bartsch, T., 'Teilbewältigung der Diskrepanz zwischen BVerfG und EGMR zur nachträglichen Verlängerung oder Anordnung der Sicherungsverwahrung', *StV*, 31 (2011), 472–80

Krey, V., 'Zur Einschränkung des Notwehrrechts bei der Verteidigung von Sachgütern', *JZ*, 34 (1979), 702–15

Krommendijk, J., 'The Use of ECtHR Case Law by the Court of Justice after Lisbon: The View of Luxembourg Insiders', *MaastJECompl*, 22 (2015), 812–35

Kromrey, H., and Morgenstern, C., 'Auslieferung bei drohender lebenslanger Freiheitsstrafe ohne Aussetzungsmöglichkeit', *ZIS*, 9 (2014), 704–15

Krumm, C., 'Bewährungswiderruf trotz Unschuldsvermutung', *NJW*, 58 (2005), 1832–6

Krzyżanowska-Mierzewska, M., 'The Reception Process in Poland and Slovakia', in Keller, H., and Stone Sweet, A., eds., *A Europe of Rights: The Impact of the ECHR on National Legal Systems* (Oxford: Oxford University Press, 2008), 531–602

Kubiciel, M., 'Das deutsche Inzestverbot vor den Schranken des EGMR', *ZIS*, 7 (2012), 282–9

Kühl, K., 'Der Einfluss der EMRK auf das Strafrecht und Strafverfahrensrecht der Bundesrepublik Deutschland (Teil II)', *ZStW*, 100 (1988), 601–44

'Der Einfluss der Menschenrechte und Grundfreiheiten der EMRK auf das deutsche und europäische Strafrecht', in Müller-Dietz, H., ed., *Festschrift für Heike Jung zum 65. Geburtstag am 23. April 2007* (Baden-Baden: Nomos, 2007), 433–44

Kühne, H.-H., 'Anmerkung zu BGH, Beschluss v. 26.8.2003 – 5 StR 145/03', *JZ*, 59 (2004), 743–4
'Anmerkung zu BGH, Urteil v. 10.06.1999 – 4 StR 87/98', *StV*, 19 (1999), 480–1
'Anmerkung zu BVerfG, Beschluss v. 15.12.2015 – 2 BvR 2735/14', *StV*, 36 (2016), 299–302
'Anmerkung zu EuGH, Urteil v. 28.9.2006 – Rs. C-150/05', *JZ*, 62 (2007), 247–8
'Anmerkung zu EuGH, Urteil v. 9.3.2006 – Rs. C-436/04', *JZ*, 61 (2006), 1019–1021
'Artikel 6 EMRK', in Pabel and Schmahl, *Internationaler Kommentar zur EMRK* (2013)
'Europäische Methodenvielfalt und nationale Umsetzung von Entscheidungen europäischer Gerichte', *GA*, 152 (2005), 195–214
Kukavica, J., and Fikfak, V., 'Strasbourg's U-Turn on Independence as Part of an Effective Investigation under Art. 2', *CLJ*, 74 (2015), 415–19
Kuty, F., 'Le sort à réserver aux actes d'un juge d'instruction légitimement suspecté de partialité', *RevDPC*, 87 (2007), 365–77
Labayle, H., and de Bruycker, P., *Towards the Negotiation and Adoption of the Stockholm Programme's Successor for the Period 2015–2019* (Brussels: EP, 2013), available at www.europarl.europa.eu/RegData/etudes/etudes/join/2013/493015/IPOL-LIBE_ET%282013%29493015_EN.pdf, last accessed 27 January 2018
Ladiges, M., 'Die notstandsbedingte Tötung von Unbeteiligten im Fall des §14 Abs. 3 LuftSiG: Ein Plädoyer für die Rechtfertigungslösung', *ZIS*, 3 (2008), 129–40
Lafourcade, M., *La réouverture des procédures juridictionnelles consécutives à un arrêt de la Cour européenne des droits de l'homme: L'éclairage français* (Paris: L.G.D.J., 2014)
Lageot, C., 'France', in Gerards, J., and Fleuren, J., eds., *Implementation of the European Convention on Human Rights and of the Judgments of the ECtHR in National Case-Law: A Comparative Analysis* (Cambridge, Antwerp and Portland: Intersentia, 2014), 145–84
Lagodny, O., 'Artikel 2 EMRK', in Pabel and Schmahl, *Internationaler Kommentar zur EMRK* (2013)
'Teileuropäisches "ne bis in idem" durch Art. 54 des Schengener Durchführungsübereinkommens (SDÜ)', *NStZ*, 17 (1997), 265–6
'Viele Strafgewalten und nur ein transnationales ne-bis-in-idem?', in Donatsch, A., Forster, M., and Schwarzenegger, C., eds., *Strafrecht, Strafprozessrecht und Menschenrechte: Festschrift für Stefan Trechsel zum 65. Geburtstag* (Zurich: Schulthess, 2002), 253–68
Lamberigts, S., 'The Directive on the Presumption of Innocence', *eucrim*, 11 (2016), 36–42
Lambert Abdelgawad, E., and Weber, A., 'The Reception Process in France and Germany', in Keller, H., and Stone Sweet, A., eds., *A Europe of Rights: The*

Impact of the ECHR on National Legal Systems (Oxford: Oxford University Press, 2008), 107–64

Last, C., '81. EGMR v. 12.3.2003 – Öcalan', in Menzel, Pierlings, and Hoffmann, *Völkerrechtsprechung* (2005), 496–500

Laue, C., 'Die Sicherungsverwahrung auf dem europäischen Prüfstand: Zugleich eine Anmerkung zu EGMR, M. vs. Deutschland v. 17. 12. 2009 – 19359/04 (in diesem Heft Seite 218 ff.)', *JR*, 82 (2010), 198–204

Lawrence, I., 'Punishment without Law: How Ends Justify the Means in Marital Rape', *DenningLJ*, 18 (2006), 37–50

Łazowski, A., and Wessel, R. A., 'When Caveats Turn into Locks: Opinion 2/13 on Accession of the European Union to the ECHR', *GLJ*, 16 (2015), 179–212

Leach, P., and Donald, A., 'Russia Defies Strasbourg: Is Contagion Spreading?', *EJIL:Talk!*, 19 December 2015, at www.ejiltalk.org/russia-defies-strasbourg-is-contagion-spreading, last accessed 27 January 2018

Lelieur, J., 'Coup d'arrêt jurisprudentiel au développement de l'espace de liberté, de sécurité et de justice', *AJP*, 11 (2014), 425–8

'"Transnationalising" Ne Bis In Idem: How the Rule of Ne Bis In Idem Reveals the Principle of Personal Legal Certainty', *ULR*, 9 (2013), 198–210

'L'Union européenne face aux coflits de compétences pénales', in Brach-Thiel, D., and Fourment, F., eds., *Questions de droit pénal international, européen et comparé: Mélanges en l'honneur du Professeur Alain Fournier* (Nancy: Presses Universitaires, 2014), 257–93

'Le dernier mot de la Cour de cassation dans l'affaire Krombach, degré zéro de la coopération judiciaire pénal dans l'UE', *AJP*, 11 (2014), 365–7

Lelieur-Fischer, J., Comments on the Green Paper on Conflicts of Jurisdiction and the Principle of Ne Bis In Idem in Criminal Proceedings (March 2006), available at https://www.mpicc.de/files/pdf2/comments_green_paper_nebisinidem.pdf, last accessed 27 January 2018

Lenaerts, K., 'Die EU-Grundrechtecharta: Anwendbarkeit und Auslegung', *EuR*, 47 (2012), 3–17

Lepsius, O., 'Human Dignity and the Downing of Aircraft: The German Federal Constitutional Court Strikes down a Prominent Anti-terrorism Provision in the New Air-Transport Security Act', *GLJ*, 7 (2006), 761–76

Letsas, G., 'The Truth in Autonomous Concepts: How to Interpret the ECHR', *EJIL*, 15 (2004), 279–305

Leverick, F., *Killing in Self-Defence* (Oxford: Oxford University Press, 2006)

Liebau, T., *'Ne bis in idem' in Europa: Zugleich ein Beitrag zum Kartellsanktionenrecht in der EU und zur Anrechnung drittstaatlicher Kartellsanktionen* (Berlin et al.: Berliner Wissenschafts-Verlag, 2005)

Ligeti, K., 'Judicial Control in the System of Mutual Recognition: The CJEU's Judgment in Mantello', *KritV*, 93 (2010), 380–90

'Rules on the Application of Ne Bis In Idem in the EU', *eucrim*, 4 (2009), 37–43

Lindner, J. F., 'Grundrechtsschutz in Europa: System einer Kollisionsdogmatik', *EuR*, 42 (2007), 160–93

'Zur grundsätzlichen Bedeutung des Protokolls über die Anwendung der Grundrechtecharta auf Polen und das Vereinigte Königreich: zugleich ein Beitrag zur Auslegung von Art. 51 EGC', *EuR*, 43 (2008), 786–99

Loos, F., 'Probleme der beschränkten Sperrwirkung strafprozessualer Entscheidungen', *JZ*, 33 (1978), 592–600

Lorenzmeier, S., 'Kartellrechtliche Geldbußen als strafrechtliche Anklage im Sinne der Europäischen Menschenrechtskonvention', *ZIS*, 3 (2008), 20–30

Lorz, R. A., and Sauer, H., 'Wann genau steht Art. 3 EMRK einer Auslieferung oder Ausweisung entgegen?', *EuGRZ*, 37 (2010), 389–407

Lubig, S., and Sprenger, J., 'Beweisverwertungsverbote aus dem Fairnessgebot des Art. 6 EMRK in der Rechtsprechung des EGMR', *ZIS*, 3 (2008), 433–40

Lüderssen, K., 'Kriegsrecht in Deutschland', *StV*, 25 (2005), 106–7

McDermott, Y., 'General Duty to Ensure the Right to a Fair and Expeditious Trial', in Sluiter, G., Friman, H., Linton, S., Vasiliev, S., and Zappalá, S., eds., *International Criminal Procedure* (Oxford: Oxford University Press, 2013), 770–818

McGoldrick, D., 'A Defence of the Margin of Appreciation and an Argument for Its Application by the HR', *ICLQ*, 65 (2016), 21–60

Macken, C., *Counter-terrorism and the Detention of Suspected Terrorists: Preventative Detention and International Human Rights Law* (London et al.: Routledge, 2011)

Maffei, S., *The European Right to Confrontation in Criminal Proceedings: Absent, Anonymous and Vulnerable Witnesses* (Groningen: Europa Law Publ., 2006)

Magiera, S., 'Bürgerrechte und justizielle Grundrechte', in Merten, D., and Papier, H.-J., eds., *Handbuch der Grundrechte in Deutschland und Europa,* vi/1: *Europäische Grundrechte I* (Heidelberg et al.: C. F. Müller, 2010), 1031–82

Mahler, F., 'Keine Sperrung der Vertrauensperson gemäß §96 StPO analog bei gleichzeitiger Verletzung des Konfrontationsrechts aus Art. 6 III 3 d EMRK', *HRRS*, 14 (2013), 333–7

Maier, S., 'Teilrechtskraft bei Aufhebung des Strafausspruchs', *NStZ*, 30 (2010), 650–2

Mangiaracina, A., 'La revisione del giudicato penale a seguito di una pronuncia della Corte Europea dei Diritti dell'Uomo', *RIDPP*, 49 (2006), 982–1009

'Verso l´affermazione del ne bis in idem nello "Spazio gindiziario europeo"', *LP*, 26 (2006), 631–51

Mansdörfer, M., *Das Prinzip des ne bis in idem im europäischen Strafrecht* (Berlin: Duncker & Humblot, 2004)

'Das Recht des Beschuldigten auf ein unverzögertes Ermittlungsverfahren', *GA*, 157 (2010), 153–68

Marchuk, I., 'Flexing Muscles (Yet Again): The Russian Constitutional Court's Defiance of the Authority of the ECtHR in the Yukos Case', *EJIL:Talk!*, 13

February 2017, at www.ejiltalk.org/flexing-muscles-yet-again-the-russian-constitutional-courts-defiance-of-the-authority-of-the-ecthr-in-the-yukos-case, last accessed 27 January 2018

Martinico, G., 'Is the European Convention Going to Be "Supreme"? A Comparative-Constitutional Overview of ECHR and EU Law before National Courts', *EJIL*, 23 (2012), 401–24

Masterman, R., 'The United Kingdom', in Gerards, J., and Fleuren, J., eds., *Implementation of the European Convention on Human Rights and of the Judgments of the ECtHR in National Case-Law: A Comparative Analysis* (Cambridge, Antwerp and Portland: Intersentia, 2014), 297–331

Masuch, T., 'Zur fallübergreifenden Bindungswirkung von Urteilen des EGMR', *NVwZ*, 19 (2000), 1266–8

Matscher, F., 'Probleme der österreichischen Strafrechtspflege im Lichte der neueren Rechtsprechung der Straßburger Konventionsorgane', *ÖRiZ*, 71 (1993), 154–66

Matt, H., 'Editorial', *eucrim*, 12 (2017), 1

'Nemo tenetur se ipsum accusare: Europäische Perspektiven', *GA*, 153 (2006), 323–8

Matz-Lück, N., 'Europäische Rechtsakte und nationaler Grundrechtsschutz', in Matz-Lück, N., and Hong, M., eds., *Grundrechte und Grundfreiheiten im Mehrebenensystem: Konkurrenzen und Interferenzen* (Heidelberg et al.: Springer, 2012), 161–202

Mavronicola, N., 'Crime, Punishment and Article 3 ECHR: Puzzles and Prospects of Applying an Absolute Right in a Penal Context', *HRLR*, 15 (2015), 721–43

Mayer, F. C., 'Einleitung', in Karpenstein, U., and Mayer, F. C., *EMRK: Konvention zum Schutz der Menschenrechte und Grundfreiheiten: Kommentar* (Munich: C. H. Beck, 2nd edn, 2015), 1–37

'Der Vertrag von Lissabon und die Grundrechte', *EuR*, 44 (2009), *Beiheft 1*, 87–102

Medina, C., *The American Convention on Human Rights: Crucial Rights and Their Theory and Practice* (Cambridge, Antwerp and Portland: Intersentia 2014)

Mehde, V., 'Gespaltener Grundrechtsschutz in der EU? Zur Bedeutung der Sonderregelung für Polen und das Vereinigte Königreich', *EuGRZ*, 35 (2008), 269–74

Mellech, K., *Die Rezeption der EMRK sowie der Urteile des EGMR in der französischen und deutschen Rechtsprechung* (Tübingen: Mohr Siebeck, 2012)

Mensching, C., 'Artikel 10 EMRK', in Karpenstein, U., and Mayer, F. C., *EMRK: Konvention zum Schutz der Menschenrechte und Grundfreiheiten: Kommentar* (Munich: C. H. Beck, 2nd edn, 2015), 310–38

Merkel, G., 'Anmerkung zu BVerfG, Beschluss v. 20.6.2012 – 2 BvR 1048/11', *ZIS*, 7 (2012), 521–3

Merkel, R., and Scheinfeld, J., 'Ne bis in idem in der Europäischen Union: Zum Streit um das "Vollstreckungselement"', *ZIS*, 7 (2012), 206–13

Merrills, J. G., *The Development of International Law by the European Court of Human Rights* (Manchester: Manchester University Press, 2nd edn, 1993)

Meyer, F., 'Die Bindung der EU-Mitgliedstaaten an die Grundrechtecharta in einer europäisierten Strafrechtspflege', *ZStW*, 128 (2016), 1089–1140

'Der EGMR als Tatsacheninstanz und das Recht auf Wahrheit', in Stuckenberg, C.-F., and Gärditz, K. F., eds., *Strafe und Prozess im freiheitlichen Rechtsstaat: Festschrift für Hans-Ulrich Paeffgen zum 70. Geburtstag am 2. Juli 2015* (Berlin: Duncker & Humblot, 2015), 793–814

'Der Grundsatz gegenseitigen Vertrauens: Konzeptualisierung und Zukunftsperspektiven eines neuen Verfassungsprinzips', *EuR*, 52 (2017), 163–86

'Die "sole or decisive"-Regel zur Würdigung nicht konfrontierter Zeugenaussagen: Not So Decisive Anymore', *HRRS*, 13 (2012), 117–20

Meyer, F., and Wohlers, W., 'Tatprovokation quo vadis: zur Verbindlichkeit der Rechtsprechung des EGMR (auch) für das deutsche Strafprozessrecht', *JZ*, 70 (2015), 761–70

Meyer-Goßner, L., '§359', in Meyer-Goßner and Schmitt, *StPO* (2016), 1490–1500

Meyer-Ladewig, J., 'Ein neuer ständiger Europäischer Gerichtshof für Menschenrechte: das 11. Protokoll zur EMRK', *NJW*, 48 (1995), 2813–17

Meyer-Ladewig, J., and Petzold, H., '50 Jahre Europäischer Gerichtshof für Menschenrechte', *NJW*, 62 (2009), 3749–54

Meysman, M., 'Quo Vadis with Vulnerable Defendants in the EU?', *EuCLR*, 4 (2014), 179–87

Michaelsen, C., 'The Renaissance of Non-refoulement? The Othman (Abu Qatada) Decision of ECHR', *ICLQ*, 61 (2012), 750–65

'"From Strasbourg, with Love": Preventive Detention before the German Federal Constitutional Court and the ECHR', *HRLR*, 12 (2012), 148–67

Milanovic, M., 'Foreign Surveillance and Human Rights, Part 3: Models of Extraterritorial Application', *EJIL:Talk!*, 27 November 2013, at www.ejiltalk.org/foreign-surveillance-and-human-rights-part-3-models-of-extraterritorial-application, last accessed 27 January 2018

'Strasbourg Judgment on the Beslan Hostage Crisis', *EJIL:Talk!*, 13 April 2017, at www.ejiltalk.org/strasbourg-judgment-on-the-beslan-hostage-crisis, last accessed 27 January 2018

'UK Investigatory Powers Tribunal Rules That Non-UK Residents Have No Right to Privacy under the ECHR', *EJIL:Talk!*, 18 May 2016, at www.ejiltalk.org/uk-investigatory-powers-tribunal-rules-that-non-uk-residents-have-no-right-to-privacy-under-the-echr, last accessed 27 January 2018

'UK to Derogate from the ECHR in Armed Conflict', *EJIL:Talk!*, 5 October 2016, at www.ejiltalk.org/uk-to-derogate-from-the-echr-in-armed-conflict, last accessed 27 January 2018

Minelli, L. A., 'Faires Verfahren im Sinne von Art. 6 Abs. 1 der EMRK', in Europäische Anwaltsvereinigung, *Das faire Verfahren nach Art. 6 EMRK. 28. Tagung der DACH in Begrenz vom 15. bis 17. Mai 2003* (Cologne: Schmidt et al., 2005), 29–50

Mitsilegas, V., 'Judicial Concepts of Trust in Europe's Multi-level Security Governance', *eucrim*, 10 (2015), 90–5

Moliner-Dubost, M., 'Le point sur la compatibilité du placement à l'isolement des détenus avec l'article 3 de la CEDH', *AJP*, 4 (2007), 160–3

Morgenstern, C., 'Krank – gestört – gefährlich: Wer fällt unter §1 Therapieunterbringungsgesetz und Art. 5 Abs. 1 lit. e EMRK?', *ZIS*, 6 (2011), 974–81

'Die Stärkung prozessualer Garantien im Recht der Untersuchungshaft in Deutschland und Polen', *ZIS*, 6 (2011), 240–7

Morsch, A., 'Die Verfahrensgarantien des Art. 6 der EMRK und das deutsche Steuerrecht', in Müller-Dietz, H., ed., *Festschrift für Heike Jung zum 65. Geburtstag am 23. April 2007* (Baden-Baden: Nomos, 2007), 601–20

Morscher, S., and Christ, P., 'Grundrecht auf öffentliche Verhandlung gem. Art. 6 EMRK', *EuGRZ*, 37 (2010), 272–80

Mosbacher, A., 'Straßburg locuta: §329 I StPO finita?', *NStZ*, 33 (2013), 312–15

Moscarini, P., 'Il silenzio dell'imputato sul fatto prorio secondo la Corte di Strasburgo e nell'esperienza italiana', *RIDPP*, 49 (2006), 611–47

Mosiek, M., 'Fremdrechtsanwendung: quo vadis?', *StV*, 28 (2008), 94–100

Mowbray, A., 'Subsidiarity and the EChR', *HRLR*, 15 (2015), 313–41

Moynihan, H., 'Principle or Pragmatism? The Supreme Court's Judgment in Keyu and Others v Secretary of State for Foreign & Commonwealth Affairs', *EJIL: Talk!*, 24 December 2015, at www.ejiltalk.org/principle-or-pragmatism-the-supreme-courts-judgment-in-keyu-and-others-v-secretary-of-state-for-foreign-commonwealth-affairs, last accessed 27 January 2018

Müller, H. E., 'Die Sicherungsverwahrung, das Grundgesetz und die Europäische Menschenrechtskonvention', *StV*, 30 (2010), 207–12

V. Müller, V. M., 'Die Verfassungsmäßigkeit des §66 b Abs. 3 StGB im Licht der Entscheidung des EGMR vom 17.12.2009', *EuR*, 46 (2011), 418–30

Müller-Terpitz, R., '80. EGMR v. 29.4.2002 – Pretty', in Menzel, Pierlings, and Hoffmann, *Völkerrechtsprechung* (2005), 489–96

Mylonopoulos, C., 'Internationalisierung des Strafrechts und Strafrechtsdogmatik. Legitimationsdefizit und Anarchie als Hauptcharakteristika der Strafrechtsnormen mit internationalem Einschlag', *ZStW*, 121 (2009), 68–93

'Strafrechtsdogmatik in Europa nach dem Vertrag von Lissabon: Zur materiellen Legitimation des Europäischen Strafrechts', *ZStW*, 123 (2011), 633–50

Nack, A., 'Deutsches Strafverfahrensrecht und Europäische Menschenrechtskonvention', in Boetticher, A., ed., *NJW-Sonderheft zur Vollendung des 65. Lebensjahres von Gerhard Schäfer am 18. Oktober 2002* (Munich et al.: C. H. Beck, 2002), 46–52

Nagler, A., 'Verteidigung gegen im Ausland gewonnene Ermittlungsergebnisse', *StV*, 33 (2013), 324–30

Nanopoulos, E., 'Killing Two Birds with One Stone? The Court of Justice's Opinion on the EU's Accession to the ECHR', *CLJ*, 74 (2015), 185–8

Naucke, W., 'Bürgerliche Kriminalität, Staatskriminalität und das Rückwirkungsverbot', in Donatsch, A., Forster, M., and Schwarzenegger, C., eds., *Strafrecht, Strafprozessrecht und Menschenrechte: Festschrift für Stefan Trechsel zum 65. Geburtstag* (Zurich: Schulthess, 2002), 505–16

Naumann, K., 'Art. 52 Abs. 3 GrCH zwischen Kohärenz des europäischen Grundrechtsschutzes und Autonomie des Unionsrechts', *EuR*, 43 (2008), 424–35

Neagu, N., 'The Ne Bis in Idem Principle in the Interpretation of European Courts: Towards Uniform Interpretation', *LJIL*, 25 (2012), 955–77

Nehm, K., 'Zur Reichweite des "ne bis in idem"-Prinzips in Art. 54 SDÜ und den Möglichkeiten seiner Fortentwicklung im Rahmen der Europäischen Union', in Pilgermair, W., ed., *Festschrift für Herbert Steininger zum 70. Geburtstag* (Vienna: Verlag Österreich, 2003), 369–86

Nergelius, J., *Constitutional Law in Sweden* (Alphen aan den Rijn: Kluwer Law International, 2011)

Nestler, N., 'Das Ende des Vollstreckungselements im (teil-)europäischen Doppelbestrafungsverbot?', *HRRS*, 14 (2013), 337–44

Neubacher, F., 'Der Bewährungswiderruf wegen einer neuen Straftat und die Unschuldsvermutung', *GA*, 151 (2004), 402–17

Niblock, R., 'Mutual Recognition, Mutual Trust? Detention Conditions and Deferring an EAW', *NJECL*, 7 (2016), 250–1

Niedobitek, M., 'Entwicklung und allgemeine Grundsätze', in Merten, D., and Papier, H.-J., eds., *Handbuch der Grundrechte in Deutschland und Europa*, vi/1: *Europäische Grundrechte I* (Heidelberg et al.: C. F. Müller, 2010), 923–78

Nieto Martín, A., 'La armonización del Derecho Penal ante el Tratado de Lisboa y el programa de Estocolmo', *RP*, 27 (2011), 78–82

Nita, B., 'Orzeczenie ETPCz jako podstawa wznowienia postępowania sądowego', *Europejski Przegląd Sądowy*, 5 (2010), No. 9, 4–10

Norouzi, A., 'Folter in Nothilfe: geboten?', *JA*, 37 (2005), 306–10

Obwexer, W., 'Der Beitritt der EU zur EMRK: Rechtsgrundlagen, Rechtsfragen und Rechtsfolgen', *EuR*, 47 (2012), 115–48

Ockelton, M., 'Article 8 ECHR, the UK and Strasbourg: Compliance, Cooperation or Clash? A Judicial Perspective', in Ziegler, K. S., Wicks, E., and Hodson, L., eds., *The UK and European Human Rights: A Strained Relationship?* (Oxford and Portland: Hart, 2015), 216–24

Ogorek, M., 'Anwendungsbereich der EU-Grundrechte-Charta: Inhalt des Grundsatzes "ne bis in idem"', *JA*, 45 (2013), 956–9

Ohler, C., 'Grundrechtliche Bindungen der Mitgliedstaaten nach Art. 51 GRCh', *NVwZ*, 32 (2013), 1433–8

Okresek, W., 'Die Umsetzung der EGMR-Urteile und ihre Überwachung', *EuGRZ*, 30 (2003), 168–74

Ostendorf, H., and Petersen, S., 'Nachträgliche Sicherungsverwahrung im Jugendstrafrecht. Rechtspolitische Folgen der Entscheidung des EGMR', *ZRP*, 43 (2010), 245–9

Oubiña Barbolla, S., 'Dilaciones indebidas', *Eunomia: Revista en Cultura de la Legalidad*, 10 (abril–septiembre 2016), 250–64

Pabel, K., '§19 Justizgrundrechte', in Grabenwarter, C. ed., *Europäischer Grundrechteschutz* (Baden-Baden: Nomos, 2014), 807–47

'86. EGMR v. 15.7.2002 – Kalashnikov', in Menzel, Pierlings and Hoffmann, *Völkerrechtsprechung* (2005), 516–21

Pache, E., and Rösch, F., 'Europäischer Grundrechtsschutz nach Lissabon: Die Rolle der EMRK und der Grundrechtecharta in der EU', *EuZW*, 19 (2008), 519–22

'Die neue Grundrechtsordnung der EU nach dem Vertrag von Lissabon', *EuR*, 44 (2009), 769–89

Paeffgen, H.-U., 'Zur historischen Entwicklung des "Beschleunigungsdenkens" im Straf(prozeß)recht', *GA*, 161 (2014), 275–93

Papier, H.-J., 'Umsetzung und Wirkung der Entscheidungen des Europäischen Gerichtshofs für Menschenrechte aus der Perspektive der nationalen deutschen Gerichte', *EuGRZ*, 33 (2006), 1–3

Paramonova, S., and Bogush, G., 'Neue Entwicklungen im Strafprozessrecht Russlands', *ZStW*, 125 (2013), 703–28

Parlato, L., 'La revisione del giudicato penale a seguito di pronuncia della Corte Europea dei Diritti dell'Uomo', *RIDPP*, 49 (2006), 1010–42

Paul, C., *Das Abwesenheitsverfahren als rechtsstaatliches Problem: Rechtsvergleichende Untersuchung deutscher, englischer, französischer, niederländischer und österreichischer Regelungen angesichts derRechtssprechung des Europäischen Gerichtshofs für Menschenrechte* (Frankfurt a.M. et al.: Peter Lang, 2007)

Paulus, A. L., 'Gedanken zur Verfassungskontrolle der Europäischen Union aus völkerrechtlicher Sicht', in Bouffier, V., Horn, H.-D., Poseck, R., Radtke, H., and Safferling, C., eds., *Grundgesetz und Europa: Liber Amicorum für Herbert Landau zum Ausscheiden aus dem Bundesverfassungsgericht* (Tübingen: Mohr Siebeck, 2016), 269–82

Pauly, J., 'Anmerkung zu EGMR, Urteil v. 3.10.2002 – 37568/97, Böhmer v. Deutschland', *StV*, 23 (2003), 85–6

'Anmerkung zu EGMR, Urteil vom 10.11.2005 – Individualbeschwerde Nr. 65745/01 – (Rechtssache Dzelili./. Deutschland)', *StV*, 26 (2006), 480–1

Payter, A., Humpherson, P., Darlow, A., Hehir, C., and Lloyd, B., 'Procedural Safeguards: The Rights of Suspects, Defendants, and Victims', in Atkinson, D., ed., *EU Law in Criminal Practice* (Oxford: Oxford University Press, 2013), 93–145

Pedain, A., 'The Human Rights Dimension of the Diane Pretty Case', *CLJ*, 62 (2003), 181–206

Peers, S., 'The EU Charter of Rights and the Right to Equality', *ERA Forum*, 11 (2011), 571–84

'The EU's Accession to the ECHR: The Dream Becomes a Nightmare', *GLJ*, 16 (2015), 213–22

Peglau, J., 'Anmerkung zu BGH, Vorlagebeschluss v. 23.8.2007 – 3 StR 50/07', *NJW*, 60 (2007), 3298–9

'Bewährungswiderruf und Unschuldsvermutung', *NStZ*, 24 (2004), 248–52

'Das BVerfG und die Sicherungsverwahrung: Konsequenzen für Praxis und Gesetzgebung', *NJW*, 64 (2011), 1924–7

'Unschuldsvermutung und Widerruf der Strafaussetzung zur Bewährung: Die neue Rechtsprechung des EGMR', *ZRP*, 36 (2003), 242–4

'Verschärfung des Rechts der Sicherungsverwahrung (§67d Abs. 3 StGB i.d.F. des SexualdelikteBekG) auf dem Prüfstand des EGMR', *jurisPR-StrafR*, 4 (2010), No. 2

Pellonpää, M., 'Der EGMR und der Aufbau des Rechtsstaats in den neuen Demokratien', in Donatsch, A., Forster, M., and Schwarzenegger, C., eds., *Strafrecht, Strafprozessrecht und Menschenrechte: Festschrift für Stefan Trechsel zum 65. Geburtstag* (Zurich: Schulthess, 2002), 79–92

Penkuhn, C., and Brill, S., 'Aktuelle Entwicklungen in der Rechtsprechung des EGMR mit Bezug zum deutschen Strafverfahren', *JuS*, 56 (2016), 682–6

Perron, W., 'Foltern in Notwehr?', in Heinrich, B., Hilgendorf, E., Mitsch, W., and Sternberg-Lieben, D., eds., *Festschrift für Ulrich Weber zum 70. Geburtstag* (Bielefeld: Gieseking, 2004), 143–54

'Rechtsvergleichende Betrachtungen zur Notwehr', in Arnold, J., Burkhardt, B., Gropp, W., Heine, G., Koch, H.-G., Lagodny, O., Perron, W., and Walther, S., eds., *Menschengerechtes Strafrecht: Festschrift für Albin Eser zum 70. Geburtstag* (Munich: C. H. Beck, 2005), 1019–40

'§32: Notwehr', in Schönke, A., Schröder, H., and Eser, A., eds., *Strafgesetzbuch: Kommentar* (Munich: C. H. Beck, 29th edn, 2014), 641–73

Peters, A., *Einführung in die Europäische Menschenrechtskonvention* (Munich: C. H. Beck, 2003)

Peukert, W., 'Artikel 5–6', in Frowein and Peukert, *EMRK-Kommentar* (2009), 140–268

'Die Bedeutung der Europäischen Menschenrechtskonvention (EMRK) für den Strafprozess', in Strafverteidigervereinigungen, eds., *Reform oder Roll-Back? Weichenstellung für das Straf- und Strafprozessrecht, 21. Strafverteidigertag vom 11.–13. April 1997 in Kassel* (Cologne: Ed. Der andere Buchladen, 1997), 231–46

Piattoli, B., 'Diritti fondamentali: obiettivi e programmi dell'UE in materia di giustizia penale', *DPP*, 13 (2007), 548–51

Pierini, J. P., 'Verletzungen der EMRK-Verfahrensgarantien und Wiedergutmachung am Beispiel des italienischen Abwesenheitsverfahrens', *ZStW*, 125 (2013), 951–73

Pinto de Albuquerque, P., and van Aaken, A., 'Punitive Damages in Strasbourg', in van Aaken, A., and Motoc, I., eds., *The ECHR and General International Law* (Oxford: Oxford University Press, forthcoming), available at https://papers.ssrn.com/sol3/papers.cfm?abstract_id=2781397, last accessed 27 January 2018

Plaza Garcia, P., 'Accession of the EU to the ECHR: Issues Raised with Regard to EU Acts on CFSP Matters', *ERA Forum*, 16 (2015), 481–94

Plöckinger, O., 'Europäisches "Ne bis in idem"', *JSt*, 4 (2003), 129

Plöckinger, O., and Leidenmühler, F., 'Zum Verbot doppelter Strafverfolgung nach Art. 54 SDÜ 1990', *wistra*, 22 (2003), 81–8

Plowden, P., and Kerrigan, K., 'Cards on the Table? Part 1', *NLJ*, 151 (2001), 735–6

Pohlreich, E., 'Die Rechtsprechung des EGMR zum Vollzug von Straf- und Untersuchungshaft', *NStZ*, 31 (2011), 560–70

Polakiewicz, J., 'Durchsetzung von EMRK-Standards mit Hilfe des EU-Rechts?', *EuGRZ*, 37 (2010), 11–20

Pollähne, H., 'Zur Erledigung der Sicherungsverwahrung gem. Art. 316e Abs. 3 EGStGB', *ZJS*, 4 (2011), 216–21

'Europäische Rechtssicherheit gegen Deutsches Sicherheitsrecht', *KJ*, 43 (2010), 255–69

'Internationale Standards gegen föderalen Wildwuchs? Neue Perspektiven für das Jugendstrafvollzugsrecht nach der BVerfG-Entscheidung', *StV*, 27 (2007), 553–8

Pollicino, O., 'The European Court of Human Rights and the Italian Constitutional Court: No "Groovy Kind of Love"', in Ziegler, K. S., Wicks, E., and Hodson, L., eds., *The UK and European Human Rights: A Strained Relationship?* (Oxford and Portland: Hart, 2015), 361–77

Pösl, M., 'Die Sicherungsverwahrung im Fokus von EGMR, BVerfG und BGH', *ZJS*, 4 (2011), 132–46

Pösl, M., and Dürr, A., 'Germany's System of Preventive Detention Considered through the European Court of Human Rights and the German Federal Constitutional Court', *EuCLR*, 2 (2012), 158–81

Postberg, R., *Das Zusammenwirken von EMRK, Grundgesetz und EU-Grundrechtecharta anhand des Art. 52 III und des Art. 53 der Charta: Eine vergleichende Untersuchung zum Schutz des Privat- und Familienlebens* (Bonn: Universität Bonn, 2008)

Prill, F., *Präventivhaft zur Terrorismusbekämpfung* (Munich: Utz, 2010)

Prosenjak, D., *Der Folterbegriff nach Art. 3 EMRK* (Hamburg: Kovač, 2011)

Puppinck, G., and de La Hougue, C., 'The Right to Assisted Suicide in the Case Law of the European Court of Human Rights,' *IJHR*, 18 (2014), 735–55

Quarthal, B., 'Nachträglich verlängerte Sicherungsverwahrung und der EGMR: Zur innerstaatlichen Rechtswirkung der Europäischen Konvention für Menschenrechte', *Jura*, 33 (2011), 495–9

Raba, K, 'The Accession of the EU to the ECHR: Overview of the Accession Agreement', *ERA Forum*, 14 (2013), 557–72

Rabe, H.-J., 'Grundrechtsbindung der Mitgliedstaaten', *NJW*, 66 (2013), 1407–9

Rackow, J., 'From Conflict to Cooperation: The Relationship between Karlsruhe and Strasbourg', in Ziegler, K. S., Wicks, E., and Hodson, L., eds., *The UK and European Human Rights: A Strained Relationship?* (Oxford and Portland: Hart, 2015), 379–99

Radtke, H. 'Anmerkung zu BGH, Beschluss v. 28.2.2001 - 2StR 458/00 (LG Gießen), *NStZ*, 21 (2001), 662–5

'Anmerkung zu EuGH, Urteil v. 9.3.2006 – C-436/04', *NStZ*, 28 (2008), 162–4

'Der Begriff der "Tat" im prozessualen Sinne in Europa', in Schneider, H., Kahlo, M., Klesczewski, D., and Schumann, H., eds., *Festschrift für Manfred Seebode zum 70. Geburtstag am 15. September 2008* (Berlin: de Gruyter, 2008), 297–316

'Der Grundsatz "Ne bis in idem" und Jurisdiktionskonflikte', in Böse, *Europäisches Strafrecht* (2013), 459–94

'Konventionswidrigkeit des Vollzugs erstmaliger Sicherungsverwahrung nach Ablauf der früheren Höchstfrist? Innerstaatliche Wirkungen und Folgen des Urteils des EGMR vom 17.12.2009', *NStZ*, 30 (2010), 537–46

'Der strafprozessuale Tatbegriff auf europäischer und nationaler Ebene', *NStZ*, 32 (2012), 479–84

'Schuldgrundsatz und Sicherungsverwahrung: Freiheitsgarantien im zweispurigen Sanktionensystem', *GA*, 158 (2011), 636–52

Radtke, H., and Busch, D., 'Transnationaler Strafklageverbrauch in den sog. Schengen-Staaten?', *EuGRZ*, 27 (2000), 421–31

'Transnationaler Strafklageverbrauch in der Europäischen Union', *NStZ*, 23 (2003), 281–8

Ramos Tapia, I., 'Effective remedies for the violation of the right to trial within a reasonable time in criminal proceedings', *eucrim*, 5 (2010), 168–72

Rech, E., 'Auswirkungen von EGMR-Urteilen zu Art. 6 EMRK auf das österreichische Strafprozessrecht', in Europäische Anwaltsvereinigung, *Das faire Verfahren nach Art. 6 EMRK. 28. Tagung der DACH in Begrenz vom 15. bis 17. Mai 2003* (Cologne: Schmidt et al., 2005), 77–92

Reding, V., 'Data Protection in the EU: Challenges Ahead', *eucrim*, 5 (2010), 25–30

Reich, A.-M., *Überlange Verfahrensdauer und andere Verfahrensfehler im Strafverfahren unter Berücksichtigung der Vollstreckungslösung des Großen Senats für Strafsachen* (Berlin: Berliner Wissenschafts-Verlag, 2011)

Reichling, T., 'Anmerkung zu LG Aachen, Beschluss v. 08.12.2009 - 52 Ks 9/08', *StV*, 30 (2010), 237

Reindl, S., *Untersuchungshaft und Menschenrechtskonvention: Der Schutz der persönlichen Freiheit und die Haft im Strafverfahren* (Vienna: Verlag Österreich, 1997)

Rekate, B., *Die Vermeidung von Jurisdiktionskonflikten und der Grundsatz einmaliger Strafverfolgung in einem Raum der Freiheit, der Sicherheit und des Rechts* (Göttingen: V & R Unipress, 2015)

Remezaite, R., 'Azerbaijan: Is It Time to Invoke Infringement Proceedings for Failing to Implement Judgments of the Strasbourg Court?', *EJIL:Talk!*, 22 March 2017, at www.ejiltalk.org/azerbaijan-is-it-time-to-invoke-infringement-proceedings-for-failing-to-implement-judgments-of-the-strasbourg-court, last accessed 27 January 2018

Renzikowski, J., 'Abstand halten! Die Neuregelung der Sicherungsverwahrung', *NJW*, 66 (2013), 1638–44

'Anmerkung zu BGH, Urteil v. 09.03.2010 - 1 StR 554/09', *NStZ*, 30 (2010), 506–8

'Das Elend mit der rückwirkend verlängerten und der nachträglich angeordneten Sicherungsverwahrung', *ZIS*, 6 (2011), 531–43

'Faires Verfahren bei rechtswidriger Tatprovokation?', in Strafrechtsprofessoren der Tübinger Juristenfakultät and Justizministerium Baden-Württemberg, eds., *Gedächtnisschrift für Rolf Keller* (Tübingen: Mohr Siebeck, 2003), 197–212

'Habeas Corpus: Probleme der Umsetzung von Art. 5 EMRK in Polen und in Deutschland', in Joerden and Szwarc, *Europäisierung des Strafrechts* (2007), 311–48

'Mala per se et delicta prohibita: rechtsphilosophische Bemerkungen zum Rückwirkungsverbot (Art. 7 EMRK)', in Amelung, K., Günther, H.-J. and Kühne, H.-H., eds., *Festschrift für Volker Krey zum 70. Geburtstag am 9. Juli 2010* (Stuttgart: Kohlhammer, 2010), 407–30

'Die nachträgliche Sicherungsverwahrung und die Europäische Menschenrechtskonvention', *JR*, 76 (2004), 271–5

'Die Zurechnung von Konventionsverletzungen bei Beweiserhebungen im Ausland und ihre Verwertbarkeit im Lichte des Anspruchs auf ein faires Verfahren', in Hellmann, U., and Schröder, C., eds., *Festschrift für Hans Achenbach* (Heidelberg et al.: C. F. Müller, 2011), 373–84

Rissing-van Saan, R., 'Neuere Aspekte der Sicherungsverwahrung im Kontext der Rechtsprechung des EGMR', in Heinrich, M., Jäger, C., Achenbach, H.,

Amelung, K., Bottke, W., Haffke, B., Schünemann, B., and Wolter, J., eds., *Strafrecht als Scientia Universalis: Festschrift für Claus Roxin zum 80. Geburtstag am 15. Mai 2011*, ii (Berlin: de Gruyter, 2011), 1173–92

Roberts, A., 'Search Warrant: Compatibility with Articles 8 and 13 of the European Convention on Human Rights: Keegan v United Kingdom Application No. 28867/03, *The Times* (9 August 2006)', *JCL*, 70 (2006), 479–81

Rogall, K., 'Ist der Abschuss gekaperter Flugzeuge widerrechtlich?', *NStZ*, 28 (2008), 1–5

Roger, B., 'Europäisierung des Strafverfahrens: oder nur der Strafverfolgung?', *GA*, 157 (2010), 27–43

Rönnau, T., and Hohn, K., '§32', in Laufhütte, Rissing-van Saan and Tiedemann, *Leipziger Kommentar StGB*, ii (2006), 353–559

Rosenau, H., 'Europäische Rechtspolitik zur Abschaffung der Todesstrafe', *ZIS*, 1 (2006), 338–43

Rostalski, F., 'Der Geltungsbereich der Unschuldsvermutung bei (freisprechendem) Urteil', *HRRS*, 16 (2015), 315–27

Roxin, C., 'Kann staatliche Folter in Ausnahmefällen zulässig oder wenigstens straflos sein?', in Arnold, J., Burkhardt, B., Gropp, W., Heine, G., Koch, H.-G., Lagodny, O., Perron, W., and Walther, S., eds., *Menschengerechtes Strafrecht: Festschrift für Albin Eser zum 70. Geburtstag* (Munich: C. H. Beck, 2005), 461–72

'Rettungsfolter?', in Griesbaum, R., Hannich, R., and Schnarr, K. H., eds., *Strafrecht und Justizgewährung: Festschrift für Kay Nehm zum 65. Geburtstag* (Berlin: Berliner Wissenschafts-Verlag, 2006), 205–18

Roxin, I., 'Ambivalente Wirkungen des Beschleunigungsgebots', *StV*, 30 (2010), 437–42 = *GA*, 157 (2010), 425–40

'Anmerkung zu BayObLG, Urteil vom 12.12.2002- 5 St RR 301/02', *StV*, 23 (2003), 377–9

'Anmerkung zu BGH, Vorlagenbeschluß v. 23.08.2007 – 3 StR 50/07', *StV*, 28 (2008), 14–18

'Wirksamer Rechtsschutz bei überlangen Strafverfahren?', *StV*, 31, 2 (2011), Editorial

Ruffert, M., 'Die Europäische Menschenrechtskonvention und innerstaatliches Recht', *EuGRZ*, 34 (2007), 245–55

Ruggeri, S., 'Inaudito Reo Proceedings, Defence Rights, and Harmonisation Goals in the EU: Responses of the European Courts and New Perspectives of EU Law', *eucrim*, 10 (2016), 42–51

'Right to Personal Participation in Criminal Proceedings and in absentia Procedures in the EU Area of Freedom, Security and Justice', *ZStW*, 128 (2016), 578–605

Rui, J. P., 'Non-conviction Based Confiscation in the EU: An Assessment of Art. 5 of the Proposal for a Directive of the EP and of the Council on the Freezing and Confiscation of Proceeds of Crime in the European Union', *ERA Forum*, 13 (2012), 349–60

Rzepka, D., *Zur Fairness im deutschen Strafverfahren* (Frankfurt a.M.: Klostermann, 2000)

Safferling, C., 'Der EuGH, die Grundrechtecharta und nationales Recht: Die Fälle Ackerberg Fransson und Melloni', *NStZ*, 34 (2014), 545–51

Towards an International Criminal Procedure (Oxford: Oxford University Press, 2003)

'Verdeckte Ermittler im Strafverfahren: deutsche und europäische Rechtsprechung im Konflikt?', *NStZ*, 26 (2006), 75–82

'Die zwangsweise Verabreichung von Brechmitteln: Die StPO auf dem menschenrechtlichen Prüfstand', *Jura*, 30 (2008), 100–8

Sagmeister, H. M., *Die Grundsatznormen in der Europäischen Grundrechtecharta: Zugleich ein Beitrag zum subjektiv-öffentlichen Recht im Gemeinschaftsrecht* (Berlin: Duncker & Humblot, 2010)

Saiz Arnaiz, A., and Torres Pérez, A., *Main Trends in the Recent Case Law of the EU Court of Justice and the European Court of Human Rights in the Field of Fundamental Rights* (Brussels: EP, 2012), available at www.europarl.europa.eu/RegData/etudes/etudes/join/2012/462446/IPOL-LIBE_ET(2012)462446_EN.pdf, last accessed 27 January 2018

Salditt, F., 'Kompensation rechtsstaatswidriger Verfahrensverzögerung', *StraFo*, 13 (2007), 513

Saliger, F., 'Absolutes im Strafprozess? Über das Folterverbot, seine Verletzung und die Folgen seiner Verletzung', *ZStW*, 116 (2004), 35–65

Sanz Hermida, A. M., 'Aplicación transnacional de la prohibición del bis in idem en la Union Europea', *RP*, 21 (2008), 126–38

Satzger, H., 'Auf dem Weg zu einer "europäischen Rechtskraft"?', in Heinrich, M., Jäger, C., Achenbach, H., Amelung, K., Bottke, W., Haffke, B., Schünemann, B., and Wolter, J., eds., *Strafrecht als Scientia Universalis: Festschrift für Claus Roxin zum 80. Geburtstag am 15. Mai 2011*, ii (Berlin: de Gruyter, 2011), 1515–36

'Der Einfluss der EMRK auf das deutsche Straf- und Strafprozessrecht', *Jura*, 31 (2009), 759–68

'Gefahren für eine effektive Verteidigung im geplanten europäischen Verfahrensrecht', *StV*, 23 (2003), 137–42

'Grund- und menschenrechtliche Grenzen für die Vollstreckung eines Europäischen Haftbefehls? "Verfassungsrechtliche Identitätskontrolle" durch das BVerfG vs. Vollstreckungsaufschub bei "außergewöhnlichen Umständen" nach dem EuGH', *NStZ*, 15 (2016), 514–22

'Sicherungsverwahrung: Europarechtliche Vorgaben und Grundgesetz', *StV*, 33 (2013), 243–9

Satzger, H., Zimmermann, F., and Eibach, M., 'Does Art. 18 ECHR Grant Protection against Politically Motivated Criminal Proceedings? Rethinking the interpretation of Art. 18 ECHR against the Background of New Jurisprudence of the ECtHR', *EuCLR*, 4 (2014), 91–113

Satzger, H., Zimmermann, F., and Eibach, M., 'Does Art. 18 ECHR Grant Protection against Politically Motivated Criminal Proceedings? Part 2: Prerequisites, Questions of Evidence and Scope of Application', *EuCLR*, 4 (2014), 248–64

Sauer, H., '"Solange" geht in Altersteilzeit: Der unbedingte Vorrang der Menschenwürde vor dem Unionsrecht', NJW, 69 (2016), 1134–8

Saul, M., 'The ECtHR's Margin of Appreciation and the Processes of National Parliaments', *HRLR*, 15 (2015), 745–74

Scalia, V., 'Protection of Fundamental Rights and Criminal Law', *eucrim*, 10 (2015), 100–11

Schaerz, P. A., 'Der Begriff des "fairen Verfahrens" gemäß Art. 6 EMRK in der schweizerischen Rechtspraxis', in Europäische Anwaltsvereinigung, *Das faire Verfahren nach Art. 6 EMRK. 28. Tagung der DACH in Begrenz vom 15. bis 17. Mai 2003* (Cologne: Schmidt et al., 2005), 51–76

Schäferskiüpper, M., and Grote, J., 'Neues aus der Sicherungsverwahrung: Eine aktuelle Bestandsaufnahme', *NStZ*, 36 (2016), 197–203

Schäferskiüpper, M., and Grote, J., 'Vollzug der Sicherungsverwahrung', *NStZ*, 33 (2013), 447–54

Schaiko, G., Lemmens, P., and Lemmens, K., 'Belgium', in Gerards, J., and Fleuren, J., eds., *Implementation of the European Convention on Human Rights and of the Judgments of the ECtHR in National Case-Law: A Comparative Analysis* (Cambridge, Antwerp and Portland: Intersentia, 2014), 95–143

Schallmoser, N.M., 'The European Arrest Warrant and Fundamental Rights: Risks of Violation of Fundamental Rights through the EU Framework Decision in Light of the ECHR', *EJCCLCJ*, 22 (2014), 135–65

Scheffler, U., 'Die Mindeststandards des Europarates vs. die Mindeststandards des Rates der EU', in Joerden and Szwarc, *Europäisierung des Strafrechts* (2007), 97–116

Schenke, W.-R., 'Die Verfassungswidrigkeit des §14 III LuftSiG', *NJW*, 59 (2006), 736–9

Schiedermair, S., 'Schwerpunktbereichsklausur: Öffentliches Recht: Individualbeschwerde vor dem EGMR: Gewaltandrohung im Verhör', *JuS*, 50 (2010), 993–8

Schilling, T., *Internationaler Menschenrechtsschutz: Das Recht der EMRK und des IPbpR* (Tübingen: Mohr Siebeck, 3rd edn, 2016)

Schlegel, S., and Wohlers, W., 'Der "Anwalt der ersten Stunde" in der Schweiz', *StV*, 32 (2012), 307–18

Schleiminger, D., *Konfrontation im Strafprozess: Art. 6 Ziff. 3 lit.d EMRK mit besonderer Berücksichtigung des Verhältnisses zum Opferschutz im Bereich von Sexualdelikten gegen Minderjährige* (Basel et al.: Helbing and Lichtenhahn, 2001)

Schlothauer, R., 'Die Flucht aus der Justizförmigkeit durch die europäische Hintertür: Zum Urteil des BGH v. 25.07.2000 – 1 StR 169/00 = StV 2000, 593', *StV*, 21 (2001), 127–31

Schmidt, W., '§359–373a', in Hannich, *Karlsruher Kommentar StPO* (2013), 2135–92

Schmitt, B., '§§151–157' and 'MRK', in Meyer-Goßner and Schmitt, *StPO* (2016), 759–820 and 2114–62

Schneider, K., '87. EGMR v. 1.7.1961 – Lawless', in Menzel, Pierlings, and Hoffmann, *Völkerrechtsprechung* (2005), 521–6

Schneiders, B., *Die Grundrechte der EU und die EMRK: Das Verhältnis zwischen ungeschriebenen Grundrechten, Grundrechtecharta und Europäischer Menschenrechtskonvention* (Baden-Baden: Nomos, 2010)

Schöch, H., 'Sicherungsverwahrung und Europäische Konvention zum Schutz der Menschenrechte und Grundfreiheiten', in Heinrich, M., Jäger, C., Achenbach, H., Amelung, K., Bottke, W., Haffke, B., Schünemann, B., and Wolter, J., eds., *Strafrecht als Scientia Universalis: Festschrift für Claus Roxin zum 80. Geburtstag am 15. Mai 2011*, ii (Berlin: de Gruyter, 2011), 1193–1214

Schöch, H., 'Das Urteil des Bundesverfassungsgerichts zur Sicherungsverwahrung', *GA*, 159 (2012), 14–31

Schomburg, W., 'Artikel 54, 55 SDÜ', in Schomburg, W., Lagodny, O., Gleß, S., and Hackner, T., eds., *Internationale Rechtshilfe in Strafsachen* (2012), 1672–92

'Criminal Matters: Transnational ne bis in idem in Europe: Conflict of Jurisdictions: Transfer of Proceedings', *ERA Forum*, 13 (2012), 311–24

'Internationales "ne bis in idem" nach Art. 54 SDÜ', *StV*, 17 (1997), 383–5

'Konkurrierende nationale und internationale Strafgerichtsbarkeit und der Grundsatz "Ne bis in idem"', in Arnold, J., Burkhardt, B., Gropp, W., Heine, G., Koch, H.-G., Lagodny, O., Perron, W., and Walther, S., eds., *Menschengerechtes Strafrecht: Festschrift für Albin Eser zum 70. Geburtstag* (Munich: C. H. Beck, 2005), 829–46

Schomburg, W., and Suominen-Picht, I., 'Verbot der mehrfachen Strafverfolgung, Kompetenzkonflikte und Verfahrenstransfer', *NJW*, 65 (2012), 1190–4

Schonard, P., 'Artikel 51 GrCh', in Lenz and Borchardt, *EU-Verträge Kommentar* (2013), 3332–9

Schorkopf, F., 'Anmerkung' (CJEU Opinion 2/13), *JZ*, 69 (2015), 781–4

'Artikel 6 EUV', in Grabitz, Hilf, and Nettesheim, *Das Recht der EU*, i (2014)

Schramm, E., 'Semesterabschlussklausur: Strafrecht: Internationales Strafrecht', *JuS*, 53 (2013), 1093–7

Schroeder, F.-C., 'Die Notwehr als Indikator politischer Grundanschauungen', in Schroeder, F.-C. and Zipf, H., eds., *Festschrift für Reinhart Maurach zum 70. Geburtstag* (Karlsruhe: C. F. Müller, 1972), 127–42

Schuhr, J. C., 'Brechmitteleinsatz als unmenschliche und erniedrigende Behandlung', *NJW*, 59 (2006), 3538–41

Schüller, A., '"Reales Risiko" der Folter oder unmenschlichen Behandlung reicht für ein Beweisverwertungsverbot', *ZIS*, 8 (2013), 245–8

Schumann, K. H., '"Brechmitteleinsatz ist Folter"?', *StV*, 26 (2006), 661–5

Schumann, S., Bruckmüller, K., and Soyer, R., 'Assessing Pre-trial Access to Legal Advice: Results of a Comparative Legal and Empirical Study', *NJECL*, 3 (2012), 31–49

Schünemann, B., 'Bürgerrechte ernst nehmen bei der Europäisierung des Strafverfahrens!', *StV*, 23 (2003), 116–22

'Der deutsche Strafprozess im Spannungsfeld zwischen Zeugenschutz und materieller Wahrheit', *StV*, 18 (1998), 391–401

'Der Richter im Strafprozess als manipulierter Dritter?', *StV*, 20 (2000), 159–65

'Mindestbedingungen einer effektiven Verteidigung in transnationalen europaischen Strafverfahren', *StV*, 36 (2016), 178–85

'Zur Reform des strafprozessualen Ermittlungsverfahrens in Europa: Kontradiktorische Ausbalancierung statt Partizipation', in Triffterer, O., ed., *Gedächtnisschrift für Theo Vogler* (Heidelberg: C. F. Müller, 2004), 81–92

Schweitzer, M., and Dederer, H.-G., *Staatsrecht III: Staatsrecht, Völkerrechtt, Europarecht* (Heidelberg et al: C. F. Müller, 11th edn, 2016)

Seher, G., 'Bewährungswiderruf wegen Begehung einer neuen Straftat', *ZStW*, 118 (2006), 101–58

Seifert, J., '§56 f I 1 StGB: Der Bewährungswiderruf infolge einer neuerlichen Straftat in der Praxis', *Jura*, 30 (2008), 684–90

Seitz, H., 'Mildeste versus punitivste Strafrechtsordnung', in Schöch, H., ed., *Recht gestalten: dem Recht dienen: Festschrift für Reinhard Böttcher zum 70. Geburtstag am 29. Juli 2007* (Berlin: De Gruyter, 2007), 675–84

Selbmann, F., 'Anpassungsbedarf der Regelungen zur Wiederaufnahme des Verfahrens an die Vorgaben der EMRK', *ZRP*, 39 (2006), 124–6

Sidhu, O., *The Concept of Equality of Arms in Criminal Proceedings under Article 6 of the European Convention on Human Rights* (Antwerp et al.: Intersentia, 2017)

Silva Sánchez, J. M., 'Constitución Europea, legalidad y derecho penal económico', in Bajo Fernández, M., ed., *Constitución Europea y derecho penal económico* (Madrid: Ed. universitaria Ramón Areces, 2006), 253–69

Simitis, S., 'Der EuGH und die Vorratsdatenspeicherung oder die verfehlte Kehrtwende bei der Kompetenzregelung', *NJW*, 62 (2009), 1782–6

Simon, O., *Die Beschuldigtenrechte nach Art. 6 Abs. 3 EMRK: Ein Vergleich zur StPO im Hinblick auf die Auswirkungen der Konventionsrechteauf die deutsche Strafrechtsprechung* (Tübingen: Medien-Verlag Köhler, 1998)

Simpson, A. W. B., *Human Rights and the End of Empire: Britain and the Genesis of the European Convention* (Oxford: Oxford University Press, 2004)

Sinn, A., 'Tötung Unschuldiger auf Grund §14 III Luftsicherheitsgesetz: Rechtmäßig?', *NStZ*, 24 (2004), 585–93

'Die Vermeidung von strafrechtlichen Jurisdiktionskonflikten in der Europäischen Union: Gegenwart und Zukunft', *ZIS*, 8 (2013), 1–9

Sinn, A., and Maly, S., 'Zu den strafprozessualen Folgen einer rechtsstaatswidrigen Tatprovokation', *NStZ*, 35 (2015), 379–84

Smith, E., 'Running before we can Walk? Mutual Recognition at the Expense of Fair Trials in Europe's Area of Freedom, Justice and Security', *NJECL*, 4 (2013), 82–98

Sokhi-Bulley, B., 'The Fundamental Rights Agency of the European Union: A New Panopticism', *HRLR*, 11 (2011), 683–706

Sommer, U., 'Strafprozessordnung und Europäische Menschenrechtkonvention', in Brüssow, R., Gatzweiler, N., Krekeler, W., and Mehle, V., eds., *Strafverteidigung in der Praxis* (Bonn: Deutscher Anwaltverlag, 4th edn, 2007), 811–56

'Die Verzögerungsrüge: "Auf der Suche nach der verlorenen Zeit"', *StV*, 32 (2012), 107–12

'Zur Frage der Einbeziehung der Europäischen Menschenrechtskonvention in den deutschen Strafprozess', *StraFo*, 16 (2010), 284–5

Sommovigo, F., 'Minimum Content and Structure of the Letter of Rights', in Arangüena Fanego, C., ed., *Garantías procesales en los procesos penales en la Unión Europea* (Valladolid: Ed. Lex Nova, 2007), 381–7

Soo, A., 'Potential Remedies for Violation of the Right to Counsel in Criminal Proceedings: Article 12 of the Directive 2013/48/EU (22 October 2013) and Its Output in National Legislation', *EuCLR*, 6 (2016), 284–307

Spaniol, M., *Das Recht auf Verteidigerbeistand im Grundgesetz und in der Europäischen Menschenrechtskonvention* (Berlin: Duncker & Humblot, 1990)

Spaventa, E., *The Interpretation of Article 51 of the EU Charter of Fundamental Rights: The Dilemma of Stricter or Broader Application of the Charter to National Measures* (Brussels: EP, 2016), available at www.europarl.europa.eu/RegData/etudes/STUD/2016/556930/IPOL_STU(2016)556930_EN.pdf, last accessed 27 January 2018

'A Very Fearful Court? The Protection of Fundamental Rights in the EU after Opinion 2/13', *MaastJECompL*, 22 (2015), 35–56

Specht, B., *Die zwischenstaatliche Geltung des Grundsatzes 'ne bis in idem': Zugleich ein Beitrag zur Auslegung des Art. 103 Abs. 3 Grundgesetz* (Berlin and Heidelberg: Springer, 1999)

Spencer, J. R., 'International Law, People Trafficking and the Power to Stay Criminal Proceedings for Abuse of Process', *CambLJ*, 73 (2014), 11–14

Spitzer, A., 'Das Rechts des Angeklagten auf Vertretung in der Beurfungshauptverhandlung', *StV*, 36 (2016), 48–55

Spronken, T., *An EU-Wide Letter of Rights: Towards Best Practice* (Antwerp et al.: Intersentia, 2010)

Staffler, L., 'Geheimdienstliches Verschwindenlassen von Terrorverdächtigen (extraordinary renditions) im Lichte der EGMR-Judikatur: Der Fall Nasr (alias Abu Omar) und Ghali gegen Italien', *EuGRZ*, 43 (2016), 344–52

Stalberg, J., *Zum Anwendungsbereich des Art. 50 der Charta der Grundrechte der Europäischen Union (ne bis in idem)* (Frankfurt a.M.: Peter Lang, 2013)

Stapper, F., 'Presse und Unschuldsvermutung', *AfP*, 27 (1996), 349–56

Stein, S., 'Grenzüberschreitendes ne bis in idem: Ein Regelungsvorschlag für die Europäische Union', *ZStW*, 115 (2003), 983–7

'Ein Meilenstein für das europäische "ne bis in idem"', *NJW*, 56 (2003), 1162–4

Zum europäischen ne bis in idem nach Artikel 54 des Schengener Durchführungsübereinkommens: Zugleich ein Beitrag zur rechtsvergleichenden Auslegung zwischenstaatlich geltender Vorschriften (Frankfurt a.M.: Peter Lang, 2004)

Steinbeiß-Winkelmann, C., 'Rechtsschutz bei überlangen Gerichtsverfahren', *ZRP*, 43 (2010), 205–9

Stewart, S., *Russland und der Europarat* (Berlin: Stiftung Wissenschaft und Politik, 2013)

Stoffers, K. F., 'Anwesenheitsrechte des Verteidigers bei Zeugenvernehmungen im Ermittlungsverfahren', *NJW*, 66 (2013), 1495–7

Stree, W., and Kinzig, J., '§56 f', in Schönke, A., Schröder, H., and Eser, A., eds., *Strafgesetzbuch: Kommentar* (Munich: C. H. Beck, 29th edn, 2014), 957–70

Streinz, R., 'Europarecht: Anwendungsbereich der EU-Grundrechtecharta', *JuS*, 53 (2013), 568–71

Stuckenberg, C.-F., 'Anmerkung zu BGH, Urteil v. 18.06.2009 – 3 StR 89/09 (LG Hannover)', *StV*, 30 (2010), 231–2

'Anmerkung' (ECtHR, *Cleve* v. *Germany*), *StV*, 36 (2016), 5–8

'Der Tatbegriff des europäischen Doppelbestrafungsverbots', in Meng, W., Ress, G., and Stein, T., eds., *Europäische Integration und Globalisierung: Festschrift zum 60-jährigen Bestehen des Europa-Instituts* (Baden-Baden: Nomos, 2011), 567–80

Sweeney, J. A., *The European Court of Human Rights in the Post-Cold War Era: Universality in Transition* (London and New York: Routledge, 2012)

Swoboda, S., 'Paying the Debts: Late Nazi Trials before German Courts', *JICJ*, 9 (2011), 243–69

'Die Pflicht zur rahmenbeschlusskonformen Auslegung im deutschen Strafverfahren', *HRRS*, 15 (2014), 10–21

'The Self-Perception of the ECJ and Its Neglect of the Defense Perspective in Its Preliminary Rulings on Judicial Cooperation in Criminal Matters', *ZIS*, 10 (2015), 361–74

Symeonidou-Kastanidou, E., 'The Right of Access to a Lawyer in Criminal Proceedings: The Transposition of Directive 2013/48/EU of 22 October 2013 on National Legislation', *EuCLR*, 5 (2015), 68–85

Szczekalla, P., '§52: Unschuldsvermutung', in Heselhaus, S. M., and Nowak, C., eds., *Handbuch der Europäischen Grundrechte* (Munich et al.: C. H. Beck et al., 2006), 1395–1413

Szydlo, M., 'Extra-territorial Application of the European Convention on Human Rights after Al-Skeini and Al-Jedda', *ICLR*, 12 (2012), 271–91

Tamietti, A., 'Le principe de légalité aux termes de l'Article 7 de la Convention européenne des droits de l'homme: Un bref aperçu de jurisprudence', *eucrim*, 10 (2015), 116–19

Tanca, A., 'Human Rights, Terrorism and Police Custody: The Brogan Case', *EJIL*, 1 (1990), 269–77

Tepperwien, I., 'Beschleunigung über alles? Das Beschleunigungsgebot im Straf- und Ordnungswidrigkeitenverfahren', *NStZ*, 29 (2009), 1–7

Terhechte, J. P., 'Rechtsangleichung zwischen Gemeinschafts- und Unionsrecht: Die Richtlinie über die Vorratsdatenspeicherung vor dem EuGH', *EuZW*, 20 (2009), 199–204

Thunberg Schunke, M., 'The Manifesto on European Criminal Procedure Law: A Commentary on the Perspective of Mutual Recognition and Violations of Defence Rights', *EuCLR*, 5 (2015), 46–53

Whose Responsibility? A Study of Transnational Defence Rights and Mutual Recognition of Judicial Decisions within the EU (Cambridge: Intersentia, 2013)

Thurnherr, D., 'The Reception Process in Austria and Switzerland', in Keller, H., and Stone Sweet, A., eds., *A Europe of Rights: The Impact of the ECHR on National Legal Systems* (Oxford: Oxford University Press, 2008), 311–92

Thym, D., 'Die Reichweite der EU-Grundrechte-Charta: Zu viel Grundrechtsschutz?', *NVwZ*, 32 (2013), 889–96

'Strafklageverbrauch bei Einstellung durch die StA: Anmerkung', *NStZ*, 23 (2003), 334–5

Tiedemann, K., '13 Thesen zu einem modernen menschenrechtsorientierten Strafprozess', *ZRP*, 23 (1992), 107–9

Tinsley, A., 'Note on the Reference in Case C-399/11 Melloni', *NJECL*, 3 (2012), 19–30

'The Reference in Case C-396/11 Radu: When Does the Protection of Fundamental Rights Require Non-execution of a European Arrest Warrant?', *EuCLR*, 2 (2012), 338–52

Tiwisina, C., *Rechtsfragen überlanger Verfahrensdauer nach nationalem Recht und der EMRK* (Baden-Baden: Nomos, 2010)

Tomás-Valiente Lanuza, C., 'Deberes positivos del Estado y Derecho penal en la jurisprudencia del TEDH', *InDret*, 17 (2016), issue 3 (July 2016), 1–73, www.indret.com/pdf/1237.pdf, last accessed 27 January 2018

Tomuschat, C., 'Der Streit um die Auslegungshoheit: Die Autonomie der EU als Heiliger Gral', *EuGRZ*, 42 (2015), 133–9

Toney, R. J., 'Disclosure of Evidence and Legal Assistance at Custodial Interrogation: What Does the European Convention on Human Rights Require?', *IJEP*, 5 (2001), 39–60

Trechsel, S., 'Akteneinsicht: Information als Grundlage des fairen Verfahrens', in Schweizer, R. J., Burkert, H., and Gasser, U., eds., *Festschrift für Jean Nicolas Druey zum 65. Geburtstag* (Zurich: Schulthess, 2002), 993–1008

Die Europäische Menschenrechtskonvention, ihr Schutz der persönlichen Freiheit und die schweizerischen Strafprozessrechte (Bern: Stämpfli, 1974)

'Die Verteidigungsrechte in der Praxis zur EMRK', *ZStrR*, 96 (1979), 337–92

Trüg, G., *Lösungskonvergenzen trotz Systemdivergenzen im deutschen und US-amerikanischen Strafverfahren: Ein strukturanalytischer Vergleich am Beispiel der Wahrheitserforschung* (Tübingen: Mohr Siebeck, 2003)

Tulkens, F., 'Criminal Procedure: Main Comparable Features of the National Systems', in Delmas-Marty, M., ed., *The Criminal Process and Human Rights* (Dordrecht et al.: Nijhoff, 1995), 5–14

Tulkens, F., and Donnay, L., 'L'usage de la marge d'appréciation par la Cour Europ. des droits de l'homme', *RSC*, 2006, 3–23

Uerpmann-Wittzack, R., 'Rechtsfragen und Rechtsfolgen des Beitritts der EU zur EMRK', *EuR*, 47 (2012), *Beiheft 2*, 167–85

UKHL EU Committee, '1st Report of Session 2004–05: Procedural Rights in Criminal Proceedings: Report with Evidence', *HL Paper*, 28 (2005)

'Ninth Report Session: 2008–09: Procedural Rights in EU Criminal Proceedings: An Update', *HL Paper*, 84 (2009)

'13th Report of Session 2012–13 – EU Police and Criminal Justice Measures: The UK's 2014 Opt-Out Decision', *HL Paper*, 159 (2013)

Ullenbruch, T., 'Das "Gesetz zur Einführung der nachträglichen Sicherungsverwahrung bei Verurteilungen nach Jugendstrafrecht": ein Unding?', *NJW*, 61 (2008), 2609–15

'Walter H. in den (soeben noch erweiterten) Rückfängen des ThUG: Nach wie vor aktueller Spaltpilz zwischen EGMR und BVerfG? Teil II', *StV*, 33 (2013), 268–78

'Walter H. in den Rückfängen des ThUG: aktuellster Spaltpilz zwischen EGMR und BVerfG?', *StV*, 32 (2012), 44–51

'Walter H. ist frei, das ThUG tot? Raffinierte Entsorgung eines europa-völkerrechtlichen Spaltpilzes in letzter Sekunde? Teil III', *StV*, 34 (2014), 174–84

Unfried, E., *Die Freiheits- und Sicherheitsrechte nach Art. 5 EMRK: Ein Vergleich mit der Strafprozessordnung im Hinblick auf die Auswirkungen der Konverntionsrechte auf die deutsche Strafrechtsprechung* (Berlin: Duncker & Humblot, 2006)

van Bockel, B., 'Case Law', *CMLR*, 45 (2008), 223–44

'The ne bis in idem Principle in the EU Legal Order: Between Scope and Substance', *ERA Forum*, 13 (2012), 325–47

van den Wyngaert, C., 'Anmerkung zu BGH, Beschluss vom 13.05.1997 – 5 StR 596/96', *NStZ*, 18 (1998), 153–4

van der Heyning, C., 'Fundamental Rights Lost in Complexity: Fundamental Rights against Violations by the Rulemaker in Converging National and European Legal Systems' (PhD thesis, University of Antwerp, 2011)

van Kalmthout, A. M., Knapen, M. M., and Morgenstern, C., eds., *Pre-trial Detention in the EU: An Analysis of Minimum Standards in Pre-trial Detention and the Grounds for Regular Review in the Member States of the EU* (Nijmegen: Wolf Legal Publishers, 2009)

van Zyl Smit, D., Weatherby, P., and Creighton, S., 'Whole Life Sentences and the Tide of European Human Rights Jurisprudence: What Is to Be Done?', *HRLR*, 14 (2014), 59–84

Velten, P., 'Der Auslandszeuge als Einbruchstelle für den Abbau von Verteidigungsrechten und Unmittelbarkeitsgrundsatz im Namen der Prozeßökonomie', *StV*, 27 (2007), 97–105

Vermeulen, G., 'Freedom from Torture and Other Inhuman or Degrading Treatment or Punishment (Article 3)', in van Dijk, P., Van Hoof, F., Van Rijn, A., and Zwaak, L., eds., *Theory and Practice of the ECHR* (2006), 405–42

Vervaele, J. A. E., 'European Criminal Law and General Principles of Union Law', in Vervaele, *European Evidence Warrant* (2005), 131–55

'Ne Bis in Idem: Towards a Transnational Constitutional Principle in the EU?', *ULR*, 9 (2013), 211–29

'The Transnational ne bis in idem Principle in the EU: Mutual Recognition and Equivalent Protection of Ruman Rights', *ULR*, 1 (2005), 100–18

Vest, H., 'Völkermord durch Tötung zweier litauischer Partisanen? Besprechung von EGMR (GC), Urt. v. 20.10.2015 – 35343/05 (Vasiliauskas v. Lithuania)', *ZIS*, 11 (2013), 487–94

Viering, M., 'Right to a Fair and Public Hearing (Article 6)', in van Dijk, P., Van Hoof, F., Van Rijn, A., and Zwaak, L., eds., *Theory and Practice of the ECHR* (2006), 511–650

Villamarín López, 'The Presumption of Innocence in Directive 2016/343/EU of 9 March 2016', *ERA Forum*, 18 (2017), 335

Voeten, E., 'Domestic Implementation of ECtHR Judgments: Legal Infrastructure and Government Effectiveness Matter: A Reply to Dia Anagnostou and Alina Mungiu-Pippidi', *EJIL*, 25 (2014), 229–38

Vogel, J., 'Editorial', *StV*, 33, 5 (2013), Editorial

'Internationales und Europäisches ne bis in idem', in Hoyer, A., Müller, H. E., Pawlik, M., and Wolter, J., eds., *Festschrift für Friedrich-Christian Schroeder zum 70. Geburtstag* (Heidelberg: C. F. Müller, 2006), 877–94

Vogel, J., and Matt, H., 'Gemeinsame Standards für Strafverfahren in der Europäischen Union', *StV*, 27 (2007), 206–14

Vogel, J., and Norouzi, A. B., 'Europäisches "ne bis in idem"', *JuS*, 43 (2003), 1059–62

Vogler, T., 'Straf- und strafverfahrensrechtliche Fragen in der Spruchpraxis der Europäischen Kommission und des EGMR', *ZStW*, 89 (1977), 761–95

von Bogdandy, A., 'Grundrechtsschutz durch die Europäische Grundrechteagentur', in Merten, D., and Papier, H.-J., eds., *Handbuch der Grundrechte in Deutschland und Europa*, vi/1: *Europäische Grundrechte I* (Heidelberg et al.: C. F. Müller, 2010), 1241–68

von Bogdandy, A., and von Bernstorff, J., 'Die Europäische Agentur für Grundrechte in der europäischen Menschenrechtsarchitektur und ihre Fortentwicklung durch den Vertrag von Lissabon', *EuR*, 45 (2010), 141–65

von Freier, F.-C., 'Verfahrensidentität und Prozessgegenstand des Verfahrens zur nachträglichen Anordnung der Sicherungsverwahrung', *ZStW*, 120 (2008), 273–330

von Hirsch, A., *Censure and Sanctions* (Oxford: Clarendon Press, 1995)

Doing Justice: The Choice of Punishments: Report of the Committee for the Study of Incarceration (Boston, MA: Northeastern University Press, 1986)

von Hirsch, A., and Ashworth, A., *Proportionate Sentencing: Exploring the Principles* (Oxford: Oxford University Press, 2005)

Vondung, J., *Die Architektur des europäischen Grundrechtsschutzes nach dem Beitritt der EU zur EMRK* (Tübingen: Mohr Siebeck, 2012)

Wagner, A., and Hacker, R.,'4 Charts Which Show the ECtHR Has Dramatically Changed Its Approach to the UK', *Rights Info*, 18 May 2016, at Rightsinfo.org/4-charts-which-show-the-european-court-of-human-rights-has-dramatically-changed-its-approach-to-the-uk, last accessed 27 January 2018

Wahl, T., 'Die EU-Richtlinien zur Stärkung der Strafverfahrensrechte im Spiegel der EMRK', *ERA Forum*, 18 (2017), 311

Walischewski, L., *Probleme des Akteneinsichtsrechts der Verteidigung im Ermittlungsverfahren im Lichte der Rechtsprechung des Bundesverfassungsgerichts und des Europäischen Gerichtshofs für Menschenrechte* (Frankfurt a.M.: Peter Lang, 1999)

Walter, T., 'Fair trial statt Nemo tenetur? Der Durchgriff auf Artikel 6 Absatz 1 EMRK bei listigen Ermittlungen', in Roth, H., ed., *Europäisierung des Rechts* (Tübingen: Mohr Siebeck, 2010), 291–308

Walther, F., 'Zur Verschränkung von Strafprozess-, Europa- und Verfassungsrecht: Zugleich Besprechung von LG Aachen StraFo 2010, 190, BGHSt 56, 11 und BVerfG NJW 2012, 1202', *ZJS*, 6 (2013), 16–23

Walther, S., 'Strafprozessuales Konfrontationsrecht – ade?', *JZ*, 59 (2004), 1107–15

'Zur Frage eines Rechts des Beschuldigten auf "Konfrontation von Belastungszeugen"', *GA*, 150 (2003), 204–25

Wang, S.-F., *Einsatz Verdeckter Ermittler zum Entlocken des Geständnisses eines Beschuldigten* (Baden-Baden: Nomos, 2015)

Wasek-Wiaderek, M., *The Principle of 'Equality of Arms' in Criminal Procedure under Article 6 of the European Convention on Human Rights and Its Functions in Criminal Justice of Selected European Countries* (Leuven: Leuven University Press, 2000)

Wasmeier, M., 'Der Europäische Haftbefehl vor dem Bundesverfassungsgericht: Zur Verzahnung des nationalen und europäischen Strafrechts', *ZEuS*, 9 (2006), 23–39

'The Principle of Ne Bis In Idem', *RIDP*, 77 (2006), 121–30

Waßmer, M. P., 'Rechtsstaatswidrige Verfahrensverzögerungen im Strafverfahren als Verfahrenshindernis von Verfassungs wegen', *ZStW*, 118 (2006), 159–201

Waszczynski, D., 'Verwerfung der Berufung wegen unentschuldigter Abwesenheit des Angeklagten', *NStZ-RR*, 19 (2014), 18–21

Wattenberg, A., and Violet, D., 'Anmerkung zu EGMR, Urteil v. 23.4.1997' – 21363/93 – Van Mechelen u.a./Niederlande (55/1996/674/861–864) (=StV 1997, 617 ff.), *StV*, 17 (1997), 620–2

Weber, K. 'Anmerkung zu BGH, Vorlageschl. des 3. Strafsenats v. 23.8.2007 – 3 StR 50/07, *JR*, 80 (2008), 36–9

Wegner, K., 'Die "Fransson"-Entscheidung des EuGH: Eine Erschütterung im System der europäischen Grundrechte?', *HRRS*, 14 (2013), 125–31

Weigend, T., 'Die Europäische Menschenrechtskonvention als deutsches Recht', *StV*, 20 (2000), 384–90

'Unverzichtbares im Strafverfahrensrecht', *ZStW*, 113 (2001), 271–304

Weiß, W., 'Grundrechtsschutz durch den EuGH: Tendenzen seit Lissabon', *EuZW*, 24 (2013), 287–92

Weitzmann, G., 'Tagung der Europäischen Rechtsakademie (ERA) am 23 und 24 Oktober 2003: Verbrechensbekämpfung in der Europäischen Union: Die Unionspolitik nach dem Konvent', *ZStW*, 116 (2004), 265–70

Wendel, M., 'Der EMRK-Beitritt als Unionsrechtsverstoß', *NJW*, 68 (2015), 921–6

Werle, G., 'Rückwirkungsverbot und Staatskriminalität', *NJW*, 54 (2001), 3001–8

Wessing, J., 'Zeugnisverweigerungsrechte ausländischer Strafverteidiger', *wistra*, 26 (2007), 171–4

Weyembergh, A., 'Approximation of Criminal Laws, the Constitutional Treaty and the Hague Programme', *CMLR*, 42 (2005), 1567–97

Widder, E., 'The Right to Challenge Witnesses: An Application of Strasbourg's Flexible "Sole and Decisive" Rule to Other Human Rights', *CJICL*, 3 (2014), 1084–97

Wiethoff, J. H., *Das konzeptionelle Verhältnis von EuGH und EGMR: Unter besonderer Berücksichtigung der aktuellen Verfassungsentwicklung der Europäischen Union* (Baden-Baden: Nomos, 2008)

Wiklund, O., 'The Reception Process in Sweden and Norway', in Keller, H., and Stone Sweet, A., eds., *A Europe of Rights: The Impact of the ECHR on National Legal Systems* (Oxford: Oxford University Press, 2008), 165–228

Winkler, S., 'Die Vermutung des "äquivalenten" Grundrechtsschutzes im Gemeinschaftsrecht nach dem Bosphorus-Urteil des EGMR', *EuGRZ*, 34 (2007), 641–54

Wohlers, W., 'Aktuelle Fragen des Zeugenschutzes: Zur Vereinbarkeit der im Strafprozessrecht des Kantons Zurich anwendbaren Zeugenschutznormen mit Art. 6 Abs. 3 lit. d EMRK', *ZStrR*, 123 (2005), 144–73

Wohlers, W., 'Art. 6 Abs. 3 (d) EMRK als Grenze der Einführung des Wissens anonym bleibender Zeugen', in Donatsch, A., Forster, M., and Schwarzenegger, C., eds., *Strafrecht, Strafprozessrecht und Menschenrechte: Festschrift für Stefan Trechsel zum 65. Geburtstag* (Zurich: Schulthess, 2002), 813–34

'Die "besonders vorsichtige Beweiswürdigung" bei gesperrten Beweismitteln', *StV*, 34 (2014), 563–9

'Das partizipatorische Ermittlungsverfahren', *GA*, 152 (2005), 11–35

'Das Strafverfahren in den Zeiten der "Eilkrankheit"', *NJW*, 63 (2010), 2470–5

Wohlers, W., and Schlegel, S., 'Zum Umfang des Rechts der Verteidigung auf Akteneinsicht gemäß §147 I StPO: Zugleich Besprechung von BGH: Urteil vom 18.6.2009 – 3 StR 89/09 (LG Hannover)', *NStZ*, 30 (2010), 486–92

Woischnik, J., *Untersuchungsrichter und Beschuldigtenrechte in Argentinien: Eine kritische Würdigung des neuen Bundesstrafverfahrensrechts anhand der rechtsstaatlichen Vorgaben der Menschenrechtskonventionen* (Freiburg i.Br.: Ed. iuscrim, Max-Planck-Institut für Ausländisches und Internationales Strafrecht, 2001)

Wollmann, S., 'Wie konventionswidrig ist die nachträgliche Sicherungsverwahrung?', *NK*, 19 (2007), 152–5

Xanthopoulou, E., 'The Quest for Proportionality for the EAW: Fundamental Rights Protection in a Mutual Recognition Environment', *NJECL*, 6 (2015), 32–52

Zacchè, F., 'Lettura di atti assunti senza contraddittorio e giusto processo (Corte europea dei diritti dell'uomo, sez. III, sent. 13 ottobre 2005)', *Indice Penale*, 9 (2006), 427–40

Zappalà, S., *Human Rights in International Criminal Proceedings* (Oxford: Oxford University Press, 2005)

Zeder, F., 'Der EuGH hat entschieden: Menschenrechtswidrige Haftbedingungen können Grund für die Ablehnung der Vollstreckung eines Europäischen Haftbefehls sein', *JSt*, 14 (2016), 262–6

Zehetgruber, C., 'Zur Unvereinbarkeit von §329 Abs. 1 S. 1 StPO mit der EMRK', *HRRS*, 14 (2013), 397–405

Zeitzmann, S., 'Zur angestrebten Reform der Vorratsdatenspeicherungsrichtlinie', *ZEuS*, 14 (2011), 433–84

Ziegenhorn, G., *Der Einfluss der EMRK im Recht der EU-Grundrechtecharta: Genuin chartarechtlicher Grundrechtsschutz gemäß Art. 52 Abs. 3 GRCh* (Berlin: Duncker & Humblot, 2009)

Zieschang, F., 'Polizeiliche Tatprovokation', in Stuckenberg, C.-F-, and Gärditz, K. F., eds., *Strafe und Prozess im freiheitlichen Rechtsstaat: Festschrift für Hans-Ulrich Paeffgen zum 70. Geburtstag am 2. Juli 2015* (Berlin: Duncker & Humblot, 2015), 423–37

'Tödliche Notwehr zur Verteidigung von Sachen und Art. 2 II a EMRK', *GA*, 153 (2006), 415–19

Zöller, M. A., 'Die Bedeutung staatlicher Schutzpflichten für das Recht auf Leben nach Art. 2 EMRK', in Esser, R., Günther, H.-L., Jäger, C., Mylonopoulos, C., and Öztürk, B., eds., *Festschrift für Hans-Heiner Kühne zum 70. Geburtstag* (Heidelberg et al.: C. F. Müller, 2013), 629–46

'Das transnationale europäische Doppelbestrafungsverbot: Luxemburgum locutum, causa finita?', *GA*, 163 (2016), 325–35

'Die transnationale Geltung des Grundsatzes ne bis in idem nach dem Vertrag von Lissabon', in Amelung, K., Günther, H.-J. and Kühne, H.-H., eds., *Festschrift für Volker Krey zum 70. Geburtstag am 9. Juli 2010* (Stuttgart: Kohlhammer, 2010), 501–22

'Grausame Tötung oder völkerrechtlich gedeckte Kriegsrepressalie? Der Fall Friedrich Engel', *Jura*, 27 (2005), 552–61

Zwaak, L., 'Right to Life (Article 2)', in van Dijk, P., van Hoof, F., van Rijn, A., and Zwaak, L., eds., *Theory and Practice of the ECHR* (2006), 351–404

'The Supervisory Task of the Committee of Ministers', in van Dijk, P., Van Hoof, F., Van Rijn, A., and Zwaak, L., eds., *Theory and Practice of the ECHR* (2006), 291–322

3

Europeanised Substantive Criminal Law in the Broader Sense (Council of Europe and EU)

1 The 'Europeanisation' of the national law of the Member States is – apart from the Union's (limited) competence to create supranational criminal law[1] – mainly brought about by Conventions of the Council of Europe (see section A below) and the the different techniques of influence of the EU (see section B).[2]

A. Council of Europe Conventions

2 As of 15 February 2018, the following substantive law conventions existed:[3]

- European Convention on the Punishment of **Road Traffic Offences** of 30 November 1964;[4]
- European Convention on the Non-applicability of Statutory Limitation to Crimes against Humanity and **War Crimes** of 25 January 1974;[5]
- European Convention on the Suppression of **Terrorism** of 27 January 1977[6] and the Protocol of Amendment of 15 May 2003;[7]
- European Convention on Offences relating to **Cultural Property** of 23 June 1985;[8]
- European Convention on Spectator **Violence and Misbehaviour at Sports Events** and in Particular at Football Matches of 19 August 1985;[9]
- European Convention for the Prevention of **Torture** and Inhuman or Degrading Treatment or Punishment of 26 November 1987,[10] supplemented by Additional Protocols I and II, both of 4 November 1993;[11]
- Convention on **Laundering**, Search, Seizure and Confiscation of the Proceeds from Crime of 8 November 1990;[12]
- Agreement on **Illicit Traffic by Sea** of 13 January 1995;[13]
- Convention on Human Rights and **Biomedicine** of 4 April 1997;[14]

- Convention on the Protection of the **Environment** through Criminal Law of 4 November 1998;[15]
- Criminal Law Convention on **Corruption** of 27 January 1999,[16] supplemented by the Additional Protocol of 15 May 2003;[17]
- Convention on **Cybercrime** of 23 November 2001,[18] supplemented by the Additional Protocol concerning the criminalisation of acts of a racist and xenophobic nature committed through computer systems of 28 January 2003;[19]
- Convention on the **Prevention of Terrorism** of 16 May 2005,[20] supplemented by Additional Protocol of 22 October 2015 (regarding foreign fighters);[21]
- Convention on Action against **Trafficking in Human Beings** of 16 May 2005;[22]
- Convention on Laundering, Search, Seizure and Confiscation of the Proceeds from Crime and on the Financing of Terrorism of 16 May 2005;[23]
- Convention on the Protection of Children against Sexual Exploitation and Sexual Abuse of 25 October 2007;[24]
- Convention on Preventing and Combating **Violence against Women and Domestic Violence** of 11 May 2011.[25]
- Convention on the **Counterfeiting of Medical Products** and similar crimes involving threats to public health of 28 October 2011.[26]
- Convention on the **Manipulation of Sports Competitions** of 18 September 2014.[27]
- Convention against Trafficking in **Human Organs** of 25 March 2015.[28]

3 The Laundering and the Cybercrime Conventions will be examined more closely here as representative examples of currently relevant substantive conventions. The **Laundering Convention** builds on the description of money laundering as a criminal offence in Art. 3 of the 1988 Vienna Convention on Illicit Drugs;[29] the offence definitions in both Conventions share *three basic elements* that characterise laundering:[30] (i) 'the conversion or transfer of property' with a particular purpose, if the origin of the property is illicit; (ii) 'the concealment or disguise of the true nature, source, location, disposition, movement, rights with respect to, or ownership of, property', and (iii) 'the acquisition, possession or use of property'. However, the Council of Europe's Laundering Convention expands the possible predicate offences – as do the relevant EU directives[31] – beyond the field of narcotics to include 'any criminal offence'.[32]

4 The **Cybercrime Convention's**[33] section on substantive criminal law[34] sets out that the contracting parties shall establish a range of criminal offences in regard to the 'confidentiality, integrity and availability of data and computer systems'; computer crime and computer fraud (cf. Art. 8) and forgery of data (Art. 7); content-related computer and Internet crime in the form of child pornography (Art. 9); and infringements of copyright (Art. 10).[35] Art. 12 requires that corporate liability be established.[36] The **Additional Protocol** concerning the criminalisation of **acts of a racist and xenophobic nature committed through computer systems** contains further offences related to criminal computer or Internet content.[37] Art. 4 covers racist and xenophobically motivated threats made through computer systems, while Art. 5 refers to racist and xenophobic insults. Art. 3 establishes that States should render the dissemination of racist and xenophobic material through computer systems a punishable offence; this raises doubts in regard to the **freedom of opinion** guaranteed by the Convention.[38] Whether the Cybercrime Convention will be able to make a more effective contribution to the approximation of national law than the Laundering Convention is doubtful, given the contracting States' broad scope for implementation (cf. e.g. the option of including additional objective or subjective requirements[39]) and the many options for making reservations.[40]

B. Approximation of Criminal Law in the Union

I. General Remarks

5 The English versions of Art. 29(2) subparagraph 3 TEU (old version)[41] and Art. 67(3) TFEU speak of the '**approximation**'[42] of the criminal laws of Member States[43] in order to 'endeavour to ensure a high level of security'. According to **Art. 83(1) TFEU** the European Parliament and Council, 'by means of directives adopted in accordance with the ordinary legislative procedure, [can] establish **minimum rules** concerning the definition of criminal offences and sanctions in the *areas of particularly serious crime* with a cross-border dimension resulting from the nature or impact of such offences or from a special need to combat them on a common basis'.[44] In addition to this, approximation may also take place to enable the effective *implementation of certain Union policies.*[45] If a Member State is of the opinion that this approximation affects 'fundamental aspects of its criminal justice system', it can implement the

emergency brake mechanism of Art. 83(3) TFEU.[46] We will return to both aspects below.

6 Taking **Art. 83(1)** TFEU as a starting point, approximation across the EU requires 'particularly **serious crime with a cross-border dimension'** (*subparagraph 1*). The areas of crime listed in *subparagraph 2* (terrorism, trafficking in human beings and sexual exploitation of women and children, illicit drug trafficking, illicit arms trafficking, money laundering, corruption,[47] counterfeiting of means of payment, computer crime and organised crime)[48] are meant to be paradigmatic, but in reality are not exhaustive,[49] as – unlike Art. 29 TEU old version[50] – according to *subparagraph 3* this list can be extended through a unanimous Council decision following the consent of the EP.[51] While cases of particularly serious crime with a cross-border dimension can be assumed to exist in the areas of crime listed, this requirement must be subjected to close scrutiny when this 'extension clause' is applied.[52] However, **the principles of subsidiarity and proportionality**[53] demand not only that extension within the meaning of subparagraph 3 be approached cautiously, but also that the above-mentioned areas of crime be interpreted strictly in respect to the severity and cross-border dimension of the crime in question;[54] at any rate, the approximation must be *necessary*.[55] The German Federal Constitutional Court, in its Lisbon judgment,[56] also demands, and rightly so, that Member States retain 'substantial scope' when implementing the directives issued as a result of Art. 83(1) TFEU.[57] Moreover, the principle of parliamentary reservation[58] also requires that **parliamentary consent** be gained prior to an extension in accordance with subparagraph 3,[59] for this rule actually represents a (hidden) *treaty-amendment clause* that cannot be reconciled with the principle of conferral[60] and the Union's lack of *competence-competence*.[61]

7 The 'definition of **minimum requirements**'[62] aims at a Union-wide minimum standard in regard to the punishability of certain *forms of conduct* and the corresponding *punishments*[63] – a kind of minimum penalty for 'minimum conduct' valid across the Union, which also authorises the Union to introduce new offences; that is, to criminalise conduct that previously was not punishable.[64] Here we can see a striking terminological reversal of what is otherwise meant by minimum requirements – namely a minimum standard under the rule of law (as it is indeed used in Art. 82(2)(b) TFEU with regard to procedural rights). Ultimately, this favours an **expansion of punishability**, for where national criminal law does not meet the (minimum) requirements set

by the EP and Council, this needs – in cases of particularly serious crime with a cross-border dimension – to be amended through an expansion of criminal law; and where these requirements have already been put into practice, national legislators are at liberty to pass even stricter criminal laws.[65] The contrary view that EU minimum rules limit the Member States' authority to adopt even stricter criminal law provisions is,[66] while certainly to be welcomed from a rights perspective, difficult to reconcile with the wording of Art. 83(1) TFEU – which does not provide for such a limitation[67] – and, more importantly, completely incompatible with the Member States' sovereign domain about their domestic criminal law. At any rate, the Union's competence also includes **penalties**,[68] mainly those of a custodial nature,[69] which – in accordance with the seminal judgment on the 'Greek maize scandal'[70] – need to be effective, proportionate and dissuasive.[71] While the specific sanction applied remains unaffected,[72] the standards of the Greek maize judgment are valid in this respect also,[73] and moreover Union law certainly provides criteria for the application of sanctions.[74]

8 As a consequence of this tendency towards criminalisation, the **protection of citizens from criminal law** through the human rights instruments of European law – that is, the ECHR, the CFREU or general legal principles (prohibition of retroactive punishment, principle of proportionality) – gains particular importance.[75] These rights constitute valid Union law[76] and thus have to be taken into account when taking recourse to Arts. 82 ff. TFEU.[77] This may even entail a decriminalising approach if otherwise a criminalisation would amount to a disproportionate restriction of Union rights or undermine the Union's basic freedoms.[78] At any rate, the Council itself acknowledges the **necessity** of **restrictions** based on the rule of law. This is evident in the basic rights focus of the Stockholm Programme[79] and the Draft Council Conclusions 2009 on criminal law, which incorporate the fundamental principles of a liberal, restrictive criminal law (*ultima ratio*, proportionality, subsidiarity, *Rechtsgutslehre*/harm principle and principle of culpability).[80]

9 The legitimising **aim** of this approximation of Member State criminalisation on as large a common denominator as possible is Art. 67(1, 3) TFEU's postulate, already mentioned above, of ensuring 'a **high level of security**' in 'an area of freedom, security and justice'.[81] This points to the autonomous function of approximation with a view to establish a – predominantly – secure area of freedom, security and justice, as opposed to a mere auxiliary function of approximation with a view to efficient co-operation in criminal matters.[82] At any rate, this once again reveals the tendency to understand (European) criminal law repressively as a *law of security and protection.*[83] The optimisation of police and judicial co-operation through as extensive a harmonisation of national criminal law as possible is a further aim of approximation.[84] This guarantees the dual criminality traditionally required for extradition,[85] although of course its significance is on the wane given the apparently unstoppable advance of the *principle of mutual recognition* previously discussed[86] and the instruments based upon it, in particular the European Arrest Warrant.[87] Also, approximation makes it possible to **prevent conflicts of jurisdiction,**[88] for these kinds of *positive* conflict of jurisdiction usually arise because there is a risk of impunity in the State of commission (*lex loci*). However, this risk would disappear if said 'minimum requirements' introduced minimum standards of punishability across the Union, as thus the territorial State's own *ius puniendi* would no longer have to be applied (extraterritorially) to prevent impunity in other Member States.[89]

10 The expansive tendency of the approximation of substantive criminal law[90] is evident not only in the extension clause of Art. 83(1) subparagraph 3, but also in the fact that the Union, pursuant to Art. 83(2) TFEU, 'may establish minimum rules with regard to the definition of criminal offences and sanctions' to **implement Union policies** if this is 'essential to ensure the effective implementation' of the policy in question.[91] Thus the **ancillary competence** already recognised by the CJEU is incorporated into primary law.[92] Criminal law becomes a mere (supposedly effective) instrument for the implementation of Union policies,[93] a means to an end, making plain the *instrumental or functional approach* of the driving forces – Commission[94] and CJEU – behind European Criminal Law.[95] The – understandable – concern here is to consistently protect legal interests and Union interests in the Member States in order to avoid adverse effects on the internal European market.[96] However, the 'serious extension' (to use the words of the German Constitutional Court) of criminal law jurisdiction that this entails is – once again – hardly compatible with the principle of conferral.[97] In any case, there needs to be a *harmonisation competence* enshrined in an *explicit legal basis* – besides Art. 83(2) TFEU – in the primary law of the policy area concerned,[98] such as, for example, Art. 191 ff. (Art. 192(1)) TFEU for environmental policy.[99] *Subsidiarity* and *proportionality* also urge caution in this respect, especially as the approximation needs to be 'essential' according to Art. 83(2) first sentence TFEU.[100] In this sense, it is required that there exist a 'serious enforcement deficit' that can only be resolved through the threat of punishment.[101] Even if this is considered overly strict with an eye towards the above-mentioned consistent implementation of Union policies,[102] in many areas the Union will not actually be able to prove the necessity, (increased) efficiency and proportionality of European *criminal* law provisions.[103] As far as the legislative procedure to adopt such measures is concerned, it is worrying that it is determined by the respective (extrapenal) harmonisation measure,[104] and that thus the EP may sometimes only have a restricted right to participation.[105]

11 At least **Art. 82(3)** and **Art. 83(3)** TFEU now make it possible for Member States that consider 'fundamental aspects of [their] criminal justice system' to be affected to apply for suspension of the ordinary legislative procedure. Thus, for example, the German Council representative has to use this possibility if instructed to do so by the Bundestag or – for state competencies – the Bundesrat.[106] However, there are three qualifications to this so-called **emergency brake procedure**. First, 'fundamental aspects' do not cover every conflict with the national legal system, but only those that affect far-reaching and fundamental principles, such as the principles of legality or culpability[107] and fundamental legislative decisions concerning the General Part of criminal law.[108] Second, the 'emergency brake' does not lead to the termination of the legislative procedure,[109] but only to its suspension, so that the European Council[110] can then deal with the matter. Even if the Council is unable to reach a consensus (in which case the matter is referred back to the Committee of Ministers),[111] the option of *enhanced co-operation* still remains.[112] If at least nine Member States are in favour of implementing the directive, they can still decide that it will be valid amongst themselves if the EP agrees.[113] Third and finally, Member States may not issue a veto for reasons unrelated to the matter at hand, for example in order to push through a different political aim. In such a case, the Commission could initiate an infringement procedure[114] due to violation of the duty of co-operation.[115] The 'emergency brake' can also be *applied analogously* if the EU issues directives on the approximation of criminal law based on other rules on competence – such as Art. 325(4) TFEU; however, it cannot be applied when the EU creates supranational criminal law,[116] as in these cases the national legal order is not directly affected by EU law.[117]

II. *Areas of Criminal Law Approximation*

12 Harmonisation mainly covers offence definitions or areas of crime – that is, the **Special Part** – while the rules of the *General Part* are at most referred to in regard to specific areas. This is due not only to the fact that national legal systems have a higher number of individual traits in the General Part than in the Special Part,[118] thus making the General Part harder to approximate and requiring special comparative preparatory work,[119] but also to the fact that the Union law competence to approximate *minimum* rules (discussed above) does not – or at least does not explicitly[120] – cover the guidelines of the structures and definitions of the General Part.[121] The following instruments were adopted:[122]

- economic and financial crime[123] (protection of the financial interests of the EU,[124] money laundering,[125] insider trading,[126] corruption,[127] protection of means of payment[128]);
- trafficking in human beings;[129]
- sexual exploitation of children and child pornography;[130]
- cybercrime;[131]
- protection of the environment;[132]
- racism and xenophobia;[133]
- smuggling of human beings (aliens).[134]

13 The areas of **organised crime,**[135] **illegal drug trafficking**[136] and **terrorism**[137] are missing from this list. These are now enumerated in Art. 83(1) subparagraph 2 TFEU, along with many other areas of crime.[138] The list in Art. 83(1) makes clear that all the areas of crime mentioned there are of equal importance; the decisive criterion is a 'cross-border dimension' within the meaning of Art. 83(1) subparagraph 1 TFEU.

14 The measures on the **protection of the Union's financial interests by means of criminal law** are of fundamental importance for all harmonising activity in the field of substantive criminal law. The legal acts issued in this context often serve as models and are in part transferred to other areas.[139] The *PIF Convention,*[140] which entered into force in 2002 and obligates Member States to punish fraudulent activity damaging to the Union,[141] forms the basis of European criminal law on financial protection.[142] Pursuant to Art. 1(1) PIF Convention, this includes – summed up roughly – intentional acts using or presenting false information that result in funds from the Union's budget[143] being wrongfully retained or illegally diminished. In addition, it covers the misapplication of funds that were originally lawfully granted.[144] Furthermore, the PIF Convention includes several fragmentary regulations on the General Part.[145] Thus Member States are also obliged to penalise the participation in, instigation of, and attempt to commit EU fraud.[146] However, these normative concepts are not defined, and thus it remains up to the Member States to specify them further. For example, national law determines when an act constitutes a punishable attempt and when it counts as a non-punishable preparatory act.[147] Accordingly, the harmonisation effects of the PIF Convention are minor in that regard.[148] Also, the guidelines regarding sanctions[149] and jurisdiction are very general.[150] The PIF Convention was supplemented by *two protocols* with respect to substantive law.[151] Protocol I,[152] which also entered into force in 2002, aims to protect the Union's finances against attacks from within. It obligates Member States to punish acts of active or passive corruption by certain officials if the acts damage or could damage the financial interests of the Union. Protocol II,[153] which became effective in 2009, on the one hand aims to create a common basis to combat money laundering[154] damaging to the Union.[155] On the other hand, it sets up minimum rules on the punishment of legal persons. When doing so, it remains up to the Member States whether they wish to hold these persons accountable under criminal or administrative law for the fraud, corruption or money laundering offences committed by their heads.[156]

15 After an extensive evaluation of the relevant legal regulations,[157] in 2012 the Commission concluded that the PIF Convention and its Protocols were not sufficient to guarantee the effective and homogeneous protection of the Union's finances.[158] Therefore it presented a proposal for a **new directive** on the fight against EU fraud by means of criminal law.[159] This proposal aimed to bring the PIF Convention and its Protocols together in slightly modified form in a single legal act and to add to them. For example, the Proposal Directive contained rules on penalising dishonest conduct in public tender procedures[160] and the misapplication of Union funds by public servants.[161] Furthermore, for the first time the Commission was seeking to introduce binding minimum minimum penalties. Thus an EU fraud involving damages of at least €100,000 should be punishable by a minimum penalty of at least six months' imprisonment and a maximum penalty of at least five years' imprisonment,[162] resulting in a binding minimum penalty range of six months to five years.[163] Furthermore, financial offences that damage the Union were to come under the statute of limitations at the earliest five years after they were committed.[164] Over the course of the legislative procedure, the Commission's proposal was debated hotly.[165] One of the main points of contention concerned the legal basis. While the Commission rightly[166] wanted to base the directive upon Art. 325(4) TFEU,[167] the Council[168] and Parliament[169] considered the ancillary competence of Art. 83(2) to be applicable. Furthermore, there was criticism that the Commission's proposals were too repressive and would interfere too strongly with the national legal systems.[170] Accordingly, the alternative proposal presented by the Council in 2013 was markedly more moderate.[171] Only the new offence of misappropriation of funds (defined more restrictively than in the Commission Proposal) appeared in addition to the classic PIF offences of fraud, active and passive corruption and money laundering.[172] Furthermore, the Council wanted to grant the Member States more scope with regard to the general conditions of punishability.[173] Of course, this would have had an adverse effect upon the harmonisation efforts especially promoted by the Commission. In the meantime, EP and Council have reached a political agreement resulting in **Directive (EU) 2017/1371**.[174] Accordingly, the distinction between fraud and fraud-related criminal offences was maintained.[175] In addition, the Directive does not resort to minimum minimum penalties, but in Art. 7(3) requires a *minimum maximum penalty* of four years in the event of serious injuries, i.e. from a damage or advantage value achieved of €100,000. The Directive also provides the 'temporary or permanent exclusion from public tender procedures' as a sanction for legal persons.[176] Last but not least regarding the limitation period, Art. 12(1) also does not include a tangible definition ('sufficient period of time').

C. The Influence of Primary and Secondary Union Law

16 Case 1

US citizen Z is giving evidence in proceedings before the Court of Justice (CJEU, Luxembourg). In doing so, he deliberately gives a false statement under oath. Has Z made himself liable to prosecution for a false-testimony offence?[177] ➔ mn. 57

17 Case 2

The animal trader T wants to import an African elephant to Germany in order to sell it to a zoo. Is T's plan permitted or is it prohibited as a punishable offence? ➔ mn. 58

18 Case 3

Karl Prantl, an Italian citizen, imported wine to Germany in so-called 'Bocksbeutel' bottles. While these bottles are commonly used in northern Italy and South Tyrol, according to the Wine Regulation valid at the time of the act in question – and enforceable by sanction – in Germany their use was only permitted for Franconian wine. Has Prantl made himself liable to prosecution?[178] → mn. 59

19 Case 4

Austrian citizen A successfully graduated in veterinary medicine from an Italian university. In France, he subsequently applied to be included in the Chamber of Veterinary Surgeons, which according to French law is a compulsory requirement for practising as a vet. However, A was denied membership as he did not possess a French diploma. He proceeded to work in France as a vet nonetheless. Has A made himself liable to prosecution according to French law?[179] → mn. 60

20 Case 5

A showman was sentenced to a fine for negligently failing to operate a tachograph in his circus motor tractor. He subsequently appealed on a point of law, and the Bavarian Supreme Regional Court submitted the matter to the German Federal Court of Justice (§121(2) GVG). The Bavarian Court was of the opinion that it could not reject the appeal because of a decision of the Higher Regional Court Düsseldorf, which referred to the applicable EC Regulation exempting 'vehicles used to transport circus and funfair equipment' from the obligation to operate a tachograph. What decision was the Federal Court of Justice obliged to reach?[180] → mn. 61

21 Case 6

Following the public prosecutor's appeal against a Regional Court verdict that acquitted the defendant of improper handling of hazardous waste (§326(1) StGB), the German Federal Court of Justice was obliged to deal with the definition of waste. To what extent does European law play a role here?[181] → mn. 62

22 Even though to date the Union has no authority to enact original criminal law – beyond the protection of its financial interests[182] – the national law of the Member States is nonetheless influenced by primary and secondary Union law in a variety of ways.[183] Before turning to the two first-mentioned forms of **reference** – from Union to national law and vice versa – a few general preliminary remarks are in order:[184] **reference norms** do not contain a (complete) definition of the offence leading to the sanction they set out, but refer to other provisions. A ('complete') offence definition thus only comes about through a *synopsis of Union law and the (national) 'blanket' criminal law.*[185] We also have to distinguish between **internal** and **external references**:[186] we speak of internal reference when both the referring and the referred-to norm were issued by *one and the same legislator*, while in cases of external reference the referring norm and the object of the reference were issued by *different* *legislators*. We can further distinguish between **static and dynamic references**: in the former, the offence definition of the reference norm refers to a different norm in a *particular* (fixed) version, while in the latter – which constitutes the broadest form of reference – the reference norm refers to a different norm in *the version currently in force*. Which type of reference applies is a matter to be determined through interpretation.[187] **'Blanket criminal laws'** represent a special case where reference is concerned.[188] We speak of blanket references when a criminal law contains a sanction, but the offence in question – at least in part – refers to another norm. The criminal law of the EU Member States is full of such provisions.[189]

I. Union Law References to National Law ('Assimilation')

23 Primary and secondary Union law contains a large number of references to national law. These references aim to place the **legal interests** of Union law – which are covered by the reference – **on an equal footing** with national legal interests in terms of the protection afforded through criminal law, and thus the aim ultimately is to **'assimilate'** the legal systems of the Member States.[190] Probably the most prominent case of such an assimilation of primary law can be found in *Art. 30 CJEU Statute*, discussed in our case 1. This provision obliges Member States to prosecute false statements made before the CJEU on a domestic level:

> A Member State shall treat any violation of an oath by a witness or expert *in the same manner as if the offence had been committed before one of its courts* with jurisdiction in civil proceedings. At the instance of the Court, the Member State concerned shall prosecute the offender before its competent court.[191]

24 This kind of construction has several consequences. First, it leads to an **expansion of the extra-territorial application of national criminal law**, as national jurisdiction is extended to include false-testimony offences committed abroad (in Luxembourg) and in supranational (Union law) proceedings.[192] Take the following example from German law: according to the relevant jurisdictional provision of the Penal Code,[193] German criminal law only applies to false-testimony offences committed abroad if they refer to a domestic proceedings, such as in the case of false testimony given before a foreign court or before a different foreign authority for the purposes of a civil case pending in Germany.[194] Without such connection, German jurisdiction formerly could be based on Art. 30 CJEU Statute in conjunction with the German false-testimony offence in question;[195] in the meantime, the legislator has extended the scope of these offences to international courts.[196]

25 This leads to a second consequence that has direct implications for substantive criminal law: if we assume, in line with prevailing opinion, that a primary law assimilation rule such as Art. 30 CJEU Statute is *self-executing* and thus constitutes directly applicable Union law,[197] then this leads to an **expansion of the national offence in question** by way of the respective primary law assimilation provision. Whether assimilation leads to 'supranational comprehensive offences' (*Gesamttatbestände*)[198] or whether 'only' national criminal laws are 'Europeanised' is of secondary importance;[199] what is decisive is the result: an **expansion of national offence definitions** in regard to both the application of the national criminal law and substantive law is achieved through supranational European law, which renders internal restrictions inoperative due to the principle of the primacy of Union law.[200] This finding is also noteworthy because the Union thereby – through expanding the scope of existing national criminal laws – is creating directly applicable **supranational Union law**[201] and thus is effectively overriding its lack of authority to legislate criminal law.[202]

26 Against this background it is unsurprising that a number of **objections** to the assimilation technique have been voiced: references to national criminal laws *re-enforce differences* in the protection of Union legal interests afforded by criminal law, as the effect of the reference depends on the existence of a national offence, which is not always given or may be repealed.[203] Furthermore, this technique constitutes a violation of the principle of *nullum crimen sine lege*, as the national (criminal) legislator has no influence on the reference made to its offences.[204] There are also cases in which the 'comprehensive offence' created through assimilation gives rise to *challenging questions regarding interpretation*.

27 Thus the primary law reference norm of Art. 194(1) EAEC Treaty states:

> Each Member State shall treat any infringement of this obligation [to maintain secrecy] as an act prejudicial to its rules on secrecy and as one falling, both as to merits and jurisdiction, within the scope of its laws relating to acts prejudicial to the security of the State or to disclosure of professional secrets.

This may lead to an expansion of national criminal law. Take the case of the German offences regarding the breach of State or official secrets[205] which are expanded by this European provision.[206] For example, if this provision is read into the legal definition of State secret given in §93(1) StGB, then this amounts to making not only the 'danger of serious prejudice to the external security of the Federal Republic of Germany' part of the offence definition, but also the danger of serious prejudice to the security of Euratom or another Member State. This raises the question whether a supranational organisation can actually have any *external* security comparable to that of a State.[207] The answer to this question used to be no, as the EU's Common Foreign and Security Policy (CFSP), as part of the 'second pillar', only existed in the form of intergovernmental co-operation and was thus not comparable to the policy of an independent State.[208] However, following the Lisbon Treaty increased supranationalisation has taken place in this regard,[209] which makes it seem at least reasonable to speak of an autonomous CFSP of the Union.[210] Similar problems arise, *mutatis mutandis*, with regard to the criminal law of other Member States.

28 Further problems arise when reference norms, such as the above-mentioned Art. 30 CJEU Statute, **refer to national criminal law globally** without specifying the norms referred to more closely.[211] There is good reason to doubt, given the *lex certa* requirement,[212] whether those addressed by the norm can justifiably be subjected to the particular difficulties of **determining the applicable norms** associated with such a blanket reference.[213] One suggested **solution** to this uncertainty is to include the extensions made to national law through assimilation in the national provisions affected.[214] However, this approach would inevitably conflict with the CJEU's case law, given that the Court expressly rejects any repetition of directly applicable Union law in national legislature in order to ensure the differentiation between (primary) Union law and the national legal systems.[215] Satzger has thus suggested not ascribing any direct effect to the reference norms, but instead seeing them only as requiring the Member States to reform their criminal laws to take the protection of the respective Union legal interests into account.[216] The principle of interpretation in conformity with Union Law (harmonious interpretation)[217] would supplement this approach.

29 Besides cases where primary Union law refers to national (criminal) law, the assimilation of the legal interests of Union law could also involve the **secondary law of the Union** (here: regulations) making references to national criminal law.[218] However, given that there are already considerable doubts concerning primary law assimilations in light of the Union's lack of competence to pass supranational criminal law, it is hardly surprising that prevailing opinion[219] **rejects** this possibility of assimilation by way of secondary Union law *a limine*. The decisive difference between primary and secondary law references is that the latter is not even based on an international treaty, unlike Art. 194 EAEC, for example.[220] The technique of secondary law references has thus rightly been abandoned.[221]

Nevertheless, the **'Customs Information System'**, a database maintained by the Commission to which the Member States' customs authorities have direct access, still works on the basis of Council Regulation (EC) No 515/97 of 13 March 1997[222] in the amended version created by Art. 1 Regulation (EC) No 766/2008 of the European Parliament and of the Council of 9 July 2008.[223] Its Art. 45(1) second sentence states in regard to the data transmitted, 'It shall be covered by the obligation of professional secrecy and shall enjoy the protection extended to like information under ... the national law of the Member States receiving it'. Thus a Council regulation is (still) making a reference with the purpose of assimilating national[224] criminal laws.[225]

II. National Law References to Union Law

30 National law frequently refers to Union law. We thus have the opposite case to that of the assimilation technique. Our case 2 deals with this situation, the problem is illustrated in Figure 5.

31 We can draw a distinction between a reference made in a national (parliamentary) *statute*[226] and one made in an *executive decree* (a provision issued by an executive authority, e.g., a minister).[227] Generally, **references from national law** to Union law[228] lead to a more intense 'Europeanisation of criminal law' than assimilation, given that **Union law directly defines** the content of national criminal norms.[229] These references give rise to a number of **questions**. First, it is doubtful whether the national (criminal) legislator is even *authorised* to sanction certain Union conduct norms according to its national criminal law at its own discretion if this is not envisaged in the Union law itself, as it would then to some extent be acting *ultra vires*.[230] Furthermore, there is a risk that the addressees of the Union norm will be subjected to *unequal treatment* – in contravention of the aim of harmonisation – if breaking certain norms is only sanctioned in criminal law in some Member States and not in

Does the import of an African elephant contrary to Art. 4(1) first sentence of Regulation (EC) No 338/97 constitute an offence pursuant to §71(1) No 2 in conjunction with §69(4) No 1 of the Federal Act for the Protection of Nature (BNatSchG)?

§ 71 BNatSchG
(1) Persons **intentionally** carrying out an **act listed in §69(4) No 1 ...** involving an animal or plant belonging to a strictly protected species **shall be punished with a custodial sentence of no more than five years or a fine**.

§ 69 IV No 1 BNatSchG
It is an administrative offence to **violate Regulation (EC) No 338/97** by intentionally or negligently
1. failing to provide an import permit, export permit or re-export certificate **contrary to Art. 4(1) first sentence**, or failing to do so correctly, completely or in a timely manner...

Art. 4 Council Regulation (EC) No 338/97 of 9 December 1996 as amended by Art. 1 Commission Regulation (EU) No 750/2013 of 29 July 2013 on the protection of species of wild fauna and flora by regulating trade therein
(1) The introduction into the Community of **specimens of the species listed in Annex A** shall be subject to completion of the **necessary checks** and the prior presentation, at the **border customs office** at the point of introduction, of an import permit issued by a **management authority** of the Member State of destination.
The **import permit** may be issued only in accordance with the restrictions established pursuant to paragraph 6 and when the following conditions have been met:
(a) the **competent scientific authority** ... has advised that the introduction into the Community:
(i) would not have a harmful effect on the conservation status of the species ...

Annex A of Council Regulation (EC) No 338/97 as amended by Art. 1 Commission Regulation (EU) No 750/2013 of 29 July 2013 lists the **African elephant** (*Loxodonta africana*).

Art.12 Council Regulation (EC) No 338/97
(1) Member States shall designate **customs offices** ... and shall state which offices are specifically intended to deal with live specimens.
...
(3) All offices designated in accordance with paragraph 1 shall be notified to the Commission which shall publish **a list of them in the Official Journal of the European Communities**.
Art.13
Similar regulations apply to the ***management and scientific authorities*** *and other competent authorities.*

Figure 5 Determining the applicable law in the case of a reference of German (criminal) law to Union law

others.[231] However, overall this argument remains unconvincing.[232] For if one – rightly – assumes that the Union lacks the competence to enact criminal law itself, then Member States should be given sovereignty over the decision to protect particular Union interests through their national criminal law, especially as the content of the Union conduct norms remains unchanged. After all, Member States are, as we will see in more detail below,[233] obliged to protect Union legal interests.[234]

32 Doubts are also voiced concerning the compliance of national reference norms with **constitutional law.**[235] Especially in cases of dynamic references, concerns are raised regarding adherence to the principle of the separation of powers, the principle of democracy and the principle of certainty (*lex certa*).[236] These concerns are particularly pertinent in cases of references to Union law, as here **two autonomous legal systems** – that of the Union[237] and that of the respective State – are **linked**. The harmonisation of Member State legal systems through such references assumes that the national reference norm (the blanket criminal norm) will incorporate the substantive legal content of the Union law norm *in the same meaning that it has in Union law*. Thus no *doubling of norms* occurs, as no prohibition or requirement of national law repeats a prohibition or requirement of Union law; rather, the thus created **national–Union law norm is Janus-faced:** it is defined by *European law* in regard to the object of reference, and by *national law* in regard to the reference or blanket norm.[238]

33 Because of the resulting accessority (accessoriness) of the blanket norm in regard to the Union law object of reference, national practice needs to appy the full provision (composed of national and Union law) in line with the **interpretation standards of Union law**;[239] however, this does not mean that **general rules of constitutional law** can be ignored. For the (conduct) norm of Union law (the object of reference) – which in principle takes priority – is formally incorporated into a national blanket criminal law norm and thus becomes part of national law, which must be measured against the respective constitution.[240] In regard to the **principle of certainty**, a twofold distinction is to be drawn: on the one hand, there is its liberty limb in the form of the *specificity* (certainty, *lex certa*) requirement of the law; on the other hand, there is its competence-related limb in the form of the *substantive* – rather than formal – *reservation of statutory powers* (*Gesetzesvorbehalt*).[241] As far as the former, the liberty limb, is concerned, the legislative authority will have to be granted a certain degree of 'typification and normativisation', especially when dealing not with core criminal law, but with special (supplementary) penal provisions ('expert criminal law') directed, for example, at particular professions.[242] The decisive factor is whether norm addressees can justifiably be expected to go to the *effort to determine the applicable law*.[243] In regard to the **reservation of statutory powers**, it should be noted that, on the basis of a substantive concept of law,[244] it is, from a constitutional perspective, admissible for blanket criminal laws to refer to infra-legal provisions (e.g. executive decrees)[245] if the (formal) blanket law sufficiently defines both the punishable conduct and the kind and extent of (penal) sanction so that the executive decree only serves as a kind of further specification.[246] The same applies, in principle, for references to *directly applicable* Union law, for it addresses citizens in the same way as, for example, the said executive decrees.[247]

34 This leads to different **consequences** for (static and dynamic) references to Union law (usually regulations, rarely directives).[248] **Static** references *to domestic law* are normally compatible with the above constitutional considerations if both the reference norm and the object of reference are sufficiently specific in themselves or can be deduced through '*overall evaluation*' (*Gesamtwertungsakt*).[249] The same goes for (static) references of national blanket criminal laws *to Union law*. Here it should be a requirement that the object of reference is always cited precisely in the reference norm because of the inherently greater effort involved for the norm addressee in determining the applicable law (*Rechtsauffindungsaufwand*).[250] The main problem concerning **dynamic references** is that the content of the object of references changes (i.e. is 'dynamic') and the effort required for the norm addressee to determine the applicable law thus increases.[251] In light of this, dynamic global references to all legal acts of the Union probably do not fulfil the criterion of cetainty.[252] The constitutional problems are aggravated further in cases of (dynamic) references *to executive decrees*.[253] Here there is first of all a risk that the *competence* to enact law reserved to the legislative is illegitimately delegated to the executive. Thus, from a constitutional perspective, it is necessary that the requirements and the kind and extent of punishment in the blanket criminal law be as closely defined as possible, so that the *legal, definitional elements* of the offence (*actus reus, Tatbestand*) are only *specified* by the object of reference.[254] As far as the *liberty limb* of the principle of certainty is concerned, it seems obvious that it is the more likely to be infringed the more difficult the process of determining the norm referred to is. Here, only 'highest demands of the reference technique' are able to help norm addressees to determine the applicable law.[255]

35 Where **dynamic (external) references to Union law** are concerned, the same applies to national executive decrees (which correspond, for that matter, to EU regulations) in regard to the *competence-safeguarding* limb of the principle of certainty. The reservation of statutory powers is thus guaranteed if or to the extent to which the authority issuing Union law regulations is only responsible for *specifying* the (complete) offence.[256] By contrast, the actual *certainty* (liberty limb) of such a blanket offence once again constitutes a more problematic issue. Beyond the flaws of dynamic references within the domestic context shown above, there is the added issue that the reference is being made to a *different* legal system, namely that of the Union. Indeed, searching for EU regulations in their applicable current version involves considerable difficulties for the (national) norm addressees, and thus this kind of a dynamic reference usually implies an **unacceptable effort in determining the applicable law.**[257] Sufficient certainty can only be assumed in exceptional cases where a norm addresses a select target group ('expert criminal law') and/or only minor sanctions are involved.[258] The German Federal Court of Justice has been somewhat more flexible in arguing that a reference is sufficiently certain when the object of reference – that is, the respective EU provision referred to – was not changed during the time period in which the offence in question was committed.[259] This is unconvincing, however, since it makes the constitutionally required *lex certa* dependent on mere coincidences – the 'if' and 'when' of a legal amendment.[260] It is even more unconvincing when the BGH in a subsequent decision even goes further to find that the *lex certa* requirement is complied with when the EU provision (*in casu* a directive) referred to is no longer valid.[261] In fact, in such a situation the very basis of criminal liability has disappeared. For, if one argues, as we have done above, that the national reference norm (the 'blanket') and the (EU) norm referred to have to be read together as one Janus-faced national–union law norm, one cannot exist without the other.[262]

36 Rule-of-law considerations require further the **due information on or publication of** the applicable (criminal law) provisions. Otherwise the guidance of social and individual behaviour through (criminal) law cannot be expected. After all, it is only possible to follow laws if those to whom the laws are addressed (the citizens) are aware of them. Accordingly, in case of the reference technique both reference norm and reference object have to be made duly public.[263] There is some dispute concerning the issue of whether, in cases of national blanket law references to Union law, the mere announcement of said Union law in the *Official Journal of the EU* is sufficient to meet these requirements.[264] The fact that Union law is directly applicable alongside national law and that the *OJEU* is thus the decisive source of law speaks in favour of this approach. Accordingly, the German Constitutional Court decided that the publication of the object of reference in the *OJEU* does not per se involve unacceptable (additional) effort on the part of the citizen subject to the Union norm, and thus can be seen as valid.[265] That determining the applicable law can entail considerable difficulties in *individual cases* – for example because foreign-language versions of a law have to be considered when interpreting it – can be taken into account within the context of the **'overall evaluation'** of blanket criminal law and reference object.[266]

III. Harmonisation by Means of Directives

37 As already mentioned above,[267] Art. 83(1) TFEU provides for a broad Union competence to approximate criminal law through directives based on primary law. Besides the areas of crime mentioned explicitly above, **areas of general policy** are also covered by this competence if approximation is deemed 'essential' for their effective implementation.[268] With the relevant Art. 83(2) TFEU the earlier controversy on the subject of **ancillary competence**[269] has been decided in favour of the latter. Previous authorisations, for example in the fields of traffic and the environment, still continue to exist.[270] Of course, it should not be forgotten that in cases where instructions are issued via directives, national criminal laws are enacted upon the sole basis of the sovereign decisions of the Member States[271] and the Union's influence thus remains indirect.[272]

38 The recognition of an ancillary competence goes, in fact, back to the **CJEU** decision on the Framework Decision on the *protection of the environment through criminal law*.[273] Here, the Court had assumed that the 'Community legislature' can already employ the harmonisation of criminal law if this is 'consider[ed] necessary' to 'ensure that the rules which it lays down on environmental protection are fully effective' when 'the application of effective, proportionate and dissuasive criminal penalties by the competent national authorities is an essential measure for combating serious environmental offences'.[274] The CJEU's line of argument was ultimately based on the assumption of competence to harmonise criminal law as **ancillary to regulatory powers**, which can thus be applied to other policy areas.[275] The CJEU confirmed this stance in its decision on the processing and transmission of *flight passenger data*,[276] for the ancillary relationship between the processing of flight passenger data (for the purposes of criminal prosecution) and the sale of flight tickets – which is open to regulation by community law – was only denied in this particular case.[277] In the same vein, on 23 October 2007 the CJEU declared invalid the Council Framework Decision to strengthen the criminal law framework for the enforcement of the law against *ship-source pollution*,[278] following the rationale of the above-mentioned precedent,[279] and in this respect invoked, in addition, a competence in the area of *joint transport policy*.[280] Despite Art. 83(2) TFEU, this approach can still be seen as watering down the principle of conferral,[281] and it reaffirms the Court's **instrumental, functional understanding of criminal law**;[282] however, admittedly this understanding has now been rubber-stamped by the Lisbon Treaty, albeit with the addition of the above-mentioned 'emergency brake'.[283]

39 At any rate, with the explicit recognition of ancillary competence in criminal matters by Art. 83(2) TFEU, the secondary law approximation of criminal law can no longer be based on judicially developed (unwritten) ancillary competence (as just discussed) or on the **general harmonisation competencies** to establish the internal market pursuant to Arts. 114 ff. TFEU.[284] Nor is it possible to draw upon the '**rounding-off competence**' or '**additional competencies rule**'[285] of Art. 352 TFEU.[286] At any rate, it is worthwhile mentioning that the EU (still as 'European Community') has made use of the said harmonisation competence in a range of areas, some of them hotly debated: weapons control,[287] waste disposal,[288] insider trading[289] and money laundering can be cited as examples.[290] In regard to the latter, the offence in question has been extensively, albeit not completely, harmonised within the EU.[291]

40 A different matter is the **scope** of Union law's competence to issue instructions (*Anweisungskompetenz*[292]). The opinions thereto differ widely:[293] while some assume that this authority also includes detailed guidelines with regard to the elements of the respective offence (*actus reus, Tatbestand*), as well as to the nature and scope of the penalty to be applied,[294] arguably the prevailing opinion is that only the specification of **aims** – in the sense of 'guiding principles' (*Zielvorgaben*) – and an 'approximation of **punitive effects**' (*Angleichung der Ahndungseffekte*) is permitted.[295] This is convincing, despite the authorisation to approximate (penal) sanctions in

Art. 83(2) TFEU. One of the factors that argues against a detailed harmonisation competence is the Union's *lack of general competence to legislate criminal law*,[296] for this would be undermined by precise secondary law specifications.[297] Furthermore, the **imperative to use criminal law in the most restrictive form possible** (*Schonungsgebot*) – based on the above-mentioned principles of proportionality and subsidiarity[298] – limits harmonisation: the Union is not permitted to enact any directly applicable criminal laws, especially none which define offence and sanction in such a detailed manner that the Member States would have no margin of discretion when implementing them.[299] Finally, it follows from Art. 288 TFEU – in respect to *directives* – that Member States must be able to choose the form and the methods by which to achieve the prescribed results (aims).[300] The scope of Union law instructions thus continues to be a matter to be decided **case-by-case**, taking the above-mentioned criteria into account.[301]

IV. Harmonisation by Means of Assimilation Based on Other Principles (Duty of Loyalty, Primacy of Union Law, Harmonious Interpretation)

1. The Duty of Loyalty or of Sincere Co-operation (Art. 4(3) TEU)

41 Even if Union legal interests that merit and require protection are not covered by the above-mentioned harmonisation techniques, national criminal law is still influenced by the Member States' duty of loyal co-operation with the Union and its institutions. The relevant Art. 4(3) TEU formulates – as did its predecessor Art. 10 TEC – Member States' **duty to fulfil their obligations** 'arising out of the treaties or resulting from the acts of the institutions of the Union'. From this follows as a direct consequence the duty to protect certain legal interests of the Union – in line with a general **duty of loyalty or 'sincere co-operation'** – and to refrain from measures endangering the aims of the Union.[302] Based on this duty, in its judgment on the Greek maize scandal,[303] the CJEU held that Member States must 'take all measures necessary to guarantee the application and effectiveness of Community law' in cases where no sanction exists for a particular (conduct) rule of Community law. The choice of sanction can be decided by the Member States, but they must ensure, in the words of the Court, 'that infringements of Community law are penalized under conditions, both procedural and substantive, which are analogous to those applicable to infringements of national law of a similar nature and importance and which, in any event, make the penalty **effective, proportionate and dissuasive**' (the so-called *Mindesttrias* or 'minimum trias').[304]

42 Art. 4(3) TEU contains a **duty** for Member States **to actively protect** the legal interests of Union law. This includes not only the protection of financial interests (to which the more specific regulation of Art. 325(1), (2) TFEU applies), but to *all (supranational) legal interests that concern the existence and functioning of the Union.*[305] Member States are also supposed to take action even when the Union takes no initiative itself; that is, when Members are not given express instruction to take concrete measures to ensure the protection of a particular legal interest.[306] Where applicable, Member States must also intervene against private persons who hinder others in the exercise of their basic freedoms under Union law.[307] In the cases of Union norms that are not already sufficiently protected in Union law, including by adequate sanctions, national legislators must determine whether it is necessary to create national criminal laws to provide effective protection. Here, it is decisive that infringements of Union norms are punished under conditions, both procedural and substantive, which are analogous to those applicable to infringements of national law of a similar nature and importance (principle of **equal treatment amounting to assimilation** of Union and national law of Member States).[308] From this perspective, Art. 325(2) TFEU, which calls for an equal protection of national and Union financial interests against fraud,[309] appears as the concretisation and consolidation of assimilation by means of criminal law.[310]

43 There are many examples of such equal treatment of national and Union interests in the criminal law of the Member States. Suffice it here to refer to some examples in German criminal law: according to §264(7) No 2 StGB (offence on subsidy fraud), 'a benefit from public funds under the law of the European Communities which is granted at least in part without market-related consideration' constitutes a subsidy within the meaning of this offence.[311] According to §370(6) AO (German Tax Statute), the offence of tax evasion also includes the reduction of import or export tax administered by another Member State or due to a State of the European Free Trade Association or an associated State; accordingly, the same goes when the act involves certain value added or consumption taxes administered by another Member State.[312] The scope of electoral offences[313] has been explicitly expanded to cover the election of Members of the European Parliament.[314]

Moreover, reference to the bribing of Members of Parliament includes Members of the European Parliament.[315]

44 Even when equal treatment does not seem sufficient reason to create national criminal law, for example if the Member State does not protect its own interests through criminal law either, this necessity of criminal law protection can arise as a result of the CJEU's **'minimum trias'** mentioned above. Accordingly, sanctions have – independently of any comparison with the situation under national criminal law – to be *effective, proportionate* and *dissuasive*.[316] With this a **minimum level of criminal law protection** is established in Union law[317] and the – in principle existing – Member States' freedom of choice and and margin of discretion is restricted.[318]

45 The duty of loyalty is (also) binding upon the **national** (criminal) courts.[319] In line with the CJEU's recent *Taricco* judgment,[320] this means that a national court may be obliged to *disapply* national provisions (*in casu* statutes of limitation) if these were to impede the imposition of criminal sanctions (regarding VAT offences affecting the Union financial interests) [321] which are necessary to adequately protect the Union's (financial) interests within the meaning of the minimum trias.[322] However, upon a referral by Italian Constitiutional Court, the CJEU decided, for the first time restricting the primacy principle, that national law cannot be disapplied if that entailed a violation of a fundamental principle such as that of legality.[323] In a more general vein, the German Federal Constitutional Court has found an obligation of national criminal courts 'to review with particular care at every stage of criminal proceedings whether there are doubts concerning the interpretation of a question of Union law that is key to the court's decision, and whether it is necessary to refer the matter to the CJEU'.[324]

2. The Primacy of Union Law

46 Prevalent opinion assumes, in line with CJEU case law,[325] that **Union law** only **overrides** national law in cases where the two collide (**primacy or precedence**),[326] not that it actually rescinds national law (declaration of invalidity).[327] This primacy goes for every branch of the law – including national constitutional law (basic rights!)[328] and criminal law.[329] The effects of this have been felt particularly in a number of cases in the field of *food law*: the prohibition of certain products subject to sanction in national law is neutralised through primary law on the free movement of goods, as long as the products do not pose a health hazard and have been produced legally in another Member State – for example, appropriately labelled beer that has not been brewed according to traditional German 'purity law'.[330] This also applied in the *Prantl* case, our case 3. In the just-quoted *Taricco* judgment the Grand Chamber held that, in line with the precedence of EU law, national provisions which would impede the effective criminal law protection of EU (financial) interests are to be disapplied and their consequences neutralised.[331]

47 In this kind of constellation, the primacy of directly applicable Union law means that the national norm, a violation of which incurs criminal sanctions, already becomes inapplicable. As a result, the national sanction loses its object of reference, as this is neutralised by Union law.[332] The CJEU judged accordingly in the case of two criminal proceedings against German-speaking foreigners in South Tyrol: here the question arose of whether they had the right to have proceedings conducted in German in line with the **prohibition of discrimination** according to Art. 12 TEC (now Art. 18 TFEU). The CJEU confirmed this and thus made the national (Italian) criminal procedural law subject to the standards of (primary) Community law.[333] While so far the neutralisation effect of EU law has favoured suspects or defendants, in *Taricco* the CJEU's finding for the first time was to the detriment of the suspect(s) since they would have benefited from the statute of limitations declared inapplicable by the Chamber.[334]

48 Furthermore, the CJEU even applies the principle of primacy concerning **directives that have not yet been implemented,**[335] as in our case 4. In fact, this is simply the (legally relevant) consequence of the assumption that even not-yet-implemented secondary law can be directly applicable in the Member States in certain cases. What is permissible under Union law cannot be criminalised in the Member States; to this extent, Union law blocks national criminalisation.[336] Of course, it should not be forgotten that directives which have an impact in the domestic sphere by way of the principle of primacy cannot form the basis for sanctioning a certain conduct without previously having been implemented internally.[337] Accordingly, it is *not* possible for a State to invoke a – not-yet-implemented – directive to the detriment of an individual person.[338] Otherwise the difference between supranational criminal legislation and Europeanisation through harmonisation[339] would be abandoned and the lack of Union law competence to enact criminal law glossed over.[340] Finally, it should be noted that the density and complexity of conduct obligations based on directives, for example in the areas of health and safety and consumer protection, can prove problematic in regard to the principle of legality (*nullum crimen sine lege*) as these obligations can form the basis of criminal liability for negligence and omission. After all, there are a growing number of directives and EU regulations that set out (new) duties of care and guarantor's obligations.[341]

49 **Art. 267 TFEU**[342] highlights the relevance of the principle of primacy for procedural law. Accordingly, the Court decides on the interpretation of treaties and the validity of institutions' actions among other things by way of a **preliminary ruling.**[343] Thus the whole of primary and secondary Union law can be the subject matter of such preliminary references.[344] As an incidental procedure, this procedure forms part of national criminal procedure[345] and protects the CJEU's exclusive power to interpret Union law.[346] Questions concerning EU law 'enjoy a presumption of relevance'; that is, the CJEU can only exceptionally refuse to rule on such questions presented within the framework of a preliminary reference.[347] There is an urgent procedure (called PPU, *procédure préjudicielle d'urgence*) where the referring court's proceedings relate to a person in custody.[348] A domestic court *can refer* one of the issues mentioned to the CJEU if it is considered to impact the outcome of the case;[349] in fact, it *must* do so if it is the domestic court of last instance[350] and the relevant point of law raises relevant doubts.[351] Thus the obligation to make a reference to the national Supreme Court[352] in matters of Union law is replaced with the **obligation to make a reference to the CJEU** (case 5).[353] The preliminary ruling binds not only the court making the reference, but also all courts of lower instance dealing with this or a similar issue (**factual precedential effect**); if an act of secondary law is declared invalid, this must be observed by all Member State courts (**factual *erga omnes* effect**).[354] With the expiry of the transitional period regarding PJCCM (five years until 1 December 2014),[355] the Commission may now also initiate infringement proceedings in this area.[356]

Accordingly, within the framework of a regulatory offence procedure for an infringement of the Foodstuffs and Commodities Act (LMBG), the Schleswig Municipal Court referred the following questions to the CJEU for preliminary ruling: whether Council Directive 89/397/EEC of 14 June 1989 on the official control of foodstuffs[357] meant that the producer of a foodstuff had a directly applicable right to a second analysis if the regulatory authorities took a sample of his or her product, and whether, if the producer had not been given the option of a second opinion, this would result in exclusion of evidence.[358] The CJEU came to the conclusion that the right to request a second opinion could be derived directly from Art. 7(1) subparagraph 2 of the Directive and that State authorities accordingly were obliged to ensure that the persons affected could exercise this right.[359] If evidence was gathered in breach of these rules (of Union law), then an **exclusionary rule** may arise **under Community law** if the fairness of the trial cannot be guaranteed in any other way.[360]

50 The possibility and obligation of a **national court** to make a preliminary reference to the CJEU may directly follow from Art. 267 TFEU (direct application) or it may be regulated in a specific national law. While several Member States take the former approach,[361] *Germany* has enacted a special Law on the CJEU (EuGHG).[362] According to its §1(1) *any* German court

> may request the Court of Justice to give a preliminary ruling on a question raised in a case pending before it and concerning the validity or interpretation of an act referred to in paragraph 1 if that court or tribunal considers that a decision on the question is necessary to enable it to give judgment.

According to §1(2) EuGHG, a court 'against whose decisions there is no judicial remedy under national law' *is obliged* to refer such cases to the CJEU for preliminary ruling 'if that court or tribunal considers that a decision on the question is necessary to enable it to give judgment.'[363] In the *UK*, Part 75 of the Criminal Procedure Rules contains a detailed procedure for prelimary reference sent to the CJEU,[364] including the possibility of a separate application for the urgent procedure if the person concerned is in custody.[365]

3. Harmonious (Conforming) Interpretation

51 The primacy of Union law forces Member States to interpret their (criminal) law in such a way that it conforms to Union law,[366] as otherwise it would be displaced by Union law in cases of collision. Interpretation in line with Union law affects not only substantive criminal law.[367] For example, if an interpretation in conformity with Union law calls for a prohibition of a particular national rule on obtaining evidence, then it is logical to assume an **exclusionary rule under Union law** if this evidence is nevertheless used in a concrete trial.[368] In contrast, a national exclusionary rule may be displaced if the use of the respective evidence is in conformity with a mutual recognition instrument on the use of transnational evidence and necessary to protect Union interests by way of criminal law.[369] Similarly, the risk of flight as ground for pre-trial detention is to be interpreted in line with the EAW, which prohibits taking into account EU foreign nationality in the context of this ground for detention.[370]

52 Moreover, the principle at hand goes not only for **regulations**, but also for **directives**.[371] Accordingly, in the *pyrolysis* decision (case 6),[372] the German Federal Court of Justice first (also) took two applicable Council directives into account when interpreting the concept of 'authorised waste' within the meaning of the relevant environmental offence,[373] and thus interpreted a particular rule of the German Criminal Code in line with an instrument of secondary Union law.[374] The Federal Court of Justice took a further step towards interpretation in line with Union law by focusing explicitly on the European origins of the rules of the *Securities Trading Act (WpHG)*, demanding that it be interpreted in a manner that conformed to EU directives.[375] Furthermore, the Court repealed a sentence for so-called *scalping*[376] issued in line with the WpHG, arguing that according to an interpretation that conformed to European directives 'self-created "facts"' could not 'be classed as insider information'.[377] This decision's special significance lies in its unmistakeable **affirmation of the interpretation** of national (here German) criminal laws **in line with Union directives**.

53 In the controversial *Pupino* decision,[378] the CJEU assumed that an obligation to interpret national law in conformity with Union law also existed in regard to – the no-longer-existing – **Framework Decisions** in the (former) PJCCM.[379] This is first and foremost the result of the wording of Art. 34(2)(b) TEU (old version), which is very closely inspired by that of the third paragraph of Art. 249 TEC (now Art. 288 TFEU).[380] Yet the Court's view is astonishing, given that an interpretation in conformity with Community law presupposes direct applicability and primacy of *Community law* but Art. 34(2)(b) second sentence TEU old version had explicitly excluded any direct effect of FDs. Thus, in fact, the CJEU converged the third pillar with the first and thus anticipated the Lisbon Treaty's dissolution of the pillar structure.[381]

54 While the interpretation in conformity with Community/Union law is also recognised in the literature in principle,[382] at the same time the principle's many **limits** are debated.[383] In *temporal* terms, an obligation to interpret in conformity with a directive only exists once the deadline for implementing said directive has passed; before this has occurred, the only option is to postulate a general obligation not to defeat the object and purpose of the directive on the basis of the principle of sincere co-operation[384] and subsidiarily pursuant to the rationale of Art. 18 VCLT.[385] The CJEU has indeed taken this view.[386] From this we can conclude, as an *argumentum a fortiori*, that any criminalising effect cannot be based upon a directive that has not yet been implemented.[387]

55 On a more fundamental level, restrictions to interpretation in line with Union law include the **general fundamental legal principles** of Union law,[388] with particular focus placed upon the *principle of certainty*[389] and the idea of the *protection of confidence* in regard to a certain legal situation.[390] The latter idea seems related to the approach of setting the limit of admissible interpretation in conformity with Union law at the point at which it would lead to a justification of or an increase in criminal liability; that is, to invoke this principle for an **interpretation that expands punishability** would not be allowed.[391] At any rate, a punishability-expanding interpretation pursuant to Union law appears to be a false problem if seen only as an *admissible interpretation* within the limits of the wording of (national) law and not as an *inadmissible analogy* that goes beyond this wording to the detriment of the defendant.[392] Under this approach the (new) interpretation only constitutes the realisation of the legislator's objective intention in light of Union law, a new jurisprudential interpretation that does not amount to retroactive punishment. From this perspective the German Federal Court of Justice's interpretation in line with Community law in the *pyrolysis* decision (case 6) should not be objected to, as the Court did nothing more than interpret the term 'waste' in conformity with Community law.[393]

56 In sum, then, interpretation in line with Union law poses no cause for concern in regard to the **constitutional principles**, especially the principle of legality (*nullum crimen sine lege*), if it remains within the scope of the wording of the law and does not amount to an inadmissible analogy.[394] The existence of such principles, however, entails that any absolute primacy or imperative meaning of the topos of interpretation in conformity with Union law must be rejected; rather, it is on an equal footing with the interpretive principles of national law, even though – as *primus inter pares* – it enjoys **relative primacy**.[395] In terms of Union law, this results from the – often mentioned – Union's lack of a general competence to legislate criminal law[396] and the principle of using criminal law in the most restrictive form possible.[397] Incidentally, the CJEU itself has recognised that the interpretation of national law in conformity with Union law 'is limited by general principles of law, particularly those of legal certainty and non-retroactivity'.[398]

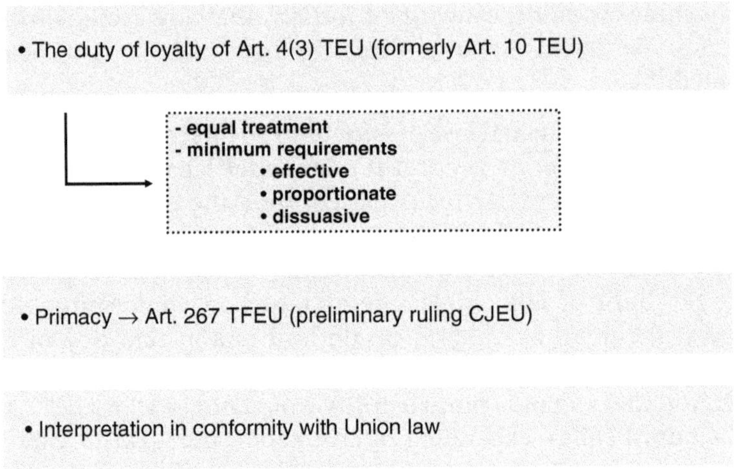

Figure 6 Harmonisation through general legal principles

57 Solution, Case 1

§154 StGB does not apply prima facie, as according to prevailing opinion it only protects the German administration of criminal justice. However, §154 StGB is *assimilated* by the (directly applicable) primary Union law of Art. 30 CJEU Statute. Union law thus expands §154 StGB, so that its definition must be read in such a way that not only national courts, but also the CJEU, is covered and – from the perspective of German jurisdiction – prosecuting Z for false testimony is not barred by the fact that there is no case of §5 No 10 StGB. §162 StGB now takes this into account including international tribunals (especially ICC, ECtHR, CJEU) in its scope of protection.

58 Solution, Case 2

Whether T's conduct is punishable as a misdemeanour according to §71(1) in conjunction with §69(4) No 1 BNatSchG depends on whether it infringes Council Regulation (EC) No 338/97 of 9 December 1996 on the protection of species of wild fauna and flora by regulating trade therein. For §69(4) No 1 BNatSchG *refers* to a violation of this regulation through importing a specimen of a species listed in the regulation. It is only possible to conclusively determine the punishable conduct after reading the regulation and its Annex A in its form amended by the further Commission Regulation (EU) No 750/2013 of 29 July 2013. However, this is problematic from the point of view of legal certainty.[399]

59 Solution, Case 3

Prantl had to be acquitted, as the German Wine Regulation was not compatible with the quantitative restrictions on imports and all measures having equivalent effect (now Art. 34 TFEU). Confusion with the

German quality wines traditionally filled in 'Bocksbeutel' bottles can be avoided by using different labels. The German judge was thus unable to apply the Wine Regulation due to the *primacy of Union law*. Of course, the matter of how this primacy is to be dealt with *exactly* and convincingly in terms of criminal law theory still requires clarification. It is conceivable, for example, that the use of traditional 'Bocksbeutel' bottles, which is contrary to the Wine Regulation (and entails the risk of confusion), could be seen as a *permissible* risk – in line with the doctrine of objective imputation (*objektive Zurechnung*) – or that the use of these bottles does not qualify as a criminal offence in regard to European wines. At any rate, there will be no way to exempt conduct permitted by Union law from the risk of sanction.

60 Solution, Case 4

The question is whether A violated a French criminal law against the unauthorised practice of veterinary medicine, even though an EC directive regulating the mutual recognition of qualifications existed at the time and had only not yet been implemented in France. In the eyes of the CJEU, A had not committed an offence, as the *EC Directive* in question *preceded* French law, even if it had not been implemented there yet.[400]

61 Solution, Case 5

The German Federal Court of Justice referred the matter back to the Bavarian Supreme Regional Court and declared itself not competent to decide on the issue referred: 'The interpretation of the EEC Regulations mentioned plays a decisive role in answering the question referred. However, the binding interpretation of the law of the EC is solely the right of the Court of the EC'.[401]

62 Solution, Case 6

The regional court took the stance that there can be no instance of 'willed' (*gewillkürter*) waste if an object can be recycled or reclaimed after being disposed of. The Federal Court of Justice opposed this, first (and mainly) by focusing on the regulations of §1(2) AbfG and subsequently by drawing on two relevant EC directives.[402] With a view to pertinent CJEU case law, the Federal Court stated that this case law needed to be taken into account by national administrative authorities and courts.[403] Thus the Federal Court changed its judicature on the concept of waste, taking the rules set out in the directives as a guideline.[404]

Notes

1. Thereto Chapter 1, mn. 19 ff.
2. Generally on this see already Chapter 1, mn. 29.
3. On the draft of a **European Model Penal Code**, cf. Ambos, *Internationales Strafrecht* (2008), §10 mn. 72. On the **APs to the ECHR** of relevance to criminal law, cf. Chapter 2, mn. 12.

4. ETS 52, Convention entered into force on 18 July 1972.
5. ETS 82, entered into force on 27 June 2003.
6. ETS 90, entered into force on 4 August 1978.
7. ETS 190, not yet entered into force.
8. ETS 119, not entered into force. See also the recent Council of Europe Convention on Offences relating to **Cultural Property** of 19 May 2017 (ETS 221). To date, this Convention is only signed by Armenia, Cyprus, Greece, Italy, Portugal, San Marino, Slovenia, Ukraine and – as observer State – Mexico.
9. ETS 120, entered into force on 1 November 1985.
10. ETS 126, amended by Prot. 1 and 2 of 4 November 1993; entered into force on 1 February 1989.
11. AP I: ETS 151, AP II: ETS 152, both entered into force on 1 March 2002.
12. ETS 141, entered into force on 1 September 1993.
13. ETS 156, entered into force on 1 May 2000.
14. ETS 164, entered into force on 1 December 1999.
15. ETS 172, not entered into force.
16. ETS 173, entered into force on 1 July 2002. Lastly, Germany ratified the Convention on 10 May 2017. On the respective critical GRECO report, cf. Hauck, *wistra*, 29 (2010), 255. On GRECO and further international mechanisms monitoring corruptions, cf. Salazar, *eucrim*, 6 (2011), 21–2.
17. ETS 191, entered into force on 1 February 2005.
18. ETS 185, entered into force on 1 July 2004.
19. ETS 189, entered into force on 1 March 2006.
20. ETS 196, entered into force on 1 June 2007.
21. ETS 217, not yet entered into force; based on SC Res. 2178/2014 and adopted by the Committee of Ministers of the CoE on 19 May 2015; cf. Bartholin, *eucrim*, 10 (2015), 124 ff.; on the Draft AP, Piacente, *eucrim*, 10 (2015), 12 ff.; crit. on SC Res. 2178/2014, Ambos, *EJIL: Talk!*, 2 October 2014; crit. also Mitsilegas, *EU Criminal Law after Lisbon* (2016), pp. 259–60.
22. ETS 197, entered into force on 1 February 2008; on the implementation and the ensuing challenges, Pietrobon, *LJIL*, 29 (2016), 485 ff.; on the protection against human trafficking offered by the ECHR, cf. Pati, *NJW*, 64 (2011), 128.
23. ETS 198, entered into force on 1 May 2008.
24. ETS 201, entered into force on 1 July 2010. On its implementation in Greece, cf. Billis and Gkaniatsos, *eucrim*, 6 (2011), 82 ff.
25. ETS 210, entered into force on 1 August 2014. On the legal situation in Portugal, cf. Ferreira, in Pływaczewski and Guzik-Makaruk, *Current Problems of the Penal Law* (2017), pp. 22 ff.
26. ETS 211, entered into force on 1 January 2016. On this, cf. Koch, in Sieber, Satzger and von Heinegg, *Europäisches Strafrecht* (2014), p. 543.
27. ETS 215, not yet entered into force. On the Recommendation CM/Rec(2011)10 on 'Promotion of the Integrity of Sport against Manipulation of Results, Notably Match-Fixing', cf. Chiaromonte, *eucrim*, 7 (2012), 30 ff.
28. ETS 216, not yet entered into force; thereto Alarcón Jiménez, *eucrim*, 10 (2015), 121 ff.
29. Convention against Illicit Traffic in Narcotic Drugs and Psychotropic Substances, UNTS 1582/1990, 95.

30. Cf. Art. 3(1)(b)(i), (ii) and (c)(i) of the Vienna Narcotics Convention and Art. 6(1) (a), (b) and (c) of the Laundering Convention; also cf. Ambos, *ZStW*, 114 (2002), 237; Herzog and Achtelik, in Herzog and Achtelik, *Geldwäschegesetz* (2014), mn. 67 ff.; Walther, in Schimansky, Bunte and Lwowski, *Bankrechts-Handbuch*, i (2017), §42 mn. 23 ff.
31. Cf. originally EC Directive 91/308/EEC of 1991 which was expanded in 2001 by Directive 2001/97/EC and 2005 by Directive 2005/60/EC, which was derogated in turn by Directive 2015/849/EU (OJ L 141 of 5 June 2015, 73), expanding the punishable conduct even further, especially with a view to terrorist financing. On the EU law, see also Walther, in Schimansky, Bunte and Lwowski, *Bankrechts-Handbuch*, i (2017), §42 mn. 23 ff.; also cf. below, n. 125.
32. Ambos, *ZStW*, 114 (2002), 237–8; on the sanctioning of money laundering in Europe, also cf. Hecker, in Görgen et al., *FS Kreuzer*, i (2009), p. 216. On the Convention's inconsistent domestic implementation, cf. Ambos, *Internationales Strafrecht* (2008), §10 mn. 70, small print.
33. On its development, cf. Schwarzenegger, in Donatsch, Forster and Schwarzenegger, *FS Trechsel* (2002), pp. 308 ff.; for a critical analysis, cf. Breyer, *DuD*, 25 (2001), 592; also cf. Gercke, *ZUM*, 54 (2010), 635 ff.; Calderoni, *CrimLSC*, 54 (2010), 339; Clough, *CLF*, 23 (2012), 363; on its implementation in Germany, Popp, *MR-Int*, 4 (2007), 84; cf. also Eisele, *ZIS*, 7 (2012), 402.
34. On the procedural instruments of the Cybercrime Convention, cf. Schnabl, *Jura*, 26 (2004), 381 ff.; Bär, *ZIS*, 6 (2011), 54–5; Clough, *CLF*, 23 (2012), 369–70.
35. On this, cf. Sieber, in Sieber, Satzger and von Heinegg, *Europäisches Strafrecht* (2014), p. 495.
36. ETS 185, Art. 12(1): 'ensure that legal persons can be held liable for a criminal offence'.
37. ETS 189, Arts. 3 ff. On this and on the implementation in Germany, cf. Hellmann and Gärtner, *NJW*, 64 (2011), 961. Also cf. Weiß, in Sieber, Satzger and von Heinegg, *Europäisches Strafrecht* (2014), pp. 473–4.
38. For a critical stance on this, cf. e.g. Kugelmann, *DuD*, 27 (2003), 345 ff., in whose opinion the broad wording of Art. 3 might lead to the risk of desirable research on racism and xenophobia becoming liable to prosecution if any computer-related communication on such topics were penalised.
39. Art. 2(2), Art. 3(2), Art. 7(2) Cybercrime Conv.
40. Cf. e.g. Art. 4(2), Art. 6(3), Art. 9(4), Art. 10(3) Cybercrime Conv.
41. On the concept's origins in the Amsterdam Treaty (Art. 29, 31(1) (e) TEU), De Bondt, *EuCLR*, 4 (2014), 148; on three phases of substantive criminal law harmonisation (post-Maastricht, post-Amsterdam and post-Lisbon), cf. Mitsilegas, *EU Criminal Law after Lisbon* (2016), p. 55.
42. But see the French (*rapprochement*) and German versions (*Annäherung* versus *Angleichung*).
43. On the umbrella term of harmonisation, cf. Chapter 1, mn. 28.
44. See Satzger, in Streinz, *EUV/AEUV* (2012), Art. 83 AEUV mn. 6. Kaiafa-Gbandi, *EuCLR*, 1 (2011), 13 ff., argues in favour of a restrictive interpretation. In the terminology used by Zöller, in Baumeister, Roth and Ruthig, *FS Schenke* (2011), pp. 587, 590, Art. 83(1), establishes an 'original competence to approximate criminal law' (orig. 'originäre Strafrechtsangleichungskompetenz'), which in contrast to the ancillary competence of the second paragraph permits the

approximation of criminal law independently of other harmonisation measures. For a critical stance on this norm's indeterminacy, which raises a number of problems for interpretation, cf. Mitsilegas, *NJECL*, 3 (2012), 225.

45. Art. 83(2) TFEU; thereto Meyer, *EuR*, 46 (2011), 175, is critical of how a distinction between the two paragraphs is to be drawn; also cf. Meyer, *Strafrechtsgenese* (2012), pp. 416 ff.
46. In the opinion of Meyer, *Strafrechtsgenese* (2012), pp. 409 ff., this norm thus goes much less far than practice prior to the Lisbon Treaty.
47. On this, cf. Badea and Buono, *ERA Forum*, 12 (2011), 346 ff.; Dannecker, in Böse, *Europäisches Strafrecht* (2013), pp. 310 ff.; from a Polish point of view, cf. Nowak, *NJECL*, 3 (2012), 366 ff. Cf. also Kubiciel, *HRRS*, 14 (2013), 213; Salazar, *eucrim*, 6 (2011), 22–3; and Stefanuc, *ERA Forum*, 12 (2011), 427, on the EU anti-corruption report which was announced for the summer of 2013 but ultimately appeared on 3 February 2014 (see http://ec.europa.eu/dgs/home-affairs/e-library/documents/policies/organized-crime-and-human-trafficking/corruption/docs/acr_2014_en.pdf, last accessed 27 January 2018). Also cf. *eucrim*, 6 (2011), 104. On further measures combating corruption, cf. Príborský, *ERA Forum*, 12 (2011), 373; Príborský, *eucrim*, 7 (2012), 34; also cf. COM (2013) 739 final, pp. 8–9; on this, cf. Beukelmann, *NJW-Spezial*, 10 (2013), 760.
48. For a critical stance on certainty, cf. Ambos and Rackow, *ZIS*, 4 (2009), 402; Meyer, *EuR*, 46 (2011), 177; Zöller, in Baumeister, Roth and Ruthig, *FS Schenke* (2011), p. 588; Brodowski, *Jura*, 36 (2013), 494; Schröder, in Hellmann and Schröder, *FS Achenbach* (2011), pp. 492 ff.; also cf. Ouwerkerk, *NJECL*, 3 (2012), 233; for a relativising stance, cf. Satzger, *Internationales und Europäisches Strafrecht* (2016), §9 mn. 34. On the individual groups of offences, cf. Satzger, in Streinz, *EUV/AEUV* (2012), Art. 83 AEUV mn. 12 ff.
49. Thus also Ouwerkerk, *NJECL*, 3 (2012), 233; for a slightly different stance, cf. Hecker, *Europäisches Strafrecht* (2015), §11 mn. 4; Safferling, *Internationales Strafrecht* (2011), §10 mn. 48; Esser, *Europäisches und Internationales Strafrecht* (2018), §2 mn. 135; Böse, in Böse, *Europäisches Strafrecht* (2013), pp. 155 f.; Satzger, in Streinz, *EUV/AEUV* (2012), Art. 83 AEUV mn. 21, who emphasises the conclusive character of the list. Cf. also Satzger, *ZIS*, 11 (2016), 773 (concluding that Art. 83(3) TFEU also concerns the general part of criminal law, since the approximation of cross-border crimes without taking it into account is not possible) and crit. on the using of 'text modules' (orig. 'Textbaustein-Methode') (774–5).
50. At the same time, Satzger, *Internationales und Europäisches Strafrecht* (2016), §9 mn. 34, sees the list as a restriction in comparison to the earlier law.
51. For a critical stance on this form of 'blanket authorisation', cf. Braum, *ZIS*, 4 (2009), 421; Nilsson, *eucrim*, 9 (2014), 21, however, considers that the 'right of extension of Union competence provided in Art. 83 is not sufficient'.
52. As argued by Zimmermann, *Jura*, 32 (2009), 846–7; Kretschmer, in Vedder and Heintschel von Heinegg, *Europäischer Verfassungsvertrag* (2007), Art. III-271 mn. 4; Satzger, *Internationales und Europäisches Strafrecht* (2016), §9 mn. 35; Esser, *Europäisches und Internationales Strafrecht* (2018), §2 mn. 136. A different opinion is put forward by Asp, *Substantive Criminal Law Competence* (2012), pp. 80 ff. ('both (a) the generic requirements and (b) the list requirement must be fulfilled' [84]); Safferling, *Internationales Strafrecht* (2011), §10 mn. 49–50; Böse, in Böse,

Europäisches Strafrecht (2013), pp. 154 f. Satzger, in Streinz, *EUV/AEUV* (2012), Art. 83 AEUV mn. 10, see this more restrictively.

53. Cf. Art. 5(1, 3, 4) TEU; Chapter 1, mn. 19 ff.
54. Zimmermann, *Jura*, 32 (2009), 847; Walter, *ZStW*, 117 (2005), 926; Satzger, *Internationales und Europäisches Strafrecht* (2016), §9 mn. 36; Hecker, *Europäisches Strafrecht* (2015), §11 mn. 8; Hecker, in Sieber, Satzger and von Heinegg, *Europäisches Strafrecht* (2014), pp. 289 ff.; Satzger, in Streinz, *EUV/AEUV* (2012), Art. 83 AEUV mn. 5. On linking the principle of *ultima ratio* with the principle of proportionality, cf. Ouwerkerk, *NJECL*, 3 (2012), 235. For a critical stance on the Commission's commonly used arguments, cf. Simon, *NJECL*, 3 (2012), 248.
55. Cf. Art. 67(3) TFEU ('if necessary'); also Satzger, *Internationales und Europäisches Strafrecht* (2016), §9 mn. 37. For a critical stance on this, cf. Mylonopoulos, *ZStW*, 123 (2011), 636, 645 ff. Simon's warning against 'legislative inflation' and 'over-criminalisation' (*NJECL*, 3 (2012), 245) goes in a similar direction. Meyer, *Strafrechtsgenese* (2012), pp. 352 ff. is highly critical of this.
56. Thereto Chapter 1, mn. 11 ff.
57. BVerfG, No 2 BvE 2/08, Judgment (30 June 2009), in *BVerfGE* 123, 267–437, para. 363; translation available at www.bundesverfassungsgericht.de/SharedDocs/Entscheidungen/EN/2009/06/es20090630_2bve000208en.html;jsessionid=67A33469EB624F3A990D068D378D95D0.2_cid361, last accessed 27 January 2018, reprinted in *CMLR*, 3 (2010), 13.
58. Art. 23(1) second sentence GG.
59. BVerfG, 2 BvE 2/08 (n. 57), para. 363. This is why §7(1) IntVG (*BGBl.* I 2009, 3822) now sets out that the German Council representative may only consent to an extension in accordance with Art. 83(1) subparagraph 3 TFEU after a corresponding parliamentary law has entered into force.
60. Cf. Art. 5(1, 2) TEU and Chapter 1, mn. 19 ff.
61. Cf. Art. 5(1, 2) TEU; also Satzger, *Internationales und Europäisches Strafrecht* (2016), §9 mn. 35; Schröder, in Hellmann and Schröder, *FS Achenbach* (2011), p. 495 is in agreement.
62. On this, cf. Simon, *NJECL*, 3 (2012), 246.
63. For a discussion of the possible combinations (minimum-maximum, minimum-minimum and maximum-maximum sanctions) and their basis in co-operation instruments with a view to the auxiliary function of approximation cf. De Bondt, *EuCLR*, 4 (2014), 149 ff. (excluding for that matter maximum-minimum sanctions).
64. Vogel, *GA*, 150 (2003), 315–16; also Weigend, *ZStW*, 116 (2004), 284–5; Tiedemann, *ZStW*, 116 (2004), 953; Hecker, *Europäisches Strafrecht* (2015), §11 mn. 4 ff.; Hecker, in Sieber, Satzger and von Heinegg, *Europäisches Strafrecht* (2014), pp. 287–8; cf. Asp, *EuCLR*, 1 (2011), 52–3; in detail Asp, *Substantive Criminal Law Competence* (2012), pp. 93 ff., 110 ff.; Satzger, in Streinz, *EUV/AEUV* (2012), Art. 83 AEUV mn. 32 ff.; a critical stance is put forward by Elholm, in Müller-Dietz, *FS Jung* (2007), pp. 147–8. Klip, *European Criminal Law* (2016), pp. 200–1, argues for an interpretation in line with the 'spirit' of the legislative act in question, as does Bock, *ZRP*, 44 (2011), 48. On the significance of comparative criminal law for harmonisation, cf. Hauck, in Beck, Burchard and Fateh-Moghadam, *Strafrechtsvergleichung als Problem und Lösung* (2011), pp. 255

ff. On the possible level of regulation: Meyer, *EuR*, 46 (2011), 179; Meyer, *Strafrechtsgenese* (2012), pp. 412–13.

65. Hecker, *Europäisches Strafrecht* (2015), §8 mn. 38, §11 mn. 5; Satzger, *Internationales und Europäisches Strafrecht* (2016), §9 mn. 42; Satzger, in Böse, *Europäisches Strafrecht* (2013), pp. 71 ff.; Klip, *European Criminal Law* (2016), p. 206; Böse, in Böse, *Europäisches Strafrecht* (2013), pp. 970 f.; crit. also Karsai, *ZIS*, 11 (2016), 31 ('increased level of repression'); for a critical stance from a Scandinavian perspective, cf. Suominen, *EuCLR*, 1 (2011), 178–9. Also cf. for earlier literature on the topic, cf. Ambos, *Internationales Strafrecht* (2008), §12 mn. 7 incl. n. 46.
66. Nilsson, *Europarättslig Tidskrift*, 14 (2011), 674–6; conc. Mitsilegas, *EU Criminal Law after Lisbon* (2016), p. 63.
67. The fact that Art. 82(2) TFEU *in fine* allows Member States to provide for a 'higher level of protection', as argued by Nilsson, *Europarättslig Tidskrift*, 14 (2011), 675, does not help in this regard since this provision does not concern substantive criminal law harmonisation.
68. Cf. Art. 83(1) first sentence, and (2) second sentence TFEU.
69. Klip, *European Criminal Law* (2016), pp. 355–9; on the other sanctions cf. ibid., pp. 359 ff.
70. Thereto main text, mn. 41.
71. Klip, *European Criminal Law* (2016), pp. 352–3. Four groups of minimum maximum penalties come into consideration: no less than 1–3 years, 2–5 years, 5–10 years or 10 years (Council Conclusions of 24/25 April 2002, Council Document 9141/02, p. 3; on this, cf. Zeder, *öAnwBl.* 70 (2008), 254; also cf. Klip, *European Criminal Law* (2016), pp. 355 ff.). Cf. Draft Council Conclusions 2009, p. 6. On the implementation on the basis of mutual recognition (Green Paper on sanctions), cf. Chapter 4, mn. 98.
72. Hecker, *Europäisches Strafrecht* (2015), §11 mn. 7; Satzger, *Internationales und Europäisches Strafrecht* (2016), §9 mn. 45; Klip, *European Criminal Law* (2016), pp. 42–3, 351. Safferling, *Internationales Strafrecht* (2011), §10 mn. 62, is critical because of this ('harmonisation is symbolic to a large extent'; orig. 'weitgehend symbolische Harmonisierung').
73. Klip, *European Criminal Law* (2016), pp. 362–3.
74. Cf. Klip, *European Criminal Law* (2016), pp. 352 ff., 362 ff.
75. Cf. Chapter 2, sections B and C.
76. Art. 6(1, 3) TEU.
77. Vogel, *GA*, 150 (2003), 316. A sceptical view is put forward by Scheffler, in Joerden and Szwarc, *Europäisierung des Strafrechts in Polen und Deutschland* (2007), pp. 112–13. On the significance of the protection of human rights for European integration, cf. Ambos and Meyer-Abich, in Parmentier and Weitekamp, *Crime and Human Rights* (2007), pp. 19 ff.; cf. also Böse, in Böse, *Europäisches Strafrecht* (2013), pp. 157–8.
78. Cf. Mitsilegas, *NJECL*, 5 (2014), 421–3; Mitsilegas, *EU Criminal Law after Lisbon* (2016), pp. 73–4 (with a view to freedom of movement).
79. Chapter 2, mn. 144.
80. Cf. Draft Council conclusions 2009, pp. 4 ff., according to which criminal law must only constitute a '*last resort*' (No 1), the principles of *subsidiarity* and *proportionality* must be observed (No 2), criminal laws must be sufficiently *precise* (No 4), actual *harm* or essential interests must be violated (No 5), and acts carried out at an

early stage or acts that only imply an abstract danger (No 5) and *negligent* conduct (Nos 6–8) should not be criminalised in principle. Also cf. Kaiafa-Gbandi, *EuCLR*, 1 (2011), 17 ff.; Böse, *EuCLR*, 1 (2011), 35 ff.; Asp, *EuCLR*, 1 (2011), 44 ff.; Zeder, *EuR*, 47 (2012), 50 ff.; Satzger, in Böse, *Europäisches Strafrecht* (2013), pp. 83 f.; on proportionality and legality pursuant to Art. 49 CFREU, Mitsilegas, *NJECL*, 5 (2014), 423–4.

81. On this, cf. Vogel, in Klip and van der Wilt, *Harmonisation and Harmonising Measures in Criminal Law* (2002), pp. 62–3. For an instructive account of the aims of European criminal law, cf. Sieber, *ZStW*, 121 (2009), 2 ff. For more detail on the area of freedom, security and justice, cf. Meyer, *EuR*, 46 (2011), 188 ff. For a critical stance on this, cf. Kaiafa-Gbandi, *EuCLR*, 1 (2011), 10.
82. For a discussion of these two functions with a preference for the auxiliary one cf. de Bondt, *EuCLR*, 4 (2014), 149 ff.
83. Vogel, *GA*, 150 (2003), 318; Satzger, *NK*, 19 (2007), 95, is in agreement. Cf. also Weyembergh, *L'harmonisation des législations: Conditions de l'espace pénal européen et révélateur de ses tensions* (2004), pp. 179–80, 264 ff. and *passim*; Weyembergh, *MaastJECompL*, 12 (2005), 155 ff., 166; a critical stance is also taken by Frisch, *GA*, 154 (2007), 272. For a more positive account of developments post-Lisbon, cf. Meyer, *Strafrechtsgenese* (2012), pp. 476 ff.
84. On the former Art. 31(c) TEU in this regard, cf. Ambos, *Internationales Strafrecht* (2008), §12 mn. 8. For a comparison of pre- and post-Lisbon, cf. Heger, *ZIS*, 4 (2009), 411–12.
85. Thereto Chapter 4, mn. 18.
86. Cf. Chapter 1, mn. 26–7; also below Chapter 4, mn. 14.
87. Thereto Chapter 4, mn. 43 ff.; also cf. Vogel, *GA*, 150 (2003), 319; Zimmermann, Glaser and Motz, *EuCLR*, 1 (2011), 64–5; more critically, Frisch, *GA*, 154 (2007), 269; Satzger, *NK*, 19 (2007), 96.
88. Art. 82(1) subparagraph 2(b) TFEU; on this, also cf. Chapter 4, mn. 3.
89. Vogel, *GA*, 150 (2003), 319; for a detailed account of conflicts of jurisdiction in the EU, cf. Hecker, *ZIS*, 6 (2011), 60.
90. On earlier law, cf. Ambos, *Internationales Strafrecht* (2008), §12 mn. 9. Cf. also Kubiciel, *ZIS*, 5 (2010), 743–4; Noltenius, *ZStW*, 122 (2010), 609 ff.
91. According to Zöller, in Baumeister, Roth and Ruthig, *FS Schenke* (2011), p. 592, this merely emphasises the principle of subsidiarity that already applies; a critical view is taken by Meyer, *EuR*, 46 (2011), 186–7 ('empty conceptual shell', orig. 'Begriffshülle ohne Kern'); Meyer, *Strafrechtsgenese* (2012), pp. 397 ff.; for a more positive take, cf. Safferling, *Internationales Strafrecht* (2011), §10 mn. 58.
92. For more detail, cf. main text, mn. 38.
93. Crit. also Satzger, *Internationales und Europäisches Strafrecht* (2016), §9 mn. 38.
94. Cf. in this regard the Commission's 'Communication on European Criminal Policy' where the 'added value' of the harmonisation of criminal law is set out, inter alia with regard to the protection and promotion of certain Union policies within the meaning of Art. 83(2) TFEU (cf. Commission, *Towards an EU Criminal Policy* (2011) (COM (2011) 573 final, pp. 9–11: 'Most importantly, it is in this field where the EU institutions need to make policy choices whether to use or not to use criminal law (instead of other measures, such as administrative sanctions) as an enforcement tool; and to determine which EU policies require the use of criminal law as an additional

enforcement tool'); crit. Mitsilegas, *EU Criminal Law after Lisbon* (2016), pp. 70–1. On the more rights-focused approach of the EP, cf. ibid., p. 71.

95. See also Mitsilegas, *NJECL*, 5 (2014), 419–20; and Mitsilegas, *EU Criminal Law after Lisbon* (2016), pp. 60–2 (speaking of 'functional criminalisation' in this context).
96. Hecker, *Europäisches Strafrecht* (2015), §8 mn. 39 incl. further references.
97. BVerfG, 2 BvE 2/08 (n. 57), para. 361; crit. also Ambos and Rackow, *ZIS*, 4 (2009), 403; Weigend, *ZStW*, 116 (2004), 284; also cf. Meyer, *Strafrechtsgenese* (2012), pp. 413–14; Satzger, in Streinz, *EUV/AEUV* (2012), Art. 83 AEUV mn. 23.
98. Cf. Art. 83(2) TFEU: 'area which has been subject to harmonisation measures'; in this vein, also Mitsilegas, *NJECL*, 5 (2014), 420.
99. Hecker, *Europäisches Strafrecht* (2015), §8 mn. 5, 43, with further bases for authorisation in mn. 41 ff.; Hecker, in Sieber, Satzger and von Heinegg, *Europäisches Strafrecht* (2014), pp. 278–9; also cf. Zeder, *EuR*, 47 (2012), 45.
100. Cf. Hecker, *Europäisches Strafrecht* (2015), §8 mn. 48 ('manifestation of the principle of subsidiarity', orig. 'Ausprägung des Subsidiaritätsgrundsatzes'); sceptically on the 'criterion of necessity' (orig. 'Unerlässlichkeitskriterium') and its restrictive potential, Satzger, *Internationales und Europäisches Strafrecht* (2016), §9 mn. 41; for a high threshold insofar, also Mitsilegas, *NJECL*, 5 (2014), 420.
101. BVerfG, 2 BvE 2/08 (n. 57), paras. 361 ff.; cf. above Chapter 1, mn. 3. For a critical stance on this, cf. Meyer, *Strafrechtsgenese* (2012), p. 414.
102. Cf. Hecker, *Europäisches Strafrecht* (2015), §8 mn. 48, who argues that overly high restrictions on the exercising of powers counteract the protective mandate of Union law.
103. Cf. Hecker, *Europäisches Strafrecht* (2015), §8 mn. 51, for whom this is only possible in cases of cross-border crime.
104. Cf. Kotzur, in Art. 83(2) second sentence TFEU: 'same . . . legislative procedure as was followed for the adoption of the harmonisation measure in question'.
105. Cf. Kotzur, in Geiger, Khan and Kotzur, *European Union Treaties: A Commentary* (2015), Article 83 TFEU mn. 11; Satzger, in Streinz, *EUV/AEUV* (2012), Art. 83 AEUV mn. 24.
106. §§9, 5(2) IntVG. On the justification for this (principle of democracy), cf. BVerfG, 2 BvE 2/08 (n. 57), para. 418; a critical stance is taken by Zimmermann, *Jura*, 32 (2009), 851; also cf. Schröder, in Hellmann and Schröder, *FS Achenbach* (2011), p. 498.
107. An instructive list of fundamental principles of criminal policy is given in the 'Manifesto on European Criminal Policy', *ZIS*, 4 (2009), 697 ff. Also cf. Mansdörfer, *HRRS*, 11 (2010), 20; Heger, *ZIS*, 4 (2009), 414; Satzger, *Internationales und Europäisches Strafrecht* (2016), §9 mn. 49; Hecker, *Europäisches Strafrecht* (2015), §8 mn. 57; Safferling, *Internationales Strafrecht* (2011), §10 mn. 64; Noltenius, *ZStW*, 122 (2010), 608–9, is also critical because of this; in favour of the States' margin of discretion, Zimmermann, *Jura*, 32 (2009), 848; Zöller, in Baumeister, Roth and Ruthig, *FS Schenke* (2011), p. 595, who considers the requirements for the emergency brake already to be met if a Member State formally issues a veto, even without giving a reason.
108. These include the punishability of attempt, the identification of the site of the crime, the limits of punishability for negligent acts (especially in regard to property offences), the punishability of participation or the punishability of

legal persons; cf. Mylonopoulos, *ZStW*, 123 (2011), 639; Hecker, in Sieber, Satzger and von Heinegg, *Europäisches Strafrecht* (2014), pp. 291–2; Hecker, in Ambos, *Europäisches Strafrecht post-Lissabon* (2011), p. 26; Satzger, in Streinz, *EUV/AEUV* (2012), Art. 83 AEUV mn. 37; on the significance of national criminal law doctrine for the definition of 'fundamental aspects', cf. Maiwald, in Freund et al., *FS Frisch* (2013), pp. 1377 ff.; on the criminal responsibility of legal persons from a comparative perspective (Germany and USA), Engelhart, *Sanktionierung von Unternehmen* (2012); on attempts in Germany to introduce the criminal responsibility of legal persons in light of the international and European framework Rönnau and Wegner, *ZRP*, 47 (2014), 158 ff.

109. Mansdörfer, *HRRS*, 11 (2010), 20; Heger, *ZIS*, 4 (2009), 413, still regard this as a 'harsh veto' (orig. 'hartes Veto').
110. Cf. Art. 15 TEU.
111. Art. 15(3), subparagraph 1 third sentence TEU.
112. Art. 15(3), subparagraph 2 TEU.
113. On the procedure, cf. Art. 20(2) TEU, Art. 329(1) TFEU; for more detail, cf. Klip, *European Criminal Law* (2016), pp. 65 ff.; Safferling, *Internationales Strafrecht* (2011), §10 mn. 99 ff.
114. Arts. 258, 259 TFEU.
115. Art. 4(3) TEU. See also Hecker, *Europäisches Strafrecht* (2015), §8 mn. 58; Satzger, *Internationales und Europäisches Strafrecht* (2016), §9 mn. 49; Satzger, in Streinz, *EUV/AEUV* (2012), Art. 83 AEUV mn. 67; Esser, *Europäisches und Internationales Strafrecht* (2018), §2 mn. 149.
116. Chapter 1, mn. 19 ff.
117. Cf. Satzger, *Internationales und Europäisches Strafrecht* (2016), §9 mn. 52 ff.; crit. of the analogous application of the emergency brake procedure as a matter of principle, Safferling, *Internationales Strafrecht* (2011), §10 mn. 67; in the same vein, Sicurella, in Klip, *Substantive Criminal law of the European Union* (2011), p. 238.
118. Cf. Ambos, *MaastJECompL*, 12 (2005), 175; on some of the sub-areas, cf. Vogel, *GA*, 150 (2003), 329 ff.; Klip, *European Criminal Law* (2016), pp. 195 ff.; Heger, *Die Europäisierung des deutschen Umweltstrafrechts* (2009), pp. 320 ff.
119. On this, cf. Ambos, in Klip, *Substantive Criminal Law of the European Union* (2011), pp. 227 ff. On the requirements for the *mens rea*, cf. Blomsma, *Mens Rea and Defences in European Criminal Law* (2012); pp. 43 ff., on offences and defences, Blomsma, *Mens Rea and Defences in European Criminal Law* (2012), pp. 285 ff. For an overview, cf. Stuckenberg, in Böse, *Europäisches Strafrecht* (2013), pp. 383–4.
120. Art. 83(1) subparagraph 1 TFEU refers to 'criminal offences and sanctions' and thus explicitly only to the Special Part. However, as the Special Part is dependent on the General Part (Ambos, *MaastJECompL*, 12 (2005), 175–6), it stands to reason to see Art. 83 as referring at least implicitly to the General Part; also cf. Satzger, *Internationales und Europäisches Strafrecht* (2016), §9 mn. 44; Satzger, *ZIS*, 11 (2016), 773–5; Safferling, *Internationales Strafrecht* (2011), §10 mn. 61. On sanctioning businesses specifically, cf. Engelhart, *eucrim*, 7 (2012), 110 ff.
121. Also cf. Hecker, *Europäisches Strafrecht* (2015), §8 mn. 38, §11 mn. 6; Satzger, Internationales und Europäisches Strafrecht (2016), §9 mn. 44; Satzger, *ZIS*, 11 (2016), 773 ff.; Esser, *Europäisches und Internationales Strafrecht* (2018), §2 mn.

140; Böse, in Böse, *Europäisches Strafrecht* (2013), p. 158; Satzger, in Streinz, *EUV/AEUV* (2012), Art. 83 AEUV mn. 34; Jähnke and Schramm, *Europäisches Strafrecht* (2017), §4 mn. 47; a more restrictive interpretation is presented in Zeder, *EuR*, 47 (2012), 46; advocating the creation of a European General Part Satzger, in Böse, *Europäisches Strafrecht* (2013), pp. 92–3.

122. In the following, I limit myself to the currently valid or still important measures; for earlier references, cf. Ambos, *Internationales Strafrecht* (2008), §12 mn. 9 incl. notes 57 ff.; for an overview, Valdés, *ERA Forum*, 16 (2015), 291, 295–8 (incl. the, in his view, 'forgotten crimes', at 299–300); Zeder, *JSt*, 4 (2017), 365 ff., with an overview on future directive proposals; on some 'Eurocrimes' and differing national implementation, cf. Klip, *European Criminal Law* (2016), pp. 231 ff., 243 ff.; also cf. COM (2011) 573 final; on this Beukelmann, *NJW-Spezial*, 8 (2011), 760. On the harmonisation of penalties and sentencing, see Asp, *BJCLCJ*, 1 (2013), 53 ff.

123. On this area from an Italian perspective, cf. Seminara, in Arnold et al., *FS Eser* (2005), p. 847; Foffani, *RP*, 27 (2011), 41; in light of the debt crisis Gómez-Jara, *EuCLR*, 3 (2013), 170.

124. Cf. **Convention** on the Protection of the European Communities' **Financial Interests** of 26 July 1995 (so-called PIF Convention), OJEC C 316 of 27 November 1995, 49; cf. also **First Protocol** of 27 September 1996 on the Convention on the Protection of the European Communities' Financial Interests, OJEC C 313 of 23 October 1996, 2; **Second Protocol** of 19 June 1997 on the Convention on the Protection of the European Communities' Financial Interests, OJEC C 221 of 19 July 1997, 11; see also the Protocol of 29 November 1996 on the Interpretation of the Convention on the Protection of the European Communities' Financial Interests, OJEC C 151 of 20 May 1997. For more details see main text, mn. 14.

125. Cf. Directive 2015/849/EU of the EP and of the Council of 20 May 2015 on the prevention of the use of the financial system for the purposes of **money laundering or terrorist financing** (OJ L 141 of 5 June 2015, 73), which shall be amended by a new directive (COM(2016) 450 final; on this Met-Domestici, *eucrim*, 11 (2016), 170 ff. ('welcome improvements' (177)); Vogel and Maillart, *eucrim*, 11 (2016), 179 ff.); crit. on the compatibility of the money-laundering register provided for in Arts. 30, 31 with the data protection regime of Arts. 7, 8 CFREU and the case law of the CJEU on the preventive retention of data Müller, *ZStW*, 128 (2016), 1021 ff., at 1023, 1084 ff.; see also the Proposal for a Directive of the EP and of the Council on countering money laundering by criminal law (COM(2016) 826 final). Regulation 2015/847/EU of the EP and of the Council of 20 May 2015 on **information accompanying transfers of funds** and repealing Regulation (EC) No 1781/2006 (OJ L 141 of 5 June 2015, 1); Directive 2014/42/EU of the EP and of the Council of 3 April 2014 on the **freezing and confiscation of instrumentalities and proceeds of crime** in the EU (OJ L 127 of 29 April 2014, 39; corrected by OJ L 138 of 13 May 2014, 114); Directive 2001/97/EC of the EP and of the Council of 4 December 2001 amending Council Directive 91/308/EEC on prevention of the use of the financial system for the purpose of **money laundering** (OJ L 344 of 28 December 2001, 76); on this Fazekas and Nanopoulos, *EJCCLCJ*, 24 (2016), 42–5 ('the answer was again sought on the legal plane, by amending parts of the relevant regime and expanding this scope to areas that were previously left unregulated'); cf. also *eucrim*, 7 (2012), 56; 8 (2013), 83. On the proposal for a directive of the EP

and Council on the prevention of the use of the financial system for the purpose of money laundering and terrorist financing (COM (2013) 45 final), cf. Zentes and Glaab, *BB*, 68 (2013), 707; Brodowski, *ZIS*, 8 (2013), 465–6; the European Data Protection Supervisor is critical in regard to data protection (at https://secure.edps.europa.eu/EDPSWEB/webdav/site/mySite/shared/Documents/Consultation/Opinions/2013/13-07-04_Money_laundering_EN.pdf, last accessed 27 January 2018). On the matter as a whole, cf. Hecker, *Europäisches Strafrecht* (2015), §8 mn. 11 ff., §11 mn. 56 ff.; Jacsó-Potyka, *Bekämpfung der Geldwäscherei in Europa* (2007), pp. 49 ff.; Stessens, *RIDP*, 77 (2006), 201 ff.; Kilchling, in Sieber, Satzger and von Heinegg, *Europäisches Strafrecht* (2011), mn. 1 ff.; Dannecker, in Böse, *Europäisches Strafrecht* (2013), pp. 322 f.; Miettinen, *Criminal Law and Policy in the European Union* (2013), pp. 146 ff.; for a comparative account, cf. Sinn, *NK*, 19 (2007), 102–3; on money laundering prevention, cf. Herlin-Karnell, *EuCLR*, 1 (2011), 153 ff.; also cf. the Stockholm Programme, p. 23; on the fight against terrorist financing see the instructive study by Sieber and Vogel, *Terrorismusfinanzierung* (2015); also Weisser, *ZIS*, 8 (2013), 343 ff.

126. Cf. Regulation 2014/596/EU of the EP and of the Council of 16 April 2014 on criminal sanctions for **market abuse** (market abuse regulation) (OJ L 173 of 12 June 2014, 1); Directive 2014/57/EU of the EP and of the Council of 16 April 2014 on criminal sanctions for **market abuse** (market abuse directive) (OJ L 173, 12 June 2014, 179). This Directive, adopted as an ancillary measure under Art. 83(2) TFEU, introduced for the first time 'criminal offences at least in serious cases and when committed intentionally' for **insider dealing and market manipulation**, including sanctions for legal persons (Arts. 3–5); thereto Cerizza, *eucrim*, 9 (2014), 85 ff.; Wilson, *ERA Forum*, 16 (2015), 427 ff.; crit. Goehler, *ZIS*, 11 (2016), 266 ff. (especially on the criminal responsibility for recommending or inducing another person in insider dealing pursuant to Art. 3(6), at 269 ff.); previously Brodowski, *ZIS*, 7 (2012), 562 f.; Brodowski, *ZIS*, 8 (2013), 464–5; Kert, *NZWiSt* (2013), 252; Schork and Reichling, *StraFo*, 19 (2012), 125; Schröder, *HRRS*, 14 (2013), 253; Wohlers, *ZStW*, 125 (2013), 454 ff. On the development of measures on financial crime, cf. Seminara, in Arnold et al., *FS Eser* (2005), pp. 868 ff.; on the implementation in Germany, cf. Park, *NStZ*, 27 (2007), 371 ff. On this as a whole, cf. Koch, in Sieber, Satzger and von Heinegg, *Europäisches Strafrecht* (2014), pp. 343 ff.

127. Joint Action 98/742/JHA of 22 December 1998 on **corruption** in the **private sector** (OJ L 358 of 31 December 1998, 2); Council FD 2003/568/JHA of 22 July 2003 on combating corruption in the private sector (OJ L 192 of 31 July 2003, 54); on this also the 'Proposal for a Directive of the EP and of the Council on the Fight against Fraud to the Union's Financial Interests by Means of Criminal Law' (COM (2012) 363 final), extending the corruption offence also to persons who administer EU funds in third States. See further Council Decision 2008/852/JHA of 24 October 2008 on a **contact-point network against corruption** (OJ L 301 of 12 November 2008, 38); Directive 2014/23/EU of the EP and of the Council of 26 February 2014 on the **award of concession contracts** (OJ L 94 of 28 March 2014, 1); cf. also Report from the Commission to the Council and the EP (EU Anti-corruption Report), COM(2014), 38 final. Directive 2014/24/EU of the EP and of the Council of 26 February 2014 on **public procurement** (OJ L 94 of 28 March 2014, 65) and Directive 2014/25/EU of the EP and of the Council of 26 February

2014 on **procurement** by entities operating in the water, energy, transport and postal services sectors (OJ L 94 of 28 March 2014, 243) provide that offers made in procurement procedures which are based on corruption are to be considered unlawful. See also Vogel, *GA*, 150 (2003), 323; Wolf, *NJW*, 59 (2006), 2737; Hecker, *Europäisches Strafrecht* (2015), §11 mn. 63 ff.; Miettinen, *Criminal Law and Policy in the European Union* (2013), pp. 148 ff.; a general account is given by Killmann, in Sieber, Satzger and von Heinegg, *Europäisches Strafrecht* (2011), mn. 1 ff.; Taseva, *NJECL*, 3 (2012), 344 ff. Cf. also the Report from the Commission COM (2011) 309 final.

128. Directive 2014/62/EU of the EP and of the Council on the protection of the euro and other currencies against **counterfeiting** by criminal law, and replacing Council FD 2000/383/JHA (OJ L 151 of 21 May 2014, 1); on the proposal, cf. Brodowski, *ZIS*, 8 (2013), 465; on the former FD, cf. Vogel, *ZRP*, 35 (2002), 8; Hecker, *Europäisches Strafrecht* (2015), §11 mn. 71 ff.; Miettinen, *Criminal Law and Policy in the European Union* (2013), pp. 153–4; also cf. Council FD 2001/413/JHA of 28 May 2001 combating fraud and counterfeiting of non-cash means of payment (OJ L 149 of 2 June 2001, 1); on this, cf. Eckstein, *ZStW*, 117 (2005), 132 ff.; Hecker, *Europäisches Strafrecht* (2015), §11 mn. 80 ff.; Killmann, in Sieber, Satzger and von Heinegg, *Europäisches Strafrecht* (2011), mn. 1 ff.; a critical stance is put forward by Duttge, in Heinrich et al., *FS Weber* (2004), pp. 288 ff. Regulation 331/2014/EU of the EP and of the Council of 11 March 2014 establishing an exchange, assistance and training programme for the protection of the euro against counterfeiting (the 'Pericles 2020' programme) (OJ L 103 of 5 April 2014, 1). Cf. on the former measures, the references in Ambos, *Internationales Strafrecht* (2014), §11 mn. 11 n. 92; cf. on the implementation in Germany, the 35th StrÄndG to amend and supplement Art. 146, 151, 152 a, 263 a StGB of 22 December 2003 (*BGBl.* I 2003, 2838). Cf. also Council Decision of 8 December 2003 concerning analysis and co-operation with regard to counterfeit euro coins (2003/861/EC) (OJ L 325 of 12 December 2003, 44), Commission Decision of 29 October 2004 establishing the European Technical and Scientific Centre (ETSC) and providing for co-ordination of technical actions to protect euro coins against counterfeiting (OJ L 19 of 21 January 2005, 73), and Council Decision 2005/511/JHA of 12 July 2005 on protecting the euro against counterfeiting by designating **Europol as the Central Office for combating euro counterfeiting**. On the issue as a whole, cf. Fontanaud, *RIDP*, 77 (2006), 249 ff.; Kuhl, in Sieber, Satzger and von Heinegg, *Europäisches Strafrecht* (2014), pp. 323 ff.

129. Directive 2011/36/EU of 5 April 2011 of the EP and of the Council on preventing and combating **trafficking in human beings** and protecting its victims, and replacing Council FD 2002/629/JHA (OJ L 101 of 15 April 2011); on this, cf. Bressan, *Eur.J.Cr.*, 20 (2012), 137; Villacampa Estiarte, *EuCLR*, 2 (2012), 291; Brand, *DRiZ* (2011), 125; Obokata and Payne, *NJECL*, 3 (2012), 198; Weißer, in Böse, *Europäisches Strafrecht* (2013), pp. 357 f.; for a critical stance, cf. Satzger, in Böse, *Europäisches Strafrecht* (2013), p. 81; from the victims' perspective, de Hoyos Sancho, in de Hoyos Sancho, *Guarantees and Rights of the Especially Vulnerable Victim in the Legal Framework of the EU* (2013), pp. 62 ff.; from an Austrian perspective on the EU influence cf. Reiter, *EU und österreichisches Strafrecht* (2008), pp. 83 ff. On the matter as a whole, cf. Eurostat, *Trafficking in human beings* (2013), at http://ec.europa.eu/dgs/home-affairs/what-is-new/news/

news/2013/docs/20130415_thb_stats_report_en.pdf, last accessed 27 January 2018; as well as the EU Strategy towards the Eradication of Trafficking in Human Beings 2012–16 (Council Document 11780/12); for the post-2016 strategy cf. Report from the Commission to the EP and to the Council on the progress made in the fight against trafficking in human beings (2016) (COM(2016) 267 final); see also Huber, in Sieber, Satzger and von Heinegg, *Europäisches Strafrecht* (2014), 394 ff.; Miettinen, *Criminal Law and Policy in the EU* (2013), pp. 162 ff., 169 ff.; from a Polish point of view, cf. Nowak, *NJECL*, 3 (2012), 374 ff.; on the implementation in Poland (Arts. 185A ff. Polish CCP) Pływaczewski et al., in Pływaczewski and Guzik-Makaruk, *Current Problems of the Penal Law* (2017), pp. 198 ff.; on the need for implementation, cf. Hecker, *Europäisches Strafrecht* (2015), §11 mn. 33. On the **Trafficking in Human Organs** see the CoE Convention, mn. 2, and the Directive 2010/45/EU on Standards of Quality and Safety of Human Organs Intended for Transplantation (OJ L 207 of 6 August 2010, 14) which contributes indirectly to combating organ trafficking by establishing competent authorities etc.; cf. Alarcón Jiménez, *eucrim*, 10 (2015), 120.

130. See Directive 2011/92/EU of the EP and of the Council of 13 December 2011 on combating the **sexual abuse and sexual exploitation of children and child pornography**, and replacing Council FD 2004/68/JHA (OJ L 335 of 17 December 2011, 1) (corrected by OJ L 18 of 21 January 2012, 7); on this, cf. Gercke, *CR*, 28 (2012), 520; Hecker, *Europäisches Strafrecht* (2015), §11 mn. 35 ff.; Ziemann and Ziethen, *ZRP* (2012), 168; Weißer, in Böse, *Europäisches Strafrecht* (2013), pp. 363 f.; from the victims' perspective, de Hoyos Sancho, in de Hoyos Sancho, *Guarantees and Rights of the Especially Vulnerable Victim in the Legal Framework of the EU* (2013), pp. 65 ff.; on the legislative procedure, Nowell-Smith, *NJECL*, 3 (2012), 383 ff.; on the draft, Meyer, *Strafrechtsgenese* (2012), pp. 436–7; on the lack of consensus re child offenders, Nowell-Smith, *NJECL*, 3 (2012), 389; on the need for implementation, Hecker, *Europäisches Strafrecht* (2015), §11 mn. 41; on the implementation regarding child pornography in Germany, Haustein, *ZIS*, 9 (2014), 348 ff. For general information, cf. Huber, in Sieber, Satzger and von Heinegg, *Europäisches Strafrecht* (2014), pp. 412 ff. On the (former) Directive 2002/629/JHA, Weyembergh, *RIDP*, 77 (2006), 211 ff.; on its national implementation, Staiger, *Eur.J.Cr.*, 13 (2005), 617 ff.; Eydner, *NStZ*, 26 (2006), 10. On the (now replaced) FD 2004/68/JHA, Vogel, *GA*, 150 (2003), 324–5; Eckstein, *ZStW*, 117 (2005), 126 ff.; Wattier, *RIDP*, 77 (2006), 223 ff.; Böse, in Hoyer et al., *FS Schroeder* (2006), pp. 751 ff.; from a criminological perspective, Staiger, *Eur.J.Cr.*, 13 (2005), 603 ff. Cf. also Council Decision 2000/375/JHA of 29 May 2000 to combat child pornography on the Internet (OJ L 138 of 9 June 2000, 1).

131. Directive 2013/40/EU of the EP and of the Council of 12 August 2013 on **attacks against information systems** and replacing Council FD 2005/222/JHA (OJ L 218 of 14 August 2013, 8); on this, cf. Naziris, *EuCLR*, 3 (2013), 338 ff.; Brodowski, *ZIS*, 5 (2010), 753; Buono, *NJECL*, 3 (2012), 332; Summers, *BJCLCJ*, 3 (2015), 55–60 (praising 'the subsidiary nature of EU criminal law' in 'modern times when criminal law is often wheeled out as a supposed remedy for all of society's ills'); Weißer, in Böse, *Europäisches Strafrecht* (2013), pp. 367–8; Miettinen, *Criminal Law and Policy in the European Union* (2013), pp. 151 ff.; Gercke, *StV*, 35 (2016), 392; on the earlier provision on FD 2005/222/JHA of 24 February 2005 on attacks against information systems (OJ L 69 of 16 March 2005, 67); Vogel, *GA*, 150 (2003), 314, 325–6 incl. notes

58–9; Hecker, *Europäisches Strafrecht* (2015), §11 mn. 86 ff.; on the EU's activities on cybercrime see Rashkoski, Naumovski and Naumovski, *EurJCrimPolicyRes*, 22 (2016), 130–2; on cybercrime in general, the FD and its implementation in Germany, cf. Sieber, in Sieber, Satzger and von Heinegg, *Europäisches Strafrecht* (2014), pp. 437 ff.; on the implementation (in Germany), Schumann, *NStZ*, 27 (2007), 675; Kainer, *EuR* 48 (2013), *Beiheft 3*, 98–9; crit. Gercke, *StV*, 35 (2016), 393–4. Also cf. the Stockholm Programme, pp. 22–3. On the Cybercrime Convention of the Council of Europe see above, mn. 4. For a good overview of EU activity in the area of online security, Bossong and Wagner, *CrimLSC*, 67 (2017), 265 ff., esp. 274 ff.

132. Directive 2008/99/EC of the EP and of the Council of 19 November 2008 on the **protection of the environment** through criminal law (OJ L 328 of 6 December 2008, 28). This directive replaced Council FD 2003/80/JHA of 27 January 2003 on the protection of the environment through criminal law (OJ L 29 of 5 February 2003, 55), which was declared invalid by the CJEU (cf. CJEU, *Commission* v. *Council*, No C-176/03 (ECLI:EU:C:2005:542), Judgment (13 September 2005), para. 48); on the FD, cf. Hecker, *Europäisches Strafrecht* (2015), §8 mn. 28–9; Mansdörfer, *Jura*, 27 (2004), 297 ff.; Vervaele, *RP*, 15 (2005), 173; Zeitler, *RIDP*, 77 (2006), 255 ff.; Heine and Ringelmann, in László and László, *Emlékkönyv, Losonczy István Professzor Halálának 25. Évfordulójára* (2005), pp. 44, esp. 48 ff.; Miettinen, *Criminal Law and Policy in the European Union* (2013), pp. 165 ff. On the current directive, cf. Zimmermann, *ZRP*, 42 (2009), 74; Fromm, *ZfW*, 48 (2009), 157; Hecker, *Europäisches Strafrecht* (2015), §8 mn. 32 ff.; Hecker, in Sieber, Satzger and von Heinegg, *Europäisches Strafrecht* (2014), pp. 520–2; Vagliasindi, *NJECL*, 3 (2012), 320; Safferling, in Streng and Kett-Straub, *Strafrechtsvergleichung* (2013), pp. 208 ff.; Behrens, *EuZW*, 22 (2011), 161 (placing the main focus on criminal liability of enterprises); from a terminological and conceptual perspective, Perini, in Ruggieri, *Languages* (2014), pp. 145 ff. (analysing the English-, French-, German-, Italian- and Spanish-language versions of the directive and finding particular translation failures in the Italian version); on EU environmental policy and the defined offences in secondary law, cf. Heger, *Die Europäisierung des deutschen Umweltstrafrechts* (2009), pp. 11, 76 ff., 275 ff., 340 ff.; Ruhs, *ZJS*, 4 (2011), 13; Hecker, in Sieber, Satzger and von Heinegg, *Europäisches Strafrecht* (2014), pp. 516 ff.; Hecker, *ZIS*, 8 (2013), 289 (focusing particularly on fraudulently granted permits); on the inadequate internal implementation, Meyer, *wistra*, 31 (2012), 371; on the implementation in the Netherlands, cf. de Rijck, *eucrim*, 6 (2011), 162; for a case solution, cf. Hecker and Zöller, *Fallsammlung zum Europäischen und Internationalen Strafrecht* (2012), pp. 111 ff. (case 11). On the (reformed) environmental criminal law in Turkey, cf. Aygörmez-Ugurlubay, in Pływaczewski and Guzik-Makaruk, *Current Problems of the Penal Law* (2017), pp. 23 ff. (arguing for an advanced reformation considering the Directive 2008/99/EC at 39–40).

133. Council FD 2008/913/JHA of 28 November 2008 on **combating certain forms and expressions of racism and xenophobia** by means of criminal law (OJ L 328 of 6 December 2008, 55) (replacing Joint Action of 15 July 1996 concerning action to combat racism and xenophobia (OJ L 185 of 24 July 1996, 5)). Crit. on the FD, Satzger, *ZRP*, 43 (2010), 139; Satzger, in Böse, *Europäisches Strafrecht* (2013), p. 79 (esp. in regard to the principle of subsidiarity); Rackow, *ZIS*, 5 (2010), 367–8; Bock, *ZRP*, 44 (2011), 46 (crit. of the planned implementation in Germany); on

the implementation, also cf. Hellmann and Gärtner, *NJW*, 64 (2011), 963 ff.; Kainer, *EuR* 48 (2013), *Beiheft 3*, 100; on the Commission Proposal, cf. Weber, *ZRP*, 41 (2008), 21. On this as a whole, cf. Hecker, *Europäisches Strafrecht* (2015), §11 mn. 116 ff.; Gualtieri, *RIDP*, 77 (2006), 263 ff.; Weiß, in Sieber, Satzger and von Heinegg, *Europäisches Strafrecht* (2014), pp. 470 ff. (on the FD, cf. pp. 477 ff.; on its implementation, cf. pp. 480 ff.); Turner, *AmJCompL*, 60 (2012), 564–74 (considering it as a paradigmatic example of the 'expressive dimension of EU criminal law'); Miettinen, *Criminal Law and Policy in the European Union* (2013), pp. 157–8; an instructive account from a Hungarian perspective is provided by Karsai, *ZStW*, 119 (2007), 1048 ff.; on the implementation in Greece, cf. Chouliaras, *eucrim*, 6 (2011), 39. As this area of crime is not mentioned in Art. 83(1) subparagraph 2 TFEU, the Union's competence has to base itself on Art. 67(3) TFEU (Hecker, *Europäisches Strafrecht* (2015), §11 mn. 4). Also cf. the Stockholm Programme, p. 9; Nilsson, *EuCLR*, 2 (2012), 121, does not consider Art. 67(3) TFEU a sufficient basis for competence (in regard to criminal law).

134. Council FD 2002/946/JHA of 28 November 2002 on the strengthening of the penal framework to prevent the facilitation of **unauthorised entry, transit and residence** (OJ L 328 of 5 December 2002); on this cf. Hecker, *Europäisches Strafrecht* (2015), §11 mn. 109 ff.; Council Directive 2002/90/EC of 28 November 2002 defining the facilitation of unauthorised entry, transit and residence (OJ L 328 of 5 December 2002, 17); on the (neutralising) impact of its Art. 11(2) – limiting the (re-)entry ban to, in principle, five years – and on opposing national law, see CJEU, *Filev and Osmani*, No C-297/12 (ECLI:EU:C:2013:569), Judgment (19 Sept. 2013); thereto conc. Hecker, *ZIS*, 9 (2014), 47 ff. (with an analysis of the relevant German law on immigration which was adjusted too late to the directive). See also on the current operative measures, Council Regulation 2007/2004/EC establishing a **European Agency for the Management of Operational Co-operation at the External Borders** (FRONTEX) (OJ L 349 of 25 November 2004, 1); last amended by Regulation 1168/2011/EU of the EP and of the Council of 25 October 2011 amending Council Regulation 2007/2004/EC establishing a European Agency for the Managemant of Operational Co-operation at the External Borders of the Member States of the EU (OJ L 304 of 22 November 2011, 1); see also Communication from the Comission to the EP and to the Council on the work of the Task Force Mediterranean (COM(2013) 869 final), assigning to the Task Force the fight against human smuggling as one of five main tasks; Directive 2008/115/EC of the EP and of the Council of 16 December 2008 on common standards and procedures in Member States for **returning** illegally staying **third-country nationals**; on this 'Returns Directive' and the CJEU's case law, Kramo, *NJECL*, 5 (2014), 34–47 ('the extension of the criminal sanction to immigration breaches such as non-compliance with a return decision runs the grave risk of infringing key values which underpin EU law, notably proportionality and respect for fundamental rights, as well as violating liberal criminal law principles'). See, on the whole, Kilchling and Herz, in Sieber, Satzger and von Heinegg, *Europäisches Strafrecht* (2011), mn. 1 ff. Also cf. the Stockholm Programme, p. 21.

135. Council FD 2008/841/JHA of 24 October 2008 on the fight against **organised crime** (OJ L 300 of 10 November 2008, 42); on the effects on Art. 129 StGB, cf. BGH, No 3 StR 277/09, Judgment (3 December 2009), in *BGHSt*, 54, pp. 216 ff.; with a commentary by Zöller, *JZ*, 65 (2010), 908–12; Kreß and Gazeas, in Paeffgen et al., *FS Puppe*

(2011), pp. 1487 ff. In this context, the **confiscation of criminal proceeds** is of particular importance, cf. e.g. Directive 2014/42/EU of the EP and of the Council of 3 April 2014 on the freezing and confiscation of instrumentalities and proceeds of crime in the EU (OJ L 127 of 29 April 2014, 39; corrected by OJ L 138 of 13 May 2014, 114) (replacing FD 2005/212/JHA of 24 February 2005); on this Simonato, *NJECL*, 6 (2015), 213 ff., who concludes that the Directive is 'far from being a breakthrough in the development of a successful EU model of "non-conviction based" confiscation' (228); for a detailed analysis of Art. 10(3) of this directive see Montaldo, *NJECL*, 6 (2015), 195 ff. (204–9); on the proposal of a Regulation on Mutual Recognition of Freezing and Confiscation orders *eucrim*, 12 (2017), 176–7. On further EU measures, Fazekas and Nanopoulos, *EJCCLCJ* 24 (2016), 42–7; Maugeri, *NJECL*, 3 (2012), 278 ff. Cf. also the Stockholm Programme, p. 21, and the Council conclusions on setting the EU's priorities for the fight against serious and organised crime between 2014 and 2017 (Council Document 12095/13). On the matter as a whole, Kreß and Gazeas, in Sieber, Satzger and von Heinegg, *Europäisches Strafrecht* (2014), pp. 356 ff.; Weißer, in Böse, *Europäisches Strafrecht* (2013), pp. 341 f.; on the models of confiscation in the national law of EU Member States, Maugeri, *NJECL*, 3 (2012), 257 ff. (distinguishing between (i) a separate criminal penalty, confiscation based on the (ii) illegal destination or (iii) origin of the assets and (iv) *actio in rem*); on the implementation in Germany, cf. Kainer, *EuR* 48 (2013), *Beiheft* 3, 99–100; focusing on the presumption of innocence Kaye, *RIDP*, 77 (2006), 323 ff.

136. Council Joint Action 96/750/JHA of 17 December 1996 concerning the approximation of the laws and practices to combat **drug addiction** and to combat **illegal drug trafficking** (OJ L 342 of 31 December 1996, 6) and Council FD 2004/757/JHA of 25 October 2004 laying down minimum provisions on the constituent elements of criminal acts and penalties in the field of illicit drug trafficking (OJ L 335 of 11 November 2004, 8); also cf. Vogel, *GA*, 150 (2003), 324; Pitto, *RIDP*, 77 (2006), 271 ff.; Böse, in Sieber, Satzger and von Heinegg, *Europäisches Strafrecht* (2014), pp. 384 ff.; and Hecker, *Europäisches Strafrecht* (2015), §11 mn. 42 ff.; as regards the definition of 'drug', COM (2013) 618 final, as well as the Proposal for a Regulation of the EP and of the Council on new psychoactive substances, COM (2013) 619 final; on this, cf. Brodowski, *ZIS*, 8 (2013), 465; also cf. the EU Drugs Strategy (2013–20) (OJ C 402 of 29 December 2012, 1; on this, cf. *eucrim*, 7 (2012), 101–2) and the Stockholm Programme, p. 24. Cf. also Gruodytė, in Pływaczewski and Guzik-Makaruk, *Current Problems of the Penal Law* (2017), pp. 452 (458–9), referring to the distinction of drug-trafficking and offences for personal need in FD 2004/757/JHA, and following, that the possession of drugs for personal need does not fall in the EU's competence.

137. Directive (EU) 2017/541 of the EP and of the Council on **combating terrorism** and replacing Council Framework Decision 2002/475/JHA and amending Council Decision 2005/671/JHA (OJ L 88 of 31 March 2017, 6); on the respective proposal Brodowski, *ZIS*, 12 (2017), 16–17; Council Decision 2015/1913/EU of 18 September 2015 on the signing, on behalf of the EU, of the Council of Europe Convention on the Prevention of Terrorism (OJ L 280 of 24 October 2015, 22); Council Decision 2015/1914/EU of 18 September 2015 on the signing, on behalf of the EU, of the Additional Protocol to the Council of Europe Convention on the Prevention of Terrorism (OJ L 280 of 24 October 2015, 24). On the fight against terrorism within the scope of the European Agenda on Security (COM(2015) 185

final), cf. Esser, in Odendahl, *Die Bekämpfung des Terrorismus mit Mitteln des Völker- und Europarechts* (2017), pp. 203 ff. On 'blacklisting' in this context, and the CJEU's *Kadi* etc. decisions, cf. Ambos, *Internationales Strafrecht* (2008), §12 mn. 10 ff.; Schmalenbach, *JZ*, 61 (2006), 349 ff.; more recently, see e.g. Rackow, *StV*, 29 (2009), 721; Rackow, *Die Polizei*, 102 (2011), 1; Meyer, *NJW*, 63 (2010), 2397; Heine, *NStZ*, 29 (2009), 428; Heun-Rehn, *ELR*, 6 (2010), 100; Schneiderhan, *DRiZ*, 87 (2009), 108; Zimmermann, *ZIS*, 4 (2009), 1; Hecker, *Europäisches Strafrecht* (2015), §11 mn. 11 ff.; Andersson, in Ambos, *Europäisches Strafrecht post-Lissabon* (2011), p. 79; Kühne, *ZRP* (2013), 243; Kreß and Gazeas, in Sieber, Satzger and von Heinegg, *Europäisches Strafrecht* (2014), pp. 367 ff.; Kainer, *EuR* 48 (2013), *Beiheft* 3, 96 ff.; Brodowski, *ZIS*, 8 (2013), 466; Weißer, in Böse, *Europäisches Strafrecht* (2013), pp. 368 f.; Oehmichen, *ZIS*, 9 (2014), 412 ff. (crit. discussing the legal basis); Hollenberg, *LJIL*, 28 (2015), 49, 62 ff. (proposing a decentralisation of the designation procedure of the targeted sanctioning regime, leaving it to the domestic system concerned, in order to overcome the due-process problems, especially the lack of access to the information relied on for the designation in the first place and the prevalence of UN Security Council resolutions); on the doctrinal classification of terrorists and the freezing of assets, cf. Pijnen, *eucrim*, 6 (2011), 167; Mitsilegas, *EU Criminal Law after Lisbon* (2016), pp. 25 ff., 236 ff. (crit. discussing the legal basis and considering terrorist sanctions as 'preventive justice'); on the concept of terrorism in the FD on the fight against terrorism, cf. Borgers, *NJECL*, 3 (2012), 68; on terrorist financing, above, n. 125; on the harmonisation from an Italian perspective, Peccioli, *DPP*, 13 (2007), 801 ff.; on the relationship between German and EU anti-terrorism, Zöller, *ZIS*, 9 (2014), 402 ff. In this context, a current **preliminary ruling of the ECJ** is worthy of mention. This ruling finds that for the exclusion of refugee status on the grounds of actions that run counter to the aims and principles of the UN (Art. 12(2)(c), (3) of Directive 2004/83/EC (OJ EU L 304 of 30 September 2004, 12)), it is not necessary for the person in question to have been sentenced for (aiding) terrorist activity; rather, it is sufficient 'that that person was a member of the leadership of that group, and there is no need to establish that that person himself or herself instigated a terrorist act or otherwise participated in it' (CJEU, *Commissaire général aux réfugiés et aux apatrides* v. *Lounani*, No C-573/14 (ECLI:EU:C:2017:71), Judgment (31 January 2017).

138. For the previous list, see Art. 31(e) TEU earlier version.
139. On the protection of the Union's financial interests as a motor of European criminal law, see Dannecker and Bülte, in Wabnitz and Janovsky, *Handbuch des Wirtschafts- und Steuerstrafrechts* (2014), mn. 383; Hecker, *Europäisches Strafrecht* (2015), §14 mn. 4; Gómez-Jara Díez, *European Federal Criminal Law* (2015), p. 76; Covolo, *L'émergence d'un droit pénal en réseau* (2015), p. 83; also Safferling, *Internationales Strafrecht* (2011), §10 mn. 19 ff.; case studies are provided in Hecker and Zöller, *Fallsammlung zum Europäischen und Internationalen Strafrecht* (2012), pp. 69 ff. (Case 8); for earlier references, cf. Ambos, *Internationales Strafrecht* (2008), §12 mn. 9 incl. n. 59.
140. Above, n. 124; thereto Council of the EU, *Explanatory Report*, 23 June 1997 (OJ C 191 of 23 June 1997, 1); Gröblinghoff, *Schutz der Interessen der EU* (1996), pp. 153 ff.; Dannecker, *ZStW*, 108 (1996), 594 ff.; Zieschang, *EuZW*, 8 (1997), 78; Ligeti, *Strafrecht und strafrechtliche Zusammenarbeit* (2005), pp. 279 ff.; Dannecker, in

Böse, *Europäisches Strafrecht* (2013), pp. 300 ff.; Killmann and Schröder, in Sieber, Satzger and von Heinegg, *Europäisches Strafrecht* (2014), pp. 310–11; in detail, Bock, *Europäisches Finanzschutzstrafrecht* (2016), Chapter 4 §2. A. III; with a specific focus upon the implementation of the PIF Convention in England and Germany, Tiegs, *Betrugsbekämpfung in der Europäischen Gemeinschaft* (2006), pp. 329 ff.

141. On the structure and magnitude of financial crime damaging to the Union, see Sieber, *ZStrR* 115 (1996), 357; Hecker, *Europäisches Strafrecht* (2015), §14 mn. 8 ff.; Bock, *Europäisches Finanzschutzstrafrecht* (2016), Chapter 2; on VAT carousel fraud from an Italian perspective, cf. Donato Toma, *eucrim*, 9 (2014), 89 ff.
142. The concept is defined by Bock, *Europäisches Finanzschutzstrafrecht* (2016), Introduction §3, who understands it as the entirety of all European and national legal norms that serve to protect the Union's financial interests by means of criminal law.
143. For a more profound account of the Union's income and expenditure, see Bock, *Europäisches Finanzschutzstrafrecht* (2016), Chapter 1 §2.
144. On the EU's concept of fraud, which is broader compared to that of the MS, cf. above Chapter 1, mn. 22 with n. 188.
145. Thereto Weißer, *GA*, 161 (2014), 444–451 (advocating not just the right but the obligation to adopt General Part rules in case of a regulation and, albeit to a minor extent, in case of a directive regarding the protection of financial interests); on criminal liability of Heads of Business, Ligeti, *eucrim*, 10 (2015), 145 ff.
146. Cf. Art. 2(1) PIF Convention.
147. See Council of the EU, *Explanatory Report*, 23 June 1997 (n. 140), p. 6; generally Weißer, *GA*, 161 (2014), 451.
148. Bock, *Europäisches Finanzschutzstrafrecht* (2016), Ch. 4 §2. D. I.
149. Art. 2 PIF Convention (punishment by 'effective, proportionate and dissuasive criminal penalties').
150. Art. 4 PIF Convention (principle of territoriality and (optional) active personality).
151. The Protocol of 29 November 1996 (above n. 124) does not contain any substantive rules, but establishes the CJEU's jurisdiction over the interpretation of the PIF Convention and Protocol I by way of preliminary rulings.
152. Above, n. 124; thereto Braum, *Europäische Strafgesetzlichkeit* (2003), pp. 180 ff.; Dannecker, in Böse, *Europäisches Strafrecht* (2013), pp. 313–14.
153. Above, n. 124; thereto Korte, *NJW*, 51 (1998), 1464; Braum, *Europäische Strafgesetzlichkeit* (2003), pp. 182–3; on the regulations on punishing legal persons, Engelhart, *eucrim*, 7 (2012), 110–11.
154. This refers to acts of money laundering where the predicate offence is an EU fraud or corruption offence within the meaning of Protocol I.
155. Art. 1 Protocol II (n. 124).
156. Art. 3 Protocol II (n. 124); see also Vogel, in Cullen, *Enlarging the Fight against Fraud in the EU* (2004), p. 63; Korte, *NJW*, 51 (1998), 1465; Fromm, *ZIS*, 2 (2007), 279; Weigend, *JICJ*, 6 (2008), 929 incl. n. 12; Stuckenberg, in Böse, *Europäisches Strafrecht* (2013), p. 388 incl. n. 42; Bock, *Europäisches Finanzschutzstrafrecht* (2016), Chapter 4 §2. B. II. incl. further references.
157. Cf. Sunderland et al., *Protection of EU Financial Interests* (2012), pp. 17 ff.

158. European Commission, *Commission Staff Working Paper*, SWD(2012) 195 final, pp. 22 ff.
159. European Commission, 'Proposal for a Directive', 11 July 2012, COM(2012) 363; thereto Kaiafa-Gbandi, *EuCLR*, 2 (2012), 319; Dannecker, in Böse, *Europäisches Strafrecht* (2013), pp. 306 ff.; BRAK, *Stellungnahme Nr. 11* (2013); Deutscher Richterbund, *Stellungnahme* (2013); Kuhl, *eucrim*, 7 (2012), 63; *Killmann and Schröder*, in Sieber, Satzger and von Heinegg, *Europäisches Strafrecht* (2014), pp. 315–16; Hecker, *Europäisches Strafrecht* (2015), §14 mn. 36 ff.; Bock, *Europäisches Finanzschutzstrafrecht* (2016), Ch. 4 §2. D.; on the definitions of the offences in particular Rheinbay, *Die Errichtung einer Europäischen Staatsanwaltschaft* (2014), pp. 132 ff.
160. Art. 4 No 1 Proposal Directive (n. 159).
161. Art. 4 No 4 Proposal Directive (n. 159).
162. Art. 8 Proposal Directive (n. 159).
163. Critically thereto BRAK, *Stellungnahme Nr. 11* (2013), no 3; Kaiafa-Gbandi, *EuCLR*, 2 (2012), 328–9.
164. Art. 12 Proposal Directive (n. 159). Kaiafa-Gbandi, *EuCLR*, 5 (2015), 13, is doubtful whether there is actually any need for harmonisation concerning the rules on the statutes of limitation. Asp, *Substantive Criminal Law Competence* (2012), p. 101, doubts whether such a regulation can be based upon the ancillary competence of Art. 83(2) TFEU, as it may no longer concern the 'definition of criminal offences and sanctions'.
165. Overview of the contentious points in Council of the EU, 'Proposal for a Directive: Preparation of the Next Triologue', 7 May 2015, 8604/15, pp. 1–2; specifically on the hotly debated question whether the directive should also include VAT tax evasion damaging to the Union, Council of the EU, 'Proposal for a Directive: Progress Report/Policy Debate', 27 May 2016, 9301/16; Council of the EU, 'Proposal for a Directive: Progress Report/Policy Debate', 3 June 2016, 9804/16.
166. Cf. above Chapter 1, mn. 22.
167. European Commission, 'Proposal for a Directive', 11 July 2012, COM(2012) 363, p. 7.
168. Council of the EU, Opinion of the Legal Service, 'Proposal for a Directive: Legal Basis', 22 October 2012, 15309/12, p. 9; Council of the EU, Note, 3 June 2013, 10232/13, p. 2.
169. EP, 'Legislative Resolution of 16 April 2014 on the Proposal for a Directive of the EP and of the Council on the Fight against Fraud of the Union's Financial Interests by Means of Criminal Law'.
170. Cf. the criticism in BR-Drs. 409/12; Swedish Parliament, *Reasoned Opinion*, 23 October 2012, Communication 86/2012; BRAK, *Stellungnahme Nr. 11* (2013), p. 6; Kaiafa-Gbandi, *EuCLR*, 2 (2012), 319; the opinion of the German Association of Judges also tended towards criticism; see Deutscher Richterbund, *Stellungnahme* (2013).
171. Council of the EU, Note, 3 June 2013, 10232/13. On 7 May 2015 the Council presented a compromise proposal that aimed to push negotiations forward; Council of the EU, 'Proposal for a Directive: Preparation of the Next Triologue', 7 May 2015, 8604/15, pp. 3 ff. A detailed comparison and critical evaluation of the different regulations suggested can be found in Bock, *Europäisches Finanzschutzstrafrecht* (2016), Ch. 4 §2. D.

172. Council of the EU, Note, 3 June 2013, 10232/13, Art. 3 (Fraud) and Art. 4 (Fraud related criminal offences).
173. See, for example, the abandonment of minimum minimum *and* minimum maximum penalties in Art. 7 and the very general guidelines on statutes of limitations in Art. 12 (prosecution 'for a sufficient period of time'), Council of the EU, Note, 3 June 2013, 10232/13.
174. Directive (EU) 2017/1371 of the EP and of the Council of 5 July 2017 on the fight against fraud to the Union's financial interests by means of criminal law (OJ L 198 of 28 July 2017, 29); on this see Juszczak and Sason, *eucrim*, 12 (2017), 80 ff. ('a cornerstone of fighting PIF crimes more effectively by means of criminal law').
175. Arts. 3 and 4 Directive (EU) 2017/1371 (n. 174).
176. Art. 9(b) Directive (EU) 2017/1371 (n. 174).
177. Case taken from Satzger, *Die Europäisierung des Strafrechts* (2001), p. 195; Satzger, *Internationales und Europäisches Strafrecht* (2016), §8 mn. 10.
178. CJEU, *Prantl* v. *Germany*, No C-16/83 (ECLI:EU:C:1984:101), Judgment (13 March 1984).
179. CJEU, *Ministère public* v. *Vincent Rodolphe Auer*, No C-271/82 (ECLI:EU:C:1983:243), Judgment (22 September 1983).
180. BGH, No 4 StR 304/88, Decision (31 January 1989), in *BGHSt*, 36, pp. 92, 94 following BGH, No 1 StR 376/84, Decision (27 November 1984), in *BGHSt*, 33, p. 76.
181. BGH, No 5 StR 444/90, Judgment (26 February 1991), in *BGHSt*, 37, pp. 333, 334, 336; also Ambos, *Fälle zum internationalen Strafrecht* (2010), p. 23 (case 2 mn. 28 ff.).
182. Cf. Chapter 1, mn. 22.
183. On the 'techniques' cf. Chapter 1, mn. 29.
184. Cf., on the following, Satzger, *Die Europäisierung des Strafrechts* (2001), pp. 216 ff. incl. further references.
185. Satzger, *Die Europäisierung des Strafrechts* (2001), p. 187.
186. On this, also cf. Moll, *Europäisches Strafrecht durch nationale Blankettstrafgesetzgebung?* (1998), pp. 28 ff., 44 ff.
187. Satzger and Langheld, *HRRS*, 12 (2011), 462.
188. On blanket references in a narrower and broader sense, cf. Moll, *Europäisches Strafrecht durch nationale Blankettstrafgesetzgebung?* (1998), pp. 46 ff.
189. See, for example, §315 a (1) No 2 **German** StGB (which makes commission dependent upon the breach of 'legal provisions relating to the safety of rail, suspension rail, ship or air traffic'); Art. 398 **Greek** PC (bankruptcy pursuant to the Greek Commercial Law as amended by the Greek Insolvency Code); §233(1) **Hungarian** PC (endangerment of railway, air and water transport systems); Art. 644(3) **Italian** PC (reference to non-criminal law as to the amount of interest in case of offence of usury); Art. 219 **Polish** PC (breach of provisions of social law); Art. 279 (1) **Portuguese** PC (environmental pollution ignoring relevant environmental laws and regulations); Art. 318bis **Spanish** PC (illegal entry defined with regard to legislation on aliens ('legislación sobre entrada o tránsito de extranjeros')). In **English** law this technique is not known under the same name but in fact cross-references to complement offence definitions are common, either within the same statute (see e.g. in the Sexual Offences Act 2003, §1 referring to §79 to define

'perpetration' etc.) or to a different statute (e.g. Weights and Measures Act 1985, §30, as to the definition of food referring to the EU FIC Regulation).

190. On assimilation and similar concepts, cf. Chapter 1, mn. 28; see also Satzger, *Die Europäisierung des Strafrechts* (2001), p. 188; Eisele, *JA*, 32 (2000), 899–900; Tiedemann, *Wirtschaftsstrafrecht* (2017), mn. 103; Hecker, *Europäisches Strafrecht* (2015), §7 mn. 6 ff.; Esser, *Europäisches und Internationales Strafrecht* (2018), §2 mn. 34 ff.; Vogel and Brodowski, in Sieber, Satzger and von Heinegg, *Europäisches Strafrecht* (2014), p. 188 ('supranational instruction to use Member State criminal law to protect the interests of the European institutions', orig. 'supranationale Anweisung, das mitgliedstaatliche Strafrecht zum Schutze der Interessen der europäischen Institutionen einzusetzen'); Asp, in Freund et al., *FS Frisch* (2013), pp. 1389 ff.
191. Emphasis added.
192. Eisele, *JA*, 32 (2000), 899–900; Satzger, *Die Europäisierung des Strafrechts* (2001), p. 192; Satzger, *Internationales und Europäisches Strafrecht* (2016), §8 mn. 13; Tiedemann, *NJW*, 46 (1993), 25; also cf. Dannecker and Freitag, *ZStW*, 116 (2004), 808; Asp, in Freund et al., *FS Frisch* (2013), p. 1389.
193. §5 No 10 StGB.
194. Ambos, in Joecks and Miebach, *Münchener Kommentar zum Strafgesetzbuch*, i (2017), §5 mn. 32.
195. §§153 ff. StGB; cf. Case 1.
196. §162(1) StGB. See also Satzger, *Die Europäisierung des Strafrechts* (2001), p. 195; Hecker and Zöller, *Fallsammlung zum Europäischen und Internationalen Strafrecht* (2012), pp. 61 ff. (Case 7).
197. Cf. BGH, No 8 StE 8/61, Judgment (1 February 1962), in *BGHSt*, 17, pp. 121, 122; Eisele, *JA*, 32 (2000), 900 incl. further references; Jescheck, in Schroeder and Zipf, *FS Maurach* (1972), p. 592; Oehler, *Internationales Strafrecht* (1983), mn. 912; Pabsch, *NJW*, 12 (1959), 2002 ff.; for different opinion, cf. Satzger, *Die Europäisierung des Strafrechts* (2001), pp. 192 ff. incl. further references; Satzger, *Internationales und Europäisches Strafrecht* (2016), §8 mn. 14–15; Satzger, in Sieber, Satzger and von Heinegg, *Europäisches Strafrecht* (2014), p. 255, who does not consider Art. 30 CJEU Statute as self-executing; for the same view, Esser, *Europäisches und Internationales Strafrecht* (2018), §2 mn. 45; left open by Jähnke and Schramm, *Europäisches Strafrecht* (2017), §4 mn. 14 (arguing that only Art. 30 CJEU Statute represents supranational European law).
198. Thus Böse, *Strafen und Sanktionen im Europäischen Gemeinschaftsrecht* (1996), p. 108 (orig. 'supranationale Gesamttatbestände'); also Vogel, in Dannecker, *Bekämpfung des Subventionsbetruges im EG-Bereich* (1993), p. 173; Dannecker, *Jura*, 29 (2006), 99–100; Hecker, *Europäisches Strafrecht* (2015), §7 mn. 6, 9–10.
199. This is how Satzger, *Die Europäisierung des Strafrechts* (2001), p. 193, interprets the view of Nehring, *Strafnormen im Atomenergierecht* (1965), p. 163, who denies the Union norm has any direct effect. Also cf. Rosenau, *ZIS*, 3 (2008), 9; Heger, in Böse, *Europäisches Strafrecht* (2013), pp. 189–90.
200. Satzger, *Die Europäisierung des Strafrechts* (2001), p. 195; a critical stance is also taken by Dannecker, *Jura*, 29 (2006), 100. On primacy in more detail, see below, mn. 46 ff.
201. Dannecker, *Jura*, 21 (1998), 81; Eisele, *JA*, 32 (2000), 900; Gröblinghoff, *Schutz der Interessen der EU* (1996), pp. 52–3; Johannes, *EuR*, 3 (1968), 69 ff., 81; Jokisch,

Gemeinschaftsrecht und Strafverfahren (2000), p. 87; Tiedemann, *NJW*, 46 (1993), 25.

202. Thereto Chapter 1, mn. 19 ff.
203. Satzger, *Die Europäisierung des Strafrechts* (2001), p. 196 incl. further references; Bacigalupo, in Dannecker, *Bekämpfung des Subventionsbetruges im EG-Bereich* (1993), pp. 146–7; Pabsch, *Der strafrechtliche Schutz der überstaatlichen Hoheitsgewalt* (1965), p. 176; Tiedemann, *ZStW*, 116 (2004), 950; Ambos, *Fälle zum internationalen Strafrecht* (2010), p. 19 (case 2 mn. 16); Jokisch, *Gemeinschaftsrecht und Strafverfahren* (2000), p. 88 (critical of this); Eisele, *JA*, 32 (2000), 900; Bacigalupo, in Schünemann, *Ein Gesamtkonzept für die europäische Strafrechtspflege* (2006), pp. 82–3.
204. Thus Jung and Schroth, *GA*, 130 (1983), 264.
205. §93(1) (concept of State secret), §203 (breach of private secrets), §353 b StGB (breach of official secrets and a special duty of confidentiality).
206. Tiedemann, *NJW*, 46 (1993), 25; also cf. Tiedemann, *Wirtschaftsstrafrecht* (2017), mn. 103; also cf. Pabsch, *Der strafrechtliche Schutz der überstaatlichen Hoheitsgewalt* (1965), pp. 153 ff.
207. Oehler, *Internationales Strafrecht* (1983), mn. 921; Oehler, in Kaufmann, Schwinge and Welzel, *Erinnerungsgabe für Max Grünhut* (1965), p. 112.
208. Satzger, *Die Europäisierung des Strafrechts* (2001), p. 197.
209. Cf. Chapter 1, mn. 9–10.
210. Also cf. Paeffgen, in Kindhäuser, Neumann and Paeffgen, *Strafgesetzbuch, Nomos Kommentar*, ii (2017), §93 mn. 28; a different opinion is put forward by Sternberg-Lieben, in Schönke, Schröder and Eser, *Strafgesetzbuch, Kommentar* (2010), §93 mn. 19.
211. Oehler, *Internationales Strafrecht* (1983), mn. 922; Satzger, *Die Europäisierung des Strafrechts* (2001), pp. 197–8.
212. Thereto main text, mn. 32.
213. Satzger, *Die Europäisierung des Strafrechts* (2001), pp. 197–8; also cf. Oehler, *Internationales Strafrecht* (1983), mn. 922.
214. Oehler, *Internationales Strafrecht* (1983), mn. 922; Pabsch, *NJW*, 12 (1959), 2004; Grasso, *Comunida des Europeas y derecho penal* (1993), pp. 163–4.
215. CJEU, *Amsterdam Bulb BV* v. *Produktschap voor Siegewassen*, No C-50/76 (ECLI: EU:C:1977:13), Judgment (2 February 1977), guiding principle 2; CJEU, *Variola* v. *Amministrazione italiana delle Finanze*, No C-34/73 (ECLI:EU:C:1973:101), Judgment (10 October 1973), para. 11. On this, cf. Satzger, *Die Europäisierung des Strafrechts* (2001), pp. 199–200.
216. Satzger, *Die Europäisierung des Strafrechts* (2001), pp. 193 ff., 198 ff., 206, 700–1.
217. Thereto main text, mn. 51 ff.
218. Examples included in Satzger, *Die Europäisierung des Strafrechts* (2001), p. 207.
219. Eisele, *JA*, 32 (2000), 900; Satzger, *Die Europäisierung des Strafrechts* (2001), p. 208; Tiedemann, *NJW*, 46 (1993), 25; Tiedemann, *ZStW*, 116 (2004), 950.
220. Tiedemann, *NJW*, 46 (1993), 25; Tiedemann, *ZStW* 116 (2004), 950.
221. Dannecker, in Ulsamer, *Lexikon des Rechts. Strafrecht/Strafverfahrensrecht* (1996), p. 303; Dannecker and Freitag, *ZStW*, 116 (2004), 808 incl. further references; Hecker, *Europäisches Strafrecht* (2015), §7 mn. 15; Heger, in Böse, *Europäisches Strafrecht* (2013), pp. 193–4.

222. Council Regulation (EC) No 515/97 of 13 March 1997 on mutual assistance between the administrative authorities of the Member States and co-operation between the latter and the Commission to ensure the correct application of the law on customs and agricultural matters (OJ L 82 of 22 March 1997, 1). See also Council Decision 2009/917/JHA of 30 November 2009 on the use of information technology for customs purposes (OJ L 323 of 10 December 2009, 20) and the recent Regulation (EU) No 2015/1525; thereto Porebska, *eucrim*, 11 (2016), 52 ff.; see also Chapter 4, n. 16 *in fine*.
223. OJ L 218 of 13 August 2008, 48 ff.
224. As to Germany, §§203, 204, 353b StGB would be relevant.
225. Satzger, *Die Europäisierung des Strafrechts* (2001), p. 207.
226. Examples in the main text, mn. 41 ff.
227. On these different reference models, cf. Rutkowski, 'Blankettvorschriften', in Erbs, Kohlhaas, Buddendiek and Rutkowski *Strafrechtliche Nebengesetze* (2006); Satzger, *Die Europäisierung des Strafrechts* (2001), pp. 235–6.
228. Rutkowski, 'Blankettvorschriften', in Erbs, Kohlhaas, Buddendiek and Rutkowski *Strafrechtliche Nebengesetze* (2006), contains a wealth of examples for references in German criminal or fine regulations to EU law; also cf. Satzger, *Die Europäisierung des Strafrechts* (2001), pp. 235–6; Satzger, in Sieber, Satzger and von Heinegg, *Europäisches Strafrecht* (2014), pp. 258–9, Hecker, *Europäisches Strafrecht* (2015), §7 mn. 82 ff.; Safferling, *Internationales Strafrecht* (2011), §11 mn. 60. Also cf. the cases in Köpferl, *Jura*, 34 (2011), 234 und Hecker and Zöller, *Fallsammlung zum Europäischen und Internationalen Strafrecht* (2012), pp. 127 ff. (Case 13).
229. Satzger, *Die Europäisierung des Strafrechts* (2001), p. 210. In detail on the problems of adaptation that can arise here and how they are compensated for, Schützendübel, *Die Bezugnahme auf EU-Verordnungen in Blankettstrafgesetzen* (2012), pp. 75 ff.
230. Oehler, *Internationales Strafrecht* (1983), mn. 933; Oehler, in Arzt et al., *FS Baumann* (1992), p. 568.
231. Oehler, in Vogler, *FS Jescheck* (1985), pp. 1405–6 note 10; Satzger, *Die Europäisierung des Strafrechts* (2001), pp. 211–12; also cf. Bacigalupo, in Dannecker, *Bekämpfung des Subventionsbetruges im EG-Bereich* (1993), pp. 149 ff.
232. Satzger, *Die Europäisierung des Strafrechts* (2001), p. 211 incl. further references.
233. Main text, mn. 41 ff.
234. Satzger, *JuS*, 44 (2004), 948 (divergence of the competence to legislate criminal and economic law).
235. Klindt, *DVBl.*, 113 (1998), 375 ff.; Satzger, in Sieber, Satzger and von Heinegg, *Europäisches Strafrecht* (2014), pp. 259–61; Mansdörfer, *Jura*, 27 (2004), 305, ascribes the high number of dropped cases in the area of environmental criminal law blanket offences (§§153, 153 a StPO) to the concerns mentioned in the text.
236. An instructive account is given by Böse, in Amelung, Günther and Kühne, *FS Krey* (2010), pp. 7 ff. Cf. also Satzger and Langheld, *HRRS*, 12 (2011), 460; Esser, *Europäisches und Internationales Strafrecht* (2018), §2 mn. 106 ff.; Hoven, *NStZ*, 36 (2016), 377, 379; Dannecker, *ZIS*, 11 (2016), 725–9.
237. Zweigert, *RabelsZ*, 28 (1964), 605 ff.
238. Satzger, *Die Europäisierung des Strafrechts* (2001), pp. 232–3 incl. further references; Hecker, *Europäisches Strafrecht* (2015), §7 mn. 77.

239. Satzger, *Die Europäisierung des Strafrechts* (2001), p. 233; also cf. Nestler, *NStZ*, 32 (2012), 672 ff. (esp. 677 ff.) using §34(4) AWG. On these interpretation standards see main text, mn. 51 ff.
240. For example, Art. 103(2), 104(1) first sentence GG, cf. Satzger, *Die Europäisierung des Strafrechts* (2001), pp. 237 ff. incl. further references; Satzger, *Internationales und Europäisches Strafrecht* (2016), §9 mn. 63.
241. BVerfG, Nos 2 BvR 234/87 and 1154/86, Decision (22 June 1986), in *BVerfGE*, 78, pp. 374, 382; also Satzger, *Die Europäisierung des Strafrechts* (2001), pp. 240–1, 241 ff., 247 ff.; Niehaus, *wistra*, 23 (2004), 208; Böse, in Amelung, Günther and Kühne, *FS Krey* (2010), p. 8; Dannecker, *ZIS*, 11 (2016), 725–9.
242. Satzger, *JuS*, 44 (2004), 943–4; Satzger, *Internationales und Europäisches Strafrecht* (2016), §9 mn. 67; Satzger, in Sieber, Satzger and von Heinegg, *Europäisches Strafrecht* (2014), pp. 259–60; Jähnke and Schramm, *Europäisches Strafrecht* (2017), §4 mn. 7 ('acceptable', orig. *hinnehmbar*); on criminal law on the protection of species in this regard, cf. Stegmann, *Artenschutz-Strafrecht* (2000), pp. 112 ff.; Mansdörfer, *Jura*, 27 (2004), 305; crit. Niehaus, *wistra*, 23 (2004), 209; on tax criminal law, cf. Ambos, *Internationales Strafrecht* (2008), §11 mn. 47 note 273.
243. Satzger, *Die Europäisierung des Strafrechts* (2001), pp. 241 ff., esp. 242, 246; Satzger, *JuS*, 44 (2004), 944.
244. As, for example, forming the foundation of Art. 103(2) GG.
245. Under German law, for example, these are based on Art. 80(2) second sentence GG.
246. BVerfG, No 2 BvL 1/15, Decision (21 September 2016), in *NJW*, 69 (2016), 3648, 3650, para. 39; crit. on the reference system in this case, also Kretschmer, *ZIS*, 12 (2016), 763–5; previously BVerfG, No 2 BvR 15/62, Judgment (3 July 1962), in *BVerfGE*, 14, pp. 174, 186; BVerfG, No 2 BvL 11/85, Decision (6 May 1987), in *BVerfGE*, 75, pp. 329, 342; BVerfG, 2 BvR 234/87 and 1154/86 (n. 241), p. 382; BVerfG, Nos 1 BvF 1/85 and 1 BvR 1/88, Judgment (5 February 1991), in *BVerfGE*, 83, pp. 238, 269; BVerfG, Nos 1 BvR 168, 1509/89 and 638, 639/90, Decision (17 November 1992), in *BVerfGE*, 87, pp. 363, 391–2; BGH, No 1 StR 745/95, Decision (16 August 1996), in *BGHSt*, 42, pp. 219, 221; Satzger, *Die Europäisierung des Strafrechts* (2001), 247–8; Stegmann, *Artenschutz-Strafrecht* (2000), pp. 120–1; Moll, *Europäisches Strafrecht durch nationale Blankettstrafgesetzgebung?* (1998), pp. 153–4; Hoven, *NStZ*, 36 (2016), 377, 379, who stresses the constitutional inadmissability of referrals as the regulatory authority would thus gain the competence to make a final decision upon the sanction decreed (at 381); Niehaus, *wistra*, 23 (2004), 210; Hecker, *Europäisches Strafrecht* (2015), §7 mn. 87; Hecker, in Sieber, Satzger and von Heinegg, *Europäisches Strafrecht* (2014), pp. 533–4; Böse, in Amelung, Günther and Kühne, *FS Krey* (2010), pp. 8 ff.
247. On §§56, 57 of the LMBG, which was annulled effective 20 May 2016, Hellmann and Beckemper, *Wirtschaftsstrafrecht* (1st edn, 2004), mn. 759, with reference to BVerfG, No 2 BvF 1/64, Decision (15 July 1969), in *BVerfGE*, 26, pp. 338, 367; not included in subsequent editions.
248. For more detail on this, cf. Satzger, *Die Europäisierung des Strafrechts* (2001), pp. 249 ff.; summarised in pp. 269–70; on directives, Eisele, *JZ*, 56 (2001), 1164.
249. Satzger, *Die Europäisierung des Strafrechts* (2001), pp. 249–50 incl. further references.

250. Satzger, *Die Europäisierung des Strafrechts* (2001), p. 253 incl. further references; Satzger, *Internationales und Europäisches Strafrecht* (2016), §9 mn. 70; Satzger, *JuS*, 44 (2004), 947. On possible impunity arising from an exchange of objects of reference, cf. Hecker, *Europäisches Strafrecht* (2015), §7 mn. 88 ff.
251. Cf. Satzger and Langheld, *HRRS*, 12 (2011), 464.
252. For a justifiably critical stance on this, cf. Hoven, *NStZ*, 36 (2016), 377, 382; Niehaus, *wistra*, 23 (2004), 207 and 210, in regard to §§12(1) first and second sentences MOG (Common Market Organisations Implementation Act). Also cf. Dannecker, *ZStW*, 117 (2005), 738–9, who states that the primacy of Union law means it does not come down to 'national constitutional guarantees, but only to Union constitutional law'.
253. Satzger, *Die Europäisierung des Strafrechts* (2001), p. 255; Hoven, *NStZ*, 36 (2016), 377, 382; also cf. BVerfG, 2 BvL 1/15 (n. 246), para. 43; Hecker, *Europäisches Strafrecht* (2015), §7 mn. 94 ff., incl. a wealth of examples.
254. Satzger, *Die Europäisierung des Strafrechts* (2001), pp. 255–6 incl. further references. Cf. also BVerfG, 2 BvL 1/15 (n. 246), paras. 43, 47.
255. Satzger, *Die Europäisierung des Strafrechts* (2001), p. 257 (orig. 'höchste Anforderungen an die Verweisungstechnik'); also cf. Dannecker, *Jura*, 29 (2006), 101.
256. Satzger, *Die Europäisierung des Strafrechts* (2001), pp. 260–1 incl. further references; Hoven, *NStZ*, 36 (2016), 377, 383 ('Here, the German legislator is not responsible for shaping the content of the decrees and prohibitions, but is indeed responsible for deciding the sanction imposed' – orig. 'Hier obliegt dem deutschen Gesetzgeber nicht die inhaltliche Ausgestaltung der Ge- und Verbote, wohl aber die Entscheidung über die angedrohte Rechtsfolge'); Niehaus, *wistra*, 23 (2004), 210; also cf. Böse, in Amelung, Günther and Kühne, *FS Krey* (2010), pp. 16 ff., who even thinks it possible that a more generous standard can be applied to references to secondary Union law than to references to domestic executive decrees.
257. Satzger, *Die Europäisierung des Strafrechts* (2001), pp. 262–3 incl. further references; Moll, *Europäisches Strafrecht durch nationale Blankettstrafgesetzgebung?* (1998), pp. 153–4; Hecker, *Europäisches Strafrecht* (2015), §7 mn. 101 ('tangle of references', orig. 'Verweisungsgestrüpp').
258. In regard to a blanket criminal law on the protection of birds of prey and owls, BGH, 1 StR 745/95 (n. 246), pp. 221–2 speaks of 'interested norm addressees' and *in concreto* emphasises that the defendant had 'studied zoology and been a hobby ornithologist for many years'. Also cf. Satzger, *Die Europäisierung des Strafrechts* (2001), pp. 263–4; Satzger, *JuS*, 44 (2004), 948; Satzger, *Internationales und Europäisches Strafrecht* (2016), §9 mn. 67; Mansdörfer, *Jura*, 27 (2004), 305; Niehaus, *wistra*, 23 (2004), 209; similarly Böse, in Amelung, Günther and Kühne, *FS Krey* (2010), pp. 14–15; Heger, in Böse, *Europäisches Strafrecht* (2013), p. 201; a different opinion can be found in Moll, *Europäisches Strafrecht durch nationale Blankettstrafgesetzgebung?* (1998), p. 154; Schützendübel, *Die Bezugnahme auf EU-Verordnungen in Blankettstrafgesetzen* (2012), p. 263 (less strict, wanting to emphasise the clear chain of reference and the specificity of the expletive norm in each individual case). For a critical stance on the issue of specificity of §34(4) AWG, Dannecker and Freitag, *ZStW*, 116 (2004), 813–14.

259. BGH, No 5 StR 543/10, Decision (17 March 2011). On changes to the object of reference, also cf. Heger, in Böse, *Europäisches Strafrecht* (2013), pp. 203 f.
260. Thus also Satzger and Langheld, *HRRS*, 12 (2011), 460.
261. BGH, No 1 StR 544/13, Decision (20 November 2013), in *NJW*, 67 (2014), 1029.
262. In the same vein (crit. of the BGH), Schuhr, *NStZ*, 34 (2014), 330–1.
263. Satzger, *Die Europäisierung des Strafrechts* (2001), pp. 264–5 incl. extensive references.
264. As rejected explicitly by Staats, in Rödig, *Studien zu einer Theorie der Gesetzgebung* (1976), pp. 244, 256–7; however, also cf. Nierhaus, in Sachs, *Grundgesetz* (2014), Art. 82 mn. 22, who claim it is sufficient if the reference to the Union norm is given precisely in the national official journal (*Bundesgesetzblatt*); on the publication of the regulations relevant to §34 AWG in the BGBl, cf. Dannecker and Freitag, *ZStW*, 116 (2004), 802.
265. Cf. BVerfG, No 2 BvR 1086/77, Decision (17 March 1978), in *ZLR*, 5 (1978), 203–4; BVerfG, No 2 BvR 618/68, Decision (13 October 1970), in *BVerfGE*, 29, pp. 198, 210; BVerfG, No 2 BvR 836/85, Decision (19 December 1991), in *NVwZ-RR*, 5 (1992), 521–2; for a more differentiated view, cf. Böse, *Strafen und Sanktionen im Europäischen Gemeinschaftsrecht* (1996), pp. 438–9; Satzger, *Die Europäisierung des Strafrechts* (2001), p. 267; Eisele, *JZ*, 56 (2001), 1164; a stricter position is taken by Niehaus, *wistra*, 23 (2004), 209, who regards the effort involved as unacceptable.
266. Satzger, *Die Europäisierung des Strafrechts* (2001), pp. 267–8.
267. Above, mn. 5–6.
268. Above, mn. 10, with n. 91.
269. Ambos, *Internationales Strafrecht* (2008), §11 mn. 30.
270. Cf. Arts. 91(1)(c), 192(1) TFEU.
271. Art. 288 subparagraph 3 TFEU.
272. Accordingly, Meyer, *EuR*, 46 (2011), 175, speaks of an 'intergovernmentalisation' (orig. 'Intergouvernementalisierung') of ancillary competence. On the difference between supranational legislation and mere instruction in this regard, cf. Ambos, *Internationales Strafrecht* (2008), §11 mn. 30 incl. further references in note 144. Merely indirect Union influence also means that individual *annulment actions*, an option made possible in principle in the Lisbon Treaty (Art. 263(4) TFEU), are doomed to fail regularly in regard to harmonisation directives; on this, cf. Gentzik, *Die Europäisierung des deutschen und englischen Geldwäschestrafrechts* (2002), pp. 61–2.
273. Council FD 2003/80/JHA of 27 January 2003 (OJ L 29 of 5 February 2003, 55 ff.).
274. CJEU, *Commission* v. *Council*, C-176/03, para. 48. This judgment annulled FD 2003/80/JHA on the grounds that it should have been adopted on the basis of the EC Treaty and not the TEU. Cf. Hecker, *Europäisches Strafrecht* (2015), §8 mn. 25 ff.; cf. on the FD 2005/667/JHA of 12 July 2005 to strengthen the criminal law framework for the enforcement of the law against ship-source pollution CJEU, *Commission* v. *Council*, No C-440/05 (ECLI:EU:C:2007:625), Judgment (23 October 2007), para. 35; for a critical stance, cf. Heger, *Die Europäisierung des deutschen Umweltstrafrechts* (2009), pp. 134 ff.; Rackow, *ZIS*, 3 (2008), 526; further references provided in Ambos, *Internationales Strafrecht* (2008), §11 note 146.

275. References on the predominantly critical response to this are given in Ambos, *Internationales Strafrecht* (2008), §11 note 147; also cf. Zimmermann, *ZRP*, 42 (2009), 74; Zimmermann, *NStZ*, 28 (2008), 662; Zöller, *ZIS*, 4 (2009), 344 ff.; Harms and Heine, in Böse and Sternberg-Lieben, *FS Amelung* (2009), p. 393; Reiling and Reschke, *wistra*, 19 (2010), 47; Hörich, *ZAR*, 30 (2010), 49; Hecker, *Europäisches Strafrecht* (2015), §8 mn. 30–1; Hecker, in Sieber, Satzger and von Heinegg, *Europäisches Strafrecht* (2014), pp. 280–3. On further policy areas, cf. Asp, *Substantive Criminal Law Competence* (2012), pp. 132 ff.
276. A different stance is taken in Zöller, *GA*, 154 (2007), 409; also cf. Jour-Schröder and Konow, *EuZW*, 17 (2006), 550–1.
277. CJEU, *Parliament* v. *Council*, Nos C-317/04 and C-318/04 (ECLI:EU:C:2006:346), Judgment (30 May 2006), para. 57; in agreement, Simitis, *NJW*, 59 (2006), 2013; also cf. Böse, *ZStW*, 119 (2007), 884; Rusteberg, *VBlBW*, 28 (2007), 174; Galli, *eucrim*, 5 (2010), 124 ff.
278. CJEU, *Commission* v. *Council*, C-440/05; on this, also cf. Hecker, *Europäisches Strafrecht* (2015), §8 mn. 31.
279. Cf. Fromm, *ZIS*, 3 (2008), 174 ('continuation of the groundbreaking case law', orig. 'Fortführung der wegweisenden Rechtsprechung'); also cf. main text, mn. 39.
280. CJEU, *Commission* v. *Council*, C-440/05, para. 69 ('those articles must be regarded as being essentially aimed at improving maritime safety, as well as environmental protection, and could have been validly adopted on the basis of Article 80(2) EC').
281. Cf. Ambos, *Internationales Strafrecht* (2008), §11 mn. 30a incl. further references in note 148.
282. As aptly noted by Sánchez Patrón, *RDP* 19 (2006), 50–1, 55 ('concepción mas instrumental'); also Šugmann Stubbs and Jager, *KritV*, 91 (2008), 65 ('criminal law as means to an end', orig. 'Strafrecht als Mittel zum Zweck').
283. Main text, mn. 11.
284. Cf. also Böse, in Böse, *Europäisches Strafrecht* (2013), p. 176 ('priority of the authorisation referring specifically to criminal procedure', orig. 'Vorrang der spezifisch auf das Strafverfahren bezogenen Ermächtigung'); Meyer, *Strafrechtsgenese* (2012), pp. 417–18; Jähnke and Schramm, *Europäisches Strafrecht* (2017), §4 mn. 49 ('barrier effect', orig. *Sperrwirkung*); left open by Miettinen, *Criminal Law and Policy in the European Union* (2013), pp. 52–3. On the former general harmonisation competence pursuant to Art. 94 ff. TEC old version, see Ambos, *Internationales Strafrecht* (2008), §11 mn. 31.
285. Cf. Geiger, in Geiger, Khan and Kotzur, *European Union Treaties: A Commentary* (2015), Art. 352 TFEU mn. 1–2.
286. Formerly Art. 308 TEC. For arguments in favour of a restrictive interpretation, cf. Ambos, *Internationales Strafrecht* (2008), §11 mn. 31 incl. n. 165. The same line is taken by Satzger, in Streinz, *EUV/AEUV* (2012), Art. 83 AEUV mn. 25 ('ruled out', orig. 'ausgeschlossen'); Safferling, *Internationales Strafrecht* (2011), §10 mn. 71 ('unjustified avoidance', orig. 'ungerechtfertigte Umgehung'); also Hecker, *Europäisches Strafrecht* (2015), §8 mn. 40 ('highly subsidiary', orig. '[h]öchst subsidiär'); a different opinion is put forward by Asp, *Substantive Criminal Law Competence* (2012), pp. 137 ff., who sees a theoretical applicability in the areas of the General Part in particular; also cf. Nilsson, *EuCLR*, 2 (2012), 121–2; Turner, *AmJCompL*, 60 (2012), 576 ff. (implied powers competence with strict procedural safeguards if the expressive purposes of criminal law – *in casu* regarding

xenophobic and racist crimes – so demand); Mitsilegas, *EU Criminal Law after Lisbon* (2016), p. 67.

287. Council Directive 91/477/EEC of 18 June 1991 on control of the acquisition and possession of weapons (OJ L 256 of 13 September 1991, 51. Amendment: OJ L 299 of 30 October 1991, 50). The Directive was most recently amended by Directive 2008/51/EC of 21 May 2008 (OJ L 179 of 8 July 2008, 5); on this, cf. Soschinka and Heller, *NVwZ*, 28 (2009), 997. See also the Proposal for a Directive of the EP and of the Council amending Directive 91/477/EEC on control of the acquisition and possession of weapons (COM(2015) 750 final).

288. Directive 2008/99/EC of the EP and of the Council of 19 November 2008 on the protection of the environment through criminal law (OJ L 328 of 6 December 2008, 28); on ship-source pollution see Directive 2005/35/EC of the EP and of the Council of 7 September 2005 on ship-source pollution and on the introduction of penalties for infringements (OJ L 255 of 30 September 2005, 11). Cf. Breuer, *Der Im- und Export von Abfällen innerhalb der Europäischen Union aus umweltstrafrechtlicher Sicht* (1998); Heine, in Müller-Dietz, *FS Jung* (2007), pp. 261 ff.

289. Directive 2014/57/EU of the EP and of the Council of 16 April 2014 on criminal sanctions for **market abuse** (market abuse directive) (OJ L 173 of 12 June 2014, 179). In detail on this with further references, cf. above n. 126. Directive 2014/57/EU replaced, together with Regulation 2014/596/EU (OJ L 173 of 12 June 2014, 1), the former Directive 2003/6/EC of the EP and of the Council of 28 January 2003 on insider dealing and market manipulation (market abuse) (OJ EC L 96 of 12 January 2003, 16), last amended by Regulation (EU) No 596/2014 of 16 April 2014 (OJ L 173 of 12 June 2014, 1); also Directive 2003/124/EC of 22 December 2003 implementing Directive 2003/6/EC of the EP (OJ L 339 of 24 December 2003, 70). Cf. Dannecker, *Jura*, 21 (1998), 82 ff. incl. further references; Achenbach, *GA*, 151 (2004), 568; on this, also cf. e.g. CJEU, *Spector Photo Group NV and Chris Van Raemdonck* v. *CBFA*, No C-45/08 (ECLI:EU:C:2009:806), Judgement (23 December 2009) with commentary by Heusel, *BKR*, 10 (2010), 77.

290. Directive 2015/849/EU of the EP and of the Council of 20 May 2015 on the prevention of the use of the financial system for the purposes of **money laundering or terrorist financing** (OJ L 141 of 5 June 2015, 73); Directive 2014/42/EU of the EP and of the Council of 3 April 2014 on the **freezing and confiscation of instrumentalities and proceeds of crime** in the EU (OJ L 127of 29 April 2014, 39; corrected by OJ L 138 of 13 May 2014, 114); Directive 2001/97/EC of the EP and of the Council of 4 December 2001 amending Council Directive 91/308/EEC on prevention of the use of the financial system for the purpose of **money laundering** (OJ EC L 344 of 28 December 2001, 76); Directive 2005/60/EC of the EP and of the Council of 26 October 2005 on the prevention of the use of the financial system for the purpose of **money laundering and terrorist financing** (OJ EU L 309 of 25 November 2005, 15, replaced by Directive 2015/849/EU); on the proposal for a directive of the EP and Council on the prevention of the use of the financial system for the purpose of money laundering and terrorist financing (COM (2016) 450 final); see already above, n. 125. In detail, Gentzik, *Die Europäisierung des deutschen und englischen Geldwäschestrafrechts* (2002), pp. 46 ff. See also the Action Plan to strengthen the fight against terrorist

financing, Esser, in Odendahl, *Die Bekämpfung des Terrorismus mit Mitteln des Völker- und Europarechts* (2017), pp. 207 ff.

291. In detail, Ambos, *ZStW*, 114 (2002), 236 ff.; already covered in Tiedemann, *NJW*, 46 (1993), 26; see also Hendel, *Bekämpfung von Geldwäsche* (2008), pp. 36 ff., 175 ff.; for a comparison with English law, see Gentzik, *Die Europäisierung des deutschen und englischen Geldwäschestrafrechts* (2002), pp. 85 ff.; on a Polish perspective, see Dlugosz, *Europäisierung des polnischen Strafrechts* (2006), pp. 118 ff.; Ochnio, *EJCCLCJ*, 24 (2016), 28–33; on the legal framework in Greece see Billis, *eucrim*, 10 (2015), 20–4.
292. Crit. of this (German) term, Safferling, *Internationales Strafrecht* (2011), §10 mn. 47, 55.
293. On the matter as a whole, cf. Satzger, *Die Europäisierung des Strafrechts* (2001), pp. 404–5; Eisele, *JZ*, 56 (2001), 1161 ff.; Mansdörfer, *Jura*, 27 (2004), 299; Hecker, *Europäisches Strafrecht* (2015), §8 mn. 55; also cf. Ligeti, *Strafrecht und strafrechtliche Zusammenarbeit* (2005), pp. 255 ff.; Simon, *NJECL*, 3 (2012), 249–50; for a summary of the case law, cf. Suhr, *ZEuS*, 11 (2008), 58 ff.
294. Böse, *Strafen und Sanktionen im Europäischen Gemeinschaftsrecht* (1996), pp. 71, 411 ff.; Hugger, *Strafrechtliche Anweisungen der Europäischen Gemeinschaft* (2000), pp. 59 ff.; Johannes, *EuR*, 3 (1968), 107–8; Jung and Schroth, *GA*, 130 (1983), 263–4; Zuleeg, in Sieber, *Europäische Einigung und Europäisches Strafrecht* (1993), pp. 54–5; Eisele, *JZ*, 56 (2001), 1162, 1164, also leans in this direction; clearly of this opinion, Eisele, *JZ*, 63 (2008), 254; also Zweigert, *RabelsZ*, 28 (1964), 617–18 and Dannecker, *ZStW* 117 (2005), 724.
295. Cf. Tiedemann, *NJW*, 46 (1993), 26; also Dieblich, *Der strafrechtliche Schutz der Rechtsgüter der Europäischen Gemeinschaften* (1985), pp. 283 ff.; Jokisch, *Gemeinschaftsrecht und Strafverfahren* (2000), pp. 84 ff.; Gröblinghoff, *Schutz der Interessen der EU* (1996), pp. 135–6, 142; Esser, *StV*, 24 (2004), 222 note 14; Hecker, *JA*, 34 (2002), 726; Oehler, in Vogler, *FS Jescheck* (1985), p. 1408; Oehler, in Arzt et al., *FS Baumann* (1992), p. 566; Perron, in Dörr and Dreher, *Europa als Rechtsgemeinschaft* (1997), pp. 140 ff.; Duttge, in Heinrich et al., *FS Weber* (2004), pp. 288–9 and 307–8; Rosenau, *ZIS*, 3 (2008), 15; Klip, *European Criminal Law* (2016), pp. 186 ff.; Hecker, in Ambos, *Europäisches Strafrecht post-Lissabon* (2011), p. 21.
296. See above, Chapter 1, mn. 19 ff.
297. Hecker, *Europäisches Strafrecht* (2015), §8 mn. 7–8, 36 ff., 55; a critical opinion is also voiced by Dannecker, *Jura*, 29 (2006), 98; Rosenau, *ZIS*, 3 (2008), 15.
298. Chapter 1, mn. 19.
299. Hecker, *Europäisches Strafrecht* (2015), §8 mn. 55; however, this is relativised in regard to cross-border crime (environment) by Heger, *Die Europäisierung des deutschen Umweltstrafrechts* (2009), pp. 17–18.
300. Dannecker, *Jura*, 21 (1998), 82; Tiedemann, *NJW*, 46 (1993), 26; Achenbach, *GA*, 151 (2004), 567, derives from Art. 249(3) TEC old version (Art. 288 TFEU), that it is 'in principle the individual States' decision' (orig. 'an sich in der Entscheidung der Einzelstaaten') whether they want to take *any* action at all. Zweigert, *RabelsZ*, 28 (1964), 616–17, is critical of the freedom to choose nature and scope.
301. Fornasier, *RMC*, 1982, 407; also Eisele, *JZ*, 56 (2001), 1163.
302. Art. 4(3) subparagraph 2 and 3 TEU states (using almost the exact same wording as Art. 10 TEC): 'The Member States shall take any appropriate measure, general

or particular, to ensure *fulfilment of the obligations* arising out of the Treaties or resulting from the acts of the institutions of the Union. The Member States shall *facilitate* the achievement of the Union's tasks and *refrain* from any measure which could jeopardise the attainment of the Union's objectives' (emphasis added). On this, cf. Geiger, in Geiger, Khan and Kotzur, *European Union Treaties: A Commentary* (2015), Article 4 TEU mn. 8 ff.; Hecker, *Europäisches Strafrecht* (2015), §7 mn. 16 ff.; Hecker, in Ambos, *Europäisches Strafrecht post-Lissabon* (2011), pp. 16–17; Hecker, in Sieber, Satzger and von Heinegg, *Europäisches Strafrecht* (2014), pp. 274–5; Safferling, *Internationales Strafrecht* (2011), §9 mn. 74 ff.; Esser, *Europäisches und Internationales Strafrecht* (2018), §2 mn. 48 ff. On the loyalty principle as the foundation of mutual trust, Meyer, *EuR*, 52 (2017), 179. It is noteworthy that the German Federal Constitutional Court does not see a conflict between its constitutional identity check and the principle of sincere co-operation but rather considers that the former is inherent in Art. 4 (2) sentence 1 TEU, BVerfG, No 2 BvR 2735/14, Decision (15 December 2015), in *NJW*, 69 (2016), 1149, 1151, para. 44; English translation available at www.bundesverfassungsgericht.de/SharedDocs/Entscheidungen/EN/2015/12/rs20151215_2bvr273514en.html, last accessed 27 January 2018; crit. on this, Sauer, *NJW*, 69 (2016), 1134, 1136 f., who accuses the BVerfG of interpreting Art. 4(2) TEU as a 'blanket authorisation' (orig. 'Blanco-Ermächtigung'); crit. also Kühne, *StV*, 36 (2016), 299, 302, who faults the BVerfG for its vague fundamental rights standards (dignity, rule of law), which mean it can review any Union law decision, thus weakening the principle of mutual recognition.

303. CJEU, *Commission* v. *Hellenic Republic*, No C-68/88 (ECLI:EU:C:1989:339), Judgment (21 September 1989), with an affirmative commentary by Tiedemann, *EuZW*, 2 (1990), 99–100; and Bleckmann, *WUR*, 2 (1991), 283 ff.; also cf. CJEU, *Commission* v. *United Kingdom*, No C-383/92 (ECLI:EU:C:1994:234), Judgment (8 June 1994).

304. CJEU, *Hellenic Republic*, C-68/88, para. 24 (emphasis added); on this, also cf. Baker, in Cullen and Jund, *Criminal Justice Co-operation in the European Union after Tampere* (2002), pp. 78–9; Satzger, *Die Europäisierung des Strafrechts* (2001), pp. 368 ff.; Hecker, *Europäisches Strafrecht* (2015), §7 mn. 24 ff.; Möhrenschlager, in Dannecker, *Bekämpfung des Subventionsbetrugs im EG-Bereich* (1993), p. 166; Tiedemann, *Wirtschaftsstrafrecht* (2017), mn. 99–100; Tiedemann, *ZStW*, 116 (2004), 951; White, *EuLRev* 31 (2006), 87–8; Zieschang, in Sieber et al., *FS Tiedemann* (2008), p. 1310; Klip, *European Criminal Law* (2016), pp. 72 ff.; Mitsilegas, *NJECL*, 5 (2014), 418–19 (considering thereby 'assimilation as a means of ensuring the effectiveness of EU law'); Dannecker, *ZIS*, 11 (2016), 723; also previously Pabsch, *Der strafrechtliche Schutz der überstaatlichen Hoheitsgewalt* (1965), pp. 160 ff.

305. For more detail, cf. Hecker, *Europäisches Strafrecht* (2015), §7 mn. 31 ff.; on the issue of legal interests, also cf. Picotti, in Ruggieri, *La protection des intérêts financiers de l'Union et le rôle de l'OLAF etc.* (2005), pp. 42 ff.

306. Gröblinghoff, *Schutz der Interessen der EU* (1996), p. 22; Deutscher, *Die Kompetenzen der EGen zur originären Strafrechtssetzung* (2000), p. 355; also cf. Baker, in Cullen and Jund, *Criminal Justice Co-operation in the European Union after Tampere* (2002), pp. 85 ff.; Möhrenschlager, in Dannecker, *Bekämpfung des*

Subventionsbetrugs im EG-Bereich (1993), p. 166; Jokisch, *Gemeinschaftsrecht und Strafverfahren* (2000), pp. 78–9; Eisele, *JZ*, 56 (2001), 1158.

307. CJEU, *Eugen Schmidberger, Internationale Transporte und Planzüge* v. *Republik Österreich*, No C-112/00 (ECLI:EU:C:2003:333), Judgment (12 June 2003); on this, cf. Dannecker, *ZStW*, 117 (2005), 722–3.
308. Gröblinghoff, *Schutz der Interessen der EU* (1996), pp. 22–3; Jokisch, *Gemeinschaftsrecht und Strafverfahren* (2000), pp. 78–9; Satzger, *Die Europäisierung des Strafrechts* (2001), p. 364; Tiedemann, *NJW*, 46 (1993), 23–4; Hecker, *Europäisches Strafrecht* (2015), §7 mn. 36, 67 ff.; on the nature and severity of the offence, cf. ibid., §7 mn. 58 ff.; on the inclusion of legal interests protected by Union law, also cf. Dannecker, *Jura*, 29 (2006), 100–1.
309. 'Member States shall take the *same* measures to counter fraud affecting the financial interests of the Union as they take to counter fraud affecting their own financial interests' (emphasis added).
310. Cf. Mitsilegas, *NJECL*, 5 (2014), 419. For the previous view of the former Art. 280(2) TEC as only of declaratory significance cf. Dannecker, *Jura*, 21 (1998), 81; Satzger, *Die Europäisierung des Strafrechts* (2001), pp. 339–40.
311. In detail, Martens, *Subventionskriminalität zum Nachteil der Europäischen Gemeinschaften* (2001), pp. 65 ff., 90 ff. and *passim*; also Hellmann and Beckemper, *Wirtschaftsstrafrecht* (2013), mn. 803, 807; Hecker, *Europäisches Strafrecht* (2015), §7 mn. 68 ff.; case studies are provided in Hecker and Zöller, *Fallsammlung zum Europäischen und Internationalen Strafrecht* (2012), pp. 53 ff. (case 6) and pp. 69 ff. (case 8); a critical stance is taken by Tiedemann, *ZStW*, 116 (2004), 951 ff.
312. In detail Thomas, *NJW*, 44 (1991), 2233 and 2236. Also cf. BGH, No 1 StR 21/11, Decision (9 June 2011), in *StV*, 32 (2012), 154. These expanded offence definitions serve to protect the financial interests of the EU, as the Union is due customs revenue and a portion of national VAT revenue, cf. Art. 2(1) of Council Decision 2007/436/EC, Euratom of 7 June 2007: on the system of the European Communities' own resources (OJ L 163 of 23 June 2007, 17).
313. Disruption of election, falsification of election results or documents, violation of secrecy of elections, blackmailing, deceiving and bribing voters, §§107–8c StGB.
314. Cf. §108d StGB; also Gröblinghoff, *Schutz der Interessen der EU* (1996), pp. 28, 43.
315. Cf. §108e StGB; also Wolf, *NJW*, 59 (2006), 2736.
316. According to the English and French versions of the judgment (*dissuasif*, 'dissuasive') this refers to negative general deterrence as grounds for punishment (cf. Gröblinghoff, *Schutz der Interessen der EU* (1996), pp. 24 ff., 26, 28–9; Jokisch, *Gemeinschaftsrecht und Strafverfahren* (2000), p. 79).
317. Hecker, *Europäisches Strafrecht* (2015), §7 mn. 36. On the Union law maximum level, which is demarcated by the general legal principles and the fundamental freedoms, cf. ibid., mn. 41 ff.
318. Klip, *European Criminal Law* (2016), pp. 19, 534–5, even considers it abolished in light of recent case law and the TFEU.
319. Dannecker, *JZ*, 41 (1996), 872.
320. CJEU, Grand Chamber, *Taricco and Others* v. *Italy*, No C-105/14 (ECLI:EU:C:2015:555), Judgment (8 September 2015), reprinted in *StV*, 37 (2017), 65, with approvingly comment by Kubiciel (preliminary ruling according to Art. 267 TFEU pursuant to a preliminary reference by the Tribunale di Cuneo, Italy, asking the Court whether EU law requires national courts of Member States 'to

refrain from certain provisions of their national law on the limitation periods applicable to the prosecution of criminal offences in order to guarantee the effective punishment of tax offences'; cf. summary by AG Kokott, Opinion of 30 April 2015, para. 1; CJEU, *Taricco*, Opinion of Advocate General Kokott (30 April 2015), para. 1; for the full four questions of the national court, cf. *Taricco*, op. cit., para. 27); cf. also the subsequent decision of the Italian Constitutional Court, available at www.giurcost.org/decisioni/2017/0024o-17.html, last accessed 27 January 2018, with an english summary, avaliable at www.penalecontemporaneo.it/d/5195-when-cooperation-means-request-for-clarification-or-better-for-revisitation, last accessed 27 January 2018.

321. The Court refers insofar to Art. 325 TFEU which, in its view, contains 'a precise obligation as to the result to be achieved'; cf. CJEU, *Taricco*, C-105/14, paras. 50–1.
322. CJEU, *Taricco*, C-105/14, para. 47 ('If the national court concludes that the application of the national provisions . . . has the effect that . . . the commission of serious fraud will escape criminal punishment, since the offences will usually be time-barred before the criminal penalty laid down by law can be imposed by a final judicial decision, it would be necessary to find that the measures laid down by national law . . . could not be regarded as being *effective and dissuasive*, which would be incompatible with Article 325(1) TFEU, Article 2(1) of the PFI Convention as well as Directive 2006/112, read in conjunction with Article 4(3) TEU'), para. 49 ('In the event that the national court concludes that the national provisions at issue do not satisfy the requirement of EU law that measures to counter VAT evasion be effective and dissuasive, that court would have to ensure that EU law is given full effect, if need be by *disapplying* those provisions and thereby *neutralising* the consequence . . . without having to request or await the prior repeal of those articles by way of legislation or any other constitutional procedure'), para. 52 ('Article 325(1) and (2) TFEU therefore have the effect, in accordance with the principle of the *precedence* of EU law . . . of rendering *automatically inapplicable*, merely by their entering into force, any conflicting provision of national law') (emphasis added). Conc. Peers, *EU Law Analysis*, 22 September 2015, available at http://eulawanalysis.blogspot.co.uk/2015/09/the-italian-job-cjeu-strengthens.html, last accessed 27 January 2018; crit. Billis, *NJECL*, 7 (2016), 20, 29 ff. (arguing that the CJEU acts as a quasi-constitutional court intervening prematurely in national proceedings and giving too little weight to the character of a statute of limitation as a procedural guarantee, thereby setting aside the principle of legality and other guarantees); crit. also Mitsilegas, *EU Criminal Law after Lisbon* (2016), pp. 74 ff., 82 (arguing, at 80, that *Taricco* 'has the effect of effectively overturning domestic criminal justice choices and in this manner lowering the level of fundamental rights protection at national level').
323. CJEU, *M.A.S. and M.B.*, No C-42/17 (ECLI:EU:C:2017:936), GC Judgment (5 December 2017), paras. 47 ff. (no non-consideration of national statute of limitation because of principle of legality).
324. BVerfG, No 2 BvR 751/89, Decision (10 July 1989), in *NJW*, 42 (1989), 2464.
325. The seminal case here is CJEU, *Van Gend & Loos* v. *Netherlands Inland Revenue Administration*, No C-26/62 (ECLI:EU:C:1963:1), Judgment (5 February 1963); and CJEU, *Costa* v. *E.N.E.L.*, No C-6/64 (ECLI:EU:C:1964:66), Judgment (15 July 1964); on this, Hecker, *Europäisches Strafrecht* (2015), §9 mn. 3; also cf. Hummrich, *DRiZ* (2005), 361–2.

326. On various collision constellations, cf. Hecker, *Europäisches Strafrecht* (2015), §9 mn. 15 ff.; Safferling, *Internationales Strafrecht* (2011), §10 mn. 22 ff.; Satzger, in Sieber, Satzger and von Heinegg, *Europäisches Strafrecht* (2014), pp. 264–6; on the distinction between 'real' and 'false' collisions, cf. Esser, *Europäisches und Internationales Strafrecht* (2018), §2 mn. 17 ff.
327. BVerfG, 2 BvR 2735/14 (n. 302), para. 38; cf. also BVerfG, No 2 BvR 687/85, Decision (8 April 1987), in *BVerfGE*, 75, pp. 223, 224; Fischer, *Europarecht* (2008), mn. 212; Herdegen, *Europarecht* (2017), §10 mn. 1; Oppermann, Classen and Nettesheim, *Europarecht* (2016), §10 mn. 32 ff.; Nicolaysen, *Europarecht*, i (2002), pp. 90 ff.; Dannecker, in Ulsamer, *Lexikon des Rechts. Strafrecht/ Strafverfahrensrecht* (1996), p. 309; Hecker, *Europäisches Strafrecht* (2015), §9 mn. 2, 8–9; Bernardi, *RSC*, 72 (2007), 717 ('negative harmonisation'); for a account of the basic issue overall, Zweigert, *RabelsZ*, 28 (1964), 639 ff.
328. On the *Solange* case law of the BVerfG, from which it derived the right to review the compatibility of Union law and Basic Law, which continues to apply even after the Lisbon Treaty: BVerfG, 2 BvE 2/08 (n. 57), paras. 331 ff.; Hecker, *Europäisches Strafrecht* (2015), §9 mn. 5 ff. It is irrelevant at which level – constitutional or ordinary legislation – the primacy is regulated or whether it is explicitly regulated at all: BVerfG, 2 BvR 2735/14 (n. 302), para. 44; on this Sauer, *NJW*, 69 (2016), 1134, 1136, according to which the BVerfG has now returned to reviewing the compatibility with basic rights as a matter of principle, as was the case prior to *Solange*.
329. Cf. Satzger, *StV*, 19 (1999), 133; Hecker, *Europäisches Strafrecht* (2015), §9 mn. 10; Dannecker, *ZStW*, 117 (2005), 703; in particular on the relationship between criminal law and the right to freedom of movement, cf. Miettinen, *Criminal Law and Policy in the European Union* (2013), pp. 125 ff.
330. Hecker, *Europäisches Strafrecht* (2015), §9 mn. 13; Hecker, *JA*, 34 (2002), 724 incl. further references; also cf. Hecker and Zöller, *Fallsammlung zum Europäischen und Internationalen Strafrecht* (2012), pp. 112 (case 11); in detail, Dannecker, *ZStW*, 117 (2005), 704 ff.; for a detailed account of neutralisation, cf. Esser, *Europäisches und Internationales Strafrecht* (2018), §2 mn. 7 ff.; Heger, in Böse, *Europäisches Strafrecht* (2013), pp. 207 f.; on the restrictions placed upon protection against fraud in (national) criminal law by Community law in the area of food law, the law against unfair competition (UWG) and the StGB; on the neutralisation of the (German) law on immigration by Directive 2008/115/EC, see already above n. 134 *in fine*.
331. CJEU, *Taricco*, C-105/14, paras. 49 and 52, quoted above n. 322.
332. Cf. CJEU, *Prantl*, C-16/83, guiding principle 8; also cf. Hecker, *JA*, 34 (2002), 725; Streinz, *Europarecht* (2016), mn. 261; Klip, *European Criminal Law* (2016), pp. 335–8; Esser, *Europäisches und Internationales Strafrecht* (2018), §2 mn. 7 ff. On the area of gambling, cf. Heine, in Nuotio, *FS Lahti* (2007), pp. 144 ff., esp. 150 ff.; and CJEU, *Engelmann*, No C-64/08 (ECLI:EU:C:2010:506), Judgment (9 September 2010), *EuZW*, 21 (2010), 821 and Heger, *ZIS*, 7 (2012), 401, who assumes a 'justification on the grounds of European law' (orig. 'Rechtfertigung kraft Europarechts').
333. CJEU, *Horst Otto Bickel and Ulrich Franz*, No C-274/96 (ECLI:EU:C:1998:563), Judgment (24 November 1998); on this, cf. Eisele, *JA*, 32 (2000), 900–1; Hecker, *Europäisches Strafrecht* (2015), §1 mn. 26, §9 mn. 14.

334. CJEU, *Taricco*, C-105/14, paras. 47 ff., as quoted above, n. 322; crit. therefore Billis, *NJECL*, 7 (2016), 29 ff.
335. Eisele, *JA*, 32 (2000), 900; Klip, *European Criminal Law* (2016), pp. 68–70; in detail Gleß, *GA*, 147 (2000), 226 ff.
336. For an instructive account on this, cf. Soyka, *wistra*, 26 (2007), 129 ff.
337. Gleß, *GA*, 147 (2000), 229.
338. CJEU, *Silvio Berlusconi et al.*, Nos C-387/02, C-391/02, C-403/02 (ECLI:EU:C:2005:270), Judgment (3 May 2005), para. 73. Of course, the directive in question had not been worded in sufficiently concrete terms to determine the culpability of Italy's then president for accounting fraud – despite a retrospective amendment of Italian law in his favour (*lex mitior*)! (thus Satzger, *JZ*, 60 (2005), 1000–1; also Dannecker, in Hoyer et al., *FS Schroeder* (2006), p. 768; Dannecker, *ZIS*, 1 (2006), 312; Hecker, *Europäisches Strafrecht* (2015), §9 mn. 19; also cf. Hecker and Zöller, *Fallsammlung zum Europäischen und Internationalen Strafrecht* (2012), pp. 113 ff. (case 11)). See further the reflections in Dannecker, in Hoyer et al., *FS Schroeder* (2006), pp. 769–70; Dannecker, *ZIS*, 1 (2006), 313–14 on the question – which is correctly answered in the negative – whether a directive is actually able to derogate a *contradictory* national norm (the *more recent* law more favourable to Berlusconi).
339. Chapter 1, mn. 18, 29.
340. Chapter 1, mn. 19 ff.
341. By way of example, Directive 2015/849/EU of the EP and of the Council of 20 May 2015 on the prevention of use of the financial system for the purposes of money laundering or terrorist financing (OJ L 141 of 5 June 2015, 73); Regulation 995/2010/EU of the EP and of the Council of 20 October 2010 laying down the obligations of operators who place timber and timber products on the market (OJ L 295 of 12 November 2010, 23); Directive 2005/29/EC of the EP and of the Council of 11 May 2005 concerning unfair business-to-consumer commercial practices in the international market (OJ L 149 of 11 June 2005, 22); Regulation 178/2002/EU of the EP and of the Council of 28 January 2002 laying down the general principles and requirements of food law, establishing the European Food Safety Authority and laying down procedures in matters of food safety (OJ L 31 of 1 February 2002, 1); Regulation (EU) 2017/821 of the EP and of the Council of 17 May 2017 laying down supply chain due-diligence obligations for Union importers of tin, tantalum and tungsten; their ores; and gold originating from conflict-affected and high-risk areas (OJ L 130 of 19 May 2015, 1); see also Hecker, *JuS*, 54 (2014), 390–3; Thomas, *NJW*, 44 (1991), 2237; further examples of EU regulations in Schröder, *NStZ*, 26 (2006), 670 ff.
342. Formerly Art. 234 TEC; see also Art. 19(3)(b) TEU.
343. For more detail on this, cf. Thiele, *Nichtigkeitsklage* (2006), pp. 59 ff.; also cf. Braum, *KritV*, 93 (2010), 319 ff.; Klip, *European Criminal Law* (2016), pp. 136 ff., 338 ff. For a critical stance on the duration of the preliminary ruling procedure (fifteen months on average in 2016), cf. press release No 17/17 of the CJEU of 17 February 2017 ('shortest duration recorded for more than 30 years'), available at http://curia.europa.eu/jcms/upload/docs/application/pdf/2017-02/cp170017en.pdf, last accessed 27 January 2018; Hecker, *Europäisches Strafrecht* (2015), §6 mn. 24, §13 mn. 22; Klip, *European Criminal Law* (2016), pp. 347. However, the urgent procedure introduced in 2008 (OJ L 24 of 29 January 2008, 42; Art. 23 CJEU Statute, Art. 104b RP CJEU) promises to improve the situation. If a person in custody is affected, the Court must decide with

a minimum of delay (Art. 267(4) TFEU; on this, cf. Thiele, *EuR*, 45 (2010), 49; Jähnke and Schramm, *Europäisches Strafrecht* (2017), §3 mn. 28; in detail Wolter, *Vorabentscheidungsverfahren und Beschleunigungsgebot in Strafsachen* (2011), pp. 104 ff. (on criticism pp. 151 ff.); also cf. Walther, *ZJS*, 6 (2013), 22–3).

344. Kotzur, in Geiger, Khan and Kotzur, *European Union Treaties: A Commentary* (2015), Article 267 TFEU mn. 8; Wolter, *Vorabentscheidungsverfahren und Beschleunigungsgebot in Strafsachen* (2011), p. 75.
345. In more detail on the integration of the preliminary reference procedure into criminal proceedings, *Hecker, Europäisches Strafrecht* (2015), §6 mn. 1–27.
346. Cf. Hecker, *Europäisches Strafrecht* (2015), §6 mn. 1–2.
347. Cf. CJEU, *Taricco*, C-105/14, para. 30 (with reference to *Halaf*, No C-528/11 (ECLI:EU:C:2013:342), Judgment (30 May 2013), para. 29 with further references). As to the exceptional possibility to 'refuse to rule on a question referred by a national court' the *Taricco* Chamber states (ibid., para. 30) that this is only possible 'where it is quite obvious that the interpretation of EU law that is sought is unrelated to the actual facts of the main action or its purpose, where the problem is hypothetical, or where the Court does not have before it the factual or legal material necessary to give a useful answer to the questions submitted to it'. Crit. of the Court's findings in the concrete case Billis, *NJECL*, 7 (2016), 27–9 (arguing that the questions referred by the Italian court have been largely speculative and unrelated to the concrete procedural stage of the case at hand).
348. Council Decision 2008/79/EC, Euratom (OJ L 24 of 29 January 2008, 42).
349. Art. 267(2) TFEU.
350. Art. 267(3) TFEU; see also Wolter, *Vorabentscheidungsverfahren und Beschleunigungsgebot in Strafsachen* (2011), pp. 81 ff. Constitutional complaints and revision requests do not count as legal remedies in this regard (Hecker, *Europäisches Strafrecht* (2015), §6 mn. 6).
351. CJEU, *Srl CILFIT und Lanificio di Gavardo SpA* v. *Ministero della Sanità*, No C-283/81 (ECLI:EU:C:1982:335), Judgment (6 October 1982), para. 16 ('acte clair principle'); cf. Hecker, *Europäisches Strafrecht* (2015), §6 mn. 6; Klip, *European Criminal Law* (2016), p. 346; Heger, *Die Europäisierung des deutschen Umweltstrafrechts* (2009), pp. 41 ff.
352. For example, in Germany to the Federal Court of Justice in line with §121(2) GVG.
353. Kühne, *Strafprozessrecht* (2015), §3 mn. 58; also cf. Heine, in Nuotio, *FS Lahti* (2007), 152; on the issue of specialist courts' power to reject matters, cf. Hummel, *NVwZ*, 27 (2008), 39.
354. Hecker, *Europäisches Strafrecht* (2015), §6 mn. 16.
355. Cf. Art. 10 Protocol 36 to the Lisbon Treaty 'on transitional provisions' (OJ C 115 of 9 May 2008) (further application of Art. 35 TEU for five years); on this, cf. Klip, *European Criminal Law* (2nd edn, 2012), pp. 128 ff.; Herlin-Karnell, *eucrim*, 5 (2010), 62; Schoppa, *Europol im Verbund der Europäischen Sicherheitsagenturen* (2013), p. 55; Wolter, *Vorabentscheidungsverfahren und Beschleunigungsgebot in Strafsachen* (2011), pp. 193 ff.; Meyer, *Strafrechtsgenese* (2012), pp. 311, 314–15. Herlin-Karnell, *EuCLR*, 1 (2011), 151, is of the opinion that this constituted one of the main reasons for the slow development of European criminal law.
356. Cf. Art. 258 TFEU.
357. OJ L 186 of 30 June 1989, 23.

358. It was not possible to clarify in the proceedings whether the authorities had informed the applicant, who was responsible for the production of 'Bockwurst' sausages, of their investigation (in such a timely manner) so that he could have cleared himself of charges of negligently placing foodstuffs on the market according to §§17(1) No 2(b), 52(1) No 9, 53(1) LMBG with a second report on the products' composition. A detailed account of the case is provided in Esser, *StV*, 24 (2004), 221 ff.; also cf. Hecker, *Europäisches Strafrecht* (2015), §6 mn. 11 with further examples and (mn. 13), a template for references for preliminary rulings.
359. CJEU, *Steffensen* v. *Germany*, No C- 276/01 (ECLI:EU:C:2003:228), Judgment (10 April 2003), paras. 45–6.
360. CJEU, *Steffensen*, C- 276/01, paras. 70–1 (para. 71: 'In this instance, since observance of the right to a second opinion guaranteed by Community law and the consequences which an infringement of that right may have as regards the admissibility of evidence in an appeal such as that in the main proceedings are at issue, *the national rules applying in relation to the taking of evidence fall within the scope of Community law. Accordingly, those rules must comply with the requirements arising from the fundamental rights*', emphasis added); on this, cf. Esser, *StV*, 24 (2004), 226–7; also Ambos, *Beweisverwertungsverbote* (2010), p. 99.
361. That is, for example, the case in **Greece** (pursuant to Art. 28(2) and (3) Constitution; thereto Billis, in Sieber, Jarvers and Silvermann, *National Criminal Law in a Comparative Legal Context*, 1.2 (2013), pp. 216–17, 224); **Hungary** (Art. 266(1)(d) CCP); **Italy** (cf. Reale and Borraccetti, *Da giudice a giudice* (2008), pp. 47 ff.), the **Netherlands, Poland** (I am indebted to Prof. A. Swiatlowski for this information), **Portugal** and **Spain** (thereto Jimeno Bulnes, *RGDP*, 16 (2008), 1 ff.); often by way of a constitutional provision which allows for the direct application of international treaties. In **Sweden** there is a specific law (2006:502) according to which the courts are to justify if they do not make a preliminary reference if so requested by a party (§1) and that they are, in certain cases, obliged to request a preliminary ruling with regard to the interpretation of international agreements concluded within the EU (§2). Otherwise the treaties are applied directly (Law 1994:1500).
362. *BGBl.* I 1998, 2035; also cf. Kühne, *Strafprozessrecht* (2015), §3 mn. 59; Suhr, in Callies and Ruffert, *Das Verfassungsrecht der Europäischen Union mit Europäischer Grundrechtecharta* (2007), Art. 35 EUV mn. 11.
363. For a recent example (harmonious interpretation regarding the element of deception in fraud, 263 StGB) where the BGH (No 2 StR 616/12, Judgment (5 March 2014), in *NJW*, 67 (2014), 2595 and No 2 StR 437/13, Judgment (28 May 2014), in *wistra*, 33 (2014), 439) did not make a preliminary reference to the CJEU crit. Heger, *HRRS*, 15 (2014), 471–3.
364. Criminal Procedure Rules and Practice Directions, Part. 44, October 2015, www.justice.gov.uk/courts/procedure-rules/criminal/docs/2015/crim-proc-rules-2015-part-44.pdf, last accessed 27 January 2018; cf. Blackstock and Tinsley, *Archbold Rev*, 8 (2015), 6; Malcom, *Archbold Rev*, 9 (2015), 5–6; explicitly welcoming this possibility, Mitsilegas, *CLR*, 63 (2016), 521, 535 ('considerable improvement'); on the previous situation, Mitsilegas, *EU Criminal Law after Lisbon* (2016), p. 48. In civil proceedings, Part 68 of the Civil Procedure Rules provides for a prelimary reference, cf. www.justice.gov.uk/courts/procedure-rules/civil/rules/part68, last accessed 27 January 2018.
365. Part 75A.5 Criminal Procedure Rules and Practice Directions.

366. CJEU, *Von Colson and Kamann* v. *Land Nordrhein-Westfalen*, No C-14/83 (ECLI: EU:C:1984:153), Judgment (10 April 1984); also cf. Hecker, *Europäisches Strafrecht* (2015), §10 mn. 1 ff., 40 ff.; Hecker, *Strafbare Produktwerbung im Lichte des Gemeinschaftsrechts* (2001), 284 and passim; Hecker, *JA*, 34 (2002), 727–8; Dannecker, in Ulsamer, *Lexikon des Rechts: Strafrecht/Strafverfahrensrecht* (1996), pp. 309 ff.; Dannecker, *Jura*, 21 (1998), 84–5; Dannecker, *JZ*, 41 (1996), 871–2; Dannecker, *Jura*, 29 (2006), 175; Vogel, *ZStW*, 109 (1997), 348 ff.; Heintschel von Heinegg, in Hoyer et al., *FS Schroeder* (2006), p. 804; Tiedemann, *ZStW*, 116 (2004), 950; Heger, in Böse, *Europäisches Strafrecht* (2013), pp. 215 f.; Esser, *Europäisches und Internationales Strafrecht* (2018), §2 mn. 67 ff.; for a more differentiated view, cf. Begemeier, *HRRS*, 14 (2013), 179; more critically, Hugger, *NStZ*, 13 (1993), 424. Cf. also (on social security legislation), BGH, No 1 StR 160/07, Judgment (24 October 2007), in *NJW*, 61 (2008), 596; and BGH, No 1 StR 44/06, Judgment (24 October 2006), in *NJW*, 60 (2007), 234 ff. with an affirmative commentary by Schulz; Zimmermann, *ZIS*, 2 (2007), 410; Hauck, *NStZ*, 27 (2007), 222, is partly of a different opinion.
367. Hecker, *Europäisches Strafrecht* (2015), §10 mn. 10 ff.
368. Satzger, *StV*, 19 (1999), 132–3; also Kühne, *JZ*, 53 (1998), 1070–1; for a different opinion, Gärditz, *wistra*, 18 (1999), 295; and BGH, No 1 StR 169/00, Judgment (25 July 2000), in *BGHSt*, 46, pp. 93, 103 (only to take into account in the assessment of the relevance and probative value of the evidence).
369. Cf. Swoboda, *HRRS*, 15 (2014), 10–13, 20–1, discussing a recent BGH decision (No 1 StR 310/12, Decision (21 November 2012), in *BGHSt*, 58, p. 32) where the Court affirmed the use of foreign evidence from telephone tapping, since this evidence was necessary to convict the defendant of tax evasion and smuggling and this conviction was necessary to protect the financial interests of the EU.
370. Cf. OLG Hamm, No 2 Ws 111/04, Decision (15 April 2004), in *StV*, 25 (2005), 35, with a critical commentary by Hilger; also Gercke, *StV*, 24 (2004), 678–9.
371. In detail, Schröder, *Europäische Richtlinien* (2002), p. 335; Satzger, *Die Europäisierung des Strafrechts* (2001), pp. 538 ff.; in detail on the interpretation of §§4(1) UWG and 263 StGB 'in the light of' Art. 18 of Directive 200/13/EC of the EP and of the Council of 20 March 2000 on the approximation of the laws of the Member States relating to the labelling, presentation and advertising of foodstuffs (OJ L 109 of 6 May 2000, 29), Hecker, *Strafbare Produktwerbung im Lichte des Gemeinschaftsrechts* (2001), pp. 292 ff.; a case study is provided in Hecker and Zöller, *Fallsammlung zum Europäischen und Internationalen Strafrecht* (2012), pp. 89 ff. (case 9) and pp. 97 ff. (case 10); Dannecker, *Jura*, 21 (1998), 84; Dannecker, *JZ*, 41 (1996), 872; Gaede and Mühlbauer, *wistra*, 24 (2005), 10; Götz, in Bröhmer, *FS Ress* (2005), pp. 487 ff.; Heintschel von Heinegg, in Hoyer et al., *FS Schroeder* (2006), p. 804; Roth, *EWS*, 16 (2005), 386 ff.; more critically, Di Fabio, *NJW*, 43 (1990), 947. In detail on interpretation in line with the Directive, Leenen, *Jura*, 35 (2012), 753 ff.
372. BGH, 5 StR 444/90 (n. 181), pp. 334, 336; on this, see Franzheim and Kreß, *JR*, 63 (1991), 402; Mansdörfer, *Jura*, 27 (2004), 300; Heger, *Die Europäisierung des deutschen Umweltstrafrechts* (2009), pp. 39–40; also see Ambos, *Internationales Strafrecht* (2008), §11 mn. 43.
373. §326(1) StGB.
374. For more detail on the 'accessority to European law' of German waste law, cf. Heger, *Die Europäisierung des deutschen Umweltstrafrechts* (2009), pp. 38 ff.

375. BGH, No 1 StR 24/03, Judgment (6 November 2003), in *BGHSt*, 48, p. 373.
376. On this term, cf. Vogel, *NStZ*, 24 (2004), 252 (a 'scalper' is a 'person able to influence the price or market value of assets traded on the capital market, particularly listed securities, through making recommendations', orig. 'Person, die in der Lage ist, durch Empfehlungen in Bezug auf kapitalmarktgehandelte Vermögenswerte, namentlich börsennotierte Wertpapiere, auf den Kurs oder Marktpreis dieser Vermögenswerte Einfluss zu nehmen'). Cf. also Hellmann and Beckemper, *Wirtschaftsstrafrecht* (2013), mn. 169 ff.
377. BGH, 1 StR 24/03 (n. 375), pp. 377–8; Vogel, *NStZ*, 24 (2004), 254, agrees; a critical opinion is put forward by Pananis, *NStZ*, 24 (2004), 287 ff.; Hellmann and Beckemper, *Wirtschaftsstrafrecht* (2013), mn. 170; Gaede and Mühlbacher, *wistra*, 24 (2005), 10 ff.
378. CJEU, *Pupino*, No C-105/03 (ECLI:EU:C:2005:386), Judgment (16 June 2005). Critical opinions are voiced by Mitsilegas, *EU Criminal Law after Lisbon* (2016), p. 202–4; Adam, *EuZW*, 16 (2005), 560–1; Herrmann, *EuZW*, 16 (2005), 437–8; Hillgruber, *JZ*, 60 (2005), 841 ff.; v. Unger, *NVwZ*, 25 (2006), 46; Rackow, *ZIS*, 3 (2008), 526; from a Spanish perspective, Morillas Cuevo and Valls Prieto, *RDFUG*, 9 (2006), 169 ff.
379. CJEU, *Pupino*, C-105/03, para. 34; conc. Swoboda, *HRRS*, 15 (2014), 11–12; cf. also Vormbaum, *Schutz der Rechtsgüter von EU-Staaten* (2005), p. 115; Ambos, *Internationales Strafrecht* (2008), §12 mn. 1 ff.
380. CJEU, *Pupino*, C-105/03, para. 34.
381. Cf. Ambos, *Internationales Strafrecht* (2008), §12 mn. 4a incl. further references for a critical assessment of this.
382. Satzger, *Die Europäisierung des Strafrechts* (2001), pp. 548–9; Hecker, *Strafbare Produktwerbung im Lichte des Gemeinschaftsrechts* (2001), pp. 284 and 308 ff.; Hecker, *ZStW*, 115 (2003), 898–9; Hecker, *Europäisches Strafrecht* (2015), §10 mn. 1 ff.; Schröder, *Europäische Richtlinien* (2002), pp. 331 ff.; Böse, *Strafen und Sanktionen im Europäischen Gemeinschaftsrecht* (1996), pp. 432 ff.; Soesters, *Insiderhandelsverbote* (2002), pp. 94 ff.; Dannecker, in Ulsamer, *Lexikon des Rechts: Strafrecht/Strafverfahrensrecht* (1996), pp. 309 ff.; Dannecker, *JZ*, 41 (1996), 872–3; Gröblinghoff, *Schutz der Interessen der EU* (1996), p. 68; Heise, *Europäisches Gemeinschaftsrecht* (1998), pp. 159 ff. esp. 166; Brechmann, *Richtlinienkonforme Auslegung* (1994), pp. 204–5; Mansdörfer, *Jura*, 27 (2004), 299 ff.; Tiedemann, *Wirtschaftsstrafrecht* (2017), mn. 102; Tiedemann, *ZStW*, 116 (2004), 950; Kühne, *GA*, 152 (2005), 197; Jens, *Der nationale Strafrechtsanwender* (2006), pp. 238 ff.; Heintschel von Heinegg, in Hoyer et al., *FS Schroeder* (2006), pp. 804 ff.; Rönnau and Wegner, *GA*, 160 (2013), 562 ff.; also cf. Vormbaum, *Schutz der Rechtsgüter von EU-Staaten* (2005), pp. 94 ff. (for a critical stance, cf. Ambos, *Internationales Strafrecht* (2008), §11 mn. 45 incl. note 259).
383. In detail, Schröder, *Europäische Richtlinien* (2002), p. 380; Hecker, *Europäisches Strafrecht* (2015), §10 mn. 35 ff., 41 ff.; Esser, *Europäisches und Internationales Strafrecht* (2018), §2 mn. 87 ff.; Safferling, *Internationales Strafrecht* (2011), §11 mn. 17 ff.; Satzger, in Sieber, Satzger and von Heinegg, *Europäisches Strafrecht* (2014), p. 267.
384. In *Inter-Environnement Wallonie ASBL* v. *Régionwallonne*, NoC-129/96 (ECLI: EU:C:1997:628), Judgment (18 Dezember 1997), para. 45 the CJEU refers to Art.

5(2) in connection with Art. 189(3) EC Treaty. On this, Herdegen, *Europarecht* (2017), §8 mn. 47; Schröder, *Grundkurs Europarecht* (2015), §6 mn. 47.

385. Hecker, *Europäisches Strafrecht* (2015), §10 mn. 30 ff.; also cf. Köhne, *Die richtlinienkonforme Auslegung* (1997), pp. 147 ff.; Karsai, *ZIS*, 11 (2016), 32–3.

386. CJEU, *Inter-Environnement Wallonie ASBL* v. *Régionwallonne*, C-129/96, para. 45 (Member States obliged to 'refrain from taking any measures liable seriously to compromise the result prescribed'); CJEU, *Werner Mangold* v. *Rüdiger Helm*, No C-144/04 (ECLI:EU:C:2005:709), Judgment (22 November 2005, para. 67 ('During the period prescribed for transposition of a directive, the Member States must refrain from taking any measures liable seriously to compromise the attainment of the result prescribed by that directive'); also CJEU, *Konstantinos Adeneler and Others* v. *Ellinikos Organismos Galaktos* [*ELOG*], No C-212/04 (ECLI:EU:C:2006:443), Judgment (4 July 2006), paras. 114–19.

387. CJEU, *Kolpinghuis Nijmegen BV*, No C-80/86 (ECLI:EU:C:1987:431), Judgment (8 October 1987); on this, cf. Hecker, *Europäisches Strafrecht* (2015), §10 mn. 41 ff. Rönnau and Wegner, *GA*, 160 (2013), 563, 567, want to take into account the not yet implemented directive, by way of *lex mitior*, if it is favourable to the defendant.

388. Böse, *Strafen und Sanktionen im Europäischen Gemeinschaftsrecht* (1996), pp. 432–3; Hecker, *Europäisches Strafrecht* (2015), §10 mn. 38.

389. Hecker, *Europäisches Strafrecht* (2015), §10 mn. 50 ff. (53).

390. Brechmann, *Richtlinienkonforme Auslegung* (1994), pp. 204–5.

391. Langenfeld, *Gleichbehandlung von Mann und Frau* (1990), p. 57; Hugger, *NStZ*, 13 (1993), 423–4; arguing against this, Schröder, *Europäische Richtlinien* (2002), pp. 327–8. Also cf. Gärditz, in Böse, *Europäisches Strafrecht* (2013), pp. 199 f.

392. In detail, Satzger, *Die Europäisierung des Strafrechts* (2001), pp. 555 ff., 556, 563–4; Satzger, in Sieber, Satzger and von Heinegg, *Europäisches Strafrecht* (2014), p. 269; also Heise, *Europäisches Gemeinschaftsrecht* (1998), pp. 165–6; Breuer, *Der Im- und Export von Abfällen innerhalb der EU aus umweltstrafrechtlicher Sicht* (1998), p. 68; Soesters, *Insiderhandelsverbote* (2002), p. 95; Dannecker, *JZ*, 41 (1996), 873; Dannecker, in Ulsamer, *Lexikon des Rechts: Strafrecht/Strafverfahrensrecht* (1996), p. 310; Hecker, *Europäisches Strafrecht* (2015), §10 mn. 61 ff.; Hecker, *JA*, 34 (2002), 727–8; Jens, *Der nationale Strafrechtsanwender* (2006), pp. 281 ff., esp. 289–90; Heintschel von Heinegg, in Hoyer et al., *FS Schroeder* (2006), p. 808; and Götz, in Bröhmer, *FS Ress* (2005), p. 489. Cf. also Ligeti, *Strafrecht und strafrechtliche Zusammenarbeit* (2005), p. 259; Vormbaum, *Schutz der Rechtsgüter* (2005), pp. 110 ff.; Esser, *Europäisches und Internationales Strafrecht* (2018), §2 mn. 91 ff.; Bielefeld, *wistra*, 26 (2007), 13, on the issue of Union law conformity in the interpretation of §370 AO.

393. Cf. Dannecker, *JZ*, 41 (1996), 873 (the 'term "waste" can also be applied to objects that have become worthless to their owner, even though they can be recycled, without going beyond the literal meaning of the word and without infringing the prohibition of analogy'; orig. 'Begriff des Abfalls kann . . . ohne Verstoß gegen das Analogieverbot auch für den Besitzer wertlos gewordene[r], gleichwohl wieder verwertbare[r] Gegenstände angewandt werden, ohne dass dadurch der mögliche Wortsinn überschritten würde').

394. Satzger, *Die Europäisierung des Strafrechts* (2001), pp. 563–4; Schröder, *Europäische Richtlinien* (2002), pp. 390, 397 ff.; Hecker, *Europäisches Strafrecht* (2015), §10 mn. 62; Hecker, *JA*, 34 (2002), 728; Mansdörfer, *Jura*, 27 (2004), 299;

also cf. Dannecker, *JZ*, 41 (1996), 873; and Tiedemann, *Wirtschaftsstrafrecht* (2017), mn. 103.

395. Cf. Hecker, *Europäisches Strafrecht* (2015), §10 mn. 26 ff.
396. Chapter 1, mn. 19 ff.
397. Above mn. 40; see also Satzger, *Die Europäisierung des Strafrechts* (2001), pp. 551, 563.
398. CJEU, *Kolpinghuis Nijmegen BV*, C-80/86, para. 13; CJEU, *Pupino*, C-105/03, paras. 44–5, 47; CJEU, *Dansk Rørindustri A/S and others* v. *Commisssion*, No C-189/02 P and others (ECLI:EU:C:2005:408), Judgment (28 June 2005), para. 220; also cf. Hecker, *Europäisches Strafrecht* (2015), §10 mn. 41 ff.; Dannecker, *JZ*, 41 (1996), 873; Karsai, *ZIS*, 11 (2016), 34 ff. (discussing, unfortunately in poor English, different scenarios regarding the impact of EU directives – either adopted, in force or implemented – on the punishability with a view to *lex praevia*).
399. See above mn. 33; also cf. Böse, in Amelung, Günther and Kühne, *FS Krey* (2010), pp. 20–1, who sees the reference technique of the BNatSchG as admissible under constitutional law; Jähnke and Schramm, *Europäisches Strafrecht* (2017), §5 mn. 31 ff.
400. CJEU, *Vincent Rodolphe Auer*, C-271/82; on this, cf. Dannecker, *Jura*, 21 (1998), 84; Eisele, *JA*, 32 (2000), 900; Soyka, *wistra*, 26 (2007), 128; Hecker, *Europäisches Strafrecht* (2015), §9 mn. 24–5.
401. BGH, 4 StR 304/88 (n. 180), p. 94 following BGH, 1 StR 376/84 (n. 180), p. 76.
402. BGH, 5 StR 444/90 (n. 178), pp. 334, 336: 'A definition of waste detached from subjective purpose is also in accordance with Council Directive 75/442/EEC . . . and Council Directive 78/319/EEC . . . which were already valid at the time of the act' (orig. 'Eine solche von subjektiven Zweckbestimmungen losgelöste Definition des Abfallbegriffs steht auch im Einklang mit den bereits zur Tatzeit geltenden RL 75/442/EWG des Rates . . . und 78/319/EWG des Rates'). For more detail on the definition of waste in Union law and on the accessoriness of §326(2) StGB to Union law, cf. Heine, in Müller-Dietz, *FS Jung* (2007), pp. 268 ff.
403. BGH, 5 StR 444/90 (n. 181), p. 336 with reference to BGH, No 3 StR 459/87, Judgment (30 August 1990), in *BGHSt*, 37, pp. 168, 175.
404. Ambos, *Internationales Strafrecht* (2008), §11 mn. 43.

Chapter Bibliography

Achenbach, H., 'Zur aktuellen Lage des Wirtschaftsstrafrechts in Deutschland', *GA*, 151 (2004), 559–74

Alarcón Jiménez, O., 'Council of Europe Convention against Trafficking of Human Organs', *eucrim*, 10 (2015), 119–24

Ambos, K., 'Comments on the Model Penal Code and European Criminal Law', in Klip, A., ed., *Substantive Criminal Law of the European Union* (Antwerp et al.: Maklu, 2011), 227–32

'Internationalisierung des Strafrechts: Das Beispiel "Geldwäsche"', *ZStW*, 114 (2002), 236–56

'Our Terrorists, Your Terrorists? The United Nations Security Council Urges States to Combat "Foreign Terrorist Fighters", but Does Not Define

"Terrorism"', *EJIL: Talk!*, 2 October 2014, at www.ejiltalk.org/our-terrorists-your-terrorists-the-united-nations-security-council-urges-states-to-combat-foreign-terrorist-fighters-but-does-not-define-terrorism, last accessed 27 January 2018

Ambos, K., and Meyer-Abich, N., 'Human Rights in Europe and the Americas: Regional Protection Systems and the Process of Regional Integration', in Parmentier, S., and Weitekamp, E. G. M., eds., *Crime and Human Rights* (Amsterdam et al.: Elsevier JAI, 2007), 11–38

Ambos, K., and Rackow, P., 'Erste Überlegungen zu den Konsequenzen des Lissabon-Urteils des Bundesverfassungsgerichts für das Europäische Strafrecht', *ZIS*, 4 (2009), 397–405

Andersson, T., 'Targeted Sanctions: How to Enforce Institutionalized Fear and Maintain the Rule of Law', in Ambos, K., ed., *Europäisches Strafrecht post-Lissabon* (Göttingen: Universitätsverlag Göttingen, 2011), 77–109

Asp, P., 'Harmonisation of Penalties and Sentencing within the EU', *BJCLCJ*, 1 (2013), 53–62

'The Importance of the Principles of Subsidiarity and Coherence in the Development of EU Criminal Law', *EuCLR*, 1 (2011), 44–55

'(More Than) Two Decades Later', in Freund, G., Murmann, U., Bloy, R., and Perron, W., eds., *Grundlagen und Dogmatik des gesamten Strafrechtssystems: Festschrift für Wolfgang Frisch zum 70. Geburtstag* (Berlin: Duncker & Humblot, 2013), 1389–1402

The Substantive Criminal Law Competence of the EU (Stockholm: Jure Bokhandel, 2012)

Bacigalupo Zapater, E., 'Möglichkeiten einer Rechtsangleichung im Strafrecht zum Schutz der Finanzinteressen der EG', in Dannecker, G., ed., *Die Bekämpfung des Subventionsbetruges im EG-Bereich* (Cologne: Bundesanzeiger, 1993), 146–61

'Die strafrechtlichen Strategien der EU', in Schünemann, B., ed., *Ein Gesamtkonzept für die europäische Strafrechtspflege* (Cologne et al.: Carl Heymanns, 2006), 81–92

Badea C., and Buono, L., 'The Recent Initiatives of the European Commission in the Area of Fraud, Corruption and Crime Victims: An Integrated Approach in EU Criminal Justice', *ERA Forum*, 12 (2011), 345–51

Bär, W., 'Transnationaler Zugriff auf Computerdaten', *ZIS*, 6 (2011), 53–9

Baker, E., 'Constitutional Rights and Duties in European Criminal Law etc.', in Cullen, P., and Jund, S., eds., *Criminal Justice Co-operation in the European Union after Tampere* (Cologne: Bundesanzeiger, 2002), 77–86

Bartholin, K., 'The Additional Protocol to the Council of Europe Convention on the Prevention of Terrorism', *eucrim*, 10 (2015), 124–8

Begemeier, M., 'Zur Reichweite der unionsrechtskonformen Auslegung im deutschen Straf- und Strafverfahrensrecht am Beispiel der "Spector Photo Group" Entscheidung des EuGH', *HRRS*, 14 (2013), 179–86

Behrens, P., 'EU führt Strafbarkeit juristischer Personen ein', *EuZW*, 22 (2011), 161

Bernardi, A., 'Le rôle du troisième pilier dans l'européanisation du droit pénal', *RSC*, 72 (2007), 713–37

Beukelmann, S., 'Europäisches Strafrecht: Update', *NJW-Spezial*, 10 (2013), 760

'Update: Europäisches Strafrecht', *NJW-Spezial*, 8 (2011), 760

Bielefeld, F., 'Fortbildung des Umsatzsteuerstrafrechts durch den EuGH? ', *wistra*, 26 (2007), 9–13

Billis, E., 'The ECJ: A "Quasi-constitutional Court" in Criminal Matters? The Taricco Judgment and Its Shortcomings', *NJECL*, 7 (2016), 20–38

'National Characteristics, Fundamental Principles, and History of Criminal Law in Greece', in Sieber, U., Jarvers, K., and Silvermann, E., eds., *National Criminal Law in a Comparative Legal Context, 1.2: Introduction to National Legal Systems: Australia, Côte d' Ivoire, Greece, South Korea* (Berlin: Dunckler & Humblot, 2013), 187–290

'Der rechtliche Rahmen zur Bekämpfung der Terrorismusfinanzierung in Griechenland', *eucrim*, 10 (2015), 19–26

Billis, E., and Gkaniatsos, P., 'Minors as Victims in the Age of Information and Communication Technologies', *eucrim*, 6 (2011), 82–7

Blackstock, J., and Tinsley, A., 'The Arrival of EU Law in Criminal Proceedings', *Archbold Rev.*, issue 8 (21 September 2015), 5–6

Bleckmann, A., 'Anmerkung zu EuGH, Urteil v. 21.9.1989 - Rs. 68/88', *WUR*, 2 (1991), 285–6

Blomsma, J., *Mens Rea and Defences in European Criminal Law* (Cambridge et al.: Intersentia, 2012)

Bock, S., *Europäisches Finanzschutzstrafrecht* (Berlin: Duncker & Humblot, 2017 forthcoming)

'Die (unterlassene) Reform des Volksverhetzungstatbestands', *ZRP*, 44 (2011), 46–9

Böse, M., 'Aufsichtsrechtliche Vorermittlungen in der Grauzone zwischen Strafverfolgung und Gefahrenabwehr', *ZStW*, 119 (2007), 848–86

'§27: Ausblick', in Böse, M., ed., *Enzyklopädie Europarecht: Europäisches Strafrecht mit polizeilicher Zusammenarbeit* (Baden-Baden: Nomos Verlagsgesellschaft, 2013), 965–77

'§20: Drogenhandel', in Sieber, U. et al., eds., *Europäisches Strafrecht* (Baden-Baden: Nomos Verlagsgesellschaft, 2014), 384–93

'Die Europäisierung der Strafvorschriften gegen Kinderpornographie', in Hoyer, A., Müller, H. E., Pawlik, M., and Wolter, J., eds., *Festschrift für Friedrich-Christian Schroeder zum 70. Geburtstag* (Heidelberg: C. F. Müller, 2006), 751–60

'§4: Kompetenzen der Union auf dem Gebiet des Straf- und Strafverfahrensrechts', in Böse, M., ed., *Enzyklopädie Europarecht:*

Europäisches Strafrecht mit polizeilicher Zusammenarbeit (Baden-Baden: Nomos Verlagsgesellschaft, 2013), 149–78

'The Principle of Proportionality and the Protection of Legal Interests', *EuCLR*, 1 (2011), 34–42

'Verweisungen auf das EU-Recht und das Bestimmtheitsgebot (Art. 103 Abs. 2 GG)', in Amelung, K., Günther, H.-J. and Kühne, H.-H., eds., *Festschrift für Volker Krey zum 70. Geburtstag am 9. Juli 2010* (Stuttgart: Kohlhammer, 2010), 7–25

Borgers, M. J., 'Framework Decision on Combating Terrorism: Two Questions on the Definition of Terrorist Offences', *NJECL*, 3 (2012), 68–82

Bossong, R., and Wagner, B., 'A Typology of Cybersecurity and Public–Private Partnerships in the Context of the EU', *CrimLSC*, 67 (2017), 265–88

Brand, T., 'Erstes EU-Strafgesetz auf Grundlage des "Lissabon-Vertrags" verabschiedet', *DRiZ*, 89 (2011), 125

Braum, S., 'Europäische Strafgesetzgebung: Demokratische Strafgesetzlichkeit oder administrative Opportunität', *wistra*, 25 (2006), 121–5

Europäische Strafgesetzlichkeit (Frankfurt a.M.: Vittorio Klostermann, 2003)

'Europäisches Strafrecht im Fokus konfligierender Verfassungsmodelle', *ZIS*, 4 (2009), 418–26

'Unabhängige Justiz: Gegengewicht zur Erosion von Grundrechten in Europa', *KritV* 93 (2010), 319–27

BRAK, *Stellungnahme Nr. 11: Zum Vorschlag für eine Richtlinie des Europäischen Parlaments und des Rates über die strafrechtliche Bekämpfung von gegen die finanziellen Interessen der Europäischen Union gerichtetem Betrug*, June 2013, at www.brak.de/zur-rechtspolitik/stellungnahmen-pdf/stellungnahmen-europa/2013/juni/stellungnahme-der-brak-2013-11.pdf, last accessed 27 January 2018

Brechmann, W., *Die richtlinienkonforme Auslegung* (Munich: C. H. Beck, 1994)

Bressan, S., 'Criminal Law against Human Trafficking within the EU: A Comparison of an Approximated Legislation', *Eur. J. Cr.*, 20 (2012), 137–63

Breuer, B., *Der Im- und Export von Abfällen innerhalb der Europäischen Union aus umweltstrafrechtlicher Sicht* (Berlin: Duncker & Humblot, 1998)

Breyer, P., 'Die Cyber-Crime-Konvention des Europarats', *DuD*, 25 (2001), 592–600

Brodowski, D., 'Innere Sicherheit in der EU', *Jura*, 36 (2013), 492–504

'Strafrechtsrelevante Entwicklungen in der Europäischen Union', *ZIS*, 7 (2012), 558–70

'Strafrechtsrelevante Entwicklungen in der Europäischen Union', *ZIS*, 8 (2013), 455–72

'Strafrechtsrelevante Entwicklungen in der Europäischen Union', *ZIS*, 12 (2017), 11–27

'Strafrechtsrelevante Entwicklungen in der Europäischen Union: Ein Überblick', *ZIS*, 5 (2010), 749–60

Buono, L., 'Gearing up the Fight against Cybercrime in the EU: A New Set of Rules and the Establishment of the European Cybercrime Centre (EC3)', *NJECL*, 3 (2012), 332–43

Calderoni, F., 'The European Legal Framework on Cybercrime: Striving for an Effective Implementation', *CrimLSC*, 54 (2010), 339–57

Cerizza, M., 'The New Market Abuse Directive', *eucrim*, 9 (2014), 85–9

Chiaromonte, C., 'Criminal Law in European Countries: Combating Manipulation of Sports Results: Match-Fixing', *eucrim*, 7 (2012), 30–3

Chouliaras, A., 'Transposing the Framework Decision on Combating Racism and Xenophobia into the Greek Legal Order', *eucrim*, 6 (2011), 39–44

Clough, J., 'The Council of Europe Convention on Cybercrime: Defining "Crime" in a Digital World', *CLF*, 23 (2012), 363–91

Commission (EU), Commission to the EP, the Council, the European Economic and Social Committee and the Committee of the Regions, 'Towards an EU Criminal Policy: Ensuring the Effective Implementation of EU Policies through Criminal Law' (Communication) COM(2011) final, 20 September 2011

Council of the EU, 'Explanatory Report on the Convention on the Protection of the European Communities' Financial Interests', 23 June 1997, EC OJ 1997 C 191/1, at http://eur-lex.europa.eu/legal-content/en/txt/?uri=uriserv:oj.c_.1997.191.01.0001.01.eng%26;toc=oj:c:1997:191:toc, last accessed 27 January 2018

'Note, Protecting the Union's Financial Interests by Means of Criminal Law', 3 June 2013, 10232/13, at http://register.consilium.europa.eu/doc/srv?l=en&f=st%2010232%202013%20init, last accessed 25 October 2016

'Opinion of the Legal Service, Proposal for a Directive of the European Parliament and of the Council on the Fight against Fraud to the Union's Financial Interests by Means of Criminal Law: Legal Basis', 22 October 2012, 15309/12, at http://db.eurocrim.org/db/en/doc/1959.pdf, last accessed 27 January 2018

'Proposal for a Directive of the European Parliament and of the Council on the Fight against Fraud to the Union's Financial Interests by Means of Criminal Law: Preparation of the next Triologue', 7 May 2015, 8604/15, at www.statewatch.org/news/2015/may/eu-council-fraud-dir-trilogue-8604-15.pdf, last accessed 27 January 2018

'Proposal for a Directive of the European Parliament and of the Council on the Fight against Fraud to the Union's Financial Interests by Means of Criminal Law: Progress Report/Policy Debate', 27 May 2016, 9301/16, at http://db.eurocrim.org/db/en/doc/2505.pdf, last accessed 27 January 2018

'Proposal for a Directive of the European Parliament and of the Council on the Fight against Fraud to the Union's Financial Interests by Means of Criminal Law: Progress Report/Policy Debate', 3 June 2016, 9804/16, at http://data.consilium.europa.eu/doc/document/st-9804-2016-init/en/pdf, last accessed 27 January 2018

Covolo, V., *L'émergence d'un droit pénal en réseau: Analyse critique du système européen de lutte antifraude* (Baden-Baden: Nomos, 2015)

Dannecker, G., 'Anforderungen des nationalen Strafverfassungsrechts an die Inbezugnahme EU-rechtlicher Verhaltensnormen und an Rückverweisungsklauseln in nationalen Rechtsverordnungen', *ZIS*, 11 (2016), 723–30

'Die Dynamik des materiellen Strafrechts unter dem Einfluss europäischer und internationaler Entwicklungen', *ZStW*, 117 (2005), 697–748

'§8: Einführung von Tatbeständen mit supranationaler Schutzrichtung (Europadelikte)', in Böse, M., ed., *Enzyklopädie Europarecht: Europäisches Strafrecht mit polizeilicher Zusammenarbeit* (Baden-Baden: Nomos Verlagsgesellschaft, 2013), 287–335

'Die Entwicklung des Strafrechts unter dem Einfluss des Gemeinschaftsrechts', *Jura*, 21 (1998), 79–87

'Europäische Gemeinschaft und Strafrecht: Juristische Personen und Personenvereinigungen', in Ulsamer, G., ed., *Lexikon des Rechts: Strafrecht/ Strafverfahrensrecht* (Neuwied et al.: Luchterhand, 2nd edn, 1996), 302–16

'Das materielle Strafrecht im Spannungsfeld des Rechts der EU', *Jura*, 29 (2006), 95–102 (Teil I) and 173–8 (Teil II)

'Strafrecht in der Europäischen Gemeinschaft', *JZ*, 41 (1996), 869–80

'Strafrechtlicher Schutz der Finanzinteressen der EG gegen Täuschung', *ZStW*, 108 (1996), 577–629

'Der zeitliche Geltungsbereich von Strafgesetzen und der Vorrang des Gemeinschaftsrechts', in Hoyer, A., Müller, H. E., Pawlik, M., and Wolter, J., eds., *Festschrift für Friedrich-Christian Schroeder zum 70. Geburtstag* (Heidelberg: C. F. Müller, 2006), 761–76

'Der zeitliche Geltungsbereich von Strafgesetzen und der Vorrang des Gemeinschaftsrechts', *ZIS*, 1 (2006), 309–17

Dannecker, G., and Bülte, J., '2. Kapitel: Die Entwicklung des Wirtschaftsstrafrechts unter dem Einfluss des Europarechts', in Wabnitz, H.-B., and Janovsky, T., *Handbuch des Wirtschafts- und Steuerstrafrechts* (Munich: C.H. Beck, 2014), 79–214

Dannecker, G., and Freitag, R., 'Zur neueren europäischen und deutschen Strafgesetzgebung im Recht der Außenwirtschaft und der Finanzsanktionen', *ZStW*, 116 (2004), 797–818

De Bondt, W., 'The Missing Link between "Necessity" and "Approximation of Criminal Sanction" in the EU', *EuCLR*, 4 (2014), 147–68

de Hoyos Sancho, M., 'The Procedural Treatment of Especially Vulnerable Victims in Current and Recent Proposed Normative Instruments in the EU', in de Hoyos Sancho, M., ed., *Guarantees and Rights of the Especially Vulnerable Victim in the Legal Framework of the EU* (Valencia: Tirant lo Banch, 2013), 47–70 de Rijck, R., 'The Isolation of Dutch Environmental Criminal Law', *eucrim*, 6 (2011), 162–7

Deutscher, J., *Die Kompetenzen der Europäischen Gemeinschaften zur originären Strafrechtssetzung* (Frankfurt a.M. et al.: Peter Lang, 2000)

Deutscher Richterbund, 'Stellungnahme zum Vorschlag für eine Richtlinie des Europäischen Parlaments und des Rates über die "strafrechtliche Bekämpfung von gegen die finanziellen Interessen der Europäischen Union gerichtetem Betrug"' KOM (2012) 363 final, January 2013, at www.drb.de/stellungnahmen/2013/rl-bekaempfung-gegen-eu-gerichtetem-betrug.html, last accessed 27 January 2018

Dieblich, F., *Der strafrechtliche Schutz der Rechtsgüter der Europäischen Gemeinschaften* (Cologne: University of Cologne, 1985)

Di Fabio, U., 'Richtlinienkonformität als ranghöchstes Normauslegungsprinzip? etc.', *NJW*, 43 (1990), 947–54

Donato Toma, G., 'VAT Carousel Fraud in the EU', *eucrim*, 9 (2014), 89–92

Duttge, G., 'Vorbereitung eines Computerbetruges: Auf dem Weg zu einem "grenzenlosen" Strafrecht', in Heinrich, B., Hilgendorf, E., Mitsch, W., and Sternberg-Lieben, D., eds., *Festschrift für Ulrich Weber zum 70. Geburtstag* (Bielefeld: Gieseking, 2004), 285–310

Eckstein, K., 'Grundlagen und aktuelle Probleme der Besitzdelikte', *ZStW*, 117 (2005), 107–42

Eisele, J., 'Arbeitnehmerüberwachung und Compliance unter Berücksichtigung der Cybercrime-Konvention', *ZIS*, 7 (2012), 402–8

'Einflussnahme auf nationales Strafrecht durch Richtliniengebung der EG', *JZ*, 56 (2001), 1157–65

'Einführung in das Europäische Strafrecht etc.', *JA*, 32 (2000), 896–902

Elholm, T., 'Strafrechtliche Maßnahmen der EU', in Müller-Dietz, H., ed., *Festschrift für Heike Jung zum 65. Geburtstag am 23. April 2007* (Baden-Baden: Nomos Verlagsgesellschaft, 2007), 135–52

Engelhart, M., *Sanktionierung von Unternehmen und Compliance* (Berlin: Duncker & Humblot, 2012)

'Unternehmensstrafbarkeit im europäischen und internationalen Recht', *eucrim*, 7 (2012), 110–23

Esser, R., 'Europäische Vorgaben für die amtliche Lebensmittelüberwachung', *StV*, 24 (2004), 221–8

European Commission, 'Commission Staff Working Paper: Impact Assessment (Part I) Accompanying the Document, Proposal for a Directive of the European Parliament and of the Council on the Protection of the Financial Interests of the European Union by Means of Criminal Law', 11 July 2012, SWD(2012) 195 final, at https://ec.europa.eu/anti-fraud/sites/antifraud/files/docs/body/impact_assessment_en.pdf, last accessed 27 January 2018

'Proposal for a Directive of the European Parliament and of the Council on the Fight against Fraud to the Union's Financial Interests by Means of Criminal Law', 11 July 2012, COM(2012) 363 final, at www.europarl.europa.eu/RegData/docs_autres_institutions/commission_europeenne/com/2012/0363/COM_COM(2012)0363_EN.pdf, last accessed 27 January 2018

European Parliament, 'Fight against Fraud to the Union's Financial Interests by Means of Criminal Law. Legislative Resolution of 16 April 2014 on the Proposal for a Directive of the European Parliament and of the Council on the Fight against Fraud to the Union's Financial Interests by Means of Criminal Law. Ordinary Legislative Procedure: First Reading, Annex to 9024/14 of 29 April 2014', at www.europarl.europa.eu/sides/getDoc.do?pubRef=-//EP//TEXT+TA+P7-TA-2014-0427+0+DOC+XML+V0//EN, last accessed 27 January 2018

Eurostat, 'Trafficking in Human Beings' (2013), at https://ec.europa.eu/anti-trafficking/sites/antitrafficking/files/trafficking_in_human_beings_-_dghome-eurostat_en_1.pdf, last accessed 27 January 2018

Eydner, J. R., 'Der neue §233 StGB: Ansätze zum Verständnis der "Ausbeutung der Arbeitskraft"', *NStZ*, 26 (2006), 10–14

Fazekas, M., and Nanopoulos, E., 'The Effectiveness of EU Law: Insights from the EU Legal Framework on Asset Confiscation', *Eur.J.C.*, 24 (2016), 39–64

Fischbeck, S., '§42: Geldwäsche', in Schimansky, H., Bunte, H.-J., and Lwowski, H.-J., eds., *Bankrechts-Handbuch*, i (Munich: C. H. Beck, 4th edn, 2011), 936–1049

Foffani, L., 'Bienes jurídicos de relevancia comunitaria y protección penal: el caso de las falsedades en las cuentas de sociedades mercantiles', *RP*, 27 (2011), 41–50

Fontanaud, D., 'Lutte contre la fraude et la contrefaçon des moyens de paiement autres que les espéces', *RIDP*, 77 (2006), 237–42

Fornasier, R., 'Le pouvoir repressif des C.E. et la protection de leurs intérêts financiers', *RMC*, 1982, 398–413

Franzheim, H., and Kreß, C., 'Die Bedeutung der EWG-Richtlinien über Abfälle für den strafrechtlichen Abfallbegriff', *JR*, 63 (1991), 402–6

Frisch, W., 'Rechtsphilosophie und Strafrecht in Europa', *GA*, 154 (2007), 250–73

Fromm, I. E., 'Anmerkung zu EuGH, Urteil v. 23.10.2007 - C-440/05', *ZIS*, 3 (2008), 168–77

'Auf dem Weg zur strafrechtlichen Verantwortlichkeit von Unternehmen/Unternehmensvereinigungen in Europa?', *ZIS*, 2 (2007), 279–91

'Bekämpfung schwerer Umweltkriminalität in der EG durch einheitliche strafrechtliche Sanktionen?', *ZfW*, 48 (2009), 157–62

Gaede, K., and Mühlbauer, T., 'Wirtschaftsstrafrecht zwischen europäischem Primärrecht, Verfassungsrecht und der richtlinienkonformen Auslegung am Beispiel des Scalping', *wistra*, 24 (2005), 9–17

Gärditz, K. F., '§6: Europäisierung des Strafrechts und nationales Verfassungsrecht', in Böse, M., ed., *Enzyklopädie Europarecht: Europäisches Strafrecht mit polizeilicher Zusammenarbeit* (Baden-Baden: Nomos Verlagsgesellschaft, 2013), 227–68

'Der Strafprozess unter dem Einfluss europäischer Richtlinien', *wistra*, 18 (1999), 293–6

Galli, F., 'Passenger Name Record Agreements: The Umpteenth Attempt to Anticipate Risk', *eucrim*, 5 (2010), 124–8

Gentzik, D., *Die Europäisierung des deutschen und englischen Geldwäschestrafrechts* (Berlin: Duncker & Humblot, 2002)

Gercke, B., 'Der Haftgrund der Fluchtgefahr bei EU-Bürgern', *StV*, 24 (2004), 675–9

Gercke, M., 'Die Entwicklung des Internetstrafrechts 2009/2010', *ZUM*, 54 (2010), 633–45

'Die EU Richtlinie zur Bekämpfung von Kinderpornographie', *CR*, 28 (2012), 520–5

'Die Harmonisierung des Europäischen Strafrechts am Beispiel des Internetstrafrechts', *StV*, 35 (2016), 391–4

Gleß, S., 'Zum Begriff des mildesten Gesetzes (§2 Abs. 3 StGB)', *GA*, 147 (2000), 224–36

Götz, V., 'Rechtsstaatliche Grundsätze des Gemeinschaftsrechts als Grund und Grenze der innerstaatlichen Anwendung von EG-Richtlinien', in Bröhmer, J., ed., *Internationale Gemeinschaft und Menschenrechte: Festschrift für Georg Ress* (Cologne et al.: Carl Heymanns, 2005), 485–96

Goehler, J., 'Europäsche Reform des Insiderstrafrechts', *ZIS*, 11 (2016), 266–80

Gómez-Jara Díez, C., *Europan Federal Criminal Law: The Federal Dimension of EU Criminal Law* (Cambridge: Intersentia, 2015)

'European Federal Criminal Law: What Can Europe Learn from the US System of Federal Criminal Law to Solve Its Sovereign Debt Crisis?', *EuCLR*, 3 (2013), 170–93

Grasso, G., *Comunida des Europeas y derecho penal* (Toledo: Ediciones de la Universidad de Castilla-La Mancha, 1993)

Gröblinghoff, S., *Die Verpflichtung des deutschen Strafgesetzgebers zum Schutz der Interessen der EU* (Heidelberg: C. F. Müller, 1996)

Gualtieri, C., 'Racism and Xenophobia', *RIDP*, 77 (2006), 263–9

Harms, M., and Heine, S., 'EG-Verordnung und Blankettgesetz: Zum Verhältnis von Gemeinschaftsrecht und nationalem Strafrecht', in Böse, M., and Sternberg-Lieben, D., eds., *Grundlagen des Straf- und Strafverfahrensrechts: Festschrift für Knut Amelung zum 70. Geburtstag* (Berlin: Duncker & Humblot, 2009), 393–412

Hauck, P., 'Anmerkung zu BGH, Urteil v. 24.10.2006 – 1 StR 44/06', *NStZ*, 27 (2007), 221–2

'Funktionen und Grenzen des Einflusses der Strafrechtsvergleichung auf die Strafrechtsharmonisierung in der EU', in Beck, S., Burchard, C., and Fateh-Moghadam, B., eds., *Strafrechtsvergleichung als Problem und Lösung* (Baden-Baden: Nomos Verlagsgesellschaft, 2011), 255–73

'Über Sinn und Widersinn der von der GRECO unterbreiteten Vorschläge zur Änderung der Korruptionstatbestände in §§108e, 299 und 331 ff. StGB', *wistra*, 29 (2010), 255–8

Haustein, B.H., 'Europarechtliche Bezüge des Kinder- und Jugenpornographiestrafrechts', *ZIS*, 9 (2014), 348–52

Hecker, B., 'Europäisches Strafrecht als Antwort auf transnationale Kriminalität', *JA*, 34 (2002), 723–30

'Europäisches Strafrecht post-Lissabon', in Ambos, K., ed., *Europäisches Strafrecht post-Lissabon* (Göttingen: Universitätsverlag Göttingen, 2011), 13–28

'Die gemeinschaftsrechtlichen Strukturen der Geldwäschestrafbarkeit', in Görgen, T., Hoffmann-Holland, K., Schneider, H., and Stock, J., eds., *Interdisziplinäre Kriminologie: Festschrift für Arthur Kreuzer zum 70. Geburtstag*, i (Frankfurt a.M.: Verlag für Polizeiwissenschaft, 2009), 216–30

'Die richtlinienkonforme und die verfassungskonforme Auslegung im Strafrecht', *JuS*, 54 (2014), 385–93

'Statement: Jurisdiktionskonflikte in der EU', *ZIS*, 6 (2011), 60–3

'§10: Harmonisierung', in Sieber, U., Satzger, H., and Heintschel von Heinegg, B., eds., *Europäisches Strafrecht* (Baden-Baden: Nomos Verlagsgesellschaft, 2014), 272–93

'§28: Umweltstrafrecht', in Sieber, U., Satzger, H., and Heintschel von Heinegg, B., eds., *Europäisches Strafrecht* (Baden-Baden: Nomos Verlagsgesellschaft, 2014), 516–28

'§29: Lebensmittelstrafrecht', in Sieber, U., Satzger, H., and Heintschel von Heinegg, B., eds., *Europäisches Strafrecht* (Baden-Baden: Nomos Verlagsgesellschaft, 2014), 529–35

'Die verspätet und fehlerhaft umgesetzte Richtlinie 2008/115/EG und ihre Auswikrungen auf das Einreise- und Aufenthaltsverbot gem. §95 Abs. 2 Nr. 1 lit. a., b AufenthG', *ZIS*, 9 (2014), 47–53

Hecker, B., and Zöller, M., *Fallsammlung zum Europäischen und Internationalen Strafrecht* (Berlin and Heidelberg: Springer, 2012)

Heger, M., 'Die Beeinflussung des deutschen Strafrechts durch EU-Recht und der Gedanke des Rechtsmissbrauchs', *ZIS*, 8 (2013), 289–96

'§5: Einwirkungen des Europarechts auf das nationale Strafrecht', in Böse, M., ed., *Enzyklopädie Europarecht: Europäisches Strafrecht mit polizeilicher Zusammenarbeit* (Baden-Baden: Nomos Verlagsgesellschaft, 2013), 179–226

Die Europäisierung des deutschen Umweltstrafrechts (Tübingen: Mohr Siebeck, 2009)

'Perspektiven des Europäischen Strafrechts nach dem Vertrag von Lissabon', *ZIS*, 4 (2009), 406–17

'Strafbarkeit von Glücksspielen, Sportwetten und Hausverlosungen via Internet im Lichte des Europarechts', *ZIS*, 7 (2012), 396–401

'Unionrechtskonforme Auslegung des Betrugstatbestandes?', *HRRS*, 15 (2014), 467–73

Heine, G., 'Die Europäisierung des Strafrechts, dargestellt am Beispiel der Verbringung von Abfällen innerhalb der EU', in Müller-Dietz, H., ed., *Festschrift für Heike Jung zum 65. Geburtstag am 23. April 2007* (Baden-Baden: Nomos Verlagsgesellschaft, 2007), 261–72

'Gemeinschaftsrecht, Strafrecht, Glücksspiele', in Nuotio, K., ed., *Festschrift in Honour of Raimo Lahti* (Helsinki: University Print, 2007), 143–56

Heine, G., and Ringelmann, C., 'Towards an European Environmental Criminal Law', in László, G. I., and László, K., eds., *Emlékkönyv, Losonczy István Professzor Halálának 25. Évfordulójára* (Pécs: PTE ÁJK, 2005), 44–56

Heine, S., 'Das Urteil des EuGH in der Rechtssache Kadi und seine Auswirkungen auf die Strafbarkeit nach §4 IV Nr. 2 AWG', *NStZ*, 29 (2009), 428–33

Heintschel von Heinegg, B., 'Gemeinschaftsrechtskonforme Auslegung des Vereinigungsbegriffs in den §§129 ff. StGB', in Hoyer, A., Müller, H. E., Pawlik, M., and Wolter, J., eds., *Festschrift für Friedrich-Christian Schroeder zum 70. Geburtstag* (Heidelberg: C. F. Müller, 2006), 799–808

Heise, F. N., *Europäisches Gemeinschaftsrecht und nationales Strafrecht* (Bielefeld: DDV, 1998)

Hellmann, U., and Beckemper, K., *Wirtschaftsstrafrecht* (Stuttgart: Kohlhammer, 1st edn, 2004)

Wirtschaftsstrafrecht (Stuttgart: Kohlhammer, 4th edn, 2013)

Hellmann, M., and Gärtner, J., 'Neues beim Volksverhetzungstatbestand: Europäische Vorgaben und ihre Umsetzung', *NJW*, 64 (2011), 961–6

Hendel, P., *Bekämpfung von Geldwäsche und Terrorismusfinanzierung* (Heidelberg: Finanz Colloquium, 2008)

Herlin-Karnell, E., 'The Development of EU Precautionary Criminalisation', *EuCLR*, 1 (2011), 149–69

'The Lisbon Treaty', *eucrim*, 5 (2010), 59–64

Herzog, F., and Achtelik, O., 'Einleitung', in Herzog, F., and Achtelik, O., eds., *Geldwäschegesetz: Kommentar* (Munich: C. H. Beck, 2nd edn, 2014)

Herrmann, C., 'Anmerkung zu EuGH, Urteil v. 16. 6. 2005 - C-105/03', *EuZW*, 16 (2005), 436–8

Heun-Rehn, S. L.-T., 'Hassan und Ayadi: Die Kadi-Rechtsprechung des Gerichtshofs und warum es spannend bleibt', *ELR*, 6 (2010), 110–23

Heusel, M., 'Zur Nutzung von Insiderinformationen', *BKR*, 10 (2010), 77–9

Hillgruber, C., 'Anmerkung zu EuGH, Urteil v. 16. 6. 2005 - C-105/03', *JZ*, 60 (2005), 841–4

Hollenberg, S., 'The Security Council's 1267/1989 Targeted Sanctions Regime and the Use of Confidential Information: A Proposal for Decentralization of Review', *LJIL*, 28 (2015), 49–71

Hörich, C., 'Die Sanktionsrichtlinie: Zündstoff zwischen EuGH und BVerfG?', *ZAR*, 30 (2010), 49–53

Hoven, E., 'Zur Verfassungsmäßigkeit von Blankettstrafgesetzen', *NStZ*, 36 (2016), 377–83

Huber, B., '§21: Menschenhandel', in Sieber, U., Satzger, H., and Heintschel von Heinegg, B., eds., *Europäisches Strafrecht* (Baden-Baden: Nomos Verlagsgesellschaft, 2014), 394–403

'§23: Schutz von Kindern und Frauen (sexuelle Ausbeutung, Pornographie, Gewalt)', in Sieber, U., Satzger, H., and Heintschel von Heinegg, B., eds., *Europäisches Strafrecht* (Baden-Baden: Nomos Verlagsgesellschaft, 2014), 412–34

Hugger, H., *Strafrechtliche Anweisungen der Europäischen Gemeinschaft* (Baden-Baden: Nomos Verlagsgesellschaft, 2000)

'Zur strafbarkeitserweiterenden richtlinienkonformen Auslegung deutscher Strafvorschriften', *NStZ*, 13 (1993), 421–4

Hummel, D., 'Die Missachtung des parlamentarischen Gesetzgebers durch die Fachgerichte unter dem Deckmantel des Anwendungsvorrangs europäischen Rechts', *NVwZ*, 27 (2008), 36–41

Hummrich, M., 'BVerfG und EuGH: Kooperation oder Konfrontation?', *DRiZ*, 83 (2005), 361–4

Jacsó-Potyka, J., *Bekämpfung der Geldwäscherei in Europa* (Berlin et al.: Berliner Wissenschafts-Verlag, 2007)

Jens, A., *Der nationale Strafrechtsanwender unter dem Einfluss des Europäischen Gemeinschaftsrechts* (Berlin: Duncker & Humblot, 2006)

Jescheck, H.-H., 'Gegenstand und neueste Entwicklung des internationalen Strafrechts', in Schroeder, F.-C., and Zipf, H., eds., *Festschrift für Reinhart Maurach zum 70. Geburtstag* (Karlsruhe: C. F. Müller, 1972), 579–95

Jimeno Bulnes, M., 'La nueva cuestión prejudicial en el espacio judicial europeo', *RGDP*, 16 (2008), 1–14

Johannes, H., 'Das Strafrecht im Bereich der Europäischen Gemeinschaften', *EuR*, 3 (1968), 63–126

Jokisch, J., *Gemeinschaftsrecht und Strafverfahren* (Berlin: Duncker & Humblot, 2000)

Jour-Schröder, A., and Konow, C., 'Die Paserelle des Art. 42 EU-Vertrag', *EuZW*, 17 (2006), 550–5

Jung, H., and Schroth, H.-J., 'Das Strafrecht als Gegenstand der Rechtsangleichung in Europa', *GA*, 130 (1983), 241–72

Kaiafa-Gbandi, M., 'The Commission's Proposal for a Directive on the Fight against Fraud to the Union's Financial Interests by Means of Criminal Law

(COM (2012) 363 final): An Assessment Based on the Manifesto for a European Criminal Policy', *EuCLR*, 2 (2012), 319–37

'The Importance of Core Principles of Substantive Criminal Law', *EuCLR*, 1 (2011), 7–34

The Post-Lisbon Approach towards the Main Features of Substantive Criminal Law: Developments and Challenges, *EuCLR*, 5 (2015), 3–18

Kainer, F., 'Strafrecht im Raum der Freiheit, der Sicherheit und des Rechts. Entwicklung und Umsetzungsprobleme des europäisierten Strafrechts in Deutschland', *EuR*, 48 (2013), *Beiheft 3*, 87–117

Karsai, K., 'The Legality of Criminal Law and the New Competences of the TFEU', *ZIS*, 11 (2016), 24–39

'Symbole als Gegenstand des ungarischen und europäischen Strafrechts: Verkehrtes Gesinnungsstrafrecht?', *ZStW*, 119 (2007), 1037–54

Kaye, N., 'Freezing and Confiscation of Criminal Proceeds', *RIDP*, 77 (2006), 323–31

Kert, R., 'Vorschläge für neue EU-Instrumente zur (strafrechtlichen) Bekämpfung von Insiderhandel und Marktmanipulation', *NZWiSt*, 2 (2013), 252–61

Kilchling, M., '§16: Geldwäsche', in Sieber, U., Satzger, H., and Heintschel von Heinegg, B, eds., *Europäisches Strafrecht* (Baden-Baden: Nomos Verlagsgesellschaft, 2014), 332–42

Kilchling, M., and Herz, A., '§22: Schleuserkriminalität', in Sieber, U., Satzger, H., and Heintschel von Heinegg, B., eds., *Europäisches Strafrecht* (Baden-Baden: Nomos Verlagsgesellschaft, 2014), 404–11

Killmann, B.-R., '§13: Bestechung, Bestechlichkeit', in Sieber, U., Satzger, H., and Heintschel von Heinegg, B., eds., *Europäisches Strafrecht* (Baden-Baden: Nomos Verlagsgesellschaft, 2014), 317–22

'§15: Unbare Zahlungsmittel', in Sieber, U., Satzger, H., and Heintschel von Heinegg, B.., eds., *Europäisches Strafrecht* (Baden-Baden: Nomos Verlagsgesellschaft, 2014), 328–31

Killmann, B.-R. and Schröder, J., '§12: Betrugs- und Finanzdelikte (inkl. Steuerstraftaten)', in Sieber, U., Satzger, H., and Heintschel von Heinegg, B., eds., *Europäisches Strafrecht* (Baden-Baden: Nomos Verlagsgesellschaft, 2014), 303–16

Klindt, T., 'Die Zulässigkeit dynamischer Verweisungen auf EG-Recht aus verfassungs- und europarechtlicher Sicht', *DVBl.*, 113 (1998), 373–80

Klip, A., 'European Integration and Harmonisation and Criminal Law', in Curtin, D. M., Smits, J. M., Klip, A., and McCahery, J. A., eds., *European Integration and Law* (Antwerp et al.: Intersentia et al., 2006), 109–50

Koch, H.-G., '§30: Arzneimittel- und Medizinprodukterecht', in Sieber, U., Satzger, H., and Heintschel von Heinegg, B., eds., *Europäisches Strafrecht* (Baden-Baden: Nomos Verlagsgesellschaft, 2014), 536–46

Koch, T., '§17: Insiderstraftaten und Marktmanipulation', in Sieber, U., Satzger, H., and Heintschel von Heinegg, B., eds., *Europäisches Strafrecht* (Baden-Baden: Nomos Verlagsgesellschaft, 2014), 343–55

Köhne, R., *Die richtlinienkonforme Auslegung: dargestellt am Abfallbegriff des §326 Abs. 1 StGB* (Trier: Universität Trier, 1997)

Köpferl, G., 'Das Badezimmerkartell: Der Vertrag von Lissabon und das deutsche Kartellordnungswidrigkeitenrecht', *Jura*, 34 (2011), 234–40

Korte, M., 'Der Schutz der finanziellen Interessen der Europäischen Gemeinschaften mit den Mitteln des Strafrechts: Das "Zweite Protokoll"', *NJW*, 51 (1998), 1464–6

Kramo, Y. A., 'The European Union's Reponse to Irregular Migration and the Problem of Criminalisation', *NJECL*, 5 (2014), 26–57

Kreß, C., and Gazeas, N., 'Europäisierung des Vereinigungsbegriffs in den §§129 ff. StGB?', in Paeffgen, H.-U., Böse, M., Kindhäuser, U., Stübinger, S., Verrel, T., and Zaczyk, R., eds., *Strafrechtswissenschaft als Analyse und Konstruktion: Festschrift für Ingeborg Puppe zum 70. Geburtstag* (Berlin: Duncker & Humblot, 2011), 1487–1500

'§18: Organisierte Kriminalität', in Sieber, U., Satzger, H., and Heintschel von Heinegg, B., eds., *Europäisches Strafrecht* (Baden-Baden: Nomos Verlagsgesellschaft, 2014), 356–65

'§19: Terrorismus', in Sieber, U., Satzger, H., and Heintschel von Heinegg, B., eds., *Europäisches Strafrecht* (Baden-Baden: Nomos Verlagsgesellschaft, 2014), 366–83

Kretschmer, B., 'Art. III-271', in Vedder, C., and Heintschel von Heinegg, W., eds., *Europäischer Verfassungsvertrag* (Baden-Baden: Nomos Verlagsgesellschaft et al., 2007), 718–28

'Rätselraten im Nebenstrafrecht', *ZIS*, 12 (2016), 763–70

Kubiciel, M., 'Der EU-Anti-Corruption Report: Ein neuer Weg zu einer kohärenten Präventionspolitik', *HRRS*, 14 (2013), 213–19

'Strafrechtswissenschaft und europäische Kriminalpolitik', *ZIS*, 5 (2010), 742–8

Kugelmann, D., 'Bekämpfung rassistischer und fremdenfeindlicher Computerstraftaten: Das Zusatzprotokoll des Europarates', *DuD*, 27 (2003), 345–7

Kuhl, L., '§14: Geldfälschung', in Sieber, U., Satzger, H., and Heintschel von Heinegg, B., eds., *Europäisches Strafrecht* (Baden-Baden: Nomos Verlagsgesellschaft, 2014), 323–7

'The Initiative for a Directive on the Protection of the EU Financial Interests by Substantive Criminal Law', *eucrim*, 7 (2012), 63–6

Kühne, H.-H., 'Anmerkung zu BVerfG, Beschluss v. 15.12.2015 – 2 BvR 2735/14', *StV*, 36 (2016), 299–302

'Anmerkung zu EuGH, Urt. v. 16.6.1998', *JZ*, 53 (1998), 1070–1

'Europäische Methodenvielfalt und nationale Umsetzung von Entscheidungen Europäischer Gerichte', *GA*, 152 (2005), 195–214

'Schwarze Listen: Bürgerlicher Tod ohne Gerichtsverfahren und ohne Beweise: Der Fall Kadi und kein Ende', *ZRP*, 46 (2013), 243–8

Langenfeld, C., *Die Gleichbehandlung von Mann und Frau im Europäischen Gemeinschaftsrecht* (Baden-Baden: Nomos Verlagsgesellschaft, 1990)

Leenen, D., 'Die Auslegung von Richtlinien und die richtlinienkonforme Auslegung und Fortbildung des nationalen Rechts', *Jura*, 35 (2012), 753–62

Ligeti, K., 'Criminal Liability of Heads of Business', *eucrim*, 10 (2015), 145–50

Strafrecht und strafrechtliche Zusammenarbeit in der Europäischen Union (Berlin: Duncker & Humblot, 2005)

Maiwald, M., 'Harmonisierung ohne Harmonie? Zur Bedeutung der Strafrechtsdogmatik für Art. 83 AEUV', in Freund, G., Murmann, U., Bloy, R., and Perron, W., eds., *Grundlagen und Dogmatik des gesamten Strafrechtssystems, Festschrift für Wolfgang Frisch zum 70. Geburtstag* (Berlin: Duncker & Humblot, 2013), 1375–88

Malcom, H., 'What Is a Preliminary Reference? And Why Should I Care?', *Archbold Rev*, 9 (19 November 2015), 5–6

Mansdörfer, M., 'Einführung in das Europäische Umweltstrafrecht', *Jura*, 27 (2004), 297–306

'Das europäische Strafrecht nach dem Vertrag von Lissabon etc.', *HRRS*, 11 (2010), 11–23

Martens, J., *Subventionskriminalität zum Nachteil der Europäischen Gemeinschaften* (Herbolzheim: Centaurus, 2001)

Maugeri, A. M., 'The Criminal Sanctions against the Illicit Proceeds of Criminal Organisations', *NJECL*, 3 (2012), 257–97

Met-Domestici, A., 'The Fight against Money Laundering in the EU: The Framework Set by the Fourth Directive and 1st Proposed Enhancements', *eucrim*, 11 (2016), 170–9

Meyer, F., 'Globale Terrorbekämpfung und nationales Nebenstrafrecht', *NJW*, 63 (2010), 2397–9

'Der Grundsatz gegenseitigen Vertrauens: Konzeptualisierung und Zukunftsperspektiven eines neuen Verfassungsprinzips', *EuR*, 52 (2017), 163–86

'Das Strafrecht im Raum der Freiheit, der Sicherheit und des Rechts', *EuR*, 46 (2011), 169–96

Strafrechtsgenese in internationalen Organisationen: Eine Untersuchung der Strukturen und Legitimationsvoraussetzungen strafrechtlicher Normbildungsprozesse in Mehrebenensystemen (Baden-Baden: Nomos, 2012)

Meyer, K., 'Führt §330d Abs. 2 StGB zur endgültigen Europarechtsakzessorietät des deutschen Umweltstrafrechts?', *wistra*, 31 (2012), 371–6

Mitsilegas, V., 'From Overcriminalisation to Decriminalisation: The Many Faces of Effectivenes in European Criminal Law', *NJECL*, 5 (2014), 416–24

'The Future of Criminalisation after Lisbon', *NJECL*, 3 (2012), 225–8

'The Uneasy Relationship between the UK and European Criminal Law: From Opt-Outs to Brexit?', *CLR*, 63 (2016), 517–36

Möhrenschlager, M., 'Einbeziehung ausländischer Rechtsgüter in den Schutzbereich nationaler Straftatbestände', in Dannecker, G., ed., *Die Bekämpfung des Subventionsbetrugs im EG-Bereich* (Cologne: Bundesanzeiger, 1993), 162–9

Moll, D., *Europäisches Strafrecht durch nationale Blankettstrafgesetzgebung?* (Göttingen: Cuvillier, 1998)

Montaldo, S., 'Directive 2014/42/EU and Social Reuse of Confiscated Assets in the EU: Advancing a Culture of Legality', *NJECL*, 6 (2015), 195–212

Morillas Cueva, L., and Valls Prieto, J., 'Hacia la nueva realidad de un derecho penal europeo', *RDFUG*, 9 (2006), 159–84

Müller, N., 'Das Geldwäscheregister nach Art. 30 und 31 der Vierten Geldwäscherichtlinie und seine Vereinbarkeit mit der Rechtsprechung des EuGH zur Vorratsdatenspeicherung', *ZStW*, 128 (2016), 1021–88

Mylonopoulos, C., 'Strafrechtsdogmatik in Europa nach dem Vertrag von Lissabon', *ZStW*, 123 (2011), 633–50

Naziris, Y., '"A Tale of Two Cities" in Three Themes: A Critique of the EU's Approach to Cybercrime', *EuCLR*, 3 (2013), 319–54

Nehring, U., *Strafnormen im Atomenergierecht* (Göttingen, Universität Göttingen, 1965)

Nestler, N., '"Umgehungshandlungen": Überlegungen zum Umgang mit Verweisungen von Blankettstrafgesetzen auf Unionsrecht am Beispiel des §34 IV AWG', *NStZ*, 32 (2012), 672–9

Niehaus, H., 'Blankettnormen und Bestimmtheitsgebot vor dem Hintergrund zunehmender europäischer Rechtssetzung', *wistra*, 23 (2004), 206–11

Nilsson, H. G., 'How to Combine Minimum Rules with Maximum Legal Certainty?', *Europarättslig Tidskrift*, 14 (2011), 665–77

'25 Years of Criminal Justice in Europe', *EuCLR*, 2 (2012), 106–22

'Where Should the EU Go in Developing Its Criminal Policy in the Future? ', *eucrim*, 9 (2014), 19–21

Noltenius, B., 'Strafverfahrensrecht als Seismograph der Europäischen Integration etc.', *ZStW*, 122 (2010), 604–26

Nowak, C., 'The Europeanisation of Polish Substantive Criminal Law', *NJECL*, 3 (2012), 363–80

Nowell-Smith, H., 'Behind the Scenes in the Negotiation of EU Criminal Justice Legislation', *NJECL*, 3 (2012), 381–93

Obokata, T., and Payne, B., 'Implementing Action against Trafficking of Human Beings under the TFEU', *NJECL*, 3 (2012), 298–319

Ochnio, A. H., 'Implementation of the New EU Directive on Confiscation in Poland: The Challenge of Overcoming the Negative Historical Experiences of Confiscation Orders', *Eur.J.C.*, 24 (2016), 19–38

Oehler, D., 'Deutsches Strafanwendungsrecht, das Recht der übernationalen Gemeinschaften und die Auslieferung eigener Staatsangehöriger', in Kaufmann, H., Schwinge, E., and Welzel, H., eds., *Erinnerungsgabe für Max Grünhut* (Marburg: Elwert, 1965), 111–27

'Der europäische Binnenmarkt und sein wirtschaftsstrafrechtlicher Schutz', in Arzt, G., Fezer, G., Weber, U., Schlüchter, E., and Rössner, D., eds., *Festschrift für Jürgen Baumann zum 70. Geburtstag am 22. Juni 1992* (1992), 561–71

'Fragen zum Strafrecht der EG', in Vogler, T., ed., *Festschrift für Hans-Heinrich Jescheck zum 70. Geburtstag* (Berlin: Duncker & Humblot, 1985), 1399–1410

Internationales Strafrecht: Geltungsbereich des Strafrechts, internationales Rechtshilferecht: Recht der Gemeinschaften, Völkerstrafrecht (Cologne: Heymanns, 2nd edn, 1983)

Oehmichen, A., 'UN-EU-Terrorist Listings: Legal Foundations and Impacts', *ZIS*, 9 (2014), 412–20

Ouwerkerk, J. W., 'Criminalisation as a Last Resort', *NJECL*, 3 (2012), 228–41

Pabsch, W. C., 'Auswirkungen der europäischen Integrationsverträge auf das deutsche Strafrecht', *NJW*, 12 (1959), 2002–4

Der strafrechtliche Schutz der überstaatlichen Hoheitsgewalt (Bonn: Röhrscheid, 1965)

Pache, E., 'Zur Sanktionskompetenz der EWG. Das EuGH-Urteil vom 27.10.1992 in der Rs. C-240/90', *EuR*, 28 (1993), 173–82

Pananis, P., 'Anmerkung zu BGH, Urteil v. 6.11.2003 – 1 StR 24/03', *NStZ*, 24 (2004), 287–9

Park, T., 'Kapitalmarktstrafrecht und Anlegerschutz', *NStZ*, 27 (2007), 369–77

Pati, R., 'Der Schutz der EMRK gegen Menschenhandel', *NJW*, 64 (2011), 128–31

Peccioli, A., 'Il terrorismo quale setore chiave per l'armonizzazione del diritto penale', *DPP*, 13 (2007), 801–7

Peers, S., 'The Italian Job: The CJEU Strengthens Criminal Law Protection of the EU's Finances', *EU Law Analysis*, 22 September 2015, available at http://eulawanalysis.blogspot.co.uk/2015/09/the-italian-job-cjeu-strengthens.html, last accessed 27 January 2018

Perini, C., 'The Influence of Directive 2008/99/EC on the Harmonization and Renewal of the Lexicon of Environmental Criminal Law', in Ruggieri, F., ed., *Criminal Proceedings, Languages and the EU* (Heidelberg et al.: Springer, 2014), 145–57

Perron, W., 'Strafrechtsvereinheitlichung in Europa', in Dörr, D., and Dreher, M., eds., *Europa als Rechtsgemeinschaft* (Baden-Baden: Nomos Verlagsgesellschaft, 1997), 135–54

Piacente, N., 'The Contribution of the Council of Europe to the Fight against Foreign Terrorist Fighters', *eucrim*, 10 (2015), 12–15

Picotti, L., 'La lutte contre la fraude communautaire das la perspective du traité établissant une constitution pour l'Europe', in Ruggieri, F., ed., *La protection des intérêts financiers de l'Union et le rôle de l'OLAF etc.* (Brussels: Bruylant, 2005), 39–86

Pietrobon, A., 'Challenges in Implementing the European Convention against Trafficking in Human Organs', *LJIL*, 29 (2016), 485–502

Pijnen, R., 'Terrorism Lists and Freezing of Assets', *eucrim*, 6 (2011), 167–72

Pitto, E., 'La lutte contre le trafic de drogue', *RIDP*, 77 (2006), 271–6

Popp, A., 'Computerstrafrecht in Europa', *MR-Int*, 4 (2007), 84–8

Porebska, E., 'Paving the Way for Improved Mutual Assistance in the Context of Customs Fraud', *eucrim*, 11 (2016), 52–5

Príborský, M., 'The European Union and the UN Convention against Corruption', *eucrim*, 7 (2012), 34–8

'The New Commission Anti-fraud Strategy: Revamped Fight against Fraud at EU Level', *ERA Forum*, 12 (2011), 373–86

Rackow, P., 'Rechtliche Rahmenbedingungen und Problemfelder europäischer Terrorismusbekämpfung', *Die Polizei*, 102 (2011), 1–32

'Strafrechtsergänzende Europäische Terrorismusbekämpfung', *StV*, 29 (2009), 721–6

'Verfasst der EuGH die Union? etc.', *ZIS*, 3 (2008), 526–37

'Was ist Verharmlosen?', *ZIS*, 5 (2010), 366–75

Rashkovski, D., Naumovski, V., and Naumovski, G., 'Cybercrime Tendencies and Legislation in the Republic of Macedonia', *Eur J Crim Policy Res*, 22 (2016), 127–51

Reale, M. C., and Borraccetti, M., *Da giudice a giudice: Il dialogo tra il giudice italiano e la Corte di Giustizia* (Milano: Giuffré Editore, 2008)

Reiling, K., and Reschke, D., 'Die Auswirkungen der Lissabon-Entscheidung des Bundesverfassungsgerichts auf die Europäisierung des Umweltstrafrechts', *wistra*, 29 (2010), 47–52

Reiter, S., *Europäische Union und österreichisches Strafrecht* (Vienna et al.: Neuer Wissenschaftlicher Verlag, 2008)

Rheinbay, S., *Die Errichtung einer Europäischen Staatsanwaltschaft* (Berlin: Duncker & Humblot, 2014)

Rönnau, H., and Wegner, K., 'Grund und Grenzen der Einwirkungen des europäischen Rechts auf das nationale Strafrecht', *GA*, 160 (2013), 561–82

'Reform des Rechts der Verbandssanktionen: europäische und internationale Vorgaben', *ZRP*, 47 (2014), 158–63

Rosenau, H., 'Zur Europäisierung im Strafrecht', *ZIS*, 3 (2008), 9–19

Roth, W.-H., 'Die richtlinienkonforme Auslegung', *EWS*, 16 (2005), 385–96

Ruhs, S., 'Europäisierung des Umweltstrafrechts', *ZJS*, 4 (2011), 13–20

Rusteberg, B., 'Die EG-Richtlinie zur Vorratsdatenspeicherung von Verkehrsdaten im System des europäischen Grund- und Menschenrechtsschutzes', *VBlBW*, 28 (2007), 171–7

Rutkowski, J., 'Blankettvorschriften' in Erbs, G., and Kohlhaas, M., eds., *Strafrechtliche Nebengesetze* (Munich: C. H. Beck, 1 January 2006)

Safferling, C., 'Strafrechtsentwicklung in der EU: Konglomerat oder Synthese?', in Streng, F., and Kett-Straub, G., eds., *Strafrechtsvergleichung als Kulturvergleich* (Tübingen: Mohr Siebeck, 2013), 187–212

Salazar, L., 'EU's Criminal Policy and the Possible Contents of a New Multi-annual Program' *eucrim*, 6 (2011), 21

Sánchez Patrón, J. M., '¿Las Comunidades Europeas tienen competencia en materia penal? La sentencia del Trib. de Justicia de 13 de sept. de 2005', *RDP*, 19 (2006), 43–55

Satzger, H., 'Anmerkung zu EuGH, Urteil v. 3.5.2005 - Rs. C-378/02', *JZ*, 60 (2005), 998

'Anmerkung zu EuGH, Urteil v. 16.6.1998', *StV*, 19 (1999), 132–3

'Das europäische Verhältnismäßigkeitsprinzip', *NK*, 19 (2007), 93–8

'§2: Grundsätze eines europäischen Strafrechts', in Böse, M., ed., *Enzyklopädie Europarecht: Europäisches Strafrecht mit polizeilicher Zusammenarbeit* (Baden-Baden: Nomos Verlagsgesellschaft, 2013), 61–95

Internationales und Europäisches Strafrecht: Strafanwendungsrecht, europäisches Straf- und Strafverfahrensrecht, Völkerstrafrecht (Baden-Baden: Nomos, 7th edn, 2016)

'Die Internationalisierung des Strafrechts als Herausforderung für den strafrechtlichen Bestimmtheitsgrundsatz', *JuS*, 44 (2004), 943–8

'Das 'Manifest zur Europäischen Kriminalpolitik'', *ZRP*, 43 (2010), 137–40

'§9: Europäisierung', in Sieber, U., Satzger, H., and Heintschel von Heinegg, B., eds., *Europäisches Strafrecht* (Baden-Baden: Nomos Verlagsgesellschaft, 2014), 251–71

'Die Zukunft des Allgemeinen Teils des Strafrechts vor dem Hintergrund der zunehmenden Europäisierung des Strafrechts', *ZIS*, 11 (2016), 771–6

Satzger, H., and Langheld, G., 'Europarechtliche Verweisungen in Blankettstrafgesetzen und ihre Vereinbarkeit mit dem Bestimmtheitsgebot', *HRRS*, 12 (2011), 460–4

Sauer, H., '"Solange" geht in Altersteilzeit: Der unbedingte Vorrang der Menschenwürde vor dem Unionsrecht', *NJW*, 69 (2016), 1134–8

Scheffler, U., 'Mindeststandards des Europarates vs. die Mindeststandards des Rates der Europäischen Union', in Joerden, J. C., and Szwarc, A. J., eds., *Europäisierung des Strafrechts in Polen und Deutschland: Rechtsstaatliche Grundlagen* (Berlin: de Gruyter, 2007), 97–113

Schmalenbach, K., 'Normentheorie vs. Terrorismus: Der Vorrang des UN-Rechts vor EU-Recht', *JZ*, 61 (2006), 349–53

Schnabl, A., 'Strafprozessualer Zugriff auf Computerdaten und die Cybercrime Konvention', *Jura*, 26 (2004), 379–85

Schneiderhan, P., 'EU-Terrorlisten: Beginn rechtsstaatlicher Verfahren?', *DRiZ*, 87 (2009), 108–9

Schoppa, K., *Europol im Verbund der Europäischen Sicherheitsagenturen* (Berlin: Duncker & Humblot, 2013)

Schork, A., and Reichling, T., 'Neues Strafrecht aus Brüssel? Europäische Kommission forciert Verschärfung des Kapitalmarktstrafrechts und Einführung eines Unternehmensstrafrechts', *StraFo*, 19 (2012), 125–8

Schröder, C., *Europäische Richtlinien und deutsches Strafrecht: Eine Untersuchung über den Einfluss europäischer Richtlinien gemäß Art. 249 Abs. 3 EGV auf das deutsche Strafrecht* (Berlin et al.: de Gruyter, 2002)

'Die Europäisierung des Strafrechts nach Art. 83 Abs. 2 AEUV am Beispiel des Marktmissbrauchsrechts: Anmerkungen zu einem Fehlstart', *HRRS*, 14 (2013), 253–63

'Perspektiven der Europäisierung des Strafrechts nach Lissabon: Neues Denken oder alte Fehler?', in Hellmann, U., and Schröder, C., eds., *Festschrift für Hans Achenbach* (Heidelberg et al.: C. F. Müller, 2011), 491–508

'Zur Europäisierung der Fahrlässigkeits- und Unterlassungsdelikte', *NStZ*, 26 (2006), 669–73

Schuhr, J., 'Anmerkung BGH 1 StR 544/13', *NStZ*, 34 (2014), 330–1

Schumann, K. H., 'Das 41. StrÄndG zur Bekämpfung der Computerkriminalität', *NStZ*, 27 (2007), 675–80

Schützendübel, C., *Die Bezugnahme auf EU-Verordnungen in Blankettstrafgesetzen* (Baden-Baden: Nomos Verlagsgesellschaft, 2012)

Schwarzenegger, C., 'Die internationale Harmonisierung des Computer- und Internetstrafrechts durch die Convention on Cybercrime vom 23. November 2001', in Donatsch, A., Forster, M., and Schwarzenegger, C., eds., *Strafrecht, Strafprozessrecht und Menschenrechte: Festschrift für Stefan Trechsel zum 65. Geburtstag* (Zürich et al.: Schulthess, 2002), 305–26

Schwedischer Reichstag, 'Begründete Stellungnahme des schwedischen Reichstags zu dem Vorschlag für eine Richtlinie des Europäischen Parlaments und des Rates über die strafrechtliche Bekämpfung von gegen die finanziellen Interessen der Europäischen Union gerichtetem Betrug (COM(2012)0363 – C7-0192/2012 – 2012/0193(COD)), 23.10.2012', Mitteilung 86/2012, at www.europarl.europa .eu/sides/getDoc.do?pubRef=-//EP//NONSGML+COMPARL+PE-498.056 +01+DOC+WORD+V0//DE&language=DE, last accessed 27 January 2018

Seminara, S., 'Die europäische Entwicklung des Strafrechts im Finanzmarktbereich aus italienischer Sicht', in Arnold, J., Burkhardt, B., Gropp, W., Heine, G., Koch, H.-G., Lagodny, O., Perron, W., and Walther, S., eds., *Menschengerechtes Strafrecht: Festschrift für Albin Eser zum 70. Geburtstag* (Munich: C. H. Beck, 2005), 847–72

Sicurella, R., 'Some Reflections on the Need for a General Theory of the Competence of the European Union in Criminal Law', in Klip, A., ed., *Substantive Criminal law of the European Union* (Antwerp et al.: Maklu, 2011), 233–49

Sieber, U., '§24: Computerkriminalität', in Sieber, U., Satzger, H., and Heintschel von Heinegg, B., eds., *Europäisches Strafrecht* (Baden-Baden: Nomos Verlagsgesellschaft, 2014), 435–68

'§26: Urheberstrafrecht', in Sieber, U., Satzger, H., and Heintschel von Heinegg, B., eds., *Europäisches Strafrecht* (Baden-Baden: Nomos Verlagsgesellschaft, 2014), 486–509

'Subventionsbetrug und Steuerhinterziehung zum Nachteil der Europäischen Gemeinschaft', *ZStrR*, 115 (1996), 357–94

'Die Zukunft des Europäischen Strafrechts', *ZStW*, 121 (2009), 1–67

Sieber, U., and Vogel, B., *Terrorismusfinanzierung: Prävention im Spannungsfeld von internationalen Vorgaben und nationalem Tatstrafrecht* (Berlin: Duncker & Humblot, 2015)

Simitis, S., 'Übermittlung der Daten von Flugpassagieren in die USA: Dispens vom Datenschutz?', *NJW*, 59 (2006), 2011–14

Simon, P., 'The Criminalisation Power of the EU after Lisbon and the Principle of Democratic Legitimacy', *NJECL*, 3 (2012), 242–56

Simonato, M., 'Directive 2014/42/EU and Non-conviction Based Confiscation: A Step Forward on Asset Recovery', *NJECL*, 6 (2015), 213–28

Sinn, A., 'Rechtsvergleichende Beobachtungen der europaweiten Strafverfolgung der organisierten Kriminalität', *NK*, 19 (2007), 100–5

Soesters, F., *Die Insiderhandelsverbote des Wertpapierhandelsgesetzes* (Frankfurt a. M. et al.: Peter lang, 2002)

Soschinka, H., and Heller, R. E., 'Verschärfungen im Waffenrecht 2009', *NVwZ*, 28 (2009), 993–8

Soyka, T., 'Einschränkungen des Betrugstatbestands durch sekundäres Gemeinschaftsrecht am Beispiel der Richtlinie 2005/29/EG über unlautere Geschäftspraktiken', *wistra*, 26 (2007), 127–33

Staats, J.-F., 'Verweisung und Grundgesetz', in Rödig, J., ed., *Studien zu einer Theorie der Gesetzgebung* (Berlin et al.: Springer, 1976), 244–60

Staiger, I., 'Trafficking in Children for the Purpose of Sexual Exploitation in the EU', *Eur. J. Cr.*, 13 (2005), 603–24

Stefanuc, R., 'Corruption, or How to Tame the Shrew with the EU Stick: The New Anti-corruption Initiative of the European Commission', *ERA Forum*, 12 (2011), 427–43

Stegmann, F., *Artenschutz-Strafrecht* (Konstanz: Hartung-Gorre, 2000)

Stessens, G., 'Money Laundering', *RIDP*, 77 (2006), 201–9

Stuckenberg, C.-F., '§10: Allgemeiner Teil eines europäischen Strafrechts', in Böse, M., ed., *Enzyklopädie Europarecht: Europäisches Strafrecht mit polizeilicher Zusammenarbeit* (Baden-Baden: Nomos Verlagsgesellschaft, 2013), 379–412

Šugmann Stubbs, K., and Jager, M., 'Europäisches Strafrecht als Instrument europäischer Integration?', *KritV*, 91 (2008), 57–72

Suhr, O., 'Strafrechtsharmonisierung in der EU etc.', *ZEuS*, 11 (2008), 45–80

Summers, S., 'EU Criminal Law and the Regulation of Information and Communication Technology', *BJCLCJ*, 3 (2015), 48–60

Sunderland, J., Balbirnie, E., Korpelainen, S., Mathis, J., Armstrong, J., 'Study on the Legal Framework for the Protection of EU Financial Interests by Criminal Law, RS 2011/07 – Final Report', 4 May 2012, at http://ec.europa.eu/justice/criminal/files/study-protection-of-eu-financial-interests_en.pdf, last accessed 27 January 2018

Suominen, A., 'The Characteristics of Nordic Criminal Law in the Setting of EU Criminal Law', *EuCLR*, 1 (2011), 170–87

Swoboda, S., 'Die Pflicht zur rahmenbeschlusskonformen Auslegung im deutschen Strafverfahren', *HRRS*, 15 (2014), 10–21

Taseva, E., 'Anti-corruption Package: Towards a More Efficient Fight against Corruption?', *NJECL*, 3 (2012), 344–62

Thiele, A., *Individualrechtsschutz vor dem Europäischen Gerichtshof durch die Nichtigkeitsklage* (Baden-Baden: Nomos Verlagsgesellschaft, 2006)

Thiele, A., 'Das Rechtsschutzsystem nach dem Vertrag von Lissabon: (K)ein Schritt nach vorn?', *EuR*, 45 (2010), 30–51

Thomas, S., 'Die Anwendung europäischen materiellen Rechts im Strafverfahren', *NJW*, 44 (1991), 2233–8

Tiedemann, K., 'Anmerkung zu EuGH, Urteil v. 21.9.1989 – Rs. 68/88', *EuZW*, 2 (1990), 100–1

'Europäisches Gemeinschaftsrecht und Strafrecht', *NJW*, 46 (1993), 23–31

'Gegenwart und Zukunft des Europäischen Strafrechts', *ZStW*, 116 (2004), 945–58

Wirtschaftsstrafrecht: Einführung und Allgemeiner Teil mit wichtigen Rechtstexten (Munich, Franz Vahlen, 4th edn, 2014)

Tiegs, H. W. A., *Betrugsbekämpfung in der Europäischen Gemeinschaft: Eine Bestandsaufnahme des englischen und deutschen Strafrechts zum Schutz der EG-Finanzinteressen* (Berlin: BWV, 2006)

Turner, J. I., 'The Expressive Dimension of EU Criminal Law', *AmJCompL*, 60 (2012), 555–83

Vagliasindi, G. M., 'The European Harmonisation in the Sector of Protection of the Environment through Criminal Law', *NJECL*, 3 (2012), 320–31

Valdés, A.R., 'The Mutual Recognition Principle in Criminal Matters: A Review', *ERA Forum*, 16 (2015), 291–303

Vervaele, J. A. E., 'La europeización del Derecho penal y la dimensión penal de la integración europea', *RP*, 15 (2005), 169–83

Villacampa Estiarte, C., 'The European Directive on Preventing and Combating Trafficking in Human Beings and the Victim-Centric Treatment of This Criminal Phenomenon', *EuCLR*, 2 (2012), 291–317

Vogel, B., and Maillart, J.B. 'Recent Developments in EU Anti-money Laundering', *eucrim*, 11 (2016), 179–83

Vogel, J., 'Criminal Responsibility: Parties to the Offence', in Cullen, P., ed., *Enlarging the Fight against Fraud in the European Union: Penal and Administrative Sanctions, Settlement, Whistleblowing and Corpus Juris in the Candidate Countries* (Cologne: Bundesanzeiger, 2004), 45–73

'Geldwäsche: Ein europaweit harmonisierter Straftatbestand?', *ZStW*, 109 (1997), 335–56

'Harmonisierung des Strafrechts in der Europäischen Union', *GA*, 150 (2003), 314

'Die Kompetenz der EG zur Einführung supranationaler Sanktionen', in Dannecker, G., ed., *Die Bekämpfung des Subventionsbetruges im EG-Bereich* (Cologne: Bundesanzeiger, 1993), 170–87

'Scalping als Kurs- und Marktpreismanipulation', *NStZ*, 24 (2004), 252–6

'Strafrechtlicher Schutz des Euro vor Geldfälschung', *ZRP*, 35 (2002), 7–11

'Why Is the Harmonisation of Penal Law Necessary?', in Klip, A., and van der Wilt, H., eds., *Harmonisation and Harmonising Measures in Criminal Law* (Amsterdam: Koninklijke Nederlandse Akademie van Wetenschappen, 2002), 55–64

Vogel, J., and Brodowski, D., '§6: Besonderer Teil des supranationalen Strafrechts (Überblick)', in Sieber, U., Satzger, H., and Heintschel von Heinegg, B., eds., *Europäisches Strafrecht* (Baden-Baden: Nomos Verlagsgesellschaft, 2014), 177–92

von Unger, M., 'Pupino: Der EuGH vergemeinschaftet das intergouvernementale Recht', *NVwZ*, 25 (2006), 46–9

Vormbaum, M., *Schutz der Rechtsgüter von EU-Staaten durch das deutsche Strafrecht* (Münster: LIT, 2005)

Walter, T., 'Inwieweit erlaubt die Europäische Verfassung ein europäisches Strafgesetz?', *ZStW*, 117 (2005), 912–33

Walther, F., 'Zur Verschränkung von Strafprozess-, Europa- und Verfassungsrecht', *ZJS*, 6 (2013), 16–23

Wattier, I., 'La lutte contre léxplotiation sexuelle des enfants et la pédopornographie et la majorité sexuelle', *RIDP*, 77 (2006), 223–35

Weber, S., 'Die Strafbarkeit der Holocaustleugnung in der Europäischen Union', *ZRP*, 41 (2008), 21–4

Weidemann, J., 'Keine strafrechtlichen Konsequenzen des Urteils des EuGH vom 3.3.2005', *wistra*, 25 (2006), 41–5

Weigend, T., 'Der Entwurf einer Europäischen Verfassung und das Strafrecht', *ZStW*, 116 (2004), 275–303

Weigend, T., 'Societas Delinquere Non Potest? A German Perspective', *JICJ*, 6 (2008), 927–45

Weiß, H., '§25: Rassismus und Fremdenfeindlichkeit', in Sieber, U., Satzger, H., and Heintschel von Heinegg, B., eds., *Europäisches Strafrecht* (Baden-Baden: Nomos Verlagsgesellschaft, 2014), 469–85

Weißer, B., '§9: Angleichung von Strafvorschriften zur grenzüberschreitenden (organisierten) Kriminalität', in Böse, M., ed., *Enzyklopädie Europarecht: Europäisches Strafrecht mit polizeilicher Zusammenarbeit* (Baden-Baden: Nomos Verlagsgesellschaft, 2013), 337–78

'Strafgesetzgebung durch die EU: Nicht nur ein Recht, sondern auch eine Pflicht?', *GA*, 161 (2014), 433–52

Weisser, N.-F., 'The Effectiveness of the Global Combat against the Financing of Terrorism for Preventing Terrorist Activity', *ZIS*, 8 (2013), 343–9

Weyembergh, A., 'The Functions of Approximation of Penal Legislation within the European Union', *MaastJECompL*, 12 (2005), 155–72

L'harmonisation des législations: Conditions de l'espace pénal européen et révélateur de ses tensions (Bruxelles: Ed. de l'Université de Bruxelles, 2004)

'La lutte contre la traite et le trafic d'êtres humains', *RIDP*, 77 (2006), 211–21

White, S., 'Harmonisation of Criminal Law under the First Pillar', *E. L. Rev.*, 31 (2006), 81–92

Wilson, S., 'The New Market Abuse Regulation and Directive on Criminal Sanctions for Market Abuse: European Capital Markets Law and New Global Trends in Financial Crime Enforcement', *ERA Forum*, 16 (2015), 427–46

Wolf, S., 'Die Modernisierung des deutschen Antikorruptionsstrafrechts durch internationale Vorgaben', *NJW*, 59 (2006), 2735–8

Wohlers, W., 'Insiderhandel und Kursmanipulation', *ZStW*, 125 (2013), 443–80

Wolter, K. M., *Vorabentscheidungsverfahren und Beschleunigungsgebot in Strafsachen* (Berlin: Ducnker & Humblot, 2011)

Zeder, F., 'Europastrafrecht: Aktueller Stand', *öAnwBl*, 70 (2008), 249–67

'Europastrafrecht, Vertrag von Lissabon und Stockholmer Programm: Mehr Grundrechtsschutz?', *EuR*, 47 (2012), 34–60

Zeitler, H. E., 'Environmental Criminal Law', *RIDP*, 77 (2006), 255–61

Zentes, U., and Glaab, S., 'Regulatorische Auswirkungen des Vorschlags der 4. EU-Geldwäscherichtlinie', *BB*, 2013, 707–14

Ziemann, S., and Ziethen, J., 'Die neue EU-Richtlinie zur Bekämpfung von Kindesmissbrauch und Kinderpornografie', *ZRP*, 45 (2012), 168–71

Zieschang, F., 'Der Einfluss der EU auf das deutsche Strafrecht', in Sieber, U., Dannecker, G., Kindhäuser, U., Vogel, J., and Walter, T., eds., *Strafrecht und Wirtschaftsrecht, Festschrift für Klaus Tiedemann zum 70. Geburtstag* (Cologne et al.: Carl Heymanns, 2008), 1303–20

'Das Übereinkommen zum Schutz der finanziellen Interessen der EG und seine Auswirkungen auf das deutsche Strafrecht', *EuZW*, 8 (1997), 78–83

Zimmermann, F., 'Die Auslegung künftiger EU-Strafrechtskompetenzen nach dem Lissabon-Urteil des Bundesverfassungsgerichts', *Jura*, 32 (2009), 844–51

'Mehr Fragen als Antworten: Die 2. EuGH-Entscheidung zur Strafrechtsharmonisierung mittels EG-Richtlinien (Rs. C-440/05)', *NStZ*, 28 (2008), 662–7

'Offene strafrechtliche Fragen im Zusammenhang mit der europäischen E-101-Bescheinigung für Wanderarbeiter', *ZIS*, 2 (2007), 407–18

'Tendenzen zur Strafrechtsangleichung in der EU: Dargestellt anhand der Bestrebungen zur Bekämpfung von Terrorismus, Rassismus und illegaler Beschäftigung', *ZIS*, 4 (2009), 1–10

'Wann ist der Einsatz von Strafrecht auf europäischer Ebene sinnvoll?', *ZRP*, 42 (2009), 74–7

Zimmermann, F., Glaser, S., and Motz, A., 'Mutual Recognition and Its Implications for the Gathering of Evidence in Criminal Proceedings', *EuCLR*, 1 (2011), 56–79

Zöller, M. A., 'Europäische Strafgesetzgebung', *ZIS*, 4 (2009), 340–9

'Neue unionsrechtliche Strafgesetzgebungskompetenzen nach dem Vertrag von Lissabon', in Baumeister, P., Roth, W., and Ruthig, J., eds., *Staat, Verwaltung und Rechtsschutz: Festschrift für Wolf-Rüdiger Schenke zum 70. Geburtstag* (Berlin: Duncker & Humblot, 2011), 579–98

'Strafrechtliche Verfolgung von Terrorismus und politischem Extremismus unter dem Einfluss des Rechts der EU', *ZIS*, 9 (2014), 402–11

'Vorratsdatenspeicherung zwischen nationaler und europäischer Strafverfolgung', *GA*, 154 (2007), 393–414

'Zur Auslegung des Begriffs der kriminellen Vereinigung in §129 StGB im europäischen Kontext', *JZ*, 65 (2010), 908–12

Zuleeg, M., 'Der Beitrag des Strafrechts zur europäischen Integration', in Sieber, U., ed., *Europäische Einigung und Europäisches Strafrecht* (Cologne et al.: Carl Heymanns, 1993), 41–60;

Zweigert, K., 'Der Einfluss des Europäischen Gemeinschaftsrechts auf die Rechtsordnungen der Mitgliedstaaten', *RabelsZ*, 28 (1964), 601–43

4

Procedural Law

Police and Judicial Co-operation

A. Foundations

Case 1

1 D lives near the German–Belgian border. After shopping in Belgium, he is followed back to his apartment on German territory by a Belgian police patrol. There it transpires that the Belgian officials had confused D's car with another German car, the driver of which had fled to the German border after being involved in a fatal traffic accident (cf. Art. 41(4)(a) indent 14 CISA). D requests that a German court determine whether the police officers' hot pursuit (Art. 41 CISA) was lawful. Will D be successful?[1] ➔ mn. 7

2 With the **Lisbon Treaty**, the police and judicial co-operation that was formerly part of the third pillar[2] became 'communitised' and transferred to the area of 'justice and home affairs'.[3] However, the measures passed under the old regime still remained valid initially and the CJEU continued to hold its only limited review competence for a transitional period of five years after the Lisbon Treaty's entry into force; that is, until 1 December 2014.[4] Within the still existing 'area of freedom, security and justice',[5] security is now to be guaranteed by the 'co-ordination and co-operation between police and judicial authorities and other competent authorities'.[6]

3 **Judicial co-operation** within the meaning of Arts. 82–6 TFEU is based on the **principle of mutual recognition.**[7] It includes measures giving this principle concrete form by laying down rules and procedures that ensure recognition[8] and *facilitating co-operation between Member States*, namely to prevent and settle conflicts of jurisdiction,[9] to support the training of the judiciary and judicial staff and to facilitate co-operation between judicial or equivalent authorities in relation to proceedings in criminal matters and the enforcement of decisions.[10] As a consequence, in the field of European **mutual legal assistance**[11] we can note a development from classic treaty-based assistance within the framework of the

Council of Europe and the third pillar of the EU towards a system of executive assistance based upon mutual recognition. Furthermore, the EP and Council can jointly lay down **minimum rules for the approximation of law** in the ordinary legislative procedure if this is necessary to facilitate the mutual recognition of judgments and judicial decisions and police and judicial co-operation in criminal matters having a cross-border dimension.[12] Finally, the judicial co-operation is complemented by the **institutionalisation** of European cross-border prosecution through *Eurojust*[13] and the *European Public Prosecutor's Office*.[14]

4 **Police co-operation** pursuant to Arts. 87–9 TFEU includes the police, customs and 'other specialised law enforcement services in relation to the prevention, detection and investigation of criminal offences'.[15] For this purpose, measures for the *exchange of information* (collection, storage, processing, and exchange of relevant information)[16] with the aim of mutual **availability**[17] as well as measures for the *training of staff* and joint *analytical work*[18] may be adopted. Measures to improve *operative* co-operation, such as the relatively successful joint investigation teams (JITs),[19] can in principle be established by the Council acting unanimously.[20] Police co-operation also includes the further development of *Europol*.[21]

5 A further important, parallel legal basis for police and judicial co-operation is the **Convention Implementing the Schengen Agreement (CISA)**.[22] The relevant regulations can be found in **Title III** ('Police and Security'), especially in Chapters 1 to 5.[23] The title 'Police and Security' is both misleading and meaningful; on the one hand, it fails to suggest that this title also contains important laws on (judicial) legal assistance, while on the other hand it draws attention to the Schengen Convention's primary orientation towards *police co-operation*.[24] This is set out in Chapter 1 (Arts. 39–47). Here, the Contracting Parties[25] undertake to ensure police exchange of information[26] and permit cross-border surveillance[27] and hot pursuit,[28] and may conclude bilateral agreements providing for the secondment of liaison officers.[29] The rules on *cross-border surveillance* and hot pursuit are of particular significance.[30] The continuation of surveillance on the territory of another Contracting Party in principle requires that Party's prior authorisation;[31] however, where there are 'particularly urgent reasons' – in the case of particularly serious crime[32] – action may be taken without authorisation, although the Contracting Party in

question must be notified immediately.[33] The officers engaged in surveillance are bound by the law of the State in whose territory they are operating (*locus regit actum*), they must be able to prove that they are acting in an official capacity and have basically no powers of intervention without the support of the officials of the territorial State (they may use their weapons only in self-defence, and entering private places is prohibited).[34] *Hot pursuit* – that is, the pursuit of a person caught in the act[35] – onto foreign territory is permissible under similar conditions: here, too, in particularly urgent cases – which presumably are the rule with criminals 'caught in the act' – action may be taken without prior authorisation of the Contracting Party in question for certain listed[36] and other extraditable offences.[37] The pursuing officers only have the right to apprehend a person in exceptional cases if the officers of the Contracting Party are not on the scene at once,[38] as long as the Schengen MS in whose territory the pursuit is taking place – such as Germany – has granted pursuing foreign officers the right to detain suspects.[39] The general conditions[40] are more or less the same as those for cross-border surveillance,[41] especially the locus rule applies once more.[42]

6 The scope of application of these options for cross-border police action and the legal problems they pose come into particular focus when the question of an **effective legal remedy** of the persons affected is raised (cf. case 1). It is not possible to derive any legal remedy *directly* from the CISA itself.[43] In particular, Art. 41(5)(a) CISA, according to which pursuing officers are bound by the law of the State on whose territory they are acting, does not imply that their actions can be made subject to the review of that State's courts.[44] Furthermore, the territorial State cannot be held liable for the actions of foreign police officers; their actions are attributed to the State they belong to.[45] Any other view would run counter to CISA's very aim, which is precisely that the feared loss of security due to the disappearance of internal borders can be countered if necessary by a State exercising its *original sovereign power on foreign territory* through hot pursuit.[46] Conversely, any civil law *claim for damages* is bound by the law of the State on whose territory the damage occurred.[47] The officers operating in the territory of another Contracting Party are regarded as officers of that Party with respect to offences committed against them or by them.[48]

Solution, case 1

7 Cross-border action within the CISA framework is *attributed to the acting officers' State*, so that *Belgian* police officers cannot exercise *German* sovereign power and hence the German legal remedies (pursuant to Art. 19(4) GG) do not apply (conversely, German legal remedies would be possible if German officers acted on foreign territory). As a result, Belgian officers thus exercised Belgian sovereign power on German territory, so that D must refer to the Belgian courts – in the same way as if he had been apprehended on Belgian territory *before* reaching the German border.[49] However, D may be able to claim damages according to German law.

B. Approximation of Procedural Law

8 The approximation[50] of procedural law[51] is possible according to **Art. 82(2) TFEU** if it is '*necessary*' to facilitate mutual recognition.[52] In this case, minimum rules can be established by means of directives adopted in accordance with the ordinary legislative procedure, which must, however, 'take into account the *differences* between the legal traditions and systems of the Member States'.[53] By contrast, if 'fundamental aspects' of a national criminal justice system are affected, MS may activate the *emergency brake procedure*.[54] Art. 82(2) lit. (a) to (c) TFEU lists three areas as the objects of approximation, although these can be added to by the unanimous[55] decision of the Council after the EP's consent has been obtained:[56]

- Lit. (a) permits the harmonisation of rules on the **admissibility of evidence**, so that evidence gathered abroad is more easily recognised in internal criminal proceedings.
- Lit. (b) provides for approximation in regard to individual procedural rights; here the '**rights of individuals**' are only to include such rights as are of *direct* benefit to the individual.[57] If one were to go beyond this, including rules that affect the legal position of the individual only indirectly, then the entirety of procedural law would become the object of approximation, as nearly all rules in criminal proceedings – from those on the judge's impartiality to those on the exclusion of evidence – impinge upon the defendant's legal position. Thus far, several Directives, already mentioned in Chapter 2, have been adopted pursuant to the Stockholm Programme and further are in preparation.[58] Even prior to the Lisbon Treaty, regulations on the treatment

of sentences *in absentia* were standardised in various framework decisions.[59]

- Finally, lit. (c) permits approximation of the **rights of the victims of crime**. The EU has already made use of this competence, rescinding the FD on the standing of victims in criminal proceedings which was passed before Lisbon and replacing it with new, more extensive regulations.[60]

C. Legal Assistance

I. Preliminary Remarks: From Classic Treaty-Based to Executive Legal Assistance Based on Mutual Recognition

9 According to a widely used **threefold distinction**, legal assistance includes the areas of *extradition*, *other mutual assistance* in criminal matters (such as the questioning of witnesses, gathering of evidence, searches and confiscation) and *enforcement assistance* (regarding the execution of foreign judgments and decisions).[61] As a State's sovereign power is restricted to its own territory,[62] mutual assistance traditionally takes place on the basis of international law treaties.[63] Thus a range of (criminal) law conventions on the above-mentioned areas were adopted in Europe under the aegis of the Council of Europe and, in accordance with Art. 34(2)(d) TEU old version, within the framework of the European Union. We will deal with the most important of these instruments in more detail in the respective sections on the different forms of legal assistance below; here, a general overview is sufficient.

10 The **CoE conventions** are, in chronological order (as of 15 February 2018), the following:

- European Convention on **Extradition** (EuCExt) of 13 December 1957[64] with AP I of 15 October 1975,[65] AP II of 17 March 1978,[66] AP III of 10 November 2010[67] and AP IV of 20 September 2012;[68]
- European Convention on **Mutual Assistance in Criminal Matters** (EuCMACM) of 20 April 1959[69] with AP I of 17 March 1978[70] and AP II of 8 November 2001;[71]
- European Convention on the **Transfer of Sentenced Persons** (TransferC) of 21 March 1983[72] with AP of 18 December 1997 and its amendment of 22 November 2017;[73]
- European Convention on the **Supervision of** Conditionally Sentenced or Conditionally Released **Offenders** of 30 November 1964;[74]
- European Convention on the **International Validity of Criminal Judgments** of 28 May 1970;[75]

- European Convention on the **Transfer of Proceedings in Criminal Matters** of 15 May 1972;[76]
- Additional Protocol of 15 March 1978 on the European Convention on **Information on Foreign Law** of 7 June 1968;[77]
- European Convention on the Control of the Acquisition and Possession of **Firearms** by individuals of 28 June 1978;[78]
- Convention on the Protection of Individuals with regard to **Automatic Processing of Personal Data** of 28 January 1981;[79]
- Convention on **Compensation to Victims of Violent Crimes** of 24 November 1983;[80]
- Convention on **Insider Trading** of 20 April 1989[81] and its AP of 11 September 1989;[82]
- Agreement on **Illicit Traffic by Sea**, implementing Art. 17 of the Vienna Drug Control Convention[83] of 31 January 1995;[84]
- Convention on **Cybercrime** of 23 November 2001[85] and concerning the Criminalisation of Acts of a Racist and Xenophobic Nature committed through Computer Systems of 28 January 2003;[86]
- Convention on **Laundering**, Search, Seizure and Confiscation of the Proceeds from Crime and on the **Financing of Terrorism** of 16 May 2005.[87]

11 At **EU level**, the relevant intergovernmental instruments enter, as a general rule, into force when adopted by at least half of the Member States.[88] Several MS have made use of the option to declare the conventions *provisionally applicable*, sometimes making reservations or declarations, although such declarations are only applicable in relation to those Contracting States that have made the same declaration. For example, for Germany, as of 27 January 2018, the following agreements and conventions were (provisionally) applicable:[89]

- the Convention of 27 September 1996 relating to **extradition** between the EU MS (EUCExt);[90]
- the Convention of 10 March 1995 on the **simplified extradition** procedure between the EU MS (EU Simplified Extradition Convention);[91]
- the Agreement between the MS of the European Communities on the Simplification and Modernisation of Methods of **Transmitting Extradition Requests** of 26 May 1989;[92]
- the Convention on **Mutual Assistance** in Criminal Matters between EU MS of 29 May 2000 (EUMAC)[93] and the AP of 16 October 2001;[94]

- The Convention between the EC Member States on the **Enforcement** of Foreign Criminal Sentences of 13 November 1991 (EC Enforcement Convention).[95]

12 The EU conventions basically supplement the corresponding CoE **'mother conventions'**,[96] such as the 1996 EUCExt which supplements the 1957 (CoE) EuCExt.[97] In a nutshell, the aim is to simplify and facilitate mutual assistance, for example making the process of extradition between Member States less complicated and harmonising the substantive conditions of extradition.[98] The CoE conventions – EuCExt, EuCMACM and the TransferC – are supplemented by the CISA;[99] this is therefore described below after the respective CoE conventions.

13 The **EU's agreements on extradition and mutual assistance with the USA** are of particular significance,[100] as they mark the first time that the Union entered into an agreement on matters of criminal law with a third State. These agreements aim to supplement the bilateral agreements of the MS with the USA.[101] Both agreements contain regulations that conflict with the EU's rights focus pursuant to Art. 6 TEU and must be seen in the context of the altered criminal justice climate following the terrorist attacks of 11 September 2001:[102] thus Art. 13 of the Extradition Agreement states that extradition *may* also take place if the requesting State, according to whose laws the person in question may also be *sentenced to death* – in this case, the USA – provides assurance that no death sentence will be passed or, even less, that it will at least not be enforced; here the ECHR comes into play as an obstacle to extradition, as we will see below.[103] Further, according to the explanatory note on Art. 9 of the Mutual Assistance Agreement, any 'categorical or systematic', refusal to transfer *personal data* on the grounds of a 'broad ... application of data protection principles' is precluded.[104] In 2010, the EU also concluded a Mutual Assistance Agreement with **Japan**, which entered into force on 2 January 2011.[105] Last but not least, the EU concluded in 2011 and 2014 two agreements on the conditions of *transfer of suspected pirates* and associated seized property with Mauritius[106] and Tanzania.[107]

14 While the above-mentioned mutual assistance agreements are characterised by a synallagmatic relationship of dependency between the requesting and the requested State, in the case of mutual assistance based on the principle of **mutual recognition**[108] the request becomes an order, the requesting State becomes the issuing State and the requested State becomes the executing State – take, for example, the terminology of the **European Arrest Warrant (EAW)**[109] as the paradigmatic instrument, to be discussed in detail below.[110] Instead of a petition (request) we are dealing with an order (warrant), an extradition becomes a surrender (with the EAW), and the tedious treaty-based process of admissibility and authorisation thus becomes an **executive transfer procedure** – at least according to the normative aspirations of the EAW and the subsequent instruments.[111] The resulting increased intertwinement of criminal and mutual assistance procedures calls for consistent and uniform basic rights standards.[112] These subsequent mutual recognition instruments were originally also adopted as Framework Decisions (FDs), but with the Lisbon Treaty they have largely been replaced by Directives. There are, on the one hand, instruments on other forms of legal assistance, especially evidence gathering, and, on the other hand, enforcement instruments. The relevant ones will be analysed in more detail below,[113] but here they are listed:[114]

15 Instruments of *other legal assistance*, especially evidence gathering:

- FD on the Execution of Orders Freezing Property or Evidence ('FD on **Freezing**');[115]
- FD on the Mutual Recognition of Confiscation Orders ('FD **Confiscation**');[116]
- FD on the **European Evidence Warrant** (FD EEW) for the Purpose of Obtaining Objects, Documents and Data for Use in Proceedings in Criminal Matters;[117] in this regard the Commission's **Green Paper** on '**obtaining evidence** in criminal matters from one Member State to another' is of fundamental importance;[118]
- Directive regarding a **European Investigation Order (EIO) in criminal matters** in 2014,[119] replacing the FD on Freezing in part (concerning the freezing of evidence) and the FD EEW as a whole;[120] consequently, the FD EEW has been repealed by Regulation (EU) 2016/95.[121]

16 Instruments of *enforcement assistance*:

- Commission **Green Paper on Sanctions**;[122]
- FD on the Mutual Recognition of Judgments in Criminal Matters for the Purpose of their Enforcement (**European Enforcement Order**);[123]
- FD on the Mutual Recognition of **Financial Penalties**;[124]
- FD on the **European Supervision Order** in pre-trial proceedings (FD ESO);[125]
- FD on **Taking Account of Convictions** in the Member States of the EU in the Course of New Criminal Proceedings;[126]

- FD on the Mutual Recognition of **Judgments and Probation Decisions** with a View to the Supervision of Probation Measures and Alternative Sanctions;[127]
- Directive on the **European Protection Order** (EPO);[128]
- Last, but not least, see also the FD on the Organisation and Content of the Exchange of Information Extracted from the **Criminal Record**,[129] concentrating the relevant information in the convicted person's Member State of nationality[130] and technically implemented by the **European Criminal Records Information System** (ECRIS).[131]

II. Extradition and Surrender

1. Extradition (Applicable European Conventions)

Case 2 (witness protection case)

17 The prosecuted person, who provided extensive testimony against a Belorussian–Lithuanian group of criminals, is in a witness protection programme in Germany. The North Rhine-Westphalian State Office of Criminal Investigation (*Landeskriminalamt*) classed the prosecuted person as at extreme risk. Lithuania requests his extradition through a European Arrest Warrant. According to the Lithuanian authorities, the prosecuted person cannot be put in witness protection in Lithuania for legal reasons. Is extradition admissible?[132] → mn. 42

a) Preliminary Remarks

18 'Extradition' concerns cases in which one State – the *requesting* State – requests that another State – the *requested* State – surrender a person who is currently staying in the requested State and is sought by the requesting State for the purposes of prosecution or – if a sentence has already been passed – enforcement.[133] The **extradition process** is thus set in motion due to the request of a foreign (requesting) State. The domestic process can be broken down into **two stages**, the (legal–judicial) admissibility and the (political–executive) authorisation procedure.[134] The combination of a legal review by a court and the actual extradition decision by an executive authority is common in all EU Member States in extradition proceedings with third (non-EAW) States, the only difference being the sequence of the two stages (either legal review or executive decision first) and the existence of procedural idiosyncrasies in some jurisdictions.

19 Thus, in **Germany** for example, in the *admissibility procedure*, the Higher Regional Court in whose district the person in question is residing[135] reviews the admissibility of the extradition in legal terms;[136] the affected person can file a *constitutional complaint* against its decision. In **Austria**, the investigative judge at the responsible court of first instance decides on the matter;[137] the person in question and the prosecution of the court of second instance can appeal against his or her decision.[138] In **Switzerland**, the authority responsible according to the law of the respective canton[139] prepares the extradition decision.[140] If the extradition is finally declared (legally) admissible, then the *authorisation procedure* follows. Here, the executive body – in Germany, the Federal or State Ministries of Justice and in Austria the Federal Ministry of Justice or an authority authorised by the ministry;[141] in Switzerland the Ministry, the Federal Department of Justice and Police[142] – decides on whether the extradition will be authorised, taking the foreign-policy implications into account.[143] Although the authorisation is an administrative act, it *cannot be challenged* in court;[144] the only condition of its lawfulness is that it was determined to be admissible *per curiam.*[145] The same two-step procedure – with the legal–judicial decision first, followed by the executive decision by the competent ministry (normally Ministry of Justice) – is applied in **Greece,**[146] **France,**[147] the **Netherlands,**[148] **Poland**[149] and **Hungary**.[150] In **Portugal**, the procedure is reversed, with the executive decision by the ministry coming first.[151] In **Italy**[152] and **Spain**[153] there is a three-step procedure with the government having to decide whether it wants to initiate extradition proceedings in the first place. In fact, however, this anticipated decision of the executive branch takes place in practically all jurisdictions, since it is the executive branch which normally receives the extradition request and thus has to take a decision on how to proceed. In the **UK**, the Extradition Act 2003 distinguishes between 'category 1' and 'category 2' territories, to be designated by the Secretary of State (§§1, 69) having a broad discretion; category 1 territories are those of the EAW system (plus Gibraltar); category 2 territories are the other countries with which the UK has an extradition treaty.[154] At any rate the UK also follows a two step judicial–executive approach with the courts (right up to the Supreme Court; on the 'appropriate judge' see §67) deciding on admissibility[155] and the Home Secretary on the authorisation (§§93 ff.),[156] albeit with a reduced role as compared to the pre-2003 situation.[157]

20 Although the EAW means that the EU conventions described in the following are only subsidiarily applicable, having a gap-closing function, it is nevertheless worth taking a closer look at them because of their remaining scope of application and the general principles of legal assistance they contain. One must not forget either that the CoE 'mother conventions' are applicable beyond the EU to all CoE Member States.

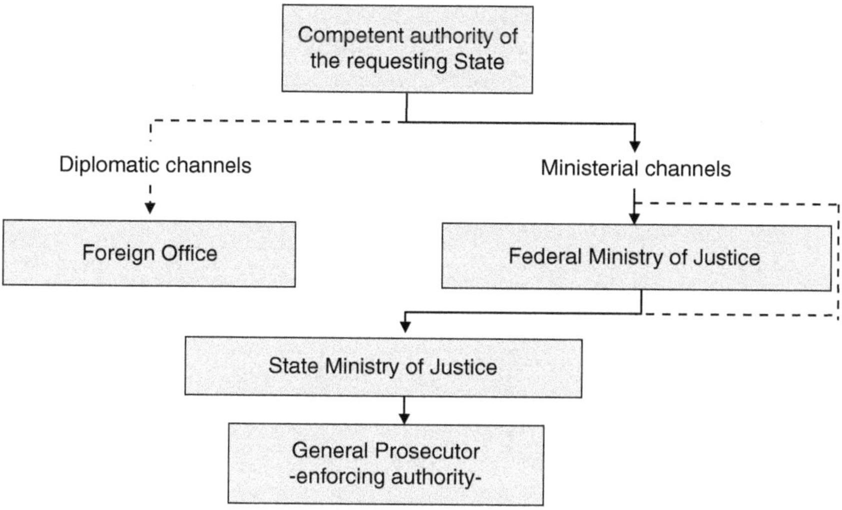

Figure 7 Extradition process according to the EuCExt – channels of communication (German case)

b) The European Convention on Extradition

21 The European Convention on Extradition (EuCExt) is the traditional European legal basis for extradition.[158] It is the **mother convention** of European treaty-based law on extradition adopted within the framework of the CoE. It sets out obligations to extradite persons for criminal prosecution and enforcement, as well as for the enforcement of reform and incapacitation measures.[159] The offence forming the basis of the extradition request must be generally extraditable – that is, constitute an offence in both the requesting and the requested State (**dual criminality**)[160] – must carry a maximum penalty (deprivation of liberty or detention order) of at least one year[161] and must not be past the statute of limitations.[162] Furthermore, there must not be any **obstacle to extradition** in the requested State.[163] *AP I* aims to restrict political offences as an obstacle to extradition; while *AP II* facilitates many aspects of extradition, such as extradition for fiscal offences;[164] and *AP III* opens up the option of a simplified extradition procedure. Figure 7 shows the process according to the Convention.

22 National extradition law generally operates in a subsidiary form with respect to international extradition treaties[165] which are part of

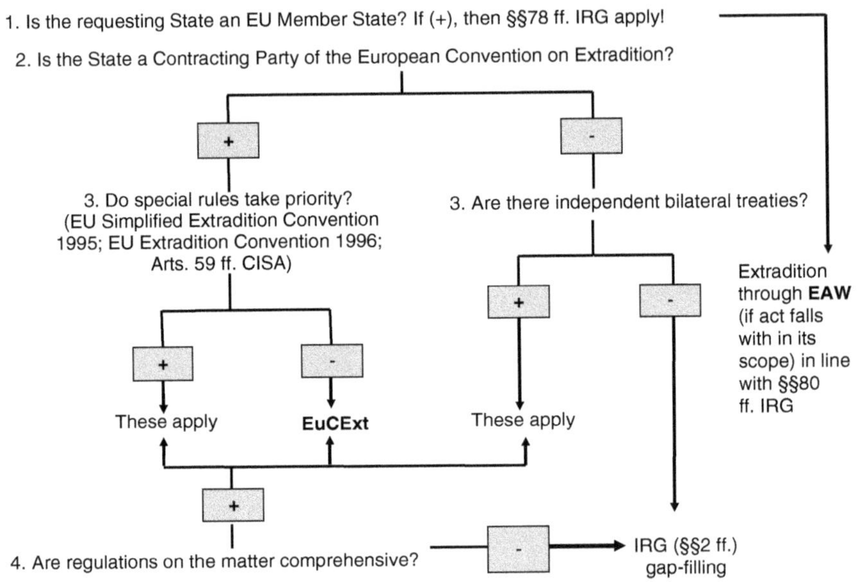

Figure 8 Review of requests for legal assistance (extradition from Germany)

internal law; accordingly, its function is to fill the gaps left by these treaties,[166] and this function applies particularly to the EuCExt.[167] Due to the large number of international extradition treaties, it is not an easy task to find the applicable law in an individual case.[168] Besides the EuCExt, further instruments may be applicable, such as the Convention's AP II and supplementary multilateral and bilateral treaties, as well as the applicable reservations and declarations and Arts. 59 ff. CISA.[169] The EuCExt goes beyond national law in particular in that it provides for a primary **obligation to extradite**, while national law normally only makes statements on the admissibility of extradition.[170] Figure 8 describes the complicated search for the right legal basis in case of an extradition requested from Germany.

23 When reviewing the admissibility of extradition, the competent national court must traditionally apply the principle of **dual criminality**[171] to ascertain whether the conduct the prosecuted person is charged with constitutes a criminal offence according to the law of both the requesting and the requested State.[172] Art. 2(1) EuCExt requires a maximum penalty of at least one year in the requesting and requested State. Yet Arts. 2 and 3 of the EU Convention on Extradition (EUCExt), to be looked at more closely at below, restrict the principle of dual criminality to the Union's area of freedom and justice. Art. 2(1) EUCExt lowers the required maximum penalty in the requested State to six months, and its Art. 3(1) further establishes exceptions for the areas of terrorism and organised crime.[173] In *treaty-based* extradition proceedings, **suspicion** is not examined, but assumed to exist on the basis of the foreign request. By contrast, for extradition without a treaty basis in the EuCExt or another agreement, reasonable suspicion needs to be established.[174] Furthermore, the extradition's admissibility depends on whether **reciprocity**[175] is guaranteed and whether the requesting State would be prepared to offer legal assistance should the situation be reversed.[176] Furthermore, in each extradition the principle of **speciality** must be observed, meaning that the extradited person will only be prosecuted for the offence on the grounds of which the extradition was granted.[177] As a consequence, speciality operates as an obstacle to prosecution and enforcement of sentences with regard to cases not included in the extradition request.[178] However, the State granting the request may dispense with adherence to the principle of speciality.[179] Furthermore, its protective function lapses if the person affected has not left the territory of the requesting State within 45 days after his final discharge or returns to this territory.[180] States may refuse to extradite their own nationals.[181]

24 Art. 16 EuCExt permits **provisional arrest** in urgent cases on the basis of the requested State's law.[182] This provisional (extradition) arrest may in no case exceed *forty days*.[183] National law may provide for a longer period in case of extradition proceedings without a treaty basis.[184] The time period *begins* the moment the person in question is apprehended and not, as was formerly advocated, at the time of the 'legal arrest'; that is, the authorisation of the provisional arrest.[185] Furthermore, the decision on whether a formal extradition detention order will be issued[186] – that is, whether the warrant for provisional arrest is converted into **one for continuous detention** (until extradition takes place) – must be reached before the deadline.[187] If the extradition documents are only received on the last working day of the time limit, or are incomplete, then no timely decision can be made and the prosecuted person is to be released.[188] Furthermore, it should be noted that due to its provisional nature Art. 16 EuCExt only refers to the **admissibility**

procedure, and therefore the decision on the (provisional) arrest[189] – such as that of the former Chilean dictator *Pinochet* in the United Kingdom based on a Spanish request – is purely legal in nature.

c) The Schengen Implementing Convention (CISA)

25 Chapter 4 (Arts. 59–66 CISA) regulates extradition and goes beyond the EuCExt (Art. 59) in that it mainly **abolishes obstacles** to extradition. Thus, as to the *statute of limitation*, the legal situation in the requesting State applies;[190] an *amnesty* and a *requirement of a formal criminal complaint* in the requested State do not form an obstacle to extradition in principle.[191] The Contracting States are obliged to extradite in the case of offences in the area of *excise taxes*.[192] The requests for extradition and transit can be made directly to the ministries responsible, listed in Art. 65(2) CISA. A **simplified extradition procedure** is possible – similarly to the EU Simplified Extradition Convention – if the extradition is not obviously inadmissible according to the law of the requested State and the wanted person *consents*.[193] The decision to relinquish the protection of the **principle of speciality** cannot be revoked.[194] Finally, an alert entered into the **Schengen Information System** (SIS)[195] shall have the same quality as a request for *provisional arrest* under Art. 16 EuCExt.[196]

26 The **SIS** is regulated extensively in Arts. 92–119 CISA;[197] the transposition of the Schengen *acquis* into Union law[198] turned the SIS into a **European information system** in which the UK and Ireland, despite their special position,[199] have also participated.[200] Essentially, the SIS is a **database** containing 'alerts on persons and property' and consisting of a centralised database in Strasbourg[201] and national databases in the Member States which connect to the central database via SIRENE (Supplementary Information Request at the National Entry).[202] Figure 9 shows how the SIS works with regard to Germany. The SIS aims to maintain public security and order in the Schengen area 'using information communicated via this system'.[203] An 'alert' – that is, an entry into this system – is made by the respective requesting Contracting Party. Alerts can be issued on persons for the purpose of extradition/surrender,[204] on aliens for the purposes of refusing entry,[205] on missing persons or persons requiring protection,[206] on witnesses and persons charged with or sentenced for an offence,[207] on persons or objects for the purposes of discreet surveillance where there is suspicion of a serious

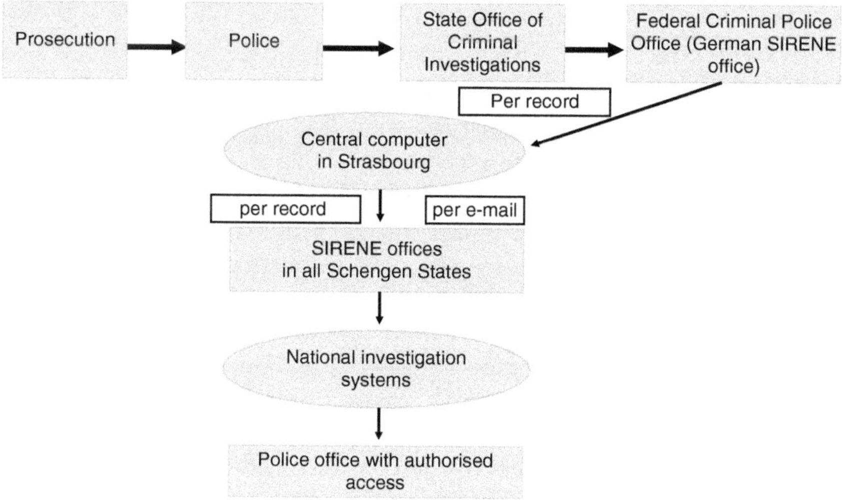

Figure 9 Searches in the Schengen Information System – the example of Germany

offence,[208] and on objects sought for the purposes of seizure or use as evidence in criminal proceedings.[209]

27 Art. 64 CISA places **alerts for the purposes of extradition**[210] on an equal footing with requests for provisional *arrest* within the meaning of traditional extradition law. This is worrying, as in the automated procedures of the SIS it is not the *requested* State that reviews the admissibility of the arrest – as is, for example, the case within the framework of Interpol;[211] instead, according to Art. 95(2) CISA, the *requesting* State ('the contracting party issuing the alert'; that is, its responsible authority, e.g. the prosecution authority) reviews whether the arrest is admissible according to the law of '*the requested*', that is, *all* (!) Contracting Parties.[212] Not only does this ask the impossible of the responsible authority in the requesting State; it also sets in motion an automated process that poses a significant risk from a perspective of fundamental rights as the requested State becomes a (blind) executive body of the requesting State,[213] although of course this only anticipates a development in extradition law that results necessarily from mutual recognition[214] and is generally extended by the EAW to arrest for the purposes of prosecution (as we will see in more detail below[215]). At any rate, the SIS II has made changes here as we will see in a moment. In terms of legal protection it is notworthy that an alert (for the purposes of arrest or of surrender based on an EAW) can be contested before domestic courts.[216]

28 Towards the end of 2006, the EU began to lay the foundations for an **SIS II** with EC Regulation 1987/2006, insofar as policies of the first pillar are implemented within its context.[217] The legal basis of SIS II was finally adopted in 2007,[218] but it came into effect, after repeated delays due to technical problems,[219] only on 9 April 2013.[220] It fully *replaces SIS I* as regulated in Title IV CISA;[221] in particular Art. 64 CISA is replaced by Art. 31 SIS II Decision 2007 giving an alert the same effect as an EAW and a request for provisional arrest,[222] and Art. 95(2) CISA is derogated, leaving it to the requested Member State to check the admissibility of an extradition.[223] Apart from a (technologically) up-to-date system, SIS II offers some *new functionalities* as compared to its predecessor: alerts on persons (to be surrendered/extradited) and objects[224] (to be seized or used as evidence) can be made directly and both can be linked (e.g. an alert on a person with an alert on a vehicle), while EAW copies can be connected with alerts on persons. SIS II can also contain supplementary information necessary for surrender or extradition, in particular biometric data (fingerprints,[225] photographs) or information on misused identity in order to prevent the misidentification of persons.[226] Each MS shall have a national SIS II office and a SIRENE bureau (responsible for the exchange of supplementary information and the quality of the information entered in SIS II). SIS II information (passport data) can be exchanged with Interpol.[227] Primary access to SIS II is by border authorities, police and customs, as well as judicial authorities in the context of criminal proceedings.[228] In a 2016 evaluation, the Commission states that 'SIS II constitutes significant EU added value, as cross-border law enforcement cooperation in such high volumes could not take place without this database';[229] at the same time, however, many suggestions for improvement and legislative proposals are made.[230]

d) The EU Convention on Extradition and Other EU Conventions

29 The EU Convention on Extradition (EUCExt)[231] facilitates extradition within the EU to a greater extent than the EuCExt, mainly because of its **abolition of a range of extradition obstacles**,[232] of which the *exception to the principle of dual criminality*[233] is probably the furthest-reaching. Thus the lack of dual criminality does not form an obstacle to extradition in the case of a 'conspiracy or an association to commit offences' if the act is not punishable according to the law of the requested State but was carried out with the aim of committing an act punishable according to the European Convention on the Suppression of Terrorism or in the field of drug trafficking and 'other forms of organised crime or other violent offences'.[234]

30 Furthermore, 'for the purposes of applying this Convention', Art. 5(1) EUCExt abolishes **political offences** as an obstacle to extradition.[235] However, Member States have the option of restricting the application of this rule to the area of terrorism by making a reservation.[236] Art. 6 abolishes **fiscal offences** as an obstacle to extradition, and Art. 7(1) denies the right to invoke the principle of **non-extradition of nationals,**[237] although in para. 2 it permits States not to grant extradition or to authorise it only under certain specific conditions. In this regard, the Dutch model seems convincing, according to which extradition is linked to transfer for the purposes of enforcement if the prosecuted person agrees to this.[238]

31 The EU **Convention on the simplified extradition procedure**[239] regulates procedural aspects not covered by the EuCExt as the 'mother convention' or by the respective additional conventions.[240] Its primary aim is to *speed up* the extradition procedure by dispensing with the admissibility procedure and certain other formalities if the prosecuted person *consents* to the extradition, having been sufficiently informed.[241] Both this Convention and the EUCExt have been largely made applicable to the non-EU MS **Norway, Iceland, Switzerland** and **Liechtenstein.**[242]

32 National law may also provide for simplified extradition procedures based on the consent of the person concerned. Thus, in Germany, §41 IRG permits 'extradition *without carrying out a formal extradition procedure*' if the prosecuted person agrees to this. If the prosecuted person is fit to stand trial and,[243] after being properly instructed, consents, then there is no need to present the documents on extradition referred to in §10 IRG if an extradition warrant has been issued. When a simple extradition request is made, the granting authority only reviews the conditions of extradition summarily, without a formal review of its admissibility. Furthermore, the accused person may choose to dispense with adherence to the *principle of speciality*.[244] Art. 1 ff. EU Simplified Extradition Convention (and other conventions) take precedence over national rules such as §41 IRG on simplified extradition to the extent that they contain more specific rules (cf. e.g. §1(3) IRG).[245] This leads to **further simplifications:** according to

Art. 3(2) EU Simplified Extradition Convention, the requirement for a formal extradition request and all required documents in line with Art. 12 EuCExt can be dropped; according to Art. 4(1) of the Simplified Extradition Convention, only certain information has to be provided by the requesting State.[246] Thus instead of 'the original or an authenticated copy of the conviction and sentence or detention order immediately enforceable or of the warrant of arrest',[247] information *on* 'the existence of an arrest warrant or other document having the same legal effect or of an enforceable judgment'[248] is sufficient.[249] Furthermore, the EU Simplified Extradition Convention sets obligatory **time limits**: thus the requesting State must be informed within ten days of the arrest of the person in question whether he or she has consented to the simplified procedure.[250] Twenty days after consent has been given at the latest, the requesting State must be informed of whether the simplified procedure will be carried out.[251]

33 The EC **Agreement on the simplification and modernisation of methods of transmitting extradition requests**[252] serves to improve co-operation in the field of extradition by making it possible for extradition requests, documents of evidence and any other official correspondence to be transmitted by fax.[253] The majority of its rules have been rendered obsolete by Art. 13 EUCExt and the EAW.[254]

e) ECHR and Additional Protocols as Obstacles to Extradition

34 In Chapter 2 we have seen how the ECHR and its APs operate on the territory of its States Parties to protect the rights of their citizens. Yet the ECHR binds its States Parties not only 'internally', but also 'externally', in that a *requested* (Convention) State may **indirectly violate** the ECHR (or an AP) through an extradition to a (third) State that commits violations of human rights.[255] Thus the treatment in the *requesting* State, which may violate human rights, can constitute an obstacle to extradition,[256] even if the ECHR does not even apply to this requesting State.[257] The reason is that the Convention binds the requested State; it has therefore to make sure that its extradition decision does not entail a violation of Convention rights in the requesting State.

35 The challenge consists of finding an appropriate balance between the *State* interest in functioning criminal prosecution, which requires a smooth extradition process, and the interest of the *individual* – which must also be recognised in the extradition process[258] – in the protection of her human rights.[259] The required **balancing of interests** *in abstracto* leads to the result that not *every* violation of the ECHR or an AP will turn into an obstacle to extradition, as otherwise there would be a risk that extraditions would practically come to a standstill. Rather, a violation of *fundamental* rights of the ECHR or an AP and (hence) a disregard for the person's *human dignity* must be involved.[260]

36 The *Soering Judgment* can be regarded as a landmark case in this context. Here, the ECtHR declared the applicant's extradition from the United Kingdom to the United States to be inadmissible as the imposition and enforcement of the **death penalty** in the US State of Virginia constituted a violation of **Art. 3 ECHR** due to the so-called *death row phenomenon.*[261] Under the current human rights regime, such an extradition would also be inadmissible due to the prohibition of capital punishment (AP VI). Extradition for the purposes of enforcing capital punishment may also be excluded due to constitutional considerations[262] and explicitly in extradition conventions.[263] In these cases, extradition is only possible following reliable **assurances** that enforcement (of the death penalty) will be suspended in the concrete case at hand.[264]

37 A **disproportionately harsh punishment** in the requesting State can also serve as grounds to refuse extradition via Art. 3 ECHR.[265] Of course, it is not the requested State's own law that is applicable, but instead it must be inquired whether the punishment imposed or to be expected in the *requesting State* must be viewed as insupportably harsh or inappropriate taking into consideration all of the circumstances of the individual case.[266] If this is the case, another obstacle to extradition arises from Art. 49(3) CFREU.[267] In light of the Grand Chamber's judgment in *Vinter*,[268] **life imprisonment** without any realistic chance of early release arguably also amounts to disproportionately harsh punishment and thus an obstacle to extradition.[269] Thus, in *Trabelsi*, the ECtHR considered the applicant's extradition from Belgium to the USA to be in violation of Art. 3 ECHR, arguing that his expected life imprisonment without parole ('maximum discretionary whole-life prison sentence') constituted a de facto irreducible sentence.[270] The 'real risk' of treatment that violates Art. 3 ECHR is sufficient.[271] Last, but not least, an extradition obstacle may arise from the risk of **torture** or **inhuman treatment** as part of the criminal procedure or of sentence enforcement.[272] Art. 3 ECHR also applies when the above-mentioned risks are posed by non-State actors.[273]

However, these risks must exist *in the individual case at hand*; general information on torture or similar acts in the requesting State is not sufficient.[274]

38 An obstacle to extradition may arise from **Art. 2(1) ECHR** if the transfer would place the life of the person involved at acute risk.[275] Here it must be noted that Art. 2 ECHR does *not* cover cases of extradition to a State where the person is at risk of being sentenced to death; however, here – apart from Art. 3 discussed above – AP VI applies.[276] **Art. 8 ECHR** can form an extradition obstacle if the provision's core element of respect for private and family life is affected.[277] **Art. 6 ECHR** can – in exceptional cases – constitute an obstacle to extradition if **no fair trial** can be expected in the requesting State, and the person in question thus cannot expect that his or her plea will be evaluated in an objective and appropriate manner.[278] This is the case, for example, in cases where there is a risk of *arbitrary arrest* and *political persecution*.[279] An extradition obstacle is also present if the right to a *review* of the sentence by a higher tribunal contained in Art. 2 AP VII does not exist (de facto) in the requesting State.[280] The opposite case may occur if, following a serious violation of the Convention in the criminal proceedings of the adjudicating State, the punishment is to be enforced by another State. In exceptional cases, an *indirect* intervention of Art. 6 or Art. 5 ECHR – that is, deriving not from the enforcement, but from the proceedings – may be a possibility.[281] There is also an obstacle to extradition if the extradition documents indicate that the acts for which extradition is requested actually form a pretext; this is suggested primarily by exaggerations, contradictions and manipulated witness statements.[282] The same applies when there are factual indications that the criminal proceedings to be carried out in the requesting State following the extradition will be based mainly on witness statements obtained through torture.[283] Conversely, the fact that the person in question was lured from his home country to the requested State through the *subterfuge* of the requesting State does not constitute an obstacle to extradition.[284]

39 If the defendant is **sentenced *in absentia***, then a violation of **Arts. 3, 6(3)(c) ECHR** is possible if this procedure violated his right to a fair hearing and appropriate defence.[285] However, this is not the case if – following extradition – the defendant has access to a legal remedy within the context of which the trial can be effectively reviewed and new exonerating material presented.[286] If there is no such legal remedy, then the decisive issue is whether the defendant knew about the trial *in absentia* and was at least able to participate in it through his defence counsel.[287] These obstacles derived from Art. 6(3)(a) ECHR also apply implicitly to extradition proceedings under the EuCExt. Thus it is worth noting that Chapter 3 of AP II of the EuCExt[288] sets out a refusal to grant extradition if minimum defence rights were not given in the proceedings leading to a judgment *in absentia*; conversely, extradition is to be granted if the person involved is assured the right to a retrial.

40 It is also inadmissible to extradite to a State that would **transfer** the person in question to a third State that violates human rights.[289] In these cases, the same rules must apply as in the constellation of (the risk of) **chain deportation**, for which the ECtHR decided that even deportation to a *Convention State* violated Art. 3 ECHR if there was a risk that this State would transfer the person in question to a third country in which she would be subjected to treatment that violated Art. 3 ECHR.[290]

41 Traditionally, qualifying the act that forms the basis of the extradition request as a **political offence** has constituted a further obstacle to extradition. According to Art. 3(1) of the EuCExt, extradition shall not be granted if the offence in respect of which it is requested is regarded by the requested State as a political offence or as an offence connected with a political offence.[291] The point and purpose of this rule is to prevent the requested State becoming involved in a political conflict in the requesting State.[292] However, against the backdrop of the political terrorism of the 1970s, the political-offence extradition obstacle came to be seen as *increasingly obstructive*.[293] Thus Arts. 1 and 2 of the European Convention on the Suppression of Terrorism[294] contain a restrictive definition of political offences.

Furthermore, Art. 1(d) and (e) of the European Convention on the Suppression of Terrorism exclude offences involving kidnapping and the use of a bomb, grenade, rocket, automatic firearm or letter or parcel bomb from the definition of political offence if the use of the mentioned devices endangers persons. In its Art. 1(a), (b) and (c), the Terrorism Convention also refers to further conventions of international law that suspend political offences as extradition obstacles, namely the Convention for the Suppression of Unlawful Seizure of Aircraft, signed at The Hague on 16 December 1970,[295] and the Convention for the Suppression of Unlawful Acts against the Safety of Civil Aviation, signed at Montreal on 23 September 1971,[296] as well as the Convention on the Prevention and Punishment of Crimes against Internationally Protected Persons, Including Diplomatic Agents, of 14 December 1973.[297] We have already seen above that AP I to the EuCExt and the EUCExt also abolished the extradition obstacle of the political offence.[298]

Solution, case 2

42 The Higher Regional Court Düsseldorf declared the request of the Lithuanian Public Prosecutor's Office for extradition to be inadmissible, as the person affected was at risk of reprisals from fellow detainees in Lithuania (including in Lithuanian prison). Even though the defendant was not at risk of being tortured by the State, the Court was of the opinion that an extradition obstacle arising from Art. 3 ECHR still exists if the person concerned may be subject to inhuman treatment by private agents being in State custody.

2. Surrender (European Arrest Warrant)

Case 3

43 Polish law-enforcement agencies accuse a German national of having pretended, in a number of individual acts in different Polish cities and towns, to supply persons with legal seasonal work in Germany, thus obtaining at least 104,890 zloty (about €24,000) by deceitful means. The granting authority makes the extradition's authorisation dependent on Poland returning the person charged to Germany for the purposes of enforcement (if appropriate) after his sentencing. Is extradition admissible?[299] ➔ mn. 74

Case 4

44 The person charged has both Polish and German citizenship. A European Arrest Warrant has been issued against him based upon a charge of embezzlement, carried out in Poland, and a charge of robbery, also carried out on Polish territory. The Public Prosecutor's Office as the responsible granting authority has stated it will not invoke any obstacles to the authorisation.[300] It justifies this decision with Poland's interest in efficiently prosecuting crimes committed on its territory. What decision will the Higher Regional Court reach?[301] ➔ mn. 75

Case 5

45 Non-EU State U is investigating German national A for espionage, treason and incitement to the betrayal of state secrets. A is charged with having published secret U state documents on military interventions and diplomatic communications on the Internet. During a business trip to the EU State S, A meets X, a citizen of State S, with whom he has consensual sexual intercourse several times. After A's departure, X goes to the police, states that A performed sexual acts upon her while she was asleep, and files charges against A for rape. Following this, an EAW is issued against A. The justification for this is that the act described clearly corresponds to the offence of Chapter 6, §II, of the Criminal Code of country S. State S requests that Germany extradite A. He denies X's representation and accuses her of being part of a plot against A instigated by State U. Even if the events described were taken to be true, they do not fall within the scope of the offence of rape according to German law or the law of State S. What decision will the responsible Higher Regional Court reach? Can A be extradited to State U following his transfer to State S?[302] → mn. 76

a) The EU Framework

46 On 13 June 2002, the Council of the EU adopted the **Framework Decision on the European Arrest Warrant** and the surrender procedures between Member States (**FD EAW**).[303] This decision harks back to the conclusions of the European Council of Tampere of 1999 and the Council's 2000 programme of measures for the implementation of the principle of **mutual recognition**[304] of judicial decisions.[305] The FD was meant to replace the outdated extradition instruments of the Council of Europe and the EU as of 1 January 2004;[306] its annex even provides a form for a 'European Arrest Warrant'. However, one must not overlook the fact that with Framework Decisions, Member States in principle can decide on the **means and manner of implementation.**[307] Even though the FD entered into force before the Lisbon Treaty, it remained valid after 1 December 2009 and has been transposed into Union law after a period of five years (i.e. 1 December 2014).[308]

47 According to Art. 1(1), (2) FD EAW, the EAW represents a **judicial decision**[309] issued by *one* Member State which is **executed** by *another* MS on the basis of the principle of *mutual recognition* for the purposes of arresting and **surrendering** a person sought for criminal prosecution or for the enforcement of a sentence.[310] The (single-stage) **surrender procedure** thus replaces the traditional two-stage extradition procedure;[311] the principle of *non-extradition of nationals* is basically abandoned.[312] The new terminology (which has already been mentioned) is also worthy of note: the concept of the **'issuing State'** (of an EAW) replaces the 'requesting State' (requesting extradition); that of the **'executing State'** replaces the 'requested State', which now (only) has, in principle, to execute the decision of the issuing State and *'surrender'* the wanted person.[313]

48 The **procedure** goes, in a nutshell, as follows: first, the EAW is to be *transmitted* to the executing judicial authority, or, if the location of the requested person is unknown, *an alert is to be issued* for them in the SIS.[314] This alert is equivalent to the EAW.[315] If necessary, the services of Interpol may be resorted

to.[316] Upon their arrest, the requested person must be *informed* of the content of the EAW; she has the right to *legal counsel* and an *interpreter*.[317] Any detention takes place according to the law of the executing State.[318] The person may *consent* to the surrender and renounce the protection offered by the principle of speciality.[319] Consent must be given voluntarily and in full awareness of the consequences;[320] it cannot be revoked as a matter of principle.[321] If the person does not consent to the surrender, he has the right to a *hearing*.[322] The executing judicial authority may request supplementary information from the issuing authority in order to reach a decision.[323] In the case of *multiple requests* – several EAWs or conflicts with the extradition request of a third country – the executing authority decides which request is to be granted primacy, taking into account the following circumstances:[324] the seriousness and locality of the offences, the dates the warrants were issued and the purposes for which they were issued.[325]

The EAW is to be dealt with 'as a **matter of urgency**'.[326] If the requested person consents to the surrender, the decision is to be reached within ten days,[327] otherwise within 60 days of the arrest.[328] In exceptional cases, the deadline can be extended by another 30 days.[329] If this time limit cannot be observed either, the Member State must inform Eurojust[330] and – in the case of repeated delays – the Council.[331] Reasons must be given for any refusal to execute an EAW.[332] The *surrender* itself is to take place 'as soon as possible', at the latest ten days after the final decision on the execution of the warrant.[333] In exceptional cases, a new date for the surrender can be agreed. Again, the surrender must take place within ten days (of the new date).[334] Surrender may be postponed for 'serious humanitarian reasons'[335] or for the prosecution of the person in question or the enforcement of her sentence in the executing State.[336] Alternatively, in the latter case the requested person may be surrendered temporarily.[337] Every Member State must in principle permit the *transit* of a requested person through its territory.[338] The (pre-trial) detention served in the executing State must be deducted.[339] Member States may generally agree to the *prosecution of other acts* than those listed in the EAW based on the principle of reciprocity.[340] In addition, in certain cases the principle of **speciality**, which applies in principle,[341] may be dispensed with.[342] The *subsequent surrender* of requested persons by the issuing State without the consent[343] of the executing State and the *handing over of property* is largely made possible.[344]

49 As far as the EAW's **scope of application** is concerned, Art. 2(2) FD EAW appears to limit it initially to acts that – according to the law of the issuing State – are 'punishable by the law of the issuing Member State by a custodial sentence or a detention order for a maximum period of at least

12 months or, where a sentence has been passed or a detention order has been made, for sentences of at least four months'. In this case, the traditional principle of **dual criminality**[345] is retained, as the executing State can make the surrender subject to the condition that the act in question (also) constitutes an offence according to its law.[346] However, this return to traditional extradition law is immediately breached by Art. 2(2) FD EAW, according to which dual criminality is not required for the **catalogue** of 'offences' listed therein if these offences are punishable in the issuing Member State by a custodial sentence or a detention order for a *maximum period of at least three years.*[347]

50 The said catalogue includes more than **32 'offences'**,[348] ranging from 'participation in a criminal organisation' (first indent) to 'corruption' (seventh indent); 'murder, grievous bodily injury' (fourteenth indent); 'environmental crime, including illicit trafficking in endangered animal species and in endangered plant species and varieties' (twelfth indent); and 'counterfeiting and piracy of products' (twenty-second indent); subsequently turning to 'rape' (twenty-eighth indent), 'crimes within the jurisdiction of the International Criminal Court' (thirtieth indent)[349] and, last but not least, an offence simply described as 'sabotage' (thirty-second indent). **No system** or guiding principle can be detected here, as the catalogue is restricted neither to cross-border crime ('terrorism', 'drug trafficking') nor to crimes that relate specifically to the Union ('protection of financial interests'), but also includes 'ordinary' offences such as fraud, arson and extortion.[350] It is also worrying that some of the 'offences' are formulated in a vague, broad manner ('corruption', 'organised or armed robbery', 'sabotage') while others rather try to capture mere criminal phenomena ('racism and xenophobia').[351] As to the latter, the combined reading of Art. 29 TEU and Art. 61(3) TFEU[352] raises doubts as to whether these phenomena can really be referred to as offences, seeing that the aforementioned regulations only serve to prevent and combat them. The fact that fraud is essentially listed twice ('fraud', 'swindling') is cause for further concern,[353] as is the parallel listing of 'counterfeiting currency, including of the euro' and the 'forgery of means of payment', given the fact that it is hard to distinguish these offences from one another in any reasonable way. The question also arises of the extent to which **effective defence** against an EAW is possible, given that the defendant's national defence counsel will, as a rule, hardly be sufficiently familiar with the language and the legal practice of the issuing Member State.[354]

51 In spite of these concerns, the **CJEU** confirmed the validity of the FD EAW[355] as part of a request for a preliminary ruling of the Belgian *Cour d'arbitrage*.[356] Unfortunately, this judgment contains *hardly any substance*: on the one hand, the empty claim of a 'high degree of trust and solidarity between the Member States'[357] is touted, although this is increasingly becoming, as the Union expands further and further, a mere Brussels or Luxembourg phantasmagoria.[358] On the other hand, the vague list of categories is supposed to satisfy the principle of legality as national law determines 'the definition of those offences'.[359] How this is compatible with the fact that no subsumption under national law is supposed to take place (as the review of dual criminality is dispensed with)[360] remains a mystery.[361] Insofar as the listed categories of the FD EAW are rendered more concrete in line with national criteria as part of their national implementation – as done, for example, by the Italian legislator[362] – this simply boils down to a retention of the requirement of dual criminality.[363] It is also criticised that obliging the executing State or the State where the act in question was committed to surrender a person accused in another MS on the grounds of the (absolute) principle of active personality violates the principle of legality if no identical offence exists in the executing State, as the conduct in question is not punishable there.[364]

52 Despite this justified criticism of the FD EAW, we should not forget that it includes **reasons for non-execution**,[365] which in fact implicitly relativises the mutual trust claimed to exist between Member States' legal systems and which serves as the basis of this endeavour.[366] If there is an amnesty, or the person requested cannot be held criminally responsible in the executing State,[367] non-execution is *mandatory* 'if' – in a parallel to Art. 54 CISA[368] –

> the executing judicial authority is informed that the requested person has been finally judged by a Member State in respect of the same acts provided that, where there has been sentence, the sentence has been served or is currently being served or may no longer be executed under the law of the sentencing Member State.[369]

While non-execution of the EAW is mandatory in these cases, its execution **may** be **refused** in a number of other cases,[370] for example when acts under Art. 2(4) FD EAW *do not constitute an offence*;[371] the requested person is *already being prosecuted*,[372] or has been *finally judged* in a third State;[373] if the criminal prosecution or punishment is *statute-barred* according to the law of the executing Member State[374] or the EAW relates to offences committed in whole or in part in the territory of the executing Member State;[375] and finally when the requested person is staying in, or is a national or a resident of, the executing Member State and that State undertakes to execute the sentence or detention order itself.[376] However, justified criticism is raised concerning the fact that the EAW does not become ineffective even if grounds for mandatory non-execution are present, but remains active (with all its detrimental effects on the person affected) until the issuing State rescinds it.[377]

53 Furthermore, execution may be made subject to certain **conditions.**[378] Thus assurances that proceedings will be resumed with the defendant present in court may be demanded if the EAW is based upon a sentence issued *in absentia*;[379] the respective Art. 4a(1)(d)(i) FD[380] may well be so interpreted as to give the person concerned a fully fledged right to a retrial.[381] Furthermore, demands may include the option of a *review* of the punishment imposed (after 20 years at the latest) or of the application of measures of clemency,[382] and – for a State's own nationals – the *return* of the surrendered person to serve the sentence passed against her.[383] Last but not least, Art. 1(3) FD EAW in conjunction with Art. 6 TEU (as well as Nos 12, 13 in the FD's Preamble) means that **a general fundamental rights reservation** applies to the entire process of surrender; here, the obstacles to extradition arising from the ECHR[384] are of particular relevance,[385] albeit not, of course, in the sense of a conflict of interest as described there, but as a *human rights-based obstacle* to the surrender of the person sought,[386] for example in case of inhumane detention conditions in the issuing State.[387] All this goes to show that the executing State still possesses the **competence to independently review and evaluate** and is more than the 'blind' executioner of the issuing State's requests for surrender.[388]

b) Problems of National Implementation: The Paradigmatic Case of Germany

54 The scope granted Member States in implementing the FD EAW has led to considerable **differences in its implementation** in the individual MS.[389] While the Council concluded in 2009 that MS have 'largely implemented' the FD EAW 'properly',[390] there have in fact been many differences in the implementation – e.g. regarding the use of terminology, the offences catalogued in Art. 2(2) FD EAW, time limits, and grounds of refusal[391] – as well as the choice of language[392] – and in 2011, seven years after the entry into force of the FD EAW, twelve MS had still not made any amendments to their legislation.[393] Those MS that have implemented the FD have done so in a manner that is by no means unanimous, not least because of constitutional problems that will be discussed in a moment. A few years later, it was still concluded, within the context of a strategic Eurojust seminar on the EAW, that 'a more stringent implementation policy in the Member States as well as the development of soft law measures and practical tools' is necessary.[394] Further, it was noted that the speciality rule could only be made superfluous by a harmonious implementation of the FD EAW.[395]

55 The German attempts to implement the FD EAW demonstrate the constitutional and technical problems in an exemplary fashion, especially with regard to (civil law) jurisdictions with a (constitutional) prohibition on extraditing nationals.[396] The legislator's first implementation attempt, the (first) EAW Act of 21 July 2004,[397] was declared unconstitutional by the German Federal Constitutional Court in July 2005. We will analyse the important reasoning of the Court in the next section. The second EAW Act was issued on 20 July 2006.[398] The difference between it and its predecessor is, as we will also see below, that the guarantees demanded by the Constitutional Court have been added.[399]

56 If the EAW's primary rationale is to replace the traditional two-step extradition procedure (admissibility and authorisation) with a **one-step, primarily judicial, procedure,**[400] it becomes plain that the German legislator has – already with the first EAW Act – made considerable use of its discretionary scope in implementing the FD EAW, considerably deviating from its guidelines.[401] This is already evident in the fact that the EAW Act I – like the EAW Act II (and other implementing legislation, e.g., the UK Extradition Act 2003)[402] – retains the traditional **terminology of extradition law**: the new §§80 ff. IRG, regulating the 'extradition to a Member State of the European Union', continue to speak of a 'requesting State' asking a 'requested State' for an 'extradition'.[403] EAW Act I[404] tended towards a retention of the 'classic' **two-stage extradition procedure** with the Higher Court as the authority deciding on admissibility[405] and the Federal or State Ministries of Justice as the granting authorities.[406] In fact, strictly speaking, the EAW Act II – due to the new regulation on 'preliminary decisions'[407] – has even created a **three-step procedural structure**, the complexity of which can only be reconciled with the FD's aim of expediting extradition with considerable difficulty.[408]

57 Conversely, the German Law on Mutual Assistance (IRG) now does in fact point towards a future in which decisions of criminal procedure will be mutually recognised in its **relinquishing** of a 'review' of **dual criminality** if one of the catalogue offences is involved[409] without any requirement for a minimum three-year custodial sentence – even though this is set out in Art. 2(2) FD EAW; instead, a custodial sentence or other sanction of *no less than twelve months* is sufficient.[410] In practice, this all means that the issuing of an arrest warrant is not barred by the fact that the requesting State has only provided an assurance that the offences the requested person is charged with may only receive the lower sentence sufficient under §81 No 1 IRG, Art. 2(1) FD EAW.[411] Of course, the problem here already lies in the FD (and in the underlying EU criminal policy as a whole), as it is taking the second step (of introducing the procedural principle of mutual recognition) before the first (harmonisation of substantive law)[412] and thus falls victim to the *fiction* of EU-wide minimum requirements that (supposedly) correspond exactly to the catalogue offences.[413] This has also been criticised by some EU MS, including Germany, which is why the legislator denied there was any 'real relinquishment of dual criminality'[414] and the FD's offence catalogue was not included in the German implementation legislation; yet a review of dual criminality is not deemed necessary if a catalogue offence is involved.[415] Thus prosecutors and judges are in fact prevented from subsumption (that is, applying the law to the facts) and the above-mentioned fiction of an EU-wide common standard is legally enforced.[416] Furthermore, it remains unclear how 'practice [is] to subsume the German offence definitions under the listed categories through development of the law'[417] if it is, as just said, prohibited from reviewing dual criminality when a catalogue offence is concerned.[418] The case law of the higher courts[419] clearly struggles with this, as it is often stated that dual criminality need not be reviewed, but that it exists nonetheless.[420] A possible solution to this problem is seen by some in the (anticipated) termination of proceedings due to lack of evidence,[421] which according to §83b(1)(b) IRG constitutes grounds to refuse extradition.[422] However, it appears doubtful whether this is really practicable, as the requested (executing) State usually only deals with the matter once the request for extradition has been made, and the granting authority cannot itself bring about a termination; furthermore, this would undermine the call not to review dual criminality.

58 It has been criticised that the relinquishing of dual criminality (in combination with the principle of mutual recognition) would result in the

most punitive European legal system being valid in each respective case: 'if the decision in criminal matters issued by *any* MS is to be enforceable and recognised in *every* MS, then a *principle of maximum punitivity* will arise of its own accord on the European level'.[423] This is, however, an overstatement. While mutual recognition and the lack of dual criminality may favour a certain repressive, transnational tendency, one must not overlook that the principle of mutual recognition also applies to favourable decisions,[424] as especially demonstrated by the recognition of a trans-European *ne bis in idem*,[425] and, more importantly, the consequences of a lack of dual criminality crucially depend on police and prosecutorial practice and the establishment of an effective defence. Furthermore, it is claimed that the principle of mutual recognition violates the **principle of democracy**, as the perpetrator of a crime committed abroad has not been able to influence the legislative process in the (foreign) jurisdiction to which he is subjected.[426] This is not convincing either:[427] as the only task of criminal law is to protect the key behavioural norms of a *particular* society, the only decisive fact is that the defendant was within the territory to which the (criminal) legal system of the requesting State applies at the time the act in question was carried out. Also, the fact that a German citizen, for example, who is sought for a crime committed abroad by the State in which the crime was carried out, has had no opportunity to shape the law to which he is to be subjected, is irrelevant; this is already evident in the example of the application of (German) criminal law to (German) minors (who, like foreign nationals, are unable to influence the law as they do not have the right to vote). However, the danger of the application of the most punitive European criminal law is of relevance for cases of crimes committed from a distance, where the locations of the act and its result are not identical, and where there is no dual criminality, for example when content that is prohibited in but can be accessed from Germany is uploaded to the Internet in a State where, for example, incitement to hatred or the glorification of violence does not constitute a criminal offence.[428] In these cases, the application of mutual recognition is indeed a cause for concern. However, the solution should be sought *de lege ferenda* in the application of criminal law. If the States' punitive authority (*ius puniendi*) were restricted to the place of commission, this problem would no longer arise.[429]

It is right that the problem of the jurisdiction and punitive authority of the requesting State should precede the question of extradition and the principle of dual criminality traditionally linked to extradition, for if the former is lacking, then this State would not (be able to) launch the extradition procedure in the first place. Accordingly, there is a natural **connection between the application of criminal law (jurisdiction) and the request for extradition:** the narrower the former, the fewer requests for extradition can be made.[430] If (European) states were to restrict their jurisdiction to their territory (principle of territoriality), requests for extradition would only be made if foreign nationals committed crimes in the territory of the requesting State but were not apprehended there. Then the requesting State, which is also a territorial State, has every right (under international law) to request that the home State extradite the offender, for punitive authority forms part of a country's exercise of sovereign power in its own territory.[431] Persons who subject themselves to this (of their own free will) by travelling to other countries must bear the consequences.[432] On the one hand, this means that a narrower concept of national jurisdiction – such as the restriction to the place where the relevant act took place (and leaving aside the place where the act took effect[433]) – is inadmissible under international law if the territorial State does not freely accept the ensuing loss of sovereignity (in the interest of a common European criminal jurisdiction, for example). On the other hand, extradition requests based upon jurisdiction that goes beyond the territoriality principle stand on less stable ground, as the requesting State cannot invoke the exercise of its territorial sovereignity as the grounds for extradition. In fact, in a common European space of freedom, security and justice, extraterritorial jurisdiction should no longer be necessary.[434]

59 Despite all of its nuances and differentiation, this debate reveals that the **relinquishing of dual criminality** represents *the* truly revolutionary innovation of the FD EAW and thus constitutes the key point of attack in current (extradition) law. The FD's other regulations either are not innovations or are unobjectionable overall. As an example of the former we can take the removal of **obstacles to extradition** for political or military offences,[435] which conform to a trend in European extradition law that was already introduced by the EuCExt and enhanced by the CISA,[436] and for which, incidentally, there are objective reasons, considering the abuse of these extradition obstacles.[437]

60 The replacement of a national with a European ***ordre public***[438] is also to be welcomed if extradition is sought via an EAW,[439] although the CJEU case law does not make the scope and limits of the rights-based rationale of such a ground for refusal entirely clear. It remains to be seen whether the Grand Chamber's more recent decision in *Aranyosi and Căldăraru* – inhumane detention conditions in the issuing State of an EAW as obstacle to surrender for the executing State[440] – marks a new trend. At any rate, if the CJEU fails to adequately protect the core of the European *ordre public*[441] – that is, the fundamental substantive and procedural rights, especially to a fair trial, as analysed in detail in Chapter 2 – national constitutional and high courts are in their full right to carry out a comprehensive **identity review** to ensure the constitutional identity of the respective Member States with regard to the EAW and other mutual recognition instruments.[442] If this delays the surrender procedure, so be it.[443] This is the price of a common area of freedom, security and justice where the protection of fundamental rights is more than mere lip service.

Of course, the exercise of the *ordre public* reservation – or recourse to the national identity review for that matter – is only possible in exceptional cases of serious rights violations or deviation from core principles of law. For example, punishing particularly serious narcotics offences with life sentences is certainly not a sufficiently important ground to invoke this reservation.[444] Thus, in most cases, mutual recognition works smoothly and efficiently, as we will see below, taking a look at EAW statistics.[445] However, there are other cases where a rights-based approach demands a hard look at the respective EAW and perhaps even the suspension of the surrender procedure. This may be the case in particular where the execution of an EAW would mean that the suspect's right to a fair trial would be violated, for example by surrendering him for the execution of a sentence based on a trial and conviction *in absentia* without the possibility of a fully fledged retrial.[446] Also, it is worth noting that in the framework of the EAW the right to an **appropriate defence** is to be granted at every stage of the procedure and not only from the time of the suspect's arrest in the executing State.[447] This applies even though – or rather, precisely because – the defence is faced with completely new problems, as the defendant is confronted with at least two legal systems, that of the issuing and that of the executing States. Accordingly, there is a need not only to co-ordinate criminal prosecution, but also to **institutionalise a co-ordinated defence**.[448]

c) The German Constitutional Court's Annulment of EAW Act I and Similar Judgments

61 From a constitutional and rights perspective, the EAW raises the question of the extent to which national or European **fundamental rights** can **bar** an **extradition** (surrender). The tendency towards a supranationalisation of co-operation in criminal matters, strengthened by the Lisbon Treaty and the principle of mutual recognition, suggests that fundamental rights have also been supranationalised. Thus their protection should now be guaranteed on a supranational level by European fundamental and human rights as set out in the

ECHR and the CFREU.[449] Those in support of a 'national solution'[450] object that, within the framework of extradition, interventions in individual legal positions (that is, of the persons to be extradited) cannot (yet) be (clearly) traced back to supranational sovereign authority; they still have an interstate character, as, for example, demonstrated by constitutional changes to facilitate extradition/ surrender within the EAW framework.[451] However, following the Lisbon Treaty and the subsequent transposition of the law of the former third pillar into Union law by 1 December 2014, this point of view has become untenable. Rather, now the legal acts of the former third pillar have to be measured (only) against the European fundamental rights. A review against national fundamental rights can be considered at most when making use of the available margin of appreciation in the course of implementation.[452]

62 The **German Federal Constitutional Court** declared the EAW Act I **invalid** in total, as it constituted, in its view, a disproportionate intervention in the freedom from extradition according to Art. 16(2) GG.[453] The legislator did not correctly perform 'the weighing . . . between the European interest in cross-border prosecution and the claim to protection that follows from the rights that stem from a person's status as a German',[454] as it failed to use the discretion opened up by Art. 4 No 7b FD EAW to refuse to 'extradit[e] a German who is charged with an offence that has a significant domestic connecting factor' (i.e. that is clearly linked to the Germany territory).[455] Furthermore, the Court regarded the lack of the possibility to challenge the decision to grant the extradition as a violation of the right to an effective remedy,[456] as the EAW Act introduced discretionary definitions into the respective authorisation procedure. While according to prevailing opinion the authorisation procedure could (also) not be contested in the past, the EAW Act I has now enshrined this in law and thus the 'legal restriction of a basic right is given concrete form'.[457] The Constitutional Court has thus clearly adopted an intergovernmental – instead of supranational – understanding of (former) police and judicial co-operation, which was already problematic even prior to the Lisbon Treaty in the light of the CJEU's *Pupino* decision.[458] Thus arises in particular the question whether the Constitutional Court would not have been better advised to declare only those parts of the EAW Act invalid that it considered to be irrecoverably problematic in terms of constitutional law, and subject the rest to interpretation in conformity with the FD EAW.[459]

Essentially identical judgments have been issued by the **Cypriot** Supreme Court and the **Polish** Constitutional Tribunal.[460] The former deemed the national law transposing the FD EAW[461] unconstitutional given that the reasons for arrest and surrender exhaustively enumerated in Art. 11 of the Cypriot Constitution did not, at the time of the decision, include the arrest of Cypriot nationals[462] with a view of their surrender to another EU Member State.[463] Consequently, Cyprus was not in a position to execute EAWs against its nationals until the Constitution was amended in 2006,[464] allowing a surrender of nationals pursuant to an EAW or international treaties.[465] In a similar manner, the Polish Consitutional Tribunal[466] held that 'the right of a Polish national' not to be extradited[467] 'is an absolute one' and 'cannot be limited by any ordinary legislative acts'.[468] For this reason, Art. 607t §1 Polish CPP, which allowed the surrender of a Polish citizen to an EU Member State on the basis of an EAW, was 'incompatible with Art. 55 Paragraph 1 of the Constitution'.[469] Nevertheless, the tribunal ruled that 'the respective provision [albeit unconstitutional] should continue to be applied'[470] for a period of 18 months after the publication of the judgment, granting the necessary time for the appropriate amendment of Art. 55.[471]

The **Czech** Constitutional Court[472] took a different route to overcome the prohibition on surrender of nationals.[473] It neither annulled the national implementation provisions nor demanded an amendment of the Constitution. Instead, it opted for a teleological interpretation which pretends to reconcile the principles of European integration, especially co-operation in the area of criminal justice, and the Constitution.[474] Accordingly, it was held that the surrender of a Czech citizen for a limited time for criminal proceedings or the enforcement of a sentence to another EU Member State 'does not and cannot constitute forcing them to leave their homeland in the sense of Art. 14 par. 4 of the Charter';[475] rather, it is demanded by the 'extensive international co-operation' 'for the investigation and suppression of criminality which takes place in the European area'; this is a consequence Czech citizens must accept given the advantages flowing from the status of EU citizenship.[476]

63 The German legislator attempted to take account of the complaints raised by the Constitutional Court first by making the **extradition of German citizens**[477] subject to (further) **complicated conditions**,[478] and second by attempting to ensure **effective legal protection**.[479] As to the former, extradition is prohibited for purely *domestic offences*,[480] while in the opposite case – for pure *foreign offences* with no domestic relevance – it is permitted without requiring dual criminality.[481] In these cases, besides the existence of a 'substantial link [of the offence] to the requesting Member State', the only requirement of extradition is that after a final conviction to a sentence of imprisonment or other sanction, the requesting State will offer to return the person sought, if she so wishes, to Germany for the purpose of enforcement (on this cf. case 3).[482] If the act in question has a 'substantial link' *neither* to a foreign State *nor* to domestic territory (so-called *mixed cases*), then extradition is subject to the existence of dual criminality and to assurances of return.[483] In sum, this legal regime prohibits extradition of nationals in case of purely domestic offences but generously permits it in case of purely foreign offences. The Polish approach – extradition in case of foreign offences only with punishability in Poland (requirement of dual criminality)[484] – shows that a more prohibitive regime is possible.

64 The concept of the **substantial link** thus forms the crux of the new legal regime; it is evident that categorising the above-mentioned *mixed cases* in particular poses a considerable challenge.[485] The legislator has tried to clarify the criterion of the **foreign link**[486] by making it dependent on whether 'essential parts' of the offence were committed abroad. In other words: a *substantial* link to a foreign State exists when *essential* parts of the act or the result occurred in the requesting State, but this is only the general rule. Not only the acts of the person to be extradited are to be considered, but also the acts of any given accomplices and participants.[487] This legal construct ultimately only replaces the concept of the substantiality of the offence's geographical link with the concept of essentiality, which calls for the same, if not a higher, degree of clarification; it is doubtful whether such a nebulous standard still meets the constitutional requirement of certainty.[488] Conversely, in order to identify a substantial **internal (domestic) link**, the legislator aims at a balancing exercise[489] whereby the competent legal authority is forced to weigh up ultimately incommensurable interests, as it is not clear how aspects as different as the weight of the charges, the practical requirements of effective prosecution, the respect for defendant rights and even the aims linked to the common European legal area[490] can be brought down to a common denominator in order to combine them in a reasonably serious methodological manner. Be this as it may, of greater import is the fact that the *extradition* of German nationals is practically *impossible* for cases with *purely domestic links* and – quite aside from the fact that this undermines the FD EAW and thus EU law[491] – there is thus a risk that other States will also refuse to extradite their nationals to Germany, invoking the principle of reciprocity.[492] From an EU perspective, this may only be mitigated by the fact that such cases are extremely rare and normally only result from domestic offences committed against nationals of the requesting State and from transnational, organised crime.

65 The regulation of §79(2) IRG, which is supposed to guarantee **effective legal protection** in line with Federal Constitutional Court requirements, is also questionable. In its first sentence, it sets out that the granting authority is to announce its intention not to raise extradition obstacles *in advance*, so that the Higher Regional Court is able to review this 'intention' *per curiam*[493] within the admissibility proceedings at the defendant's request[494] (on this, cf. case 4).[495] While this guarantees a legal remedy,[496] the procedure is somewhat confusing,[497] and also questions the traditional extradition procedure to the extent that the competent court is unable to comprehensively review the (foreign-) policy discretion of the granting authority *ex post*.[498] In any case, this basically turns the FD's aim of simplifying and expediting the extradition procedure on its head, given that with the preliminary expression of an intent by the granting authority a preliminary stage to the traditionally two-stage extradition procedure is introduced and thus it is turned into a **three-step procedure**:[499] preliminary decision of the granting authority[500] – decision on admissibility by the Higher Regional Court[501] – (final) decision on whether to grant extradition.[502]

66 Another problematic issue is that the EAW Act II treats **Germans** and **foreign nationals** living in Germany **differently**.[503] For foreign nationals resident in Germany, the criterion of substantial internal or external links of the Act does not constitute an element of the decision on admissibility, but instead is only one aspect that needs to be taken into account within the context of an authorisation procedure.[504] This could constitute a violation of the **non-discrimination principle** of European law,[505] at least as far as EU citizens are concerned.[506] The new regulation also means that the discretionary decision of the granting authority is made more complicated.[507] Last, but not least, the grounds for refusing the extradition of a foreign national resident in Germany[508] mean that the extradition of such persons to an EU State can be refused, but not – even under otherwise identical conditions – their extradition to a non-EU State.[509] In this regard, too, the FD's purpose is turned on its head; it is simply unconvincing that a non-EU State is treated more favourably than an EU Member State as far as extradition requests are concerned.[510]

d) The Concrete Analysis of Extradition Requests under the EAW System

67 The FD EAW significantly altered the process of extradition within the EU,[511] creating, first of all, an **obligation to grant extradition** following an EAW as a matter of principle. This has been translated into the respective national legislation, such as the EAW Act II.[512] Accordingly, it is only possible to refuse to grant an admissible request for extradition under limited conditions.[513] A refusal must be well-reasoned.[514] Further, the EAW prevails over other extradition rules,[515] and this is also reflected in national law;[516] exceptionally the old law may be more favourable and thus still applicable.[517]

68 Given the precedence of the EAW rules, as implemented in national law, **extradition requests within the EU** are to be analysed in the **following sequence**: first it must be ascertained whether the respective national EAW rules are applicable;[518] if this is the case, then the respective procedural and time-limit requirements must be observed.[519] If national EAW rules are not applicable, then it needs to be ascertained whether the pertinent extradition conventions apply. Where appropriate, it may be necessary to refer back to the general regulations of the relevant national law. Under the EAW, the review of the **admissibility** of an extradition following an EAW request by the issuing Member State remains in the hands of the competent national court;[520] its decision is followed – in line with the traditional two-step procedure – by the *executive* **authorisation procedure.**[521]

69 As we have seen above, the German EAW Act II has now complicated this procedure, turning it into a *threefold* one, with (i) the granting authority to declare in advance 'whether it intends to raise objections under §83b',[522] followed by (ii) the legal-admissibility decision and (iii) the executive authorisation.[523] If the granting authority does *not* wish to raise objections (in advance), then it needs to provide reasons.[524] The granting authority continues to enjoy a broad discretion, which can also include non-justiciable foreign-policy considerations.[525] The preliminary decision of the granting authority remains subject to review by the higher regional court to the extent that the court subsequently has to decide on the admissibility and even has to review the decision not to raise objections to extradition;[526] however, the preliminary decision as such restricts the court's scope for review at least in factual terms.[527]

e) Evaluation of the EAW

70 While there have been some shortcomings in the implementation of the FD EAW in the Member States, as we saw at the beginning of this section, its use since 2005 has been rapidly increasing – from 6,894 EAWs issued in 2005 to 16,144 in 2015[528] – and its impact of the efficiency of extradition/surrender within the EU has been clearly positive.[529] This follows first of all from the considerably reduced time in EAW surrender proceedings as compared to pre-EAW traditional extradition proceedings, i.e. from the previous one-year average to less than two months under the EAW and even, in case of consent to surrender by the person concerned (50 per cent of all surrenders), to 14 to 16 days.[530] Further, it follows from the available statistics on the actual execution of the EAWs; that is, the effective surrender of the person sought or at least her arrest or identification.[531]

71 There is, however, another side of the coin and that is the EAW's (potential) negative impact upon fundamental rights, especially the rights to liberty and to an adequate defence. These rights are affected by the EAW's excessive use even for minor offences,[532] accompanied by (pre-trial) detention where such detention would not occur in normal domestic cases and the difficulty of finding adequate legal representation.[533] A possible response to these rights deficiencies is to take recourse to the **proportionality principle**[534] – as part of the above-mentioned[535] European *ordre public* pursuant to Art. 1(3) FD EAW[536] – and thus introduce a general *proportionality test* when issuing and executing an EAW.[537] Such a general test would also make it possible to harmonise the otherwise diverse national law of the Member States.[538] In fact, the Commission itself recommended such a test in its 2011 EAW Report, invoking a 'general agreement' among Member States that an EAW should not be sought for 'very minor offences', since that would undermine trust in the instrument and create 'a disproportionate effect on the liberty and freedom of requested persons'.[539] As a consequence, the Council decided to include a proportionality check in the EAW Handbook,[540] and the Commission concluded that 'it is essential that all MS apply a proportionality test'.[541] In fact, to invoke Art. 1(3) FD EAW as the legal basis of such a proportionality test shows clearly that this provision is to be interpreted as a rights reservation to EAW surrenders.[542]

72 In more concrete terms, the issuing State would have to check whether an EAW would not be disproportionate in light of the seriousness of the offence at stake; judicial control could ensure that the proportionality requirement is taken seriously.[543] The executing State would have to consider whether proportionality would operate as a bar to surrender, either within its exercise of discretion[544] or as an autonomous bar. In this regard, rights considerations may, in line with the above considerations on a European *ordre public* and the constitutional identity review,[545] operate as a bar to surrender either by rendering it disproportionate or in their own right. Thus, as recently held by the CJEU,[546] the (inhumane) detention conditions in the issuing State may constitute a bar to surrender. Interestingly, in its 2011 EAW Report, the Commission took exactly this view, stating that it is 'clear' that the FD EAW 'does not mandate surrender where an executing judicial authority is satisfied . . . that such surrender would result in a breach of a requested person's fundamental rights arising from unacceptable detention conditions'.[547]

Further, in order to bring Art. 2(1) FD EAW into line with the proportionality principle, a *minimum sentence*, e.g. one year, to be expected or executed should be required.[548] Concerning the catalogue of offences of Art. 2(2) FD EAW, a restrictive interpretation is called for, especially with regard to those which are described in rather vague terms and rather constitute phenomena of criminality.[549] Furthermore, alternatively, less intrusive measures should be used if possible, especially if no flight risk exists and it can be expected that the suspect will voluntarily appear pursuant to a summons. In such cases, an SIS alert pursuant to Art. 98 CISA to communicate the place of residence of the person concerned[550] may be sufficient.[551] Other alternative measures based on mutual recognition, e.g. the trans-European use of supervision orders[552] or the transfer of prisoners,[553] have to be developed further and implemented.[554]

73 Last, but not least, the effective co-ordination of a **trans-European defence**, already mentioned above,[555] gains particular importance in the context of the EAW.[556] To make effective use of any judicial remedy and to invoke the rights objections mentioned above, the suspect must have an adequate defence. In order to effectively defend his liberty in the executing State, he must be assisted by counsel immediately.[557]

Solution, case 3

74 The Higher Regional Court has to take the admissibility decision on the basis of §80(1) IRG as this case deals with the requested extradition of a *German* citizen for a crime allegedly carried out only in Polish territory, so that a 'substantial link to the requesting Member State' (Poland) exists and we are thus dealing with *a purely foreign offence*. In these cases it must be ensured that the requesting MS (Poland) will, if necessary, return the sought person.[558] *In casu* the OLG Düsseldorf affirmed this precondition. Furthermore, the acts in question constitute extraditable offences in regard to the fraud cited,[559] especially as the acts correlate with a list category of Art. 2(2) FD EAW and under Polish law carry a maximum punishment of detention of no less than three years; moreover, no review of dual criminality was required. Accordingly, the Higher Regional Court was able to declare the extradition admissible.[560]

Solution, case 4

75 Here, the OLG has to review the granting authority's *preliminary decision on authorisation*.[561] Even though this gives the granting authority broad discretion, its decision must show plausibly *that* a *comprehensive evaluation process* has indeed taken place. *In casu* the OLG was unable to confirm this, and thus decided in an interlocutory order that the intended authorisation of extradition was based on incorrect assessment.[562]

Solution, case 5

76 Rape constitutes an *extraditable offence*.[563] The extradition is not prevented by the fact that A is a German citizen, as the act in question relates to a purely foreign offence since it has been committed on a foreign (non-German) territory (in S). As far as A claims that X's description of events is untruthful, a review as to whether there are reasonable grounds to believe that the person sought has committed the offence with which he is charged is only a possibility in justified exceptional cases.[564] In any case, a simple denial is irrelevant. The principle of *dual criminality* does not apply here since rape falls under one of the 32 offence categories listed in Art. 2(2) FD EAW.[565] Here, the law of the issuing State (S) is decisive in determining whether an act correlates to one of the offence categories. The issuing State is also responsible for legally evaluating the act; this is not reviewed by the executing State as a matter of principle. In order to prevent improper issuing of EAWs, it should at least be possible to demand that the categorisation of the act as a catalogue offence be logical and convincing. Here, we could criticise the fact that it is only ascertained that the act clearly conforms to the defined offence of rape, without addressing the obvious question of consent. Probably the competent Higher Court will thus initially refuse to execute the EAW and request further information from the issuing authority. The principle of *speciality* could act as an obstacle to *chain extradition* to U following extradition to S. According to Arts. 27, 28 FD EAW it is only the requesting State (S) that needs to observe the principle of speciality. Accordingly – subject to the exceptions that do not apply here – S may only transfer A to U if the responsible authorities in Germany have agreed to this. However, Germany will not agree, given the prohibition of extraditing its own nationals to the non-EU State U.[566] Thus transfer to U is not possible.[567]

III. Other Forms of Legal Assistance, Particularly Cross-border Gathering of Evidence

1. Preliminary Remarks

77 Other forms of mutual legal assistance primarily refer to investigative measures.[568] In this field, too, there is a plethora of applicable CoE/EU agreements and EU instruments of mutual recognition that make the legal situation extremely confusing for both students and practitioners. We will analyse them in detail below.[569] Against this background, the Commission's attempt at **harmonisation**, which forms the basis of its Green Paper on obtaining evidence in criminal matters, is to be welcomed in principle. We will also take a closer look at the Green Paper below.

78 At any rate, any attempt at harmonisation along the lines of the Commission proposals is confronted with the **principled criticism of mutual recognition.**[570] This criticism can be specified in regard to legal assistance concerning evidence gathering, in that evidence consists of 'unfinished products' created as part of the complex process of ascertaining the truth that cannot without further ado be taken out of their usual environment – that is, the national system of criminal procedure – and implanted into a foreign procedural system.[571] It is a unique feature of legal assistance concerning evidence that any gathering of such evidence is inextricably linked with the procedural law of the respective legal system and goes through a process encompassing several stages. Accordingly, the differences in both the structure and the details of European systems of criminal procedure affect the respective mutual assistance.[572] In addition, legal assistance to obtain evidence by way of mutual-recognition instruments not only requires common minimum standards as regards technical procedural rules on evidence, but also needs a **minimum standard of fundamental rights** that promotes mutual trust[573] and guarantees a fair trial and effective defence.[574] Indeed, the importance of a minimum fair-trial standard is confirmed by the US experience in inter-state co-operation where the fair-trial rights guaranteed under the US Constitution provide for a baseline harmonisation of state criminal procedures that undergird and enhance mutual trust.[575] Quite aside from this, we already count several mutual-recognition instruments going far beyond traditional legal assistance agreements, which have yet to prove themselves in practice. Of particular relevance in the evidentiary context is the *European Investigation Order* (EIO),[576] which may overcome the existing fragmentation.

2. European Agreements on Mutual Legal Assistance (CoE and EU)

79 The **European Convention on Mutual Assistance in Criminal Matters** (EuCMACM) of the CoE is – similarly to the European Convention on Extradition for extradition – the '*mother convention*' for other European treaty-based *legal assistance*; that is, all forms of legal assistance that are not related to extradition and enforcement.[577] Art. 1 sets out the right of the Contracting Parties to 'afford each other . . . the widest measure of mutual assistance', although restrictions are to be observed concerning political and fiscal offences, based on the national *ordre public* and,[578] where applicable, national reservations.[579] Arts. 3–6 EuCMACM regulate requests for legal assistance by way of the traditional *letters rogatory*. Arts. 7–12 cover individual legal assistance measures.[580] Arts. 14–20 regulate interstate procedure. The **AP I** facilitates legal assistance in fiscal offences[581] and extends the Convention's scope of application to further legal-assistance measures in the service of documents and the execution of a sentence in the requesting State.[582] **AP II** contains further measures to facilitate legal assistance, e.g. the temporary transfer of detained persons to the requested Party,[583] hearings by video or telephone conference,[584] or specific investigation measures, especially cross-border observations, permission of controlled delivery, covert investigations and JITs.[585]

80 Chapter 2 of the **CISA** (Arts. 48–53) supplements[586] the EuCMACM. Arts. 49 and 50 CISA go beyond the EuCMACM, *extending* the *obligation to provide legal assistance* to certain areas, such as proceedings for administrative offences; proceedings for claims for damages arising from prosecution; clemency proceedings; and – of the greatest practical significance – proceedings for infringement of laws regarding excise duties, value added tax and customs duties.[587] At the same time, the *requirements* for legal assistance are essentially restricted to the need for the conduct forming the basis of the request for mutual assistance to be subject to some form of sanction according to the law of both Contracting Parties, including in some cases even only as an administrative sanction.[588] Procedural *documents* can be *sent* directly to natural persons or corporate entities by post;[589] each Schengen State has made a list of the respective documents.[590] Furthermore, requests for legal assistance can be made *directly* between judicial authorities,[591] although requests for transfer or transit need to go through the normal channels of communication in the ministries of justice.[592] Direct communication between judicial authorities, especially the direct sending of procedural documents, can safely be called a revolutionary novelty of the CISA, given that in traditional legal assistance such contact with foreign judicial authorities must go through the relevant legal-assistance departments of the executive (normally the Ministry of Justice).[593] Last, but not least, Art. 73 CISA provides for the possibility of *controlled deliveries* in the context of illicit drug trafficking.

81 The **EU Mutual Assistance Convention** (EUMAC) entered into force on 23 August 2005.[594] It repealed Arts. 49(a), 52, 53 and 73 CISA,[595] and made the Schengen-related provisions applicable to Norway and Iceland.[596] Art. 3 states that legal assistance shall also be provided in proceedings brought by administrative authorities and against legal persons. Art. 4(1) displaces, for the first time in a European instrument,[597] the *lex loci* in favour of the *lexi fori* (*forum regit actum*)[598] with regard to 'formalities and procedures' indicated by the requesting State and to be complied with by the requested State.[599] Arts. 5–7 simplify the procedure; in particular the procedural documents to be sent directly to a foreign judicial authority must no longer be defined by way of national lists as under Art. 52 CISA.[600] Furthermore, regulations are set out on hearings by video or telephone conference,[601] controlled deliveries,[602] joint investigation teams (JITs),[603] covert investigations[604] and the interception of telecommunications.[605]

3. Gathering of Evidence: From Traditional Mutual Legal Assistance to Mutual Recognition

a) Preliminary Remarks

82 Above (mn. 15) we have listed all relevant instruments on other mutual assistance, especially evidence gathering.[606] This matter is now, within the EU, with more than one MS involved, comprehensively regulated by the Directive on the European Investigation Order (EIO).[607] With effect from 22 May 2017, it has replaced[608] the FD on the European Evidence Warrant (FD EEW),[609] as well as the corresponding provisions of the EuCMACM,[610] of the CISA,[611] of the EUMAC,[612] and of the FD on Freezing.[613] The FD EEW had already been repealed by the Regulation (EU) 2016/95.[614]

b) Freezing of Evidence and Property

83 The FD on freezing property or evidence[615] applied to freezing orders issued for purposes of *securing evidence* and the subsequent *confiscation of property*.[616] A 'freezing order' issued by a judicial authority of one Member State, the '*issuing State*', is to be recognised and executed by another Member State, the '*executing State*'.[617] The 'competent judicial authorities' shall recognise the freezing order without any further formality and forthwith take all measures necessary for its execution.[618] However, the FD initially applied only to the freezing order of the issuing State;[619] the actual transmission of the frozen object from the (requested) executing State to the (requesting) issuing State required a request to this effect[620] and thus followed traditional rules of legal assistance.[621] This has been criticised in several Member States and given rise to the EIO[622] to be analysed below.[623] *Dual criminality* was relinquished for certain offences – the catalogue is the same as that of the EAW[624] – if these are punishable in the issuing State by a custodial sentence of a maximum period of at least three years.[625]

c) European Evidence Warrant

84 The European Evidence Warrant (EEW)[626] was linked with the FD on Freezing and made it possible for Member States to have *objects, documents and data* confiscated in one MS and transmitted to another. It represented the '*judicial decision*' of one Member State, the 'issuing State', which was to be 'executed' by another Member State, the 'executing State'.[627] The *issuing State* had to have 'reasonable grounds' to believe that 'relevant objects, documents or data' are located in the territory of the executing State.[628] It could specify procedural rules and formalities (*forum regit actum*),[629] as long as these did not conflict with the fundamental legal principles of the executing State.[630] The warrant had to be proportionate[631] and legally admissible under the law of the issuing State in a comparable case.[632] The '*executing authorities*' should recognise the freezing order without any further formality and at once take all measures necessary for its execution according to their law (*locus regit actum*).[633] Deadlines served to expedite the process.[634] *Double* *criminality* was relinquished unless it was necessary to carry out a search or seizure[635] or unless offences of the EAW catalogue[636] were involved,[637] as long as these were punishable by a custodial sentence or a detention order for a maximum period of at least three years.[638]

85 However, there is a range of reasons to **criticise** the EEW.[639] Initially, it covered – as its name already suggests – only *certain, already extant, evidence.*[640] This excludes, for example, personal evidence (hearings of witnesses and suspects)[641] and evidence that is present but can only be accessed through indirect means, such as DNA samples.[642] Nor were included real-time information, the gathering of communication data and the examination of already present objects (covered by the EEW), documents or data.[643] Accordingly, the traditional form of legal assistance had to be used for all of these types of evidence.[644] The EEW could only be applied to criminal or administrative proceedings with judicial protection.[645] The broad definition of the issuing authority as 'any other judicial authority as defined by the issuing State'[646] is incompatible with the exclusive *judicial competence* in such matters (*Richtervorbehalt*).[647] Thus many jurisdictions, e.g. Germany, had to refuse to execute a warrant not issued by a judge, a court, an investigating magistrate or a public prosecutor as a matter of principle,[648] and make a declaration to this effect.[649] And while the *division of legal remedies* – against the execution of an EEW in the executing State, against its issue in the issuing State[650] – appeared to be consistent, it may have forced the person affected having to take legal action in a foreign country.[651] Furthermore, legal remedies could be restricted to cases using coercive measures.[652] The FD did not determine how *evidence was to be handled*; ultimately, the issuing State decided on this.[653]

d) The Commission's Green Paper on Evidence

86 The Commission already endorsed the application of the principle of mutual recognition of evidence in the **2001 Green Paper on Establishing a European Public Prosecutor,**[654] and thus encouraged the idea of EU-wide evidence; that is, evidence that can, along the lines of the principle of freedom of movement of goods, move freely throughout the Union.[655] In light of the above critique,[656] it should be clear, however, that only a common (supranational or harmonised) European criminal procedure,[657] or at least a **European system for the admission of evidence**, would create an adequate basis for supranational legal assistance in matters of evidence.[658]

87 With the **Green Paper** on '**obtaining evidence in criminal matters from one Member State to another**',[659] the Commission proposed the replacement of traditional legal assistance by the transnational gathering of evidence based upon the principle of mutual recognition. To that effect, the existing instruments, which, as we have seen above, are based either on classic legal assistance or on mutual recognition (especially the EEW), are to be *summarised* in one instrument, given that the legal situation 'may cause confusion among practitioners';[660] the fact that the respective individual instruments can only be applied to certain aspects renders their practical application difficult.[661] In particular, legal assistance shall be made more *efficient* through mutual recognition,[662] and the actual *use* of the evidence gathered shall be ensured.[663] Going beyond the EEW, real-time information is to be transmitted between the MS. Finally, '*non-legislative measures*' such as guidelines and training for practitioners are suggested.

e) The European Investigation Order (EIO)

88 Even though the Green Paper has been strongly criticised (also within the Member States[664]) the Council and EP adopted a Directive regarding a **European Investigation Order (EIO) in criminal matters** in 2014, which entered into force on 22 May 2017.[665] This created a unified legal assistance instrument that covers all investigative actions – with the exception of joint investigation teams[666] and cross-border surveillance pursuant to Art. 40 CISA[667] – and thus aims to overcome the existing fragmentation,[668] albeit to a large extent following the principles of traditional mutual assistance.[669] The directive covers, *ratione materiae*, not only criminal proceedings in the narrower sense, but all proceedings by administrative or judicial authorities 'in respect of acts which are punishable under the national law of the issuing State by virtue of being infringements of the rules of law and where the decision may give rise to proceedings before a court having jurisdiction, in particular, in criminal matters'.[670] As with the EEW, the issuing authority can be not only a court, but also 'any other judicial authority as defined by the issuing State and, in the specific case ... acting in its capacity as an investigating authority in criminal proceedings with competence to order the gathering of evidence in accordance with national law';[671] however, in this case the EIO must be validated by an (investigative) judge or prosecutor prior to transmission to the executing authority.[672] Thus the directive creates a general judicial reservation (*Justizvorbehalt*)

which, although not to be equated with a judge's reservation *stricto sensu* (that is, the requirement of authorisation by a judge, *Richtervorbehalt*),[673] is a novelty in (European) mutual assistance and may from now on be considered the new European minimum standard in other mutual legal assistance.[674] At any rate, the executing authority may have to be a judge if this is so required by national law;[675] otherwise, however, if national law is more flexible, administrative authorities, in particular the police, may execute the EIO.[676] Thus, overall, an EIO may be issued and executed without judicial control *stricto sensu* (i.e. control by a judge at either the issuing or executing stage).[677] A request to issue an EIO may also be filed by a suspect/accused or his lawyer, in line with the applicable defence rights of national law.[678]

89 The order must be executed by the executing State, as a rule, within 120 days.[679] Similarly to the EAW, the aim is to make the EIO subject to **strict deadlines** in order to render its execution more efficient. When undertaking the requested investigative action, the executing authority must comply with the '**formalities and procedures**' indicated by the issuing authority,[680] thereby ensuring – in line with the principle of *forum regit actum*[681] – that the evidence gathered can be admitted and used in the issuing State;[682] if, in turn, the executing authority does not comply with these procedural rules of the issuing State, the *exclusion of the relevant evidence* may ensue (thereto also below mn. 94).[683] Thus the issuing authority can primarily request the executing authority to comply with such 'formalities and procedures' that serve the said admission of evidence in the issuing State and, in line with the rights focus of the directive,[684] aim to protect the rights of the suspect;[685] under such a restrictive interpretation an incompatibility with 'the fundamental principles of law'[686] of the executing State may safely be avoided.[687] At any rate, the executing authority will largely apply its own law (*locus regit actum*)[688] and the Directive explicitly enables it to take recourse to different measures or indeed refuse to execute the order completely in exceptional cases.[689]

90 Recourse to **different measures**[690] is possible if the requested investigative measure does not exist under the law of the executing State or would not be available in a similar domestic case;[691] yet the executing State has to make a minimum standard and number of (non-coercive)[692] measures available.[693] Further, the executing State may take recourse to a less intrusive but equally effective measure to obtain the relevant evidence.[694] This is reminiscent of the second step in the

proportionality test; that is, the necessity of the measure with a view to the objective pursued.[695] Indeed, the principle of proportionality is explicitly recognised in Art. 6(1)(a) EIO Directive according to which the *issuing* authority is obliged to review the proportionality of the investigative measure in question. While this rule only provides for a proportionality test by the issuing authority, the *executing* authority may also take into account the proportionality of the measure. This follows from several considerations. On a general level, it arises from the executing authority's right to refuse execution in case of rights violations[696] – we will return to this most general ground for refusal below – since the principle of proportionality belongs to these rights as part of a European *ordre public*.[697] Further, more specifically it results from the right – just mentioned – of the executing authority to take recourse to different (less intrusive) measures and, most specifically, to consult the issuing authority if it has reason to believe that the measure is, inter alia, not necessary or proportionate.[698] This right to consult presupposes that the executing authority actually examines the proportionality of the measure, at least in a summary fashion, in the first place.[699] The Directive's recourse to proportionality is to be welcomed[700] and confirms the approach taken above with regard to the EAW;[701] that is, to invoke proportionality against an excessive application of a mutual-recognition instrument disregarding fundamental rights. Last, but not least, the investigative measure can only be ordered if it is possible to do so 'under the same conditions in a similar domestic case'.[702] This ensures that the issuing State does not use an EIO for '**forum shopping**'; that is, request a measure from another MS which it could not actually order under its own law.[703]

91 If a 'different' measure in the sense mentioned above is not available at all, the executing authority shall notify the issuing authority that it cannot provide the requested assistance.[704] This almost converts the lack of availability into a general ground for refusal[705] and indeed only a restrictive interpretation of Art. 10(5) EIO Directive, limiting its application to the specific requirements of lawfulness of the relevant measure,[706] can avoid this result and ensure a reasonable delimitation with regard to Art. 11 EIO Directive.[707] The actual **grounds for refusal** – grounds for 'non-recognition or non-execution' in the Directive's language[708] – differ from those of other instruments, such as the FD EAW and the FD on the European Supervision Order (ESO),[709] which could in individual cases lead to partly contradictory results.[710] Also, refusing to execute an EIO on the ground, already included in the FD EEW, that 'its execution would harm essential national security interests',[711] seems somewhat anachronistic.[712] By contrast, while the draft Directive did not provide for a *general* ground for refusal,[713] such a general ground of sorts is now – apart from several specific grounds[714] – foreseen in Art. 11(1)(f), according to which the execution can be refused if otherwise the executing State were to violate its human rights obligations under Art. 6 TEU and the CFREU.[715] This *rights-based ground for refusal* is a welcome novelty in a mutual-recognition instrument and shows that the EU seems to take its rights obligations and programmatic discourse since Stockholm seriously.[716] Of course, given its broad *ratione materiae* scope (essentially all relevant individual rights), the application of this ground makes significant demands on the executing authority. In fact, it has, *proprio motu*, to carry out an *ex ante* assessment of likely rights violations which an execution of the relevant request would produce;[717] the scarce and schematic information contained in the EIO form may not suffice to be able to make such an assessment, which means that the executing authority will have to consult the issuing authority.[718] Also, while this ground refers to the executing State's rights obligations, the underlying separation between action by the issuing and the executing States is somewhat artificial and certainly untenable if the issuing authority already commits a rights violation so serious that it also affects the execution of an EIO.[719] **Dual criminality** is relinquished, as is now standard in the mutual-recognition instruments, if the conduct in question falls under one of the offences of the EAW catalogue and is punishable with a minimum maximum sentence of three years in the issuing State.[720]

92 The Directive contains a series of regulations on **specific investigative measures**, such as the temporary transfer of a detained person for the purposes of investigation, video or telephone conferences and information on bank accounts and transactions (including their monitoring and real-time information),[721] as well as – under a separate chapter – interception of telecommunications.[722] These measures cannot be analysed in detail here, but scholarly analysis is increasingly covering this area.[723] In this context, the importance of effective remedies becomes readily apparent. In fact, the Directive provides for a **bifurcated system of remedies** with the possibility to challenge the 'substantive reasons for issuing the EIO' in the issuing State[724] and the 'recognition or execution of an EIO' in the executing State. The latter remedy is not granted explicitly but follows from three considerations: (i) the Member State's general obligation to provide for remedies;[725] (ii) the obligation of both the issuing and the *executing authority* to 'inform each other about the legal remedies sought against the issuing, the *recognition* or the *execution* of an EIO';[726] and lastly (iii) the fact that the issuing State 'shall take into account a successful challenge against the *recognition or execution* of an EIO'.[727] Thus, in the executing State, a challenge can be brought against the recognition or execution – as opposed to the substantive reasons (given by the issuing State and therefore to be challenged there) – of the respective EIO.[728] This **division of labour** between the issuing and the executing States confirms the underlying idea of shared, transnational proceedings where the execution is part of the procedure led by the issuing State[729] and, thus, the execution State trusts in the lawfulness of the issuing State's measure and only examines its formal legality.[730] Such a division of labour in transnational criminal proceedings and the ensuing necessity of mutual trust presuppose, of course, certain common minimum standards with respect to both the requirements of evidence gathering and the protection of defence rights. Indeed, this is acknowledged by primary Union law itself, especially Art. 82(2)(a) TFEU, but the procedural law of the Member States, in general and in regard to evidence gathering, is far from harmonised.[731] This is, in fact, the reason why the EIO Directive allows the executing State to take recourse to different measures (mentioned above) to comply with the EIO of the issuing State.

93 Apart from that, the bifurcated system of judicial remedies makes the life of a suspect difficult, since she is necessarily forced to deal with at least one foreign legal system and language.[732] Adequate legal advice to account for this additional difficulty, e.g. by way of a **transnational defence** team,[733] is not provided. In this sense, it is fair to say that the EIO Directive – like previous mutual-recognition instruments – fails to address the particular problems of a defence in transnational proceedings. It is positive, though, that an EIO can be challenged in both the issuing and the executing State and, in particular, that the former must take into account a successful challenge in the latter.[734] This collaboration of the issuing and executing States paves the way for a **concentration** of the legal remedy in the executing State, which then should also decide on the lawfulness (substantial reasons) of the ordering of the measure by the issuing State.[735] This would at least avoid the suspect having to challenge the EIO in two jurisdictions. Of course, a challenge would only have a practical impact if the execution of the EIO were – contrary to Art. 14(6) EIO Directive –

suspended, i.e. if the respective evidence were not handed over to the issuing State until a final decision on the challenge has been taken.[736]

94 At any rate, given that the issuing State must take a successful challenge in the executing State into account in its proceedings as forum State, an **exclusion** of the respective **evidence** may ensue if the unlawfulness identified by the court of the executing State is serious enough;[737] similarly, a rights violation by the executing State itself – in the course of the execution of the EIO – may also entail an exclusion of the respective evidence in the proceedings in the issuing State.[738] On the other hand, as already argued above,[739] the executing authority's non-compliance with the formalities and procedures indicated by the issuing authority pursuant to Art. 9(2) EIO Directive may also entail the exclusion of the relevant evidence. All this shows that the EIO Directive does not do away with the **forum rule**[740] as to the admission and use of evidence; that is, it accepts the general rule that it is for the forum State to decide, pursuant to its national law, whether and how it accept evidence gathered abroad.[741] This, in turn, shows that there are clear limits to mutual recognition in the field of gathering evidence. In fact, the issuing (requesting) forum State does not automatically accept the evidence gathered by the executing (requested) State, although there may be a presumption of trust given that this State is an EU Member State.[742] Yet this trust clearly finds its limits, as in other areas of police and judicial co-operation, in the European or national (identity review!) *ordre public*.[743]

IV. Enforcement Assistance

1. Transfer and Enforcement Agreements

95 The scope of the **CoE's** Convention on the Transfer of Sentenced Persons (TransferC)[744] goes beyond the borders of Europe.[745] Its purpose is that sentenced persons may serve their **sentence in their home country** in order to facilitate their **rehabilitation** and render enforcement more humane. However, this Convention does not constitute any obligation to transfer. Rather, a transfer will be based upon a *consensus* between the sentencing and the home State and requires the consent of the person affected.[746] The Convention also regulates enforcement following the transfer, whereby the sentence is either continued or converted into an equivalent one;[747] in the latter case, Art. 11 TransferC provides for some rules, especially that the deprivation of liberty already served by the sentenced person must be deducted.[748] The enforcement following transfer, including any suspension of the sentence, takes place according to the law of the administering State.[749] The **AP**[750] permits enforcement in the home State without the consent of the person affected if he seeks to avoid its execution by fleeing from the sentencing State to the home State.[751] Furthermore, enforcement is shifted to the State to which the person in question is deported.[752]

96 The TransferC is supplemented by Arts. 67–9 **CISA** on the **transfer of the enforcement** of criminal judgments.[753] Art. 68(1) CISA sets out the option of requesting that the home State of the convict take over enforcement of the sentence if said convict has fled to this State and 'is within its territory'. The person in question does *not* have to consent to this transfer of enforcement.[754]

97 The Convention between the EC Member States on the Enforcement of Foreign Criminal Sentences of 13 November 1991 (**EC Enforcement Convention**)[755] links to the TransferC and Arts. 67–9 CISA, although according to its preamble the TransferC is only to be 'considered' and is not regarded as the mother convention.[756] The key issue that the Enforcement Convention is concerned with is the extent to which the consent of the affected person can be dispensed with in transfer for the purposes of enforcement (along the lines of Art. 69 CISA just referred to). Its Art. 3 – similarly to Art. 3 TransferC and Art. 68 CISA – requires that the sentenced person is in the territory of the executing State. Its purpose is the *removal of obstacles to enforcement*; the main concern is with *rendering prosecution more effective*, not with rehabilitation and humanisation of enforcement like the TransferC. A further **specific convention** is the Convention of 17 June 1998 on *Driving Disqualifications*.[757]

2. Instruments on the Basis of Mutual Recognition

98 The Commission's **Green Paper on Sanctions**[758] examined whether the differences in the Member States' systems of sanctions constituted an obstacle to the creation of an area of freedom, security and justice, and which areas required that further action be taken in this regard.[759] The Commission considers the approximation of laws in the field of sanctions to be particularly useful and necessary in order to give the general public a shared sense of justice, to prevent offenders from taking advantage of divergences between penalties and to promote the acceptance of a pan-European application of the *ne bis in idem* principle.[760] Furthermore, removing differences between the laws on penalties and their enforcement is supposed to enhance mutual trust and thus help to secure acceptance of the mutual recognition of judgments.[761] Following an analysis of the pertinent European legal instruments, the Commission states that thanks to the FD EAW and the (then) proposals for legal instruments in the area of the mutual recognition of fines and financial penalties, confiscations and decisions on the annulment of rights, progress has already been made, but that action is still needed concerning the recognition of sanctions involving the deprivation of liberty and their enforcement.[762] In regard to the considerable divergences in Member States' law on penalties,[763] the Commission considers it desirable especially to determine a common penalty for participation in a criminal organisation[764] and also encourages the introduction of common maximum penalties, even envisaging the abolition of lifelong imprisonment;[765] minimum rules should be issued to define the offence and the (financial) penalty.[766] Further approximation of laws in the areas of sanctions applied to legal persons[767] and the use of alternative sanctions[768] is also seen as desirable. Based on this, proposals are made for the mutual recognition and enforcement of custodial penalties and alternative sanctions.[769]

99 The FD **European Enforcement Order** (EEO),[770] which was to have been implemented by 5 December 2011,[771] aims to facilitate the social rehabilitation of sentenced EU nationals by having the sentence executed in their familiar (domestic) environment[772] and thus to reduce the number of foreign EU nationals in domestic prisons.[773] The practical relevance of the FD cannot be overestimated given that tens of thousands of EU citizens are prosecuted per year in other MS[774] and thus the question of the place of the execution of the sentence arises.[775] The FD applies if the sentenced person is in the sentencing ('issuing') or the enforcing ('executing') MS.[776] While in practice the issuing MS may take the initiative,[777] both the issuing and the executing MS are entitled to request to 'forward the judgment' in order to have its enforcement transferred;[778] the sentenced person may also make the request.[779] The executing State is obliged – absent a relevant ground for refusal[780] – to recognise the foreign judgment and enforce it;[781] in doing so it applies its own law.[782] As a rule, the executing State should be the sentenced person's State of nationality or residence,[783] or in exceptional cases any other MS[784] if both this State and the sentenced person consent.[785] In any case, the issuing State must satisfy itself, in line with the FD's aim, enunciated above, that the enforcement of the sentence by the executing State would serve the purpose of facilitating the social rehabilitation of the sentenced person.[786] The requirement of *double criminality* is dispensed with for certain offences – which conform to the EAW catalogue[787] – if these are punishable in the issuing State by deprivation of liberty for a maximum period of at least three years[788] and no declaration is made that the catalogue of Art. 7(1) EEO will not be applied.[789] As a matter of principle, the sentenced person may only be prosecuted or sentenced for those acts that form the basis for the transfer (*principle of speciality*).[790] The executing State is permitted to adapt the kind and duration of the penalty to its law under certain narrowly defined conditions but may not aggravate it.[791] In any case, the 'full period' of the deprivation of liberty already served must be deducted.[792] The FD must be applied duly taking into account the European *ordre public*.[793]

100 The FD on the application of the principle of mutual recognition to **financial penalties**[794] regulates the recognition of financial penalties – to be understood broadly[795] – across the EU, especially in the area of road traffic offences.[796] It has a high practical importance.[797] The financial penalty is to be imposed on a natural or legal person by a decision of the competent authority in the issuing State; this may be a court[798] but also an administrative authority, provided that the person concerned has had an opportunity to have the case tried by a criminal court;[799] otherwise there is no decision within the FD's meaning and it is not applicable in the first place.[800] The decision, together with a certificate (standard form),[801] is to be transmitted to the suspect's Member State (executing State) and thus constitutes the actual legal assistance request.[802] The executing MS is obliged to recognise and enforce this decision 'without any further formality',[803] taking the information contained in the certificate as the basis for the execution.[804] Yet it may invoke one of the grounds for refusal listed in Art. 7,[805] in particular if the certificate 'is incomplete or manifestly does not correspond to the decision'.[806] It is also noteworthy that the execution can be refused if the financial penalty is below €70.[807] This is certainly of practical significance and important in light of the *proportionality* principle, although one wonders why the financial threshold is not higher.[808] Proportionality and other fundamental rights and principles (European *ordre public*) are to be taken into account.[809] If this is taken seriously, Member States honouring the culpability principle will have problems executing decisions based on pure owner liability (*Halterhaftung*) in road traffic cases, since this kind of strict liability does not care whether the owner or another person drove the relevant vehicle.[810] *Double criminality* does not require verification for the (administrative) offences[811] listed in Art. 5,[812] which adds seven types of minor offence, particularly traffic offences, to the EAW catalogue.[813] Monies obtained from the enforcement of decisions shall accrue to the executing State unless otherwise agreed.[814]

101 In Germany, the FD was implemented without any major changes in July 2010 by the **EU Financial Penalties Act.**[815] The Act is traditional in its distinction between admissibility and authorisation,[816] whereby there is a basic obligation to grant authorisation that does not apply only when the act was committed (also) in Germany or outside the territory of the requesting MS.[817] The central granting authority is the Federal Office of Justice in Bonn.[818] The legislator included the other (optional) grounds for refusal in Art. 7 FD as *obligatory* grounds for inadmissibility in §87b IRG[819] and added strict liability as a further reason for refusal.[820] The person concerned may file an objection against authorisation with the competent district court.[821] Unlike the FD (Art. 10), the German implementation does not contain any alternative custodial sentences.[822]

102 The FD on the **European Supervision Order (ESO) in pre-trial proceedings**[823] is based upon the concept of the mutual recognition of supervision measures in order to *avoid provisional (pre-trial) detention.*[824] At the same time, the general public is to be protected by the option of supervision, seeing as previously there was only the option of either provisional detention or unsupervised movement.[825] More concretely speaking, the FD, providing for a series of obligatory and facultative supervision measures,[826] aims to ensure equal treatment of persons subject to criminal proceedings resident in the trial state and those not so resident,[827] as the latter are imprisoned more often on a regular basis on the grounds of their flight risk.[828] Take the case of Polish citizen P who commits a burglary in Spain: if he were Spanish he would normally not be detained but being a foreigner (EU) he will probably be detained given the flight risk. Thus if the FD worked properly it could considerably diminish the significant number of EU foreigners in pre-trial detention in Member States[829] and it would be yet another example where mutual recognition would work in favour of suspects.[830] Unfortunately, the FD's implementation is slow and far from uniform,[831] and it may produce unintended consequences, especially the issuing of an ESO by a Member

State which would otherwise not opt for pre-trial detention given the limited seriousness of the offence. Thus, in such a case, the ESO would produce a result detrimental to the suspect and it may be necessary to take recourse to *ordre public* and/or proportionality considerations to avoid it.[832] At any rate, the suspect has to agree to the issuing of an ESO[833] but she cannot claim it by right.[834] A legal remedy exists primarily in the issuing MS given that its decision triggers the proceedings;[835] yet the suspect may file a remedy against the executing Member State's recognition decision.[836] The executing MS must inform the issuing authority 'immediately' in case of a breach of an ESO.[837] *Double criminality* is not required for 32 offences, which, in essence,[838] correspond to the EAW catalogue, if punishable with a maximum minimum sentence of three years;[839] yet MS may declare the ESO not applicable to 'some or all' of these offences out of constitutional considerations.[840]

103 The FD on **taking account of convictions** in the EU Member States **in the course of new criminal proceedings**[841] determines the conditions under which existing convictions must be taken into account when convicting a person of another act in another MS.[842] Previous convictions handed down in foreign EU States are to have the same effect as internal convictions.[843]

104 The FD on the Mutual Recognition of Judgments and Probation Decisions with a View to the **Supervision of Probation Measures and Alternative Sanctions**[844] – like the EEO, which takes primacy[845] – aims first and foremost to improve the chances of rehabilitating the person affected.[846] At the same time, the monitoring of compliance with probation measures is to be improved, thus preventing recidivism.[847] This is to take place in the areas of the measures listed in the FD (e.g. obliging the sentenced person to avoid certain localities and persons or to report to a specific authority at a specific time);[848] the MS can also take over the supervision of further measures.[849] Any enforcement and subsequent decisions will take place according to the law of the executing State.[850] The measure ordered may be *adapted* if it is otherwise incompatible with the law of the executing State;[851] it may not be made more severe or longer than the measure originally imposed.[852] The executing State may *refuse* to execute the measure if there is no *dual criminality*; however, the requirement for dual criminality does not apply to the EAW's catalogue of offences[853] if the principle of *ne bis in idem* would be violated, if there is immunity, or if the enforcement of the sentence is statute-barred according to the law of the executing State and relates to an act which falls within its competence according to that law.[854]

Notes

1. Case taken from Gleß and Lüke, *Jura*, 22 (2000), 402.
2. Art. 29 ff. TEU old version. On its historical development from the various forms of co-operation within the framework of the EC since the 1970s, cf. Ambos, *Internationales Strafrecht* (2008), §12 mn. 2.
3. See already above Chapter 1, mn. 9.
4. Cf. Art. 10 Protocol No 36 to the Lisbon Treaty 'On Transitional Provisions' (OJ C 115 of 9 May 2008, 322). On the CJEU's review competence before and after Lisbon, cf. Skouris, *EuCLR*, 1 (2011), 108 ff.; Skouris, in Meng, Ress and Stein, *FS Europa-Institut* (2011), pp. 545 ff.; de Amicis, *EuCLR*, 2 (2012), 47–8.
5. Title V, Art. 67(1) TFEU. On the genesis, see e.g. Leanza, in Acuña, *Il mandato di arresto europeo* (2004), pp. 7 ff.
6. Art. 67(3) TFEU.
7. Art. 82(1) subparagraph 1 TFEU; on this, cf. Chapter 1, mn. 25 ff.
8. Art. 82(1) subparagraph 2(a) TFEU.
9. As to the Union's competence to 'prevent and settle conflicts of jurisdiction' pursuant to Art. 82(1) subparagraph 2(b) TFEU, both Böse, in Zöller et al., *FS Wolter* (2013), p. 1313; and Asp, *Procedural Criminal Law Cooperation* (2016), p. 36, rightly criticise the tension between this possibility and the jurisdictional expansion implicit in Art. 83 TFEU and in many secondary-law instruments. See generally Asp, *Procedural Criminal Law Cooperation* (2016), pp. 27–8 (quoting Art. 10 of the Market Abuse Directive as an example of a jurisdiction provision in the sense of Art. 82(1) subpara. 2(b) TFEU).
10. Art. 82(1) subparagraph 2(b)–(d) TFEU. See also Satzger, in Streinz, *EUV/AEUV* (2012), Art. 82 AEUV mn. 2 ff. On the former legal regime according to Art. 31 TEU old version, cf. Ambos, *Internationales Strafrecht* (2008), §12 mn. 20. On conflicts of competence, cf. Ambos, *Internationales Strafrecht* (2014), §4 mn. 1 ff.; as well as Sinn, *ZIS*, 8 (2013), 3; Eisele, *ZStW*, 125 (2013), 1 ff.; Satzger, in Streinz, *EUV/AEUV* (2012), Art. 82 AEUV mn. 39 ff.; Caeiro, in Correia, Machado and Loureiro, *Estudos homenagem Gomes Canotilho*, iii (2012), pp. 194 ff.
11. Thereon main text, mn. 9 ff.
12. Art. 82(2) TFEU; on this, cf. main text, mn. 8.
13. Art. 85 TFEU, on this cf. Chapter 5, mn. 16 ff.
14. Art. 86 TFEU, Chapter 5, mn. 24 ff.
15. Art. 87(1) TFEU. On the distinction between police and judicial co-operation, cf. Vermeulen, *Free Gathering and Movement of Evidence* (2011), pp. 17 ff.
16. In this regard, cf. also Council Decision 2003/335/JHA of 8 May 2003 (OJ L 118 of 14 May 2003, 12) on the investigation and prosecution of **genocide, crimes against humanity** and **war crimes** (on this, cf. also Ryngaert, *EJCCLCJ*, 14 (2006), 70 ff.) and the **Prüm Convention** (Convention between the Kingdom of Belgium, the Federal Republic of Germany, the Kingdom of Spain, the French Republic, the Grand Duchy of

Luxembourg, the Kingdom of the Netherlands and the Republic of Austria on the Stepping Up of Cross-border Cooperation, particularly in Combating Terrorism, Cross-border Crime and Illegal Migration of 27 May 2005, available at https://ec.europa.eu/anti-fraud/sites/antifraud/files/docs/body/prumtr.pdf, last accessed 27 January 2018; on this, cf. Hetzer, in Sieber, Satzger and von Heinegg, *Europäisches Strafrecht* (2014), pp. 748 ff.). The Prüm Convention originally specified the exchange of data in three areas (DNA analysis, fingerprints and motor vehicles) between the Contracting Parties and was transposed into EU law in June 2008 (Council Decision 2008/616/JHA, OJ L 210 of 6 August 2008, 1–11, the so-called **Prüm Decision**; and Council Decision 2006/616/JHA, OJ L 210 of 6 August 2008, 12–72); for a detailed account on this, cf. Böse, *Grundsatz der Verfügbarkeit* (2007), pp. 42 ff.; also de Biolley, *RIDP*, 77 (2006), 35 ff.; Hummer, *EuR*, 42 (2007), 527 ff.; Niemeier and Zerbst, *ERA Forum*, 8 (2007), 535 ff.; Meyer, *NStZ*, 28 (2008), 190; Krüßmann, *Transnationales Strafprozessrecht* (2009), pp. 456 ff.; Schoppa, *Europol* (2013), pp. 89 ff.; on the implementation, *eucrim*, 5 (2010), 55, 142; *eucrim*, 6 (2011), 16–17, 110, 115, 150; *eucrim*, 7 (2012), 104–5; *eucrim*, 8 (2013), 11–12, 46–7, 122; see also Council Document 5074/7/13. The **UK** and **Ireland** have opted in to apply the rules of the Prüm Convention (Commission Decision (EU) 2016/809 of 20 May 2016, OJ L 132 of 25 May 2016, 105), while **Denmark** has made use of the opt-out clause (*eucrim*, 5 (2010), 142; on Danish opt-outs in general, cf. already Chapter 1, mn. 11). The non-EU states **Norway** and **Iceland** are taking part in some parts of the Prüm Convention (Council Decision 2010/482/EU of 26 July 2010, OJ L 238 of 9 September 2010, 1). Cf. also Council FD 2006/960/JHA of 18 December 2006 on **simplifying the exchange of information and intelligence** between law enforcement authorities of the MS of the EU (OJ L328 of 20 December 2006, 89), which can be traced back to a Swedish initiative, according to which Member States' prosecution authorities should have access to data under the same conditions as national authorities (on this, cf. Böse, *Grundsatz der Verfügbarkeit* (2007), pp. 39 ff.; Meyer, *NStZ*, 28 (2008), 189–90; Eisele, in Sieber, Satzger and von Heinegg, *Europäisches Strafrecht* (2014), pp. 890–1); Council Decision 2008/633/JHA of 23 June 2008 concerning access for consultation of the **Visa Information System** (VIS) by designated authorities of MS and by Europol for the purposes of the prevention, detection and investigation of terrorist offences and of other serious criminal offences (OJ L 128 of 13 August 2008, 129); Regulation (EU) No 603/2013 of the EP and of the Council of 26 June 2013 on the establishment of 'Eurodac' for the **comparison of fingerprints** for the effective application of Regulation (EU) No 604/2013 etc. (OJ L 180 of 29 June 2013, 1); cf. also Communication from the Commission on 'Strengthening Law Enforcement Cooperation in the EU: the European Information Exchange Model (EIXM)', COM (2012) 735 final; for a detailed account of the exchange of criminal prosecution data, cf. Zöller, *ZIS*, 6 (2011), 64; Esser, in Böse, *Europäisches Strafrecht* (2013), pp. 743–7; from a Polish perspective, cf. also Buczma, *ERA Forum*, 12 (2011), 465 ff. On information exchange with regard to **traffic offences**, cf. Directive 2011/82/EU of the EP and of the Council of 25 October 2011 facilitating the cross-border exchange of information on road-safety-related traffic offences (OJ L 288 of 5 October 2011, 1); replaced by Directive 2015/413/EU of the EP and of the Council of 11 March 2015 facilitating cross-border exchange of information on road-safety traffic offences (OJ L 68 of 13 March 2015, 9); on the respective litigation before the CJEU regarding the right legal basis – according to the CJEU Art. 91(1)(c) TFEU – cf. Mitsilegas, *EU Criminal Law* *after Lisbon* (2016), pp. 21–5; crit. also Langheld, *EuCLR*, 2 (2012), 276 ff. On information exchange with regard to **customs fraud**, cf. Regulation (EU) 2015/1525 of the EP and of the Council of 9 September 2015 amending Council Regulation (EC) No 515/97 on mutual assistance between the administrative authorities of the MS and co-operation between the latter and the Commission to ensure the correct application of the law on customs and agricultural matters (OJ L 243 of 18 September 2015, 1); the previous Regulation 515/97 which was limited to the co-operation in administrative proceedings has been complemented by the Convention on mutual assistance and co-operation between customs administrations (Naples II) (OJ C 24 of 23 January 1998, 1) with a view to criminal proceedings (otherwise Art. 6 EUMAC, main text, mn. 80, was applicable); on the new Regulation 2015/1525, cf. Porebska, *eucrim*, 11 (2016), 52 ff.; crit. Schulz, *eucrim*, 11 (2016), 55, 58–60 (arguing that especially its Art. 12 abolishes the previous separation between administrative and criminal proceedings, allowing for the admission of evidence gathered by a requested State in proceedings of both kinds in the requesting State and thus giving rise to human rights concerns). On information exchange with regard to **criminal records**, see main text, mn. 15 *in fine*.

17. For a basic account of this principle – which is based on mutual recognition (Chapter 1, mn. 25 ff.) – cf. Böse, *Grundsatz der Verfügbarkeit* (2007); cf. also Safferling, *Internationales Strafrecht* (2011), §10 mn. 38–9; Eisele, in Sieber, Satzger and von Heinegg, *Europäisches Strafrecht* (2014), pp. 892–3; Hauck, in Böse, *Europäisches Strafrecht* (2013), p. 433; cf. *in concreto* the corresponding Draft FD COM (2005) 490 final of 12 October 2005 and its amendment under the German Council Presidency (Council Doc. 7315/07); on this, cf. Esser, in Böse, *Europäisches Strafrecht* (2013), pp. 711–13. On **data protection** in this context, cf. Council FD 2008/977/JHA of 27 November 2008 on the protection of personal data processed in the framework of police and judicial co-operation in criminal matters (OJ L 350 of 30 December 2008, 60 (on this, cf. Esser, in Böse, *Europäisches Strafrecht* (2013), pp. 705–7)) and the Proposal for a Directive of the EP and of the Council on the protection of individuals with regard to the processing of personal data by competent authorities for the purposes of prevention, investigation, detection or prosecution of criminal offences or the execution of criminal penalties, and the free movement of such data, COM (2012) 10 final; Council Doc. 6002/13; on this, see also de Busser, *eucrim*, 8 (2013), 17 ff.; Esser, in Böse, *Europäisches Strafrecht* (2013), p. 708; on its scope, Hörauf, *ZIS*, 8 (2013), 276 ff. On data protection in the EU in general, cf. Eisele, in Sieber, Satzger and von Heinegg, *Europäisches Strafrecht* (2014), pp. 894 ff.; Esser, in Böse, *Europäisches Strafrecht* (2013), pp. 703–5; cf. also Nalewajko, *Grundsatz der gegenseitigen Anerkennung* (2010), pp. 284 ff.; Klip, *European Criminal Law* (2016), pp. 395–6; Braum and Covolo, in Ligeti, *Prosecutor for the EU*, i (2013), pp. 1111 ff.; Satzger, *Europäisches und Internationales Strafrecht* (2016), §10 mn. 75 ff. For a critical stance on the general availability of data, cf. also Böse, *Grundsatz der Verfügbarkeit* (2007), pp. 137 ff.; Meyer, *NStZ*, 28 (2008), 192 ff.; Brodowski, *ZIS*, 7 (2012), 474; Brodowski, *Jura*, 35 (2013), 497.
18. Art. 87(2) TFEU.
19. Cf. Art. 13 EUMAC and Council FD 2002/465/JHA (OJ L 162 of 20 June 2002, 1); an instructive take on this issue is given by Sensburg, *Kriminalistik*, 62 (2008), 661; on a draft model agreement, *eucrim*, 5 (2010), 17–18; also see the 'Joint Investigations Teams Practical Guide', Council Doc. 6128/1/17 of 14 February 2017; from a practical perspective, Zaharieva, *ERA Forum*, 18 (2017), 397 ff.

20. Art. 87(3) subparagraph 1 TFEU. On the possible procedure of *enhanced co-operation* between at least nine MS, cf. Art. 87(3) subparagraphs 2 and 3 TFEU and Chapter 3, mn. 11 *in fine*.
21. Art. 88 TFEU; for more detail, cf. Chapter 5, mn. 7 ff.
22. On its development and scope, cf. Chapter 1, mn. 34–6.
23. For a comprehensive analysis (with changes), cf. Huybreghts, *ERA Forum*, 16 (2015), 386–95.
24. For a critical stance on this, cf. Gleß, in Schomburg et al., *Internationale Rechtshilfe in Strafsachen* (2012), p. 1637.
25. The **UK** and **Ireland** opted in, but the UK only with regard to Arts. 39, 40 (and Arts. 42, 43 as related to Art. 40), 44, 46, 47, and Ireland only with regard to Arts. 39, 44 (cf. Council Decision 2004/926/EC of 22 December 2004 on the putting into effect of parts of the Schengen *acquis* by the United Kingdom of Great Britain and Northern Ireland (OJ L 395 of 31 December 2004, 70–80); on this Frenz, *Handbuch Europarecht*, vi (2011), mn. 2747–9; cf. also Huybreghts, *ERA Forum*, 16 (2015), 386, 388). **Norway** and **Iceland** take part via the Prüm Convention (above n. 16); generally on police co-operation from a Scandinavian point of view, cf. Boucht, *EuCLR*, 2 (2012), 203. In this regard, cf. also the **German–Swiss Police Treaty** of 27 April 1999 (*BGBl.* II 2001, 946); on this, cf. Hecker, *Europäisches Strafrecht* (2015), §5 mn. 77 ff.; Krüßmann, *Transnationales Strafprozessrecht* (2009), pp. 453 ff.
26. Art. 39 CISA, also Art. 46(2)(a) CISA. Note, however, that these provisions have been largely replaced by FD 2006/960/JHA and the Prüm Decision (above n. 16); cf. Huybreghts, *ERA Forum*, 16 (2015), 387; for more detail, see also Böse, *Grundsatz der Verfügbarkeit* (2007), pp. 30 ff.; Hetzer, in Sieber, Satzger and von Heinegg, *Europäisches Strafrecht* (2014), pp. 741–2; Esser, in Böse, *Europäisches Strafrecht* (2013), pp. 702–3.
27. Art. 40 CISA.
28. Art. 41 CISA. Thereto see also OLG Koblenz, No 1 OWi 3 SsBs 63/14, Decision (30 October 2014), in *NStZ*, 37 (2017), 108, according to which evidence must be assumed inadmissible under international law (!) if the police embark upon investigative measures without any international legal agreement or the consent of the state whose territory is concerned; with crit. commentary by Radtke, *NStZ*, 37 (2017), 108, who criticises that the nature of the violation of sovereignty, which is not concerned with individual protection, has not been taken into consideration.
29. Art. 47 CISA. On this from a French perspective, cf. Aubert, *RSC*, 77 (2012), 434 ff.
30. On this, cf. Hetzer, in Sieber, Satzger and von Heinegg, *Europäisches Strafrecht* (2014), p. 742; Krüßmann, in Böse, *Europäisches Strafrecht* (2013), pp. 691–2.
31. Art. 40(1) CISA.
32. Cf. Art. 40(7) CISA: murder, manslaughter, rape, arson, forgery of money, aggravated burglary, robbery, receiving stolen goods, extortion, kidnapping, hostage taking, trafficking in human beings, illicit trafficking in narcotic drugs and psychotropic substances, breach of the laws on arms and explosives, wilful damage through the use of explosives, illicit transportation of toxic and hazardous waste.
33. Art. 40(2) CISA. Critical of the practicability of this Hecker, *Europäisches Strafrecht* (2015), §5 mn. 39; on Art. 40 CISA, cf. also Gleß, *Beweisrechtsgrundsätze* (2006), pp. 123–4; Gleß, *Internationales Strafrecht* (2015), mn. 526–7.
34. Art. 40(3) CISA.
35. Art. 41(1) CISA. On the necessary degree of suspicion Soiné, *ZIS*, 11 (2016), 322–3.

36. Cf. Art. 41(4)(a) CISA, which contains the same offences as Art. 40(7) (see above n. 32) as well as 'failure to stop and give particulars after an accident which has resulted in death or serious injury'.
37. Art. 41(4) CISA.
38. *Ex* Art. 41(2) CISA. On obligations to inform and instruct the suspect, cf. Soiné, *ZIS*, 11 (2016), 323.
39. Hecker, *Europäisches Strafrecht* (2015), §5 mn. 42. On Art. 41(2) CISA in regard to German–French relations, cf. Goy, *Vorläufige Festnahme* (2002), esp. p. 202 and *passim*. On ensuing obligations to inform and instruct the suspect, on his identification and interrogation, as well as on evidentiary rules (especially with a view to the exclusion of evidence obtained by interrogation), cf. Soiné, *ZIS*, 11 (2016), 323–9.
40. Cf. Art. 41(5) CISA. On the reporting obligation to the competent local authorities pursuant to lit. (g), cf. Soiné, *ZIS*, 11 (2016), 321.
41. On cross-border surveillance and hot pursuit, cf. Heinrich, *NStZ*, 16 (1996), 365–6; Gleß and Lüke, *Jura*, 20 (1998), 73–4; Würz, *Das Schengener Durchführungsübereinkommen* (1997), mn. 82 ff.; and Kattau, *Strafverfolgung* (1993), pp. 112 ff.
42. Cf. Art. 41(5)(a) CISA; also Soiné, *ZIS*, 11 (2016), 328.
43. Goy, *Vorläufige Festnahme* (2002), p. 249; Hecker, *Europäisches Strafrecht* (2015), §5 mn. 106.
44. Gleß and Lüke, *Jura*, 22 (2000), 402; Harings, *Grenzüberschreitende Zusammenarbeit* (1998), pp. 259 ff., esp. 261.
45. Cf. Gleß and Lüke, *Jura*, 22 (2000), 402 incl. further references; Hecker, *Europäisches Strafrecht* (2015), §5 mn. 108, 110.
46. Gleß and Lüke, *Jura*, 22 (2000), 402; in detail, Harings, *Grenzüberschreitende Zusammenarbeit* (1998), pp. 251 ff., esp. 258; on the lack of international arrangements for mutually 'borrowing institutions and agencies' (*Organleihe*), cf. Gleß and Lüke, *Jura*, 22 (2000), 403; also Goy, *Vorläufige Festnahme* (2002), p. 252.
47. Cf. Art. 43(2) CISA. See also Gleß and Lüke, *Jura*, 22 (2000), 403; Gleß, in Schomburg et al., *Internationale Rechtshilfe in Strafsachen* (2012), p. 1637; Würz, *Das Schengener Durchführungsübereinkommen* (1997), mn. 149; cf. also Hecker, *Europäisches Strafrecht* (2015), §5 mn. 46–7.
48. Art. 42 CISA. cf. also Hecker, *Europäisches Strafrecht* (2015), §5 mn. 44–5.
49. Gleß and Lüke, *Jura*, 22 (2000), 403; Goy, *Vorläufige Festnahme* (2002), pp. 254 ff.
50. On the difficulty of distinguishing clearly between approximation and harmonisation, cf. already Chapter 1, mn. 28.
51. On the alleged distinction between national procedural and co-operation laws in this regard, see previously Chapter 1, mn. 10 with n. 76.
52. Cf. also Satzger, *Europäisches und Internationales Strafrecht* (2016), §10 mn. 79 ('complementary remedy', orig. 'komplementäres Hilfsmittel'); Satzger, in Streinz, *EUV/AEUV* (2012), Art. 82 AEUV mn. 3, 11, 55; Esser, *Europäisches und Internationales Strafrecht* (2018), §5 mn. 32; Asp, *Procedural Criminal Law Cooperation* (2016), pp. 29–30. On the link between harmonisation and recognition, see Capus, *Strafrecht und Souveränität* (2010), pp. 394 ff.
53. Art. 82(2) subparagraph 1, second sentence TFEU, added emphasis.
54. Art. 82(3), TFEU; on this, cf. Chapter 3, mn. 11.

55. Although the European Council may unanimously decide that a qualified majority is sufficient in this regard (Art. 48(7) TEU). However, in Germany, Parliament would have to be involved in such a case (BVerfG, Nos 2 BvE 2/08 et al., Judgment (30 June 2009), in *NJW*, 62 (2009), 2267, 2289, 2295, paras. 366, 419; cf. also §§4, 7 IntVG; see also Zöller, in Baumeister, *FS Schenke* (2011), p. 593; Esser, *Europäisches und Internationales Strafrecht* (2018), §5 mn. 29).
56. Art. 82(2)(d) TFEU. Mansdörfer, *HRRS*, 11 (2010), 15, lists as further regulatory areas: declaring individual types of procedure invalid in principle, specifying basic procedural rights (e.g. those of Art. 6 ECHR) and regulating 'transnational investigations' (orig. 'Ermittlungsverfahren mit transnationalem Charakter').
57. Thus also BVerfG, 2 BvE 2/08 et al. (n. 55), 2288, para. 358; Satzger, *Europäisches und Internationales Strafrecht* (2016), §10 mn. 83; Satzger, in Streinz, *EUV/AEUV* (2012), Art. 82 AEUV mn. 60. A summary and evaluation of defendants' rights can be found in Esser, in Zöller et al., *FS Wolter* (2013), pp. 1335 ff.
58. Cf. Chapter 2, mn. 146 ff.
59. Council FD 2009/299/JHA (OJ L 81 of 27 March 2009, 24); Kirsch, *StraFo*, 21 (2008), 457, is critical of this in regard to the rights of the accused; as is Esser, *Europäisches und Internationales Strafrecht* (2018), §5 mn. 41; Wahl, *eucrim*, 10 (2015), 75–6; cf. also ECPI, *ZIS*, 8 (2013), 444–5. On this, cf. also Hauck, *JR* 2009, 141 ff. However, Böse, in Ambos, *Europäisches Strafrecht post-Lissabon* (2011), pp. 61–2, welcomes the fact that the treatment of sentences *in absentia* is standardised in all framework decisions.
60. Directive 2012/29/EU of the EP and of the Council of 25 October 2012 establishing Minimum Standards on the Rights, Support and Protection of Victims of Crime, and Replacing Council FD 2001/220/JHA (OJ L 315 of 14 November 2012, 5); on the negotiations, Nowell-Smith, *NJECL*, 3 (2012), 383 ff.; welcoming the directive but concerned regarding implementation, Rasquete, Ferreira and Moyano Marques, *ERA Forum*, 15 (2014), 119 ff.; crit. of the directive, Bock, *ZIS*, 8 (2013), 203 ff.; crit. in regard to upholding the principle of subsidiarity, ECPI, *ZIS*, 8 (2013), 444; also crit. in this regard, Öberg, *EuCLR*, 5 (2015), 33 ff.; on the geographical scope of the protection, Nowell-Smith, *NJECL*, 3 (2012), 385–7; crit. regarding the legal basis Mitsilegas, *EU Criminal Law* (2016), pp. 196–8, 210. See also the European Commission, *Communication Strengthening Victims' Rights* (2011); on the draft directive, cf. Fichera, *eucrim*, 6 (2011), 79 ff.; Schünemann, *ERA Forum*, 12 (2011), 445 ff.; Anders, *ZStW*, 124 (2012), 384 ff.; Wieczorek, *EuCLR*, 2 (2012), 144 ff.; Tamarit Sumalla, in de Hoyos Sancho, *Guarantees and Rights of the Especially Vulnerable Victim* (2013), pp. 42–3; de Hoyos Sancho, in de Hoyos Sancho, *Guarantees and Rights of the Especially Vulnerable Victim* (2013), pp. 55 ff.; on the needs of the victims of cyberstalking, Maple and Lang, *NJECL*, 3 (2012), 208 ff.; on stalking in general, cf. Van der Aa and Römkens, *EuCLR*, 3 (2013), 232 ff. On the (now rescinded) FD 2001/220/JHA, see CJEU, *Pupino*, No C-105/03 (ECLI:EU:C:2005:386), Judgment (16 June 2005); CJEU, *György Katz* v. *István Roland Sós*, No C-404/07 (ECLI:EU:C:2008:553), Judgment (9 October 2008); CJEU, *Giovanni Dell'Orto*, No C-467/05 (ECLI:EU:C:2007:395), Judgment (28 June 2007) and CJEU, *Emil Eredics and Mária Vassné Sápi*, No C-205/09 (ECLI:EU:C:2010:623), Judgment (21 October 2010); with a commentary by Bock, *JZ*, 66 (2011), 469–71; Ouwerkerk, *Mutual Recognition* (2011), pp. 98–9. On the implementation of the directive in Germany, Meier, in Zöller et al., *FS Wolter* (2013), pp. 1387 ff.; on the

implementation of the FD in Slovenia, cf. Zgaga, *eucrim*, 6 (2011), 88 ff. An overview of the Europeanisation of victims' rights can be found in Bock, in Barton and Kölbel, *Ambivalenzen der Opferzuwendung des Strafrechts* (2012), pp. 67 ff.; generally on the place of the victim in Europe's area of criminal justice also Mitsilegas, *EU Criminal Law* (2016), pp. 185 ff.; on the procedural standing of victims from a comparative perspective (France, Germany, Italy and Spain), de Hoyos Sancho, *Ejercicio de la Acción Penal* (2016), pp. 81 ff., 125 ff.

61. Cf. Hackner and Schierholt, *Internationale Rechtshilfe* (2017), mn. 2; Hecker, *Europäisches Strafrecht* (2015), §2 mn. 62; in detail on the problem of striking a balance between efficiency and the protection of individual rights in mutual assistance, Gleß and Spencer, *StV*, 26 (2006), 269 ff.; on mutual assistance within the CIS, and on the USA and Canada, Krüßmann, *Transnationales Strafprozessrecht* (2009), pp. 460 ff., 481 ff., 509 ff.
62. Cf. in detail Capus, *Strafrecht und Souveränität* (2010), pp. 107 ff.
63. On the development of mutual assistance, Capus, *Strafrecht und Souveränität* (2010), pp. 266 ff.
64. ETS No 24; entry into force 18 April 1960; ratified by all 47 CoE MS and three non-Member States (Israel, Korea and South Africa).
65. ETS No 86; entry into force 20 August 1979.
66. ETS No 98; entry into force 5 June 1983.
67. ETS No 209; entry into force 1 May 2012.
68. ETS No 212; entry into force 1 June 2014.
69. ETS No 30; entry into force 12 June 1962.
70. ETS No 99; entry into force 12 April 1983.
71. ETS No 182; entry into force 1 February 2004.
72. ETS No 112; entry into force 1 July 1985; for the 2017 Protocol amending the AP see ETS No 222.
73. ETS No 167; entry into force 1 June 2000.
74. ETS No 51; entry into force 22 August 1975.
75. ETS No 70; entry into force 26 July 1974.
76. ETS No 73; entry into force 30 March 1978.
77. ETS No 97; entry into force 31 August 1979.
78. ETS No 101; entry into force 1 July 1982.
79. ETS No 108; entry into force 1 October 1985.
80. ETS No 116; entry into force 1 February 1988.
81. ETS No 130; entry into force 1 October 1991.
82. ETS No 133; entry into force 1 October 1991.
83. Cf. Chapter 3, mn. 3 with n. 29.
84. ETS No 156; entry into force 1 May 2000.
85. ETS No 185; entry into force 1 July 2004.
86. ETS No 189; entry into force 1 March 2006.
87. ETS No 198; entry into force 1 May 2008.
88. Art. 34(2)(a) TEU old version.
89. Cf. the constantly updated information on www.consilium.europa.eu/en/documents-publications/agreements, last accessed 27 January 2018.
90. OJ C 313 of 23 October 1996, 11; on 17 April 2007, the Convention was ratified by 20 MS and applied as of 16 July 2007 by 14 of them in their mutual relations (cf. www.consilium.europa.eu/en/documents-publications/agreements-conventions/agreement/?aid=1996063, last accessed 27 January 2018).

91. OJ C 78 of 30 March 1995, 2; on 17 April 2007, the Convention was ratified by 20 MS and as of 16 July 2007 applied early by 14 of them in their mutual relations (cf. www.consilium.europa.eu/en/documents-publications/treaties-agreements/agreement/?id=1995104, last accessed 27 January 2018).
92. The Agreement (available at www.consilium.europa.eu/en/documents-publications/treaties-agreements/agreement/?id=1989025, last accessed 27 January 2018) was signed on 26 May 1989 in San Sebastian by nine of the 12 EC MS with the exception of Germany and the UK, which signed it later (23 December 1992 and 8 November 1995 respectively), and Ireland, which never signed it; cf. www.consilium.europa.eu/en/documents-publications/treaties-agreements/agreement/?id=1989025, last accessed 27 January 2018.
93. OJ C 197 of 12 July 2000, 3; entry into force 23 August 2005, following ratification by eight States; on this, Kreß, *ZStW*, 116 (2004), 468–9; Vervaele, *RP*, 15 (2005), 175–6; Vermeulen, *RIDP*, 77 (2006), 81 ff.; on video and telephone hearings and telecommunications surveillance, Gleß, *Beweisrechtsgrundsätze* (2006), pp. 113 ff.; on telecommunications surveillance, cf. also Schuster, *NStZ*, 26 (2006), 657 ff. The EU Mutual Assistance Convention and its AP have been applicable to Iceland and Norway since 1 January 2013 (OJ L 26 of 24 January 2004, 3; OJ L 322 of 21 November 2012, 1).
94. OJ C 326 of 21 November 2001, 1; entry into force 5 October 2005.
95. Available at www.consilium.europa.eu/en/documents-publications/treaties-agreements/agreement/?id=1991074&DocLanguage=en, last accessed 15 February 2018; pursuant to its Art. 21(3), as of 16 May 2005 the Convention has been applied provisionally between the Netherlands (for the Netherlands Antilles and Aruba) and Latvia and Germany; an instructive overview can be found in Schomburg and Hackner, in Schomburg et al., *Internationale Rechtshilfe in Strafsachen* (2012), p. 1470.
96. Cf. Hackner and Schierholt, *Internationale Rechtshilfe* (2017), mn. 15; Asp, *Procedural Criminal Law Cooperation* (2016), pp. 40–1; Gleß, *Internationales Strafrecht* (2015), mn. 494; a critical stance is taken by Klip, in Curtin et al., *European Integration and Law* (2006), p. 129; Klip, *European Criminal Law* (2016), pp. 352–3; a similar view is taken by Frank, *DRiZ*, 84 (2006), 10. On links back on the level of the Council of Europe, cf. Gilmore and Harris, in Cullen and Jund, *Criminal Justice Co-operation in the EU after Tampere* (2002), p. 113.
97. Vogel, *JZ*, 56 (2001), 938.
98. Cf. also Asp, *Procedural Criminal Law Cooperation* (2016), pp. 40–2 (enumeration four advantages).
99. Cf. Arts. 59, 48, 67 CISA.
100. Council Decision of 6 June 2003 (OJ L 181 of 18 July 2003, 25, 27 and 34); both agreements entered into force on 1 February 2010 (OJ L 325 of 11 December 2009, 4).
101. Kaiafa-Gbandi, *KritV*, 87 (2004), 14–15; on this, cf. also Krüßmann, *Transnationales Strafprozessrecht* (2009), pp. 507 ff.; Mylonopoulos, *ZStW*, 121 (2009), 75–6; Raphael, *ERA Forum*, 11 (2011), 569; Schröder and Stiegel, in Sieber, Satzger and von Heinegg, *Europäisches Strafrecht* (2014), pp. 616 ff. On the requirement of dual criminality, cf. Capus, *Strafrecht und Souveränität* (2010), pp. 365–6. Possible former MS–US treaties were harmonised with the

new EU treaties; on Germany, for example, cf. Rackow and Birr, *GoJIL*, 2 (2010), 1124.

102. In detail on this matter as a whole, Spinellis, in Arnold et al., *FS Eser* (2005), pp. 873 ff.; more critically, Kaiafa-Gbandi, *EJCCLCJ*, 13 (2005), 489.
103. Main text, mn. 33 ff. For a critical stance on this, cf. Kaiafa-Gbandi, *KritV*, 87 (2004), 15–16; Spinellis, in Arnold et al., *FS Eser* (2005), pp. 878 and 888, is more reticent; on transatlantic co-operation in the fight against terrorism, cf. Mitsilegas, *eucrim*, 5 (2010), 111 ff.
104. OJ L 181 of 19 July 2003, 41; Kaiafa-Gbandi, *KritV*, 87 (2004), 17; for a differentiated take on the problematic issue of data protection, cf. Spinellis, in Arnold et al., *FS Eser* (2005), pp. 881 ff.; Krüßmann, *Transnationales Strafprozessrecht* (2009), pp. 645 ff. (on the different 'philosophies of data protection'); on an EU–USA data protection agreement, *eucrim*, 6 (2011), 13. On the JITs envisaged in Art. 5, cf. Plachta, *EJCCLCJ*, 13 (2005), 294 ff. The SWIFT Agreement (Council Document 16110/09, Parliament Document P7_TA(2010)0029), which was rejected by the EP on 11 February 2010, and the Agreement on the Use and Transfer of Passenger Name Records (PNR) (OJ L 215 of 11 August 2012, 5) run along the same lines as the Mutual Assistance Convention. For more detail on the SWIFT Agreement and the Passenger Name Records Agreement of 2007, cf. Tamm, *VuR*, 25 (2010), 215 ff.; on the latter, cf. also Galli, *eucrim*, 5 (2010), 124 ff. and *eucrim*, 6 (2011), 14–15. There is also a PNR Agreement between the EU and Australia (OJ 2012 L 186 of 14 July 2012, 4). A further one with Canada was signed on 25 June 2014 (Council Doc. 12657/1/13 REV 1, Brussels, 20 November 2013) but has not yet been adopted due to the lack of the EP's consent, which depends on the opinion of the CJEU, requested by the EP on 10 April 2015; on 26 July 2017, the CJEU declared the Agreement – following essentially AG Mengozzi's Opinion of 8 September 2016 – incompatible with Arts. 7, 8, 21 and Art. 52(1) of the CFREU; cf. CJEU, *Opinion 1/15* (ECLI:EU:C:2017:592), Judgment (26 July 2017), paras. 119 ff. Furthermore, on 23 June 2015 the Council mandated the Commission to negotiate a PNR agreement with Mexico; cf. thereon *eucrim*, 10 (2015), 86. Regarding the harmonisation of the PNR system within the EU, Directive (EU) 2016/681 was adopted (on the use of PNR Data for the Prevention, Detection, Investigation and Prosecution of Terrorist Offences and Serious Crime (OJ L 119 of 4 May 2016, 132–49); thereon *eucrim*, 11 (2016), 14, 78).
105. On this, cf. *eucrim*, 5 (2010), 143–4; Rackow and Birr, *GoJIL*, 2 (2010), 1126–7; Schröder and Stiegel, in Sieber, Satzger and von Heinegg, *Europäisches Strafrecht* (2014), pp. 621 ff.
106. OJ L 254 of 30 September 2011, 3–6; cf. also Council Decision 2011/640/CFSP of 12 July 2011 on the signing and conclusion of the Agreement between the EU and the Republic of Mauritius on the conditions of transfer of suspected pirates and associated seized property (OJ L 254 of 30 September 2011, 1–2).
107. OJ L 108 of 11 April 2014, 3–8; cf. also Council Decision 2014/198/CFSP of 10 March 2014 on the signing and conclusion of the Agreement between the EU and the United Republic of Tanzania on the conditions of transfer of suspected pirates and associated seized property from the EU-led naval force to the United Republic of Tanzania (OJ L 108 of 11 April 2014, 1–2).
108. See already Chapter 1, mn. 26–7.

109. FD 2002/584/JHA (OJ L 190 of 18 July 2002).
110. Main text, mn. 46 ff.; see also Klip, *European Criminal Law* (2016), pp. 381 ff., 394–5, 400 ff.
111. Cf. Spencer, *ZIS*, 5 (2010), 602 ff.; Ambos, *ZIS*, 5 (2010), 557–8; Suominen, *Mutual Recognition in Cooperation* (2011), pp. 60–1, also stresses that the strict time limits and the leading idea of a unified area of freedom, security and justice are forms of mutual recognition.
112. Cf. Böse, in Tiedemann et al., *Die Verfassung moderner Strafrechtspflege* (2016), pp. 216 ff.
113. Cf. Main text, mn. 82 ff. and 98.
114. Cf. http://db.eurocrim.org/db (last accessed 27 January 2018) for an up-to-date list.
115. FD 2003/577/JHA (OJ L 196 of 2 August 2003, 45); see main text, mn. 82.
116. FD 2006/783/JHA (OJ L 328 of 24 November 2006, 59); amended by Art. 4 FD 2009/299/JHA of 26 February 2009 (OJ L 81 of 26 March 2009, 24–36); on this see also Klimek, *Mutual Recognition* (2017), pp. 365 ff. The prosecutor is the issuing and executing authority (*eucrim*, 5 (2010), 143). The FD applies to final decisions on the confiscation of assets (including items acquired through crime, value replacement and instrumentalities) and in this regard supplements the FD on Freezing; cf. EU, *Green Paper on Sanctions* (2004), p. 27; cf. also Juppe, *Gegenseitige Anerkennung strafgerichtlicher Entscheidungen* (2007), pp. 66–7; Gleß, in Sieber, Satzger and von Heinegg, *Europäisches Strafrecht* (2014), pp. 722 ff. In Germany, the FD 2006/783/JHA was implemented in §§88 ff. IRG, cf. also *BGBl.* I 2009, 3214; on this, cf. Morgenstern, in Böse, *Europäisches Strafrecht* (2013), pp. 606–7; Lelieur, *EuCLR*, 5 (2015), 288–94. In this context, cf. also **Directive** of the EP and of the Council on the freezing and confiscation of instrumentalities and proceeds of crime in the EU (OJ L 127 of 29 April 2014, 39), which aims to simplify international co-operation in this area by approximating substantive laws on freezing and confiscation; see also the German implementation through the Asset Recovery through Criminal Law Act of 13 April 2007 (*BGBl.* I 2017 S. 872); on the proposal, cf. COM (2012), 85, on this, cf. Brodowski, *ZIS*, 8 (2013), 467; cf. also *eucrim*, 7 (2012), 151; *eucrim*, 8 (2013), 84. Lastly, see recently on the common position on a proposal of a **Regulation** on Mutual Recognition and Confiscation Orders of 8 December 2017 *eucrim*, 12 (2017), 176–7.
117. FD 2008/978/JHA (OJ L 350 of 18 December 2008, 74); see main text, mn. 83–4.
118. COM (2009) 624 final; on this see main text, mn. 86; cf. also Busemann, *ZIS*, 5 (2010), 552 ff; Ambos, *ZIS*, 5 (2010), 557 ff.; Schierholt, *ZIS*, 5 (2010), 567 ff.; Allegrezza, *ZIS*, 5 (2010), 569 ff.; Bachmaier Winter, *ZIS*, 5 (2010), 580 ff.; Lelieur, *ZIS*, 5 (2010), 590 ff.; and Spencer, *ZIS*, 5 (2010), 602 ff.; also Ormazábal Sánchez, *La Ley Penal*, 7 (2010), no 74, 26–7.
119. Directive 2014/41/EU (OJ L 130 of 1 May 2014, 1); see main text, mn. 87 ff.
120. Art. 34 EIO Directive.
121. Cf. recital 11 and Art. 1 Regulation (EU) 2016/95 of 20 January 2016 repealing certain acts in the field of police co-operation and judicial co-operation in criminal matters (OJ L 26 of 2 February 2016, 9); on this Brodowski, *ZIS*, 12 (2017), 25. See also main text, mn. 82.
122. EU, *Green Paper on Sanctions* (2004), COM (2004) 334 final; for an analysis, see main text, mn. 98.
123. FD 2008/909/JHA (OJ L 327 of 5 December 2008, 27); amended by FD 2009/299/JHA (OJ L 81 of 27 March 2009, 24); for an analysis, see main text, mn. 99.

124. FD 2005/214/JHA (OJ L 76 of 22 March 2005, 16); amended by FD 2009/299/JHA (OJ L 81 of 27 March 2009, 24); for an analysis, see main text, mn. 99–100.
125. FD 2009/829/JHA (OJ L 294 of 11 November 2009, 20); for an analysis, see main text, mn. 102.
126. FD 2008/675/JHA (OJ L 220 of 15 August 2008, 32); see main text, mn. 103. The Belgian Initiative with a view to the adoption of an FD on the recognition and enforcement of prohibitions arising from convictions for sexual offences committed against children (Council Document 14207/04, 14207/04 ADDa/04, 15121/07) was approved by the EP in 2006 (TA(2006)0236), but has not yet been resumed following the entry into force of the Lisbon Treaty. On the proposal, cf. Plachta, *ICLR*, 7 (2007), 436–7; Sajonz, *RIDP*, 77 (2006), 163 ff.
127. FD 2008/947/JHA (OJ L 337 of 16 December 2008, 102); amended by FD 2009/299/JHA (OJ L 81 of 27 March 2009, 24); for an analysis, see main text, mn. 104. On the implementation in the individual Member States, cf. Flore et al., *Probation Measures and Alternative Sanctions* (2012), pp. 7 ff.; Council Document 7334/1/12 REV 1; on this, see *eucrim*, 7 (2012), 151.
128. Directive 2011/99/EU of 13 December 2011 (OJ 2011 L 338 of 21 December 2011, 2); on this, cf. Bock, *ZIS*, 8 (2013), 210; Mitsilegas, *EU Criminal Law* (2016), pp. 189–90; Klimek, *Mutual Recognition* (2017), pp. 461 ff.; on the draft, Brodowski, *ZIS*, 5 (2010), 384; Jiménez Becerril and Romero Lopez, *eucrim*, 6 (2011), 76 ff.; crit. with regard to the invoked legal basis (Art. 82(1)(a) and (d) TFEU) BR-Drs. 43/10; Mitsilegas, *EU Criminal Law* (2016), pp. 195–7.
129. FD 2009/315/JHA of 26 February 2009 (OJ L 93 of 6 April 2009, 23). Thereon Hochmayr and Ligocki, *ZIS*, 11 (2016), 159 ff. This FD incorporated the provisions of, and replaced, Council Decision 2005/876/JHA of 21 November 2005 on the exchange of information extracted from the criminal record (OJ L 322 of 9 December 2005, 33); thereto Plachta, *ICLR*, 7 (2007), 433–4; see recital 13 and Art. 12 FD 2009/315/JHA.
130. Cf. Arts. 4 and 5 FD 2009/315/JHA; thereon crit., Hochmayr and Ligocki, *ZIS*, 11 (2016), 163 ff. (deploring a one-sided application of mutual recognition as only information detrimental to the convicted person is to be stored by his MS, which may lead to a rights violation and have a stigmatising effect undermining his resocialisation).
131. Council Decision 2009/316/JHA of 6 April 2009 in application of Article 11 of FD 2009/315/JHA (OJ L 93 of 7 April 2009, 33); on ECRIS, Albers, in Albers et al., *Evaluation Framework* (2013), pp. 48–9; Brodowski, *ZIS*, 12 (2017), 24–5.
132. Case according to OLG Düsseldorf, Nos III-4 Ausl. (A) 16/05 – 44/06 III et al., Decision (9 February 2006), in *NStZ*, 26 (2006), 692.
133. Weigend, *JuS*, 40 (2000), 105 ff.; on the terminology, cf. also Henzelin, in Zen-Ruffinen, *Du monde pénal* (2006), p. 194; a fundamental overview is provided in García Sánchez, *La extradición* (2005), pp. 5 ff. Capus, *Strafrecht und Souveränität* (2010), pp. 218–19, refers to extradition and other (ancillary) legal assistance as secondary legal assistance and to the taking over of prosecution and enforcement as primary legal assistance.
134. Cf. Rackow, in Ambos, König and Rackow, *Rechtshilferecht in Strafsachen* (2015), p. 97; Schomburg et al., *Internationale Rechtshilfe in Strafsachen* (2012), pp. 5–6; Schomburg, Lagodny and Schallmoser, in Böse, *Europäisches Strafrecht* (2013), pp. 500–1; Hackner and Schierholt, *Internationale Rechtshilfe* (2017), mn. 66 ff.;

Lagodny, in Widmaier, *Münchener Anwaltshandbuch Strafverteidigung* (2014), pp. 943–4; Schwaighofer and Ebensperger, *Internationale Rechtshilfe* (2001), p. 14; Hecker, *Europäisches Strafrecht* (2015), §2 mn. 76 ff.

135. For an instructive account of local jurisdiction in extradition proceedings, cf. OLG Koblenz, No 1 Ausl. 2/05, Decision (9 February 2005), in *NStZ*, 26 (2006), 110.
136. §§13, 14 IRG. Thereon König, in Ambos, König and Rackow, *Rechtshilferecht in Strafsachen* (2015), pp. 213 ff.
137. §31(5) ARHG.
138. §31(6) ARHG.
139. Art. 16 IRSG.
140. Art. 52 ff. IRSG; for an extensive account on the Swiss legal assistance procedure, cf. Donatsch et al., *Internationale Rechtshilfe* (2015), pp. 124 ff.
141. Cf. §74(1)1 and (2) IRG, §34(1) ARHG. In Germany, the State Ministries of Justice are responsible in treaty-based extraditions (agreement on competence of 28 April 2004, available at www.verwaltungsvorschriften-im-internet.de/bsvwvbund_28042004_935021713162004.htm, last accessed 27 January 2018); they have in part delegated responsibility to the State's central public prosecutor's office.
142. Art. 17(1) and Art. 55 IRSG.
143. Schomburg et al., *Internationale Rechtshilfe in Strafsachen* (2012), p. 5; Weigend, *JuS*, 40 (2000), 109. On the legal situation in Spain, cf. García Sánchez, *La extradición* (2005), pp. 77 ff.
144. BVerfG, Nos 2 BvR 483/95, 2 BvR 2501/95 and 2 BvR 2990/95, Decision (18 June 1997), in *BVerfGE*, 96, pp. 100, 118; crit. Lagodny, *JZ*, 53 (1998), 568–70.
145. Schomburg et al., *Internationale Rechtshilfe in Strafsachen* (2012), p. 5.
146. Cf. Arts. 436–356 CCP (legal admissibility decision by judicial council, consisting of three Court of Appeals judges, Art. 448; authorisation decision by Minister of Justice, Art. 452).
147. Cf. Arts. 696–47 CPP, especially Arts. 696–9, 696–15, 696–18 (transmission of extradition request from Foreign/Justice Ministry to competent *procureur général; chambre de l'instruction* decides about admissibility of request; executive authorisation by prime minister, briefed by minister of justice).
148. Cf. Arts. 28, 33 Extradition Act (district court decides on admissibility of extradition request, minister of justice on authorisation).
149. Cf. Arts. 602–7 CPC (admissibility decision taken by provincial court, with possible appeal to higher court (*Sąd Apelacyjny*); executive decision by the government, normally represented by the Ministry of Justice).
150. Cf. Arts. 11–30 Hungarian Act Nr XXXVIII of 1996 on International Legal Assistance in Criminal Matters (the Budapest Regional Court (*Fővárosi Törvényszék'*) decides on admissibility of extradition request, the minister of justice on authorisation).
151. Cf. Lei 144/99 (31 August 1999) (Lei da Cooperação Judiciária em Matéria Penal), especially Arts. 21 and 24, available at www.pgdlisboa.pt/leis/lei_mostra_articulado.php?artigo_id=295A0021%26;nid=295%26;tabela=leis%26;pagina=1%26;ficha=1%26;nversao=#artigo, last accessed 27 January 2018 (if the Minister of Justice finds that the extradition request may proceed, then it is for a high court

(*relação*) to seize the case and decide. The positive decision of the ministry is not binding on the court).

152. Cf. Arts. 697–722 CPP, esp. Arts. 703, 704, 708 (minister of justice decides whether it rejects request or initiates extradition proceedings by sending it to the general prosecutor of the Appeal Court; the court decides on admissibility of extradition; minister of justice decides about authorisation of extradition).
153. Cf. Ley 4/1985 (21 March 1985) de extradición pasiva (political decision by government, normally Ministry of Justice, whether extradition proceedings shall be initiated; legal admissibility decision by investigative court (*juzgado central de instrucción*); final executive decision again by government).
154. For the current list cf. Grange and Niblock, *Extradition Law* (2015), pp. 4–5; on the history and rationale of the distinction, cf. Nicholls, Montgomery and Knowles, *Extradition and Mutual Assistance* (2013), pp. 37–40.
155. On the extradition hearing in category 1 and 2 cases, cf. Nicholls, Montgomery and Knowles, *Extradition and Mutual Assistance* (2013), pp. 69 ff., 105 ff.
156. For a good overview, cf. Gibbins, in Jones, *Extradition and Mutual Assistance* (2010), pp. 18–22; see also Grange and Niblock, *Extradition Law* (2015), pp. 134 ff., 147–8.
157. Cf. Nicholls, Montgomery and Knowles, *Extradition and Mutual Assistance* (2013), pp. 147 ff.; on the reduced role of the Home Secretary at the beginning of extradition proceedings, cf. ibid., pp. 64–7.
158. Heger and Wolter, in Ambos, König and Rackow, *Rechtshilferecht in Strafsachen* (2015), p. 497; Weigend, *JuS*, 40 (2000), 106.
159. Art. 1 EuCExt.
160. For more detail, see main text, mn 23.
161. Art. 2(1) EuCExt.
162. Art. 10 EuCExt.
163. Cf. Arts. 3 ff. EuCExt; on such obstacles, cf. main text, mn. 33 ff.
164. Chapter 2 in conjunction with Art. 5 EuCExt; see also Schomburg, in Schomburg et al., *Internationale Rechtshilfe in Strafsachen* (2012), p. 665.
165. Cf. e.g. §1(3) IRG, §1 ARHG and Art. 1(1) IRSG (subordinate to international treaties).
166. Heger and Wolter, in Ambos, König and Rackow, *Rechtshilferecht in Strafsachen* (2015), p. 498; Lagodny, in Schomburg et al., *Internationale Rechtshilfe in Strafsachen* (2012), p. 72; on Switzerland, cf. also Henzelin, in Zen-Ruffinen, *Du monde pénal* (2006), p. 195.
167. Lagodny, in Schomburg et al., *Internationale Rechtshilfe in Strafsachen* (2012), p. 72.
168. Lagodny, in Schomburg et al., *Internationale Rechtshilfe in Strafsachen* (2012), pp. 72–6.
169. See main text, mn. 24–7.
170. Heger and Wolter, in Ambos, König and Rackow, *Rechtshilferecht in Strafsachen* (2015), pp. 499–500; Schomburg, in Schomburg et al., *Internationale Rechtshilfe in Strafsachen* (2012), p. 631. Thus, for example, §§10 ff. ARHG and Art. 2 ff., 32 ff. IRSG, which formulate the requirements and obstacles to admissibility (such as prohibiting the extradition of their own citizens, cf. §12 ARHG, Art. 7 IRSG), delimit extradition comparatively tightly, although these limits are superseded by international obligations to extradite (cf. Schwaighofer and Ebensperger,

Internationale Rechtshilfe (2001), pp. 5–6). Art. 1(4) IRSG explicitly sets out that 'no claim to interstate cooperation in criminal matters can be deduced' from the IRSG. On the reservations to legal assistance under Swiss law, cf. Gleß, *Internationales Strafrecht* (2015), mn. 339–40; Donatsch et al., *Internationale Rechtshilfe* (2015), pp. 80 ff.

171. For a basic account of this principle, cf. Keijzer, in Blekxtoon and Van Ballegooij, *Handbook on the EAW* (2005), pp. 140 ff.; García Sánchez, *La extradición* (2005), pp. 205 ff. (who distinguishes it from the principle of legality, pp. 198 ff.); Pohl, *Vorbehalt und Anerkennung* (2009), pp. 145 ff.; Lagodny, in Sieber, Satzger and von Heinegg, *Europäisches Strafrecht* (2014), p. 556; Suominen, *Mutual Recognition in Cooperation* (2011), pp. 175 ff.; on its significance and foundations, Nalewajko, *Grundsatz der gegenseitigen Anerkennung* (2010), pp. 176 ff.; Zeidler, *Der Grundsatz der beiderseitigen Strafbarkeit im Auslieferungsrecht* (2008); cf. also Capus, *Strafrecht und Souveränität* (2010), pp. 335–6, 340 ff., 432 ff.; on the protective function for individual rights, cf. ibid, pp. 410 ff.

172. Cf. Art. 2(1) EuCExt; for national law see e.g. §§2, 3 IRG (§3(2): maximum penalty of deprivation of liberty for at least one year) and §11(1) ARHG; thereon Schwaighofer and Ebensperger, *Internationale Rechtshilfe* (2001), p. 8. The national court's competence also includes reviewing whether the foreign laws were actually in force at the time in question; cf. OLG Brandenburg, No 2 Ausl. (A) 17/09, Decision (5 November 2009), in *NStZ*, 30 (2010), 709; on dual criminality in the case of desertion OLG Hamm, No 2 Ausl. 65/10, Decision (11 May 2010), in *NStZ*, 30 (2010), 708; from a Swedish perspective, Cameron et al., *ICL from a Swedish Perspective* (2011), pp. 173 ff.

173. See main text, mn. 29.

174. See e.g. §10(2) IRG; cf. Hecker, *Europäisches Strafrecht* (2015), §2 mn. 70.

175. On this principle in general, Van der Wilt, in Blekxtoon and Van Ballegooij, *Handbook on the EAW* (2005), pp. 71 ff.

176. See e.g. §5 IRG; cf. Heger and Wolter, in Ambos, König and Rackow, *Rechtshilferecht in Strafsachen* (2015), p. 502; Lagodny, in Schomburg et al., *Internationale Rechtshilfe in Strafsachen* (2012), pp. 94–5; Weigend, *JuS*, 40 (2000), 107; Hecker, *Europäisches Strafrecht* (2015), §2 mn. 69.

177. Cf. Art. 14 EuCExt.

178. See, for an example, BGH, No 1 StR 218/14, Decision (25 May 2014), in *NStZ*, 34 (2014), 590 (non-enforcement of sentence regarding conduct not included in an EAW issued by German court and executed by Irish authorities).

179. Cf. Art. 14 (1)(a) EuCExt.

180. Cf. Art. 14 (1)(b) EuCExt; see also Hackner and Schierholt, *Internationale Rechtshilfe* (2017), mn. 28; Hecker, *Europäisches Strafrecht* (2015), §2 mn. 72; García Sánchez, *La extradición* (2005), pp. 242 ff.; Nalewajko, *Grundsatz der gegenseitigen Anerkennung* (2010), pp. 202–3; Miettinen, *NJECL*, 4 (2013), 100 ff.; in detail, Capus, *Strafrecht und Souveränität* (2010), pp. 244 ff.; Suominen, *Mutual Recognition in Cooperation* (2011), p. 47, thus regards speciality as a form of 'temporary immunity'. For an example of the lapse of the speciality protection because of return, cf. BGH, No 1 StR 165/12, Decision (19 December 2012), in *BGHSt* 58, p. 76; for a lapse in appeal proceedings, BGH, No 1 StR 148/11, Decision (9 December 2012), in *BGHSt* 57, p. 138; BGH, No 1 StR 165/12, Decision (25 October 2012), in *NStZ-RR*, 18 (2013), 251.

181. Cf. Art. 6 EuCExt; for more detail on this 'nationality exception', see Deen-Racsmány and Blekxtoon, *EJCCLCJ*, 13 (2005), 318 ff., 322 ff.; García Sánchez, *La extradición* (2005), pp. 259 ff. On such prohibitions in national law, see main text, n. 396.
182. Cf. Art. 16(1) EuCExt.
183. Art. 16(4) EuCExt.
184. Cf. e.g. §16(2) IRG: two months, and three months for non-European States; see also Schomburg, in Schomburg et al., *Internationale Rechtshilfe in Strafsachen* (2012), p. 648.
185. Heger and Wolter, in Ambos, König and Rackow, *Rechtshilferecht in Strafsachen* (2015), p. 517; Schomburg, in Schomburg et al., *Internationale Rechtshilfe in Strafsachen* (2012), pp. 648–9 incl. further references.
186. Cf. e.g. §15 IRG.
187. BGH, No 4 ARs 6/78, Decision (3 May 1978), in *BGHSt*, 28, p. 31; BGH, No 4 ARs 10/85, Decision (10 September 1985), in *BGHSt*, 33, p. 310; cf. also Hackner and Schierholt, *Internationale Rechtshilfe* (2017), mn. 73.
188. OLG Hamm, No 4 Ausl. 67/02 (39/02), Decision (12 April 2002), in *NStZ*, 22 (2002), 665.
189. Ambos, *JZ*, 54 (1999), 18.
190. Cf. Hecker, *NStZ*, 22 (2002), 664 incl. further references; BGH, No 4 ARs 16/09, Decision (18 February 2010), in *NStZ-RR*, 15 (2010), 177.
191. Art. 62(2), (3) CISA.
192. Art. 63 in conjunction with Art. 50(1) CISA.
193. Art. 66(1) CISA.
194. Art. 66(2) CISA.
195. Cf. Art. 95 CISA; thereon European Commission, *Staff Working Document* (2011) (complementing European Commission, *Report Implementation EAW* (2011)), p. 14).
196. Cf. Art. 64 CISA; on this, see also main text, mn. 26.
197. Cf. Gleß, in Schomburg et al., *Internationale Rechtshilfe in Strafsachen* (2012), pp. 1700–13; Hackner and Schierholt, *Internationale Rechtshilfe* (2017), mn. 59 ff.; Hecker, *Europäisches Strafrecht* (2015), §2 mn. 75, §5 mn. 48 ff.; De Capitani, *ERA Forum*, 15 (2014), 104–6; also Mörbel, in Cullen and Jund, *Criminal Justice Co-operation in the EU after Tampere* (2002), pp. 50, 53–4; Kattau, *Strafverfolgung* (1993), pp. 135 ff.; Würz, *Das Schengener Durchführungsübereinkommen* (1997), mn. 152 ff.; Vervaele, *RP*, 15 (2005), 179, 183; de Biolley, *RIDP*, 77 (2006), 26–7; Eisele, in Sieber, Satzger and von Heinegg, *Europäisches Strafrecht* (2014), pp. 880 ff.; Esser, in Böse, *Europäisches Strafrecht* (2013), pp. 725–8; for the changes cf. Huybreghts, *ERA Forum*, 16 (2015), 396–8.
198. See above Chapter 1, mn. 34 ff.
199. Cf. Chapter 1, mn. 34.
200. Hecker, *Europäisches Strafrecht* (2015), §5 mn. 49; but see below, n. 205.
201. Art. 92(3) CISA. There is a backup in Sankt Johann im Pongau (Austria).
202. Art. 92(1), (2) CISA. Each MS shall set up its own national section 'for its own national account and at its own risk'; see also Gusy and Gimbal, in Baldus and Soiné, *Rechtsprobleme der internationalen polizeilichen Zusammenarbeit* (1999), pp. 125–6; Meyer and Hüttemann, *ZStW*, 128 (2016), 398–9 (regarding SIS II); on the special solution for Liechtenstein using the Swiss entry, cf. Huybreghts, *ERA Forum*, 16 (2015), 396.

203. Art. 93 CISA.
204. Art. 95 CISA.
205. Art. 96 CISA. The UK and Ireland, which do not take part in the common border policies, do not use this provision; cf. Huybreghts, *ERA Forum*, 16 (2015), 396, 402.
206. Art. 97 CISA.
207. Art. 98 CISA.
208. Art. 99 CISA.
209. Art. 100 CISA. On this, cf. Gusy and Gimbal, in Baldus and Soiné, *Rechtsprobleme der internationalen polizeilichen Zusammenarbeit* (1999), pp. 131 ff.
210. Art. 95 CISA.
211. Generally on Interpol, searches via Interpol and legal remedies, Meyer and Hüttemann, *ZStW*, 128 (2016), 399–400, 408–12, 428–44. Interpol is displaced by SIS II if the latter is applicable, cf. ibid., 399.
212. For a critical stance on this, cf. Gleß, in Schomburg et al., *Internationale Rechtshilfe in Strafsachen* (2012), p. 1704.
213. Scheller, *JZ*, 47 (1992), 908.
214. Cf. already Chapter 1, mn. 26–7.
215. Main text, mn. 46 ff.
216. In Germany, it is recognised that the alert can be challenged before the district court pursuant to an analogy to §98(2) StPO as it constitutes a coercive measure based on §131 StPO; cf. OLG Celle, No 2 VAs 3/09, Decision (16 April 2009), in *NStZ*, 30 (2010), 534 incl. further references. On the complex issue of legal remedies as to SIS II (mainly based on privacy and data protection violations), cf. Meyer and Hüttemann, *ZStW*, 128 (2016), 418–28.
217. Cf. third recital of Regulation 1987/2006 of 20 December 2006 on the establishment, operation and use of the second-generation Schengen Information System (SIS II) (OJ L 381 of 28 December 2006, 4). The matter dealt with is 'the entry and processing in SIS II of alerts in respect of third country nationals . . . for the purpose of refusing entry into, or a stay in, a Member State' (Art. 2(1) of the Regulation). Cf. also EC Regulation 1988/2006 (OJ L 411 of 30 December 2006, 1); and Council Decision 2006/1007/JHA of 21 December 2006 amending Decision 2001/886/JHA on the development of the second generation Schengen Information System (SIS II) (OJ L 411 of 30 December 2006, 78). Cf. also Commission Decision 2008/333/EC adopting the SIRENE Manual and other implementing measures for the second-generation Schengen Information System (SIS II) (OJ L 123 of 8 May 2008) and Commission Decision 2010/261/EU on the Security Plan for Central SIS II and the Communication Infrastructure (OJ L 112 of 5 May 2010); cf. also David, *Eléments de droit pénal international et européen* (2009), mn. 10.3.32–3; Schoppa, *Europol* (2013), pp. 76 ff.; Albers, in Albers et al., *Evaluation Framework* (2013), pp. 47–8; Eisele, in Sieber, Satzger and von Heinegg, *Europäisches Strafrecht* (2014), p. 883; Esser, in Böse, *Europäisches Strafrecht* (2013), pp. 727–8; Meyer and Hüttemann, *ZStW*, 128 (2016), 396, 397–9, 403–8, 418–28.
218. Council Decision 2007/533/JHA of 12 June 2007 on the establishment, operation and use of the second-generation Schengen Information System (SIS II) (OJ L 205 of 7 August 2007, 63).
219. On the repeated delays cf. *eucrim*, 2 (2007), 70 ff.; *eucrim*, 3 (2008), 8; *eucrim*, 4 (2009), 3–4; *eucrim*, 4 (2009), 64; *eucrim*, 5 (2010), 3; *eucrim*, 6 (2011), 4; *eucrim*, 8 (2013), 35.

220. Huybreghts, *ERA Forum*, 16 (2015), 393 with n. 57; cf. also 'From the Schengen Information System (SIS 1+) to the Second Generation Schengen Information System (SIS II)', available at http://eur-lex.europa.eu/legal-content/EN/TXT/?uri=uriserv:jl0010, last accessed 27 January 2018; *eucrim*, 8 (2013), 35.
221. Cf. Arts. 68, 69 and 71 Council Decision 2007/533/JHA (with Art. 68(1) explicitly referring to Arts. 64, 92–119 CISA); cf. also Regulation 1104/2008 of 24 October 2008 on migration from the Schengen Information System (SIS 1+) to the second generation Schengen Information System (SIS II) (OJ L 299 of 8 November 2008, 1–8) and Council Decision 2008/839/JHA of 24 October 2008 on migration from the Schengen Information System (SIS 1+) to the second-generation Schengen Information System (SIS II) (OJ L 299 of 8 November 2008, 43–49), both of which have now expired.
222. Cf. Art. 31 Council Decision 2007/533/JHA (execution of action based on an alert on a person wanted for arrest with a view to surrender or extradition): '1. An alert entered in SIS II in accordance with Article 26 in conjunction with the additional data referred to in Article 27, shall constitute and have the same effect as a EAW ... 2. Where FD 2002/584/JHA does not apply, an alert entered in SIS II in accordance with Articles 26 and 29 shall have the same legal force as a request for provisional arrest under Article 16 of the European Convention on Extradition of 13 December 1957 or Article 15 of the Benelux Treaty concerning Extradition and Mutual Assistance in Criminal Matters of 27 June 1962.' Thereto Meyer and Hüttemann, *ZStW*, 128 (2016), 407–8.
223. On this see Art. 24(1) Council Decision 2007/533/JHA: 'Where a MS considers that to give effect to an alert entered in accordance with Articles 26, 32 or 36 is incompatible with its national law, its international obligations or essential national interests, it may subsequently require that a flag be added to the alert to the effect that the action to be taken on the basis of the alert will not be taken in its territory. The flag shall be added by the SIRENE Bureau of the MS which entered the alert.'
224. On alerts on firearms, cf. *eucrim*, 10 (2015), 133.
225. Cf. thereon *eucrim*, 9 (2014), 95–6.
226. European Commission, *Memo SIS II* (2013), p. 2; cf. also *eucrim*, 8 (2013), 35; *eucrim*, 10 (2015), 2; Meyer and Hüttemann, *ZStW*, 128 (2016), 398.
227. On the connection of Europol with SIS II, cf. *eucrim*, 10 (2015), 4.
228. For more information, cf. also European Commission, *Memo SIS II* (2013), p. 2; cf. also *eucrim*, 8 (2013), 35; *eucrim*, 10 (2015), 2.
229. Commission report COM(2016) 880 final, pp. 7 ff. (10), see also 19 ff. (20: 'outstanding operational and technical success').
230. Commission report COM(2016) 880 final, pp. 10 ff.; on new legislative proposals see Brodowski, *ZIS*, 12 (2017), 702.
231. OJ C 313 of 23 October 1996, 12.
232. Heger and Wolter, in Ambos, König and Rackow, *Rechtshilferecht in Strafsachen* (2015), p. 321; Schomburg and Gleß, in Schomburg et al., *Internationale Rechtshilfe in Strafsachen* (2006), pp. 924 ff.; Vogel, *JZ*, 56 (2001), 938–9.
233. Art. 3 EUCExt.
234. Art. 3(1)(a) and (b) EUCExt. Cf. the Explanatory Report (OJ C 191 of 23 June 1997, 13), cited in Schomburg and Gleß, in Schomburg et al., *Internationale Rechtshilfe in Strafsachen* (2006), p. 930.

235. Heger and Wolter, in Ambos, König and Rackow, *Rechtshilferecht in Strafsachen* (2015), p. 322; Baier, *GA*, 148 (2001), 443; Vogel, *JZ*, 56 (2001), 938–9; in detail on non-extradition for political offences from a Belgian perspective, cf. David, *Eléments de droit pénal international et européen* (2009), mn. 7.1.26 ff.
236. Cf. the Explanatory Report (OJ C 191 of 23 June 1997, 13), cited in Schomburg and Gleß, in Schomburg et al., *Internationale Rechtshilfe in Strafsachen* (2006), p. 932.
237. Cf. Vogel, *JZ*, 56 (2001), 939; Deen-Racsmány and Blekxtoon, *EJCCLCJ*, 13 (2005), 325–6; for a fundamental account of the extradition of nationals, cf. Pohl, *Vorbehalt und Anerkennung* (2009), pp. 225 ff.; on the extradition of German nationals, cf. also Ambos, *Fälle zum internationalen Strafrecht* (2010), pp. 7 (case 1 mn. 15–16), 9 (case 1 mn. 22 ff.) and 11 (case 1 mn. 30).
238. Cf. Heger and Wolter, in Ambos, König and Rackow, *Rechtshilferecht in Strafsachen* (2015), p. 322; Baier, *GA*, 148 (2001), 443–4; Schomburg, *NJW*, 54 (2001), 802.
239. See above, mn. 11 with n. 91.
240. Hackner and Schierholt, *Internationale Rechtshilfe* (2017), mn. 86 n. 186.
241. Heger and Wolter, in Ambos, König and Rackow, *Rechtshilferecht in Strafsachen* (2015), p. 323; Hackner and Schierholt, *Internationale Rechtshilfe* (2017), mn. 86; Vogel, *JZ*, 56 (2001), 939.
242. Cf. Council Decision 2003/169/JHA of 27 February 2003 determining which provisions of the 1995 convention on simplified extradition procedure between the MS of the EU and of the 1996 convention relating to extradition between the MS of the EU constitute developments of the Schengen *acquis* in accordance with the agreement concerning the Republic of **Iceland's** and the Kingdom of **Norway's** association with the implementation, application and development of the Schengen *acquis* (OJ L 67 of 12 March 2003, 25); Art. 2(2) and Annex B of the agreement between the EU, the EC and the **Swiss Confederation** on the Swiss Confederation's association with the implementation, application and development of the Schengen *acquis* (OJ L 53 of 27 February 2008, 52–79); cf. also protocol between the EU, the EC, the Swiss Confederation and the Principality of **Liechtenstein** on the accession of the Principality of Liechtenstein to the agreement between the EU, the EC and the Swiss Confederation on the Swiss Confederation's association with the implementation, application and development of the Schengen *acquis* (OJ L 160 of 18 June 2011, 21–25); thereon Huybreghts, *ERA Forum*, 16 (2015), 393–4.
243. Lagodny, in Schomburg et al., *Internationale Rechtshilfe in Strafsachen* (2012), pp. 245–6 incl. further references; on the decision on the costs involved in the case of §41 IRG, cf. OLG Karlsruhe, No 1 AK 4/05, Decision (21 March 2005), in *NStZ*, 26 (2006), 112.
244. Hackner and Schierholt, *Internationale Rechtshilfe* (2017), mn. 86 ff.; on the principle of speciality in Art. 14(1) European Convention on Extradition, cf. LG Bielefeld, No Qs 323+324/06 II, Decision (25 July 2006), in *StV*, 26 (2006), 642.
245. Hackner and Schierholt, *Internationale Rechtshilfe* (2017), mn. 88.
246. Hackner and Schierholt, *Internationale Rechtshilfe* (2017), mn. 89.
247. Art. 12(2)(a) EuCExt.
248. Art. 4(1)(c) EU Simplified Extradition Convention.
249. For a critical stance on this, cf. Hackner et al., *Internationale Rechtshilfe* (2003), mn. 89: 'fragile foundation for deprivation of liberty' (orig. 'zerbrechliche Grundlage einer Freiheitsentziehung').

250. Art. 8 EU Simplified Extradition Convention.
251. Art. 10 EU Simplified Extradition Convention. Cf. on individual aspects Hackner and Schierholt, *Internationale Rechtshilfe* (2017), mn. 88. On the process of the simplified extradition procedure, cf. also Ambos, *Internationales Strafrecht* (2008), Figures 22, 23, pp. 470–1.
252. See above, mn. 11 with n. 92.
253. Art. 2 of the agreement on transmitting extradition requests.
254. Cf. Schomburg and Gleß, in Schomburg et al., *Internationale Rechtshilfe in Strafsachen* (2006), p. 951.
255. See Chapter 2, mn. 124–5.
256. Peters and Altwicker, *EMRK* (2012), pp. 66 ff.; on the 'extraterritorial effect' (orig. 'extraterritorialen Wirkung') of Convention guarantees, cf. Matscher, in Donatsch, Forster and Schwarzenegger, *FS Trechsel* (2002), pp. 28 ff.; Ziegenhahn, *Schutz der Menschenrechte* (2002), pp. 402 ff.; Ress, *ZaöRV*, 69 (2009), 304–5; Janik and Kleinlein, *GoJIL*, 1 (2009), 468 ff.; in regard to the prosecution of pirates, Esser and Fischer, *JR*, 82 (2010), 514 ff.; from a Swiss perspective, Donatsch, Heimgartner, Meyer and Simonek, *Internationale Rechtshilfe* (2015), pp. 80 ff.; especially on fundamental rights as grounds for refusal in the EAW, see Mitsilegas, *EU Criminal Law* (2016), pp. 131–6. On the relationship between extradition and asylum procedure, Hackner and Schierholt, *Internationale Rechtshilfe* (2017), mn. 118. From the case law, cf. OLG Frankfurt a.M., No 2 Ausl. A 36/06, Decision (23 August 2006), *StV*, 27 (2007), 142 (on the inadmissibility of extradition in the case of conviction by a Turkish state security court). For an instructive overview of the (traditional) substantive conditions of legal assistance, cf. Lagodny, in Widmaier, *Münchener Anwaltshandbuch Strafverteidigung* (2014), p. 943; on further extradition obstacles, cf. Lagodny, in Sieber, Satzger and von Heinegg, *Europäisches Strafrecht* (2014), p. 558.
257. OLG Frankfurt a.M., No 2 Ausl. A 73/06, Decision (1 March 2007), in *NStZ*, 28 (2008), 166.
258. On the rationale of this, cf. García Sánchez, *La extradición* (2005), pp. 145 ff.
259. On the dilemma of this trade-off, cf. Böse, *NStZ*, 22 (2002), 670–1; Keijzer, in Blekxtoon and Van Ballegooij, *Handbook on the EAW* (2005)), pp. 186–7.
260. Cf. Böse, *NStZ*, 22 (2002), 672; in greater detail, Lagodny, in Schomburg et al., *Internationale Rechtshilfe in Strafsachen* (2012), pp. 421–2.
261. ECtHR, *Soering* v. *the UK*, No 14038/88, Judgment (7 July 1989), para. 111: 'having regard to the very long period of time spent on death row in such extreme conditions, with the ever present and mounting anguish of awaiting execution of the death penalty ... the applicant's extradition to the United States would expose him to a real risk of treatment going beyond the threshold set by Article 3'. *Soering* was extradited following assurances that the death penalty would not be enforced, and has been in prison ever since (cf. Soering's autobiographical account). For further references, cf. Ambos, *Internationales Strafrecht* (2008), §10 mn. 82 incl. n. 549. On Art. 3 ECHR in this context, cf. also Safokolov, *OstEuR*, 10 (2009), 167 ff.; Michaelsen, *ICLQ*, 61 (2012), 753.
262. Cf. Arts. 102 and 2(2) first sentence GG, and §8 IRG; see also §20 ARHG and Art. 37(3) IRSG.
263. E.g. Art. 11 EuCExt; also Hackner and Schierholt, *Internationale Rechtshilfe* (2017), mn. 119; Schomburg, in Schomburg et al., *Internationale Rechtshilfe in*

Strafsachen (2012), p. 642; on this in general, García Sánchez, *La extradición* (2005), pp. 338 ff.

264. Cf. e.g. §8 IRG; also Hackner and Schierholt, *Internationale Rechtshilfe* (2017), mn. 119–20; cf. also OLG Frankfurt a.M., 2 Ausl. A 73/06 (n. 257) with a commentary by Schneider et al.; OLG Dresden, No OLG Ausl. 108/07, Decision (25 August 2008), in *NStZ*, 29 (2009), 462; ECtHR, *Othman (Abu Qatada)* v. *the UK*, No 8139/09, Judgment (17 January 2012); on this, Michaelsen, *ICLQ*, 61 (2012), 752, 759 ff., 762–3; on the parallel law in Austria (critically) Schwaighofer and Ebensperger, *Internationale Rechtshilfe* (2001), p. 11; cf. ibid., p. 128, for the reservations of Austria and Switzerland on Art. 11 EuCExt. On the EU–US extradition agreement in this regard, cf. main text, mn. 13 above.

265. In detail on the *Sholam Weiss* case (sentenced to 845 years' imprisonment for property offences by an American district court), cf. Peukert, in Triffterer, *GS Vogler* (2004), pp. 151 ff., 155 ff.; also Böse, *NStZ*, 22 (2002), 672; Hecker, *Europäisches Strafrecht* (2015), §3 mn. 45 ff. According to OLG Wien, No 22 Ns 2/01, Decision (11 September 2001), in *NStZ*, 22 (2002), 669 with commentary by Böse, *NStZ*, 22 (2002), 670–2, an extradition obstacle based on Art. 2 AP VII ECHR (right to review by a higher tribunal) also comes into question; on repealing an extradition warrant due to the disproportionality of the provisional arrest, cf. OLG Düsseldorf, No III-3 Ausl. 75/10, Decision (8 September 2010), in *StV*, 31 (2011), 170. Cf. also European Commission, *Report Implementation EAW* (2011), p. 7; in agreement, Thomas, *ERA Forum*, 13 (2013), 587; cf. also Smith, *NJECL*, 4 (2013), 86–7; ECPI, *ZIS*, 8 (2013), 431–2, 437–8.

266. Hackner and Schierholt, *Internationale Rechtshilfe* (2017), mn. 122 incl. references from case law. Examples of insupportably harsh treatment following extradition, which thus would conflict with fundamental principles of German law, can be found in OLG Karlsruhe, No 1 AK 1/06, Decision (10 August 2006), in *StV*, 27 (2007), 145–6.

267. OLG Stuttgart, No 1 Ausl. (24) 1246/09, Decision (25 February 2010), in *NJW*, 63 (2010), 1617. In any case, the applicability of the charter derives – as the OLG rightly assumes – from Art. 51(1) first sentence of the charter, as extradition on the basis of an EAW is initiated by Union law, and Germany is thus implementing EU law (cf. also Chapter 2, mn. 154).

268. ECtHR, *Vinter et al.* v. *the UK*, Nos 66069/09, 130/10 and 3896/10, GC Judgment (9 July 2013), paras. 107 ff.; thereon Chapter 2, mn. 119.

269. In this vein Mavronicola, *HRLR*, 15 (2015), 742–3; on the previous case law see Kromrey and Morgenstern, *ZIS*, 9 (2014), 710–11.

270. ECtHR, *Trabelsi* v. *Belgium*, No 140/10, Judgment (4 September 2014), paras. 121 ff.; thereon (in agreement) Kromrey and Morgenstern, *ZIS*, 9 (2014), 711–12, 714–15.

271. ECtHR, *Saadi* v. *Italy*, No 37201/06, Judgment (28 February 2008), para. 108; ECtHR, *Trabelsi*, 140/10, para. 116.

272. Hackner and Schierholt, *Internationale Rechtshilfe* (2017), mn. 123; Ziegenhahn, *Schutz der Menschenrechte* (2002), pp. 412 ff.; Johnston, *ICLR*, 11 (2011), 1 ff., with special reference to assurances that torture will not be applied; similarly for inhuman detention conditions BVerfG, No 2 BvR 26/04, Decision (3 March 2004), in *NStZ-RR*, 9 (2004), 308; on the risk of torture, OLG Karlsruhe, No 1 AK 40/03, Decision (27 May 2004), in *StV*, 24 (2004), 442; on an extradition

obstacle due to (possible) detention conditions that violate human rights in Belorussian prisons, OLG Hamm, No (2) 4 Ausl. A 29/2003 (173/04), Decision (12 July 2004), *StV*, 25 (2005), 286; on Egyptian detention conditions, OLG Köln, No 6 Ausl. A 106/08, Decision (21 June 2010), in *NStZ*, 30 (2010), 706; on detention conditions in Greece, Mansell, *EuCLR*, 2 (2012), 39–40. From an Austrian perspective, cf. Murschetz, *Auslieferung* (2007), pp. 187 ff. In regard to Turkish prisons, cf. also OLG Köln, No 6 Ausl. A 3/09, Decision (4 June 2009) and No 6 Ausl. A 88/09, Decision (4 October 2009).

273. On the inadmissibility of extradition when the requesting State (Lithuania) is unable to protect the person in question from the feared reprisals of organised criminals, OLG Düsseldorf, III-4 Ausl. (A) 16/05 – 44/06 III et al. (n. 132) ('extradition obstacle of Art. 3 ECHR, 25 GG'). Crit. on the recent case law of the UK Supreme Court, Allen, *EJIL:Talk!*, 28 July 2017 (arguing that the Supreme Court misunderstands the ECtHR's case law and an individual application 'would provide the ECtHR with an opportunity to correct the Supreme Court's misapplication of its jurisprudence and to reaffirm the general applicability of the Saadi test in extradition cases involving detention'. On the ECtHR's judgment in *Saadi* v. *Italy*, n. 271.
274. OLG Köln, No 6 Ausl. A 4/07, Decision (22 August 2008), in *NStZ-RR*, 14 (2009), 140.
275. Hackner and Schierholt, *Internationale Rechtshilfe* (2017), mn. 111.
276. Ziegenhahn, *Schutz der Menschenrechte* (2002), pp. 406 ff.; Hecker, *Europäisches Strafrecht* (2015), §3 mn. 40 ff. On the specific Art. 19(2) CFREU, cf. Beltrán de Felipe and Nieto Martín, *JICJ*, 10 (2012), 583–4. According to BVerfG, No 2 BvR 2259/04, Decision (6 July 2005), in *BVerfGE*, 113, p. 154, the risk of a life sentence without parole is no obstacle to the admissibility of extradition.
277. OLG Karlsruhe, No 1 AK 23/04, Decision (14 February 2005), in *NStZ*, 25 (2005), 351 (separation of an underage child from its mother and the possible onset of life-threatening illness); cf. also OLG Hamm, No (2) 4 Ausl. A 163/08 (89/09), Decision (25 February 2010), in *StV*, 31 (2011), 173. Cf. also Mansell, *EuCLR*, 2 (2012), 42–3; and Smith, *NJECL*, 4 (2013), 90–1, for the case that extradition takes place before sufficient preparations have been made for the criminal proceedings.
278. Cf. Lagodny, in Schomburg et al., *Internationale Rechtshilfe in Strafsachen* (2012), p. 425; Ziegenhahn, *Schutz der Menschenrechte* (2002), pp. 429–30; in this context, cf. also Matscher, in Donatsch, Forster and Schwarzenegger, *FS Trechsel* (2002), pp. 35–6; in detail on Art. 6 as an obstacle to extradition and deportation, Hailbronner, in Bröhmer, *FS Ress* (2005), pp. 997 ff.; cf. also OLG Karlsruhe, No 1 AK 68/08, Decision (8 December 2008), in *NStZ*, 30 (2010), 41; OLG Hamm, 2 Ausl. 65/10 (n. 172). But, cf. also BVerfG, No 2 BvR 890/16, Decision (6 September 2016), where the fact that the accused's silence may be used to her detriment in criminal proceedings does not hinder extradition to the UK; see thereto already in the context of the constitutional identity review above Chapter 2, mn. 156 with n. 904. On a violation of Art. 6 on the grounds of the *circumstances of the extradition procedure*, see Ziegenhahn, *Schutz der Menschenrechte* (2002), pp. 426 ff.
279. References in Böse, *NStZ*, 22 (2002), 671.
280. Cf. OLG Wien, 22 Ns 2/01 (n. 265); Austrian Supreme Court of Justice, No 14 Os 8/02, Decision (9 April 2002) and No 14 Os 30/03, Decision (9 September 2003)

can be challenged; crit. Peukert, in Triffterer, *GS Vogler* (2004), pp. 155 ff.; UNHRC, 'Views of the Human Rights Committee under article 5, paragraph 4, of the Optional Protocol to the International Covenant on Civil and Political Rights', annexed to UN Doc. CCPR/C/77/D/1086/2002 (15 May 2003), is also critical (available at www.worldlii.org, last accessed 27 January 2018). On the guaranteed judicial review of a decision deriving from Art. 6 ECHR (here in connection with the Convention on Transfer), cf. ECtHR, *Buijen* v. *Germany*, No 27804/05, Judgment (1 April 2010), para. 43.

281. Matscher, in Donatsch, Forsters and Schwarzenegger, *FS Trechsel* (2002), pp. 41 ff. On this, cf. also ECtHR, *Buijen* v. *Germany*, 27804/05 (n. 280), paras. 40–3.
282. KG, No (4) Ausl. A 522/03 (139–40/07), Decision (30 January 2009), in *NStZ-RR*, 14 (2009), 242.
283. ECtHR, *Othman (Abu Qatada)*, 8139/09 (n. 264), paras. 236 ff.
284. BVerfG, No 2 BvR 1243/03, Decision (5 November 2003), in *BVerfGE*, 109, p. 13; with critical commentary by Dickersbach, *StV*, 24 (2004), 435 ff.
285. ECtHR, *Krombach* v. *France*, No 29731/96, Judgment (13 February 2001), paras. 82 ff.; on extradition in *in absentia* trials, cf. also BVerfG, No 2 BvR 283/05, Decision (4 July 2005), in *NStZ*, 26 (2006), 102; BGH, No 4 ARs 4/01, Decision (16 October 2001), *BGHSt*, 47, pp. 120, 123–7; cf. also OLG Stuttgart, No 3 Ausl. 76/03, Decision (28 January 2005), in *StV*, 25 (2005), 284 (Hungarian sentence *in absentia*), commented upon critically by Karsai, *ZIS*, 1 (2006), 443 ff.; OLG Zweibrücken, No 1 Ausl. 16/05, Decision (7 August 2006), in *NStZ*, 27 (2007), 109 (Belgian sentence *in absentia*); and OLG Stuttgart, No 3 Ausl. 147/2005, Decision (21 April 2006), in *NStZ*, 26 (2006), 693 (Czech sentence *in absentia*); OLG Koblenz, No (1) Ausl. – III/1/06, Decision (6 September 2007), in *NStZ-RR*, 13 (2008), 111 (Albanian sentence *in absentia*); Hackner and Schierholt, *Internationale Rechtshilfe* (2017), mn. 129 incl. n. 399; Ziegenhahn, *Schutz der Menschenrechte* (2002), pp. 431–2; cf. also FD 2009/299/JHA amending FD 2002/584/JHA, 2005/214/JHA, 2006/783/JHA and 2008/947/JHA, on enhancement of the procedural rights of persons and fostering of the application of the principle of mutual recognition in respect of decisions rendered in the absence of the person (trials *in absentia*) (OJ L 81 of 27 March 2009, 24); on this, cf. Klitsch, *ZIS*, 4 (2009), 11 ff.; cf. also the case in Mansell, *EuCLR*, 2 (2012), 37–8.
286. Hackner and Schierholt, *Internationale Rechtshilfe* (2017), mn. 129.
287. BVerfG, 2 BvR 26/04 (n. 272), 309–10; cf. also BGH, 4 ARs 4/01 (n. 285), pp. 123 ff.; OLG Karlsruhe, No 1 AK 29/02, Decision (27 February 2003), in *StV*, 24 (2004), 444; Hackner and Schierholt, *Internationale Rechtshilfe* (2017), mn. 130.
288. *BGBl.* II 1990, 118; *BGBl.* II 1991, 874; cf. also Schomburg, in Schomburg et al., *Internationale Rechtshilfe in Strafsachen* (2017), pp. 665–71; also Wahl, *eucrim*, 10 (2015), 71 (arguing that Art. 3 AP II EuCExt establishes a European *ordre public*, given a more concrete form by the FD EAW).
289. Cf. Royer, *AJP*, 4 (2007), 188, on a related decision of the Cour de cassation of 7 February 2007. On this, using the example of the Assange case, Marauhn and Simon, *ZJS*, 5 (2012), 594–5.
290. ECtHR, *T. I.* v. *the UK*, No 43844/98, Decision (7 March 2000). However, this does not apply when the person in question is able to appeal against further deportation in the transit country: ECtHR, *K. R. S.* v. *the UK*, No 32733/08, Decision (2 December 2008).

291. This is also reflected in national law, cf. §6(1) IRG §14 ARHG and Art. 3 IRSG.
292. Weigend, *JuS*, 40 (2000), 108; more detail on this extradition obstacle can be found in García Sánchez, *La extradición* (2005), pp. 361 ff.
293. Cf. Grützner, Pötz and Kreß, *Internationaler Rechtshilfeverkehr*, v (2017), 43rd update, Preliminary Remarks on the European Convention on the Suppression of Terrorism, mn. 6.
294. European Convention on the Suppression of Terrorism of 27 January 1977 (ETS No 90); entry intro force 4 August 1978.
295. UNTS 12325, Vol. 860, pp. 105–11; entry into force 14 October 1971.
296. UNTS 14118, Vol. 974, pp. 178–84; entry into force 26 January 1973.
297. UNTS 15410, Vol. 1035, pp. 167–72; entry into force 20 February 1977.
298. See above, mn. 20 and 29.
299. OLG Düsseldorf, No III-4 Ausl. (A) 80/06, Decision (6 November 2011), in *NStZ-RR*, 12 (2007), 113.
300. Cf. §79(2) IRG (giving the authorising institution the possibility to invoke obstacles to a surrender request).
301. OLG Stuttgart, No 3 Ausl. 52/06, Decision (6 March 2007), in *StV*, 27 (2007), 258–9.
302. Based on Ambos and Bock, *JuS*, 52 (2012), 437 ff., modelled on the case of Wikileaks founder Julian Assange.
303. FD 2002/584/JHA (OJ L 190 of 18 July 2002, 1). On the legislative history, cf. Fichera, *Implementation of the EAW* (2011), pp. 70 ff. The EAW was made applicable to **Norway** and **Iceland** by way of a specific agreement between them and the EU, which was signed in 2006 but concluded only in 2014 (cf. agreement between the EU and the Republic of Iceland and the Kingdom of Norway on the surrender procedure between the MS of the EU and Iceland and Norway (OJ L 292 of 21 October 2006, 2–14); thereon Huybreghts, *ERA Forum*, 16 (2015), 394; and Council Decision 2014/835/EU of 27 November 2014 on the conclusion of the agreement between the EU and the Republic of Iceland and the Kingdom of Norway on the surrender procedure between the MS of the EU and Iceland and Norway (OJ L 343 of 28 November 2014, 1–2). For the **Nordic countries** (Denmark, Finland, Iceland, Norway and Sweden) the EAW applies for surrender procedures with 'third' EU MS, while for surrender procedures between them the **Nordic Arrest Warrant** (NAW) is applicable (Convention of 15 December 2005 on Surrender on the Basis of an Offence between the Nordic States (the Nordic Arrest Warrant), entry into force 16 November 2012). This is in conformity with the FD EAW, which provides in Art. 31(2) that 'MS may continue to apply bilateral or multilateral agreements or arrangements in force . . . so far as . . . [they] allow the objectives of this FD to be extended or enlarged and help to simplify or facilitate further the procedures for surrender of persons who are the subject of European arrest warrants'; on the NAW, cf. Strandbakken, *eucrim*, 2 (2007), 139 ff.; Mathisen, *NJIL*, 79 (2010), 5 ff., 11 ff., 16 f.; Cameron et al., *ICL from a Swedish Perspective* (2011), pp. 237–8; Suominen, *Mutual Recognition in Cooperation* (2011), pp. 81 ff.; Suominen, *EuCLR*, 4 (2014), 41–5; Tolttila, *NJECL*, 2 (2011), 376 ff.; Asp, *Procedural Criminal Law Cooperation* (2016), pp. 40–1. **Switzerland** declared in 2009 that 'an EAW issued by a foreign State is considered, according to these Conventions [the EuCExt of 13 December 1957 and the Schengen Convention of 19 June 1990] and the domestic law, as a valid basis for a request for provisional arrest and extradition', cf. Council doc. 8501/09 ('Article 95 of the

Schengen Convention, European Arrest Warrant (EAW), Brussels, 6 April 2009'); thereon also Huybreghts, *ERA Forum*, 16 (2015), 394. On the relationship between the FD EAW and other forms of extradition between EU MS, cf. CJEU, *Ignacio Pedro Santesteban Goicoechea*, No C-296/08 PPU (ECLI:EU:C:2008:457), Judgment (12 August 2008), paras. 48 ff. ('Article 31 of the FD must be interpreted as referring only to the situation in which the European arrest warrant system is applicable, which is not the case where a request for extradition relates to acts committed before a date specified by a MS in a statement made pursuant to Article 32 of the FD' (para. 63)); on this, cf. European Commission, *Staff Working Document* (2011), pp. 18–19; Klimek, *EAW* (2015), pp. 277–83.

304. On its significance and development, see already Chapter 1, mn. 26 with n. 215.
305. Heger and Wolter, in Ambos, König and Rackow, *Rechtshilferecht in Strafsachen* (2015), p. 324; Wehnert, *StraFo*, 16 (2003), 356 ff.; Plachta and Van Ballegooij, in Blekxtoon and Van Ballegooij, *Handbook on the EAW* (2005), pp. 32 ff.; Deen-Racsmány and Blekxtoon, *EJCCLCJ*, 13 (2005), 333 ff.; Hüttemann, *European Criminal Procedure* (2012), pp. 72–3; for further references, cf. Ambos, *Internationales Strafrecht* (2008), §12 mn. 56 incl. n. 321.
306. Recitals nos 1, 11, and Art. 31 FD EAW; see also OLG Stuttgart, No 3 Ausl. 80/04, Decision (7 September 2004), in *NJW*, 57 (2004), 3437–8; von Heintschel-Heinegg and Rohlff, *GA*, 150 (2003), 45; Wehnert, *StraFo*, 16 (2003), 356 ff.; Combeaud, *RIDP*, 77 (2006), 131 ff.; Krüßmann, *Transnationales Strafprozessrecht* (2009), pp. 589 ff.
307. Cf. also Klip, *European Criminal Law* (2016), pp. 82 ff.
308. Cf. above, mn. 2.
309. Its legal nature is controversial; for the nature of a 'European judicial title', Arangüena Fanego, *RDP*, 20 (2007), 17–18; cf. also Heger and Wolter, in Ambos, König and Rackow, *Rechtshilferecht in Strafsachen* (2015), p. 336. See also CJEU, *Bob-Dogi*, No C-241/15 (ECLI:EU:C:2016:385), Judgment (1 June 2016), paras. 56–8 ('that Article 8(1)(c) of the Framework Decision is to be interpreted as meaning that the term "arrest warrant", as used in that provision, must be understood as referring to a national arrest warrant that is distinct from the European arrest warrant'); confirmed in CJEU, *Özçelik*, No C-453/16 PPU (ECLI:EU:C:2016:860), Judgment (10 November 2016), para. 27; on this Brodowski, *ZIS*, 12 (2017), 22.
310. Cf. also Heger and Wolter, in Ambos, König and Rackow, *Rechtshilferecht in Strafsachen* (2015), p. 336; OLG Köln, No 6 Ausl. 63/05 – 31/05, Decision (16 August 2005), in *NStZ*, 26 (2006), 112 (EAW not only a request for arrest, but also for extradition; a different opinion is put forward by KG, No (4) Ausl. A. 803/05 (174/05), Decision (3 November 2005), in *StV*, 26 (2006), 91); for further references, cf. Ambos, *Internationales Strafrecht* (2008), §12 mn. 58 n. 353. On the admissibility of a warrant issued by a judicial authority that is not a court, cf. Marauhn and Simon, *ZJS*, 5 (2012), 594; on the autonomous interpretation of the concept of 'issuing judicial authority' (to be distinguished from pure executive organs), CJEU, *Poltorak*, No C-452/16 PPU (ECLI:C:2016:858), Judgment (10 November 2016), paras. 31 ff., and CJEU, *Kovalkovas*, No C-477/16 PPU (ECLI:C:2016:861), Judgment (10 November 2016), paras. 24 ff.; on this Brodowski, *ZIS*, 12 (2017), 697–8; cf. also Thomas, *ERA Forum*, 13 (2013), 586–7.
311. Cf. Art. 9 ff. FD EAW; also OLG Stuttgart, 3 Ausl. 80/04 (n. 306), 3437–8; von Heintschel-Heinegg and Rohlff, *GA*, 150 (2003), 46; Wehnert, *StraFo*, 16 (2003),

357–8; Satzger and Pohl, *JICJ*, 4 (2006), 689; Lagodny, in Blekxtoon and Van Ballegooij, *Handbook on the EAW* (2005), pp. 43–4, sees the relinquishing of the authorisation procedure as the most important innovation; a critical stance is taken by Van der Wilt, in Blekxtoon and Van Ballegooij, *Handbook on the EAW* (2005), pp. 76 ff.; de Groot, in Blekxtoon and Van Ballegooij, *Handbook on the EAW* (2005), p. 95. On the different terms 'extradition' and 'surrender', cf. also Cameron et al., *ICL from a Swedish Perspective* (2011), pp. 212–13.

312. Ex Arts. 4 No 6, 5 No 3 FD EAW. In detail on this, cf. Deen-Racsmány, *EJCCLCJ*, 14 (2006), 272 ff.; also García Sánchez, *La extradición* (2005), pp. 441 ff.; on the implementation problems involved, Fichera, *Implementation of the EAW* (2011), pp. 128 ff. On EU citizenship and the EAW, Mitsilegas, *EU Criminal Law* (2016), pp. 213–20. Cf. also CJEU, *Petruhhin*, No C-182/15 (ECLI:EU:C:2016:630), Judgment (6 September 2016), paras. 25 ff., where the Court held that there is no violation of Union law by distinguishing between nationals and EU citizens; on this Brodowski, *ZIS*, 12 (2017), 12–13.

313. Heger and Wolter, in Ambos, König and Rackow, *Rechtshilferecht in Strafsachen* (2015), p. 324; Wehnert, *StraFo*, 16 (2003), 357; cf. also Schomburg, *NJW*, 56 (2003), 3393; Vierucci, *JICJ*, 2 (2004), 275, 279; Deen-Racsmány, *EJCCLCJ*, 14 (2006), 274; Mackarel, *EJCCLCJ*, 15 (2007), 43–4; Murschetz, *Auslieferung* (2007), p. 310. Nevertheless, this is still only a variant of classic extradition; in particular, there is no 'intervention' on the part of the issuing State in the sense that it is not able to directly obligate the authorities of the executing State. In this regard, it is rather national laws on implementation that are applicable; cf. Globke, *GA*, 158 (2011), 412 ff., 423.

314. Art. 9(1), (2) FD EAW; cf. above, mn. 24–7.

315. Art. 9(3) FD EAW. For the domestic implementation in Germany, see §83 a(2) IRG new version; on this, cf. OLG Stuttgart, 3 Ausl. 80/04 (n. 306), 3437–8; OLG Karlsruhe, No 1 AK 20/04, Decision (26 October 2004), in *NJW*, 57 (2004), 3789–90; OLG Braunschweig, No Ausl. 5/04, Decision (3 November 2004), in *NStZ-RR*, 10 (2005), 18–19; OLG Karlsruhe, No 1 AK 4/05, Decision (10 February 2005), in *StV*, 25 (2005), 232; OLG Karlsruhe, No 1 AK 39/06, Decision (31 August 2006), in *NJW*, 59 (2006), 3510; OLG Köln, No 6 Ausl. A 54/12 - 45, Decision (13 July 2012), in *StV*, 33 (2013), 99; Ahlbrecht, *StV*, 25 (2005), 42; Hackner, *NStZ*, 25 (2005), 314. A different opinion is put forward in OLG Köln, 6 Ausl. 63/05 - 31/05 (n. 310) (alert in the SIS only represents a request for arrest).

316. Art. 10(3) FD EAW.

317. Art. 11 FD EAW. For more detail on these and other minimum rights, cf. Arangüena Fanego, *RDP*, 20 (2007), 46 ff.; Ouwerkerk, *Mutual Recognition* (2011), pp. 95 ff.; on the right to defence, Jiménez-Villarejo Fernández, in Arangüena Fanego, *Garantías procesales en los procesos penales en la Unión Europea* (2007), pp. 121 ff.; Mansell, *EuCLR*, 2 (2012), 43 ff.

318. Art. 12 FD EAW. For a critical stance on this, cf. Arangüena Fanego, *RDP*, 20 (2007), 60 ff.

319. Art. 13(1) FD EAW. While consenting to surrender does not constitute renunciation of the requirement of speciality per se (BGH, No 1 StR 314/12, Decision (7 August 2012), in *NStZ-RR*, 17 (2012), 345), returning to the country despite being informed of the consequences of doing so can provide grounds for revoking this principle (BGH, 1 StR 165/12 (n. 180), pp. 76 ff.).

320. Art. 13(2) FD EAW.
321. Art. 13(4) FD EAW.
322. Art. 14 FD EAW.
323. Art. 15(2) FD EAW.
324. Art. 16(1) FD EAW.
325. González Cano, Acuña, *Il mandato di arresto europeo* (2004), pp. 179 ff.; Berni, in Acuña, *Il mandato di arresto europeo* (2004), pp. 278 ff.; García Sánchez, *La extradición* (2005), pp. 461–2. cf. Ambos, in Esser et al., *FS Kühne* (2013), p. 509.
326. Art. 17(1) FD EAW. On this Heger and Wolter, in Ambos, König and Rackow, *Rechtshilferecht in Strafsachen* (2015), p. 357.
327. Art. 17(2) FD EAW.
328. Art. 17(3) FD EAW.
329. Art. 17(4) FD EAW.
330. On this, cf. Chapter 5, mn. 16 ff.
331. Art. 17(7) FD EAW.
332. Art. 17(6) FD EAW.
333. Art. 23(1), (2) FD EAW.
334. Art. 23(3) FD EAW. Thereon cf. CJEU, *Vilkas*, No C-640/15 (ECLI:EU:C:2017:39), Judgment (25 January 2017) (*in casu* the surrender failed due to the resistance of the person to be surrendered; the Court decided that a new date for the surrender could be agreed, 'in so far as, on account of exceptional circumstances, that resistance could not have been foreseen by those authorities and the consequences of the resistance for the surrender could not have been avoided in spite of the exercise of all due care by those authorities'). On the German implementation of the time limits in §83 c IRG, cf. Ambos, *Internationales Strafrecht* (2006), Figure 28.
335. Art. 23(4) FD EAW.
336. Art. 24(1) FD EAW.
337. Art. 24(2) FD EAW; crit. thereof Eurojust, *Strategic Seminar EAW* (2014), p. 7: 'The provision on temporary surrender is useful, but its practical implementation is considered cumbersome and therefore should be developed further.'
338. Art. 25 FD EAW.
339. Art. 26 FD EAW.
340. Art. 27(1) FD EAW.
341. Art. 27(2) FD EAW.
342. Art. 27(3) FD EAW. On this, cf. CJEU, *Leymann and Pustovarov*, No C-388/08 PPU (ECLI:EU:C:2008:669), Judgment (1 December 2008); thereon European Commission, *Staff Working Document* (2011), pp. 19–20; Klimek, *EAW* (2015), pp. 253–8; de Amicis, *EuCLR*, 2 (2012), 53 ff. cf. also Castillejo Manzanares, in Acuña, *Il mandato di arresto europeo* (2004), pp. 109 ff.; Gaito, in Acuña, *Il mandato di arresto europeo* (2004), pp. 213 ff.; Fichera, *Implementation of the EAW* (2011), pp. 82 ff.; Burchard, in Böse, *Europäisches Strafrecht* (2013), pp. 562–3; cf. also OLG Köln, No 6 Ausl. A 85/10, Decision (6 October 2010), in *NStZ*, 31 (2011), 471. For a complete renunciation of this principle, cf. Henke, *Der europäische Haftbefehl* (2008), p. 35. On the issue of a possible legal remedy (appeal with suspensive effect) under national law against the consent of the executing State (Art. 27(4) FD EAW), cf. CJEU, *Jeremy F. v. Premier ministre*, No C-168/13 PPU (ECLI:EU:C:2013:358), Judgment (30 May 2013) (affirming, at paras. 38, 74, that the lack of an explicit provision in the FD EAW to that effect 'does not mean' that MS cannot provide for

such a remedy as long as the time limits of Art. 17 FD EAW are complied with); on this Klimek, *EAW* (2015), pp. 262–5; Mitsilegas, *EU Criminal Law* (2016), pp. 135–6.

343. On the unproblematic subsequent surrender with the consent of the executing State, cf. Miettinen, *NJECL*, 4 (2013), 105. On this, also using the example of the *Assange* case, Marauhn and Simon, *ZJS*, 5 (2012), 594–5; Ambos, in Esser et al., *FS Kühne* (2013), pp. 507–8; Cameron et al., *ICL from a Swedish Perspective* (2011), p. 191. In the case of several European arrest warrants carried out one after the other, only the consent of the State that carried out the last surrender is decisive, CJEU, *Melvin West*, No C-192/12 PPU (ECLI:EU:C:2012:404), Judgment (28 June 2012); on this, cf. Klimek, *EAW* (2015), pp. 258–62; Miettinen, *NJECL*, 4 (2013), 109 ff.

344. Arts. 28, 29 FD EAW.

345. Schomburg et al., *Internationale Rechtshilfe in Strafsachen* (2012), p. 7; Lagodny, in Schomburg et al., *Internationale Rechtshilfe in Strafsachen* (2012), pp. 85–6; cf. also Gualtieri, in Acuña, *Il mandato di arresto europeo* (2004), pp. 56 ff.; Castillejo Manzanares, in Acuña, *Il mandato di arresto europeo* (2004), pp. 112 ff.; Colvin, in Acuña, *Il mandato di arresto europeo* (2004), p. 339; for a critical view of its abolition, cf. Manacorda, *CassP*, 47 (2007), 4349 ff.

346. Art. 2(4) FD EAW. See also von Heintschel-Heinegg and Rohlff, *GA*, 150 (2003), 47–8; Schaper, *Verfassungsrechtliche Probleme* (2009), p. 79, who claims that the principle of dual criminality has only been renounced in part; Ouwerkerk, *Mutual Recognition* (2011), pp. 93–4, is of the same opinion; more critically, Nalewajko, *Grundsatz der gegenseitigen Anerkennung* (2010), pp. 196 ff. On the relationship between dual criminality and fundamental rights, Mitsilegas, *EU Criminal Law* (2016), pp. 131–2.

347. Heger and Wolter, in Ambos, König and Rackow, *Rechtshilferecht in Strafsachen* (2015), pp. 327–8; Deiters, *ZRP*, 36 (2003), 359 ff.; Rohlff, *Der Europäische Haftbefehl* (2003), pp. 85–6; Huber, in Wolter et al., *Festgabe Hilger* (2003), p. 143; Delmas-Marty, *CYELS*, 7 (2004/2005), 20–1; a critical stance is taken in particular by Schünemann, *ZIS*, 2 (2007), 532; also Rosi, in Acuña, *Il mandato di arresto europeo* (2004), pp. 77 ff.; on the problems arising from the *simultaneous* abolition of dual criminality and the non-extradition of nationals, cf. Deen-Racsmány and Blekxtoon, *EJCCLCJ*, 13 (2005), 336 ff., cf. also n. 383; in favour from an Italian perspective *Picotti*, in Bargis and Selvaggi, *Mandato d'arresto europeo* (2005), pp. 41 ff. (dual criminality serves sovereignity but not rights of the suspect). For further references, esp. from an Italian perspective and on the draft regulations of transnational criminal procedure in the EU, cf. Schünemann, *Gesamtkonzept für die europäische Strafrechtspflege* (2006); cf. also Ambos, *Internationales Strafrecht* (2008), §12 mn. 60 n. 367.

348. For more detail, cf. Heger and Wolter, in Ambos, König and Rackow, *Rechtshilferecht in Strafsachen* (2015), pp. 338 ff.; Keijzer, in Blekxtoon and Van Ballegooij, *Handbook on the EAW* (2005), pp. 152 ff.; Fichera, *Implementation of the EAW* (2011), pp. 93 ff.; in detail on the 32 'offences', Klimek, *Mutual Recognition* (2017), pp. 501 ff. (concluding that the 32 'offences' 'have never been harmonised at the EU level as a united "piece of work"' (at p. 562)).

349. For a detailed account of this scope of application of the EAW, cf. Vierucci, *JICJ*, 2 (2004), 275, esp. 277 ff.

350. Von Heintschel-Heinegg and Rohlff, *GA*, 150 (2003), 48; critically Wehnert, *StraFo*, 16 (2003), 357; Deen-Racsmány and Blekxtoon, *EJCCLCJ*, 13 (2005), 362; Mackarel, *EJCCLCJ*, 15 (2007), 40, 44; Arangüena Fanego, *RDP*, 20 (2007),

30 ff.; Capus, *Strafrecht und Souveränität* (2010), p. 357; Fichera, *Implementation of the EAW* (2011), pp. 118 ff.; Mavany, *Die europäische Beweisanordnung* (2012), pp. 120 ff.; ECPI, *ZIS*, 8 (2013), 441–2. On CJEU case law, cf. de Amicis, *EuCLR*, 2 (2012), 49–50.

351. Crit. on this Nalewajko, *Grundsatz der gegenseitigen Anerkennung* (2010), p. 197; von Heintschel-Heinegg, in Sieber, Satzger and von Heinegg, *Europäisches Strafrecht* (2014), p. 673; ECPI, *ZIS*, 8 (2013), 441–2; Böse, in Albers et al., *Evaluation Framework* (2013), p. 366; Vormbaum, *Schutz der Rechtsgüter von EU-Staaten durch das deutsche Strafrecht* (2005), p. 92. On the need for legal assistance due to the unclear offence definitions, cf. OLG Karlsruhe, No 1 AK 30/05, Decision (18 August 2005), in *StV*, 25 (2005), 676.
352. Formerly Art. III-257(3) Treaty Establishing a Constitution for Europe.
353. Accurately criticised in Wehnert, *StraFo*, 16 (2003), 358. BT-Drs. 15/1718, 18, contains a plea for understanding: 'The list was negotiated primarily in French. The offences of both "fraude" and "escroquerie" were included in line with French law. It must be the reserve of practice to subsume the German offence definitions under the list categories through development of the law' (Orig.: 'Die Liste wurde überwiegend in französischer Sprache verhandelt. Entsprechend dem französischen Recht wurden sowohl die Tatbestände des "fraude" als auch der "escroquerie" aufgenommen. Es muss der Praxis vorbehalten bleiben, die deutschen Tatbestände unter die Listenkategorien im Wege der Rechtsfortbildung zu subsumieren').
354. Nestler, *ZStW*, 116 (2004), 340–1; Fuchs, *ZStW*, 116 (2004), 370; Heine, *Die Rechtsstellung des Beschuldigten* (2009), pp. 121 ff.; in favour of 'dual legal representation', Mansell, *EuCLR*, 2 (2012), 43 ff.; for dual and early defence, Anagnostopoulos, *ERA Forum*, 15 (2014), 15–16; in favour of a 'public defender' to co-ordinate dual defence, Salditt, *StV*, 23 (2003), 136–7. In Germany, the suspect requested by an EAW is to be informed immediately that he is entitled to appoint a lawyer in the issuing State (§83c(2) IRG) (para. 2 was adopted by the Act of 27 August 2017; *BGBl*. I 2017, 3295).
355. CJEU, *Advocaten voor de Wereld VZW* v. *Leden van de Ministerraad*, No C-303/05 (ECLI:EU:C:2007:261), Judgment (3 May 2007); on this, cf. European Commission, *Staff Working Document* (2011), pp. 16–17; Klimek, *EAW* (2015), pp. 41 ff., 222–5; Mitsilegas, *EU Criminal Law* (2016), pp. 131–3; Asp, *Procedural Criminal Law Cooperation* (2016), pp. 116–21; Braum, *wistra*, 26 (2007), 401 ff.; Michalke, *EuZW*, 18 (2007), 377–8; Fennelly, *ERA Forum*, 8 (2007), 519 ff.; Manacorda, *CassP*, 47 (2007), 4346 ff.; Manacorda, *RSC*, 72 (2007), 900–1; Mylonopoulos, *ZStW*, 121 (2009), 72 ff.; Suelmann, *HumFoR*, 14 (2009), 122 ff.; Ebert and Pinkel, *StudZR*, 5 (2008), 361 ff.; Tinkl, *ZIS*, 2 (2007), 419 ff.
356. Belgian Constitutional Court, No 124/2005, Judgment (13 July 2005), available at www.const-court.be, last accessed 27 January 2018. On this, cf. Satzger and Pohl, *JICJ*, 4 (2006), 690; Weyembergh, *eucrim*, 1 (2006), 27–8.
357. CJEU, *Advocaten voor de Wereld VZW*, C-303/05, para. 57: due to this trust, it can be assumed that 'the categories of offences in question feature among those the seriousness of which in terms of adversely affecting public order and public safety justifies dispensing with the verification of double criminality'. On the link between trust and mutual recognition, cf. also Capus, *Strafrecht und Souveränität* (2010), pp. 394 ff.
358. Thus BVerfG, No 2 BvR 2236/04, Judgment (18 July 2005), in *BVerfGE 113*, pp. 297–8, is justifiably reticent on this issue. A symptomatic example is furnished

by OLG Stuttgart, No 3 Ausl. 6/2007, Decision (7 March 2007), in *StV*, 27 (2007), 260, guiding principle 2: 'The mutual recognition of European Arrest Warrants must be based upon a high degree of mutual trust, *for which there must also be an acceptable basis in individual cases*' (emphasis added). Cf. also OLG Karlsruhe, No 1 AK 72/06, Decision (18 June 2007), in *StV*, 27 (2007), 650–1, according to which, first, a 'factual description' in the EAW is required that 'allows a reasonable conclusion to be drawn in the sense of an examination of whether it is warranted to describe the defendant's conduct as an offence from this catalogue', and second, under certain special circumstances even an examination of the evidence for the charge must be carried out; cf. also BVerfG, No 2 BvR 2115/09, Decision (9 October 2009), in *StraFo*, 22 (2009), 458. A sceptical point of view is also put forward by Klip, in Curtin et al., *European Integration and Law* (2006), p. 137; Leutheusser-Schnarrenberger, *StraFo*, 20 (2007), 269; Gleß, *Beweisrechtsgrundsätze* (2006), p. 164; differentiating according to offence, Schmahl, *DVBl.*, 122 (2007), 1468; on the need for measures to enhance trust (esp. the creation of minimum standards of criminal procedure) Nalewajko, *Grundsatz der gegenseitigen Anerkennung* (2010), pp. 101 ff.; Suominen, *Mutual Recognition in Cooperation* (2011), pp. 46 ff.; restrictively Mavany, *Die europäische Beweisanordnung* (2012), pp. 64 ff.; on the relationship between the right to liberty and mutual recognition see Mancano, *CYELS*, 18 (2016), 215 ff.; on the relationship between mutual recognition and trust, see also previously Chapter 1, mn. 26 with further references.

359. CJEU, *Advocaten voor de Wereld VZW*, C-303/05, para. 53.
360. As it can be omitted due to mutual trust; cf. once again CJEU, *Advocaten voor de Wereld VZW*, C-303/05, para. 57; Klimek, *EAW* (2015), pp. 222–5.
361. Crit. also Braum, *wistra*, 26 (2007), 405; conc. with the CJEU, however, Fennelly, *ERA Forum*, 8 (2007), 533–4; for a more fundamental treatment, cf. Asp, *Procedural Criminal Law Cooperation* (2016), pp. 173 ff. (calling for a flexible approach according to which it suffices if the executing State can criminalise the respective conduct – even if it has not explicitly done so – i.e., if there are no opposing values or *ordre public* considerations which would make the execution of the request impossible (177–80); in fact, an *ordre public* clause may operate as a substitute for double criminality (180) since a strict double-criminality requirement cannot be justified within the EU (181); at any rate, 'some version' of legality may pose an obstacle to extradition/surrender, especially in case of such vague 'offences' as in the EAW (186)).
362. Art. 8(1), Legge 69/2005 (22 April 2005) ('*Disposizioni per confermare il diritto interno alla decisione quadro 2002/584/GAI del Consiglio, del 13. 6. 2002, relative al mandato d'arresto europeo e alle procedure di consegna tra Stati membri*'), *Gazetta Ufficiale*, No 98, 29 April 2005. On this, cf. also Lagodny, in Lagodny, Wiederin and Winkler, *Probleme des Rahmenbeschlusses* (2007), p. 145.
363. For detailed analysis, see Impalà, *ULR*, 1 (2005), 56 ff.; Satzger and Pohl, *JICJ*, 4 (2006), 689–90, both taking the idiosyncratic Italian legal situation into account.
364. Mylonopoulos, *ZStW*, 123 (2011), 641. On this, cf. also the restrictive German regulations on the extradition of nationals to be discussed in the next subsection. Of course, this problem is mitigated if only a limited active principle of personality is seen as admissible, cf. Ambos, *Treatise ICL III* (2016), pp. 218–19.
365. Cf. Zypries, *RuP*, 40 (2004), 6; Gleß, *ZStW*, 116 (2004), 360; Marchetti, in Acuña, *Il mandato di arresto europeo* (2004), pp. 133 ff.; García Sánchez, *La extradición* (2005), pp. 443 ff.; Böhm, *StraFo*, 26 (2013), 178 (no '"arrest warrant" justifying

surrender, but merely a modern "detection tool'"); on the different grounds for refusal, cf. Freund, *Untersuchungshaft gegen EU-Ausländer* (2010), pp. 206 ff.; Schork, *Auslieferungsverfahren* (2009), pp. 226–7; Burchard, in Böse, *Europäisches Strafrecht* (2013), pp. 555–69; Suominen, *Mutual Recognition in Cooperation* (2011), pp. 111 ff.; Ouwerkerk, *Mutual Recognition* (2011), pp. 102 ff.; Arangüena Fanego, *RDP*, 20 (2007), 62 ff., 80 is critical of the Framework Decision's varying implementation in the Member States.

366. Cf. also Royer, *AJP*, 4 (2007), 188; Böse, in Ambos, *Europäisches Strafrecht post-Lissabon* (2011), p. 60; by contrast, Suominen, *Mutual Recognition in Cooperation* (2011), pp. 87–8, sees the codification of grounds for refusal as a prerequisite of mutual trust.
367. Art. 3(1), (3) FD EAW.
368. Thereon Chapter 2, mn. 167 ff. On the effect of the FD EAW on the implementation of the Schengen *aquis*, CJEU, *Kretzinger*, No C-288/05 (ECLI:EU:C:2007:441), Judgment (18 July 2007), paras. 53 ff. ('the fact that a Member State in which a person has been sentenced by a final and binding judgment under its national law may issue a European arrest warrant for the arrest of that person in order to enforce the sentence under the Framework Decision cannot affect the interpretation of the notion of enforcement within the meaning of Article 54 of the CISA' (para. 64)); European Commission, *Staff Working Document* (2011), pp. 27–8; Klimek, *EAW* (2015), pp. 231–5.
369. Art. 3(2) FD EAW. Cf. Klimek, *EAW* (2015), pp. 225–35; Van der Wilt, in Blekxtoon and Van Ballegooij, *Handbook on the EAW* (2005), pp. 101 ff.; Marchetti, in Acuña, *Il mandato di arresto europeo* (2004), pp. 138 ff.; Fichera, *Implementation of the EAW* (2011), pp. 122 ff.; OLG Köln, No 6 Ausl. A 77/09, Decision (28 October 2009); cf. also CJEU, *Mantello*, No C-261/09 (ECLI:EU:C:2010:683), Judgment (16 November 2010); thereon, European Commission, *Staff Working Document* (2011), p. 22; Klimek, *EAW* (2015), pp. 225–31; on the concept of 'the same acts' within the meaning of Art. 3(2) FD EAW (OLG Stuttgart, No 3 Ausl. 175/08, Decision (29 June 2009), in *eucrim*, 5 (2010), 140), according to which there are no grounds to refuse to execute an EAW if the issuing judicial authority has explicitly ascertained, in line with national law and taking consideration of Art. 3(2) FD EAW, that the judgment previously passed by its judiciary does not constitute a final judgment on the acts referred to in the arrest warrant; on this, cf. also de Amicis, *EuCLR*, 2 (2012), 57–8. Cf. also Chapter 2, mn. 187.
370. Art. 4 FD EAW.
371. Art. 4(1) FD EAW.
372. Art. 4(2) FD EAW.
373. Art. 4(5) FD EAW. On this, cf. OLG Köln, 6 Ausl. A 77/09 (n. 369).
374. Art. 4(4) FD EAW. On this, cf. OLG Karlsruhe, No 1 AK 102/11, Decision (25 March 2013), in *NStZ*, 33 (2013), 602.
375. Art. 4(7)(a) FD EAW. On this, cf. Keijzer, in Blekxtoon and Van Ballegooij, *Handbook on the EAW* (2005), pp. 160 ff.; González Cano, in Acuña, *Il mandato di arresto europeo* (2004), pp. 159 ff. This makes dual criminality a prerequisite for such offences, as the executing State is able to refuse to execute an EAW on the grounds that the prosecuted act does not constitute an offence according to its law (cf. also Lensing, in Blekxtoon and Van Ballegooij, *Handbook on the EAW* (2005), pp. 211). According to Art. 4(7)(b) FD, extradition can be refused if the EAW

refers to offences committed outside the territory of the issuing State and the law of the executing State does not allow prosecution for the same offences when committed outside its territory; on Art. (7)(a) and (b), cf. Deen-Racsmány and Blekxtoon, *EJCCLCJ*, 13 (2005), 354–5.

376. Art. 4(6) FD EAW; on the relationship of this provision with EU citizenship law, Mitsilegas, *EU Criminal Law* (2016), pp. 213–20. In this regard, the CJEU emphasises that Art. 4(6) FD EAW must be interpreted 'to the effect that it precludes legislation of a MS implementing that provision which, in a situation where the surrender of a foreign national in possession of a residence permit of indefinite duration in the territory of that MS is sought by another MS in order to execute a custodial sentence imposed on that national by a decision which has become final, first, does not authorise such a surrender, and secondly, merely lays down the obligation for the judicial authorities of the first MS to inform the judicial authorities of the second MS that they are willing to take over the enforcement of the judgment, where, on the date of the refusal to surrender, the execution has not in fact been taken over and where, furthermore, in the event that taking over that execution subsequently proves to be impossible, such a refusal may not be challenged' (CJEU, *Popławski*, No C-579/15 (ECLI:C:2017:503), Judgment, 29 June 2017, para. 24). Moreover the Court explains that Art. 4(6) FD EAW 'does not authorise a MS to refuse to execute an EAW issued with a view to the surrender of a person who has been finally judged and given a custodial sentence, on the sole ground that that MS intends to prosecute that person in relation to the same acts as those for which that judgment was pronounced' (ibid., para. 48).

377. Smith, *NJECL*, 4 (2013), 87–8; Satzger, *NStZ*, 15 (2016), 521.

378. On this, cf. Suominen, *Mutual Recognition in Cooperation* (2011), pp. 261 ff.

379. Art. 4a FD EAW. In the old version amended by FD 2009/299/JHI (expungement of the old Art. 5(1)); cf. also CJEU, *I. B.*, No C-306/09 (ECLI:EU:C:2010:626), Judgement (21 October 2010) (return of the surrendered person as the condition of executing an EAW against a person sentenced *in absentia*); on this, cf. also *eucrim*, 5 (2010), 144–5; European Commission, *Staff Working Document* (2011), p. 22; Klimek, *EAW* (2015), pp. 243–7; Wahl, *eucrim*, 10 (2015), 71 ff.; Mitsilegas, *EU Criminal Law* (2016), pp. 133 ff.; de Amicis, *EuCLR*, 2 (2012), 55 ff.; on the autonomous interpretation of Art. 4a FD EAW CJEU, *Dworzecki*, No C-108/16 PPU (ECLI:C:2016:346), Judgment (24 May 2016), paras. 25 ff.; cf. also CJEU, *Tupikas*, No C- 270/17 PPU (ECLI:C:2017:628), Judgment (10 August 2017), para. 98, according to which the concept of 'trial resulting in the decision' (Art. 4a(1)(a)(i) FD EAW) 'must be interpreted as relating only to the instance at the end of which the decision is handed down which finally rules on the guilt of the person concerned and imposes a penalty on him, such as a custodial sentence, following a re-examination, in fact and in law, of the merits of the case'.

380. The relevant part reads that the person 'will be expressly informed of his or her right to a retrial, or an appeal, in which the person has the right to participate and which allows the merits of the case, including fresh evidence, to be re-examined, and which may lead to the original decision being reversed'.

381. Cf. BVerfG, No 2 BvR 2735/14, Decision (15 December 2015), in *NJW*, 69 (2016), 1149, paras. 86–90; English translation available at www.bundesverfassungsgericht.de/SharedDocs/Entscheidungen/EN/2015/12/rs20151215_2bvr273514en.html, last accessed 27 January 2018. As a consequence, a judgment *in absentia* may amount

to an obstacle to surrender, cf. main text, mn. 38, and OLG Köln, No 6 Ausl. A 69/11 – 56, Decision (2 September 2011), in *StV*, 33 (2013), 100 (Polish sentence *in absentia*); OLG Düsseldorf, No III-3 Ausl. 92/12, Decision (4 September 2012), in *StV*, 33 (2013), 101 (Dutch sentence *in absentia*); OLG Karlsruhe, No 1 AK 51/10, Decision (4 January 2011), in *StV*, 31 (2011), 426–8 (Romanian sentence *in absentia*); but see also OLG Celle, 1 Ausl. 56/12, Decision (18 December 2012), in *StV*, 33 (2013), 315 (judgment *in absentia* based on a deal between the prosecution and the defendant pursuant to Art. 335 PolishCCP does not constitute an obstacle to surrender).

382. Art. 5(2) FD EAW. Cf. OLG Stuttgart, 3 Ausl. 80/04 (n. 306), 3439.

383. Art. 5(3) FD EAW. On this, cf. Lensing, in Blekxtoon and Van Ballegooij, *Handbook on the EAW* (2005), pp. 209–10; more critically, Deen-Racsmány and Blekxtoon, *EJCCLCJ*, 13 (2005), 336 ff., who draw attention to the problem that the State of the prosecuted person may not actually be able to execute the punishment, as the act is not punishable according to its law; critically, from a defence lawyer's perspective, Wehnert, in Widmaier, *FS Dahs* (2005), p. 529. No new court decision is needed for return; cf. OLG Hamm, No 2 Ausl. 66/13, Decision (23 May 2013), in *NStZ*, 33 (2013), 603.

384. See above, mn. 29 ff.

385. Cf. Garlick, in Blekxtoon and Van Ballegooij, *Handbook on the EAW* (2005), pp. 167 ff.; Keijzer, in Blekxtoon and Van Ballegooij, *Handbook on the EAW* (2005), pp. 192–3; Morgan, in Blekxtoon and Van Ballegooij, *Handbook on the EAW* (2005), pp. 197 ff.; in greater depth, Pohl, *Vorbehalt und Anerkennung* (2009), pp. 122 ff.; Chiavario, *RIDPP*, 48 (2005), 981–2, is critical of the loss of procedural guarantees; Tinkl, *Rechtsstellung des Einzelnen* (2008), p. 204, is also critical, claiming that the FD does not meet the ECHR's requirements.

386. Keijzer, in Blekxtoon and Van Ballegooij, *Handbook on the EAW* (2005), p. 193, formulates this aptly: 'bars a[n] EAW from being executed'; cf. also Thomas, *ERA Forum*, 13 (2013), 587–8.

387. On this cf. *Aranyosi and Căldăraru* main text, mn. 60. See in this context also Niblock, *NJECL*, 7 (2016), 251 (arguing that the requirement for the requesting State to provide information to the executing judicial authority regarding the detention conditions 'marks a shift away from an overreliance on mutual trust').

388. Cf. also OLG Stuttgart, 3 Ausl. 6/2007 (n. 358); Böhm, *StraFo*, 26 (2013), 180–1; OLG Karlsruhe, No 1 AK 46/06, Decision (21 November 2006), in *NStZ*, 27 (2007), 412, on the issue that decisions on suspending the arrest warrant are solely up to the requested (executing) State. On the question of an absolute limitation for pre-trial detention in the context of an EAW issued by the Municipal Court Hanau and to be executed in Italy, cf. Nino, *JCL*, 71 (2007), 501 ff. On the courts' review competence in cases of provisional arrest for the purpose of extradition in general, cf. BVerfG, No 2 BvR 1608/07, Decision (16 September 2010), in *StV*, 31 (2011), 170.

389. For an overview see Heger and Wolter, in Ambos, König and Rackow, *Rechtshilferecht in Strafsachen* (2015), p. 331; Krüßmann, *Transnationales Strafprozessrecht* (2009), pp. 596 ff.; on different time limits and language requirements, cf. Hackner, *NStZ*, 25 (2005), 314–15; crit. von Heintschel-Heinegg and Rohlff, *GA*, 150 (2003), 44 n. 5; Deen-Racsmány and Blekxtoon, *EJCCLCJ*, 13 (2005), 340 ff.; Mackarel, *EJCCLCJ*, 15 (2007), 46 ff.; Arangüena Fanego, *RDP*, 20 (2007), 20 ff. On the **English** and **Irish** declaration that an EAW may not be executed only for purposes of investigation (with pre-trial detention), cf. Conway, *EJCCLCJ*, 13 (2005), 256–7, 258 ff.; on the

implementation in **Austria** through the EU-JZG (whose §1(2) states that the regulations of the ARHG continue to apply *mutatis mutandis* as long as the EU-JZG does not affect any other regulation), cf. Murschetz, *Auslieferung* (2007), pp. 309 ff.; Sautner, in östBMJ, *Fortbildungsseminar aus Strafrecht und Kriminologie* (2006), pp. 96 ff.; Sautner, *ÖJZ*, 9 (2005), 328 ff.; Lagodny, *StV*, 25 (2005), 518–19; Hinterhofer, in Lagodny, Wiederin and Winkler, *Probleme des Rahmenbeschlusses* (2007), pp. 205 ff.; on **Croatia**, see Sokol, *EJCCLCJ*, 23 (2015), 258 ff.; on **Denmark**, cf. Geraci, in Pansini and Scalfati, *Il mandato d'arresto europeo* (2005), pp. 237 ff.; on **Sweden**, Cameron et al., *ICL from a Swedish Perspective* (2011), pp. 214 ff.; on **Scandinavia**, Suominen, *EuCLR*, 1 (2011), 179 ff.; Suominen, *Mutual Recognition in Cooperation* (2011), pp. 83 ff., 112 ff.; on **France**, cf. Delmas-Marty, *CYELS*, 7 (2004/2005), 22 incl. further references; Confalonieri, in Pansini and Scalfati, *Il mandato d'arresto europeo* (2005), pp. 245 ff.; Pfützner, *eucrim*, 1 (2006), 29 ff.; Errera, in Guild, *Constitutional Challenges to the EAW* (2006), pp. 145 ff.; on **Hungary**, cf. Petra, *EAW in Hungary* (2015); on **Italy** Panebianco, in Acuña, *Il mandato di arresto europeo* (2004), pp. 189 ff.; Diddi, in Pansini and Scalfati, *Il mandato d'arresto europeo* (2005), pp. 3 ff.; Fichera, *Implementation of the EAW* (2011), pp. 136 ff., 157 ff.; on the **Netherlands**, Van der Hulst, *eucrim*, 9 (2014), 64 ff.; on **Spain**, Romano, in Pansini and Scalfati, *Il mandato d'arresto europeo* (2005), pp. 273 ff.; Arangüena Fanego, *RDP*, 20 (2007), 38 ff., 48 ff.; Löber, *Ablehnung der Vollstreckung* (2017), pp. 220 ff.; on **Slovakia**, Klimek, *EJCCLCJ*, 20 (2012), 181 ff.; on **Slovenia**, Šugman Stubbs, *eucrim*, 2 (2007), 133 ff.; on the **United Kingdom**, Geraci, in Pansini and Scalfati, *Il mandato d'arresto europeo* (2005), pp. 257 ff.; MacCormick, in Müller-Dietz, *FS Jung* (2007), pp. 536–7; Mackarel, *EJCCLCJ*, 15 (2007), 52 ff., 58 ff.; Spencer, *StatuteLR*, 30 (2009), 184 ff.; Fichera, *Implementation of the EAW* (2011), pp. 148 ff., 162 ff.; on the question of why the EAW's implementation has not led to constitutional problems there, Padfield, *EuConst*, 3 (2007), 253 ff. On the (constitutional) legal situation in **Italy** and **Poland**, cf. Carducci, in Acuña, *Il mandato di arresto europeo* (2004), pp. 91 ff.; Impalà, *ULR*, 1 (2005), 56 ff.; Manacorda, *eucrim*, 1 (2006), 33 ff.; and Kowalik-Bańczyk, *GLJ*, 6 (2005), 1358 ff.; Nalewajko, *ZIS*, 2 (2007), 113 ff.; Nita, *eucrim*, 1 (2006), 36 ff.; Weigend and Górski, *ZStW*, 117 (2005), 194 ff.; Bem, in Guild, *Constitutional Challenges to the EAW* (2006), pp. 125 ff.; Grasso, *NJECL*, 4 (2013), 120 ff.; on **Belgian** (constitutional) case law, Weyembergh, *eucrim*, 1 (2006), 26 ff.; on Belgium in general, David, *Eléments de droit pénal international et européen* (2009), mn. 7.1.17 ff.; on the **Nordic Arrest Warrant** and its relationship with the surrender agreement between the EU and **Norway/Iceland**, see already n. 303; cf. also Klimek, *EAW* (2015), pp. 191 ff.; for a **European** comparison: Van Sliedregt, *EuConst*, 3 (2007), 244 ff.; Henke, *Der europäische Haftbefehl* (2008), pp. 22 ff.; Fichera, *Implementation of the EAW* (2011), pp. 168 ff.; Suominen, *eucrim*, 6 (2011), 24 ff. Cf. also the 'Replies to Questionnaire on Quantitive Information on the Practical Operation of the EAW', Council Doc. 7551/4/10; *eucrim*, 5 (2010), 97. On the effects on **Switzerland**, cf. Schork, *Auslieferungsverfahren* (2009), pp. 278 ff.

390. Presidency, 'Final Report on the Fourth Round of Mutual Evaluations: The Practical Application of the EAW and Corresponding Surrender Procedures between MS', Council 8302/2/09, REV 2, Brussels 18 May 2009, p. 6.
391. Cf. Klimek, *EAW* (2015), pp. 204 ff., concluding that it has 'not been implemented in a uniform way' (216).

392. Some MS accept the EAW only in their own language, others in several languages and still others only in certain languages; cf. Annex IV (pp. 112–13) to the 2017 version of the EAW Handbook (European Commission, 2017), available at https://ejustice.europa.eu/fileDownload.do?id=db28c045-9f92-472e-9452-518b4ce84712, last accessed 15 February 2018; crit. Spiezia, in Ruggieri, *Languages* (2014), pp. 35–7.

393. European Commission, *Report Implementation EAW* (2011), pp. 5, 9; for more details see European Commission, *Staff Working Document* (2011), pp. 3 ff., 33 ff. According to Klimek, *EAW* (2015), p. 204 only 13 MS have met the deadline for implementation.

394. Cf. Eurojust, *Strategic Seminar EAW* (2014), p. 7.

395. Eurojust, *Strategic Seminar EAW* (2014), p. 13: 'In an ideal world where the FD EAW had been implemented in the same way in all MS, the speciality rule would not be needed.'

396. Such prohibitions are common in civil law jurisdictions far beyond Europe. For the EU, see e.g. Art. 16(2) clause 1 **German** GG ('No German may be extradited to a foreign country', translation in Tomuschat and Currie, *Basic Law for the Federal Republic of Germany* (2012), p. 23); but now extradition (surrender) is allowed pursuant to international treaties. The same goes for **Cyprus** (Art. 11(2)(f) Constitution, in more detail main text, mn. 62 with n. 461 ff.), **Italy** (Art. 26 Constitution), **Portugal** (Art. 33(3) Constitution; also Law 144/99, Art. 32) and **Poland** (Art. 55(1) Constitution with exception in paras. 2 and 3; see main text, n. 467 ff.). In **Spain**, the extradition of nationals is prohibited by the Act of Passive Extradition (Ley de Extradición Pasiva) of 1985 (Art. 3) unless based on an international treaty (Art. 1); then it is admissible on the basis of reciprocity (Art. 13.3. Spanish Constitution). In **Hungary**, the extradition of nationals is only allowed if the person sought for extradition has double nationality and has his permanent residence in the foreign State (Sect. 13(1) Act XXXVIII of 1996 on International Legal Assistance in Criminal Matters). In the **Netherlands**, the extradition of nationals is prohibited by both the extradition and surrender (EU) Act for the execution of a sentence, but allowed for prosecution upon the condition that the person concerned will be returned to the Netherlands for execution. In **France**, the Constitution is silent on the matter. The Conseil d'état held in its opinion (*avis*) No 356–641 of 24 November 1994 that the principle of non-extradition of French nationals has a basis neither in an individual right of the Déclaration des droits de l'homme de 1789 or the Préambule de la Constitution of 1946, nor as a 'principe fondamental reconnu par les lois de la République' which has constitutional rank according to the Préambule de la Constitution of 1946. Yet Art. 696-2 CPP excludes extradition proceedings against French nationals ('n'ayant pas la nationalité française'). A procedural prohibition also exists in **Greece** (Art. 438(a) Greek CPP). See generally Deen-Racsmány, *LJIL*, 20 (2007), 170 (before the EAW 14 of 25 Member States prohibited extradition of nationals).

397. *BGBl.* I 2004, 1748; draft and explanatory statement in BT-Drs. 15/1718; cf. also Ahlbrecht, *StV*, 25 (2005), 41 ff.; Vogel, *JZ*, 60 (2005), 802–3. The EAW Act also applies to pending trials, the *prohibition of retroactivity* does not intervene (OLG Stuttgart, 3 Ausl. 80/04 (n. 306), 3437–8; Hackner, *NStZ*, 25 (2005), 312; crit. Ahlbrecht, *StV*, 25 (2005), 43). §§78 ff. IRG, implementing the FD EAW, are not subject to any *condition of reciprocity* (OLG Karlsruhe, No 1 AK 6/04, Decision

(15 September 2004), in *StV*, 24 (2004), 547–8; OLG Karlsruhe No 1 AK 42/03, Decision (22 September 2004), in *StV*, 25 (2005), 31 and 32).

398. *BGBl.* I 2006, 1721.
399. Cf. also Heger and Wolter, in Ambos, König and Rackow, *Rechtshilferecht in Strafsachen* (2015), pp. 330–1; Hecker, *Europäisches Strafrecht* (2015), §12 mn. 41; Burchard, in Böse, *Europäisches Strafrecht* (2013), pp. 544–6.
400. Böse, in Momsen, Bloy and Rackow, *Fragmentarisches Strafrecht* (2003), p. 241; Klimek, *EAW* (2015), p. 315.
401. For a critical stance on this, cf. OLG Stuttgart, 3 Ausl. 80/04 (n. 306), 3439; on this, cf. n. 406 below; approvingly, Ahlbrecht, *StV*, 25 (2005), 43.
402. Cf. Part 1 UK Extradition Act 2003 referring to category 1 territories (i.e. EAW MS) and speaking of 'extradition'.
403. BT-Drs. 15/1718, 5 ff.; cf. also Wehnert, *StraFo*, 16 (2003), 359; Vogel, *JZ*, 60 (2005), 803; and Heger, *ZIS*, 2 (2007), 223 on EAW Act II. From a comparative perspective on the terminology used, see Klimek, *EAW* (2015), pp. 208–10, 312.
404. For more detail, cf. Ambos, *Internationales Strafrecht* (2011), §12 mn. 45–6.
405. On administrative courts' denial of jurisdiction over EAWs within the meaning of §40 VwGO: OVG Hamburg, No 5 So 194/09, Decision (11 December 2009); BVerwG, No 1 B 1.10, Decision (18 May 2010), in *DÖV*, 63 (2010), 743.
406. Cf. BT-Drs. 15/1718, 11 left col., 15 right col.; also Schünemann, *StV*, 23 (2003), 531 ff.; Wehnert, *StraFo*, 16 (2003), 359; Seitz, *NStZ*, 24 (2004), 546–7, 549; Lagodny, in Arnold et al., *FS Eser* (2005), p. 781. OLG Stuttgart, 3 Ausl. 80/04 (n. 306), 3439, is critical in this regard: 'it is incompatible with the FD EAW . . . that the Federal Republic of Germany . . . has retained a non-judicial (ministerial) granting procedure that is not restricted to the administrative transfer and receipt of European Arrest Warrants' (orig. 'mit dem RbEuHb unvereinbar . . . dass die BR Deutschland . . . ein nicht justizielles (ministerielles) Bewilligungsverfahren beibehalten hat, welches sich nicht auf die administrative Übermittlung und Entgegennahme Europäischer Haftbefehle beschränkt').
407. Cf. the complicated §79(2) IRG providing that the executive authority granting the extradition shall decide before the admissibility decision of the Higher Regional Court if it intends to invoke obstacles to extradition/surrender.
408. For a rightly critical stance, cf. Hackner et al., *NStZ*, 26 (2006), 665; Heger, *ZIS*, 2 (2007), 224; Geyer, in Guild, *Constitutional Challenges to the EAW* (2006), p. 122; Böhm, *StraFo*, 26 (2013), 178.
409. §81 No 4 IRG in conjunction with Art. 2(2) FD EAW.
410. §81 No 1 IRG. Cf. Seitz, *NStZ*, 24 (2004), 546–7; also Nestler, *ZStW*, 116 (2004), 337.
411. OLG Stuttgart, 3 Ausl. 80/04 (n. 306), 3437–8; however, OLG Karlsruhe, No 1 AK 30/06, Decision (10 August 2006), in *NStZ*, 27 (2007), 111–12, demands that the events described can 'plausibly be described as a catalogue offence'. On the issue that the expectation of a high sanction when *§15(1) No 1 IRG is interpreted in conformity with the FD* can support an arrest warrant issued against a German national, cf. OLG Stuttgart, No 3 Ausl. 52/06, Decision (26 October 2006), in *NStZ*, 27 (2007), 410–11.
412. A critical stance is also taken by Wehnert, *StraFo*, 16 (2003), 358; Hassemer, *ZStW*, 116 (2004), 317–18; Fuchs, *ZStW*, 116 (2004), 368–9; Schwaighofer and Ebensperger, *Internationale Rechtshilfe* (2001), p. 15; Vander Beken, in Klip and

Van der Wilt, *Harmonisation* (2002), p. 97; de Hoyos Sancho, *RDPP*, 18 (2007), 118; Bernardi, *RSC*, 72 (2007), 725; Manacorda, *RSC*, 72 (2007), 904 ff.; Hefendehl, *ZIS*, 1 (2006), 230–1; Gilmore, *RIDP*, 77 (2006), 20, is more sympathetic.

413. Seitz, *NStZ*, 24 (2004), 546–7; Hackner, *NStZ*, 25 (2005), 312 ('fiction of Union-wide harmonisation', orig. 'Fiktion unionsweiter Harmonisierung').
414. BT-Drs. 15/1718, 17 right col.
415. §81 No 4 IRG.
416. On this matter, cf. OLG Stuttgart, 3 Ausl. 80/04 (n. 306), 3437–8, in reference to the assurances given by the Greek investigative judge; further on the examination of the evidence for a given charge in line with §10(2) IRG in cases of '(suspected) abuse of the right to extradition' (orig. '(vermutetem) Missbrauch des Auslieferungsanspruchs'), cf. Ahlbrecht, *StV*, 25 (2005), 43.
417. Thus BT-Drs. 15/1718, 18 left col.
418. Also criticised in Wehnert, *StraFo*, 16 (2003), 359.
419. Cf. OLG Karlsruhe, No 1 AK 64/15, Decision (4 January 2016), in *StV*, 36 (2016), 236; OLG Karlsruhe, No 1 AK 111/14, Decision (10 November 2015), para. 49; OLG Celle, No 1 Ausl. 7/10, Decision (14 June 2010), in *StraFo*, 23 (2010), 431; OLG Zweibrücken, No 1 Ausl. 17/08, Decision (2 November 2009), in *OLGSt*, IRG §10 No 3, para. 34; OLG Köln, No 6 Ausl. A 41/09 – 52, Decision (31 August 2009), in *OLGSt*, IRG §83b No 1, para. 46; OLG Köln, No 6 Ausl. A 25/08, Decision (27 April 2009), in *OLGSt*, IRG §83 No 2, para. 11; OLG Nürnberg, No 1 OLG Ausl. 130/07, Decision (23 June 2009), in *StV*, 30 (2010), 233.
420. Cf. Hackner, *NStZ*, 25 (2005), 312 left col.
421. Cf. §170(2) StPO.
422. Wehnert, *StraFo*, 16 (2003), 360, argues along these lines; for a different view see Seitz, *NStZ*, 24 (2004), 547–8, 549, who is concerned that the FD EAW will be undermined by anticipated terminations according to §170(2) StPO.
423. Schünemann, *ZRP*, 36 (2003), 187; Schünemann, *StV*, 23 (2003), 532; Schünemann, *ZIS*, 5 (2010), 736; in reference to the FD EAW, Schünemann, *ZStW*, 116 (2004), 383; conc. Albrecht, *KritV*, 91 (2008), 53; Freund, *Untersuchungshaft gegen EU-Ausländer* (2010), p. 227; a similar view is taken by Nestler, *ZStW*, 116 (2004), 335–6; Broß, in Griesbaum, Hannich and Schnarr, *FS Nehm* (2006), p. 34; Capus, *Strafrecht und Souveränität* (2010), pp. 129–30; crit. also Wehnert, *StraFo*, 16 (2003), 359; cf. also Buruma, *ZStW*, 116 (2004), 424 ff. In favour of combining the principle of the most-favourable legal situation (*Meistbegünstigung*) and the 'Swiss model', according to which the procedural law of the investigating prosecution applies on principle except in cases of severe violations of basic rights, Art. III-171(1) AE-Europäische Strafverfolgung (Schünemann, *Alternativentwurf Europäische Strafverfolgung* (2004)); on this, Schünemann, *ZStW*, 116 (2004), 384–5; critically, Vogel, *ZStW*, 116 (2004), 407 ff.; on the primacy of the forum rule, cf. also Ambos, *ZIS*, 5 (2010), 565–6.
424. Wasmeier, *ZStW*, 116 (2004), 321–2: against this argument Schünemann, *ZStW*, 116 (2004), 383; cf. also Schünemann, *StV*, 26 (2006), 364.
425. Cf. Chapter 2, mn. 165 ff.
426. Schünemann, *StV*, 23 (2003), 532; Vogel, *ZStW*, 116 (2004), 400 ff., is of a different opinion.
427. Deiters, *ZRP*, 36 (2003), 360–1; contra Schünemann, *StV*, 23 (2003), 532; also Hecker, *Europäisches Strafrecht* (2015), §12 mn. 37; arguing against recoursing to

the principle of democracy, Gleß, *ZStW*, 116 (2004), 360; and Kreß, *ZStW*, 116 (2004), 463–4.

428. On the *Töben* case (Holocaust denial punishable according to §§130, 131 StGB, but not in Australia), cf. Ambos, *Internationales Strafrecht* (2018), §1 mn. 8, 22.
429. Deiters, *ZRP*, 36 (2003), 361; cf. also Buruma, *ZStW*, 116 (2004), 430 ff.: the State in which the act was committed has primacy.
430. Gleß, *ZStW*, 116 (2004), 361–2 argues along these lines, calling for a 'unified – and thus curbed – European law on criminal jurisdiction' (orig. 'vereinheitlichtes – und dadurch gezügeltes – europäisches Strafanwendungsrecht'); cf. also Fuchs, *ZStW*, 116 (2004), 369; Vogel, *ZStW*, 116 (2004), 411; Kreß, *ZStW*, 116 (2004), 465 ff.; Juppe, *Gegenseitige Anerkennung strafgerichtlicher Entscheidungen* (2007), pp. 136–7.
431. Ambos, *Treatise ICL III* (2016), pp. 206 ff.
432. As argued by Gleß, *ZStW*, 116 (2004), 360; Meyer, in Arnold, *FS Eser* (2005), p. 804.
433. On the effects principle in international (criminal) law, cf. Ambos, *Treatise ICL III* (2016), pp. 213–16.
434. Cf. also Nestler, *ZStW*, 116 (2004), 338–9.
435. They are removed since they are not mentioned in the FD as grounds for refusal. For the German law, see §82 in conjunction with §§6, 7 IRG.
436. Cf. Art. 5 EuCExt and Art. 62 CISA as well as above, mn. 25 ff., 29 ff.
437. Too one-sided, Schünemann, *StV*, 23 (2003), 531 ff.; cf. also Cameron et al., *ICL from a Swedish Perspective* (2011), pp. 176 ff.
438. Cf. Art. 1(3) FD EAW (especially referring to the rights as enshrined in Art. 6 TEU) and, as an example of national law, §73 second sentence IRG (referring also to Art. 6 TEU, i.e. the EU rights standard).
439. Cf. Zypries, *RuP*, 40 (2004), 6; Vogel, *ZStW*, 116 (2004), 412; Kreß, *ZStW*, 116 (2004), 467; Tinkl, *Rechtsstellung des Einzelnen* (2008), pp. 209 ff.; cf. also OLG Braunschweig, Ausl. 5/04 (n. 315), 18–19; also Billing, *EuCLR*, 2 (2012), 83 ff. (taking into account the comparable situation in asylum law); cf. also Suominen, *Mutual Recognition in Cooperation* (2011), pp. 290 ff., 339 ff.; Mitsilegas, *EU Criminal Law* (2016), pp. 136–40; Satzger, *NStZ*, 15 (2016), 514 ff.; Böse, in Tiedemann et al., *Die Verfassung moderner Strafrechtspflege* (2016), pp. 212.
440. CJEU, *Pál Aranyosi and Robert Căldăraru*, Nos C-404/15 and C-659/15 PPU (ECLI: EU:C:2016:198), GC Judgment (5 April 2016); thereon Chapter 2, mn. 156 *in fine*. See also Eurojust, *Outcome Report of the College Thematic Discussion* (16 May 2017), Council-Doc. 9197/17, pp. 2 ff. (in favour of a comprehensive balancing of the interests involved; thereto Brodowski, *ZIS*, 12 (2017), 696–7).
441. Crit. of the CJEU's 'missing perspective' on human rights and the 'shadow side' of its political engagement as 'driving force' of EU integration, Swoboda, *ZIS*, 10 (2015), 361, 373–4.
442. Cf. thereon already Chapter 2, mn. 156.
443. In the same vein BVerfG, 2 BvR 2735/14 (n. 381), para. 105 ('Arising delays . . . are to be accepted', orig. 'Entstehende Verzögerungen . . . sind hinzunehmen'). Crit. of the decision for these very delays and the general difficulty it will cause for an efficient execution of an EAW, Kühne, *StV*, 36 (2016), 302; similarly, Sauer, *NJW*, 69 (2016), 1137 ('Communitarisation of extradition law . . . reversed', orig. 'Vergemeinschaftung des Auslieferungsrechts . . . rückgängig macht').
444. OLG Stuttgart, 3 Ausl. 80/04 (n. 306), with reference to the legal situation in France, the UK, Austria, Luxembourg, Ireland and Greece. Conversely,

Ahlbrecht, *StV*, 25 (2005), 43, has concerns regarding the lack of a legal remedy with respect to the granting decision according to §74b IRG old version (which was subsequently declared void by the BVerfG, cf. main text, mn. 55). A critical stance is also taken by Braum, *GA*, 152 (2005), 694.

445. In this section, mn. 69.

446. Cf. BVerfG, 2 BvR 2735/14 (n. 381), paras. 51 ff. (reversing and remanding a decision of the Düsseldorf Higher Regional Court to surrender a US citizen, pursuant to an EAW, to Italy, where he had been sentenced in his absence to a custodial sentence of thirty years; the BVerfG stated that the Higher Court had not sufficiently inquired and clarified whether the complainant's substantive submission – namely that in Italy he would not have the opportunity of a new evidentiary hearing at which he would be able to be present – would render his surrender violatory of the principle of culpability, which belongs to Germany's constitutional identity); thereon Brodowski, *JR*, 2016, 415 ff. (criticising the collateral damages the 'nuclear option' of the identity review may have). On national case law, see already above, n. 381.

447. In this sense Art. 11(2) FD EAW; crit. on this also Wehnert, *StraFo*, 16 (2003), 358; in detail on the rights of the accused person, cf. Morgan, in Blekxtoon and Van Ballegooij, *Handbook on the EAW* (2005), pp. 197–8.

448. On this, cf. already Chapter 1, mn. 32.

449. Möstl, *Die staatliche Garantie für die öffentliche Sicherheit und Ordnung* (2002), p. 568, argues in favour of a replacing of German basic rights.

450. Pechstein, *EuR*, 34 (1999), 12; Streinz, *Europarecht* (2008), mn. 476; Zimmermann, *JZ*, 56 (2001), 234; cf. also Böse, *Grundsatz der Verfügbarkeit* (2007), pp. 51–2.

451. With regard to Art. 16(2) second sentence GG, cf. Wolff, *StV*, 24 (2004), 155; critically, Schünemann, *ZStW*, 116 (2004), 385–6 incl. further references. On the changes to the Polish constitution, cf. Guzik Makaruk, *ZStW*, 116 (2004), 374–5; for a critical stance on the position taken by the BVerfG from a Polish perspective, cf. Komárek, *CMLR*, 44 (2007), 25.

452. Gärditz, in Böse, *Europäisches Strafrecht* (2013), pp. 263–4.

453. BVerfG, 2 BvR 2236/04 (n. 358), p. 304; on the many commentaries and discussion, including from a foreign perspective, cf. Ambos, *Internationales Strafrecht* (2008), §12 mn. 69 n. 445, Heger and Wolter, in Ambos, König and Rackow, *Rechtshilferecht in Strafsachen* (2015), p. 330; and Schork, *Auslieferungsverfahren* (2009), pp. 255 ff.; on the constitutionality of the transfer of sovereign powers in general, using the example of the FD EAW, cf. Schaper, *Verfassungsrechtliche Probleme* (2009), pp. 173 ff. On the legal situation between the EAW Act I being declared invalid and the entry into force of EAW Act II, cf. OLG Hamburg, No Ausl. 13/05, Decision (15 August 2005), in *NStZ*, 26 (2006), 111; OLG Köln, 6 Ausl. 63/05 – 31/05 (n. 310); OLG Karlsruhe, No 1 AK 31/04, Decision (7 September 2005), in *StV*, 25 (2005), 673 and 674. Following the BVerfG Judgment (which referred to a Spanish request for extradition), the Spanish Audiencia Nacional treated German extradition requests as normal extradition requests, invoking the principle of reciprocity (Arangüena Fanego, *RDP*, 20 (2007), 24). Generally on the sovereignity objection, cf. Królikowski and Znojek, *RSC*, 71 (2006), 551 ff., esp. 560.

454. BVerfG, 2 BvR 2236/04 (n. 358), p. 307 (official translation); concurring, Knopp, *JR*, 77 (2005), 450 ff.; a critical stance is taken by Vogel, *JZ*, 60 (2005), 806, who correctly points out that Art. 16(2) second sentence GG could also be understood

as a restriction of protective scope and that the Court should have discussed this; in a similar vein, Gas, *EuR*, 41 (2006), 287 ff.; and Gas, *RPDP*, 10 (2007), 813 ff.; also Hufeld, *JuS*, 45 (2005), 867; and Tomuschat, *EuGRZ*, 32 (2005), 454–5.

455. BVerfG, 2 BvR 2236/04 (n. 358), p. 306. On this, cf. also OLG Hamm, No 4 Ausl. A 12/07, Decision (7 May 2009), in *NStZ-RR*, 15 (2010), 209. On the potential consequences of the Constitutional Court's decision for the application of criminal law, cf. Böse and Meyer, *ZIS*, 6 (2011), 339. For a critical stance on this, cf. Gleß, *EuCLR*, 1 (2011), 120 ff., who under certain circumstances wants to assume an inevitable mistake of law if the person in question was unable to predict that a certain legal system would apply.
456. Art. 19(4) GG.
457. BVerfG, 2 BvR 2236/04 (n. 358), pp. 309, 312.
458. Cf. Chapter 3, mn. 53.
459. Cf. the dissenting opinion of Gerhardt, *NJW*, 58 (2005), 2301–2. On this, see Baddenhausen and Pietsch, *DVBl.*, 120 (2005), 1566; Satzger and Pohl, *JICJ*, 4 (2006), 693; critically on the result of complete invalidity also Vogel, *JZ*, 60 (2005), 804; Tomuschat, *EuGRZ*, 32 (2005), 460; Tams, *JA*, 38 (2006), 179; Hufeld, *JA*, 39 (2007), 42; Van Ooyen, *Die Staatstheorie des Bundesverfassungsgerichts und Europa* (2006), p. 54; Van Ooyen, in Möllers and Van Ooyen, *Europäisierung und Internationalisierung der Polizei* (2006), p. 67; Schmahl, *DVBl.*, 122 (2007), 1466; in agreement with the BVerfG Schünemann, *StV*, 25 (2005), 683.
460. For a summary of the relevant case law regarding the legal challenging of the validity of the EAW before national Courts, cf. Mackarel, *EJCCLCJ*, 15 (2007), 55 ff.; see also Henke, *Der europäische Haftbefehl* (2008), pp. 17 ff.; Mitsilegas, *CMLR*, 43 (2006), 1297–9.
461. Law No 133(I)/2004. This law was later amended by Laws 112(I)/2006, 30(I)/2014, and 183(I)/2014.
462. Art. 11(2)(f) Cypriot Constitution old version explicitly limited its application to non-nationals ('the arrest or detention . . . of an alien against whom action is being taken with a view to deportation or extradition').
463. Supreme Court of Cyprus, *General Attorney* v. *Konstantinou*, No 294/2005, Judgment (7 November 2005); for a summary of the judgment in English, see Council, *Decisions of Supreme Courts and Constitutional Courts Concerning the European Arrest Warrant* (11 November 2005) (Council Doc. 14281/05 COPEN 176), pp. 2–3; thereon, cf. also European Commission, *Report Implementation EAW* (2007), pp. 5–6; Deen-Racsmány, *EJCCLCJ*, 14 (2006), 290–2; Mitsilegas, *CMLR*, 43 (2006), 1298–9; Klimek, *EAW* (2015), pp. 301–4.
464. Fifth Amendment of the Cypriot Constitution 127(1)/2006.
465. Art. 11(2)(f) Cypriot Constitution (new version) reads, 'the arrest or detention . . . of a national of the Republic with a view to extraditing or surrendering him, subject to the following provisions: (i) The arrest or detention of a national of the Republic for the purpose of surrendering him under a European arrest warrant is possible solely in relation to events that occurred or acts done subsequent to the date of accession of the Republic to the European Union. (ii) The arrest or detention of a national of the Republic for the purpose of extraditing or surrendering him pursuant to an international agreement binding the Republic is possible solely in relation to events that occurred or acts done subsequent to the publication of the Fifth Amendment of the Constitution Law of 2006'.

466. Constitutional Tribunal of the Polish Republic (Trybunał Konstytucyjny w Polsce), No P 1/05, Judgment (27 April 2005), available in English at http://trybunal.gov.pl/fileadmin/content/omowienia/P_1_05_full_GB.pdf, last accessed 27 January 2018; thereon cf. European Commission, *Report Implementation EAW* (2007), p. 5; Deen-Racsmány, *EJCCLCJ*, 14 (2006), 278–82; Brandt, *EuR*, 44 (2009), 135–7, 141 ff.; Klimek, *EAW* (2015), pp. 286–90.
467. Art. 55(1) Polish Constitution (old version): 'The extradition of a Polish citizen is prohibited.'
468. Trybunał Konstytucyjny w Polsce, P 1/05 (n. 466), para. 4.2.
469. Trybunał Konstytucyjny w Polsce, P 1/05 (n. 466), para. 4.4.
470. Trybunał Konstytucyjny w Polsce, P 1/05 (n. 466), para. 5.4.
471. It was amended on 8 September 2006. Art. 55(1) now reads, 'Extradition of a Polish citizen is prohibited, except for a situation foreseen by paragraph 2'; for Art. 55(2), see below, n. 484.
472. Constitutional Court of the Czech Republic (Ústavní Soud), 2006/05/03 – No Pl. ÚS 66/04: EAW, Judgment (3 May 2006), available in English at www.usoud.cz/en/decisions/20060503-pl-us-6604-european-arrest-warrant-1, last accessed 27 January 2018; cf. thereon European Commission, *Report Implementation EAW* (2007), p. 6; Komárek, *CMLR*, 44 (2007), 26 ff.; Klimek, *EAW* (2015), pp. 296–300.
473. Cf. Art. 14(4) second sentence Czech Charter of Fundamental Rights and Freedoms: 'No citizen may be forced to leave her homeland'.
474. Ústavní Soud, 2006/05/03 – No Pl. ÚS 66/04 (n. 472), para. 83.
475. Ústavní Soud, 2006/05/03 – No Pl. ÚS 66/04 (n. 472), para. 72.
476. Ústavní Soud, 2006/05/03 – No Pl. ÚS 66/04 (n. 472), para. 71.
477. On nationality reservations with mutual recognition in general, cf. Suominen, *Mutual Recognition in Cooperation* (2011), pp. 27 ff.
478. Cf. §80 IRG.
479. Cf. §79(2) IRG.
480. *Argumentum e contrario ex* §80(2) No 2 IRG.
481. Hackner *et al.*, *NStZ*, 26 (2006), 666; cf. also OLG Düsseldorf, III-4 Ausl. (A) 80/06 (n. 299), 113–14.
482. Cf. §80(1) first sentence No 1 IRG. However, OLG Karlsruhe, No 1 AK 46/06, Decision (20 December 2006), in *StV*, 27 (2007), 149–50, also wants to weigh up individual cases when there is a substantial link to a foreign State. A narrower view is taken by Hufeld, *JA*, 39 (2007), 42.
483. Cf. §80(2) IRG. See Hackner et al., *NStZ*, 26 (2006), 667; cf. also OLG Karlsruhe, No 1 AK 39/08, Decision (6 July 2009), in *NStZ*, 30 (2010), 708. On the correlation between jurisdiction reservations and the relinquishing of dual criminality, cf. Suominen, *Mutual Recognition in Cooperation* (2011), p. 173.
484. Cf. Art. 55(2) Polish Constitution: 'Extradition of a Polish citizen may be granted upon a request made by a foreign state or an international judicial body if such a possibility stems from an international treaty ratified by Poland or a statute implementing a legal instrument enacted by an international organisation of which the Republic of Poland is a member, provided that the act covered by a request for extradition: (1) was *committed outside the territory* of the Republic of Poland, and (2) constituted an *offence under the law in force in the Republic of Poland* or would have constituted an offence under the law in force in the Republic of Poland if it had been committed within the territory of the Republic of Poland,

both at the time of its commitment and at the time of the making of the request' (emphasis added).

485. Hackner et al., *NStZ*, 26 (2006), 667, accurately criticise the idiosyncratic, more or less mirror-inverted version of the conditions for extradition according to §80(1), (2) IRG; this is taken even further in Schünemann, *StV*, 26 (2006), 366; Schünemann, in Joerden and Szwarc, *Europäisierung des Strafrechts* (2007), pp. 272–3; crit. also Ahlbrecht, *eucrim*, 1 (2006), 42 ff.; Weigend, in Müller-Dietz, *FS Jung* (2007), pp. 1079 ff.; Tinkl, *Rechtsstellung des Einzelnen* (2008), pp. 170 ff.
486. Cf. §80(1) second sentence IRG.
487. OLG Hamm, 4 Ausl. A 12/07 (n. 455); OLG Karlsruhe, No 1 AK 3/07, Decision (11 May 2007), in *NJW*, 60 (2007), 2567; OLG Karlsruhe, 1 AK 39/08 (n. 483).
488. Hackner et al., *NStZ*, 26 (2006), 667, are rightly critical of this; as are Böhm, *NJW*, 59 (2006), 2592 ff.; and Rosenthal, *ZRP*, 39 (2006), 108.
489. Cf. §80(2) second sentence IRG.
490. Rightly sharply criticised by Schünemann, *StV*, 26 (2006), 366; crit. also Rosenthal, *ZRP*, 39 (2006), 108; Arangüena Fanego, *RDP*, 20 (2007), 25; Michalke, *EuZW*, 18 (2007), 378; however, cf. also Heger, *ZIS*, 2 (2007), 224: the legislator 'understandably only copied the Karlsruhe reflections' (orig. 'verständlicherweise – nur die Karlsruher Überlegungen abgeschrieben').
491. Demetrio Crespo, *Diario La Ley*, no 6641 (2006), 1305 ff., is critical in this regard. Cf. also Suominen, *Mutual Recognition in Cooperation* (2011), p. 154; Weigend, in Müller-Dietz, *FS Jung* (2007), pp. 1073 and 1078, rightly interprets the non-extradition of nationals as an 'imperative of prudence in the relationship between States' and not as an 'insurmountable constitutional rule', and sees 'points of conflict with the regulations of the FD' (orig. 'Klugheitsregel im Verhältnis der Staaten untereinander … unüberwindliches verfassungsrechtliches Gebot … Konfliktpunkte mit den Vorgaben des Rahmenbeschlusses').
492. Just like the Spanish Audiencia Nacional following the Judgment of the Constitutional Court; cf. n. 455 above. Interestingly, Sweden does not apply this principle; cf. Cameron et al., *ICL from a Swedish Perspective* (2011), p. 102.
493. §79(2) third sentence IRG: 'subject to review'.
494. §§29, 41 IV IRG. This review can be dispensed with only in cases of simplified extradition (§79(2) fourth sentence IRG); that is, when the requested person agrees (§41(1) IRG).
495. On this, cf. OLG Karlsruhe, 1 AK 46/06 (n. 482); OLG Stuttgart, 3 Ausl. 52/06 (n. 301); KG, No (4) Ausl. A 378/06 (149/06), Decision (14 August 2006), in *NStZ*, 27 (2007), 110.
496. Otherwise, the request for extradition contained in an EAW constitutes a legal administrative act that is not attributable to Germany and thus cannot be challenged before German courts pursuant to §§23 ff. EGGVG; cf. OLG Celle, 2 VAs 3/09 (n. 216). Cf. also Schomburg, Lagodny and Schallmoser, in Böse, *Europäisches Strafrecht* (2013), pp. 501–2.
497. Rosenthal, *ZRP*, 39 (2006), 108; Ahlbrecht, *eucrim*, 1 (2006), 42; Weigend, in Müller-Dietz, *FS Jung* (2007), p. 1078; by contrast, Sinn and Wörner, *ZIS*, 2 (2007), 212, are supportive.
498. Rosenthal, *ZRP*, 39 (2006), 108–9.

499. Crit. Hackner et al., *NStZ*, 26 (2006), 665; Böhm, *StraFo*, 26 (2013), 178; Heintschel von Heinegg, in Sieber, Satzger and von Heinegg, *Europäisches Strafrecht* (2014), p. 670; Lagodny, *StV*, 25 (2005), 518 (previously arguing in favour of abolishing the authorisation procedure).
500. §79(2) first sentence IRG.
501. §§12–14 IRG.
502. Ex §74 IRG.
503. In detail on this, cf. Tinkl, *ZIS*, 5 (2010), 320 ff.; Heintschel von Heinegg, in Sieber, Satzger and von Heinegg, *Europäisches Strafrecht* (2014), pp. 671–2.
504. On this, see also OLG Karlsruhe, No 1 AK 51/07, Decision (16 December 2008), in *NStZ-RR*, 14 (2009), 107; OLG Hamburg, No Ausl. 3/08, Decion (20 March 2008), in *NStZ*, 29 (2009), 460; OLG Köln, 6 Ausl. A 41/09 (n. 419).
505. On the non-discrimination principle, cf. Klip, *European Criminal Law* (2016), pp. 97 ff.; Herdegen, *Europarecht* (2017), §6 mn. 17 ff. incl. further references.
506. Thus Reinhardt and Düsterhaus, *NVwZ*, 25 (2006), 433–4; crit. also with regard to the Constitutional Court's decision, Wasmeier, *ZEuS*, 9 (2006), 36 ff.; for a different view Heger, *ZIS*, 2 (2007), 225 (no violation of the non-discrimination principle); for a case-by-case inquiry, Freund, *Untersuchungshaft gegen EU-Ausländer* (2010), pp. 277 ff., 299; Zimmermann, *ZIS*, 12 (2017), 223 ff., wants to extend the protection of Art. 16(2) GG to all citizens of the Union. On this, see also CJEU, *Wolzenburg*, No C-123/08 (ECLI:EU:C:2009:616), Judgment (6 October 2009); CJEU, *João Pedro Lopes Da Silva Jorge*, No C-42/11 (ECLI:EU:C:2012:517), Judgment (5 September 2012); on this, see Klimek, *EAW* (2015), pp. 247–52; Montag and von Bonin, *NJW*, 66 (2013), 3488. See also the recent preliminary reference to the CJEU by LG Berlin, No 28 O 111/14, Decision (18 March 2016), reprinted in *EuZW*, 27 (2016), 400.
507. Schmidt, *StraFo*, 20 (2007), 9 ff.
508. Cf. §83b(2) IRG. See CJEU, *Szymon Kozlowski*, No C-66/08 (ECLI:EU:C:2008:437), Judgment (17 July 2008); thereon CJEU, *Wolzenburg*, C-123/08; thereon see European Commission, *Staff Working Document* (2011), pp. 18 (*Kozlowski*), 20–2 (*Wolzenburg*); Klimek, *EAW* (2015), pp. 236–40 (*Kozlowski*), 240–3 (*Wolzenburg*); de Amicis, *EuCLR*, 2 (2012), 50 ff.
509. More detail in Schmidt, *StraFo*, 20 (2007), 8 ff.; cf. also Vogel, *JZ*, 60 (2005), 805.
510. Crit. also Schmidt, *StraFo*, 20 (2007), 8 (citing numbers from the case law of the OLG Köln from 2005 in n. 17).
511. On the review of EAWs, cf. also Safferling, *Internationales Strafrecht* (2011), §12 mn. 59.
512. Cf. §79(1) IRG.
513. Cf. §83b IRG.
514. §79(1) second sentence IRG.
515. Cf. Art. 31 FD EAW.
516. Cf. e.g. §78 IRG (in conjunction with §1(4) IRG), giving primacy to the 'specific regulations' of this part (§§78 ff. IRG), including regarding international agreements (§78(3) in conjunction with §1(3) IRG).
517. Cf. BT-Drs. 15/1718, 13 right col. (application of EAW rules 'as far as' they 'constitute the more favourable law, which will regularly be the case'). We can probably assume that 'more favourable' in this context refers to the simplified

process of dealing with requests and the easier combating of crime; cf. once again the explanatory notes on §78 IRG in BT-Drs. 15/1718, 15 left col.; against an 'automatism' regarding the most favourable option (orig. 'Meistbegünstigungsautomatismus') Hackner, *NStZ*, 25 (2005), 311–12. Apart from that, it can be assumed that §§78 ff. IRG are final, cf. BT-Drs. 15/1718, 15.

518. E.g. §§80 ff. IRG.

519. Cf. §§83a and c IRG in particular; on this, see Ambos, *Internationales Strafrecht* (2006), Figure 28; Hackner, *NStZ*, 25 (2005), 314–15. As far as the length of the extradition or transit detention is concerned, the 40-day limit of Art. 16(4) EuCExt applies, as this is not detailed in §§78 ff. IRG. On the possibility of *repairing* breaches of essential procedural requirements, cf. OLG Karlsruhe, No 1 AK 2/07, Decision (26 July 2007), in *StV*, 27 (2007), 654. On Spanish law on this matter, cf. Jimeno Bulnes, *RP*, 16 (2005), 106 ff.

520. See already above, mn. 18–19. For Germany, see §§13, 14 IRG (here the EAW Act has not changed anything), and BT-Drs. 15/1718, 11 left col.

521. For Germany, see BT-Drs. 15/1718, 15 right col.; on the authorisation procedure, cf. Schomburg et al., *Internationale Rechtshilfe in Strafsachen* (2012), pp. 5–6; Hackner and Schierholt, *Internationale Rechtshilfe* (2017), mn. 68 ff.; Hackner, in Lagodny, Wiederin and Winkler, *Probleme des Rahmenbeschlusses* (2007), p. 197; now cf. also OLG Karlsruhe, No 1 AK 72/06, Decision (18 June 2007), in *StV*, 27 (2007), 650, according to which issuing an extradition arrest warrant on the basis of an EAW is precluded if no authorisation can to be expected.

522. Cf. §79(2) first sentence IRG.

523. Crit. Hackner, in Lagodny, Wiederin and Winkler, *Probleme des Rahmenbeschlusses* (2007), p. 198; Hackner, in Schomburg et al., *Internationale Rechtshilfe in Strafsachen* (2012), pp. 469–70.

524. §79(2) second sentence IRG.

525. BT-Drs. 16/1024, 12; crit. Hackner et al., *NStZ*, 26 (2006), 665, in regard to §79(1) first sentence IRG; on EAW Act I cf. also BT-Drs. 15/1718, 15 right col.

526. §79(2) third sentence IRG.

527. Cf. Hackner *et al.*, *NStZ*, 26 (2006), 665–6; see also the *travaux* in BT-Drs. 16/1024, 13 ('a very broad discretionary scope of the granting authority').

528. Cf. https://e-justice.europa.eu/content_european_arrest_warrant-90-en.do?clang=en, last accessed 27 January 2018.

529. For a similar positive assessment, Klimek, *EAW* (2015), pp. 323 ff., 337–8 ('most successful mutual recognition instrument ever', summarising and relying on the Commission's evaluation in 2005, 2007 and 2011 and the Council's 2009 report), 366; see also Albert and Merlin, *eucrim*, 10 (2015), 61.

530. Cf. European Commission, *Report Implementation EAW* (2011), pp. 3, 11, 12 (statistics from 2005 to 2009); for more recent statistics (until 2015), cf. https://e-justice.europa.eu/content_european_arrest_warrant-90-en.do?clang=en, last accessed 27 January 2018; generally thereon, also Klimek, *EAW* (2015), p. 318.

531. As to effective surrender, the listing on the e-justice-homepage shows an increase from 836 persons (2005) to 4,431 (2009) and 5,304 (2015), which is approximately one-third as compared to the number of issued EAWs insofar as there is registered an increase from 6,894 (2005) to 15,827 (2009) and 16,144 (2015); cf. https://e-justice.europa.eu/content_european_arrest_warrant-90-en.do?clang=en, last accessed 27 January 2018.

532. For a ranking of offences for issuing an EAW based on information from EJN contact points interviewed by Albers, see Albers, in Albers et al., *Evaluation Framework* (2013), p. 309; for France, cf. Beauvais, in Albers et al., *Evaluation Framework* (2013), p. 157; for the Netherlands, cf. Blesgraaf and Langbroek, in Albers et al., *Evaluation Framework* (2013), p. 201; for Germany, cf. Wahl, in Albers et al., *Evaluation Framework* (2013), p. 269; indicating especially Poland and Romania as MS issuing EAWs for petty offences, Beauvais and Giannoulis, in Albers et al., *Evaluation Framework* (2013), p. 150; and Van den Brink et al., in Albers et al., *Evaluation Framework* (2013), p. 196; for a defence perspective, Wahl, in Albers et al., *Evaluation Framework* (2013), p. 321 (Poland). This problem is understated by Klimek, *EAW* (2015), p. 365 ('does not apply to petty crime'); crit. also Schallmoser, *EJCCLCJ*, 22 (2014), 161–2 (regarding proportionality); Albert and Merlin, *eucrim*, 10 (2015), 62; Anagnostopoulos, *ERA Forum*, 15 (2014), 16; Xanthopoulou, *NJECL*, 6 (2015), 48; Swoboda, *ZIS*, 10 (2015), 363.

533. Cf. European Commission, *Report Implementation EAW* (2011), pp. 3, 6; for a defence perspective, cf. Wahl, in Albers et al., *Evaluation Framework* (2013), pp. 320–1 (lack of proportionality regarding nature of offence and restriction of liberty), 323 ff. (inter alia, lack of effective legal representation); listing possible rights violations, also Schallmoser, *EJCCLCJ*, 22 (2014), 161–4.

534. Proportionality is, of course, a complex principle derived from constitutional law theory and case law (especially the one of the German Constitutional Court), which has invaded criminal law and procedure, international humanitarian and criminal law as well as human rights law (see e.g. Ambos, *Treatise ICL I* (2013), pp. 15, 63, 83, 290–1, 333, 420–1; Ambos, *Treatise ICL II* (2014), pp. 160, 173, 285 ff.; Ambos, *Treatise ICL III* (2016), pp. 397–9, 543; on the principle in Arts. 49(3), 52(1) CFREU, see already Chapter 2, mn. 160). Being a general principle, it needs to be structured and refined, as most convincingly done by the **three-step test** employed by the German Constitutional Court, distinguishing between (i) the suitability of the means employed with a view to the objective pursued, (ii) the necessity of these means or the possibility of less onerous means and (iii) the balancing of the interests involved (proportionality *stricto sensu*) (cf., among others, BVerfG, No 1 BvR 665/66, Judgment (16 March 1971), in *BVerfGE*, 30, p. 316; BVerfG, No 2 BvR 636/72, Judgment (8 May 1974), in *BVerfGE* 37, pp. 201, 212; BVerfG, Nos 2 BvL 43, 51, 63, 64, 70, 80/92, 2 BvR 2031/92, Judgment (9 March 1994), in *BVerfGE* 90, pp. 145, 200; cf. also Klatt and Meister, *Constitutional Structure of Proportionality* (2013), pp. 7 ff.; in basically the same vein, CJEU, *The Queen* v. *the Minister for Agriculture, Fisheries and Food, Ex p Fedesa*, No C-331/88 (ECLI:EU:C:1990:391), Judgment (13 November 1990); for a detailed account of proportionality in EU law, cf. UK Supreme Court, *R (on the application of Lumsdon and others)* v. *Legal Services Board (Respondent)*, No [2015] UKSC 41, Judgment (24 June 2015), paras. 23 ff.). In **human rights law**, this three-step test has been converted into a four-step one, adding the issue of the legitimacy of the measure's objective as a first, more fundamental question (ECtHR, *Handyside* v. *the UK*, No 5493/72, Judgment (7 December 1976), paras. 49–50; ECtHR, *Keegan* v. *the UK*, No 28867/03, Judgment (18 July 2006), paras. 29–30; for such a four-step test, Xanthopoulou, *NJECL*, 6 (2015), 36–7; on the distinction between the EU and human rights test in that regard, Bjorge and Williams, *CLJ*, 75 (2016), 187, discussing the judgment quoted above in *Lumsdon*). At any rate, hard cases have to be resolved at the last stage, as famously summarised in

Robert Alexy's 'law of balancing' (*Abwägungsgesetz*), according to which 'the permissible level of non-satisfaction of, or detriment to, one principle depends on the importance of satisfying the other' (for the full definition cf. Alexy, *Theorie der Grundrechte* (1986), p. 146; English translation by Rivers, *Theory of Constitutional Rights* (2002), p. 102).

535. Above, mn. 60.
536. Cf. Böse, in Albers et al., *Evaluation Framework* (2013), pp. 85, 335 ff.; also Anagnostopoulos, *ERA Forum*, 15 (2014), 18, 19.
537. Cf. generally Fichera and Herlin-Karnell, *EuPubL*, 19 (2013), 771 (offering 'fragments of proportionality' with the 'exact impact of proportionality . . . to be crystallised' as an 'answer for a Europe of Rights'). The proportionality test has also been advocated by Lord Philips in UK Supreme Court, *Assange* v. *the Swedish Prosecution Authority*, No [2012] UKSC 22, Judgment (30 May 2012), para. 90 ('scheme of the EAW should be reconsidered in order to make express provision for consideration of proportionality'); dismissing the *Radu* and *Melloni* decisions of the CJEU (thereon Chapter 2, mn. 156) measured against a (four-tiered) proportionality test, Xanthopoulou, *NJECL*, 6 (2015), 38–47; in favour also Anagnostopoulos, *ERA Forum*, 15 (2014), 16, 19; Mitsilegas, *EU Criminal Law* (2016), pp. 142–6, advocating 'two *loci* of proportionality' but also cautious regarding the 'added value of the proportionality test based on the severity of the alleged conduct . . . if the scope of the mutual recognition instruments – and the EAW FD in particular – is not limited to include fewer, only serious offences' (at 146). On proportionality as a general principle and regarding the issuing and execution of EAWs in three MS, cf. Beauvais and Giannoulis, in Albers et al., *Evaluation Framework* (2013), pp., 107 ff., 111 ff. (France); Van den Brink et al., in Albers et al., *Evaluation Framework* (2013), pp. 165 ff., 172 ff. (Netherlands); and Böse and Wahl, in Albers et al., *Evaluation Framework* (2013), pp. 213 ff., 220 ff. (Germany); summarising, Böse, in Albers et al., *Evaluation Framework* (2013), pp. 343 ff. Yet defence lawyers complain that courts are reluctant to accept a disproportionality objection; cf. Wahl, in Albers et al., *Evaluation Framework* (2013), p. 321.
538. Cf. Eurojust, *Strategic Seminar EAW* (2014), p. 9: 'While several MS introduced an explicit ground for refusal on fundamental rights in their national implementation law on the EAW, others rely on general constitutional safeguards, including the ECHR and the CFREU.'
539. Cf. European Commission, *Report Implementation EAW* (2011), pp. 7–8.
540. European Council, *Follow-up to the recommendations in the final report on the fourth round of mutual evaluations, concerning the EAW, during the Spanish Presidency of the Council of the EU* (31 May 2010) (Council 8436/2/10 REV 2), p. 3, inserting the following modification in the EAW Handbook (Council 17195/1/10 REV 1 COPEN 275, available at http://register.consilium.europa.eu/doc/srv?l=EN&f=ST%208436%202010%20REV%202%20COR%201, last accessed 27 January 2018): 'It is clear that the FD on the EAW does not include any obligation for an issuing MS to conduct a proportionality check and that the legislation of the MS plays a key role in that respect. Notwithstanding that, considering the severe consequences of the execution of an EAW with regard to restrictions on physical freedom and the free movement of the requested person, the competent authorities should, *before deciding to issue a warrant, consider proportionality* by assessing a number of important factors. In particular these

will include an assessment of the seriousness of the offence . . . the possibility of the suspect being detained, and the likely penalty imposed if the person sought is found guilty of the alleged offence. Other factors also include ensuring the effective protection of the public and taking into account the interests of the victims of the offence' (underlining in the original, italics added). See also the 2017 version of the Handbook (Eur. Commission, 2017), pp. 19, 49 (sect. 2.4., 5.7.).

541. European Commission, *Report Implementation EAW* (2011), p. 8; in favour of a 'mandatory proportionality check' are also the EJN contact points interviewed by Albers, in Albers et al., *Evaluation Framework* (2013), p. 316.

542. In this line see also BVerfG, 2 BvR 2735/14 (n. 381), paras. 93–5 (futher referring to recitals 10, 12, 13 and 14 FD EAW). Therefore Schallmoser, *EJCCLCJ*, 22 (2014), 136, 145, 160–1, criticising the FD EAW's lack of an *explicit* human rights clause, is somewhat overstated, being too positivist.

543. For a judicial control *ex ante* and and judicial review *ex post*, Böse, in Albers et al., *Evaluation Framework* (2013), p. 365. A judicial remedy could also make sure that the EAW is actually suspended and the person concerned would not be arrested in another MS on the basis of the respective EAW; cf. ibid., pp. 365–6.

544. Cf. Böse, in Albers et al., *Evaluation Framework* (2013), pp. 84–5 (proportionality to be considered as part of the exercise of discretion by the executing authority with regard to the options of refusal pursuant to Art. 4, 4bis, 5 FD EAW).

545. Above, mn. 60.

546. *Aranyosi and Căldăraru*, above, n. 440 and main text.

547. European Commission, *Report Implementation EAW* (2011), p. 7.

548. Cf. Böse, in Albers et al., *Evaluation Framework* (2013), p. 366; in a similar vein against the issuing for 'minor offences', Xanthopoulou, *NJECL*, 6 (2015), 50; see in this regard also UK Court of Appeal (Criminal Division), *Criminal Practice Directions Amendment No 2*, [2014] EWCA Crim 1569 (23 July 2014), paras. 17. A.3 and 17.A.5 (indicating minor offences which do not justify extradition), available at www.judiciary.gov.uk/wp-content/uploads/2014/07/Criminal-Practice-Directions-Amendment-No.2.pdf, last accessed 27 January 2018.

549. Cf. Böse, in Albers et al., *Evaluation Framework* (2013), p. 366 (no 'excessive labelling').

550. See already above, mn. 25–8.

551. Cf. Wahl, in Albers et al., *Evaluation Framework* (2013), p. 321; Böse, in Albers et al., *Evaluation Framework* (2013), p. 366.

552. On the relevant FD 2009/829/JHA, see main text, mn. 102.

553. On the transfer of prisoners pursuant to FD 2008/909/JHA, cf. also Eurojust, *Strategic Seminar EAW* (2014), p. 10 ('should also help to overcome shortcomings in the application of the EAW').

554. See generally Böse, in Albers et al., *Evaluation Framework* (2013), p. 366; Xanthopoulou, *NJECL*, 6 (2015), 51. On a model for granting the citizen the power to hold MS liable for their use of EAWs in cases ending with acquital or non-prosecution, see Sørensen, *EuCLR*, 5 (2015), 194 ff.

555. Cf. Chapter 1, mn. 32.

556. See in more detail Wahl, in Albers et al., *Evaluation Framework* (2013), pp. 327–9, 331.

557. Cf. Böse, in Albers et al., *Evaluation Framework* (2013), p. 367 ('right of first adive by a defence counsel').

558. §80(1) No 1 IRG.
559. §81 No 4 IRG.
560. OLG Düsseldorf, III-4 Ausl. (A) 80/06 (n. 299).
561. Cf. §79(2) third sentence IRG.
562. OLG Stuttgart, 3 Ausl. 52/06 (n. 301), 258–9.
563. Cf. §81 No 1 IRG in conjunction with Art. 2(1) FD EAW.
564. Cf. §10(2) IRG.
565. Cf. §81 No 4 IRG in conjunction with Art. 2(2) FD EAW.
566. Art. 16(2) GG.
567. In detail, with further references, Ambos and Bock, *JuS*, 52 (2012), 437 ff.
568. On the many other objects of mutual assistance, cf. Capus, *Strafrecht und Souveränität* (2010), pp. 238 ff.
569. For a brief summary from a rights perspective (regarding coercive measures), cf. Ruggeri, in Ruggieri, *Languages* (2014), pp. 220–4.
570. Cf. Chapter 1, mn. 26–7.
571. Meyer, *GA*, 154 (2007), 17 ff., 31 ff. (concerned that the principle of mutual recognition entails the acceptance of evidence by the MS even if it violates fundamental rights such as the *nemo tenetur* principle); see also Sanz Hermida, *RP*, 21 (2008), 136.
572. For a principled criticism, cf. Ambos, *ZIS*, 5 (2010), 557, 559; cf. also Ahlbrecht, *StV*, 33 (2013), 118. In detail on the 'legal connotation' (orig. 'Rechtskonnotation') of evidence, cf. Gleß, *ZStW*, 125 (2013), 575 ff.
573. On mutual trust as the basis of mutual recognition see already above, n. 358. See also in this context on the refusal of an EAW because of failing mutual trust in lieu of (successfully) invoking fundamental rights, Meysman, *EuCLR*, 6 (2016), 199.
574. In the same vein, Anagnostopoulos, *ERA Forum*, 15 (2014), 19. From a rights perspective, advocating an 'inter-level approach' with a new transnational 'ad hoc procedure' for gathering evidence, Ruggeri, in Ruggieri, *Languages* (2014), pp. 233–6.
575. Cf. Turner, *EuCLR*, 4 (2014), 114, 146.
576. See main text, mn. 87–94.
577. European Convention on Mutual Assistance in Criminal Matters of 20 April 1959, ETS No 30, entry into force 12 June 1962; Kubiciel, in Ambos, König and Rackow, *Rechtshilferecht in Strafsachen* (2016), p. 934. A summary is provided in Schomburg, in Schomburg et al., *Internationale Rechtshilfe in Strafsachen* (2012), p. 621; cf. also Gleß, *Beweisrechtsgrundsätze* (2006), pp. 109–10; Gleß, *Internationales Strafrecht* (2015), mn. 493 ff.; Krüßmann, *Transnationales Strafprozessrecht* (2009), pp. 433 ff.; Zimmermann, Glaser and Motz, *EuCLR*, 1 (2011), 58; on interrogations in the presence or with the participation of officers of the requesting State, cf. BGH, No 1 StR 421/06, Decision (8 November 2006), in *JR*, 79 (2007), 260; with commentary by Lagodny, *JR*, 79 (2007), 260–2.
578. Art. 2 EuCMACM.
579. Cf. Art. 5 EuCMACM.
580. On enforcing an arrest warrant with the assurance of safe passage according to Art. 12, cf. LG Regensburg, No 1 Qs 38/2012, Decision (24 May 2012), in *StV*, 33 (2013), 167.
581. Arts. 1, 2 AP EuCMACM.
582. A summary is provided in Lagodny and Schomburg, in Schomburg et al., *Internationale Rechtshilfe in Strafsachen* (2012), p. 732.

583. Arts. 3, 13 AP II.
584. Arts. 9, 10 AP II.
585. Arts. 17–20 AP II.
586. Cf. Art. 48 CISA.
587. Art. 50 CISA.
588. Art. 51(a) CISA; on the intended abolition by the EEW, cf. Huybreghts, *ERA Forum*, 16 (2015), 390–1.
589. Art. 52 CISA; thereon Roth, *NStZ*, 34 (2014), 552–3.
590. Cf. on the national, especially (long) German list, cf. Roth, *NStZ*, 34 (2014), 555–6. The German list contains all kinds of announcements from the various phases of the criminal procedure, including appeal proceedings, enforcement proceedings, accessorial and private accusation and ancillary proceedings.
591. Art. 53 CISA.
592. Art. 53(3) CISA; on this, cf. de Biolley, *RIDP*, 77 (2006), 29–30.
593. The sending of procedural documents to foreign judicial authorities is not the exercise of (national) criminal justice but mutual legal assistance; this is still visible in Art. 7 EuCMACM (communication between requested and requesting Party); see also Roth, *NStZ*, 34 (2014), 552.
594. Council Act of 29 May 2000 establishing in accordance with Article 34 of the Treaty on EU the Convention on Mutual Assistance in Criminal Matters between the MS of the EU (OJ C 197 of 12 July 2000, 1). The German Implementation Act inserted, inter alia, §61 IRG a on the 'transmission of personal data without request' and §83 k IRG on the creation of joint investigation teams from different EU States; on this, cf. BT-Drs. 15/4232; also Rinio, *NStZ*, 24 (2004), 189 n. 3; and Gleß, *Beweisrechtsgrundsätze* (2006), pp. 124 ff. At the time of writing (January 2018), the EUMAC has not entered into force in Croatia, Greece, Ireland and Italy; see www.consilium.europa.eu/en/documents-publications/agreements-conventions/agreement/?aid=2000023, last accessed 27 January 2018.
595. Cf. Art. 2(2) EUMAC. Cf. also Huybreghts, *ERA Forum*, 16 (2015), 388.
596. Cf. Art. 2(1) EUMAC. The EUMAC itself was made applicable to Norway and Iceland by a specific agreement in 2010; it was also extended to Switzerland and Liechtenstein once in force in all contracting parties, albeit with an opt-out possibility in case of future changes of Art. 51 CISA regarding tax offences; cf. Huybreghts, *ERA Forum*, 16 (2015), 389, 391.
597. At the international level, a similar, albeit less explicit rule has been proposed by Art. 6 UN Model Treaty on Mutual Assistance in Criminal Matters (A/RES/45/117, 14 December 1990): 'requests for assistance shall be carried out promptly, *in the manner provided for by the law and practice of the requested State*. To the extent consistent with its law and practice, the requested State shall *carry out the request in the manner specified by the requesting State*' (emphasis added).
598. Generally on the *locus* and *forum* rule, cf. Krüßmann, *Transnationales Strafprozessrecht* (2009), pp. 281 ff., 623 ff.; Gleß, *ZStW*, 125 (2013), 592 ff.
599. Ruggeri, in Ruggieri, *Languages* (2014), p. 221, calls this 'a huge cultural change in the field of judicial assistance'. See also Gleß and Schomburg, in Schomburg et al., *Internationale Rechtshilfe in Strafsachen* (2012), p. 1229.
600. Cf. Art. 5 EUMAC; thereon Roth, *NStZ*, 34 (2014), 553 (however, giving the relevant documents in this provision a different meaning than in Art. 52 CISA,

focusing on the German version ('Verfahrensurkunden' instead of 'gerichtliche Urkunden', Art. 52 CISA)).

601. Arts. 10, 11 EUMAC. On audiovisual hearings, cf. e.g. BGH, No 5 StR 344/07, Decision (9 October 2007), in *NStZ*, 28 (2008), 232–3.

602. Art. 12 EUMAC.

603. Art. 13 EUMAC. On this, cf. Plachta, *EJCCLCJ*, 13 (2005), 288 ff.; Rijken, *ULR*, 2 (2006), 100 ff.; Riegel, *eucrim*, 4 (2009), 99 ff.; Neumann, in Sieber, Satzger and von Heinegg, *Europäisches Strafrecht* (2014), pp. 610–11; Kugelmann, in Böse, *Europäisches Strafrecht* (2013), pp. 667–9; Krüßmann, in Böse, *Europäisches Strafrecht* (2013), pp. 682–9; Klip, *European Criminal Law* (2016), pp. 496 ff.; Jähnke and Schramm, *Europäisches Strafrecht* (2017), §7 mn. 5–6; from a Swedish perspective, Cameron et al., *ICL from a Swedish Perspective* (2011), pp. 138 ff.; with a particular focus on combating narcotics crime, Nestler, *GA*, 157 (2010), 653–4.

604. Art. 14 EUMAC. The provision needs to be implemented by bilateral agreements between the requesting and the requested State (cf. Art. 14(2) EUMAC) and is complemented by ad hoc agreements in the context of particular events, e.g. a NATO or G8 summit (thereon Barczak, *StV*, 32 (2012), 183, referring to the co-operation between the German police and the British Association of Chief Police Officers). At any rate, the provision confirms the *locus regit actum* rule as to the applicable law and procedure (Art. 14(3) EUMAC) and thus leaves the details to the relevant State Parties (crit. Aquilina, *eucrim*, 8 (2013), 64); it does not limit (transnational) covert investigations to particular (serious) offences (crit. Barczak, *StV*, 32 (2012), 187); for a further analysis of the legal status of the covert investigator, his limited powers and possible exclusionary rules, cf. Barczak, *StV*, 32 (2012), 186–8. Interestingly, the Council called already in 2007 for a simplified cross-border deployment of undercover officers, albeit limited to the fight against 'serious cross-border crime'; cf. Council, *Council Resolution on simplifying the cross-border deployment of undercover officers in order to step up MS' cooperation in the fight against serious cross-border crime* (25 May 2007) (No 6678/3/07 REV 3); cf. also the overview of the replies to the relevant questionnaire, Council, *Replies to questionnaire on undercover officers: Discussion paper* (13 February 2008) (Council Doc. 6323/08). Art. 14 EUMAC was replaced by Art. 29 EIO Directive on 22 May 2017; it essentially repeats it, the only difference being that there is no general reservation clause for the MS; cf. thereon Peers, *EU Justice and Home Affairs Law*, ii (2016), p. 333; on the confirmation of the *locus regit actum* rule as to the applicable law and procedure, cf. also Belfiore, in Ruggeri, *Transnational Evidence* (2014), p. 96; on the exception from the mutual recognition principle by the provision about covert investigations, see Ruggeri, in Ruggeri, *Transnational Evidence* (2014), p. 10; Maggio, in Ruggeri, *Transnational Evidence* (2014), p. 146.

605. Arts. 17 ff. EUMAC. Cf. also Schomburg, *NJW*, 54 (2001), 802; on the main trial by video conference based on Art. 10 EUMAC, cf. Rinio, *NStZ*, 24 (2004), 189; from a French perspective, see Aubert, *RSC*, 77 (2012), 438 ff.

606. Above, mn. 15.

607. Directive 2014/41/EU (OJ L 130 of 1 May 2014, 1). For an analysis, see main text, mn. 87–94.

608. Art. 34 EIO Directive. For an overview of this transition, see Bachmaier, *eucrim*, 10 (2015), 47.

609. See main text, mn. 83–4.
610. See above, mn. 79.
611. See above, mn. 80.
612. See above, mn. 81.
613. See main text, mn. 83.
614. See above, mn. 15.
615. FD 2003/577/JHA (OJ L 196 of 2 August 2003, 45); on this, cf. Heger, *ZIS*, 2 (2007), 554 ff.; Gleß, in Sieber, Satzger and von Heinegg, *Europäisches Strafrecht* (2014), pp. 696 ff.; Gleß, in Böse, *Europäisches Strafrecht* (2013), pp. 624–5; Suominen, *Mutual Recognition in Cooperation* (2011), pp. 92 ff.; Miettinen, *Criminal Law and Policy in the EU* (2013), pp. 188–9; Lelieur, *EuCLR*, 5 (2015), 281 ff.; on opposing rights of third parties (legal persons) pursuant to Art. 11(1) cf. Lagodny, in Joerden and Schmoller, *Rechtsstaatliches Strafen, FS Yamanaka* (2017), pp. 581 ff. On implementation in Germany, cf. *BGBl.* I 2008, 995; on implementation in Sweden, cf. Cameron et al., *ICL from a Swedish Perspective* (2011), pp. 149 ff.; on the implementation in Scandinavia, Suominen, *Mutual Recognition in Cooperation* (2011), pp. 94 ff.; for an evaluation of the implementation within the EU, cf. COM (2008) 885 final; *eucrim*, 5 (2010), 53–4, 143.
616. Art. 3(1) FD 2003/577/JHA.
617. Arts. 1, 2 FD 2003/577/JHA.
618. Art. 5(1) FD 2003/577/JHA. On grounds for refusal, cf. Kubiciel, in Ambos, König and Rackow, *Rechtshilferecht in Strafsachen* (2015), p. 852; Gleß, in Sieber, Satzger and von Heinegg, *Europäisches Strafrecht* (2014), pp. 701–2.
619. Art. 1, 5(1) FD 2003/577/JHA. On the transmission of the freezing order, cf. Arts. 4, 9 FD on Freezing.
620. Art. 10 FD 2003/577/JHA.
621. Gleß, in Sieber, Satzger and von Heinegg, *Europäisches Strafrecht* (2014), pp. 696, 705; Zimmermann, Glaser and Motz, *EuCLR*, 1 (2011), 65; Lelieur, *EuCLR*, 5 (2015), 283–4.
622. Belgium, Bulgaria, Estonia, Spain, Austria, Slovenia and Sweden presented the Initiative for a Directive of the EP and of the Council regarding the EIO in criminal matters of 29 April 2010, Council Document 9145/10, 3; thereon also Vernimmen-Van Tiggelen and Surano, *Future of Mutual Recognition in Criminal Matters in the EU* (2008), pp. 17, 32. On the deficiencies of the EU legal framework, making the relevant instruments for freezing and confiscation ineffective, see also Fazekas and Nanopoulos, *EJCCLCJ*, 24 (2016), 47 ff. On the transition from the FD on Freezing and the FD on Confiscation orders to the EIO, as a transition from mutual recognition to harmonisation, see Albert and Merlin, *eucrim*, 10 (2015), 61–2. On the new procedures of freezing and confiscating criminal assets under the new EIO Directive, see Lelieur, *EuCLR*, 5 (2015), 296 ff.; Fazekas and Nanopoulos, *EJCCLCJ*, 24 (2016), 42 ff.
623. Main text, mn. 87–94.
624. Above, mn. 48–9.
625. Art. 3(2) FD 2003/577/JHA.
626. FD 2008/978/JHA (OJ L 350 of 18 December 2008, 74); on this, cf. Hüttemann, *European Criminal Procedure* (2012), pp. 113 ff.; Roger, *GA*, 157 (2010), 27 ff.: Hecker, in Marauhn, *Bausteine eines europäischen Beweisrechts* (2007), p. 32; Krüßmann, *StraFo*, 21 (2008), 458 ff.; Krüßmann, *Transnationales*

Strafprozessrecht (2009), pp. 602 ff.; Gleß, *Internationales Strafrecht* (2015), mn. 500–1; Gleß, in Sieber, Satzger and von Heinegg, *Europäisches Strafrecht* (2014), pp. 680–2; Gleß, in Böse, *Europäisches Strafrecht* (2013), pp. 621–4; on the draft, Ahlbrecht, *NStZ*, 26 (2006), 70 ff.; from a Greek perspective, Spinellis, in Joerden et al., *FS Szwarc* (2009), pp. 701 ff.; on the development, Mavany, *Die europäische Beweisanordnung* (2012), pp. 79 ff. Crit. of the lukewarm support of Germany (waiting for 'further developments on the European level', cf. BT-Drs. 17/702, 31–2 and BT-Drs. 17/1543, 1 ff.), Vogel, *JZ*, 67 (2012), 26–7; for an implementation proposal, cf. Mavany, *Die europäische Beweisanordnung* (2012), pp. 177 ff.

627. Arts. 1, 2 FD EEW.
628. Art. 8(1) FD EEW. On this, cf. Mavany, *Die europäische Beweisanordnung* (2012), pp. 104 ff.
629. See already above, mn. 81.
630. Art. 12 FD EEW.
631. Art. 7(1)(a) FD EEW.
632. Art. 7(1)(b) FD EEW.
633. Art. 11 FD EEW; on the *locus* rule in the CISA see already above, mn. 5. On the (few) grounds for refusal, Gleß, in Sieber, Satzger and von Heinegg, *Europäisches Strafrecht* (2014), pp. 687–9; Mavany, *Die europäische Beweisanordnung* (2012), pp. 127 ff.
634. Art. 15 FD EEW.
635. Art. 14(1) FD EEW.
636. Above, mn. 49–50.
637. Cf. also Germany's Declaration pursuant to Art. 23 IV FD, printed as an annex to the FD; on this, cf. Zimmermann, Glaser and Motz, *EuCLR*, 1 (2011), 67.
638. Art. 14(2) FD EEW.
639. Cf. among others Kubiciel, in Ambos, König and Rackow, *Rechtshilferecht in Strafsachen* (2015), pp. 835–6; Heger, *ZIS*, 2 (2007), 547 ff.; Krüßmann, *StraFo*, 21 (2008), 458 ff.; Roger, *GA*, 157 (2010), 27 ff.; Klip, *European Criminal Law* (2016), pp. 435 ff.; Gleß, in Sieber, Satzger and von Heinegg, *Europäisches Strafrecht* (2014), pp. 680–2; Rackow, in Ambos, *Europäisches Strafrecht post-Lissabon* (2011), pp. 118–19; Lelieur, *EuCLR*, 5 (2015), 284 ('failure'); particularly from a defence perspective, Heine, *Die Rechtsstellung des Beschuldigten* (2009), pp. 129 ff.; cf. also the somewhat critical contributions of Busemann, *ZIS*, 5 (2010), 552 ff.; Ambos, *ZIS*, 5 (2010), 557 ff.; Allegrezza, *ZIS*, 5 (2010), 569 ff.; Spencer, in *ZIS*, 5 (2010), 602 ff.; and Nalewajko, *Grundsatz der gegenseitigen Anerkennung* (2010), pp. 254 ff. For a more favourable view, Bachmaier Winter, *ZIS*, 5 (2010), 580 ff. For a survey on the future of the EEW, *eucrim*, 5 (2010), 54; for alternative and supplementary suggestions for a solution, cf. Nalewajko, *Grundsatz der gegenseitigen Anerkennung* (2010), pp. 248 ff.
640. Art. 4(2) FD EEW; also Kubiciel, in Ambos, König and Rackow, *Rechtshilferecht in Strafsachen* (2015), p. 835; Williams, *RIDP*, 77 (2006), 155 ff.; Claverie-Rousset, *EuCLR*, 2 (2012), 153; Zimmermann, Glaser and Motz, *EuCLR*, 1 (2011), 66; Mavany, *Die europäische Beweisanordnung* (2012), pp. 97 ff.
641. The only exception is the (more or less accidental) receipt of statements from persons present during the execution of the EEW and directly related to the subject of the EEW (Art. 4(6)). For a critical stance on this, cf. Roger, *GA*, 157 (2010), 27, 33–4.

642. Satzger, *Europäisches und Internationales Strafrecht* (2016), §10 mn. 44.
643. Williams, *RIDP*, 77 (2006), 155–6.
644. Cf. Belgium et al., *Directive Initiative EIO* (2010), Council Document 9145/10, 3; Zeder, *ÖJZ*, 64 (2009), 992, 994–5, 997; Nalewajko, *Grundsatz der gegenseitigen Anerkennung* (2010), p. 243.
645. Art. 5 FD EEW.
646. Art. 2(c) FD EEW.
647. For a critical stance on this, cf. Gleß, *StV*, 24 (2004), 679, 681; Leutheusser-Schnarrenberger, *StraFo*, 20 (2007), 269, 271; Roger, *GA*, 157 (2010), 27, 34; ECPI, *ZIS*, 8 (2013), 442.
648. Art. 11(4) FD EEW.
649. Art. 11(5) FD EEW.
650. Cf. Art. 18(1) and (2) FD EEW.
651. Roger, *GA*, 157 (2010), 41; for a critical stance on the FD on Freezing, Krüßmann, *Transnationales Strafprozessrecht* (2009), p. 601; cf. also Gleß, in Sieber, Satzger and von Heinegg, *Europäisches Strafrecht* (2014), pp. 690–1; Mavany, *Die europäische Beweisanordnung* (2012), pp. 72 ff., 145 ff.; critically, Hauck, in Böse, *Europäisches Strafrecht* (2013), p. 438. On legal remedies in cases of legal assistance in Germany, cf. OLG Dresden, No OLG Ausl. 74/10, Decision (30 November 2010), in *StV*, 31 (2011), 430; crit. also ECPI, *ZIS*, 8 (2013), 442. On legal remedies, cf. also Vermeulen, *Free Gathering and Movement of Evidence* (2011), pp. 21–2.
652. Art. 18(1) second sentence FD EEW.
653. Cf. Ambos, *Beweisverwertungsverbote* (2010), pp. 81 ff.; Roger, *GA*, 157 (2010), 42; Claverie-Rousset, *EuCLR*, 2 (2012), 158, 162–3; Mavany, *Die europäische Beweisanordnung* (2012), pp. 93, 159 ff.
654. COM (2001) 715 final, 7 ff.; on this cf. Ambos, *Internationales Strafrecht* (2011), §13 mn. 19 ff.; Stiegel, *ZRP*, 36 (2003), 175; Hecker, *Europäisches Strafrecht* (2015), §14 mn. 38 ff.
655. On the basics of this, cf. Sieber, *ZStW*, 103 (1991), 963; Sieber, *ZRP*, 33 (2000), 190; also Gleß, *ZStW*, 115 (2003), 136 ff.; Wolter, in Wolter et al., *Festgabe Hilger* (2003), p. 277.
656. Chapter 1, mn. 26–7 and, in this chapter, mn. 77.
657. Chiavario, *RIDPP*, 48 (2005), 987; and Bachmaier Winter, *ZIS*, 5 (2010), 587–8, are rightly sceptical of the feasibility of this. However, cf. the EU Model Rules developed in the meantime, available at www.eppo-project.eu/index.php/EU-model-rules, last accessed 27 January 2018.
658. On this, cf. Biehler et al., *Criminal-Law Protection of the Financial Interests of the Community* (2002), p. 29; Gleß, *ZStW*, 115 (2003), 148 ff. (on her further proposal, cf. Ambos, *Internationales Strafrecht* (2008), §12 mn. 57c); Radtke, *GA*, 151 (2004), 19–20; Braum, *ZRP*, 35 (2002), 513; Tiedemann, in Arnold, *FS Eser* (2005), pp. 894 ff.; Brüner and Hetzer, *NStZ*, 23 (2003), 117–18; Hecker, *Europäisches Strafrecht* (2015), §12 mn. 68; Roger, *GA*, 157 (2010), 32–3; Claverie-Rousset, *EuCLR*, 2 (2012), 156, 164 ff.; on the positive effect on the (further) harmonisation of criminal procedural law, cf. Catalano, *DPP*, 13 (2007), 529–30; Gaede, *ZStW*, 115 (2003), 876–7, is sceptical, favouring the creation of a 'self-contained European constitutional criminal procedural law'.
659. COM (2009) 624 final; cf. also the references in n. 118 above.

660. COM (2009) 624 final, p. 4.
661. Cf. also Zeder, *EuR*, 47 (2012), 38: 'It should be criticised that the regulations are complicated and casuistic and moreover diverge on analogue objects of regulation' (orig. 'Zu kritisieren ist . . . dass . . . Regelungen kompliziert und kasuistisch sind und überdies zu analogen Regelungsgegenständen voneinander abweichen'); Claverie-Rousset, *EuCLR*, 2 (2012), 152–3; cf. also *eucrim*, 6 (2011), 68–9; and Rackow, in Ambos, *Europäisches Strafrecht post-Lissabon* (2011), p. 119.
662. For a critical stance on this, cf. Ambos, *ZIS*, 5 (2010), 558 incl. further references.
663. For a basic account of the problem of using evidence in transnational criminal proceedings, cf. Krüßmann, *Transnationales Strafprozessrecht* (2009), pp. 333 ff., 628 ff.
664. Cf. e.g. Busemann, *ZIS*, 5 (2010), 552 ff.; Ambos, *ZIS*, 5 (2010), 557 ff.; Allegrezza, *ZIS*, 5 (2010), 569 ff.; Spencer, in *ZIS*, 5 (2010), 602 ff.; all incl. further references.
665. Directive 2014/41/EU (OJ L 130 of 1 May 2014, 1); on this cf. Klimek, *Mutual Recognition* (2017), pp. 421 ff. At the date of writing (January 2018) 16 MS (Belgium, Croatia, Estonia, Finland, France, Germany, Greece, Hungary, Italy, Latvia, Lithuania, Malta, the Netherlands, Portugal, Slovakia and the UK) have communicated national implementing measures to the European Commission; cf. www.ejn-crimjust.europa.eu/ejn/EJN_Library_StatusOfImpByCat.aspx?CategoryId=120, last accessed 27 January 2018. Germany introduced §§91a -98e IRG on 5 January 2017 (*BGBl.* I 2017, p. 31), transposing the EIO into national law; thereto Rackow, *KriPoZ*, 2 (2017), 79 ff., who notes that the changes made by the EIO could also have been achieved by reforming the Convention on Mutual Assistance in Criminal Matters (at 87); see also Jähnke and Schramm, *Europäisches Strafrecht* (2017), §6 mn. 44 (welcoming the German implementation); Brahms and Gut, *NStZ*, 37 (2017), 388 ff.

For the **first proposal**, cf. Belgium et al., *Directive Initiative EIO* (2010), Council Document 9145/10. This proposal was broadly supported by the Commission; the Council adopted the joint proposal on 21 December 2011 (Council Document 18918/11). On the proposal, cf. Rackow and Birr, *GoJIL*, 2 (2010), 1110 ff.; Brand, *DRiZ*, 88 (2010), 317; Burchard, in Beck, Burchard and Fateh-Moghadam, *Strafrechtsvergleichung* (2011), pp. 278 ff.; Ahlbrecht, *StV*, 33 (2013), 114 ff.; cf. also the statements of the German Judges Association (DRiB) Nos 29/10, 59/10 and 27/11, available at www.drb.de/stellungnahmen.html, last accessed 27 January 2018; crit. Heydenreich, *StraFo*, 25 (2012), 442–3; generally crit. of the EIO as premature, as no experience with the EEW has been gained as yet, Zimmermann, Glaser and Motz, *EuCLR*, 1 (2011), 70.

On the **actual directive**, cf. Böse, *ZIS*, 9 (2014), 152 ff., concluding that the novelty of the directive is its standardised and accelerated procedure, but that it still does not fully meet the challenge of granting adequate defence rights in the framework of its transnational procedure (163–4); in the same vein, Belfiore, *EuCLR*, 5 (2015), 313 ff. ('flexible' and 'comprehensive system' but the 'fair balance between efficient legal assistance and the respect of individual rights has been disregarded', 324); Bachmaier, *eucrim*, 10 (2015), 47 ff. ('very positive to have a single instrument', but 'the defence still does not have the same opportunities to challenge transnational and national evidence', 56, 58); Schuster, *StV*, 35 (2015), 393 ff. (concluding that, while providing for an accelerated, standardised procedure, the directive maintains the protective mechanism of traditional mutual assistance, 398–9); Daniele, *NJECL*, 6 (2015), 179 ff.

(arguing that the directive while, sticking to a traditional horizontal approach to evidence gathering, has 'operative implications' that may change the structure of national evidentiary provisions, 'turning many of them from rigid "rules" into flexible "principles"', 180; see also 184–5); Zimmermann, *ZStW*, 127 (2015), 143 ff. (with an overall positive assessment at 174–5: 'very flexible instrument', better balancing of opposing interests than previous instruments, 'model'); Ronsfeld, *Rechtshilfe, Anerkennung und Vertrauen* (2015), pp. 126 ff.; from a rights perspective, crit. Armada, *NJECL*, 6 (2015), 9 ff. (focusing on the right to privacy); also from a rights perspective and with regard to the Italian law, Ruggeri, *ZIS*, 10 (2015), 456 ff.; from a language perspective, Camaldo, in Ruggieri, *Languages* (2014), pp. 204–5, 209–11, 212–13.

666. Cf. Art. 3 and also recitals 7 and 8 of the EIO Directive; on JITs, see already above, mn. 4. For a critical stance on this, cf. Vermeulen, *Free Gathering and Movement of Evidence* (2011), pp. 33 ff.; from the point of view of data protection, European Data Protection Supervisor, *eucrim*, 5 (2010), 146; also Ahlbrecht, *StV*, 33 (2013), 117; Heydenreich, *StraFo*, 25 (2012), 444; for a comparison of the EIO and JITs from a practical perspective, Zaharieva, *ERA Forum*, 18 (2017), 397 ff. (stressing the advantages of JITs regarding the participation of non-EU MS and the 'common investigative environment' (406)).

667. Cf. recital 9 EIO Directive; on Art. 40 CISA, see already above, mn. 5 with n. 27.

668. In the same vein, Böse, *ZIS*, 9 (2014), 152 ff.; Zimmermann, *ZStW*, 127 (2015), 148, 174; Armada, *NJECL*, 6 (2015), 9 ('comprehensive system'); Ruggeri, *ZIS*, 10 (2015), 461; Belfiore, *EuCLR*, 5 (2015), 316, 324; Bachmaier, *eucrim*, 10 (2015), 47; crit. Huybreghts, *ERA Forum*, 16 (2015), 390 (simplification 'failed'). But note that **Ireland** and **Denmark** opted out of the directive, while it applies – subject to the Brexit negotiations – to the **UK**; cf. recitals 44 (for Ireland), 45 (for Denmark) and 43 (for the UK) EIO Directive; thereon also Huybreghts, *ERA Forum*, 16 (2015), 391.

669. In the same vein, Böse, *ZIS*, 9 (2014), 163–4; Schuster, *StV*, 35 (2015), 398–9; Daniele, *NJECL*, 6 (2015), 179, 180.

670. Art. 4(b), (c) EIO Directive. The application regarding tax and customs offences also follows *e contrario* from Art. 11(3). Critically, taking aspects of proportionality into account, Zimmermann, Glaser and Motz, *EuCLR*, 1 (2011), 70–1; from the perspective of procedural economy, Rackow, in Ambos, *Europäisches Strafrecht post-Lissabon* (2011), p. 125.

671. Art. 2(c)(ii) EIO Directive. This includes general administrative authorities, including the police (as already noted by Rackow and Birr, *GoJIL*, 2 (2010), 1112, on the first draft; cf. also Erbežnik, *EuCLR*, 2 (2012), 6–7; Vermeulen, *Free Gathering and Movement of Evidence* (2011), pp. 13 ff.; in favour of this 'broad definition of "issuing authority"', Bachmaier, *eucrim*, 10 (2015), 48–9 ('strike[s] the right balance between eficiency and respect for the diversity of the different legal orders involved in the judicial cooperation', albeit recognising that 'its implementation is not devoid of problems'); critically, Heydenreich, *StraFo*, 25 (2012), 443; Zimmermann, Glaser and Motz, *EuCLR*, 1 (2011), 74; Rackow, in Ambos, *Europäisches Strafrecht post-Lissabon* (2011), pp. 126 ff.). According to a Commission survey (*eucrim*, 5 (2010), 145), only five MS had the intention to give administrative authorities the competence to issue an EIO (Austria, Finland, Lithuania, Slovenia and Sweden).

672. Art. 2(c)(ii) EIO Directive. On this, cf. ECPI, *ZIS*, 8 (2013), 442. On judicial discretion in mutual recognition in general, cf. Weyembergh, in Ligeti, *Prosecutor for the EU*, i (2013), pp. 945 ff.

673. Cf. Böse, *ZIS*, 9 (2014), 158 (validation 'no equivalent substitute for judge's reservation', orig. 'kein gleichwertiger Ersatz für einen Richtervorbehalt'); crit. also Ruggeri, *ZIS*, 10 (2015), 462. On the maintenance of the judge's reservation in the national (German) implementation of the directive, cf. Zimmermann, *ZStW*, 127 (2015), 168; on differentiating between 'gerichtlicher und justizieller' decision in the issuing procedure, Ronsfeld, *Rechtshilfe, Anerkennung und Vertrauen* (2015), pp. 138 ff., according to whom the responsibility for reviewing the condition for issuing the EIO lies with the judge (at 145).
674. Böse, *ZIS*, 9 (2014), 153.
675. Cf. Art. 2(d) second sentence EIO Directive ('court authorisation'). Schuster, *StV*, 35 (2015), 396, sees no problem with a 'judge reservation' as provided for in German law.
676. Cf. Armada, *NJECL*, 6 (2015), 13 (taking police execution in the UK as an example).
677. Therefore crit. Armada, *NJECL*, 6 (2015), 11–13, 31.
678. Art. 1(3) EIO Directive. Thus, in civil law (judge-led) proceedings this right would follow from the right to request the gathering of certain evidence ('Beweisantragsrecht', cf. §244(3)–(6) StPO; thereon Schuster, *StV*, 35 (2015), 394).
679. Art. 12(3), (4) EIO Directive. Crit. of the 30-day recognition limit of Art. 12(3), Camaldo, in Ruggieri, *Languages* (2014), p. 208.
680. Art. 9(2) EIO Directive. This, of course, implies that the executing authority has some knowledge of the law of the issuing State; on this problem of *Fremdrechtsanwendung* ('application of foreign law') see previously Ambos, *ZIS*, 5 (2010), 561; regarding the EIO, cf. Ruggeri, *ZIS*, 10 (2015), 462.
681. Cf. already above, mn. 81; and in this context, Zimmermann, Glaser and Motz, *EuCLR*, 1 (2011), 71 ff.; Vermeulen, *Free Gathering and Movement of Evidence* (2011), pp. 41 ff.; also Gleß, *ZStW*, 125 (2013), 590; Zerbes, *EuCLR*, 5 (2015), 309–11 ('compromise between coherence of the entire procedure and the protection of essential rights'); Rackow, in Ambos, *Europäisches Strafrecht post-Lissabon* (2011), pp. 133–4; Böse, *ZIS*, 9 (2014), 152; Armada, *NJECL*, 6 (2015), 19–21 (correctly arguing, at 20–1, that the forum rule is, in principle, incompatible with mutual recognition since this principle implies that the forum State accepts the measures taken in the executing State under the *locus regit actum rule*); the latter point is also made by Ruggeri, *ZIS*, 10 (2015), 462.
682. Cf. Böse, *ZIS*, 9 (2014), 153–4.
683. In this sense, Art. 9(2) EIO Directive reaffirms the general principle that the requested State's non-compliance with conditions imposed by the requesting State pursuant to international (or European) law may entail an exclusion of the relevant evidence in the latter; cf. Schuster, *ZIS*, 11 (2016), 568; generally on exclusionary rules pursuant to violations of international law, Ambos, *Beweisverwertungsverbote* (2010), pp. 85 ff.
684. Cf. esp. recitals 12 and 18 EIO Directive.
685. Cf. Zimmermann, *ZStW*, 127 (2015), 150–1; Bachmaier, *eucrim*, 10 (2015), 55.
686. On the ambiguous and controversial meaning of this reservation clause in Art. 9(2) EIO Directive, cf. Armada, *NJECL*, 6 (2015), 21.
687. For a different view, Ruggeri, *ZIS*, 10 (2015), 462 (arguing that the executing authority even has to apply procedural rules of the issuing State if they interfere with individual rights, but this interpretation would almost certainly give rise to a

conflict with the executing State's fundamental principles and is therefore to be rejected). See also Ronsfeld, *Rechtshilfe, Anerkennung und Vertrauen* (2015), p. 161, who sees deadlines and mutual recognition as having a cumulative effect leading to the acceleration and increased efficiency of mutual assistance.

688. See also Schuster, *ZIS*, 11 (2016), 565.
689. Arts. 10, 11 EIO Directive.
690. See generally on Art. 10 Zimmermann, *ZStW*, 127 (2015), 162 ff. (welcoming it as a positive novelty which dismisses 'automatic' recognition).
691. Art. 10(1) EIO Directive.
692. On the non-coercive character of these measures, cf. Armada, *NJECL*, 6 (2015), 17 with n. 49.
693. Cf. 10(2) EIO Directive (e.g. hearing of witness, expert, victim, suspected or accused person, any non-coercive investigative measure, identification of persons by certain means). Crit. Böse, *ZIS*, 9 (2014), 155–6 (while generally not very invasive measures, protection may still be lowered compared to national law); also crit. Belfiore, *EuCLR*, 5 (2015), 320–1, 324 (no 'clear-cut distinction between coercive and non-coercive measures'); Zimmermann, *ZStW*, 127 (2015), 163 (considering this as a 'hidden' harmonisation obligation outside the framework of Art. 82(2)(d) TFEU, but this is unconvincing since the Council and the EP are in their rights to harmonise *via* specific directives; apart from that, harmonisation is necessary to make mutual recognition instruments more effective; see thereon below, n. 731 with main text).
694. Art. 10(3) EIO Directive; crit. of the optional ('may') character of the provision, Armada, *NJECL*, 6 (2015), 17.
695. See above, n. 534. In this context, see also Böse, *ZIS*, 9 (2014), 158; Zimmermann, *ZStW*, 127 (2015), 164; Depauw, *EuCLR*, 6 (2016), 86 ff.; Belfiore, *EuCLR*, 5 (2015), 318–19; Bachmaier, *eucrim*, 10 (2015), 51–2.
696. Cf. Art. 11(1)(f) EIO Directive; see also Art. 14(2) referring to the 'fundamental rights in the executing State' and thus making clear they have in any case ('without prejudice') to be observed.
697. See already main text above, mn. 71.
698. Cf. Art. 6(3) in connection with Art. 6(1)(a) EIO Directive.
699. In the same vein, Böse, *ZIS*, 9 (2014), 158; Bachmaier, *eucrim*, 10 (2015), 52; for a more restrictive interpretation stressing that the final decision is taken by the issuing authority, Armada, *NJECL*, 6 (2015), 15–16, but ultimately also finding that the executing authority may review proportionality by way of 'other mechanisms' (p. 16) and even arguing that the wide discretion inherent in the proportionality test may entail that it replaces the assessment of the issuing authority (p. 30).
700. Cf. also Zimmermann, Glaser and Motz, *EuCLR*, 1 (2011), 69; Gleß, in Böse, *Europäisches Strafrecht* (2013), pp. 626–7; Ruggeri, *ZStW*, 125 (2013), 416 ff.; Böse, *ZIS*, 9 (2014), 153; Schuster, *StV*, 35 (2015), 396; Daniele, *NJECL*, 6 (2015), 186–7, 189–90.
701. Main text above, mn. 71.
702. Art. 6(1)(b) EIO Directive.
703. Cf. Böse, *ZIS*, 9 (2014), 153; Armada, *NJECL*, 6 (2015), 18; for an early participation of the suspect/the defence to avoid forum shopping, Anagnostopoulos, *ERA Forum*, 15 (2014), 14; expressing doubts as to the practical importance of forum

shopping, Träskman, *EuCLR*, 5 (2015), 63–4; on the problem of forum shopping with regard to Art. 7 ECHR, see already Chapter 2, mn. 127 *in fine*.

704. Art. 10(5) EIO Directive.
705. On the lack of availability as a 'hidden' ground for refusal separate from those set out in Article 10 and based on the application of the principle of proportionality previously (on the draft Directive), see also Mangiaracina, *ULR*, 10, 1 (2014), 127–8.
706. Cf. recital 10 EIO Directive, referring to lawful availability 'in certain situations, for example where the investigative measure can only be carried out for offences of a certain degree of seriousness, against persons for whom there is already a certain level of suspicion or with the consent of the person concerned'. Thereon also Zimmermann, *ZStW*, 127 (2015), 164–7; Bachmaier, *eucrim*, 10 (2015), 53–4.
707. On further problems of delimitation, cf. Böse, *ZIS*, 9 (2014), 156–7.
708. Art. 11 EIO Directive; thereon Thunberg Schunke, *EuCLR*, 5 (2015), 52 ('encouraging development'); Zimmermann, *ZStW*, 127 (2015), 152 ff. (critical of their facultative nature, at 153); equally crit. of the facultative nature of the grounds for refusal and distinguishing between three groups (traditional obstacles, Union minimum standards and obstacles derived from the law of the issuing State), Böse, *ZIS*, 9 (2014), 154 ff.
709. Thereon main text, mn. 102.
710. For a critical stance on this, cf. ECPI, *ZIS*, 8 (2013), 443; Zimmermann, Glaser and Motz, *EuCLR*, 1 (2011), 78 ff. Böse, in Ambos, *Europäisches Strafrecht post-Lissabon* (2011), pp. 61 ff., is generally critical of the different ways the principle of mutual recognition is implemented in the different legislative acts.
711. Art. 11(1)(b) EIO Directive.
712. Zimmermann, Glaser and Motz, *EuCLR*, 1 (2011), 69 ('bit outmoded').
713. Crit. on the draft, Ahlbrecht, *StV*, 33 (2013), 117. Critically, as national laws have only been harmonised to a small degree, Zimmermann, Glaser and Motz, *EuCLR*, 1 (2011), 75–6; cf. also Ouwerkerk, *Mutual Recognition* (2011), p. 113.
714. Thus the execution may be refused in case of opposing immunities or privileges (Art. 11(1)(a) EIO Directive), a violation of *ne bis in idem* (Art. 11(1)(d)), a limitation of the respective investigative measure to certain (catalogue) offences in the executing State, none of which is included in the respective EIO (Art. 11(1)(h); on this, cf. Vermeulen, *Free Gathering and Movement of Evidence* (2011), pp. 32–3.
715. On the genesis, especially the FRA's role, Armada, *NJECL*, 6 (2015), 25.
716. In a similar vein, Zimmermann, *ZStW*, 127 (2015), 157–8 (yet critical of the implicit limitations); also Daniele, *NJECL*, 6 (2015), 183–4 (quoting several provision referring to fundamental rights, e.g. Art. 1(4), 14(7)) and 190 ff. (examing the directive with a view to the right of confrontation regarding witnesses and the right to privacy); while ultimately welcoming this ground still generally critical because of shortcomings with regard to the right to privacy, Armada, *NJECL*, 6 (2015), 9, 11, 24–7, 31 (calling for a procedural legality requirement in the sense of the ECtHR's case law at 18–19, 22); for Bachmaier, *eucrim*, 10 (2015), 54, this provision does not amount to a 'European ordre public clause', but 'it represents a specific safeguard for the protection of the fundamental rights in the AFSJ'; according to Ronsfeld, *Anerkennung, Rechtshilfe und Vertrauen* (2015), pp. 175 ff., a reservation based on fundamental rights is not necessary in principle; only obviously unlawful procedures constitute an

exception (at 177–8); generally crit. of the lack of sufficient guarantees, Camaldo, in Ruggieri, *Languages* (2014), p. 208; in favour of a general rights clause previously, Ruggeri, in Ruggieri, *Languages* (2014), p. 233.

717. Cf. Armada, *NJECL*, 6 (2015), 25–7.
718. Cf. Art. 11(4) EIO Directive; see also Armada, *NJECL*, 6 (2015), 27.
719. See also Zimmermann, *ZStW*, 127 (2015), 158–9.
720. Art. 11(1)(g) with Annex D EIO Directive. Cf. thereon Böse, *ZIS*, 9 (2014), 154; Zimmermann, *ZStW*, 127 (2015), 160–1 (esp. noting the replacement by *Diebstahl* with *Raub* in the German version of the offences catalogue); on the draft versions, cf. Bachmeier, *ZIS*, 5 (2010), 585; Rackow and Birr, *GoJIL*, 2 (2010), 1117; Ahlbrecht, *StV*, 33 (2013), 117; Heydenreich, *StraFo*, 25 (2012), 440–1; Vermeulen, *Free Gathering and Movement of Evidence* (2011), p. 32.
721. Arts. 22–9 EIO Directive.
722. Arts. 30, 31 EIO Directive.
723. Zimmermann, *ZStW*, 127 (2015), 170 ff.; Schuster, *StV*, 35 (2015), 394 ff. For a critical stance on the inclusion in the EIO, cf. Claverie-Rousset, *EuCLR*, 2 (2012), 155. Ruggeri, *ZStW*, 125 (2013), 425 ff., is also critical of the incoherent categorisation as 'coercive measures'.
724. Art. 14 (2) EIO Directive.
725. Cf. Art. 14(1) EIO Directive.
726. Cf. Art. 14(5) EIO Directive (emphasis added).
727. Cf. Art. 14(7) first sentence EIO Directive (emphasis added).
728. Critically on legal supervision by the executing State, Garcimartín Montero, *eucrim*, 12 (2017), 47–8 and 49.
729. See in this regard also Art. 9(4) EIO Directive, according to which the issuing authority may request to participate in the execution of the EIO; thereon Schuster, *StV*, 35 (2015), 394 (novelty).
730. Cf. Böse, *ZIS*, 9 (2014), 153, 157; also, more generally, Zimmermann, *ZStW*, 127 (2015), 169; Schuster, *StV*, 35 (2015), 394.
731. Cf. Böse, *ZIS*, 9 (2014), 157–8 (especially referring to the different degrees of suspicion in MS necessary to issue investigation measures within the meaning of the EIO Directive); crit. of the directive's lack of harmonisation, Camaldo, in Ruggieri, *Languages* (2014), p. 208.
732. Crit. also Heydenreich, *StraFo*, 25 (2012), 439 ff.; Schuster, *StV*, 35 (2015), 398 ('little transparent'); see also the similar criticism voiced on the FD EEW, above, mn. 84.
733. Calling for 'enhanced protection' and 'appropriate universal due process standards' to be put in place generally in transnational investigations, Vogler, in Ruggieri, *Transnational Inquiries* (2013), p. 39; calling for 'multinational defence teams' or 'double defence', Böse, *ZIS*, 9 (2014), 160; in a similar vein, Thunberg Schunke, *EuCLR*, 5 (2015), 52–3 ('perspective must be on the *transnational setting*', emphasis in the original); Löfgren, *EuCLR*, 5 (2015), 57 ('EU defence organisation'); Belfiore, *EuCLR*, 5 (2015), 321–3, 324 ('enhancing the role of the accused in criminal proceedings having a cross-border dimension. Even if the accused persons and defence lawyers are taken into consideration *expressis verbis* in the EIO Directive, their chances to benefit from legal assistance and be part of it are minimal and only occasional'); Bachmaier, *eucrim*, 10 (2015), 57–8 ('a mechanism to grant an efficient transnational defence'); also Armada, *NJECL*, 6

(2015), 29; in favour of a participation of private parties to enhance the defence Ruggeri, in Ruggieri, *Languages* (2014), p. 232.

734. Art. 14 (7) first sentence EIO Directive, as quoted a moment ago in the main text.
735. See for such a concentration Böse, *ZIS*, 9 (2014), 160; Camaldo, in Ruggieri, *Languages* (2014), p. 208.
736. Cf. Böse, *ZIS*, 9 (2014), 160–1. In detail on the EIO from the perspective of fundamental rights, Garcimartín Montero, *eucrim*, 12 (2017), 45 ff., who sees a tension between the effective handling of evidence on the basis of the principle of mutual recognition and rights protection.
737. Thereon Böse, *ZIS*, 9 (2014), 161; Zimmermann, *ZStW*, 127 (2015), 170; Schuster, *StV*, 35 (2015), 398; apparently more cautiously Ruggeri, *ZIS*, 10 (2015), 463 (no exclusionary rule 'with certainty'); similarly Anagnostopoulos, *ERA Forum*, 15 (2014), 21 (no automatic admissibility of evidence in issuing State).
738. Cf. Böse, *ZIS*, 9 (2014), 161–3.
739. Above, mn. 89 with n. 683.
740. Cf. already above, mn. 81.
741. On the general rule, cf. Schuster, *Verwertbarkeit* (2006), pp. 29, 105; Schuster, *ZIS*, 11 (2016), 566–7; also Ambos, *Beweisverwertung* (2010), p. 81 with further references in n. 466; see also Art. 37 Regulation EPPO 2017; Chapter 5, mn. 29. This is also the position of national case law, see e.g. BGH, No 1 StR 310/12, Decision (21 November 2012), in *BGHSt*, 58, p. 32; Cour de cassation (France), No 02–85379, Chambre criminelle arrêt (23 October 2002) (free admission of foreign evidence in French courts; see esp. Art. 472 CPC). While in some MS the lawfulness of the foreign gathering of evidence, pursuant to the locus rule, is presumed (for Hungary, cf. Karsai, in Gropp et al., *Entwicklung von Rechtssystemen* (2014), pp. 160–1; for Spain, cf. Ormazábal Sánchez, *La Ley Penal*, 7 (2010), no 74, 32–4), the case law has normally not dealt with cases where this presumption could be problematic. Arguably, MS courts will not admit evidence if the admission were to (fundamentally) violate their legal order (see in this vein Art. 359a Dutch CPC providing in para 1(c) for a bar to prosecution where as a result of non-observance of procedural rules there can be no more fair trial, thereon District Court of The Hague (*Rechtbank's-Gravenhage*), No 09/748801-09 (English translation), Judgment (21 October 2011), 12 ff.; also Art. 587 Polish CPC: admission of foreign evidence if it 'does not conflict with the principles of the legal order in the Republic of Poland'; thereon Nita-Światlowska, in Hofmański, Szumiło-Kulczycka and Czarnecki, *Außerprozessuale Beweiserhebung* (2015), pp. 309 ff.; for Italy cf. Constitutional Court (Corte Costituzionale), No 379/1995, Sentenza (13 July 1995); and Ubertis, *CassP*, 54 (2014), 696 ff.; for Spain, cf. Ormazábal Sánchez, *La Ley Penal*, 7 (2010), no 74, 34–5, who himself advocates the forum rule in the absence of a harmonised procedural law, at 40–2).
742. Cf. BGH, 1 StR 310/12 (n. 741) (third guiding principle: the gathering of the evidence in and by an EU MS can only be subjected to a limited review of lawfulness by the forum MS (Germany), at least if it has not formally requested the gathering of this evidence); in the same vein, BGH, No 1 StR 39/14, Decision (9 April 2014), in *NStZ*, 34 (2014), 608; crit. Schuster, *ZIS*, 11 (2016), 571–3 (advocating a broader review by the forum State).
743. For a recent analysis of exclusionary rules from a German perspective, see Schuster, *ZIS*, 11 (2016), 566 ff. with further references (basically advocating an exclusion of

the respective evidence if (i) the requested State's gathering of evidence entails rights violations under its own law, (ii) the requested State fails to comply with conditions imposed by the requesting State based on international law and (iii) the use of the evidence in the requesting State, albeit lawful in the requested State, would violate fundamental individual/human rights in the former); previously Ambos, *Beweisverwertung* (2010), pp. 81 ff. with further references. See, with regard to the mutual assistance in customs offences in light of the new Regulation 2015/1525 (above, n. 16), Schulz, *eucrim*, 11 (2016), 60 (national criminal courts may not admit evidence gathered abroad in the framework of administrative proceedings); note that in case of criminal proceedings the EIO Directive applies from the start, above, n. 670 and main text.

744. Above, n. 72; summarised in Schomburg and Hackner, in Schomburg et al., *Internationale Rechtshilfe in Strafsachen* (2012), p. 886.
745. Kubiciel, in Ambos, König and Rackow, *Rechtshilferecht in Strafsachen* (2015), pp. 690–1.
746. Art. 3(1)(d) and (f), Art. 7 TransferC.
747. Arts. 8, 9 TransferC.
748. Art. 11(1)(c) TransferC; thereon BGH, No 4 ARs 9/13, Decision (13 January 2014), in *BGHSt*, 59, p. 136 (conversion of Japanese sentence pursuant to TransferC, which displaces German IRG).
749. Art. 9(3) TransferC; see also OLG Karlsruhe, No 2 Ws 224/11, Decision (24 November 2011), in *StV*, 32 (2012), 546; Kubiciel, in Ambos, König and Rackow, *Rechtshilferecht in Strafsachen* (2015), p. 699 ff.
750. Above, n. 73; summarised in Schomburg and Hackner, in Schomburg et al., *Internationale Rechtshilfe in Strafsachen* (2012), p. 886.
751. Art. 2 AP TransferC. On the definition of flight, cf. OLG Dresden, No Ausl. 184/10, Decision (9 June 2011), in *NStZ*, 32 (2012), 102; Kubiciel, in Ambos, König and Rackow, *Rechtshilferecht in Strafsachen* (2015), p. 692.
752. Art. 3 AP TransferC.
753. Art. 67 CISA.
754. Art. 69(1) CISA.
755. Above, n. 95.
756. A summary is provided in Schomburg and Hackner, in Schomburg et al., *Internationale Rechtshilfe in Strafsachen* (2012), p. 1477.
757. OJ C 216, 10 July 1998, 2.
758. EU, *Green Paper on Sanctions* (2004).
759. EU, *Green Paper on Sanctions* (2004), p. 2.
760. EU, *Green Paper on Sanctions* (2004), pp. 9–10; on *ne bis in idem*, see Chapter 2, mn. 165 ff.
761. EU, *Green Paper on Sanctions* (2004), p. 10.
762. EU, *Green Paper on Sanctions* (2004), p. 28. On this, cf. the FD European Enforcement Order to be dealt with in the main text, mn. 99.
763. EU, *Green Paper on Sanctions* (2004), pp. 26 ff. and Annexes I–III.
764. Cf. Joint Action 8/733/JHA of 21 December 1998 on making it a criminal offence to participate in a criminal organisation in the Member States of the European Union (OJ L 351 of 29 December 1998, 1).
765. EU, *Green Paper on Sanctions* (2004), pp. 51 ff.
766. EU, *Green Paper on Sanctions* (2004), p. 52.

767. EU, *Green Paper on Sanctions* (2004), p. 52.
768. EU, *Green Paper on Sanctions* (2004), pp. 54–5.
769. EU, *Green Paper on Sanctions* (2004), pp. 57 ff.
770. Council FD 2008/909/JHA of 27 November 2008 on the application of the principle of mutual recognition to judgments in criminal matters imposing custodial sentences or measures involving deprivation of liberty for the purpose of their enforcement in the European Union (OJ L 327 of 5 December 2008, 27); amended by FD 2009/299/JHA (OJ L 81 of 27 March 2009, 24); on this, cf. Brodowski, *ZIS*, 12 (2017), 23–4; Morgenstern, in Böse, *Europäisches Strafrecht* (2013), pp. 592–8; Jähnke and Schramm, *Europäisches Strafrecht* (2017), §8 mn. 6 ff.; Klimek, *Mutual Recognition* (2017), pp. 261 ff.; Hüttemann, *StV*, 36 (2016), 519 ff. (focusing on the German implementation with an overall positive assessment despite concerns with regard to an effective protection of the rights of the sentenced person); on the draft FD, cf. Morgenstern, *ZIS*, 3 (2008), 76 ff.
771. On the status of implementation, see https://www.ejn-crimjust.europa.eu/ejn/EJN_Library_StatusOfImpByCat.aspx?CategoryId=36, last accessed 27 January 2018. Many MS did not comply with this deadline. In Germany, for example, it was only implemented on 11 July 2015, *BGBl.* I 2015, p. 1349 (introducing §§84–84n IRG); in detail on the procedure with Germany as executing State, cf. Hüttemann, *StV*, 36 (2016), 520 ff. At the time of writing (27 January 2018) the FD has been implemented in all Member States, with the exception of Bulgaria. If a MS has stated pursuant to Art. 18(2) sentence 1 FD EEO that it is not applying the FD to final judgments issued by 5 December 2011 at the latest, the law only applies to such previous *final* decisions (CJEU, *Van Vemde*, No C-582/15 (ECLI:EU:C:2017:37), Judgment (25 January 2017), paras. 27 ff.).
772. Cf. recital 9 and Arts. 3(1), 4(2) EEO; also Hüttemann, *StV*, 36 (2016), 519, 521.
773. Cf. Morgenstern, *ZIS*, 3 (2008), 76 ff.; Plachta, in Jareborg, *Double Criminality* (1989), pp. 84, 96 incl. further references.
774. Report from the Commission to the EP and the Council on the implementation by the Member States of the FD 2008/909/JHA, 2008/947/JHA and 2009/829/JHA on the mutual recognition of judicial decisions on custodial sentences or measures involving deprivation of liberty, on probation decisions and alternative sanctions and on supervision measures as an alternative to provisional detention, COM (2014) 57 final, 5 February 2014, p. 5.
775. On the practical relevance see also Hüttemann, *StV*, 36 (2016), 519 ff.
776. Art. 3(2) EEO.
777. See also Hüttemann, *StV*, 36 (2016), 520.
778. Cf. Art. 4(2), (5) first sentence EEO; see also Hüttemann, *StV*, 36 (2016), 520.
779. Art. 4(5) second sentence EEO.
780. Cf. Art. 9 EEO; e.g. the *ne bis in idem* principle is violated (Art. 9(1)(c)), or the person's immunity or age constitutes an obstacle (subparas. (f), (g)); thereon also Hüttemann, *StV*, 36 (2016), 525–6 (crit. of the lack of a clear system of Art. 9 EEO). Art. 9(1)(i) has been amended by Art. 5 of FD 2009/299/JHA.
781. Art. 3(1) EEO.
782. Art. 17 EEO. Note, however, that the issuing State may still grant an amnesty or pardon or decide on a review of the respective judgment, Art. 19 EEO; thereon also Hüttemann, *StV*, 36 (2016), 528–9; on taking into account specific enforcement rules of the issuing State, ibid., 527–8.

783. Art. 4(1)(a,b), recital 17 EEO.
784. Art. 4(1)(c) EEO.
785. Art. 4(3) second sentence, Art. 6(1) EEO. In turn, the consent of the sentenced person is not required if enforcement shall be transferred to his State of nationality/residence or to which she will be deported pursuant to an expulsion or deportation order or to which she has fled or otherwise returned, Art. 6(2) EEO; crit. Mitsilegas, *EU Criminal Law* (2016), pp. 220–3 ('maximum automaticity' which 'disregards any consequences of an enforced transfer for the right to private and family life').
786. Art. 4(2) EEO.
787. Above, mn. 50.
788. Art. 7(1) EEO.
789. Art. 7(4) EEO. In this context, the CJEU set a precedent with its decision that double criminality – to the extent that a MS can use it as grounds not to carry out an enforcement order pursuant to Art. 7(3), Art. 9(1)(d) FD EEO – must also be seen as fulfilled 'where the factual elements underlying the offence . . . would also, per se, be subject to a criminal sanction in the territory of the executing State if they were present in that State' (CJEU, *Grundza*, No C-289/15 (ECLI:EU:C:2017:4), Judgment (11 January 2017), paras. 33 ff.); on this cf. Brodowski, *ZIS*, 12 (2017), 698.
790. Art. 18 EEO.
791. Art. 8 EEO.
792. Art. 17(2) EEO. If this means a one-to-one deduction (here, the French version is unclear: 'déduit *intégralement* la période de privation de liberté déjà subie', emphasis added), in regard to the otherwise customary flexible deduction according to the court's discretion (cf. e.g. §51(4) StGB), this would lead to an unequal treatment of EU and non-EU foreign nationals if the deprivation of liberty is credited more highly in non-EU States (crit. also Morgenstern, *ZIS*, 3 (2008), 81). Aside from this issue, the principle of mutual recognition would thus be used to feign an equality of detention conditions across the EU that does not correspond with reality (cf. EP, *Report on Prison Conditions in the European Union of 22 October 1998*, Parliamentary Document A4–0369/98, produced before the Union's enlargement to the East!). Cf. also the Commission's doubts in EU, *Green Paper on the Application of EU Criminal Justice Legislation in the Field of Detention* (14 June 2011), COM (2011) 327 final, pp. 5 ff.; and Mansell, *EuCLR*, 2 (2012), 41. A critical stance is also taken by Morgenstern, in Böse, *Europäisches Strafrecht* (2013), pp. 596–7. On the possibilities of deviation, cf. also Ouwerkerk, *Mutual Recognition* (2011), pp. 100 ff.
793. Cf. Art. 3(4) EEO.
794. FD 2005/214/JHA (OJ L 76 of 22 March 2005, 16); amended by FD 2009/299/JHA (OJ L 81 of 27 March 2009, 24). For more detail on this, cf. Karitzky and Wannek, *NJW*, 63 (2010), 3393 ff.; Hackner and Trautmann, *DAR*, 80 (2010), 71 ff.; Burhoff, *ZAP*, 22 (2010), *Fach 22*, 539 ff.; Schünemann and Roger, *ZIS*, 5 (2010), 515 ff.; Böse, *ZIS*, 5 (2010), 607 ff.; Bönke, *NZV*, 19 (2006), 19 ff.; Albrecht, *SVR*, 7 (2007), 361 ff.; Gleß, *Internationales Strafrecht* (2015), mn. 504; Gleß, in Sieber, Satzger and von Heinegg, *Europäisches Strafrecht* (2014), pp. 707 ff.; Johnson and Plötzgen-Kamradt, *eucrim*, 6 (2011), 33 ff.; Morgenstern, in Böse, *Europäisches Strafrecht* (2013), pp. 603–5; Miettinen, *Criminal Law and Policy in the EU* (2013), pp. 190–1; Jähnke and Schramm, *Europäisches Strafrecht* (2017), §8 mn. 21 ff.;

Klimek, *Mutual Recognition* (2017), pp. 331 ff. At the time of writing (27 January 2018), the FD 2005/214/JHA was implemented in 26 MS; the implementation process is ongoing in Ireland, while there is no notification from Greece; on the implementation, cf. Report from the Commission based on Article 20 of the Council FD 2005/214/JHA of 24 February 2005 on the application of the principle of mutual recognition to financial penalties, 22 December 2008, COM (2008) 888 final; General Secretariat of the Council, 'Implementation of Council FD 2005/214/JHA of 24 February 2005 on the application of the principle of mutual recognition to financial penalties: Information provided to the General Secretariat', 5 June 2015 Council Doc. 9667/15; on the implementation in Austria, cf. Pronebner, *DAR-Extra*, 80 (2010), 748 ff.; Johnson, *ZIS*, 8 (2013), 361 ff.

795. Cf. Art. 1(b) FD 2005/214/JHA; thereon Riedmeyer, *NZV*, 27 (2014), 20.
796. Cf. recital 4 FD 2005/214/JHA. For a critical stance on the application to road traffic offences, cf. Schünemann and Roger, *ZIS*, 5 (2010), 522–3. Besides the fine, the legal costs can also be claimed, but only if the trial ended with the issuing of a financial penalty and not a penalty involving deprivation of liberty; Johnson, *eucrim*, 8 (2013), 66.
797. According to Johnson, *ZIS*, 10 (2015), 121 ff., in Germany alone there are more than 40,000 requests (thereof 26,464 are incoming requests from MS) since the entry into force of the German implementation Act on 28 October 2010. In August 2016 the number of incoming requests amounted to 44,990 and outgoing ones to 25,792 (Dr C. Johnson, email to the author, 15 August 2016); for a detailed analysis of the respective case law, cf. Johnson, *SVR*, 16 (2016), 449 ff.
798. Art. 1(a)(i) FD 2005/214/JHA.
799. Art. 1(a)(ii), (iii) FD 2005/214/JHA.
800. See, for an example, Scholz, *VRR*, 6 (2014), 8–9 (Italian penalty by administrative authority for traffic offence).
801. Cf. Art. 4(2) FD 2005/214/JHA and the Annex. The certificate has been amended by Art. 3(3) FD 2009/299/JHA; therefore there exist currently two different certificates; cf. Johnson, *ZIS*, 10 (2015), 479.
802. Cf. Art. 4 FD 2005/214/JHA (with a special rule for the UK and Ireland in para. 7); thereon also Johnson, *ZIS*, 10 (2015), 478–9.
803. Art. 6 FD 2005/214/JHA. Crit. of the automatism in the execution, Riedmeyer, *NZV*, 27 (2014), 19.
804. See, in this vein, OLG Düsseldorf, No III-3 Ausl. 59/14, Decision (2 June 2015), in *ZIS*, 10 (2015), 477 (competent German authority must take information contained in the certificate as basis of its decision; cf. §87a no 2 IRG).
805. Art. 7 has been amended by Art. 3 FD 2009/299/JHA.
806. Art. 7(1) FD 2005/214/JHA. It is controversial how to interpret Art. 7(1)(f) according to which the execution may be refused if the person concerned cannot be held criminally liable in the executing State due to her age. Does this ground only limit execution regarding the age of criminal responsibility (in this vein, Johnson, *ZIS*, 10 (2015), 122–3) or may it be broadly read as showing the FD's consideration of the suspect's age in general, thereby accounting for the more lenient sanctions in the youth criminal law of some MS (in this vein, OLG Hamburg, No 1 Ws 69/14, Decision (10 September 2014), in *ZIS*, 10 (2015), 119, 121).
807. Art. 7(2)(h) FD 2005/214/JHA.

808. Cf. e.g. OLG Düsseldorf, III-3 Ausl. 59/14 (n. 804), where the execution of a Dutch penalty of €102 for a traffic offence (12 km/h above speed limit) involved, apart from the executing authority, five full-time judges (twice the single full-time judge at the Municipal Court and the three full-time judges of the Higher Regional Court in appeal).
809. Cf. Art. 3 FD 2005/214/JHA.
810. Crit. also Riedmeyer, *NZV*, 27 (2014), 21; on the legal situation in Austria and the even stricter one in the Netherlands and the ensuing right to refuse the execution in Germany, cf. Scholz, *VRR*, 6 (2014), 10–13.
811. For a critical stance on the implementation in some MS, which is restricted to criminal offences, cf. Johnson, *eucrim*, 8 (2013), 66–7. On owner liability, cf. KG, No 4 Ws 2/13 - 122 Ss 149/12, Decision (16 January 2013), in *NStZ*, 33 (2013), 603.
812. On the limits of mutual recognition, cf. among others FG Hamburg, *DAR*, 80 (2010), 281 ('It is not possible (at present) to enforce Austrian financial penalties as the driver is not named'); cf. also Gleß, in Sieber, Satzger and von Heinegg, *Europäisches Strafrecht* (2014), pp. 713–15; on the extended catalogue of (39) 'offences', cf. Klimek, *Mutual Recognition* (2017), pp. 393 ff.
813. These are: 'conduct which infringes road traffic regulations, including breaches of regulations pertaining to driving hours and rest periods and regulations on hazardous goods'; 'smuggling of goods'; 'infringements of intellectual property rights'; 'threats and acts of violence against persons, including violence during sport events'; 'criminal damage'; (petty) 'theft'; and 'offences established by the issuing State and serving the purpose of implementing obligations arising from instruments adopted under the EC Treaty or under Title VI of the EU Treaty'. On this, cf. also the declaration of Germany, BT-Drucks 17/1288, 24; thereon, cf. Schmidt, *NZWiSt*, 1 (2012), 97.
814. Art. 13 FD 2009/299/JHA. On scope and first practical experiences, cf. Johnson, *eucrim*, 8 (2013), 65, 67.
815. Act to Implement the FD 2005/214/JI of 8 July 2010, *BGBl.* I 2010, 1408, incorporated into §§87–87p IRG. On the deadline contrary to the FD in §98 IRG, cf. Trautmann, *NZV*, 24 (2011), 62; Trautmann and Hackner, in Schomburg et al., *Internationale Rechtshilfe in Strafsachen* (2012), p. 580. An overview of the implementation and first practical experiences can be found in Johnson, *eucrim*, 8 (2013), 65 ff.; highly critical, Schünemann and Roger, *ZIS*, 5 (2010), 515 ff., esp. 517 (Act should never have been passed; 'a Bundestag that felt itself to be the "lackey of Brussels"', orig. 'ein sich als "Lakai von Brüssel" fühlender Bundestag'); riposte by Böse, *ZIS*, 5 (2010), 607 (609: 'completely exaggerated', orig. 'völlig überzogen'); rejoinder by Schünemann, *ZIS*, 5 (2010), 735 ff.; for a relativising view Vogel, *JZ*, 67 (2012), 27.
816. §§87b, 87d IRG.
817. Cf. also Art. 7(2)(d) FD 2009/299/JHA.
818. On the advantages of a central authority, cf. Johnson, *eucrim*, 8 (2013), 66; in favour also Riedmeyer, *NZV*, 27 (2014), 19.
819. For more detail, cf. Schmidt, *NZWiSt*, 1 (2012), 96 ff. However, in practice the grounds for refusal are irrelevant; Johnson, *eucrim*, 8 (2013), 67.
820. §87b(3) No 9 IRG. This rule was deemed necessary as some MS set out the strict liability of the vehicle owner; on this, cf. Scholz, *VRR*, 6 (2014), 10–13; cf. also OLG Köln, No 2 SsRs 2/12, Decision (21 May 2012), in *NZV*, 25 (2012), 450; OLG

Düsseldorf, No III-3 AR 6/11, Decision (9 February 2012), in *ZIS*, 7 (2012), 78; AG Bochum, No 29 Gs 2/12, Decision (27 Feburary 2012), in *DAR*, 82 (2012), 222.

821. §87h IRG. On the (perceived) lack of legal remedies, Schünemann and Roger, *ZIS*, 5 (2010), 519–20.
822. Cf. BT-Drs. 17/1288, 17.
823. FD 2009/829/JHA (OJ L 294 of 11 November 2009, 20); for a detailed analysis, Morgenstern, *ZIS*, 9 (2014), 216 ff.; Klimek, *Mutual Recognition* (2017), pp. 393 ff.; see also Esser, in Joerden and Szwarc, *Europäisierung des Strafrechts* (2007), pp. 244 ff.; Kazele, *NJ*, 64 (2010), 1 ff.; also Satzger, *Europäisches und Internationales Strafrecht* (2016), §10 mn. 40; on the historical development, cf. Neveu, *NJECL*, 4 (2013), 134 ff.; on procedure, ibid., pp. 146 ff.
824. Art. 8 FD 2009/829/JHA.
825. Recital 3 FD 2009/829/JHA.
826. Cf. Art. 8 FD 2009/829/JHA, distinguishing between six measures which 'shall' be applied (e.g. information of change of residence, obligation to avoid certain localities and contact with specific persons, para. 1) and others which a MS may apply ('prepared to monitor', para. 2, e.g. obligation not to engage in specific activies); thereon Morgenstern, *ZIS*, 9 (2014), 223–5 (arguing that the 'obligation to undergo therapeutic treatment or treatment for addiction' violates the presumption of innocence, at 224). On the great number and great variety of supervision measures recognised in the various MS and the resulting problems of translation, cf. Flore et al., *Probation Measures and Alternative Sanctions* (2012), p. 3; Neveu, *NJECL*, 4 (2013), 143.
827. Recital 5 FD 2009/829/JHA.
828. Cf. e.g. the German ground for detention of 'risk of flight' (§112(2) No 2 StPO), which is indicated in particular when the person charged is resident abroad (Graf, in Hannich, *Karlsruher Kommentar StPO* (2013), §112 StPO mn. 21).
829. On available statistics, cf. Morgenstern, *ZIS*, 9 (2014), 216–19, 235 (table).
830. For an overall positive assessment, Morgenstern, *ZIS*, 9 (2014), 232–3 (complex measure but with potential to reduce pre-trial detention). By contrast, Heine, *Die Rechtsstellung des Beschuldigten* (2009), p. 152, takes a critical stance, claiming that the supervision order does not 'really create any added value for the accused' (orig. 'wirklichen Mehrwert für den Beschuldigten').
831. Cf. Morgenstern, *ZIS*, 9 (2014), 219–20 and *passim* (showing the differences in several MS, especially focusing on Austria).
832. See also Morgenstern, *ZIS*, 9 (2014), 225–7 (discussing issuing of EAW in case of non-compliance with ESO), 231–2 (possible net-widening effect).
833. This follows from the presumption of innocence and Art. 9(1) FD 2009/829/JHA; cf. Morgenstern, *ZIS*, 9 (2014), 228–9.
834. Cf. Art 2(2) FD 2009/829/JHA ('does not confer any right on a person'); for a critical discussion see Morgenstern, *ZIS*, 9 (2014), 229 (arguing that the proportionality of an ESO must also be examined in light of fundamental rights, especially Art. 5 ECHR); crit. regarding the suspect's lack of influence, also Neveu, *NJECL*, 4 (2013), 145–6.
835. Cf. Art. 19(5) FD 2009/829/JHA (referring to a remedy in the issuing MS) and the certificate annexed to the FD which shall accompany the decision of the issuing MS (Art. 10(1)) and which has to indicate whether a remedy was filed; for a discussion see Morgenstern, *ZIS*, 9 (2014), 230–1.

836. Cf. Arts. 12(2) and 20(2)(d) FD 2009/829/JHA.
837. Art. 19(3) FD 2009/829/JHA; thereon Morgenstern, *ZIS*, 9 (2014), 231.
838. Apart from the factually irrelevant difference in the offence of trade in organs, where the FD 2009/829/JHA includes the adjective 'human' before 'organs' also.
839. Art. 14 FD 2009/829/JHA.
840. Cf. Art. 14(4) FD 2009/829/JHA; thereon Morgenstern, *ZIS*, 9 (2014), 228.
841. FD 2008/675/JHA (OJ L 220 of 15 August 2008, 32); for an example with regard to a German/Polish case, cf. Hochmayr and Ligocki, *ZIS*, 11 (2016), 162–3; on the implementation in Germany, *BGBl.* I 2009, 3214; thereon BGH, No 5 StR 432/09, Decision (27 October 2010), in *NJW*, 63 (2010), 2677; on the recognition of criminal convictions from EU MS in the UK, see Mujuzi, *EuCLR*, 5 (2015), 87 ff.
842. Art. 1 FD 2008/675/JHA.
843. Art. 2 FD 2008/675/JHA.
844. FD 2008/947/JHA (OJ L 337 of 16 December 2008, 102); amended by FD 2009/299/JHA (OJ L 81 of 27 March 2009, 24); on this, cf. Staudigl and Weber, *NStZ*, 28 (2008), 17 ff.; Morgenstern, in Böse, *Europäisches Strafrecht* (2013), pp. 559–602; Klimek, *Mutual Recognition* (2017), pp. 303–4; crit. on the German implementation, because of the missed opportunity to make use of the FD's focus on resocialisation, Jähnke and Schramm, *Europäisches Strafrecht* (2017), § 8 mn. 14 ff.
845. Art. 1(3)(b) FD 2008/909/JHA.
846. Art. 1 FD 2008/947/JHA.
847. Recital 8 FD 2008/947/JHA.
848. Art. 4(1) FD 2008/947/JHA.
849. Art. 4(2) FD 2008/947/JHA.
850. Arts. 13, 14 FD 2008/947/JHA.
851. Art. 9(1) FD 2008/947/JHA.
852. Art. 9(3) FD 2008/947/JHA.
853. Art. 10 FD 2008/947/JHA.
854. Art. 11 FD 2008/947/JHA.

Chapter Bibliography

Ahlbrecht, H., 'Die Europäische Ermittlungsanordnung – oder: EU-Durchsuchung leicht gemacht', *StV*, 33 (2013), 114–20

'Europäische Haftbefehl im Interim', *eucrim*, 1 (2006), 39–44

'Freier Personenverkehr innerhalb der EU in Auslieferungssachen', *StV*, 25 (2005), 40–7

'Der Rahmenbeschluss-Entwurf der Europäischen Beweisanordnung', *NStZ*, 26 (2006), 70–5

Albers, P., 'Institutional Aspects Related to Mutual Trust between EU Member States', in Albers et al., 'Evaluation Framework' (2013), 32–55

'Results Survey Contact Points of the European Judicial Network in Criminal Matters', in Albers et al., 'Evaluation Framework' (2013), 302–17

Albert, J., and Merlin, J.-B., 'Is the EU Ready for Automatic Mutual Recognition . . . in the Fight Against Crime?', *eucrim*, 10 (2015), 60–4

Albrecht, F., 'Die grenzüberschreitende Verfolgung von Verkehrsverstößen: Ein Überblick', *SVR*, 7 (2007), 361–8

Albrecht, P.-A., 'Eine unabhängige Judikative als Gegengewicht zur Erosion europäischer Strafrechtsprinzipien?', *KritV*, 91 (2008), 39–56

Alexy, R., *Theorie der Grundrechte* (Frankfurt: Suhrkamp, 1986)

A Theory of Constitutional Rights, translation by J. Rivers (Oxford: Oxford University Press, 2002)

Allegrezza, S., 'Critical Remarks on the Green Paper on Obtaining Evidence from One Member State to Another and Securing Its Admissibility', *ZIS*, 5 (2010), 569–79

Allen, S., 'Non-state Actors and Non-refoulement: The Supreme Court's Decision in Zain Taj Dean', *EJIL:Talk!*, 28 July 2017, available at www.ejiltalk.org/non-state-actors-and-non-refoulement-the-supreme-courts-decision-in-zain-taj-dea, last accessed 21 November 2017.

Ambos, K., 'Der Fall des Julian Assange: Europäischer Haftbefehl versus diplomatisches Asyl', in Esser, R., et al., eds., *Festschrift für Hans-Heiner Kühne zum 70. Geburtstag* (Heidelberg et al.: C. F. Müller, 2013), 503–18

'Der Fall Pinochet und das anwendbare Recht', *JZ*, 54 (1999), 16–24

'Transnationale Beweiserlangung: 10 Thesen zum Grünbuch der EU-Kommission "Erlangung verwertbarer Beweise in Strafsachen aus einem anderen Mitgliedstaat"', *ZIS*, 5 (2010), 557–66

Ambos, K., and Bock, S., 'Europäischer Haftbefehl und Jurisdiktionskonflikte: Grenzenlose Strafverfolgung', *JuS*, 52 (2012), 437–42

Anagnostopoulos, I., 'Criminal Justice Cooperation in the EU after the First Few "Steps": A Defence View', *ERA Forum*, 15 (2014), 9–24

Anders, R. P., 'Straftheoretische Anmerkungen zur Verletztenorientierung im Strafverfahren', *ZStW*, 124 (2012), 374–410

Aquilina, K., 'Fighting Corruption in Malta and at European Union Levels', *eucrim*, 8 (2013), 61–4

Arangüena Fanego, C., 'La situación actual de la orden europea de detención y entrega', *RDP*, 20 (2007), 11–87

Armada, I., 'The EIO and the Lack of European Standards for Gathering Evidence', *NJECL*, 6 (2015), 8–31

Aubert, B., 'Droit de l'Union européenne', *RSC*, 77 (2012), 433–43

Bachmaier, L., 'Transnational Evidence: Towards the Transposition of Directive 2014/41 Regarding the European Investigation Order in Criminal Matters', *eucrim*, 10 (2015), 47–60

Bachmaier Winter, L., 'European Investigation Order for Obtaining Evidence in the Criminal Proceedings', *ZIS*, 5 (2010), 580–89

Baddenhausen, H., and Pietsch, J., 'Rahmenbeschlüsse der Europäischen Union', *DVBl.*, 120 (2005), 1562–6

Baier, H., 'Die Auslieferung von Bürgern der Europäischen Union an Staaten innerhalb und außerhalb der EU', *GA*, 148 (2001), 427–46

Barczak, T., 'Der verdeckte Einsatz ausländischer Polizisten in Deutschland: Rechtsrahmen, Rechtsprobleme und Reformbedarf', *StV*, 32 (2012), 182–89

Beauvais, P., 'Annex to the Country Report France: Statistics', in Albers et al., 'Evaluation Framework' (2013), 156–63

Beauvais, P., and Giannoulis, V., 'Country Report France', in Albers et al., 'Evaluation Framework' (2013), 106–55

Belfiore, R., 'Critical Remarks on the Proposal for a European Investigation Order and Some Considerations on the Issue of Mutual Admissibility of Evidence', in Ruggeri, S., ed., *Transnational Evidence and Multicultural Inquiries in Europe: Developments in EU Legislation and New Challenges for Human Rights-Oriented Criminal Investigations in Cross-border Cases* (Heidelberg et al: Springer, 2014), 91–105

'The European Investigation Order in Criminal Matters: Developments in Evidence-Gathering across the EU', *EuCLR*, 5 (2015), 312–24

Beltrán de Felipe, M., and Nieto Martín, A., 'Post 9/11 Trends in International Judicial Cooperation: Human Rights as a Constraint on Extradition in Death Penalty Cases', *JICJ*, 10 (2012), 581–604

Bem, K., 'The European Arrest Warrant and the Polish Constitutional Court Decision of 27 April 2005', in Guild, E., ed., *Constitutional Challenges to the European Arrest Warrant* (Nijmegen: Wolf Legal Publishers, 2006), 125–36

Bernardi, A., 'Le rôle du troisième pilier dans l'européanisation du droit pénal', *RSC*, 72 (2007), 713–37

Berni, G., 'Concorrenza del mandato, richieste di estradizione, obblighi internazionali ed il concorso di processi penali tra i vari Stati membri', in Acuña, R., *Il mandato di arresto europeo* (2004), 277–84

Biehler, A., Gleß, S., Parra, N., and Zeitler, H. E., *Criminal-Law Protection of the Financial Interests of the Community and the Establishment of a European Prosecutor: Analysis of the European Commission's Green Paper* (Luxemburg: European Parliament, 2002), at www.europarl.europa.eu/RegData/etudes/etudes/join/2003/319291/DG-4-JOIN_ET(2003)319291_EN.pdf, last accessed 27 January 2018

Billing, F., 'The Parallel between Non-removal of Asylum Seekers and Non-execution of a European Arrest Warrant on Human Rights Grounds: The CJEU Case of N. S. v. Secretary of State for the Home Department', *EuCLR*, 2 (2012), 77–91

Bjorge, E., and Williams, J. R., 'The Protean Principle of Proportionality: How Different Is Proportionality in EU Contexts?', *CLJ*, 75 (2016), 186–89

Blesgraaf, M., and Langbroek, P., 'Annex to the Country Report The Netherlands: Statistics', in Albers et al., 'Evaluation Framework' (2013), 200–11

Bock, S., 'Anmerkung: EuGH, Urteil v. 21. 10. 2010 – C-205/09 Eredics, Sápi'. *JZ*, 66 (2011), 469–71

'Das europäische Opferrechtspaket: Zwischen substantiellem Fortschritt und blindem Aktionismus', *ZIS*, 8 (2013), 201–11

'Opferrechte im Lichte europäischer Vorgaben', in Barton, S., and Kölbel, R., eds., *Ambivalenzen der Opferzuwendung des Strafrechts* (Baden-Baden: Nomos, 2012), 67–88

Böhm, K. M., 'Der Europäische Haftbefehl im Lichte des Grundsatzes der gegenseitigen Anerkennung und die praktische Umsetzung im nationalen Auslieferungsrecht', *StraFo*, 26 (2013), 177–83

'Das neue Europäische Haftbefehlsgesetz', *NJW*, 59 (2006), 2592–6

Bönke, D. O., 'Grenzüberschreitende Ahndung von Verkehrsverstößen', *NZV*, 19 (2006), 19–24

Böse, M., 'Anmerkung zu OLG Wien, Beschluss v. 11.9.2001 - 22 Ns 2/01', *NStZ*, 22 (2002), 670–2

'Comparative Overview of the Country Reports and Surveys', in Albers et al., 'Evaluation Framework' (2013), 334–62

'Die Ermittlung der "besten" Strafgewalt im Spannungsfeld von Strafanwendungsrecht und internationaler Zuständigkeit', in Zöller, M. A., Hilger, H., Küper, W., and Roxin, C., eds., *Gesamte Strafrechtswissenschaft in internationaler Dimension: Festschrift für Jürgen Wolter zum 70. Geburtstag am 7. September 2013* (Berlin: Duncker & Humblot, 2013), 1311–28

'Die Europäische Ermittlungsanordnung: Beweistransfer nach neuen Regeln? ', *ZIS*, 9 (2014), 152–64

'Der Grundsatz der gegenseitigen Anerkennung unter dem Vertrag von Lissabon', in Ambos, *Europäisches Strafrecht post-Lissabon* (2011), 57–75

Der Grundsatz der Verfügbarkeit von Informationen in der strafrechtlichen Zusammenarbeit der Europäischen Union (Göttingen: V & R Unipress et al., 2007)

'Legitimität des europäischen Kooperationsrechts: Menschenrechtliche Standards zwischen Freiheitsschutz und Effektivitätsdenken', in Tiedemann, K., Sieber, U., Satzger, H., Burchard, C., and Brodowski, D., eds., *Die Verfassung moderner Strafrechtspflege: Erinnerung an Joachim Vogel* (Baden-Baden: Nomos, 2016), 211–20

'The Pilot Project: The Principle of Proportionality and the European Arrest Warrant', in Albers et al., 'Evaluation Framework' (2013), 80–104

'Das Prinzip der gegenseitigen Anerkennung in der transnationalen Strafrechtspflege der EU', in Momsen, C., Bloy, R., and Rackow, P., eds., *Fragmentarisches Strafrecht: Beiträge zum Strafrecht, Strafprozessrecht und zur Strafrechtsvergleichung* (Frankfurt a.M.: Peter Lang, 2003), 233–50

'Der Rechtsstaat am Abgrund? Zur Skandalisierung des EU-Geldsanktionengesetzes', *ZIS*, 5 (2010), 607–13

'Recommendations on Making Proportionate Use of the European Arrest Warrant', in Albers et al., 'Evaluation Framework' (2013), 364–7

Böse, M., and Meyer, F., 'Die Beschränkung nationaler Strafgewalten als Möglichkeit zur Vermeidung von Jurisdiktionskonflikten in der Europäischen Union', *ZIS*, 6 (2011), 336–44

Böse, M., and Wahl, T., 'Country Report Germany', in Albers et al., 'Evaluation Framework' (2013), 212–67

Boucht, J., 'Cross-border Use of Police Powers within the EU: A Finnish, Norwegian and Swedish Perspective', *EuCLR*, 2 (2012), 203–35

Brahms, K., and Gut, T., 'Zur Umsetzung der RL EEA in das deutsche Recht: Ermittlungsmaßnahmen auf Bestellschein?', *NStZ*, 37 (2017), 388–95

Brand, T., '(Grundrechts-)Freie Fahrt für Beweisanordnungen?', *DRiZ*, 88 (2010), 317

Brandt, W., 'Verfassungsrecht in Polen: Verfassungsbeschwerde und Rechtsprechung des polnischen Verfassungsgerichtshofs zu Fragen der EU-Mitgliedschaft', *EuR*, 44 (2009), 131–45

Braum, S., 'Der Europäische Haftbefehl: Motor europäischer Strafrechtspflege?', *wistra*, 26 (2007), 401–5

'Europäisches Strafrecht im administrativen Rechtsstil', *ZRP*, 35 (2002), 508–14

'Das Prinzip der gegenseitigen Anerkennung', *GA*, 152 (2005), 681–99

Braum, S., and Covolo, V., 'From Proven Fragmentation to Guaranteed Data Protection within the Virtual Criminal Law Enforcement Area', in Ligeti, *Prosecutor for the EU*, i (2013), 1011–46

Brodowski, D., 'Die drohende Verletzung von Menschenrechten bei der Anerkennung Europäischer Haftbefehle auf dem Prüfstand: Die zweifelhafte Aktivierung der Verfassungsidentität durch das BVerfG und eine Kurskorrektur in der Rechtsprechung des EuGH', *JR*, 2016, 415–32

'Der "Grundsatz der Verfügbarkeit" von Daten zwischen Staat und Unternehmen', *ZIS*, 7 (2012), 474–9

'Innere Sicherheit in der EU', *Jura*, 35 (2013), 492–504

'Strafrechtsrelevante Entwicklungen in der EU', *ZIS*, 12 (2017), 688–703

'Strafrechtsrelevante Entwicklungen in der Europäischen Union', *ZIS*, 5 (2010), 376–86

'Strafrechtsrelevante Entwicklungen in der Europäischen Union', *ZIS*, 8 (2013), 455–72

'Strafrechtsrelevante Entwicklungen in der Europäischen Union', *ZIS*, 12 (2017), 11–27

Broß, S., 'Konstruktive Probleme bei der Einigung Europas: Dargestellt am Beispiel des Europäischen Haftbefehls', in Griesbaum, R., Hannich, R., and Schnarr, K. H., eds., *Strafrecht und Justizgewährung: Festschrift für Kay Nehm zum 65. Geburtstag* (Berlin: Berliner Wissenschafts-Verlag, 2006), 27–40

Brüner, F.-H. and Hetzer, W., 'Nationale Strafverfolgung und Europäische Beweisführung?', *NStZ*, 23 (2003), 113–18

Burchard, C., '§14: Auslieferung (Europäischer Haftbefehl)', in Böse, *Europäisches Strafrecht* (2013), 537–72

'Die europäische Ermittlungsanordnung', in Beck, S., Burchard, C., and Fateh-Moghadam, B., eds., *Strafrechtsvergleichung als Problem und Lösung* (Baden-Baden: Nomos, 2011), 275–306

Buczma, S. R., 'ECRIS: A Step Leading to the Establishment of a Coherent European Platform for Exchange of Information: Remarks from a Polish Perspective', *ERA Forum*, 12 (2011), 465–78

Burhoff, D., 'Die Vollstreckung ausländischer Geldsanktionen', *ZAP*, 22 (2010), *Fach 22*, 539–46

Buruma, Y., 'Radikale Toleranz: Auf dem Weg zu einem zweidimensionalen Raum der Freiheit, der Sicherheit und des Rechts', *ZStW*, 116 (2004), 424–35

Busemann, B., 'Strafprozess ohne Grenzen?', *ZIS*, 5 (2010), 552–6

Caeiro, P., 'A jurisdição penal da união europeia como meta-jurisdição: Em especial, a compêtencia para legislar sobre as bases de jurisdição nacionais', in Correia, F. A., Machado, J. M., and Loureiro, J. C., eds., *Estudos em homenagem ao Prof. Doutor José Joaquim Gomes Canotilho*, iii (Coimbra: Coimbra Editora, 2012), 179–210

Camaldo, L., 'The European Investigation Order', in Ruggieri, F., ed., *Criminal Proceedings, Languages and the EU: Linguistic and Legal Issues* (Berlin and Heidelberg: Springer, 2014), 203–14

Cameron, I., Thunberg-Schunke, M., Påle-Bartes, K., Wong, C., and Asp, P., *International Criminal Law from a Swedish Perspective* (Cambridge and Portland: Intersentia, 2011)

Capus, N., *Strafrecht und Souveränität* (Bern: Stämpfli, 2010)

Carducci, M., 'Interrogativi costituzionali sul mandato di arresto europeo', in Acuña, R., *Il mandato di arresto europeo* (2004), 91–6

Castillejo Manzanares, R., 'El objetivo de la orden europea de detención', in Acuña, R., *Il mandato di arresto europeo* (2004), 99–131

Catalano, E. M., 'Molto incertezze e piccoli passi nel percorso di europeizzazione del diritto processuale penale', *DPP*, 13 (2007), 522–30

Chiavario, M., 'Cooperazione giudiziaria e di polizia in materia penale a livello Europeo', *RIDPP*, 48 (2005), 974–89

Claverie-Rousset, C., 'The Admissibility of Evidence in Criminal Proceedings between EU Member States', *EuCLR*, 3 (2013), 152–69

Colvin, A., 'Mandato di arresto Europe: Una prospettiva inglese', in Acuña, R., *Il mandato di arresto europeo* (2004), 335–43

Combeaud, S., 'Première réussite pour le principe de reconnaissance mutuelle: Le mandat d'arrêt européen', *RIDP*, 77 (2006), 131–42

Confalonieri, A., 'La legislazione in Francia', in Pansini, G., and Scalfati, A., eds., *Il mandato d'arresto europeo* (Napoli: Jovene, 2005), 245–55

Conway, G., 'Judicial Interpretation and the Third Pillar', *EJCCLCJ*, 13 (2005), 255–83

Daniele, M., 'Evidence Gathering in the Realm of the EIO', *NJECL*, 6 (2015), 179–94

De Amicis, G., 'Initial Views of the Court of Justice on the European Arrest Warrant: Towards a Uniform Pan-European Interpretation?', *EuCLR*, 2 (2012), 47–60

de Biolley, S., 'Les débuts: L'acquis Schengen', *RIDP*, 77 (2006), 23–38
de Busser, E., 'The Data Protection Gap', *eucrim*, 8 (2013), 17–22
De Capitani, E., 'The Schengen System after Lisbon: From Cooperation to Integration', *ERA Forum*, 15 (2014), 101–18
Deen-Racsmány, Z., 'The European Arrest Warrant and the Surrender of Nationals Revisited: The Lessons of Constitutional Challenges', *EJCCLCJ*, 14 (2006), 271–306
'Lessons of the European Arrest Warrant for Domestic Implementation of the Obligation to Surrender Nationals to the ICC', *LJIL*, 20 (2007), 167–91
Deen-Racsmány, Z., and Blekxtoon, R., 'The Decline of the Nationality Exception in European Extradition', *EJCCLCJ*, 13 (2005), 317–63
de Groot, S., 'Mutual Trust in (European) Extradition Law', in Blekxtoon and van Ballegooij, *Handbook on the EAW* (2005), 83–97
de Hoyos Sancho, M., 'Acerca de la necesidad de armonizar las garantías procesales de los sospechosos en la union europea', *RDPP*, 18 (2007), 117–42
El Ejercicio de la Acción Penal por la Víctimas (Cizur Menor, Navarra: Aranzadi, 2016)
'The Procedural Treatment of Especially Vulnerable Victims in Current and Recent Proposed Normative Instruments in the EU', in de Hoyos Sancho, M., ed., *Guarantees and Rights of the Especially Vulnerable Victim in the Legal Framework of the EU* (Valencia: Tirant lo Blanch, 2013), 47–70
Deiters, M., 'Gegenseitige Anerkennung von Strafgesetzen in Europa', *ZRP*, 36 (2003), 359–62
Delmas-Marty, M., 'Towards an Integrated European Criminal Law', *CYELS*, 7 (2004–5), 17–31
Demetrio Crespo, E., 'El caso Darkazanli', *Diario La Ley*, no 6641 (2006), 1305–10
Depauw, S., 'A European Evidence (Air)Space? Taking Cross-border Legal Admissibility of Forensic Evidence to a Higher Level', *EuCLR*, 6 (2016), 82–98
Dickersbach, A., 'Anmerkung zu BVerfG, Beschluß vom 05.11.2003 - 2 BvR 1243/03, 2 BvR 1506/03', *StV*, 24 (2004), 435–8
Diddi, A., 'Premesse e contenuti della riserva di giurisdizione con riferimento alla disciplina attuativa', in Pansini, G., and Scalfati, A., eds., *Il mandato d'arresto europeo* (Napoli: Jovene, 2005), 3–20
Donatsch, A., Heimgartner, S., and Simonek, M., *Internationale Rechtshilfe* (Zürich et al.: Schulthess, 2011)
Ebert, F. C., and Pinkel, T., 'Der EuGH zwischen Europäischem Haftbefehl und europäischen Grundrechten', *StudZR*, 5 (2008), 361–73
Eisele, J., '§49: Datenverkehr im Rahmen der PJZS', in Sieber, Satzger and von Heinegg, *Europäisches Strafrecht* (2014), 877–93
'§50: Datenschutz im Rahmen der PJZS', in Sieber, et al., eds., *Europäisches Strafrecht* (2014), 894–900

'Jurisdiktionskonflikte in der Europäischen Union: Vom nationalen Strafanwendungsrecht zum Europäischen Kollisionsrecht?', *ZStW*, 125 (2013), 1–33

Erbežnik, A., 'The Principle of Mutual Recognition as a Utilitarian Solution and the Way Forward', *EuCLR*, 2 (2012), 3–19

Errera, R., 'The Relationship of Extradition Law in International Treaties with the European Arrest Warrant and Its Application in France', in Guild, E., ed., *Constitutional Challenges to the European Arrest Warrant* (Nijmegen: Wolf Legal Publishers, 2006), 141–62

Esser, R., '§19: Daten- und Informationsaustausch in Strafsachen in der Europäischen Union', in Böse, *Europäisches Strafrecht* (2013), 697–748

'Europäische Initiativen zur Begrenzung der Untersuchungshaft', in Joerden, J. C., and Szwarc, A. J., eds., *Europäisierung des Strafrechts in Polen und Deutschland: Rechtsstaatliche Grundlagen* (Berlin: de Gruyter, 2007), 233–54

'Initiativen der EU zur Harmonisierung der Beschuldigtenrechte: Zugleich eine kritische Analyse der Richtlinie 2012/13/EU zum Recht auf Belehrung und Unterrichtung in Strafverfahren', in Zöller, M. A., Hilger, H., Küper, W., and Roxin, C., eds., *Gesamte Strafrechtswissenschaft in internationaler Dimension: Festschrift für Jürgen Wolter zum 70. Geburtstag am 7. September 2013* (Berlin: Duncker & Humblot, 2013), 1329–54

Esser, R., and Fischer, S., 'Menschenrechtliche Implikationen der Festnahme von Piraterieverdächtigen', *JR*, 82 (2010), 513–26

Eurojust, *Strategic Seminar 'The EAW: Which Way Forward' and 7th Meeting of the Consultative Forum: The Hague, 10–11 June 2014 – Report and Conclusions* (24 September 2014), Council 13581/14, COPEN 231

European Commission, *Commission Staff Working Document* (11 April 2011), SEC (2011) 430 final

Communication from the Commission to the European Parliament, the Council, the Economic and Social Committee and the Committee of the Regions: Strengthening Victims' Rights in the EU (18 May 2011), COM (2011) 274 final

Memo – Questions and Answers: Schengen Information System (SIS II (9 April 2013)

Handbook on How to Issue and Execute a European Arrest Warrant (28 September 2017), C(2017) 6389 final, available at https://e-justice.europa.eu/fileDownload.do?id=db28c045-9f92-472e-9452-518b4ce84712, last accessed 15 February 2018

Report from the Commission to the EP and the Council: On the Implementation since 2007 of the Council FD of 13 June 2002 on the EAW (11 April 2011), COM (2011) 175 final

Report on the Implementation since 2005 of the Council FD of 13 June 2002 on the EAW and the Surrender Procedures between MS (11 July 2007), COM (2007) 407 final

European Criminal Policy Initiative, 'Manifesto on European Criminal Procedure Law', *ZIS*, 8 (2013), 430–46

Fazekas, M., and Nanopoulos, E., 'The Effectiveness of EU Law: Insights from the EU Legal Framework on Asset Confiscation', *EJCCLCJ*, 24 (2016), 39–64

Fennelly, N., 'The European Arrest Warrant', *ERA Forum*, 8 (2007), 519–34

Fichera, M., *The Implementation of the European Arrest Warrant in the European Union* (Cambridge, Antwerp and Portland: Intersentia, 2011)

'The Status of the Victim in European Union Criminal Law', *eucrim*, 6 (2011), 79–82

Fichera, M., and Herlin-Karnell, E., 'The Margin of Appreciation Test and Balancing in the Area of Freedom Security and Justice: A Proportionate Answer for a Europe of Rights?', *EuPubL*, 19 (2013), 759–87

Flore, D., Bosly, S., Honhon, A., and Maggio, J., eds., *Probation Measures and Alternative Sanctions in the European Union* (Cambridge and Portland: Intrersentia, 2012)

Frank, C., 'Strafverfolgungskompetenz der Länder im Licht der Entwicklung eines Raumes der Freiheit, der Sicherheit und des Rechts: Ein Bericht der AG Europa der Justizministerkonferenz', *DRiZ*, 84 (2006), 10–11

Freund, O., *Die Anordnung von Untersuchungshaft wegen Flucht und Fluchtgefahr gegen EU-Ausländer* (Baden-Baden: Nomos, 2010)

Fuchs, H., 'Bemerkungen zur gegenseitigen Anerkennung justizieller Entscheidungen', *ZStW*, 116 (2004), 368–71

Gaede, K., 'Nullum judicium sine lege', *ZStW*, 115 (2003), 846–79

Garcimartín Montero, R., 'The EIO and the Respect for Fundamental Rights in Criminal Investigations', *eucrim*, 12 (2017), 45–50

Gärditz, K. F., '§6: Europäisierung des Strafrechts und nationales Verfassungsrecht', in Böse, *Europäisches Strafrecht* (2013), 227–68

Gaito, A., 'La vigenza del principio di "specialità"', in Acuña, R., *Il mandato di arresto europeo* (2004), 213–27

Galli, F., 'Passenger Name Record Agreements: The Umpteenth Attempt to Anticipate Risk', *eucrim*, 5 (2010), 124–8

Garlick, P., 'The European Arrest Warrant and the ECHR', in Blekxtoon and van Ballegooij, *Handbook on the EAW* (2005), 167–82

Gas, T., 'L'inconstitutionnalitè de la loi Allemande sur le mandat d'arrêt européen', *RPDP*, 10 (2007), 813–28

'Die Verfassungswidrigkeit des Europäischen Haftbefehlsgesetzes', *EuR*, 41 (2006), 285–98

Geraci, R. M., 'La disciplina nel Regno Unito', in Pansini, G., and Scalfati, A., eds., *Il mandato d'arresto europeo* (Napoli: Jovene, 2005), 257–71

'La normativa danesa', in Pansini, G., and Scalfati, A., eds., *Il mandato d'arresto europeo* (Napoli: Jovene, 2005), 237–44

Gerhardt, M., 'Sondervotum zu BVerfG, Beschluss v. 18.7.2005 – 2 BvR 2236/04', *NJW*, 58 (2005), 2301–3

Geyer, F., 'The European Arrest Warrant in Germany', in Guild, E., ed., *Constitutional Challenges to the European Arrest Warrant* (Nijmegen: Wolf Legal Publishers, 2006), 101–23

Gibbins, B., 'Overview', in Jones, J. R. W. D., and Davidson, R., *Extradition and Mutual Assistance Handbook* (Oxford: Oxford University Press, 2nd edn, 2010), 15–23

Gilmore, B., 'Introduction', *RIDP*, 77 (2006), 15–22

Gilmore, W. C., and Harris, L. M., 'Mutual Legal Assistance, Organised Crime and the EU: Reflections on Progress Achieved to Date', in Cullen, P., and Jund, S., eds., *Criminal Justice Co-operation in the European Union after Tampere* (Cologne: Bundesanzeiger, 2002), 107–13

Gleß, S., 'Grenzüberschreitende Beweissammlung', *ZStW*, 125 (2013), 573–608

'Kommentar zum Vorschlag für einen Rahmenbeschluss über eine "Europäische Beweisanordnung"', *StV*, 24 (2004), 679–83

'A New Test for Mens Rea? Safeguarding Legal Certainty in a European Area of Freedom, Security and Justice', *EuCLR*, 1 (2011), 114–22

'§16: Beweisrechtshilfe', in Böse, *Europäisches Strafrecht* (2013), 611–29

'§38: Europäische Beweisanordnung', in Sieber, Satzger and von Heinegg, *Europäisches Strafrecht* (2014), 677–95

'§39: Sicherstellung von Vermögensgegenständen oder Beweismitteln in der EU', in Sieber, Satzger and von Heinegg, *Europäisches Strafrecht* (2014), 696–706

'§39a: Gegenseitige Anerkennung von Geldstrafen und Geldbußen', in Sieber, Satzger and von Heinegg, *Europäisches Strafrecht* (2014), 707–21

'§40: Anerkennung von Einziehungsentscheidungen', in Sieber, Satzger and von Heinegg, *Europäisches Strafrecht* (2014), 722–8

'Die "Verkehrsfähigkeit von Beweisen" im Strafverfahren', *ZStW*, 115 (2003), 131–50

'Zum Prinzip der gegenseitigen Anerkennung', *ZStW*, 116 (2004), 353–67

Gleß, S., and Lüke, M., 'Rechtsschutz gegen grenzüberschreitende Strafverfolgung in Europa', *Jura*, 22 (2000), 400–6

'Strafverfolgung über die Grenzen hinweg', *Jura*, 20 (1998), 70–9

Gleß, S., and Spencer, J., 'Effizienz und Individualrechtsschutz im Dreiecksverhältnis der sonstigen Rechtshilfe', *StV*, 26 (2006), 269–74

Globke, C., 'Die Wirkung des Europäischen Haftbefehls', *GA*, 158 (2011), 412–23

González Cano, M. I., 'La orden de detención europea: ejecución condicionada del mandamiento y concurso de solicitudes y procedimientos', in Acuña, R., *Il mandato di arresto europeo* (2004), 151–88

Goy, B., *Vorläufige Festnahme und grenzüberschreitende Nacheile* (Berlin: Duncker & Humblot, 2002)

Graf, J.-P., '§112 StPO', in Hannich, *Karlsruher Kommentar StPO* (2013), 634–54

Grange, E., and Niblock, R., *Extradition Law: A Practioner's Guide* (London: LAG, 2015)

Grasso, C., 'The European Arrest Warrant under the Scrutiny of the Italian Constitutional Court', *NJECL*, 4 (2013), 120–33

Gualtieri, P., 'I reati perseguibili con il mandato d'arresto europeo', in Acuña, R., *Il mandato di arresto europeo* (2004), 51–64

Gusy, C., and Gimbal, A., 'Rechtliche Schranken der polizeilichen Zusammenarbeit im Rahmen des Schengener Informationssystems', in Baldus, M., and Soiné, M., eds., *Rechtsprobleme der internationalen polizeilichen Zusammenarbeit* (Baden-Baden: Nomos, 1999), 124–44

Guzik Makaruk, E. M., '"Ne bis in idem", Europäischer Haftbefehl und der Verfassungsentwurf für Europa aus polnischer Sicht', *ZStW*, 116 (2004), 372–5

Hackner, T., 'Der Europäische Haftbefehl in der Praxis der Staatsanwaltschaften und Gerichte', *NStZ*, 25 (2005), 311–15

'Probleme der Umsetzung des Europäischen Haftbefehls in Deutschland', in Lagodny, O., Wiederin, E., and Winkler, R., eds., *Probleme des Rahmenbeschlusses am Beispiel des Europäischen Haftbefehls* (Vienna: Neuer Wissenschaftlicher Verlag, 2007), 193–203

Hackner, T., and Schierholt, C., *Internationale Rechtshilfe in Strafsachen* (Munich: C. H. Beck, 2012)

Internationale Rechtshilfe in Strafsachen: Ein Leitfaden für die Praxis (Munich: C.H. Beck, 3rd edn, 2017)

Hackner, T., Schomburg, W., Lagodny, W., and Gleß, S., 'Das 2. Europäische Haftbefehlsgesetz', *NStZ*, 26 (2006), 663–9

Hackner, T., Schomburg, W., Lagodny, W., and Wolf, N., *Internationale Rechtshilfe in Strafsachen* (Munich: C. H. Beck, 2003)

Hackner, T., and Trautmann, S., 'Die Vollstreckung ausländischer Geldstrafen und Geldbußen nach dem Gesetzesentwurf der Bundesregierung zu einem Europäischen Geldsanktionengesetz', *DAR*, 80 (2010), 71–6

Hailbronner, K., 'Art. 6 EMRK als Hindernis der Auslieferung und Abschiebung', in Bröhmer, J., ed., *Internationale Gemeinschaft und Menschenrechte: Festschrift für Georg Ress zum 70. Geburtstag am 21. Januar 2005* (Cologne et al.: Carl Heymanns, 2005), 997–1010

Harings, L., *Grenzüberschreitende Zusammenarbeit der Polizei- und Zollverwaltungen und Rechtsschutz in Deutschland* (Berlin: Duncker & Humblot, 1998)

Hassemer, W., 'Strafrecht in einem europäischen Verfassungsvertrag', *ZStW*, 116 (2004), 304–19

Hauck, P., 'Richterlicher Anpassungsbedarf durch den EU-Rahmenbeschluss zur Anerkennung strafgerichtlicher Entscheidungen in Abwesenheit des Angeklagten?', *JR*, 81 (2009), 141–7

'§11: Europarechtliche Vorgaben für nationale Strafverfahren', in Böse, *Europäisches Strafrecht* (2013), 413–58

Hecker, B., 'Anmerkung zu BGH, Beschluss v. 6.6.2002 - 4 ARs 3/02', *NStZ*, 22 (2002), 663–4

'Die Europäische Beweisanordnung', in Marauhn, T., ed., *Bausteine eines europäischen Beweisrechts* (Tübingen: Mohr Siebeck, 2007), 27–38

Hefendehl, R., 'Europäisches Strafrecht: Bis wohin und nicht weiter?', *ZIS*, 1 (2006), 229–36

Heger, M., 'Europäische Beweissicherung: Perspektiven der strafrechtlichen Zusammenarbeit in Europa', *ZIS*, 2 (2007), 547–56

'Der Europäische Haftbefehl: Zur Umsetzung europäischer Vorgaben in Deutschland', *ZIS*, 2 (2007), 221–5

Heine, H., *Die Rechtsstellung des Beschuldigten im Rahmen der Europäisierung des Strafrechts* (Frankfurt a.M. et al.: Peter Lang, 2009)

Heinrich, B., 'Die Nacheile im Rahmen von Strafverfolgungsmaßnahmen', *NStZ*, 16 (1996), 361–6

Heintschel von Heinegg, B., '§37: Europäischer Haftbefehl', in Sieber, Satzger and von Heinegg, *Europäisches Strafrecht* (2014), 661–76

Heintschel von Heinegg, B., and Rohlff, D., 'Der Europäische Haftbefehl', *GA*, 150 (2003), 44–51

Henke, J. N., *Der europäische Haftbefehl: Entwicklung und Schwierigkeiten* (Munich: Akademischer Verlag, 2008)

Janik, C., and Kleinlein, T., 'When Soering Went to Iraq ...: Problems of Jurisdiction, Extraterritorial Effect and Norm Conflicts in Light of the European Court of Human Rights' Als-Saadoon Case', *GoJIL, 1* (2009), 459–518

Hetzer, W., '§41: Zusammenarbeit der Polizeibehörden', in Sieber, Satzger and von Heinegg, *Europäisches Strafrecht* (2014), 729–53

Henzelin, M., 'L'état requerant en matiere de cooperation judiciaire: extensions et limites de l'approche pragmatique', in Zen-Ruffinen, P., ed., *Du monde pénal: Mélanges en l'honneur de Pierr-Henri Bolle* (Basel et al.: Helbing & Lichtenhahn, 2006), 193–204

Heydenreich, C. W., 'Die Europäische Ermittlungsanordung', *StraFo, 25* (2012), 439–44

Hinterhofer, H., 'Die Umsetzung des Rahmenbeschlusses über den Europäischen Haftbefehl in Österreich', in Lagodny, O., Wiederin, E., and Winkler, R., eds., *Problème des Rahmenbeschlusses am Beispiel des Europäischen Haftbefehls* (Vienna: Neuer Wissenschaftlicher Verlag, 2007), 205–26

Hochmayr, G., and Ligocki, D, 'Der Strafregisteraustausch in der EU und das Recht auf Resozialisierung', *ZIS*, 11 (2016), 159–72

Hörauf, D., 'Ordnungswidrigkeiten und der europäische Straftatenbegriff: Subkategorie oder aliud-Verhältnis?', *ZIS*, 8 (2013), 276–9

Huber, B., 'Die polizeiliche und justizielle Zusammenarbeit in Europa', in Wolter, J., Schenke, W.-R., Rieß, P., and Zöller, M. A., eds., *Datenübermittlungen und Vorermittlungen: Festgabe für Hans Hilger* (Heidelberg: Müller, 2003), 135–52

Hüttemann, S. D., 'Das neue Vollstreckungshilferecht im Bereich der freiheitsentziehenden Sanktionen innerhalb der EU', *StV*, 36 (2016), 519–30

Principles and Perspectives of European Criminal Procedure (Florence: European University Institute, 2012)

Hufeld, U., 'Art. 16 GG: Ausbürgerung und Auslieferung im Kontext', *JA*, 39 (2007), 41–3

'Der Europäische Haftbefehl vor dem Bundesverfassungsgericht', *JuS*, 45 (2005), 865–71

Hummer, W., 'Der Vertrag von Prüm: "Schengen III"?', *EuR*, 42 (2007), 517–30

Huybreghts, G., 'The Schengen Convention and the Schengen Acquis: 25 Years of Evolution', *ERA Forum*, 16 (2015), 379–426

Impalà, F., 'The European Arrest Warrant in the Italian Legal System', *ULR*, 1 (2005), 56–78

Jiménez Becerril, T., and Romero Lopez, C., 'The European Protection Order', *eucrim*, 6 (2011), 76–8

Jiménez-Villarejo Fernández, F., 'Armonización de la garantías procesales etc.', in Arangüena Fanego, C., ed., *Garantías procesales en los procesos penales en la Unión Europea* (Valladolid: Ed. Lex Nova, 2007), 119–54

Jimeno Bulnes, M., 'La adopción de medidas cautelares de carácter personal con motivo de la ejecución de una orden europea de detención y entrega', *RP*, 16 (2005), 106–22

Johnson, C., 'Anmerkung', *ZIS*, 10 (2015), 121–3

'Anmerkung', *ZIS*, 10 (2015), 478–9

'First Experiences in Germany with Mutual Recognition of Financial Penalties', *eucrim*, 8 (2013), 65–8

'Rechtsprechungsübersicht: Anerkennung und Vollstreckung von EU-Geldsanktionen nach dem Rahmenbeschluss 2005/214/JI', *SVR*, 16 (2016), 450–3

'Zur Anerkennung und Vollstreckung von EU-Geldsanktionen in Österreich', *ZIS*, 8 (2013), 361–3

Johnson, C., and Plötzgen-Kamradt, S., 'Gegenseitige Anerkennung von Geldstrafen und Geldbußen in Deutschland', *eucrim*, 6 (2011), 33–9

Johnston, J. G., 'The Risk of Torture as a Basis for Refusing Extradition and the Use of Diplomatic Assurances to Protect against Torture after 9/11', *ICLR*, 11 (2011), 1–48

Juppe, M., *Die gegenseitige Anerkennung strafgerichtlicher Entscheidungen in Europa* (Frankfurt a.M.: Peter Lang, 2007)

Kaiafa-Gbandi, M., 'Europäisches Strafrecht', *KritV*, 87 (2004), 3–23

'The Treaty Establishing a Constitution for Europe and Challenges for Criminal Law', *EJCCLCJ*, 13 (2005), 483–514

Karitzky, H., and Wannek, F., 'Die EU-weite Vollstreckung von Geldstrafen und Geldbußen', *NJW*, 63 (2010), 3393–7

Karsai, K., 'Grenzuebrschreitende Beweisverbote', in Gropp, W., Öztürk, B. Sozüer, A., and Wörner, L. eds., *Die Entwicklung von Rechtssystemen in ihrer gesellschaftlichen Verankerung* (Baden-Baden: Nomos, 2014), 153–62

'Ungeschicktes und folgenreiches Vorgehen in der transnationalen Rechtshilfe', *ZIS*, 1 (2006), 443–6

Kattau, T., *Strafverfolgung nach Wegfall der europäischen Grenzkontrollen* (Pfaffenweiler: Centaurus, 1993)

Kazele, N., 'Änderungen im Recht der Untersuchungshaft', *NJ*, 64 (2010), 1–6

Keijzer, N., 'The Double Criminality Requirement', in Blekxtoon and van Ballegooij, *Handbook on the EAW* (2005), 137–63

'Extradition and Human Rights: A Dutch Perspective', in Blekxtoon and van Ballegooij, *Handbook on the EAW* (2005), 183–94

Kirsch, S., 'Schluss mit lustig!', *StraFo*, 21 (2008), 449–58

Klatt, M., and Meister, M., *The Constitutional Structure of Proportionality* (Oxford: Oxford University Press, 2013)

Klimek, L., *European Arrest Warrant* (Cham et al.: Springer, 2015)

'New Law on the European Arrest Warrant in the Slovak Republic: Does It Fulfil Standards at the Level of the EU?', *EJCCLCJ*, 20 (2012), 181–92

Klip, A., 'European Integration and Harmonisation and Criminal Law', in Curtin, D. M., Smits, J. M., Klip, A., and McCahery, J. A., *European Integration and Law* (Antwerp: Intersentia, 2006), 109–53

Klitsch, S., 'Der neue EU-Rahmenbeschluss zu Abwesenheitsverurteilungen: Ein Appell zur Revision', *ZIS*, 4 (2009), 11–21

Knopp, L., 'Bundesverfassungsgericht contra EU-Haftbefehl: Zum Urteil des Bundesverfassungsgerichts vom 18. Juli 2005', *JR*, 77 (2005), 448–53

Komárek, J., 'European Constitutionalism and the European Arrest Warrant', *CMLR*, 44 (2007), 9–40

Kowalik-Bańczyk, K., 'Should We Polish It Up? The Polish Constitutional Tribunal and the Idea of Supremacy of EU Law', *GLJ*, 6 (2005), 1355–66

Kreß, C., 'Das Strafrecht auf der Schwelle zum europäischen Verfassungsvertrag', *ZStW*, 116 (2004), 445–74

Królikowski, M., and Znojek, M., 'L'argument de la souveraineté en contestation du mandat d'arrêt européen', *RSC*, 71 (2006), 551–66

Kromrey, H., and Morgenstern, C., 'Auslieferung bei drohender lebenslanger Freiheitsstrafe ohne Aussetzungsmöglichkeit', *ZIS*, 9 (2014), 704–15

Krüßmann, T., 'Grenzüberschreitender Beweistransfer durch Europäische Beweisanordnung?', *StraFo*, 21 (2008), 458–63

'§18: Besondere Formen der grenzüberschreitenden Zusammenarbeit', in Böse, *Europäisches Strafrecht* (2013), 679–96

Kühne, H.-H., 'Anmerkung zu BVerfG, Beschluss v. 15.12.2015 - 2 BvR 2735/14', *StV*, 36 (2016), 299–302

Kugelmann, D., '§17: Europäische Polizeiliche Kooperation', in Böse, *Europäisches Strafrecht* (2013), 631–78

Lagodny, O., 'Anmerkung zu BGH v. 8. 11. 2006 - 1 StR 421/06', *JR*, 79 (2007), 260–2

'Anmerkung zu BVerfG, Beschluss v. 18.6.1997 - 2 BvR 483/95 et al.', *JZ*, 53 (1998), 568–70

'Eckpunkte für die zukünftige Ausgestaltung des deutschen Auslieferungsverfahrens', *StV*, 25 (2005), 515–19

'"Extradition" without a Granting Procedure: The Concept of Surrender', in Blekxtoon and van Ballegooij, *Handbook on the EAW* (2005), 39–45

'Konstellationen transnationaler Strafverfolgung von Konzerngesellschaften', in Joerden, J. C., and Schmoller, K., eds., *Rechtsstaatliches Strafen: Festschrift für Keiichi Yamanaka zum 70. Geburtstag am 16. März 2017* (Berlin: Duncker und Humblot, 2017), 575–88

'§22: Transnationales Strafverfahren', in Widmaier, G., ed., *Münchener Anwaltshandbuch Strafverteidigung* (Munich: C. H. Beck, 2nd edn, 2014), 932–56

'§31: Traditionelles Auslieferungs- und Rechtshilferecht (horizontale Rechtshilfe)', in Sieber, Satzger and von Heinegg, *Europäisches Strafrecht* (2014), 549–68

'Überlegungen zu einem menschengerechten transnationalen Straf- und Strafverfahrensrecht', in Arnold, J., Burkhardt, B., Gropp, W., Heine, G., Koch, H.-G., Lagodny, O., Perron, W., and Walther, S., eds., *Menschengerechtes Strafrecht: Festschrift für Albin Eser zum 70. Geburtstag* (Munich: C. H. Beck, 2005), 777–96

'Die Umsetzung der materiellen Übergabe- bzw. Auslieferungsvoraussetzungen und der Verfahrensregelungen in den Mitgliedsstaaten im Überblick', in Lagodny, O., Wiederin, E., and Winkler, R., eds., *Probleme des Rahmenbeschlusses am Beispiel des Europäischen Haftbefehls* (Vienna: Neuer Wissenschaftlicher Verlag, 2007), 143–9

'Konstellationen transnationaler Strafverfolgung von Konzerngesellschaften', in Joerden, J. C., and Schmoller, K., eds., *Rechtsstaatliches Strafen: Festschrift für Prof. Dr. Dr. h.c. mult. Keiichi Yamanaka zum 70. Geburtstag am 16. März 2017* (Berlin: Duncker & Humblot, 2017), 575–88

Langheld, G. C., 'Has European Union Begun to Drive Criminal Law down a Slippery Road?', *EuCLR*, *2* (2012), 276–90

Leanza, U., 'La creazione di uno spacio unico europeo di libertà, sicurezza e giustizia', in Acuña, R., *Il mandato di arresto europeo* (Padova: CEDAM, 2004), 7–24

Lelieur, J., 'L'application de la reconnaissance mutuelle à l'obtention transnationale de preuves pénales dans l'Union européenne: une chance pour un droit probatoire français en crise?', *ZIS*, 5 (2010), 590–601

'Freezing and Confiscating Criminal Assets in the European Union', *EuCLR, 5* (2015), 279–303

Lensing, H., 'The European Arrest Warrant and Transferring Execution of Prison Sentences', in Blekxtoon and van Ballegooij, *Handbook on the EAW* (2005), 209–16

Leutheusser-Schnarrenberger, S., 'Der Europäische Beschuldigte', *StraFo, 20* (2007), 267–77

Löfgren, O., 'A Manifesto for European Criminal Procedure Law: A Prosecutorial Perspective', *EuCLR*, 5 (2015), 54–9

MacCormick, N., 'A Common Approach to Crime? Observations on the European Arrest Warrant and the Democratic Deficit', in Müller-Dietz, H., ed., *Festschrift für Heike Jung zum 65. Geburtstag am 23. April 2007* (Baden-Baden: Nomos, 2007), 535–42

Mackarel, M., 'The European Arrest Warrant. The Early Years: Implementing and Using the Warrant', *EJCCLCJ*, 15 (2007), 37–65

Maggio, P., 'The EIO Proposal for a Directive and Mafia Trials: Striving for Balance between Efficiency and Procedural Guarantees', in Ruggeri, S., ed., *Transnational Evidence and Multicultural Inquiries in Europe: Developments in EU Legislation and New Challenges for Human Rights-Oriented Criminal Investigations in Cross-border Cases* (Heidelberg et al: Springer, 2014), 139–49

Manacorda, S., 'La deroga alla doppia punibilità nel mandato di arresto europeo etc.', *CassP*, 47 (2007), 4346–63

'Notes sur la loi italienne portant mise en ouvre du mandat d'arrêt européen (loi du 22 avril 2005, n° 69)', *eucrim*, 1 (2006), 33–6

'La consolidation de l'espace de liberté, de sécurité et de justice: etc.', *RSC*, 72 (2007), 899–909

Mancano, L., 'The Right to Liberty in European Union Law and Mutual Recognition in Criminal Matters', *CYELS*, 18 (2016), 215–38

Mangiaracina, A., 'A New and Controversial Scenario in the Gathering of Evidence at the European Level: The Proposal for a Directive on the European Investigation Order', *ULR*, 10, 1 (2014), 113–33

Mansdörfer, M., 'Das Europäische Strafrecht nach dem Vertrag von Lissabon – Oder: Europäisierung des Strafrechts unter nationalstaatlicher Mitverantwortung', *HRRS*, 11 (2010), 11–23

Mansell, D., 'The European Arrest Warrant and Defence Rights', *EuCLR*, 2 (2012), 36–46

Maple, C., and Lang, R., 'Vulnerability, Victims and Free Movement: The Case of Cyberstalking', *NJECL*, 3 (2012), 208–22

Marauhn, T., and Simon, S., 'Diplomatisches Asyl für Julian Assange?', *ZJS*, 5 (2012), 593–601

Marchetti, M. R., 'Il diniego obbligatorio e facoltativo del mandato', in Acuña, R., *Il mandato di arresto europeo* (2004), 133–44

Mathisen, G., 'Nordic Cooperation and the EAW: Intra-Nordic Extradition, the Nordic Arrest Warrant and Beyond', *NJIL*, 79 (2010) 1–33

Matscher, F., 'Bemerkungen zur extraterritorialen oder indirekten Wirkung der EMRK', in Donatsch, A., Forster M., and Schwarzenegger, C., eds., *Strafrecht, Strafprozessrecht und Menschenrechte: Festschrift für Stefan Trechsel zum 65. Geburtstag* (Zurich et al.: Schulthess, 2002), 25–46

Mavany, M., *Die europäische Beweisanordnung und das Prinzip der gegenseitigen Anerkennung* (Heidelberg et al.: Müller, Verlagsgruppe Hüthig, Jehle, Rehm, 2012)

Mavronicola, N., 'Crime, Punishment and Article 3 ECHR: Puzzles and Prospects of Applying an Absolute Right in a Penal Context', *HRLR*, 15 (2015), 721–43

Meier, B.-D., 'Neues aus Europa? Die Opferschutzrichtlinie der EU', in Zöller, M. A., Hilger, H., Küper, W., and Roxin, C., eds., *Gesamte Strafrechtswissenschaft in internationaler Dimension: Festschrift für Jürgen Wolter zum 70. Geburtstag am 7. September 2013* (Berlin: Duncker & Humblot, 2013), 1387–1400

Meyer, F., 'Die Aussagefreiheit und das Prinzip der gegenseitigen Anerkennung', *GA*, 154 (2007), 15–35

'Der Grundsatz der Verfügbarkeit', *NStZ*, 28 (2008), 188–94

Meyer, F., and Hüttemann, S. D., 'Internationale Fahndung nach Personen: Von Steckbriefen, Rotecken und Funksprüchen', *ZStW*, 128 (2016), 394–445

Meyer, J., 'Die künftige Europäische Verfassung und das Strafrecht', in Arnold, J., ed., *Menschengerechtes Strafrecht: Festschrift für Albin Eser zum 70. Geburtstag* (Munich: C. H. Beck, 2005), 797–806

Meysman, M., 'Belgium and the European Arres Warrant: Is European Criminal Cooperation under Pressure?', *EuCLR*, 6 (2016), 186–210

Michaelsen, C., 'The Renaissance of Non-refoulement? The Ozhman (Abu Qatada) Decision of the European Court of Human Rights', *ICLQ*, 61 (2012), 750–66

Michalke, R., 'Anmerkung zu EuGH, Urteil v. 3 5.2007 – C-303/05', *EuZW*, 18 (2007), 377–8

Miettinen, S., 'Onward Transfer under the European Arrest Warrant: Is the EU Moving towards the Free Movement of Prisoners?, *NJECL*, 4 (2013), 99–119

Mitsilegas, V., 'The Constitutional Implications of Mutual Recognition in Criminal Matters in the EU', *CMLR*, 43 (2006), 1277–1311

Mitsilegas, V., 'Transatlantic Counter-terrorism Cooperation after Lisbon', *eucrim*, 4 (2010), 111–17

Mörbel, R. K., 'Die Bekämpfung der internationalen Kriminalität: Perspektiven aus der Sicht des BKA', in Cullen, P., and Jund, S., eds., *Criminal Justice Co-*

operation in the European Union after Tampere (Cologne: Bundesanzeiger, 2002), 49–57

Möstl, M., *Die staatliche Garantie für die öffentliche Sicherheit und Ordnung* (Tübingen: Mohr Siebeck, 2002)

Montag, F., and von Bonin, A., 'Die Entwicklung des Unionsrechts bis Mitte 2013', *NJW*, 66 (2013), 3487–91

Morgan, C., 'The European Arrest Warrant and Defendants Rights: An Overview', in Blekxtoon and van Ballegooij, *Handbook on the EAW* (2005), 195–208

Morgenstern, C., 'Die Europäische Überwachungsanordnung', *ZIS*, 9 (2014), 216–35

'§15: Vollstreckungshilfe', in Böse, *Europäisches Strafrecht* (2013), 573–610

'Strafvollstreckung im Heimatstaat: der geplante EU-Rahmenbeschluss zur transnationalen Vollstreckung von Freiheitsstrafen', *ZIS*, 3 (2008), 76–83

Mujuzi, J. D., 'The Recognition of Foreign Convictions from Member States of the European Union in Criminal Trials in the United Kingdom: Emerging Issues', *EuCLR*, 5 (2015), 86–106

Mylonopoulos, C., 'Internationalisierung des Strafrechts und Strafrechtsdogmatik: Legitimationsdefizit und Anarchie als Hauptcharakteristika der Strafrechtsnormen mit internationalem Einschlag', *ZStW*, 121 (2009), 68–93

'Strafrechtsdogmatik in Europa nach dem Vertrag von Lissabon: Zur materiellen Legitimation des Europäischen Strafrechts', *ZStW*, 123 (2011), 633–50

Nalewajko, P., 'Der Europäische Haftbefehl: aktuelle Entwicklungen in Polen', *ZIS*, 2 (2007), 113–17

Grundsatz der gegenseitigen Anerkennung: Eckstein der justiziellen Zusammenarbeit in Strafsachen in der Europäischen Union? (Berlin: Duncker & Humblot, 2010)

Nestler, C., 'Europäisches Strafprozessrecht', *ZStW*, 116 (2004), 332–52

Nestler, N., 'Der Mandatsbereich von Europol im Lichte grenzüberschreitender Betäubungsmittelkriminalität', *GA*, 157 (2010), 645–58

Neumann, D., '§34: Gemeinsame Ermittlungsteams', in Sieber, Satzger and von Heinegg, *Europäisches Strafrecht* (2014), 610–14

Neveu, S., 'Probation Measures and Alternative Sanctions in Europe: From the 1964 Convention to the 2008 Framework Decision', *NJECL*, 4 (2013), 134–53

Niblock, R., 'Mutual Recognition, Mutual Trust? Detention Conditions and Deferring an EAW', *NJECL*, 7 (2016), 250–1

Nicholls, C, Montgomery, C., Knowles, J. B., Doobay, A., and Summers, M., *The Law of Extradition and Mutual Assistance* (Oxford: Oxford University Press, 3rd edn, 2013)

Niemeier, M., and Zerbst, P., 'Der Vertrag von Prüm: Vertiefte grenzüberschreitende Zusammenarbeit zur Kriminalitätsbekämpfung in der EU', *ERA Forum*, 8 (2007), 535–47

Nino, M., 'Court of Cassation, United Criminal Sections (Corte di Cassazione, Sezioni Unite Penali)', *JCL*, 71 (2007), 501–5

Nita, B., 'Das Urteil des polnischen Verfassungsgerichtshofs über den Europäischen Haftbefehl', *eucrim*, 1 (2006), 36–9

Nita-Światlowska, B., 'Einschränkungen der Verwertbarkeit von den durch fremde Organe durchgeführten Beweisaufnahmen in Strafverfahren', in Hofmański, P., Szumiło-Kulczycka, D., and Czarnecki, P., eds., *Ausserprozessuale Beweiserhebung und ihre Verwertung im Strafprozess* (Warsaw: Beck, 2015), 309–20

Nowell-Smith, H., 'Behind the Scenes in the Negotiation of EU Criminal Justice Legislation', *NJECL*, 3 (2012), 381–93

Ormazábal Sánchez, G., 'La prueba penal en el espacio judical europeo', *La Ley Penal*, 7, no 74 (2010), 5–42

Ouwerkerk, J., *Quid pro quo? A Comparative Law Perspective on the Mutual Recognition of Judicial Decisions in Criminal Matters* (Cambridge et al.: Intersentia, 2011)

Öberg, J., 'Subsidiarity and EU Procedural Criminal Law', *EuCLR*, 5 (2015), 19–45

Padfield, N., 'The Implementation of the European Arrest Warrant in England and Wales', *EuConst*, 3 (2007), 253–68

Panebianco, M., 'L'esecuzione della decision quadro del 13-06-2002 nell' ordinamento italiano', in Acuña, R., *Il mandato di arresto europeo* (2004), 189–209

Pechstein, M., 'Die Justitiabilität des Unionsrechts', *EuR*, 34 (1999), 1–26

Peers, S., *EU Justice and Home Affairs Law, II: EU Criminal Law, Policy and Civil Law* (Oxford: Oxford University Press, 4th edn, 2016)

Petra, B., *Az európai elfogatóparancs Magyarországon: The European Arrest Warrant in Hungary* (OKRI: Budapest, 2015)

Peukert, W., 'Auslieferung zur Verbüßung einer Gefängnisstrafe von 845 Jahren wegen reiner Vermögensdelikte konventionskonform?', in Triffterer, O., ed., *Gedächtnisschrift für Theo Vogler* (Heidelberg: C. F. Müller, 2004), 151–62

Pfützner, P., 'Der Europäische Haftbefehl und seine Umsetzung in das französische Recht', *eucrim*, 1 (2006), 29–33

Picotti, L., 'Il mandato d'arresto europeo fra principio di legalità e doppia incriminazione', in Bargis, M., and Selvaggi, E., eds., *Mandato d'arresto europeo: Dall'estradizione alle procedura di consegna* (Turin: Giappichelli, 2005), 33–69

Plachta, M., 'Criminal Records in an Era of Globalization: Identifying Problems and Conceptualizing Solutions within the EU', *ICLR*, 7 (2007), 425–47

'Joint Investigation Teams', *EJCCLCJ*, 13 (2005), 284–302

'The Role of Double Criminality in International Cooperation in Penal Matters', in Jareborg, N., ed., *Double Crminality* (Uppsala: Iustus Förlag, 1989), 84–134

Plachta, M., and van Ballegooij, W., 'The Framework Decision on the European Arrest Warrant and Surrender Procedures between Member States of the EU', in Blekxtoon and van Ballegooij, *Handbook on the EAW* (2005), 13–38

Pohl, T., *Vorbehalt und Anerkennung: Der Europäische Haftbefehl zwischen Grundgesetz und europäischem Primärrecht* (Baden-Baden: Nomos et al., 2009)

Pronebner, V., 'Warum werden ausländische Verkehrssünder nach wie vor nicht verfolgt?', *DAR-Extra*, 80 (2010), 748–51

Porebska, E., 'Paving the Way for Improved Mutual Assistance in the Context of Customs Fraud', *eucrim*, 11 (2016), 52–5

Rackow, P., 'Das Anerkennungsprinzip auf dem Prüfstein der Beweisrechtshilfe', in Ambos, König and Rackow, *Europäisches Strafrecht post-Lissabon* (2011), 117–36

'Überlegungen zu dem Gesetz zur Änderung des IRG vom 5.1.2017', *KriPoZ*, 2 (2017), 79–87

Rackow, P., and Birr, C., 'Recent Developments in Legal Assistance in Criminal Matters', *GoJIL*, 2 (2010), 1087–1128

Radtke, H., 'Anmerkung zu EuGH, Urteil v. 9.3.2006, C-436/04', *NStZ*, 28 (2008), 162–4

'Der Europäische Staatsanwalt: Ein Modell für Strafverfolgung in Europa mit Zukunft?', *GA*, 151 (2004), 1–21

Raphael, M., 'Tracing and Confiscating Illicit Proceeds: The Perspective of the Defence', *ERA Forum*, 11 (2011), 545–70

Rasquete, C., Ferreira, A., and Moyano Marques, F., 'Why Do We Need Concrete Measures for Victims at EU Level? A View from the Coalface', *ERA Forum*, 15 (2014), 119–29

Reinhardt, J., and Düsterhaus, D., 'Verfassungsgemäß, aber gemeinschaftswidrig? Zur Neufassung des deutschen Gesetzes über den Europäischen Haftbefehl und der damit einhergehenden Inländerprivilegierung', *NVwZ*, 25 (2006), 432–4

Ress, G., 'Der Europäische Gerichtshof für Menschenrechte als pouvoir neutre', *ZaöRV*, 69 (2009), 289–309

Riedmeyer, O., 'Die Vollstreckung von verkehrsrechtlichen Geldstrafen und Geldbußen aus EU-Mitgliedstaaten in Deutschland', *NZV*, 27 (2014), 18–21

Riegel, R., 'Gemeinsame Ermittlungsgruppen: Herausforderungen und Lösungen', *eucrim*, 4 (2009), 99–106

Rijken, C., 'Joint Investigation Teams', *ULR*, 2 (2006), 99–118

Rinio, C., 'Hauptverhandlung per Videokonferenz im Wege der internationalen Rechtshilfe in Strafsachen', *NStZ*, 24 (2004), 188–91

Roger, B., 'Europäisierung des Strafverfahrens: oder nur der Strafverfolgung?', *GA*, 157 (2010), 27–43

Rohlff, D., *Der europäische Haftbefehl* (Frankfurt a.M.: Peter Lang, 2003)

Romano, M., 'La leggi spagnole', in Pansini, G., and Scalfati, A., eds., *Il mandato d'arresto europeo* (Napoli: Jovene, 2005), 273–8

Ronsfeld, P., *Rechtshilfe Anerkennung und Vertrauen: die Europäische Ermittlungsanordnung* (Berlin: Duncker & Humblot, 2015)

Rosenthal, M., 'Europäisches Haftbefehlsgesetz, zweiter Versuch', *ZRP*, 39 (2006), 105–9

Rosi, E., 'L'elenco dei reati nella decisione-quadro sul mandato d'arresto europeo etc.', in Acuña, R., *Il mandato di arresto europeo* (Padova: CEDAM, 2004), 71–90

Roth, A., 'Direkte Korrespondenz deutscher Staatsanwaltschaften und Strafgerichte mit Verfahrensbeteiligten im Ausland', *NStZ*, 34 (2014), 551–8

Royer, G., 'Observations Cour de cassation, crim., 7.2.2007', *AJP*, 4 (2007), 187–88

Ruggeri, S., 'Beweisrechtshilfe und Grundrechtseingriffe am Beispiel des Richtlinienvorschlags einer europäischen Ermittlungsanordnung (RlV EEA)', *ZStW*, 125 (2013), 407–34

'Introduction to the Proposal of a European Investigation Order: Due Process Concerns and Open Issues', in Ruggeri, S., ed., *Transnational Evidence and Multicultural Inquiries in Europe: Developments in EU Legislation and New Challenges for Human Rights-Oriented Criminal Investigations in Cross-border Cases* (Heidelberg et al: Springer, 2014), 3–25

'Multiculturalism, Coercive Measures, Human Rights in EU Judicial Cooperation in Criminal Matters', in Ruggieri, F., ed., *Criminal Proceedings, Languages and the EU: Linguistic and Legal Issues* (Berlin, Heidelberg: Springer, 2014), 215–36

'Die Vewertung im Ausland erhobener Beweise im europäischen Rechtsraum', *ZIS*, 10 (2015), 456–67

Ryngaert, C., 'Universal Jurisdiction in an ICC Era', *EJCCLCJ*, 14 (2006), 46–80

Safokolov, Y., 'Die Rechtsprechung des EGMR zum Folterverbot', *OstEuR*, 10 (2009), 167–83

Sajonz, C., 'Peines privatives de liberté et ransfert des personnes condamnées', *RIDP*, 77 (2006), 163–8

Salditt, F., 'Doppelte Verteidigung im einheitlichen Raum', *StV*, 23 (2003), 136–7

Sanz Hermida, A. M., 'Aplicación transnacional de la prohibición del bis in idem en la Unión Europea', *RP*, 21 (2008), 126–38

Satzger, H., 'Grund- und menschenrechtliche Grenzen für die Vollstreckung eines Europäischen Haftbefehls? "Verfassungsrechtliche Identitätskontrolle" durch das BVerfG vs. Vollstreckungsaufschub bei "außergewöhnlichen Umständen" nach dem EuGH', *NStZ*, 15 (2016), 505–22

Satzger, H., and Pohl, T., 'The German Constitutional Court and the European Arrest Warrant', *JICJ*, 4 (2006), 686–701

Sauer, H., '"Solange" geht in Altersteilzeit: Der unbedingte Vorrang der Menschenwürde vor dem Unionsrecht', *NJW*, 69 (2016), 1134–8

Sautner, L., 'Aktuelle Tendenzen der Europäisierung des Strafrechts', in Österreichisches Bundesministerium für Justiz, ed., 34. *Ottensteiner Fortbildungsseminar aus Strafrecht und Kriminologie: 20. bis 24. Februar 2006* (Vienna et al.: Neuer Wissenschaftlicher Verlag, 2006), 79–101

'Die Vollstreckung eines Europäischen Haftbefehls nach dem EU-JZG', *ÖJZ*, 9 (2005), 328–43

Schallmoser, N. M., 'The EAW and Fundamental Rights', *EJCCLCJ*, 22 (2014), 135–65

Schaper, T., *Verfassungsrechtliche Probleme bei der Übertragung von Hoheitsrechten zur Schaffung eines Europäischen Strafrechts* (Berlin: Duncker & Humblot, 2009)

Scheller, S. M., 'Das Schengener Informationssystem: Rechtshilfeersuchen "per Computer"', *JZ*, 47 (1992), 904–11

Schierholt, C., 'Stellungnahme zum Grünbuch der Europäischen Kommission zur Erlangung verwertbarer Beweise in Strafverfahren aus einem anderen Mitgliedstaat', *ZIS*, 5 (2010), 567–8

Schmahl, S., 'Der Europäische Haftbefehl vor dem EuGH', *DVBl.*, 122 (2007), 1463–70

Schmidt, J., 'Die transnationale Vollstreckung von Geldstrafen nach dem Europäischen Geldsanktionsgesetz', *NZWiSt*, 1 (2012), 95–101

Schmidt, U., 'Die Auslieferung nichtdeutscher Staatsangehöriger nach der Neufassung des Europäischen Haftbefehlsgesetzes', *StraFo*, 20 (2007), 7–11

Scholz, C. J., 'Auswirkungen des Rahmenbeschlusses zur Geldsanktionenvollstreckung von 2005 und des Gesetzes über die internationale Rechtshilfe in Strafsachen auf die deutsche Rechtspraxis', *VRR*, 6 (2014), 8–13

Schomburg, W., 'Internationale vertragliche Rechtshilfe in Strafsachen', *NJW*, 56 (2003), 3392–5

'Ein neuer Start! Internationale vertragliche Rechtshilfe in Strafsachen', *NJW*, 54 (2001), 801–6

Schomburg, W., Lagodny, O., and Schallmoser, N. M., '§13: Grundlagen der Zusammenarbeit', in Böse, *Europäisches Strafrecht* (2013), 495–536

Schoppa, K., *Europol im Verbund der Europäischen Sicherheitsagenturen* (Berlin: Duncker & Humblot, 2013)

Schork, A., *Das Auslieferungsverfahren in der Schweiz und in Deutschland unter Einbeziehung des Europäischen Haftbefehls* (Frankfurt a.M.: Peter Lang, 2009)

Schröder, J., and Stiegel, U., '§35: Zusammenarbeit mit Drittstaaten', in Sieber, Satzger and von Heinegg, *Europäisches Strafrecht* (2014), 615–29

Schünemann, B., 'Die Entscheidung des Bundesverfassungsgerichtes zum Europäischen Haftbefehl', *StV*, 25 (2005), 681–85

'Europäischer Haftbefehl und EU-Verfassungsentwurf auf schiefer Ebene: Die Schranken des Grundgesetzes', *ZRP*, 36 (2003), 185–89

'Europäischer Sicherheitsstaat = europäischer Polizeistaat?', *ZIS*, 2 (2007), 528–34

'Grundzüge eines Alternativ-Entwurfs zur europäischen Strafverfolgung', *ZStW*, 116 (2004), 376–99

'Die Implementation des Europäischen Haftbefehls in Polen und Deutschland im Vergleich', in Joerden, J. C., and Szwarc, A. J., eds., *Europäisierung des Strafrechts in Polen und Deutschland: Rechtsstaatliche Grundlagen* (Berlin: de Gruyter, 2007), 265–77

'Noch einmal: Zur Kritik der rechtsstaatlichen Bresthaftigkeit des EU-Geldsanktionengesetzes, des europatümelnden strafrechtlichen Neopositivismus und seiner Apologie von Böse', *ZIS*, 5 (2010), 735–41

'Die parlamentarische Gesetzgebung als Lakai von Brüssel? Zum Entwurf des Europäischen Haftbefehlsgesetzes', *StV*, 23 (2003), 531–3

'Verteidigung in Europa', *StV*, 26 (2006), 361–8

'Die Vorschläge der Europäischen Kommission für eine Opferschutzrichtlinie', *ERA Forum*, 12 (2011), 445–63

Schünemann, B., and Roger, B., 'Die Karawane der Europäisierung des Strafrechts zieht weiter', *ZIS*, 5 (2010), 515–23

Schulz, U., 'Können die Regelungen über die Zusammenarbeit der EU-Mitgliedstaaten bei der Strafverfolgung kurzerhand aufgehoben werden? ', *eucrim*, 11 (2016), 55–60

Schuster, F. P., 'Telekommunikationsüberwachung in grenzüberschreitenden Strafverfahren nach Inkrafttreten des EU-Rechtshilfeübereinkommens', *NStZ*, 26 (2006), 657–63

Verwertbarkeit im Ausland gewonnener Beweise im deutschen Strafprozess (Berlin: Duncker and Humblot, 2006)

'Die Europäische Ermittlungsanordnung: Möglichkeiten einer gesetzlichen Realisierung', *StV*, 35 (2015), 393–9

'Verwertbarkeit von Beweismitteln bei grenzüberschreitender Strafverfolgung', *ZIS*, 11 (2016), 564–73

Seitz, H., 'Das Europäische Haftbefehlsgesetz', *NStZ*, 24 (2004), 546–9

Sensburg, P. E., 'Rechtliche Rahmenbedingungen von Joint Investigation Teams', *Kriminalistik*, 62 (2008), 661–5

Sieber, U., 'Bekämpfung des EG-Betrugs und Perspektiven der europäischen Amts- und Rechtshilfe', *ZRP*, 33 (2000), 186–92

'Europäische Einigung und Europäisches Strafrecht', *ZStW*, 103 (1991), 957–79

Sinn, A., 'Die Vermeidung von strafrechtlichen Jurisdiktionskonflikten in der Europäischen Union', *ZIS*, 8 (2013), 1–9

Sinn, A., and Wörner, L., 'The European Arrest Warrant and Its Implementation in Germany', *ZIS*, 2 (2007), 204–20

Skouris, V., 'Criminal Law Issues in the Case-Law of the European Court of Justice: A General Overview', *EuCLR*, 1 (2011), 108–13

'Zum Rechtsschutz in der EU nach Lissabon', in Meng, W., Ress, G., and Stein, T., eds., *Europäische Integration und Globalisierung: Festschrift zum 60-jährigen Bestehen des Europa-Instituts* (Baden-Baden: Nomos, 2011), 545–54

Smith, E., 'Running before We Can Walk? Mutual Recognition at the Expense of Fair Trials in Europe's Area of Freedom, Justice and Security', *NJECL*, 4 (2013), 82–98

Soiné, M., 'Identitätsfeststellung und Vernehmung festgenommener Personen im Anschluss an grenzüberschreitende Nacheile im Schengen-Raum', *ZIS*, 11 (2016), 319–29

Sokol, T., 'Implementation of EAW in Croatia: A Risk for the Functioning of Judicial Cooperation in Criminal Matters in the EU?, *EJCCLCJ*, 23 (2015), 258–80

Sørensen, H. B. F. M., 'Mutual Recognition and the Right to Damages for Criminal Investigations', *EuCLR*, 5 (2015), 194–208

Spencer, J. R., 'The Green Paper on Obtaining Evidence from One Member State to Another and Securing Its Admissibility: The Reaction of One British Lawyer', *ZIS*, 5 (2010), 602–6

'Implementing the European Arrest Warrant', *StatuteLR*, 30 (2009), 184–202

Spinellis, D., 'Das Auslieferungs- und das Rechtshilfeabkommen zwischen EU und USA', in Arnold, J., Burkhardt, B., Gropp, W., Heine, G., Koch, H.-G., Lagodny, O., Perron, W., and Walther, S., eds., *Menschengerechtes Strafrecht: Festschrift für Albin Eser zum 70. Geburtstag* (Munich: C. H. Beck, 2005), 873–88

Spinellis, D., 'Die (geplante) Europäische Beweisanordnung (aus der Sicht des griechischen Rechts)', in Joerden, J. C., Scheffler, U., Sinn, A., and Wolf, G, eds., *Vergleichende Strafrechtswissenschaft: Frankfurter Festschrift für Andrzej J. Szwarc zum 70. Geburtstag* (Berlin: Duncker & Humblot, 2009), 701–12

Spiezia, F., 'Linguistic Regimes and Judicial Cooperation in the Eurojust's Perspective', in Ruggieri, F., ed., *Criminal Proceedings, Languages and the EU: Linguistic and Legal Issues* (Berlin, Heidelberg: Springer, 2014), 23–42

Staudigl, U., and Weber, S., 'Europäische Bewährungsüberwachung', *NStZ*, 28 (2008), 17–20

Stiegel, U., 'Grünbuch der Kommission zur Schaffung einer Europäischen Staatsanwaltschaft', *ZRP*, 36 (2003), 172–5

Strandbakken, A., 'The Nordic Answer to the European Arrest Warrant: The Nordic Arrest Warrant', *eucrim*, 2 (2007), 138–40

Suelmann, S., 'Der Europäische Haftbefehl: Kompetenz der EU, Regelungsgegenstand und Anwendungsprobleme', *HumFoR*, 14 (2009), 122–39

Šugman Stubbs, K., 'The Implementation of the European Arrest Warrant in the Republic of Slovenia', *eucrim*, 2 (2007), 133–8

Suominen, A., 'The Characteristics of Nordic Criminal Law in the Setting of EU Criminal Law', *EuCLR*, 1 (2011), 170–87

'Different Implementations of Mutual Recognition Framework Decisions', *eucrim*, 6 (2011), 24–7

'The Nordic Arrest Warrant Finally in Force', *EuCLR*, 4 (2014), 41–5

The Principle of Mutual Recognition in Cooperation in Criminal Matters (Cambridge and Portland: Intersentia, 2011)

Swoboda, S., 'The Self-Perception of the ECJ and Its Neglect of the Defense Perspective in Its Preliminary Rulings on Judicial Cooperation in Criminal Matters', *ZIS*, 10 (2015), 361–74

Tamarit Sumalla, J., 'European Policy on Victims of Crime', in de Hoyos Sancho, M., ed., *Guarantees and Rights of the Especially Vulnerable Victim in the Legal Framework of the EU* (Valencia: Tirant lo Blanch, 2013), 31–46

Tamm, M., 'Rückwirkungen des gescheiterten SWIFT-Abkommens auf das Abkommen über Fluggastdaten?', *VuR*, 25 (2010), 215–23

Tams, C. J., 'Anmerkung zu BVerfG NJW 2005, 2289: Europäischer Haftbefehl', *JA*, 38 (2006), 177–9

Thomas, J., 'The Principle of Mutual Recognition: Success or Failure?', *ERA Forum*, 13 (2013), 585–88

Thunberg Schunke, M., 'The Manifesto on European Criminal Procedure Law: A Commentary on the Perspective of mutual Recognition and Violations of Defence Rights', *EuCLR*, 5 (2015), 46–53

Tiedemann, K., 'Bemerkungen zur Zukunft des europäischen Strafprozesses', in Arnold, J., ed., *Menschengerechtes Strafrecht: Festschrift für Albin Eser zum 70. Geburtstag* (Munich: C. H. Beck, 2005), 889–99

Tinkl, C., 'Anmerkung zu EuGH, Urteil v. 3.5.2007 - C-303/05', *ZIS*, 2 (2007), 419–21

Die Rechtsstellung des Einzelnen nach dem Rahmenbeschluss über den Europäischen Haftbefehl (Frankfurt a.M.: Peter Lang, 2008)

'Die Ungleichbehandlung eigener und fremder Staatsangehöriger im deutschen Auslieferungsrecht', *ZIS*, 5 (2010), 320–6

Tolttila, K., 'The Nordic Arrest Warrant: What Makes for Even Higher Mutual Trust', *NJECL*, 2 (2011), 368–77

Tomuschat, C., 'Ungereimtes: Zum Urteil des Bundesverfassungsgerichts vom 18. Juli 2005 über den Europäischen Haftbefehl', *EuGRZ*, 32 (2005), 453–60

Trautmann, S., 'Das neue Europäische Geldsanktionsgesetz: Vollstreckung ausländischer Geldsanktionen zur Ahndung von Verkehrsverstößen', *NZV*, 24 (2011), 57–62

Träskman, O., '"A Nordic Academic Perspective" to the European Criminal Policy Initiative: A Manifesto for European Criminal Procedure Law', *EuCLR*, 5 (2015), 60–7

Turner, J. I., 'Interstate Conflict and Cooperation in Criminal Cases: An American Perspective', *EuCLR*, 4 (2014), 114–46

Ubertis, G., 'La prova acquisita all'estero e la sua utilizzabilità in Italia', *CassP*, 54 (2014), 696–706

van der Aa, S., and Römkens, R., 'The State of the Art in Stalking Legislation: Reflections on European Developments', *EuCLR*, 3 (2013), 232–356

van den Brink, T., Langbroek, P., Marguery, T., and Sluijs, O., 'Country Report The Netherlands', in Albers et al., 'Evaluation Framework' (2013), 164–98

vander Beken, T., 'Freedom, Security and Justice in the European Union', in Klip, A., and van der Wilt, H., eds., *Harmonisation and Harmonising Measures in Criminal Law* (Amsterdam: Koninklijke Nederlandse Akad. van Wetenschappen, 2002), 95–102

van der Hulst, J., 'Extradition and the European Arrest Warrant in the Netherlands', *eucrim*, 9 (2014), 64–8

van der Wilt, H., 'The Principle of Reciprocity', in Blekxtoon and van Ballegooij, *Handbook on the EAW* (2005), 71–81

'The European Arrest Warrant and the Principle Ne Bis in Idem', in Blekxtoon and van Ballegooij, *Handbook on the EAW* (2005), 99–117

van Ooyen, R. C., Die Staatstheorie des Bundesverfassungsgerichts und Europa (Baden-Baden: Nomos, 2006)

'(K)ein Raum der Freiheit, der Sicherheit und des Rechts? Die Entscheidung des Bundesverfassungsgerichts zum EU-Haftbefehl', in Möllers, M. H., and van Ooyen, R. C., eds., *Europäisierung und Internationalisierung der Polizei* (Frankfurt a.M.: Verlag für Polizeiwissenschaft, 2006), 59–68

van Sliedregt, E., 'The European Arrest Warrant: Extradition in Transition', *EuConst*, 3 (2007), 244–52

Vermeulen, G., 'EU Conventions Enhancing and Udpating Traditional Mechanisms for Judicial Cooperation in Criminal Matters', *RIDP*, 77 (2006), 59–95

Free Gathering and Movement of Evidence in Criminal Matters in the EU (Antwerp et al.: Maklu, 2011)

Vernimmen-Van Tiggelen, G., and Surano, L., *Analysis of the Future of Mutual Recognition in Criminal Matters in the EU, Final Report* (20 November 2008), at http://ec.europa.eu/justice/criminal/files/mutual_recognition_en.pdf, last accessed 27 January 2018

Vervaele, J. A. E., 'La europeización del Derecho penal y la dimensión penal de la integración europea', *RP*, 15 (2005), 169–84

Vierucci, L., 'The European Arrest Warrant: An Additional Tool for Prosecuting ICC Crimes', *JICJ*, 2 (2004), 275–85

Vogel, J., 'Abschaffung der Auslieferung?', *JZ*, 56 (2001), 937–43

'Europäischer Haftbefehl und deutsches Verfassungsrecht', *JZ*, 60 (2005), 801–9

'Licht und Schatten im Alternativ-Entwurf Europäische Strafverfolgung', *ZStW*, 116 (2004), 400–23

'Strafrecht und Strafrechtswissenschaft im internationalen und europäischen Rechtsraum', *JZ*, 67 (2012), 25–31

Vogler, R., 'Transnational Inquiries and the Protection of Human Rights in the Case-Law of the European Court of Human Rights', in Ruggeri, S., *Transnational Inquiries and the Protection of Fundamental Rights in Criminal Proceedings: A Study in Memory of Vittorio Grevi and Giovanni Tranchina* (Heidelberg et al.: Springer, 2013), 27–40

Vormbaum, M., *Schutz der Rechtsgüter von EU-Staaten durch das deutsche Strafrecht* (Münster: LIT, 2005)

Wahl, T., 'Annex to the Country Report Germany: Statistics', in Albers et al., 'Evaluation Framework' (2013), 268–300

'Der Rahmenbeschluss zu Abwesenheitsentscheidungen Brüsseler EU-Justizkooperation als Fall für Straßburg?', *eucrim*, 10 (2015), 70–6

'Summary of the Defence Lawyers' Views on the European Arrest Warrant and Mutual Trust', in Albers et al., 'Evaluation Framework' (2013), 318–32

Wasmeier, M., 'Der Europäische Haftbefehl vor dem Bundesverfassungsgericht: Zur Verzahnung des nationalen and europäischen Strafrechts', *ZEuS*, 9 (2006), 23–39

'Stand und Perspektiven des EU-Strafrechts', *ZStW*, 116 (2004), 320–5

Wehnert, A., 'Deutsches und Europäisches Strafrecht: Fragen und Widersprüche', in Widmaier, G., ed., *Festschrift für Hans Dahs* (Cologne: Schmidt, 2005), 523–42

'Europäischer Haftbefehl', *StraFo*, 16 (2003), 356–60

Weigend, E., and Górski, A., 'Die Implementierung des Europäischen Haftbefehls in das polnische Strafrecht', *ZStW*, 117 (2005), 193–207

Weigend, T., 'Der Eckstein als Stein des Anstoßes', in Müller-Dietz, H., ed., *Festschrift für Heike Jung zum 65. Geburtstag am 23. April 2007* (Baden-Baden: Nomos, 2007), 1069–84

'Grundsätze und Probleme des deutschen Auslieferungsrechts', *JuS*, 40 (2000), 105–11

Weyembergh, A., 'Les jurisdictions belges et le mandat d'arrêt européen', *eucrim*, 1 (2006), 26–9

'Transverse Report on Judicial Control in Cooperation in Criminal Matters', in Ligeti, *Prosecutor for the EU*, i (2013), 945–85

White, S., 'Harmonisation of criminal law under the first pillar', *E.L. Rev.*, 31 (2006), 81–92

Wieczorek, I., 'A Needed Balance between Security, Liberty and Justice: Positive Signals Arrive from the Field of Victims' Rights', *EuCLR*, 2 (2012), 141–57

Williams, C., 'The European Evidence Warrant', *RIDP*, 77 (2006), 155–62

Wolff, H. A., 'Die verfassungsrechtlichen Auslieferungsverbote', *StV*, 24 (2004), 154–9

Wolter, J., 'Polizeiliche und justizielle Datenübermittlungen in Deutschland und der Europäischen Union: Polizei und Europol, Staatsanwaltschaft und Eurojust', in Wolter, J., et al., eds., *Datenübermittlungen und Vorermittlungen: Festgabe für Hans Hilger* (Heidelberg: Müller, 2003), 275–90

Würz, K., *Das Schengener Durchführungsübereinkommen: Einführung, Erläuterungen, Vorschriften* (Stuttgart et al.: Boorberg, 1997)

Xanthopoulou, E., 'The Quest for Proportionality for the EAW: Fundamental Rights Protection in a Mutual Recognition Environment', *NJECL*, 6 (2015), 32–52

Zaharieva, R., 'The European Investigation Order and the Joint Investigation Team: Which Road to Take', *ERA Forum*, 18 (2017), 397–408

Zeder, F., 'Europastrafrecht, Vertrag von Lissabon und Stockholmer Programm: Mehr Grundrechtsschutz? ', *EuR*, 47 (2012), 34–60

'Gegenwart und Zukunft der gegenseitigen Anerkennung in Strafsachen in der EU', *ÖJZ*, 64 (2009), 992–1002

Zeidler, A., *Der Grundsatz der beiderseitigen Strafbarkeit im Auslieferungsrecht* (Hamburg: Kovač, 2008)

Zerbes, I., 'Legal Issues of Transnational Exchange of Electronic Evidence in Criminal Proceedings', *EuCLR*, 5 (2015), 304–11

Zgaga, S., 'Rights of Victims in Slovenian Criminal Law According to the EU Framework Decision on the Standing of Victims in Criminal Proceedings', *eucrim*, 6 (2011), 88–92

Ziegenhahn, D., *Der Schutz der Menschenrechte bei der grenzüberschreitenden Zusammenarbeit in Strafsachen* (Berlin: Duncker & Humblot, 2002)

Zimmermann, A., 'Die Auslieferung Deutscher an Staaten der EU und an internationale Gerichtshöfe', *JZ*, 56 (2001), 233–8

Zimmermann, F., 'Die Europäische Ermittlungsanordung: Schreckgespenst oder Zukunftsmodell für grenzüberschreitende Strafverfahren?', *ZStW*, 127 (2015), 143–75

Zimmermann, F., Glaser, S., and Motz, A., 'Mutual Recognition and Its Implications for the Gathering of Evidence in Criminal Proceedings: A Critical Analysis of the Initiative for a European Investigation Order', *EuCLR*, 1 (2011), 56–80

Zimmermann, T., 'Der Fall "Pisciotti" vor dem EuGH. Oder: Vom Wert der Unionsbürgerschaft im Auslieferungsrecht', *ZIS*, 12 (2017), 220–9

Zöller, M. A., 'Der Austausch von Strafverfolgungsdaten zwischen den Mitgliedstaaten der Europäischen Union', *ZIS*, 6 (2011), 64–9

'Neue unionsrechtliche Strafgesetzgebungskompetenzen nach dem Vertrag von Lissabon', in Baumeister, P., ed., *Staat, Verwaltung und Rechtsschutz: Festschrift für Wolf-Rüdiger Schenke zum 70. Geburtstag* (Berlin: Duncker & Humblot, 2011), 579–98;

Zypries, B., 'Rechtspolitik in der Europäischen Union: Rückblick und Ausblicke', *RuP*, 40 (2004), 3–12

5

Institutionalisation

1 In this chapter the relevant institutions applying, implementing and supervising European Criminal Law will be analysed. This analysis confirms the remarkably repressive tendency of the European criminal justice project, providing for an avalanche of repressive institutions which, as already analysed in Chapter 1,[1] operate in a compound network (*Verbund*) of criminal prosecution and thereby exercise a considerable, albeit not very explicit, influence at the operational level of European criminal justice. As if this were not enough, the European Public Prosecutor Office (EPPO), to be operational not before end of 2020, though, lurks around the corner and all this is not – what a stark contrast! – matched by a proper European criminal defence institution.[2] Indeed, as we have seen throughout this book,[3] so far criminal defence across Europe has been organised on a private level with the European Criminal Bar Association (ECBA) as its only visible representative.[4] This situation is, of course, difficult to reconcile with the strong normative recognition of defence rights in the European instruments, especially the ECHR and the CFREU, as analysed in detail in Chapter 2 of this book.

A. L'Office européen de lutte anti-fraude (OLAF)

2 OLAF was established by Commission Decision 1999/352/EC, ESCS, Euratom ('**OLAF Decision**')[5] and Regulations 1073/99 (EC) and 1074/99 (Euratom)[6] in 1999 as an independent Commission agency and the successor of the *Unité de coordination de la lutte anti-fraude* (UCLAF).[7] Pursuant to Art. 9 of Protocol No 36,[8] the two regulations remained valid after the Lisbon Treaty, but in 2013 they were replaced by Regulation (EU, Euratom) No 883/2013 ('**OLAF Regulation 2013**').[9] An evaluation has been carried out in October 2017.[10]

OLAF was founded by the Commission as an **independent** investigative office, as the previous inclusion of UCLAF in the Commission's hierarchy and its resulting dependence on instructions had led to the very real risk of the suppression of internal investigations.[11] While OLAF is assigned to the Commission in terms of organisational structure, the Office is completely autonomous as far as investigative operations are concerned ('**dual function**'),[12] and its investigations are thus a direct execution of Union authority.[13] OLAF is headed by a director general appointed for a seven-year, non-renewable term.[14] If he considers the Office's independence to have been violated by the Commission, he can bring this matter before the CJEU.[15] OLAF's independence is also safeguarded by an external Supervisory Committee, which regularly checks upon the Office's investigative activities.[16]

3 The Office's key task is to investigate **fraud, corruption and other illegal activity** affecting the financial interests of the Union.[17] Besides this repressive task, OLAF is also obliged to present preventive **strategies and legislative initiatives** with the objective of fraud prevention and the prevention of counterfeiting the euro,[18] and to support and co-ordinate Member States' co-operation to protect the financial interests of the Union against fraud.[19] Concerning OLAF's investigations, it should be noted that the Office is an administrative authority and its activity thus does not, in principle, fall within the field of criminal procedure but rather represents **preliminary investigative action of an administrative nature.**[20] Of course, this does not exclude the possibility that an OLAF report could trigger a criminal investigation and thus form part of criminal proceedings in a broad sense.[21] Yet the extent to which OLAF's findings can be used in criminal proceedings is controversial.[22] Pursuant to Art. 11(2) OLAF Regulation, OLAF's final reports 'shall constitute admissible evidence … in the same way and under the same conditions as administrative reports drawn up by national administrative inspectors'.

4 A distinction is to be made between external and internal investigations.[23] **External investigations** are linked to the work carried out by UCLAF; here, OLAF is dependent on the competent national investigative authorities, at least in factual terms. When carrying out an 'on-the-spot check' of an economic operator, for example, OLAF must observe the procedural law of the respective Member State and is *not* permitted to adopt any *coercive measures.*[24] However, national authorities are obliged to co-operate with OLAF to a large extent; in particular, they must support the Office in gathering relevant information.[25] **Internal investigations** refer to irregularities within the institutions, offices and agencies of the Union.[26] In this respect, OLAF holds a much stronger position than UCLAF (going beyond its director general's independence): OLAF may carry out investigations within the sphere of an EU institution against that institution's will, examining and if necessary confiscating documents and data media and gathering information from EU officials and servants.[27] OLAF may also be obliged to hand proceedings over to national justice authorities, who then continue these as criminal investigation proceedings.[28] Any 'pre-investigation measure' carried out by OLAF concludes with a **report** providing information on the investigation's legal basis, the procedural steps followed, the facts established and their preliminary legal evaluation, including any financial effects. Furthermore, the report documents compliance with procedural guarantees. Annexed to the report are the recommendations of the director general concerning whether any measures are to be taken and, if so, which ones.[29] While the nature of a recommendation leaves a margin of appreciation to the Member States whether to initiate an investigation, they are obliged to co-operate in good faith,[30] and have to admit the OLAF reports as evidence in their national proceedings.[31]

5 Despite these extensive powers, we should not forget that OLAF has to operate within an **area of political tension**. This can be seen, for instance, through the fact that the above-mentioned authorisation to investigate even against an EU institution's will was created against the (initial) resistance of the Commission. Initially it was unclear whether OLAF also had the authority to carry out investigations in the European Central Bank and the European Investment Bank; however, in the meantime, following legal action brought by the Commission, the CJEU has declared decisions of the ECB and EIB that claimed the prevention of fraud to be the remit of their respective internal audit alone[32] to be invalid.[33] OLAF's extensive investigative powers towards Members of the EP stand in a tense relationship with the open mandate of the MEPs, who according to Art. 1(2) of the parliamentary implementation decision[34] are 'required to cooperate fully with the Office' in internal investigations.[35]

6 Unlike earlier versions,[36] the current OLAF Regulation for the first time also contains a list of mandatory **procedural guarantees**.[37] This can be seen as a response to widespread rights violations in the course of OLAF investigations.[38] First, OLAF is obliged to be objective; the Office must investigate facts both for and against the person concerned.[39] Persons interviewed shall have the right to avoid self-incrimination (*nemo tenetur* principle).[40] The presumption of innocence applies to the persons affected by the investigation (that is, those who may subsequently be charged in later criminal proceedings).[41] If they are to be questioned, they must be given ten days' notice. The summons must inform the person concerned of their rights. In particular, they may be assisted by a person of their choice.[42] Furthermore, they have the right to comment on the facts concerning them.[43] The application of the procedural guarantees in practice is to be monitored by the Supervisory Committee.[44] Even though the introduction of procedural guarantees should be welcomed wholeheartedly, it seems doubtful whether the catalogue in Art. 9 OLAF Regulation already suffices for investigation results to be used in a comprehensive manner that is unobjectionable under the rule of law in any subsequent proceedings. This is the background against which the Commission's Proposals to create a 'controller of procedural safeguards' and stronger rights for searches and confiscations should be read,[45] seeing as here the concern is to ensure the unrestricted use of the information established by OLAF by the EPPO (to be dealt with in the last section of this Chapter).[46]

B. Europol

7 Europol became operational as the successor to the **European Drugs Unit (EDU)** on 1 July 1999.[47] Both institutions originate the reflections of the EC Summit of Luxembourg (1991) on establishing a European central criminal investigation department.[48]

In 1992, the Maastricht Treaty enshrined the creation of a 'European Police Office (Europol)' in Art. K.1 No 9 TEU (Art. 29(2) first indent TEU old version). However, as establishing Europol required a long period of preparation, the EDU was founded in 1993. Its aim was initially to improve the exchange of information and operative co-operation in the area of drug-related crime, and simultaneously prepare the ground for Europol; its remit was later expanded substantially.[49] The *legal foundations* of the *EDU's* activities were laid first by a 'Ministerial Agreement on the establishment of the European Drugs Unit' of 2 June 1991[50] and later by a Joint Action.[51]

8 On 26 July 1995, the EU Member States enacted the Convention on the establishment of a **European Police Office (Europol Convention)**[52] on the basis of Art. 29(2), Art. 34(2)(d) TEU old version. The Convention entered into force on 1 October 1998,[53] and Europol commenced its operations on 1 July 1999 on this legal basis.[54] The Council Decision of 6 April 2009 ('**Council Decision 2009**')[55] established a new foundation in secondary law,[56] replacing the Europol Convention.[57] The decision

granted Europol legal personality and the 'most extensive' legal and contractual capacity in the Member States.[58] The **Lisbon Treaty** refers to Europol in connection with Eurojust[59] and the EPPO,[60] giving it a prominent role in supporting and strengthening police co-operation in cross-border 'serious crime affecting two or more Member States, terrorism and forms of crime which affect a common interest covered by a Union policy'.[61] According to the Council's concepts as set out in the **Stockholm Programme**,[62] Europol should also become 'a hub for information exchange' and facilitate European co-operation in the area of prosecution.[63] In the meantime, the new **Europol Regulation** was adopted on 11 May 2016 (**Europol Regulation 2016**), replacing and repealing the former 2009 Decisions.[64] Unlike the Commission Proposal which suggested that Europol and the European Police College (CEPOL)[65] should be merged,[66] it is now envisaged that these two institutions should merely co-operate.[67] In addition, on 1 January 2013 the European Cybercrime Centre (EC3) was established within Europol. The EC3 serves as a focal point and pool for information on cybercrime and for specialist knowledge, supporting Member States' investigations and serving as 'the collective voice' of all investigators dealing with cybercrime.[68]

9 Europol's **tasks** derive from Art. 88(2) TFEU[69] and Art. 4 Europol Regulation 2016. Accordingly, Europol is tasked with the collection, analysis and exchange of information on the one hand, and with the co-ordination, organisation and execution of investigations together with the Member States or within the framework of joint investigative teams (JITs, to which we will return in a moment) on the other hand.[70] Europol is still not permitted to independently carry out any *operational actvities*, but only 'in liaison and in agreement' with the Member States; *coercive measures* remain the exclusive responsibility of the national authorities.[71] Demands for a 'European FBI' and an upgrading of Europol to an operative agency with coercive powers[72] have thus been denied.[73] The former distinction between 'principal tasks' and 'additional tasks'[74] has been given up in Art. 4 Europol Regulation 2016, providing instead for a comprehensive list of basically equal tasks. These essentially correspond to the former Art. 5 Europol Decision 2009, although greater emphasis is laid on supporting Member State investigations, analyses and other measures.

The tasks include the collection, storage, processing, analysis and exchange of information, including criminal intelligence,[75] notifying national authorities of information concerning them,[76] providing analytical support to MS in connection with major international events,[77] and combating cybercrime,[78] as well as preparing threat assessments, strategic analyses and general situation reports.[79] Furthermore, in cases where co-ordinated action in several MS is necessary, Europol may recommend the setting up of JITs.[80] Europol may itself participate in such a team,[81] supporting it especially in the collection and analysis of intelligence.[82] Moreover, Europol is to develop specialist knowledge for national authorities, and to provide advice on investigations[83] and strategic intelligence to assist the efficient and effective use of the resources available for operational activities and the support of such activities. In order to fulfil all of these tasks, Europol is to maintain a comprehensive information system,[84] which may also incorporate a significant amount of personal data,[85] as will be seen in the following. MS have regulated their co-operation with Europol in specific Acts,[86] in their international co-operation laws[87] or as part of general police law.[88]

10 In performing these tasks, Europol is bound by the **objectives** and **subject matter jurisdiction** set out in Art. 3 Europol Regulation 2016. Its *objective* is to prevent and combat organised crime, terrorism and other forms of serious crime listed exhaustively in an annex to the Decision.[89] According to this annex, Europol's *competence* includes drug trafficking, money laundering, swindling and fraud, corruption, trafficking in human beings, murder and computer crime.[90] However, it is required that the crimes in question affect two or more Member States in such a way that joint action is necessary.[91] Europol's jurisdiction also extends to so-called 'related criminal offences',[92] including criminal offences committed in order to procure the means of perpetrating acts, to facilitate commission or to prevent punishment.[93] Otherwise, the priorities are to be decided by the Council.[94]

11 The main focus of Europol's activity thus remains the gathering and analysis of intelligence using an **automated information processing system**, consisting of the 'Europol Information System' and the 'Analysis work files'.[95] The flow of information between Europol and the Member States takes place via their respective **national units**,[96] which in turn second their own **Europol liaison officers** (ELOs) to Europol, as shown in Figure 10;[97] as 'ambassadors' of the Members States these liaison officers enjoy *diplomatic status*.[98]

The national units are the only liaison bodies between Europol and the Member State authorities,[99] and are Europol's most important source

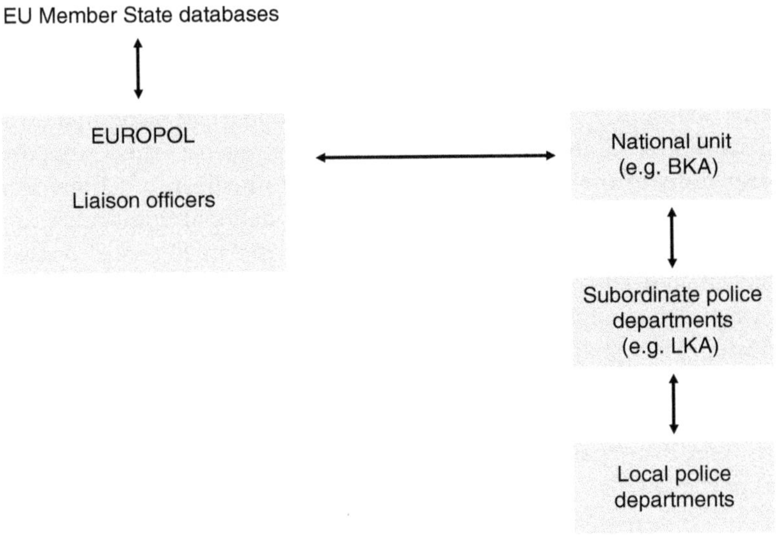

Figure 10 National liaison officers – information flow

of information.[100] They may refuse to supply information because of (essential) national security interests.[101] Europol inputs data from third States or deriving from its own analyses itself.[102] The fact that data are gathered and processed by national authorities according to national law,[103] but can subsequently be accessed by every (other) Member State via its national unit, is a cause for concern.[104] For this makes it possible for a national unit to access data which it would not have been allowed to collect in the first place or would have been forced to erase in the meantime according to its national law.[105] Thus the **transfer of data throughout the Union** is permitted without a prior harmonisation of the rules on the gathering and use of data,[106] thereby risking a lowering of the standard of data protection.[107] Also, the transfer of data to third States or third parties[108] deserves critical examination.[109]

12 Pursuant to the above-mentioned information processing system, Europol has extensive **informational rights** and has been compared to a 'mega-search engine'.[110] First, Europol is able to process 'such data as are necessary for the performance of Europol's tasks'[111] via a specific information system.[112] The *(personal) data* include the attributes suitable for identifying not only persons who are suspected of having committed or taken part in a criminal offence in respect of which Europol is competent according to Art. 4 Europol Regulation 2016 or who have been convicted of such an offence,[113] but also 'persons regarding whom there are factual indications or reasonable grounds under the national law of the Member State concerned to believe that *they will commit* criminal offences in respect of which Europol is competent'.[114] Data retrieval is admissible insofar as it is required for the tasks of an individual case and is otherwise subject to the legal and administrative regulations of the retrieving unit.[115] However, only national liaison bodies and officers and (duly empowered) Europol officials have the **right to retrieve data**;[116] that is, as a rule, the competent national police authorities.[117] The possibility of an extension of retrieval rights to 'competent authorities designated to that effect by the Member States' does not ultimately change the police's control over the data, for the authority making the enquiry is only told whether the data are available, and is still forced to refer to the respective national unit for its actual content.[118] As a result, we have a full **police control over the data** which is difficult to reconcile with the prosecutorial/judicial control over the criminal proceedings (including the relevant data) as envisaged in the procedural systems of most Member States.[119]

Take the case of Germany, where the Federal Criminal Police (BKA) and the State Criminal Police Offices (*Landeskriminalämter*, LKAs) are able to retrieve data.[120] From a procedural perspective, this violates the principle that the prosecutorial authority is in charge of proceedings,[121] as it is only able to access information via the mentioned federal and state criminal police authorities.[122] The BKA is obliged to inform the prosecuting authorities without undue delay, but can exercise discretion concerning the *transmission* of data to them.[123] This dubious legal situation is not rendered any better by the fact that the (German) public prosecutor's office does not have direct access to the Inpol police information system in national investigations either.[124]

13 **Personal data** may be processed, inter alia, for the purpose of 'cross-checking aimed at identifying connections or other relevant links' with regard to 'persons who are suspected of having committed or taken part in a criminal offence . . . or who have been convicted of such an offence' and with regard to 'persons regarding whom there are factual indications or reasonable grounds to believe that they will commit criminal offences'.[125] As a result, *any EU citizen* can thus become a Europol target.[126] These darker sides of European integration in the field of internal security have given rise to the criticism, in regard to Europol (and Eurojust), that '[W]ith so-called "international" data transmissions, it is no longer possible for citizens to know who knows what

about them at any given time'.[127] The Europol Regulation 2016 pretends to remedy this, covering the issue of data protection extensively in Arts. 34 ff. Besides time limits for the storage and erasure of personal data having been introduced,[128] the persons affected are to be granted the right to information, rectification, erasure and blocking.[129] Furthermore, an independent data protection officer is to be appointed, who will ensure that data protection regulations are complied with.[130]

14 As far as the **monitoring of Europol** is concerned,[131] it should first be noted that Europol's activity can only affect fundamental rights through interventions in the *right to informational self-determination* (right to privacy) as the agency does not have, as we have seen above, any operative authority to go beyond this[132] – which is certainly reassuring from the point of view of fundamental rights.[133] At any rate, the right to privacy is important enough and it is particulary the task of the European Data Protection Supervisor (EDPS) to ensure that it is respected.[134] In addition, *national supervisory bodies* are to be established to monitor the input, the retrieval and any communication to Europol of personal data by the Member State concerned.[135] Any person shall have the right to request the national supervisory body.[136] *Political* control is to be exercised by the EP together with the national *parliaments* and specified further in regulations.[137] In this vein, Europol Regulation 2016 now provides for a *Joint Parliamentary Scrutiny Group (JPSG)*, to be set up by the EP together with the national parliaments.[138] The JPSG shall 'politically' monitor Europol's 'activities in fulfilling its mission';[139] it can request the chairperson of the management board, the executive director or the respective deputies to appear before it to discuss relevant matters;[140] it may also request the EDPS to appear before it to discuss issues of fundamental rights.[141] Moreover, Europol is of its own accord to place certain information, including threat assessments and strategic analyses, at the parliaments' disposal. The EP is also to have access to classified information processed by or through Europol.[142] However, the effectiveness of Europol's obligation to provide information and be accountable to the parliaments is limited by its obligations of discretion and confidentiality.[143]

15 The *judicial* control of concrete measures can now – after the five-year transitional period has expired[144] – be exercised by the CJEU pursuant to Art. 263(4) TFEU, as it (now) also monitors the legality of the actions of the 'bodies, offices or agencies of the Union'.[145] The Europol Regulation 2016 provides for a series of remedies.[146] The usual immunity regulations that apply to the officials and servants of the EU[147] also apply to Europol and its staff,[148] so that they are almost completely exempt from Member State jurisdiction concerning their acts carried out in an official capacity.[149] Of course, we should bear in mind that the rationale of immunity for international organisations is or should be primarily to maintain their functioning and not to protect their officials from (valid) prosecution.[150]

C. Eurojust

16 In parallel to OLAF's activity as a kind of 'preliminary investigation authority' for fraud related to the Union and police-specific co-operation within the context of Europol, the necessity of cross-border crime fighting has also grown stronger on a judicial level. This started[151] with the exchange of **liaison magistrates** and **liaison prosecutors**[152] and the establishment of a **European Judicial Network (EJN)**.[153]

The *liaison magistrates* and *prosecutors* are tasked with encouraging and accelerating all forms of judicial co-operation by establishing direct links.[154] The *EJN* goes beyond this, establishing a network of judicial points of contact that are usually located in the Member States' ministries of justice and are available as 'active intermediaries' – without any investigative authority of their own – facilitating co-operation.[155] They co-operate both with one another and with local authorities. The aim is to create 'the most appropriate direct contacts',[156] establishing networks of personal contacts (an 'old-boys' network'). Besides creating these 'appropriate contacts', periodic meetings of the national representatives are to be held and basic information on the national legal system is to be made available.[157]

17 However, it soon became evident that the decentralised co-ordination arising from this form of organisation resulted in a vast number of contact points and thus a loss of personal closeness.[158] In any case, **centrally co-ordinating cross-border prosecution** must inevitably stretch a *decentralised* network of *national* contact points to its limits in structural terms.[159] It was thus deemed necessary to create an *additional* central body in which the representatives of the judicial authorities of all Member States are located. Accordingly, the Council Decision of 14 December 2000 first established a provisional judicial co-operation unit with its seat in Brussels **(Pro-Eurojust)**.[160] Pro-Eurojust became **Eurojust**, based in The Hague, following the *Council Decision* of 28 February 2002.[161] This decision was amended in 2008 ('**Council**

Decision 2008').[162] Art. 85 TFEU[163] initially formed the basis for Eurojust's activity in primary EU treaty law. In the meantime, the Commission has submitted a Proposal for a Regulation based upon Art. 85 TFEU ('**Regulation Proposal Eurojust 2013**'), which aims to provide Eurojust with a new, more modern and more effective legal framework.[164] Should it be adopted, the regulation would apply directly, rendering national implementation acts obsolete.[165] Yet it has been criticised that the proposal does not fully exploit the potential of Art. 85 TFEU, especially as regards binding powers for Eurojust to initiate criminal investigations and resolve conflicts of jurisdiction.[166] In addition, there is still no role for the **defence** and no access to Eurojust services.[167] At any rate, with the adoption of the EPPO Regulation (to be discussed below) Eurojust's legal framework needs to be adjusted.

18 In **organisational** terms, Eurojust was conceptualised as an independent,[168] collegial[169] judicial institution of the Union, possessing legal personality.[170] Eurojust's **tasks** are the *initiation* of criminal investigations and proposing the initiation of prosecutions, the *co-ordination* of investigations and prosecutions in the Member States, and the strengthening of judicial *co-operation*, including with the EJN;[171] in summary, Eurojust thus *supports* and improves co-operation in cross-border prosecution as a kind of **documentation centre and clearing house with a service function**,[172] although its ability to **initiate investigations**[173] clearly shows the Lisbon Contracting Parties' willingness to grant Eurojust the right of initiative.[174] At any rate, the right to launch formal proceedings remains the prerogative of the national authorities.[175] Eurojust's **subject matter jurisdiction** covers serious crime with a cross-border dimension affecting two or more Member States.[176] This is rendered more concrete in Art. 4(1) Council Decision 2008, which defines Eurojust's jurisdiction by referring to the above-mentioned[177] catalogue of Europol.[178] In addition, Eurojust may assist in investigations and prosecutions concerning other kinds of crime at the request of a competent Member State authority.[179] By contrast, the Regulation Proposal for the first time wants to define Eurojust's subject matter jurisdiction independently of Europol.[180] Furthermore, the 'extension of competence by request' is to be abolished.[181] In order to fulfil the above-mentioned objectives, Eurojust usually acts through one or more of the **national members** concerned[182] or – when requested or in cross-border investigations – as a **College**.[183] In both cases, Eurojust may *take the initiative* in many cases by directing requests at the Member States, for example to undertake investigations of certain offences[184] or to set up JITs.[185] Furthermore, Eurojust is authorised to *process personal data*;[186] in that regard there exist similar data protection problems as with Europol.[187] Eurojust also co-operates with non-EU States, who may second liaison magistrates to Eurojust for this purpose.[188]

19 Since 2002, the number of cases has risen steadily.[189] The main focus of Eurojust's practical casework is evident in the **Eurojust Annual Report** 2016:[190] around 11 per cent of cases were in the area of drug trafficking (254 cases); fraud offences made up around 28.4 per cent of casework (657 cases). Numbers rose slightly in the area of trafficking in human beings to 4 per cent (from 79 to 93 cases),[191] while the area of cybercrime dropped to 2.5 per cent (from 62 to 60 cases). Terrorism offences (67 cases) represented 2.9 per cent while corruption offences (74 cases) dropped to 3.2 per cent[192] and illegal immigration (66 cases) constituted 2.8 per cent. A further 8.6 per cent are made up of other cases related to organised crime (199 cases).

20 While Art. 9(1), (3) Eurojust Council Decision still left it up to Member States to decide which **internal powers** they wished to grant the national members,[193] the above-mentioned Art. 85(2) TFEU now sets clear bounds as far as **formal proceedings** are concerned. Regardless of this, the Regulation Proposal Eurojust 2013 envisages granting national members comparatively extensive powers. Thus they shall facilitate or otherwise support mutual legal assistance themselves, exchange information with national competent authorities or participate in joint investigation teams. In urgent cases they shall even be competent to independently order investigative measures.[194] They shall be granted access to a wide range of national registers.[195]

21 Member States have **implemented**[196] the Eurojust Decision by way of special Acts[197] or special provisions in existing legislation,[198] or in a mere practical administrative manner.[199] *Germany* opted for a special law, the *Eurojust Act* (EJA).[200] In its first paragraph, §4 EJA (communication of information) sets out an obligation to communicate information to Eurojust, which is then curtailed considerably in the second paragraph: its no 2 permits German offices to omit to share information if 'the disclosure of information leads to the risk of serious damage to the detriment of the Federal Republic of Germany'.[201] It is also striking that the key norm of §4 EJA ('communication of information'), according to the wording of its first paragraph, requires German authorities to review, in the case of Eurojust requests, whether this sharing of information 'is necessary for Eurojust to carry out its tasks'. However, as the German authority will not be able to carry out such a necessity review due to its limited perspective – as compared to Eurojust, where all the information converges – it will simply have to trust that the national member's assessment of the data communication's necessity is indeed accurate.[202] It can been seen clearly here that the transfer of 'informational sovereignty' to a European agency goes hand in hand with an 'advance' of trust, for which the only solid foundation probably is the relationship between criminal lawyers from the same Member State; that is, their sharing of the same legal and cultural preconceptions. At the same time, one does wonder whether the mentioned national 'review clause' ('to the extent as is necessary to carry out tasks') could not have been dispensed with, seeing as the requested national authorities are unable to evaluate the necessity of the informational intervention independently anyway. Despite these inconsistencies, this phrasing was retained in the most recent amendments to the EJA.

22 Eurojust maintains close **relations** with existing co-operation structures.[203] There is a particularly close and complementary relationship between Eurojust and the **EJN** which is backed up by primary law,[204] making clear that the latter continues to exist besides the former.[205] The close relationship is also evident in spatial terms as the EJN secretariat is located in Eurojust. The EJN contact points are – metaphorically speaking – the 'extended arm of the national members (of Eurojust) in the Member States',[206] but there are problems of delimitation, as is especially manifest in the allocation of cases.[207] Eurojust co-operates with **OLAF** to combat crimes affecting the financial interests of the Union.[208] **Europol** and Eurojust co-operate closely with a view to increasing their effectiveness in combating serious forms of international crime.[209] They represent two complementary elements of pan-European prosecution,[210] focusing especially on information exchange/analysis[211] and co-ordinating the establishment and operation of JITs.[212] However, structural differences between the two institutions lead to tensions and problems of delimitation, especially at the investigation stage.[213] Also, as we have seen above, the investigative powers and executive competences remain – at least at present – with the national police and prosecutorial authorities. How the relationship develops in future will depend on the regulation to be issued pursuant to Art. 85(1) subparagraph 2 TFEU. On the one hand, the Lisbon Treaty codified Eurojust's position purely as a

service and co-ordination unit[214] – in contrast to earlier movements towards extending its competences[215] – while on the other hand the Treaty promises to increase Eurojust's powers in regard to the initiation of investigations.[216] This discrepancy is reflected in the current Regulation Proposal, which on the one hand emphasises Eurojust's supportive and co-ordinating function,[217] but on the other hand grants the national members extensive competences.[218] The idea of Eurojust as the **nucleus of a European Public Prosecutor's Office** expressed in Art. 86 TFEU ('from Eurojust')[219] seems to have been abandoned. Rather, Eurojust and the (emerging) EPPO are to stand side by side as independent institutions connected by a 'special relationship' and close co-operation.[220] We will return to the envisaged relationship below.[221]

D. The Court of Justice of the European Union (CJEU)

23 The CJEU includes the Court of Justice, the General Court and specialised courts.[222] The Court of Justice may sit as a full court, in a Grand Chamber of 13 judges, or in chambers of three or five judges.[223] Its jurisdiction encompasses ruling 'on actions [for annulment] brought by a MS, an institution or a natural or legal person', giving 'preliminary rulings' and ruling 'in other case provided for in the Treaties',[224] especially infringement proceedings.[225] As we have seen throughout this book, the CJEU has generally taken a pro-EU, integrationist stance,[226] and advocated the principle of mutual recognition, often assuming mutual trust without a solid basis in national law or practice.[227] This has not only led to the characterisation of the Court as a driving force of EU integration,[228] but also, more importantly, attracted criticism from a rights perspective which so far – despite recent positive developments[229] – has been neglected by the Court.[230] The Lisbon Treaty has strengthened its role as the sole interpreter (preliminary rulings) and enforcer (infringement proceedings) of Union law also in the field of European criminal law and procedure:[231]

- With the incorporation of the CISA into Union law with the 1997 Amsterdam Treaty the CJEU gained *jurisdiction over CISA*.[232]
- Through the 'communitisation' of the former third pillar, the CJEU's jurisdiction has been extended to the area of *police and judicial co-operation* now part of 'justice and home affairs',[233] including extended enforcement powers with regard to pre-Lisbon Acts in this area.[234]
- By way of the *preliminary reference* procedure[235] and the ensuing preliminary rulings the CJEU is the sole interpreter of Union

law;[236] by the incorporation of the CFREU into Union law[237] and the CJEU's Opinion 2/13 on the EU accession to the ECHR the CJEU has reaffirmed its *monopoly of interpretation* also with regard to human rights law.[238]

- The national implementation of directives is – in contrast to the (previous) framework decisions – subject to review by the CJEU as part of *infringement proceedings*.[239]
- Union Acts in the field of criminal law and procedure may also be the object of an *annulment action*, inter alia instituted by individuals if they are directly affected by them.[240]

E. The European Public Prosecutor's Office (EPPO)

24 The institution of a 'European Public Prosecutor's Office' (EPPO), with a view to **improving the criminal law protection of the financial interests** of the Union,[241] was originally proposed by the 'Corpus Juris' in 1998[242] and was the object of a Commission **Green Paper** in 2001.[243] It has been included in primary Union law by way of **Art. 86 TFEU**,[244] according to which the EPPO shall be established 'from Eurojust' by unanimous decision of the Council after obtaining the EP's consent.[245] However, the establishment of the institution has proven to be more difficult than expected and former Commissioner Reding's target date of 1 January 2015[246] turned out to be unrealistic.[247] In the meantime a 2013 Commission Regulation Proposal[248] has been replaced[249] by a 2017 Council Proposal.[250] The sheer number of square brackets and footnotes in the 2016 Regulation Proposal,[251] demonstrating the lack of agreement among Member States in multiple areas, did not give cause for optimism; thus the Council's registration of absence of unanimity in terms of Art. 86 (1) TFEU on 7 February 2017 came as no surprise.[252] The establishment of the EPPO is now taking place within the framework of enhanced co-operation according to Art. 86(1) subparagraph 3 TFEU,[253] thereby for the first time making first use of this option. The 2017 Council Proposal just mentioned formed the basis of the recently adopted regulation (**'Regulation EPPO 2017'**).[254] The EPPO shall assume its work at earliest three years after the entry into force of the Regulation, i.e., 31 October 2020.[255]

25 In terms of its **organisation**, the EPPO is conceived as an independent, decentralised body of the Union with legal personality;[256] it shall not receive instructions from persons external to the Office but generally be accountable to the EP, Council and Commission.[257] It is organised at a *central and a decentralised level*, the former essentially consisting of the Central Office at The Hague and the latter of the European Delegated Prosecutors coming from and located in the Member States.[258] This corresponds to the hybrid or so-called '*two-hat model*' already given preference in the above-mentioned Green Paper,[259] relying on a combination of European and national staff. The *Central Office*[260] includes the College, the Permanent Chambers, the European Chief Prosecutor plus two deputies,[261] the European Prosecutors (one per Member State)[262] and the Administrative Director.[263] The *College*[264] is the policy and general oversight organ, without any operational responsibility, connecting the central level (chief prosecutor) and the European delegated prosecutors (that is, the ones of the Member States).[265] The *permanent chambers*, to be set up by the College,[266] are responsible for the 'equal distribution of workload' and 'the proper functioning of the Office';[267] they monitor and direct the investigations of the European delegated prosecutors,[268] taking the relevant procedural decisions upon a proposal by the former[269] or *proprio motu*[270] and giving instructions to the delegated prosecutor handling the case 'in compliance with applicable national law'.[271] The permanent chambers may delegate their decision-making power to the European prosecutor[272] responsible for the supervision of the case handled by the delegated prosecutor;[273] she may then give instructions to the delegated prosecutor, also 'in compliance with applicable national law'.[274] The delegated prosecutor is to follow these instructions.[275] The ensuing hierarchy between the central level (permanent chambers/European prosecutors) and the decentralised Member State level (delegated prosecutors) may, despite the reference to the national law of the competent delegated prosecutor and the liaison function of the European prosecutors,[276] turn into a source of tension and conflict.[277]

26 The EPPO's **material competence** (subject matter jurisdiction) generally follows from Art. 86(1) TFEU ('crimes affecting the financial interests of the Union'), but needs to be translated into concrete offences to be taken from the recently adopted[278] *PIF-Directive*.[279] Thus, in fact, the respective Art. 22(1) of the 2017 Regulation creates a kind of (dynamic) blanket criminal law provision[280] aggravated by the fact that it does not define any element of any offence. As we have already seen above, such a legal technique is difficult to reconcile with the legality principle (*nullum crimen sine lege*).[281] At any rate, there is no cross-border element; the

EPPO's competence derives exclusively from the offence's impact on the financial interests of the Union.[282] This also follows from the rules on **formal** (territorial and personal) **competence** according to which it suffices that the offence was committed in the territory of one Member State or by a national of one Member State (provided that this MS has extra-territorial jurisdiction in such cases).[283] In addition, the material competence also extends to 'participation in a criminal organisation', if its activity is directed against the Union's financial interests,[284] and to offences which are 'inextricably linked' to offences against the financial interests of the Union.[285] Also, the Council may extend the Office's competence to serious cross-border crimes.[286]

The EPPO's broad material competence is not without problems with regard to the principles of subsidiarity and proportionality[287] – all the more as the Member States by and large have criminal law systems that function well and in most cases are able to ensure proportionate and effective prosecution. Against this background a kind of '*complementarity model*' modelled after the ICC's Rome Statute[288] seems preferable. Accordingly, the EPPO would only intervene if the national authority responsible 'is unable or not in a position to sufficiently protect the EU's financial interests itself'.[289] At any rate, it follows from the rules on the **exercise of the EPPO's competence** – which is limited in case of less serious offences[290] – that the MS still retain their (original) competence,[291] and thus the Regulation follows the model of a **shared** (instead of an exclusive) **competence.**[292] If the relevant conduct falls within its material competence, however, the EPPO may set aside the national competence[293] by either initiating an investigation right away[294] or making use of its right of evocation.[295] This is, of course, another source of tension between the EPPO and the competent MS authorities, although, in case of 'disagreement', the ultimate decision is to be taken by competent authority of the MS.[296]

27 An **investigation** is initiated 'where there are reasonable grounds to form the view[297] that an offence within the competence of the European Public Prosecutor's Office is being or has been committed.'[298] The information on relevant conduct will normally come from the competent authorities of the Member State.[299] The investigation is to be handled by the European delegated prosecutor[300] of the competent Member State;[301] she may be instructed to do so.[302] Under certain conditions a case may be reallocated to another delegated prosecutor,[303] or the supervising European prosecutor (central level) may herself conduct the investigation.[304] In line with the principle of availability, as known from the EIO,[305] Member States shall ensure that a series of investigation **measures** – apart from the ones existing under national law[306] – are available,[307] albeit subject to conditions under national law.[308] This entails a de facto *minimum harmonisation.*[309] At any rate, such measures may only be ordered – by the handling delegated prosecutor, but subject to a judicial authorisation[310] in line with the *lex loci*[311] – where there are 'reasonable grounds to believe' that it might provide 'useful' information or evidence, and where there is 'no less intrusive measure available which could achieve the same objective'.[312] In cross-border investigations a close co-operation between the delegated prosecutor handling the case and the one assigned in another Member State (where the investigative measure needs to be carried out) – the assisting delegated prosecutor – is necessary,[313] entailing the same problems as known from mutual-recognition instruments.[314] While for the enforcement of investigative measures in principle the *lex loci* applies,[315] the handling delegated prosecutor may indicate 'formalities and procedures' to be complied with[316] in line with a limited *lex fori* rule as known from the mutual-assistance instruments.[317] The handling delegated prosecutor may issue an EAW if she considers that the arrest and surrender of a suspect not present in her MS is necessary.[318]

28 Once the **investigation** is **completed**, the handling delegated prosecutor prepares a draft decision – to be submitted to the central level (supervising European prosecutor and competent permanent chamber) – to either prosecute the case or not.[319] In case of a **non-prosecution decision** there are several options: referral to the national prosecutorial authorities of a Member State (which has jurisdiction), dismissal of the case or prosecution pursuant to a simplified procedure.[320] The situation of *referral* (or rather deferral) largely corresponds to the above-mentioned non-exercise of competence in case of less serious offences which do not constitute a sufficiently relevant attack on the financial interests of the Union.[321] The permanent chamber may *dismiss* the case if prosecution is impossible, for example due to the death of the suspected person, expiry of the statute of limitations or the risk of violating the prohibition of double jeopardy.[322] Prosecution pursuant to a *simplified procedure* presupposes that such a procedure exists in the law of the competent MS in the first place.[323] Further, its application has three basic conditions: (i) limited seriousness of the offence, in particular with regard to the financial damage caused; (ii) the suspect's willingness to repair the damage;[324] and (iii) its compatibility with the 'general objectives and basic principles' of the EPPO.[325] In case of a **prosecution decision** (to be taken by the permanent chamber),[326] first the **trial court** has to be determined. As a rule, this will be the competent court of the MS of the handling delegated prosecutor, even if there are other Member States with jurisdiction,[327] unless 'there are sufficiently justified grounds' to bring the case to prosecution in another MS, taking into account the criteria set out in Art. 26(4) and (5) Regulation 2017.[328] This rule–exception relationship and the listed criteria diminish the possibility of *forum shopping* which gave rise to severe criticism of the 2013 Regulation Proposal.[329] Several cases may be joined to be prosecuted in a Member State which has jurisdiction for all the individual cases.[330] The competent court *within* the respective MS will then be determined according to its law.[331] The delegated prosecutor may propose the competent permanent chamber to lodge an **appeal**.[332]

29 Given that there is no common European criminal procedure, the **applicable procedural law** is the one of the trial court of the competent Member State (*lex fori*). Thus the national procedural law of the forum MS ultimately becomes the foundation or rather the substitute for the – lacking – 'European' criminal procedure[333] – although, arguably, the very idea of an EPPO calls for the parallel creation of a common European law on criminal procedure.[334] The separate provision on **evidence**[335] does not change the situation since it is in fact a mere provision on the *admissibility* of evidence.[336] In substance, it confirms the *lex fori* rule since it leaves it to the trial court to freely assess the evidence[337] (according to its national law), and while the evidence gathered in another Member State 'shall not be denied admission' for the mere fact of its foreign origin,[338] the trial court is to make sure that the admission would not be incompatible with a fair trial in a broad sense.[339] The respect for a fair trial and rights of suspects/accused generally is confirmed by a **comprehensive rights provision** which, apart from a general recourse to the CFREU[340] and procedural rights available under national law,[341] attempts to establish the Union rights, especially as set out in the relevant directives,[342] as a minimum standard.[343] This is complemented by *detailed data protection rules*,[344] which attempt to contain the EPPO's extensive informational rights somewhat,[345] and a (new) provision on **judicial review**.[346] It subjects the EPPO's procedural acts – which produce legal effects vis-à-vis third parties[347] – to a review by national courts[348] and selected acts to a review by the CJEU pursuant to Art.

263 TFEU,[349] including dismissal decisions;[350] in addition, the provision gives the CJEU further review rights, especially to issue preliminary rulings pursuant to Art. 267 TFEU with regard to the validity of EPPO acts.[351]

30 Last, but not least, the EPPO's **relationship** with existing institutions – especially OLAF, Eurojust and Europol – and the reasonable **delimitation** of their competences remains open to debate.[352] As far as **OLAF** is concerned, its (external) investigations in the field of financial irregularities affecting the Union's interests would overlap with those of a future EPPO.[353] In light of this, there is some debate around having OLAF assist the EPPO and making it subject to the EPPO's instructions, equipping it with extended investigative powers if necessary (similarly to the role of the police towards the public prosecutor's office in continental European legal systems),[354] or merging it with the EPPO straight away.[355] The 2017 Regulation favours the former solution, assigning to OLAF basically a complementary and supporting role vis-à-vis the EPPO,[356] giving the latter prevalence in the case of parallel investigations[357] and leaving OLAF only with 'administrative action' where the EPPO has decided not to conduct an investigation or to dismiss the case anyway.[358] This is in any case more convincing than a merger of OLAF with the EPPO, since the former must continue to investigate administrative irregularities, including with regard to the EPPO.[359] As to **Eurojust**, the wording of Art. 86(1) TFEU ('from Eurojust') seems to imply that the EPPO will incorporate Eurojust, at least in the long run, and indeed the fact that the former shall 'rely on the support and resources' of the latter[360] seems to confirm that the EPPO shall grow out of Eurojust. On the other hand, however, Art. 85 TFEU reaffirms the existence of Eurojust as an institution of horizontal co-operation, while the EPPO is designed as a vertical-investigation agency.[361] Pursuant to the Regulation, both institutions shall have 'a close relationship . . . based on mutual cooperation within their respective mandates',[362] and the EPPO 'may associate' Eurojust with its operational activities.[363] All this speaks in favour of a coexistence of both institutions.[364] In relation to **Europol**, the obvious solution that suggests itself is for the EPPO to control proceedings (as is functionally the case anyway), taking precedence over Europol, in line with the continental European model of a prosecutorial direction of the police.[365] Of course, the problem with this solution is that a prosecuting authority designed to have only sectoral authority, i.e. with regard to the financial interests of the Union, cannot

go beyond this authority by interfering with another institution's (Europol's) much broader competence. The Regulation, while leaving the detail of the 'close relationship' between Europol and the EPPO to a future arrangement,[366] at least acknowledges the information and analytical support the latter can receive from the former.[367] All in all, in the long term, improving co-operation between the various institutions by extending the EPPO's powers to the fight against serious, cross-border crime might be worth consideration;[368] this would bring the EPPO into line with Eurojust[369] and Europol.[370]

Notes

1. Chapter 1, mn. 18 with nn. 154–371.
2. See previously crit. Chapter 2, mn. 149 and Chapter 4, mn. 60, 72, 93.
3. Cf. the private proposals mentioned in Chapter 1, mn. 32.
4. Cf. www.ecba.org/content last accessed 27 January 2018.
5. OJ L 136 of 31 May 1999, 20; amended by Commission Decision 2013/478/EU of 27 September 2013 (OJ L 257 of 28 September 2013, 19).
6. OJ L 136 of 31 May 1999, 1 and 8.
7. On the historical development, cf. Brüner and Spitzer, in Sieber, Satzger and von Heinegg, *Europäisches Strafrecht* (2014), pp. 776–7; Zöller, in Böse, *Europäisches Strafrecht* (2013), pp. 844–7; Strobel, *Untersuchungen* (2012), pp. 31 ff.
8. Protocol (No 36) on Transitional Provisions (OJ C 326 of 26 October 2012, 326).
9. OJ L 248 of 18 September 2013, 1; on this, cf. Simonato, *eucrim*, 11 (2016), 136–40 ('far from an exhaustive code to regulate the powers to investigate irregularities and fraud against the EU budget' (139–40)); Brodowski, *ZIS*, 8 (2013), 463; on the draft, cf. Lingenthal, *ZEuS*, 15 (2012), 195; Met-Domestici, *eucrim*, 7 (2012), 25; on the attempts at reform in general, cf. Zöller, in Böse, *Europäisches Strafrecht* (2013), pp. 861–4. On the regulation's (further) legal foundations, cf. Brüner and Spitzer, in Sieber, Satzger and von Heinegg, *Europäisches Strafrecht* (2014), pp. 780–5.
10. See on this Report from the Commission to the EP and the Council, *Evaluation of the application of Regulation (EU, EURATOM) No 883/2013 of the EP and of the Council of 11 September 2013 concerning investigations conducted by the European Anti-Fraud Office (OLAF) and repealing Regulation (EC) No 1073/1999 of the EP and of the Council and Council Regulation (Euratom) No 1074/1999*, COM(2017) 589 final. Thereto and on possible reforms Janda and Panait, *eucrim*, 12 (2017), 182 ff.; Boven'Eerdt, *eucrim*, 12 (2017), 188 ff.
11. On this, cf. Ambos, *Internationales Strafrecht* (2008), §13 mn. 1; see also Strobel, *Untersuchungen* (2012), p. 33.
12. Von Bubnoff, *ZEuS*, 5 (2002), 197; European Anti-fraud Office, *Annual Report 2010* (2010), p. 7; on the issue of independence, also cf. Beukelmann, *NJW*, 63 (2010), 2085; Heine, *Rechtsstellung des Beschuldigten* (2009), pp. 221–2; Cretin, in Espina Ramos and Vicente Carbajosa, *The Future EPPO* (2009), p. 59; Schoppa, *Europol* (2013), pp. 80–1; however, Esser, *Europäisches und Internationales Strafrecht* (2018), §3 mn. 15, remains critical. On the inter-

institutional relationship between OLAF, Europol, Eurojust and the EPPO, see Marletta, *eucrim*, 11 (2016), 141–5.

13. Hecker, *Europäisches Strafrecht* (2015), §4 mn. 20, speaks of 'unionsunmittelbare[r] Vollzug'; on the advantages of the ensuing supranationality of OLAF in terms of investigation and co-operation cf. Panait, *eucrim*, 10 (2015), 65, 66.
14. Art. 17(1) OLAF Regulation 2013.
15. Cf. von Bubnoff, *ZEuS*, 5 (2002), 197; Gleß, *EuZW*, 10 (1999), 619; Hallmann-Häbler and Stiegel, *DRiZ*, 81 (2003), 242.
16. Art. 15 OLAF Regulation 2013.
17. Art. 1(4) OLAF Regulation 2013. See also Hallmann-Häbler and Stiegel, *DRiZ*, 81 (2003), 242; Hetzer, *EJCCLCJ*, 14 (2006), 27 ff.; Kinzel, *Braucht Europa eine gemeinsame Staatsanwaltschaft?* (2008), pp. 22 ff. Among other tasks, von Bubnoff, *ZEuS*, 5 (2002), 198, enumerates customs fraud, misuse of subventions, tax evasion on a scale that impacts the Union budget and the misconduct of EU staff when carrying out their professional duties. Also cf. the OLAF Report 2016, pp. 9–10 (available at https://ec.europa.eu/anti-fraud/sites/antifraud/files/olaf_report_2016_en.pdf, last accessed 27 January 2018). In 2016, OLAF completed 1, 157 procedures and recommended a total of €631.1 million for recovery.
18. Art. 2(4) OLAF Decision.
19. Art. 1(2) OLAF Regulation 2013. See also Hallmann-Häbler and Stiegel, *DRiZ*, 81 (2003), 242–3. On the co-operation with Europol und Eurojust, cf. Covolo, *eucrim*, 7 (2012), 85–6; on the co-operation with third States cf. Panait, *eucrim*, 10 (2015), 65, 68.
20. Hallmann-Häbler and Stiegel, *DRiZ*, 81 (2003), 241–2; von Bubnoff, *ZEuS*, 5 (2002), 196 and 198; Cretin, in Espina Ramos and Vicente Carbajosa, *The Future EPPO* (2009), p. 54; Zöller, in Böse, *Europäisches Strafrecht* (2013), pp. 847–8; Brüner and Spitzer, in Sieber, Satzger and von Heinegg, *Europäisches Strafrecht* (2015), p. 769.
21. In a similar vein Stojanovski, *eucrim*, 6 (2011), 128, 139; also cf. Brüner and Spitzer, *EuR*, 43 (2008), 860, who point out the relevance of OLAF's investigative activity for criminal law, and Esser, *Europäisches und Internationales Strafrecht* (2018), §3 mn. 11 ('a "hybrid" institution in nature', orig. 'Charakter einer "hybriden" Institution'); Panait, *eucrim*, 10 (2015), 67–8 ('OLAF as a European Hybrid Body'); Strobel, *Untersuchungen (OLAF)* (2012), pp. 231 ff., goes even further, claiming that OLAF investigations are always also criminal ones (p. 321).
22. Cf. *Green Paper EPPO* (2001), pp. 17–18; on this, also cf. von Bubnoff, *ZEuS*, 5 (2002), 201–2; González-Herrero and Butincu, *eucrim*, 4 (2009), 90; Hetzer, *EJCCLCJ*, 14 (2006), 28, argues in favour of a general applicability.
23. Arts. 3 and 4 OLAF Regulation 2013. Cf. also Heine, *Rechtsstellung des Beschuldigten* (2009), pp. 223–4; Cretin, in Espina Ramos and Vicente Carbajosa, *The Future EPPO* (2009), p. 54; Gless, *Internationales Strafrecht* (2015), mn. 482; Covolo, *eucrim*, 7 (2012), 83–4; Brüner and Spitzer, in Sieber, Satzger and von Heinegg, *Europäisches Strafrecht* (2014), pp. 785 ff.; Zöller, in Böse, *Europäisches Strafrecht* (2013), pp. 852–3; Esser, *Europäisches und Internationales Strafrecht* (2018), §3 mn. 18; and the case studies in European Anti-fraud Office, *Annual Report 2010* (2010), pp. 9 ff.; also the overview of the distribution and sharing of the Office's workload on p. 14; in detail, cf. Strobel, *Untersuchungen* (2012), pp. 120 ff., who distinguishes between external horizontal, external sectoral and internal investigations.

24. Von Bubnoff, *ZEuS*, 5 (2002), 199; Hallmann-Häbler and Stiegel, *DRiZ*, 83 (2005), 174; Vervaele, *RP*, 15 (2005), 174; Stojanovski, *eucrim*, 6 (2011), 128. On external investigations, cf. the case study in Hallmann-Häbler and Stiegel, *DRiZ*, 81 (2003), 243; Weitendorf, *Die interne Betrugsbekämpfung* (2007), p. 128. Hauck, *ZStW*, 124 (2012), 478, is critical of the vague wording used on investigative actions.
25. Art. 3(4)–(6) OLAF Regulation 2013; see in detail on information sharing between OLAF and Member States, Panait, *eucrim*, 10 (2015), 65–7, 68.
26. Cf. Hallmann-Häbler and Stiegel, *DRiZ*, 81 (2003), 242–3; Satzger, *Internationales und Europäisches Strafrecht* (2016), §10 mn. 20; Kuhl and Spitzer, in Sieber, Satzger and von Heinegg, *Europäisches Strafrecht* (2014), pp. 235–6; for an extensive account of OLAF's internal investigative authority, cf. Weitendorf, *Die interne Betrugsbekämpfung* (2007), pp. 82 ff.
27. Art. 4(2) OLAF Regulation 2013. See also Gleß, *EuZW*, 10 (1999), 619 (doubtful whether any authorisation to formally question witnesses can be derived from this); going further von Bubnoff, *ZEuS*, 5 (2002), 198 (arguing that the said EU officials are obliged to assist in the required manner); cf. also Hallmann-Häbler and Stiegel, *DRiZ*, 81 (2003), 242–3. Be this as it may, according to the new version, the right to formally interrogate persons in (both internal and external) investigations can probably be derived from Art. 9(2) OLAF Regulation 2013.
28. Art. 12(2) subparagraph 1 OLAF Regulation 2013. See also Gleß, *EuZW*, 10 (1999), 619; von Bubnoff, *ZEuS*, 5 (2002), 198–9.
29. Art. 11(1) OLAF Regulation 2013. See also von Bubnoff, *ZEuS*, 5 (2002), 200; Hallmann-Häbler and Stiegel, *DRiZ*, 81 (2003), 243; Panait, *eucrim*, 10 (2015), 67–8 ('power to recommend').
30. On the respective duty of loyalty or of sincere co-operation (Article 4(3) TEU), see Chapter 3, mn. 41 ff.
31. Cf. Art. 11(2) OLAF Regulation 2013 ('shall constitute admissible evidence'); cf. also Panait, *eucrim*, 10 (2015), 68; Jähnke and Schramm, *Europäisches Strafrecht* (2017), §4 mn. 11.
32. Cf. Art. 2 Decision ECB/1999/5 of the ECB of 7 October 1999 (OJ L 291 of 13 November 1999, 36); and the unpublished Decision of the EIB 1999/352 (on this, cf. ECJ, *Commission* v. *European Investment Bank*, No C-15/00 (ECLI:EU:C:2003:396), Judgment (10 July 2003), paras. 42 ff.).
33. ECJ, *Commission* v. *European Central Bank*, No C-11/00 (ECLI:EU:C:2003:395), Judgment (10 July 2003) and ECJ, *Commission* v. *European Investment Bank*, C-15/00; in this context, also cf. Hallmann-Häbler and Stiegel, *DRiZ*, 81 (2003), 242; and von Bubnoff, *ZEuS*, 5 (2002), 199.
34. EP Decision concerning the terms and conditions for internal investigations in relation to the prevention of fraud, corruption and any illegal activity detrimental to the Communities' interests (OJ C 189 of 7 July 2000, 210).
35. On this, cf. ECJ, *Rothley* v. *Parliament*, No T-17/00 (ECLI:EU:T:2002:39), Judgment (26 February 2002), para. 68; Hetzer, *NJW*, 57 (2004), 3749–50, is in agreement; a critical stance is taken by Berner, *Untersuchungsbefugnisse* (2004), pp. 153 ff., 241 ff. and *passim*.
36. On the criticism voiced on these, cf. Gleß, *EuZW*, 10 (1999), 620–1; Hetzer, *EJCCLCJ*, 14 (2006), 30–1; for a different view cf. von Bubnoff, *ZEuS*, 5 (2002), 203; on legal remedies, cf. Kuhl and Spitzer, in Sieber, Satzger and von Heinegg, *Europäisches Strafrecht* (2014), pp. 240–1.

37. Cf. Art. 9 OLAF Regulation 2013. On data protection, cf. Laudati, *eucrim*, 8 (2013), 14.
38. Cf. Stojanovski, *eucrim*, 6 (2011), 128 ff. (with case law references).
39. Art. 9(1) OLAF Reg.
40. Art. 9(2) subparagraph 1 OLAF Reg.
41. Art. 9(1) OLAF Reg.
42. Art. 9(2) subparagraphs 2–3 OLAF Reg.
43. Art. 9(4),(5) OLAF Reg.
44. Art. 15(1) subparagraph 2 OLAF Reg. Cf. Esser, *Europäisches und Internationales Strafrecht* (2018), §3 mn. 20. On the monitoring of OLAF in general, cf. Brüner and Spitzer, in Sieber, Satzger and von Heinegg, *Europäisches Strafrecht* (2014), pp. 794–801.
45. COM (2013) 533 final.
46. On concerns with regard to data protection cf. Stojanovski, *eucrim*, 6 (2011), 131.
47. OJ C 185 of 1 July 1999, 1; also cf. Milke, *Europol und Eurojust* (2003), p. 45; Ellermann, *ZEuS*, 5 (2002), 562; Ellermann, *Europol und FBI* (2005), pp. 52 ff.; Felgenhauer, in Wolter et al., *Festgabe Hilger* (2003), p. 76; Storbeck and Felgenhauer, in Möllers and van Ooyen, *Europäisierung und Internationalisierung der Polizei* (2006), p. 16 incl. n. 3; Hecker, *Europäisches Strafrecht* (2015), §5 mn. 59; David, *Eléments de droit pénal international et européen* (2009), mn. 6.2.7; Ubah, Nwebo and Ezeanyika, in Pływaczewski and Guzik-Makaruk, *Current Problems of Penal Law and Criminology* (2017), pp. 795–6.
48. For a comprehensive account of this development, cf. Milke, *Europol und Eurojust* (2003), pp. 23 ff.; Korrell, *Europol* (2005), pp. 11 ff.; also cf. Storbeck, *Kriminalistik*, 50 (1996), 18; Zachert, *Kriminalistik*, 46 (1992), 7; Martínez Soria, *VerwArch*, 89 (1998), 416; Martínez Soria, in Baldus and Soiné, *Rechtsprobleme* (1999), pp. 52 ff., 64–5; Conroy, in Regan, *The New Third Pillar* (2000), pp. 126–7; Nunzi, *RIDP*, 77 (2006), 286; Schoppa, *Europol* (2013), pp. 175 ff.; Ruthig, in Böse, *Europäisches Strafrecht* (2013), pp. 752–5. On earlier and subsequent forms of police co-operation, especially Interpol, cf. Milke, *Europol und Eurojust* (2003), pp. 116 ff.; Martínez Soria, in Baldus and Soiné, *Rechtsprobleme* (1999), pp. 52 ff.; Hecker, *Europäisches Strafrecht* (2015), §5 mn. 3.
49. Gleß, *NStZ*, 21 (2001), 623; Storbeck, *Kriminalistik*, 48 (1994), 201–2; Zieschang, *ZRP*, 29 (1996), 427; Daub, in Baldus and Soiné, *Rechtsprobleme* (1999), pp. 87–8; Ellermann, *Europol und FBI* (2005), pp. 37 ff.; Vervaele, *RP*, 15 (2005), 176.
50. Notification of the Federal Ministry of the Interior of 29 December 1994, *BGBl.*, II 1995, 154.
51. Joint Action of 10 March 1995 (OJ L 62 of 20 March 1995, 1). On the criticism of these foundations, cf. Ambos, *Internationales Strafrecht* (2008), §13 mn. 5 small print.
52. OJ C 316 of 27 November 1995, 1.
53. Art. 45 Europol Convention (OJ C 316 of 27 November 1995, 1); also cf. Mokros, in Denninger and Rachor, *Handbuch des Polizeirechts* (2012), mn. 30 ff.
54. Milke, *Europol und Eurojust* (2003), pp. 45 ff., listing the legal acts and further implementing provisions; Satzger, *Internationales und Europäisches Strafrecht* (2016), §10 mn. 3.
55. Council Decision of 6 April 2009 establishing the European Police Office (Europol), 2009/371/JHA (OJ L 121 of 15 May 2009, 37).

56. Cf. Art. 34(2)(c) TEU old version.
57. Cf. Art. 1(1) Europol Decision 2009.
58. Art. 2 Europol Decision 2009. On Europol's earlier hybrid position, cf. Ambos, *Internationales Strafrecht* (2008), §13 mn. 6a; and on its structural incorporation, cf. Niemeier and Walter, *Kriminalistik*, 64 (2010), 18; Wandl, *Europol* (2008), p. 46, sees Europol's legal personality as confirmed even prior to the Europol Decision 2009.
59. Art. 85(1) subparagraph 1 TFEU.
60. Art. 86(2) TFEU.
61. Art. 88(1) TFEU. See also Satzger, *Internationales und Europäisches Strafrecht* (2016), §10 mn. 5. On Art. 88 TFEU, cf. Ruthig, in Zöller et al., *FS Wolter* (2013), pp. 1472 ff.
62. Cf. Chapter 2, mn. 144–5.
63. Stockholm Programme, p. 20; on this, cf. Niemeier, *ERA Forum*, 11 (2010), 200 ff.; Ruthig, in Böse, *Europäisches Strafrecht* (2013), pp. 750 ff.
64. Regulation (EU) 2016/794 of the EP and of the Council of 11 May 2016 on the European Union Agency for Law Enforcement Co-operation (Europol) and replacing and repealing Council Decision 2009/371/JHA, 2009/934/JHA, 2009/935/JHA, 2009/936/JHA and 2009/968/JHA (OJ L 135 of 24 May 2016, 53).
65. Cf. Decision 2005/681/JHA (OJ L 256 of 1 October 2005, 63).
66. COM (2013) 173 final, 4 ff.; on this, cf. Brodowski, *ZIS*, 8 (2013), 463–4; Esser, in Sinn and Zöller, *Neujustierung des Strafrechts* (2013), pp. 74–5. Also cf. *eucrim*, 7 (2012), 51; 2013, 36–7. On the debate preceding the regulation proposal, cf. Ruthig, in Böse, *Europäisches Strafrecht* (2013), pp. 771–4. The German *Bundesrat* raised a subsidiarity objection against this, as the EU does not have the competence to regulate the training and professional development of law-enforcement officials; cf. BR-Drs. 346/13.
67. Art. 4(1)(i) Europol Regulation 2016 ('in co-ordination with CEPOL').
68. COM (2012) 140 final; Council Doc. 10603/12; on this, cf. Buono, *NJECL*, 3 (2012), 332 ff.; Esser, in Odendahl, *Bekämpfung des Terrorismus* (2017), p. 228; on data protection requirements in particular, cf. Drewer and Ellermann, *ERA Forum*, 2012, 381 ff.; also cf. *eucrim*, 7 (2012), 57, 94, 103–4.
69. On Art. 3 Europol Convention, cf. Ambos, *Internationales Strafrecht* (2008), §13 mn. 7.
70. Cf. also Neumann, in Sieber, Satzger and von Heinegg, Europäisches Strafrecht (2014), pp. 807 ff.; Ruthig, in Böse, *Europäisches Strafrecht* (2013), 765, 769–70; on Europol's tasks relating to combating of terrorism Esser, in Odendahl, *Bekämpfung des Terrorismus* (2017), p. 228 (also on the distinction between the European Counter Terrorism Center (ECTC) and the European Gendarmerie Force (Eurogendfor) at pp. 223 ff.).
71. Cf. Art. 88(3) TFEU. In the same vein Hecker, *Europäisches Strafrecht* (2015), §5 mn. 64; Esser, *Europäisches und Internationales Strafrecht* (2018), §3 mn. 42; Esser, in Odendahl, *Bekämpfung des Terrorismus* (2017), p. 215; Böse, *ZIS*, 5 (2010), 82; Bauer, in Weidenfeld, *Lissabon* (2008), p. 108. For more detail on the terminology, cf. Hauck, *ZStW*, 124 (2012), 475 ff.; on the different interpretations of this guideline, cf. Ruthig, in Zöller et al., *FS Wolter* (2013), pp. 1482–3.
72. Cf. Ambos, *Internationales Strafrecht* (2008), §13 mn. 12–13.
73. Ratzel, *Kriminalistik*, 61 (2007), 285.

74. Cf. Art. 5(1) and (2) versus Art. 5(3) Europol Decision 2009. On the previous situation according to the Europol Convention, cf. Ambos, *Internationales Strafrecht* (2008), §13 mn. 7–8.
75. Art. 4(1)(a) Europol Regulation 2016.
76. Art. 4(1)(b) Europol Regulation 2016.
77. Art. 4(1)(e) Europol Regulation 2016.
78. Art. 4(1)(l), (m) Europol Regulation 2016.
79. Art. 4(1)(f) Europol Regulation 2016.
80. Arts. 4(1)(d), 5(5) Europol Regulation 2016. The details of this are regulated in FD 2002/465/JHA on joint investigation teams; thereto already above Chapter 4, mn. 4, 81. Regarding Europol's function in this regard cf. Weyembergh, Armada and Brière, *NJECL*, 6 (2015), 272–3.
81. On this, cf. Riegel, *eucrim*, 4 (2009), 101–2; Arts. 4(1)(d), 5 Europol Regulation 2016. On the potential role of OLAF in these investigation teams, cf. de Moor, *eucrim*, 4 (2009), 94; Cretin, in Espina Ramos and Vicente Carbajosa, *The Future EPPO* (2009), p. 58; on the potential role of Eurojust, cf. Lopes da Mota, *eucrim*, 4 (2009), 88.
82. Art. 5(2)–(4) Europol Regulation 2016.
83. Arts. 4(1)(g) Europol Regulation 2016.
84. Art. 17 ff. Europol Regulation 2016.
85. Annex II to the Europol Regulation 2016 (OJ L 135 of 24 May 2016, 109).
86. Cf. e.g. **Austria** (EU–Police Co-operation Act, *BGBl.* I No 132/2009, last amended *BGBl.* I No 61/2016); **Germany** (Europol Act, *BGBl.*, 1997 II, 2150; 2006 II, 250; thereto Neumann, in Sieber, Satzger and von Heinegg, *Europäisches Strafrecht* (2014), pp. 808–9). In **Greece**, the Europol Convention was ratified by Law 2605/1998 as amended by Laws 3002/2002, 3294/2004 and 3295/2004. Art. 8(6) of the Presidential Decree 178/214 (31 December 2014) regulates the co-operation with Europol of the competent national authority, i.e. the Europol Section of the Hellenic Police International Police Co-operation Division.
87. This is, for example, the case in **Hungary** (cf. Law No CXXX of 2013 on International Co-operation with EU Member States, which creates the 'International Criminal Co-operation Centre' NEBEK (*Nemzetközi Bűnügyi Együttműködési Központ*)).
88. This is, for example, the case in **France** (where the national Europol unit is located in the 'direction central' of the 'Police judiciaire', cf. Art. D8-2 no 4 CPP and details are regulated in executive decrees), **Italy** (cf. Ministerial Decree of 21 February 1996 creating the 'National Unit Europol' within the International Co-operation Service of the National Criminal Police; also Law 93/1998 of 23 March implementing the Europol Convention), **Poland** (Ch. 10 Police Act (Ustawa o Policji) locating Europol in the main police headquarters), **Portugal** (cf. Art. 12 of the Law on the Organisation of the Criminal Investigation (Lei de Organização da Investigação Criminal, Lei no 49/2008, de 27 Agosto), which creates the International Co-operation Unit linking the national police with Europol) and **Spain** (cf. Art. 11 Orden INT/28/2103 of 18.1.2013, BOE-A-2013-662 creating a Division of International Co-operation providing, inter alia, for the national unit of Europol). In the **UK** the 'International Crime Bureau' of the 'National Crime Agency' facilitatesco-operation with Europa and is the UK SIRENE office; cf. www.nationalcrimeagency.gov.uk/about-us/working-in-partnership/international-cooperation, last accessed 27 January 2018. In the non-Member State **Switzerland** co-

operation is based on an agreement with Europol of 24.9.2004 (cf. www.admin.ch/opc/de/classified-compilation/20020040/index.html, last accessed 27 January 2018) and an organisational regulation for the police of 17 November 1999 (as of 1 November 2015); according to its Art. 10 the national Europol office is located in the Federal Police in Bern. On the Member States' commitment to, and information sharing with, Europol in general, Disley et al., *Evaluation of the Implementation of the Europol Council Decision and of Europol's Activities* (2012), pp. 47 ff.

89. OJ L 135 of 24 May 2016, 108. On Europol's fight against organised crime and terrorism cf. Esser, in Sinn and Zöller, *Neujustierung des Strafrechts* (2013), pp. 64–70.
90. Schubert, *Europol* (2008), pp. 37 ff.; for an overview of the work of the different sections of Europol's department of serious crime, cf. Ratzel, *Kriminalistik*, 61 (2007), 428 ff.; on the 'shift in emphasis' in competence, cf. Niemeier and Walter, *Kriminalistik*, 64 (2010), 19; on the legal situation under the Europol Convention, cf. Ambos, *Internationales Strafrecht* (2008), §13 mn. 8; in greater depth on Europol's activities in the area of cross-border drugs crime, Nestler, *GA*, 157 (2010), 651 ff.
91. Art. 3(1) Europol Regulation 2016.
92. Art. 3(2) Europol Regulation 2016.
93. Art. 3(2)(a)–(c) Europol Regulation 2016. Also cf. Felgenhauer, in Wolter et al., *Festgabe Hilger* (2003), p. 76.
94. Consideration (13) Europol Regulation 2016 ('priorities set by the Council'); previously Art. 4(2) Europol Decision 2009.
95. Cf. Art. 17 ff. Europol Regulation 2016. On this, cf. Hecker, *Europäisches Strafrecht* (2015), §5 mn. 62; Satzger, Internationales und Europäisches Strafrecht (2016), §10 mn. 7; Ratzel, *Kriminalistik*, 61 (2007), 287; Niemeier and Walter, *Kriminalistik*, 64 (2010), 19–20; David, *Eléments de droit pénal international et européen* (2009), mn. 6.28; Gleß, *Internationales Strafrecht* (2015), mn. 458; Ruthig, in Böse, *Europäisches Strafrecht* (2013), pp. 766–7; Esser, in Sinn and Zöller, *Neujustierung des Strafrechts* (2013), pp. 70–1; also cf. Arts. 17 ff. Europol Regulation 2016. The Prüm Convention of 27 May 2005 (Chapter 4, mn. 4 n. 16) already set out increased co-operation; on this, cf. Hummer, *EuR*, 42 (2007), 517 ff.; Böse, *Grundsatz der Verfügbarkeit* (2007), pp. 42 ff.; on Europol's retention of data, cf. Schubert, *Europol* (2008), pp. 82 ff.
96. In **Austria** and **Germany** this is the Bundeskriminalamt (BKA); for other MS see above, n. 88.
97. In detail, Milke, *Europol und Eurojust* (2003), pp. 68 ff.; also cf. Conroy, in Regan, *The New Third Pillar* (2000), p. 129; Qubain, Kattge, Wandl and Gamma, *Kriminalistik*, 61 (2007), 364–5; Satzger, *Internationales und Europäisches Strafrecht* (2016), §10 mn. 6; on co-operation with Switzerland, cf. Gleß, *Internationales Strafrecht* (2015), mn. 604 ff.
98. Cf. Art. 6(5) Europol Regulation 2016; also Freyer, *Kriminalistik*, 57 (2003), 81.
99. Cf. Art. 7(2) Europol Regulation 2016; more explicitly Art. 8(2) subparagraph 1 Europol Decision 2009.
100. Cf. Art. 7(6) Europol Decision 2009.
101. Art. 7(7)(a)–(c) Europol Regulation 2016.
102. Art. 38(2)(b) Europol Regulation 2016.
103. Art. 38(2)(a) Europol Regulation 2016.

104. Also cf. Hecker, *Europäisches Strafrecht* (2015), §5 mn. 65.
105. This criticism is taken further by Weichert, in Baldus and Soiné, *Rechtsprobleme* (1999), pp. 79 ff.; crit. also Esser, in Sinn and Zöller, *Neujustierung des Strafrechts* (2013), p. 71; a different opinion is put forward by Aulehner, in Baldus and Soiné, *Rechtsprobleme* (1999), p. 103.
106. Zieschang, *ZRP*, 29 (1996), 429, is critical of this, as is Klip, *European Criminal Law* (2016), p. 492–3. By contrast, Ruthig, in Wolter et al., *Festgabe Hilger* (2003), pp. 204–5, sees this as a standard that correlates more or less with that of German data protection law.
107. Weichert, in Baldus and Soiné, *Rechtsprobleme* (1999), pp. 82–3; de Busser, *eucrim*, 8 (2013), 20; crit. also Heine, *Rechtsstellung des Beschuldigten* (2009), p. 203; Noltenius, *ZStW*, 122 (2010), 616–17; Esser, in Sinn and Zöller, *Neujustierung des Strafrechts* (2013), p. 71; Esser, *Europäisches und Internationales Strafrecht* (2018), §3 mn. 44; endorsed by Aulehner, in Baldus and Soiné, *Rechtsprobleme* (1999), p. 104; this is contradicted explicitly, for example, by Daub, in Baldus and Soiné, *Rechtsprobleme* (1999), p. 95; for more on information exchange from a police perspective, also Del Moral Torres, *ARI*, 6 (2010), no 50. On data protection at the EU level, especially the new General Data Protection Regulation, cf. Chapter 2, mn. 152–3.
108. Cf. Art. 23(1), (2) Europol Regulation 2016 and Council Decision 2009/935/JHA of 30 November 2009 determining the list of third States and organisations with which Europol shall conclude agreements (OJ L 325 of 11 December 2009, 12).
109. Cf. Esser, in Sinn and Zöller, *Neujustierung des Strafrechts* (2013), p. 72; for more flexibility, Disley et al., *Evaluation of the Implementation of the Europol Council Decision and of Europol's Activities* (2012), p. 113 ('In seven interviews ... it was suggested that Europol should find a more flexible way to exchange information with third parties'); previously Ambos, *Internationales Strafrecht* (2008), §13 mn. 9 small print. For more information on the exchange of data between the EU, Eurojust and Europol on the one hand and the USA on the other, cf. de Busser, *eucrim*, 5 (2010), 30. Crit. on Europol's participation in non-EU working groups of police co-operation, Esser, in Sinn and Zöller, *Neujustierung des Strafrechts* (2013), p. 73.
110. Sénat (France), *Rapport d'information, Europol et Eurojust: Perspectives d'avenir*, No 477, 17.4.2014, p. 10 ('méga-moteur de recherches').
111. Art. 18(1) Europol Regulation 2016.
112. Cf. previously Art. 11 Europol Decision 2009 ('Europol Information System'). On the previous Art. 6 Europol Convention, cf. Milke, *Europol und Eurojust* (2003), pp. 74 ff.; Ellermann, *Europol und FBI* (2005), pp. 54 ff.
113. Art. 18(2)(a)(i) Europol Regulation 2016.
114. Art. 18(2)(a)(ii) Europol Regulation 2016 (emphasis added). Justified criticism of Art. 8(2) Europol Convention has been voiced, for example, by Ellermann, *ZEuS*, 5 (2002), 565 incl. further references; Weichert, in Baldus and Soiné, *Rechtsprobleme* (1999), pp. 75–6; Böse, *Grundsatz der Verfügbarkeit* (2007), pp. 34–5, 99 ff.
115. Art. 20(1) Europol Regulation 2016.
116. Arts. 20(1), (2), 21(1) Europol Regulation 2016.
117. See above, n. 96.
118. Cf. Art. 21(1) Europol Regulation 2016.
119. Cf. §101 **Austrian** CCP; Art. 148 **Dutch** CCP; §162 **German** CCP; Art. 327 **Italian** CCP; Art. 326 **Polish** CCP; Arts. 48, 263 no 1 **Portuguese** CCP; §3, Chapter 23

Swedish CCP. In contrast, in **England and Wales** the police are in charge of the investigation and the CPS is (only) in charge of the prosecution; as a matter of fact, for historic reasons (the CPS was only created in 1986) it is fair to say that the (local) police are more powerful than the local prosecutor. See also the national reports by Cornils and Verch, Voß, Huber and Rabenstein, Leblois-Happe and Barth, Faure, van Riel and Ubachs, Caianiello and Orlandi, and Zerbes, in Gleß, Grote and Heine, *Justizielle Einbindung und Kontrolle von Europol*, i (2001), pp. 37 ff., 111 ff., 190 ff., 276 ff., 350 ff., 420 ff., 478 ff.

120. For the LKAs see §3(1) first sentence Europol Act.
121. Cf. §161 StPO.
122. A critical stance is also taken by Wolter, in Wolter et al., *Festgabe Hilger* (2003), pp. 286, 288.
123. Cf. §2(1) second sentence Europol Act; also Martínez Soria, *VerwArch*, 89 (1998), 423–4.
124. Cf. Ambos, *Jura*, 25 (2003), 680 incl. further references in n. 100. For this reason, Ellermann, *Europol und FBI* (2005), p. 302, does not consider the situation in Europol to constitute a 'striking anomaly' (orig. 'krasse Besonderheit').
125. Cf. Art. 18(2), (5) in conjunction with Annex II B(1) Europol Regulation 2016. On Art. 10 Europol Convention, cf. Tolmein, *StV*, 19 (1999), 110; Ellermann, *ZEuS*, 5 (2002), 565–6, according to whom even information on these persons' sex lives is not out of question (however, this is relativised in ibid., n. 21: only possible if essential to the investigation). Furthermore, cf. the criticism in Zieschang, *ZRP*, 29 (1996), 428, on the regulation of data erasure in Art. 8(5) Europol Convention.
126. For a critical stance, cf. Ellermann, *ZEuS*, 5 (2002), 566; also Bechthold, *Betrifft JUSTIZ*, 13 (1997), 120.
127. Cf. Wolter, in Wolter et al., *Festgabe Hilger* (2003), p. 288; crit. also Paeffgen, *ZStW*, 118 (2006), 332–3; Nestler, *GA*, 157 (2010), 652; Ruthig, in Zöller et al., *FS Wolter* (2013), p. 1480 takes a more positive view.
128. Art. 31 Europol Regulation 2016.
129. Arts. 36, 37 Europol Regulation 2016.
130. Art. 43 Europol Regulation 2016.
131. For more detail on the previous debate surrounding this and the possible options, cf. Ambos, *Internationales Strafrecht* (2008), §13 mn. 14 ff.
132. See also Art. 88(3) TFEU.
133. Safferling, *Internationales Strafrecht* (2011), §12 mn. 14, remains critical nonetheless. On the recently established Europol Internet Referral Unit (EU IRU) and its relationship with the data protection regime of Europol Regulation 2016, see Ellermann, *ERA Forum*, 17 (2016), 562 ff., arguing at 578 that the EU IRU 'must operate on the basis of Europol's robust data protection regime'; on the EU IRU also Esser, in Odendahl, *Bekämpfung des Terrorismus* (2017), pp. 226–7.
134. Art. 43 Europol Regulation 2016.
135. Art. 42(1) Europol Regulation 2016.
136. Art. 42(4) Europol Regulation 2016.
137. Cf. Art 88(2) subparagraph 2 TFEU. On this, see *eucrim*, 6 (2011), 5; Albrecht and Janson, *EuR*, 47 (2012), 230. Ruthig, in Zöller et al., *FS Wolter* (2013), p. 1473, does not consider the present monitoring options to be sufficient.
138. Art. 51 Europol Regulation 2016. On the former Joint Supervisory Body (JSB), Satzger, *Internationales und Europäisches Strafrecht* (2016), §10 mn. 9; Hecker,

Europäisches Strafrecht (2015), §5 mn. 60; Ruthig, in Böse, *Europäisches Strafrecht* (2013), pp. 780–5.

139. Art. 51(1), (2) Europol Regulation 2016. On the previous situation, crit. Esser, in Sinn and Zöller, *Neujustierung des Strafrechts* (2013), pp. 73–4; previously also Ambos, *Internationales Strafrecht* (2008), §13 mn. 15, 17.
140. Art. 51(2)(a) Europol Regulation 2016; cf. previously Art. 34(4) Europol Decision 2009. On the Management Board, see Art. 37; and Ambos, *Internationales Strafrecht* (2008), §13 mn. 15.
141. Art. 51(2)(b) Europol Regulation 2016.
142. Art. 52 Europol Regulation 2016.
143. Council Decision 2009/968/JHA of 30 November 2009 adopting the rules on the confidentiality of Europol information (OJ L 332 of 17 December 2009, 17).
144. Cf. Art. 10(1) and (3) Protocol No 36 to the Lisbon Treaty (n. 8); therefore crit. regarding the intensity of judicial control, Hecker, *Europäisches Strafrecht* (2015), §5 mn. 61; a similar stance is taken by Heine, *Rechtsstellung des Beschuldigten* (2009), pp. 204 ff.; for a different opinion, cf. Ruthig, in Zöller et al., *FS Wolter* (2013), pp. 1475 ff.; Ruthig, in Böse, *Europäisches Strafrecht* (2013), p. 782, who assumes that control can be exercised immediately.
145. Cf. Art. 263(1) TFEU; also cf. Recital 21 Europol Decision 2009 with reference to Art. 35 TEU old version; see also Thiele, *EuR*, 45 (2010), 49; Saurer, *EuR*, 45 (2010), 63; Everling, *EuR*, 44 (2009) supplement 1, 79; on the problems of effective legal remedies prior to the decision, cf. von Arnauld, *JA*, 40 (2008), 332. A positive view is also taken by Brodowski, *Jura*, 35 (2013), 503–4; Schoppa, *Europol* (2013), pp. 238 ff. (241: 'groundbreaking', orig. 'bahnbrechend').
146. Cf. Art. 47 ff. Europol Regulation 2016: right to lodge a complaint with the EDPS (Art. 47), right to a judicial remedy against the EDPS before the CJEU (Art. 48), and liability for incorrect personal data processing and the right to compensation (Art. 50). See also Art. 65(3): 'decisions taken by Europol under Art. 8 of Regulation (EC) No 1049/2001 may be the subject of a complaint to the European Ombudsman or of an action before the Court of Justice of the European Union, in accordance with Articles 228 and 263 TFEU respectively'.
147. Cf. Protocol No 7 on Privileges and Immunities of the EU (OJ C 310 of 16 December 2004, 261).
148. Art. 63(1) Europol Regulation 2016. On the Europol Immunity Protocol replaced by Art. 51(1) and (2) Europol Decision 2009, cf. Ambos, *Internationales Strafrecht* (2008), §13 mn. 14.
149. Cf. Art. 11 of Protocol No 7 on the Privileges and Immunities of the EU. On immunity, also cf. Schoppa, *Europol* (2013), pp. 246 ff.; Ruthig, in Zöller et al., *FS Wolter* (2013), pp. 1478–9; Ruthig, in Böse, *Europäisches Strafrecht* (2013), pp. 784–5.
150. Cf. more generally Hölscheidt and Schotten, *NJW*, 52 (1999), 2852–3 and 2854; also Kremer, *Immunität für Europol-Bedienstete?* (2003), pp. 71 ff.
151. Cf. Milke, *Europol und Eurojust* (2003), pp. 277–8; von Langsdorff, *StV*, 23 (2003), 472–3; Vervaele, *RP*, 15 (2005), 176.
152. Joint Action 96/277/JHA of 22 April 1996 (OJ L 105 of 27 April 1996, 1).
153. Joint Action 98/428/JI of 29 June 1998 (OJ L 191 of 7 July 1998, 4), replaced by Decision 2008/976/JHA of 16 December 2008 on the EJN (OJ L 348 of 24 December 2008, 130); for an instructive account of this, cf. Galgo, *RIDP*, 77

(2006), 299 ff.; also cf. Klip, *European Criminal Law* (2016), pp. 502–4; Zöller, in Böse, *Europäisches Strafrecht* (2013), pp. 812 ff.; Hecker, *Europäisches Strafrecht* (2015), §5 mn. 66; Zwiers, *EPPO* (2011), pp. 278 ff.; Nehm, *DRiZ*, 78 (2000), 356–7; Stiegel, in Sieber, Satzger and von Heinegg, *Europäisches Strafrecht* (2014), pp. 831 ff.; Weyembergh, Armada and Brière, *NJECL*, 6 (2015), 279–80. On the co-operation between the EJN and Eurojust, cf. Dannecker, in Streinz, *EUV/AEUV* (2012), Art. 85 AEUV mn. 27.

154. Cf. Art. 2(1) Joint Action 96/277. However, von Langsdorff, *StV*, 23 (2003), 472, reports that so far Germany has only sent a 'liaison prosecutor' to Paris. This has not changed to date (information provided by the BMJ via email on 27 March 2014).
155. Cf. Arts. 1, 4(1) Joint Action 98/428.
156. Cf. Art. 4(1) Joint Action 98/428.
157. Arts. 3, 5 ff. Joint Action 98/428.
158. There are contact points in 41 States outside the EU, the most recent ones set up in Algeria, Chile, Colombia, Iraq, Jordan, Lebanon, Libya, the Palestinian Authorities, Saudi Arabia; cf. Eurojust, *Annual Report 2016* (2017), p. 44. On Eurojust's co-operation with third States in general, cf. also Eurojust, *Annual Report 2016* (2017), pp. 42 ff.
159. For a critical stance on this, cf. von Langsdorff, *StV*, 23 (2003), 473; also cf. Zwiers, *EPPO* (2011), p. 251.
160. OJ L 324 of 14 December 2000, 2; cf. von Langsdorff, *StV*, 23 (2003), 473–4; Dieckmann, *NStZ*, 21 (2001), 620; Suominen, *MJECL*, 15 (2008), 219; Grotz, in Sieber, Satzger and von Heinegg, *Europäisches Strafrecht* (2014), pp. 819–20; Zöller, in Böse, *Europäisches Strafrecht* (2013), pp. 789 ff. On the creation of Pro-Eurojust, cf. Ambos, *Internationales Strafrecht* (2008), §13 mn. 20 small print.
161. OJ L 63 of 6 March 2002, 1; amended by OJ L 196 of 25 July 2002, 63.
162. Council Decision 2009/426/JHA of 16 December 2008 (OJ L 138 of 4 June 2009, 14).
163. Previously Art. 31(2) TEU old version.
164. COM (2013) 535 final; thereto Mitsilegas, *EU Criminal Law* (2016), pp. 96–100; subsequently the EU Council has adopted its 'General Approach', cf. Council Doc. 6643/15 of 27 February 2015; on this Brodowski, *ZIS*, 11 (2016), 111–12; Mitsilegas, *EU Criminal Law* (2016), pp. 101–3.
165. Satzger, *Internationales und Europäisches Strafrecht* (2016), §10 mn. 16; also cf. Weyembergh, *eucrim*, 8 (2013), 127.
166. Cf. Mitsilegas, *EU Criminal Law* (2016), pp. 95–6, 97–8 with further references; the Council's General Approach (above, n. 164) does not change the matter; cf. Mitsilegas, *EU Criminal Law* (2016), p. 103 ('powers of Eurojust remain limited').
167. Crit. Esser, in Sinn and Zöller, *Neujustierung des Strafrechts* (2013), p. 84.
168. Art. 30(3) Council Decision 2008.
169. Art. 5(1)(b), 7 Council Decision 2008. On the 'college', see main text, mn. 18. This collegial structure is an important difference to the hierarchical structure of Europol, cf. Weyembergh, Armada and Brière, *NJECL*, 6 (2015), 263.
170. Art. 1 Council Decision 2008. Also cf. von Bubnoff, *ZEuS*, 5 (2002), 207–8; Fawzy, *Die Errichtung von Eurojust* (2005), p. 35; Kretschmer, *Jura*, 29 (2007), 173; in more detail on Eurojust's organisational structure, Zwiers, *EPPO* (2011), pp. 261 ff.
171. Art. 85(1) subparagraph 2 TFEU; cf. also Council Doc. 9579/16 + COR, p. 5.

172. Art. 85(1) TFEU, Art. 3 Council Decision 2008. The French Senate (above, n. 110), p. 39, has compared it to a 'control tower' alluding to its right to intervene in complex cross-border cases ('Eurojust est une "tour de contrôle" qui constitue une indispensable structure de coordination et de coopération entre les autorités judiciaires des États membres'). See also Satzger, *Internationales und Europäisches Strafrecht* (2016), §10 mn. 13; Hecker, *Europäisches Strafrecht* (2015), §5 mn. 72; Esser, *Europäisches und Internationales Strafrecht* (2018), §3 mn. 70–1; Dannecker, in Streinz, *EUV/AEUV* (2012), Art. 85 AEUV mn. 3 ff.; also cf. von Bubnoff, *ZEuS*, 5 (2002), 205 ff.; von Langsdorff, *StV*, 23 (2003), 475; Kapplinghaus and Milke, *DRiZ*, 82 (2004), 267; Kapplinghaus, in Eser and Rabenstein, *Strafjustiz im Spannungsfeld von Effizienz und Fairness* (2004), pp. 164 and 166–7; Dieckmann, *NStZ*, 21 (2001), 620; Schomburg, *DRiZ*, 78 (2000), 343; Suominen, *MJECL*, 15 (2008), 220–1; Frenz, *wistra*, 29 (2010), 433; Suhr, *ZEuS*, 12 (2009), 700; Böse, *Grundsatz der Verfügbarkeit* (2007), pp. 29–30; Spiezia, *ERA Forum*, 11 (2011) 390 ff.; Grotz, in Sieber, Satzger and von Heinegg, *Europäisches Strafrecht* (2014), pp. 821–3; Zöller, in Böse, *Europäisches Strafrecht* (2013), pp. 794 ff.; on Eurojust's co-ordinating activity in particular, cf. Serzysko, *ERA Forum*, 11 (2011), 594–5. Art. 16(2) FD EAW specifies that Eurojust's advice may be sought in regard to requests; further references in Ambos, *Internationales Strafrecht* (2008), §13 mn. 21 n. 141.
173. Cf. Art. 85(1) subparagraph 2 (a) TFEU.
174. A different opinion is put forward by Dannecker, in Streinz, *EUV/AEUV* (2012), Art. 85 AEUV mn. 10–11. Art. 2(1) Regulation Proposal Eurojust 2013 gives Eurojust a much more limited competence, namely to support and strengthen the co-ordination and co-operation between the national authorities.
175. Art. 85(2) TFEU.
176. Art. 85(1) subparagraph 1 TFEU.
177. Above, mn. 9.
178. On Eurojust's repressive fight against terrorism, cf. Esser, *GA*, 151 (2004), 711; Esser, in Sinn and Zöller, *Neujustierung des Strafrechts* (2013), pp. 80–2 (including organised crime); Esser, in Odendahl, *Bekämpfung des Terrorismus* (2017), pp. 231 ff.; arguing in favour of extending its competence to include crimes under international law, Ryngaert, *EJCCLCJ*, 14 (2006), 72 ff.
179. Art. 4(2) Council Decision 2008.
180. Art. 3 Regulation Proposal Eurojust 2013. On the co-operation problems that may arise from this, cf. Weyembergh, *eucrim*, 8 (2013), 128–9.
181. Weyembergh, *eucrim*, 8 (2013), 129–30.
182. Art. 6(1) Council Decision 2008; Arts. 5(1)(a), 6(a) Regulation Proposal Eurojust 2013.
183. Art. 7 Council Decision 2008; Arts. 5(1)(b), 10 Regulation Proposal Eurojust 2013. For more detail, cf. von Bubnoff, *ZEuS*, 5 (2002), 208–9; Fawzy, *Die Errichtung von Eurojust* (2005), pp. 37 ff.; Thwaites, *RIDP*, 77 (2006), 294; Serzysko, *ERA Forum*, 11 (2011), 588 ff.; Zöller, in Böse, *Europäisches Strafrecht* (2013), pp. 792 ff. For more detail on the national members, cf. Grotz, in Sieber, Satzger and von Heinegg, *Europäisches Strafrecht* (2014), pp. 824–7 (on the college, pp. 826–7). Art. 7 ff. Regulation Proposal Eurojust 2013 aims to strengthen the national members; on this, cf. Brodowski, *ZIS*, 8 (2013), 462; also cf. Weyembergh, *eucrim*,

8 (2013), 127–8. On the importance of one common language (English), Spiezia, in Ruggieri, *Languages* (2014), pp. 37–40.

184. Cf. Arts. 6(1)(a)(i) and 7(1)(a)(i) Council Decision 2008; Art. 7(1)(a) Regulation Proposal Eurojust 2013.
185. Arts. 6(1)(a)(iv) and 7(1)(a)(iv) Council Decision 2008; thereto Weyembergh, Armada and Brière, *NJECL*, 6 (2015), 271–2.
186. Cf. Arts. 14–25 Council Decision 2008; Arts. 27–37 Regulation Proposal Eurojust 2013. On the question of legal remedy given the intervention in the right to informational self-determination involved herein, cf. Milke, *Europol und Eurojust* (2003), pp. 286 ff.; Esser and Herbold, *NJW*, 57 (2004), 2423–4; Dannecker, in Streinz, *EUV/AEUV* (2012), Art. 85 AEUV mn. 17 ff.; von Bubnoff, *ZEuS*, 5 (2002), 212, thinks any monitoring beyond the obligation to provide reports (Art. 32 Eurojust Decision) unnecessary. Also cf. Eurojust, *Annual Report 2003* (2004), pp. 15 ff. A critical stance is taken by Wolter, in Wolter et al., *Festgabe Hilger* (2003), p. 288. Also cf. the expansion of the data protection regulations in Arts. 31–7 Regulation Proposal Eurojust 2013.
187. Cf. above, mn. 10–12; and Esser, in Sinn and Zöller, *Neujustierung des Strafrechts* (2013), p. 83.
188. Thus far, **Norway, Switzerland** and the **USA** have made use of this option; cf. http://eurojust.europa.eu/about/structure/college/Pages/liaison-magistrates.aspx (accessed 27 January 2018). In June 2013 **Liechtenstein** signed a co-operation treaty with Eurojust, which also permits the exchange of liaison magistrates; cf. *eucrim*, 8 (2013), 40. Cf. also Grotz, in Sieber, Satzger and von Heinegg, *Europäisches Strafrecht* (2014), pp. 829–30; Esser, in Sinn and Zöller, *Neujustierung des Strafrechts* (2013), p. 83.
189. According to Thwaites, *RIDP*, 77 (2006), 295, from 202 (2002) to 588 (2005). The Eurojust Annual Report for 2008 states that 1,193 cases were dealt with; in 2009, 1,372 cases were registered, which represented an increase of 15 per cent from the previous year; in 2010 the number rose to 1,424 cases, in 2011 to 1,441 cases. In 2015, 2,214 cases, and in 2016 2,306 cases, have been reported, an increase of 14 per cent on the previous year. Eurojust, *Annual Report 2016* (2017), pp. 9–10.
190. Eurojust, *Annual Report 2016* (2017), pp. 27 ff.
191. In this context, also see the Final Evaluation Report on the Implementation of the Eurojust Action Plan against THB 2012–2016 of 17 January 2017, www.eurojust.europa.eu/Practitioners/operational/THB/Documents/2017-01-31-THB-FINAL.pdf, last accessed 27 January 2018.
192. In detail on corruption cases, Spiezia, *ERA Forum*, 11 (2011), 393 ff.
193. Von Langsdorff, *StV*, 23 (2003), 474.
194. Art. 8 Regulation Proposal Eurojust 2013.
195. Art. 9 Regulation Proposal Eurojust 2013.
196. Cf. generally Eurojust, *Evaluation of the Eurojust Council Decision* (2015), pp. 17 ff.
197. See e.g. for **Portugal** Law 36/2003 of 22 August as amended by Law 20/2014 of 15 April; for **Italy** the Law of 14 March 2005, Gazzetta Ufficiale n. 72 of 29 March 2005, available at www.camera.it/parlam/leggi/05041l.htm, accessed 27 January 2018 (thereto also cf. Manzione, *LP*, 25 (2005), 243 ff.); for **Greece**, Law 3663/2008 (Eurojust, JITs and Other Provisions, 28 May 2008) as amended by Law 3904/2010; a further amendment is in preparation; for **Spain** the most recent Law 16/2015 of 7 July, BOE No 162, 8.7.2015, p. 56554.

198. See e.g. for **Austria** §§63 ff. of the Law on Judicial Co-operation in Criminal Matters with MS of the EU, *BGBl.* O No 36/2004, last amended *BGBl.* I No 107/2014; for **France** Art. 17 of Law 2004-204 of 9 March introducing Arts. 695-4 to 695-9 CCP (for more details see Bulletin officiel du Ministère de la justice, Circulaire du 18 février 2014, BOMJ n° 2014-02 du 28 février 2014 – JUSD1404290C); for **Hungary** Law No CLXXX of 2012 on Co-operation with EU MS in criminal matters (regarding the Council Decision 2008). In **Poland**, there is a mixture of provisions in special laws and executive decrees, for example the Ordinances of the Minister of Justice of 30 April 2012 (co-operation of prosecutor's office with international organizations) and of 23 December 2015, Chapter 6 (co-operation with national members of Eurojust).
199. In **England and Wales** it has been implemented basically by administrative action without a proper statutory basis; searching legislation one only finds a reference to Eurojust in para. 41 of the Explanatory Note to the Crime (International Co-operation) Act 2003. In the **Netherlands**, for example, the minister of security and justice saw no pressing need for a full implementation; only two minor amendments regarding data have been made (Art. 17 §4 Act on Police Data and Art. 8 §6 Act of Judicial and Criminal Justice Data). In the non-MS **Switzerland** there is an agreement with Eurojust of 27 November 2008, cf. www.admin.ch/opc/de/classified-compilation/20092002/index.html, accessed 27 January 2018.
200. Act Implementing Council Decision (2002/187/JHA) of 28 February 2002 setting up Eurojust with a view to reinforcing the fight against serious crime (Eurojust Act – EJA) of 12 May 2004, *BGBl.*, I 2004, 902; last amended by Art. 1 Amendment Act of 7 June 2012 (*BGBl.*, I 2012, 1270); cf. also BR-Drs. 545/03; BT-Drs. 15/1719; BT-Drs. 15/1719; 15/2484; 15/2717; 15/2832 and BR-Drs. 255/04; on this, cf. Zöller, in Böse, *Europäisches Strafrecht* (2013), pp. 805–11; Dannecker, in Streinz, *EUV/AEUV* (2012), Art. 85 AEUV mn. 14 ff.
201. The Draft Act (cf. BR-Drs. 545/03, 4; BT-Drs. 15/1719, 6) originally planned to restrict the option of not sharing information pursuant to §4(2) No 2 to cases where 'the communication of information would compromise foreign political interests of the Federal Republic of Germany'. However, the Bundesrat was unable to reach consensus on this (BT-Drs. 15/2717, 1, 3). Also cf. Esser and Herbold, *NJW*, 57 (2004), 2423.
202. Thus the response of the (former) deputy German member Kapplinghaus when asked by the author (in an email of 14 June 2004).
203. Cf. Art. 26 Council Decision 2008; and Eurojust, *Annual Report 2016* (2017), pp. 41 ff.; also Kapplinghaus, in Eser and Rabenstein, *Strafjustiz im Spannungsfeld von Effizienz und Fairness* (2004), pp. 169 ff. (including the relationship to States outside the EU); Fawzy, *Die Errichtung von Eurojust* (2005), pp. 93 ff.; Thwaites, *RIDP*, 77 (2006), 297; Serzysko, *ERA Forum*, 11 (2011), 596–7.
204. Art. 85(1)(c) TFEU; see also Art. 25a Council Decision 2008.
205. See also Weyembergh, Armada and Brière, *NJECL*, 6 (2015), 280.
206. Von Langsdorff, *StV*, 23 (2003), 474; Kapplinghaus, in Eser and Rabenstein, *Strafjustiz im Spannungsfeld von Effizienz und Fairness* (2004), pp. 169–70; on this issue, also cf. von Bubnoff, *ZEuS*, 5 (2002), 209; on the number of contact points, cf. n. 158 above.
207. Cf. Weyembergh, Armada and Brière, *NJECL*, 6 (2015), 281–3.

208. Art. 26(4) Council Decision 2008. Critically thereto Eurojust, *Annual Report 2003* (2004), p. 36; on 'frictions' also cf. Kapplinghaus, in Eser and Rabenstein, *Strafjustiz im Spannungsfeld von Effizienz und Fairness* (2004), p. 169; also Eurojust, *Annual Report 2004* (2005), p. 17; for a more positive view, cf. Eurojust, *Annual Report 2012* (2013), p. 48. On co-operation also cf. Spiezia, *ERA Forum*, 11 (2011), 392–3; Esser, in Böse, *Europäisches Strafrecht* (2013), p. 723; Dannecker, in Streinz, *EUV/AEUV* (2012), Art. 85 AEUV mn. 26.
209. Art. 2 of the Co-operation Agreement between Eurojust and Europol of 1 October 2009, cf. www.eurojust.europa.eu/doclibrary/Eurojust-framework/agreements/Agreement%20between%20Eurojust%20and%20Europol%20(2010)/Eurojust-Europol-2010-01-01-EN.pdf, accessed 27 January 2018. The agreement entered into force on 1 January 2010 and repealed the first co-operation agreement of 9 June 2004. It has not been published in the OJ.
210. Described aptly in Milke, *Europol und Eurojust* (2003), p. 289; Kapplinghaus and Milke, *DRiZ*, 82 (2004), 268; Kapplinghaus, in Eser and Rabenstein, *Strafjustiz im Spannungsfeld von Effizienz und Fairness* (2004), p. 169; Esser and Herbold, *NJW*, 57 (2004), 2421; crit. Esser, *GA*, 151 (2004), 721. For more details, cf. Weyembergh, Armada and Brière, *NJECL*, 6 (2015), 261 ff. (analysing the historical and structural differences but also stressing common features as 'service providers' and demanding greater respect for the different objectives, greater awareness and transparency, giving a key role to the EP, 284–7); also Fawzy, *Die Errichtung von Eurojust* (2005), pp. 134 ff.; Spiezia, *ERA Forum*, 11 (2011), 393; Esser, in Böse, *Europäisches Strafrecht* (2013), p. 724; Dannecker, in Streinz, *EUV/AEUV* (2012), Art. 85 AEUV mn. 24–5; Eurojust, *Annual Report 2016* (2017), p. 41.
211. Cf. Weyembergh, Armada and Brière, *NJECL*, 6 (2015), 275–9. According to Art. 85(1) subparagraph 1 TFEU, Eurojust shall receive information from Europol.
212. See already above, nn. 80 and 372 with main text; also cf. Weyembergh, Armada and Brière, *NJECL*, 6 (2015), 271–4 (considering them a 'good example' of co-operation but highlighting tensions regarding funding).
213. Cf. Weyembergh, Armada and Brière, *NJECL*, 6 (2015), 267 ff.
214. This follows from Art. 85(2) TFEU *e contrario*; see also von Bubnoff, *ZEuS*, 5 (2002), 204; von Langsdorff, *StV*, 23 (2003), 475; Vervaele, *RP*, 15 (2005), 180.
215. Cf. Eurojust, *Annual Report 2008* (2009), p. 37 (closer co-operation with Europol, including in operations). In regard to Art. III-273 (1) (a) VerfV Esser, *GA*, 151 (2004), 721. In favour of an extended competence Jähnke and Schramm, *Europäisches Strafrecht* (2017), §7 mn. 23 (stating that Eurojust was assigned a new task with the CJEU's decision in *Aranyosi* and *Caldararu* (Ch 4 mn. 60), namely to make the execution of an EAW possible in cases where it is suspended because cases of inhuman detention conditions in the issuing State).
216. Art. 85(1) subparagraph 2 (a) TFEU.
217. Art. 2(1) Regulation Proposal Eurojust 2013.
218. Above, mn. 20.
219. Also cf. Satzger, *Internationales und Europäisches Strafrecht* (2016), §10 mn. 17; de Gouttes, in Espina Ramos and Vicente Carbajosa, *The Future EPPO* (2009), pp. 103–4; de Angelis, *eucrim*, 7 (2012), 76. For earlier references, cf. Ambos, *Internationales Strafrecht* (2008), §13 mn. 23 n. 160. Espina Ramos, in Klip, *Substantive Criminal Law of the European Union* (2011), p. 37, is critical of this because of the different aims of Eurojust (strengthening co-operation between

Member States) and EPPO (European investigations), as are Hamran and Szabova, *NJECL*, 4 (2013), 46 ff., who show that there is no consensus on what 'from Eurojust' actually means. Csúri, *eucrim*, 7 (2012), 80, interprets this wording to mean that Eurojust will either turn into the EPPO or be merged with it. On further possible interpretations, cf. Grünewald, *HRRS*, 14 (2013), 509–10; Zöller, in Böse, *Europäisches Strafrecht* (2013), pp. 829–31.

220. Cf. Art. 41 Regulation Proposal Eurojust 2013.

221. Below, mn. 30.

222. Art. 19(1) TEU. See also Jähnke and Schramm, *Europäisches Strafrecht* (2017), §3 mn. 2. On the establishment of these specialised courts, cf. Art. 257 TFEU.

223. Arts. 251 TFEU, 16 CJEU Statute, 60 RP CJEU. Normally, the Court assigns any case brought before it to the chambers of three and of five judges (Arts. 16(1) CJEU Statute, 60(1) RP CJEU). If the difficulty or importance of the case or particular circumstances so require, or when a MS or an institution of the Union that is party to the proceedings so requests, the Court shall sit in a grand chamber (Arts. 16(3) CJEU Statute, 60(1) RP CJEU). As a full Court it shall sit in cases of exceptional importance (Arts. 16(5) CJEU Statute, 60(2) RP CJEU), or when deciding the waiving of immunity from legal proceedings of one of its judges (Art. 3 CJEU Statute), or where cases are brought before it pursuant to Art. 228(2) TFEU (dismissal of the European Ombudsman) or Arts. 245(2), 247 (deprivation of pension rights or other benefits and compulsory retirement of Members of Commission) or 286(6) TFEU (deprivation of office, pension rights or other benefits of Member of the Court of Auditors) (Arts. 16(4) CJEU Statute, 60(2) RP CJEU). The Court shall be assisted by advocates general, cf. Art. 252 TFEU; on the election of judges and the Advocates-General, cf. Art. 253–5 TFEU.

224. Art. 19(3) TEU; see also Art. 17(1) TEU (Commission oversight of Union law 'under the control of the CJEU').

225. Thereto cf. Art. 258 TFEU. For a brief summary of the relevant proceedings, cf. Lelieveldt and Princen, *Politics of the EU* (2015), pp. 69–70 (annulment action, infringement procedure, preliminary ruling). Cf. also Jähnke and Schramm, *Europäisches Strafrecht* (2017), §3 mn. 4, 15 ff. (considering the infringment proceeding as the 'institutionally and politically most important instrument to protect the law' (orig. *institutionell und politisch wichtigste Instrument zur Wahrung des Rechts*)). On the jurisdiction of the General Court, cf. Art. 256 TFEU.

226. Cf. above, Chapter 1, mn. 4; Chapter 2, mn. 9, 156; Chapter 3, mn. 10, 46–8.

227. This is in particular true with regard to procedural mutual-recognition instruments, especially the EAW; cf. for a critique Chapter 4, mn. 56–7, 59, 77; yet the CJEU also invoked mutual trust to preserve its autonomy vis-à-vis the ECtHR; cf. Opinion 2/13 as discussed in Chapter 2, mn. 9. See also Ostropolski, *NJECL*, 6 (2015), 168, 177–8 (praising the CJEU for its 'resolute defence' of mutual trust, converting it into the 'strongest fortress of defence of mutual trust') and 171 ff. (discussing CJEU case law on *ne bis in idem* and the EAW as well as Opinion 2/13).

228. Cf. Hinarejos, *EuLRev*, 36 (2011), 420–3 ('catalyst for integration', 'strong judicially driven inegration'); Swoboda, *ZIS*, 10 (2015), 361 ('driving force', jurisprudence as 'powerful weapon of integration'); Mitsilegas, *EU Criminal Law* (2016), p. 51 ('Court's readiness to see criminal justice competence subsumed within other fields of EU action'). Cf. also Jähnke and Schramm, *Europäisches Strafrecht* (2017), §3 mn. 30 ('motor of integration').

229. On the grand chamber's judgment in *Aranyosi and Căldăraru*, Nos C-404/15 and C-659/15 PPU; above, Chapter 2, mn. 156 *in fine*.
230. See e.g. Hinarejos, *EuLRev*, 36 (2011), 420–1, 423–30 (convincingly arguing that the fundamental difference between integration in economic and criminal matters and the different role that rights play in the latter demand from the CJEU to operate 'as a check on integration, rather than its champion'; it may only push for integration in this area if this benefits individual rights); Swoboda, *ZIS*, 10 (2015), 361 ff. (complaining of the CJEU's missing defence perspective); calling for a stronger commitment of the Court, also Mitsilegas, *EU Criminal Law* (2016), p. 184 ('task of the Court to develop an effective level playing-field of fundamental rights protection'); see also Chapter 4, mn. 60.
231. Cf. in particular De Busser, *ERA Forum*, 16 (2015), 280, 284–6. On the general complaint possibility in case of alleged violation of the principle of subsidiarity, cf. Art. 8 Subsidiarity Protocol (Lisbon Treaty, Protocol (No 2) on the Application of the Principles of Subsidiarity and Proportionality (OJ C 326 of 26 October 2012, 206)), in conjunction with Art. 263 TFEU; thereto above, Chapter 1, mn. 19.
232. Cf. Chapter 1, mn. 34; see in particular for the CJEU's extensive case law on Art. 54 CISA, Chapter 2, mn. 172 ff.
233. Cf. Chapter 1, mn. 34; see also Hinarejos, *EuLRev*, 36 (2011), 420; Böse, in Sieber, Satzger and von Heinegg, *Europäisches Strafrecht* (2014), pp. 993–4.
234. Cf. Chapter 1, mn. 9 with further details on the transitional period and exceptions.
235. Cf. Schorkopf, *Staatsrecht* (2017), §8 mn. 168 ff.; Böse, in Sieber, Satzger and von Heinegg, *Europäisches Strafrecht* (2014), pp. 993–8; Klip, *European Criminal Law* (2016), pp. 133–46. Member States use this possibility to a quite varying degree: in 2016 the total of 470 preliminary references of 28 MS have mainly come from Germany (84), Italy (62), Spain (47), the Netherlands (26), Belgium (26), France and the UK (both 23). For the full period from 1961 to 2016 there have been 9,616 preliminary references, coming mainly from Germany (2,300), Italy (1,388), the Netherlands (975), France (954), Belgium (820) and the UK (612); see CJEU, *Annual Report 2016* (2017), pp. 107–8, available at http://curia.europa.eu/jcms/upload/docs/application/pdf/2017-04/ragp-2016_final_en_web.pdf (accessed 27 January 2018). For the full period one has to take into account, of course, that important MS only joined the EU long after the 1960s (especially Spain).
236. Cf. Art. 19(3)(b) TEU and Arts. 256(3), 267 TFEU; see for more details Chapter 3, mn. 49–51.
237. Art. 6(1) TEU; see also Chapter 1, mn. 31 and Chapter 2, mn. 1, 6, 154 ff.
238. Cf. Chapter 2, mn. 9; on the increasing importance of the CFREU in the CJEU's case law, cf. Chapter 2, mn. 154 ff.; on the use of ECtHR case law by the CJEU after the Lisbon Treaty, cf. Krommendijk, *MJ*, 22 (2015), 812 ff.
239. Arts. 258–60 TFEU; see Chapter 1, mn. 33 with further references; also Böse, in Sieber, Satzger and von Heinegg, *Europäisches Strafrecht* (2014), pp. 1008–10. The CJEU's 'unlimited jurisdiction with regard to penalties' pursuant to Art. 261 TFEU has no specific criminal law relevance but rather refers to regulations which provide for financial penalties against natural persons; cf. Cremer, in Calliess and Ruffert, *EUV/AEUV* (2016), Art. 261 AEUV, mn. 1–2.
240. Cf. Art. 19(3)(b) TEU and Art. 263(4) TFEU; thereto Chapter 3, mn. 37 with n. 272; also Böse, in Sieber, Satzger and von Heinegg, *Europäisches Strafrecht* (2014), pp. 999–1008; Schorkopf, *Staatsrecht* (2017), §8 mn. 158 ff. This may also

become relevant regarding procedural acts of the future EPPO; cf. Art. 36(3) Regulation Proposal EPPO 2017 (below, n. 250); and Mitsilegas, *EU Criminal Law* (2016), pp. 44, 117. Annulment actions regarding OLAF reports have repeatedly been considered inadmissible by the CJEU; cf. Stojanovski, *eucrim*, 6 (2011), 129.

241. For a critical stance on this, cf. Kempf, *StV*, 23 (2003), 128–9; Hecker, *Europäisches Strafrecht* (2015), §14 mn. 49 ff.; Albrecht, *ZRP*, 37 (2004), 2–3; Schünemann, *StV*, 23 (2003), 116; Satzger, *StV*, 23 (2003), 137–8; more reticently in regard to its necessity, Wright, in Espina Ramos and Vicente Carbajosa, *The Future EPPO* (2009), pp. 64–5; Heger, *ZIS*, 4 (2009), 416; Radtke, *GA*, 151 (2004), 4 ff. (agrees in principle); Castaldo, *StV*, 23 (2003), 123; Suhr, *ZEuS*, 12 (2009), 701; Sieber, *ZStW*, 121 (2009), 48–9; Scheuermann, *Prinzip der gegenseitigen Anerkennung* (2009), pp. 105 ff.; Ligeti and Simonato, *NJECL*, 4 (2013), 8 ff.; Wade, *CrimLSC*, 59 (2013), 444 ff. (including an evaluation of the EuroNeedsProjects), www.mpicc.de/shared/data/pdf/euroneeds_report_jan_2011.pdf, accessed 27 January 2018; on the EPPO's role as a guardian of the European taxpayers' money and the EU legislator's duty to ensure the EPPO's material competence, cf. Jourová, *eucrim*, 11 (2016), 94 ff. On the position of the Scandinavian states, cf. Suominen, *EuCLR*, 1 (2011), 183–4; on the Dutch position, Van der Hulst, *eucrim*, 11 (2016), 99 ff.

242. 'Corpus Juris introducing penal provisions for the purpose of the financial interests of the European Union'; cf. Delmas-Marty, *Corpus Juris der strafrechtlichen Regelungen zum Schutz der finanziellen Interessen der Europäischen Union* (1998); thereto Csúri, *CYELS*, 18 (2016), 128–34; Vervaele, in Espina Ramos and Vicente Carbajosa, *The Future EPPO* (2009), pp. 135 ff.; de Angelis, *eucrim*, 7 (2012), 75; and Ambos, *Internationales Strafrecht* (2008), §13 mn. 24 small print. On the EPPO's history based on the Corpus Juris cf. Bösch, in Espina Ramos and Vicente Carbajosa, *The Future EPPO* (2009), p. 25; Pinto Monteiro, in Espina Ramos and Vicente Carbajosa, *The Future EPPO* (2009), pp. 97 ff.; Hamran and Szabova, *NJECL*, 4 (2013), 41 ff.; Ligeti, *EuCLR*, 1 (2011), 123 ff.; Killmann and Hofmann, in Sieber, Satzger and von Heinegg, *Europäisches Strafrecht* (2014), pp. 865–9.

243. Green Paper EPPO (2001).

244. For a comparative-language interpretation (Italian, German and English) of the primary law, cf. Ruggieri, in Ruggieri, *Languages* (2014), pp. 109 ff.

245. Art. 86(1) TFEU.

246. Cf. Justice Commissioner Reding, press release IP/13/709 of 17 July 2013, http://europa.eu/rapid/press-release_IP-13-709_en.htm, last accessed 27 January 2018.

247. In the same vein, previously Grünewald, *HRRS*, 14 (2013), 509; Espina Ramos, in Klip, *Substantive Criminal Law of the EU* (2011), p. 39; see also Mitsilegas, *EU Criminal Law after Lisbon* (2016), p. 103 ('main battlefield between EU institutions with regard to the relationship between EU law and national criminal law'); on the subsidiarity objections by national parliaments, cf. ibid., pp. 41–3.

248. COM (2013) 534 final of 17 July 2013; on this, cf. Beukelmann, *NJW-Spezial*, 10 (2013), 568; Brodowski, *ZIS*, 8 (2013), 460 ff.; Damaskou, *NJECL*, 6 (2015), 138 ff.; Mitsilegas, *EU Criminal Law after Lisbon* (2016), pp. 104 ff.; Asp, *Procedural Criminal Law Cooperation* (2016), pp. 192 ff.; crit. Csúri, *CYELS*, 18 (2016), 137–42 ('the proposal has lost sight of the original objectives' (140)); a highly critical stance is also taken by Erbežnik, *EuCLR*, 5 (2015), 214–21 (pointing to the lack of democratic control, of judicial (court) oversight and of rules regarding measures and admissibility of evidence, and concluding that 'the EPPO proposal is legally a

highly problematic proposal that might potentially even endanger the EU area of Freedom, Security and Justice' (220)); also cf. *eucrim*, 8 (2013), 41–2; Killmann and Hofmann, in Sieber, Satzger and von Heinegg, *Europäisches Strafrecht* (2014), pp. 875.

249. For an overview of the proposals discussed before the Lisbon Treaty, cf. Ligeti, in Klip, *Substantive Criminal Law of the EU* (2011), pp. 55 ff.; Zwiers, *EPPO* (2011), pp. 355 ff.; on the 2014 Greek and Italian proposal, Damaskou, *NJECL*, 6 (2015), 143–9 (shift of power to Member States); Csúri, *CYELS*, 18 (2016), 145; also cf. Safferling, *Internationales Strafrecht* (2011), §12 mn. 27 ff.
250. Council of the EU, Presidency, Proposal for a Regulation on the establishment of the EPPO – Draft Regulation, 5766/17, 31 January 2017; it then became the Draft Regulation implementing enhanced co-operation on the establishment of the EPPO – Presidency text, Council Doc. 7761/17 of 3 April 2017. The additions are restricted in the main to adaptations of the rules on the financing and entering into force of the regulation proposal in the MS in the procedure of enhanced co-operation (see Arts. 49(6) and (7), 75(2) and (3)). Between the 2013 and 2017 proposals, 92 official documents have been produced; see the listing by the *eurocrim* database (as of 27 January 2018), available at https://db.eurocrim.org/db/en/vorgang/306, accessed 27 January 2018. On the recent developments, see Brodowski, *ZIS*, 12 (2017), 11–15; Brodowski, *ZIS*, 12 (2017), 689–90.
251. Council of the EU, Presidency, Proposal for a Regulation on the Establishment of the EPPO – Consolidated Text, 15200/16, 2 December 2016.
252. On this, see press release 48/17 of 7 February 2017 ('EPPO has been part of the Treaties since 2009. However, as the last six and a half years have shown its establishment has been elusive'), available at www.statewatch.org/news/2017/feb/eu-council-eppo-prel.pdf, accessed 27 January 2018.
253. Notification to the EP, the Council and the Commission with a view to establishing enhanced co-operation of 16 MS (Belgium, Bulgaria, Croatia, Cyprus, Czech Republic, Finland, France, Germany, Greece, Lithuania, Luxembourg, Portugal, Romania, Slovakia, Slovenia, Spain) on the draft Regulation on the establishing of the EPPO in accordance with the third subparagraph of Article 85(1) of the TFEU, Council Doc. 8027/17 of 5 April 2017; Latvia and Estonia also decide to participate: Council-Doc 9546/17 of 24 May 2017 and Doc. 10053/17 of 7 June 2017.
254. Council Regulation (EU) 2017/1939 of 12 October 2017 implementing enhanced cooperation on the establishment of the European Public Prosecutor's Office ('the EPPO') (OJ L 283 of 31 October 2017, 1). In addition to the MS mentioned in the previous n., Austria and Italy also joined the measure (ibid., preamble para. (8)).
255. Art. 120(2) Regulation EPPO 2017.
256. Arts. 3, 6, 8(1) Regulation EPPO 2017; see also Killmann and Hofmann, in Sieber, Satzger and von Heinegg, *Europäisches Strafrecht* (2014), pp. 869–70.
257. Art. 6(2) Regulation EPPO 2017.
258. Art. 8(2)–(4) Regulation EPPO 2017; see also Art. 13. There shall be at least two delegated prosecutors per MS.
259. On this, cf. Hamran and Szabova, *NJECL*, 4 (2013), 49–50; also Klip, in Klip, *Substantive Criminal Law of the EU* (2011), p. 27; in detail on alternative proposals, Ligeti and Simonato, *NJECL*, 4 (2013), 13 ff.; Ligeti, in Ligeti, *Toward a Prosecutor for the EU*, i (2013), p. 3; Sicurella, in Ligeti, *Toward a Prosecutor for the EU*, i (2013), pp. 872 ff.; White, *eucrim*, 7 (2012), 67 ff.; White, *NJECL*, 4 (2013), 22 ff.;

Damaskou, *NJECL*, 6 (2015), 132–6; on the organisation cf. also Brodowski, *StV*, 37 (2017), 685. De Angelis, *eucrim*, 7 (2012), 77–8, favours a central EPPO, supported by a college of three delegated prosecutors from each nation, and the directors or presidents of Europol, Eurojust and OLAF; on this note, also cf. the (previous) preference of some States, Council Doc. 18120/13, p. 4.

260. Art. 8(3) Regulation EPPO 2017.
261. Thereto Art. 11 Regulation EPPO 2017. The chief prosecutor shall be appointed by the EP and council for a non-renewable period of seven years (cf. Art. 14), the two deputies by the college for a renewable period of three years from among the European prosecutors (cf. Art. 15). Their number was controversial, as can be seen from the use of squared brackets with regard to 'two' in Art. 13a(1) Regulation Proposal EPPO 2016 (Council-Doc. 10830/16 of 11 July 2016).
262. Cf. Art. 12 Regulation EPPO 2017; on their appointment and dismissal, cf. Art. 16 (three candidates from each Member State; non-renewable selection for six years but still controversial).
263. On the status and responsibilities of the administrative director, cf. Arts. 18–19 Regulation EPPO 2017.
264. Cf., for details, Art. 9 Regulation EPPO 2017.
265. The Regulation uses 'European Delegated Prosecutor' (e.g. Art. 5(3)) and 'European Prosecutor per MS' (e.g. Art. 9(1)) synonymously. On them in more detail, cf. Art. 13; on appointment and dismissal, cf. Art. 17.
266. Art. 9(3) Regulation EPPO 2017.
267. Art. 10(1) Regulation EPPO 2017.
268. Art. 10(2) Regulation EPPO 2017.
269. E.g. bringing a case to judgment, dismissing it, applying a simplified procedure; cf. Art. 10(3) Regulation EPPO 2017 ('reviewing a draft decision' of the delegated prosecutor) with references to relevant procedural provisions.
270. E.g. instructing the delegated prosecutor to initiate an investigation, cf. Art. 10(4) Regulation EPPO 2017 with references to relevant procedural provisions.
271. Art. 10(4) Regulation EPPO 2017; on the permanent chamber's right to instruction, see also Art. 22(2).
272. Art. 10(7) Regulation EPPO 2017.
273. Art. 12(1) Regulation EPPO 2017.
274. Art. 13(3) Regulation EPPO 2017.
275. Art. 13(1) subparagraph 2 second sentence Regulation EPPO 2017.
276. Art. 12(5) Regulation EPPO 2016 ('liaisons and channels of information between the Permanent Chambers and the European Delegated Prosecutors').
277. Crit. on the hierarchy (as provided for in the previous proposal), also Nieto Martín, Wade and Muñoz de Morales, in Ligeti, *Toward a Prosecutor for the EU*, i (2013), pp. 787 ff. (considering it 'surprising' that the EPPO system is strongly hierarchical, unlike the majority of federal criminal law systems).
278. On the PIF Directive (OJ L 198 of 28 July 2017, 29) and the PIF Convention as its basis, see Chapter 3, mn. 14–15 with further references. Thereto Csúri, *CYELS* 18 (2016), 134–45 (calling the scope of the Union's financial interests 'the Achilles heel of the negotiations'); crit. regarding the EPPO's common criminal law, de Angelis, *eucrim*, 7 (2012), 76–7 ('il serait paradoxal d'instituer un Parquet européen ayant vocation à exercer ses fonctions sur tout le territoire de l'Union

mais contraint à agir selon des législations diversifiées en ce qui concerne les comportements punissables' (77)).

279. Cf. Art. 22(1) Regulation Proposal EPPO 2017. In detail Brodowski, *StV*, 37 (2017), 686–7. On the need to further elaborate upon Art. 86 Abs. 1 TFEU, cf. Ligeti, in Ligeti, *Toward a Prosecutor for the EU*, i (2013), 2; Csúri, *CYELS*, 18 (2016), 137–42, 146–9; in detail, Sicurella, in Ligeti, *Toward a Prosecutor for the EU*, i (2013), 875 ff.; on the possibilities for expansion, cf. ibid., 888 ff.; crit. Conway, *CLF*, 24 (2013), 396 ff.
280. On the concept, see already above, Chapter 3, mn. 22.
281. Cf. Chapter 3, mn. 26–7; crit. also Vervaele, *ERA Forum*, 15 (2014), 85 ff. (calling for the definition of the offences in the Regulation itself).
282. Ligeti and Simonato, *NJECL*, 4 (2013), 10–11, emphasise that no restriction to cross-border cases derives from the phrasing 'from Eurojust' in Art. 86(1) TFEU. On the conflicts of competence that may nevertheless arise, cf. Nieto Martín, Wade and Muñoz de Morales, in Ligeti, *Toward a Prosecutor for the EU*, i (2013), pp. 797–8.
283. Cf. Art. 23 Regulation EPPO 2017. The EPPO further has competence if the suspect is employed by the Union, 'provided that a MS' has extraterritorial jurisdiction.
284. Cf. Art. 22(2) Regulation EPPO 2017.
285. Cf. Art. 22(3) Regulation EPPO 2017.
286. Cf. Art. 86(4) TFEU ('serious crime having a cross-border dimension'). Damaskou, *NJECL*, 6 (2015), 137, wants to distinguish this wording from the notion of cross-border crime ('somewhat different'), but gives no further explanation.
287. Cf. European Criminal Policy Initiative, *ZIS*, 8 (2013), 427; Conway, *CLF*, 24 (2013), 399–400; Asp, *Procedural Criminal Law Cooperation* (2016), p. 203 (subsidiarity); cf. also the subsidiarity objections of 15 Member States (Council Doc. 16624/13); on this, cf. Lörcher and Petersen, *NJW*, 66 (2013), *NJW-aktuell*, issue 47, 16; also cf. *eucrim*, 8 (2013), 117–18; a different opinion is put forward by Gómez-Jara, *EuCLR*, 3 (2013), 177, 178–9, 187 ff., in light of the financial crisis.
288. On this, in detail Ambos, *Treatise ICL III* (2016), pp. 266 ff.
289. Satzger, *NStZ*, 33 (2013), 210 ff.; in a similar vein previously Klip, in Klip, *Substantive Criminal Law of the EU* (2011), p. 29; also Damaskou, *NJECL*, 6 (2015), 130.
290. Cf. Art. 25(2) and (3) Regulation EPPO 2017. Art. 22(3) explicitly refers to Art. 25(3), but this is rather confusing since Art. 25(3) establishes a general rule of non-exercise of the EPPO's competence (leaving it to the competent Member State jurisdiction) with regard to *all* offences within its material competence pursuant to Art. 22 if one of its conditions is fulfilled. For a €100,000 threshold, see also Arts. 27(8), 34(3).
291. See previous note and also Art. 25(1) second sentence Regulation EPPO 2017 ('competent national authorities shall not exercise their *own competence* in respect of the same criminal conduct' (emphasis added)). On the exercise of jurisdiction see also Brodowski, *StV*, 37 (2017), 687–8.
292. On the discussion between an exclusive and shared competence (the former favoured by the Commission, the latter by the Council/Member States) cf. Asp, *Procedural Criminal Law Cooperation* (2016), pp. 198 ff. (favouring a shared competence if the EPPO's aim is to fight financial crime with more, centralised resources, 200–3, 207, but, at any rate, making it dependent on the EPPO's objectives).

293. Cf. Art. 25(1) first sentence Regulation EPPO 2017('If the EPPO decides to exercise its competence'). See also the reporting/information obligations of Member States pursuant to Art. 24.
294. Cf. Art. 25(1) first sentence in conjunction with Art. 26 Regulation EPPO 2017.
295. Cf. Art. 25(1) first sentence in conjunction with Art. 27 Regulation EPPO 2017. The right to evocation may even be exercised by a European delegated prosecutor (Art. 22a (5)); this may create a difficult situation for her since she is closely linked to the national prosecution service and thereby forced to act against her (former) national colleagues.
296. Cf. Art. 25(6) Regulation EPPO 2017 (albeit with a somewhat awkward wording).
297. The somewhat awkward formulation 'form the view' replaces the previous, more common 'believe'.
298. Cf. Art. 26(1) Regulation EPPO 2017.
299. The former reporting obligation contained in Art. 15 ('sources of investigation') of the 2013 Proposal is now contained in Art. 24(1) Regulation EPPO 2017.
300. Cf. Art. 26(1) Regulation EPPO 2017.
301. On the jurisdictional criteria to be taken into account to decide on the competent Member States, cf. Art. 25(1) and (4) Regulation EPPO 2017.
302. Cf. Art. 26(3) Regulation EPPO 2017.
303. Cf. Art. 28(3) Regulation EPPO 2017 (if the handling delegated prosecutor cannot perform the investigation or fails to follow instructions).
304. Cf. Art. 28(4) subparagraph 1 Regulation EPPO 2017 (e.g. in case of the seriousness of the offence and its impact at the EU level).
305. Cf. Art. 10(2) EIO Directive, thereto Chapter 4, mn. 88.
306. Cf. Art. 30(4) Regulation EPPO 2017.
307. Cf. Art. 30(1) Regulation EPPO 2017 (e.g. searching of premises, property etc.; production of relevant objects and computer data; freezing instrumentalities or proceeds of crimes; interception). On the lifting of privileges or immunities, cf. Art. 29; on the disposition of confiscated assets, cf. Art. 38. Crit. Matt, *eucrim*, 12 (2017), 1 (who points out that the regulation proposal does not include any reparation for wrongfully imposed coercive measures such as imprisonment).
308. Cf. Art. 30(2) and (3) Regulation EPPO 2017 (distinguishing between general conditions and 'further' conditions regarding specific investigative measures).
309. See also Zerbes, *ZIS*, 10 (2015), 146–7.
310. See on this the explicit reference in Art. 31(3) Regulation EPPO 2017. For a detailed account of the (lack of) judicial control in EPPO investigations (regarding the 2013 proposal), see Đurđević, in Ligeti, *Toward a Prosecutor for the EU*, i (2013), pp. 986 ff.; Grünewald, *HRRS*, 14 (2013), 511–12, fears that this will result in a softening of judicial discretion and thus in a deterioration of the rights of the accused. Böse, *RW*, 3 (2012), 172 ff., thus suggests introducing a European investigative judge.
311. Cf. Art. 30(5) second sentence Regulation EPPO 2017 ('The procedures and detailed rules for taking the measures shall be governed by the applicable national law'); thereto (regarding the 2013 Proposal), crit. Zerbes, *ZIS*, 10 (2015), 147–8.
312. Cf. Art. 30(5) first sentence Regulation EPPO 2017.
313. Cf. Art. 31(1) Regulation EPPO 2017.
314. Cf. esp. Art. 31(5) Regulation EPPO 2017 (impossibility of carrying out assigned measure by assisting delegated prosecutor due to lack of information or other defects).
315. Cf. generally Art. 30(5) second sentence and specifically Art. 32 first sentence Regulation EPPO 2017.

316. Art. 32 second sentence Regulation EPPO 2017.
317. Cf. Chapter 4, mn. 80, 82, 87; also in favour in this context, Zerbes, *ZIS*, 10 (2015), 148, 154.
318. Cf. Art. 33(2) Regulation EPPO 2017.
319. Cf. Art. 35(1) Regulation EPPO 2017.
320. Cf. Art. 35(1) first sentence Regulation EPPO 2017.
321. Cf. Art. 34(2) Regulation EPPO 2017 with reference to Art. 25(2) and (3), thereto above n. 289.
322. Cf. Art. 39 Regulation EPPO 2017.
323. Cf. Art. 40(1) Regulation EPPO 2017.
324. This condition comes from the former Art. 29 Proposal Regulation EPPO 2013 on a 'transaction'.
325. Cf. Art. 40(2) Regulation EPPO 2017.
326. It may deviate from the draft decision; cf. Art. 35(2) Regulation EPPO 2017.
327. Cf. Art. 36(1) first sentence Regulation EPPO 2017.
328. Namely (i) place of the suspect's habitual residence, (ii) suspect's nationality and (iii) place of the main financial damage.
329. See e.g. Damaskou, *NJECL*, 6 (2015), 143; Mitsilegas, *EU Criminal Law after Lisbon* (2016), p. 93 (crit. of lack of judicial control in that regard); Faletti, *eucrim*, 12 (2017), 26; for previous references, cf. Ambos, *Internationales Strafrecht* (2014), §13 mn. 23.
330. Cf. Art. 36(4) Regulation EPPO 2017.
331. Art. 36(5) Regulation EPPO 2017.
332. Cf. Art. 36(7) Regulation EPPO 2017. Note, in particular, the practical problem of compliance with varying national deadlines indicated in the provision.
333. Crit. Klip, *MJ*, 12 (2005), 117; Zöller, in Böse, *Europäisches Strafrecht* (2013), p. 839. Crit. in regard to the principle of equality, Faletti, *eucrim*, 12 (2017), 25–6.
334. Cf. also Satzger, *Internationales und Europäisches Strafrecht* (2016), §10 mn. 22. For an attempt to create such a common procedural minimum standard, see the 'Model Rules for the Procedure of the EPPO', available at www.eppo-project.eu/index.php/EU-model-rules, accessed 27 January 2018; on the preparatory country reports, cf. Ligeti, *Strafrecht und strafrechtliche Zusammenarbeit in der EU* (2005), pp. 9 ff. De Angelis, *eucrim*, 7 (2012), 76, assumes that only a procedure that is 'essentiellement accusatoire' meets the requirements of Art. 86 TFEU and demands that the role of the police and court be adapted accordingly.
335. Art. 37 Regulation EPPO 2017.
336. More correctly, therefore, the title of the respective Art. 30 Regulation Proposal EPPO 2013 ('admissibility of evidence').
337. Art. 37(2) Regulation EPPO 2017.
338. Cf. Art. 37(1) Regulation EPPO 2017 ('not be denied admission on the mere ground that the evidence was gathered in another Member State or in accordance with the law of another Member State').
339. Cf. Recital 80 Regulation EPPO 2017 referring to 'fairness', 'rights of the defence' and other rights of the CFREU in line with Art. 6 TEU. Crit. on the 2013 proposal, Zerbes, *ZIS*, 10 (2015), 149–53 (albeit acknowledging the 'potential' of the fairness reservation); cf. also Ambos, *Internationales Strafrecht* (2014), §13 mn. 24 with further references.
340. Cf. Art. 41(1) Regulation EPPO 2017.
341. Cf. Art. 41(3) Regulation EPPO 2017.

342. Thereto Chapter 2, mn. 146 ff.
343. Cf. Art. 41(2) Regulation EPPO 2017. The 2013 proposal has attracted much criticism in that regard; cf. Damaskou, *NJECL*, 6 (2015), 141–2; for previous references see Ambos, *Internationales Strafrecht* (2014), §13 mn. 25.
344. Cf. Arts. 47 ff. Regulation EPPO 2017. These rules seem to be largely modelled after the recently adopted General Data Protection Regulation, thereto Chapter 2, mn. 152 ff.
345. Cf. Arts. 43 ff. Regulation EPPO 2017. On the relevance of good information networks, cf. Nieto Martín, Wade and Muñoz de Morales, in Ligeti, *Toward a Prosecutor for the European Union: A Comparative Analysis*, i (2013), pp. 790 ff.
346. Art. 42 Regulation EPPO 2017. Crit. of the lack of judicial review by the CJEU under the 2013 proposal, Damaskou, *NJECL*, 6 (2015), 142; Böse, *JZ*, 72 (2017), 82 ff.; for a good discussion of the options preferring a control by the CJEU Mitsilegas, *EU Criminal Law after Lisbon* (2016), pp. 113–19.
347. This does not affect a broader judicial review for any procedural act under national law; cf. Art. 42(1) Regulation EPPO 2016 (n. 261) with n. 56.
348. Art. 42(1) Regulation EPPO 2017. Crit. thereto Böse, *JZ*, 72 (2017), 85, who sees the jurisdictions of national courts as incompatible with primary law; also see Faletti, *eucrim*, 12 (2017), 26, according to whom ECJ jurisdiction would be preferable ('national courts are unlikely to waive their own jurisdiction and to refer the case to a jurisdiction in another Member State').
349. Art. 42(3) Regulation EPPO 2017. The Regulation Proposal 2016 (Art. 36(3)) contained further decisions, (some of) which are now, however, included in Art. 42(2).
350. See, for a thoughtful study on the judicial review of the EPPO's dismissal decisions, Göhler, *NJECL*, 6 (2015), 102 ff. (convincingly advocating a supranational review mechanism pursuant to Art. 86(3) TFEU, with the appropriate forum still to be defined, and a standing by EU citizens in order to strengthen the EPPO's 'accountability and confirm the legality of its dismissal decisions' (118) and ensure confidence in the institution).
351. Cf. Art. 42(2) and – regarding Arts. 268, 272 and 270 TFEU – Art. 42(4)–(6) Regulation EPPO 2017.
352. Cf. e.g. Suominen, *MJECL*, 15 (2008), 230–1; Bösch, in Espina Ramos and Vicente Carbajosa, *The Future EPPO* (2009), pp. 27–8; and Brüner, in Espina Ramos and Vicente Carbajosa, *The Future EPPO* (2009), p. 50, according to whom the EPPO should form 'a complement to existing institutions at the EU level'; in a similar vein Damaskou, *NJECL*, 6 (2015), 152 ('not established to the detriment of the existing EU entities'). By contrast, others hold that Eurojust will continue first and foremost to coordinate national investigations even after the EPPO has been established, cf. Brezigar, in Espina Ramos and Vicente Carbajosa, *The Future EPPO* (2009), p. 95; and Vervaele, in Espina Ramos and Vicente Carbajosa, *The Future EPPO* (2009), p. 152.
353. Cf. von Bubnoff, *ZEuS*, 5 (2002), 222–3; Hetzer, *EJCCLCJ*, 14 (2006), 42; Klement, *eucrim*, 12 (2017), 196 ff.
354. See COM (2013) 532, 9; COM (2013), 533; on this, cf. Esser, *Europäisches und Internationales Strafrecht* (2018), §3 mn. 24–5; as well as Biehler, Gleß, Parra and Zeitler, *Strafrechtlicher Schutz der finanziellen Interessen der EG* (2002), pp. 46–7; Espina Ramos, in Klip, *Substantive Criminal Law of the EU* (2011), p. 42; also cf. the case studies on pp. 69 ff.; a similar stance is taken by von Bubnoff, *ZEuS*, 5 (2002), 223; see also Brüner and Spitzer, *NStZ*, 22 (2002), 397–8; Bösch, in Espina

Ramos and Vicente Carbajosa, *The Future EPPO* (2009), p. 27; Kallas, in Espina Ramos and Vicente Carbajosa, *The Future EPPO* (2009), pp. 71–2; Covolo, *eucrim*, 7 (2012), 86–7; further ideas in Dannecker, in Streinz, *EUV/AEUV* (2012), Art. 86 AEUV mn. 18; Zwiers, *EPPO* (2011), p. 399.

355. Also cf. Conway, *CLF*, 24 (2013), 390. OLAF's area of internal investigations (mn. 2) could then be allocated to the European Court of Auditors (Art. 285 TFEU).
356. Art. 101(1) and (3) Regulation EPPO 2017; previously Killmann and Hofmann, in Sieber, Satzger and von Heinegg, *Europäisches Strafrecht* (2014), pp. 871–2; in a similar vein Venegoni, *eucrim*, 12 (2017), 193 ff.; Klement, *eucrim*, 12 (2017), 196 ff.
357. Art. 101(2) Regulation EPPO 2017.
358. Art. 101(4) Regulation EPPO 2017.
359. See also Art. 110 Regulation EPPO 2017 (on OLAF's auditing function together with the European Court of Auditors). On OLAF's continuing function in this area, see also Damaskou, *NJECL*, 6 (2015), 129, 149–50.
360. Cf. Art. 100(4) Regulation EPPO 2017. The details of this 'arrangement' shall be regulated by separate agreement.
361. In this vein see also Asp, *Procedural Criminal Law Cooperation* (2016), p. 193 ('something more than Eurojust').
362. Cf. Art. 100(1) Regulation EPPO 2017.
363. Cf. Art. 100(2) Regulation EPPO 2017.
364. In the same vein Damaskou, *NJECL*, 6 (2015), 131–2, 150; cf. also Killmann and Hofmann, in Sieber, Satzger and von Heinegg, *Europäisches Strafrecht* (2014), p. 871; see also above, mn. 22.
365. On this, see already above, mn. 11 Cf. also Dannecker, in Streinz, *EUV/AEUV* (2012), Art. 86 AEUV mn. 16; Damaskou, *NJECL*, 6 (2015), 151 (assistance).
366. Cf. Art. 102(1) Regulation EPPO 2017 ('working arrangement').
367. Cf. Art. 102(2) Regulation EPPO 2017.
368. Art. 86(4) TFEU. On this, cf. Zimmermann, *Jura*, 31 (2009), 845; Zwiers, *EPPO* (2011), pp. 391 ff.
369. Cf. Art. 85(1) TFEU.
370. Cf. Art. 88(1) TFEU.

Chapter Bibliography

Albrecht, J. P., and Janson, N. J., 'Die Kontrolle des Europäischen Polizeiamtes durch das Europäische Parlament nach dem Vertrag von Lissabon und dem Europol-Beschluss', *EuR*, 47 (2012), 230–40

Albrecht, P.-A., 'Europäischer Strafrechtsraum: Ein Albtraum?', *ZRP*, 37 (2004), 1–4

Ambos, K., 'Staatsanwaltschaftliche Kontrolle der Polizei, Verpolizeilichung des Ermittlungsverfahrens und organisierte Kriminalität', *Jura*, 25 (2003), 674–82

Aulehner, J., 'Europol und das Recht auf informationelle Selbstbestimmung', in Baldus, M., and Soiné, M., eds., *Rechtsprobleme der internationalen polizeilichen Zusammenarbeit* (Baden-Baden: Nomos Verlagsgesellschaft, 1999), 99–123

Bauer, M., 'Organisation und rechtlicher Rahmen des Politikfeldes Inneres und Justiz nach dem Vertrag von Lissabon', in Weidenfeld, W., ed., *Lissabon in der Analyse* (Baden-Baden: Nomos Verlagsgesellschaft, 2008), 99–114

Bechthold, I., 'Europol: was steckt dahinter?', *Betrifft JUSTIZ*, 13 (1997), 118–20

Berner, A., *Die Untersuchungsbefugnisse des Europäischen Amtes für Betrugsbekämpfung (OLAF) gegenüber dem Europäischen Parlament* (Frankfurt a.M. et al.: Peter Lang, 2004)

Beukelmann, S., 'Die Europäische Staatsanwaltschaft', *NJW-Spezial*, 10 (2013), 568

'Europäisierung des Strafrechts: Die neue strafrechtliche Ordnung nach dem Vertrag von Lissabon', *NJW*, 63 (2010), 2081–6

Biehler, A. et al., *Strafrechtlicher Schutz der finanziellen Interessen der EG und Schaffung einer Europäischen Staatsanwaltschaft* (Luxemburg: Europäisches Parlament, 2002), at http://edz.bib.uni-mannheim.de/daten/edz-ma/ep/02/budg111_de.pdf, accessed 28 October 2016

Bösch, H., in Espina Ramos, J. A., and Vicente Carbajosa, I., eds., *The Future European Public Prosecutor's Office* (Madrid: Boletín Oficial del Estado, 2009), 24–9

Böse, M., 'Die Entscheidung des Bundesverfassungsgerichts zum Vertrag von Lissabon und ihre Bedeutung für die Europäisierung des Strafrechts', *ZIS*, 5 (2010), 76–91

'Die Europäische Staatsanwaltschaft "als" nationale Strafverfolgungsbehörde?', *JZ*, 72 (2017), 82–7

'Ein europäischer Ermittlungsrichter: Perspektiven des präventiven Rechtsschutzes bei Errichtung einer Europäischen Staatsanwaltschaft', *RW*, 3 (2012), 172–96

Der Grundsatz der Verfügbarkeit von Informationen in der strafrechtlichen Zusammenarbeit der Europäischen Union (Göttingen: V & R Unipress et al., 2007)

Boven'Eerdt, K., 'Learning Lessons: Reflecting on Regulation 883/2013 through Comparative Analysis', *eucrim*, 12 (2017), 188–92

Brezigar, B., in Espina Ramos, J. A., and Vicente Carbajosa, I., eds., *The Future European Public Prosecutor's Office* (Madrid: Boletín Oficial del Estado, 2009), 94–6

Brodowski, D., 'Innere Sicherheit in der EU', *Jura*, 35 (2013), 492–504

'Strafrechtsrelevante Entwicklungen in der Europäischen Union', *ZIS*, 8 (2013), 455–72

'Strafrechtsrelevante Entwicklungen in der Europäischen Union', *ZIS*, 11 (2016), 106–20

'Strafrechtsrelevante Entwicklungen in der Europäischen Union', *ZIS*, 12 (2017), 11–27

Brüner, F.-H., in Espina Ramos, J. A., and Vicente Carbajosa, I., eds., *The Future European Public Prosecutor's Office* (Madrid: Boletín Oficial del Estado, 2009), 48–52

Brüner, F.-H., and Spitzer, H., 'Der Europäische Staatsanwalt: ein Instrument zur Verbesserung des Schutzes der EU-Finanzen oder ein Beitrag zur Verwirklichung eines Europas der Freiheit, der Sicherheit und des Rechts?', *NStZ*, 22 (2002), 393–8

'OLAF-REFORM II: Kosmetischer Eingriff oder Großer Wurf?', *EuR*, 43 (2008), 859–73

'§43: OLAF', in Sieber, U., Satzger, H., and Heintschel von Heinegg, B., eds., *Europäisches Strafrecht* (Baden-Baden: Nomos Verlagsgesellschaft, 2014), 677–700

Buono, L., 'Gearing Up the Fight against Cybercrime in the EU: A New Set of Rules and the Establishment of the European Cybercrime Center (EC3)', *NJECL*, 3 (2012), 332–43

Caianiello, M., and Orlandi, R., 'Landesbericht Italien', in Gleß, S., Grote, R., and Heine, G., eds., *Justitielle Einbindung und Kontrolle von Europol*, i: *Nationale und europäische Strafverfolgung* (Freiburg i.Br.: Ed. iuscrim, 2001), 329–82

Castaldo, A. R., 'Der strafrechtliche Schutz der Finanzinteressen der EG durch Schaffung einer europäischen Staatsanwaltschaft und die italienische Rechtsordnung', *StV*, 23 (2003), 122–6

Conroy, N., 'Police cooperation and Europol', in Regan, E., ed., *The New Third Pillar: Cooperation against Crime in the European Union* (Dublin: Institute for European Affairs Dublin, 2000), 118–33

Conway, G., 'Holding to Account a Possible European Public Prosecutor: Supranational Governance and Accountability across Diverse Legal Traditions', *CLF*, 24 (2013), 371–401

Cornils, K., and Verch, U., 'Landesbericht Dänemark', in Gleß, S., Grote, R., and Heine, G., eds., *Justitielle Einbindung und Kontrolle von Europol*, i: *Nationale und europäische Strafverfolgung* (Freiburg i.Br.: Ed. iuscrim, 2001), 9–74

Covolo, V., 'From Europol to Eurojust: Towards a European Public Prosecutor', *eucrim*, 7 (2012), 83–8

Cretin, T., 'The Future European Prosecutor', in Espina Ramos, J. A., and Vicente Carbajosa, I., eds., *The Future European Public Prosecutor's Office* (Madrid: Boletín Oficial del Estado, 2009), 53–9

Csúri, A., 'Naming and Shaping', *eucrim*, 7 (2012), 79–83

'The Proposed European Public Prosecutor's Office: From a Trojan Horse to a White Elephant?', *CYELS*, 18 (2016), 122–51

Damaskou, A., 'The EPPO: A Ground-Breaking New Institution of the EU Legal Order', *NJECL*, 6 (2015), 126–52

Daub, I., 'Das Europäische Polizeiamt: Gefahr für den Föderalismus?', in Baldus, M., and Soiné, M., eds., *Rechtsprobleme der internationalen polizeilichen Zusammenarbeit* (Baden-Baden: Nomos Verlagsgesellschaft, 1999), 86–98

de Angelis, F., 'L'espace judiciaire pénal européen: Une vision se concrétise', *eucrim*, 7 (2012), 75–8

de Busser, E., 'The Data Protection Gap', *eucrim*, 8 (2013), 17–22

'The Lisbon After-Burn Effect', *ERA Forum*, 16 (2015), 277–89

'Transatlantic adequacy and a certain degree of perplexity', *eucrim*, 5 (2010), 30–6

de Gouttes, R., in Espina Ramos, J. A., and Vicente Carbajosa, I., eds., *The Future European Public Prosecutor's Office* (Madrid: Boletín Oficial del Estado, 2009), 101–5

Delmas-Marty, M., ed., *Corpus Juris der strafrechtlichen Regelungen zum Schutz der finanziellen Interessen der Europäischen Union* (Cologne et al.: Carl Heymanns, 1998)

'Towards an Integrated European Criminal Law', *CYELS*, 7 (2004–5), 17–31

Del Moral Torres, 'La cooperación policial en la UE', *ARI*, 6 (2010), no 50, 1–12

de Moor, S., 'The Difficulties of Joint Investigation Teams and the Possible Role of OLAF', *eucrim*, 4 (2009), 94–9

Dieckmann, J., 'Europäische Kooperation im Bereich der Strafrechtspflege', *NStZ*, 21 (2001), 617–23

Disley, E., Irving, B., Hughes, W., and Patruni, B., 'Evaluation of the Implementation of the Europol Council Decision and of Europol's Activities' (2012), at www.rand.org/pubs/technical_reports/TR1264.html, last accessed 28 October 2016

Drewer, D., and Ellermann, J., 'Europol's Data Protection Framework as an Asset in the Fight against Cybercrime', *ERA Forum*, 13 (2012), 381–95

Đurđević, Z., 'Judicial Control in Pre-trial Criminal Procedure Conducted by the European Public Prosecutor's Office', in Ligeti, K., ed., *Toward a Prosecutor for the European Union: A Comparative Analysis*, i (Oxford et al.: Hart Publishing, 2013), 986–1010

Ellermann, J., *Europol und FBI: Probleme und Perspektiven* (Baden-Baden: Nomos Verlagsgesellschaft, 2005)

'Terror Won't Kill the Privacy Star: Tackling Terrorism Propaganda Online in a Data Protection Compliant Manner', *ERA Forum*, 17 (2016), 555–82

'Vom Sammler zum Jäger: Europol auf dem Weg zu einem "europäischen FBI"?', *ZEuS*, 5 (2002), 528–85

Erbežnik, A., 'European Public Prosecutor's Office (EPPO): Too Much, Too Soon, and without Legitimacy?', *EuCLR*, 5 (2015), 209–21

Espina Ramos, J. A., 'Towards a European Public Prosecutor's Office: The Long and Winding Road', in Klip, A., ed., *Substantive Criminal Law of the European Union* (Antwerp et al.: Maklu, 2011), 35–50

Esser, R., 'Der Beitrag von Eurojust zur Bekämpfung des Terrorismus in Europa', *GA*, 151 (2004), 711–21

'Internationale und europäische strafrechtliche Zusammenarbeit im Bereich der Terrorismusbekämpfung', in Odendahl, K., ed., *Die Bekämpfung des Terrorismus mit Mitteln des Völker- und Europarechts* (Berlin: Duncker und Humblot, 2017), 203–47

'Die Rolle von Europol und Eurojust bei der Bekämpfung von Terrorismus und organisierter Kriminalität', in Sinn, A., and Zöller, M. A., *Neujustierung des Strafrechts durch Terrorismus und Organisierte Kriminalität* (Heidelberg: C. F. Müller, 2013), 61–87

Esser, R., and Herbold, A. L., 'Neue Wege für die justizielle Zusammenarbeit in Strafsachen: Das Eurojust-Gesetz', *NJW*, 57 (2004), 2421–4

Eurojust, *Eurojust-Jahresbericht 2003* (2004), at http://eurojust.europa.eu/doclibrary/corporate/eurojust%20Annual%20Reports/Annual%20Report%202003/Annual-Report-2003-EN.pdf, last accessed 26 June 2017

Eurojust-Jahresbericht 2004 (2005), at http://eurojust.europa.eu/doclibrary/corporate/eurojust%20Annual%20Reports/Annual%20Report%202004/Annual-Report-2004-EN.pdf, last accessed 26 June 2017

Annual Report 2005 (2006), at http://eurojust.europa.eu/doclibrary/corporate/eurojust%20Annual%20Reports/Annual%20Report%202005/Annual-Report-2005-EN.pdf, last accessed 26 June 2017

Eurojust-Jahresbericht 2008 (2009), at http://eurojust.europa.eu/doclibrary/corporate/eurojust%20Annual%20Reports/Annual%20Report%202008/Annual-Report-2008-EN.pdf, last accessed 26 June 2017

Eurojust-Jahresbericht 2012 (2013), at http://eurojust.europa.eu/doclibrary/corporate/eurojust%20Annual%20Reports/Annual%20Report%202012/Annual-Report-2012-EN.pdf, last accessed 26 June 2017

Annual Report 2015 (2016), at http://eurojust.europa.eu/doclibrary/corporate/eurojust%20Annual%20Reports/Annual%20Report%202015/Annual-Report-2015-EN.pdf, last accessed 26 June 2017

'Evaluation of the Eurojust Council Decision and the activities carried out by Eurojust, Final Report' (30 June 2015), avaliable at http://www.eurojust.europa.eu/doclibrary/Eurojust-framework/ejlegalframework/Evaluation%20of%20the%20implementation%20of%20the%20Eurojust%20Council%20Decision%20-%20Final%20Report/Evaluation%20of%20the%20implementation%20of%20the%20Eurojust%20Council%20Decision%20-%20Final%20Report.pdf, accessed 28 October 2016

European Criminal Policy Initiative, 'Manifest zum Europäischen Strafverfahrensrecht', *ZIS*, 8 (2013), 412–29

Everling, U., 'Rechtsschutz in der EU nach dem Vertrag von Lissabon', *EuR*, 44 (2009), *Beiheft 1*, 71–86

Faletti, F., 'The European Public Prosecutor's Office and the Principle of Equality', *eucrim*, 12 (2017), 25–7

Faure, M., van Riel, B., and Ubachs., S., 'Landesbericht Niederlande', in Gleß, S., Grote, R., and Heine, G., eds., *Justitielle Einbindung und Kontrolle von Europol*, i: *Nationale und europäische Strafverfolgung* (Freiburg i.Br.: Ed. iuscrim, 2001), 383–444

Fawzy, O. M., *Die Errichtung von Eurojust: Zwischen Funktionalität und Rechtsstaatlichkeit* (Baden-Baden: Nomos Verlagsgesellschaft, 2005)

Felgenhauer, H., 'Grundlagen der institutionalisierten Polizeizusammenarbeit in der EU', in Wolter, J. et al., eds., *Datenübermittlungen und Vorermittlungen: Festgabe für Hans Hilger* (Heidelberg: Müller, 2003), 75–90

Frenz, W., 'Von Eurojust zur Europäischen Staatsanwaltschaft', *wistra*, 29 (2010), 432–4

Freyer, H., 'Europol', *Kriminalistik*, 57 (2003), 80–4

Galgo, A., 'La Red Judicial Europea', *RIDP*, 77 (2006), 299–305

Gleß, S., 'Das Europäische Amt für Betrugsbekämpfung (OLAF)', *EuZW*, 10 (1999), 618–21

'Europol', *NStZ*, 21 (2001), 623–8

Göhler, J., 'To Continue or Not: Who Shall Be in Control of the EPPO's Dismissal Decisions?', *NJECL*, 6 (2015), 102–25

Gómez-Jara, C., 'European Federal Criminal Law: What Can Europe Learn from the US System of Federal Criminal Law to Solve Its Sovereign Debt Crisis?', *EuCLR*, 3 (2013), 170–93

González-Herrero, J., and Butincu, M.-M., 'The Collection of Evidence by OLAF and Its Transmission to the National Judicial Authorities', *eucrim*, 4 (2009), 90–4

Grotz, M., '§45: Eurojust', in Sieber, U., Satzger, H., and Heintschel von Heinegg, B., eds., *Europäisches Strafrecht* (Baden-Baden: Nomos Verlagsgesellschaft, 2014), 716–27

Grünewald, A., 'Eine Europäische Staatsanwaltschaft nach den Vorstellungen der Europäischen Kommission', *HRRS*, 14 (2013), 508–15

Hallmann-Häbler, U., and Stiegel, U., 'Das Europäische Amt für Betrugsbekämpfung (OLAF)', *DRiZ*, 81 (2003), 241–45

Hamran, L., and Szabova, E., 'European Public Prosecutor's Office: Cui Bono?', *NJECL*, 4 (2013), 40–58

Hauck, P., 'Heimliche Ermittlungsmaßnahmen im Prozessrecht der internationalen Strafgerichtsbarkeit (EU- und Völkerstrafrecht)', *ZStW*, 124 (2012), 473–98

Heger, M., 'Perspektiven des Europäischen Strafrechts nach dem Vertrag von Lissabon', *ZIS*, 4 (2009), 406–17

Heine, H., *Die Rechtsstellung des Beschuldigten im Rahmen der Europäisierung des Strafverfahrens* (Frankfurt a.M. et al.: Peter Lang, 2009)

Hetzer, W., 'Fight against Fraud and Protection of Fundamental Rights in the EU', *Eur. J. Cr.*, 14 (2006), 20–45

Hetzer, W., 'Korruptionsbekämpfung in Europa', *NJW*, 57 (2004), 3746–50

Hinarejos, A., 'Integration in Criminal Matters and the Role of the Court of Justice', *EuLRev*, 36 (2011), 420–30

Hölscheidt, S., and Schotten, T., 'Immunität für Europol-Bedienstete: Normalfall oder Sündenfall?', *NJW*, 52 (1999), 2851–5

Huber, B., and Rabenstein, C., 'Landesbericht England und Wales', in Gleß, S., Grote, R., and Heine, G., eds., *Justitielle Einbindung und Kontrolle von Europol, i: Nationale und europäische Strafverfolgung* (Freiburg i.Br.: Ed. iuscrim, 2001), 161–238

Hummer, W., 'Der Vertrag von Prüm: "Schengen III"?', *EuR*, 42 (2007), 517–30

Janda, M., and Panait, R., 'The OLAF Regulation: Evaluation and Future Steps', *eucrim*, 12 (2017), 182–8

Jourová, V., 'The Cost(s) of Non-Europe in the Area of Freedom, Security and Justice', *eucrim*, 11 (2016), 94–8

Kallas, S., in Espina Ramos, J. A., and Vicente Carbajosa, I., eds., *The Future European Public Prosecutor's Office* (Madrid: Boletín Oficial del Estado, 2009), 67–73

Kapplinghaus, J., 'Strafrechtliche Zusammenarbeit in Europa: Aus der Sicht einer Europäischen Einrichtung: Eurojust', in Eser, A., and Rabenstein, C., eds., *Strafjustiz im Spannungsfeld von Effizienz und Fairness* (Berlin: Duncker & Humblot, 2004), 163–76

Kapplinghaus, J., and Milke, T., 'Eurojust: Eine Serviceeinheit für die nationalen Strafverfolgungsbehörden', *DRiZ*, 82 (2004), 265–8

Kempf, E., 'Der Europäische Staatsanwalt: Freier Fuchs im freien Hühnerstall?', *StV*, 23 (2003), 128–30

Killmann, B.-R., and Hofmann, M., '§48: Perspektiven für eine Europäische Staatsanwaltschaft', in Sieber, U., Satzger, H., and Heintschel von Heinegg, B., eds., *Europäisches Strafrecht* (Baden-Baden: Nomos Verlagsgesellschaft, 2011), 757–66

Kinzel, P., *Die Europäische Verfassung: Braucht Europa eine gemeinsame Staatsanwaltschaft?* (Saarbrücken: VDM Müller, 2008)

Klement, P., 'OLAF at the Gates of Criminal Law', *eucrim*, 12 (2017), 196–200

Klip, A., 'The Constitution for Europe and Criminal Law: A Step Not Far Enough', *MJ*, 12 (2005), 115–24

'Towards a General Part of Criminal Law for the European Union', in Klip, A., ed., *Substantive Criminal Law of the European Union* (Antwerp et al.: Maklu, 2011), 15–34

Korrell, V., *Europol: Polizei ohne rechtsstaatliche Bindungen?* (Frankfurt a.M. et al.: Peter Lang, 2005)

Kremer, B., *Immunität für Europol-Bedienstete? Eine Untersuchung der Aufgaben und Befugnisse von Europol unter besonderer Berücksichtigung der Immunitätsproblematik* (Frankfurt a.M. et al.: Peter Lang, 2003)

Kretschmer, J., 'Europol, Eurojust, OLAF: Was ist das und was drüfen die?', *Jura*, 29 (2007), 169–75

Krommendijk, J., 'The Use of ECtHR Case Law by the Court of Justice after Lisbon', *MJ*, 22 (2015), 812–35

Kuhl, L., and Spitzer, H., '§8: Die Verordnungen (Euratom, EG) 2185/1996 und (EG) 1073/99 betreffend die Untersuchungen des Europäischen Amts für Betrugsbekämpfung (OLAF) zum Schutz der finanziellen Interessen der Europäischen Union', in Sieber, U., Satzger, H., and Heintschel von Heinegg, B., eds., *Europäisches Strafrecht* (Baden-Baden: Nomos Verlagsgesellschaft, 2011), 213–28

Laudati, L., 'Data Protection at OLAF', *eucrim*, 8 (2013), 14–17

Leblois-Happe, J., and Barth, H., 'Landesbericht Frankreich', in Gleß, S., Grote, R., and Heine, G., eds., *Justitielle Einbindung und Kontrolle von Europol*, i: *Nationale und europäische Strafverfolgung* (Freiburg i.Br.: Ed. iuscrim, 2001), 239–328

Ligeti, K., 'The European Public Prosecutor's Office: How Should the Rules Applicable to Its Procedure be Determined?', *EuCLR*, 1 (2011), 123–48

'The European Public Prosecutor's Office: Which Model?', in Klip, A., ed., *Substantive Criminal Law of the European Union* (Antwerp et al.: Maklu, 2011), 51–65

'Introduction', in Ligeti, K., ed., *Toward a Prosecutor for the European Union: A Comparative Analysis*, i (Oxford et al.: Hart Publishing, 2013), 1–6

Ligeti, K., and Simonato, M., 'The European Public Prosecutor's Office: Towards a Truly European Prosecution Service?', *NJECL*, 4 (2013), 7–21

Lingenthal, L., 'Die OLAF-Reform: Der aktuelle Änderungsentwurf und dessen Auswirkungen auf die Effektivität der Kontrollen und die Verfahrensrechte der Betroffenen', *ZEuS*, 15 (2012), 195–232

Lopes da Mota, J. L., 'Eurojust and Its Role in Joint Investigation Teams', *eucrim*, 4 (2009), 88–90

Lörcher H., and Petersen, H., '"Gelbe Karte" der Mitgliedstaaten für den Europäischen Staatsanwalt', *NJW*, 66 (2013), *NJW-aktuell*, issue 47, 16–18

Manzione, D., 'L'attuazione italiana (e "all'italiana"?) di Eurojust', *LP*, 25 (2005), 243–52

Marletta, A., 'Interinstitutional Relationship of European Bodies in the Fight against Crimes Affecting the EU's Financial Interests', *eucrim*, 11 (2016), 141–45

Martínez Soria, J., 'Die polizeiliche Zusammenarbeit in Europa und der Rechtsschutz des Bürgers', *VerwArch*, 89 (1998), 400–38

'Die polizeiliche Zusammenarbeit in Europa zwischen traditionellem völkerrechtlichem Vertragsrecht und Vergemeinschaftung', in Baldus, M., and Soiné, M., eds., *Rechtsprobleme der internationalen polizeilichen Zusammenarbeit* (Baden-Baden: Nomos Verlagsgesellschaft, 1999), 50–71

Matt, H., 'Editorial', *eucrim*, 12 (2017), 1

Met-Domestici, A., 'The Reform of the EU's Anti-corruption Mechanism', *eucrim*, 7 (2012), 25–30

Milke, T., *Europol und Eurojust: Zwei Institutionen zur internationalen Verbrechensbekämpfung und ihre justitielle Kontrolle* (Göttingen: V & R Unipress, 2003)

Mokros, R., 'O. Polizei und Justiz auf der Ebene der Europäischen Union', in Lisken, H., and Denninger, E., eds., *Handbuch des Polizeirechts* (Munich: C. H. Beck, 4th edn, 2007), 1321–84

Nehm, K., 'Zusammenarbeit der Strafverfolgungsorgane in Europa', *DRiZ*, 78 (2000), 355–64

Nestler, N., 'Der Mandatsbereich von Europol im Lichte grenzüberschreitender Betäubungsmittelkriminalität', *GA*, 157 (2010), 645–58

Neumann, D., '§44: Europol', in Sieber, U., Satzger, H., and Heintschel von Heinegg, B., eds., *Europäisches Strafrecht* (Baden-Baden: Nomos Verlagsgesellschaft, 2011), 701–15

Niemeier, M., 'Nach dem Vertrag von Lissabon: Die polizeiliche Zusammenarbeit in der EU', *ERA Forum*, 11 (2010), 197–206

Niemeier, M., and Walter, M., 'Neue Rechtsgrundlage für Europol', *Kriminalistik*, 64 (2010), 17–22

Nieto Martín, A., Wade, M., and Muñoz de Morales, M, 'Federal Criminal Law and the European Public Prosecutor's Office', in Ligeti, K., ed., *Toward a Prosecutor for the European Union: A Comparative Analysis*, i (Oxford et al.: Hart Publishing, 2013), 781–802

Noltenius, B., 'Strafverfahrensrecht als Seismograph der Europäischen Integration', *ZStW*, 122 (2010), 604–26

Nunzi, A., 'Europol', *RIDP*, 77 (2006), 285–92

Ostropolski, T., 'The CJEU as a Defender of Mutual Trust', *NJECL*, 6 (2015), 166–78

Paeffgen, H.-U., 'Haus ohne Hüter?', *ZStW*, 118 (2006), 275–357

Panait, R. 'Information Sharing between OLAF and National Judicial Authorities', *eucrim*, 10 (2015), 64–70

Pinto Monteiro, F., in Espina Ramos, J. A., and Vicente Carbajosa, I., eds., *The Future European Public Prosecutor's Office* (Madrid: Boletín Oficial del Estado, 2009), 97–100

Qubain, A., Kattge, L., Wandl, C., and Gamma, M., 'Europol: Das Europäische Polizeiamt', *Kriminalistik*, 61 (2007), 363–9 (Teil 2)

Radtke, H., 'Der Europäische Staatsanwalt: Ein Modell für Strafverfolgung in Europa mit Zukunft?', *GA*, 151 (2004), 1–21;

Ratzel, M.-P., 'Europol: Das Europäische Polizeiamt', *Kriminalistik*, 61 (2007), 284–91 (Teil 1), 67 (2007), 428–34 (Teil 3)

Riegel, R., 'Gemeinsame Ermittlungsgruppen', *eucrim*, 4 (2009), 99–106

Ruggieri, F., 'The Future of the EPPO in the Framework of Art. 85 and 86 TFEU: A Comparison between the Italian, German, and English versions', in F.

Ruggieri, *Criminal Proceedings, Languages and the EU: Linguistic and Legal Issues* (Heidelberg: Springer, 2014), 109–20

Ruthig, J., 'Europol als Baustein eines Europäischen Polizeirechts: Gestaltungsmöglichkeiten bei der EuropolVO', in Zöller, M. A. et al., eds., *Gesamte Strafrechtswissenschaft in internationaler Dimension, Festschrift für Jürgen Wolter zum 70. Geburtstag am 7. September 2013* (Berlin: Duncker & Humblot, 2013), 1469–93

'Verfassungsrechtliche Grenzen der transnationalen Übermittlung personenbezogener Daten', in Wolter, J. et al., eds., *Datenübermittlungen und Vorermittlungen: Festgabe für Hans Hilger* (Heidelberg: Müller, 2003), 183–210

Ryngaert, C., 'Universal Jurisdiction in an ICC Era', *Eur. J. Cr.*, 14 (2006), 46–80

Satzger, H., 'Gefahren für eine effektive Verteidigung im geplanten europäischen Verfahrensrecht', *StV*, 23 (2003), 137–42

'Die potentielle Errichtung einer Europäischen Staatsanwaltschaft: Plädoyer für ein Komplementaritätsmodell', *NStZ*, 33 (2013), 206–13

Saurer, J., 'Individualrechtsschutz gegen das Handeln der Europäischen Agenturen', *EuR*, 45 (2010), 51–67

Scheuermann, S., *Das Prinzip der gegenseitigen Anerkennung im geltenden und künftigen Europäischen Strafrecht: Zugleich eine Abhandlung über die Notwendigkeit einer Europäischen Staatsanwaltschaft* (Hamburg: Kovač, 2009)

Schomburg, W., 'Auf dem Weg zu einem Europäischen Rechtsraum!', *DRiZ*, 78 (2000), 341–44

Schoppa, K., *Europol im Verbund der Europäischen Sicherheitsagenturen* (Berlin: Duncker & Humblot, 2013)

Schubert, I., *Europol und der virtuelle Verdacht: Die Suspendierung des Rechts auf informationelle Selbstbestimmung* (Frankfurt a.M.: Peter Lang, 2008)

Schünemann, B., 'Bürgerrechte ernst nehmen bei der Europäisierung des Strafverfahrens!', *StV*, 23 (2003), 116–22

Sénat (France) *Rapport d'information, fait au nom de la Commission des affaires européennes (1) sur Europol et Eurojust: Perspectives d'avenir*, No 477, 17 April 2014

Serzysko, A., 'Eurojust and the European Judicial Network on a New Legal Basis', *ERA Forum*, 12 (2011), 585–600

Sicurella, R., 'Setting Up a European Criminal Policy for the Protection of EU Financial Interests: Guidelines for a Coherent Definition of the Material Scope of the European Public Prosecutor's Offices', in Ligeti, K., ed., *Toward a Prosecutor for the European Union: A Comparative Analysis*, i (Oxford et al.: Hart Publishing, 2013), 870–904

Sieber, U., 'Die Zukunft des Europäischen Strafrechts', *ZStW*, 121 (2009), 1–67

Simonato, M., 'OLAF Investigations in a Multi-level-System', *eucrim*, 11 (2016), 136–40

Spiezia, F., 'How to Improve Cooperation between Member States and EU Institutions so as to Better Ensure the Protection of Whistleblowers', *ERA Forum*, 12 (2011), 387–407

'Linguistic Regimes and Judicial Cooperation in the Eurojust's Perspective', in F. Ruggieri, ed., *Criminal Proceedings, Languages and the European Union: Linguistic and Legal Issues* (Berlin, Heidelberg: Springer, 2014), 23–42

Stiegel, U., '§46: EJN und Verbindungsrichter/-staatsanwälte', in Sieber, U., Satzger, H., and Heintschel von Heinegg, B., eds., *Europäisches Strafrecht* (Baden-Baden: Nomos Verlagsgesellschaft, 2011), 728–38

Stojanovski, V., 'Procedural Rights of Persons under Investigation by OLAF', *eucrim*, 6 (2011), 127–32

Storbeck, J., 'EUROPOL: Probleme und Lösungen', *Kriminalistik*, 50 (1996), 17–21

'EUROPOL: Symbol ihrer Zeit', *Kriminalistik*, 48 (1994), 201–4

Storbeck, J., and Felgenhauer, H., 'Kooperation im Bereich Innere Sicherheit in Europa', in Möllers, M. H., and van Ooyen, R. C., eds., *Europäisierung und Internationalisierung der Polizei* (Frankfurt a.M.: Verlag für Polizeiwissenschaft, 2006), 11–20

Strobel, S., *Die Untersuchungen des Europäischen Amtes für Betrugsbekämpfung (OLAF)* (Baden-Baden: Nomos Verlagsgesellschaft, 2012)

Suhr, O., 'Die polizeiliche und justizielle Zusammenarbeit nach dem "Lissabon"-Urteil des Bundesverfassungsgerichts', *ZEuS*, 12 (2009), 687–715

Suominen, A., 'The Characteristics of Nordic Criminal Law in the Setting of EU Criminal Law', *EuCLR*, 1 (2011), 170–87

'The Past, Present and the Future of Eurojust', *MJECL*, 15 (2008), 217–34

Swoboda, S., 'The Self-Perception of the ECJ and Its Neglect of the Defense Perspective in Its Preliminary Rulings on Judicial Cooperation in Criminal Matters', *ZIS*, 10 (2015), 361–74

Thiele, A., 'Das Rechtsschutzsystem nach dem Vertrag von Lissabon: (K)ein Schritt nach vorn?', *EuR*, 45 (2010), 30–51

Thwaites, N., 'EUROJUST: Beacon in EU Judicial Co-operation', *RIDP*, 77 (2006), 293–8

Tolmein, O., 'Europol', *StV*, 19 (1999), 108–16

Trentmann, C., 'Eurojust und Europäische Staatsanwaltschaft: Auf dem richtigen Weg?', *ZStW*, 129 (2017), 108–45

Ubah, C. B. A., Nwebo, O. E., and Ezeanyika, S., 'Transnational Crime and International Organization: The Challenge of Internal and International Security', in Pływaczewski, E. W., and Guzik-Makaruk, E. M., eds., *Current Problems of the Penal Law and Criminology* (Warszawa: Wydawnictwo C. H. Beck, 2017), 781–802

van der Hulst, J., 'No Added Value of the EPPO?', *eucrim*, 11 (2016), 99–104

Venegoni, A., 'The New Frontier of PFI Investigations', *eucrim*, 12 (2017), 193–6

Vervaele, J. A. E., 'La europeización del Derecho penal y la dimensión penal de la integración europea', *RP*, 15 (2005), 169–83

'From Eurojust to the European Prosecution Service in the European Judicial Area', in Espina Ramos, J. A., and Vicente Carbajosa, I., eds., *The Future European Public Prosecutor's Office* (Madrid: Boletín Oficial del Estado, 2009), 125–62

'The Material Scope of Competence of the EPPO: *Lex Uncerta* and *Unpraevia*?', *ERA Forum*, 15 (2014), 85–99

von Arnauld, A., 'Die Europäisierung des Rechts der inneren Sicherheit', *JA*, 40 (2008), 327–35

von Bubnoff, E., 'Institutionelle Kriminalitätsbekämpfung in der EU', *ZEuS*, 5 (2002), 185–237

von Langsdorff, H., 'Maßnahmen der Europäischen Union zur Vereinfachung und Beschleunigung der Rechtshilfe und insoweit vorgesehene Beschuldigten- und Verteidigerrechte', *StV*, 23 (2003), 472–7

Voß, T., 'Landesbericht Deutschland', in Gleß, S., Grote, R., and Heine, G., eds., *Justitielle Einbindung und Kontrolle von Europol*, i: *Nationale und europäische Strafverfolgung* (Freiburg i.Br.: Ed. iuscrim, 2001), 75–160

Wade, M. L., 'A European Public Prosecutor: Potential and Pitfalls', *CrimLSC*, 59 (2013), 439–86

Wandl, C., *Europol: Unterstützung der Kriminalpolizei im Kampf gegen schwere internationale Kriminalität* (Linz: ProLibris.at, 2008)

Weichert, T., 'Das Europäische Polizeiamt: Gefahr für den Föderalismus?', in Baldus, M., and Soiné, M., eds., *Rechtsprobleme der internationalen polizeilichen Zusammenarbeit* (Baden-Baden: Nomos Verlagsgesellschaft, 1999), 72–85

Weitendorf, S., *Die interne Betrugsbekämpfung in den Europäischen Gemeinschaften durch das Europäische Amt für Betrugsbekämpfung (OLAF)* (Münster: Lit., 2007)

Weyembergh, A., 'An Overall Analysis of the Proposal for a Regulation on Eurojust', *eucrim*, 8 (2013), 127–31

Weyembergh, A., Armada, I., and Brière, C., 'Competition or Cooperation? State of Play and Future Perspectives on the Relations between Europol, Eurojust and the EJN', *NJECL*, 6 (2015), 261–87

White, S., 'A Decentralised European Public Prosecutor's Office', *eucrim*, 7 (2012), 67–75

Wolter, J., 'Polizeiliche und justizielle Datenübermittlungen in Deutschland und der Europäischen Union: Polizei und Europol, Staatsanwaltschaft und Eurojust', in Wolter, J. et al., eds., *Datenübermittlungen und Vorermittlungen: Festgabe für Hans Hilger* (Heidelberg: Müller, 2003), 275–90

Wright, R., in Espina Ramos, J. A., and Vicente Carbajosa, I., eds., *The Future European Public Prosecutor's Office* (Madrid: Boletín Oficial del Estado, 2009), 60–5

Zachert, H.-L., 'EUROPOL', *Kriminalistik*, 46 (1992), 7–11

Zerbes, I., 'Fragmentiertes Strafverfahren: Beweiserhebung und Beweisverwertung nach dem Verordnungsentwurf zur EStA', *ZIS*, 10 (2015), 148–55

'Landesbericht Österreich', in Gleß, S., Grote, R., and Heine, G., eds., *Justitielle Einbindung und Kontrolle von Europol*, i: *Nationale und europäische Strafverfolgung* (Freiburg i.Br.: Ed. iuscrim, 2001), 445–529

Zieschang, F., 'Der Austausch personenbezogener Daten mittels Europol', *ZRP*, 29 (1996), 427–9

Zimmermann, F., 'Die Auslegung künftiger EU-Strafrechtskompetenzen nach dem Lissabon-Urteil des Bundesverfassungsgerichts', *Jura*, 31 (2009), 844–51

Zwiers, M. W., *The European Public Prosecutor's Office: Analysis of a Multilevel Criminal Justice System* (Cambridge et al.: Intersentia, 2011).

GENERAL BIBLIOGRAPHY

Albers, P., Beauvais, P., Bohnert, J.-F., Böse, M., Langbroek, P., Renier, A., and Wahl, T., 'Final Report: Towards a Common Evaluation Framework to Assess Mutual Trust in the Field of EU Judicial Cooperation in Criminal Matters' (March 2013), at www.government.nl/documents/reports/2013/09/27/final-report-towards-a-common-evaluation-frame work-to-assess-mutual-trust-in-the-field-of-eu-judicial-cooperation-in-criminal-m, accessed 30 September 2016

Ambos, K., *Beweisverwertungsverbote, Grundlagen und Kasuistik: Internationale Bezüge – Ausgewählte Probleme* (Berlin: Duncker & Humblot, 2010)

ed., *Europäisches Strafrecht post-Lissabon* (Göttingen: Universitäts-Verlag Göttingen, 2011)

Fälle zum internationalen Strafrecht (Munich: C. H. Beck, 2010)

Internationales Strafrecht (Munich: C. H. Beck, 1st edn, 2006)

Internationales Strafrecht (Munich: C. H. Beck, 2nd edn, 2008)

Internationales Strafrecht (Munich: C. H. Beck, 3rd edn, 2011)

Internationales Strafrecht (Munich: C. H. Beck, 4th edn, 2014)

Internationales Strafrecht (Munich: C. H. Beck, 5th edn, 2018)

Treatise on International Criminal Law, i: Foundations and General Part (Oxford: Oxford University Press, 2013)

Treatise on International Criminal Law, ii: The Crimes and Sentencing (Oxford: Oxford University Press, 2014)

Treatise on International Criminal Law, iii: International Criminal Procedure (Oxford: Oxford University Press, 2016)

Ambos, K., König, S., and Rackow, P., eds., *Rechtshilferecht in Strafsachen* (Baden-Baden: Nomos Verlagsgesellschaft, 2015)

Arndt, H.-W., *Europarecht* (Heidelberg et al.: C. F. Müller, 7th edn, 2004)

Arndt, H.-W., Fischer K., and Fetzer, T., *Europarecht* (Heidelberg et al.: C. F. Müller, 11th edn, 2015)

Asp, P., *The Procedural Criminal Law Cooperation of the EU* (Stockholm: Stiftelsen Skrifter utgivna av Juridiska fakulteten vid Stockholms universitet, 2016)

The Substantive Criminal Law Competence of the EU (Stockholm: Jure Bokhandel, 2012)

Bieber, R., Epiney, A., Haag, M., and Kotzur, M., *Die Europäische Union: Europarecht und Politik* (Baden-Baden: Nomos Verlagsgesellschaft et al., 12th edn, 2016)

Blekxtoon, R., and van Ballegooij, W., eds., *Handbook on the European Arrest Warrant* (The Hague: T. M. C. Asser Press, 2005)

Böse, M., ed., *Enzyklopädie Europarecht Band 9: Europäisches Strafrecht mit polizeilicher Zusammenarbeit* (Baden-Baden: Nomos, 2013)

Strafen und Sanktionen im Europäischen Gemeinschaftsrecht (Cologne et al.: Carl Heymanns, 1996)

Callies, C., and Ruffert, M., eds., *Verfassung der Europäischen Union: Kommentar der Grundlagenbestimmungen*, i (Munich: C. H. Beck, Vienna: Manzsche Verlags- und Universitätsbuchhandlung, 2006)

eds., *EUV/AEUV: Das Verfassungsrecht der Europäischen Union mit Europäischer Grundrechtecharta. Kommentar* (Munich: C. H. Beck, 5th edn, 2016)

Chalmers, D., Davies, G., and Monti, G., *European Union Law* (Cambridge: Cambridge University Press, 3rd edn, 2014)

Corstens, G., and Pradel, J., *European Criminal Law* (The Hague et al.: Kluwer Law International, 2002)

Craig, P., *The Lisbon Treaty: Law, Politics, and Treaty Reform* (Oxford: Oxford University Press, 2013)

Craig, P., and de Búrca, G., eds., *The Evolution of EU Law* (Oxford: Oxford University Press, 2nd edn, 2011)

Dannecker, G., ed., *Die Bekämpfung des Subventionsbetrugs im EG-Bereich* (Cologne: Bundesanzeiger, 1993)

Dannecker, G., and Jansen, O., eds., *Steuerstrafrecht in Europa und in den Vereinigten Staaten* (Stuttgart et al.: Boorberg et al., 2007)

Dashwood, A., Dougan, M., Rodger, B., Spaventa, E., and Wyatt, D., *Wyatt and Dashwood's European Union Law* (Oxford and Portland: Hart, 6th edn, 2011).

David, E., *Eléments de droit pénal international et européen* (Bruxelles: Bruylant, 2009)

Delmas-Marty, M., ed., *Corpus Juris der strafrechtlichen Regelungen zum Schutz der finanziellen Interessen der EU* (Cologne et al.: Carl Heymanns, 1998)

Delmas-Marty, M., and Spencer, J. R., eds., *European Criminal Procedures* (Cambridge: Cambridge University Press, 2002)

Delmas-Marty, M., and Vervaele, J. A. E., eds., *The Implementation of the Corpus Juris in the Member States*, 4 Vols. (Antwerp et al.: Intersentia, 2000–1)

Demko, D., *'Menschenrecht auf Verteidigung' und Fairness des Strafverfahrens auf nationaler, europäischer und internationaler Ebene* (Bern: Stämpfli, 2014)

Dörr, O., Grote, R., and Marauhn, T., eds., *EMRK/GG: Konkordanzkommentar zum europäischen und deutschen Grundrechtsschutz* (Tübingen: Mohr Siebeck, 2nd edn, 2013)

Erb, V., Esser, R., Franke, U., Graalmann-Scheerer, K., Hilger, H., and Ignor, A., eds., *Löwe-Rosenberg, Die Strafprozessordnung und das Gerichtsverfassungsgesetz: Großkommentar* (Berlin: de Gruyter, 26th edn, 2012)

Esser, R., *Auf dem Weg zu einem europäischen Strafverfahrensrecht* (Berlin: de Gruyter, 2002)

Europäisches und Internationales Strafrecht (Munich: C. H. Beck, 2nd edn, 2018)

EU, *Follow-up-Mitteilung, Grünbuch zum strafrechtlichen Schutz der finanziellen Interessen der Europäischen Gemeinschaften und zur Schaffung einer Europäischen Staatsanwaltschaft, KOM(2003) 128 endgültig* (Brussels, 19 March 2003)

from the Commission: Procedural Safeguards for Suspects and Defendants in Criminal Proceedings throughout the European Union, 19 February 2003 COM(2003) 75 final

on Conflicts of Jurisdiction and the Principle of ne bis in idem in Criminal Proceedings, 23 December 2005 COM(2005) 696 final

on Criminal-Law Protection of the Financial Interests of the Community and the Establishment of a European Prosecutor, 11 December 2001 COM(2001) 715 final

die Angleichung, die gegenseitige Anerkennung und die Vollstreckung strafrechtlicher Sanktionen in der Europäischen Union, KOM(2004) 334 endgültig (Brussels, 30 April 2004)

Trust in the European Judicial Area: A Green Paper on the Application of EU Criminal Justice Legislation in the Field of Detention, 14 June 2011 COM(2011) 327 final

EuAlÜbk., Europäisches Auslieferungsübereinkommen vom 13. 12. 1957

EU-AuslÜbk., EU-Auslieferungsübereinkommen (Übereinkommen vom 27. 9. 1996 aufgrund von Artikel K.3 des Vertrages über die EU über die Auslieferung zwischen den Mitgliedstaaten der EU)

EUBestG, Gesetz zu dem Protokoll v. 27. 9. 1996 zum Übk. über den Schutz der finanziellen Interessen der EGen (EU-Bestechungsgesetz) v. 10. 9. 1998, BGBl. II S. 2340

EuGHG, Gesetz betreffend die Anrufung des Gerichtshofes der EGen im Wege des Vorabentscheidungsverfahrens auf dem Gebiet der polizeilichen Zusammenarbeit und der justiziellen Zusammenarbeit in Strafsachen nach Art. 35 des EU-Vertrages v. 6. 8. 1998, BGBl. I 1998 S. 2035; BGBl. I 1999 S. 728

EuHbG, Europäisches Haftbefehlsgesetz (Gesetz zur Umsetzung des Rahmenbeschlusses über den Europäischen Haftbefehl und die Übergabeverfahren zwischen den Mitgliedstaaten der EU vom 21. Juli 2004)

EU-JZG, (Austrian) Bundesgesetz über die justizielle Zusammenarbeit in Strafsachen mit den Mitgliedsstaaten der EU (EU-JZG), (Austrian) BGBl. I 2004/36

EuRhÜbk., Europäisches Rechtshilfeübereinkommen (Europäisches Übereinkommen vom 20. April 1959 über die Rechtshilfe in Strafsachen)

Europäische Anwaltsvereinigung e. V., ed., *Das faire Verfahren nach Art. 6 EMRK* (Cologne: Schmidt et al., 2005)

European Committee on Crime Problems, *Extraterritorial Criminal Jurisdiction* (Strasbourg: Council of Europe, 1990)

EuropolG, Gesetz zu dem Übereinkommen vom 26. Juli 1995 auf Grund von Artikel 31 des Vertrags über die EU über die Errichtung eines Europäischen Polizeiamts: Europol-Gesetz: vom 16. Dezember 1997

Europol-Immunitätsprotokoll, Protokoll über die Vorrechte und Immunitäten für Europol, die Mitglieder der Organe, die stellvertretenden Direktoren und die Bediensteten von Europol v. 19. 6. 1997 (Abl. EG C 221 v. 19. 7. 1997, 2; BGBl. II 1998 S. 975)

EuropolK, Übereinkommen vom 26. Juli 1995 auf Grund von Artikel 31 des Vertrags über die EU über die Errichtung eines Europäischen Polizeiamts: Europol-Übereinkommen

EuTerrÜbk., Europäisches Übereinkommen zur Bekämpfung des Terrorismus vom 27. Januar 1977, BGBl. II 1978 S. 321, 907

EU-VereinfAuslÜbk., Übereinkommen über das vereinfachte Auslieferungsverfahren zwischen den Mitgliedstaaten der Europäischen Union vom 10. März 1995

Fischer, G., *Europarecht* (Cologne et al.: Carl Heymanns, 2nd edn, 2008)

Fischer, H.-G., *Europarecht: Grundlagen des Europäischen Gemeinschaftsrechts in Verbindung mit deutschem Staats- und Verwaltungsrecht* (Munich: C. H. Beck, 3rd edn, 2001)

Fischer, K. H., *Der Vertrag von Lissabon* (Baden-Baden: Nomos Verlagsgesellschaft et al., 2008)

Flore, D., *Droit pénal européen: Les enjeux d'une justice pénale européenne* (Brussels: Larcier, 2009)

Frenz, W., *Handbuch Europarecht,* iv: *Europäische Grundrechte* (Berlin: Springer, 2009)

Handbuch Europarecht, vi: *Institutionen und Politiken* (Berlin: Springer, 2011)

Frowein, J. A., and Peukert, W., *Europäische Menschenrechtskonvention: EMRK-Kommentar* (Kehl: N. P Engel, 3rd edn, 2009)

García Sánchez, Beatriz, *La extradición en el ordenamiento interno español, internacional y comunitario* (Albolote: Comares, 2005)

Geiger, R., *Grundgesetz und Völkerrecht mit Europarecht: Die Bezüge des Staatsrechts zum Völkerrecht und Europarecht. Ein Studienbuch* (Munich: C. H. Beck, 6th edn, 2013)

Geiger, R., Khan, D.-E., and Kotzur, M., *European Union Treaties: Treaty on European Union, Treaty on the Functioning of the European Union* (Munich et al.: C. H. Beck et al., 2015)

Gleß, S., *Beweisrechtsgrundsätze einer grenzüberschreitenden Strafverfolgung* (Baden-Baden: Nomos Verlagsgesellschaft, 2006)

Internationales Strafrecht: Grundriss für Studium und Praxis (Basel: Helbing und Lichtenhahn, 2nd edn, 2015)

Gollwitzer, W., *Menschenrechte im Strafverfahren: MRK und IPBPR* (Berlin: de Gruyter, 2005)

Grabenwarter, C., *European Convention on Human Rights: Commentary* (Munich: C. H. Beck et al., 2014)

Grabenwarter, C., and Pabel, K., *Europäische Menschenrechtskonvention* (Munich: C. H. Beck et al., 6th edn, 2016)

Grabitz, E., Hilf, M., and Nettesheim, M., *Das Recht der Europäischen Union, EUV/AEUV*, i (Munich: C. H. Beck, 2013)

Grützner, H., Pötz, P.-G., and Kreß, C., eds., *Internationaler Rechtshilfeverkehr in Strafsachen* (Heidelberg: C. F. Müller, 40. Aktualisierung, December 2016)

Guild, E., ed., *Constitutional Challenges to the European Arrest Warrant* (Nijmegen: Wolf Legal Publishers, 2006)

Haager Programm, Haager Programm zur Stärkung von Freiheit, Sicherheit und Recht in der EU, Mitteilung der Kommission an den Rat und das EP: Das Haager Programm, KOM(2005), 184 endgültig, Abl. EU C v. 3. 3. 2005

Haltern, U., *Europarecht: Dogmatik im Kontext* (Tübingen: Mohr Siebeck, 2nd edn, 2007)

Hannich, R., ed., *Karlsruher Kommentar zur Strafprozessordnung: Mit GVG, EGGVG und EMRK* (Munich: C. H. Beck, 7th edn, 2013)

Harris, D., O'Boyle, M., and Warbrick, C., *Law of the European Convention on Human Rights* (Oxford: Oxford University Press, 3rd edn, 2014)

Hecker, B., *Europäisches Strafrecht* (Berlin: Springer, 1st edn, 2005)

Europäisches Strafrecht (Berlin: Springer, 5th edn, 2015)

Strafbare Produktwerbung im Lichte des Gemeinschaftsrechts (Tübingen: Mohr Siebeck, 2001)

Hecker, B., and Zöller, M. A., *Fallsammlung zum Europäischen und Internationalen Strafrecht* (Berlin et al.: Springer, 2012)

Heger, M., *Die Europäisierung des deutschen Umweltstrafrechts* (Tübingen: Mohr Siebeck, 2009)

Herdegen, M., *Europarecht* (Munich: C. H. Beck, 19th edn, 2017)

Völkerrecht (Munich: C. H. Beck, 16th edn, 2017)

Herlin-Karnell, E., *The Constitutional Dimension of European Criminal Law* (Oxford: Hart Publishing, 2012)

Heselhaus, S., and Nowak, C., eds., *Handbuch der Europäischen Grundrechte* (Munich et al.: C. H. Beck et al., 2006)

Horder, J., *Ashworth's Principles of Criminal Law* (Oxford: OUP, 8th edn, 2016)

Jähnke, B., and Schramm, B., *Europäisches Strafrecht* (Berlin: De Gruyter, 2017)

Jarass, H. D., *Charta der Grundrechte der Europäischen Union* (Munich: C. H. Beck, 3rd edn, 2016)

Jarass, H. D., *EU-Grundrechte: Ein Studien- und Handbuch* (Munich: C. H. Beck, 2005)

Jeschek, H.-H., and Weigend, T., *Lehrbuch des Strafrechts: Allgemeiner Teil* (Berlin: Duncker & Humblot, 5th edn, 1996)

Joecks, W., and Miebach, K., eds., *Münchener Kommentar zum Strafgesetzbuch*, 8 volumes (Munich: C. H. Beck, 2nd edn, 2011–2015)

Joerden, J. C., and Szwarc, A. J., eds., *Europäisierung des Strafrechts in Polen und Deutschland: Rechtsstaatliche Grundlagen* (Berlin: Duncker & Humblot, 2007)

Kindhäuser, U., *Strafgesetzbuch: Lehr- und Praxiskommentar* (Baden-Baden: Nomos, 7th edn, 2017)

Kindhäuser, U., Neumann, U., and Paeffgen, H.-U., eds., *Nomos Kommentar: Strafgesetzbuch,* i: *Allgemeiner Teil: §§1–79b* (Baden-Baden: Nomos, 5th edn, 2017)

Klip, A., *European Criminal Law: An Integrative Approach* (Cambridge et al.: Intersentia, 1st edn, 2009)

European Criminal Law: An Integrative Approach (Cambridge et al.: Intersentia, 2nd edn, 2012)

European Criminal Law: An Integrative Approach (Cambridge, Antwerp and Portland: Intersentia, 3rd edn, 2016)

Materials on European Criminal Law (Cambridge and Antwerp: Intersentia, 2nd edn, 2014)

ed., *Substantive Criminal Law of the European Union* (Antwerp et al.: Maklu, 2011)

Krüßmann, T. M., *Transnationales Strafprozessrecht* (Baden-Baden: Nomos Verlagsgesellschaft, 2009)

Kühne, H.-H., *Strafprozessrecht: Eine systematische Darstellung des deutschen und europäischen Strafverfahrensrechts* (Heidelberg et al.: C. F. Müller, 9th edn, 2015)

Lagodny, O., *Empfiehlt es sich, eine europäische Gerichtskompetenz für Strafgewaltskonflikte vorzusehen?, Gutachten im Auftrag des Bundesministeriums der Justiz, Berlin* (2001), at www.uni-salzburg.at/filead min/oracle_file_imports/460066.PDF, accessed 27 June 2017

Lagodny, O., Wiederin, E., and Winkler, R., eds., *Probleme des Rahmenbeschlusses am Beispiel des Europäischen Haftbefehls: Ein neues Instrument der europäischen Integration aus Sicht von Europarecht, Strafrecht, Verfassungsrecht und Völkerrecht* (Vienna: Neuer Wissenschaftlicher Verlag, 2007)

Lasok, K. P. E., *Law and Institutions of the EU* (London: Butterworths, 7th edn, 2001)

Laufhütte, H.-W., Rissing-van Saan, R., and Tiedemann, K., eds., *Strafgesetzbuch, Leipziger Kommentar* (12th edn, Berlin: de Gruyter, 2006 ff.)

Lelieveldt, H., and Princen, S., *The Politics of the European Union* (Cambridge: Cambridge University Press, 2nd edn, 2015)

Lenz, C. O., and Borchardt, K.-D., eds., *EU-Verträge Kommentar nach dem Vertrag von Lissabon: EUV - AEUV - GRCh* (Cologne: Bundesanzeiger, Vienna: Linde, 6th edn, 2013)

Ligeti, K., *Strafrecht und strafrechtliche Zusammenarbeit in der Europäischen Union* (Berlin: Duncker & Humblot, 2005)

ed., *Toward a Prosecutor for the European Union: A Comparative Analysis* (Oxford et al.: Hart Publishing, 2013)

Mayer, M., *Ne-bis-in-idem-Wirkung europäischer Strafentscheidungen* (Frankfurt a. M.: Peter Lang, 1992)

Menzel, J., Pierlings, T., and Hoffmann, J., eds., *Völkerrechtsprechung* (Tübingen: Mohr Siebeck, 2005)

Meyer, J., ed., *Charta der Grundrechte der Europäischen Union* (Baden-Baden: Nomos Verlagsgesellschaft, 4th edn, 2014)

Meyer-Goßner, L., and Schmitt, B., *Strafprozessordnung: Gerichtsverfassungsgesetz, Nebengesetze und ergänzende Bestimmungen* (Munich: C. H. Beck, 60th edn, 2017)

Meyer-Ladewig, J., Nettesheim, M., and von Raumer, S., eds., *Europäische Menschenrechtskonvention: Handkommentar* (Baden-Baden: Nomos, Basel: Helbing Lichtenhahn, Vienna: Manz, 4th edn, 2017)

Miettinen, S., *Criminal Law and Policy in the European Union* (Abingdon, Oxon: Routledge, 2013)

Mitsilegas, V., *EU Criminal Law* (Oxford and Portland: Hart Publishing, 2009)

EU Criminal Law after Lisbon (Oxford and Portland: Hart Publishing, 2016)

Mitsilegas, V., Bergström, M., and Konstadinides, T., eds., *Research Handbook on EU Criminal Law* (Cheltenham and Northampton: Edward Elgar Publishing, 2016)

Murschetz, V., *Auslieferung und Europäischer Haftbefehl: Kontinentaleuropäische und anglo-amerikanische materielle Prinzipien des Auslieferungsrechts im Vergleich zum Europäischen Haftbefehl und dessen Umsetzung in Österreich* (Vienna et al.: Springer, 2007)

Nicolaysen, G., *Europarecht: Die Europäische Integrationsverfassung*, i (Baden-Baden: Nomos Verlagsgesellschaft, 2nd edn, 2002)

Oehler, D., *Internationales Strafrecht* (Cologne et al.: Carl Heymanns, 2nd edn, 1983)

Oppermann, T., *Europarecht* (Munich: C. H. Beck, 3rd edn, 2005)

Oppermann, T., Classen, C. D., and Nettesheim, M., *Europarecht* (Munich: C. H. Beck, 7th edn, 2016)

Pabel, K., and Schmahl, S., eds., *Internationaler Kommentar zur Europäischen Menschenrechtskonvention: Mit einschlägigen Texten und Dokumenten* (Cologne et al.: Carl Heymanns, 1994)

Pache, E., ed., *Die Europäische Union: Ein Raum der Freiheit, der Sicherheit und des Rechts?* (Baden-Baden: Nomos Verlagsgesellschaft, 2006)

Peers, S., Hervey, T., Kenner, J., and Ward, A., *The EU Charter of Fundamental Rights* (Oxford and Portland: Hart, 2014)

Peters, A., and Altwickler, T., *Europäische Menschenrechtskonvention: Mit rechtsvergleichenden Bezügen zum deutschen Grundgesetz* (Munich: C. H. Beck, 2nd edn, 2012)

Radtke, H., and Hohmann., O., eds., *Strafprozessordnung: Kommentar* (Munich: Vahlen, 2011)

RbEuHb, Rahmenbeschluss des Rates vom 13. Juni 2002 über den Europäischen Haftbefehl und die Übergabeverfahren zwischen den Mitgliedstaaten

Regan, E., *The New Third Pillar* (Dublin: Institute of European Affairs Dublin, 2000)

Reid, K., *A Practitioner's Guide to the European Convention on Human Rights* (London: Thomson, Sweet & Maxwell, 3rd edn, 2007)

Roxin, C., *Strafrecht: Allgemeiner Teil*, i (Munich: C. H. Beck, 4th edn, 2006)

Strafrecht: Allgemeiner Teil, ii (Munich: C. H. Beck, 2003)

Roxin, C., and Schünemann, B., *Strafverfahrensrecht* (Munich: C. H. Beck, 28th edn, 2014)

Rozo Acuña, E., ed., *Il mandato di arresto europeo e l'estradizione: Profili costituzionali, penali, processuali ed internazionali* (Padova: Cedam, 2004)

Sachs, M., eds., *Grundgesetz, Kommentar* (Munich: C. H. Beck, 7th edn, 2014)

Safferling, C., *Internationales Strafrecht* (Berlin et al.: Springer, 2011)

Sanders, A., and Young, R., *Criminal Justice* (Oxford et al.: Oxford University Press, 4th edn, 2010)

Satzger, H., *Die Europäisierung des Strafrechts* (Cologne et al.: Carl Heymanns, 2001)

International and European Criminal Law (Munich: C. H. Beck, Oxford: Hart, Baden-Baden: Nomos, 2nd edn, 2018)

Internationales und Europäisches Strafrecht (Baden-Baden: Nomos Verlagsgesellschaft, 7th edn, 2016)

Schimansky, H., Bunte, H.-J., and Lwowski, H.-J., eds., *Bankrechts-Handbuch*, i (Munich: C. H. Beck, 5th edn, 2017)

Schomburg, W., Lagodny, O., Gleß, S., and Hackner, T., *Internationale Rechtshilfe in Strafsachen* (Munich: C. H. Beck, 5th edn, 2012)

Schorkopf, F., *Staatsrecht der internationalen Beziehungen* (Munich: C. H. Beck, 2017)

Schröder, C., *Europäische Richtlinien und deutsches Strafrecht: Eine Untersuchung über den Einfluß europäischer Richtlinien gemäß Art. 249 Abs. 3 EGV auf das deutsche Strafrecht* (Berlin et al.: de Gruyter, 2002)

Schroeder, W., *Grundkurs Europarecht* (Munich: C. H. Beck, 4th edn, 2015)

SchÜbk., Übereinkommen von Schengen vom 14. Juni 1985 zwischen den Regierungen der Staaten der Benelux-Wirtschaftsunion, der

Bundesrepublik Deutschland und der Französischen Republik betreffen den schrittweisen Abbau der Kontrollen an den gemeinsamen Grenzen

Schünemann, B., ed., *Alternativentwurf Europäische Strafverfolgung* (Cologne et al.: Carl Heymanns, 2004)

ed., *Ein Gesamtkonzept für die europäische Strafrechtspflege* (Cologne et al.: Carl Heymanns, 2006)

Schütz, H.-J., Bruha, T., and König, D., *Casebook Europarecht* (Munich: C. H. Beck, 2004)

Schütze, R., *European Union Law* (Cambridge: Cambridge University Press, 2015)

Schwaighofer, K., and Ebensperger, S., *Internationale Rechtshilfe in strafrechtlichen Angelegenheiten* (Vienna: WUV Universitätsverlag, 2001)

Schwarze, J., ed., *EU-Kommentar* (Baden-Baden: Nomos et al., 3rd edn, 2012)

Sieber, U., Satzger, H., and Heintschel von Heinegg, B., eds., *Europäisches Strafrecht* (Baden-Baden: Nomos, 2nd edn, 2014)

Simester, A. P., Spencer, J. R., Stark, F., Sullivan, G. R., and Virgo, G. J., *Simester and Sullivan's Criminal Law: Theory and Doctrine* (Oxford: Hart, 6th edn, 2016).

Streinz, R., ed., *EUV/AEUV: Vertrag über die Europäische Union und Vertrag über die Arbeitsweise der Europäischen Union* (Munich: C. H. Beck, 2nd edn, 2012)

Europarecht (Heidelberg: C. F. Müller, 10th edn, 2016)

Streinz, R., Ohler, C., and Hermann, C., *Der Vertrag von Lissabon zur Reform der EU: Einführung mit Synopse* (Munich: C. H. Beck, 3rd edn, 2010)

Tettinger, P. J., and Stern, K., *Kölner Gemeinschaftskommentar zur Europäischen Grundrechte-Charta* (Munich: C. H. Beck, 2006)

Tiedemann, K., *Wirtschaftsstrafrecht* (Munich: Vahlen, 5th edn, 2017)

Tochilovsky, V., *The Law and Jurisprudence of the International Criminal Tribunals and Courts: Procedure and Human Rights Aspects* (Cambridge, Antwerp and Portland: Intersentia, 2nd edn, 2014)

Ulsamer, G., ed., *Lexikon des Rechts: Strafrecht/Strafverfahrensrecht* (Neuwied et al.: Luchterhand, 2nd edn, 1996)

van Dijk, P., van Hoof, F., van Rijn, A., and Zwaak, L., eds., *Theory and Practice of the European Convention on Human Rights* (Antwerp, Oxford: Intersentia, 4th edn, 2006)

Vedder, C. W., and Heintschel von Heinegg, W., eds., *Europäischer Verfassungsvertrag, Handkommentar* (Baden-Baden: Nomos Verlagsgesellschaft, 2007)

Vervaele, J. A. E., ed., *European Evidence Warrant: Transnational Judicial Inquiries in the EU* (Antwerp et al.: Intersentia, 2005)

Vest, H., *Gerechtigkeit für Humanitätsverbrechen? Nationale Strafverfolgung von staatlichen Systemverbrechen mit Hilfe der Radbruchschen Formel* (Tübingen: Mohr Siebeck, 2006)

Villiger, M. E., *Handbuch der Europäischen Menschenrechtskonvention (EMRK) unter besonderer Berücksichtigung der schweizerischen Rechtslage* (Zürich: Schulthess et al., 2nd edn, 1999)

Wasmeier, M., and Möhlig, A., *Strafrecht der Europäischen Union (Textsammlung)* (Baden-Baden: Nomos Verlagsgesellschaft, 2nd edn, 2008)

Wolter, J., ed., *Systematischer Kommentar zur Strafprozessordnung, mit GVG und EMRK* (Cologne: Carl Heymanns, 4th edn, 2012)

INDEX

Lightning Source UK Ltd.
Milton Keynes UK
UKHW052142251120
373740UK00026B/689

9 781107 552135